BAD BOYS

BAD BOYS

The Actors
of Film Noir

KAREN BURROUGHS
HANNSBERRY

McFarland & Company, Inc., Publishers
Jefferson, North Carolina, and London

LIBRARY OF CONGRESS CATALOGUING-IN-PUBLICATION DATA

Hannsberry, Karen Burroughs, 1962–
Bad boys : the actors of film noir / Karen Burroughs Hannsberry.
p. cm.
Includes bibliographical references and index.

ISBN 0-7864-1484-7 (illustrated case binding : 50# alkaline paper)

1. Motion picture actors and actresses— United States—
Biography— Dictionaries. 2. Male actors— United States—
Biography— Dictionaries. 3. Film noir— United States. I. Title.
PN1998.2.H36 2003 791.43'028'092273 — dc21 2002156688

British Library cataloguing data are available

On the cover: James Cagney

Manufactured in the United States of America

*McFarland & Company, Inc., Publishers
Box 611, Jefferson, North Carolina 28640
www.mcfarlandpub.com*

For all those I love, and all of those who love me.

ACKNOWLEDGMENTS

There are so many individuals without whom this book truly could not have been completed.

For their roles in helping to make my accounts of the actors in this volume come alive, I am most humbly grateful to Ed Begley, Jr., Jay Bernstein, Andrea Bershad (daughter of Sheldon Leonard), the late Jeff Corey, Kirk Douglas, Peter Ford (son of Glenn Ford), Farley Granger, Coleen Gray, June Lockhart, Michael Macready (son of George Macready), and Robert Wise.

I cannot find the words to express my appreciation for my tireless research assistants, Alan David Burroughs and Diane Sippl, who served as my eyes, heart, and mind on the East and West coasts. I am also indebted to Theresa Henderson Burroughs, who provided invaluable aid in countless ways, including compiling the index for this book. For their various forms of support and assistance, it is a pleasure to thank Evelyn Mildred Henderson, Veronica and Jessica Hannsberry, Imani Walton, Kevin Hamilton Smith, Bob King of *Classic Images* and *Films of the Golden Age*, James J.J. Wilson of *Filmfax*, Karin Dagneau, Evelin Past, Jane Kellogg, DeeDee E. Dellos, David Lee Guss, Judy Walters, Billy Long, Bob J. Robison, Jack Harnedy, Alvin Peterson, Adam Zanders, Ismaila Goudiaby, Keith Rogers, Alan K. Rode, Diane Karg, Janet Lorenz of the Margaret Herrick Library of the Academy of Motion Picture Arts and Sciences, the staff of the performing arts section of the Harold Washington Library in Chicago, and the staff of the Library of the Performing Arts in New York.

For assisting me in securing the striking photographs that provide a visual depiction of noir's bad boys, I express sincere gratitude to Ron Harvey and Bruce Donnella of the Everett Collection in New York City; Jim Shepard of the Collectors Bookstore in Hollywood, California; Movie Star News in New York City; T. Gene Hatcher; and David Wentick.

Finally, for helping me to obtain the hundreds of films in which it was a pleasure and privilege to lose myself during countless hours, I am truly indebted to Nick Lapetina, Dan Van Neste, and Marc Dolezal.

CONTENTS

PREFACE

He hails from the dark side of the
screen.

He can be vicious or violent, as likely
to slap a dame's face as kiss her. Or a daunt-
less protector of the law, nabbing hoods
with a combination of instinct, fortitude,
and grit. He might be vulnerable and gul-
lible, apt to succumb to the whims of a
conniving cutie at the drop of the proverbial hat. He can be inexorably hardened by
life's unforeseen knocks, brimming with
cynicism, suspicion, and doubt. Or overcome with desperate disillusionment,
caught up in circumstances beyond his control and urgently seeking a way out of a
seemingly hopeless plight.

More so than his feminine counterpart,
this man represents every type of persona,
occupying all social and economic strata,
and spanning the occupational gamut from
the vilest petty criminal to the most upstanding judge. He is an indefatigable gumshoe in *The Big Sleep* (1946), a carnival
sharpshooter in *Gun Crazy* (1949), an
unscrupulous newspaper photographer in
Shakedown (1950), a hard-working truck
driver in *Desperate* (1947), a prize-fighter
in *The Set-Up* (1949), a priest in *Edge of
Doom* (1950). He pumps gas in *The Postman
Always Rings Twice* (1946), sells insurance
in *Double Indemnity* (1944), drives a taxicab in *99 River Street* (1953), writes short
stories in *Danger Signal* (1945), picks pockets in *Pickup on South Street* (1953). He is
an endless number of syndicate chiefs, assistant district attorneys, private dicks, gun-
toting henchmen, and prison inmates.

He dwells in the world of the film
noir.

From Philip Marlowe and Sam Spade
to Johnny Rocco and Cody Jarrett, the film
noir male is a unique, fascinating, and infinitely watchable being, displaying a wide
range of emotions, behaviors, and motivations. Some of the films from the era depict
men who are almost mindlessly violent,
such as Neville Brand's Chester in *D.O.A.*
(1950), whose sole enjoyment in life seems
to be derived from inflicting pain on others. Other films noirs contain flawed
authority figures, as in *The Glass Key* (1942),
in which Senator Ralph Henry (Moroni
Olsen) conceals his role in his son's death;
Guilty Bystander (1950), which features
alcoholic ex-cop Max Thursday (Zachary
Scott); or *Detective Story* (1951), where law-

man Jim McLeod (Kirk Douglas) is ruled by an inflexible moral code that costs him his marriage and, ultimately, his life. Some focus on hapless males whose lives are turned upside down because of their unquenchable desire for a woman, such as insurance agent John Forbes (Dick Powell) in *Pitfall* (1948), garage mechanic Dan Brady (Mickey Rooney) in *Quicksand* (1950), or Mike Lambert (Glenn Ford), the unemployed engineer in *Framed* (1947). Then there are films in which ruthless, powerful crime bosses rule with a steel will and an iron fist, including the brutal Mr. Brown (Richard Conte) in *The Big Combo* (1955) and Neil Eichelberger (Ed Begley) in *The Turning Point* (1952), who sacrifices a building of innocent people in the pursuit of his personal objectives. And on the right side of the law, film noir offers numerous portraits of courageous officers, from undercover agents such as Lawrence Trumble (William Bendix) in *Macao* (1952), to beat cops including Rocky Barnes (Mark Stevens) in *Between Midnight and Dawn* (1950). From the most imposing gumshoe to the meekest elevator operator, each man in film noir plays a role in weaving the fabric of this dim and murky universe.

> "The poor boy — he's psychopathic. He likes the sight of blood." — Luther Adler in *D.O.A.* (1950)

The era of film noir is one that disdains absolute definitions, flaunts exceptions, and welcomes interpretations. The movies that comprise this category of filmmaking were released approximately between 1940 and 1959, but were first identified as "film noir" (literally, "black film") in 1946 by French critics who became aware of a dark, cynical tone that was prevalent in a growing number of American motion pictures. As I wrote in my previous book, *Femme Noir:*

Bad Girls of Film, these films depict a world of pessimism, corruption, and hopelessness, and are distinguished by their shadowy, dim appearance and dark overtones. These films also commonly contain specific elements of plot, setting, and characterization, including urban locales, the commission of crimes, the presence of femmes fatales, betrayal between characters, and the use of flashback and narration. In addition, films noirs frequently include such visual details as dimly lit rooms, unusual camera angles, and rain-slick streets.

Alongside these elements, films noirs are also noted for scenes of brutal or unusual forms of violence. In *Raw Deal*, Raymond Burr douses his mistress with a bucket containing flaming cognac. Scalding coffee is thrown by Lee Marvin into Gloria Grahame's face in *The Big Heat* (and she later returns the favor). In *Red Light* (1949), Raymond Burr (again!) kicks a jack supporting a truck trailer, crushing Gene Lockhart beneath and, similarly, Nick Dennis is flattened by a car in *Kiss Me Deadly* (1955). A priest in *Edge of Doom* (1950) is bludgeoned to death with a heavy brass crucifix. Luther Adler's character in *Cornered* (1945) unloads several bullets in a man's face so as to render him unrecognizable. Joseph Cotten is hit by a train in *Shadow of a Doubt* (1943), George Murphy is run over by a tractor in *Border Incident* (1949), and William Talman in *Armored Car Robbery* (1950) is struck and killed by an airplane. A trio of inmates in *Brute Force* (1947) threatens a fellow convict with a blow torch until the luckless man is crushed by a grinding machine, and in the same film, a sadistic guard is tossed from a tower and killed by a swarm of angry prisoners. No fewer than four cast members in *Angel Face* (1953) perish in their cars by careening backwards over a cliff. And in *Suspense* (1946), Albert

Dekker is shot, stuffed into a rolltop desk, and incinerated.

Despite its commonalities—and unlike such screen genres as westerns, comedies, or horror—film noir cannot be absolutely defined or succinctly described, and countless exceptions abound. For example, while nearly all of the features from this period are filmed in black and white, several Technicolor films fall into the category of film noir, including *House of Bamboo* (1955), *Leave Her to Heaven* (1945), and *Slightly Scarlet* (1956). Films noirs are typically set in large American cities, but the titles of such features as *Berlin Express* (1948), *Calcutta* (1947), *Macao* (1952), and *The Shanghai Gesture* (1941) clearly reveal their deviation from this standard. And while many of these films depict a duplicitous and often deadly female character who leads to the downfall of the male protagonist, numerous film noir features contain no such individual, including *Crossfire* (1947), *In a Lonely Place* (1950), *On Dangerous Ground* (1951), *Shadow of a Doubt* (1943), and *Touch of Evil* (1958). Yet, while each of these films represents a departure from the norm, all are, nonetheless, film noir.

This gripping era of filmmaking is perhaps more passionately and extensively discussed than any other, particularly with regard to which films are actually considered to be film noir. Because of the era's widely encompassing denotation and a frequently subjective nature based more on tone and mood than setting, the classification of the films is sometime more a matter of personal opinion than irrefutable fact. Not every film with looming shadows on the wall, light filtering through window blinds, flashing neon signs, and stark shots staring down spiral staircases is film noir. Nor is every film that contains a double-crossing female, a relentless detective, or

a luckless, misguided family man. But most noirs contain some, if not all, of these elements.

Perhaps more than any other quality, however, it is the feeling that makes the film noir what it is—the atmosphere of hopelessness, the ambience of doom, the aura of pessimism and cynicism, greed and distrust. (Interestingly, as difficult as film noir is to define, one can glean an understanding of the period by examining the titles of the films themselves. A number of words are used repeatedly in film noir titles—examined collectively, they provide a simplistic, yet revealing and accurate reflection of the era's overall tone, including "fear," "dark," "night," "kill," "big," "city," "crime," "guilty," "strange," "lady," "kiss," "street," and "cry." Another effective indicator of the spirit of film noir comes from those features with one-word titles, such as *Desperate, Cornered, Pitfall, Conflict, Tension, Nightmare, Framed, Possessed, Convicted,* and *Caught*.)

"What does a dame like you want with a guy like me?"—Burt Lancaster in *Sorry, Wrong Number* (1948)

Bad Boys: The Actors of Film Noir shines a spotlight on the male characters who populated the films noirs of the 1940s and 1950s, and profiles the private and public lives of the actors who portrayed them. Some of the actors are such popular, well-known personages as Humphrey Bogart, James Cagney, Kirk Douglas, Burt Lancaster, Edward G. Robinson, and Robert Mitchum. Others are less familiar, particularly to today's audiences, including Gene Lockhart, Moroni Olsen, and Harold Vermilyea. This volume also includes an appendix that focuses on some of the era's lesser players, those who were frequently seen in the classic film noir features, but usually in only minor roles. These actors include Jay Adler, Whit Bissell, Harry Shannon, Art Smith, and Tito Vuolo.

Most of the actors in this book appeared in at least four films noirs during the 1940s and 1950s. The six exceptions to this criterion are those actors who were seldom seen in film noir features, but starred in some of the most noted offerings from the era: James Cagney in *White Heat* (1949), John Dall in *Gun Crazy* (1950), Fred MacMurray in *Double Indemnity* (1944), Ralph Meeker in *Kiss Me Deadly* (1955), Tom Neal in *Detour* (1945), and Clifton Webb in *Laura* (1944). Aside from these performers, I adhered strictly to my self-imposed criterion which, as it turned out, forced me to leave out such performers as Richard Basehart, Ward Bond, Jack Elam, Sam Jaffe, Lee Marvin, George Sanders, and James Whitmore.

Writing this book has been a labor of love and a journey of discovery. I have been a classic movie fan since childhood, but the realm of film noir has always been something special. Because it was necessary for me to view — at least once — each of the 240 films noirs discussed in this book, it was with sheer delight that I was introduced to such gems as *Desperate* (1947), *The Devil Thumbs a Ride* (1947), *Drive a Crooked Road* (1954), *The Enforcer* (1951), *The Hitch-Hiker* (1953), *Kiss the Blood Off My Hands* (1948), *The Mob* (1951), *New York Confidential* (1955), *Plunder Road* (1957), *Shakedown* (1950), *Ride the Pink Horse* (1947), and *Roadblock* (1951). It has also been a rewarding sojourn to delve into the off-screen lives of the actors who performed in these films. There were actors — including Lee J. Cobb, Richard Conte, and William Holden — whose talent I grew to cherish even more. There were performers whose personal struggles, triumphs, and sacrifices served to invoke a genuine admiration, including Dana Andrews, Raymond Burr, Jeff Corey, Kirk Douglas, J.C. Flippen, Lloyd Nolan, and William Talman. I learned about actors such as Steve Cochran, Wallace Ford, Robert Mitchum, and Tom Neal, whose personal experiences served to support the adage that truth is stranger than fiction. And there were those whom I encountered for the first time, including Fred Clark, Douglas Fowley, John Hoyt, and Regis Toomey. They have all become like old friends — instantly recognized, appreciated, and treasured.

It is with pleasure that I invite you now to proceed, with caution, into cinema's darkest milieu — a world peopled by wiseguys and gunsels, shysters and stoolies, heroes and heels — the bad boys of film noir.

THE ACTORS

——— LUTHER ADLER ———

"The next time you must indulge your hot, Spanish passion for dramatics, put on a uniform with polished boots and stomp around your wife's bedchamber. Do not attempt brilliant decisions."— Luther Adler in *Cornered* (1945)

Luther Adler had show business in his blood. Son of stage performer parents, he was also the brother of actress and coach Stella and actor Jay (who once labeled his sibling "the golden boy of the family"). Rather than being overshadowed by the fame of his kin, however, Luther Adler emerged as one of the most well-respected character actors of his time. Known mostly for his work on the Broadway stage, Adler was seen in fewer than 30 films, but he distinguished himself in five films from the noir era: *Cornered* (1945), *House of Strangers* (1949), *Kiss Tomorrow Goodbye* (1950), *D.O.A.* (1950), and *M* (1951).

Adler was born on May 4, 1903, in New York City, one of seven children of famed Yiddish theater pioneer Jacob Adler and his actress wife, Sarah. Adler made his stage debut at the young age of five, performing at Manhattan's Thalia Theatre in the Yiddish drama, *Schmendrick*, which starred his father. After receiving his schooling in New York and Chicago, Adler honed his acting craft performing in numerous plays for his father's company, The Yiddish Theatre Company, and while still in his teens, he toured with the troupe to London, Vienna, and South Africa.

Adler made his Broadway debut in 1923 in *Humoresque*, co-starring Laurette Taylor, and was later seen in *Money Talks* in 1925, *Monkey Business* and *We Americans* in 1926, *The Music Makers* in 1927, and *Street Scene* and *Red Dust* in 1929. And his reputation blossomed in 1932 when he joined the celebrated Group Theatre, appearing in such productions as *Night Over Taos*, *Success Story*, *Awake and Sing*, and *Alien Corn*, opposite Katherine Cornell. He performed with the Group Theatre throughout the 1930s, and earned rave reviews in 1937 for his portrayal of violinist-turned-boxer Joe Bonaparte in *Golden Boy*—famed drama critic Brooks Atkinson noted that Adler played "the part of the headlong fighter with the speed and energy of an open-field runner." During this period, the actor also continued working with his father's troupe — in 1936, he was seen with his entire family in *Millions*, a Yiddish adaptation of a German play.

Also in the late 1930s, Adler attracted the attention of 20th Century-Fox studio talent scouts, and was cast in his debut film, *Lancer Spy* (1937), starring Dolores Del Rio and George Sanders. The following year, Adler married actress Sylvia Sidney, and the couple later had a son, Jacob. But after less than a decade, in 1947, the marriage ended in divorce. He later remarried, this time to Julie Roche, to whom he remained married until his death. (Shortly after Adler's death in the mid-1980s, his son, Jacob, would die of amyotrophic lateral sclerosis, better known as Lou Gehrig's disease.)

Unfazed by Hollywood's charms, Adler returned to the Broadway stage after his brief film appearance, where he was seen in such productions as *Men in White* and *Paradise Lost*. He also toured in 1943 with then-wife Sylvia Sidney in *Jane Eyre*. By the mid-1940s, the actor was ready to give films another try, and he returned to the big screen in the first of his five film noir features, *Cornered* (1945). Starring Dick Powell, this tense manhunt drama focused on the efforts of Canadian airman Lawrence Gerard (Powell) to track down the Nazi collaborators who murdered his wife. Adler portrayed the small, but key role of Marcel Jarnac, the object of Powell's search. Jarnac, who is also being hunted by a group of expatriates, plans to effectively disappear by passing off a petty informant, Melchior Incza (Walter Slezak), as himself. Making his entrance near the film's end, Jarnac shoots Incza several times in the face and wryly remarks: "That face will be very difficult to recognize now." Jarnac also plans to murder Gerard, but the airman overtakes him and beats him to death. Despite his brief appearance on screen, Adler was applauded by critics, with Jim Henaghan of the *Los Angeles Examiner* writing that the actor "will thrill you with his splendid reading of a great, meaning speech," and the *New York Times'* critic labeling his performance "well done."

"I liked *Cornered*, although it wasn't a big role in the Hollywood interpretation of a big role," Adler said later. "You heard all about me from the other characters. Actually I had only a few minutes before the camera."

Another three years passed before Adler appeared before the camera again—in 1948, he was seen with Alan Ladd and Veronica Lake in *Saigon*, an adventure film set in the Orient. After the film's release, the actor explained his lengthy absence from the screen scene.

"The only reason I've waited so long between pictures is because I've been busy in New York," he said. "An actor goes where he has to work. It happened that I had signed for a show to go into rehearsal the moment I finished my first movie. So I didn't stick around Hollywood. And to be honest, nobody asked me. It's as simple as that."

Following this pronouncement, Adler continued to divide his time between coasts, busy with such stage productions as *A Flag is Born*, in which he starred as well as directed, and films with some of Hollywood's biggest names, including *The Loves of Carmen* (1948) with Rita Hayworth and Glenn Ford, *Wake of the Red Witch* (1949) with John Wayne, and his second film noir, *House of Strangers* (1949), starring Edward G. Robinson and Susan Hayward. The latter film told the story of Italian-American banker Gino Monetti (Robinson) and his four sons, petulantly ruthless Joe (Adler), weak and pliable Tony (Efrem Zimbalist, Jr.), dull-witted Pietro (Paul Valentine), and the favorite of the group, shrewd lawyer Max (Richard Conte). When Gino goes on trial for illegal banking practices, Max tries to bribe a juror to ensure his father's release, but he is betrayed by Joe and spends seven years in prison. Vowing revenge on his brothers after his release, Max later experiences a change of heart, but the jealous and embittered Joe continues to suspect his motives: "Who do you think you're talking to? You're no different than the old man," Joe tells his brother. "Pa never changed and neither will you. You've both got the same blood. Well, so have I. That's one thing you forgot." After ordering Pietro to pummel Max into near-unconsciousness, Joe then directs his brother to toss Max from a balcony to his death, but Pietro refuses, turning on Joe when he employs an oft-repeated putdown—"Dumbhead!"—that was coined by their father. Saving Joe from Pietro, Max leaves his quarreling siblings behind, joining his long-suffering girlfriend (Hayward) to make a new start. Among a cast of fine performances, Adler's Joe was a standout, and the actor earned mention from a number of critics, who noted his "able" and "effective" portrayal.

Adler's four films in 1950 included two noirs, *Kiss Tomorrow Goodbye* and *D.O.A.* In the former, the actor portrayed Keith "Cherokee" Mandon, a shyster lawyer who teams with escaped convict Ralph Cotter (James Cagney) to blackmail a pair of crooked cops. Described by one character as an "evil man," Mandon not only supervises the successful blackmailing scheme, but he also secures a legal gun permit for Cotter and arranges for his lengthy prison record to be expunged. Mandon backs out of the lucrative arrangement, however, when Cotter ignores his advice, romancing and later marrying the daughter of a high-powered official. ("I can protect myself even if it means throwing you to the wolves," Mandon tells Cotter, "and believe me, after the way you've behaved in this matter, nothing would give me greater pleasure.") Ironically, it is not through the law that Cotter's schemes come to an end, but at the hands of his old girlfriend, Holiday (Barbara Payton), who grimly tells him to "kiss tomorrow goodbye" before she guns him down.

The actor's second noir of the year, *D.O.A.*, told the fast-paced story of accountant Frank Bigelow (Edmond O'Brien), who learns that he has been poisoned and has only days to live. Determined to find the persons responsible for his demise, Bigelow ultimately tracks down a series of individuals involved with the crime, including a local racketeer, Majak (Adler), whose connection centered on the purchase of a stolen shipment of iridium. Refined and soft-spoken, with a benevolent veneer, Majak apologetically informs Bigelow that he will have to kill him: "Under other circumstances, you could go home … but now, you present a problem," Majak says. "You know I can go to jail for 10 years for this little business? At my age, that's my life — that means my entire life. With my life, I do

not take chances. I am sorry, believe me. Goodbye, Mr. Bigelow — and forgive me." Bigelow manages to escape from Majak's psychotic gunman, however, and later tracks down the man who poisoned him, gunning him down and reporting the entire incident to police before he himself dies.

Adler earned praise for both of his 1950 noirs; of his performance in *Kiss Tomorrow Goodbye*, he was labeled "tops" by Edwin Schallert of the *Los Angeles Times*, and after the release of *D.O.A.*, Earl H. Donovan of the *Los Angeles Examiner* wrote: "As chief menace, Luther Adler is superlative, but when isn't he?" The actor remained in the realm of film noir the following year, appearing in his final offering from the era, *M* (1951). A remake of Fritz Lang's 1931 hit starring Peter Lorre, this grim feature focused on the simultaneous efforts of police and a wide-reaching group of organized criminals to find a serial murderer of young girls. Adler portrayed Dan Langley, an alcoholic ex-lawyer who provides legal advice to the head of the gang, Marshall

(Martin Gabel). The hoods get the jump on police in finding the hood, cornering him in a parking garage where he is surrounded by a mob of angry citizens. Marshall, who wants to take credit for the capture in order to divert the attention of police from his own nefarious activities, turns to Langley to stall the bloodthirsty crowd, telling him to "talk and keep talking until the press gets here." But when Langley first addresses the evils of society and later blames Marshall for his own descent into alcoholism and corruption, Marshall guns him down, just as police arrive to cart the killer off to prison. Although most critics focused their praise on David Wayne's outstanding performance as the child-killer, Adler was singled out by Philip K. Scheuer of the *Los Angeles Times*, who wrote that the actor was "theatrically triumphant as the drink-sodden attorney."

Throughout the remainder of the decade, Adler stayed busy in such films as *The Desert Fox* (1951), in which he was seen in a memorable cameo as Adolph Hitler; *The Tall Texan* (1953), a mediocre western starring Lloyd Bridges and Lee J. Cobb; *The Girl in the Red Velvet Swing* (1955), which depicted the celebrated 1906 murder of playboy-architect Stanford White; and *The Last Angry Man* (1959), a first-rate drama that marked Paul Muni's return to film after a 13-year absence. Adler was also seen in such stage productions as *Tovarich* in 1952 and *The Merchant of Venice* in 1953, and *A Month in the Country* in 1956; directed the stage productions of *Angel Street* and *A View From the Bridge*; and appeared in a number of television series including *The United States Steel Hour*, *Naked City*, *Westinghouse Desilu Playhouse*, *The Untouchables*, and *The Twilight Zone*.

After *The Last Angry Man*, Adler focused most of his attention on his stage career, with notable performances in the 1964 production of Paddy Chayevsky's *The Passion of Josef D*, and the following year in *Fiddler on the Roof*, in which he replaced star Zero Mostel. He returned to films in 1966 in *Cast a Giant Shadow*, an overblown biopic of World War II hero Col. David "Mickey" Marcus, and two

years later was seen in *The Brotherhood*, a Mafia-themed feature that bombed at the box office despite fine performances from Adler, Kirk Douglas, and Alex Cord.

Now in his 70s, Adler continued to appear in films during the next decade — the best of these were *Murf the Surf* (1974), an offbeat crime drama starring Robert Conrad, and *The Man in the Glass Booth* (1975), which focused on the exploits of Nazi war criminal Adolph Eichmann. Less successful were such features as *Crazy Joe* (1974), a weak biography of Mafia mobster Joe Gallo; *Voyage of the Damned* (1976), which was notable primarily for its spate of cameos from such veterans as Orson Welles, James Mason, Julie Harris, Jose Ferrer, and Wendy Hiller; and *Mean Johnny Barrows* (1976), directed and produced by actor Fred Williamson. Adler's last film appearance was in the well-received Paul Newman starrer, *Absence of Malice* (1981), in which he played the star's mobster uncle.

On December 8, 1984, at the age of 81, Luther Adler died at his home in Kutztown, Pennsylvania. After his death, a letter signed by such cinematic luminaries as Marlon Brando, Paul Newman, and Alexander Scourby appeared in the *New York Times*, praising Adler's accomplishments in film and on stage.

"Throughout his long career he gave a glamour, a touch of something larger than life, to every part he played," the letter read. "The American public knew him for what he was — not an idol of the moment, but an actor of enduring value. He was respected and loved by his colleagues and by the people. He has done his work. He has had his time. He will never be forgotten as long as there are actors to honor his memory."

Film Noir Filmography

Cornered. Director: Edward Dmytryk. Producer: Adrian Scott. Running time: 102 minutes. Released by RKO, December 25, 1945. Cast: Dick Powell, Walter Slezak, Micheline Cheirel, Nina Vale, Morris Carnovsky, Edgar Barrier, Steven Geray, Jack La Rue, Luther Adler, Gregory Gay.

House of Strangers. Director: Joseph L. Mankiewicz. Producer: Sol C. Siegel. Running time: 101 minutes. Released by 20th Century-Fox, July 1, 1949. Cast: Edward G. Robinson, Susan Hayward, Richard Conte, Luther Adler, Paul Valentine, Efrem Zimbalist, Jr., Debra Paget, Hope Emerson, Esther Minciotti, Diana Douglas, Tito Vuolo, Albert Morin, Sid Tomack, Thomas Henry Brown, David Wolfe, John Kellogg, Ann Morrison, Dolores Parker.

Kiss Tomorrow Goodbye. Director: Gordon Douglas. Producer: William Cagney. Running time: 102 minutes. Released by Warner Bros., August 4, 1950. Cast: James Cagney, Barbara Payton, Helena Carter, Ward Bond, Luther Adler, Barton Mac-Lane, Steve Brodie, Rhys Williams, Herbert Heyes, John Litel, William Frawley, Robert Karnes, Kenneth Tobey, Dan Riss, Frank Reicher, John Halloran, Neville Brand.

D.O.A. Director: Rudolph Mate. Producer: Harry M. Popkin. Running time: 83 minutes. Released by United Artists, April 30, 1950. Cast: Edmond O'Brien, Pamela Britton, Luther Adler, Beverly Campbell, Lynn Baggett, William Ching, Henry Hart, Neville Brand, Laurette Luez, Jess Kirkpatrick, Cay Forrester, Virginia Lee, Michael Ross.

M. Director: Joseph Losey. Producer: Seymour Nebenzal. Running time 87 minutes. Released by Columbia, June 10, 1951. Cast: David Wayne, Howard Da Silva, Martin Gabel, Luther Adler, Steve Brodie, Glenn Anders, Norman Lloyd, Walter Burke, Raymond Burr.

References

Biography of Luther Adler. Paramount Studios, December 1946.

Biography of Luther Adler. Paramount Studios, circa 1948.

Biography of Luther Adler. American Film Theatre, circa 1975.

Letter to the Editor. *New York Times*, March 10, 1985.

"Luther Adler, Stage & Film Actor, a Group Theater Founder, Dies." *Variety*, December 12, 1984.

"Luther Adler, Actor Who Starred in 'Fiddler.'" *New York Times*, December 10, 1984.

Obituary. *The Hollywood Reporter*, December 14, 1984.

Obituary. *Variety*, December 11, 1984.

LEON AMES

"It's you or her. If you didn't have anything to do with killing Nick Smith, you'd better sign this because if you don't, I'll know and so will the judge. And so will the jury. And so will that guy that gives you the business in the poison gas chamber in San Quentin. And so will the boys who bury you out there alongside all the others who were too dumb to make a deal while they still had a chance to save their necks."—Leon Ames in ***The Postman Always Rings Twice*** (1946)

More likely to be seen portraying a wise and sympathetic paternal figure or upstanding military leader, Leon Ames proved during the era of film noir that he could be as dark and menacing as the toughest villain. In two first-rate noirs, *The Postman Always Rings Twice* (1946) and *Angel Face* (1953), he portrayed calculating attorneys who displayed a facade of compassion that masked an implacable core of steel. He was also a memorable contributor to three additional films from the era: *Lady in the Lake* (1947), *The Velvet Touch* (1948), and *Scene of the Crime* (1949).

Ames was born Leon Wycoff on January 20, 1903, in Portland, Indiana, son of Russian immigrants Charles Elmer Wycoff, a furniture manufacturer and farmer, and his wife, Cora Alice deMasse. Educated in the elementary schools of neighboring Logansport, Fowler, and Delphi, Indiana, Wycoff graduated from Delphi High School and held a series of jobs ranging from lumberjack to store detective. Following a stint with the National Guard, the young man decided to indulge his lifelong interest in acting and set out for New York, but the closest he came to Broadway was selling shoes on 42nd Street and visiting theatrical agencies during his lunch hours. His determination finally paid off in 1925 when he landed a job with the Charles K. Champlin Players in Lansford, Pennsylvania.

"I told all kinds of lies about my experience and he hired me at $40 a week. I was a 'general business man,' that is, I played small character roles," the actor explained in a 1961 interview. "[Champlin] wanted me to stay all night and drive to Lansford with him the next morning, but I told him I had to go back to New York that night. I wanted to talk to the only actors I knew — two chorus boys in Queen High."

Usually cast as an older man, Wycoff began appearing in a new play each week, including *She Got What She Wanted*, *East is West*, and *Twin Beds*, and later was cast for the road companies of *The Cat and the Canary*, *Love 'em and Leave 'em*, *Broadway*, and *Tomorrow and Tomorrow*. When the latter production played in Los Angeles, the actor was selected from the cast to portray a detective in his film debut, *The Murders in the Rue Morgue* (1932), in which he was credited as Leon Waycoff. He remained in Hollywood for three more years, playing small roles in a series of all-but-forgotten films. Surpassing the actor's appearances on-screen, however, were his activities behind the scenes. In 1933,

he joined with 18 fellow actors, including James Gleason, Alan Mowbray, Boris Karloff, C. Aubrey Smith, and Charles Starrett and, in a secret meeting, formed the Screen Actors Guild (SAG), a union designed to protect the rights of actors in Hollywood. The actor would go on to serve for more than 30 years on the Guild's board of directors, as national president from 1957 to 1958, and as the first president emeritus. At the time that the SAG was established, Ames' Guild membership card number was 15; as of this writing, the group's membership numbered more than 98,000.

Meanwhile, the actor returned to the stage in 1934 to tour in *Tobacco Road* with Henry Hull, then returned to the screen for a small roles in *Strangers All* (1935), the first film in which he was billed as Leon Ames, and *Reckless* (1935), starring Jean Harlow. Back in New York, Ames made his Broadway debut in 1936 in *Bright Honor* which, although panned by critics, earned favorable notices for the actor.

For the next several years, Ames continued to divide his talents between New York and Hollywood, appearing in such stage productions as *The Land Is Bright* and *Guest in the House*, and films including *Murder in Greenwich Village* (1937), a weak mystery starring Richard Arlen and Fay Wray; *Charlie Chan on Broadway* (1937), an above-average entry in the long-running series; *Suez* (1938), a lavish historical romance featuring the popular team of Tyrone Power and Loretta Young; and *The Mysterious Mr. Moto* (1938), the second of eight films in the series starring Peter Lorre.

Off screen, Ames managed to squeeze romance into his increasingly hectic performing schedule; in 1937, he had met actress Christine Gossett on a Hollywood soundstage. Married on June 25, 1938, the two welcomed a daughter, Shelley, on October 26, 1940, and a son, Leon, Jr., on May 12, 1943, and remained together until Ames' death 55 years later.

With the advent of the 1940s, Ames was seen in feature films of varying quality, including *No Greater Sin* (1941), a turgid drama about the evils of syphilis; *Ellery Queen and the Murder Ring* (1941), another lackluster entry in the Columbia Studios series; and *The Iron Major* (1943), a well-done biopic starring Pat O'Brien as Frank Cavanaugh, hero of World War I and successful football coach at Dartmouth, Fordham and other colleges.

While appearing in a tour of *Silk Hat Harry* in 1943, Ames inked a seven-year contract with MGM, appearing the following year as Alonzo Smith, the bewildered patriarch in the popular musical *Meet Me in St. Louis* (1944), starring Judy Garland and Margaret O'Brien. The actor would later offer a half-joking comment about child performers, saying that they were "all as sweet as sugar until the director says 'action.' And then they'll cut your throat with a dull saw." He was next seen in such winners as *Twelve Seconds Over Tokyo* (1944), a box-office hit starring Van Johnson; *The Thin Man Goes Home* (1944), the fifth film in the William Powell–Myrna Loy series; *Weekend at the Waldorf* (1945), a remake of *Grand Hotel* (1932) with an all-star cast that included Lana Turner, Van Johnson, Ginger Rogers, and Walter Pidgeon; *Anchors Aweigh* (1945), an entertaining musical featuring Frank Sinatra and Gene Kelly; and *They Were Expendable* (1945), a John Ford–directed epic about torpedo boat crews during World War II. He was also seen in his initial foray into film noir, *The Postman Always Rings Twice* (1946).

Directed by Tay Garnett, *Postman* starred Lana Turner as the beautiful but unhappily married Cora Smith, who uses her charms to coax a drifter, Frank Chambers (John Garfield), into killing her middle-aged spouse (Cecil Kellaway). After botching a clumsy first attempt, Cora and Frank succeed in their murderous plan, but they are instantly suspected of the crime, and Frank is pressured into signing a confession against his lover. Frank is ultimately set free and Cora receives a suspended sentence for manslaughter, but although they later marry, Frank's betrayal has left Cora bitter and vengeful. Near the film's end, Frank and Cora realize their love for each other, but it is too late — a tragic car accident leaves Cora dead and Frank sentenced to the gas chamber for her murder.

In a supporting role, Ames portrayed Kyle Sackett, the cunningly ruthless district attorney who corners Frank after his arrest, soothingly calling him "laddie," and manipulating him into turning on Cora. ("Maybe you didn't have anything to do with it," Sackett tells him. "Maybe *she* did it. Listen, laddie, she *did* do it.") In this departure from most of his roles, Ames was at once savvy, devious, and perceptive, and earned praise from several critics, including *Film Daily*'s reviewer, who said he "assists the stars capitally," and the critic for *The Hollywood Review*, who wrote that Ames "provide[d] mordant humor in [his] sharp characterization."

Ames remained in the realm of noir the following year, with a featured role in *Lady in the Lake* (1947), starring and directed by Robert Montgomery in the unusual "camera I" method. With the camera providing Montgomery's point of view, ads touting the film gleefully announced: "YOU accept an invitation to a blonde's apartment! YOU get socked in the jaw by a murder suspect!"

In this complex noir, Ames is Derace Kingsby, president of Kingsby Publications, which churns out such popular rags as "Lurid Detective" and "Murder Masterpieces." When Kingsby's wife, Crystal (described by one character as "a liar, a cheat, and a thief") turns up missing, his attractive assistant, Adrienne Fromsett (Audrey Totter) hires private detective Philip Marlowe (Montgomery). Adrienne's motives are less than honorable, however — she has designs on Kingsby herself — but when she suggests that his wife may have been involved in the murder of a local gigolo, Kingsby makes it clear where his loyalties lie: "If you think you're going to harm Crystal, you're very much mistaken," he tells Adrienne. "And please understand this clearly: if I've ever said anything endearing to you, Miss Fromsett, it was because I was lonely. And I don't ever intend to say anything endearing to you again. Now or any time." In addition to the gigolo's killing, Marlowe's investigation unearths two additional murders — including

Kingsby's wife, who is the luckless "lady in the lake" of the film's title. Despite obstacles that include a frame-up for drunken driving, Marlowe ultimately learns that the killer is a neurotic former nurse (Jayne Meadows) — but she gets knocked off herself in the film's climax by her embittered ex-lover (Lloyd Nolan). All ends well for Marlowe, however, who winds up in a final clinch with Adrienne Fromsett.

The release of *Lady in the Lake* found many moviegoers disappointed at the few glimpses they were given of Robert Montgomery, but critics were impressed with the film's "seeing eye" camera — in *Time* magazine, the film was labeled "unusual, effective and clever," and the critic for *Variety* raved that the subjective point of view transformed "what otherwise would have been a fair whodunit into socko screen fare."

In the next two years, Ames added to his reputation as cinema's favorite father figure, portraying Elizabeth Taylor's dad in *A Date with Judy* (1948), and the patriarch of the March family in *Little Women* (1949). He countered these features, however, with a pair of appearances on the dark side of the screen in *The Velvet Touch* (1948) and *Scene of the Crime* (1949). In the first of the two, Ames portrayed domineering Broadway producer Gordon Dunning, whose outlook on life is revealed early on when he pronounces, "Love — that's a business proposition. Something you sell over the footlights and the suckers eat it up. Success and money — that's what rules the world." As the film opens, Gordon is in the midst of a heated argument with his protégée, famed stage comedienne Valerie Stanton (Rosalind Russell), whose career he has successfully guided for the last 10 years. When Valerie announces her plan to abandon her lucrative teaming with Gordon in favor of a starring role in a drama, Gordon threatens to expose their "more than professional" relationship to Valerie's fiancé, and in a fit of anger, Valerie bludgeons Gordon to death. Police, however, suspect that the murderer is Gordon's ex-lover, actress Marion Webster (Claire Trevor), who was found

in a state of shock next to Gordon's body. When the distraught Marion later commits suicide, Valerie appears to be in the clear, but she grows increasingly tortured by her conscience, as well as by the presence of a crafty homicide detective, Capt. Danbury (Sidney Greenstreet). On the opening night of her dramatic play, Valerie is informed by the detective that the case has been closed, but she writes a note of confession and, following an acclaimed performance, prepares to give herself over to authorities.

Produced by Independent Artists, the film company established by Rosalind Russell and her husband, Frederick Brisson, *The Velvet Touch* was met with mixed reviews from critics. On the positive side, the reviewer for *Variety* found that the film had "a little of everything that goes to make up entertainment," and *The Hollywood Reporter*'s critic wrote that it was "an unusual and excellent mystery melodrama." But the East coast critics were less impressed with the feature, with the *New York Times*' reviewer judging that the story was "not very fetching," and the critic from *The New Yorker* noting the film's "several dreary scenes." Ames, however, was favorably mentioned in several notices; the critic for *Variety* wrote that he "scores soundly," and the review in *The Hollywood Reporter* labeled him as "ideally cast."

In his next noir, *Scene of the Crime*, Ames was seen as A.C. Forster, the shrewd and level-headed captain of detectives who is among the first to arrive on the scene where an off-duty officer has been killed. To head up the investigation into the killing, Forster taps Mike Conovan (Van Johnson), a dedicated cop known for his passion for the job. ("Grab on to that temper," Forster admonishes Conovan in one scene. "You think being mad makes you a better detective?") Conovan's investigation into the crime is not an easy one — he is injured in an attempted hit on his life, and later caves to pressures from his wife (Arlene Dahl) to quit the force. But when another cop takes his place and winds up dead, Conovan returns to the force, cozying up to a nightclub singer (Gloria DeHaven) who inadvertently leads him to the killer of the two officers. A box-office hit — due in large part to the star power of Van Johnson — *Scene of the Crime* was noted primarily by critics for its documentary style and view into the inner-workings of the mob; in a typical review, the *New York Times'* Bosley Crowther wrote, "We've been quickly treated to a refresher course in the detection of crime, a glossary of underworld lingo, and a couple of odes to the nobility of cops."

After appearances in such features as *The Skipper Surprised His Wife* (1950), a lightweight domestic comedy with Robert Walker and Jan Sterling; *Dial 1119* (1950), a taut thriller starring Marshall Thompson; and *It's a Big Country* (1951), a box-office flop despite its massive, all-star cast, Ames' contract with MGM ended. His first film as a freelancer was his final film noir, the gripping *Angel Face* (1953), starring Robert Mitchum and Jean Simmons. Here, Ames portrayed Fred Barrett, a cunning defense attorney who defends Diane Tremayne (Simmons) and her lover, Frank (Mitchum) when they are charged with the murder of her father and stepmother. As it turns out, Diane alone was responsible, but Barrett pulls out all the stops in defending the pair, even suggesting that they get married in order to play on the sympathies of the jury. ("It's very simple — all the world loves a lover," Barrett says. "Juries are no exception.") After Barrett wins an acquittal, Frank announces his plans to leave his new wife, but the "Angel Face" has other ideas — offering to drive her spouse to the bus station, she throws the car in reverse, sending the couple over the cliff to their deaths. Upon its release, *Angel Face* earned mixed reviews, with one critic terming it "a study in morbid depravity," and another calling it "an exasperating blend of genuine talent, occasional perceptiveness, and turgid psychological claptrap." Critics were divided in their opinions of Ames as well; the reviewer for the *New York Times* found him "unduly roguish and altruistic," but he was hailed as "quite magnificent" in the *Hollywood Citizen-News*, and Philip K. Scheuer wrote in the *New York Times* that the actor

was "a suave, conniving shyster and a disgrace to the bar (though Ames makes him understandable)."

Ames was only seen in a handful of films during the remainder of the decade, including *By the Light of the Silvery Moon* (1953), in which he played Doris Day's father; *Sabre Jet* (1953), a routine melodrama starring Robert Stack; and *Peyton Place* (1957), a box-office smash based on the best-selling novel by Grace Metalious. Instead, he divided his talents between the stage and the small screen, portraying Clarence Day, Sr., in the television series *Life with Father*, playing a featured role in a road tour in *The Moon Is Blue* in 1952, and appearing on Broadway in 1958 in the short-lived comedy, *Howie*. Aside from performing, his energies were focused on his duties as national president of the Screen Actors Guild, member of the board of directors of the Motion Picture Health and Welfare Fund, and as honorary mayor, for two terms, of Studio City, California. The actor also owned and operated a profitable Ford franchise that he'd launched in 1945 with a single Studio City dealership and expanded into one of the largest automobile franchises in the west.

"Actors are not artists with their heads in the clouds," Ames once said. "They have as much common sense and business acumen as anyone. They can become as expert in reading a financial statement as in reading a script."

During the 1960s, Ames played another television patriarch, this time on *Father of the Bride*, which played for one season on CBS, and from 1963 to 1965, portrayed Gordon Kirkwood, the neighbor of Mr. Ed's owner, Wilbur Post. He was also seen in guest spots on such series as *The Beverly Hillbillies*, *My Three Sons*, *The Virginian*, and *Bewitched*, and in several family-oriented feature films from the Disney Studios, including *The Absent-Minded Professor* (1961), *Son of Flubber* (1963), *The Misadventures of Merlin Jones* (1964), and *The Monkey's Uncle* (1965).

In the midst of Ames' busy performing schedule, the actor experienced a bizarre, real-life encounter that, in terms of sheer drama, eclipsed the plot of any of his movies. The

Jean Simmons and Leon Ames in *Angel Face* (1953).

incident began during the breakfast hour on February 12, 1964, when 21-year-old Lynn Wayne Benner rang the doorbell at Ames' home, forced his way inside, and held Ames and his wife, Christine, at gunpoint. Aware of Ames' thriving automobile dealerships, Benner, an unemployed mechanic and father of three, demanded $50,000 from the actor, who instructed a business associate to withdraw the money from the bank and bring it to the home. Meanwhile, a houseguest visiting the Ames, Herbert F. Baumgarteker, was held captive as well.

"He drank six cups of coffee and he smoked all my cigarettes," Ames later told the press. "[And my] bulldog just sat there licking the guy's hands."

When the manager of Ames' Encino dealership, Ralph Williams, arrived with the money, Benner reportedly forced Williams to bind Ames' wrists, feet, and mouth with surgical tape, then locked Williams and Baumbarteker in the trunk of Ames' car and drove off in his own car, with Christine Ames as a hostage. Ten minutes later, Benner was stopped by police, who had been alerted by a bank manager.

"I was frightened," Christine Ames said. "When he saw the police closing in, he pushed the gun into my side. I said, 'Please don't do that.' He dropped it and put his hands up. He was very handsome. He didn't look like the type at all. I told him so."

Benner later pleaded guilty to the robbery-kidnapping and was sentenced to life in prison. His probation report indicated that Ames and his wife had promised to communicate with Benner in prison "in order to encourage him to become a useful citizen."

Meanwhile, following a five-year absence

from films, Ames returned to the screen in *On a Clear Day You Can See Forever* (1970), starring Barbra Streisand, and *Tora! Tora! Tora!* (1970), a wartime actioner whose massive cast included Joseph Cotten, Martin Balsam, Jason Robards, James Whitmore, E.G. Marshall, Neville Brand, and George Macready. He also appeared in *Hammersmith Is Out* (1972), a tiresome Elizabeth Taylor-Richard Burton vehicle; *The Meal* (1975), an interesting character study set during a dinner party; *Just You and Me, Kid* (1979), an unfunny comedy starring George Burns and Brooke Shields; *Peggy Sue Got Married* (1986), a box-office hit in which Ames portrayed the deceased grandfather of the title character; and the actor's final film, *Jake Speed* (1986), a mediocre comedy-adventure featuring Ames, fittingly, as "Pop."

After suffering a stroke in the early 1990s, Ames was admitted to a rest home in Laguna Beach, California, but a second, massive stroke on October 12, 1993, resulted in the actor's death. At the age of 91, he had been the last surviving member of the 19 founders of the Screen Actors Guild.

One of Hollywood's most enduring, beloved, and respected performers, Leon Ames demonstrated his versatility in countless roles on stage and television, and in more than 100 films, creating a legacy that leaves no doubt regarding his talent and durability. Looking back at his career, the actor himself once acknowledged his good fortune and expressed appreciation for both his personal life and his professional accomplishments.

"I have never reached stardom, but what could I ask for, beyond what I have?" he said. "I get good roles—as many as I can take. I have a home, a family, happiness, and security.

"Is anything better?"

Film Noir Filmography

The Postman Always Rings Twice. Director: Tay Garnett. Producer: Carey Wilson. Running time: 113 minutes. Released by MGM, May 2, 1946. Cast: Lana Turner, John Garfield, Cecil Kellaway, Hume Cronyn, Leon Ames, Audrey Totter, Alan Reed.

Lady in the Lake. Director: Robert Montgomery. Producer: George Haight. Running time: 105 minutes. Released by MGM, January 23, 1947. Cast: Robert Montgomery, Lloyd Nolan, Audrey Totter, Tom Tully, Leon Ames, Jayne Meadows, Morris Ankrum, Lila Leeds, Richard Simmons.

The Velvet Touch. Director: John Gage. Producer: Frederick Brisson. Running time: 97 minutes. Released by RKO, 1948. Cast: Rosalind Russell, Leo Genn, Claire Trevor, Leon Ames, Frank McHugh, Walter Kingsford, Dan Tobin, Lex Barker, Nydia Westman, Theresa Harris, Irving Bacon, Esther Howard, Harry Hayden, Walter Erwin, Martha Hyer, Michael St. Angel, Louis Mason, James Flavin, Charles McAvoy, Dan Foster, Bess Flowers, Jim Drum, Allan Ray, Bill Wallace, Russell Hicks, James Todd, Joyce Arling, Ida Schumaker, Phillip Barnes, Bessie Wade.

Scene of the Crime. Director: Roy Rowland. Producer: Harry Rapf. Released by MGM, July 28, 1949. Running time: 94 minutes. Cast: Van Johnson, Gloria DeHaven, Tom Drake, Arlene Dahl, Leon Ames, John McIntire, Norman Lloyd, Donald Woods, Richard Benedict, Anthony Caruso, Tom Powers, Jerome Cowan.

Angel Face. Director and Producer: Otto Preminger. Running time: 91 minutes. Released by RKO, February 2, 1953. Cast: Robert Mitchum, Jean Simmons, Mona Freeman, Herbert Marshall, Leon Ames, Barbara O'Neil, Kenneth Tobey, Raymond Greenleaf.

References

"Ames Kidnaper Sentenced to Life in Prison." *Los Angeles Times*, May 1, 1964.

"Ames Kidnap Suspect Admits Armed Holdups." *Los Angeles Times*, February 14, 1964.

"Ames, Past Prexy, Anti SAG Merger." *Variety*, April 14, 1982.

"Ames Wins Honor SAG Denies Reagan." *Variety*, February 4, 1981.

"Film-Television Fund Honor for Leon Ames." *Variety*, May 20, 1986.

Gehman, Richard. "The World's Luckiest 'Father.'" *TV Guide*, May 19, 1962.

Greene, Patterson. "Ames Refuses 'Dirty' Plays." *Los Angeles Examiner*, September 2, 1956.

Greenletter, Horace. "Big Business Nothing New to Actor." *Los Angeles Daily News*, October 21, 1952.

Grimes, William. "Leon Ames, Actor and Unionist, 91; Roles in 100 Films." *New York Times*, October 15, 1993.

"Guilty Plea in Actor Ames Kidnap." *Los Angeles Herald-Examiner*, March 25, 1964.

"Hail Ames, Not Reagan." *Variety*, March 21, 1979.

Hoaglin, Jess L. "The Face Is Familiar." *Hollywood Studio Magazine*, August 1972.

Holbrook, Walter. "It Has Not Been Easy Sledding, But Ames at Last Has Arrived." *New York Herald-Tribune*, March 17, 1940.

"Leon Ames Opens New Ford Agency." *Los Angeles Times,* February 15, 1968.

Obituary. *Variety*, October 25, 1993.

Oliver, Myrna. "Leon Ames; Last Surviving Screen Actors Guild Founder." *Los Angeles Times*, October 14, 1993.

Palmer, Zuma. "Ames Refused New Series Until

'Father of the Bride' Came Along." *Hollywood Citizen-News*, September 11, 1961.

_____. "Repertory Greatest Training for Acting, Leon Ames Believes." *Hollywood Citizen-News.* September 12, 1961.

"Parents of Three Held in Kidnapping." *Los Angeles Herald-Examiner*, February 13, 1964.

"Screen Actors to Install Leon Ames." *Los Angeles Times*, November 15, 1957.

Toy, Steve. "Ames Turning Tables; Seeking Indie Candidates For SAG Board." *Variety*, September 4, 1974.

Trimborn, Harry. "Wife of Leon Ames Kidnapped, Rescued." *Los Angeles Times*, February 13, 1964.

DANA ANDREWS

"I got everything by talking fast in a world that goes for talking. And ended up with exactly nothing."— Dana Andrews in *Fallen Angel* (1945)

Ambitious and determined, candid and committed, Dana Andrews led a life comprised of the stuff from which movies were made. The legend of his start in pictures reads more like fiction than fact, and while he enjoyed great success as an actor, behind the scenes he battled alcoholism and suffered through the tragic deaths of both his first wife and the oldest of his four children. Still, in his later years, he emerged triumphant, launching a second career as a real estate mogul, winning the battle of the bottle, and becoming an outspoken champion against drunk driving as well as a respected advocate on the behalf of his fellow actors. With acclaimed performances to his credit in such first-rate features as *The Ox-Bow Incident* (1943) and *The Best Years of Our Lives*, Andrews also starred in six films from the noir era: *Laura* (1944), *Fallen Angel* (1945), *Where the Sidewalk Ends* (1950), *Edge of Doom* (1950), *While the City Sleeps* (1956), and *Beyond a Reasonable Doubt* (1956).

Born on January 1, 1909 (some sources say 1912), Carver Dana Andrews was the third of nine children of Rev. Charles Forrest Andrews, a Baptist minister, and his wife, Annis Speed — one of his siblings would grow up to be actor Steve Forrest. His father's ministerial duties caused frequent relocations; shortly after his birth, Andrews' family moved from his birthplace in Collins, Mississippi, to Louisville, Kentucky, and later to several cities throughout the state of Texas, including San Antonio, Uvalde, and Huntsville, where Andrews graduated in 1926 from Huntsville High School. Enrolling in Sam Houston Teachers College in Huntsville as a business administration major, Andrews got his first taste of performing when he appeared in two dramas there, but he left school in 1929 and became a "jack of all trades," working in a series of jobs that included working as an accountant for the Gulf Oil Corporation in Austin, Texas, and serving as publicity man for a movie theater. It was during the latter job that Andrews, as he claimed, "got bitten by the acting bug."

"I doubled inside the theater at night — we had a sound film, *Wings* ... I had to watch the picture all the way through the run," the actor said in a 1945 interview with columnist Hedda Hopper. "I got so I knew the story by heart, so I concentrated on the actors. Just to entertain myself, I'd reconstruct how they played the parts and imagine how I'd do it.

That's when I began to feel I had acting talent. Since being fired from a job, or quitting one, never bothered me, I just took my hat and started for Hollywood."

Hitchhiking his way west, the young man ended up in Van Nuys, California, landing a job pumping gas and signing on with the Van Nuys Amateur Theater, where he met his first wife, Janet Murray. Married in 1932, the couple had a son, David Curran Andrews, but in 1935, Janet was suddenly stricken with pneumonia, and died three days after contracting the illness.

Meanwhile, according to legend, Andrews borrowed money from friends in order to finance voice lessons, but a local agent reportedly advised him, "Singers can be had for two bits a dozen — learn to act!" Andrews took the recommendation to heart and was accepted at the famed Pasadena Community Playhouse, making his first stage appearance there as a spear carrier in a Shakespearean drama. He also dropped his surname and became professionally known as Dana Andrews. Two years later, while appearing with Florence Bates in *Oh Evening Star* at the Pasadena Playhouse, Andrews was spotted by a talent scout for Samuel Goldwyn and was signed to a contract.

"I was so excited that I told all of my friends of my good luck," Andrews later recalled. "But I never made a movie and I had the feeling they thought I wasn't telling the truth. I was plenty embarrassed."

Although Andrews' career appeared to be at a virtual standstill, his personal life was not. While working at the Pasadena Playhouse, he met actress Mary Todd, and the two married on November 17, 1939. Todd immediately abandoned her budding career, and the couple went on to have three children, Kathryn in 1942, Stephen in 1944, and Susan in 1948.

Career-wise, things began looking up for Andrews when he was cast in a minor role in a top-notch western, *The Westerner* (1940), produced by Sam Goldwyn, directed by William Wyler, and starring Gary Cooper. Andrews later recalled with amusement the impact of his appearance in the film.

"Probably my biggest 'sheer chance' thing happened right down there on 44th Street [in New York]," the actor said. "I had just made my first movie [and] they put up a huge sign — 'The Westerner,' it said, 'starring Gary Cooper and Dana Andrews.' I had exactly four lines in the picture. Nobody had ever heard of me. But the publicity department had done that for all the billboards. They thought Dana was a girl's name, and was the girl in the picture, and that it looked more exciting to have Cooper and a girl. If I'd used my real first name, Carver, maybe I'd never have made it."

After *The Westerner*, Sam Goldwyn sold half of Andrews' contract to 20th Century-Fox — according to Andrews, Goldwyn did not want to pay him a large salary, and opted to "share" him with Fox, which promptly cast him in *Sailor's Lady* (1940), a programmer starring Nancy Kelly and Jon Hall; *Lucky Cisco Kid* (1940), with Cesar Romero in the title role; *Tobacco Road* (1941), the first of five films in which he would appear with Gene Tierney; and *Swamp Water* (1941), director Jean Renoir's first American film and one of Andrews' favorites. During the next three years, Andrews stayed busy, splitting his time between such Goldwyn vehicles as *Ball of Fire* (1941), where he portrayed the gangster boyfriend of Barbara Stanwyck, and features at Fox including *Crash Dive* (1943), a tribute to the submarine service, and *The Ox-Bow Incident* (1943), in which Andrews was featured as one of three men condemned to death by a vigilante mob for a crime they didn't commit. Although the latter film was lauded by critics, however, it didn't do well at the box office.

"People expected to see a western and it was not a western," Andrews suggested years later. "It was an indictment of what happens when men take the law into their own hands."

Despite the disappointing audience reception from this feature, however, Andrews starred the following year in the film that would make his popularity shoot through the roof — the hauntingly riveting *Laura* (1944). In this classic film noir, Andrews

starred as Mark McPherson, a no-nonsense, unflappable cop who begins the film with an investigation into the murder of Laura Hunt (Gene Tierney), who has been killed by a single shotgun blast to the face. The parties involved in McPherson's probe include Waldo Lydecker (Clifton Webb in, arguably, the best role of his career), an effete, acerbic columnist who is in love with Laura; Shelby Carpenter (Vincent Price), Laura's playboy fiancé; and Anne Treadwell (Judith Anderson), Laura's aunt, who wants Shelby for herself. As McPherson delves into Laura's life in the search for her killer, he finds himself inexplicably drawn to her. ("Did it ever strike you that you're acting very strangely?" Lydecker snipes in one scene. "It's a wonder you don't come here like a suitor, with roses and a box of candy.") Later, McPherson's interest in Laura further heightens when she shows up alive and well, and the detective learns the murdered woman was actually a model with whom Shelby was having an affair. Although he briefly suspects Laura herself of the crime, McPherson ultimately fingers Lydecker as the killer, and guns him down in Laura's apart-ment as the writer tries to kill his would-be lover for the second time.

Andrews was universally hailed for his portrayal of the relentless flatfoot — the reviewer for *Variety* praised his "intelligent, reticent performance," and Alton Cook of the *New York World-Telegram* gushed, "In a brief career, Dana Andrews has consistently outdone each of his successive performances. The smoldering force with which he plays the detective leaves one pretty sure the chain of topping himself will be broken with this picture — unless he turns out to be just about the finest actor of our time." Ironically, the film — a blockbuster at the box office — could have turned out much differently. Rouben Mamoulian was originally hired by Darryl F. Zanuck to direct the film, but was later replaced by Otto Preminger, who threw out his predecessor's costumes, sets, and footage, and began from scratch. Further, Zanuck envisioned Jennifer Jones or Hedy Lamarr in the title role, but they both turned it down. The Fox chief also wanted Laird Cregar for the Waldo Lydecker role and John Hodiak as Mark McPherson. Fortunately, Preminger had other plans.

After *Laura*, Andrews' fame skyrocketed — he signed a new contract with Sam Goldwyn and 20th Century-Fox that would earn him $1.5 million over five years, and among the roster of Fox actors receiving fan mail, he rose from 12th to the number one slot. Some of the letters from fans had their humorous aspects, Andrews recalled.

"A lot of the people who write want a photograph," Andrews said in a 1945 interview. "And once in a while someone writes who you know darn well has never seen you in a picture but is just trying to build up a big collection of photographs. Several times I have received letters that have begun, 'Dear Miss Andrews, I have seen your pictures and I …' Of course, under those circumstances I get a particular kick out of sending my photo."

Andrews was next seen in a string of successful features, including *A Walk in the Sun* (1945), a World War II feature co-starring

Richard Conte and John Ireland, and *State Fair* (1945), a delightful musical in which Andrews played opposite Jeanne Crain. Although Andrews possessed a pleasant baritone voice and had received a year of voice training, however, he declined to sing in the latter film, insisting that his songs be dubbed.

"I could have saved the studio some money and sung the tune a lot better," Andrews said later, "but I kept my mouth shut. I don't like what happens to singers in Hollywood — nobody will accept you as an actor."

In his third film of 1945, Andrews returned to the realm of film noir, starring with Linda Darnell and Alice Faye in *Fallen Angel*. In this feature, Andrews portrays Eric Stanton, a cynical, down-on-his-luck press agent who falls for a money-grubbing waitress named Stella (Darnell), whose shallow demeanor is revealed when she tells Eric that she wants "a ring and a home." Despite Stella's obvious materialism, Eric cooks up a scheme to marry a wealthy small-town girl (Faye) for her money, then quickly divorce her in order to wed Stella. When Stella winds up dead, however, Eric is immediately suspected of her murder — he goes on the lam with his loyal wife tagging along, but later returns to the scene of the crime when he realizes that Stella's death came at the hands of a retired policeman (Charles Bickford), with whom Stella had also been involved. Despite stylish direction from Otto Preminger and good performances from the stars, the film was a disappointment at the box office.

During the remainder of the decade, Andrews starred in a number of well-received features, the most memorable of which was the post–World War II drama, *The Best Years of Our Lives* (1946), which won the Academy Award for Best Picture, and was labeled by Andrews as "the best film I ever made." He was also seen in *Canyon Passage* (1946), an action-packed western based on a *Saturday Evening Post* story by Ernest Haycox; *Daisy Kenyon* (1947), a glossy soaper co-starring Joan Crawford and Henry Fonda; and *My Foolish Heart* (1949), a first-rate tear-jerker

with Susan Hayward. His less stellar features during these years included the mawkish melodrama *Night Song* (1948), where Andrews portrayed a bitter pianist who abandons his brilliant concerto after being blinded in an accident, and *The Forbidden Street* (1949), a creaky Victorian-era drama with Andrews playing the dual roles of an art teacher and a barrister.

By now, in the midst of his propitious film career, signs had started to appear which indicated that Andrews was dealing with a drinking problem behind the scenes. In October 1945, the actor was arrested on suspicion of assault with a deadly weapon when he and a friend, Lt. Leo Nomis, were caught throwing rocks at the window of a police officer. The officer, Sgt. Fred Collani, reported that he had discovered Andrews and Nomis throwing stones and "disturbing" a row of mailboxes in front of his home. Collani further stated that the two men threw stones at him when he confronted them, forcing him to retreat to the safety of his home.

"It's all just a misunderstanding," Andrews explained. "I was driving Lt. Nomis home and my car stalled near Sgt. Collani's house. I knocked at the door to see if I could use the telephone, but nobody answered. Then I threw some pebbles at the window, hoping to wake them up so I could call a garage." The charges were dropped.

Three years later, in January 1948, the actor was detained for suspected drunk driving and refused to get into the police car when informed that he was under arrest. According to the arresting officers, Andrews told them, "You can't arrest me. When I appear before the judge, I will be sober, so how can he decide whether I am drunk now or not?" After initially entering a plea of not guilty, Andrews later pleaded guilty and was fined $25. Later that year, while in London for the filming of *The Forbidden Street*, the actor admitted to columnist Louella Parsons that he'd been cautioned by Sam Goldwyn about his behavior.

"Sam Goldwyn warned me to be careful of everything I say," Andrews said. "I made a vow not to touch one drop of liquor while I'm here in Europe, and I like being on the wagon so much I may stay right on it."

With that, Andrews appeared to refocus his energies on his career, and of his three features the following year, two took him back to the realm of film noir— *Where the Sidewalk Ends* (1950) and *Edge of Doom* (1950). In the first, he again starred with Gene Tierney, this time as Mark Dixon, a hotheaded, physically over-aggressive police detective who, as the film opens, is being reprimanded for his temper by his superior, Inspector Foley (Robert Simon). Although Dixon sarcastically claims that he will "try not to hate hoodlums," Foley downgrades his position to a second-grade detective, telling him: "You don't hate hoodlums—you like to beat them up. You get fun out of it." Later, when Dixon accidentally kills a murder suspect, he disposes of the body and unsuccessfully tries to pin the crime on Tommy Scalise (Gary Merrill), a gangleader who was actually responsible for the original murder. Instead, police suspect that the killer is local cabdriver Jiggs Taylor (Tom Tully) whose daughter, Morgan (Tierney), was married to the man killed by Dixon. As Dixon grows increasingly fond of Morgan, he becomes consumed by guilt and confronts Scalise in an effort to both exonerate Jiggs and ensure Scalise's capture. Ultimately, Scalise surrenders and Dixon confesses his crime, comforted by the knowledge that Morgan will be waiting for him. Upon its release, *Where the Sidewalk Ends* was hailed by audiences and critics alike, with the reviewer from *Variety* singling out Andrews for his "excellent" performance.

Next, in *Edge of Doom* (the first of his films noirs that was not directed and produced by Otto Preminger), Andrews portrayed Father Roth, a compassionate clergyman who takes over the parish in an impoverished neighborhood after the former priest (Harold Vermilyea) is found bludgeoned to death. Before long, Roth suspects that the murder was committed by Martin Lynn (Farley Granger), a troubled local boy coping with the recent death of his mother.

Although the chief detective on the case (Robert Keith) suspects Martin, however, he lacks the evidence needed for an arrest. Later, unable to cope with his burden of guilt, Martin seeks help from Roth and, accompanied by the priest, finally turns himself in to the authorities.

After the preview of *Edge of Doom* was poorly received by audiences, Sam Goldwyn hired writer Ben Hecht to enlarge Andrews' relatively minor role and add a prologue and epilogue, which framed Roth's experience with Martin as a flashback. In the revised version, Roth is telling the story to a disillusioned young priest who is planning to leave the parish; after sharing the details of Martin's circumstances, Roth concludes: "I know now I saw God in Martin Lynn ... conscience had triumphed over fear and despair. I don't think I helped Martin Lynn as much as he helped me. To see and understand that faith is a part of a human soul, even when the soul wars against it." Hecht's changes were apparently just what the film needed; after its general release, *Edge of Doom* earned mostly good reviews, with Wylie Williams of the *Hollywood Citizen-News* terming it "an adult film with a believable message," and Philip K. Scheuer conceding in the *Los Angeles Times* that Hecht's changes made the picture "more readily acceptable as a whole to filmgoers."

Despite Andrews' previous successes on screen, both the quality and quantity of his assignments began to decline as the 1950s unfolded. Although he ended his contracts with Sam Goldwyn and 20th Century-Fox in 1952 in order to freelance, few of the 17 films in which he appeared during the decade were memorable — the best of these were *Assignment: Paris* (1952), an espionage drama; *Duel in the Jungle* (1954), an offbeat western costarring Donna Reed; *Elephant Walk* (1954), a big-budget feature climaxed by a herd of elephants destroying a tea plantation; and his final two films noirs, *While the City Sleeps* (1956) and *Beyond a Reasonable Doubt* (1956).

As Edward Mobley in *While the City Sleeps*, Andrews plays a ruthlessly ambitious television anchor at Kyne Enterprises, a sweeping communications corporation whose new president announces that he will award the job of executive director to the employee who unearths the identity of the city's "Lipstick Killer." Vying with Mobley for this prize are wire service manager Mark Loving (George Sanders), newspaper editor John Day Griffith (Thomas Mitchell), photo service editor Harry Kritzer (James Craig), and local reporter Mildred Donner (Ida Lupino). By convincing his fiancée (Sally Forrest) to act as bait for the murderer, Mobley ultimately solves the crime — only to give the coveted position to the more-deserving Griffith. Favorably described by one critic as "full of sound and fury, murder, sacred and profane love and a fair quote of intramural intrigue," *While the City Sleeps* also earned accolades for Andrews, who was included in the *New York Times'* sweeping praise of the film's principal characters as "[doing] justice to their assignments."

In *Beyond a Reasonable Doubt*, Andrews' final entry in the era of film noir, he portrays Tom Garrett, a writer who, after witnessing an execution, cooks up a scheme with publisher Austin Spencer (Sidney Blackmer) to test the theory of circumstantial evidence: Tom will allow himself to be incriminated in the unsolved murder of a young girl, with Spencer withholding the evidence that will prove Tom's innocence. The plan appears to be a success until Spencer — who is also the father of Tom's fiancée, Susan (Joan Fontaine) — is killed in an automobile accident shortly before the jury returns a guilty verdict. Unable to locate the evidence compiled by Spencer, Susan rallies public support for Tom through her father's newspaper, but the ambitious district attorney is unmoved and Tom is scheduled for execution. At the 11th hour, Tom is cleared when a letter from the dead publisher is located, but in an ironic twist, during a conversation with Susan just prior to his pardon, Tom inadvertently reveals that he really is the killer. Despite direction from Fritz Lang (his last film), and a first-rate cast, the implausible plot of *Beyond of a Reasonable Doubt* failed to register with crit-

ics or audiences, who stayed away from the film in large numbers.

Between film assignments during the 1950s, Andrews toured with his wife, Mary, in a stage version of *The Glass Menagerie*, and later, made his Broadway debut when he replaced Henry Fonda in *Two for the Seesaw*, co-starring Anne Bancroft. He complained at one point that he was unable to find good film roles because "they want top box office names for blockbusters and I'm not in that category." But it was becoming increasingly apparent that Andrews' dwindling assignments were directly linked with his continued struggles with the bottle.

In July 1955, newspapers reported that the actor had lacerated two of his fingers when he "accidentally" broke a pane of glass in a local bar that was not yet opened. Six months later, Andrews called a Studio City police station from a restaurant to complain that he was having difficulty finding change to pay his tab — when police arrived, the restaurant's owner reported that the actor had become "loud and boisterous, but simmered down when he found his change absent-mindedly in another pocket." In September 1956, Andrews made news again when he contacted police in Santa Barbara to report that his car had been stolen — when police located the car, Andrews was unable to find his keys and was forced to take a 100-mile taxicab ride back to Hollywood. And on December 29, 1956, the actor was arrested for drunk driving when his car rammed into the back of a vehicle that had stopped at a red light. Police reported that Andrews had been driving "in an erratic manner" just before the accident occurred.

"I was under the influence but was not drunk," Andrews was quoted by the officers. "Fools drive while drinking. I'm lucky I did not kill someone. I'm thankful for that." As with his drunk driving arrest in the late 1940s, Andrews first pleaded not guilty and was slated for a jury trial, but later changed his plea. This time, the actor was sentenced to 15 days in jail or a fine of $263. (Andrews paid the fine, but the matter didn't end there. The passenger of the car, an 18-year-old blind woman, sued the actor for $100,000. She was later awarded $5,000 in damages.)

The fallout from Andrews' obvious drinking problem reached its peak in 1958 when he was slapped with a breach-of-contract suit by Waverly Productions, Inc., and producer Benedict Bogeaus, who sought $159,769 from the actor. In November 1957, the actor had signed a contract to star in *Enchanted Island* (1958) — the suit charged that, while traveling to Acapulco, Mexico, for the on-location shooting, Andrews "consumed excessive amounts of alcoholic beverages and was repeatedly in a state of extreme and severe self-induced intoxication." The suit went on to cite 20 instances during which Andrews was unable to work, claiming that he demonstrated "infrequent and occasional periods of sobriety."

"His appearance was that of a person under the influence of alcohol and was inconsistent with the healthy, robust character he was supposed to portray," the suit stated, adding that, while in Mexico, Andrews was "insulting, offensive and abusive" toward Mexican citizens and twice was involved in incidents involving physical violence. Finally, in violation of his contract, the suit charged, Andrews returned to Los Angeles on January 1, 1958.

Andrews responded that the charges were "ridiculous."

"I think this was deliberately done as a surprise," he said of the lawsuit. "The whole thing is an argument over money." The lawsuit was ultimately dropped and the film was completed later that year, but the damage to Andrews' reputation and career was significant.

With the dawn of a new decade, Andrews continued to appear sporadically in films, and returned to Broadway in 1961 for *The Captains and the Kings*, but his interests had taken a new direction — real estate. In November 1960, he revealed that he had purchased two three-unit apartment houses in Anaheim, California, and a $300,000 apartment building in North Hollywood, which he renovated

and later sold for a profit of $150,000. Four years later, he and his partner, Hollywood builder Jack M. Okean, unveiled a new $2.5 million, 126-unit apartment complex in Garden Grove, California.

"You've got to become interested in something that makes money for you instead of costing money," Andrews told columnist Hedda Hopper, adding that he had taken night courses in real estate at UCLA. "I studied and learned how to appraise property and how to use other people's money. I could kick myself that I didn't learn it sooner; I'd have a lot more of my earnings left."

Also during this period, Andrews entered the realm of television, although years earlier he had echoed director Fritz Lang's label of television as a "moronoscope," saying that his "business is to sell entertainment, not to sell products." After an apparent change of heart, the actor was seen on such programs as *The Twilight Zone*, *Playhouse 90*, and the *Alcoa Premiere Theater* production of "The Boy Who Wasn't Wanted."

Then, in November 1963, Andrews turned his talents to the political arena when he was elected as president of the Screen Actors Guild. As head of the guild, Andrews became an outspoken champion on behalf of his peers; one of his many causes was his support of pay-television — a precursor to today's pay-per-view concept.

"The actor is being pushed out of the business," Andrews told columnist Hal Humphrey in 1963. "There are too many actors out of work. It's very serious. We used to pick up money on TV, but the networks take advantage of the job scarcity to cut the actor's salary. When they learn he's hungry, they start slashing the price. Not until we have pay TV can actors hold up their heads with other artists and get roles worthy of their ability. The great hope of pay TV is that it would be entertainment, not an advertising medium — as it is, television is an adjunct of the advertising business."

In later years, the actor headed a campaign to ban nudity in all films, claiming that women were being exploited because "greedy" producers had decided they could make money "by having performers do something they cannot do on television." Andrews' support of actors continued long after he stepped down from the presidency of SAG — in 1981, he joined a number of film luminaries, including Mickey Rooney, Rock Hudson, Lana Turner, and Jane Powell, in a class-action suit against eight major film studios, seeking television residuals for films in which the stars had appeared before February 1960. Also that year, he threw his support behind the candidacy of actor Edward Asner for the SAG presidency, counteracting the endorsement of incumbent president William Schallert by another former SAG president Dennis Weaver, who contended that Schallert had more experience.

"No amount of experience can replace respect, credibility, and determination ... experience is valuable, but experience can be acquired by anyone," Andrews said. "Natural leadership is limited to very few and without leadership, there can be no strength." Asner won the post.

Sadly, tragedy struck Andrews' life in 1964 when his oldest son, David, suffered a cerebral hemorrhage. After five hours of brain surgery, the 30-year-old musician and radio announcer remained in a coma and he died less than a month later. The actor's personal life declined further as it became apparent that his drinking problem was continuing to plague him — in January 1968, while touring in a road production of *The Odd Couple*, Andrews fell in a hotel bathtub and suffered a skull fracture. He was in critical condition for nearly a week. Days later, columnist Harrison Carroll reported in the *Los Angeles Herald-Examiner* that the 28-year marriage of Andrews and Mary Todd was "on a shaky basis," and that Mary was helping to nurse the actor to health after his fall, but "they are not on good terms."

"We are neither one thing or the other right now," the columnist quoted Mary. "I can't bear for Dana to be sick alone so I am here part of the time. The rest I spend at my father's house. We are not planning a divorce.

Maybe we can work out our problems." But four months after making that statement, Mary Todd filed for divorce, accusing Andrews of causing her "great mental and physical suffering." It was later revealed that Mary had informed her husband that would not come back to him unless he stopped drinking.

Apparently, that was the impetus Andrews needed to turn his life around. The actor stopped drinking, reconciled with his wife, and candidly discussed his battle with the bottle, beginning with a public service announcement in 1971.

"I'm Dana Andrews and I'm an alcoholic," he said. "I don't drink anymore, but I used to — all the time. I attended [Alcoholics Anonymous] meetings for a time, but in the long run I had to work out my problem for myself." The actor also acknowledged that his drinking problem had negatively impacted his career: "No one ever said anything to me about my drinking," he said. "But word gets around, and the pictures dried up."

Andrews joined the Advisory Board of the Alcoholism Council of Greater Los Angeles, and became a spokesperson against the dangers of drunk driving. Ten years later, after the deaths of film stars William Holden and Natalie Wood, Andrews took to task those individuals who condemned the press for reporting that the deaths were alcohol-related.

"How can you not mention it? [Alcohol] is the number three cause of death in the United States," Andrews said in December 1981. "Alcoholism is no disgrace. If a man had heart disease, you wouldn't say you are being unfaithful to the memory of that person to report that. Well, alcoholism is another disease. If only one partygoer at this [holiday] season, invited to take that last and maybe fatal drink for the road, says, 'No thanks,' remembering what [the media] have reported about the death of William Holden and Natalie Wood, and remembering, too, that what happened to these celebrated people could just as easily happen to him ... then I suggest their deaths will surely not have been in vain."

While Andrews' activities behind the scenes took up a great deal of his time, he had continued to appear in films and on television — in the late 1960s, he was seen in such features as *Brainstorm* (1965), a well-done suspensor starring Jeffrey Hunter and directed by actor William Conrad, and *Johnny Reno* (1966), a western in which Andrews starred in the title role. And on the small screen, he signed on to star in an NBC-TV daytime soap opera, *Bright Promise*. Portraying a college president, Andrews said that he was "impressed after reading the first five scripts and felt I had to accept the part."

"Some people in my profession seem to have a low opinion of daytime TV because its major audience is women," the always-candid actor said. "Well, I think women have a great deal more taste and knowledge of theater than men. Another aspect that I like is that this show is taped live, the nearest thing to a live performance. It gives you the chance to create as if it were happening right now." Andrews appeared on the serial during its entire run, from 1969 to 1972.

Andrews added radio to his performing repertoire during the 1970s, recording several programs for broadcast on the American Armed Forces Radio Network, including *Call Northside 777* with Thomas Gomez, *Swamp Water* with Anne Baxter, and *The Token* with Ann Blyth. He was also seen in such made-for-TV movies as *The Failing of Raymond* (1971), *A Shadow in the Streets* (1975), *The First 36 Hours of Dr. Durant* (1975), and *The Last Hurrah* (1977). On the silver screen, he appeared in *Airport 1975* (1975), *The Last Tycoon* (1976), the Chuck Norris actioner *Good Guys Wear Black* (1979), and his last film, *Prince Jack* (1984).

In 1990, it was reported that Andrews had suffered a series of small strokes and was living in the John Douglas French Center for Alzheimer's Disease in Los Alamitos, California, where he was receiving treatment for multi-infarct dementia, a condition similar to Alzheimer's disease. Despite his condition, his wife said, "people would make a fuss over him and ask him for his autograph." Two years later, on December 17, 1992, the 83-year-old actor died from heart failure and pneumonia.

Although his struggle with alcoholism was likely a leading factor in Dana Andrews' decline in feature films, and not only threatened his marriage, but his life as well, the actor did not "go gentle into that good night." Both professionally and personally, he proved himself to be a man of talent, integrity, determination, and dedication. Andrews was never nominated for an Academy Award — despite first-rate performances in a range of films — and he never rose to the rank of stardom that his abilities deserved, but he was the personification of perseverance, as he overcame obstacles, survived setbacks, and conquered demons.

In the early 1970s, the entertainment writer for an Oklahoma publication asked his readers to respond to the question, "Who is Dana Andrews?" The best reply to the paper's query offers a fitting description for the legacy of the actor's life and career:

"As a very young teenager back in World War II, happiness for me was a bag of popcorn and a Dana Andrews movie," the reader said. "So I thought I would share with you the memories that his name evokes. He belonged to that era of the true romantic hero: the Tyrone Powers, the Robert Taylors, the Spencer Tracys; all idealists who believed and fought for a cause — and got the girl at the close of the movie."

Film Noir Filmography

Laura. Director and Producer: Otto Preminger. Running time: 88 minutes. Released by 20th Century-Fox, October 11, 1944. Cast: Gene Tierney, Dana Andrews, Clifton Webb, Vincent Price, Judith Anderson, Dorothy Adams, James Flavin, Clyde Fillmore, Ralph Dunn, Grant Mitchell, Kathleen Howard. Awards: Academy Award for Best Cinematography (Joseph LaShelle). Academy Award nominations for Best Director (Otto Preminger), Best Supporting Actor (Clifton Webb), Best Screenplay (Jay Oratler, Samuel Hoffenstein, Betty Reinhardt), Best Art Direction (Lyle Wheeler, Leland Fuller, Thomas Little).

Fallen Angel. Director and Producer: Otto Preminger. Running time: 98 minutes. Released by 20th Century-Fox February 6, 1946. Cast: Alice Faye, Dana Andrews, Linda Darnell, Charles Bickford, Anne Revere, Bruce Cabot, John Carradine, Percy Kilbride.

Where the Sidewalk Ends. Director and Producer: Otto Preminger. Running time: 95 minutes. Released by 20th Century-Fox, July 7, 1950. Cast: Dana Andrews, Gene Tierney, Gary Merrill, Bert Freed, Tom Tully, Karl Malden, Ruth Donnelly, Craig Stevens, Robert Simon, Harry von Zell, Don Appell, Neville Brand, Grace Mills, Lou Krugman, David McMahon, David Wolfe, Steve Roberts, Phil Tully, Ian MacDonald, John Close, John McGuire, Lou Nova.

Edge of Doom. Director: Mark Robson (with additional scenes by King Vidor). Producer: Samuel Goldwyn. Running time: 99 minutes. Released by RKO, September 27, 1950. Cast: Dana Andrews, Farley Granger, Joan Evans, Robert Keith, Paul Stewart, Mala Powers, Adele Jergens, Harold Vermilyea, John Ridgeley, Doulas Fowley, Mabel Paige, Howland Chamberlain, Houseley Stevenson, Sr., Jean Innes, Ellen Corby, Ray Teal, Mary Field, Virginia Brissac, Frances Morris.

While the City Sleeps. Director: Fritz Lang. Producer: Bert Friedlob. Running time: 99 minutes. Released by RKO, May 16, 1956. Cast: Dana Andrews, Rhonda Fleming, George Sanders, Howard Duff, Thomas Mitchell, Vincent Price, Sally Forrest, John Barrymore, Jr., James Craig, Ida Lupino, Robert Warwick, Ralph Peters, Vladimir Sokoloff, Mae Marsh, Sandy White.

Beyond a Reasonable Doubt. Director: Fritz Lang. Producer: Bert Friedlob. Running time: 80 minutes. Released by RKO, September 5, 1956. Cast: Dana Andrews, Joan Fontaine, Sidney Blackmer, Philip Bourneur, Shepperd Strudwick, Arthur Franz, Edward Binns, Robin Raymond, Barbara Nichols, William Leicester, Dan Seymour, Rusty Lane, Joyce Taylor, Carleton Young, Trudy Wroe, Joe Kirk, Charles Evan, Wendell Niles.

References

"Actor Dana Andrews in Guilty Plea." *Los Angeles Times*, January 31, 1957.

"Actor Dana Andrews Seized on Drunk Charge." *Los Angeles Times*, December 30, 1956.

"Actor Hits Initiative to Ban Pay TV." *Hollywood Citizen-News*, April 21, 1964.

"Actors Guild Approves Strike by 1,499–1 Vote." *Los Angeles Times*, November 19, 1963.

"Actors Guild Nominates Dana Andrews to Replace George Chandler as Prez." *Variety*, September 11, 1963.

"Alcoholism Council Lauds Shore, Lund." *Variety*, March 8, 1977.

"Andrews Sued by Waverly Productions." *Hollywood Citizen-News*, March 12, 1958.

"A Serious Situation." *Los Angeles Times*, January 20, 1965.

Bacon, James. "Andrews Delighted with Soap Opera." *Los Angeles Herald-Examiner*, April 16, 1970.

_____. "Dana Bounces Back." *Los Angeles-Examiner*, May 30, 1977.

Biography of Dana Andrews. 20th Century Fox, July 15, 1944.

"Blind Girl Wins Verdict from Actor." *Los Angeles Times*, May 28, 1963.

"Book Dana Andrews as Auto Drunk." *Los Angeles Herald Express*, December 29, 1956.

"Both Goldwyn and 20th Century Plan Boost for Dana Andrews." *Los Angeles Examiner*, March 17, 1943.

Carrithers, Joe. "Dana Andrews, Star." *Classic Images*, May 1984.

Carroll, Harrison. "Long Marriage May Be Ending." *Los Angeles Herald-Examiner*, January 29, 1968.

"Dana Andrews Arrested on Drunk Charge." *Los Angeles Times*, January 12, 1948.

"Dana Andrews' Battle with Alcohol Lends Credence to Role in 'Pilot.'" *Boxoffice*, January 15, 1979.

"Dana Andrews Dies; Actor Was a Success but Not a Star." *Los Angeles Times*, December 18, 1992.

"Dana Andrews Ends Night in Jail on Drunk Charge." *Los Angeles Examiner*, January 12, 1948.

"Dana Andrews Fan Pities Teenagers, Anti-Heroes." *Boxoffice*, December 20, 1971.

"Dana Andrews Goes Into Warners 'Brainstorm' Pic." *The Hollywood Reporter*, January 7, 1965.

"Dana Andrews Held as Drunk After Crash." *Los Angeles Mirror*, December 29, 1956.

"Dana Andrews Injured in Fall." *Hollywood Citizen-News*, January 11, 1968.

"Dana Andrews in Lockup for Stone-Throwing." *Los Angeles Times*, August 31, 1945.

"Dana Andrews in 'Small Step.'" *The Hollywood Reporter*, March 21, 1975.

"Dana Andrews in Tab Change Row." *Los Angeles Times*, February 18, 1956.

"Dana Andrews Locked Out of Car, So Taxis 100 Miles." *Los Angeles Times*, September 27, 1956.

"Dana Andrews OK, But in Hosp After 'Odd' Tour Fall." *Variety*, January 12, 1968.

"Dana Andrews Passes Cigars." *Los Angeles Examiner*, circa July 1942.

"Dana Andrews Pleads Innocent to Drunk Driving." *Los Angeles Times*, January 1, 1957.

"Dana Andrews' Son Dies at 30." *Los Angeles Times*, February 16, 1964.

"Dana Andrews' Son in Critical Condition." *Los Angeles Times*, January 23, 1964.

"Dana Andrews Stars in Daytime Series." *Los Angeles Herald-Examiner*, August 15, 1969.

"Dana Andrews USOing." *Variety*, April 18, 1970.

Davis, Charles E., Jr. "Actor Finds Success— as Real Estate Operator." *Los Angeles Times*, May 24, 1964.

Denunzio, Marie. "Dana Andrews Won't Let Them Die in Vain." *Los Angeles Herald-Examiner*, December 5, 1981.

"Drunk Count Costs Dana Andrews $25." *Los Angeles Times*, January 17, 1948.

Garrison, Maxine. "Lucky Stiff or Fall Guy? Dana Wonders." *Pittsburgh Press*, June 4, 1945.

Greene, Patterson. "Curtain Call for Dana Andrews." *Los Angeles Examiner*, December 7, 1958.

Hale, Wanda. "Film Star and Financier." *Los Angeles Daily News*. March 1, 1965.

Henry, Marilyn. "Let's Not Forget ... Dana Andrews." *Classic Film Collector*, Winter 1977.

Hopper, Hedda. "Andrews Seeking Script for His Dream Picture." *Los Angeles Times*, September 7, 1947.

_____. "Andrews Starring in Broadway Play." *Los Angeles Times*, August 11, 1961.

_____. "Artful Actor Hits Zenith by 'Tricks.'" *Los Angeles Times*, August 12, 1945.

_____. "Dana Andrews Father Again." *Los Angeles Times*, January 30, 1948.

_____. "Dana 'Jack of All Trades.'" *Miami Daily News*, August 5, 1945.

Hull, Bob. "Dana Andrews Bemoans Today's Heroes with Their Clayed Feet." *Los Angeles Herald-Examiner*, June 5, 1962.

Humphrey, Hal. "Andrews Attacks 'Moronoscope.'" *Los Angeles Times*, April 24, 1963.

"In This Case, Serving Two Masters Paid Off." *New York Times*, March 12, 1944.

Lindsley, James. "Hollywood Story of Texan and with Different Twist." *Dallas Times Herald*, February 18, 1944.

Manners, Dorothy. "Andrews' Smashing Comeback." *Los Angeles Herald-Examiner*, June 15, 1977.

McClay, Howard. "Actor Andrews Figures to Do Own Bookkeeping." *Los Angeles Daily News*, circa 1952.

Meade, James. "Dana Andrews Learned Craft from Early Films." *The [Warren, Ohio] Tribune Chronicle*, October 21, 1977.

"Mrs. Andrews Sues Dana for Divorce." *Hollywood Citizen-News*, May 29, 1968.

Obituary. *Variety*, December 21, 1992.

Page, Don. "Dana Andrews Has Promise." *Los Angeles Times*, October 4, 1969.

"Pane Breaks; Actor Hurt." *Los Angeles Times*, July 12, 1955.

Parsons, Louella O. "Dana Andrews." *Los Angeles Examiner*, September 5, 1948.

_____. "Gas Station Men Who Staked Dana Andrews Reap Harvest." *Los Angeles Examiner*, January 8, 1944.

_____. "'Papa May Spank'— but Dana Andrews Still Wants to Play Lead Role." *Los Angeles Examiner*, May 16, 1943.

"Pornographic Movie Trend Is on Way Out, Actor Dana Andrews Believes." *Boxoffice*, September 25, 1972.

Ranney, Omar. "A Visit with Dana Andrews, One of the Top Young Stars." *Cleveland Press*, December 8, 1945.

Redelings, Lowell E. "Closeup of an Actor." *Hollywood Citizen-News*, June 3, 1947.

"Rooney Files Suit Over TV Residuals." *Variety*, June 26, 1981.

Scheuer, Philip K. "Precedent-Shattering Deal Made by Andrews." *Los Angeles Times*, October 23, 1945.

_____. "Town Called Hollywood." *Los Angeles Times*, December 14, 1941.

Scott, John L. "Dana Andrews Lauds Broadway Stint." *Los Angeles Times*, December 27, 1959.

Severo, Richard. "Dana Andrews, Film Actor of 40's, Is Dead at 83." *New York Times*, December 19, 1992.

Shaffer, Rosalind. "Dana Andrews Wrapped Up in Family." *St. Paul Pioneer Press*, August 6, 1944.

Sharpe, Howard. "The Remarkable Andrews." *Photoplay*, April 1943.

"Studio Sues Andrews in Film Failure." *Los Angeles Examiner*, March 12, 1958.

Steele, Joseph Henry. "Portrait of a Minister's Son." *Photoplay*, July 1944.

"Tender Tough Guy." *People*, January 11, 1993.

Townsend, Dorothy. "Dana Andrews Defends Death Stories." *Los Angeles Times*, December 5, 1981.

Tusher, Will. "Dana Andrews Throws Support Behind Ed Asner for SAG Prez." *Variety*, October 12, 1981.

ED BEGLEY

"Make up your mind to be a cop — not a gangster with a badge." — Ed Begley in *On Dangerous Ground* (1951)

Ed Begley had to act.

"I could no more control that than I could breathing," he once said. And his compulsion was apparent in his countless film, stage, and television appearances. Burly, blustering, and boisterous, Ed Begley was renowned for his versatility — whether he was portraying a bigoted political boss, an alcoholic businessman, an indulgent father, or a crusading officer of the law, Begley delivered. He was also the recipient of numerous awards for his acting ability, including an Academy Award for his outstanding performance in *Sweet Bird of Youth* (1962), and he appeared during his career in a total of seven films noirs: *The Street with No Name* (1948), *Sorry, Wrong Number* (1948), *Convicted* (1950), *Dark City* (1950), *On Dangerous Ground* (1952), *The Turning Point* (1952), and *Odds Against Tomorrow* (1959).

Edward James Begley was born on March 25, 1901, in Hartford, Connecticut, one of four children of Hannah Clifford Begley and her husband Michael, an Irish immigrant hod carrier (a laborer who carries supplies to bricklayers, stonemasons, and similar craftsmen). Young Ed was attracted to show business from an early age — he could often be found haunting local circuses and vaudeville theatres — and at age 11, he ran away from home to join a traveling carnival.

"I was always running away from home," he recalled later. "I always wanted to become an actor. I knew I was causing my parents a great deal of worry, but off I'd go."

At the age of 13, Begley abandoned the notion of a formal education and entered the school of life — wandering the country and landing a wide variety of jobs over the years that included working as a night cook in a hospital, night elevator boy in a hotel, steel pusher in an iron foundry, pick and shovel laborer, Western Union messenger, horse and wagon driver for a department store, and boiler operator in a Philadelphia insane asylum. But his only brush with acting had taken place shortly after he'd left home as a teenager — he'd imitated Charlie Chaplin to win first place in a Hartford department store contest.

"A fly-by-night movie company producer asked me to come over and work for him, but I was much too shy," Begley said. "I had a tremendous urge to act, but I had a very low opinion of my own talent."

While Begley was bouncing from job to job, he managed to find time to get married, on April 1, 1922, to radio actress Amanda Huff, with whom he would remain until her 1957 death. In 1947, however, the actor became romantically involved with an NBC page, Allene Jeanne Sanders, and the couple went on to have two children, Allene in October 1948, and Edward Begley, Jr. in September 1949. According to Begley, Jr., his parents ended their relationship when he was about a year old.

"I was told that Amanda was my mother — she passed away when I was seven," Begley, Jr., said in 2002. "I discovered that Allene Sanders was, in fact, my mother when I was 16 years old. We became fairly close by the time I hit my 20s and remained so until she died." (Edward Begley, Jr., grew up to find fame as the Emmy-nominated star of the acclaimed television series *St. Elsewhere* and star in such feature films as *The Accidental Tourist* [1988] and *Best in Show* [2000].) Meanwhile, it wasn't until Begley was 31 years old and working in a Hartford steel mill that he decided to take the plunge into the acting profession, asking his boss for an afternoon off so that he could try out for the stock company at local radio station WTIC. After landing a small part in a dramatic broadcast, Begley secured full-time work at the radio station, taking on a variety of positions, including actor, announcer, writer and disc jockey. While there, Begley honed his talent for dialects— an ability he said he'd inherited from his "frustrated actor" father— and his ability to take on any role became legendary. In one play alone, he portrayed an old Mexican, a young Mexican, and a Chinese cook.

In the early 1940s, after 10 years as a "big fish in the little pond" at WTIC, Begley traveled to New York to try his hand at the "big time." Before long, he landed his first role, on a program called *David Harding, Counterspy,* and was soon one of radio's busiest actors— according to the *Los Angeles Herald-Examiner,* it was "easier to name the shows on which he didn't act." Among other roles, Begley was the first Charlie Chan, and was also heard on such programs as *Amanda of Honeymoon Hill*; *Mr. Keen, Tracer of Lost Persons*; the *Kate Smith Show*; the *Philip Morris Playhouse*; *Steve Graham, Family Doctor*; and *The Aldrich Family.*

Between radio jobs, Begley made his Broadway debut in 1943 as a Nazi general in *Land of Fame.* But the play was panned by critics— one reviewer labeled it "amateurish in plot, structure, and dialogue"— and audiences were unimpressed. He fared a little better in his next stage venture—for his role as a film producer in *Get Away, Old Man,* he was singled out in the *New York Herald Tribune* for "[doing] his best to give some dimensions to the part," and in the *Christian Science Monitor* for his "unflagging vitality and unction." But when his next play, *Pretty Little Parlor,* closed after a week, Begley returned his focus to his successful radio career.

After making a short film for Universal and supplying voices for a Paramount Pictures cartoon, Begley made his feature film debut in 1947 in *Boomerang!*, a semi-documentary melodrama. His success in this film led to his casting in the Broadway production of *All My Sons,* by Arthur Miller, in which he portrayed a manufacture who knowingly produces defective airplane parts during World War II. Begley's performance was hailed by critics and audiences alike.

After a small role in the forgettable *Big Town* (1947), starring Hillary Brooke and Phillip Reed, Begley appeared in his first film noir, *The Street with No Name* (1948), a fast-moving semi-documentary starring Richard Widmark as a sadistic gang leader and Mark Stevens as the undercover FBI agent who infiltrates Widmark's mob. Although one critic claimed the film was "worth your breathless attention," the fifth-billed Begley had little to do in his role as a police chief, and can be chiefly spotted rounding up his officers or standing to the side observing the main action. But the actor landed more screen time later that year in his second film noir, *Sorry, Wrong Number* (1948).

This riveting feature centered on Leona Stevenson (Barbara Stanwyck), a spoiled, hypochondriac heiress who overhears a murder plot, learns too late that she is the intended victim, and realizes that her husband, Henry (Burt Lancaster), is the mastermind behind the scheme. Playing Leona's overindulgent father, James Cotterell, Begley's best scene was a confrontation with Henry, which followed one of Leona's patented "heart" attacks: "Leona can't stand being treated the way you did this morning— she never has been before and she's not going to be now," Cotterell vehemently informs his son-in-law. "I don't give a hoot about your opinions— have them. Think anything you like. But while you're in this house, you'll do what my daughter tells you to do." The movie received critical raves, and Begley was singled out by a number of critics, including Howard Barnes of the *New York Herald Tribune,* who praised the actor's "commanding characterization of a drug store tycoon."

During this period, Begley made two rare comedy appearances, in *Sitting Pretty* (1948), starring Clifton Webb as the prissy babysitter Lynn Belvidere, and *It Happens Every Spring* (1949), an amusing tale about a chemist who changes the game of baseball when he invents a solution that repels wood. He was also seen in small roles as a racketeer in the underrated Alan Ladd starrer, *The Great Gatsby* (1949); an ill-fated oil baron in *Tulsa*

(1949), starring Susan Hayward and Preston Foster; and a rancher in the western saga, *Saddle Tramp* (1950), before returning to film noir with back-to-back features, *Convicted* (1950) and *Dark City* (1950).

The first, *Convicted*, starred Glenn Ford as Joe Hufford, a luckless broker sentenced to prison for the death of a man killed in a barroom brawl. A model prisoner, Joe is hired as the chauffeur for the prison warden (Broderick Crawford) who, as district attorney, had been reluctantly responsible for Joe's conviction. But when Joe refuses to implicate his roommate in the murder of a prison stoolie, he is himself suspected of the killing. All ends well, however, when the roommate confesses to the killing, and the compassionate warden arranges Joe's parole. *Convicted* was a modest success and earned good reviews, with one critic writing that it "has several off-beat twists to its development, keeping it from being routine," but in a relatively minor part as the head of the parole board, Begley barely registered.

The actor was seen to better advantage his second noir of 1950, *Dark City*, co-starring Charlton Heston and Jack Webb. In this feature, businessman Arthur Winant (Don DeFore) commits suicide after being fleeced out of his money by a trio of con men — Danny Haley (Heston, in his screen debut), Augie (Webb), and Barney (Begley). After Winant's death, the men begin to believe that they are being stalked, and Barney — the most paranoid of the group — is the first to suspect that something is amiss: "This whole thing gives me the creeps," he tells his pals. "All day long I've had the feeling that I was being followed." Barney's fears are realized when Winant's mentally unbalanced brother, Sidney (Mike Mazurki) undertakes a plan of revenge to systematically murder each of the men responsible for Arthur's death, beginning with Barney. When Augie becomes the killer's second victim, Haley teams up with police to trap Sidney, who is ultimately gunned down while trying to murder Haley. As the ulcer-suffering, milk-drinking confidence man, Begley turned in a memorable perfor-

mance and was mentioned by one reviewer for his contribution to the film's "generally okay storytelling."

Begley's nine film appearances during the next two years included *Lone Star* (1951), a star-studded, big-budget epic featuring Clark Gable, Ava Gardner, and Lionel Barrymore; *You're in the Navy Now* (1951), a lightweight naval comedy notable as providing the film debuts for both Charles Bronson and Lee Marvin; *Boots Malone* (1952), a horseracing saga starring William Holden in the title role; and *Deadline U.S.A.*, which featured Begley in a well-received role as a crusading newspaper editor. Also during the early 1950s, Begley added two more films noirs to his credit, *On Dangerous Ground* (1951), and *The Turning Point* (1952). In the former, Begley had the small and rather thankless role of a police captain who dispatches a volatile cop (Robert Ryan) to the country to investigate a murder. The film did poorly at the box office and was panned by Bosley Crowther in the *New York Times* for its "flimsy material."

Begley fared far better with *The Turning Point*, based on the 1951 hearings of Senator

Estes Kefauver and starring Edmond O'Brien as John Conroy, the head of a commission investigating organized crime. Here, Begley was featured as Neil Eichelberger, a vicious crime boss who ruled his organization with an iron fist and a steel will: "We've built a great outfit—almost foolproof," he tells his henchmen in one scene. "But we've got the same weak links any business has. People. If we've got one or 500 people, we've got that many weak links." The mobster's sinister nature is most blatantly revealed when he orders the burning of a building containing a set of damaging papers—despite the fact that the building also houses several apartments. (When his own men express disbelief and horror at the idea, Eichelberger coolly smiles, assuring them that not even "a jury would believe we would do it.") Although Eichelberger succeeds in obliterating the damaging evidence—and killing numerous innocents in the process—he is unable to escape justice and is finally brought down by the film's final reel. For his performance as the vicious mob boss, Begley was singled out by several critics, including the reviewer for the *New York Times*, who termed him "excellent."

Despite his busy filming schedule, Begley found time to appear in two stage productions, *What Price Glory?* and *John Loves Mary*, as well as to launch his prolific television career. Beginning in 1950 with *The Armstrong Circle Theatre*, Begley starred in countless small-screen programs over the next two decades, including *Lights Out, Cameo Theatre, Big Town, Danger, Leave it to Larry, The Guiding Light, Philco Television Playhouse, Medallion Theatre, Robert Montgomery Presents, You Are There, The Big Story*, and *T-Men in Action*. In 1954, Begley was praised for his "superb" performance in the Broadway production of *All Summer Long*, and the following year received rave reviews—and a Tony award—for his portrayal of Matthew Harrison Brady in *Inherit the Wind*. The critic from the *New York Herald Tribune* called Begley "an actor of range, variety and scale," adding that his performance "has been widely praised, but is likely never to be

praised quite enough." Begley played the role for more than two years and 789 performances, and when illness forced his co-star, Paul Muni, to leave the show, Begley stepped into his role. The act was considered to be Begley's tour-de-force, and he was further applauded by reviewers, including the critic for *Newsweek*, who observed, "The versatile Mr. Begley eased himself out of the role of the fundamentalist prosecutor and became the free-thinking defense counsel as though he were changing suits."

Begley received additional accolades in 1955 for a pair of outstanding television performances; in the first, the Rod Serling production of *Patterns*, Begley earned an Emmy nomination (and praise from the *New York Times* reviewer, who wrote, "As Andy, Mr. Begley abjured the maudlin, yet caught the tragedy of the executive who is the victim of personality and policy conflict"). Begley was also a memorable contributor to the first-rate production of *Twelve Angry Men*, in which he played Juror #10. He recreated both roles on the big screen, in 1956 and 1957, respectively.

In his last and, perhaps, his best film noir role, Begley starred in 1959 with Robert Ryan and Harry Belafonte in *Odds Against Tomorrow*, a hard-hitting story about three desperate men who team up to rob a bank. Here, Begley portrayed David Burke, a crooked ex-cop who recruits a racially prejudiced ex-convict (Ryan) and a black singer (Belafonte) to help carry out his elaborate scheme to rob a New York bank. Despite the underlying racial tension, the men succeed in stealing the cash, but the plan begins to fall apart when Burke is shot outside the bank by police, and ultimately, all three men end up dead. For his performance, Begley received unanimous acclaim from critics, including the *New York Times'* Bosley Crowther who said the actor "comes out a solid, scheming, cold-blooded corrupted cop ... the sheer build-up of the contemplation of a crime is of an artistic caliber that is rarely achieved on the screen."

During the next several years, Begley

continued his frequent stage and television appearances and in 1962 received an Academy Award for Best Supporting Actor for his portrayal of "Boss" Finley, a corrupt politician, in *Sweet Bird of Youth*. Off-screen, the actor remarried in 1961, to Dorothy Reeves, but the couple divorced two years later. ("Didn't work," the actor told a *TV Guide* reporter.) Shortly after his divorce, however, he eloped to Las Vegas with Helen Jordan, the 38-year-old secretary of Begley's agent. The following year, the couple had a daughter, Maureen, and the actor frequently joked with the media about the incongruity of having an infant child at his age.

"My oldest son just became a grandfather, making me a great-grandfather," he said in the *Corpus Christi Caller-Times*. "Someday, my youngest daughter, Maureen, may be baby-sitting for that baby. Who will she be caring for? What relation?" And he jovially told another reporter, "I have a son older than my wife and I'm older than my mother-in-law!"

Begley's follow-up to his Oscar-winning role in *Sweet Bird of Youth* was a significant departure—he was seen, as he termed it "singing and jigging for dear life" in the Debbie Reynolds starrer *The Unsinkable Molly Brown* (1964). He continued his non-stop performing schedule throughout the remainder of the decade, appearing in such films as *The Oscar* (1966), *Hang 'Em High* (1967), *Wild in the Streets* (1968), and *The Dunwich Horror* (1970); teleplays including *The Silent Gun* (1969) with Lloyd Bridges; such television series as *The Name of the Game, The High Chaparral, My Three Sons*, and the *Donald O'Connor Show*; and stage plays including *Never Too Late* (1969) which, fittingly, told the story of an elderly father of a baby.

Sadly, in the midst of his continuing professional achievements, and his contentment on the homefront, Ed Begley's life came to an end on April 28, 1970, while attending a party at the home of his publicist, Jay Bernstein. Although the actor's obituaries stated that he died from an apparent heart attack, Bernstein later said Begley choked while eating.

"I was giving the party for Susan Hayward and Ed, who's really one of the sweetest men I've ever known," Bernstein recalled in a 2001 interview. "He choked on a piece of steak. We took him into the kitchen—[singer] Mac Davis gave him mouth-to-mouth resuscitation, and Ed Ames, the singer, was working on him, and Scoey Mitchell was looking for the paramedics. Ed died in my kitchen. I felt so badly. He was just always nice, always had a smile, always warm. Never had a star kind of temperament, always the life of the party, always had something fun to say. Always the one who was making everyone else feel good."

Although Ed Begley specialized in portraying corrupt, vicious, and even murderous characters, he was, by all accounts, a loving, loyal, and universally-admired man. His great body of work in radio, television, film, stage, and audio recordings stands for itself—perhaps the greatest tribute to Begley as a man, however, came after his death from actor Tony Randall, who co-starred with Begley in the stage production of *Inherit the Wind*:

"People seem surprised to learn that in life he was a merry soul, very funny, much given to practical jokes," Randall said. "He had known his roaring days and the admiration of the ladies. He had known his sad days, too, but he was not capable of bitterness. He had a wonderful energy that showed in his great blue eyes and forced him to enjoy every minute of life, whether he willed it or not. Herman Shumlin once called him 'clean-hearted Ed Begley' and that's what he was."

Film Noir Filmography

Street with No Name. Director: William Keighley. Producer: Samuel G. Engel. Running time: 91 minutes. Released by 20th Century–Fox, July 14, 1948. Cast: Mark Stevens, Richard Widmark, Lloyd Nolan, Barbara Lawrence, Ed Begley, Donald Buka, Joseph Pevney, John McIntire, Howard Smith, Walter Greaza, Joan Chandler, Bill Mauch, Sam Edwards, Don Kohler, Rober McGee, Vincent Donahue, Phillip Pine, Buddy Wright, Larry Anzalone, Robert Karnes, Robert Patten.

Sorry, Wrong Number. Director: Anatole Litvak. Producers: Hal B. Wallis, Anatole Litvak. Running time: 98 minutes. Released by Paramount, September 1, 1948. Cast: Barbara Stanwyck, Burt Lancaster, Ann Richards, Wendell Corey, Harold Vermilyea, Ed Begley, Leif Erickson, William Conrad, John Bromfield, Jimmy Hunt, Dorothy Neumann, Paul Fierro. Awards: Academy Award nomination for Best Actress (Barbara Stanwyck).

Convicted. Director: Harry Levin. Producer: Jerry Bresler. Running time: 91 minutes. Released by Columbia, August 1950. Cast: Glenn Ford, Broderick Crawford, Millard Mitchell, Dorothy Malone, Carl Benton Reid, Frank Faylen, Will Geer, Martha Stewart, Henry O'Neill, Douglas Kennedy, Ronald Winters, Ed Begley, Frank Cady, John Doucette, Ilka Gruning, John A. Butler, Peter Virgo, Whit Bissell.

Dark City. Director: William Dieterle. Producer: Hal Wallis. Running time: 98 minutes. Released by Paramount, October 18, 1950. Cast: Charlton Heston, Lizabeth Scott, Viveca Lindfors, Dean Jagger, Don DeFore, Jack Webb, Ed Begley, Henry Morgan, Walter Sande, Mark Keuning, Mike Mazurki, Stanley Prager, Walter Burke.

On Dangerous Ground. Director: Nicholas Ray. Producer: John Houseman. Running time: 82 minutes. Released by RKO, February 12, 1952. Cast: Ida Lupino, Robert Ryan, Ward Bond, Charles Kemper, Anthony Ross, Ed Begley, Ian Wolfe, Sumner Williams, Gus Schilling, Frank Ferguson, Cleo Moore, Olive Carey, Richard Irving, Pat Prest.

The Turning Point. Director: William Dieterle. Producer: Irving Asher. Running time: 85 minutes. Released by Paramount, November 14, 1952. Cast: William Holden, Edmond O'Brien, Alexis Smith, Tom Tully, Ed Begley, Dan Dayton, Adele Longmire, Ray Teal, Ted De Corsia, Don Porter, Howard Freeman, Neville Brand.

Odds Against Tomorrow. Director: Robert Wise. Producer: Robert Wise. Running time: 96 minutes. Released by United Artists, October 15, 1959. Cast: Harry Belafonte, Robert Ryan, Gloria Grahame, Shelley Winters, Ed Begley, Willi Kuluva, Mae Barnes, Carmen DeLavallade, Richard Bright, Lou Gallo, Fred J. Scollay, Lois Thorne.

References

Adams, Antony. "Jack of All Trades, But Master Of One." *Long Island Sunday Press*, June 26, 1955.

"Begleys to Biscuit Tallow for Tots." *Variety*, March 5, 1965.

Biography of Ed Begley. Paramount Studios, May 1966.

Carlson, Barbara. "Ed Begley Dies; Actor of Many Roles." *Hartford Courant*, April 30, 1970.

"Drama Teacher Begley-ed." *Variety*, August 12, 1970.

"Dropout Drops In for His Diploma." *Variety*, July 3, 1969.

"Ed Begley, Actor, Dead at 69; Noted for Character Portrayals." *New York Times*, April 30, 1970.

"Ed Begley Dies of Heart Attack." *Variety*, April 30, 1970.

"Funeral Rites Conducted for Ed Begley." *Los Angeles Herald-Examiner*, May 2, 1970.

Gould, J. "Patterns Is Hailed as a Notable Triumph." *New York Times*, January 17, 1956.

Greenberg, Abe. "'Dropout' Ed Begley — Gets Ph.D. — In Film!" *Hollywood Citizen News*, May 20, 1969.

Hopper, Hedda. "Stork Causes Ed Begley to Cancel Tour." *Los Angeles Times*, May 14, 1964.

_____. "Why Ed Begley, Dean of Actors, Never Became Singer for the Met." *Los Angeles Times*, December 8, 1963.

Langley, Frank. "Begley Strong At 70." *Corpus Christi Caller-Times*, February 15, 1970.

McGinley, Art. "Actor Ed Begley; a Man Of Warmth and Humility." *The Hartford Times*, May 1, 1970.

Nathanson, Mort. Biography of Ed Begley. United Artists Corp., circa 1957.

Nicola, J.D. "The Theater's His Home." *Long Island Catholic*, October 11, 1962.

Obituary. *Newsweek*, May 11, 1970.

Obituary. *New York Times*, April 30, 1970.

Obituary. *Time*, May 11, 1970.

Parsons, Louella O. "Life Begins at 62." *Los Angeles Herald-Examiner*, May 3, 1964.

Randall, Tony. "Ed Begley 1901–1970." *New York Times*, May 17, 1970.

Rich, Allen. "Ed Begley — A Very Remarkable Fella." *Citizen News*, October 2, 1968.

Ronnie, Art. "Ed Begley: No. One Radio Dialectician." *Los Angeles Herald-Examiner*, May 8, 1965.

Ryan, Bill. "Ed Begley, Actor, 1901–1970; Anguish, Acclaim, Serenity." *The Hartford Times*, April 29, 1970.

"Services Set for Actor Ed Begley." *Los Angeles Times*, April 30, 1970.

Taylor, T. "Stage Right, Stage Left." *Cue*, June 8, 1957.

"The Man Has Right to Dance." *Los Angeles Times*, June 18, 1964.

Whitney, Dwight. "He Needed No School of Acting." *TV Guide*, August 2, 1964.

Zunser, Jesse. "An Actor's Actor." *Cue*, August 3, 1963.

WILLIAM BENDIX

"I've got just the place for me and you. A little room upstairs that's too small for you to fall down in. I can bounce you around off the walls — that way we won't be wasting a lot of time while you get up off the floor." — William Bendix in *The Glass Key* (1942)

Brash and burly, with a broad face and a nose that appeared to have been haphazardly fashioned from clay, William Bendix was well-deserving of the moniker "The Mug." The actor, who himself once remarked, "I'm about as handsome as a mud fence," was hardly of leading man stock, but his talent as a character actor made him one of Hollywood's most dependable and likable stars. Perhaps best known for his long-running title role on the radio, television, and film versions of *The Life of Riley*, Bendix was also a standout in six examples from the film noir era: *The Glass Key* (1942), *The Dark Corner* (1946), *The Blue Dahlia* (1946), *Calcutta* (1947), *Detective Story* (1951), and *Macao* (1952).

William Bendix was born on January 14, 1906, on the East side of New York City, the only child of Oscar and Hilda Carnell Bendix. Although Bendix was not musically inclined, he descended from a strong musical background — his father was a musician who played with local bands, his uncle was Max Bendix, a violinist who once conducted the Metropolitan Opera Orchestra, and he was distantly related to composer Felix Mendelssohn (whose compositions included "The Wedding March," commonly used for wedding recessionals). According to Bendix, "My misguided mother wanted me to play the violin, but I preferred to be a ball player."

Bendix got his first taste of acting at the age of five, when his father arranged for him to have a small role in a silent Lillian Walker film made at Brooklyn's Vitagraph Studios, and as a teenager he appeared in several productions with the Henry Street Settlement Playhouse on New York's lower East side — but he participated in these theatrical activities for amusement only. Instead, Bendix was single-mindedly focused on the game of baseball. When his family moved to a more fashionable area in the uptown section of New York, the youngster landed a job as a bat boy for the New York Giants and New York Yankees at the Polo Grounds, where the teams played at the time. Bendix would later fondly recall "rushing hot dogs" to Yankee great Babe Ruth: "One day he really ran me," Bendix said of the ballplayer. "Twenty-four dogs and you'd thought that woulda killed him, but he hit two home runs." His baseball aspirations ended when the Giants went south for spring training and his parents refused to allowed Bendix to accompany them (although a few years later, he did do a stint as a semi-professional second baseman). Instead, Bendix dropped out of high school after two years at the Townsend Harris preparatory school, and took on a series of odd jobs, including delivering movie films for $12 a week. He also earned $10 weekly playing semi-professional football for a team known as the Westchesters.

The future actor's first "real" job was a branch manager of a wholesale grocery company in Orange, New Jersey. His solid income allowed him to marry his childhood sweetheart, Therese Stefanotti, in 1928. The couple went on to have a daughter, Lorraine, and adopt a second daughter, Stephanie; their marriage lasted until Bendix's death.

Meanwhile, Bendix was forced into another career move when the Depression and the development of larger "supermarket" chains forced his store to close. To make ends meet, he worked for a while as a singing waiter in Greenwich Village, then renewed his old interest in acting when he landed a job with the WPA Federal Theatre Project, earning $17.50 a week. Years later, the actor would explain the reason behind his career change: "I didn't go to high school, so how could I be a doctor or a lawyer?" he asked. "I was a semi-

pro in baseball, a semi-pro in football, and got the gate as a grocery clerk. I can't sing, I can't dance, I can't play an instrument. What's left but acting?"

After three years with the Federal Theatre Project, Bendix was seen in six successive Broadway plays, but each was a flop. Meanwhile, he honed his craft by working summer stock in towns throughout the East, including Ivorytown, Connecticut; Newport, Rhode Island; Maplewood, New Jersey; and Buck County, Pennsylvania.

Bendix's big break finally came in 1939, when he played the role of Krupp, the policeman, in the Broadway hit *The Time of Your Life*. The actor remained with the play throughout its year-long run and its road tour. His well-received performance in the production caught the attention of film producer Hal Roach, whose studio created the Laurel and Hardy and Our Gang features, as well as films starring such notables as Thelma Todd, Zasu Pitts, and Patsy Kelly. Bendix signed a contract with Hal Roach Studios for $300 ("work or no work"), but his film debut was in the MGM production of *Woman of the Year* (1942). Although it was a small role, Bendix's performance was noted by one re-

viewer who wrote that he made it "superior to what may have been originally intended."

The actor was seen in five additional movies that year, including an Abbott and Costello comedy, *Who Done It?* (1942); a mediocre programmer for Hal Roach, *The Brooklyn Orchid* (1942); and a rousing wartime drama, *Wake Island* (1942), which earned the actor an Academy Award nomination for Best Supporting Actor (he lost to Van Heflin for *Johnny Eager*). Ironically, the actor later said that his first experience before the camera had left him panic-stricken: "I didn't know where the camera was until after the first scene was over," he recalled. "Never been so scared in my life."

After his appearance in *The Brooklyn Orchid*, Bendix signed a non-exclusive contract with Paramount Studios and entered the realm of film noir in *The Glass Key* (1942). In this hard-hitting Dashiell Hammett tale, Bendix portrayed the henchman of a seedy casino owner. Although the film starred the popular teaming of Alan Ladd and Veronica Lake, Bendix all but stole the show with his performance of the sadistic strongman. He is particularly vicious in one scene, in which he mercilessly beats Ladd's character, and then remarks with a sense of admiration, "You can't croak him — he's tough. He likes this. Dontcha, baby?" The scene was memorable for its off-screen reality, as well. According to author Beverly Linet, Bendix accidentally hit the diminutive Ladd firmly on the jaw during one take of the scene, knocking him unconscious. The film's director, Stuart Heisler, ordered that the shot be printed, and it appears in the film. However, Bendix was extremely upset by his action and Ladd awoke to find the hulking actor crying. He was touched by Bendix's reaction, the two became close friends, and Ladd would later specifically request that the actor appear in many of his future films, including *China* (1943), *Skirmish on the Home Front* (1944), *The Blue Dahlia* (1946), *Two Years Before the Mast* (1946), and *The Deep Six* (1957).

The following year, Bendix continued to offer top-notch performances in films such as *Hostages* (1943), which told the story of the Czech underground movement during the Nazi occupation. The reviewer for the *New York Times* lauded his portrayal of a Czech saboteur, saying the actor "brought a heartening vigor" to the role, and the *New York World-Telegram*'s critic wrote that Bendix had given "the most sensitively detailed performance of his brief and brilliant career." And for his appearance in *Guadalcanal Diary* (1943), one critic raved that Bendix "comes closest to dominating the performances as an ex–taxi driver from Brooklyn who adds humor and meaning to every scene in which he appears." The actor topped off this exceptional year with a nomination from the Motion Picture Exhibitors for the actor "most likely to succeed."

With top billing, Bendix received mixed reviews for the "title role" of *The Hairy Ape* (1944), playing a simple-minded ship worker, but he earned a slew of accolades with his portrayal of a dull-witted but compassionate ship's stoker in Alfred Hitchcock's *Lifeboat* (1944). Of his performance, the reviewer for the *New York World-Telegram* wrote that Bendix, "who has never been bad in a movie, never has been better." Bendix would later recall the experience on the film as one of his most memorable.

"All of us in the cast of *Lifeboat* were supposed to be survivors from a torpedoed ship, you remember, and we were fished out of the sea all dripping with oil," Bendix said. "Every day for three weeks I was dunked in crankcase oil. At the end of each day's work I'd take three showers [but they] didn't do any good. Crankcase oil kept oozing out of my pores. When my wife and I went to a restaurant for dinner, people would ask if they could change tables, to get as far away from Bendix as possible. It was six months before I got that stuff out of my system."

During this time, the actor began to spread his dramatic wings, landing a role that would be associated with him for the rest of his career. In 1944, he replaced veteran actor Lionel Stander (who would gain television fame late in his life on the popular series *Hart*

to Hart) on the radio program *The Life of Riley*, portraying the bumbling and bewildered Chester A. Riley. Married, and the father of two, Chester was known for stumbling his way through life in a series of minor disasters, and popularized the catchphrase, "What a revolting' development this is." Bendix would remain with the show until 1951.

On screen, Bendix continued his busy film schedule, appearing as himself in such lightweight fare as *It's in the Bag* (1945) and *Duffy's Tavern* (1945), then returning to more somber stuff in the first-rate wartime drama, *A Bell for Adano* (1945), with John Hodiak and Gene Tierney. Of his six films in 1946, two were films noirs—in the first, *The Dark Corner*, he portrayed "White Suit," a mysterious man hired by a wealthy art dealer (Clifton Webb) to make life miserable for private detective Bradford Galt (Mark Stevens). The art dealer—Hardy Cathcart—first orders White Suit to goad Galt into killing attorney Tony Jardine (Kurt Krueger), who is having an affair with Cathcart's wife. When this ploy fails, White Suit takes matters into his own hands, killing Jardine and framing Galt for the crime. Despite the satisfactory completion of his duties, however, White Suit meets an ignominious end when Cathcart arranges a meeting to pay him off and, instead, pushes him from an upper story window to his death. But Cathcart gets his just deserts in the film's climax when his own wife guns him down after learning that he was responsible for her lover's death. In a cast that included excellent performances by Stevens and Webb, Bendix was again a standout—the *New York Times* reviewer found that he played his role with "rugged naturalness," and in the *Los Angeles Examiner*, James O'Farrell gushed: "There is a splendid treat in the delivery by William Bendix of a wonderful performance of the role of a cold-blooded killer, with not a moment of comedy in the characterization. He's never been better."

In Bendix's second film noir of the year, *The Blue Dahlia*, he gave an outstanding performance as Buzz Wanchek, an ex–Navy man whose wartime head injury nearly drives him

insane. When the duplicitous wife of his wartime pal Johnny Morrison (Alan Ladd) is
found murdered, Buzz finds himself among
those being investigated, along with Johnny
and his wife's lover, Eddie Harwood (Howard
Da Silva). Buzz becomes the chief suspect,
however, when he reveals that he was with
Mrs. Morrison shortly before her death, and
is unable to remember the details of the evening. With police close to forcing a confession out of the confused veteran, Buzz experiences a moment of illumination ("I wouldn't
dirty my hands on her," he says), and it is
ultimately revealed that the real killer was a
blackmailing house detective (Will Wright).
The film's screenplay — by Raymond Chandler (who also penned the novels on which
noir classics *The Big Sleep* [1946] and *Lady in
the Lake* [1946] were based) — had originally
had fingered Bendix's character as the killer.
However, representatives from the U.S. Navy
reportedly objected to the depiction of one of
their men succumbing to murder as a result
of a battle injury. As a result, Chandler altered
the film's climax, resulting in a rather unexpected conclusion.

Continuing his non-stop film schedule,
Bendix appeared in six features in 1947, including, *Where There's Life*, a Bob Hope starrer; *The Web*, a suspenseful crime drama with
Edmond O'Brien and Vincent Price; *I'll Be
Yours*, a so-so musical remake of Preston
Sturges' *The Good Fairy* (1935); and his fourth
film noir, *Calcutta*. Set in the exotic locale of
the film's title, this feature depicts Bendix
and co-star Alan Ladd as Pedro Blake and
Neale Gordon, two commercial plane pilots
who set out to find the killer of their buddy,
Bill Cunningham (John Whitney). Of the
two, Bendix's character is the more impulsive; in one scene, frustrated by the "double-
talk" of a suspect in the case, Blake suggests
that they "get him outside and slap him up
against a wall." And later, when he is arrested
after an altercation with police officers, he
explains, "Sure I socked 'em. How'd I know
they were cops? When I come out a door and
two guys jump on me, I take a pop at 'em and
save the explanations for later." Blake and

Gordon's quest to find Cunningham's killer
leads them to a jewelry smuggling ring and
a murderous Indian smuggler, but they are
stunned to ultimately learn that a major
player in the scheme is none other than Cunningham's sweet-faced fiancée (Gail Russell),
who is turned over to police in the final reel.
Despite his supporting role, Bendix made his
presence a memorable one, but reviews were
mixed; the critic for *Variety* complained that
the actor was "somewhat ignored in [the] picture," while the *New York Times* reviewer —
although he labeled the picture a "sorry mess
indeed"— noted that Ladd was "nicely abet-
ted" by Bendix.

Coming full circle in his career, Bendix
starred in 1948 in *The Time of Your Life*, based
on the stage play in which he'd gotten his first
big break. Rather than portraying the policeman, however, this time he portrayed Nick,
the bartender, and was hailed in the *New
York Herald Tribune* for being "commanding, as always." But later that year, he starred
in what he considered the worst flop of his
career — the title role in *The Babe Ruth Story*.
Although the film was a box-office hit and
Bendix turned in a superb performance, critics were not kind, and the actor later told a
reporter: "I knew the Babe real well and I was
thrilled when I was asked to play the lead in
the story of his life. But it was a terrible movie.
I was so sick about it that I went to the hospital with ulcers when we finished it."

Bendix returned to more friendly ground
with the film version of his radio hit, *The Life
of Riley* (1949), a successful comedy co-starring Rosemary DeCamp as Riley's long-suffering wife, Peg. He next starred in a rare western, *Streets of Laredo* (1949), played a guard
in a juvenile detention home in *Johnny Holiday* (1949), starred opposite Robert Mitchum
and Jane Greer in a chase thriller, *The Big
Steal* (1949), and donned bangs and a suit of
armor for his role as a knight in the delightful musical comedy, *A Connecticut Yankee in
King Arthur's Court* (1949). In the latter, which
starred Bing Crosby and Rhonda Fleming,
Bendix was required to do his first on-screen
singing. "The [Metropolitan Opera] seems to

be doing alright this season, and I guess Crosby can still handle Sinatra without any help," Bendix jokingly said of his singing part. "But I'm happy to tackle a tune when they need some laughs, especially on a movie set where everything handy seems to be securely nailed to the floor."

In 1950, Bendix signed a seven-year contract with Howard Hughes, which allowed him to seek outside work, but he only appeared in two films that year, *Kill the Umpire*, a lightweight comedy with Una Merkel, and *Gambling House*, where he played a crime boss opposite Victor Mature. He rebounded from these run-of-the-mill features with a first-rate performance in his fifth film noir, *Detective Story* (1951). Termed "bruisingly real" by critics, this gritty film focuses on a day in the life of a New York City squad room of plainclothes detectives, and depicts a mélange of fascinating characters, including a feeble-minded shoplifter (Lee Grant), a callous abortionist (George Macready), and an upstanding young man (Craig Hill) jailed for stealing to hold on to his materialistic, would-be girlfriend. Bendix played Lou Brody, a tough cop with a heart of gold, who provided a much-needed balance for co-worker Jim McLeod (superbly played by Kirk Douglas), known for his inflexibility and fierce moral stance. Brody's character is especially poignant when he appeals to McLeod to drop the charges against the young man, and later offers sage advice to his friend when a conflict with his wife threatens to end McLeod's marriage. It is also Brody who remains by McLeod's side in the final reel, reciting the Acts of Contrition as the detective lay dying from a gunshot wound. As always, Bendix was singled out for his performance by critics, and was lauded by the film's director, William Wyler, as well, who said, "He's quite an actor, and I hope that this may prove an opportunity for him to remind people of that fact."

Bendix followed up this first-rate feature with a role in his final film noir, *Macao* (1952). In this film, Bendix portrayed Lawrence Trumble, one of three Americans who happen to find themselves on the same boat to the "quaint and bizarre" colony of the film's title. Also along are Nick Cochran (Robert Mitchum), an ex–GI wanted for a minor offense back home in the United States, and Julie Benton (Jane Russell), a singer with a questionable past and a penchant for pick pocketing. Posing as a salesman, Trumble is actually a New York detective on the trail of casino owner Vincent Halloran (Brad Dexter), who is safe from the law as long as he remains within the borders of Macao. In an effort to lure Halloran outside of the colony's 3-mile limit, Trumble enlists the aid of Cochran, but the plan has a disastrous outcome for the detective — not only does Halloran figure out Cochran's intentions, but when his henchman go after Cochran, they accidentally kill Trumble instead. Before he dies, however, Trumble reveals to Cochran the real reason for his presence in Macao, and the ex–GI later works with Julie to successfully carry out Trumble's mission. Despite good individual performances, *Macao* was a box office dud and was trashed by critics — the acerbic Bosley Crowther of the *New York Times* called it "a flimflam designed for but one purpose and that is to mesh" Mitchum and Russell, and the critic for *Variety* merely dismissed it as a "routine formula pic."

Bendix fared little better with his next two pictures, *A Girl in Every Port* (1952), starring Groucho Marx (sans brothers), and a tiresome pirate adventure, *Blackbeard the Pirate* (1952). With his film choices dwindling, Bendix turned to the medium of television, where he'd appeared since the late 1940s in such programs as *Philco Television Playhouse* and *Lights Out*. But this time he was on the small screen for the third incarnation of his popular series, *The Life of Riley*. The show had initially been seen on NBC-TV from 1949 to 1950, starring Jackie Gleason — at that time, Bendix's film obligations had prevented him from appearing in the series. But in 1953, freed from his contracts, the actor gladly accepted the role, appearing opposite Marjorie Reynolds as his wife. Five years later, however, the actor had had enough.

"I just got sick of it and it was time to quit," Bendix told columnist Joe Hyams in 1958. "It became an absolute grind day after day, the same story week after week. How far can you go after 220 pictures with the same family. I told … my agents several months ago that I didn't want to do the show next year. I saw no point in keeping at it once the fun had gone out of it…. I guess it will take a while before people stop thinking of me as Riley whenever they see me on the motion picture screen." A few years later, however, after returning to series television in the short-lived Western drama *Overland Trail*, Bendix's view of the *Riley* series appeared to have softened. "I enjoyed playing Riley," he told a reporter in 1961. "He was a good-hearted, stupid character, and I thought the series was a lot of fun."

Meanwhile, in between filming for *The Life of Riley*, Bendix had appeared in a handful of forgettable films, including *Dangerous Mission* (1954), a weak, would-be thriller filmed in 3-D; *Crashout* (1955), a so-so actioner about six convicts who break out of prison in search of a cache of gold; *Battle Stations* (1956), which focused on life aboard a World War II aircraft carrier; and *The Deep Six* (1957), another mediocre wartime drama. With the cancellation of *The Life of Riley* in 1958, Bendix stepped up his appearances on such television drama showcases as *Westinghouse Television Playhouse*, as well as regular series including *The Untouchables, Wagon Train*, and *Mister Ed*. He also returned to the stage in 1960, as an end-run replacement for Jackie Gleason in the musical comedy *Take Me Along*.

The actor continued his work on the big screen but, sadly, his best roles were behind him. The eight films in which he appeared between 1959 and 1963 were mediocre at best, and included the mildly amusing *Idol on Parade* (1959), which featured the actor as a blustering sergeant, and *For Love or Money* (1963), a weak comedy that could not be salvaged despite the talents of such veterans as Kirk Douglas and Thelma Ritter. His best film during these years was *Boys' Night Out*

(1962), starring Kim Novak, James Garner, and Tony Randall, but Bendix had only a small role.

After the release of the latter film, Bendix spent time performing on a daytime radio show and appearing in the stage production of *Take Her, She's Mine* in St. Charles, Illinois. Early the following year, he was in the news because of a lawsuit he filed against CBS-TV for cancelling *Bill and Martha*, a television series in which he was slated to star with actress Martha Raye; since a 1955 operation for stomach ulcers, the actor had been plagued by illness, and the network had reportedly judged him physically incapable of doing the show. Disagreeing with this decision, Bendix sought $2.5 million in damages, but the case ended abruptly with what he termed an "amicable" out-of-court settlement. The actor spent most of the remainder of that year on a road tour of the play *Never Too Late*.

Then, on December 8, 1964, Bendix was rushed to Good Samaritan Hospital in Los Angeles, where he was diagnosed with lobar pneumonia. Eight days later, still hospitalized, his condition complicated by malnutrition, William Bendix died. He was 58 years old. (Two low-budget westerns in which Bendix had appeared — *Johnny Nobody* [1965] and *Young Fury* [1965] — were released after his death.)

William Bendix possessed a genuine and undeniable talent that lives on in countless memorable films and outstanding roles. While the actor often downplayed his acting ability ("I just read the lines … I try to understand the guy I'm to play," he once said), he enjoyed a stellar career with more than 50 film appearances. And his was a career not only appreciated by audiences and critics, but also, according to the actor, by Bendix himself:

"I've had a long, varied, pleasant, eventful career," he said in 1960. "I started out without any advantages, but I've been lucky and successful and I've had fun."

Film Noir Filmography

The Glass Key. Director: Stuart Heisler. Producer: B.G. DeSylva. Running time: 85 minutes.

Released by Paramount, October 15, 1942. Cast: Brian Donlevy, Veronica Lake, Alan Ladd, Bonita Graville, Joseph Calleia, Richard Denning, Moroni Olsen, William Bendix, Margaret Hayes, Arthur Loft, George Meader, Eddie Marr, Frances Gifford, Joe McGuinn, Frank Hagney, Joseph King.

The Dark Corner. Director: Henry Hathaway. Producer: Fred Kohlmar. Running time: 99 minutes. Released by 20th Century–Fox, April 9, 1946. Cast: Mark Stevens, Lucille Ball, Clifton Webb, William Bendix, Kurt Kreuger, Cathy Downs, Reed Hadley, Constance Collier, Eddie Heywood and His Orchestra, Molly Lamont.

The Blue Dahlia. Director: George Marshall. Producer: John Houseman. Running time: 98 minutes. Released by Paramount, April 19, 1946. Cast: Alan Ladd, Veronica Lake, William Bendix, Howard Da Silva, Doris Dowling, Tom Powers, Hugh Beaumont, Howard Freeman, Don Costello, Will Wright, Frank Faylen, Walter Sande. Awards: Academy Award nomination for Best Original Screenplay (Raymond Chandler).

Calcutta. Director: John Farrow. Producer: Seton I. Miller. Running time: 83 minutes. Released by Paramount, May 30, 1947. Cast: Alan Ladd, Gail Russell, William Bendix, June Duprez, Lowell Gilmore, Edith King, Paul Singh, Gavin Muir, John Whitney, Benson Fong.

Detective Story. Director and Producer: William Wyler. Running time: 105 minutes. Released by Paramount, November 6, 1951. Cast: Kirk Douglas, Eleanor Parker, William Bendix, Cathy O'Donnell, George Macready, Horace McMahon, Gladys George, Joseph Wiseman, Lee Grant, Gerald Mohr, Frank Faylen, Craig Hill, Michael Strong, Luis Van Rooten, Bert Freed, Warner Anderson, Grandon Rhodes, William "Bill" Phillips, Russell Evans. Awards: Academy Award nominations for Best Actress (Eleanor Parker), Best Supporting Actress (Lee Grant), Best Director (William Wyler), Best Original Screenplay (Philip Yordan and Robert Wyler).

Macao. Director: Josef von Sternberg. Producer: Alex Gottlieb. Running time: 81 minutes. Released by RKO, April 30, 1952. Cast: Robert Mitchum, Jane Russell, William Bendix, Thomas Gomez, Gloria Grahame, Brad Dexter, Edward Ashley, Philip Ahn, Vladimir Sokoloff, Don Zelaya.

References

"Actor William Bendix Dies." *San Francisco Chronicle*, December 15, 1964.

"Bendix, CBS in Suit Settlement." *The Hollywood Reporter*, October 2, 1964.

"Bendix Gets Important Role in 'Detective Story.'" *New York Herald Tribune*, January 4, 1951.

"Bendix's D.C. Citation." *Variety*, March 26, 1958.

"Bendix Sues CBS for $2,658,000 Over Nixed Series." *The Hollywood Reporter*, May 12, 1964.

"Bill and Babe Get Together as One Man." *New York Herald Tribune*, July 25, 1948.

"Bill Bendix Loses Battle for His Life." *Los Angeles Herald-Examiner*, December 15, 1964.

Biography of William Bendix. General Artists Corporation, August 1961.

Biography of William Bendix. Paramount Studios, January 14, 1948.

Biography of William Bendix. Paramount Studios, February 1951.

Boyle, Hal. "Bill's 6 Rules for Long Marriage." *Los Angeles Evening Mirror News*, July 9, 1959.

Branigan, Alan. "Return of a Prodigal." *Newark Evening News*, June 11, 1961.

Curtis, Olga. "Bendix, Husband Who Says It with Diamonds." *New York Journal-American*, August 10, 1963.

Darbyshire, Martha B. "The New Life of 'Riley.'" *The American Home*, March 1958.

DuBrow, Rick. "Bendix Says Some Actors Forget They Are People." *Newark Evening News*, January 11, 1959.

Glover, William. "Bendix Gets Stage Role — and the Girl." *Los Angeles Times*, October 23, 1960.

Henry, Marilyn. "Let's Not Forget … William Bendix." *Classic Film Collector*, Summer 1978.

Hyams, Joe. "The New Life of Riley." Publication Unsourced, circa 1958.

Humphrey, Hal. "If You Say 'Health' to Bendix — Smile." *Los Angeles Times*, June 26, 1964.

"Life of Riley: Fact or Fiction?" *TV Guide*, circa 1955.

Linet, Beverly. *Ladd: A Hollywood Tragedy*. New York: Berkley Publishing Corporation, 1979.

"Movie Man." *Cue*, April 17, 1943.

Nelsen, Don. "A Most Valuable Player." *New York Sunday News*, December 25, 1960.

Oppenheimer, Peer J. "Meet Bill Bendix — Country Gentleman." *Hollywood Citizen-News*, August 14, 1959.

Shane, Ted. "Hollywood's Magnificent Mug." *The Saturday Evening Post*, September 2, 1944.

Talbott, Earl G. "William Bendix Dies: Actor Lived the Life of Riley." *New York Herald Tribune*, December 15, 1964.

"The Other Bendix." *New York Herald Tribune*, January 26, 1950.

"The Role I Liked Best." *The Saturday Evening Post*, February 2, 1946.

"William Bendix, Actor, 58, Is Dead." *New York Times*, December 15, 1964.

"William Bendix Is Dead at 58; Versatile Actor Created Riley." *New York Times*, December 15, 1964.

"Wm. Bendix Dies." *Los Angeles Times*, December 15, 1964.

BRUCE BENNETT

"Don't kid me, Early—you never had a mother. You were put together in some machine shop. You can think, but you can't feel…. You're no good. You're no good at all."
— Bruce Bennett in *Shakedown* (19505)

What's in a name? For Bruce Bennett, the difference between obscurity and fame.

For the first nine years of his screen career the actor languished, as Herman Brix, in such lackluster vehicles as *Death on the Diamond* (1934), *Amateur Crook* (1937), and *Tarzan and the Green Goddess* (1938). But within a decade of his moniker modification to Bruce Bennett, this handsome Olympic medalist found himself in the cinematic company of such luminaries as Bette Davis in *A Stolen Life* (1946), Ida Lupino in *The Man I Love* (1946), Humphrey Bogart in *The Treasure of the Sierra Madre* (1948), and Errol Flynn in *Silver River* (1948). As Bruce Bennett, the actor also made his mark on the noir era, with featured roles in seven films from the period: *Mildred Pierce* (1945), *Danger Signal* (1945), *Nora Prentiss* (1947), *Dark Passage* (1947), *Mystery Street* (1950), *Shakedown* (1950), and *Sudden Fear* (1952).

Herman Brix was born on May 19, 1906, in Tacoma, Washington, the son of a lumberman and one of five children. After attending elementary and high school in Tacoma, Brix enrolled in the University of Washington, where he distinguished himself as a top athlete; a member of the crew, hockey, track, golf, and swimming teams, he was also all-American tackle on the school's football team, which played in the 1926 Rose Bowl championship (losing by one point to the University of Alabama, whose team included future matinee idol Johnny Mack Brown). He was also a national champion in the shot-put and the javelin throw, and a silver medalist in the shot-put at the 9th Olympic games in Amsterdam in 1928.

More than one theory exists to explain Brix's leap from track and field to the streets of Hollywood. According to one, Brix trained for the Olympics at the home of actor Doug-

las Fairbanks, Sr., who persuaded him to give acting a try. A more detailed version maintains that Brix got his start after pitching an idea to MGM to produce a series of athletic film shorts. Spotted in one of the shorts by talent scouts from Paramount Pictures, Brix was cast in his screen debut, a football yarn called *Touchdown* (1931). Before filming on *Touchdown* was completed, Brix was tapped for the title role in MGM's upcoming adventure, *Tarzan, the Ape Man* (1932), but fate intervened. While filming a football scene in his first feature, Brix sustained a broken shoulder and was hospitalized for four months. By the time he recovered, the role had been given to former Olympic swimming champion, Johnny Weismuller.

Down, but not out, Brix appeared in a series of bit parts, playing a "Klopstokian Athlete" in *Million Dollar Legs* (1932), a wrestler in *Madison Square Garden* (1932), and Hercules in *Student Tour* (1934). He was also briefly seen in a barroom scene in *Riptide* (1934), a box-office hit starring MGM favorite, Norma Shearer. Then, in 1935, he earned a second opportunity to play Tarzan, this time in *The New Adventures of Tarzan*, co-starring Ula Vale. In this instance, the actor was handpicked by *Tarzan* author Edgar Rice Burroughs, who had reportedly grown disillusioned with the screen portrayals of his hero and was determined to more accurately depict the ape man as the erudite former nobleman of the novel. Produced by the author's company, Burroughs-Tarzan Enterprises, Inc., the movie was released as a 265-minute, 12-chapter serial set in the jungles of Guatemala. But while filming this feature, Brix once again discovered the hazards of moviemaking when he was supposed to swing down a jungle vine to rescue a damsel in distress.

"I ran for the rope, which of course gave

it an extra push," the actor recalled in a 1999 interview in the *Christian Science Monitor.* "I swung way too far out and dropped way beyond the pool. I still have the scars from that fall."

Meanwhile, as Brix was endeavoring to secure a firm foothold in the movie business, he had found love off-screen. After a brief courtship, he married Jeannette Braddock on January 31, 1933, and the couple later had two children, Christine, on June 4, 1944, and Christopher, on May 13, 1947. They remained married for 68 years, until Jeannette's death in 2001.

During the next several years, Brix took on larger roles in a series of mediocre films for independent studios, including *Silks and Saddles* (1937) for Victory Pictures, *Land of Fighting Men* (1938) for Monogram, and *Hawk of the Wilderness* (1938) for Republic. He also reprised his role as the ape man in *Tarzan and the Green Goddess* (1938), and spent a year studying in the acting workshop of Austrian theatrical director/producer Max Reinhardt.

"It's a good thing I learned to take it in sports competition, or I might have given up," the actor said. But his luck was about to change.

In late 1939, Brix signed a contract with Columbia Studios and changed his name to the more marquee-friendly Bruce Bennett. The following year, he was seen in a whopping 20 movies, including *West of Abilene*, a "B" western starring Don Beddoe; *Girls of the Road,* featuring a mostly female cast headed by Ann Dvorak and Helen Mack; *Café Hostess*, a cliché-ridden melodrama set in the world of underground nightclub owners; *The Secret Seven*, a so-so thriller about a group of crime-busting scientists; and *Before I Hang*, starring Boris Karloff as a condemned doctor who sets out to prove that old age is a curable disease. Bennett continued his frenetic shooting schedule over the next two years, but few of his films made an impact at the box-office and in 1944, he asked to be released from his Columbia contract. Promptly picked up by Warner Bros., who reportedly promised Bennett stardom if he "delivered," the actor hit

the jackpot with his first assignment — and his first film noir — *Mildred Pierce* (1945).

Here, Bennett plays Bert Pierce, an unemployed real estate broker whose homemaker wife, Mildred (Joan Crawford, in her first Oscar-winning role), helps make ends meet by baking and selling pies. Frustrated by Mildred's concentration on their two children, the snobbish and affected Veda (Ann Blyth) and sweet, precocious Kay (Jo Ann Marlowe), Bert leaves his family, challenging his wife to "see how well you can get along without me." To his surprise, Mildred gets along just fine, first taking on a job as a waitress, and then opening a chain of successful restaurants. Along the way, she meets and marries a penniless aristocrat, Monte Beragon (Zachary Scott); her youngest daughter dies from a sudden attack of pneumonia; and Mildred becomes even more determined to please her increasingly pretentious daughter, Veda. Ultimately, Mildred's thriving business is bankrupted by Monte, and Veda repays her mother's years of sacrifice by seducing her husband. Monte scoffs at Veda's plans for a future with him, however, and an enraged Veda shoots and kills him. Ever the devoted mother, Mildred tries to take the blame for the crime, but detectives arrest Veda as she is attempting to flee, and the film's conclusion finds Mildred and Bert reunited.

In a film that included such standout roles as those played by Crawford, Blyth, and Scott, Bennett nonetheless managed to turn in a well-done portrayal of a husband disillusioned, frustrated, and nearly defeated by circumstances beyond his control. His efforts were recognized by several critics after the film's release, including *Variety*'s reviewer, who noted his "effective" performance, and the critic for *The Hollywood Reporter*, who wrote: "Bruce Bennett is awfully good in the script's only colorless role, and it must be admitted that its very colorlessness is a spoke in the wheel that turns its staggering drama."

After the success of this film, Bennett was quickly cast in his second film noir, *Danger Signal* (1945), starring Faye Emerson and Zachary Scott. A minor entry in the noir cycle, this feature follows the activities of Ronald Mason (Scott), a charming, cultured writer — who also happens to be the murderer of a young New York housewife. When he flees the scene of his crime and heads west, he finds a safe haven as a boarder in the Los Angeles home of Hilda Fenchurch (Emerson) and her younger sister, Anne (Mona Freeman). Hilda, a stenographer in a doctor's office, falls in love with Ronald, but he sets his sights on Anne after learning that she will inherit a sizable trust fund when she marries. Discovering Ronald's plans, Hilda plots his murder, stealing a vial of poison from the office of her employer, Dr. Andrew Lang (Bennett), and planning to dispense the lethal liquid during a dinner at the beach house of a friend, Dr. Silla (Rosemary DeCamp). Although Hilda is psychologically unable to carry out her scheme, Ronald gets his just desserts when the husband of the dead New York housewife tracks him to the beach house. Running from the irate spouse, Ronald trips over an exposed tree root and plunges over a cliff to his death.

As the rather absent-minded scientist, Bennett's Lang was mostly seen admiring Hilda from afar or effecting ill-timed attempts to pursue a relationship with her. It is only when he believes that Hilda is in danger that Lang really comes to life — driving at top speed to the beach house with Dr. Silla, he narrowly avoids several crack-ups and craftily eludes a traffic cop, prompting Dr. Silla to admiringly comment, "I would never have believed it of you, Andrew!" However, although the film earned favorable notices from several critics (including the reviewer for *Independent*, who called it a "corking good dramatic tale"), audiences disagreed, and stayed away in droves. But Bennett rebounded from this disappointment with appearances in *A Stolen Life* (1946), starring Bette Davis, *The Man I Love* (1947), with Ida Lupino, and his third venture into film noir, the underrated *Nora Prentiss* (1947). A fascinating tale, this feature stars Kent Smith as Richard Talbot, a successful San Francisco doctor and family man who is increasingly disheartened by his humdrum existence. Looking for a little spice, he visits a nightclub while his wife and children are out of town, and soon becomes involved with a sultry singer, Nora Prentiss (Ann Sheridan). When Nora realizes that she has no future with the married doctor, she ends their affair and moves to New York, but when a patient dies of a heart attack in his office, Richard finds a way to have his cake and eat it, too. Disguising the dead man's body as his own, Richard sets the car on fire, sends it plummeting over a cliff, and happily joins Nora in New York. Before long, however, he is plagued by paranoia and increasing suspicions over Nora's friendship with her boss, Phil Dinardo (Robert Alda). After Richard exchanges blows with Dinardo, knocking him unconscious, he flees in a panic, becoming involved in a fiery auto accident that leaves his face burned beyond recognition. Richard's downward spiral continues when, ironically, he is tied to the murder of "Dr. Talbot" in San Francisco and arrested for his own death. Plagued with remorse over his duplicitous behavior, Richard refuses to reveal his true identity and is convicted of murder. Bidding Nora farewell in the grim finale, Richard tells her, "I'm no possible good to anybody ... besides, I am guilty. I killed Richard Talbot."

In this riveting film, Bennett played the pivotal role of Richard's co-worker, Dr. Joel Merriam, whose footloose-and-fancy-free lifestyle (he lives at the local YMCA and often stays out all night) serves as an unconscious impetus for Richard's misdeeds. And later, after Richard's disappearance, it is Merriam who pieces together the clues left behind, leading police to suspect Richard of murder. Despite the good performances from the cast and the unusual story, however, *Nora Prentiss* was released to widely varying reviews; while the *New York Times*' Bosley Crowther dismissed the feature as "major picture-making at its worst," William Weaver praised the film in *Motion Picture Herald*, calling it a "feat of melodramatic story-telling which achieves also the result of maintaining suspense of unique intensity down to the final sequence."

In his follow-up to this memorable noir, Bennett was seen in his fourth feature from the period, *Dark Passage* (1947). Here, Humphrey Bogart starred as Vincent Parry, a convict wrongfully convicted of his wife's murder, who escapes from prison, only to be picked up on the highway by Irene Jansen (Lauren Bacall). A wealthy artist who had followed Parry's trial and championed his claim of innocence, Irene opens her home to him, furnishing money and clothes. While there, Parry learns that Irene's neighbor is Madge Rapf (Agnes Moorehead), a friend of his late wife, whose trial testimony was instrumental in his conviction. Meanwhile, Parry arranges to undergo plastic surgery, planning to recuperate at the home of a friend, but when his pal winds up dead, Parry finds himself the subject of a police manhunt. Realizing that Madge is the real murderer of both his wife and his friend, Parry confronts her, demanding a confession. Madge refuses to admit her guilt, however, and, during an hysterical rant, she accidentally falls from a window to her death. Faced with the hopelessness of his situation, Parry flees to South America, where he is later joined by Irene, and they begin a new life together.

Despite his third-billing, Bennett's role as Irene's former beau was a minor one; he made the most of his single scene, however, offering a memorable rant against Madge: "Why don't you leave people alone?" he asks her. "You're not satisfied unless you're bothering people. If it isn't your family you're pestering, it's your friends, it's people you don't even know — it's me!" He rebounded from this brief screen appearance the following year, with a showy role in one of the best films of his career, *The Treasure of the Sierra Madre* (1948). In this feature, starring Humphrey Bogart, Walter Huston, and Tim Holt as three rogues who try to get rich on a gold strike in Mexico, Bennett was memorable as a wily drifter who attempts to muscle his way into the group.

During the remainder of the decade, Bennett appeared in a series of mostly forgettable features, including *Silver River* (1948), a humdrum western starring Errol Flynn; *Smart Girls Don't Talk* (1948), in which he was featured as a villainous nightclub owner; *The Doctor and the Girl* (1949), a soaper set in a hospital; *The House Across the Street* (1949), a tiresome drama about a crime-solving newspaperman; and *Task Force* (1949), an overly talky World War II drama featuring Gary Cooper. By now, Bennett was growing weary of his mundane roles, and complained to the press that he would "rather kiss a horse" than continue in the romantic leads in which he had been cast.

"In the first place, I'm tired of getting lip paint on my face and working on stuffy sound stages with temperamental actresses," Bennett said in 1949. "I want to get into the open air."

Fortunately for the actor, his cinematic luck began to change with the onset of the 1950s, when he was seen in back-to-back films noirs, *Mystery Street* (1950) and *Shakedown* (1950). In *Mystery Street*, Bennett played his third noir doctor, a Harvard scientist named Dr. McAdoo, who uses his forensic expertise to aid police in solving the murder of a local "B" girl. Working only from the victim's skeleton, McAdoo is able to ascertain her age, height, and hair color — and even that she was a former toe dancer. Ultimately, McAdoo and the police team, led by Lt. Morales (Ricardo Montalban), follow the doctor's initial clues to James Joshua Harkley (Edmon Ryan), a respected descendant of one of the city's oldest families.

After earning praise for his "likeable" portrayal of the research scientist, Bennett moved on to his second noir of the year, *Shakedown* (1950). Grim and action-filled, this feature tells the story of Jack Early (Howard Duff), a ruthlessly ambitious newspaper photographer who believes in stopping at nothing to "get the picture." Befriending a local mobster, Nick Palmer (Brian Donlevy), Early gets a tip about a robbery planned by a rival gang member known as Coulton (Lawrence Tierney). Early uses the negative to blackmail Coulton who, learning of Palmer's betrayal, plants a bomb in his car — providing Early with another golden photo opportunity. The conscienceless shutterbug continues to demonstrate the drastic lengths to which he will go for a photograph, but his iniquities finally catch up to him when he is shot by Coulton and, as his last act before he dies, takes a picture of his killer.

In a strong supporting role, Bennett portrayed newspaper photo editor, David Glover, whose grudging appreciation for Early's attention-grabbing pictures was surpassed by his disdain for the man's techniques. "He's got such a terrible driving ambition," Glover says in one scene. "The feeling I get from Early is that he'd stop at nothing — and that's not a virtue." For his efforts, Bennett earned mixed reviews — while he was singled out by several critics for his "good" performance, Darr Smith of the *Los Angeles Daily News* wrote that Bennett "appeared to have trouble with [his] material, though [he] occasionally rises above it," and the critic for the *New York Times* labeled the actor's performance "indecisive." The film itself, however, earned mostly good notices, with the *Los Angeles Times* critic praising the "crisp and clear" direction, and the reviewer from the *Los Angeles Herald-Examiner* noting the "well-told, exigent story."

The following year, fulfilling his desire for more outdoor work, Bennett was loaned out for a pair of well-done westerns, Paramount's *The Great Missouri Raid* (1951) and *The Last Outpost* (1951), and made a rare comedic appearance in the entertaining MGM feature *Angels in the Outfield* (1952), before returning to Warners for his final film noir, *Sudden Fear* (1952). In this gripping thriller, Bennett portrayed Steve Kearney, attorney to wealthy San Francisco playwright, Myra Hudson (Joan Crawford). When Myra falls in love with and marries a young actor, Lester Blaine (Jack Palance), Steve wastes no time drafting a new will that gives her new spouse $10,000 a year for life, or until he remarries. Objecting to the idea of "hanging on to him from the grave," Myra outlines a new will on her voice-activated dictaphone. Later, while listening to the playback, Myra is horrified to hear a conversation recorded by her husband and his lover, Irene (Gloria Grahame), in which they discuss their plans for Myra's murder. After recovering from her initial shock and sorrow, Myra decides to turn the tables on the devious duo, plotting an elaborate scheme to kill Lester and implicate Irene. Ultimately, Myra is unable to carry out the actual murder, but Lester discovers her plot and tries to run her down with his car. Unfortunately for him — and his lover — Myra and Irene are dressed in similar clothing (in keeping with Myra's original scheme), and Lester mistakenly crashes his car into Irene, killing them both.

Upon its release, *Sudden Fear* was a box-office hit and was universally hailed by critics; in a typical review, the *Los Angeles Examiner*'s Ruth Waterbury gushed: "*Sudden Fear* is a smashing, searing thunderbolt of entertainment. No production of the year equals it in its wracking suspense, its awesome emotion, its romantic force and pathos." And although the role of the steadfast attorney was a relatively subdued role for Bennett, the actor earned mention in *The Hollywood Reporter* for his "fine job," and was praised by Edwin Schallert in the *Los Angeles Times*, who wrote that Bennett "shines briefly as a Rock of Gibraltar attorney."

Following appearances in a disappointing battle-of-the-sexes comedy, *Dream Wife* (1953), and a mediocre war film, *Dragonfly Squadron* (1953), Bennett asked to be released from his contract with Warners and turned his attentions to the small screen, appearing throughout the remainder of the decade on such programs as *Stories of the Century, Science Fiction Theater, Playhouse 90, West Point, Perry Mason,* and *Laramie.* After a year away from feature films, Bennett returned as a freelancer in 1955, appearing mostly in such westerns as *Robber's Roost* (1955), in which he portrayed a wheelchair-bound rancher; *The Three Outlaws* (1956), with Neville Brand and Alan Hale, Jr. (who would later achieve fame as the Skipper on TV's *Gilligan's Island*); and *Daniel Boone, Trail Blazer* (1956), which featured Bennett in the title role. A significant departure from these oaters was the box-office smash *Strategic Air Command* (1955), a wartime drama notable for its breathtaking airplane footage.

Relegated by the end of the decade to roles in such low-budget offerings as *The Cosmic Man* (1959) and *The Alligator People* (1959), Bennett attempted to change the course of his career by writing his own movie — the result was a dismal actioner, *Fiend of Dope Island* (1961), with a cast of unknowns that included Robert Bray, Tania Velia, and Ralph Rodriguez. It would be his last feature film for more than a decade. Turning his back on Hollywood, Bennett sought a completely new livelihood, working for a time as western sales manager for a local corporation, and later turning to real estate, selling property for the Beverly Hills firm of Wallace Moir. Initially, the actor used his given name of Herman Brix, but he admitted that he was still frequently identified by his clients.

"[They'd say] 'Who are you hiding from? We know who you are,'" Bennett said in 1984. "It's kind of humorous. Halfway through a deal, some of them will say, 'Oh, my God.' Some recognize me right away, and others never do."

Bennett made a brief return to films in 1972, with a small role in *Deadhead Miles,* starring Alan Arkin, but the film would not be released until more than 10 years later. His final performance was in *The Clones* (1974) a routine thriller starring Michael Greene and Gregory Sierra, although the actor said in 1984 that he would resume his acting career "if the right part came along."

"At this point, I'd be kind of choosy," Bennett said. "There have been a few times that I've come close to doing something, but now I wouldn't do it unless it was something that was going to do credit to me."

No such roles have emerged, but at the age of 94, Bennett made an appearance at the players practice for the Rose Bowl game on January 1, 2001, between the Purdue Boilermakers and Bennett's alma mater, the University of Washington. The actor told players that, 75 years later, the game in which he'd played remained a well-remembered and highly treasured moment in his life.

Since the death of his wife, Jeannette, in 2001, Bennett has lived quietly in his Los Angeles home, away from the glaring spotlight of Tinseltown. He continues to be remembered and appreciated, however, for his contribution to the annals of Hollywood in such memorable features as *Mildred Pierce* and *The Treasure of the Sierra Madre,* where his performances make film-lovers grateful that Herman Brix became Bruce Bennett.

Film Noir Filmography

Mildred Pierce. Director: Michael Curtiz. Producer: Jerry Wald. Running time: 113 minutes. Released by Warner Brothers, September 28, 1945. Cast: Joan Crawford, Jack Carson, Zachary Scott, Eve Arden, Ann Blyth, Bruce Bennett, Lee Patrick, Moroni Olsen, Jo Ann Marlowe, Barbara Brown, Charles Trowbridge, John Compton, Butterfly McQueen. Awards: Academy Award for Best Actress (Joan Crawford). Academy Award nominations for Best Picture, Best Supporting Actress (Ann Blyth and Eve Arden), Best Black and White Cinematography (Ernest Haller), Best Screenplay (Ranald MacDougall).

Danger Signal. Director: Robert Florey. Producer: William Jacobs. Running time: 78 minutes.

Released by Warner Bros., November 14, 1945. Cast: Faye Emerson, Zachary Scott, Dick Erdman, Rosemary DeCamp, Bruce Bennett, Mona Freeman, John Ridgely, Mary Servoss, Joyce Compton, Virginia Sale.

Nora Prentiss. Director: Vincent Sherman. Producer: William Jacobs. Running time: 111 minutes. Released by Warner Brothers, February 22, 1947. Cast: Ann Sheridan, Kent Smith, Bruce Bennett, Robert Alda, Rosemary DeCamp, John Ridgely, Robert Arthur, Wanda Hendrix, Helen Brown, Rory Mallinson, Harry Shannon, James Flavin, Douglas Kennedy, Don McGuire, Clifton Young.

Dark Passage. Director: Delmar Daves. Producer: Jerry Wald. Running time: 106 minutes. Released by Warner Bros., September 27, 1947. Cast: Humphrey Bogart, Lauren Bacall, Bruce Bennett, Agnes Moorehead, Tom D'Andrea, Clifton Young, Douglas Kennedy, Rory Mallinson, Houseley Stevenson.

Mystery Street. Director: John Sturges. Producer: Frank E. Taylor. Running time: 94 minutes. Released by MGM, July 27, 1950. Cast: Ricardo Montalban, Sally Forrest, Bruce Bennett, Elsa Lanchester, Marshall Thompson, Jan Sterling, Edmon Ryan, Betsy Blair, Wally Maher, Ralph Dumke, Willard Waterman, Walter Burke, Don Shelton, Brad Hatton. Awards: Academy Award nomination for Best Original Screenplay (Leonard Spigelgass).

Shakedown. Director: Joe Pevney. Producer: Ted Richmond. Running time: 80 minutes. Released by Universal-International, September 23, 1950. Cast: Howard Duff, Brian Donlevy, Peggy Dow, Lawrence Tierney, Bruce Bennett, Anne Vernon, Stapleton Kent, Peter Virgo, Charles Sherlock.

Sudden Fear. Director: David Miller. Producer: Joseph Kaufman. Running time: 110 minutes. Released by RKO, August 7, 1952. Cast: Joan Crawford, Jack Palance, Gloria Grahame, Bruce Bennett, Virginia Huston, Touch [Mike] Conners. Awards: Academy Award nominations for Best Actress (Joan Crawford), Best Supporting Actor (Jack Palance), Best Black and White Cinematography (Charles B. Lang, Jr.), Best Costume Design, Black and White (Sheila O'Brien).

References

"All-American Bennett." Chamberlain and Lyman Brown Theatrical Agency, circa 1947.
"Athletes in Films." *New York Times*, February 10, 1947.
Biography of Bruce Bennett. Paramount Studios, May 1956.
Biography of Bruce Bennett. RKO Radio Studios, circa 1952.
"Bruce Bennett." *Hollywood Studio Magazine*, December 1973.
Goodale, Gloria. "He Tarzan, Lord of the Jungle." *The Christian Science Monitor*, June 18, 1999.
"Herman Brix, aka Bruce Bennett, as Tarzan!" Internet resource: http://www.briansdriveintheater. com/hermanbrix.html.
"Long Arm of TV." *Variety*, February 25, 1953.
Mosby, Aline. "Bruce Bennett Prefers Horses to Glamorous Leading Ladies." *Hollywood Citizen-News*, January 3, 1949.
Neumeyer, Kathleen. "Twinkle, Twinkle, Former Star." *Los Angeles Magazine*, January 1984.
"Olympic Champion Once; Now Learning to Act." *New York Times*, January 4, 1939.
"On the Town." *Hollywood Citizen-News*, September 30, 1952.
"Tarzan Is Always Good for Some Chest-Thumping." *Los Angeles Times,* December 21, 2000.
"Where Are They Today?" *The Hollywood Reporter*, January 27, 1971.

HUMPHREY BOGART

"You know, you're the second guy today that thinks a gat in the hand means the world by the tail." — Humphrey Bogart in *The Big Sleep* (1946)

Unconventionally handsome, undeniably masculine, and unapologetically self-assured, Humphrey Bogart was, if not the prototypic noir actor, then certainly the quintessential noir *star*. With a single look, he could melt a female's knees, cause a male foe to cower, or bring a smile to the lips of a crying child. In a body of nearly 100 films that ranged from the superior (*Casablanca, The African Queen*) to the fairly ludicrous (*The Return of Dr. X*), Bogart demonstrated his prowess in drama as well as comedy, and excelled in 11 films noirs: *High Sierra* (1941), *The Maltese Falcon* (1941), *Conflict* (1945), *The Big Sleep* (1946),

Dark Passage (1947), *Dead Reckoning* (1947), *Key Largo* (1948), *Knock on Any Door* (1949), *In a Lonely Place* (1950), *The Enforcer* (1951), and *The Harder They Fall* (1956).

Humphrey DeForest Bogart was born in New York City, the son of Belmont De-Forest Bogart, a Manhattan surgeon, and his wife Maud Humphrey, a prominent illustrator and artist. The exact date of Bogart's birth, however, is in question. Many sources claim that he was born on January 23, 1899, but his birth certificate and an announcement in a local newspaper list the date as December 25, 1899, and his studio biography from Warner Brothers claims that he entered the world on December 25, 1900. The future star was educated at the Trinity School in New York City and later at the Phillips Academy in Andover in Massachusetts, where his father had enjoyed a celebrated baseball career. Young Humphrey's experience at the school was not as prestigious, however — he was expelled for engaging in a mischievous prank.

"I thought it would be a good idea to duck an assistant professor, a very unpopular gent, in a fountain," Bogart recalled years later. "There was a whole gang of us in on the plot, but it was a dark night and he didn't recognize anybody but me. The school asked me to leave."

Because he "loved boats and water," Bogart joined the Navy after his expulsion from Phillips, where he served as a seaman on the destroyer *Santa Olivia*, and as a helmsman on the troopship *Leviathan*. It is believed that during his service on the latter ship, the actor sustained a lip wound that resulted in his trademark lisp. The circumstances that led to the injury remain in question, however. According to one version, Bogart was wounded by a piece of shrapnel (or wood) during the shelling of the *Leviathan*. Another account maintains that the actor was assigned to escort another sailor to the Port Smith Prison in Massachusetts (or the Portsmouth Prison in New Hampshire), and while changing trains, the sailor struck Bogart in the mouth with his handcuffs. Bogart, the story claims, still managed to safely deliver the prisoner,

but his resulting surgery was botched, resulting in the permanent lisp.

Bogart was honorably discharged from the Navy after the end of World War I, and found employment as a tug and lighter inspector for a Pennsylvania company, as an office boy for the brokerage firm of S.W. Strauss & Co., and doing clerical work for producer William A. Brady, a neighbor of the Bogart family. Later, Brady promoted Bogart to stage manager of his film studio, World Pictures, in New Jersey. However, as with Bogart's correct birthdate and the manner in which he earned his lisp, the story of how he got his start in acting is a hazy one. Some sources claim that Brady asked Bogart to direct an unfinished film, but the future actor did such a poor job that Brady was forced to finish the task himself. At the urging his daughter, actress Alice Brady, the producer gave Bogart a job as road manager and understudy to the actors, which led to his being cast in minor parts. Others maintain that Bogart became interested in acting when he began frequenting local theaters after the war and asked Brady to give him a part in a play, *Experience,* when a bit actor was fired. Because he was already receiving a salary as the play's road manager, Bogart offered to play the part at no extra cost to the producer, and Brady agreed. Another account holds that Alice Brady thought Bogart had acting potential and gave him a small role in *Drifting*, a play in which she was the star. And still another version states that Bogart, while working as road manager on the play *The Ruined Lady*, was dared by actor Neil Hamilton to go on stage one night in his place. Bogart did and, although the experiment was a disaster, William Brady suggested that he try for a career on the stage because "actors earn good money."

The circumstances surrounding his entry into acting notwithstanding, it is agreed that Bogart spent the next 13 years appearing in a variety of plays, including *Swifty* (1922), for which he was panned as "inadequate," *Meet the Wife* (1923), *Nerves* (1924), *Candle Snatchers* (1925), *Baby Mine* (1927), *Saturday's*

Children (1928), *It's a Wise Child* (1929), *After All* (1931), *I Loved You Wednesday* (1932), *Our Wife* (1933), *Invitation to Murder* (1934), and *The Petrified Forest* (1935). The latter production was a smash hit, and the play's star, Leslie Howard, promised that if it were ever made into a film, he would ensure that Bogart reprised his role. Meanwhile, during this period, Bogart was also gaining experience on the silver screen. In 1930, he debuted in *A Devil with Women*, starring Victor McLaglen, and was later seen in such forgettable fare as *Up the River* (1930), which was notable as Spencer Tracy's first film and which began a lifelong friendship between the two men; *Bad Sister* (1931), Bette Davis' movie debut; *A Holy Terror* (1931), Bogart's first western; *Love Affair* (1932), in which the actor portrayed his first leading role; and *Three on a Match* (1932) where, in a small role as a racketeer boss, Bogart demonstrated a hint of the menacing persona that would come to serve him well in future films.

In 1936, when Warner Brothers acquired the rights to *The Petrified Forest*, studio executives planned to cast contract player Ed-

ward G. Robinson as Duke Mantee, the vicious gangster that Bogart had played to such acclaim on Broadway. True to his word, Leslie Howard insisted that the part be given to Bogart, and even went so far as to refuse to star in the film unless Bogart was cast as Mantee. Bogart was given the role and it proved to be the break for which he had been waiting. The film was a critical and financial success and Bogart was signed to a studio contract with Warner Brothers. After more than a decade, Humphrey Bogart had finally arrived.

While his acting career was taking off, Bogart had been busy behind the scenes as well. In May 1926, the actor married stage star Helen Menken, whom he had met two years earlier while stage managing a road production of *Drifting*. The marriage was doomed from the start, however. Bogart reportedly married the actress to further his career, and the union was characterized by frequent arguments and physical altercations. The couple split after less than a year. Then in May 1928, Bogart gave marriage another try — this time he was wed to stage actress Mary Phillips, with whom he had appeared in *Nerves*. The two began a long-distance relationship when Bogart began appearing in films and his wife refused to abandon her screen career. This marriage, too, would ultimately end in divorce, in 1937.

Despite his success in *The Petrified Forest*, Bogart found himself once again languishing in a series of "B" movies, including *Isle of Fury* (1936), which the actor later claimed he never remembered making; *Swing Your Lady* (1938), a silly musical comedy; *The Oklahoma Kid* (1939), a second-rate western costarring James Cagney; and *The Return of Dr. X* (1939), an odd horror film in which the actor portrayed a doctor who was put to death in the electric chair, is later brought back to life, and spends his time in search of fresh blood to stay alive. Bogart later referred to the film as "this stinking movie." The actor continued to be disillusioned about his screen roles, but later explained his reasons for never turning one down: "I'm known as the guy who always squawks about roles, but never refuses to play one," he said. "I've never forgotten a piece of advice [silent actor] Holbrook Blinn gave me when I was a young squirt and asked him how I could get a reputation as an actor. He said, 'Just keep working.' The idea is that if you're always busy, sometime somebody is going to get the idea that you must be good." And indeed, there were a number of memorable films made by Bogart during this period, including *Dead End* (1937), which saw the actor in a small but showy role as a callous gangster; *Angels with Dirty Faces* (1938), a James Cagney starrer with Bogart portraying a corrupt attorney; *Dark Victory* (1939), where the actor played a horse trainer for doomed star Bette Davis; and *They Drive By Night* (1941), starring Bogart as George Raft's truck driver brother.

After the release of the latter film, Bogart's career received a monumental boost when he was cast in a starring role in his first film noir, *High Sierra* (1941). It was pure fate that the actor was cast in the role of ruthless gangster Mad Dog Roy Earle — the part had previously been offered to, and rejected by, both George Raft and Paul Muni. As Earle, Bogart portrayed an aging gangleader who, upon his release from a lengthy prison stretch, embarks on a final caper. He enlists two young hoods as his partners in the job, and finds himself the object of unwanted affection from Marie Garson (outstandingly played by Ida Lupino), the girlfriend of one of the men. Meanwhile, Earle fancies himself in love with a young crippled girl, Velma (Joan Leslie), but after he finances an operation that successfully repairs her clubfoot, he realizes that his love for the young girl is unrequited. Over time, he falls in love with the ever-faithful Marie, but their relationship is doomed — the well-planned robbery scheme is botched when Earle kills a guard in self-defense, the two others in on the heist die in a fiery car accident, and Earle is forced to go on the lam. Ultimately, he flees into the Sierra Mountains, but he is trapped there by police and is killed by a sharpshooter's bullet. This stellar film marked the turning point in Bogart's

career and was praised by such critics as the *New York Times'* Bosley Crowther, who said that the actor "plays the leading role with a perfection of hard-boiled vitality."

Bogart was firmly established as a star later in 1941 with the release of his second film noir entry, *The Maltese Falcon*, which marked the directorial debut of John Huston and was nominated for Best Picture (losing to *How Green Was My Valley*). Here, Bogart is Sam Spade, a private detective hired to find the famed Maltese Falcon, a jewel-encrusted black bird that was, according to legend, stolen by pirates in 1539, while the statuette was en route from the Knights of Templar of Malta to Charles V of Spain. Along the way, Spade encounters a medley of quirky characters all in search of the bird, including the ruthless and single-mindedly mercenary "Fat Man" (Sidney Greenstreet), his ineffectual and ill-fated gunman, Wilmer (Elisha Cook, Jr.), and femme fatale extraordinare, Brigid O'Shaunessy (Mary Astor), with whom Spade begins an affair. A typically complicated and action-packed noir entry, the film ends with the famed bird still not found, and Spade turning his lover into the police for murder: "Yes, angel, I'm going to send you over," Spade tells her. "But chances are, you'll get off with life. That means if you're a good girl, you'll be out in 20 years. I'll be waiting for you. If they hang you, I'll always remember you." *The Maltese Falcon* was a hit with audiences and critics alike, with one reviewer calling it "no ordinary tale of crime and detection" and claiming that Bogart "was never given a part more suitable to his talents."

While Bogart was riding high on his "overnight success," his off-screen life was becoming as dramatic as any of his films. In 1937, on the set of the Bette Davis vehicle *Marked Woman*, Bogart met actress Mayo Methot, who portrayed one of the film's nightclub "hostesses" (a 1930s euphemism for prostitute). Notorious for her hard drinking and violent temper, Methot married Bogart in August 1938, but the relationship was a volatile one from the start — during their honeymoon stay at New York's Algonquin

Hotel, the couple got into a huge fight, causing $400 in damage to their room. The duo became known as the "Battling Bogarts," and more than lived up to their name. They were frequently embroiled in both public and private brawls, including one occasion when Methot stabbed Bogart in the back, and another when she fired a gun at him. The couple's raucous battles became almost commonplace among their friends as well as the press—in the *New York Times*, columnist Earl Wilson recounted a phone conversation he'd had with the actor, during which a crashing sound could be heard in the background. "My wife just missed me with an ashtray," Wilson quoted Bogart. "I don't know what's wrong with her aim lately."

On screen, Bogart was continuing to rack up screen hits, including *All Through the Night* (1942), an entertaining spy spoof, and *Across the Pacific* (1942), a wartime espionage adventure described by one critic as "a delightfully fear-jerking picture." But the actor far exceeded these pictures with his next screen role—café proprietor Rick Blaine in *Casablanca* (1942). An outstanding drama that combines romance, intrigue, and heroism, with a touch of humor thrown in for good measure, *Casablanca* is perhaps Bogart's best-known and best-loved film. For his outstanding performance, Bogart received his first Academy Award nomination for Best Actor, but lost to Paul Lukas for *Watch on the Rhine*. The film itself also garnered a number of awards, including Best Picture and Best Director.

During the filming of *Casablanca*, Mayo Methot became increasingly jealous of her husband's beautiful co-star, Ingrid Bergman, frequently visiting the set and complaining that the love scenes between Bogart and Bergman were far too convincing. After the film's release, Methot reportedly attempted suicide, and a stay in an institution was prescribed, but Bogart instead took her with him on a U.S.O. tour of troops stationed in the Pacific. It was only a temporary solution to a problem that was spiraling out of control.

Bogart followed *Casablanca* with a series of wartime pictures—*Action in the North Atlantic* (1943), *Sahara* (1943), and *Passage to Marseille* (1944)—before returning to film noir in *Conflict* (1945). In this suspenseful feature, Bogart portrayed a rare "bad guy" role as Richard Mason, a successful architect who is secretly in love with the younger sister (Alexis Smith) of his shrewish wife (Rose Hobart). When he is temporarily wheelchair-bound following a car accident, he develops a near-flawless scheme to murder his wife, making way—he hopes—for his pursuit of her sister. After he successfully carries out the murder, with his wife's body hidden in a car beneath a pile of logs, Mason begins to experience a number of strange occurrences—finding her handkerchiefs and other personal effects and spotting a woman dressed in the clothes his wife wore when he killed her. Finally, doubting his own sanity, he returns to the scene of the crime, only to discover that his wife's body has been removed and that police had known of his guilt all along. The film's final reel finds him being led off by police, his face bathed in an expression of bewilderment. Upon its release, *Conflict* was well-received by critics; the reviewer from *Variety* called it "a convincing study," and the *New York Times*' Bosley Crowther found that it had "considerable melodramatic grit." Bogart earned equally good notices, with one labeling him "appropriately callous and cold, brutish without being sulphurous."

Bogart next starred in *To Have and Have Not* (1945), a wartime drama where he played a cabin cruiser proprietor who makes his living by taking wealthy tourists on fishing trips off the island of Martinique. The film's topnotch cast, plot, and direction aside, *To Have and Have Not* is better known for its intrigue behind the scenes. It was on this film that Bogart met Lauren Bacall, an 18-year-old New York model making her screen debut. Reportedly, when Bogart first met the young beauty, he told her, "We'll have a lot of fun together." Before long, the two were embroiled in a passionate affair, Bogart divorced Mayo Methot later that year, and 11 days after his divorce was finalized, he married Bacall.

Left to right: Jack Perry, Humphrey Bogart and Bob Steele in *The Big Sleep* (1946).

They would go on to have two children — Stephen Humphrey in 1949, and in 1952, Leslie Howard, named after the actor whose intervention had given Bogart his big break in Hollywood. The couple's marriage would last until Bogart's death in 1957. ("I was never happy until I met this one," the actor once said.)

On-screen, Bogart next starred opposite his wife in his fourth film noir, the often-confusing *The Big Sleep* (1946), which was labeled by one critic as "wakeful fare for folks who don't care what is going on, or why, so long as the talk is hard and the action harder." As Philip Marlowe, Bogart plays a no-nonsense private eye who is hired by a wealthy invalid, General Sternwood (Charles Waldron), to find out who is blackmailing his thumb-sucking, nymphomanic daughter,

Carmen (Martha Vickers). Along the way, Marlowe unearths a series of murders and encounters Carmen's older sister, Vivian (Bacall), described by her father as "spoiled, exacting, smart, and ruthless," as well as a motley crew of characters that include steely gambling house owner Eddie Mars (John Ridgely). By the film's end, Marlowe has discovered that Mars is the key to the spate of killings and confronts him in the climax at a remote house in the woods: "You're pretty smart, but I've been waiting for this one," Marlowe tells him. "You came in here without a gun — you were going to sit there and agree to everything, just like you're doing now. But when I went out that door, things were going to be different — that's what those boys are doing out there. But everything's changed, Eddie, because I got here first…. What'll they do to

Humphrey Bogart, Dudley Dickerson and Lizabeth Scott in *Dead Reckoning* (1947).

the first one that goes out that door? Who's it going to be, Eddie — you or me?" After repeatedly firing at Mars, Marlowe forces the gambler from the house, where he is gunned down by his own men, and Marlowe winds up in a clinch with Vivian in the final reel. The film was another hit for Bogart — critics raved about his portrayal of Marlowe, including the reviewer for *Film Daily*, who wrote that he "wears the tailored role in a manner that is calculated to be one of the best performances of the season."

Bogart was back in the realm of noir the following year when he starred in two features from the era, *Dead Reckoning* (1947) and *Dark Passage* (1947). In the first, Bogart is Rip Murdock, a war hero who is determined to unearth the whereabouts of his combat buddy, Johnny Drake (William Prince), who disap-

peared just before he was about to receive the Congressional Medal of Honor. Murdock's search leads him to Johnny's hometown, where he learns that his friend has been murdered. He also locates Johnny's girlfriend, Coral Chandler (Lizabeth Scott), a former nightclub singer, and discovers that Johnny had been accused before the war of murdering the singer's first husband. Against his better judgment, Murdock falls under her spell, but he later learns that Coral is married to a cold-blooded gangster and nightclub owner, Martinelli (Morris Carnovsky), and that the two were responsible for the deaths of both Coral's first husband and Johnny. In the film's climax, Murdock informs Coral that he is turning her in to police, despite his love for her: "That's the tough part of it," he says. "But it'll pass. Those things do, in time.

And then there's one other thing. I loved [Johnny] more." During the drive to the station, however, Coral shoots Murdock, causing an accident that results in her death. Bogart once again earned raves for his performance, with a typical review coming from Mandel Herbstman in *Motion Picture Herald*, who wrote that "it is the slugging, grimacing performance of Humphrey Bogart that dominates throughout" the film.

In his next noir, *Dark Passage*, Bogart portrays Vincent Parry, a prison escapee who was wrongfully convicted for the murder of his wife. The first 40 minutes of the film are presented in a first-person point of view, showing only Bogart's hands and forearms until his character undergoes plastic surgery to alter his looks. Harbored by a wealthy artist, Irene Jansen (Lauren Bacall), who picked him up on the road after his escape, Parry is determined to solve his wife's killing, but succeeds only in being charged for a second homicide. Ultimately, Parry learns that the real killer was Marge Rapf (Agnes Moorehead), a friend of both his late wife and Irene, and tells her in a heated confrontation, "I'm the pest now. You've always been the pest, but now I'm going to be because I know you killed Gert and I know you killed George. And I've got to make you confess it. And there's no way you can get away." But Marge refuses to admit her guilt, and in an unexpected occurrence, she accidentally falls from a window to her death, crushing Parry's last chance for proving his innocence. Faced with the hopelessness of his situation, Parry flees the country and, later, Irene joins him. The actor earned only mixed reviews from this film, however — the reviewer from *Variety* complained of his "general passiveness," while the *Film Daily* critic raved that the performance of the actor and his wife "gives every indication of boosting the pair's stock even higher."

With Bogart's popularity at an all-time high, the actor used his celebrity to support a cause that could have resulted in the demise of his career. In 1947, when the United States House Un-American Activities Committee began its investigation of Communism in the motion picture industry, Bogart traveled to Washington, D.C., with his wife and such luminaries as Gene Kelly, Danny Kaye, Ira Gershwin, and John Huston, to protest the treatment of the writers, directors, and actors who were appearing before the committee. In a radio address, Bogart stated that he "sat in the committee room and heard it happen."

"We saw American citizens denied the right to speak by elected representatives of the people," Bogart said. "We saw police take citizens from the stand like criminals. We saw the gavel of the committee chairman cutting off the words of free Americans."

Reportedly, Bogart's stance had a swift effect on his career. Box receipts for *Dark Passage* plummeted and studio head Jack Warner insisted that the actor offer a retraction. Before long, the actor did just that, telling reporters that his trip to the nation's capital had been "ill-advised, even foolish," but "at the time it seemed like the right thing to do." Although many of Bogart's fellow actors understood his public reversal, his friend and director John Huston, did not.

"I was surprised ... to read that Bogie had recanted," Huston said in a 1994 documentary. "I talked to him about it when he came back out — he said that we'd made a mistake in this. I regard it as a mistake that Bogie did this. He should've stuck to his guns."

Career-wise, Bogart's biggest successes lay just ahead. In 1948, he starred with Walter Huston and Tim Holt in *The Treasure of the Sierra Madre*, portraying Fred C. Dobbs, a good-natured prospector whose greed for gold drives him to murder. He followed this first-rate offering with a starring role in his seventh film noir, *Key Largo* (1948). Here, Bogart is Frank McCloud, a former Army major who travels to a small hotel in the title location to pay his respects to the family of a deceased war buddy. McCloud soon finds that the hotel, operated by the dead man's father, James Temple (Lionel Barrymore), and widow, Nora (Lauren Bacall), has been taken over by a notorious gangster, Johnny

Rocco (Edward G. Robinson), deported from the United States years earlier as an "undesirable alien." Accompanied by his gang, Rocco plans to sell a stack of counterfeit bills he has imported from Cuba, and regain his former prominence in America, but McCloud is determined to stop him. When Rocco forces McCloud to pilot a boat for his escape, the war veteran kills the gangster and his henchmen and returns, triumphant, to Nora's waiting arms. Yet another hit for the actor, this moody and intense drama racked up universal accolades from critics, including one who praised Bogart for his "usual strong performance.... It is an excellent portrayal that gains stature because of the absence of overdone heroics."

Bogart's next noir, *Knock on Any Door* (1949), was the first film produced by Santana Pictures Corporation, the production company the actor had established two years earlier and had named for his beloved boat, *Santana*. In this feature, the actor portrays Andrew Morton, a crusading attorney who defends a young hoodlum, Nick Romano (John Derek), accused of murdering a policeman. Believing Romano's claim that he has been framed on the basis of his lengthy criminal record, Morton passionately defends him, telling jurors during the trial, "In every man's life, there are pinpoints of time that govern his destiny. In his adolescence and his youth, a push to the right — a life of honor and credit. A push to the left — a life like Nick Romano's." Throughout the trial, Morton examines the circumstances in Romano's life that led to his life of crime, including his commission of petty thefts in a desperate effort to support his pregnant young wife, and his despair when she commits suicide. Under cross-examination by a relentless prosecutor, however, Romano ultimately admits his guilt, revealing that he had lied to Morton all along. Although it was based on the best-selling Willard Motley novel, *Knock on Any Door* was a disappointment on the big screen; Frank Eng of the *Los Angeles Daily News* thought the feature was "a forthright and engrossing study," but most critics disagreed, with the *Los Angeles Times*' Philip K. Scheuer judging it "sporadically exciting, but uneven," and Lloyd L. Sloan of the *Hollywood Citizen-News* finding that Bogart "does not register as convincingly as he has in many past roles." And the *New York Times*' Bosley Crowther was apparently so offended by the film that he felt compelled to write two separate reviews; in one, he blasted the feature's "inconsistencies and flip flops," and in the second, written four days later, he dismissed it as "hokum from the start."

Off-screen, Bogart was making a name for himself as a hard-drinking, fun-loving character — a reputation that grew after a 1949 incident involving two models and a stuffed panda bear. Reportedly, during the early morning hours of September 25, 1949, Bogart was at the El Morocco nightclub, where he purchased the large bear from a cigarette girl with plans to present it to his young son, Stephen. Two models approached the actor, and when one of the women tried to take the panda, Bogart pushed her to the floor. The parties involved were taken into custody, but the case was later thrown out of court. Asked whether he had been drunk at the time of the incident, however, Bogart jovially replied, "Isn't everybody at three o'clock in the morning?"

Meanwhile, Bogart followed *Knock on Any Door* with a starring role as an ex-flyer in *Tokyo Joe* (1949), the second feature produced under the Santana Pictures banner, and played another former pilot in his next feature, *Chain Lightning* (1950). He was then seen in back-to-back, top-notch films noirs, *In a Lonely Place* (1950), his third film for Santana, and *The Enforcer* (1950). As Dixon Steele in *In a Lonely Place*, Bogart is a hot-tempered screenwriter who finds himself accused of murder when a young hatcheck girl is murdered shortly after leaving his apartment. Steele is released from suspicion when a neighbor, Laurel Gray (the always fascinating Gloria Grahame), provides him with an alibi, and the two soon fall in love and plan to marry. But Dix begins to exhibit increasingly disturbing behavior — in one scene, he nearly kills a motorist who sideswipes his car, and in another, he eerily directs a re-enactment of the hatcheck girl's murder while dining with a detective friend, Brub Nicolai (Frank Lovejoy) and his wife. (Suggesting that the murder was committed in a car, Dix instructs Brub to put his arm around his wife's neck: "You get to a lonely place in the road and you begin to squeeze ... you love her and she's deceived you. You hate her patronizing attitude, she looks down on you, she's impressed with celebrity. She wants to get rid of you. Squeeze harder, harder. Squeeze harder. It's wonderful to feel her throat crush under your arm.") Dix's life continues its downward spiral when he angrily attacks his loyal agent (Art Smith) in a restaurant and later learns that Laurel — suspecting that he actually did kill the hatcheck girl — plans to end their engagement. Minutes after she reveals this news, however, Laurel receives a call from police and is informed that the real killer has been caught: "Yesterday, this would have meant so much to us," she says. "Now, it doesn't matter."

After this outstanding feature, Bogart starred in his last film under his Warner Bros. contract, *The Enforcer* (1951), as Martin Ferguson, a district attorney who is determined to convict a seemingly untouchable gang leader, Albert Mendoza (Everett Sloane). When the key witness against the gangster, Joseph Rico (Ted De Corsia), falls to his death while attempting to escape from police, Ferguson re-examines the case in an effort to unearth evidence that could be used against Mendoza. ("You ever have a tune run through your head and you can't remember the words?" Ferguson asks the captain of police. "Somewhere in that testimony, somebody said something that's stuck in my brain. It got lost in the shuffle because we didn't need it — we had Rico.") As Ferguson and the police captain spend the night reviewing the evidence, a series of flashbacks, told from the point of view of four men who worked for the gangster, reveal that Mendoza was the top man of an organized, murder-for-hire racket. Finally, at the end of the grueling night, Ferguson picks

up on a clue that he'd missed throughout the investigation, and searches for a young woman, Angela Vetto (Patricia Joiner), who had been an eyewitness to a murder Mendoza had committed years earlier. At the same time that Ferguson is looking for Vetto, however, Mendoza's hoods are tracking her as well, and trail her to a busy downtown mall. Through the use of a loudspeaker, Ferguson tells Vetto that her life is in danger and directs her to a meeting place — although the killers follow Ferguson, the district attorney later guns down one of the men and the other is captured by police.

Both *In a Lonely Place* and *The Enforcer* were hits at the box office and racked up good reviews; for his performance in the former, Bogart was labeled "excellent" in *Variety*, and *The Enforcer* was described by one critic as "tense, taut, big-time melodramatic entertainment."

After his final Santana picture, *Sirocco* (1951), a Middle East drama co-starring Lee J. Cobb and Everett Sloane, Bogart starred in what may have been the greatest triumph of his career, *The African Queen* (1951). As Charley Allnut, a scruffy, gin-swilling ship captain who falls in love with a prim missionary (Katharine Hepburn), Bogart offered an outstanding and memorable characterization that earned him his first Academy Award as Best Actor. In his acceptance speech for the long-deserved award, Bogart humbly stated, "I've been around a long time — maybe they like me."

As his career continued at its successful pace, Bogart always managed to find time for recreation. He was known for his frequent gatherings with friends at the popular restaurant Romanoff's, which led to the creation of the Rat Pack — the precursor to the group later made famous by Frank Sinatra and his cronies. Reportedly, the group of friends, which included Sinatra, Judy Garland and her then-husband Sid Luft, David Niven, director John Huston, humorist Nathaniel Benchley, and songwriter Jimmy Van Heusen, would gather at Romanoff's daily around 12:30 P.M. According to legend, on one occasion, Lauren Bacall took a look at the mischievous crew and cracked, "I see the rat pack is all here." And, thus, the original Rat Pack was born. Soon after, columnist Joe Hyams reported the event in the *New York Herald Tribune,* naming the "elected officers" as Frank Sinatra, pack master; Judy Garland, first vice-president; Lauren Bacall, den mother; Sid Luft, cage master; and Humphrey Bogart, rat in charge of public relations. Bogart even created a "coat of arms" for the group — a rat gnawing on a human hand — and a motto, "Never rat on a rat."

"The Holmby Hills Rat Pack held its first annual meeting last night at Romanoff's restaurant in Beverly Hills," Hyams wrote in his column. "Membership is open to free-minded, successful individuals who don't care what anyone thinks about them.... A motion concerning the admittance of Claudette Colbert was tabled at the insistence of Miss Bacall, who said that Miss Colbert 'is a nice person, but not a rat.'"

While he wasn't carousing with his Rat Pack crew, Bogart continued to star in a series of first-rate films, including *Deadline U.S.A.* (1952), portraying an embattled newspaper editor; *Beat the Devil* (1954), a comedy-drama directed by John Huston; *Sabrina* (1954), a popular Billy Wilder comedy co-starring William Holden and Audrey Hepburn; *The Barefoot Contessa* (1954), featuring Bogart as a world-weary film director; and *The Caine Mutiny* (1954), which earned the actor a third Academy Award nomination for his outstanding portrayal of an unstable ship's captain (he lost to Marlon Brando for *On the Waterfront*).

After playing a vicious escaped convict in *The Desperate Hours* (1955), Bogart was seen in the final film noir of his career, *The Harder They Fall* (1956). In this saga of the seedy side of the boxing world, Bogart is Eddie Willis, an unemployed sportswriter who is hired as a press agent by an unscrupulous promoter, Nick Benko (Rod Steiger). Willis' primary job is to foster publicity for Benko's latest acquisition, a huge South American fighter, Toro Moreno (Mike Lane), but

Willis soon discovers that Moreno is a "powder puff" in the ring. Despite his increasing qualms about the exploitation of the dim-witted boxer, Willis effectively guides him through a lengthy series of fixed fights to the heavyweight championship. Later, after learning that Moreno's contract has secretly been sold, and unable to stomach the dirty business any longer, Willis gives Moreno the $26,000 he has earned as his press agent and sends the young man back to his home in South America. Incensed by Willis' disloyalty, Benko threatens his life, but the agent reveals his plan to write a series of articles exposing the racket, telling him, "You can't scare me and you can't buy me."

Hailed by one critic as "a lively and stinging film," *The Harder They Fall* was a hit at the box-office, probably enhanced by the amount of publicity given to the film — in December 1955, Columbia Studios announced that because of "lack of cooperation from the International Boxing Commission," it had been unable to gain permission to use any stadium in the country for filming and was forced to combine two stages to make a boxing arena. The film garnered more press in May 1956, when former heavyweight boxing champion Primo Carnera filed a $1.5 million lawsuit against the studio, claiming that the movie paralleled his "rise and fall in the ring" and that, as a result, he had been "subjected to ridicule" and "has lost the admiration, respect, and friendship of neighbors and business acquaintances." In August of that year, the ex-fighter, who later became a wrestler and a restauranteur, lost his case when Judge Stanley Mosk, of the Santa Monica Superior Court, ruled that "one who became a celebrity or public figure waived the right of privacy and did not regain it by changing his profession."

Sadly, this first-rate film would be Bogart's last. During the filming of *The Harder They Fall,* the actor had complained of fatigue and frequently suffered from a sore throat and chronic cough. Diagnosed with cancer of the esophagus, the actor underwent an eight-hour surgery, during which his esophagus was removed. The actor continued his daily habits of smoking and drinking, however, and despite chemotherapy, the cancer spread. His weakening condition notwithstanding, Bogart held court at his home every day, during which he would receive visits from his long-time pals. One friend, actress Doris Johnson, recalled one of her visits to the house during Bogart's last days.

"That day we went to see him, he had lost so much weight. He seemed so frail," Johnson said in a 2001 documentary on the actor's life. "He loved his friends coming in to visit him. He liked keeping in touch. He didn't want to retire to the death bed. But he knew his time was very limited."

Bogart succumbed to his illness on January 14, 1957, bringing to a close one of the most successful and admired careers in the annals of Hollywood. Although his death came nearly a half-century ago, however, the actor has continued to be remembered and honored in the decades since. In 1993, Bogart's character from *Casablanca* was inserted via computer into a popular soft drink commercial; in 1997 a United States postage stamp was issued bearing his likeness; and in 1999, he was named the greatest male screen legend by the American Film Institute.

In a screen career that spanned six decades and consisted of nearly 100 films, Humphrey Bogart is truly deserving of the status he still maintains as a film icon. Off-screen, the actor was, by all accounts, beloved by family and friends, and this melding of his personal relationships and his professional impact was fittingly immortalized by director John Huston at Bogart's memorial service.

"When you live and work with a man, you get to know him pretty well. The better I got to know Humphrey Bogart, the more I admired him," Huston said. "He was a very sincere, a deeply humble man, a very faithful man. Faithful to his work, his friends and, finally, his family. He was a devoted father and he loved his wife most dearly. It's a loss to the world, of course — that great talent — but the world can refer to it in the pictures that re-main behind. The loss to his family and to his friends is, therefore, all the greater.

"There'll never be another Bogart."

Film Noir Filmography

High Sierra. Director: Raoul Walsh. Producer: Hal B. Wallis. Running time: 100 minutes. Released by Warner Brothers, January 4, 1941. Cast: Humphrey Bogart, Ida Lupino, Alan Curtis, Arthur Kennedy, Joan Leslie, Henry Hull, Barton MacLane, Henry Travers, Elisabeth Risdon, Cornel Wilde, Minna Gombell, Paul Harvey, Donald MacBride, Jerome Cowan, John Eldredge, Isabel Jewell, Willie Best, Arthur Aylsworth, Robert Strange, Wade Boteler, Sam Hayes.

The Maltese Falcon. Director: John Huston. Producer: Hal B. Wallis. Running time: 100 minutes. Released by Warner Brothers, October 3, 1941. Cast: Humphrey Bogart, Mary Astor, Gladys George, Peter Lorre, Barton MacLane, Sydney Greenstreet, Ward Bond, Jerome Cowan, Elisha Cook, Jr., James Burke, Murray Alper, John Hamilton, Emory Parnell. Awards: Academy Award nomination for Best Picture, Best Supporting Actor (Sidney Greenstreet), Best Screenplay (John Huston).

Conflict. Director: Curtis Bernhardt. Producer: William Jacobs. Running time: 86 minutes. Released by Warner Brothers, June 15, 1945. Cast: Humphrey Bogart, Alexis Smith, Sydney Greenstreet, Rose Hobart, Charles Drake, Grant Mitchell, Patrick O'Moore, Ann Shoemaker, Frank Wilcox, James Flavin, Edwin Stanley, Mary Servoss.

The Big Sleep. Director: Howard Hawks. Producer: Howard Hawks. Running time: 118 minutes. Released by Warner Brothers, August 31, 1946. Cast: Humphrey Bogart, Lauren Bacall, John Ridgeley, Martha Vickers, Dorothy Malone, Patricia Clarke, Regis Toomey, Charles Waldron, Charles D. Brown, Louis Jean Heydt, Elijah Cook, Jr., Sonia Darrin, Bob Steele, James Flavin, Thomas Jackson, Thomas Rafferty, Theodore Von Eltz, Dan Wallace, Joy Barlowe.

Dark Passage. Director: Delmar Daves. Producer: Jerry Wald. Running time: 106 minutes. Released by Warner Brothers, September 27, 1947. Cast: Humphrey Bogart, Lauren Bacall, Bruce Bennett, Agnes Moorehead, Tom D'Andrea, Clifton Young, Douglas Kennedy, Rory Mallinson, Houseley Stevenson.

Dead Reckoning. Director: John Cromwell. Producer: Sidney Biddell. Running time: 100 minutes. Released by Columbia, January 22, 1947. Cast: Humphrey Bogart, Lizabeth Scott, Morris

Carnovsky, Charles Cane, William Prince, Marvin Miller, Wallace Ford, James Bell, George Chandler, William Forrest, Ruby Dandridge.

Key Largo. Director: John Huston. Producer: Jerry Wald. Running time: 100 minutes. Released by Warner Brothers, July 16, 1948. Cast: Humphrey Bogart, Edward G. Robinson, Lauren Bacall, Lionel Barrymore, Claire Trevor, Thomas Gomez, Harry Lewis, John Rodney, Marc Lawrence, Don Seymour, Monte Blue, Jay Silver Heels, Rodric Redwing. Awards: Academy Award for Best Supporting Actress (Claire Trevor).

Knock on Any Door. Director: Nicholas Ray. Producer: Robert Lord. Running time: 100 minutes. Released by Columbia, February 22, 1949. Cast: Humphrey Bogart, John Derek, George Macready, Allene Roberts, Susan Perry, Mickey Knox, Barry Kelley, Cooley Wilson, Cara Williams, Jimmy Conlin, Sumner Williams, Sid Melton, Pepe Hern, Dewey Martin, Robert A. Davis, Houseley Stevenson, Vince Barnett, Thomas Sully, Florence Auer, Pierre Watkins, Gordon Nelson, Argentina Brunetti, Dick Sinatra, Carol Coombs, Joan Baxter.

In a Lonely Place. Director: Nicholas Ray. Producer: Robert Lord. Running time: 94 minutes. Released by Columbia, May 17, 1950. Cast: Humphrey Bogart, Gloria Grahame, Frank Lovejoy, Carl Benton Reid, Art Smith, Jeff Donnell, Martha Stewart, Robert Warwick, Morris Ankrum, William Ching, Steven Geray, Hadda Brooks, Alice Talton, Jack Reynolds, Ruth Warren, Ruth Gillette, Guy Beach, Lewis Howard.

The Enforcer. Director: Bretaigne Windust. Producer: Milton Sperling. Running time: 88 minutes. Released by Warner Brothers, February 24, 1951. Cast: Humphrey Bogart, Zero Mostel, Ted De Corsia, Everett Sloane, Roy Roberts, Lawrence Tolan, King Donovan, Robert Steele, Patricia Joiner, Don Beddoe, Tito Vuolo, John Kellogg, Jack Lambert, Adelaide Klein, Susan Cabot, Mario Siletti.

The Harder They Fall. Director: Mark Robson. Producer: Philip Yordan. Running time: 108 minutes. Released by Columbia May 9, 1956. Cast: Humphrey Bogart, Rod Steiger, Jan Sterling, Mike Lane, Max Baer, Sr., Jersey Joe Walcott, Edward Andrews, Harold J. Stone, Carlos Montalban, Nehemiah Persoff, Felice Orlandi, Herbie Faye, Rusty Lane, Jack Albertson, Val Avery, Tommy Herman, Vinnie De Carlo, Pat Comiskey, Matt Murphy,

Abel Fernandez, Marian Carr, Joe Greb. Awards: Academy Award nomination for Best Black and White Cinematography (Burnett Guffey).

References

Asher, Jerry. "This Is Bogart." *Photoplay*, January 1944.

"Battling Bogart." *Screen Greats Series No. 2*, Barven Publications, 1971.

"Bogie & Bacall." *Screen Greats Series No. 2*, Barven Publications, 1971.

"Bogie Became a Star Playing the Roles These Guys Turned Down." *Screen Greats Series No. 2*, Barven Publications, 1971.

Cooke, Alistair. "Mr. Bogart Defends His Own." *The Guardian*, October 1, 1949.

Dolven, Frank. "The Man Called 'Bogart.'" *Classic Images*, March 1993.

Fagen, Herb. "Bogart Remembered." *Films of the Golden Age*, Spring 1997.

Fidler, Jimmie. "Bogart's Stock Booms After Ten Long Years." *The Dallas Morning News*, June 29, 1943.

"His Knock-Down, Drag-Out Marriages." *Screen Greats Series No. 2*, Barven Publications, 1971.

"Katie, Oscar and the African Queen." *Screen Greats Series No. 2*, Barven Publications, 1971.

McCarty, Clifford. "Humphrey Bogart." *Films in Review*, May 1957.

Pryor, Thomas M. "Carnera Charges Studio with Foul." *The New York Times*, May 1, 1956.

Rudin, Max. "Fly Me to the Moon: Reflections on the Rat Pack." *American Heritage*, December 1998.

Wilson, Earl. "Please, Bogie and Sluggy, Go Back Together Again." *New York Post*, October 20, 1944.

Documentaries

"Bogart." A Flaum-Grinberg Production. Copyright 1962.

"Bogart: The Untold Story." An Iambic Production, in association with TNT. Copyright 1996.

"Humphrey Bogart: Behind the Legend." Produced by Millenial Entertainment and Archive Films, in association with Arts & Entertainment Networks. Copyright 1994.

NEVILLE BRAND

*"You ain't scared yet, are you, Bigelow? But you'll be scared. Good and scared. I think
I'll give it to you in the belly…. Takes longer when you get it in the belly. That's the way
I want to see you go, Bigelow. Nice and slow."— Neville Brand in* D.O.A. *(1950)*

Neville Brand was once told that his face looked as though the entire Russian Army had conducted a three-day battle on it in their mountain climbing boots. The actor with the craggy kisser and villainous reputation wasn't offended.

"Guys like me will be around this town a lot longer than the pretty boys because we are … one of a kind," he said. "We may produce nightmares instead of pleasant dreams, but we aren't forgotten."

A bonafide hero of World War II who waged and won a hard-fought battle against alcoholism, Brand was typed throughout his film and television career as a "heavy," but was able to show his versatility in roles such as the kind-hearted guard in *Birdman of Alcatraz* (1962) and the loud-mouthed, good-hearted Texas Ranger in TV's *Laredo*. But it is the roles that called for a gun in his hand and a sneer on his lips that stand out in the memory — and these were the roles that he played in his six films noirs: *D.O.A.* (1950), *Where the Sidewalk Ends* (1950), *Kiss Tomorrow Goodbye* (1950), *The Mob* (1951), *The Turning Point* (1952), and *Kansas City Confidential* (1952).

One of seven children, Neville Brand was born on August 13, 1920 (some sources say 1921), in Griswold, Iowa. His father, Leo, a bridge builder, moved the family to Kewanee, Illinois, when Brand was seven and divorced his wife, Helen, a few years later. To help support his large family, Brand landed a series of jobs, including soda jerk, waiter, and shoe salesman.

"I even worked in a bookie joint," he told a *TV Guide* reporter in 1966.

According to Brand's Paramount Studio biography and other published reports, the future actor joined the First Ranger Battalion at the age of 16 and was one of only 99 sur-

vivors of a 3,000-man unit that fought at Dieppe, on the coast of France. There is no evidence that Brand was ever a member of the Rangers, however, and his brother, Bryce Brand, later said that "there was a lot they printed about Nev that wasn't true." Other sources state that Brand graduated from high school, entered the Illinois National Guard, and was later inducted into the U.S. Army. Regardless of his origins of service, it is a fact that Brand distinguished himself during World War II; among his many medals, he was awarded the Silver Star for his bravery during an encounter with German soldiers. When his unit came under a machine-gun attack from a hunting lodge being used as a German command post, Brand dodged the enemy fire, entered the lodge from a rear door, and sprayed the occupants with a Tommy gun.

"I must have flipped my lid," Brand later said of his actions.

Shortly before the war's end, in April 1945, Brand was felled by a gunshot to his upper right arm and nearly bled to death while penned by enemy fire. ("I knew I was dying," he said in 1966. "It was a lovely feeling, like being half-loaded.") After his rescue, Brand was awarded the Purple Heart, and received a series of other decorations, including the Good Conduct Medal, the Combat Infantryman's Badge, the American Defense Service Ribbon, and the European/African/Middle Eastern Theater Ribbon with three Battle Stars. His honors earned him the status of the fourth most decorated soldier of World War II.

Following his honorable discharge from the Army, Brand got his first taste of acting with his appearance in a 1946 U.S. Army Signal Corps propaganda film, which featured another future star, Charlton Heston. After

this experience, Brand took advantage of the G.I. Bill of Rights to study acting in New York and began appearing in a series of off–Broadway plays, including Jean-Paul Sartre's *The Victors*. He was spotted in this production by Hollywood producer Harry Popkin, who gave Brand a small role in his film, *D.O.A.* (1950).

Brand's initial foray into the shadowy world of film noir, *D.O.A.* tells the riveting story of Frank Bigelow (Edmond O'Brien), a businessman who discovers that he has ingested a poison for which there is no antidote, and spends the remainder of his now-shortened life in a frantic effort to unearth his killer. In a small but memorable part, Brand is featured as a psychotic, lip-licking henchman — one character describes him as "an unfortunate boy who is unhappy unless he gives pain. He likes to see blood." Despite his limited screen time, Brand was noticed by several reviewers, including George H. Spires, who wrote in *Motion Picture Herald* that Brand "gives a performance that will undoubtedly win many plaudits from both the public and the industry," and the *Los Angeles Examiner*'s Earl H. Donovan, who termed the actor "a psychopathic killer who will make your flesh creep."

Later in the year, Brand was seen in small roles in two more films noirs; in *Where the Sidewalk Ends* (1950), he was 12th billed as a gangleader's henchman, and in *Kiss Tomorrow Goodbye* (1950), he played an escaping convict who was killed off during the first few minutes by his partner in the prison break (James Cagney). His brief appearance in the latter film notwithstanding, Brand's character played a pivotal role; his sister (Barbara Payton) later becomes involved with Cagney's Ralph Cotter, but when she learns he murdered her brother, she kills Cotter in the final reel.

The following year, Brand was seen in a mixture of films from memorable to mildly diverting, including *Only the Valiant* (1951), a fairly interesting western with Gregory Peck, and a war adventure, *Halls of Montezuma* (1951), in which Brand portrayed a blinded Marine. To prepare for the role, the actor reportedly spent parts of each day, for four weeks, with his eyes covered. After this well-done feature, he was seen in a string of three consecutive films noirs, *The Mob* (1951), *The Turning Point* (1952), and *Kansas City Confidential* (1952).

The first, *The Mob*, was a tautly written and directed feature focusing on a cop, Johnny Damico (Broderick Crawford), who goes undercover to successfully infiltrate a waterfront racket. Cast as Gunner, Brand played a henchman who first tangles with Damico on behalf of his boss, Castro (Ernest Borgnine), and later is the first to realize that Damico is a cop. ("Castro shoulda let me get you the other night," Gunner tells the detective. "You gonna knock me off or pinch me?)" Described — rather inexplicably — by one critic as a "college-type killer," Brand earned mention in several reviews, with praise ranging from "good" to "excellent." Brand's next noir, *The Turning Point*, starred Edmond O'Brien as John Conroy, a crusading attorney hired to break up a crime syndicate. When Conroy's boyhood pal, Jerry McKibbon (William Holden), aids the cause by writing a series of newspaper exposes, he is targeted for execution by the syndicate. To get rid of the bothersome reporter, the head of the mob hires a skilled gunman known only as Red (Brand). In the film's tension-filled climax, Red stalks Holden's character throughout a crowded boxing arena, finally succeeding in fatally wounding the reporter before he himself is gunned down by police. One reviewer, Margaret Harford of the *Hollywood Citizen-News*, called this scene the best in the film.

In his final film noir, *Kansas City Confidential*, Brand was featured as Boyd Kane, one of a trio of felons blackmailed by an embittered former police captain, Timothy Foster (Preston Foster), into committing an armored car robbery. Although Kane is initially reluctant to go along with the plan ("What makes you think I can't go on doin' alright?" he sneers), he eventually signs up for the intricate scheme. Only after a shootout leaves two of the men dead — including Kane — is it revealed that Foster's true plan was to turn over the three ex-cons to police, collect the reward money, and embarrass his former department. Labeled in one review as "a fast-moving, suspenseful entry for the action market," *Kansas City Confidential* also featured actress Coleen Gray as the former captain's daughter, who years later described Brand as "the steely-eyed, evil person of all time."

"I only had one scene with him, but I was very impressed — he was mean," Gray said in 2001. "But he was a nice person, and an intelligent person. That always appealed to me."

Next, Brand was seen as a prisoner of war in one of the best films of his career, *Stalag 17* (1953), top-billed by Brand's *Turning Point* victim, William Holden. The year also saw him in four other films, including *The Charge at Feather River* (1953), a western starring Guy Madison and filmed in 3-D, and *Man Crazy* (1953), in which he played his first starring role. He continued his busy film schedule during the next three years, receiving acclaim for his performance as a inmate who leads a prison uprising in *Riot in Cell Block 11* (1954), and portraying a Viking warrior chief in *Prince Valiant* (1954). And — having complained years earlier that he was

always cast as a solider or a killer and never got to "kiss a girl" — Brand also starred in his first romantic lead in *Return from the Sea* (1954), opposite Jan Sterling. But most of his pictures during this period were such clunkers as *The Lone Gun* (1954), a cliché-ridden western with George Montgomery and Dorothy Malone; the big-budget flop, *The Prodigal* (1955), starring Lana Turner; and *Bobby Ware Is Missing* (1955), a tiresome drama about a kidnapped boy.

Off screen, Brand had developed a growing penchant for alcohol during his years in Hollywood, and its effects were beginning to reach the press. In May 1954, he was arrested for drunk driving after he reportedly drove his foreign sports car into the rear of another vehicle. He told police officers that he wasn't drunk — he was just "acting" like it. The driver of the other vehicle, a 20-year-old Los Angeles City College student, sued Brand for $11,000 in damages, alleging that he had suffered back and neck injuries, but the suit was later dropped. Brand was finding better luck career-wise, however — in the early 1950s, he discovered the medium of television, which provided him with the greatest success of his performing career.

"Television was very good to me," Brand told *TV Guide* in 1966. "Movies never made me a star. The stage never did it. But from the beginning, I've been a star on television."

Throughout the remainder of the decade, Brand would be featured on countless small-screen programs, including *The United States Steel Hour, Westinghouse Desilu Playhouse, Zane Grey Theater, Naked City, Wagon Train, The Twilight Zone,* and *Bonanza*. He turned in an outstanding performance in 1957, in the teleplay of *All the King's Men*, earning a Sylvania Award for his portrayal of the corrupt politician, Willie Stark, and was also hailed for his menacing depiction of Al Capone in 1959 on the popular series *The Untouchables*.

With his focus now on the small screen, Brand began appearing in only a handful of feature films each year — the best of these were the box office hit, *Love Me Tender*

(1956), which served as the film debut of Elvis Presley; *Tin Star* (1957), a well-written western with Henry Fonda and Anthony Perkins; *Cry Terror* (1958), a fast-paced thriller starring James Mason; *The Adventures of Huckleberry Finn* (1960), featuring Brand as Huck's often-inebriated father, Pap; *The Last Sunset* (1961), an off-beat but fascinating western directed by Robert Aldrich; *Birdman of Alcatraz* (1962), in which Brand played a compassionate prison guard; *That Darn Cat* (1965), an entertaining Disney picture; and *Tora! Tora! Tora!* (1970), which won an Academy Award for Best Special Visual Effects.

Brand offered one of his most memorable television portrayals on the light-hearted weekly western series, *Laredo,* which ran on NBC from 1965 to 1967. Brand was featured as Reese Bennett, a tough — if not very bright — member of the Texas Rangers. Despite his popularity on the show, however, Brand became known for his heavy drinking, lack of discipline, and frequent run-ins with the show's directors and co-stars.

"I missed a lot of days I should have been on the set and wasn't," Brand said in 1966. "It was the first steady job I ever had in my life, and it took some adjusting to. I've seen the light."

But Brand's bad behavior continued, and just a year later, with *Laredo* facing cancellation, he was abruptly suspended by the series' producer, and did not appear in the show's last several episodes.

"You can't shoot an hour show in five days, like they were doing most of the time, without losing something," Brand told a *Los Angeles Times* columnist following the termination of the show. "I started giving them a bad time, because there were some scenes I just wouldn't do. One week I stayed locked in my dressing room the whole week until they rewrote the script. Sure, I got drunk, but there were reasons."

Brand's struggle with the bottle wasn't the only issue he faced behind the scenes; for several years he'd experienced an unstable — and complex — love life, as well. The first of Brand's three wives was one Jean Enfield, with whom he had a daughter, Mary, and who, according to news accounts, was just 18 years old when she married Brand in the early 1950s. In 1955, Jean sued Brand for divorce and he counter sued, filing a cross complaint for mental cruelty and testifying that his wife had left him to become a bullfighter in Mexico.

Brand married his second wife, Laura Rae, on April 6, 1957, in Emilano Zapata, state of Morales, Mexico, and the couple had two daughters, Michelle and Katrina. But this union, too, was destined for failure. In 1961, the actor reportedly obtained a divorce in Chihuahua, Mexico, but one article stated that he and Laura "resumed living together as man and wife [that] same year," and finally separated in 1964. Five years after this split, in June 1969, Laura was back in court, claiming that the 1961 Mexican divorce and accompanying property settlement agreement should be declared null and void, and asking the Superior Court to dissolve her marriage. This complicated request was granted a month later, when Brand agreed to a monthly child support and alimony settlement.

Little is known about Brand's third wife, Ramona — one account states that the couple met in Schwab's drug store, and that they separated in 1965. Of course, in light of the court's decision that Brand's 1961 Mexican divorce was invalid, this would mean that Brand's marriage to Ramona overlapped the marriage to Laura!

Meanwhile, Brand's film choices had taken a turn for the worse. After the popular *Tora! Tora! Tora!* in 1970, the actor was seen in a string of low-budget timewasters, including *The Mad Bomber* (1972), in which he played a psychotic rapist; *This Is a Hijack* (1974), a humdrum actioner; and *Psychic Killer* (1975), starring Jim Hutton as a vengeful ex-con who murders his victims by using his powers of astral projection.

This downward spiral of Brand's film roles was mirrored by his life off-screen — since the early 1960s, his drinking had continued to escalate, he'd started taking drugs, and his weight ballooned from 175 pounds to

250. Finally, in the mid-1970s, he was forced to take stock of his life.

"I lost my head, man," he told a reporter from the *Los Angeles Times*. "I became a mess. Suddenly you're not drinking to get drunk anymore — the booze became medicine.... I began to miss my work a lot. And my kids. And my reading. Because I couldn't read, couldn't concentrate. I wouldn't take walks. I hated the sunlight. I didn't want to see nobody laugh. I couldn't watch television. I couldn't do a damn thing but stay drunk."

Brand admitted that he entered several rehabilitation programs before he was finally able to remain sober. "I was like a little kid," he said. "I had to learn to take one step at a time. I'm still doing it. Only I'm taking big steps now.... This here is my last shot. I can never get that lost again. Because I don't have the time, the chances."

Although the studios were no longer lined up at his door, Brand managed to find work in such feature films as *Eaten Alive* (1976), in which he portrayed a sexually repressed hotel owner who murders his guests with a scythe and feeds them to his alligator; *Five Days from Home* (1978), where he was featured as a police detective pursuing a prison escapee; *Angels' Brigade* (1979), a low-budget quickie about drag racers; and a number of made-for-television movies including *Captains and the Kings* (1976), *Captains Courageous* (1977), and *The Seekers* (1979).

Brand was cast in four feature films in 1980 — including one, *The Return*, that was so sub-par that it never received a theatrical release — but he was not seen on screen again for another five years, when he starred with Aldo Ray and Tina Louise in *Evils of the Night* (1985), a rather silly science fiction/horror film about space creatures kidnapping teen campers. It was Brand's last film.

On April 16, 1992, Brand died of emphysema at Sutter General Hospital in Sacramento, California. Most of his newspaper obituaries mentioned that, in addition to his three daughters, he was survived by his wife, Rae — it is not known whether this was his fourth wife, or if newspapers were referring to Brand's second wife, Laura Rae.

Although he never became a household name, Neville Brand certainly distinguished himself as a fine character actor, both on the big screen and on television. The key to the actor's success may have been best explained by Brand himself: "I need to act," he said. "I need applause. I need the approval of a public. When the audience applauds, it is saying, in effect, 'I love you.' I need this."

Film Noir Filmography

D.O.A. Director: Rudolph Mate. Producer: Harry M. Popkin. Running time: 83 minutes. Released by United Artists, April 30, 1950. Cast: Edmond O'Brien, Pamela Britton, Luther Adler, Beverly Campbell, Lynn Baggett, William Ching, Henry Hart, Neville Brand, Laurette Luez, Jess Kirkpatrick, Cay Forrester, Virginia Lee, Michael Ross.

Where the Sidewalk Ends. Director and Producer: Otto Preminger. Running time: 95 minutes. Released by 20th Century-Fox, July 7, 1950. Cast: Dana Andrews, Gene Tierney, Gary Merrill, Bert Freed, Tom Tully, Karl Malden, Ruth Donnelly, Craig Stevens, Robert Simon, Harry von Zell, Don Appell, Neville Brand, Grace Mills, Lou Krugman, David McMahon, David Wolfe, Steve Roberts, Phil Tully, Ian MacDonald, John Close, John McGuire, Lou Nova.

Kiss Tomorrow Goodbye. Director: Gordon Douglas. Producer: William Cagney. Running time: 102 minutes. Released by Warner Brothers, August 4, 1950. Cast: James Cagney, Barbara Payton, Helena Carter, Ward Bond, Luther Adler, Barton MacLane, Steve Brodie, Rhys Williams, Herbert Heyes, John Litel, William Frawley, Robert Karnes, Kenneth Tobey, Dan Riss, Frank Reicher, John Halloran, Neville Brand.

The Mob. Director: Robert Parrish. Producer: Jerry Bresler. Running time: 87 minutes. Released by Columbia, October 17, 1951. Cast: Broderick Crawford, Betty Buehler, Richard Kiley, Otto Hulett, Matt Crowley, Neville Brand, Ernest Borgnine, Walter Klavun, Lynne Baggett, Jean Alexander, Ralph Dumke, John Marley, Frank De Kova, Jay Adler, Duke Watson, Emile Meyer, Carleton Young.

The Turning Point. Director: William Dietele. Producer: Irving Asher. Running time: 85 minutes. Released by Paramount, November 14, 1952. Cast: William Holden, Edmond O'Brien, Alexis Smith, Tom Tully, Ed Begley, Dan Dayton, Adele

Longmire, Ray Teal, Ted De Corsia, Don Porter, Howard Freeman, Neville Brand.

Kansas City Confidential. Director: Phil Karlson. Producer: Edward Small. Running time: 98 minutes. Released by United Artists, November 28, 1952. Cast: John Payne, Coleen Gray, Preston Foster, Dona Drake, Jack Elam, Neville Brand, Lee Van Cleef, Mario Seletti, Howard Negley, Ted Ryan, George Wallace, Vivi Janiss, Helen Keeb.

References

"Actor Brand to Pay Wife $1000 Monthly." *Los Angeles Herald-Examiner*, July 11, 1969.

"Actor in Crash Drunk, Says Suit." *Los Angles Examiner*, October 12, 1954.

"Actor 'Just Acting' but Police Book His 'Act' at Jail." *Los Angeles Examiner*, May 25, 1954.

"Actor's Wife Challenges Old Divorce." *Hollywood Citizen-News*, June 12, 1969.

Biography of Neville Brand. Paramount Studios, March 1956.

"Divorce Granted Film Actor Brand." *Hollywood Citizen-News*, October 6, 1955.

Hano, Arnold. "Wallace Beery, Humphrey Bogart and Me." *TV Guide*, June 25, 1966.

"Heavies? Who Is?" *TV Guide*, April 30, 1960.

Henniger, Paul. "Neville Brand Has That Saving Habit." *Los Angeles Times*, April 21, 1965.

Hopper, Hedda. "Ex-Villain Brand Wins Romantic Role." *Los Angeles Times*, February 27, 1954.

Humphrey, Hal. "Brand — Maverick of the Boone Lot." *Los Angeles Times*, June 1, 1967.

_____. "Niche for Neville? Try and Find One." *Los Angeles Times*, November 30, 1965.

Lambert, Bruce. "Neville Brand, 71, Craggy Actor Known for Many Roles as Villains." *New York Times*, April 19, 1992.

McClay, Howard. "It Took Wilder and 'Stalag 17' to Land Brand in Prison Camp." *Los Angeles Daily News*, August 3, 1953.

Morehouse, Ward. "Menacing Brand Gentle in Person." *New Haven Reporter*, December 16, 1962.

"Neville Brand to Star in Allied Artists' 'Riot' Film." *The Folsom Observer*, August 27, 1953.

"Neville Brand; Tough-Guy Actor, Decorated War Hero." *Los Angles Times*, April 18, 1992.

"Neville Brand, Tough Guy, Dies." *The Hollywood Reporter*, April 20, 1992.

Obituary. *The London Times*, May 9, 1992.

Obituary. *People*, May 4, 1992.

Obituary. *Variety*, April 20, 1992.

Obituary. *Variety*, April 27, 1992.

Pam, Jerry. "Neville Brand Seen Hit in Prison Film." *Beverly Hills Newslife*, February 10, 1954.

Roosevelt, Edith. "Finds Acting Most Exciting." *New York Morning Telegraph*, April 18, 1952.

Smith, Bea. "Brand Likes Tough Roles." *Newark Evening News*, December 2, 1962.

Smith, Cecil. "Big Al Takes a Train Ride." *Los Angeles Times*, January 5, 1961.

Thirer, Irene. "Neville Brand Lived with Killers." *New York Post*, February 25, 1954.

STEVE BRODIE

"Gimme ten minutes alone with 'em and they'll rat on their mother."— Steve Brodie in *M* (1951)

According to friends, Steve Brodie could have been a star.

"I don't think he pushed hard enough to really become big," fellow actor Walter Reed once said. "He didn't realize how good he was."

Brodie, who appeared in more than 100 feature films and television shows during his 50-year career, was best known for his roles in "B" westerns and action films, but also made an impact in six first-rate features from the film noir era: *Desperate* (1947), *Crossfire* (1947), *Out of the Past* (1947), *Armored Car Robbery* (1950), *Kiss Tomorrow Goodbye* (1950), and *M* (1951).

Brodie was born John Stephens in Eldorado, Kansas, on November 25, 1919, son of Alexander and Lena Stephens. As a child, Stephens, along with his five siblings, moved to Wichita, Kansas, where he attended elementary and high school and got his first job working as an assistant golf pro at the city's Meadowlark Country Club. For a while, the young man aspired toward a career in the field of law, but his interests soon changed.

"Clarence Darrow was a hero of mine,"

the actor said once. "I asked myself, 'What profession offers the same kind of excitement as defending somebody in a sensational jury trial?' So I decided to be an actor, since lawyers and actors both have to render colorful performances."

Two versions exist regarding the actor's leap from Wichita to Hollywood. In one, he gained his initial brush with the stage as a property boy with a stock company in nearby Salina, then worked during a summer with the Colonel Fairchild's Stock Players in a traveling tent show, playing a range of characters from young boys to old men. He later signed on with a stock company in Spring Lake, Michigan, where he specialized in playing heavies. When opportunities in the theater slowed down, Stephens worked for a while in the oil fields of Texas and California, but returned to Wichita with the advent of World War II for work as a welder at the Swallow Aircraft Plant. By 1942, he was back in California, where he landed a part in a stage show and was spotted by talent scouts from MGM who signed him to a contract in February 1943.

According to the second, more colorful version, the young man headed straight for New York where, still using his given name of John Stephens, he spent a year in a series of mostly unsuccessful auditions.

"I couldn't get arrested in New York," the actor reportedly said. "Then I got an idea, 'Why not come up with a name that people will remember and possibly even want to exploit?'" He adopted the name of Steve Brodie, a real-life New York saloon keeper who claimed to have survived a 1886 leap from the Brooklyn Bridge into the East River, leading to the catchphrase "pulling a brodie."

"The next time I went to a tryout, I told the fella taking names that I was Steve Brodie. 'Are you any relation to the guy who jumped off the Brooklyn Bridge?' 'Yes,' I answered. 'He was my uncle. We're both considered the black sheep of the family.' And the following morning I received a phone call telling me I had a job. One thing led to another, until one night a talent scout from MGM saw me in a play and brought me to Hollywood."

Regardless of the path he took, the newly named Steve Brodie made his film debut in *Thirty Seconds Over Tokyo* (1944), a box office smash that recreated the World War II bombing of Tokyo and Yokohama. During the next two years, Brodie appeared in such films as *Ladies Courageous* (1944), a Loretta Young starrer about the Women's Auxiliary Ferrying Squad; Universal's *Follow the Boys* (1945), a rousing, all-star tribute to the war effort; and *Anchors Aweigh* (1945), an entertaining musical starring Frank Sinatra and Gene Kelly. Dropped by MGM, Brodie freelanced for a year before being picked up by RKO which, for the actor, offered a more pleasant atmosphere than the one he'd experienced at MGM.

"MGM ... was like a factory," Brodie said in a 1984 interview. "Everybody was afraid that if you told somebody something, it was going to get to the front office. It was like a family at RKO."

For his new studio, Brodie appeared in a series of mostly "B" westerns, including *Badman's Territory* (1946), *Sunset Pass* (1946), *Code of the West* (1947), *Trail Secret* (1947), and *Thunder Mountain* (1947). In addition to these oaters, Brodie was also featured in a number of film noir features released by the studio, including three in 1947: *Desperate*, *Crossfire*, and *Out of the Past*.

In the first, *Desperate*— described in *Variety* as a "ripsnorting gangster meller"— Brodie took on one of the few starring roles of his career, portraying Steve Randall, a newlywed truck driver with a baby on the way. To earn extra cash, Steve accepts a job hauling perishables for a boyhood friend, Walt Radak (Raymond Burr), but he quickly learns that the load actually consists of stolen goods and he signals a passing cop. A shootout between police and Radak's gang leaves the officer dead and Radak's kid brother, Al (Larry Nunn), sentenced to death for murder. Steve goes on the lam with his wife, but Walt eventually tracks him down, planning to murder him at the moment of his brother's execution. Managing to escape, Steve becomes the hunter, rather than the hunted, and stalks Walt through an apartment house until he kills him.

After turning in a fine performance as the family man on the run for his life, Brodie was featured in his second noir, *Crossfire*, which centered on the murder of Joseph Samuels (Sam Levene), a Jewish ex-serviceman. The crime investigation, headed by Detective Finlay (Robert Young), focuses on four army buddies who met Samuels in a bar shortly before the murder. Brodie played one of the servicemen, Floyd Bowers (Brodie), who was present when his racist army pal, Montgomery (Robert Ryan), beat Samuels to death. Despite his promise to keep mum, Floyd is obviously distraught over the incident, and Montgomery murders him by hanging him with a necktie. Later told that Floyd is still alive, Montgomery returns to the scene of his crime and is gunned down by police when he tries to flee. Released just weeks before another film with an anti–Semitic theme, *Gentleman's Agreement* (1947), *Crossfire* earned acclaim from critics, including the reviewer for *Variety*, who wrote: "Here is a hard-hitting film whose whodunit aspects are fundamentally incidental to the overall thesis of bigotry and race prejudice."

Brodie's final noir of the year, *Out of the Past*, stands today as one of the quintessential films of the era. Complex and riveting, it uses an extensive flashback to reveal a core of distinctive characters, including no-nonsense private eye Jeff Bailey (Robert Mitchum); Jeff's mercenary partner, Jack Fisher (Brodie); callous racketeer Whit Sterling (Kirk Douglas); and Whit's murderous girlfriend, Kathie Moffett (Jane Greer), with whom Jeff falls in love. By the time the film finishes tracking these individuals through a series of frame-ups and double-crosses, all four are dead. The demise of Brodie's character comes at the hands of Kathie, who shoots him while he is in the midst of a fierce scuffle with Jeff Bailey.

"Jacques Tourneur, the director of *Out of the Past*, was very concerned with how the fight between Bob Mitchum and myself was staged," Brodie later recalled. "He didn't want it to be like a majority of movie fights, with wide swings and Sunday punches, but rather like professional sparring which would be photographed mostly in silhouette. My friend, Robert Ryan, who used to be a boxer, worked out with me for a couple of weeks beforehand, and I think it really paid off. Because it's the kind of a scene that stays with an audience."

Off-screen, Brodie had found time for romance when, in 1946, he attended a party given by N. Peter Rathvon, who had recently taken over as president at RKO. At the event, he met 23-year-old actress Lois Andrews, who had been married in her teens to vaudevillian George Jessel, and later to radio singer and film actor David Street. After a month-long, whirlwind courtship, Brodie and Andrews eloped to Tijuana, Mexico, just six days after Andrews had obtained an annulment of her marriage to Street. A year later, in October 1947, they were married a second time, in a church ceremony.

"We wanted to make it legal as far as California is concerned — although we want it understood we were perfectly free to marry when we did last year," Andrews explained to the press.

Despite their precautions, however, the marriage didn't last, and in 1950, Brodie married again, this time to Barbara Savitt, widow of orchestra leader Jan Savitt. Two years later, Brodie and Savitt had a son, Kevin (who later became involved with films as an actor, writer, director, and producer), but this union, too, ended in divorce.

Career-wise, Brodie continued to appear in a spate of westerns for RKO; the best of these were *Station West* (1948), a witty and well-directed feature starring Dick Powell and Brodie's *Out of the Past* co-star, Jane Greer, and *Return of the Badmen* (1948), the sequel to Brodie's earlier *Badman's Territory*. In May 1948, RKO was taken over by tycoon Howard Hughes, who fired nearly 700 employees of the studio. Brodie was among the casualties.

"He quickly turned the studio into a parking lot," the actor once remarked.

Brodie's sudden status as a freelancer had little effect on the number of movies he made; in 1949, he appeared in nine films, including *I Cheated the Law* for 20th Century–Fox, which featured the actor as a gangster who is acquitted of a murder; Lippert's *Treasure of Monte Cristo*, starring Glenn Langan and his soon-to-be real-life wife, Adele Jergens; and United Artists' *Home of the Brave*, a hard-hitting racial drama in which Brodie offered a believable portrait of a racist soldier. (After Brodie's 1992 death, a number of newspaper obituaries would erroneously report that he had been nominated for an Academy Award for Best Supporting Actor for the role.)

In 1950, after such films as *Winchester '73*, a top-notch western starring James Stewart, and *The Great Plane Robbery*, a tiresome drama featuring Brodie in yet another villainous role, the actor returned to film noir in *Armored Car Robbery* and *Kiss Tomorrow Goodbye*. Produced by Brodie's former studio, RKO, *Armored Car Robbery* is a fast-paced, often-overlooked noir gem that opens with the brilliant heist of an armored car at a baseball park. Masterminded by Dave Purvis (William Talman), the gang involved in the robbery is rounded out by Al Mapes (Brodie), Ace Foster (Gene Evans), and Benny McBride (Douglas Fowley), who is wounded during a

shootout and later finished off by Dave. Conflicts between the gang members escalate when Mapes learns of Purvis' plan to give McBride's share of the stolen loot to his widow, showgirl Yvonne LeDoux (Adele Jergens) — with whom Purvis has been having a secret affair: "Well, ain't that just dandy," Mapes says. "Big-hearted Purvis playing Santa Claus to his pal's widow. A burlesque queen…. You know, she *is* a pretty slick number. And I understand her heart didn't exactly belong to Benny. Maybe you owe her that dough, huh, Purvis?" A short time later, Purvis flees with the entire take when the gang's hideout is surrounded by police; Ace is gunned down and Mapes escapes in a boat, but he is nabbed by police when he goes to Yvonne's theater in search of Purvis. The last remaining member of the gang, Purvis, nearly makes a clean getaway from the local airport, but he ultimately meets a shocking end when he is struck by a departing airplane.

After being praised along with several co-stars for "back[ing] Talman's robbery play expertly," Brodie appeared with James Cagney and Barbara Payton in his second film noir of 1950, *Kiss Tomorrow Goodbye*. Here, the actor played a radio technician known as Jinx, who teams with escaped convict Ralph Cotter (Cagney) to blackmail a pair of corrupt small-town cops (Ward Bond and Barton MacLane). After several jobs, however, Jinx finds that he is repelled by the actions of the conscienceless Cotter, and tries to back out of the gang: "I felt like a man on the top floor of a house that's on fire," he later says. "You run for a window to jump out, and there's no ladder. You jump, you get killed. If you stay where you are, you get killed. That's how it was." Ultimately, however, Jinx's choice to "stay" or "jump" is taken out of his hands — he is apprehended by police and put on trial, along with the two lawmen, a shrewd shyster (Luther Adler), and an unctuous garage attendant (Rhys Willams), and Cotter meets his end at the hands of his jealous girlfriend, Holiday (Payton). Upon its release, the film was dismissed by the reviewer for the *New York Times* for its "snarling, mangling, triple-crossing, and exterminating," and the *Los Angeles Times'* Edwin Schallert, while singling out Brodie as "tops," warned his readers: "After seeing it, you are of a mood to say that, engrossing as it is, this is enough!"

The following year, Brodie was seen in his final film noir appearance, *M* (1951), a sordid tale focusing on the efforts to apprehend a former mental patient (David Wayne) who is driven to abduct and kill young girls. Working on the side of the law are police detectives Carney (Howard Da Silva) and Becker (Brodie), a hard-nosed lieutenant who, despite his penchant for using brawn over brains to solve cases, identifies the vital clue that leads to the killer's identity. Before the police can locate the suspect, however, a local mobster sees the opportunity to divert attention from his own troubles with the law and mobilizes his forces to hunt down the child-killer. Surrounded by a mob of angry citizens, the killer nearly loses his life, but police arrive in time to take him in. Although Brodie was mostly ignored by critics, this remake of the 1931 Fritz Lang classic earned good reviews, with the *Los Angeles Times'* Philip K. Scheuer calling the film "provocative and stirring," and Lowell E. Redelings writing in the *Hollywood Citizen-News* that it "hasn't lost any of its basic suspense in a new version."

At this point in his career, Brodie expanded his performing repertoire to include the medium of television. From the early 1950s through the late 1970s, Brodie appeared in guest spots on countless television series, including *Adventures of Wild Bill Hickok, Alfred Hitchcock Presents, Wanted: Dead or Alive, The Rough Riders, Perry Mason, Rawhide, Pony Express, The Deputy, Stagecoach West, Maverick, Cheyenne, Gunsmoke, The Dakotas, The Twilight Zone, The Virginian, Bonanza, Police Woman, The Beverly Hillbillies, Police Story,* and *CHiPs.* Brodie also served as the narrator of *High Road to Danger,* and played a recurring character on the series *The Life and Legend of Wyatt Earp* from 1959 to 1961.

Despite his spate of performances on the small screen, Brodie found time to continue his feature film appearances in such movies as *The Story of Will Rogers* (1952), starring the famed humorist's son, Will Rogers, Jr., in the title role; *Lady in the Iron Mask* (1952), in which he was seen as Athos, one of the Three Musketeers; *Donovan's Brain* (1953), an interesting science-fictioner about a scientist who preserves the brain of a dead multimillionaire; *The Caine Mutiny* (1954), a first-rate naval drama starring Humphrey Bogart as the unstable ship captain, Phillip Queeg; *The Far Country* (1955), a well-done western with James Stewart and Ruth Roman; *The Crooked Circle* (1958), a so-so boxing drama where Brodie portrayed a crusading sportswriter; and *Arson for Hire* (1959), a timewasting action feature starring Brodie as a fire inspector.

In the late 1950s and early 1960s, Brodie, who was once described as a man who "always likes to have a good time," was in the news on several occasions for his off-screen activities. In 1959, several of his neighbors signed a petition that listed a variety of complaints against the actor, including that he frequently used an electric saw and hammer at 3 A.M., that he had a radio hooked up to a loudspeaker that he played at all hours of the night, that there was "constant shouting, loud voices, and laughter from his house," and that a horseshoe game that the actor played with friends each weekend "created sounds like an iron foundry." When one neighbor, an England native, complained about the horseshoes, Brodie reportedly "asked her why she didn't go back to England." The rather amusing case ended peaceably, however, with the city attorney's office charging the parties to "try to be good neighbors."

Two years later, Brodie was involved in a less humorous incident when he drove into a parked car and was charged with drunk driving. The actor pleaded guilty in the Van Nuys Municipal Court and was fined $226. And the actor was in the news again in 1966, when his wife, Barbara, sued him for divorce, claiming that he would disappear from their home for hours or days on end.

"He would go out to mail a letter and I

wouldn't see him for six or seven hours," Barbara testified in court. "I was always looking for him."

By now, the actor's film career was winding down; his appearances during the 1960s and 1970s included small roles in two Elvis Presley vehicles, *Blue Hawaii* (1961) and *Roustabout* (1964), and featured parts in three low-budget horror films, *The Wild Wild World of Batwoman* (1966), *The Giant Spider Invasion* (1975), and *Frankenstein Island* (1981). In one of his last performances, he was also seen in *Mugsy's Girls* (1985), a sorority house romp that was written, directed, and produced by Brodie's son, Kevin. The actor's final big-screen appearance came three years later in *The Wizard of Speed and Time* (1988), a bizarre film about "dreams and reality, corruption and idealism," in which he portrayed a Hollywood film director named Lucky Straeker.

In the later years of his career, Brodie primarily used his talents for voice-over work on commercials for a variety of products and companies, including Conoco Oil. He also made live appearances at such events as the 1991 Western Film Festival in Knoxville, Tennessee, where he delighted fans with his reminisces of his acting heyday. Not long after this event, on January 9, 1992, Brodie died of cancer. He was 72 years old.

In his vast assemblage of Hollywood features, Steve Brodie seldom took on starring roles, but he managed to make a significant on-screen impact in a variety of memorable films, including *Desperate*, *Out of the Past*, and *Home of the Brave*. As demonstrated by the vastly diverse characterizations he offered in these features and many others, Brodie possessed a versatile talent and an unaffected screen presence that has provided him with a solid place in the history of the silver screen.

"Everybody wants to be a leading man," Brodie said once, "but early on I discovered it is much better to be a heavy because you work more. I loved doing them all. When a part was given to me, I went at it hard…. And if I had my life to live over again, I wouldn't change a thing.

"I have had a ball."

Film Noir Filmography

Desperate. Director: Anthony Mann. Producer: Michel Kraike. Running time: 73 minutes. Released by RKO, May 20, 1947. Cast: Steve Brodie, Audrey Long, Raymond Burr, Douglas Fowley, William Challee, Jason Robards, Sr., Freddie Steele, Lee Frederick, Paul E. Burns, Ilka Gruning.

Crossfire. Director: Edward Dmytryk. Producer: Adrian Scott. Running time: 85 minutes. Released by RKO, July 22, 1947. Cast: Robert Young, Robert Mitchum, Robert Ryan, Gloria Grahame, Paul Kelly, Sam Levene, Jacqueline White, Steve Brodie, George Cooper, Richard Benedict, Richard Powers, William Phipps, Lex Barker, Marlo Dwyer. Awards: Academy Award nominations for Best Picture, Best Director (Edward Dmytryk), Best Supporting Actor (Robert Ryan), Best Supporting Actress (Gloria Grahame), Best Original Screenplay (John Paxton).

Out of the Past. Director: Jacques Tourneur. Producer: Warren Duff. Running time: 96 minutes. Released by RKO, November 25, 1947. Cast: Robert Mitchum, Jane Greer, Kirk Douglas, Rhonda Fleming, Richard Webb, Steve Brodie, Virginia Huston, Paul Valentine, Dickie Moore, Ken Niles.

Armored Car Robbery. Director: Richard Fleischer. Producer: Herman Schlom. Running time: 67 minutes. Released by RKO, June 8, 1950. Cast: Charles McGraw, Adele Jergens, William Talman, Douglas Fowley, Steve Brodie, Don McGuire, Don Haggerty, James Flavin, Gene Evans.

Kiss Tomorrow Goodbye. Director: Gordon Douglas. Producer: William Cagney. Running time: 102 minutes. Released by Warner Brothers, August 4, 1950. Cast: James Cagney, Barbara Payton, Helena Carter, Ward Bond, Luther Adler, Barton MacLane, Steve Brodie, Rhys Williams, Herbert Heyes, John Litel, William Frawley, Robert Karnes, Kenneth Tobey, Dan Riss, Frank Reicher, John Halloran, Neville Brand.

M. Director: Joseph Losey. Producer: Seymour Nebenzal. Running time 87 minutes. Released by Columbia, June 10, 1951. Cast: David Wayne, Howard Da Silva, Martin Gabel, Luther Adler, Steve Brodie, Glenn Anders, Norman Lloyd, Walter Burke, Raymond Burr.

References

Biography of Steve Brodie. General Service Studios, October 6, 1959.

Biography of Steve Brodie. RKO Radio Studios, circa 1947.

"Brodie Fined in Drunk Case." *Hollywood Citizen-News*, October 10, 1962.

"Brodie's Son Can Play Ball — but No Bats." *Los Angeles Times*, August 12, 1959.

Carney, Alan. "Remembering Steve Brodie and Steve McQueen." *The Big Reel*, May 1992.

Carroll, Harrison. "Lois Andrews Remarriage to Mark Wedding Anniversary." *Los Angeles Herald Express*, October 14, 1947.

Collura, Joe. "Steve Brodie: Better to Be Bad." *Classic Images*, April 1992.

"Lois, Brodie Marry Again." *Los Angeles Examiner*, October 15, 1947.

"Mrs. Steve Brodie Divorces Actor." *Los Angeles Herald-Examiner*, April 1, 1966.

"Neighbor's Rap Actor's 'Noise.'" *Hollywood Citizen-News*, August 12, 1959.

Nielsen, Ray. "Steve Brodie and Out of the Past." *Classic Images*, March 1984.

Obituary. *The Big Reel*, March 1992.

Obituary. *Variety*, January 20, 1992.

"S. Brodie Sued for Divorce." *Hollywood Citizen-News*, July 29, 1965.

"Steve Brodie; Actor in 200 Action Films." *Los Angeles Times*, January 11, 1992.

"Steve Brodie Weds Barbara Savitt in Las Vegas Chapel." *Los Angeles Times*, September 11, 1950.

"Steve Brodie Weds Lois Andrews Again." *Los Angeles Times*, October 15, 1947.

"Steve Brodie, Wife Divide in Divorce." *Hollywood Citizen-News*, April 4, 1966.

RAYMOND BURR

"You dumb ox. I oughta knock your brains out. You musta studied to get that stupid."— Raymond Burr in *Desperate* (1947)

Perry Mason. Ironside. Two fictional characters with whom the name of Raymond Burr is instantly and inextricably linked. But the handsome, hefty actor of stage, screen, and television led a life off-screen that was far more fascinating and complex than even the most fanciful script could supply. An intensely private man, Burr apparently invented much of his past, including several wives, a son, and service in World War II. Renowned for his generosity, numerous accounts abound of the actor's demonstrations of his compassion for loved ones and strangers alike. And in contrast with his somber television persona, Burr was a notorious practical joker who left his co-workers never knowing what next to expect.

Although he was on the right side of the law during his prolific television career, in films Burr was almost always cast as a villain, and lent his commanding presence to 10 features from the film noir era: *Desperate* (1947), *Pitfall* (1948), *Sleep, My Love* (1948), *Raw Deal* (1948), *Abandoned* (1949), *Red Light* (1950), *M* (1951), *His Kind of Woman* (1951), *The Blue Gardenia* (1953), and *Crime of Passion* (1957).

Raymond William Stacy Burr was born on May 21, 1917, in New Westminster, British Columbia, the oldest of three children. His father, William, worked as a hardware store salesman, and his mother, Minerva, a native of Chicago, Illinois, studied music and played the piano in the local symphony orchestra. Minerva also played the piano to accompany the silent movies that were shown at the town's movie theater, which may have spurred Burr's initial interest in an acting career.

When Burr was six years old, his mother moved the family to Vallejo, California, where her parents owned a small hotel. Unable to find employment in California, William Burr returned to Canada after eight months, and the couple later divorced. (Some 30 years later, in 1955, William and Minerva would remarry and remain together until Minerva's death in 1974). After several years, Burr was sent to the San Rafael Military School in Northern California, but it was a miserable experience for the youngster. Burr, who would struggle with a weight problem for most of his life, was ostracized and teased by his classmates, and was reportedly barred by school officials from riding horses in the school's cavalry parades because of his size. He would later refer to his tenure at the school as "purgatory."

At the age of 17, Burr dropped out of school to join the Civilian Conservation Corps (CCC), a federally-funded project of the Franklin D. Roosevelt administration that was designed to put unemployed youths to work in forests, parks, and range lands. During his time with the CCC, Burr worked at a variety of jobs, including fighting forest fires and planting trees.

Up until this point, Burr's acting experiences had been limited to church plays and school productions, but after leaving the CCC, he reportedly met film director Anatole Litvak, who arranged for Burr to act in a summer theater in Toronto. Later, according to published reports, Burr traveled with a repertory company in Britain, then landed a job singing in a Paris nightclub, Le Ruban Bleu. Back in the United States, Burr signed on with the famed Pasadena Playhouse, for which he appeared in several productions, then headed for New York to try his luck on Broadway.

In 1940, Burr debuted on Broadway in *Crazy with the Heat,* but the play was a flop and his performance went virtually unnoticed. Undaunted, the actor remained in New York, earning his keep by working a series of odd jobs. Three years later, he was back on Broadway, portraying the French patriot, Voulain, in *The Duke in Darkness.* His critically acclaimed performance attracted the notice of Hollywood agent Lester Salkow, who arranged for a screen test at RKO Studios, where Burr signed a contract.

Burr's life at this point becomes somewhat of a mystery. The actor later claimed that he enlisted in the United States Navy in 1943, was assigned to counter-intelligence, and was wounded while aboard a ship in the Pacific that was bombed by Japanese Kamikaze planes. After undergoing several operations, Burr said, he was awarded the Purple Heart. Other published reports declare that Burr was shot in the stomach while in Okinawa. However, no records exist to indicate that Raymond Burr ever served in the United States Navy at all.

This unexplained gap in time notwithstanding, Burr made his film debut in 1946 in

RKOs *Without Reservations,* a rather bland comedy starring John Wayne and Claudette Colbert. He followed this feature with his first role as a villain, portraying an escaped convict in *San Quentin* (1947), then attracted notice from critics for his performance as a sinister heavy in *Code of the West* (1947). Later that year, he turned in another menacing performance in his first film noir, *Desperate* (1947). The film's star, Steve Brodie, said that he was responsible for Burr's casting in the role.

"Ray was ... testing for a biblical part, so I suggested his name to the producer, Michael Kraike, for our picture," Brodie said. "Kraike liked the idea, and for the next decade villain roles were about the only parts Raymond Burr played."

This gripping, Anthony Mann–directed thriller focuses on Steven Randall (Brodie), who drives a truck and whose newlywed wife, Anne (Audrey Long), is expecting their first child. Anxious to add to his income, Steve is enticed by an old neighborhood chum, Walt Radak (Burr), into hauling a shipment of perishables, but balks at the job when he learns that his cargo consists of stolen goods.

When Steve signals a passing cop, gunfire is exchanged, killing the policeman and leaving Walt's kid brother, Al (Larry Nunn), charged with murder. Steve flees from Walt and his gang and goes on the lam with his pregnant wife, tracked relentlessly by Walt, who finally catches up to Steve just minutes before Al's scheduled execution. Planning to exact revenge by killing Steve at the same moment of Al's death, Walt offers Steve a "last meal," telling him: "I'm sorry I can't give you a choice of food, but it won't make much difference. You're not going to live long enough to get any nourishment out of it." Steve manages to escape, however, and after stalking Walt at gunpoint up the winding staircases of an apartment building, he shoots Walt, sending him catapulting — in a shockingly memorable scene — to his death at the base of the stairs. Although a small film, *Desperate* did modest business at the box office, and Burr's menacing characterization of Walt was one of the highlights of the picture.

After small roles in such films as *I Love Trouble* (1947), a passable thriller starring Franchot Tone, *Station West* (1948), a tautly directed western, and *Walk a Crooked Mile* (1948), a spy thriller with Dennis O'Keefe and Louis Hayward, Burr was seen in three films noirs, *Sleep, My Love* (1948), *Raw Deal* (1948), and *Pitfall* (1948).

In the first of Burr's 1948 noirs, *Sleep, My Love*, the actor was only briefly seen as a police sergeant, but he logged more screen time in his next noir of the year, *Raw Deal*. This well-done feature starred Dennis O'Keefe as Joe Sullivan, a gangster imprisoned for a crime committed by his boss, Rick Coyle (Burr). It is Coyle who aids Joe's escape from prison, but his motivation is far from chivalrous: "He was screaming he wanted out," Coyle tells his underlings. "When a man screams, I don't like it. Especially a friend. He might scream loud enough for the D.A. to hear. I don't want to hurt the D.A.'s ears. He's sensitive." Learning of Coyle's deception, Joe manages to avoid a four-state dragnet and, accompanied by his faithful girlfriend, Pat (Claire Trevor), goes after his former boss.

During a gun battle, Rick is shot and falls from a window to his death, but Joe, too, has been mortally wounded and later dies.

As Coyle, Burr portrayed a brutish and violent character whose persona was best illustrated in an early scene, in which he first learns that Joe has slipped through the wide net cast by police. As he digests this disturbing information, Coyle's mistress jostles against him and spills champagne on his jacket. Coyle picks up a bucket of flaming cognac and flings it on the screaming woman: "Take her away," he says. "She shoulda been more careful." Although this Anthony Mann–directed feature was praised for its taut action, however, Burr's notices were mixed — the critic for the *Motion Picture Herald* noted his "good performance [as] a sinister and sadistic criminal boss," but the actor was dismissed in *Variety* as "reminiscent of the late Laird Cregar in bulk and manner but … deficient in a sinister quality." But Burr elicited none of these ambiguities in his final noir of the year, *Pitfall*, where he was a standout as a psychotic private detective named Mack MacDonald. The film's action centers on married insurance agent Johnny Forbes (Dick Powell), whose dull, suburban life gets an unexpected jolt when he meets a beautiful blond, Mona Stevens (Lizabeth Scott). Planning to retrieve stolen items Mona received from her embezzler boyfriend (Byron Barr), Johnny falls for her instead, becoming ensnared in a web of lies at home, and running afoul of MacDonald, whose pursuit of Mona knows no bounds. Although Mona firmly tells him, "I don't like you — I don't want you around," MacDonald continues to stalk her and later tries unsuccessfully to set up Johnny's murder. But MacDonald meets an unexpected end when he shows up at Mona's house and starts packing her clothes, planning to force her to accompany him to Reno — Mona pulls out a gun and shoots him dead.

Burr was universally hailed for his portrayal of the nefarious detective — in the *Los Angeles Daily News*, Frank Eng wrote that the character was "beautifully underplayed to its unctuous hilt by Raymond Burr," and the critic for the *New York Times* raved: "As the heavy, literally and figuratively, a newcomer named Raymond Burr does a sinister and fascinating job. He is a big man and unless we are mistaken, his weight, histrionically and otherwise, will make an impression on the screen in days to come."

During the next three years, Burr was seen in a variety of features, including such films as *Key to the City* (1950), an MGM comedy with Clark Gable and Loretta Young; *Unmasked* (1950), in which he was a standout as a murderous scandal sheet editor; *Bride of the Gorilla* (1951), a campy, low-budget horror film which saw the actor transform into a gorilla-man; and *A Place in the Sun* (1951), which featured one of the screen performances for which he is best remembered — the unyielding district attorney whose vehement prosecution sends Montgomery Clift to the electric chair. Also during this period, Burr added four more noirs to his dark repertoire: *Abandoned* (1949), *Red Light* (1950), *M* (1951), and *His Kind of Woman* (1951). The first of these, *Abandoned* (touted as "the year's most sensational picture"), focused on a baby-stealing racket headed by a kindly-looking middle-aged woman, Mrs. Donner (Marjorie Rambeau), and Kerric (Burr), described by one character as "the cheapest private detective in town, [who] specializes in framing divorces and frightening little children." When a local reporter, Mark Sitko (Dennis O'Keefe), closes in on the truth about Donner and Kerric's activities, the detective tries to double-cross his partner and leave town, but his efforts only serve to earn him a drawer at the morgue. Ultimately, all ends well when Sitko obtains the evidence needed to expose the racket and Donner is apprehended by authorities. Although *Abandoned* was perhaps the weakest of Burr's nine films noirs, it was labeled "a melodrama with sock" by one reviewer, and Burr was singled out for his "magnificent performance of [a] sharply etched character."

Burr's next noir, *Red Light*, begins with a foreword that tells the audience: "A prison is a place where crime usually ends, but in our story this is where it began." The mastermind of the crime in question is Nick Cherney (Burr), who was sent to prison for embezzling from his former boss, trucking magnate Johnny Torno (George Raft). With the assistance of a soon-to-be-paroled buddy (Henry Morgan), Nick exacts revenge on Torno by arranging the murder of his beloved brother, an Army chaplain who recently returned from the war. An extensive search for his brother's killer leads Torno to Nick, who bitterly admits his crime: "I paid for the job. Paid for it with your money — money you sent me to prison for taking. Your cash paid for the gun that killed your own brother. How do ya like that for a payoff, Torno? Yeah, it hurts, doesn't it?" Bent on vindicating his sibling's senseless death, Torno chases Nick onto the roof of a building during a driving rainstorm, where Nick steps on a wire and is electrocuted. Once again, Burr was lauded for his performance — John L. Scott of the *Los Angeles Times* found that he made "an impression as the villain," and in the *Los Angeles Examiner*, Sara Hamilton gushed: "A special line goes to Raymond Burr for his superb work as the scheming embezzler. Here's an actor you'll be asking about long after you've come out of the theater, so let's have more of Burr in roles like these, please."

The actor was mostly overlooked, however, in his seventh noir, *M* (1951), the remake of the 1931 Fritz Lang classic. A rather sordid feature, this film centers on a psychologically damaged man who is tortured by his compulsion to abduct and murder little girls. Although police efforts are basically ineffectual, a local mobster sees a chance to "take the heat off" of his pending indictment and mobilizes his vast network of underlings to finally catch the killer. As a whispery-voiced mob captain, Burr was overshadowed both on screen and in reviews by David Wayne's role of the child-killer, but he played a more significant role in his next film noir, *His Kind of Woman*. Here, Burr was Nick Ferraro, a syndicate boss exiled in Italy, who conjures a plot to murder and assume the identity of professional gambler Dan Milner (Robert Mitchum). Disposing of a federal immigration official (Tim Holt) who has learned of his scheme, Ferraro has Milner abducted and spirited aboard his yacht; in a particularly vicious scene, Ferraro prepares to shoot Milner, and beats his semi-conscious victim in the head, telling him, "I want you to see it coming." But Ferraro's well-laid plans are foiled by a vacationing actor (Vincent Price, in a picture-stealing performance), who rallies local authorities, storms the ship, and clears the way for Milner to fatally shoot his captor. Despite a first-rate cast, *His Kind of Woman* was a disappointment at the box office, and critics were generally unimpressed, with the reviewer from the *New York Times* labeling it "one of the worst Hollywood pictures in years ... probably the only one since the advent of Vitaphone that needs sub-titles."

Around this time, Burr embarked on the first of seven overseas USO tours to visit soldiers fighting in the Korean War. He took the trips during the next four years, often turning down lucrative film roles, and in 1953, he headed a contingent that remained in the Far East for six months, longer than any other group. During these visits, Burr not only emceed the nightly shows, but also insisted on going to front lines, according to Army commander Maj. Stan McClellan, who said that the actor went "in and out of bunkers, weapons positions, half-destroyed trenches, ammo supply points."

"I can't describe the open-mouthed amazement with which he was greeted by every soldier we met!" McClellan said in *The Saturday Evening Post*. "He stopped and talked to each of them. It did more than anything else to convince the men of this fighting outfit that the 'folks at home' were really not so far away after all." After returning home from his overseas visits, Burr would frequently telephone the parents of the soldiers he had visited, in order to tell them how their sons were doing. And when the conflict ended in 1955, Burr continued his commitment to the country's servicemen, coordinating shows for bases along with West Coast and visiting veterans hospitals on a regular basis. Asked on

one occasion why he engaged in such activities, Burr replied that it was "because I think it should be done, and there aren't enough people doing it."

Career-wise, Burr was seen in a mixed-bag collection of films, including *Mara Maru* (1952), an Errol Flynn starrer described in *Variety* as a "deep-sea treasure hunt with whodunit overtones"; *Tarzan and the She-Devil* (1953), a tiresome entry in the jungle-man series; *The Bandits of Corsica* (1953), the rather disappointing sequel to *The Corsican Brothers* (1941); and *Fort Algiers* (1953), a silly spy thriller that saw the actor portraying an Arab leader called Amir. Burr fared better, however, with roles in *Meet Danny Wilson* (1952), in which he played a tough racketeer promoter, and his ninth film noir, *The Blue Gardenia* (1953).

In this feature, Burr essayed yet another bad-guy role, playing a sleazy ladies' man named Harry Prebble. The film's action begins when Norah Larkin (Anne Baxter), recently dumped by her serviceman beau, impulsively accepts a date with Harry, who plies her with liquor, takes her to his home, and tries to seduce her. During a struggle to fight off Harry's insistent advances, Norah passes out and is later unable to remember the night's events until she reads in the newspaper that Harry was found murdered. Tortured by guilt, Norah finally arranges to turn herself in to a local reporter, Casey Mayo (Richard Conte), but after her arrest, Mayo continues his investigation, finally unearthing the real killer — another woman who had fallen under the spell of the suave Harry Prebble.

Directed by Fritz Lang, *The Blue Gardenia* earned modest reviews, with one reviewer calling it "a contribution that has both mood and intenseness, and that is so good much of the way that you can almost stand for a banal and quite-to-be-expected climax." Although Burr's relatively minor role earned little mention, he was singled out by Edwin Schallert of the *Los Angeles Times*, who wrote that the actor was "particularly successful as a heavy."

The following year, Burr played perhaps the best role of his screen career, a henpecked jewelry salesman who strangles and dismembers his wife in *Rear Window* (1954). In addition to this first-rate feature, Burr was seen in *Gorilla At Large* (1954), an entertaining 3-D melodrama in which the actor portrayed another wife-killer; *Casanova's Big Night* (1954), a mildly amusing Bob Hope vehicle; *You're Never Too Young* (1954), one of the less popular Dean Martin–Jerry Lewis comedies; *A Man Alone* (1955), an excellent western that marked the directorial debut of actor Ray Milland; *Godzilla, King of the Monsters!* (1956), the classic Japanese monster movie, in which Burr held the distinction of being the only non–Japanese cast member; *A Cry in the Night* (1956), featuring Burr in a standout role as the psychotic kidnapper of Natalie Wood; and *Crime of Passion* (1957), the actor's film noir swan song. This feature starred Barbara Stanwyck as Kathy Doyle, a bored housewife who becomes preoccupied with furthering the career of her police detective husband, Bill (Sterling Hayden). When Kathy learns that Bill's boss, Inspector Tony Pope (Burr), plans to retire, she seduces him, using the occasion of their one-night stand to exact a vow that he will name Bill as his successor. But when Kathy insists that Pope live up to his promise, the inspector coldly refuses: "We haven't fooled each other," he tells her. "You dealt the cards, I played them as they came. The game's over. In my book, you wind up with enough chips. Now pick them up and go home." Enraged, Kathy fatally shoots Pope, but her role in the crime is eventually discovered by her husband, who reluctantly turns her over to authorities. For his standout performance as Pope, Burr earned high praise from critics, including the reviewer from the *New York Times*, who wrote: "In a mighty ticklish role, Mr. Burr, as a man with a conscience, is excellent."

By now, Burr had expanded his performing repertoire to include both radio and television. Since 1947, he had been on numerous radio broadcasts, including *Dragnet*, *Pat Novak for Hire*, and a starring role in 1956 on the CBS radio production of *Fort Laramie*. And beginning in the early 1950s, he guested on such television shows as *Family Theatre*, *Sound-Off Time*, and *Lux Video Theatre*. But in 1957, he accepted the television role for which is perhaps best associated — the unbeatable, implacable defense attorney, Perry Mason, based on the series written by Erle Stanley Gardner. Ironically, though, Burr was not the first choice for the role — he was originally considered for the role of district attorney Hamilton Burger.

"Fortunately for us, he said he would test for Burger only if we tested him for Mason, too," former actress and show producer Gail Patrick Jackson said in a 1959 *Saturday Evening Post* article. "When Erle saw Ray's tests, he said, 'That's Perry Mason.'"

For the next nine years, Burr starred in 271 episodes of the popular series, appearing on-screen in 90 percent of each episode, and earning Emmy Awards in 1958-59 and 1960-61 for Outstanding Performance by an Actor in a Series (Lead). Throughout the run of *Perry Mason*, the conscientious actor lived primarily in a bungalow on the studio where the show was shot, rising at 3:30 A.M. to learn his numerous lines, and working until 7:30 P.M. each weekday.

"To live at the studio was the only way I could do the job," Burr said in a 1988 interview with *TV Guide*. "I had no life whatsoever, except the show. We did 39 shows in our first season alone.... The tension to make it right week after week could get to you."

To lighten the often-stressful atmosphere on the set, Burr became notorious for playing practical jokes on his co-stars. A favorite target was Barbara Hale, who played Mason's faithful secretary, Della Street. According to the actress, Burr's pranks included putting a baby alligator in a drawer that she opened during a courtroom scene, having all of her dressing room furniture removed and deposited at her house, hiding a small white mouse in the toe of a stocking that Hale had washed and hung up to dry, and nailing her shoes to the floor.

"Someday I shall get even," Hale said in 1959. "But you know, seriously, the show is of a serious nature, and with work being like it is, these little gags break the tension that otherwise would be absolutely unbearable."

During his tenure on the Perry Mason show, instances of Burr's overwhelming generosity and compassion continued to mount. In one case, Burr learned that a veteran screen actor, George E. Stone, had fallen ill and had not worked for several years. Burr, who had not previously met the actor, arranged for him to be hired as the court clerk on Perry Mason, a steady job that required no exertion. In another case, Burr heard of a little girl in Worcester, Massachusetts, who had been severely burned in a fire, and had requested a picture of her favorite television character, Perry Mason. The following weekend, Burr flew to Massachusetts to visit the child in the hospital and, incensed when the press showed up, refused to be photographed. Another instance involved the show's makeup man, who collapsed on the set one day, suffering from a hemorrhaging ulcer.

"Who took him to the hospital? Ray," Gail Patrick Jackson told *TV Guide*. "And was up all night with him."

Cast member William Talman, who portrayed prosecutor Hamilton Burger, relayed yet another story.

"How many guys do you know who would throw their houses open to refugees? Two years ago, when they had the big Malibu fire, Ray insisted on them bringing people to [his house]," Talman said in a 1961 interview. "This is just an open-hearted guy. His personal life reflects his utter dedication to causes, to serving his fellow man."

As the popularity of the show increased with each passing season, Burr began to receive thousands of fan letters on a weekly basis, was frequently asked to address lawyer's conventions, and was awarded an honorary law degree from the McGeorge School of Law in Sacramento. Not all litigators were fans, however. Many lawyers objected to Mason's unbeaten track record, claiming that the show made prosecuting attorneys look "ridiculous." (Contrary to popular belief, Mason did not win all of his cases on the show; in a fall 1963 episode, entitled "The Case of the Deadly Ver-

dict," the jury found Mason's client guilty.) And in a well-publicized case, a North Carolina judge once refused to attend a local Bar Association convention because Burr was scheduled as the featured speaker.

In concert with Burr's exploding popularity with the public, countless articles began to appear about the actor, providing details of his professional career and his personal life. Nearly every published account of Burr focused on the tragedies of his troubled personal life, stating that the actor had been married three times. According to these articles, Burr's first wife, Annette Sutherland, was a British (or Scottish) actress with whom he had a son, Michael Evan. Sutherland is said to have died in the 1943 plane crash that also killed actor Leslie Howard and young Michael was sent to relatives in England, but he died of leukemia in 1953, at the age of 10. Meanwhile, the reports state, Burr married again in 1947, this time to Isabella Ward, whom he had met while both were performing at the Pasadena Playhouse. This marriage later ended in divorce. And Burr's third wife, Laura Andrina Morgan, reportedly died of cancer just weeks after their wedding in 1950 (or 1954, depending on the account).

This chronicling of Burr's tragic loves and losses makes for engrossing reading, but there is considerable doubt as to its veracity. According to Burr's sister, Geraldine Fuller, the actor was married only once, to Isabella Ward, but the union was annulled after just three weeks. And none of the actor's friends or relatives ever reported having met or even seen a photograph of his son. (Still, although Burr seldom revealed details about his private life, he discussed his son's death with a reporter as late as 1991, telling him, "When I knew my boy was going to die ... I didn't accept it, but I knew it.... If there had been any way I could have stopped it from happening to him, stopped leukemia from killing him and others, if I could stop it today, I would.") While the entire truth may never be known, a logical rationale for these reportedly contrived tales was that they served to cover up the reality of Burr's personal life.

"It was an open secret towards the middle and end of his career that he was gay.... That was a time in Hollywood history when homosexuality was not countenanced," celebrity biographer Bob Thomas said in a 2000 documentary on Burr's life. "To have that revealed would be a career-ending move. Ray was not a romantic star by any means, but he was a very popular figure.... If it were revealed at that time in Hollywood history, it would have been very difficult for him to continue."

Rather than the marriages described in Burr's biographical accounts, the actor had a longtime relationship with actor Robert Benevides, who met Burr in 1955 when he delivered a script to his house. The two formed a business and personal partnership that would last until Burr's death in 1993. In 1965, Burr and Benevides purchased a remote island in Fiji, on which they raised dairy and beef cattle, became part-owners of a local newspaper, and established a business cultivating rare orchids. With his typical compassion, Burr also built a school for the native children of the island and in later years, he arranged for 30 Fijians to come to the United States, where he paid for their education. In the mid-1980s, Burr would sell the island and, with Benevides, purchase a vineyard in Sonoma, California, where he would continue to raise his orchids and eventually begin cultivating wine. The Raymond Burr Vineyards is still in operation today.

Career-wise, after nearly a decade, Perry Mason finally defended his last case in 1966. Despite his lengthy association with the show, however, Burr did not experience a pleasant parting. Burr later revealed that, after urging from CBS executives, he had verbally agreed to a 10th and final season, only to read in the newspaper that the series had been cancelled.

"Nothing about the end was nice," he told *TV Guide* in 1988. "I remember finishing my last scene at 10 in the morning and going to my dressing room to take my makeup off. I had a watch on that they'd bought for Mason five or six years before, which I wore on the show, and I was in my dressing room for no

more than 10 minutes before they came over and asked for the watch.... I thought it was bad manners [to ask for it] before I even had my face washed — like I was going to steal it.... I gave them the watch and never saw any of them again."

Burr wasted little time before leaping into another television series. In 1967, he was back on the small screen in the title role of *Ironside*, an hour-long series about a former chief of detectives who was confined to a wheelchair after being paralyzed during an assassination attempt. Like *Perry Mason*, the show was a runaway hit. *Ironside* co-star Don Galloway, who portrayed Det. Sgt. Ed Brown, placed the success of the series squarely on Burr's shoulders.

"He had two great qualities as an actor — one you can learn and the other, you can't," Galloway said in a 2000 documentary. "The first is economy — he was an economic actor. He did what needed to be done and let the power of his personality do the rest of it. And the second thing, which I don't think you can really learn, is to make good choices — and he had an uncanny instinct for doing so."

Ironside ran for eight successful seasons, finally ending in January 1975 after 199 episodes. Two years later, Burr embarked on another series, *Kingston: Confidential*, on which he portrayed investigative reporter R.B. Kingston. But for Burr, the third time wasn't the charm, and the series was cancelled after 13 episodes.

During the late 1960s and 1970s, in addition to his work on *Ironside*, Burr managed to find time for other television projects, guesting on such programs as *It Takes a Thief, The Andy Williams Show, The ABC Comedy Hour*, and *The Love Boat*. He also formed his own company, Harbour Productions, producing and starring in, among other projects, the 1973 made-for-television movie, *A Man Whose Name Is John*, based on the life of Pope John XXIII.

In 1985, at age 68 and nearly three decades after filming the final episode of *Perry Mason*, Burr reprised his role as the daunting defense attorney in a two-hour television movie, *The Return of Perry Mason*. He was joined by Barbara Hale, who had played his secretary, and Hale's real-life son, actor William Katt (best known for his roles in *Carrie* [1976] and on television's *The Greatest American Hero*), portrayed the son of Mason's private investigator Paul Drake. (William Hopper, the actor who played Drake in the series, and who was also the son of famed columnist Hedda Hopper, suffered a fatal heart attack in 1970; William Talman, who played Hamilton Burger, died of lung cancer in 1968; and Ray Collins, who portrayed Lt. Tragg, left the series in 1964, dying the following year from emphysema.)

"I like to work," Burr said in 1988 of his return to the role. "And I like the growth in Mason, the change in him and his personality…. I think people always like seeing their system of justice affirmed — and it always is with Mason. The innocent go free. The guilty get caught. And Mason is the guy who does it all."

The Return of Perry Mason was the highest-rated television movie of 1985, and Burr went on to star in 25 more Perry Mason movies over the next eight years. By 1992, however, Burr's health had begun to fail, and in January 1993 he was diagnosed with kidney cancer. With his typical selflessness, Burr delayed an operation in order to complete filming on two television movies, another in the Perry Mason series and *The Return of Ironside*.

"He wanted to make sure that he finished the show for everybody else," Robert Benevides said in 2000. "He was an amazing man."

By the time the movies were completed, however, Burr's cancer had spread and was inoperable. The actor spent the next several months at his home in Sonoma, overseeing the dispersal of his estate through various charities, gifts to friends, and the creation of grant and trust programs. During the last several weeks of his life, Burr hosted farewell parties for his friends and family, as well as for the approximately 23 foster children whom he had supported over the years.

On September 12, 1993, with his life companion Robert Benevides at his side, Raymond Burr died at his Sonoma Valley home. His death saw the end not only to a fine acting career that had spanned six decades and encompassed radio, stage, screen, and television but, more importantly, the life of a man who thought more of others than he did himself. As a testament to his outstanding career and his unmatched contributions to others, Burr's hometown of New Westminster, British Columbia, in 1996 established The Raymond Burr Performing Arts Society. The Society is in the process of engaging in a capital campaign to restore and remodel the city's historic Columbia Theatre, which will be renamed The Raymond Burr Performing Arts Centre, housing a performance theater, rehearsal space, and teaching rooms. The center will serve as a fitting tribute to a man described by Robert Benevides as "the most generous man I'll ever know."

"He worked with Errol Flynn at one point, and Flynn told him, 'If I die with more than $10 in my pocket, I haven't done a good job.' I'm paraphrasing, but that's basically what he said," Robert Benevides said. "And Raymond lived by that. And when he died, he didn't have any money. He had nothing. Because he had given everything away. He had done so much, for so many people — it's amazing…. I'll never know another man like that."

Film Noir Filmography

Desperate. Director: Anthony Mann. Producer: Michel Kraike. Running time: 73 minutes. Released by RKO, May 20, 1947. Cast: Steve Brodie, Audrey Long, Raymond Burr, Douglas Fowley, William Challee, Jason Robards, Sr., Freddie Steele, Lee Frederick, Paul E. Burns, Ilka Gruning.

Pitfall. Director: Andre de Toth. Producer: Samuel Bischoff. Running time: 86 minutes. Released by United Artists, August 24, 1948. Cast: Dick Powell, Lizabeth Scott, Jane Wyatt, Raymond Burr, John Litel, Byron Barr, Jimmy Hunt, Ann Doran, Selmer Jackson, Margaret Wells, Dick Wassel.

Sleep, My Love. Director: Douglas Sirk. Producer: Charles Buddy Rogers, Ralph Cohn. Running time: 96 minutes. Released by United Artists, February 18, 1948. Cast: Claudette Colbert, Robert Cummings, Don Ameche, Rita Johnson, George Coulouris, Hazel Brooks, Queenie Smith, Keye Luke, Fred Nurney, Maria San Marco, Raymond Burr, Lillian Bronson, Ralph Moran.

Raw Deal. Director: Anthony Mann. Producer: Edward Small. Running time: 79 minutes. Released by Eagle-Lion, July 8, 1948. Cast: Dennis O'Keefe, Claire Trevor, Marsha Hunt, John Ireland, Raymond Burr, Curt Conway, Chili Williams, Richard Fraser, Whitner Bissell.

Abandoned. Director: Joseph M. Newman. Producer: Jerry Bresler. Running time: 78 minutes. Released by Universal-International, October 28, 1949. Cast: Dennis O'Keefe, Gale Storm, Jeff Chandler, Meg Randall, Raymond Burr, Marjorie Rambeau, Jeanette Nolan, Mike Mazurki, Will Kuluva, David Clarke, William Page, Sid Tomack, Perc Launders, Steve Darnell, Clifton Young, Ruth Sanderson.

Red Light. Director and Producer: Roy Del Ruth. Running time: 84 minutes. Released by United Artists, January 15, 1950. Cast: George Raft, Virginia Mayo, Gene Lockhart, Barton MacLane, Henry Morgan, Raymond Burr, Arthur Franz, Arthur Shields, Frank Orth, Philip Pine, Movita Castenada, Paul Frees, Claire Carleton, Soledad Jiminez.

M. Director: Joseph Losey. Producer: Seymour Nebenzal. Running time 87 minutes. Released by Columbia, June 10, 1951. Cast: David Wayne, Howard Da Silva, Martin Gabel, Luther Adler, Steve Brodie, Glenn Anders, Norman Lloyd, Walter Burke, Raymond Burr.

His Kind of Woman. Director: John Farrow. Producer: Robert Sparks. Running time: 120 minutes. Released by RKO, August 1951. Cast: Robert Mitchum, Jane Russell, Vincent Price, Tim Holt, Charles McGraw, Marjorie Reynolds, Raymond Burr, Leslye Banning, Jim Backus, Philip Van Zandt, John Mylong, Carleton G. Young, Erno Verebes, Dan White, Richard Bergren, Stacy Harris, Robert Cornthwaite.

The Blue Gardenia. Director: Fritz Lang. Producer: Alex Gottlieb. Running time: 90 minutes. Released by Warner Brothers, March 28, 1953. Cast: Anne Baxter, Richard Conte, Ann Sothern, Raymond Burr, Jeff Donnell, Richard Erdman, George Reeves, Ruth Storey, Ray Walker, Nat "King" Cole, Celia Lovsky, Frank Ferguson, Alex Gottlieb.

Crime of Passion. Director: Gerd Oswald. Producer: Herman Cohen. Running time: 85 minutes. Released by United Artists, January 9, 1957. Cast: Barbara Stanwyck, Sterling Hayden, Raymond Burr, Fay Wray, Royal Dano, Virginia Grey, Dennis Cross, Robert Griffin, Jay Adler, Malcolm Atterbury, John S. Launer, Brad Trumbull, Skipper McNally, Jean Howell, Peg La Centra, Nancy Reynolds, Marjorie Owens, Robert Quarry, Joe Conley, Stuart Whitman.

References

Barber, Mary. "Perry Mason: The Champion of Orchids." *Los Angeles Times*, May 26, 1988.

Battelle, Phyllis. "Perry Mason Deserves Accolade; TV Proves It." *Los Angeles Herald-Examiner*, May 4, 1962.

Brady, James. "In Step With: Raymond Burr." *Parade*, October 29, 1989.

Burr, Raymond. "Down on the Farm." *Los Angeles Times*, January 19, 1986.

Efron, Edith. "A Caldron of Frustrations, Part I." *TV Guide*, February 15, 1969.

_____. "A Caldron of Frustrations, Part II." *TV Guide*, February 22, 1969.

Gehman, Richard. "The Case of the Oversize Actor." *TV Guide*, March 17, 1961.

_____. "TV's Perry Mason." Publication Unsourced, circa 1962.

Hopper, Hedda. "Burr to Give Up 'Law Practice.'" *Los Angeles Times*, July 26, 1964.

Jennings, C. Robert. "Burr for the Prosecution." *TV Guide*, September 16, 1967.

Johnson, Robert. "TV's Make-Believe Lawyer." *The Saturday Evening Post*, October 3, 1959.

Lowry, Cynthia. "Ray Burr Crusading for the Handicapped." *Los Angeles Herald-Examiner*, September 8, 1971.

McClay, Howard. "Burr's Future is Brighter Now." *Los Angeles Daily News*, October 6, 1953.

Murphy, Mary. "With Raymond Burr During His Final Battle." *TV Guide*, September 25, 1993.

"Perry Mason's Prisoner." *Look*, September 2, 1958.

Podolsky, J.D. "The Defense Rests." *People*, September 27, 1993.

Rader, Dotson. "The Private Trials of Raymond Burr." *Parade*, February 3, 1991.

"Raymond Burr Talks of Island Paradise." *Hollywood Citizen-News*, October 9, 1967.

Richman, Alan. "Raymond Burr Booms Back to Court as Perry Mason, but He Regrets Ever Taking the Role That Made Him Famous." *People*, May 26, 1986.

Rubin, Sam. "Perry Mason ... Dead or Alive?" *Classic Images*, January 1994.

"The Case of the Reluctant Perry Mason." *TV Guide*, June 3, 1961.

"Those Perry Mason Days Were a Real Trial." *TV Guide*, May 14, 1988.

Townley, Roderick. "Raymond Burr." *US*, March 19, 1990.

Whitney, Dwight. "And Now The Man Who Became Pope John." *TV Guide*, April 21, 1973.

Documentary

"Raymond Burr: The Case of the TV Legend." Produced by ABC News for A&E Networks. Copyright 2000.

JAMES CAGNEY

"What's the matter, Parker? I ain't gonna do anything. Not now. I'm gonna let you stay awake nights. Sweat it out. And when I get ready, good and ready, I'll pay you back."
— James Cagney in *White Heat* (1949)

During his film career, James Cagney proffered some of the most enduring images and memorable characters ever to appear on celluloid—callously shoving a grapefruit into the face of his mistress in *Public Enemy* (1931) and later, in the same movie, suffering a grisly demise as a "mummified" corpse; deliberately tarnishing his tough-guy reputation by pretending to "turn yellow" on his way to the electric chair in *Angels with Dirty Faces* (1938); demonstrating his considerable prowess as a song-and-dance man in his portrayal of George M. Cohan in *Yankee Doodle Dandy* (1942); depicting a neurotic, palm tree-loving ship's captain in *Mister Roberts* (1955). The multi-talented performer also provided what is perhaps his best-known cinematic portrait in one of his two film noir appearances, perishing in a fiery, apocalyptic explosion in *White Heat* (1949).

"Everything he does is *big*," actor-director Orson Welles once remarked, "and yet it's never for a moment unbelievable, because it's *real*. It's true."

A native of New York's Lower East Side, James Francis Cagney, Jr., was born on July 17, 1899, the second of seven children (two siblings died in infancy) of Irish-American bar owner James Francis Cagney and his Irish-Norwegian wife, Carolyn Nelson Cagney.

"My father had a saloon at Eighty-first Street and First Avenue, just a little place," Cagney recalled in a 1982 *Rolling Stone* magazine interview, "and he was known as the 'two for one' bartender, meaning that he drank two for every one he served. Not a wise way to make a living. In those days, my father thought he had something going simply by running the place, but he was wrong, unfortunately. He was a bookkeeper, originally—that was the irony of it. He also liked to play the horses and ran through a lot of what little money we had."

To help boost the family coffers, young Cagney landed his first professional job at the age of 14, working as an office boy at the *New York Sun*. At various times between his studies at Stuyvesant High School, he also held down posts as a switchboard operator and a pool hall attendant, earned cash wrapping bundles at Wanamaker's Department Store, and sold tickets for the Hudson Riverboat Line. With the little time he had left, Cagney developed considerable skills as a boxer, becoming runner-up for the New York State lightweight amateur boxing title, and indulged his budding interest as a performer in several productions at the local Lenox Hill Settlement House.

After graduating from high school, Cagney enrolled at Columbia University, but he dropped out to work full-time after the 1918 death of his father, a victim of an influenza epidemic and "the inroads of all that booze," the actor said. Seeking a larger income than he was earning at his $14-a-week job at Wanamaker's, Cagney jumped at the opportunity to double his salary by auditioning for a vaudeville act called *Every Sailor* at Keith's Eighty-first Street Theatre. Although he learned, to his "great surprise," that the production was a female impersonation act, Cagney landed the part and the following year won a slot in the chorus of a Broadway musical, *Pitter Patter*.

"I didn't know the highland fling from a sailor's hornpipe, and I couldn't even sing *Sweet Adeline*, but I needed that job," Cagney once said of his tryout for his Broadway debut. "Fifty applicants assembled. I watched the fellow's feet next to me and did what he did."

Also in the chorus of *Pitter Patter* were actor Allen Jenkins, who would appear alongside Cagney in a number of his Hollywood productions, and a dancer from Iowa named Frances Willard Vernon.

"We met backstage," Cagney said in 1985. "She could dance, but I could not. She was also cute. I said 'Hello,' and she said, 'Hello,' and that was the beginning of a love relationship that has spanned 63 years, and still exists today. Because her name is Willard, I call her Willie, or Bill, for short. If you want to call it love at first sight, then I guess that's what it was."

Cagney and "Bill" married in 1922, later adopted two children, James and Kathleen, and remained together until the actor's death in 1986. After their run in *Pitter Patter*, they hit the vaudeville circuit together, performing in *Lew Fields' Ritz Girls* and sometimes appearing in their own act, billed as Vernon and Nye. In the late 1920s, "Bill" retired from performing and, along with her husband, opened the Cagney School of Dance in Elizabeth, New Jersey.

In addition to his appearances with his wife, Cagney was seen in numerous productions throughout the 1920s, including *Dot's My Boy* (1921); *Outside Looking In* (1925), where he played one of his first tough-guy roles; *Women Go on Forever* (1927); *The Grand Street Follies of 1928* (1928); and *Maggie the Magnificent* (1929), in which he was paired for the first time with actress Joan Blondell. The two were teamed again the following year in *Penny Arcade* (1930), but although the play closed after 24 performances, it attracted the attention of Broadway star Al Jolson, who bought it for the screen and sold it to Warner Bros., stipulating that Cagney and Blondell reprise their roles for the film. A short time later, Cagney was on his way to Hollywood.

"I came out for three weeks," the actor once said, "and I stayed, to my absolute amazement, for 31 years!"

Retitled *Sinner's Holiday*, Cagney's screen debut ran only 55 minutes but it earned favorable reviews for the actor, including a mention from the *New York Times* critic who remarked, "The most impressive acting is done by James Cagney." Studio head Jack Warner wasted no time in signing Cagney to a three-year, $400-a-week contract, and the actor made four pictures in the next six months, including *The Doorway to Hell* (1930), a bootlegging drama; *Other Men's Women* (1930), his second of six films with Joan Blondell; and *The Millionaire* (1931), a comedy starring George Arliss. After these features, Cagney was cast in the film that would transform him into an overnight sensation, *The Public Enemy* (1931).

"The story was about two street pals— one soft-spoken, the other a really tough little article," Cagney once recalled. "For some incredible reason, I was cast as the quiet one; Eddie Woods, a fine actor but a boy of gentle background, well-spoken and educated, became the tough guy. Fortunately, Bill Wellman, the director ... quickly became aware of the obvious casting error. He knew at once that I could project that direct gutter quality, so Eddie and I switched roles after Wellman made an issue out of it with [production head] Darryl Zanuck."

It was in *The Public Enemy* that Cagney offered the first of his string of memorable movie moments, ramming a half-grapefruit in the mug of his moll (Mae Clarke) after telling her, "I wish you was a wishing well — so that I could tie a bucket to ya and sink ya!"

"That half-grapefruit has become a piece of Americana," Cagney said of the scene. "It was just about the first time, if not the very first, that a woman had been treated like a broad on the screen instead of like a delicate

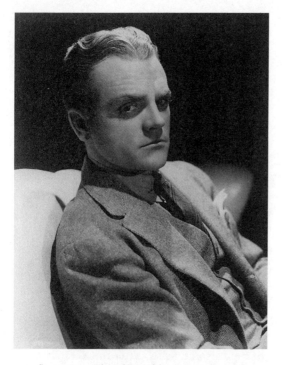

flower.... That bit of business became so identified with me that years afterward when I'd go into a restaurant, people would send me half-grapefruits with their compliments and I got so tired of that deal I began to duck eating in public. It was hard for me to get used to the idea that in *The Public Enemy* I had hit the jackpot overnight."

After his triumph in *The Public Enemy*, Cagney was cast opposite Joan Blondell in *Blonde Crazy* (1931) and with Edward G. Robinson in *Smart Money* (1931), but before the films were released, Cagney fired what would become the initial salvo in an ongoing battle with Jack Warner.

"[The studio] had a couple of people on the lot who were stars, and they were getting $125,000 a picture," Cagney later recalled. "And here I was up above the title just as they were, and I was getting $400 a week. That didn't last long—I walked out."

During Cagney's retreat to New York, audiences turned out in droves for *Blonde Crazy* and *Smart Money*, and three months later, Warners renegotiated the actor's contract, increasing his weekly salary to $1,400 and allowing for "periodic reappraisals" of his

worth. Cagney's first picture after his brief walkout was another hit, *Taxi!* (1932), co-starring Loretta Young, followed by *The Crowd Roars* (1932), where he played a race car driver, and *Winner Take All* (1932), in which he demonstrated his boxing skills. After the latter feature, Cagney staged another walkout, telling the press, "A player should be in a position to demand what he is worth as long as he is worth it. My employers can't see my way so I'm through." This time, it took the studio six months to see Cagney's way — he returned to the lot later that year with an agreement for four pictures a year at $3,500 a week, to increase to $4,500 weekly by 1935.

Cagney's highly publicized battles for adequate compensation were not limited to his own career; his reputation as a Hollywood rebel also encompassed his struggles on behalf of his peers. In October 1933, the actor became one of the first major stars to join the fledgling Screen Actors Guild (SAG), later serving as First Vice President, President, and member of the Board of Directors. More than four decades after receiving his SAG card, the actor would be honored with the organization's lifetime achievement award.

"He was respected on both sides of the bargaining table and was personally involved in solving his fellow actors' problems," former SAG Executive Secretary John L. Sales said in 1986. "He'd often call at 1 or 2 A.M. with stories of an actor's troubles, and we'd often hold emergency meetings at his home. He was a marvelous example to Guild members."

Over the next few years, Cagney starred in such hits as *Lady Killer* (1933), in which he again abused co-star Mae Clarke, this time by dragging her across a room by her hair; *Footlight Parade* (1933), where he was given the opportunity to display his talent as a hoofer; *Here Comes the Navy* (1934), the first of Cagney's eight features with lifelong friend Pat O'Brien; *Jimmy the Gent* (1934), co-starring Bette Davis; and *'G' Men* (1935), which found the actor on the right side of the law as an FBI agent. In one of his few clunkers during this period, Cagney also appeared in the lavish production of Shakespeare's *A Midsummer Night's Dream* (1935), portraying Bottom, a weaver who is transformed by fairies into a donkey. A box-office disappointment, the film earned a handful of good reviews upon its release, but Cagney was universally panned, with the critic for the *New York Times* writing that he "belabors the slapstick of his part beyond endurance."

Despite his status as a top box-office draw, Cagney's fight with his studio heated up again in 1935 when he was seen in five releases—one more than his agreement called for. The actor walked out again, this time suing Warners for breach of contract and succeeding in earning a release from the studio.

"I used to like to walk out on [Jack Warner], frankly, whenever my contract didn't suit me," Cagney said in 1982. "I'd cuss him out in Yiddish, which I had learned from Jewish friends in my days at Stuyvesant High. Drove him wild. 'What'd he *say*?' he'd yell. '*What'd he just call me?*' People now see me as being tough, but it had nothing to do with being tough and everything to do with being stubborn. The point in life is to get what you want. There's no gain in getting things you don't want, and there's no gift in settling for something."

Following his defection from Warners, Cagney signed with the newly-formed Grand National studio, but after only two features there, he was once again lured back to Warner Bros., which offered him the phenomenal deal of $150,000 per film against 10 percent of the gross, story refusal rights, and a "happiness clause," which allowed the actor to terminate his contract if he judged his relationship with the studio to be "obnoxious or unsatisfactory to him." It was a deal Cagney couldn't refuse, and he returned to the studio in back-to-back features with Pat O'Brien, *Boy Meets Girl* (1938), an amusing screwball comedy, and the box-office smash *Angels with Dirty Faces* (1938). In the latter, Cagney earned a Best Actor Academy Award nomination for his portrayal of street tough Rocky Sullivan, wowing audiences in the scene where, on the way to his execution, he feigns cowardice in order

to tarnish the image held by the hero-worshipping delinquents from his neighborhood (played by the Dead End Kids). Also in this film, Cagney first demonstrated the quirky, often-imitated mannerisms that would become such an indelible part of his screen persona. In his autobiography, the actor wrote that he drew on his childhood experiences in his development of the character.

"Rocky Sullivan was in part modeled on a fella I used to see when I was a kid," Cagney recalled. "He was a hophead and a pimp, with four girls on his string. He worked out of a Hungarian rathskeller on First Avenue between 77th and 78th Streets.... All day long he would stand on that corner, hitch up his trousers, twist his neck and move his necktie, lift his shoulders, snap his fingers, then bring his hands together in a soft smack. His invariable greeting was 'Whaddya ya hear? Whaddya ya say?' So I recalled this fella and his mannerisms and gave them to Rocky Sullivan just to bring some modicum of difference to this roughneck. I did that gesturing maybe six times in the picture—that was over 30 years ago—and the impressionists are still doing me doing him."

Although Cagney lost the Oscar to Spencer Tracy in *Boys Town* (1938), he received the New York Film Critics' Award and was hailed by critics, including Kate Cameron of the *New York Daily News*, who judged that his performance was "one of the most impressive he has ever given"; the critic for *Variety*, who noted his "swagger and aw-go-to-hell pugnacity"; and the *New York Post*'s Archer Winston, who wrote, "It's an all-Cagney portrait, crackling with nervous energy and excellent."

Cagney followed this top-notch feature with a series of hits, including *The Roaring Twenties* (1939), where he was seen with Humphrey Bogart as a ruthless bootlegger; *Each Dawn I Die* (1939), co-starring George Raft; *City for Conquest* (1940), in which he turned in what one critic termed a "stunning performance" as a semi-blinded pugilist; and *The Fighting 69th* (1940), an all-male wartime drama with Pat O'Brien and George Brent.

(After the latter feature, the actor once again tangled with Warner Bros., filing suit when the marquee at the film's premiere initially listed O'Brien's name, instead of Cagney's, in the top-billing slot.)

At this point in his career, however, Cagney's squabbles with his studio faded into insignificance when he faced highly publicized charges of Communism. Several years earlier, Cagney had contributed to a fund aiding striking cotton pickers in California which, unbeknownst to the actor, was backed by an organization with left-wing leanings. He'd also donated money to the defense of the Scottsboro boys, nine black youths in Alabama who had been falsely accused of rape, and his check wound up hanging on the wall of a Communist Party office in San Francisco. As a result of his contributions to these and similar causes, Cagney was named as a Communist — along with such notables as Humphrey Bogart and Fredric March — by former Communist Party leader John R. Leech. Cagney vehemently denied the charges, attributing them to "West Coast political aspirants," and in August 1940 appeared before a congressional committee headed by Martin Dies. Reportedly, after only 15 minutes, Dies cleared the actor of all charges.

"[Dies] went in to interview Cagney and he came out with Cagney's autographed picture," Warner Bros. screenwriter Julius Epstein said years later. "That was the big laugh around the studio."

With this scare behind him, Cagney starred in two successful comedies, The Strawberry Blonde (1941) with Olivia deHavilland and Rita Hayworth, and The Bride Came C.O.D. (1941) opposite Bette Davis, before being cast in one of his best-loved films, Yankee Doodle Dandy (1942). Portraying Broadway hoofer George M. Cohan — who reportedly hand-picked the actor for the role — Cagney turned in a memorable, multifaceted performance that allowed him to showcase his dancing talent and display a wide range of emotion, from humor to pathos.

"There was a scene that he did that was so remarkable, everyone on the lot, I think was affected by it," Cagney's co-star Joan Leslie recalled in a 1992 documentary. "It was when he said goodbye to his dying father. [Director] Mike Curtiz spoiled a take because of crying so loud he couldn't control it. The script girl cried so much that she blurred the ink on the notes on her script. It was quite a moment."

Nominated for his second Academy Award for Best Actor, Cagney went home with the golden statuette this time around, beating out such formidable opposition as Ronald Colman in Random Harvest (1942), Gary Cooper in Pride of the Yankees (1942), Walter Pidgeon in Mrs. Miniver (1942), and Monty Woolley in The Pied Piper (1942). In his brief acceptance speech (which followed a rambling monologue delivered by Greer Garson for her Mrs. Miniver win), Cagney told the assembled guests, "An actor is only as good as people think he is and as bad as people think he is. I am glad so many thought I was so good."

Yankee Doodle Dandy was Cagney's last film under his Warner Bros. contract, and he turned down offers to re-sign with the studio in order to form a production company with his brother, Bill, who had for years served as his agent and manager. Under the Cagney Productions banner, the siblings produced three films, Johnny Come Lately (1943), a mediocre period piece that one critic labeled "not dreadful"; Blood on the Sun (1945), an anti–Japanese actioner co-starring Sylvia Sidney; and The Time of Your Life (1948), based on the Pulitzer Prize-winning play by William Saroyan and co-starring Cagney's baby sister, Jeanne. Between features, Cagney found time to contribute to the war effort by serving as chairman of the Hollywood Victory Committee, heading up bond-raising tours alongside such stars as Pat O'Brien, Judy Garland, Charles Boyer, and Bing Crosby. He also performed at overseas military bases, lent his Martha's Vineyard estate to the Army for maneuvers, appeared in recruiting trailers for the Allied war effort, and narrated the 1944 documentary short, Battle Stations.

Despite the critical success of Cagney's

James Cagney and Edmond O'Brien in *White Heat* (1949).

The Time of Your Life, the actor's production company took a financial blow ("We lost a half-million dollars ... it was a very unhappy situation," the actor said), and Cagney returned the following year to his old home studio, appearing in six Warners features over the next four years. The first of these contained the actor's standout performance in the film noir classic *White Heat* (1949).

In this fast-paced, tautly directed feature, Cagney starred as Cody Jarrett, a psychotic gangster characterized by incapacitating headaches and an abnormally close relationship with his mother, Ma Jarrett (Margaret Wycherly). As one character explains, "His mother has been the prop that's held him up. He's got a fierce, psychopathic devotion for her. All his life whenever he got into a jam, he just put out his hand and there was Ma

Jarrett." The film opens with a daring train robbery executed by Jarrett and his gang, resulting in a haul of $300,000 — and four deaths. Early on, Jarrett's penchant for violence is clearly demonstrated when his name is recklessly revealed by one of his henchmen. After the train's hapless engineer remarks, "You won't get away with it, Cody," the gangster responds, "Cody, huh? You've got a good memory for names. Too good." And he promptly shoots the engineer to death.

Sought by police, Jarrett devises a scheme to confess to a minor crime committed in another state at the same time as the train heist, but he is unaware that federal authorities are on to his plan and have assigned an undercover agent, Hank Fallon (Edmond O'Brien), as his prison cellmate. Once inside, Fallon gains Jarrett's trust by saving his life when a fellow inmate tries to kill him and later acting as a soothing surrogate mother when Jarrett suffers one of his excruciating headaches. Meanwhile, Ma Jarrett visits her son to inform him that his wife, Verna (Virginia Mayo), has run off with one of his underlings, Big Ed Somers (Steve Cochran). Ma vows revenge on the deceitful couple, but Jarrett soon learns that she has been killed and, in a memorable scene, becomes completely unglued, crawling across the prison dining table and slugging several guards before being subdued and carried off, howling and moaning.

After the death of his mother, Jarrett stages a prison break along with several other prisoners— including Fallon — kills Big Ed, and reunites with his gang to plan a heist at a huge gas facility. Fallon manages to alert his contact of the upcoming caper, but his cover is blown during the robbery when he is recognized by a member of the gang, a revelation that pushes Jarrett close to the brink of madness. "A *copper*. A *copper*. How do ya like that, boys? A *copper*," Jarrett says. "And we went for it. *I* went for it. Treated him like a kid brother. And I was going to split 50–50 with a copper." When police converge on the plant, Fallon escapes and Jarrett's gang are picked off one by one, but Jarrett climbs to the top of a huge storage tower and fires into the huge gas tank, shouting, "Made it, Ma! Top of the world!" just before the tank explodes.

Although Cagney's portrait of Cody Jarrett is viewed today as a tour-de-force, a few critics seemed slightly overwhelmed by his performance after the film's release. The reviewer for *Cue* seemed particularly affected, writing that Cagney, "heavier in voice, body, and jowl, plays a homicidal paranoiac with a mother fixation — a crazy killer who mixes train robbery with murder, bestiality with sadism, and tops the whole unsavory mess with a slobbering, shuddering series of epileptic fits the like of which I hope I may never again see in the fearful darkness of a movie theatre." The *New York Times*' Bosley Crowther took a far more favorable view, however, opining that the actor "achieves the fascina-tion of a brilliant bull-fighter at work, deftly engaged in the business of doing violence with economy and grace. His movements are supple and electric, his words are as swift and sharp as swords and his whole manner carries the conviction of confidence, courage and power."

The following year, Cagney starred in the second of his two films noirs, *Kiss Tomorrow Goodbye* (1950), once again turning in a well-done portrait of a ruthless killer. This time the actor portrayed Ralph Cotter, who is first seen breaking out of prison with a fellow inmate named Carleton (Neville Brand). When Carleton is shot by guards, Cotter finishes him off before being picked up in the getaway by Carleton's sister, Holiday (Barbara Payton), and a radio operator known as Jinx (Steve Brodie). Setting up shop in the small town where Holiday lives, Cotter wastes no time in resuming his criminal activities, teaming with Jinx to rob the payroll of a local grocery store and killing an employee in the process. When a pair of crooked cops, Weber (Ward Bond) and Reece (Barton MacLane), show up to demand that the men turn over the stolen money to them, Cotter and Jinx make a recording of the shakedown attempt, using it to blackmail the lawmen into aiding them with another heist. Meanwhile, although he has become romantically involved with Holiday, Cotter falls for Margaret Dobson (Helena Carter), the daughter of one of the town's most prominent citizens, and secretly marries her. But Cotter's crimes and misdeeds finally catch up to him when Holiday not only learns of his marriage, but also that he killed her brother, and she confronts him at the film's end, telling him to "kiss tomorrow goodbye," just before she guns him down.

Produced by Cagney's brother, Bill, *Kiss Tomorrow Goodbye* garnered a mixed reaction from critics; Bosley Crowther of the *New York Times* acknowledged that the film offered "a slick veneer, some lively episodes, and a couple of neat secondary performances," but he judged that, "as a whole, [it] comes off as a poor man's carbon copy of *The Asphalt Jungle*." But the *Los Angeles Times*' Edwin

Schallert wrote that "Cagney provides one of his slickest scoundrels ever … [and] does a thorough job of it." Even Schallert admitted, though, that "it's probably just about time for Cagney to quit this kind of picture."

During the remainder of the decade, Cagney turned in some of his best performances in films such as *Come Fill the Cup* (1951), where he played an alcoholic newsman; *Mister Roberts* (1955), in which he was seen in the memorable role of a hard-nosed ship's captain with an unusual fondness for his palm tree plant; *Love Me or Leave Me* (1955), where his portrayal of 1920s gangster Martin "The Gimp" Snyder" earned the actor his third Academy Award nomination (he lost to Ernest Borgnine in *Marty*); and *Man of a Thousand Faces* (1957), in which he was applauded for his "superb" depiction of actor Lon Chaney, Sr. The decade also saw Cagney's appearance in *A Lion Is in the Streets* (1953), a relatively forgettable drama that was notable primarily because it employed Cagney's brother, Bill, as producer, sister Jeanne in a supporting role, and another brother, Ed, as story editor. And later in the decade, Cagney went behind the camera for his sole directorial effort on the poorly received *Short Cut to Hell* (1957), earning mention in *Time* magazine for "manag[ing] to beauty-spot a few of the bare places with some characteristically Cagney touches." Between feature films, the actor also made a handful of rare television appearances, including a re-enactment of a scene from *Mister Roberts* on the *Ed Sullivan Show* in 1955, and a role in an episode of *Robert Montgomery Presents* called "Soldiers from the War Returning" in 1956.

In 1961, Cagney was cast in a supporting role in what would turn out to be his last film for the next three decades, *One, Two Three*. Although this Billy Wilder comedy earned a cool reception from audiences, Cagney's performance as a fast-talking Coca-Cola salesman landed the actor a number of favorable notices, including one from the critic for *Esquire* magazine, who wrote: "He plays it fortissimo all the way, as is right, and his vulgar vitality is just what is needed to keep the act

from falling off the high wire." But by now, Cagney decided that acting had "become something of a bore instead of an exciting thing."

"It was a very personal decision. I had had it, but I'll tell you exactly what I meant by that," Cagney said in his 1982 interview in *Rolling Stone*. "Most of the shooting [on *One, Two, Three*] took place at Bavaria Studios outside of Munich, right in the middle of the German countryside. Being a city boy, I've always loved the country, and this landscape was magnificent. I began to realize that I was happiest when I was outside, roaming around the hills. One day, after finishing a scene, I walked out of the studio to get some exercise. A few moments later, one of the crew yelled, 'Ready, Mr. Cagney!' I walked back into this cavernous studio, which was pitch black, and on impulse, I turned back to look at the sunshine I had left behind. I stood there, very upset, thinking, 'Darkness before me, sunlight behind me. This is it; no more. I want to be in that light.' A man can't earn his living walking into darkness, separated from the real world and its beauty. I followed my heart, away from acting. I love to make people happy, but Cagney has to come first, right?"

Although Cagney provided the narration for an anti–Communist government documentary, *Road to the Wall* (1962), an NBC-TV special, *Smokey the Bear* (1966), and the western *Arizona Bushwhackers* (1968), the actor remained out of the limelight for nearly 15 years, spending most of his time on Martha's Vineyard or his farm near Millbrook, New York, indulging his interests in farming, painting, collecting antique carriages, and raising horses. Then, in 1974, at the age of 75, Cagney made a triumphant return to the Hollywood community to accept the Life Achievement Award from the American Film Institute (AFI), becoming the second individual to receive the honor (director John Ford was the first). The event was a star-studded affair, featuring tributes from such cinematic notables as John Wayne, Bob Hope, Joan Blondell, Mae Clarke, George Raft, and Doris Day.

Along with clips from the actor's impressive career, and a performance by Frank Gorshin, who became known for his Cagney impersonations, the evening was highlighted by Cagney's acceptance speech, during which he offered thanks to his old nemesis, Jack Warner, who had, the actor said, dubbed him "The Professional Againster." Cagney also evoked a roaring ovation when he addressed the numerous imitations that had cropped up over the years.

"Just in passing, I never said, 'You dirty rat,'" Cagney quipped. "What I actually said was, 'Judy, Judy, Judy!'"

After the AFI tribute, Cagney resumed his life out of the public eye, reportedly rejecting numerous film offers, including *Kotch* (1971) and *The Godfather, Part II* (1974). But he was seen on television in 1980, when he received a Kennedy Center Lifetime Achievement Award, and the following year returned to the big screen in a much-heralded performance in Milos Forman's *Ragtime* (1981), which starred Howard Rollins. Although the actor had been debilitated by diabetes and a mild stroke in 1977, he was a standout in his role as a wily New York police commissioner and the film was a critical and financial success. Three years later, shortly after being presented with the Presidential Medal of Freedom, Cagney was seen as an aging prizefighter in the made-for-television movie *Terrible Joe Moran* (1984), but by this time, the actor was suffering from dysphasia, which caused his speech to slur, and his entire role was reportedly dubbed by another actor.

On Easter Sunday 1986, his body weakened by heart and circulatory ailments and diabetes, James Cagney died at his home in upstate New York, with his wife of 64 years, Bill, at his side. His passing invited a spate of tributes from former co-stars, including James Stewart, who called him "one of the biggest names of all in motion pictures," and Bob Hope, who said, "I'd be selfish to say I'm going to miss him because all the whole world's going to miss him." The Requiem Mass held at the New York church where Cagney once served as an altar boy was attended by a ver-

itable "who's who" of Hollywood stars and such local notables as Governor Mario Cuomo, Mayor Richard Koch, and Cardinal O'Connor, and his pallbearers included boxer Floyd Patterson, dancer Mikhail Baryshnikov, actor Ralph Bellamy, and director Milos Forman.

While James Cagney is commonly thought of in terms of his performances in gangster films, his wide-ranging talent and versatility was well-demonstrated in such features as *Yankee Doodle Dandy*, *Mister Roberts*, and *Man of a Thousand Faces*. Although numerous descriptions have been offered to account for Cagney's enormous and long-lasting appeal, perhaps the best was furnished by actor-turned-president Ronald Reagan, who said that Cagney was "the best at whatever he did — a hero, a villain, a comic, or a dancer."

"America has lost one of her finest artists," Reagan said in a statement released after Cagney's death. "Jimmy burst upon our movie screen with an energy and a talent we have never seen before and we will never see again."

Film Noir Filmography

White Heat. Director: Raoul Walsh. Producer: Lou Edelman. Running time: 114 minutes. Released by Warner Bros., September 2, 1949. Cast: James Cagney, Virginia Mayo, Edmond O'Brien, Margaret Wycherly, Steve Cochran, John Archer, Wally Cassell, Fred Clark, Ford Rainey, Fred Coby, G. Pat Collins, Mickey Knox, Paul Guilfoyle, Robert Osterloh, Ian MacDonald, Ray Montgomery.

Kiss Tomorrow Goodbye. Director: Gordon Douglas. Producer: William Cagney. Running time: 102 minutes. Released by Warner Bros., August 4, 1950. Cast: James Cagney, Barbara Payton, Helena Carter, Ward Bond, Luther Adler, Barton MacLane, Steve Brodie, Rhys Williams, Herbert Heyes, John Litel, William Frawley, Robert Karnes, Kenneth Tobey, Dan Riss, Frank Reicher, John Halloran, Neville Brand.

References

Alexander, Shana. "Cagney." *Newsweek*, February 4, 1974.

Amory, Cleveland. "The Incredible James Cagney — Tough Enough to Be Gentle." *Parade*, August 5, 1984.

Arnold, Gary. "James Cagney Dies at 86; Won Fame in Gangster Roles. *Washington Post*, March 31, 1986.

Benson, Sheila. "Lessons from a Man Named Jimmy." *Los Angeles Times*, April 6, 1986.

Biography of James Cagney. William Cagney Productions, circa 1947.

Brock, Alan. "James Cagney: A Personal Friendship." *Classic Images*, August 1993.

"Cagney at 79: He's a Yankee Doodle Dandy." *Los Angeles Times*, July 19, 1978.

"Cagney Hailed for 40-Year Career." *Boxoffice*, April 15, 1974.

Cagney, James. *Cagney by Cagney*. New York: Doubleday, 1976.

_____. "I'm Glad I Had Trouble." *This Week Magazine*, June 7, 1959.

_____, as told to Pete Martin. "How I Got This Way." *Saturday Evening Post*, January 7, 1956.

"Cagney Suffers Minor Stroke." *Los Angeles Times*, May 14, 1977.

Chute, David. "Cagney's Career Was 'Top of the World.'" *Los Angeles Herald-Examiner*, March 31, 1986.

Clooney, Nick. "How James Cagney Got Burned — Politically." *American Movie Classics Magazine*, July 1997.

DuBrow, Rick. "James Cagney: Song-and-Dance Tough Guy Enters His 80s with a Paint Brush." *Los Angeles Herald-Examiner*, July 15, 1979.

"Famed Actor James Cagney Dies at Age 85." *The Hollywood Reporter*, March 31, 1986.

Flint, Peter B. "James Cagney Is Dead at 86; Master of Pugnacious Grace." *New York Times*, March 31, 1986.

Haber, Joyce. "The Cagney Touch: Always Leave Them Liking." *Los Angeles Times*, March 17, 1974.

Harmetz, Aljean. "Cagney — The Man Who Got Away." *New York Times*, March 3, 1974.

Hildebrand, Harold. "Cagney Stars in 59th Film." *Los Angeles Examiner*, June 5, 1960.

"In Memoriam: James Cagney." *Screen Actor*, Spring 1986.

"James Cagney Enters Hospital." *Los Angeles Herald-Examiner*, March 29, 1979.

"James Cagney, Legend of Movies, Dies at 86." *Los Angeles Times*, March 31, 1986.

"Kennedy Center to Honor Cagney." *The Hollywood Reporter*, December 5, 1980.

Krohn, Lewis G. "Cagney's Book May Have Omitted Much." *Classic Film Collector*, Winter 1977.

Lacayo, Richard. "It Was All Big — and It Worked." *Time*, April 14, 1986.

McCarthy, Todd. "James Cagney, 86, Dies in N.Y. From Diabetic Complications." *Variety*, March 31, 1986.

Osborne, Robert. "New 'Cagney' Bio Leaves Dark Side Underexposed." *The Hollywood Reporter*, January 8, 1998.

Pryor, Thomas M. "James Cagney: A Remembrance." *Variety*, April 3, 1986.

Reed, Susan K. "'I Always Wanted to be a Farmer.'" *Saturday Review*, December 1981.

Roura, Phil, and Poster, Tom. "Cagney: A 'Tough Guy' Fights Back." *New York Daily News*, circa 1980.

Speck, Gregory. "James Cagney." *Interview*, December 1985.

Squarini, Peter. "The Original Rocky: James Cagney." *Classic Images*, December 1983.

"So Long, Jimmy." *Milwaukee Journal*, February 3, 1963.

Schickel, Richard. "Some Kind of Genius." *Time*, November 16, 1981.

Steele, Joseph Henry. "Portrait of a Shy Guy." *Photoplay*, October 1943.

"Where Are They Now?" *Newsweek*, April 22, 1968.

White, Timothy. "Looking Backward." *Rolling Stone*, February 18, 1982.

MORRIS CARNOVSKY

"You place me in an extremely distasteful position, Mr. Murdock. By nature, I am a gentleman. Truly gentle. Brutality has always revolted me as a weapon of the witless."
— Morris Carnovsky in *Dead Reckoning* (1947)

Morris Carnovsky was, above all else, an actor.

"I began by adoring words," he said once. "I've learned to use them for all their juiciness and malleability."

Highly acclaimed for his work on the stage, Carnovsky was a founder of New York's famed Group Theatre and was seen throughout his career in contemporary plays as well as Shakespearean dramas. With appearances

"It was a stick of greasepaint that made me an actor. I played ... in *Disraeli*, and until then, I had never smelled greasepaint," he said in 1943. "Somebody came to make me up, and when he took a stick of greasepaint and began to spread it on my face, the smell must have got into my blood. I could never get away from it."

After high school, Carnovsky studied languages and literature at Washington University, where he continued to nurture his affinity for the stage by joining the school's Thyrsus Dramatics Society and performing in a number of student productions. Upon his graduation in 1920, Carnovsky moved to Boston, where he joined the Henry Jewett Players, then returned to New York two years later to appear with the Provincetown Players in *The God of Vengeance*. Carnovsky signed up with the Theater Guild Acting Company in 1924, and remained with the group for six years, appearing in such productions as *The Brothers Karamazov*, *Saint Joan*, *Marco's Millions*, and *Volpone*. In 1929, he played his first lead when he portrayed the title role in Chekhov's *Uncle Vanya*. Two years after this acclaimed performance, Carnovsky joined with Lee Strasberg as one of the founders of the famed Group Theater.

"We founded the Group because we were sick and tired of the old romantic theater and encrusted star system," Carnovsky said. "We weren't interested in stars. We were looking for real, living drama. I'd always had a nagging sense that I wasn't altogether the craftsman I wanted to be. I knew acting was more than just walking on, being inspired. Listening to Lee, I was eager to reduce all this to a science of acting of the highest degree. This new thing was exciting."

Alongside such future notables as John Garfield, Franchot Tone, Elia Kazan, Frances Farmer, Luther and Stella Adler, Lee J. Cobb, and Sylvia Sidney, Carnovsky appeared in a variety of productions over the next decade, including *Waiting for Lefty*, *Awake and Sing*, *Night Music*, *Paradise Lost*, *Men in White*, and *Golden Boy*. Of Carnovsky's performance in the latter production, Brooks Atkinson

in fewer than 25 films, however, his face is not as familiar on the silver screen, but he was seen in such successful movies as *The Life of Emile Zola* (1937), *Rhapsody in Blue* (1945), and *Our Vines Have Tender Grapes* (1945), and was featured in five films from the noir era: *Cornered* (1945), *Dead Reckoning* (1947), *Thieves' Highway* (1949), *Gun Crazy* (1950), and *The Second Woman* (1951).

Carnovsky, the third of seven children, was born on September 5, 1897, in St. Louis, Missouri, to Issac and Jennie Carnovsky, Lithuanian immigrants who moved to the United States shortly after their marriage. For many years, the couple operated a neighborhood grocery store on 13th Street, over which the family lived.

"It was a tough neighborhood," Carnovsky recalled years later. "In fact, I ran away from kindergarten the first day I was sent."

The future actor attended Jefferson Elementary School and Yeatman High School, where he "got the bug of the theater" and made his debut in 1914 playing Benjamin Disraeli in a high school play. His experience with playing this part convinced the 17-year-old that he was destined for an acting career.

wrote in the *New York Times* that the actor "beautifully conveys the silent grief of the affectionate father who realizes that he is losing his boy." *Golden Boy* was also significant to Carnovsky for personal reasons— the cast of the production included a young actress, Phoebe Brand. Carnovsky and Brand married in the early 1940s and later had a son, Stephen. The union lasted until Carnovsky's death in 1992.

Meanwhile, Hollywood had discovered Carnovsky's talents, and in 1937, he made his film debut in the box-office hit, *The Life of Emile Zola*, starring Paul Muni in the title role. Later that year, he was seen in a witty comedy, *Tovarich*, starring Claudette Colbert and Charles Boyer, then returned to New York, where he continued to perform in Group Theater productions until the company was disbanded in 1941. Back on the west coast, Carnovsky appeared in such films as *Edge of Darkness* (1942), a well-done wartime drama starring Errol Flynn; *Address Unknown* (1944), a tautly directed anti–Nazi feature; *Rhapsody in Blue* (1945), in which he portrayed the father of composer George Gershwin; *Our Vines Have Tender Grapes* (1945), a moving drama centered on life in a small Wisconsin town; and his first film noir, *Cornered* (1945).

Cornered, which features a complex plot even by film noir standards, starred Dick Powell as Laurence Gerard, a Canadian pilot and former prisoner of war who is determined to find the killers of his French wife. Although he is informed that the murderer, Marcel Jarnac (Luther Adler) is dead, Gerard soon unearths evidence to the contrary. As he continues his search, Gerard encounters a series of shady individuals, including Jarnac's mysterious wife (Micheline Cheirel); a wealthy expatriate, Tomas Comargo (Steven Geray); Tomas' uncle, Santana (Carnovsky); and a hotel valet, Diego (Jack LaRue). Suspicious of the entire lot, Gerard later discovers that Santana and Diego are part of an organization dedicated to finding Nazi collaborators and that they, too, are hot on Jarnac's trail. The level-headed Santana warns Gerard that there's "no room for murderous revenge," but the pilot continues his reckless quest, ultimately locating Jarnac and beating him to death. *Cornered* was hailed by critics after its release; in one of the film's best notices, the *New York Times*' reviewer called it "a drama of smoldering vengeance and political scheming which builds purposefully and with graduating tension to a violent climax, a committing of murder that is as thrilling and brutal as any you are likely to encounter in a month of moviegoing." The same critic singled out Carnovsky for praise as well, applauding the actor for his "well done" performance.

After appearing in *Miss Susie Slagle's* (1946), a lightweight period piece starring Veronica Lake and Sonny Tufts, Carnovsky returned to the dark side of the screen for his second film noir, *Dead Reckoning* (1947). This feature starred Humphrey Bogart as paratrooper Rip Murdock, who travels to a small town seeking the truth behind the disappearance of his army buddy, Johnny Drake (William Prince). After learning that Drake has been killed in a fiery auto crash, Murdock encounters Johnny's old flame, Coral Chandler (Lizabeth Scott), and Martinelli (Carnovsky), a powerful gangster to whom Coral is inexplicably bound. Almost against his will, Murdock falls for Coral, but in time he discovers that Martinelli and Coral have been secretly married for years, that Coral's first husband was killed for his money, and that Martinelli possesses the gun that can prove his wife's guilt. Later, Coral kills Martinelli, and when Rip reveals his plan to drive Coral to the local police station, she shoots him as well, causing a car crash that ends her life. As Martinelli, the best of Carnovsky's film noir roles, the actor was hailed by critics; the reviewer for *Variety* praised his "suavely unscrupulous" portrayal, and Jack D. Grant of *The Hollywood Reporter* wrote: "The supporting cast is distinguished by several highlights, chiefly those delivered by Morris Carnovsky as the gambler...."

Between movie assignments, Carnovsky frequently returned to New York for roles in such productions as *My Sister Eileen*, *Café Crown*, and *Counterattack*. He also worked for five years as a teacher and director for the Actor's Laboratory in Hollywood, helming such productions as *Volpone*, *The Dragon*, and *Monday's Heroes*. On screen, he was seen in such features as *Saigon* (1948), the last and least successful teaming of Alan Ladd and Veronica Lake; *Siren of Atlantis* (1948), an unintentionally campy film starring Maria Montez in one of her final roles; and *Man-Eater of Kumaon* (1948), a tedious adventure saga starring Sabu and Wendell Corey. Carnovsky fared better, however, with his third film noir, *Thieves' Highway* (1949).

Here, the actor portrayed Yanko Garcos, a former truck driver whose encounter with a corrupt merchant, Mike Figlia (Lee J. Cobb) has left him wheelchair-bound. When Yanko's war veteran son, Nick (Richard Conte), learns that Figlia was responsible for the truck accident that crippled his father, he determines to exact revenge. Traveling cross-country to San Francisco, Nick teams with a hard-working trucker, Ed Kenny (Millard Mitchell); gets picked up by a seemingly hard-boiled refugee, Rica (Valentina Cortesa); and is beaten and robbed by a pair of thugs in Figlia's employ. Seemingly bested by Figlia and his underlings, Nick reaches the breaking point when his partner is killed in a fiery accident on the road and Figlia hires local truckers to retrieve the dead man's load of produce. After taking a hatchet to Figlia, Nick beats the merchant into confessing his role in Yanko's accident and Figlia is taken to jail. Although Carnovsky's small but pivotal role was mostly overlooked by reviewers, *Thieves' Highway* was a commercial and critical success, with Bosley Crowther writing in the *New York Times* that the film was "stunningly played by a top-form cast [and] one of the best melodramas—one of the sharpest and most taut—we've had this year."

After an appearance in the sole oater of his screen career, *Western Pacific Agent*, Carnovsky was back to more familiar ground with his appearance in his fourth film noir, the classic *Gun Crazy* (1950), which opens as a gun-obsessed youngster, Bart Tare (Rusty Tamblyn), breaks into a store window to steal a firearm and promptly finds himself in trouble with the law. Brought before Judge Willoughby (Carnovsky), the young man is sentenced to a reform school. "We're not trying you here today because you like to shoot, Bart," the judge tells him. "We're trying you because the thing you like so well has turned into a dangerous mania with you…. We all want things, Bart, but our possession of them has to be regulated by law." After several years at the out-of-town school, Bart returns as an adult (John Dall), only to fall for carnival sharpshooter Annie Laurie Starr (Peggy Cummins). Before long, Bart and Annie are married, but when their money runs out, they commit a series of hold-ups and find themselves on the run from the law. Although Bart is reluctant to take part in the crimes, he is motivated by his love for Annie, even when she displays a reckless disregard for life that leaves more than one corpse behind. At the film's end, the luckless lovers are cornered in the mountains by police and as Annie prepares to fire on the approaching officers, Bart kills her just before he himself is gunned down.

Singled out for portraying his role as a juvenile court judge with "dignity and understanding" in *Gun Crazy*, Carnovsky was next seen as Le Bret in *Cyrano deBergerac* (1950), starring Jose Ferrer in his Oscar-winning title performance, followed by his final film noir, *The Second Woman* (1951). Here, Carnovsky portrays Dr. Hartley, a general practitioner who suspects that local architect Jeff Cohallan (Robert Young) is a paranoiac suffering from delusions of persecution following the auto crash death of his fiancée, Vivian Sheppard. Hartley's concern increases when Jeff experiences a series of unfortunate occurrences, including a devastating fire at his house, and he warns his would-be girlfriend, Ellen (Betsy Drake), that Jeff might be unconsciously causing the incidents. As it turns out, the man behind the acts is Ben Sheppard—Jeff's boss and Vivian's father, who blames Jeff for his daughter's death. Ironically, Ben's hatred is misplaced; the car was actually driven by a local playboy with whom Vivian was having an affair, and Jeff kept the truth from Ben in order to salvage his daughter's reputation.

Off screen, Carnovsky's personal life began to resemble a movie plot when he became embroiled in the "witch-hunt" initiated by the House Un-American Activities Committee to ferret out Communism in the motion picture industry. Carnovsky was thrust into the maelstrom of paranoia and finger-pointing when he was named by actor Larry Parks and director Elia Kazan as being involved in Communist activities. (Kazan also named several others who had been involved with New York's Group Theater, including Clifford Odets and Carnovsky's wife, Phoebe Brand.)

Called before the committee, Carnovsky refused to answer questions or label any others as Communists, telling committee members: "There is no force in government which can compel a citizen to reveal his political, religious, or social affiliations."

Although the actor's stance was courageous and admirable, it nonetheless left him unable to find work in Hollywood. Returning to familiar ground in New York, Carnovsky in 1953 began a two-year run in the off–Broadway stage production of *The World of Sholem Aleichem*. Then, in 1956, director and producer John Houseman recruited the actor to appear in his American Shakespeare Festival in Stratford, Connecticut. According to Carnovsky, Houseman "did not give a damn about the blacklist."

For the next seven summers, Carnovsky played a wide range of Shakespearean characters at the Stratford Festival, including the Earl of Salisbury in *King John*, the Provost in *Measure for Measure*, and Gremio in *The Taming of the Shrew*. He also played opposite Katharine Hepburn in *The Merchant of Venice*, earning high praise from one critic who said his portrayal of Shylock was "rich in understanding, proud to the very end and infinitely moving." In 1965, Carnovsky took on the title role in *King Lear*, delivering such a dynamic performance that several performances of other productions at the festival

were canceled in ordered to give *King Lear* a longer run. During this period, Carnovsky also appeared in the television productions of *Medea* (1959) and *The World of Sholom Aleichem* (1959).

Meanwhile, after a 10-year absence from the silver screen, Carnovsky quietly returned to feature films in *Vu du pont* (1961), a Sidney Lumet–directed drama also known as *A View from the Bridge*. He would appear in only one more production for the silver screen, the 1974 feature, *The Gambler*, starring James Caan and Paul Sorvino. Also during this period, Carnovsky headed the drama department at Brandeis University in Massachusetts, and served as actor-director at Ohio's Oberlin College. In 1969, showing no signs of slowing down, Carnovsky, at age 72, joined director Tyrone Guthrie in a highly acclaimed, 33-city tour of *Lamp at Midnight*, a drama about the famed astronomer Galileo.

During the 1970s, Carnovsky kept active in such projects as directing a production of *Volpone* for the Lab Theatre in New York, and appearing in *Awake and Sing* in which he recreated the role of the Jewish-American grandfather than he had originated on Broadway during the 1935-36 season. Toward the end of the decade, Carnovsky's accomplishments in the theater were honored when he was inducted into the Theater Hall of Fame.

In 1983, Carnovsky was seen in his final stage production, Chekhov's *The Cherry Orchard* at the Long Wharf Theater in New Haven, Connecticut. Nine years after this farewell performance, at the age of 94, the actor died of natural causes at his home in Easton, Connecticut.

Although Morris Carnovsky could have suffered a career-ending blow during the Communist paranoia of the 1950s, the actor refused to let the circumstances derail his course or alter his vision. While he refused to dwell on the impact of the blacklist, however, Carnovsky did speak of the HUAC hearings, stating that "as an experience, it was revolting, injurious, hurtful." But he managed to turn these negative aspects into qualities that enhanced him, both professionally and personally.

"From the point of view of the entire picture, in an odd way it nurtured me, strengthened me, made me hard, objective, even resigned," Carnovsky said in 1965. "And to that degree, I think it fed me as an actor."

Producer: Harry M. Popkin. Running time: 91 minutes. Released by United Artists, February 1, 1951. Cast: Robert Young, Betsy Drake, John Sutton, Florence Bates, Morris Carnovsky, Henry O'Neill, Jean Rogers, Raymond Largay, Shirley Ballard, Vici Raaf, John Galludet, Jason Robards, Sr., Steven Geray, Jimmy Dodd, Smokey Whitfield, Cliff Clark.

Film Noir Filmography

Cornered. Director: Edward Dmytryk. Producer: Adrian Scott. Running time: 102 minutes. Released by RKO, December 25, 1945. Cast: Dick Powell, Walter Slezak, Micheline Cheirel, Nina Vale, Morris Carnovsky, Edgar Barrier, Steven Geray, Jack La Rue, Luther Adler, Gregory Gay.

Dead Reckoning. Director: John Cromwell. Producer: Sidney Biddell. Running time: 100 minutes. Released by Columbia, January 22, 1947. Cast: Humphrey Bogart, Lizabeth Scott, Morris Carnovsky, Charles Cane, William Prince, Marvin Miller, Wallace Ford, James Bell, George Chandler, William Forrest, Ruby Dandridge.

Thieves' Highway. Director: Jules Dassin. Producer: Robert Bassler. Running time: 94 minutes. Released by 20th Century-Fox, September 23, 1949. Cast: Richard Conte, Valentina Cortesa, Lee J. Cobb, Barbara Lawrence, Jack Oakie, Millard Mitchell, Morris Carnovsky, Tamara Shayne, Kasia Orzazewski, Norbert Schiller, Hope Emerson, George Tyne, Edwin Max, David Clarke, Walter Baldwin, David Opatoshu.

Gun Crazy. Director: Joseph H. Lewis. Producer: Frank and Maurice King. Running time: 87 minutes. Released by United Artists, as *Deadly Is the Female* on January 26, 1950; re-released as *Gun Crazy* on August 24, 1950. Cast: Peggy Cummins, John Dall, Berry Kroeger, Morris Carnovsky, Anabel Shaw, Harry Lewis, Nedrick Young, Trevor Bardette, Mickey Little, Rusty Tamblyn, Paul Frison, Dave Bair, Stanley Prager, Virginia Farmer, Anne O'Neal, Frances Irwin, Don Beddoe, Robert Osterloh, Shimen Ruskin, Harry Hayden.

The Second Woman. Director: James V. Kern.

References

Barron, James. "Morris Carnovsky Is Dead at 94; Acting Career Spanned 60 Years." *New York Times*, September 2, 1992.

Biography of Morris Carnovsky. Paramount Pictures, April 5, 1946.

"Carnovsky and Others for Arts Awards." *Variety*, May 27, 1981.

"Carnovsky Scorns Life of Roaming." *New York Journal American*, December 26, 1937.

Folkart, Burt A. "Morris Carnovsky; Acted in Modern, Classic Roles." *Los Angeles Times*, September 3, 1992.

Funke, Lewis. "Carnovsky Finds Lear a Symbol of Humanity's Power to Endure." *New York Times*, June 25, 1963.

Hewes, Henry. "Broadway Postscript." *Saturday Review*, July 27, 1957.

Hughes, Charlotte. "Of Morris Carnovsky." *New York Times*, February 22, 1942.

"Morris Carnovsky Directs in Lab Theatre Opener." Howard Atlee Publicity, September 26, 1975.

"Morris Carnovsky Joins McCarter Co. for 40th Anniversary of 30s 'Awake and Sing.'" McCarter Theatre Company, February 17, 1978.

"Morris Carnovsky to Play 'Rabbi Azrael' in 'The Dybbuk.'" 4th Street Theatre, November 26, 1954.

Obituary. *The Hollywood Reporter*, September 11, 1992.

Obituary. *The London Times*, September 12, 1992.

Obituary. *Time*, September 14, 1992.

Obituary. *Variety*, September 7, 1992.

Ormsbee, Helen. "Carnovsky Finds Soviet Hero New Type on American Stage." *New York Times*, February 21, 1942.

FRED CLARK

"I don't like blackmailers — nor would you, if you were in my business. They constitute a very bad industrial hazard." — Fred Clark in *Ride the Pink Horse* (1947)

Although few balding actors made a name for themselves in Hollywood, Fred Clark parlayed his smooth pate into a career that lent itself equally to portrayals of bungling funny men and the most ruthless villains.

"What's wrong with being bald?" Clark once queried. "It makes a man look more mature. Toupees are silly. Besides, when a man is minus hair, he makes an extra effort at charm to overcome it."

Clark, a regular for two years on TV's popular *Burns and Allen Show*, appeared during his 22-year film career alongside some of Hollywood's biggest luminaries, including Robert Montgomery, William Holden, James Stewart, Joan Crawford, and Bob Hope. He also was featured in five outstanding examples from the film noir era: *The Unsuspected* (1947), *Ride the Pink Horse* (1947), *Cry of the City* (1948), *White Heat* (1949), and *Sunset Boulevard* (1950).

Frederic Leonard Clark was born on March 9, 1914, in Lincoln, California, where his father, Fred, Sr., worked for the county. After attending Lincoln Elementary School, Menlo School for Boys, and Lincoln High School, Clark enrolled as a psychology student at Stanford University, with plans to pursue a medical career. The course of his future changed, however, during his senior year at Stanford, when Clark appeared in a school production of *Yellow Jack*. After his graduation, Clark won a scholarship to the American Academy of Dramatic Arts, where he studied for two years, then honed his craft in small parts in such Broadway plays as *Schoolhouse on the Lot*, *Ringside Seat*, *What a Life*, and *See My Lawyer*, and stock productions in New London, Connecticut, and Brattleboro, Vermont.

"I was also in 'bootleg stock' on Staten Island and in Mt. Vernon, New York, where we changed our names and the plays' names, and passed the hat between the first and second acts and split the take," Clark recalled later. "I averaged $2.50 a performance, four days a week."

In 1940, Clark returned to California, where he toured Northern California and Nevada in repertory theater, and the following year appeared in two stock productions with veteran actress Judith Anderson.

"I met people who talked me into trying Hollywood," Clark said, "except nothing happened. Couldn't crack pictures."

After two more years in stock, Clark took a break from the stage to enlist in the Army. Stationed in Salt Lake City, Utah, and Sacramento, California, the actor interviewed inductees and conducted tests in the Army Specialized Training Program, then became company clerk in a replacement company that traveled to England, France, Germany, and Czechoslovakia.

Upon his discharge from the Army, Clark planned to return to Vermont for more stock work when he finally got the break he'd been seeking for nearly a decade. After being recommended by a fellow actor, Clark signed on with the Gryphon Players, a little theater group in Laguna, California. While appearing in one of the company's productions, *Angel Street*, he was spotted by famed director Michael Curtiz, who signed him to a personal contract.

Clark's first feature for Curtiz was also his entry into the world of film noir — *The Unsuspected* (1947). A complex and sometimes bewildering example from the era, *The Unsuspected* stars Claude Rains as Victor Grandison, a popular radio personality who hangs his secretary in his study and stages the death to appear a suicide. As the film continues,

This feature, Clark's second film noir, begins as the film's protagonist, Lucky Gaugin (played by Montgomery, who also directed), emerges from a bus into a dusty Mexican town — it turns out that he is in town planning to blackmail a racketeer, Frank Hugo (Clark), who'd ordered the murder of Lucky's friend, Shorty. Along the way, he encounters such memorable characters as Pila (Wanda Hendrix), a mysterious Mexican girl who shadows Lucky's every movement, Pancho (Thomas Gomez, in an Oscar-winning performance), a jovial carousel operator, and Retz (Art Smith), a relentless FBI agent who is determined to nab Hugo for his crimes.

As the cruel and callous mobster, whose hearing impediment requires him to wear an auditory aid, Clark delivered a knockout performance that was hailed by numerous critics, including Bosley Crowther, who wrote in the *New York Times* that he played "a big-time crook in a thoroughly convincing manner," and William Weaver of *Motion Picture Herald*, who said Clark "sets a new pattern for screen heavies."

Continuing his successful string of film noir appearances, Clark was next seen in *Cry of the City* (1948), where he was third-billed after stars Victor Mature and Richard Conte. Here, Clark plays Lt. Jim Collins, a homicide detective who teams with his partner, Vittorio Candella (Mature) to capture small-time hood Martin Rome (Conte), killer of a police officer and an unscrupulous lawyer. In Clark's best scene, Collins confronts Rome in the hospital, where he is recovering from injuries he received in the gun battle with the officer he killed: "If you're looking for sympathy, Rome, save it," Collins tells him. "I just left Mrs. McCready, the wife of the guy you killed, you murdering rat. She looked fine. Eyes all red, tears streaming down her face. And here you sit, getting shaved." Ruthlessly using and discarding a series of people — including the prison hospital trustee and a local doctor — Rome tries to flee the country, but his efforts are thwarted when Candella tracks him to a neighborhood church, where he has gone to meet his girlfriend,

Grandison continues to rack up more bodies, including his trampy niece, Althea (Audrey Totter), who learns that the radio star has been spending the fortune belonging to his ward (Joan Caulfield). He also causes the death of Althea's alcoholic husband (Hurd Hatfield) and later tries to do away with his ward as well. A beacon of normalcy among this concoction of quirky characters, Clark portrayed Richard Donovan, chief of the local homicide bureau, who is a key in exposing Grandison's crimes.

Regarded today as a first-rate example of film noir, *The Unsuspected* earned dismal reviews upon its release; in a typical review, John McCarten of *The New Yorker* called it "a seedy mystery in which the corpses of murdered people are piled around like buns in a bakery's day-old shop." While Clark was mostly overlooked by critics, however, his appearance in the film had a fortuitous result.

"From [*The Unsuspected*], I got that *really* lucky break," Clark recalled. "Audrey Totter was in it, and recommended me to Bob Montgomery, who was looking for a new face to play the deaf heavy in *Ride the Pink Horse*."

Teena (Debra Paget, in her film debut), and he is shot down in the street when he tries to escape.

After the release of *Cry of the City*, for which Clark earned a mention for his "stand-out performance as Mature's cynical side-kick," Michael Curtiz dissolved his production company and Clark signed on with Warner Brothers. But after appearing in only one film, *Two Guys from Texas* (1948), he cancelled his contract and opted for freelance work. During the next two years, he was seen in a variety of features, including *Fury at Furnace Creek* (1948), a well-done western starring Victor Mature and Coleen Gray; *Alias Nick Beal* (1949), which was applauded by critics but failed to click with moviegoers; and his fourth film noir, *White Heat* (1949).

This noir classic centers on Cody Jarrett (James Cagney), a violent and conscienceless gang leader whose character traits include blinding headaches and an Oedipal attachment to his mother (Margaret Wycherly). Aside from its cast of fascinating characters, including Cody's duplicitous wife (Virginia Mayo), a back-stabbing hood (Steve Cochran), and an undercover detective (Edmond O'Brien), *White Heat* contains one of the most memorable scenes in film noir. After escaping from prison to hunt down the killers of his mother, Cody goes on a shooting spree that ends atop an oil refinery where, just before he is blown to bits in a fiery explosion, he shouts, "Made it, Ma — top of the world!" A box office hit, *White Heat* was described by the *Los Angeles Examiner*'s Ruth Waterbury as "a melodrama loaded with sex, double-crossing, violent death, and absolutely agonizing suspense," and Bosley Crowther wrote in the *New York Times* that it was "one of the most explosive pictures that [Cagney] or anyone has ever played." Along with the liberal praise heaped upon the film's principal characters, Clark was applauded for his supporting role by Waterbury, who called him "powerfully sinister" in his role as Cody's fence for stolen bills, known as "The Trader."

In 1950, the busiest year of Clark's screen career, he was featured in *Mrs. O'Malley and Mr. Malone*, a fast-paced comedy-thriller starring James Whitmore and Marjorie Main; *Treasure Island*, a well-done Technicolor Disney production; *Return of the Frontiersman*, a tiresome oater with Gordon MacRae and Julie London; *The Jackpot*, in which he played James Stewart's boss; and *The Eagle and the Hawk*, a passable western with John Payne and Rhonda Fleming. Also that year, Clark was seen in the final film noir of his career, *Sunset Boulevard*.

An outstanding entry from the film noir era, *Sunset Boulevard* observes the relationship between aging silent movie actress Norma Desmond (Gloria Swanson) and the down-on-his-luck, unemployed writer, Joe Gillis (William Holden), who becomes her lover. With its vivid depiction of Norma's pitiful attempts at a screen comeback, Joe's reluctant acceptance of his role as a kept man and, finally, the writer's murder by the deranged former star, *Sunset Boulevard* earned deserved praise from one reviewer as "that rare blend of pungent writing, expert acting, masterly direction, and unobtrusively artistic photography which quickly casts a spell over an audience and holds it enthralled to a shatter climax." Offering a bit of comic relief in an otherwise grim film, Clark played Sheldrake, described as "a smart producer with a set of ulcers to prove it." Although the part was a relatively minor one, Clark made the most of his brief time on-screen and was singled out by the critic for the *New York Times*, who wrote that he "makes a strong impression."

After *Sunset Boulevard*, Clark was seen in a series of blockbusters, including *A Place in the Sun* (1951), starring Montgomery Clift and Elizabeth Taylor; *The Lemon-Drop Kid* (1951), a vehicle for Bob Hope; and *Meet Me After the Show* (1951), a Betty Grable starrer. He also turned his talents to the small screen, appearing from 1951 to 1953 as Harry Morton in The *George Burns and Gracie Allen Show*.

"[It was the] happiest working conditions and employers of my life," Clark said later, "but I finally decided I'd better get out or I'd be typed for the rest of my life."

Throughout his run on the *Burns and Allen Show*, Clark continued his appearances on the big screen in such films as *Three for Bedroom C* (1952), a box-office flop starring Gloria Swanson, and *The Caddy* (1953), a mildly amusing Dean Martin–Jerry Lewis vehicle. He also found time to play in a number of stock productions, including *Dear Ruth, Room Service, The Petrified Forest, Our Town, Anything Goes,* and *Light Up the Sky*. In the latter production, Clark co-starred with a young film and stage actress, Benay Venuta — what he later called "the luckiest break" — and on February 15, 1952, the two were married. The couple went on to become a popular husband-and-wife team on the stage, but they divorced in the early 1960s and Clark would later remarry in 1965.

Throughout the remainder of the decade, Clark stayed busy in such successful vehicles as *How to Marry a Millionaire* (1953), a hit comedy starring Lauren Bacall, Marilyn Monroe, and Betty Grable; *Daddy Long Legs* (1955), featuring Fred Astaire and Leslie Caron; *The Solid Gold Cadillac* (1956), an amusing comedy with Judy Holliday; and one of his best-remembered features, *Don't Go Near the Water* (1957), in which he portrayed an apoplectic Navy commander. On the small screen, he was seen in guest spots on such popular television series as *The Untouchables, The Twilight Zone, The Dick Van Dyke Show, Petticoat Junction,* and *The Beverly Hillbillies,* on which he played the recurring role of Dr. Roy Clyburn. Also during this period, Clark returned to Broadway, appearing in *Romanoff and Juliet* in 1957 and *Absence of a Cello* in 1963.

In the early 1960s, Clark appeared in several foreign films, including *Mi Mujer Me Gusta Más* (1961) and *A Porte Chiuse* (1961), but back in the United States, he signed on for a series of duds, including *Zotz!* (1962), an insipid comedy featuring such screen veterans as Mike Mazurki, Cecil Kellaway, and Margaret Dumont; *Curse of the Mummy's Tomb* (1964), a low-budget horror film with a virtually unknown cast; *Sergeant Deadhead* (1965), a lame Frankie Avalon vehicle; *Dr.*

Goldfoot and the Bikini Machine (1965), whose title alone accurately indicates its level of quality; and *Skidoo* (1968), an abysmal comedy that was, amazingly, directed and produced by Otto Preminger, and wasted the talents of such screen stars as Groucho Marx, Jackie Gleason, George Raft, and Burgess Meredith. Between films, Clark earned extra spending cash appearing in a series of dog food commercials.

In November 1968, Clark, who had suffered with back problems for several years, entered St. John's Hospital in Los Angeles for treatment of a back spasm. While there, he developed a liver ailment and died three weeks later, on December 5, 1968. He was 54 years old. (Released after his death, his final film, *I Sailed to Tahiti with an All Girl Crew* [1969], again failed to live up to his previous successes.)

During his prolific career on the silver screen, Fred Clark became one of Hollywood's most dependable character actors, with topnotch performances in some of the finest offerings on film. Although he became most closely associated in his later years with the type of cantankerous character he portrayed in the *Burns and Allen Show* and in the film, *Don't Go Near the Water*, the actor viewed this typecasting with typical humor.

"It's a losing battle which I don't regret," Clark said once. "I've made a handsome living out of that role."

Film Noir Filmography

The Unsuspected. Director: Michael Curtiz. Producer: Charles Hoffman. Running time: 103 minutes. Released by Warner Brothers, October 3, 1947. Cast: Joan Caufield, Claude Rains, Audrey Totter, Constance Bennett, Hurd Hatfield, Michael North, Fred Clark, Harry Lewis, Jack Lambert, Ray Walker, Nana Bryant, Walter Baldwin.

Ride the Pink Horse. Director: Robert Montgomery. Producer: Joan Harrison. Running time: 101 minutes. Released by Universal-International, October 8, 1947. Cast: Robert Montgomery, Thomas Gomez, Rita Conde, Iris Flores, Wanda Hendrix, Grandon Rhodes, Tito Renaldo, Richard Gaines, Andrea King, Art Smith, Martin Garralaga, Edward Earle, Harold Goodwin, Maria Cortez, Fred Clark. Awards: Academy Award nomination for Best Supporting Actor (Thomas Gomez).

Cry of the City. Director: Robert Siodmak. Producer: Sol Siegel. Running time: 96 minutes. Released by 20th Century-Fox, September 29, 1948. Cast: Victor Mature, Richard Conte, Fred Clark, Shelley Winters, Betty Garde, Barry Kroeger, Tommy Cook, Debra Paget, Hope Emerson, Roland Winters, Walter Baldwin, June Storey, Tito Vuolo, Mimi Aguglia, Konstantin Shayne, Howard Freeman.

White Heat. Director: Raoul Walsh. Producer: Lou Edelman. Running time: 114 minutes. Released by Warner Brothers, September 2, 1949. Cast: James Cagney, Virginia Mayo, Edmond O'Brien, Margaret Wycherly, Steve Cochran, John Archer, Wally Cassell, Fred Clark, Ford Rainey, Fred Coby, G. Pat Collins, Mickey Knox, Paul Guilfoyle, Robert Osterloh, Ian MacDonald, Ray Montgomery. Awards: Academy Award nomination for Best Motion Picture Story (Virginia Kellogg).

Sunset Boulevard. Director: Billy Wilder. Producer: Charles Brackett. Running time: 115 minutes. Released by Paramount, August 10, 1950. Cast: William Holden, Gloria Swanson, Erich von Stroheim, Nancy Olson, Fred Clark, Lloyd Gough, Jack Webb, Cecil B. DeMille, Hedda Hopper, Buster Keaton, Anna Q. Nilsson, H.B. Warner, Franklyn Farnum, Sidney Skolsky, Ray Evans, Jay Livingston. Awards: Academy Awards for Best Art Direction-Set Decoration, B/W (Hans Dreier, John Meehan, Sam Comer, Ray Moyer), Best Score, Drama or Comedy (Franz Waxman), Best Story and Screenplay (Charles Brackett, Billy Wilder, D.M. Marshman Jr.). Academy Award nominations for Best Picture, Best Director (Billy Wilder), Best Actor (William Holden), Best Supporting Actor (Erich Von Stroheim), Best Actress (Gloria Swanson), Best Supporting Actress (Nancy Olson), Best B/W Cinematography (John F. Seitz), Best Film Editing (Arthur Schmidt, Doane Harrison).

References

Biography of Fred Clark. General Artists Corporation, circa 1962.

Biography of Fred Clark. Margaret Ettinger and Company, circa 1947.

Biography of Fred Clark. Paramount Studios, August 1950.

"Fred Clark, Movie, TV Actor, Dies." *Los Angeles Times*, December 6, 1968.

Greene, Patterson. "'Joey' Stars Are Real-Life Team." *Los Angeles Examiner*, September 30, 1956.

Mosby, Aline. "Being Bald O.K., Says Fred Clark." *Hollywood Citizen-News*, December 10, 1949.

"Newcomer Scores Big Hit in Hazard." *Paca News*, March 29, 1948.

Obituary. *Hollywood Reporter*, December 10, 1968.

Obituary. *Time*, December 13, 1968.

Obituary. *Variety*. December 9, 1968.

———————— LEE J. COBB ————————

"Don't you threaten me — I'm not some little cloak-and-suiter you can push around. You're dealing with Walter Mitchell!"— Lee J. Cobb in *The Garment Jungle* (1957)

Lee J. Cobb was a survivor.

During his 40-year acting career, he weathered a massive heart attack, years of persecution because of his association with the Communist Party, and near-bankruptcy, only to emerge as what playwright Arthur Miller labeled "the best dramatic actor I ever saw." A veteran of stage, screen, and television, Cobb saw his greatest triumph as the original Willy Loman in *Death of a Salesman* and fulfilled a lifelong dream in the late 1960s portraying King Lear on Broadway. He was also a standout in such superb films as *On the Waterfront* (1954), *12 Angry Men* (1957), and *The Brothers Karamazov* (1958), attracted a new generation of fans during a four-year stint on TV's *The Virginian*, and was seen in seven films from the noir era: *Johnny O'Clock* (1947), *The Dark Past* (1948), *Call Northside 777* (1948), *Thieves' Highway* (1949), *The Man Who Cheated Himself* (1950), *The Garment Jungle* (1957), and *Party Girl* (1958).

The beefy actor with the distinctive voice was born Leo Jacoby on December 8, 1911, on the Lower East Side of New York, where his father, Benjamin, worked as a compositor for the *Jewish Daily Forward* newspaper. Considered to be a musical prodigy, Cobb was a virtuoso on the harmonica and studied to be a concert violinist, but his plans for a musical career ended when a fall shattered his wrist at the age of 17, just before his scheduled debut at Carnegie Hall. Cobb turned instead to acting.

"At 17, the things that attracted me about acting were the good old glamour, the superficial things," Cobb told *Cue* magazine in 1949. "I wanted to make movies to be a big star."

Against the wishes of his parents — who wanted the boy to be an accountant — Cobb headed for Hollywood, but his only appearance before the camera was in a screen test for another performer. Discouraged, he returned to New York, got a job selling radios for the Davega company, and studied accounting at night school at NYU.

"I didn't get very far because accounting and I became mortal enemies," Cobb quipped years later. "I survived, but I didn't kill accounting — it's still around, isn't it?"

Cobb's dreams of an acting career never wavered and, resigned to his ambition, his parents allowed him to return to California, where he signed on with the Pasadena Playhouse. The actor would later recall that it was his once-reluctant father who gave him the idea for his stage name, suggesting that he break his last name, Jacoby, into two parts, resulting in Lee J. Cobb.

"When my father did this for me, I knew that, finally, he believed in me as an actor," Cobb said.

The actor appeared for two years in a variety of small parts for the Pasadena Playhouse, and was seen in a bit part in *The Vanishing Shadow* (1934), a 12-episode serial produced by Universal Studios. He returned to New York at the age of 23 and ultimately signed on with The Group Theatre, appearing in such productions as *Waiting for Lefty* and *Golden Boy*. Because of his massive build and a hairline that had begun to recede when

Cobb was still a teenager, he was consistently cast in character roles playing older men. In between plays, Cobb traveled to California, where he was seen in a pair of low-budget westerns, *North of the Rio Grande* (1937) and *Rustler's Valley* (1937).

"I used to come out and make a couple of 'Hopalong Cassidy' films for Harry Sherman," Cobb recalled in 1947, "collect my checks, then go back and be perfectly happy to accept IOUs from the Group."

Cobb got his first big break in Hollywood when Columbia Pictures tapped him to reprise his role as Papa Bonaparte in the screen version of *Golden Boy* (1939) — at age 27, he played the father of star William Holden. He remained in Hollywood for *This Thing Called Love* (1940), a sophisticated comedy starring Rosalind Russell and Melvyn Douglas. Also that year, Cobb found time to marry actress Helen Beverly, with whom he had two children, Vincent and Julie. (The couple divorced 12 years later, however, with Helen charging that Cobb made her feel "inferior and inadequate.")

Cobb was back on stage in New York later in 1940 for *The Fifth Column*, with Franchot Tone, and appeared in 1941 opposite Tallulah Bankhead in *Clash by Night*, then returned to Hollywood for good, signing a contract with 20th Century-Fox. For Fox, the actor was seen in such features as *Tonight We Raid Calais* (1943), a well-crafted war adventure with John Sutton and Annabella; *The Song of Bernadette* (1943), starring Jennifer Jones as the real-life French peasant girl who sees a vision of the Virgin Mary; and *The Moon Is Down* (1943), a somber portrait focusing on the German invasion of Norway. Cobb then enlisted in the Army Air Forces, with hopes of becoming a pilot, but was assigned instead to a radio unit. He was also seconded from duty to appear in Moss Hart's Broadway stage hit *This Is the Army*, recreating his role the following year for the screen version, *Winged Victory* (1944), alongside several other enlisted actors, including Edmond O' Brien, Lon McCallister, Don Taylor, and Mark Daniels.

After the war, Cobb played Kralahome, the Prime Minister of Siam, in *Anna and the King of Siam* (1946), starring Rex Harrison and Irene Dunne, followed by a steady stream of film noir appearances, beginning with *Johnny O'Clock* (1947). Here, Cobb played Inspector Koch, a hard-nosed lawman investigating the murder of a crooked cop, Chuck Blayden (Jim Bannon), and his naïve girlfriend, Harriet (Nina Foch). Koch centers his investigation on Johnny O'Clock (Dick Powell) and Pete Marchettis (Thomas Gomez), co-owners of a profitable gambling casino that Blayden was trying to muscle his way into. Although he is certain of Marchettis' involvement, however, Koch is frustrated by Johnny's refusal to help him get the evidence he needs to nab him: "When I first met you, I though maybe you had some feelings," he tells him. "I see now I was wrong. You're a hood. A cheap hood, a cop-hater. I should've treated you like one." Later, Marchettis' realization that his wife, Nelle (Ellen Drew), is in love with Johnny, sets off a chain of events; Marchettis makes an unsuccessful attempt on Johnny's life, Johnny confronts him in the casino and kills his partner in self-defense, and Nelle accuses Johnny of killing her husband in cold blood when he rejects her. Cornered in the casino, Johnny prepares to shoot his way out, but he is persuaded by his love for Harriet's sister, Nancy (Evelyn Keyes) to give himself up to Koch. Although it was a hit with moviegoers, the film garnered mixed reactions from critics; the reviewer from *Motion Picture Herald* offered high praise, terming it "an exciting, expertly acted thriller" but, inexplicably, Bosley Crowther disagreed in the *New York Times*, saying "the slowness and general confusion of the plot for two-thirds of the film does not make for notable excitement."

The following year, Cobb was seen in the semi-documentary noir thriller, *Call Northside 777* (1948). Here, he played Brian Kelly, a blustering Chicago newspaper editor who assigns reporter Jim McNeal (James Stewart) to investigate a newspaper ad offering $5,000 for the killers of a police officer 11 years be-

fore. ("It wouldn't hurt to check it," Kelly quips when McNeal balks at the assignment. "You might get your name in the papers.") It turns out that the ad was placed by the mother of Frank Wiecek (Richard Conte), whom she insists was wrongly imprisoned for the crime. Initially, McNeal and Kelly are interested only in the increased readership that the resulting stories evoke, but they eventually come to believe in the man's innocence, and McNeal works tirelessly to track down evidence that will back up their claim. Although a key witness in the case refuses to admit that she gave false testimony, McNeal comes through at the 11th hour, providing proof that Wiecek did not commit the crime and ultimately securing his release.

While he was off-screen for most of *Northside 777*, Cobb was singled out by Crowther in the *New York Times*, who said his role was "winningly acted." He was seen in a far more substantial role, however, in his third film noir, *The Dark Past* (1948). This feature opens as police psychiatrist Andrew Collins (Cobb), shares a personal experience with a colleague in order to illuminate the benefits of psychiatric treatment for criminals. A flashback shows that, years earlier, Collins, his wife, and three friends were held hostage in the doctor's lakeside cabin by notorious escaped convict, Al Walker (William Holden), and his gang. While confined in the cabin, Collins uses his psychiatric background to unearth the root of Walker's murderous tendencies, and the frightening incident is peacefully resolved when Walker gives himself up to police. Cobb turned in an admirable performance as the unflappable psychiatrist, who tells Walker at one point, "I don't kill sick people, I cure them." Lavished with high praise by critics, Cobb was termed "near-excellent" in *Motion Picture Herald*; the critic for *Newsweek* praised his "expert playing"; and Lloyd L. Sloan raved in the *Hollywood Citizen-News*: "Lee J. Cobb, one of Hollywood's finest actors, maintains high standards with a first-rate performance."

Following this triumph, Cobb remained on the dark side of the screen for his fourth film noir appearance in *Thieves' Highway* (1949). In this gritty, Jules Dassin–directed feature, Cobb was featured as Mike Figlia, an unscrupulous merchant responsible for an accident that crippled the father of war veteran Nick Garcos (Richard Conte). When Nick arrives in town seeking retribution, he promptly encounters Figlia, who demonstrates his unprincipled practices by hiring a local girl to keep Nick off the streets while he sells his shipment of produce from under him. Although Nick later shows up for the money Figlia received, the merchant endeavors to give him only a portion, turning vicious when Nick demands the full amount: "Hey, listen, you cheap peddler—I was in this business when you were still sucking out of a bottle," Figlia rants. "I'm giving you more money than you've ever seen in your life. When'd you ever make more than a day's pay?" Forced to turn over the profits, Figlia is undaunted—he pays a pair of his hoods to beat Nick and retrieve the cash. Later, after Nick's partner is killed in a truck accident and Figlia pays two local peddlers to collect the dead man's merchandise, Nick confronts him, attacking him with a hatchet and beating him until he confesses his role in the accident involving Nick's father. After its release, *Thieves' Highway* was hailed as "one of the best melodramas—one of the sharpest and most taut—we've had this year," and Cobb earned his usual good notices, with Bosley Crowther writing in the *New York Times*: "This Figlia is a beauty—and, as played by Lee J. Cobb, he grows on the screen to the full dimensions of a believable rascal of the business world."

Although Cobb was by now developing a following for his standout character performances on screen, his greatest stage triumph was just ahead.

"[Director] Elia Kazan sent me the script of Arthur Miller's play, *Death of a Salesman*," Cobb recalled, "and I knew there was no living for me unless I played the Willy Loman part."

Over the objections of executives at 20th Century–Fox, Cobb opened on Broadway in the coveted role on February 10, 1949, and earned raves from critics, who called his performance "epic" and "a towering accomplishment." He would play the grueling part—for which he won the Donaldson Award for Best Actor—for more than 300 performances. After 11 months, the exhausted actor was finally forced to bow out of the play.

"What happened ... was that I folded. It was as simple as that," Cobb said in 1950. "Willy Loman is the greatest opportunity any actor could have in the theater. Leaving him isn't something you do with equanimity. The miracle was that I ever got to play him—after eight years away from Broadway! And for a long while, the [studio's] resistance was so formidable it looked like a hopeless case."

After leaving the play, Cobb revealed his desire to play Willy Loman in a planned film version of *Death of a Salesman*, saying he was "dying to do it" and "wouldn't leave a stone unturned to get the role." But when the film was made by Columbia Pictures in 1951, the part was given to veteran actor Fredric March. (Cobb was somewhat compensated nearly 15 years later when he reprised the role of Willy Loman in a televised version of the play, earning an Emmy nomination for best actor. However, although Emmys were given to the production for Outstanding Dramatic Program, and to the director, Alex Segal, Cobb lost to Peter Ustinov in *Barefoot in Athens*.)

Meanwhile, back in Hollywood, Cobb concluded his contract with 20th Century–Fox with a starring role in his fifth film noir, *The Man Who Cheated Himself* (1951). In yet another showy performance, Cobb starred as Lt. Ed Cullen, a veteran cop whose illicit affair with a married woman, Lois (Jane Wyatt), leads to his undoing. When Lois shoots and kills her husband, Cullen craftily covers up her involvement in the crime, but he is assigned to work the case along with his kid brother and partner, Andy (John Dall). An enthusiastic rookie detective, Andy persistently pursues the case, rejecting his brother's theory that the murder was committed by a local street hood and turning up clues that finally point to Cullen. But when

Andy shows up to reluctantly arrest his brother, Cullen continues to feign innocence: "You drunk? You sure can dream 'em up," he says. "You know, if the same thing didn't happen to a lot of rookies, I'd knock your ears down. Give 'em one break and suddenly they're masterminds— running around like hot-tailed beavers, arresting the whole population. You're blowin' your top again — go on home." When Andy refuses to back down, Cullen knocks him out and attempts to flee with Lois, but he is eventually tracked down by his brother and arrested. Once again, Cobb was applauded for his performance, with the *Los Angeles Examiner*'s Kay Proctor terming him "restrained and effective as always," and the *New York Times*' reviewer praising his "solid and effective performance." But shortly after this release of the film, and in the midst of his soaring career, Cobb became ensnared in a nightmarish experience that would last for the next several years.

Since the late 1940s, the Hollywood community had functioned under a cloud of suspicion and paranoia, hatched by the House Un-American Activities Committee's (HUAC) investigation into Communism in the motion picture industry. In 1951, during secret testimony before the committee, actor Larry Parks claimed that Cobb, along with several others (including Morris Carnovsky, John Garfield, Sterling Hayden, Sam Jaffe, Edward G. Robinson, Anne Revere, and Howard Da Silva), had been involved with the Communist Party. Cobb unequivocally denied the charge.

"I should like to make it clear that I am not a Communist, have never been a Communist, and have never joined nor sponsored any organization which I knew to be subversive," Cobb said.

But two years later, Cobb reversed his position. Testifying in a closed session before the House committee, Cobb admitted that he had joined the Communist Party in New York in the early 1940s at the invitation of fellow Group Theatre members Phoebe Brand and Morris Carnovsky. He further testified that he had developed "a general disenchantment

with the Party methods" and discontinued his membership in 1946. Cobb also identified several individuals that had also been Party members, including actors Lloyd Bridges, Jeff Corey, Marc Lawrence, Anne Revere, Rose Hobart, and Gale Sondergaard.

In later years, Cobb rarely discussed the HUAC testimony and his motivations for reversing his stance, but in a 1968 interview with the *New York Times*, he frankly revealed the impact that the incident had on his life.

"I could speak a torrent of words on the subject," he said, "but it would hurt so many people and what is the use now that so much time has gone by? I like to hope there is more perspective and less bitterness now. They kept after me for three years ... they took away my passport so I couldn't travel. They kept at me and at me. Oh, they have unspeakable ways— very special ways I couldn't describe to you — to force you to do what they want.... My personal life was shattered. When I finally went to the Committee, they already knew what I had to tell them, so the whole thing was a farce. But I had to make the gesture — to survive. Afterwards, it meant starting a new life, making a new set of friends. When I realized what I had to do, I set about doing it and I felt strong again."

After Cobb's initial denial of Party involvement, he had only appeared in one film, *The Fighter* (1952), but he returned to the screen after his 1953 testimony and was seen in such films as *Yankee Pasha* (1954), a swashbuckler with Jeff Chandler and Rhonda Fleming. Also during this period, he offered one of his best screen characterizations, gangster union boss Johnny Friendly in *On the Waterfront* (1954), earning his first Academy Award nomination for best supporting actor. (The film won an Oscar for Best Film, as did Elia Kazan for Best Director, Marlon Brando for Best Actor, and Eva Marie Saint for Best Supporting Actress, but the vote for Best Supporting Actor was split between fellow *Waterfront* nominees Rod Steiger and Karl Malden, and the statuette went to Edmond O'Brien for *The Barefoot Contessa*.)

Shortly after his triumphant performance

in *Waterfront*, however, Cobb's personal life took another dive. In May 1955, while working on the film *The Houston Story* (released in 1956 with Gene Barry in the starring role), Cobb suffered a massive, near-fatal heart attack, which he later attributed to his non-stop performing schedule and the stress he had experienced because of the HUAC investigation. Unable to work, the actor went into debt (due, in part, by an affinity for gambling, he later acknowledged), but he was bailed out by actor Frank Sinatra, with whom he had appeared in *Miracle of the Bells* (1948).

"Frank and I hadn't seen each other since years before, but there he was, saying my life," Cobb said in 1968. "After he'd helped me, he disappeared again and I don't believe I've talked with him since. I would still like to thank him."

Fortune came into Cobb's life in another form as well — while recovering during his hospital stay, he was visited on a regular basis by Mary Hirsch, a 26-year-old elementary school teacher who'd met the actor at a party a short time before. On June 28, 1957, Cobb and Mary were married, and went on to have two sons. The couple would remain together until Cobb's death in 1976.

Professionally, Cobb was seen in some of his best films during the last half of the 1950s, including *The Three Faces of Eve* (1957), an outstanding drama in which he played the doctor of a woman (Joanne Woodward) suffering from multiple personality disorder; *12 Angry Men* (1957), where Lee J. Cobb was a standout among of cast of excellent performances given by such veterans as Henry Fonda, Ed Begley, Martin Balsam, and E.G. Marshall; and *The Brothers Karamazov* (1957), earning his second Academy Award nomination for his role as the film's implacable father (he lost this time to Burl Ives in *The Big Country*). Cobb was also seen during this period in his final two films noirs, *The Garment Jungle* (1957) and *Party Girl* (1958).

In the first, Cobb was top-billed as Walter Mitchell, a powerful clothing manufacture who adamantly rejects his workers' desires to join a union. For years, Mitchell has been paying local mobster Artie Ravidge (Richard Boone) to keep the unionists at bay, and he finds himself at odds with his son, Alan (Kerwin Matthews), who joins the company and grows increasingly sympathetic toward the union's cause. The father-son relationship further erodes when Mitchell refuses to believe Alan's claim that Ravidge is responsible for the deaths of several union organizers, but when Mitchell later realizes the truth and tries to disassociate himself from Ravidge, he meets with resistance: "For 15 years I kept the unions off your back and you never asked me how!" Ravidge tells him. "All you did was grab the benefits…. If you wanna play games—remember how I play!" When Mitchell fires him, Ravidge makes good on his veiled threat, and guns Mitchell down in his office. Determined to avenge his father's death, Alan unearths evidence that leads to Ravidge's arrest, and he later redeems the family name when he takes over the business. Directed by Vincent Sherman, *The Garment Jungle* was brimming with first-rate performances, including Cobb's, which was labeled "superior," and the film itself was praised in the *New York Times* as "the garment sector's most savagely pictorial screen appraisal to date."

Next, in *Party Girl*, a rare color noir released late in the era, Cobb portrayed a 1930s-era gangster, Rico Angelo, who is characterized by his hard-drinking and unpredictable brutality. In a scene that provides a clear illustration of his persona, Rico presides over a mob gathering during which he honors a member of his gang, Frankie Gasto (Aaron Saxon), by presenting him with a silver pool cue. Although Frankie attempted to take over Rico's organization, the mob leader says, "that's ambition for you. And a guy that's got ambition has got something coming. I could've asked anybody else to give this to Frankie, but me—I like to do things personally." And Rico proceeds to beat Frankie to death with the pool cue. Helmed by Nicholas Ray, the film's action centers on Rico and his shrewd mouthpiece, attorney Thomas Farrell (Robert Taylor), who tries to distance himself from his corrupt lifestyle after falling for local showgirl Vicki Gaye (Cyd Charisse). Rico balks at this proposed defection ("Nobody ever quit me. I got rid of a few guys, but nobody ever quit," he tells Farrell), and he later abducts Vicki, threatening to disfigure her with acid unless Farrell recants damaging information on Rico that he provided to police. Rico is unable to carry out his plan, however — when police gunfire erupts, the mobster is shot, accidentally douses himself with acid, and falls through an upper-story window to his death.

While *Party Girl* holds up today as a fairly interesting feature with a number of notable performances, it was savaged by most critics upon its release; in one of the few favorable reviews, Lynn Bowers of the *Los Angeles Examiner* called it "quite well done with the help of a top cast." In the more typical notices, A. H. Weiler wrote in the *New York Times* that there was "little novel or exciting" about the film, and in the *Los Angeles Mirror-News*, Margaret Harford said that "nearly everyone is wasted in such a picture." As for Cobb, he was labeled "good" by one reviewer, but the *Los Angeles Times*' Philip K. Scheuer quipped: "Not all the corn is on the Cobb in *Party Girl*, but Lee J. shucks his share of it."

In addition to his feature film appearances, Cobb was also enjoying success on the small screen during this period. In 1958, he earned an Emmy nomination for his performance in the *Studio One* presentation of "No Deadly Medicine" (losing to Peter Ustinov for *The Life of Samuel Johnson*). He also received rave reviews for his portrayal of the title role in *I, Don Quixote* in 1959, followed by another Emmy nod in 1961 for "Project Immortality," which appeared on *Playhouse 90* (he lost to Laurence Olivier in *The Moon and Sixpence*).

With the onset of the 1960s, Cobb was seen in *Exodus* (1960), a box-office hit based on Leon Uris' best-selling novel; *Four Horsemen of the Apocalypse* (1961), a dismal remake of the 1921 Rudolph Valentino classic; and *How the West Was Won* (1962), a big-budget hit whose all-star cast included John Wayne, Henry Fonda, Debbie Reynolds, James Stewart, Gregory Peck, Richard Widmark, and Thelma Ritter. After this feature, Cobb stunned the film community by accepting the role of Judge Henry Garth on the television series The *Virginian*. He would remain with the show for the next four years.

"It's always the uncreative people who wonder why I played Judge Garth on television for so long. I played it partly so my epitaph won't read 'Cobb died waiting to play Lear,'" Cobb said with typical frankness in 1968. "Actors can't wait for anybody or anything anymore. There isn't time and the competition is too keen. This is the era of name actors doing voice-overs and selling deodorant and playing in industrials and TV series to live. But it never was my intention to die pure, because suffering for your art can be pretty degrading. I know this from past experience. Now I just want to keep on living to fight another day."

During a press junket to publicize the series, Cobb once again displayed his penchant for straightforward, no-holds-barred commentary when he took the opportunity to speak out against television critics, saying that they are "fawned on by the agencies and networks."

"Who the hell are they to criticize?" he asked in a 1963 *Variety* article. "I don't know what the hell function they serve. Except for a few who have taken on the laudable task of elevating standards through their criticism, I don't concur with their tastes personally."

Just a year later, the infinitely quotable actor took a stand on another favorite issue — censorship of the arts— blasting critics who "like to assume a noble stance and proclaim in blanket fashion that all films which are unsuitable for the kindergarten class are dirty."

"I think it is a pretense of nobility to say that all films should also be equally suitable for all the children," Cobb said in *The Hollywood Reporter*. "A so-called family film made in poor taste is by far a greater wrong than an adult film with a daring theme made in impeccable taste.... I suppose the film theater is often a convenient place in which to stash the children, but surely parents, with a little effort, can find a better sanctuary for them without resorting to a campaign to make all theaters safe for toddlers."

After the end of *The Virginian*, Cobb starred with James Coburn in the popular spy spoof, *Our Man Flint* (1966), and its sequel, *In Like Flint* (1967), and reprised his role as Judge Garth in a television movie, *The Meanest Men in the West* (1967). And in 1968, he realized a long-time dream when he returned to Broadway to star in *King Lear*, earning rave reviews for his portrayal, including one describing it as "the finest performance in a distinguished career."

During the following decade, Cobb was seen in several foreign films and such television movies as *Heat of Anger* (1971), *Double Indemnity* (1973)— in which he played the role portrayed by Edward G. Robinson in the 1944 film —*Dr. Max* (1974), and *The Great Ice Rip-Off* (1974). He also appeared in a handful of feature films; the best of these were *The Man Who Loved Cat Dancing* (1973), in which he played a bounty hunter tracking

down the film's star, Burt Reynolds; and *The Exorcist* (1973), one of the most financially successful horror films in movie history. His last two films were both released in 1975, *That Lucky Touch*, a dim-witted comedy starring Roger Moore, and *Blood, Sweat and Fear*, in which Cobb played the boss of an international narcotics ring.

Now in his early 60s, Cobb was showing no signs of slowing down, and was reportedly in the process of considering a return to the stage. Sadly, although he had been in good health since his massive heart attack 20 years earlier, Cobb suffered another attack on February 11, 1976, and later died at his home in Woodland Hills, California, bringing to an end a career that remains one of the most highly acclaimed in the annals of Hollywood. In addition to his own successes, Cobb left behind a legacy of acting in his children and grandchildren. His daughter, Julie, made her acting debut on the television series *The D.A.* in 1971, and has since appeared as a regular on two series, *A Year at the Top* and *Charles in Charge*; several made-for-television movies including *Salem's Lot* (1979); and such feature films as *Defending Your Life* (1991) and *Dr. Jekyll and Mrs. Hyde* (1995). Cobb's oldest son, Vincent, and his granddaughter, Jennifer, have several acting credits as well.

Even after his death, Lee J. Cobb continued to be recognized as one of most significant performers of his time; in 1981, he was inducted into the Theatre Hall of Fame, along with other notables including Jose Ferrer, Leslie Howard, Maureen Stapleton, Margaret Sullavan, Jule Styne, and Gwen Verdon. The talent, energy, and commitment that he brought to every role were once ideally described by a colleague, who said:

"There is a theory that regardless of who co-stars with Lee J. Cobb in a film, the character he plays is the one which stays with the audience. They may forget the title of the film, the beauty of the women, or the name of the handsome male star, but the less glamorous role of scientist, doctor, father or grandfather played by Cobb remains unforgettable."

Film Noir Filmography

Johnny O'Clock. Director: Robert Rossen. Producer: Edward G. Nealis. Running time: 95 minutes. Released by Columbia, March 27, 1947. Cast: Dick Powell, Evelyn Keyes, Lee J. Cobb, Ellen Drew, Nina Foch, Thomas Gomez, John Kellogg, Jim Bannon, Mabel Paige, Phil Brown, Jeff Chandler, Kit Guard.

The Dark Past. Director: Rudolph Mate. Producer: Buddy Adler. Running time: 74 minutes. Released by Columbia, December 22, 1948. Cast: William Holden, Nina Foch, Lee J. Cobb, Adele Jergens, Stephen Dunne, Lois Maxwell, Barry Kroeger, Steven Geray, Wilton Graff, Robert Osterloh, Kathryn Card, Bobby Hyatt, Ellen Corby, Charles Cane, Robert B. Williams.

Call Northside 777. Director: Henry Hathaway. Producer: Otto Lang. Running time: 111 minutes. Released by 20th Century-Fox. Cast: James Stewart, Richard Conte, Lee J. Cobb, Helen Walker, Betty Garde, Kasia Orzazewski, Joanne de Bergh, Howard Smith, Moroni Olsen, John McIntire, Paul Harvey, George Tyne, Richard Bishop, Otto Waldis, Michael Chapin, E.G. Marshall, Truman Bradley.

Thieves' Highway. Director: Jules Dassin. Producer: Robert Bassler. Running time: 94 minutes. Released by 20th Century-Fox, September 23, 1949. Cast: Richard Conte, Valentina Cortesa, Lee J. Cobb, Barbara Lawrence, Jack Oakie, Millard Mitchell, Morris Carnovsky, Tamara Shayne, Kasia Orzazewski, Norbert Schiller, Hope Emerson, George Tyne, Edwin Max, David Clarke, Walter Baldwin, David Opatoshu.

The Man Who Cheated Himself. Director: Felix E. Feist. Producer: Jack M. Warner. Running time: 81 minutes. Released by 20th Century-Fox, February 8, 1951. Cast: Lee J. Cobb, John Dall, Jane Wyatt, Lisa Howard, Alan Wells, Harlan Warde, Tito Vuolo, Mimi Aguglia, Charles Arnt, Marjorie Bennett, Bud Wolfe, Morgan Farley, Howard Negley.

The Garment Jungle. Director: Vincent Sherman. Producer: Harry Kleiner. Running time: 88 minutes. Released by Columbia, May 22, 1957. Cast: Lee J. Cobb, Kerwin Matthews, Gia Scala, Richard Boone, Valerie French, Robert Loggia, Joseph Wiseman, Adam Williams, Harold J. Stone, Wesley Addy, Willis Bouchey, Robert Ellenstein, Celia Lovsky.

Party Girl. Director: Nicholas Ray. Producer: Joe Pasternak. Running time: 99 minutes. Released by MGM, October 28, 1958. Cast: Robert Taylor, Cyd Charisse, Lee J. Cobb, John Ireland, Kent Smith, Claire Kelly, Corey Allen, Lewis Charles, David Opatoshu, Kem Dibbs, Patrick McVey, Barbara Lang, Myrna Hansen, Betty Utey, Jack Lambert.

References

"Actor Cobb Admits Red Cell Membership in '43." *Hollywood Citizen-News*, September 30, 1953.
"Actor Divorced." *Los Angeles Herald Express*, July 28, 1952.
"Actor Lee J. Cobb Dies at 64." *The (Philadelphia) Evening Bulletin*, February 12, 1976.
Bosworth, Patricia. "Lee J.'s New Life." *New York Times*, November 17, 1968.
"Broadway Tribute Inducts 26 into Theatre Hall of Fame." *The Hollywood Reporter*, March 12, 1981.
"Bulk of Cobb's Estate Left to Second Wife." *Variety*, February 23, 1976.
Cobb, Lee J. "Lee J. Cobb Speaks His Mind on Many Things." *Los Angeles Times*, September 23, 1962.
"Fox Studios Deny Actor's Claim of Broken Contract and Back Pay." *Hollywood Citizen-News*, October 8, 1946.
Goodman, Ezra. "Lee J. Cobb." *Los Angeles Daily News*, April 6, 1951.
Greenberg, Abe. "Lee J. Cobb Set for Movie Return." *Hollywood Citizen-News*, April 29,1964.
"He Wears Well." *Newsweek*, January 26, 1959.
"Julie Cobb in 'D.A.'" *Variety*, June 7, 1971.
"Julie Cobb Set for 'Cannon' Seg." *Variety*, November 16, 1972.
Kaufman, Dave. "Lee Cobb 'Resents' Critics; Brands Ratings a 'Fraud.'" *Variety*, June 25, 1962.
"Lee Cobb Admits He Was Red Member for Five Years." *Los Angeles Examiner*, November 30, 1953.
"Lee Cobb Married to Teacher." *Los Angeles Times*, June 28, 1957.
"Lee Cobb Tells Probe He Quit Reds in 1946." *Variety*, September 30, 1953.
"Lee J. Cobb, 64, Gained Fame on Stage, Screen and TV." *Philadelphia Inquirer*, February 12, 1976.
"Lee J. Cobb, Actor, Sued for Divorce." *Los Angeles Times*, June 19, 1952.
"Lee J. Cobb Cracks At Critics Who Crack Non-Family Fare." *The Hollywood Reporter*, July 29, 1964.
"Lee J. Cobb Creates the Grand Illusion." *Cue*, March 5, 1949.
"Lee J. Cobb Denies All Commie Party Charges." *The Hollywood Reporter*, April 7, 1951.
"Lee J. Cobb Gets Young Roles at Last." *Stage and Cinema*, February 4, 1968.
"Lee J. Cobbs Parents of Son." *Los Angeles Times*, March 26, 1960.
"Lee J. Cobb, the Actor, Is Dead at 64." *New York Times*, February 12, 1976.
"Losing Sight of Creative Forces." *The Hollywood Reporter*, July 1, 1964.

Obituary. *Newsweek*, February 23, 1976.

Parsons, Louella O. "Lee J. Cobb in Collapse." *Los Angeles Examiner*, May 10, 1955.

_____. "Lee J. Cobb Speaks from the Heart." *Los Angeles Examiner*, November 17, 1957.

_____. "Lee J. Cobb Weds Teacher." *Los Angeles Examiner*, June 28, 1957.

Scheuer, Philip K. "Another Discovery! Cobb 'Grows Young.'" *Los Angeles Times*, June 22, 1947.

Smith, Cecil. "Lee J. Cobb: His Stage, Screen Roles Bear Stamp of Greatness." *Los Angeles Times*, November 28, 1958.

"Victory by Ridicule." *Time*, November 23, 1959.

"View from a Star." *New York Times*, August 10, 1958.

STEVE COCHRAN

"Plug him and he drops, same as anybody else."— Steve Cochran in *White Heat* (1949)

With his swarthy good looks and tough-guy demeanor, Steve Cochran was a natural for the hoods and cutthroats he so often portrayed in the movies, and he was seen to good advantage in five entries from the film noir era: *The Chase* (1946), *White Heat* (1949), *The Damned Don't Cry* (1950), *Private Hell 36* (1954), and *The Beat Generation* (1959). Despite a career that included more than 40 films during a span of three decades, however, Cochran frequently found himself in the press more often for his off-screen exploits than his cinematic performances—from his numerous run-ins with the law to his bizarre death in the middle of the Pacific, Cochran led a life that surpassed even the most creative Hollywood script.

Named for his lumberman father, Robert Alexander Cochran was born May 25, 1917, in Eureka, California, the eldest of two children. When Cochran was eight, his family set out by automobile to visit relatives living in Denver, but after they were delayed for a week by a snowstorm in Laramie, Wyoming, the elder Cochran was so taken with the city that he moved the family there. After attending Fremont Grammar School, Cochran's family pulled up stakes again, and the young man attended high school in Cheyenne, where he won letters in basketball, football, and boxing. Although Cochran hadn't settled on a career choice, he showed an interest in commercial art, cartooning, and architecture. But when he was kicked off the school basketball team after missing training practice, Cochran turned his sights toward dramatics. He never looked back.

Following high school, Cochran enrolled in Wyoming University, but he quit after a year to join the Federal Theatre Project in Detroit, playing leads in *It Can't Happen Here* and *The Road to Rome*. In 1937, he decided to try his luck in Hollywood, but couldn't even manage to get a screen test. Undaunted, he stayed in California, gaining more experience through little theater groups; while appearing in one production, *There's Always Juliet*, he adopted the name of one of the characters, and Steve Cochran was born.

Returning to his hometown of Laramie, Cochran converted a barn into a playhouse and produced a number of little theater plays such as *East Lynne* and *Ten Nights in a Barroom*. He later moved to Carmel, California, and organized another little theater group, which he funded by working on a nearby ranch. While in Carmel, he played in *Twelfth Night* and *Macbeth* as part of a Shakespearean festival held in the open-air Forest Theatre. During the next several years, Cochran continued his travels, acting and directing for the Junior League's children's theatre in San Francisco, performing on a number of radio shows in Hollywood, playing in Army camps on the Pacific Coast, landing the lead in a road company of *My Sister Eileen*, and playing stock at the Greenwood Theatre at Peak's Island near Portland, Maine. In between acting jobs,

he made ends meet by performing various jobs, including firing the steam plant at a sand pit near Del Monte, California, and working as a private policeman at Macy's department store in New York.

After nearly seven years of futile attempts to make it into the "big time," Cochran finally got his break in the mid-1940s, when the Theatre Guild in New York cast him in the lead in *Without Love.* Soon after, he caught the attention of producer Sam Goldwyn, who took an option on his services. Cochran toured Columbus, Ohio, Milwaukee, and Chicago in the play before hitting Los Angeles, where Goldwyn exercised the option and cast Cochran in a popular Danny Kaye vehicle, *The Wonder Man* (1945). He also appeared that year in *The Gay Senorita,* a mediocre bit of fluff starring Jinx Falkenburg; and two entries in the Boston Blackie series, *Boston Blackie Booked on Suspicion* and *Boston Blackie's Rendezvous,* in which he starred as a crazed killer who escapes from a lunatic asylum.

In terms of box-office receipts, Cochran hit the jackpot in 1946, with featured roles in a pair of money-makers, *The Kid from Brooklyn,* another Danny Kaye starrer, and *The Best Years of Our Lives,* which won a slew of Academy Awards, including nods for Best Picture, Best Actor, Best Supporting Actor, and Best Director. Also that year, Cochran leapt into the domain of film noir, portraying a suave racketeer in *The Chase.* Here, Robert Cummings was top-billed as Chuck Scott, an ex-G.I. hired as the chauffeur for Eddie Roman (Cochran), who lives in an opulent Miami mansion with his unhappy wife, Lorna (Michele Morgan), and his inscrutable sidekick, Gino (Peter Lorre). Before long, Chuck and Lorna fall in love and run away together to Cuba, but soon after they arrive, Lorna is fatally stabbed in a nightclub and Chuck is arrested for her murder. Escaping from police, Chuck conducts his own investigation and learns that the actual murderer is Gino, who kills him. It turns out that the entire adventure was merely a fever-induced nightmare suffered by Chuck, but his plan to flee

with Lorna was not; when Roman learns of the plan, he speeds toward the local docks to stop them, but he is killed, along with Gino, when his car is hit by a speeding train.

Sometimes confusing and often bizarre, *The Chase* was highlighted by the performance turned in by Cochran; his character's persona is strikingly revealed in an early scene, where Roman is seen receiving a manicure in his home. When the manicurist accidentally nicks his finger, she quickly apologizes: "Oh, I'm sorry, Mr. Roman — you moved," she says. "But you didn't," Roman rejoins, slapping her from her stool onto the floor, "quick enough." The woman leaves the room crying, leaving Roman to comment, "Stupid dame." For his picture-stealing portrayal, Cochran was lauded by reviewers; John L. Scott of the *Los Angeles Times* praised the actor's "impressive performance," and the critic from the *New York Times* wrote: "Amid [the] welter of dreams ... are some solid and entertaining portrayals. Count as best among these that of Steve Cochran."

In the next two years, Cochran made only two films, *Copacabana* (1947), a vehicle for Groucho Marx and Carmen Miranda, and *A Song Is Born* (1948), a hit musical starring

Danny Kaye. Instead, he took time off from his budding screen career to appear on Broadway with the legendary Mae West in the revival of *Diamond Lil*. Upon his return to California, he signed with Warner Brothers and was cast in his second film noir, *White Heat* (1949). In this top-notch feature, Cochran played Big Ed Somers, a rebellious, outspoken member of a gang headed by the psychologically disturbed Cody Jarrett (James Cagney). The film opens as Cody's gang pulls off a lucrative train robbery that results in the deaths of four men — sought by authorities for the heist, Cody craftily confesses to a lesser crime and is sentenced to prison for a short term. While in prison, however, Cody not only learns that Big Ed has run off with his wife, Verna (Virginia Mayo), but also that his beloved mother (Margaret Wycherly) has been killed. Breaking out of prison, Cody goes after Big Ed and Verna, and when he confronts his wife, she tells him that Big Ed shot his mother in the back. Not knowing that Verna was the real killer, Cody guns down Big Ed and reunites his gang for another robbery, but his plan is foiled by the efforts of an undercover cop (Edmond O'Brien) and he dies in the famed scene atop an oil refinery tank, shouting, "Made it, Ma — top of the world!" before he is incinerated in a fiery explosion. Despite the overwhelming performance provided by Cagney, Cochran was mentioned by several reviewers, including Lloyd L. Sloan of the *Hollywood Citizen-News*, who termed him "excellent."

The following year, Cochran continued racking up the bad-guy roles with starring parts in *Dallas*, an above-average western starring Gary Cooper; *Highway 301*, a gritty cops-and-robbers saga, and *Storm Warning*, co-starring Doris Day and Ginger Rogers. In this gripping feature (which also starred president-to-be Ronald Reagan), Cochran played a bigoted family man who is a member of the Ku Klux Klan. He later called the role his favorite of his career.

"To me, one source of satisfaction in playing the role of Hank in *Storm Warning* was the feeling that I might be making a small contribution toward racial tolerance," he told the *Saturday Evening Post*. "As a youngster in Wyoming, I had seen the fiery crosses of the Ku Klux Klan burning near my home and even then I sensed their frightening menace. As Hank in this picture, I had a chance to show how basically shabby such demonstrations are."

Cochran's final film of 1950 was his third film noir, *The Damned Don't Cry*, with Joan Crawford, David Brian, and Kent Taylor. Here, Cochran was again cast as a gangster, this time playing Nick Prenta, a renegade syndicate member who tries to take over the entire organization from his ruthless boss, George Castleman (Brian). While planning his strategy from his base on the West coast, Nick falls for a wealthy society woman, Lorna Hansen Forbes (Crawford), not knowing that she is Castleman's mistress and has been dispatched by Castleman to set a trap for him. Despite his love for Lorna, however, Nick indicates in a telling exchange that business comes first; Lorna coyly asks Nick, "If you couldn't trust me, would you have me killed?" and Nick solemnly responds, "No. I'd do that myself." Over time, Lorna grows to return Nick's feelings and deliberately delays the plan to ensnare him, but Castleman senses Lorna's change of heart, unexpectedly shows up in town, beats Lorna savagely, and kills Nick in a shootout.

A well-made and often gripping film, *Damned* nonetheless earned mixed reviews — the critic for *Variety* wrote that "Vincent Sherman's direction spots quite a bit of tension and sound dramatics," and he praised Cochran for his "forceful portrayal," but the *New York Times*' Bosley Crowther found that Sherman's direction was "as specious as the script" and charged that "a more artificial lot of acting could hardly be achieved." There was no such dissension over Cochran's performance, however; the critic for *Trade Show* said the actor "has a field day in a colorful spot," *Film Daily*'s reviewer labeled him "vivid and compelling," and in the *Los Angeles Times*, Dorothy Manners wrote: "Next to [Joan Crawford], Steve Cochran makes the best

Joan Crawford, Steve Cochran, and Selena Royle in *The Damned Don't Cry* (1950).

impression as the diamond-in-the-rough who dares to break with the syndicate — and winds up just in the rough."

The year 1951 would be Cochran's busiest of his career — the best of his five films that year were *Jim Thorpe — All American*, a first-rate biopic about the Native American Olympic star, and *Inside the Walls of Folsom Prison*, a prison film set in the 1920s, which starred Cochran as a tough inmate who leads an escape. Also that year, Cochran played a rare good-guy role, in *The Tanks Are Coming*, as a rugged soldier who leads his troop into battle after their master sergeant is killed.

Off-screen, Cochran became embroiled in the first of many brushes with the law when, on New Year's Day 1952, he was involved in an altercation with Lenwood "Buddy" Wright, an aircraft worker and for-

mer professional boxer. According to Wright's version of the incident, he was a guest at a party given at Cochran's house, and after leaving, discovered that he had left behind an overcoat. When he returned, Wright charged, Cochran met him at the door and "brutally and violently" struck him over the head with a baseball bat. According to Cochran, however, Wright had come to the house "as an intruder looking for a fight and had his fists raised," forcing the actor to use the bat in self-defense. Cochran wasn't charged, but three months later, Wright filed a $405,000 suit for assault and battery damages against the actor, claiming that he had suffered serious head injuries and was forced to take a sick leave from his aircraft job. Following a two-week trial in June 1953, a jury awarded Wright $16,000 in general and punitive damages. (The award was reduced to $7,500 the following month by a Superior Court Judge.)

Cochran was back in the news in October 1953 when he arrested for reckless driving and evading arrest after an automobile chase with police. According to newspaper accounts, Cochran ran a red light while driving his new $6,000 German sports car, but when police flagged him over, the actor sped off, leading officers on a chase for five miles. The pursuit came to an end only after the cops fired a warning shot. "You are a poor sport," Cochran reportedly told police after the incident. "You wouldn't have caught me if you hadn't shot." He later pleaded guilty and paid a minor fine, but insisted that the chase was just a "lark," adding, "I just wanted to show my friends how my new sports car would corner."

During the next two years, Cochran played starring roles in six films, including a secret Communist agent in *Operation Secret* (1952), a cowboy in *The Lion and the Horse* (1952), and a stage director in *She's Back on Broadway* (1953). All were forgettable. He was also featured in the dreadful musical *The Desert Song* (1953), which was his final film under his Warner Brothers contract. Meanwhile, in 1953, Cochran started his own production company, Robert Alexander Productions, and enthusiastically discussed his new venture in the press.

"Working behind as well as in front of the cameras gives one such a feeling of growth as an artist," he said. "I left Warner Bros. recently because I wasn't growing. I had some pleasant assignments there ... but the last few parts were so bad I had to get out. This new producing-acting venture is my most exciting experience yet."

Then in 1954, the actor starred with Ida Lupino and her then-husband Howard Duff in the tense film noir, *Private Hell 36*, produced by Lupino's production company, Filmakers. In this feature, Cochran played Cal Bruner, a police detective who, along with his partner, Jack Farnham (Howard Duff), finds a steel box filled with cash following a car crash. Rather than turning over the entire

amount, Bruner talks his partner into splitting a portion of the money, which he craves in order to provide material possessions for his nightclub singer girlfriend, Lili (Lupino). The simple scheme grows more complex, however, characterized by Farnham's conscience-stricken behavior and a mysterious blackmailer who demands the stolen money. Later, even Lili suggests that they don't need the things that the money could buy, but Bruner insists, telling her, "That's what you say today. But tomorrow you'll see something in the window. Something with a price tag on it. A big price tag. And you'll want it. And even if you don't, I will. And we're gonna have those things." Meanwhile, Farnham insists on turning over the cash to the unseen blackmailer, but Bruner has no intention of giving the money back — when the two men arrive at the planned meeting place, Bruner shoots his partner in the back, and he is, in turn, gunned down by his superior (Dean Jagger), who reveals he'd known about the theft all along. Although *Private Hell 36* stands up today as a fine example of the film noir era, it received mixed reviews upon its release; while the critic for *Variety* labeled it a "good entry" and cited Cochran's "suitable" performance, Bosley Crowther dismissed it in the *New York Times* as "just an average melodrama about cops."

After portraying a seedy circus advance man in *Carnival Story* in 1954, Cochran was off-screen for a year, returning instead to the stage, where he starred as Starbuck in a production of *The Rainmaker*. He was back to feature films in 1956 in *Slander*, a fast-paced drama that starred the actor as the ruthless publisher of a tabloid magazine, and *Come Next Spring*, the first film produced by Cochran's production company. In this well-made film, Cochran starred opposite Ann Sheridan as a farmer who redeems himself for his past drinking and wild ways. The feature was well-received by critics and audiences alike — a letter to *Filmland* magazine by one fan praised the actor's favorable characterization: "I hope Steve Cochran succeeded in *Come Next Spring* in getting away from being typed as a criminal-villain-tough guy. Let's see Steve in more roles like this real soon." During this time, Cochran also began appearing on various television programs, including *Zane Grey Theater* and *The Naked City*.

Between acting assignments, Cochran was busy making headlines for his off-screen exploits. In October 1956, he earned the dubious distinction of receiving the first flying ticket issued by a police helicopter. The adventure-loving actor — who had been flying for about two years, and had approximately 100 hours of flying time behind him — was cited by officers when he dipped over his mountaintop home in Studio City and rocked his wings. Claiming that he did not see the police helicopter trailing behind him, Cochran initially pleaded not guilty, but he later reversed his plea and was fined $500, grounded for 90 days, and given a suspended sentence of 30 days in jail.

The actor was in only one film in 1957, a well-crafted thriller entitled *The Weapon*, about a boy who accidentally shoots a playmate with a gun used to kill an Army officer 10 years before. He spent much of the year on a five-month picture-making junket to Europe, scouting locations for his upcoming film project, *Il Grido*. The picture, in which Cochran co-starred with Alida Valli and Betsy Blair, was filmed and released later that year in Italy, but wasn't released in the United States until 1962. Meanwhile, Cochran starred as a Confederate officer in *Quantrill's Raiders* (1958), a fairly entertaining low-budget western, and as an underworld kingpin in *I, Mobster* (1958), in which he suffered his 25th on-screen death. Shortly after the release of the latter film, Cochran discussed his success in playing villains on the silver screen.

"I don't act like a hood [in my films]," Cochran told Hollywood columnist Joe Hyams. "I'm basically a decent person and I let this come through in my portrayals. After all, a guy has to make a living some way, even if he's a gangster. The big secret in playing a gangster in movies is to really believe that the character you are playing is doing no wrong."

Cochran followed *I, Mobster* with a rare heroic role in the first-rate suspenser, *The Big Operator* (1959), as a man who goes up against a tyrannical labor boss, chillingly portrayed by Mickey Rooney. Interestingly, Cochran's next film, *The Beat Generation* (1959), featured the same director and producer, and many of the same actors as *The Big Operator*, but the result was not nearly as effective. In *The Beat Generation*, Cochran's final film noir, he stars as Dave Culloran, a woman-hating cop searching for a rapist known as "The Aspirin Kid." When his own wife, Francie (Fay Spain), is attacked by the molester, Culloran "treats her like a suspect," and when she later learns she is pregnant, his marriage falls apart, characterized by Culloran's suspicion that the child was fathered by the rapist. ("What if it is his child?" Francie asks. "Could you look at it? Could you love it?") Eventually, Francie leaves Culloran, who insists on continuing with his dogged quest for the Aspirin Kid, finally tracking him down among a group of beach-dwelling, bongo-banging beatniks, and reuniting with his wife — and newborn baby — in the final reel.

Clearly the weakest of Cochran's five noir features, *The Beat Generation* contains a few good moments, but they are overshadowed by the film's "hep" dialogue and quirky characters, including a woman who presents a poetry reading while smoking a cigarette and holding a large, white rat. (In one of the film's unintentionally funny scenes, Culloran announces to a trio of party-going beatniks that he is a policeman. One of the women sprays him with a stream of water from the bar and gleefully rejoins, "I'm a fireman!") The feature was a disaster at the box office and was slammed by critics, including the reviewer for the *New York Times*, who labeled it "downright embarrassing" and announced, "*The Beat Generation* is enough to make any member or non-member walk outside the theater and butt his head against the wall. This excruciating and tasteless little entertainment package arrived at neighborhood showcases yesterday, courtesy of Metro-Goldwyn-Mayer — if courtesy is the right word."

In 1960, Cochran had a brush with disaster when his yacht crashed into a Los Angeles Harbor breakwater in heavy fog. The actor and the boat's other occupants—18-year-old Heddie Grasberg, 19-year-old Nicole Makay, two dogs, and a monkey — were forced to dive out of the boat. All escaped without injury. It was the second sailing mishap of the actor's life. Several years earlier, he had spent a grim night in the Catalina Channel, bailing out his 35-foot ketch until a U.S. Coast Guard patrol boat towed the actor in. Tragically, this would not be the actor's last misfortune on the water.

Around this time, after two brief marriages earlier in his career, Cochran gave the institution another try in 1961, marrying Danish actress Jonna Jensen in Las Vegas on March 18th. But the third time would not be the charm. The two separated in November, and the actress filed for divorce on January 5, 1962. Meanwhile, Cochran continued his television appearances in programs that included *The Untouchables*, *The Twilight Zone*, and *The Virginian*, and was seen in such big-screen features as *The Deadly Companions* (1961), notable primarily as the directorial debut of famed director Sam Peckinpah, and *Of Love and Desire* (1963), a poorly scripted film that marked Merle Oberon's return to pictures after a seven-year absence.

In August 1964, while shooting his next film, *Mozambique*, in South Africa, Cochran once again found himself the topic of unflattering press coverage when he was arrested on a civil court order brought by a local jockey who accused him of adultery. The jockey, Arthur Cecil Miller, sought $5,000 in damages, claiming that Cochran had been having an affair with his wife, who had a small role in the film. The following month, a high court judge cleared Cochran of all charges and threw out the jockey's claim. Cochran angrily stressed his innocence to *Los Angeles Herald Examiner* columnist Harrison Carroll.

"It didn't happen and the fellow didn't have a shred of evidence," the actor said. "He submitted what he said was a love letter [to his wife] from me. You know what it said? 'To Heather, nice to have worked with you.

Aloha, Steve.' I gave autographs like that to a number of kids who worked in the film."

Having successfully dodged yet another scandal, Cochran was back in the newspapers just three months later when a 23-year-old singer, displaying a bruised and swollen face, told police that Cochran had beaten and gagged her during a quarrel at his Hollywood Hills home. The singer, Ronie Rae, told authorities that Cochran invited her to his home to audition for a part in a new film he was producing, *Captain O'Flynn*. After she accidentally spilled a drink on Cochran's floor, Rae claimed, a quarrel ensued, during which Cochran tied her hands and feet with neckties, beat her, and gagged her with a towel. She was able to eventually free herself, and arrange for her father and grandmother to pick her up, Rae said.

Cochran's account of the incident was vastly different. He agreed that Rae was at his home for an audition, and he also admitted that he had bound her with neckties, but he said that it was for her own protection because she has "hurtling herself about." The violence was initiated, Cochran stated, after Rae had consumed her second drink and took exception to the fact that the actor was ignoring a tape of her songs.

"I didn't want to embarrass her by saying, 'Horrible. Awful. Can't stand it. Go home!'" he explained. So instead, he went upstairs, the actor said, and Rae threw herself to the floor, smashed furniture, and butted her head against the fireplace. "She appeared to be on some kind of pills," Cochran said, adding that when her father arrived to pick Rae up, his first words were, "She's been on those pills again." Just five days after the news broke, Cochran was cleared of all charges. In fact, officials declared that the actor "may have done [Rae] a great service, by tying her up."

Although Cochran had emerged from this potential disaster virtually unscathed, the uproar involving Rae was a tragic omen of things to come. The film for which the actress was auditioning, *Captain O'Flynn*, was to be based on the real-life adventures of Lee

Quinn, a ship captain who in 1963 began a voyage in the Pacific aboard his ketch with an all-girl crew. Cochran was intrigued with the idea of bringing Quinn's story to the big screen, and in 1965 the actor decided to enact a first-hand tryout of the adventure. Out of a pool of nearly 200 female applicants, he hired three Mexican women, Eva Montero Castellano, 25, a seamstress; Eugenia Bautista Zacarias, 19, a laundress; and Lorenza de la Rosa, 14, to accompany him on an eight-day sailing trip from Acapulco down the Pacific Coast to Costa Rica, where the picture was to be filmed on location.

Cochran and his "crew" set sail on June 5, 1965. It would be his last adventure. Three weeks later, on June 26, 1965, the actor's 40-foot schooner was towed into the Guatemala port of Champerico. On board were the three Mexican women — and the dead body of Steve Cochran. Officials later determined that the 49-year-old actor had fallen ill from acute infection edema — a paralyzing lung ailment — during the voyage and died 10 days after departing from Acapulco. For nearly two weeks, the Mexican women drifted helplessly in the schooner until being rescued in Guatemala.

The Hollywood community was stunned by Cochran's strange and sudden death. But his 23-year-old estranged wife, Jonna Jensen, wasted no time in laying claim to his money. Just four days after the actor's body was discovered, Jensen filed a petition in Los Angeles Superior Court for letters of administration over his estate, estimated to be worth $150,000. The following day, the actor's 79-year-old mother, Rose Cochran, filed a similar petition of her own, pointing out the fact that her son's widow had filed for divorce. She also cited a post-nuptial agreement signed by her son and his wife which stipulated that all of their property was to remain separate. The agreement further stated that Jensen would receive one-third of his estate — only if there was no action pending for divorce for separate maintenance. In July, a Superior Court judge appointed both Jensen and Cochran's mother as temporary administrators of his estate, but three months later, Jensen was

named sole administrator. It was a seedy footnote to an already-gruesome set of circumstances. (After his death, Cochran's last two films were released — *Mozambique* [1966], the picture he made in South Africa, and *Tell Me in the Sunlight* [1967], which marked the actor's big-screen directorial debut.)

Although Steve Cochran was typed as the heavy throughout his career, he nonetheless demonstrated in numerous movies that he had a genuine talent, and he will be remembered for his unforgettable portrayals in films such as *White Heat*, *Storm Warning*, and *Inside the Walls of Folsom Prison*. Despite his brushes with the law in his personal life, Cochran seemed to be more of a reckless adventurer than any kind of real menace, and while his acting career appeared to be waning at the time of his death, he was just starting in a new director as a director and producer. Because of these realities, his premature end is that much more tragic.

Film Noir Filmography

The Chase. Director: Arthur Ripley. Producer: Seymour Nebenzal. Running time: 86 minutes. Released by United Artists, November 22, 1946. Cast: Michele Morgan, Robert Cummings, Steve Cochran, Lloyd Corrigan, Jack Holt, Don Wilson, Alexis Minotis, Nina Koschetz, Peter Lorre, Yolanda Lacca, James Westerfield, Jimmy Ames, Shirley O'Hara.

White Heat. Director: Raoul Walsh. Producer: Lou Edelman. Running time: 114 minutes. Released by Warner Bros., September 2, 1949. Cast: James Cagney, Virginia Mayo, Edmond O'Brien, Margaret Wycherly, Steve Cochran, John Archer, Wally Cassell, Fred Clark, Ford Rainey, Fred Coby, G. Pat Collins, Mickey Knox, Paul Guilfoyle, Robert Osterloh, Ian MacDonald, Ray Montgomery. Awards: Academy Award nomination for Best Motion Picture Story (Virginia Kellogg).

The Damned Don't Cry. Director: Vincent Sherman. Producer: Jerry Wald. Running time: 103 minutes. Released by Warner Bros., May 13, 1950. Cast: Joan Crawford, David Brian, Steve Cochran, Kent Smith, Hugh Sanders, Selena Royle, Jacqueline de Wit, Morris Ankrum, Sara Perry, Richard Egan, Jimmy Moss, Edith Evanson, Eddie Marr.

Private Hell 36. Director: Don Siegel. Producer: Collier Young. Running time: 81 minutes. Released by Filmakers, September 3, 1954. Cast: Ida Lupino, Steve Cochran, Howard Duff, Dean Jagger, Dorothy Malone, Bridget Duff.

The Beat Generation. Director: Charles Haas. Producer: Albert Zugsmith. Running time: 93 minutes. Released by MGM, October 21, 1959. Cast: Steve Cochran, Mamie Van Doren, Ray Danton, Fay Spain, Louis Armstrong and his All Stars, Maggie Hayes, Jackie Coogan, Jim Mitchum, Cathy Crosby, Ray Anthony, Dick Contino, Irish McCalla, Vampira, Billy Daniels, Maxie Rosenbloom, Charles Chaplin, Jr., Anne Anderson.

References

"$405,000 Suit Charges Actor Beat Up Guest." *Los Angeles Times*, March 5, 1952.

"Actor Called Adulterer in Jockey's Suit." *Los Angeles Times*, August 17, 1964.

"Actor Steve Cochran Cleared in 'Beating.'" *Los Angeles Herald Examiner*, December 9, 1964.

"Actor Cleared of Adultery." *Los Angles Herald Examiner*, September 13, 1964.

"Actor Denies Flying Plane Recklessly." *Los Angeles Times*, October 6, 1956.

"Actor Denies Guilt in Race with Police." *Los Angeles Daily News*, November 19, 1953.

"Actor's Mother Seeks Control of His Estate." *Los Angeles Times*, July 1, 1965.

"Astor Handles 'Il Grido' at 35%." *Variety*, July 26, 1961.

Bowe, Edwina. "Singer's Own Fault She Was Hurt, Says Cochran." *Los Angeles Herald-Examiner*, December 6, 1964.

"Cochran's Widow Asks Estate Post." *Hollywood Citizen-News*, June 30, 1965.

Cochran, Steve. "The Role I Liked Best." *Saturday Evening Post*, circa 1951.

Glass, George. Biography of Steve Cochran. Samuel Goldwyn Productions, circa 1945.

"Damages Won from Actor Cochran Cut." *Los Angeles Times*, July 16, 1953.

"Ex-Pug Suing Steve Cochran Wins $16,000." *Los Angeles Times*, June 6, 1953.

Hyams, Joe. "Steve Cochran — 'Nice Thug.'" *New York Herald Tribune*, August 18, 1958.

"Jockey Links Wife and Actor." *New York Daily News*, August 17, 1964.

"Kin Await Cochran's Body." *Los Angeles Herald-Examiner*, June 28, 1965.

Letter to the Editor. *Filmland*, December 1956.

"Mom, Widow Administer Actor Estate." *Hollywood Citizen-News*, July 24, 1965.

"Police Bullet Brings Halt to Steve Cochran's Auto." *Hollywood Citizen-News*, November 9, 1953.

Salazar, Ruben. "Actor's Sea Death to Lung Attack." *Los Angeles Times*, June 28, 1965.

Scott, Vernon. "Steve Cochran Declined Film Offer from Yugoslavian Reds." *New York Morning Telegraph*, May 14, 1957.

"Screen Actor Greets Press." *Newark Evening News*, September 16, 1954.

"Steve Cochran's Car Halted by Police Gunfire." *Los Angeles Times*, November 9, 1953.

"Steve Cochran Fined $500 for Reckless Flying." *Los Angeles Times*, October 25, 1956.

"Steve Cochran Gagged, Beat Her, Singer Says." *Los Angeles Times*, December 4, 1964.

"Steve Cochran Widow Administers Estate." *Variety*, October 12, 1965.

"Testing New Auto, He Says." *Los Angeles Daily News*, November 9, 1953.

Thompson, Howard. "Plans Discussed by Steve Cochran." *New York Times*, October 21, 1962.

WILLIAM CONRAD

"Things have changed around here ... I'm 60 percent legitimate now. I'm what you might call a pretty big man. You know, big men don't scare easily." — William Conrad in *Cry Danger* (1951)

Most familiar to modern audiences for his television roles in the popular series *Cannon* and *Jake and the Fatman*, William Conrad possessed talents that stretched far beyond his portrayals of stocky lawmen. During his 50-year career, he served in such varied capacities as producer, director, and even lyricist; he portrayed characters on an estimated 7,500 radio broadcasts; and his distinctive baritone voice can be heard on numerous television programs including *The Adventures of Bullwinkle and Rocky* and *The Fugitive*. While Conrad's screen career consisted of less than 40 features, the actor nonetheless offered a memorable presence in six films noirs: *The Killers* (1946), *Body and Soul* (1947), *Sorry, Wrong Number* (1948), *Tension* (1949), *Cry Danger* (1951), and *The Racket* (1951).

The portly, mustachioed actor was born William Cann in Louisville, Kentucky, on September 27, 1920. The son of a theater owner, he once maintained that a career in the field of entertainment was almost inevitable.

"It all came about so naturally that I was never consciously aware of my desire for 'showbiz' until I had fallen right in the middle of it," Conrad said in 1971. "My father, from the time I was two years old, had been a motion picture exhibitor, and I suppose it never occurred to me to do anything else but be an actor."

When young William was seven years old, his family moved to Los Angeles, California, and after his graduation from Excelsior High School in nearby Bellflower, he enrolled as a literature and drama major at Fullerton Junior College. It was while he was a student at the latter institution that William got his first taste of performing.

"I started hanging around a small radio station hidden behind a gas station in Beverly Hills," Conrad once recalled. "That station was and is today KMPC, but it took a long time to really land a job there. I hung around and did odd jobs here and there. Finally, one guy said, 'We gotta give the kid something.' I'll never forget that first check. I should have saved it. But in those days I needed the money. The stub said, 'For the two-week period ending so-and-so for acting, writing, producing, directing, and singing.' I think the amount was $2.75!"

Changing his last name to Conrad, the actor was heard on numerous radio broadcasts, and in his spare time, he took signing lessons that revealed an impressive bass voice with a three-octave range. But with the onset of World War II in 1942, Conrad's burgeoning radio career was interrupted and he signed up with the United States Air Force, serving in World War II for the next four years as a fighter pilot. During a 1943 furlough, Conrad

married a non-professional, June Nelson, but the couple later divorced. The actor married again in 1958, to former fashion model Susan Randall, with whom he later had a son, Charles. He would remain married to Susan until her death in 1979, after a two-year battle with cancer. The following year, Conrad would take a final trip down the aisle, marrying Tippy Huntley, the widow of famed newsman Chet Huntley.

Meanwhile, after his release from the service, Conrad was immediately thrust into the world of film noir, debuting on the big screen in *The Killers* (1946). In this tautly directed thriller, Conrad plays a hired assassin by the name of Max who, along with his partner, Al (Charles McGraw), opens the picture with a literal bang. Searching for a small-town gas station attendant known as "the Swede" (Burt Lancaster), Max and Al terrorize a trio of men inside a local diner where the Swede is a regular customer. ("I'll tell you what's going to happen. We're gonna kill the Swede," Max nonchalantly reveals. "He never had a chance to do anything to us, he never even seen us. We're killin' him for a friend.") When he doesn't show, the men find the Swede in his apartment and wordlessly gun him down as he lies in bed. The remainder of the film focuses on a series of flashbacks that reveal the reasons behind the Swede's murder, including his obsession with the duplicitous Kitty (Ava Gardner), his association with a double-crossing gang leader, "Big Jim" Colfax (Albert Dekker), and a $250,000 payroll heist. In his small but pivotal role, Conrad was mostly overlooked by critics, but the reviewer for *Variety* wrote that the "performances without exception are top quality," and in *Motion Picture Herald*, William R. Weaver labeled the film "an elaborate and cunningly wrought expansion of the Ernest Hemingway short story of the same title."

The following year, Conrad remained in the realm of noir with his sole screen appearance of 1947, *Body and Soul*. This riveting feature told the story of prizefighter Charlie Davis (John Garfield), following his triumphant climb from amateur fighter to boxing champion, and the loved ones he steps over to reach the top, from his best pal, Shorty Polaski (Joseph Pevney), to his faithful, long-time girlfriend, Peg (Lilli Palmer). As Quinn, Conrad portrayed a corrupt promoter who first encounters the boxer in a neighborhood saloon, but is unmoved by Shorty's efforts to sell him on Charlie's merits: "I've seen knock-outs before," Quinn says. "So what. Kids win this and that everyday. Thousands of 'em. One out of a hundred fights professionally, one out of a thousand's worth watching. One out of a million's worth coffee and doughnuts. Tell your boy to get an honest job." It doesn't take long, however, for Quinn to recognize Charlie's talent in the ring, and he becomes his manager, benefiting from the boxer's rise to fame and fortune, then betraying him by making a deal with another promoter for Charlie to take a dive in his title fight. Along with the other members of the film's supporting cast, Conrad earned mention from several reviewers, including Lowell E. Redelings of the *Hollywood Citizen-News*, who noted his "credible work," the *Los Angeles Daily News*' Virginia Wright, who praised his "effective" performance, and Bosley Crowther of

the *New York Times*, who found the actor "revolting as a punk."

After roles in such pictures as *Four Faces West* (1948), a well-done western starring Joel McCrea, and *To the Victor* (1948), a drama set in post–World War II France, Conrad returned to film noir, with appearances in *Sorry, Wrong Number* (1948) and *Tension* (1949). The first, hailed by one critic as a "real chiller," begins as a bedridden heiress, Leona Stevenson (Barbara Stanwyck), overhears a telephone conversation in which two men plot a woman's murder. Although the call is disconnected before the name of the woman is revealed, Leona discovers through a series of frantic telephone calls that her husband, Henry (Burt Lancaster), has been involved in a scheme to steal from the drug company owned by her father and that Henry is being blackmailed by a former partner — played by Conrad — for $200,000. Leona also learns that she is the intended victim of the murder plot — which has been engendered by her husband. Although Henry later has a change of heart, it is too late for Leona, and Henry is forced to listen to his wife's horrified screams as the murderer enters her bedroom.

In his sole scene in the film, Conrad's character, Morano, offers a menacing presence cloaked beneath a façade of amiability as he informs Henry and his partner, a drug company chemist (Harold Vermilyea), that his organization has "unanimously" voted to kill them. "You see, Stevenson, since you went into business for yourself, we've suffered quite a loss," Morano tells him. "Now — if you were to turn back what you've accumulated and pay us, say, $200,000 — for our injured feelings — I might get the board to reconsider their decision. Provided, of course, that both of you continue working under our humble supervision."

After his sinister role as the blackmailer in *Sorry, Wrong Number*, Conrad switched to the right side of the law for his fourth film noir, *Tension*. Here, the actor portrayed Lt. Edgar "Blackie" Gonsales who, along with his partner, Collier Bonnabel (Barry Sullivan), investigates the murder of a wealthy local man, Barney Deager (Lloyd Gough). The complex case hinges on an unassuming drug store manager, Warren Quimby (Richard Basehart), and his gold-digging wife, Claire (Audrey Totter). Although the detectives soon focus their investigation on a man known as Paul Sothern, they discover that locating him is more difficult than they would have imagined: "There is no Paul Sothern," Gonsales informs his partner. "Get a load of this—not in the phone directories, has no car ownership, he's not on any payroll, no hotel registry, no hospital cards on him, no charge accounts, never took out any insurance, he doesn't take milk from a milkman, doesn't have a newspaper delivered, and he's got no police record. All we've gotta do is find him." It turns out that Sothern is actually Warren Quimby, whose wife was having an affair with the dead man—and who is trapped by Bonnabel into confessing that she is the real killer. Although the film is a memorable offering from the noir era, it was panned upon its release; in a typical review, Floyd Stone wrote in *Motion Picture Herald*: "Its story is simple, and if the pace had been rapid and the length shorter, there might have emerged an excellent program film."

During the next two years, Conrad played such varied roles as a police lieutenant in *East Side, West Side*, a so-so soaper with Barbara Stanwyck and James Mason; a crooked dice shooter in *Any Number Can Play* (1949), starring Clark Gable; an ill-fated bartender named Chuckles in *Dial 1119* (1950); and a French major in the swashbuckling adventure *The Sword of Monte Cristo* (1951). He also added two more features to his noir repertoire, *Cry Danger* (1951) and *The Racket* (1951). In the first, he played Castro, an unctuous racketeer who is marked for revenge by ex-con Rocky Mulloy (Dick Powell), recently released after a five-year prison stretch for a murder and $100,000 robbery he didn't commit. The other principal players in the story are Nancy Morgan (Rhonda Fleming), the wife of Rocky's still-imprisoned partner, Danny; Delong (Richard Erdman), an ami-

able, hard-drinking marine who manufactured the alibi that earned Rocky's release; Darlene (Jean Porter), Delong's girlfriend, whom he describes as "a part-time model and a full-time pickpocket"; and Lt. Gus Cobb (Regis Toomey), a dogged police detective who teams with Rocky to discover that Castro hired Danny to commit the robbery, framed Rocky for the crime, then tried to murder him—resulting in the death of Darlene. As Castro, the third-billed Conrad played his most distinctive film noir appearance; in a chillingly memorable scene, he is forced to confess to his crimes when Rocky repeatedly fires a gun at his head in "Russian Roulette" fashion. For his standout performance, Conrad was singled out in the *New York Times* for "play[ing] the heavy with unctuous delight," and the critic for *Variety* praised the feature as possessing "all the ingredients for a suspenseful melodrama.

In *The Racket*, the last of Conrad's films noirs, the actor was featured as Sgt. Turck, a member of the state's attorney's special investigations department who is far less upstanding and far more corrupt than his impressive title might suggest. On the payroll of the city's powerful organized crime mob, Turck works to stymie the efforts of police captain Tom McQuigg (Robert Mitchum) to nab his nemesis, Nick Scanlon (Robert Ryan), a seemingly untouchable mobster. Scanlon's increasingly violent tendencies contrasts with his more business-like superiors, however, and when mob bosses determine that he is expendable, it is Turck who gets the nod to get rid of him—while in custody, as Scanlon tries to escape from an open window, Turck shoots and kills him. Conrad's portrayal of the intelligent but deadly official represented a fitting conclusion to his film noir career.

Between films during this period, Conrad provided the narration for a short-lived television anthology series, *Escape*, and lent his distinctive speaking voice to numerous radio programs, including *Johnny Modero: Pier 23*, *Nightbeat*, *Suspense*, *Strange Wills*, and *Jeff Regan, Investigator*. In 1952, he took on the role of Marshal Matt Dillon on the

William Conrad, Robert Mitchum, and Ray Collins in *The Racket* (1951).

popular radio series *Gunsmoke*, which ran until 1961. Throughout the remainder of the 1950s, Conrad divided his time between his radio projects and such feature films as *The Desert Song* (1953), a horrid musical starring Raymond Massey as a dastardly sheik; *Cry of the Hunted* (1953), a chase film with Barry Sullivan and Vittorio Gassman; *The Conqueror* (1956), a notoriously bad epic starring John Wayne as Genghis Khan; and *The Ride Back* (1957), in which Conrad portrayed a law enforcement officer who tracks down a fugitive played by Anthony Quinn. In addition to its first-rate performances, the latter film was notable as Conrad's first outing as a feature film producer. The following year, the actor further expanded his repertoire when he added directing to his growing list of abilities.

"Directing always held a certain fascination for me and the thought of one day producing seemed like an impossible dream," Conrad said in 1971. "Acting, at that time, struck me as a kind of child's play and that a man should have more responsibility in life than just being an actor. With this in mind I decided to set my goals toward becoming a director and a producer. I wanted the business end of television and motion pictures."

Conrad began his career behind the camera at Ziv Studios, one of the top 10 production companies during the early days of television. In his directorial debut, he helmed an episode of the television show *Target*, hosted by veteran screen star Adolphe Menjou, then agreed to perform in five episodes of the popular western series *Bat Masterson* on the condition that he be allowed to direct five episodes. As it turned out, Conrad retired from acting after appearing in only one segment of the show, and went on to serve as director on such television series as *This Man Dawson* (which he also produced), *General Electric True* (produced by fellow actor Jack Webb), the TV version of *Gunsmoke* (he was rejected for the screen role of Marshal Dillon because of his balding pate and ever-increasing girth), *Naked City*, *Men Into Space*, and *Temple Houston*. He was also brought in as producer and director in an effort to boost the sagging ratings of the "hip" detective series, *77 Sunset Strip*, which was produced by Warner Brothers television. Following Conrad's work on the series, he was hired to direct several feature films for Warners.

"I was producing *77 Sunset Strip* and my contract expired on a Friday. I was putting my junk in my car when I was told Jack Warner was calling me," Conrad recalled in a 1966 *Los Angeles Times* interview. "Since I had seen Mr. Warner only once or twice in two years, I thought one of the guys was putting me on. But it was really Mr. Warner, who got me at home about two hours later and said, 'I want you to act, to direct, to produce — do anything you want.'"

Conrad went on to direct several films for Warners, including *The Man from Galveston* (1965), which was the pilot for the series *Temple Houston* and was originally slated for television airing, and *My Blood Runs Cold* (1965), a tepid thriller starring Joey Heatherton and Troy Donahue. He was both producer and director for the horror film *Two on a Guillotine* (1965), and *Brainstorm* (1965), a suspenser with Jeffrey Hunter, Anne Francis, and Dana Andrews; and producer for *An American Dream* (1966), *Covenant with Death* (1967), *The Cool Ones* (1967), *First to Fight* (1967), and *Chubasco* (1968), for which he also served as lyricist. During this period, Conrad was also hired as executive producer for Warner Brothers television.

"I'm having an absolute ball," Conrad said in 1966. "I can't stand doing nothing."

In addition to his work behind the scenes during the 1960s, Conrad kept a hand in the performing end of the business, providing narration for such series as *The Adventures of Bullwinkle and Rocky*, *The Fugitive*, *The Invaders*, *The March of Time*, *George of the Jungle*, and *The Dudley-Do-Right Show*. But late in the decade, he was convinced by a friend to step back in front of the camera, which led to a second acting career. After playing the role of a longshoreman's union boss in the hit television series *In the Name of the Game*, Conrad was tapped for the lead role in a new detective series, *Cannon*. Unlike most television detectives up until that time, Frank Cannon was — as described by Conrad — "a nonglamorous, rather portly private eye who has a weight problem and doesn't always outwit the villain."

"I guess Cannon is the kind of guy a lot of people can identify with," he said.

Despite his many years in the entertainment business, Conrad earned the honor of "Most Promising New Male TV Star" from *Motion Picture Daily-Television Today* after the first season of *Cannon*. Although the show enjoyed a successful run on CBS-TV from 1971 to 1976, however, Conrad later expressed disappointment with the series.

"Most of television is crap. *Cannon* was crap," he said shortly after the show left the air. "I was delighted to see it cancelled."

After *Cannon*, Conrad appeared in two short-lived television series, *Keefer*, where he played a Lisbon bar owner during World War II, and *Nero Wolfe*, in which he portrayed the title role of the orchid-loving detective. He was also seen in such made-for-television movies as *Night Cries* (1978), *The Return of Frank Cannon* (1980), *Shocktrauma* (1982), and *The Mikado* (1982), the Gilbert and Sullivan musical in which he surprised viewers with his singing ability. Briefly returning to the big screen, Conrad played the head of a local syndicate in *Moonshine Country Express* (1977), and later provided the narration for three television series, *Tales of the Unexpected* (1977), *Buck Rogers in the 25th Century* (1979) and *Manimal* (1983).

Then, in 1987, Conrad landed the lead

role in his second successful series, *Jake and the Fatman*, a spinoff of an episode of the popular Andy Griffith legal series, *Matlock*. As Jason Lochinvar "Fatman" McCabe, Conrad portrayed a curmudgeonly, slovenly former cop turned Honolulu district attorney with a weakness for Hawaiian shirts and baseball caps. Although the series was a modest hit, Conrad soon became disillusioned with the writing of the show, and said at one point, "I want to get out. When I say what I think, I get in trouble." Still, the actor remained with the series throughout its five-year run, and was later praised by the show's executive producer.

"[Conrad] could be irascible and very blunt and direct in his opinions," said Dean Hargrove, "but underneath it all he was a very decent, thoughtful, and considerate gentleman."

Prior to the cancellation of *Jake and the Fatman*, Conrad was tapped as the narrator for *Hudson Hawk* (1991), a critical and financial disaster starring Bruce Willis. It would be his last feature film performance. On February 11, 1994, the actor suffered a heart attack at his home and died later at the North Hollywood Medical Center. He was 73 years old.

William Conrad will primarily be remembered for his television series roles, but his prolific radio appearances earned him a posthumous induction in 1997 in the Radio Hall of Fame. In addition to his radio and television work, however, he should also be honored for the versatility that allowed him to wear the hats of producer, director, executive, and one of the greatest screen heavies of film noir.

"You get a guy like Bill, he simply wasn't concerned about whether he was successful or not," Conrad's wife, Tippy, said after his death. "He just had a strong notion about what he wanted and he went ahead and did it."

Film Noir Filmography

The Killers. Director: Robert Siodmak. Producer: Mark Hellinger. Running time: 105 minutes. Released by Universal, August 28, 1946. Cast: Edmond O'Brien, Ava Gardner, Albert Dekker, Sam Levene, John Miljan, Virginia Christine, Vince Barnett, Burt Lancaster, Charles D. Brown, Donald MacBride, Phil Brown, Charles McGraw, William Conrad, Queenie Smith, Garry Owen, Harry Hayden, Bill Walker, Jack Lambert, Jeff Corey, Wally Scott, Gabrielle Windsor, Rex Dale. Awards: Academy Award nominations for Best Director (Robert Siodmak), Best Film Editing (Arthur Hilton), Best Score/Drama or Comedy (Miklos Rozsa), Best Screenplay (Anthony Veiller).

Body and Soul. Director: Robert Rossen. Producer: Bob Roberts. Running time: 105 minutes. Released by United Artists, August 22, 1947. Cast: John Garfield, Lilli Palmer, Hazel Brooks, Anne Revere, William Conrad, Joseph Pevney, Canada Lee, Lloyd Goff, Art Smith, James Burke, Virginia Gregg, Peter Virgo, Joe Devlin, Shirmin Rushkin, Mary Currier, Milton Kibbie, Tim Ryan, Artie Dorrell, Cy Ring, Glen Lee, John Indrisano, Dan Tobey. Awards: Academy Award for Best Film Editing (Francis Lyon, Robert Parrish). Academy Award nominations for Best Actor (John Garfield), Best Original Screenplay (Abraham Polonsky).

Sorry, Wrong Number. Director: Anatole Litvak. Producers: Hal B. Wallis, Anatole Litvak. Running time: 98 minutes. Released by Paramount, September 1, 1948. Cast: Barbara Stanwyck, Burt Lancaster, Ann Richards, Wendell Corey, Harold Vermilyea, Ed Begley, Leif Erickson, William Conrad, John Bromfield, Jimmy Hunt, Dorothy Neumann, Paul Fierro. Awards: Academy Award nomination for Best Actress (Barbara Stanwyck).

Tension. Director: John Berry. Producer: Robert Sisk. Running time: 95 minutes. Released by MGM, January 11, 1950. Cast: Richard Basehart, Audrey Totter, Cyd Charisse, Barry Sullivan, Lloyd Gough, Tom D'Andrea, William Conrad, Tito Renaldo.

Cry Danger. Director: Robert Parrish. Producers: Sam Wiesenthal and W.R. Frank. Running time: 79 minutes. Released by RKO, February 21, 1951. Cast: Dick Powell, Rhonda Fleming, Richard Erdman, William Conrad, Regis Toomey, Jean Porter, Jay Adler, Joan Banks, Gloria Saunders, Hy Averback, Renny McEvoy, Lou Lubin, Benny Burt.

The Racket. Director: John Cromwell. Producer: Edmund Grainger. Running time: 88 minutes. Released by RKO, December 12, 1951. Cast: Robert Mitchum, Lizabeth Scott, Robert Ryan, William Talman, Ray Collins, Joyce MacKenzie, Robert Hutton, Virginia Huston, William Conrad, Walter Sande, Les Tremayne, Don Porter, Walter Baldwin, Brett King, Richard Karlan, Tito Vuolo.

References

Biography of William Conrad. Paramount Studios, circa 1954.

Biography of William Conrad. Warner Bros. Studios, August 1966.

Bourdain, G.S. "William Conrad, Actor, Is Dead; Star of Fatman Series Was 73." *New York Times*, February 13, 1994.

Conrad, William. "30 Years in Showbiz." *The Hollywood Reporter*, circa 1971.

Corwin, Miles. "William Conrad; Star of Cannon, Fatman." *Los Angeles Times*, February 12, 1994.

Davies, Jonathan. "Conrad into Hall of Fame as Radio's Marshal Dillon." *The Hollywood Reporter*, August 12, 1997.

Fury, David. "Many Careers of William Conrad." *Classic Images*, November 1988.

"Hall of Famers." *Los Angeles Times*, August 15, 1997.

Laurent, Lawrence. "Cannon Guns Down Rivals." *The Washington Post*, July 30, 1975.

"Man of Substance." *People*, February 28, 1994.

McClay, Howard. "Conrad Has Top Spot in RKO's Conqueror." *Los Angeles Daily News*, June 10, 1954.

Natale, Richard. "Heart Attack Claims Conrad, 73." *Variety*, February 14, 1994.

Obituary. *The London Times*, February 14, 1994.

Obituary. *Variety*, February 21, 1994.

Smith, Cecil. "A Private Eye Steals the Show." *Los Angeles Times*, December 5, 1974.

_____. "Conrad Stars in Nero Wolfe." *Los Angeles Times*, January 3, 1981.

_____. "Eight-Course Series for Epicurean Eye." *Los Angeles Times*, August 7, 1980.

Thomas, Kevin. "Conrad Sees Green in Future." *Los Angeles Times*, July 6, 1966.

"William Conrad, Cannon, Dies." *The Hollywood Reporter*, February 14, 1994.

RICHARD CONTE

"He used to be my boss. Now I'm his.... First is first and second is nobody." — Richard Conte in *The Big Combo* (1955)

Swarthy and sophisticated, with an intense gaze and an enigmatic smile, Richard Conte was made for the big screen. But his path to Hollywood contained a number of detours — before finally setting his sights on an acting career, Conte worked such widely varying jobs as truck driver, waiter, floor walker, stock boy, Wall Street messenger, and piano player — and even cut hair at 35 cents a head. Once he made it to Tinseltown, the handsome Italian actor was seen in such memorable features as *I'll Cry Tomorrow* (1955), *Full of Life* (1956), *Ocean's Eleven* (1960), and *The Godfather* (1972), and played opposite some of the screen's top stars, including Susan Hayward, Anne Baxter, and Gene Tierney. He was also featured in an impressive collection of 10 features from the film noir era: *Somewhere in the Night* (1946), *Call Northside 777* (1948), *Cry of the City* (1948), *House of Strangers* (1949), *Thieves' Highway* (1949), *The Sleeping City* (1950), *The Blue Gardenia* (1953), *New York Confidential* (1954),

The Big Combo (1955), and *The Brothers Rico* (1957).

Nicholas Peter Conte was born on March 24, 1910, in Jersey City, New Jersey, one of two children of Julie and Pasquale Conte, a neighborhood barber who insisted that his son take piano and art lessons. As a child, however, Conte lacked direction; at P.S. 32 and, later, at Dickinson High School, he was only a mediocre student, spending more time drawing pictures than on his studies. Away from school, he played the piano and organized a jazz band known as the Moonlight Rhythm Boys.

"It took me five years to finish the four-year [high school] course," Conte admitted.

After graduating, Conte took the first job that came along, working as a messenger on Wall Street. Later, he worked a long and varied series of jobs, quitting when he got bored or getting fired for failing to perform his duties — he once recalled losing a floor walker job at a department store for "permitting women to wear more clothes out of the store than they had when they entered."

But Conte's life took on a focused direction during the summer of 1935, when he landed a position waiting tables at the Pinebrook Country Club in Connecticut. In addition to his other duties, Conte learned, he was required to entertain the guests.

"The Group Theatre from New York was putting on a play a week for the camp clientele. Joe Pevney was entertainment director," Conte recalled in a 1953 *Los Angeles Times* interview. "One day he says to me, 'You're going to be in a musical.' I said he was out of his mind, that I couldn't sing or dance. His only answer to that was, 'It's part of your job!'"

Conte was given a few lines to read from a play about a man unjustly accused of murder. During the reading, the actor said that he "became very moved by what I was reading and started trembling and crying." Impressed by his performance, one of the Group Theatre members suggested that Conte pursue a career in acting, and later arranged a scholarship for him to attend the Neighborhood Playhouse in New York.

"When I went to that school, you couldn't understand a word I said from a diction point of view," Conte said. "It was like my whole head was opened up and all this was poured in — Shakespeare, Moliere, Euripides, Ibsen, all the arts! I studied piano, painting, dancing — yes, with Martha Graham! I had found something at last with which I could make an emotional connection, and a new world opened up. I knew then that I didn't care whether I would eat or make any money. I just wanted to act."

Conte stayed at the Neighborhood Playhouse for two years, performing in stock during the summer at the Brattleboro Theatre in Massachusetts. He made his Broadway debut in *My Heart's in the Highlands*, the first play written by William Saroyan, then landed the title role in the road company of *Golden Boy*. Deciding to give Hollywood a try, Conte was immediately signed by 20th Century-Fox and given fourth-billing in his first film, a west-

ern called *Heaven with a Barbed Wire Fence* (1939). But after the film's release, he was unceremoniously dumped by the studio.

Undaunted, Conte returned to New York, spending the next several years in a succession of plays, including *Night Nurse, Heavenly Express, Somewhere in France, Press Time, Walk Into My Parlor*, and *Jason*. In 1942, after his performance in the latter production, famed critic George Jean Nathan proclaimed Conte "the year's most outstanding actor."

Conte's promising career on the stage was interrupted when he enlisted in the Army during World War II, where he spent most of his time in the entertainment detail. After nine months, he was given an honorable medical discharge and immediately returned to the stage, starring opposite Judith Anderson in the 1943 Broadway production of *The Family*. Although the play's run was short-lived, Conte's performance led to offers from several Hollywood studios. Ironically, the best offer came from 20th Century-Fox, which had dropped him less than four years earlier. Fox executives wanted to "Americanize" Conte's name by changing it to "Conty," but he refused. He compromised, however, by changing his first name — and Richard Conte was born.

Conte's first film under his new moniker was *Guadalcanal Diary* (1943), a first-rate wartime feature co-starring Preston Foster, Lloyd Nolan, and William Bendix. During filming, Conte married Ruth Strohm, a New York radio actress whom he had been dating for several years. In 1948, the couple adopted a baby, Mark, who would grow up to become a film editor on numerous feature films, including *Turner and Hooch* (1989), *Double Impact* (1991), *Posse* (1993), and *On the Sixth Day* (2000), and such television movies as *Hiroshima* (1995), *Too Rich: The Secret Life of Doris Duke* (1999), and *Sex, Lies and Obsession* (2001).

On-screen, Conte was next seen in *The Purple Heart* (1944), a harrowing war drama about a group of U.S. airmen tried as war criminals by the Japanese; *A Walk in the Sun* (1945), another well-done film set during the war, this time focusing on infantrymen assigned to capture an isolated farmhouse from the Germans; *The Spider* (1945), in which Conte was top-billed as a tough private detective in New Orleans; and *Somewhere in the Night* (1946), the first of his 10 films noirs.

This complex story focuses on an amnesiac, George Taylor (John Hodiak), who goes in search of his past with only two leads: a briefcase containing a gun and $5,000 from a man named Larry Cravat, and a note from a woman that reads in part: "I despise you now, and the memory of you. I'm ashamed for having loved you." Traveling to Los Angeles, Taylor is befriended by a nightclub singer, Christy Smith (Nancy Guild), who solicits the help of her boss, club owner Mel Philips (Conte). After meeting a series of unsavory characters—including a man, Anzelmo (Fritz Kortner), who describes himself as "once a great thief and magnificent scoundrel"—Taylor finally learns the truth: that *he* is Larry Cravat, that Mel Philips was his former partner, and that he stole $2 million from Philips before disappearing from town. He also learns that Philips wants his money back: "I've thought about you a lot ... for three years, about you and the money you stole from me," Philips tells Taylor/Cravat. "You're going to be a poor man now ... a dead man is a poor man." Before Philips can collect his money and make good his threat, however, he is stopped by a cunning detective (Lloyd Nolan), who shoots him after tracking him down at the local docks. For his performance as the duplicitous nightclub owner, Conte earned mostly good reviews; he was no doubt included in the *Los Angeles Examiner* critic's praise of the "fine characterization by the supporting actors" in the film, and in the *New York Times*, Bosley Crowther opined: "Lloyd Nolan, Richard Conte ... and several others are competent as varied pawns. Their performances are interesting; it's only too bad that they have such turbid and inconclusive things to do."

As Conte continued to add to his acting repertoire, he was also demonstrating his talent in other areas. Having maintained his longtime interest in drawing, the actor exhibited a collection of his paintings in the late 1940s at the Beverly Hills Hall of Art. He also signed a three-year contract with the Hallmark company to supply paintings for their greeting cards, earning $500 for each painting, and five percent of the gross sales on all cards that used his artwork. Conte continued to paint and exhibit his work throughout his career.

"It's a matter of self-use," Conte once said. "No matter how much talent you have at anything, you still have to work very hard at it to be good."

Meanwhile, after playing a murderous double agent in the spy thriller *13 Rue Madeleine* (1947), and a carefree race driver on loan to United Artists in *The Other Love* (1947), Conte appeared in five films noirs during the next three years: *Call Northside 777* (1948), *Cry of the City* (1948), *House of Strangers* (1949), *Thieves' Highway* (1949), and *The Sleeping City* (1950).

In the first of the five, *Call Northside 777* (1948), Conte played the supporting role of Frank Wiecek, whose false imprisonment for the murder of a policeman has sparked an ongoing campaign by his mother, Tillie (Kasia Orzazewski), to win his freedom. Tillie's efforts finally pay off when local reporter Jim McNeal (James Stewart) is assigned to investigate an advertisement Tillie placed in his newspaper, offering a $5,000 reward for the police officer's killers. Initially, McNeal is interested only in the increased readership engendered by the series of articles he pens, but his opinion begins to change when he is confronted by Wiecek at the prison: "I don't want you to write anymore about me and my family.... I'll stay here a thousand years, but you must not write any more about my wife, and my mother, and my boy. My mother is doing this for me — not to sell your papers." After later becoming convinced of Wiececk's innocence, McNeal works vigorously to earn his freedom and, after a series of dead-ends, succeeds in employing a police technique to refute the testimony of the chief witness in the case. Finally released from prison after 11 years, Wiecek announces to his family and McNeal, "It's a good world outside."

After earning praise for his "intensely sincere performance" as the wrongfully imprisoned man in *Northside*, Conte played a character whose guilt was never in question — Martin Rome in *Cry of the City* (1948). This tightly scripted feature focuses on a slew of distinctive characters, including Rome, a small-time hood who, according to one character, "has been committing crimes for the last five years" and, most recently, killed a cop during a botched robbery attempt; Teena (Debra Paget, in her film debut), Rome's innocent and unflaggingly loyal girlfriend; Niles (Berry Kroeger), an unscrupulous attorney; Rose Given (Hope Emerson), a local masseuse with a lethal technique; and Lt. Vittorio Candella (Victor Mature), a detective who is determined to bring Rome to justice. The lives of the various characters intermingle when Niles tries to force Rome into confessing to a jewel theft he didn't commit and Rome kills the attorney in self-defense, swipes the stolen goods, and tries to trade them to Rose in exchange for $5,000 in cash and tickets to South America. Rose endeavors to obtain the jewels by strangling Rome during a massage, but the hood double-crosses her and she is later arrested by police. Meanwhile, Candella catches up to Rome at a neighborhood church, where he has gone to meet Teena; when Rome tries to escape, he is gunned down in the street.

Conte earned raves for his standout portrait of the callous hoodlum in *Cry of the City*; Kay Proctor of the *Los Angeles Examiner* labeled him "excellent"; the *Los Angeles Times'* critic went a step further and judged that he was "perhaps too good"; and in the *New York Times*, Bosley Crowther raved: "Richard Conte's Martin Rome is not the flashy, gun-toting braggart. But as the indomitable and cruel killer he neatly uses his lines to accentuate a subdued characterization of a truly dangerous renegade." The actor earned similar accolades in his fourth film noir, *House of Strangers* (1949), described by one critic as a "rich, colorful, full-bodied drama of New

York's East Side." Here, Conte played attorney Max Monetti, the favorite son of Gino (Edward G. Robinson), a prominent, if unconventional, bank owner. When Max's father is arrested for his illegal banking practices, his three brothers refuse to help and Max winds up in jail for trying to bribe a juror. Max emerges from prison seven years later, bitterly vowing revenge on his siblings and refusing to heed the pleas of his faithful, long-time lover, Irene Bennett (Susan Hayward), who wants him to move with her to San Francisco. ("Vengeance is a rare wine," Max says. "I'm gonna get drunk on it.") After he reviews the events of his past, Max decides to abandon his vendetta, but his suspicious brothers refuse to believe Max's sudden change of heart and come close to murdering him. He manages to escape, however, when his brothers begin to turn on each other, and he ultimately leaves his past behind to make a new start with Irene. After the release of the film, Conte was hailed for his performance by several critics; the reviewer for *The Hollywood Reporter* labeled him "magnificent," and although Lloyd L. Sloan of the *Hollywood Citizen-News* gave a lukewarm review to the film itself, he found the acting to be "above average" and wrote that Conte "helps cover the poor story development with his interpretation of the young lawyer role."

In Conte's next noir, *Thieves' Highway* (1949), the actor portrayed Nick Garcos, a war veteran who returns from service to learn that his truck driver father (Morris Carnovsky) has been crippled following an accident on the road. Discovering that a corrupt San Francisco merchant, Mike Figlia (Lee J. Cobb), was responsible for the accident, Nick purchases a truckload of apples and drives across the country. Once there, Nick gets more than he bargained for — the exhausted veteran gets picked up by an attractive refugee, Rica (Valentina Cortesa), not knowing that she has been paid $50 by Figlia for the job. While Nick is sleeping in Rica's apartment, Figlia sells his cargo of prized apples, and although Nick forces the merchant to return the money, he is later beaten and robbed by a pair of Figlia's thugs. Ultimately, Nick beats Figlia into confessing that he caused the truck accident that maimed his father, Figlia is carted off to jail, and Nick prepares to begin a new life with Rica.

Conte, who was applauded in the *New York Times* for his "superb" performance, later named his role as Nick Garcos as one of his favorites, calling the character "an understandable, sympathetic character who faced a tough problem — the type of role that is very satisfying to play." After this feature, his last under his Fox contract, the actor signed with Universal and was promptly cast in his fifth consecutive noir, *The Sleeping City* (1950). Filmed on location at New York's Bellevue Hospital, this film opens with the shocking murder of a doctor, who is shot in the face at point-blank range. Posing as an intern, Detective Fred Rowan (Conte) is assigned to the case, but along the way he falls for Ann Sebastian (Coleen Gray), a hospital employee who is preoccupied with the illness of her young niece. When a second doctor at the hospital commits suicide, Rowan suspects a tie-in to the earlier murder, and his hunch proves correct — as it turns out, both doctors were in debt to the hospital's seemingly innocuous elevator operator, Pop Ware (Richard Taber), who supplemented his income by hustling doctors into placing bets for horse races. Rowan later learns that the deceased doctors had been forced to steal and sell hospital pharmaceuticals to cover their gambling losses, and that Ann Sebastian had signed the prescriptions necessary to obtain the drugs. Although Ann rationalizes her involvement by insisting that she needed the money to pay for her niece's treatments, Rowan reluctantly turns her over to police at the film's end.

Once again, Conte earned accolades for his performance; the critic for *Variety* judged that he "gives his usually plausible performance, underplaying in contrast to a number of the Broadway-recruited players with their tendency to overact," and Bosley Crowther wrote in the *New York Times* that the actor "does a thoroughly commendable job with the role.... He makes the ingenious detective

a remarkably sympathetic chap whose feeling for tired, impoverished interns is quite as sensitive as his quick deductive powers." Despite his spate of rave notices over the last several years, however, Conte was by now becoming increasingly outspoken in his views on moviemaking and acting. In a 1948 interview with columnist Lowell E. Redelings, Conte addressed the tendency of actors to pass off "stoicism" as a form of emoting.

"There's entirely too much 'brave' acting on the screen. It seems to be the fashion to go through fire, storm, war, and heartbreak with the same stoic expression," Conte said. "And you can't put over real drama with a face completely devoid of feeling. You'll find more drama on Hollywood Boulevard than on the sound stages. Too many actors are afraid they'll seem hammy if they act like people really do."

Conte put his theory to use in his next film, *Under the Gun* (1950), earning good reviews for his portrayal of a gambler sent to prison for murder. He followed this intriguing drama with roles as a racketeer in *The Raging Tide* (1951); a movie producer in *Hollywood Story* (1951); a rebellious goldminer in *The Raiders* (1952); a Mexican boxer in *The Fighter* (1952); and an Arab prince in *Desert Legion* (1953), which concluded his commitment with Universal. Now a freelancer, he returned to film noir, starring with Anne Baxter in *The Blue Gardenia* (1953).

In this feature — the weakest of the actor's 10 noirs — Conte played Casey Mayo, a newspaper reporter whose latest assignment focuses on the murder of a local artist and well-known womanizer, Harry Prebble (Raymond Burr). After unearthing a series of leads — including the fact that the killer is a blonde female — Casey pens an open letter to the "unknown murderess" in his newspaper: "By now, you must be frightened out of your wits," the letter reads. "You don't know which way to turn, there's no place to hide, nowhere to run. Except to me." Casey is soon contacted by Norah Larkin (Baxter), who tells him that her "friend" committed the crime, but cannot remember the details. As she grows to trust

the reporter, Norah meets Casey at a local diner and tells him the truth — jilted by her serviceman boyfriend in a "Dear Jane" letter, Norah had gone on a blind date with Prebble on the night of the murder. A half-dozen "Blue Gardenia" cocktails later, Norah accompanied Prebble to his house, where he tried to attack her, but she passed out and awakened to find him dead. During Norah's confession to Casey, she is overheard by a waiter at the diner, who contacts the authorities, and when police show up to arrest her a short time later, Norah accuses Casey of setting a "dirty trap." Feeling responsible for Norah's capture, Casey continues to pursue the case and ultimately learns that the murder was actually committed by Prebble's pregnant girlfriend, who killed him while Norah was passed out on the floor.

Helmed by Fritz Lang, *The Blue Gardenia* was greeted with mixed reviews upon its release; Lowell E. Redelings of the *Hollywood Citizen-News* termed the film "an average murder drama," and while David Bongard of the *Los Angeles Daily News* praised Conte's "seasoned performance," he found that if "Lang had been given a better script to direct,

it would have been a better movie." But Edwin Schallert disagreed in the *Los Angeles Times*, finding that the film "has both mood and intenseness, and is so good much of the way that you can almost stand for a banal and quite-to-be-expected climax."

During the next few years, Conte languished in a series of run-of-the-mill features, including *Slaves of Babylon* (1953), a biblical drama about the overthrow of Babylon; *A Race for Life* (1954), an automobile racing yarn; *Highway Dragnet* (1954), a low-budget crime feature; and *Target Zero*, a Korean War drama. He fared far better, however, with his next film noir appearance, in *New York Confidential* (1955).

Grim, fascinating, and unrelentingly violent, this feature centered on Charlie Lupo (Broderick Crawford), the head of a powerful New York syndicate boss; Lupo's daughter, Kathy (Anne Bancroft), who despises her father's work and claims that "decent people don't want me around — it's as if I had a disease"; and Nick Magellan (Conte), Lupo's right-hand man, aptly described by Kathy as "not like the rest of Papa's hoodlums. Like a cobra — always relaxed, yet always ready to strike." The action in the film depicts the ultimate demise of all three characters — increasingly disturbed by her status as a gangster's daughter, Kathy commits suicide; Lupo decides to expose the syndicate to the F.B.I. rather than take the rap for a high-profile murder, and is marked for death as a result; and Nick, who reluctantly accepts the assignment of killing his boss, is himself shot down by an unseen gunman after he carries out the job.

Following the release of *Confidential*, for which he was singled out for his "skillful acting," Conte starred opposite Susan Hayward in one of his best films, *I'll Cry Tomorrow* (1955), based on the life of singer Lillian Roth. He followed this first-rate feature with *The Big Tip-Off* (1955), a confusing crime drama, and *The Case of the Red Monkey* (1955), a tedious spy feature with a virtually unknown cast. In an interview with *New York Mirror-News* columnist Kendis Rochlen, Conte admitted that he had not been living up to his potential in his recent films.

"I think I'm a better actor than I've been shown to be on the screen so far," Conte said. "I'd say up to now I've only used 40 percent of my talent."

The actor used a considerably higher percentage of his abilities, however, when he starred with Cornel Wilde and Jean Wallace in his ninth film noir, *The Big Combo* (1955). Here, the actor starred as a vicious hood known as Mr. Brown, who was characterized by his sadistic treatment of his society girlfriend, Susan Lowell (Jean Wallace), and his contentious, cat-and-mouse relationship with police detective Leonard Diamond (Cornel Wilde). Diamond, who is not only obsessed with bringing Brown to justice, but is also in love with Susan, tries a number of unsuccessful approaches in his effort to nab the gangster, but succeeds only in being abducted by Brown and his hoods. In a particularly horrific scene, Brown mercilessly tortures the detective, first by blasting the volume in a hearing aid device that he places in Diamond's ear, and then by forcing Diamond to drink hair tonic containing 40 percent alcohol. ("Look at the drunken cop," Brown wryly observes. "Isn't that a shame.") Undeterred in his resolve to apprehend Brown, Diamond finally uncovers evidence that proves the mobster's role in the murder of his former boss. After learning that Brown plans to flee the country, Diamond confronts him in an isolated airplane hangar and, as Susan helps by continuously focusing a large spotlight on her lover, Diamond finally places him under arrest. Although *The Big Combo* stands up today as a superbly acted and tautly directed offering from the film noir era, critics were unimpressed upon the film's release; the reviewer for the *New York Times* acknowledged that Conte "does his level best as a cardboard-cut sadist," but he added that "it would have been wonderful to have heard someone simply ask for the time and get a straight answer. Both [screenwriter Philip Yordan] and director Joseph Lewis share responsibility for the open-throttle monotonous serving of

mayhem." The critic for *Variety* took a slightly less dim view; while dismissing the plot as "rambling" and "not too credible," he admitted that the film featured "grim dramatics that are hard-hitting ... [and] cut out to order for the meller fan who likes his action rough and raw."

The following year, Conte starred in another standout film of his career, *Full of Life* (1956), a touching comedy-drama in which he played the husband of Judy Holliday. And in 1957, he was seen in his final film noir appearance, *The Brothers Rico*. This late entry in the cycle starred Conte as Eddie Rico, an ex-gangster who has turned his life around, becoming the successful owner of a laundry business, and settling down with wife Alice (Dianne Foster), with whom he plans to adopt a baby. Eddie's blissful existence is rocked, however, with a dual punch—first, he learns that his kid brothers Gino (Paul Picerni) and Johnny (James Darren) were involved in a recent mob hit and have both disappeared. A short time later, Eddie is contacted by mob boss Sid Kubik (Larry Gates), whom Eddie regards as a trusted father figure. Kubik asks Eddie to locate Johnny, claiming that he wants to ensure his brother's safe exit from the country until the heat from the mob hit dies down. Reluctantly agreeing, Eddie later learns that he has been double-crossed by Kubik, who has already killed Gino, and wants Johnny found so that he can dispense the same fate. Unable to save the life of his second brother, Eddie kills Kubik during a gun battle, exposes the organized crime syndicate to authorities, and, in the final reel, is seen arriving at an orphanage with Alice to pick up their new baby. As had become the norm for Conte, he was applauded for his role in *The Brothers Rico*; in a typical review, the critic for the *Los Angeles Times* wrote that the performances in the film were "first-class," citing Conte as a "standout as the man who is finally disillusioned."

In 1960, Conte announced that he had formed an independent theatrical and television company, named Pinebrook after the Connecticut resort where he was first inspired to become an actor. He told reporters that the initial film produced by the company would be *Paradise Below*, in which he planned to star, but the film was never made, and the company was later dissolved. Instead, Conte was seen in small roles throughout the decade in such films as *Ocean's Eleven* (1960), a box-office smash featuring Frank Sinatra, Dean Martin, Sammy Davis, Jr., Angie Dickinson, and Cesar Romero; *Who's Been Sleeping in My Bed?* (1963), a sex comedy starring Dean Martin; *The Greatest Story Ever Told* (1965), a star-studded Biblical epic in which Conte portrayed the role of Barabbas; *Hotel* (1967), based on Arthur Hailey's best-selling novel; and *Tony Rome* (1967), an entertaining private-eye tale starring Frank Sinatra in the title role. Conte was also seen in *Extrana Invasion* (1965), one of more than 20 foreign films in which he appeared during the next decade; guested on several television series, including *Alfred Hitchcock Presents*, *The Untouchables*, and *Naked City*; and played an ex-gangster in the cast of the short-lived sitcom *The Jean Arthur Show*.

In 1963, Conte revealed that, after 20 years of marriage, he and his wife, Ruth, were divorced. The actor remarried in 1972; his second wife Colleen, appeared with him occasionally in his European films under the name of Shirlee Garner. Also in 1972, Conte made a rare appearance in an American film when he portrayed the role of Barzini in the Academy Award-winning hit, *The Godfather*. It would be the actor's last U.S. film.

On April 3, 1975, just four weeks after completing work on his latest foreign film, *La Encadenada* (1975), Conte suffered a heart attack and was admitted to the UCLA Medical Center. Two weeks later, while still in the hospital, Conte had a second, massive attack, and he died on April 15, 1975, at the age of 61. At the time of his death, Conte had reportedly been working on several projects, including a semi-autobiographical account of his experiences in Hollywood, a biography of the late actor John Garfield, and a new exhibition of his paintings.

Multi-talented, industrious, and always

professional, Richard Conte may have started out with a lack of direction, but he certainly didn't end up that way. Instead, he developed into an accomplished, confident actor who appreciated his ability and the responsibility he had to the public — and wasn't afraid to say so.

"I know my business and I think I have a certain sincerity and feeling that comes across," Conte said once. "This is important. With today's audiences you must have that quality of sincerity and truth. The people don't want actors who try to fool them anymore."

Film Noir Filmography

Somewhere in the Night. Director: Joseph L. Mankiewicz. Producer: Anderson Lawler. Running time: 110 minutes. Released by 20th Century-Fox, June 12, 1946. Cast: John Hodiak, Nancy Guild, Lloyd Nolan, Richard Conte, Josephine Hutchinson, Fritz Kortner, Margo Woode, Sheldon Leonard, Lou Nova, John Russell, Houseley Stevenson, Charles Arnt, Al Sparlis.

Call Northside 777. Director: Henry Hathaway. Producer: Otto Lang. Running time: 111 minutes. Released by 20th Century-Fox. Cast: James Stewart, Richard Conte, Lee J. Cobb, Helen Walker, Betty Garde, Kasia Orzazewski, Joanne de Bergh, Howard Smith, Moroni Olsen, John McIntire, Paul Harvey, George Tyne, Richard Bishop, Otto Waldis, Michael Chapin, E.G. Marshall, Truman Bradley.

Cry of the City. Director: Robert Siodmak. Producer: Sol Siegel. Running time: 96 minutes. Released by 20th Century-Fox, September 29, 1948. Cast: Victor Mature, Richard Conte, Fred Clark, Shelley Winters, Betty Garde, Barry Kroeger, Tommy Cook, Debra Paget, Hope Emerson, Roland Winters, Walter Baldwin, June Storey, Tito Vuolo, Mimi Aguglia, Konstantin Shayne, Howard Freeman.

House of Strangers. Director: Joseph L. Mankiewicz. Producer: Sol C. Siegel. Running time: 101 minutes. Released by 20th Century-Fox, July 1, 1949. Cast: Edward G. Robinson, Susan Hayward, Richard Conte, Luther Adler, Paul Valentine, Efrem Zimbalist, Jr., Debra Paget, Hope Emerson, Esther Minciotti, Diana Douglas, Tito Vuolo, Albert Morin, Sid Tomack, Thomas Henry Brown, David Wolfe, John Kellogg, Ann Morrison, Dolores Parker.

Thieves' Highway. Director: Jules Dassin. Producer: Robert Bassler. Running time: 94 minutes. Released by 20th Century-Fox, September 23, 1949. Cast: Richard Conte, Valentina Cortesa, Lee J. Cobb, Barbara Lawrence, Jack Oakie, Millard Mitchell, Morris Carnovsky, Tamara Shayne, Kasia Orzazewski, Norbert Schiller, Hope Emerson, George Tyne, Edwin Max, David Clarke, Walter Baldwin, David Opatoshu.

The Sleeping City. Director: George Sherman. Producer: Leonard Goldstein. Running time: 85 minutes. Released by Universal-International, September 20, 1950. Cast: Richard Conte, Coleen Gray, Peggy Dow, John Alexander, Alex Nicol, Richard Taber, James J. Van Dyk, Hugh Reilly, Michael Strong, Frank M. Thomas, Richard Kendrick, Henry Hart, Robert Strauss, Herbert Ratner, Mickey Cochran, Ernest Sarracino.

The Blue Gardenia. Director: Fritz Lang. Producer: Alex Gottlieb. Running time: 90 minutes. Released by Warner Brothers, March 28, 1953. Cast: Anne Baxter, Richard Conte, Ann Sothern, Raymond Burr, Jeff Donnell, Richard Erdman, George Reeves, Ruth Storey, Ray Walker, Nat "King" Cole, Celia Lovsky, Frank Ferguson, Alex Gottlieb.

New York Confidential. Director: Russell Rouse. Producer: Clarence Greene. Running time: 87 minutes. Released by Warner Bros., February 18, 1955. Cast: Broderick Crawford, Richard Conte, Marilyn Maxwell, Anne Bancroft, J. Carrol Naish, Onslow Stevens, Barry Kelley, Mike Mazurki, Celia Lovsky, Herbert Heyes, Steven Geray.

The Big Combo. Director: Joseph Lewis. Producer: Sidney Harmon. Running time: 89 minutes. Released by Allied Artists, February 13, 1955. Cast: Cornel Wilde, Richard Conte, Brian Donlevy, Jean Wallace, Robert Middleton, Lee Van Cleef, Earl Holliman, Helen Walker, Jay Adler, John Hoyt, Ted De Corsia, Helen Stanton, Roy Gordon, Whit Bissell, Steve Mitchell, Baynes Barron, James McCallion, Tony Michaels, Brian O'Hara, Rita Gould, Bruce Sharpe, Michael Mark, Philip Van Zandt, Donna Drew.

The Brothers Rico. Director: Phil Karlson. Producer: Lewis J. Rachmil. Running time: 92 minutes. Released by Columbia, September 1957. Cast: Richard Conte, Dianne Foster, Kathryn Grant, Larry Gates, James Darren, Argentina Brunetti, Lamont Johnson, Harry Bellaver, Paul Picerni, Paul Dubov, Rudy Bond, Richard Bakalyn, William Phipps, Mimi Aguglia, Maggie O'Byrne, George Cisar, Peggy Maley, Jane Easton.

References

"Actor Conte Eulogized as Good Friend, Gentle Man." *Los Angeles Times*, April 20, 1975.

Alpert, Don. "Conte Has Own Method." *Los Angeles Times*, February 14, 1960.

Berg, Louis. "A Star Comes Home." *This Week*, May 5, 1950.

Biography of Richard Conte. Paramount Studios, September 1965.

Carroll, Harrison. "Actor Conte, Wife Reveal Divorce." *Los Angeles Herald-Express,* July 12, 1963.

"Conte Forms Indie Pix, TV Company." *Variety*, January 1, 1960.

Conte, Richard. "The Role I Liked Best." *Saturday Evening Post*, circa 1950.

Gaver, Jack. "Along the Great White Way." *Los Angeles Daily News*, February 10, 1951.

Jones, Jack. "Richard Conte, Cold-Eyed Movie Gangster, Dies at 61." *Los Angeles Times*, April 16, 1975.

MacPherson, Virginia. "Love-Making in Films a Rough Deal." *Hollywood Citizen-News*, July 8, 1949.

McClay, Howard. "If You're Getting the Fan Mail, Stop Screaming, Son." *Los Angeles Daily News*, June 15, 1953.

Pryor, Thomas M. "Conte in the Sun." *New York Times*, March 3, 1946.

Redelings, Lowell E. "An Actor's Beliefs on Acting." *Hollywood Citizen-News*, September 29, 1959.

_____. "Opinions of an Actor." *Hollywood Citizen-News*, March 3, 1948.

"Richard Conte Dies at 61; Was in Films Since 1944." *Boxoffice*, April 21, 1975.

"Richard Conte Dies In Hollywood at 65." *Variety*, April 23, 1975.

"Richard Conte Left No Will, 70G Estate." *Variety*, April 30, 1975.

"Richard Conte Services Held." *Los Angeles Herald-Examiner*, April 20, 1975.

"Rites Set For Actor Richard Conte." *Los Angeles Herald-Examiner*, circa April 16, 1975.

Rochlen, Kendis. "Conte the Confusing." New York Mirror-News, September 16, 1955.

Scheuer, Philip K. "Conte May Return to Stage as Prince, Not Bark of Dog." *Los Angeles Times*, March 29, 1953.

ELISHA COOK, JR.

"Keep on ridin' me. They're gonna be pickin' iron out of your liver." — Elisha Cook, Jr., in *The Maltese Falcon* (1941)

Short in stature with a baby face, Elisha Cook, Jr., specialized in portraying shady characters.

"Funny, isn't it, that I thought I'd be playing romantic juveniles when I went into movies, and ended up doing pimps, informers, rats, and heels," Cook once said. "That's okay. I love 'em. They're much more interesting than straight people."

Although he once declared that he had appeared in "more bombs than I care to remember," Cook was seen in a number of cinematic blockbusters, including *Sergeant York* (1941), *Shane* (1953), and *Rosemary's Baby* (1968). But it was in the realm of film noir that the actor made his mark. Portraying such colorfully named characters as "Skeets," "Bobo," and "Oval," he was one of the era's most familiar character performers, with appearances in *Stranger on the Third Floor* (1940), *The Maltese Falcon* (1941), *I Wake Up Screaming* (1942), *Phantom Lady* (1944), *The Big Sleep* (1946), *The Gangster* (1947), *Born to Kill* (1947), *Fall Guy* (1947), *Don't Bother to Knock* (1952), *I, the Jury* (1953), *The Killing* (1956), *Baby Face Nelson* (1957), and *Plunder Road* (1957).

The diminutive actor, known to his friends as "Cookie," was born in San Francisco, California, on December 26, 1903 (some sources place his year of birth as early as 1902 and as late as 1907), but he moved with his parents to Chicago just weeks before the San Francisco earthquake of 1906. Following in the footsteps of his stage actress mother, Helen Henry, Cook got his first taste of acting during his teen years while selling programs for the play, *Lightning*, in the lobby of the Blackstone Theater. A chance encounter one evening with the play's star, Frank Bacon, set an irrevocable course for Cook's future.

"Frank Bacon put me in the business," Cook recalled. "I went down to meet him and he said, 'Would you like to go on the stage?' I said, 'Sure, I guess so.' I did a walk-on in the courtroom scene. I did pretty good, so later he says to me, 'Want to go to New York?' He was quite a guy, Mr. Bacon was."

After his rather inauspicious debut in *Lightning*, Cook spent the next several years honing his craft with a repertory company that toured the East and Midwest, performing with a tent show, and even appearing in vaudeville. He also made his debut on Broadway in 1926 in *Henry — Behave*, joining a cast that included Edward G. Robinson, but Cook once said that his favorite experience during this period was in a stock company production entitled *Thank You*.

"I was getting $25 a week," Cook recalled in a 1978 interview. "Then the property man gave me five bucks to load the baggage car and I did it all the rest of the tour — I made more money loading the goddamn baggage than I did on salary."

Cook made his film debut in 1930 in *Her Unborn Child* — a low-budget soaper shot on location in a garage on New York's East Side — but he didn't appear on screen again for another six years. Instead, he continued his stage work and in 1933 he finally got his big break — while Cook was appearing in a production in Skowhegan, Maine, the play's director informed him that the famed Theater Guild in New York had expressed an interest in his acting services.

"I said, 'You puttin' me on?'" Cook said. "He said, 'No. Eugene O'Neill's written a play called *Ah, Wilderness!* You get the hell outta here, go on down there.' I drove all the way to New York in my Model A."

Cast as a young man wending his way toward manhood, Cook caused a minor sensation in the play, and was singled out for his performance by several critics, including Eugene Burr of *Billboard*, who praised the actor's "sensitive and fine portrayal." Later, during a break from the two-year run of the play, Cook decided to give Hollywood another try. Before his departure, he was given a valuable piece of advice from Pulitzer Prize–winning playwright Owen Davis, whose son, Owney, was Cook's close friend.

"He said to me, 'Junior, you're going to go out there and make a lot of real bad pictures," Cook recalled. "'Now, if you want to be intelligent, you play small parts—because then they can never blame you.' That's what I've been doing ever since."

Cook found no trouble finding screen work, and after the close of *Ah, Wilderness!*, he was seen in a series of films that might qualify for the "real bad pictures" category, including two in which he portrayed a jockey, *Two in a Crowd* (1936) and *Thoroughbreds Don't Cry* (1937) ("I had never been on a horse in my life," he later said); *Life Begins in College* (1937), a football romp starring the Ritz Brothers; *The Devil Is Driving* (1937), which railed against the evils of drunk driving; *My Lucky Star* (1938), a Sonja Henie vehicle; and *Grand Jury Secrets* (1939), a programmer about a crusading reporter. The best of his features from this period were *Pigskin Parade* (1936), an entertaining musical in which Judy Garland made her film debut, and *Submarine Patrol* (1938), a sea adventure helmed by John Ford. Cook later recalled that the latter film was memorable for more than its good box office.

"I'm on this mock-up bridge, see, and they used to hold the water over us and then let it go when they were ready to shoot. Well the water knocked me off the deck, and I grabbed the piano wire that was holding the bridge up. Sliced the top of my thumb off," Cook recalled in a 1985 interview. "So Ford comes running up to me and says, 'Jesus, that was a good scene.' I said, 'Great, Mr. Ford, but I cut my thumb off.' He takes one look and passes out. Later, he gave me a made-up Navy Cross and took me out on his yacht — but he never employed me again."

The onset of the 1940s also saw Cook's introduction into the world of film noir; in 1940, he was featured in a pioneering entry in the noir cycle, *Stranger on the Third Floor*, starring Peter Lorre. Here, Cook was fifth-billed as Joe Briggs, a luckless taxi driver who is arrested after he is spotted fleeing the scene of a throat-slashing murder. On the stand during his trial, Joe desperately proclaims his innocence, but he is convicted and sentenced to death on the strength of testimony from reporter Michael Ward (Joe McGuire), who saw Joe leaving the crime scene. After Joe is led screaming from the courtroom, both Michael and his girlfriend, Jane (Margaret Tallichet), begin to have doubts about his guilt, and Michael suspects a mysterious stranger in a white scarf (Peter Lorre) after his neighbor is also found with his throat cut. Michael reports his suspicions to police, but finds himself arrested for the crime, leaving his girlfriend to search for the white-scarfed man. In a local diner, Jane has a chance encounter with the man, and although he later admits to Jane that he is the killer, he tries to make her his third victim. Jane flees from the man, who gives chase and is struck and killed by a truck, and the film's final end shows Michael and Jane entering a taxicab following their wedding — with Joe Briggs serving as the driver.

After being singled out as "satisfying in the role of the innocent man railroaded to jail" in *Stranger*, Cook was seen in small roles in pictures such as *Public Deb No. 1* (1940), a weak comedy starring George Murphy, and *Tin Pan Alley* (1940), a pleasant musical with Alice Faye and Betty Grable. He enjoyed one of the best years of his career in 1941, appearing in *Love Crazy*, a witty William Powell-Myrna Loy comedy; *Ball of Fire*, starring Barbara Stanwyck as a burlesque dancer; and *Sergeant York*, the true story of World War I hero Alvin C. York. He was also seen that year in his second — and most successful — film noir, *The Maltese Falcon*.

In this classic feature, Cook played the role for which he is perhaps best remembered — a hapless gunsel named Wilmer Cook. The film's story centered on the efforts of Brigid O'Shaugnessy (Mary Astor), Joel Cairo (Peter Lorre), and Kasper Gutman (Sydney Greenstreet) to find an elusive statuette of a bird that is crested with jewels. Ruthlessly determined, each of the principal players turns to private detective Sam Spade (Humphrey Bogart) for assistance in their quest, but they leave a slew of bodies in their wake, including O'Shaugnessy's partner, Floyd Thursby, who is never seen on screen; Spade's partner, Miles Archer (Jerome Cowan); and Jacoby (Walter Huston), a ship's captain who delivers to Spade what is believed to be the coveted falcon. When Spade determines that it is necessary to provide police with a "fall guy" for the trio of murders, Gutman reluctantly offers up Wilmer, whom he regards "as a son." Wilmer manages to escape, however, when the dead captain's bundle arrives and the group's frantic examination of the bird reveals that it is a fake. While Cairo and Gutman depart, planning to continue their search, Spade forces Brigid to confess to the murder of his partner and, despite his feelings for her, he turns her over to police.

As Gutman's faithful but distinctly inept gunman, Cook offered one of the film's many superb performances; although he is disarmed by Spade on more than one occasion, he continuously endeavors to project a tough exterior, telling Spade in an early scene, "Keep askin' for it, and you're gonna get it. Plenty." For his performance in this box-office smash, the actor earned praise from a number of reviewers, including Bosley Crowther of the *New York Times*, who termed him "stunning," and James Francis Crow of the *Hollywood Citizen-News*, who singled out several of the film's supporting cast members, adding, "I mention all of them because they are all at advantage under [John] Huston's directorial guidance — particularly Lorre, Greenstreet, and Cook."

Years after the release of the film, Cook would proclaim *The Maltese Falcon* as his favorite picture. "There wasn't one decent person in the whole film," he said. "This guy [Wilmer] is a nothin' — but he's a deadly nothin'!"

The following year, Cook was featured in his third noir, *I Wake Up Screaming* (1942), as Harry Williams, a socially-inept switchboard operator in a building whose most famous resident, model and would-be actress Vicky Lynn (Carole Landis), has just been murdered. The woman's promoter, Frankie Christopher (Victor Mature), is promptly suspected of the crime, but he narrowly avoids capture with the help of Vicky's sister, Jill (Betty Grable, in a rare non-singing role), and goes on the lam to find the real killer. Despite his declarations of innocence, Frankie is constantly hounded by police detective Ed Cornell (Laird Cregar), who insists that Frankie is guilty of the crime and tells him in one scene, "When I get all my evidence together, I'm going to have you tied up like a pig at a slaughterhouse." Ultimately, Frankie's quest for the murderer leads him to Harry Williams, and he tricks the young man into confessing: "I didn't know what I was doing, I swear," Harry admits. "She screamed and I lost my head." Harry also reveals, however, that he'd already confessed his guilt to Cornell, who "told me to just come back here and keep quiet, and forget all about it." As it turns out, Cornell, who was obsessed with the famed model, has maintained a veritable shrine to her in his apartment and was jealous of her relationship with Frankie — but before Frankie can turn him over to his fellow officers, Cornell drinks a vial of poison and dies in the final reel. Upon its release, *I Wake Up Screaming* was met with widely varying opinions from critics; while the *New York Times'* Bosley Crowther dismissed the feature as "a pretty obvious whodunit and a strangely unmoving affair," the critic for *Variety* wrote, "Most murder mysteries are 'Bs' regardless of budget, but this one is an exception to the rule. The director, H. Bruce Humberstone, has been equipped with a good script and from his cast has obtained results that are all that may be asked in a murder meller with a romantic strain of more than ordinary strength."

While Cook was boosting his performing repertoire, he also found time for romance. In 1929, while still living in New York, he married dancer and actress Mary Lou McMichael who, along with her three brothers, performed as the Merry Macs. Cook and Mary divorced in 1942, and the following year, he would marry again. His second wife, Peggy, was a stand-in for actress Carole Landis, and the two met on the set of Cook's 1942 film with Landis, *A Gentleman at Heart.* Although Cook and Peggy remained together for more than 40 years, their romance got off to a shaky start when the actor enlisted in the Army Air Corps shortly after they met.

"World War II was going on, and I was feeling patriotic," Cook said in 1985. "I was sent to Will Rogers Field — what were they going to do with a 40-year-old actor, for Christ's sake? They needed me like a toothache. They made me business manager of the base newspaper. I ended up pushing newspapers around the base — on a bicycle, if you can beat that."

After the war, Cook and Peggy settled in Bishop, California, where they remained together until Peggy's death in the late 1980s: "We wanted kids, but it didn't happen," Cook said. "Oh, listen — we had a ball!"

On-screen, despite his well-done per-formance in *The Maltese Falcon*, Cook spent the next two years in a series of duds, including *Wildcat* (1942), a drama about rival oil prospectors; *A-Haunting We Will Go* (1942), a Laurel and Hardy vehicle that paled in comparison to their earlier work; and *In This Our Life* (1942), which was directed by John Huston and starred Bette Davis as a woman who steals her sister's husband. (The best part of the latter production was an "inside joke" cameo appearance by several of the cast members from *The Maltese Falcon*, including Cook, Humphrey Bogart, Mary Astor, Sydney Greenstreet, and Peter Lorre.) Cook fared better, however, with *Manila Calling* (1942), a war adventure starring Lloyd Nolan and Cornel Wilde; *Up in Arms* (1944), a lavish musical that served as the debut of Danny Kaye; and *Phantom Lady* (1944), the actor's fifth film noir.

In this feature, Cook was jazz drummer Cliff Milburn, who is characterized by his penchant for leering at female audience members and his self-described image as a "hep cat." When civil engineer Scott Henderson (Alan Curtis) is arrested for the murder of his wife, Cliff is among the series of individuals he turns to for an alibi; it turns out that, on the night of the murder, Scott was in the company of young woman he'd met in a bar and taken to the local musical revue where Cliff performed. Unable to identify the woman by name, Scott tells police that she was seen by several individuals on the evening in question, but each deny ever seeing her. After Scott is convicted and sentenced to die for the crime, his loyal secretary, Carol Richman (Ella Raines), works with a police inspector, Burgess (Thomas Gomez), to prove Scott's innocence. As part of her quest, Carol makes a date with Cliff, allowing him to paw her until he drunkenly reveals that he was paid to keep quiet about the mysterious woman. ("Five hundred smackeroos," he says, "just for lookin' at the dame and sayin' that I didn't!") A short time later, Carol contacts Burgess, but when they return to Cliff's apartment, they find that he has been murdered. Continuing her search, Carol finally tracks down the "phantom lady" and discovers that the murders were committed by Scott's best friend, Jack Marlow (Franchot Tone), who admits that he killed Scott's wife after she broke off their affair. As Marlow prepares to make Carol his third victim, however, Burgess arrives, and Marlow falls to his death from a window while trying to flee.

After earning a number of favorable notices for his memorable performance in *Phantom Lady*, Cook was next seen in *Why Girls Leave Home* (1945), a low-budget programmer starring Lola Lane; *Dillinger* (1945), starring Lawrence Tierney in the title role; *Two Smart People* (1946), a mediocre comedy-crime feature; *Blonde Alibi* (1946), a time-wasting whodunit about an aviator wrongly accused of murder; and *Cinderella Jones* (1946), a dull musical comedy notable only for the brush with danger that Cook experienced during filming.

"I was supposed to be jumping a white charger across a stream," Cook said. "They shot it in a studio tank with a wire guide through the horse's nose. The horse got excited and put his hoof up over the wire, dragged me underneath him, and I had to cut myself loose. It didn't hurt the horse any. The animals were always better protected than the actors."

With the exception of *The Falcon's Alibi* (1946), in which Cook was a standout as a menacing radio disc jockey, the actor's films during these years were mostly forgettable. With his typically philosophical view of life, however, Cook seemed to take this reality in stride.

"When I was first breaking into pictures, I learned the most important thing is to do your work — always do the conscientious best you can," he said once. "In the great days of the movies, you've got to remember that there were six, seven major studios and a few independents, and the main object was to keep the theaters filled up. The material ... now and then, it's marvelous, but mostly it's a lot of crap."

But Cook's next film — *The Big Sleep* (1946) — definitely did not fit the "crap" de-

scription. A box-office smash directed and produced by Howard Hawks, this feature was a riveting contribution to the film noir era, despite a complex and often confusing plot that began with a blackmail scheme and ended with more than a half-dozen murders. Starring Humphrey Bogart as private detective Philip Marlowe, *The Big Sleep* also featured Martha Vickers as the thumb-sucking nymphomaniac who was the target of the blackmail; Lauren Bacall as her older, sensible sister; and John Ridgeley as a hard-boiled gambling house owner. And in a relatively minor, but memorable role, Cook portrayed Harry Jones, who becomes a part of Marlowe's investigation after offering information to the private detective in exchange for a cash payoff: "I ain't tried to pull anything," Harry complains when Marlowe threatens to contact the police. "I came here with a straight proposition. Take it or leave it. One right guy to another. You start wavin' cops at me. You oughta be ashamed of yourself." Marlowe and Harry later strike a deal, planning to meet later to complete the transaction, but Harry never makes it — forced to drink poison by one of Ridgeley's underlings, he winds up as one of the film's spate of corpses. Cook's brief appearance on screen was noted in the review by *Los Angeles Times* critic Edwin Schallert, who wrote that he "help[ed] to build up the picture's impact." Schallert also heaped praise on the entire cast of the film, opining that "the ensemble works consistently on a thrill and horror schedule, each helping to fill out part of the very large and complicated patterns."

The following year, 1947, would see Cook's most prolific contribution to the era of the dark; of his four films that year, three were film noir: *The Gangster*, *Fall Guy*, and *Born to Kill*. His roles in the first two were little more than bit parts; in *The Gangster*, he was seen in only one scene, playing a small-time hood who warns a rival mobster (Barry Sullivan) that he is "out of business," only to end up picking himself off the ground for his troubles. And in *Fall Guy*, he played the part of Joe Marcello, whose involvement with a hapless war veteran leads to a young woman's murder. Cook's third noir of the year, however, offered the actor the meaty role of Marty Waterman, the best friend of psychotic killer Sam Wild (Lawrence Tierney). Aware of his friend's volatile temper and penchant for violence, Marty serves as a constant calming influence, even as Sam murders his girlfriend, Laury Palmer (Isabel Jewell), and the man he found her with. Although Sam appears to settle down by marrying a wealthy San Francisco woman, Georgia Staples (Audrey Long), he promptly becomes involved with Georgia's foster sister, Helen Trent (Claire Trevor), who knows about the murders Sam committed and is perversely drawn to his deadly nature. But even Helen is repulsed when Sam kills Marty after mistakenly suspecting him of having an affair with Helen, and she contacts the authorities. Learning of her deception, Sam adds Helen to his growing list of corpses before he himself is shot and killed by police.

After *Born to Kill*— which was hailed by one critic as a "sexy, suggestive yarn of crime with punishment"— Cook portrayed a piano player in *The Great Gatsby* (1949), which starred Alan Ladd in the title role. Shortly after the film's release, however, the actor encountered a stumbling block in his career. Despite the development of what he termed a "good relationship" with the Warner Brothers studio over the last several years, Cook clashed with studio heads following his appearance in the 1949 crime drama, *Flaxy Martin.*

"They wanted to cut my pay to $500 a week. I refused to work for that," Cook recalled. "We argued back and forth, and they decided to freeze me out, and before long I couldn't turn up a job anywhere in Hollywood. In a few months, we ran completely out of money."

To make ends meet, Cook took a job "shoveling gravel" on the nearby Owens Valley pipeline.

"Peg would go out and pick up pop bottles for the two cents. On weekends I'd go out and shoot deer just to put some meat on the table," Cook said. "I went to my job on the pipeline every day, and Peggy stood by me. A year and a half went by, and I didn't know if I'd ever work as an actor again."

After an absence from the screen during 1950, Cook managed to land a minor role in his sole film of 1951, *Behave Yourself*, starring Farley Granger and Shelley Winters. The following year also saw Cook in a single feature, but the role was more significant and the film was of higher quality — his seventh film noir, *Don't Bother to Knock* (1952). Here, Cook portrayed Eddie Forbes, whose niece, Nell (Marilyn Monroe), has been recently released from a mental hospital after a suicide attempt following the death of her fiancé. Relatively assured that she has recovered from her trauma, Eddie arranges for Nell to babysit a young girl in the hotel where he works as an elevator operator, but when the young woman begins to dress in the negligee and jewels belonging to the child's mother, it becomes obvious that she is still unwell. ("Are you actin' that way again? I been an elevator jockey for 14 years— ain't that enough to get outta life without any more trouble?" Eddie asks Nell when he stops by the room to check on her. "Why are you so restless? You're ticking like a clock. I thought everything was clearing up. I thought you were getting better. Now, I wonder about everything.") Nell's illness further manifests itself when she flirts with a hotel guest named Jed (Richard Widmark), confusing him with her dead lover and accusing her charge of coming between them. When Eddie arrives at the room at the end of his shift, Nell knocks him unconscious with a heavy floor ashtray, and the child's mother later returns to find her daughter bound and gagged in the bedroom. In a daze, Nell wanders to the hotel lobby, purchasing a razor blade from the counter with plans to finish the task she'd started three years before, but before she can carry out the deed, Jed makes his way through the gathered crowd and convinces Nell to surrender to police. While *Don't Bother to Knock* stands up well today, and is of particular interest because of Monroe's striking performance, the film was panned on its release; in a typical review, the critic for *Variety* found that the performances of Cook and several co-stars were "okay," but judged that the film itself was "produced in too haphazard and leisurely a fashion."

Cook was next seen in his first western, the classic *Shane* (1953), in which he portrayed the rare good guy role of a defiant homesteader. The actor later recalled his experience on the film with amusement.

"We're getting ready to shoot my big scene, where Jack Palance wastes me on the steps outside the saloon…. Just before the shot, [director George] Stevens takes me aside and says, 'Cookie, you're the worst actor I've ever seen, but I'm stuck with you.' Then we shoot the scene," Cook said. "Well, at the end of the day, I'm sitting at the bar and Stevens comes in and what do you think he says? 'Cookie,' he says, 'that was the greatest footage I've ever seen.' He'd just wanted to have fear and respect showing in my face when he shot. And I can tell you, by God, he got it."

Cook followed *Shane* with the second western of his career, *Thunder Over the Plains* (1953), then returned to film noir for a minor role in *I, the Jury* (1953), playing a half-wit known as Bobo who was characterized by his fondness for insects. ("I'm learnin' all about bees," he says in his first scene. "Look—I got me a library book and a card.") Although his part was limited to only two scenes, however, Cook was mentioned in *Variety*, along with several other supporting players, as "good for the characters to be presented."

The actor's films during the next several years were mostly forgettable; the best was the 1955 release, *Trial* (the first film in which he was credited with the "Jr." dropped from his name), which focused on the murder trial of a Mexican youth (Rafael Campos) charged with murder. And Cook scored again the following year with a first-rate performance in the eighth film noir feature of his career, *The Killing* (1956).

In this film, arguably one of the best of the noir era, Cook portrayed mild-mannered cashier George Peatty, who becomes part of a plan to knock off a race track in an effort to please his materialistic wife, Sherry (Marie Windsor): "I seem to recall you made a memorable statement," Sherry mockingly tells George in one scene. "Something about hitting it rich, and having an apartment on Park Avenue, and a different car for every day of the week. Not that I really care about such things, understand—as long as I have a big, handsome, intelligent brute like you." Rounded out by petty criminal Johnny Clay (Sterling Hayden), a cop who owes money to the mob (Ted De Corsia), and a bartender with an invalid wife (Joe Sawyer), the group successfully carries out the elaborate scheme, but before they can celebrate their triumph, Sherry's lover (Vince Edwards) tries to steal the cache, resulting in a shootout that leaves most of the men dead. The only survivors are Clay, whose arrival at the meeting place was delayed, and George, who manages to summon enough strength to struggle home in time to kill his duplicitous wife. Clay later tries to flee with his girlfriend (Coleen Gray) from the local airport, but fate steps in when the suitcase full of money falls from a baggage cart and the group's mastermind is nabbed by police.

"*The Killing* was one of the classiest suspense thrillers ever made, and it also had an exceptional cast," Cook later said of the film. "Marie Windsor and I … both had the feeling afterwards that maybe we had reached a little beyond our normal range. Parts like that don't sift down too often."

The year following the release of *The Killing* saw Cook's appearance in his final two films from the noir era, *Baby Face Nelson* (1957) and *Plunder Road* (1957). The first, starring Mickey Rooney in the title role, told the story of the notorious gangster, tracking his rise and fall as a gangleader. As one of the members of his gang, Cook was only briefly on screen, tangling with his trigger-happy boss over the counting of their latest haul. Cook didn't have a high opinion of *Baby Face Nelson*, recalling that during filming, he was outfitted with a bulletproof vest and fired upon with live ammunition.

"Sheer idiocy," Cook commented. "I don't know who the director was … Don Siegel? Whoever. It was a hack picture."

He fared better in the last film noir of his career which, reminiscent in theme to *The Asphalt Jungle* (1950) and *The Killing* (1956), centered on the intricate robbery of a train carrying $10 million in gold. For the first 13 minutes of this interesting feature, as the heist is being carried out, none of the characters speak — the first time that their voices are heard is when the gang of five men finish the job and begin to laugh with a sense of mixed triumph and relief. In addition to Eddie (Gene Raymond), the college-educated mastermind of the theft, the gang consists of Frankie (Steven Rich), a race-car driver; Roly (Stafford Rep), who is known for his obsessive gum-chewing; and Commando (Wayne Morris), a former movie stuntman. The final member of the group, Skeets (Cook), has been in and out of prison for 23 years and dreams of using his proceeds from the job to move to Rio with his 17-year-old son. (Although he admits that he has never been to Rio, Skeets speaks almost nostalgically about the country's "white sand, blue sea, plenty of room to move around.") In three separate trucks, the men head for Los Angeles, but before long, Roly is killed by police and Skeets and Commando are captured after shooting a gas station attendant. The remaining two gang members, Eddie and Frankie, make it safely to their destination, a huge foundry where they are greeted by Eddie's waiting girlfriend, Fran (Jeanne Cooper, who would later earn fame in a long-running role on the popular television soaper *The Young and the Restless*). Over the next several hours, the trio carry out the plan's artful next step, which involves melting the gold bricks, molding them into car parts, and attaching them to a Cadillac. After successfully completing the job, and with little time to spare, Eddie, Frankie, and Fran prepare to have the car shipped overseas, but on the traffic-heavy highway, the carefully planned caper comes apart at the seams. When a motorist rams into the rear of the Cadillac, the two cars become locked together, a passing cop notices the Cadillac's gold bumpers, and the dream ends as Frankie is gunned down, Fran is captured, and Eddie

jumps from an overpass to his death. Although it was mostly overlooked upon its release, the little-known *Plunder Road* is an excellent example of the film noir era, offering taut direction, well-drawn characterizations, and fine performances from the entire cast.

With the exception of the bleakly powerful western *Day of the Outlaw* (1959), the amusing comedy *Papa's Delicate Condition* (1963), and the Roman Polanski–directed horror classic *Rosemary's Baby* (1968), most of Cook's films throughout the remainder of the 1950s and the 1960s were mediocre at best. He had better luck on the small screen, however; from the mid-1950s through the 1980s, the actor would be a frequent guest on numerous programs, including *Alfred Hitchcock Presents, Gunsmoke, Bat Masterson, Rawhide, The Fugitive, Perry Mason, The Wild, Wild West, Bonanza, Star Trek, Batman, The Odd Couple, The Bionic Woman,* and *Magnum P.I.,* on which he played a recurring role as Francis "Ice Pick" Hofstetler. He also appeared in several made-for-television movies, including *The Night Stalker* (1972), *Salem's Lot* (1979), and *It Came Upon a Midnight Clear* (1984), and returned to his roots on the stage in 1963 for the Broadway production of *The Resistible Rise of Arturo Ui.*

Despite his prolific television career, Cook continued to appear in feature films during the next two decades, including *The Great Northfield, Minnesota Raid* (1972), an offbeat western about the Cole Younger–Jesse James gang; *Blacula* (1972), a popular entry in the "blaxploitation" genre; *The Black Bird* (1975), an amusing spoof of The Maltese Falcon, in which Cook reprised his role as Wilmer; *1941* (1979), a big-budget comedy directed by Steven Spielberg (whom Cook termed "a nice kid"); *Carny* (1980), an atmospheric look at carnival life; and *Hammett* (1982), a fictionalized account of the life of writer Dashiell Hammett. The latter film, in which he portrayed a taxi driver, would be Cook's last.

In the mid-1980s, after decades of heavy drinking (or what he called "cutting the touches"), Cook stopped quit alcohol cold turkey. The actor said that the sudden cessation of his longtime habit had been easy.

"Everybody said it was gonna be a helluva problem, it wasn't at all," he said in 1985. "I'll tell you why I gave it up. I got a 300-mile trip, 600 miles to go to work from here to Bishop and back. Suddenly I realized I had my nip in Mojave, it was 175 miles to Bishop and I'd stop in Lone Pine and have my nip, in my car. Then at 60 miles to Bishop I found that single line [on the highway] was getting doubled, and I said, 'uh oh — look out.' And I quit — boom."

In the early 1990s, Cook suffered a stroke which rendered him unable to speak, and on May 18, 1995, after several years of failing health, the actor died. The last surviving cast member of *The Maltese Falcon*, Cook was 91 years old.

In a memorable screen career rife with portrayals of small-time hoods to ex-convicts, stoolies to psychotic killers, and hustlers to petty thieves, Elisha Cook, Jr., was a gem. Although he was never a leading man, he made a significant mark on the silver screen, appearing in nearly 100 features over a span of seven decades. Perhaps part of his popularity and longevity stemmed from his sincere affection for his craft and his love of the movies.

"I just love acting — always loved it, because it seemed to make people happy," Cook said once. "Most people's lives are pretty dreary, you know? What else do they have to come home to? No sir, I've had my times. I wouldn't trade places with any man, high, low, or jack."

Film Noir Filmography

Stranger on the Third Floor. Director: Boris Ingster. Producer: Lee Marcus. Running time: 64 minutes. Released by RKO, September 1, 1940. Cast: Peter Lorre, John McGuire, Margaret Tallichet, Charles Waldron, Elisha Cook, Jr., Charles Halton, Ethel Griffies, Cliff Clark, Oscar O'Shea, Alec Craig, Otto Hoffman.

I Wake Up Screaming. Director: H. Bruce Humberstone. Producer: Milton Sperling. Running time: 82 minutes. Released by 20th Century-Fox, January 16, 1942. Cast: Betty Grable, Victor Mature, Carole Landis, Laird Cregar, William Gargan, Alan Mowbray, Allyn Joslyn, Elisha Cook, Jr., Chick Chandler, Morris Ankrum, May Beatty.

The Maltese Falcon. Director: John Huston. Producer: Hal B. Wallis. Running time: 100 minutes. Released by Warner Brothers, October 3, 1941. Cast: Humphrey Bogart, Mary Astor, Gladys George, Peter Lorre, Barton MacLane, Sydney Greenstreet, Ward Bond, Jerome Cowan, Elisha Cook, Jr., James Burke, Murray Alper, John Hamilton, Emory Parnell. Awards: Academy Award nomination for Best Picture, Best Supporting Actor (Sydney Greenstreet), Best Screenplay (John Huston).

Phantom Lady. Director: Robert Siodmak, Producer: Joan Harrison. Running time: 87 minutes. Released by Universal, February 17, 1944. Cast: Franchot Tone, Ella Raines, Alan Curtis, Thomas Gomez, Fay Helm, Elisha Cook, Jr., Andrew Tombes, Jr., Regis Toomey, Virginia Brissac, Milburn Stone.

The Big Sleep. Director: Howard Hawks. Producer: Howard Hawks. Running time: 118 minutes. Released by Warner Brothers, August 31, 1946. Cast: Humphrey Bogart, Lauren Bacall, John Ridgeley, Martha Vickers, Dorothy Malone, Patricia Clarke, Regis Toomey, Charles Waldron, Charles D. Brown, Louis Jean Heydt, Elisha Cook, Jr., Sonia Darrin, Bob Steele, James Flavin, Thomas Jackson, Thomas Rafferty, Theodore Von Eltz, Dan Wallace, Joy Barlowe.

The Gangster. Director: Gordon Wiles. Producers: Maurice and Frank King. Running time: 84 minutes. Released by Allied Artists, October 1947. Cast: Barry Sullivan, Belita, Joan Lorring, Akim Tamiroff, Henry Morgan, John Ireland, Fifi D'Orsay, Virginia Christine, Sheldon Leonard, Leif Erickson, Charles McGraw, John Kellogg, Elisha Cook, Jr., Ted Hecht, Jeff Corey.

Born to Kill. Director: Robert Wise. Producer: Sid Rogell. Running time: 92 minutes. Released by RKO, May 3, 1947. Cast: Claire Trevor, Lawrence Trevor, Walter Slezak, Philip Terry, Audrey Long, Elisha Cook, Jr., Isabel Jewell, Esther Howard, Kathryn Card, Tony Barrett, Grandon Rhodes.

Fall Guy. Director: Reginald LeBorg. Producer: Walter Mirisch. Running time: 64 minutes. Released by Monogram, March 15, 1947. Cast: Clifford Penn, Teala Loring, Robert Armstrong, Virginia Dale, Elisha Cook, Jr., Douglas Fowley, Charles Arnt, Harry Strang.

Don't Bother to Knock. Director: Roy Ward Baker. Producer: Julian Blaustein. Running time: 76 minutes. Released by 20th Century-Fox, July 1952. Cast: Richard Widmark, Marilyn Monroe,

Anne Bancroft, Donna Corcoran, Jeanne Cagney, Lurene Tuttle, Elisha Cook, Jr., Jim Backus.

I, the Jury. Director: Harry Essex. Producer: Victor Saville. Running time: 88 minutes. Released by United Artists, August 14, 1953. Cast: Biff Elliott, Preston Foster, Peggie Castle, Margaret Sheridan, Alan Reed, Frances Osborne, Robert Cunningham, Elisha Cook, Jr., Paul Dubov, Mary Anderson, Tani Seitz, Dran Seitz, Robert Swanger, John Qualen.

The Killing. Director: Stanley Kramer. Producer: James B. Harris. Running time: 84 minutes. Released by United Artists, May 20, 1956. Cast: Sterling Hayden, Coleen Gray, Vince Edwards, Jay C. Flippen, Marie Windsor, Ted De Corsia, Elisha Cook, Jr., Joe Sawyer, Timothy Carey, Jay Adler, Kola Kwarian, Joseph Turkell, James Edwards.

Baby Face Nelson. Director: Don Siegel. Producer: Al Zimbalist. Running time: 85 minutes. Released by United Artists, November 1957. Cast: Mickey Rooney, Carolyn Jones, Sir Cedric Hardwicke, Leo Gordon, Ted De Corsia, Anthony Caruso, Jack Elam, Chris Dark, Emile Meyer, Dan Terranova, Dabbs Greer, Bob Osterloh, Dick Crocett, Paul Baxley, Thayer David, Ken Patterson, Sol Gorse, Gil Perkins, Tom Fadden, Lisa Davis, John Hoyt, Elisha Cook, Jr., Murray Alper, George E. Stone, Hubie Kerns, Paul and Richard Donnelly.

Plunder Road. Director: Hubert Cornfield. Producers: Leon Chooluck, Laurence Stewart. Running time: 82 minutes. Released by 20th Century-Fox, December 5, 1957. Cast: Gene Raymond, Jeanne Cooper, Wayne Morris, Elisha Cook, Jr., Stafford Repp, Steven Ritch, Nora Hayden.

References

"Elisha Cook, Jr., Has Staged and Won a One-Man Strike." Publication Unsourced, circa 1933.

Folkart, Burt A. "Elisha Cook, Jr., 91; Classic Movie Villain." *Los Angeles Times*, May 20, 1995.

Goodman, Mark. "Give 'Em the Gunsel." *G.Q.,* April 1985.

Lewis, Grover. "Cook's Tour." *New West*, June 2, 1980.

_____. "Humphrey Bogart, Bathtub Gin but No Incest with Marilyn." *The Washington Post*, November 3, 1985.

Obituary. *The London Times*, May 22, 1995.

Thomas, Robert M. "Elisha Cook, Jr., Villain in Many Films, Dies at 91." *New York Times*, May 21, 1995.

Title Unknown. *New York Times*, May 25, 1979.

Young, Jordan R. "Bit Parts Hit for Elisha Cook." *Los Angeles Times*, May 8, 1978.

———— JEFF COREY ————

"You can't lock men up and expect 'em to stay put. Not even if you feed 'em off gold plates. They'll always fight to get out — and take the gold plates with 'em." — Jeff Corey in *Canon City* (1948)

There was nothing conventional about Jeff Corey. Not his distinctively craggy looks, nor his exceptional talent, and certainly not his experience in Hollywood.

Blacklisted in the 1950s due to accusations of Communist leanings, Corey saw his promising film career diminish virtually overnight, but the indomitable actor refused to allow the experience to derail his life — he not only went on to become one of Hollywood's most respected acting coaches, but he returned to the big screen after an absence of more than a decade to appear in such memorable films as *The Cincinnati Kid* (1965), *True Grit* (1969),

Butch Cassidy and the Sundance Kid (1969), and *Little Big Man* (1970). Noted for his versatility as a character actor, Corey also appeared in six outstanding — and widely varying — examples from the film noir era: *Somewhere in the Night* (1946), *The Killers* (1946), *The Gangster* (1947), *Brute Force* (1947), *Canon City* (1948), and *Follow Me Quietly* (1949).

The third of four children, Jeff Corey was born in New York City on August 10, 1914, to Nathan Corey, owner of a sash, door, and trim business in the Bronx, and his wife, Mary. According to the actor, his childhood was a pleasant one.

"It was a very close neighborhood — people didn't move. They lived where they lived, and they'd stay put," Corey recalled in a 2000 interview. "I always had good friends, played punchball on the street — although we had to worry about the horse manure, because there were practically no automobiles then."

Corey first became interested in acting one summer while attending Camp Mohaph in the Catskill Mountains. His first role was in a medieval farce. "I was so excited, with the footlights on me, and to wear makeup," he said. "I really caught the bug. I've still got the bug." Later, as a student at New Utrecht High School, Corey's fascination with the stage continued to flourish.

"I was not a terribly good student," Corey admitted, "but I was the best actor in the productions that they put on."

The plays in which he appeared — which were directed by the school's biology teacher — included Shelley's adaptation of *Faust*, with Corey in the lead role as Mephisto. In addition to enjoying the experience of performing on stage, the budding thespian found that acting had another benefit: "I thought I was funny looking," he said, "but the girls liked me."

Because his high school grades did not qualify Corey for enrollment at a city college, the future actor turned to the world of work, selling sewing machines door-to-door. "I got six dollars for expenses and gave up after a week," he said. But fate was soon to intervene. Shortly after abandoning his brief vocation as a sewing machine salesman, Corey was notified that he had been awarded the two-year Milward Adams scholarship at the Feagin School of Dramatic Arts in New York. While there, Corey also received permission to work with Percy Vivian's Shakespeare Repertory Company, where he played small parts in *Julius Caesar*.

"I was a little too eager, and some of the leading actors objected to this young man taking center stage," he said, "but their reaction was flattering to me."

When he graduated from Feagin, Corey toured for two years in Clare Tree Major's Children's Theater, appearing in such productions as *Aladdin and His Magic Lamp* and *Robin Hood*. Upon his return to New York he landed a job playing a spear carrier in *Hamlet*, starring Leslie Howard. "When we toured, [Howard] needed a replacement for the part of Rosencrantz," Corey said. "I auditioned and I got the part." He was 22 years old.

Acting did not consume all of Corey's time, however. In September 1937, he found Hope — the woman who would become his lifelong partner. "I was rehearsing with a friend for a play," Corey recalled. "After rehearsal, I volunteered to walk [my friend] home, and I was introduced to her roommate, Hope. We really liked each other. I courted her in Central Park." Corey and Hope married in February 1938 and later had three daughters, Evie, Jane, and Emily. The couple remained together for more than 60 years, until Corey's 2002 death.

Career-wise, Corey found work with the Federal Theatre Project in New York, a component of President Franklin D. Roosevelt's Works Progress Administration (WPA) that was designed to provide work for unemployed professionals in the theater during the Depression. When funding for the project was eliminated in 1939, however, Corey found himself unable to secure a job.

"I was going to quit acting — I even enrolled at Brooklyn Technological College to learn blueprint reading," Corey recalled. But once again, Corey's fate steered him in a different direction. At the time, the actor and his wife possessed a Ford Model A car that they had purchased at an auction from the Department of Street Cleaning. In their bank account was a total of $180.

"My wife suggested that we go to California," Corey said. "Our car had no headlights, so we couldn't drive by night. It took us 18 days."

Once the couple was settled in Los Angeles, Corey's first order of business was finding an agent. "The only jacket I had was a Harris tweed, but I put it on one day and I walked to Sunset Boulevard," Corey said. "I went to one agent who didn't want me, another said he'd get back to me, and the third said, 'I like you, kid.' I was working at MGM the next day."

The actor's first role was Johann, a Swedish newlywed in the Myrna Loy-Melvyn Douglas comedy, *Third Finger, Left Hand* (1940). "I went to Swedish neighborhoods to learn the accent, but they all spoke perfect English!" Corey recalled. "So one of my fellow actors, Greta Grandsted, taught me the accent."

During the next three years, Corey appeared in a series of mostly forgettable films, including *Small Town Deb* (1941), a mediocre comedy starring Jane Withers; *Paris Calling* (1941), a war movie featuring Elisabeth Bergner and Randolph Scott; and *North to the Klondike* (1942), a so-so oater for Universal. Several of his roles during this period were in box-office hits, however, such as *The Moon Is Down* (1943), based on John Steinbeck's novel about the World War II Nazi occupation of a Norwegian village, and *My Friend Flicka* (1943), the heartwarming tale of the friendship between a boy, played by Roddy McDowall, and his horse. And although it was not successful at the time of its release, *The Devil and Daniel Webster* (1941), where Corey portrayed local farmer Tom Sharp, is today considered first-rate.

Two weeks after the birth of his first daughter, Evie, in 1943, Corey enlisted in the United States Navy, where he served as a combat motion picture photographer in 14 major engagements. Upon his release, he was honored with three citations for his work. Returning to Hollywood, Corey entered the realm of film noir in back-to-back features from the era. The first, *Somewhere in the Night* (1946), was directed by Joseph Mankiewicz and focuses on the story of George Taylor (John Hodiak), an ex–Marine suffering from amnesia. In a bit part as a bank teller, however, Corey barely registered.

The actor was seen to better advantage in his second film noir, *The Killers* (1946), a top-notch feature that opens with the murder of a small-town gas station attendant known as "the Swede" (Burt Lancaster). After the

killing, insurance investigator Jim Reardon (Edmond O'Brien) determines to uncover the circumstances that led to the Swede's demise, and encounters a number of individuals who were connected to him, including his conniving girlfriend, Kitty (Ava Gardner), and Big Jim Colfax (Albert Dekker), the leader of a gang of hoods that carried out a payroll heist. Reardon also runs across the path of a fidgety character known as Blinky Franklin (Corey), a member of Big Jim's gang. In Corey's best scene in the film, his character is seen on his deathbed, hallucinating about his role in the payroll robbery — Corey later recalled that it was this scene that served as his audition for the picture.

"Afterward, the film's director, Robert Siodmak, whispered to me, 'you got the part,'" Corey said. "It was a thrilling thing to do. An interesting part — a wonderful movie."

After bit parts in several films — including the Barbara Stanwyck–Ray Milland western, *California* (1946), and the holiday classic, *Miracle on 34th Street* (1947) — Corey was seen in another small noir role, this time in *The Gangster* (1947), starring Barry Fitzgerald. Here, Corey was seen only briefly as one of three garage owners who unmercifully beat their brother-in-law (John Ireland), a gambling addict who has stolen from them. He logged considerably more screen time, however, in his next film noir, *Brute Force* (1947). A brutal prison drama that is chock-full of noir regulars, *Brute Force* focuses on a group of prison inmates who are brutalized by a sadistic guard and plan an intricate escape. Despite the large cast of such actors as Burt Lancaster, Howard Duff, Sam Levene, and John Hoyt, Corey was memorable as Freshman, who meets a grisly death when his fellow inmates discover that he has double-crossed them. In return for his betrayal, he is strapped to the front of a dump car that the inmates are using to escape through a tunnel, and he is riddled with machine gun bullets by prison guards waiting at the end of the tunnel.

Corey later recalled that the film's director, Jules Dassin, "didn't particularly like *Brute Force*, but he said I was good in it. I thought it was a sensational movie — what a horrific thing it was." Critics agreed — Harrison Carroll wrote in the *Los Angeles Evening Herald Express*, "For ferocity and suspense, Hollywood has never filmed a jail-break equaling the one in this picture," and the reviewer for *Newsweek* termed the film "a forceful, even sadistic melodrama with moments of terrifying action and a climax that will raise the hackles on your neck." And Corey was singled out by several reviewers, including Lloyd L. Sloan of the *Los Angeles Citizen-News*, who stated that his performance was among those that "deserves to be lauded," and *The Hollywood Reporter*'s Jack D. Grant, who found that Corey's portrayal had "merit."

After his shocking role in *Brute Force*, Corey returned to tamer fare, playing such small parts as a cavalry officer in the Red Skelton comedy *A Southern Yankee* (1948), and a "cigarette smoker" in the box-office hit, *Homecoming* (1948), starring Clark Gable and Lana Turner. But he was back to prison with a starring role in his fourth film noir, *Canon City* (1948). Based on the real-life 1947 prison break from the Canon City prison in Colorado, the film offered a documentary-style approach and featured a number of the prison's actual inmates, as well as the prison's real-life warden playing himself. Corey starred as Carl Schwartzmiller, the ringleader of the break, who was still in prison at the time of the movie's on-location filming.

"That was some experience — the most awful thing was the smell of the uniforms and the dust on the floor — everything smelled of formaldehyde," Corey recalled. "I had a chance to talk to Schwartzmiller. He was in solitary, in a dark room, about a 4 × 4 aperture with bars through them. Schwartzmiller thought I would be good for the part. At one point when the chief of the guards' face was turned away, [Schwartzmiller] pointed to the pencil in my shirt pocket and whispered, 'pencil.' I gave it to him. On Saturday, I rented a car to visit relatives of my mother in Denver — when I drove back the next night, the PR man said, 'Did you hear about Schwartzmiller? He killed himself.' I asked him how he did it. The PR man said he'd broken a pencil and jabbed it into his vein and bled to death. I was so upset. I said to myself, 'How do I live with this?'

"And then the guy said he was just kidding."

After being singled out as "impressive" and "convincing" for his role in *Canon City*, Corey was seen in featured roles as a seaman in *Wake of the Red Witch* (1949), a rousing adventure starring John Wayne and Gail Russell; a double-crossing gang member in *Hideout* (1949); and a psychiatrist in the Stanley Kramer–directed *Home of the Brave* (1949), which Corey called his favorite film. He then starred as a police sergeant with William Lundigan and Dorothy Patrick in his final film noir, *Follow Me Quietly* (1949). Focusing on a series of murders committed by a psychotic known only as "The Judge," this 59-minute feature shows the painstaking efforts of the frustrated police to identify the killer by creating a life-size model of him, based on clues he leaves behind. Corey, who said he was "intrigued" with the film, later recalled an amusing exchange he had with director Richard Fleischer about his performance. "I watched myself in the rushes — one time I said I liked

Jeff Corey, Dorothy Patrick, and William Lundigan in *Follow Me Quietly* (1949).

what I was doing. I thought my performance was so economical," Corey said. "And Fleischer said, 'If it was any more economical, we wouldn't even see you!'"

During the next two years, Corey continued his busy filming schedule, appearing in a total of 14 features, including *Bright Leaf* (1950), starring Gary Cooper and Lauren Bacall, and *The Next Voice You Hear* (1950), which told the story of a couple who hears the voice of God on the radio, as well as such western dramas as *Rawhide* (1951), with Tyrone Power and Susan Hayward; *Red Mountain* (1951), with Alan Ladd; and *Only the Valiant* (1951), with Gregory Peck.

But by now, Corey had more pressing matters than learning his lines or being fitted for costumes. In 1947, the House Un-American Activities Committee had initiated an in-

vestigation into Communism in the motion picture industry, resulting in the imprisonment of a group of individuals who became known as the Hollywood Ten. Four years later, the committee began another round of hearings in an effort to root out Communists in Hollywood, leading to a "Red Scare" in which numerous actors, directors, writers, and other Hollywood workers provided names to the committee of individuals who were suspected of Communist activities. The committee's efforts resulted in the blacklisting of more than 320 Hollywood workers—including Jeff Corey.

According to the actor, he had participated in left-wing meetings several years earlier, but had long since dissociated himself from the movement. "Many of our friends were absolutely disenchanted with what the

American Communist Party turned out to be," Corey said. "We had not been politically involved for five years when this thing occurred." Despite this, Corey was named by actor Marc Lawrence, and almost immediately, his career as an actor came to a halt. The pilot for a television series co-starring Ann Harding was scrapped—"I was called in and told that all the advertising agencies had said they couldn't go on and support the show if I was going to be in it," Corey said. Next, the actor lost the starring role in the film *Angels in the Outfield* (1951). "I was thrilled to be able to play this part—an all–American boy," he recalled, "and that was taken away."

While frustrated by his inability to work in films and television, however, the resilient actor refused to be beaten. "It was an ugly thing, but I didn't go into mourning," he said. Instead, Corey got a job as a carpenter to support his family and enrolled at UCLA under the G.I. Bill of Rights. "I had a perfect average—unlike my high school experience," Corey recalled with amusement. "So there was something wrong with my high school— not me."

Before long, Corey was asked by a group of young actors to start a class teaching acting techniques. "They started coming to my house—Carol Burnett was one of them — and I took plywood and boards, and with very little money, I turned my garage into a theater. I never advertised, I was never in the phone book. It was all word-of-mouth." Corey began teaching seven classes a week, plus a children's class on Saturday mornings, and his pupils eventually included such notables as James Dean, Jack Nicholson, Rita Moreno, Robert Blake, Sheree North, and Richard Chamberlain.

"It became *the* place," he said. Over time, studios began assigning their actors to work with Corey, and the school was later described in *The National Observer* as "a major influence in the motion picture industry."

"I think I can honestly say that I was an actor's actor," Corey said. "Actors like me and respected me. And by teaching, it helped me sustain whatever talent I have as an actor."

As the years went on, Corey began to reacquaint himself with his acting career. He appeared at the Mark Taper Theater in *In the Matter of J. Robert Oppenheimer*, played Polonius in the Taper production of *Hamlet*, and appeared in *A View from the Bridge* in LaJolla, California, with Martin Balsam and Rita Moreno. He also began making television appearances in such series as *The Adventures of Superman*, *The Untouchables*, *Bonanza*, *Perry Mason*, and *Rawhide*.

Then, in 1963—12 years after his last film — Corey finally returned to the big screen. The film was *The Yellow Canary*, starring Pat Boone, Barbara Eden, and Steve Forrest.

"Pat Boone wanted me for that role — I was coaching him on a part, and we got along marvelously," Corey recalled. "One day he came to my house, saying, 'We did it, we did it, we did it!'"

Later that year, Corey was seen in *The Balcony* (1963), with Shelley Winters, Peter Falk, and another blacklisted star, Lee Grant. This was followed by *Lady in a Cage* (1964), where he was seen in the standout role of a wino who breaks into the house of a semi-invalid; *Once a Thief*, (1964), with Alain Delon and Jack Palance; and *Mickey One* (1965), a crime drama starring Warren Beatty. He also traveled to Germany to portray Abraham Lincoln in *Der Schatz der Azteken* (1965), helmed by the director of *The Killers*, Robert Siodmak.

"Nineteen years after *The Killers*, I got a telegram from Siodmak, asking me to play the part, and of course I was thrilled to do it," Corey recalled. He laughingly added that when he arrived at the airport, he put on a beard—"I looked like Alley Oop in the comics. The Berlin headlines said, 'Abraham Lincoln Has Come to Berlin.' I went to Siodmak and told him it was a ridiculous beard — and then I took out a five dollar bill and had them reconstruct it!"

Throughout the remainder of the decade, Corey was seen in a series of blockbusters, including *The Cincinnati Kid* (1965), with Steve McQueen and Edward G. Robinson; *In Cold Blood* (1967), with former student

Robert Blake; *True Grit* (1969), starring John Wayne; and the Robert Redford–Paul Newman starrer *Butch Cassidy and the Sundance Kid* (1969). "Couldn't do better than that," Corey said modestly.

As the 1970s began, Corey expanded his talents into the field of directing, overseeing episodes of such programs as *Night Gallery, Alias Smith and Jones, The Bob Newhart Show,* and *The Sixth Sense.* He also continued his guest appearances in front of the television camera, and appeared during the next three decades on some of the most popular series on network television, including *The Streets of San Francisco, Mission Impossible, Kojak, One Day at a Time, Starsky and Hutch, The Bionic Woman, Little House on the Prairie, Lou Grant, Night Court, The A-Team, Picket Fences, Murphy Brown, Babylon 5, Charmed,* and — in November 2000 — *The District.* He was also seen in such made-for-television movies as *Shootout* (1971), *Something Evil* (1972), *Curse of the Black Widow* (1977), *The Pirate* (1978), *Homeward Bound* (1980), *Father of Hell Town* (1985), *The Rose and the Jackal* (1990), and *The Lottery* (1996).

In between his television appearances, Corey found time for feature films as well — the most popular of these included *Little Big Man* (1970), *The Last Tycoon* (1976), *Oh, God!* (1977), and *Conan the Destroyer* (1984), directed by Richard Fleischer, who had directed Corey in *Follow Me Quietly.* His feature film roles continued throughout the 1990s.

And as if his jobs in front of and behind the camera did not consume enough of his time, the actor also held a number of education-related posts through the years. He was appointed Professor of Theatre Arts at California State University in Northridge; Artist in Residence at Ball State University in Indiana, the University of Illinois at Bloomington, the University of Texas at Austin, and the Graduate School of Creative Writing at New York University; and conducted seminars at Emory University in Atlanta and for the Canadian Film Institute.

Then, nearly five decades after he was blacklisted, and on the 50-year anniversary of the Hollywood Ten, an event took place that served in part to compensate Corey for the years he lost in Hollywood. On October 27, 1997, the Academy of Motion Picture Arts and Sciences in Beverly Hills, California, hosted "Hollywood Remembers the Blacklist," a commemoration organized by the American Federation of Television and Radio Artists, the Directors Guild of America, the Screen Actors Guild, and the Writers Guild of America, west. The occasion was designed to not only honor the professional and personal lives of the individuals blacklisted in the 1950s, but also to acknowledge the culpability of the four guilds in failing to provide their support. The event featured readings of HUAC testimonies by such luminaries as Kevin Spacey, James Cromwell, Billy Crystal, Alfre Woodard, Kathy Baker, John Lithgow, and David Hyde Pierce.

"The presidents of the guilds all got up and apologized — it was wonderful to see them get up and apologize, because they knew that none of us were criminals. We were exemplary citizens," Corey said. "It was an extraordinary meeting. All of the blacklisted people were invited — it was really a great event. So we were redeemed."

Corey — who died in August 2002 following complications from a fall in his Santa Monica home — added, however, that he neither forgave nor forgot about the men and women who testified at the hearings and named their colleagues.

"I loathe the informers," he said. "And they loathe themselves, and there's no forgiving them. You can't do that to another human being." Still, this stance didn't prevent the actor from acknowledging that he enjoyed an exceptional career and lived a full, happy, and fortuitous existence.

"I found my own way," he said in 2000. "We have wonderful children who understand and respect us. And six grandchildren. I'm still teaching. I have four union pensions. We have the greatest view in all Los Angeles.

"I feel good about my life."

Film Noir Filmography

Somewhere in the Night. Director: Joseph L. Mankiewicz. Producer: Anderson Lawler. Running time: 110 minutes. Released by 20th Century-Fox, June 12, 1946. Cast: John Hodiak, Nancy Guild, Lloyd Nolan, Richard Conte, Josephine Hutchinson, Fritz Kortner, Margo Woode, Sheldon Leonard, Lou Nova, John Russell, Houseley Stevenson, Charles Arnt, Al Sparlis, Jeff Corey, Henry Morgan.

The Killers. Director: Robert Siodmak. Producer: Mark Hellinger. Running time: 105 minutes. Released by Universal, August 28, 1946. Cast: Edmond O'Brien, Ava Gardner, Albert Dekker, Sam Levene, John Miljan, Virginia Christine, Vince Barnett, Burt Lancaster, Charles D. Brown, Donald MacBride, Phil Brown, Charles McGraw, William Conrad, Queenie Smith, Garry Owen, Harry Hayden, Bill Walker, Jack Lambert, Jeff Corey, Wally Scott, Gabrielle Windsor, Rex Dale. Awards: Academy Award Nominations for Best Director (Robert Siodmak), Best Film Editing (Arthur Hilton), Best Score/Drama or Comedy (Miklos Rozsa), Best Screenplay (Anthony Veiller).

The Gangster. Director: Gordon Wiles. Producers: Maurice and Frank King. Running time: 84 minutes. Released by Allied Artists, October 6, 1947. Cast: Barry Sullivan, Belita, Joan Lorring, Akim Tamiroff, Henry Morgan, John Ireland, Fifi D'Orsay, Virginia Christine, Sheldon Leonard, Leif Erickson, Charles McGraw, John Kellogg, Elisha Cook, Jr., Ted Hecht.

Brute Force. Director: Jules Dassin. Producer: Mark Hellinger. Running time: 95 minutes. Released by Universal-International, June 6, 1947. Cast: Burt Lancaster, Hume Cronyn, Charles Bickford, Yvonne DeCarlo, Ann Blyth, Ella Raines, Anita Colby, Sam Levene, Howard Duff, Art Smith, Roman Bohnen, John Hoyt, Richard Gaines, Frank Puglia, Jeff Corey, Vince Barnett, James Bell, Jack Overman, Whit Bissell, Sir Lancelot, Ray Teal, Jay C. Flippen, James O'Rear, Howland Chamberlain, Kenneth Patterson, Crane Whitley, Charles McGraw, John Harmon, Gene Stutenroth, Wally Rose, Carl Rhodes, Guy Beach, Edmund Cobb, Tom Steele.

Canon City. Director: Crane Wilbur. Producer: Bryan Foy. Running time: 82 minutes. Released by Eagle-Lion, June 30, 1948. Cast: Scott Brady, Jeff Corey, Whit Bissell, Stanley Clements, Charles Russell, DeForest Kelley, Ralph Byrd, Warden Roy Best, Henry Brandon, Alfred Linder, Ray Bennett, Bob Bice, Bob Kellard, Richard Irving, Bud Wolfe, Mabel Paige, Reed Hadley.

Follow Me Quietly. Director: Richard Fleischer. Producer: Herman Schlom. Running time: 59 minutes. Released by RKO, July 7, 1949. Cast: William Lundigan, Dorothy Patrick, Jeff Corey, Nestor Paiva, Charles D. Brown, Paul Guilfoyle, Edwin Max, Frank Ferguson, Marlo Dwyer, Michael Brandon, Douglas Spencer.

References

Benson, Rex. "Actor–Director–Teacher Jeff Corey: 'I Believe Acting Should Be Playful, Enjoyable; Keep Many Irons in Fire." *Drama-Logue*, May 4, 1979.

Biography of Jeff Corey. Paramount Pictures, December 1950.

Biography of Jeff Corey. Paramount Pictures, circa 1969.

Canayay, Jan. "An Interview." *Film Criticism*, Summer 1976.

"Corey Coming." *Christian Science Monitor*, February 17, 1973.

Drennan, Kathryn M. "A Test of Character." *Starlog*, December 1989.

Gauguin, Lorraine. "Jeff Corey: Shadowy Actor 'Overlooked, Not Neglected.'" *Los Angeles Times*, September 10, 1967.

Greenberg, Abe. "Jeff Corey Becomes an Acting Institution." *Hollywood Citizen-News*, January 12, 1970.

Harmetz, Aljean. "When the Government Said, 'Let's Put on a Show.'" *New York Times*, July 10, 1989.

"Jeff Corey Comeback." *The Hollywood Reporter*, January 6, 1961.

MacPherson, Virginia. "Actors Not Versatile Enough." *New York Morning Telegraph*, July 18, 1950.

Schumach, Murray. "TV Role for Actor Blacklisted in '50." *New York Times*, January 10, 1961.

Scott, Vernon. "Acting Coach: Nothing to It." *New Jersey Record*, January 2, 1975.

"'Seconds' Filming." *New York Daily News*, June 11, 1965.

Teal, James. "Interviews." *Dramatics*, May 1981.

Thomas, Bob. "Jeff Corey Is Back from 10-Year Exile." *Los Angeles Mirror*, January 20, 1961.

WENDELL COREY

"She's a stupid little tramp. I'm betting even money we'll have to get rid of her....
She'll go unremembered by the end of the week."—Wendell Corey in *The Big Knife*
(1955)

Wendell Corey was renowned for his versatility. In any given film, he could be seen as a demented killer, a cuckolded husband, a faithful chum, or the guy who never gets the girl—and play them all with equal skill. In a span of 22 years, Corey appeared in only 40 features, but he was seen opposite some of Hollywood's most luminous leading ladies, including Joan Crawford, Barbara Stanwyck, and Loretta Young. His brief but prestigious career included such screen classics as *Rear Window* (1954) and *The Rainmaker* (1956), and—although seldom cast as the heavy—he appeared in six notable offerings from the era of film noir: *I Walk Alone* (1948), *Sorry, Wrong Number* (1948), *The Accused* (1949), *The File on Thelma Jordon* (1950), *The Big Knife* (1955), and *The Killer Is Loose* (1956).

The reliable actor with the ice-blue eyes was born on March 20, 1914, in Dracut, Massachusetts, one of four children of a Congregational minister. Although his parents wanted Corey to follow his father into the ministry, the young man balked at the idea. Still, a career in acting was the furthest thought from his mind.

"I didn't just turn actor," Corey recalled in a 1946 interview. "As a matter of fact, I didn't have any idea of it. I got out of high school right in the teeth of the Depression. Money was short—and I went right after a job. Had quite a few of them around Springfield [Massachusetts] for three or four years."

Among Corey's jobs was a stint selling washing machines for a local department store. Taking a break one day from his salesman duties, he dropped by a rehearsal of the Springfield Repertory Players, where a friend was performing in *Street Scene*. Learning that the cast was in need of an actor to portray a Swedish janitor, Corey auditioned and won the part.

"Not much money in it. In fact, no money at all," Corey later said. "They'd gotten hold of me out of sheer desperation. No one else wanted the part. So I was selling refrigerators during the day and playing the janitor at night."

After this chance introduction to the theater, Corey never looked back. He remained with the Springfield company for a year, then toured in several productions throughout New England with the Federal Theater Project. While appearing at the Copley Theater in Boston in 1942, Corey fell for his co-star, Alice Wylie, and just three weeks later, the two were married by Corey's father. Corey and his wife later had four children, Robin, Jonathan, Jennifer, and Bonnie, and enjoyed a marriage that lasted until Corey's 1968 death.

Meanwhile, Corey played with a variety of stock companies, and appeared opposite Gertrude Lawrence in the road company of *Errand for Bernice*. Before long, he made his way to Broadway, appearing in a string of productions, including *Strip for Action, The First Million, Follow the Girls, Comes the Revelation, Manhattan Nocturne,* and *But Not Goodbye*. They were all flops. But Corey got his long-awaited break in 1946 when he was cast opposite Betty Field in Elmer Rice's *Dream Girl*.

"It was really a fluke the way I caught on with this," Corey said during the run of the successful play. "I tried for *The Rugged Path*, but I wasn't right for the part. Bob Sherwood, Garson Kanin, and Spencer Tracy were awfully nice about it, however. They agreed that I was a natural for this stint in *Dream Girl*. They went so far as to tell Elmer Rice that I'd fit into this. I read twice for him—and here I am in a dressing room that's a suite. I've even got a kitchenette and a bath!"

While Corey was performing in *Dream Girl*, Hollywood beckoned, and he signed a contract with producer Hal Wallis. But before heading for California, Corey fulfilled a dream he'd had for several years. Leasing a local community hall for the summer, he organized his own stock theater, for which he produced, directed, and starred in a repertory of 10 plays. Among the members of the company was actress Betsy Drake, who would later marry (and divorce) Cary Grant.

Once in Hollywood, Corey made his film debut in *Desert Fury* (1947) as a combination servant, strong-arm friend, and Svengali to a gambler, portrayed by John Hodiak. The following year, he was seen in *Man-Eater of Kumaon* (1948), a jungle adventure in which he starred as a doctor tracking down a man-eating tiger; *The Search* (1948), a sensitive portrait of the relationship between a soldier (Montgomery Clift) and a homeless Czech boy; and his first two films noirs: *I Walk Alone* (1948) and *Sorry, Wrong Number* (1948).

In *I Walk Alone*, Corey played Dave Turner, whose brother, Frankie (Burt Lancaster), has just been released from prison after a 14-year stretch for bootlegging. Despite his plans for the future, Frankie soon learns that his former partner, nightclub owner Noll "Dink" Turner (Kirk Douglas), has no intention of honoring the profit-sharing agreement they'd made before Frankie's arrest. He also discovers that Dink has not only hired Dave as his accountant, but that together they have created an intricate corporate structure that virtually guarantees Frankie's exclusion. Later, when Frankie stages an unsuccessful takeover of the club and Dink has him roughed up by his thugs, Dave decides that he's had enough: "When I saw Frankie take his beating, I got my stomach full — 100 percent full," he tells Dink. "There's not a fraction left for anything else.... There's not even enough room for me to be afraid anymore." When Dave threatens to expose Dink's corrupt dealings to police, however, Dink has him killed, but Frankie later forces a confession from the nightclub owner, who is gunned down by police while trying to flee.

Dismissed by one reviewer for his "wan" performance in *I Walk Alone*, Corey fared little better in his second noir of the year, *Sorry Wrong Number*. Here, he played the rather thankless role of the doctor to Leona Stevenson (Barbara Stanwyck), a domineering heiress described by Corey's character as a "cardiac neurotic" who suffers physical attacks brought on by "her emotions, her temper, and her frustrations." As this first-rate thriller begins, the bedridden Leona overhears a telephone conversation in which two men discuss the murder of an unidentified woman. By the time the feature reaches its nail-biting finale, Leona has learned that *she* is the woman being discussed, and that her weak-willed husband, Henry (Burt Lancaster), was the impetus behind the crime. Despite Henry's last-minute change of heart, and his frantic efforts to warn his wife, Leona is forced to watch in horror as her killer's shadowy figure moves furtively up the stairs to her room. Upon its release, *Sorry, Wrong Number* was a hit at the box office, earning high praise for the performances of Stanwyck and Lancaster; Corey's role as the mild-mannered physician, however, was mostly overlooked.

The following year, Corey appeared with Clark Gable and Alexis Smith in the moderately popular *Any Number Can Play* (1949); vied with Robert Mitchum for the affections of Janet Leigh in *Holiday Affair* (1949); and added another feature to his noir repertoire, *The Accused* (1949). This tense film starred Loretta Young as Dr. Wilma Tuttle, a prim psychology professor who is attacked by one of her students (Douglas Dick) and kills him, then covers up her crime by making his death appear as a diving accident. Although an inquest rules that the student's death was caused by drowning, a persistent detective, Ted Dorgan (Corey), refuses to accept this verdict. Only slightly hampered by his growing feelings for the professor, Dorgan continues to pursue the case, and his dogged investigation ultimately results in Tuttle's arrest for murder. Although the film's end is weakened by the professor's subsequent acquittal, *The Accused* was a tautly directed feature throughout, and was applauded by critics, including one who said it "exploits fear and emotional violence into a high-grade melodrama." Along with co-stars Young and Robert Cummings, Corey earned praise as well, with the reviewer from *Variety* writing that his "matter-of-fact police officer portrayal has a human quality that catches on," and the *New York Times* critic declaring that he "brings a high degree of conviction" to the role.

Corey remained in the dark realm of noir with his first release of 1950, *The File on Thelma Jordon*, starring Barbara Stanwyck. Here, Corey turned in a memorable performance as assistant district attorney Cleve Marshall, a devoted family man who gets far more than he bargained for when he falls in love with the appealing femme of the film's title. When Thelma is arrested for the murder of her elderly aunt, Cleve blindly believes her pleas of innocence — he not only finances the services of a top-flight defense attorney, but he also risks his career by deliberately bungling the prosecution of her case. Thelma is ultimately acquitted, but afterward, Cleve is stunned to learn that she was indeed guilty of killing her aunt, and also that she plans to run away with her long-time lover, Tony Laredo (Richard Rober). While later fleeing with Laredo, however, Thelma has a change of heart and causes the car to crash, resulting in both their deaths. Managing to cling to life until Cleve's arrival at the hospital, Thelma tells him, "I couldn't go on with him. You did that for me."

Two of Corey's four children, Robin and Jonathan, were also seen in small roles in *Thelma Jordon*—the actor later said he'd let himself "be talked into [it]," but he added that the experience was an illuminating one.

"I watched them — and since then, other children — start out fresh and enthusiastic and then saw the fatigue and frustration in their eyes when they had to do scenes over and over again," Corey said in 1956. "When people ask my advice about getting children into the movies, I tell them, 'If you want to be Fagins, go ahead. If you love your kids, don't subject them to working in pictures.'"

Also that year, Corey starred in a pair of first-rate features, *Harriet Craig* (1950), in which he played the long-suffering husband of the title character, and *The Furies* (1950), a moody western where he was seen as the lover of Barbara Stanwyck. During the next several years, he appeared in such successful features as *Rich, Young and Pretty* (1951), an enjoyable musical starring Jane Powell; *Carbine Williams* (1952), a crime drama with James Stewart and Jean Hagen; *My Man and I* (1952), a interesting melodrama with Ricardo Montalban and Shelley Winters; and, in what was arguably the best film of his career, Alfred Hitchcock's *Rear Window* (1954), starring James Stewart and Grace Kelly. In this riveting feature, Stewart starred as a wheelchair-bound photographer who suspects one of his neighbors of a gruesome murder; Corey played Stewart's sardonic detective friend, who initially disregards his theories. (Years later, he would recall the experience of acting with Grace Kelly, who retired from films two years later to marry Prince Rainier of Monaco: "When we made that picture, I predicted that Miss Kelly would get whatever she wanted out of life," Corey said in 1958. "She was a wonderful girl, and was so sure of where she was going, I predicted she would make it. She did.")

After *Rear Window*, Corey portrayed a rare dastardly role in the engrossing and often disturbing film noir *The Big Knife* (1955). With the incongruous moniker of Smiley Coy, Corey portrayed the shallow, disingenuous lackey of studio chief Stanley Hoff (Rod Steiger), who is willing to go to any lengths to protect the studio's cinematic investments— even murder. Of particular interest to Coy and Hoff is Charlie Castle (Jack Palance), a self-absorbed, philandering film star whose refusal to re-sign with the studio serves as the catalyst for a series of luckless events, including the threatened exposure of his auto accident that resulted in a child's death. In one of the film's most memorable scenes, Coy focuses his attentions on the starlet who has been "shooting her mouth off" about the accident, detailing his idea to ensure her silence: "Take her home, give her some martinis ... the gin is doctored," Coy calmly instructs Charlie. "Leave the minute she passes out —from that moment on, you're in the clear.... Everything you are this minute depends on a few drinks in a trollop's guts." Although he balks at Smiley's reprehensible scheme, Charlie's world begins to collapse after he recklessly insults Hoff, and he ultimately commits suicide because, according to one character, because he "just couldn't go on hurting those he loved." Described by a reviewer as "a candidly toadying hypocrite," Corey was a first-rate addition to the film's outstanding cast.

The following year, Corey starred in another high point of his film career, *The Rainmaker* (1956), playing the patient, would-be boyfriend of Katharine Hepburn, who almost loses her to a charismatic con man played by Burt Lancaster. Later that year, he was back on the dark side of the screen — and, this time, the wrong side of the law — in his final film noir, *The Killer Is Loose* (1956). As this feature begins, police detective Sam Wagner (Joseph Cotten) accidentally shoots and kills the spouse of bank robber Leon Poole (Corey). After spending three years in prison for the robbery, Poole escapes, vowing revenge on the detective by killing his wife, Lila (Rhonda Fleming). Craftily evading a police dragnet, Poole murders a local farmer and forces his way into the home of Otto Flanders (John Larch), an old army "pal" who'd given Poole the hated nickname of "Foggy" during their time together in the service. Flanders is added to the killer's list of victims after he foolishly tells Poole, "I could take you myself if I had to ... and I'm just one guy without a gun." (After fatally shooting Flanders, Poole quietly asks the dead man's hysterical wife, "What else could I do?") With single-minded determination, Poole manages to reach the detective's house and nearly succeeds in his plan of revenge before he is shot by police. Although Corey turned in a frighteningly memorable performance as the bespectacled killer, the feature was panned by the *New York Times'* Bosley Crowther, who wrote: "The only thing remarkable about this picture is that it could be so absolutely dull with Mr. Cotten and Mr. Corey in it."

During the remainder of the 1950s, Corey appeared in a handful of mostly forgettable fare; his best was a rare comedy portrayal of the title character in *Alias Jesse James* (1959), produced by and starring Bob Hope. Instead, the actor focused most of his energies during the decade on the small screen. In October 1951, Corey had his first major television role in a production of "Susan and God" on *Celanese Theatre*, and starred on the same series two years later in "A Tale of Two Cities." He moved into series television in 1957, portraying as a U.S. Coast Guard captain on the short-lived half-hour series, *Harbor Command*, and in 1959 played the father of Patsy McCormack (of *The Bad Seed* [1956] fame) in *Peck's Bad Girl*.

"I decided to appear in a series for just one reason — money," Corey once said. "I'd have to make two pictures a year to earn as much loot as I will on [television]. This way I can do both."

Also during the 1950s, and continuing in the 1960s, Corey returned to his roots in the theater, appearing in the London cast of

Voice of the Turtle opposite Margaret Sullavan; *Sabrina Fair* with Diana Lynn; the seven-
month national company tour of *The Caine
Mutiny Courtmartial*; the Broadway production of *Night of the Auk* with Christopher
Plummer and Claude Rains; and *Jolly's Progress* with Eartha Kitt for the Theatre Guild.
Corey also starred opposite his wife in a production in Ogunquit, Maine, and appeared
with his entire family in *Our Town* at Elitch's
Gardens in Denver. To accommodate his frequent stage and television appearances, Corey
moved his family to New Canaan, Connecticut.

"Los Angeles is more smoggy than sunny.
It's no place to raise kids," Corey said in 1956.
"As for their being more space for kids to play
in out there ... Los Angeles kids live in their
backyards. There's much more 'country' in
the East." The family lived at their "country"
home in Connecticut for the next several
years before relocating back to "smoggy" California.

From January to July 1961, Corey starred
opposite Nanette Fabray in the NBC television series, *Westinghouse Playhouse* (also
known as the *Nanette Fabray Show* or *Yes Yes
Nanette*), and the following year was seen in
another NBC series, this time a medical drama
called *The Eleventh Hour*. Corey starred as a
court-appointed psychiatrist, Dr. Theodore
Bassett, but left the show after a year to return
to films and was replaced by Ralph Bellamy.

"I'm not one of those guys who knock
making movies," Corey said once. "I guess
that's because I'm not stage-struck. Don't get
me wrong — acting is a good life, the best. But
I'd just as soon stick to pictures."

Back in Hollywood, Corey was seen in
only one feature, *Blood on the Arrow* (1964),
a western starring Dale Robertson, before he
took up another interest — politics. A one-
time president of the Academy of Motion Picture Arts and Sciences and a director of the
Screen Actors Guild, Corey had also previously participated in several political activities, including introducing President Dwight
D. Eisenhower at the ball for his second in-
auguration in 1956, and serving as chairman

at the 1959 San Francisco Republican convention. Then, in 1965, the actor took his political leanings a step further when he won a seat
on the Santa Monica city council, saying that
he was "interested in the things that are going on."

"I got tired of hearing myself say why
don't they do something about such-and-such
a problem. Or when are they going to do such
and so?" Corey told columnist Vernon Scott
in 1965. "My friends grew weary of hearing
me talk about 'they' all the time. It turns out
'they' is me, and the rest of the city's citizens."

Although Corey insisted in the 1965 interview that he had no aspirations for higher
political office ("Politics start at the local level
and that's as far as I want to go," he said), he
threw his hat in the ring the following year for
the United States House of Representatives
from the 28th District in Santa Monica. He
took time out during the campaign, however,
to co-star with Howard Keel and Joan Caulfield in *Red Tomahawk* (1967), a well-done
depiction of the battle of Little Big Horn, and
his bid for Congress was ultimately unsuccessful.

In 1968, after his failed campaign for
Congress, Corey was seen as a villainous cattle baron in *Buckskin*, with Barry Sullivan and
Joan Caulfield, and later that year he was cast
as an FBI agent in *The Astro-Zombies* (1969),
whose name alone provides a fairly accurate
indication of its quality. But Corey would not
live to see the film's release.

In October 1968, shortly after filming his
role for *The Astro-Zombies*, Corey began complaining to friends that he felt ill. Admitted
to the Motion Picture Country Home and
Hospital, Corey died there on November 8,
1968, of a liver ailment. He was only 54 years
old.

One of Hollywood's unsung leading men,
Wendell Corey demonstrated his talent and
versatility in widely varying roles in such films
as *Rear Window*, *The Rainmaker*, and *The
Killer Is Loose*. Although his entry into the
acting world was strictly by chance, it was a
fortuitous accident that benefited his legions
of fans.

Film Noir Filmography

I Walk Alone. Director: Byron Haskin. Producer: Hal B. Wallis. Running time: 98 minutes. Released by Paramount, January 22, 1948. Cast: Burt Lancaster, Lizabeth Scott, Kirk Douglas, Wendell Corey, Kristine Miller, George Rigaud, Marc Lawrence, Mike Mazurki, Mickey Knox, Roger Neury.

Sorry, Wrong Number. Director: Anatole Litvak. Producers: Hal B. Wallis, Anatole Litvak. Running time: 98 minutes. Released by Paramount, September 1, 1948. Cast: Barbara Stanwyck, Burt Lancaster, Ann Richards, Wendell Corey, Harold Vermilyea, Ed Begley, Leif Erickson, William Conrad, John Bromfield, Jimmy Hunt, Dorothy Neumann, Paul Fierro. Awards: Academy Award nomination for Best Actress (Barbara Stanwyck).

The Accused. Director: William Dieterle. Producer: Hal B. Wallis. Running time: 101 minutes. Released by Paramount, January 12, 1949. Cast: Loretta Young, Robert Cummings, Wendell Corey, Sam Jaffe, Douglas Dick, Suzanne Dalbert, Sara Allgood.

The File on Thelma Jordan. Director: Robert Siodmak. Producer: Hal B. Wallis. Running time: 100 minutes. Released by Paramount, January 18, 1950. Cast: Barbara Stanwyck, Wendell Corey, Paul Kelly, Joan Tetzel, Stanley Ridges, Richard Rober, Minor Watson, Barry Kelley, Laura Elliott, Basil Ruysdael, Jane Novak, Gertrude W. Hoffman, Harry Antrim, Kate Lawson, Theresa Harris, Byron Barr, Geraldine Wall, Jonathan Corey, Robin Corey.

The Big Knife. Director and Producer: Robert Aldrich. Running time: 111 minutes. Released by United Artists, November 8, 1955. Cast: Jack Palance, Ida Lupino, Wendell Corey, Jean Hagen, Rod Steiger, Shelley Winters, Ilka Chase, Everett Sloane, Wesley Addy, Paul Langton, Nick Dennis, Bill Walker, Mike Winkelman, Mel Welles, Robert Sherman, Strother Martin, Ralph Volkie, Michael Fox, Richard Boone.

The Killer Is Loose. Director: Budd Boetticher. Producer: Robert L. Jacks. Running time: 73 minutes. Released by United Artists, March 2, 1956. Cast: Joseph Cotten, Rhonda Fleming, Wendell Corey, Alan Hale, Jr., Michael Pate, Virginia Christine, John Larch, John Beradino, Paul Bryar, Dee J. Thompson.

References

"Corey Meets An Old Boss." *The Louisville Courier-Journal*, September 21, 1958.
Corey, Wendell. "I Never Dry the Dishes." Publication Unsourced, circa 1949.
Francis, Robert. "Minister's Son, Wendell Corey by Name, Hits the Big Jackpot." *Brooklyn Daily Eagle*, February 10, 1946.
"Gastric Disorder Hits Actor Corey." *New York Mirror-News*, November 2, 1958.
"Grass Roots Campaign?" *New York Morning Telegraph*, May 31, 1966.
Okon, May. "They'll Take the East." *Sunday News*, July 8, 1956.
"Wendell Corey Hurts Arm in Fall." *New York Post*, September 22, 1963.
"Who's Who in the Cast." *Playbill*, The Wind Is Ninety, August 26, 1945.
Scott, Vernon. "Film Salaries and the System." *New York World Telegram*, January 10, 1959.
_____. "New Politico." *Newark Evening News*, June 11, 1965.
Shaffer, Rosalind K. Biography of Wendell Corey, circa 1961.
"The New Corey." *New York Herald-Tribune*, October 28, 1949.
"Wendell Corey, Actor by Chance, Dead at 54." *New York Post*, November 9, 1968.
"Wendell Corey, 54, Dead." *New York Times*, November 9, 1968.

JOSEPH COTTEN

"The whole world is a joke to me." — Joseph Cotten in *Shadow of a Doubt* (1943)

Joseph Cotten's film career was fruitful but curious. In a span of four decades, he appeared in nearly 100 films, including such classics as *Citizen Kane* (1941), *The Magnificent Ambersons* (1942), and *Gaslight* (1944), and earned a lasting reputation of film excellence. The bulk of his many films, however, ranged from slightly-better-than-mediocre to downright awful ("Everyone flirts now and then with a little trash," he once said). Still, although most of his quality productions were released early in his lengthy career, Cotten possessed an unquestionable talent, elegant good looks, and suave demeanor that combined to make him a star of Hollywood's Golden Age and a memorable contributor to film noir in five features from the era: *Journey into Fear* (1941), *Shadow of a Doubt* (1943), *The Third Man* (1949), *Niagara* (1953), and *The Killer is Loose* (1956).

The tall, urbane actor was born on May 15, 1905, in Petersburg, Virginia, where his father, Joseph Cotten, Sr., worked as assistant postmaster. Receiving his schooling in the Petersburg educational system, Cotten's first job was working for his father, disbursing special delivery mail by bicycle.

"I had the best pair of legs in the world," Cotten once remarked. "I pedaled a million miles if I pedaled a yard."

After getting his first taste of acting while performing in high school productions, Cotten became so enamored with the stage that he dropped out of school, borrowed $150 from a banker relative, and enrolled at the Hickman School of Expression in Washington, D.C. In retrospect, however, the actor was not impressed with his formal training.

"Mr. Hickman's voice lessons were invaluable," he wrote in his 1987 autobiography, *Vanity Will Get You Somewhere*. "Beyond that, I learned that private acting instruction should be prohibited by law.... It is the audience who teaches [an actor] to act, and that can take place only in a theater."

A year later, Cotten moved to New York where, unable to find stage work, he eked out a living as a paint salesman. In 1925, after "wearing out a half-dozen pairs of shoes tramping Broadway," Cotten was lured by a real estate boom to Miami, Florida, landing a job as an advertising salesman at the *Miami Herald* newspaper, and finally gaining some acting experience in numerous productions at the Miami Civic Theatre. He also found time to start the Tip Top Salad Company, for which he packaged and sold potato salad to area drug stores.

"It was a good life for a lazy fellow like

me," Cotten recalled in a 1979 *Los Angeles Times* interview. "I managed to spend many days on the beach getting a suntan."

Armed with a letter of introduction from a patron of the Miami Civic Theatre, Cotten returned to New York and found work as assistant stage manager for producer David Belasco. While working with Belasco, Cotten also understudied Melvyn Douglas in the 1930 stage play *Tonight or Never*, and later spent a season with the Copley Theater Players in Boston, appearing in close to 30 productions. While in Boston, Cotten married Lenore Kip, an associate editor for *Harper's Bazaar* magazine whom he had met in Miami. The two would remain married until Lenore's death from leukemia nearly 30 years later.

Back in New York, Cotten found work modeling and acting in one-reel industrial films. He also met the man who would introduce him to Hollywood — Orson Welles. According to Cotten, the two became fast friends after being thrown out of a New York radio studio for laughing inappropriately during a live broadcast. Outside the studio, Welles reportedly told Cotten, "You seem to like the same things I do. How'd you like to work with me on the stage?"

"Up to then, I hadn't really much stage experience. But [Orson] took a chance on me and gave me my first starring role," Cotten later recalled. "Pretty soon I was doing all kinds of jobs for him, and other actors started calling me 'assistant genius.' Orson and I had rooms next door to each other in a basement in Greenwich Village. We had holes in our shoes, but smoked dollar cigars."

Cotten joined the "boy genius" for two plays in Welles' Unit 891 of the Federal Theatre, and when Welles and John Houseman established the Mercury Theater in 1937, Cotten was cast in three productions, including *Julius Caesar*. Later, Cotten won the coveted role of C.K. Dexter Haven opposite Katharine Hepburn in the hit stage play *The Philadelphia Story*, but while he garnered favorable reviews for his performance, the actor was overlooked in favor of Cary Grant when the film rights were bought in 1940. Down, but not out, Cotten instead made his screen debut in what is now considered one of the best films ever made: *Citizen Kane* (1941). Notwithstanding his admission that he was "scared to death of the camera," Cotten earned widespread accolades for his portrayal of the film's cynical drama critic Jedidiah Leland; in a typical review, the *New York Times*' Bosley Crowther wrote that Cotten's portrayal "puts to shame the surface posturing of some of our more popular stars."

"I'd have never gotten into movies if Orson Welles hadn't been making *Citizen Kane*," Cotten said once. "Orson had all his old Mercury actors in *Citizen Kane*, so I jumped at the chance to be in it."

Following a role as the romantic lead opposite Merle Oberon in Alexander Korda's *Lydia* (1942), and earning praise for his "fine and sensitive acting" in Welles' *The Magnificent Ambersons* (1942), Cotten was cast in the film that would serve as his initiation into the world of film noir —*Journey Into Fear* (1941). Produced by Welles and co-written by Cotten, this early noir entry centers on munitions expert Howard Graham (Cotten), who is nearly killed by an assassin's bullet while visiting a nightclub in Istanbul. Informed that

he is the target of a Nazi conspiracy, Graham returns to America aboard a cargo ship, where one of the passengers is a Turkish agent, Kuvetli (Edgar Barrier), assigned to ensure Graham's safe passage. Also on board are Muller (Eustace Wyatt), the brains behind the Nazi plot, and Banat (Jack Moss), the trigger man from the nightclub. Later, Kuvetli turns up dead, Graham is captured by — and ultimately escapes from — the Nazis, and Muller is killed during a shootout atop a rain-slick building.

After being singled out in the *New York Times* for his "deftly suggestive performance" in *Journey to Fear*, Cotten signed a long-term contract with producer David O. Selznick, who promptly loaned him out for his second noir, Alfred Hitchcock's *Shadow of a Doubt* (1943). Here, Cotten turned in a subtle performance as Charlie Oakley, a self-described "promoter [who has] done a little bit of everything," who pays a visit to the small town of Santa Rosa, California. During Oakley's stay with his sister's family, which includes his adoring niece and namesake, Charlie (Teresa Wright), it is revealed that the out-of-towner is suspected of murdering a series of wealthy widows. Despite Oakley's charming demeanor, he reveals a darker side during a mealtime diatribe on his female peers: "The cities are full of women — middle-aged, widows, husbands dead," Oakley says. "Husbands who've spent their lives making fortunes. Working and working. And they die and leave their money to their wives.... And what do the wives do, these useless women? You see them in the hotels, the best hotels, every day by the thousands. Drinking the money, eating the money. Losing the money at bridge, playing all day and all night. Smelling of money. Proud of their jewelry but of nothing else. Horrible, faded, fat, greedy women." Although young Charlie ultimately comes to believe that her uncle is guilty, another suspect in the "Merry Widow" murders is killed while fleeing police and the case is officially closed. A short time later, Oakley abruptly decides to leave town, but as the train departs the city, he forces his niece to remain on board and tries to kill her by throwing her from the moving vehicle.

During the struggle, however, Charlie hangs on to the side of the train, and Oakley falls to his death instead. For his role as the frightening uncle, Cotten was labeled "excellent" by the critic for *Variety*, and Bosley Crowther raved in the *New York Times*: "As the progressively less charming Uncle Charlie, Joseph Cotten plays with smooth, insinuating ease while injecting a harsh and bitter quality which nicely becomes villainy."

After *Shadow of a Doubt*, Cotten was seen in a series of romantic leads, including the wartime hit *Since You Went Away* (1943), starring Claudette Colbert and Shirley Temple, and *I'll Be Seeing You* (1943), in which he played a shell-shocked war veteran who is nursed back to health by Ginger Rogers. He also co-starred with Ingrid Bergman and Charles Boyer in the outstanding *Gaslight* (1944); *Love Letters* (1945) and *Duel in the Sun* (1945), both opposite Jennifer Jones; *The Farmer's Daughter* (1947), co-starring Loretta Young in her Academy-Award winning title role; and *Portrait of Jennie* (1948), a ghostly love story for which Cotten received the Venice Film Festival award for best actor. The actor finished the decade with *Under Capricorn* (1949), a rather disappointing offering from Alfred Hitchcock, and two more films noirs, *The Third Man* (1949) and *Beyond the Forest* (1949).

In the first, Cotten starred as Holly Martins, a writer of "cheap novelettes" who journeys to Vienna to join his friend, Harry Lime (Orson Welles). Upon his arrival, however, Holly is shocked to learn that Harry has been killed after being struck by a car, and he endeavors to unearth the circumstances after he receives conflicting stories about the accident. One version maintained that, after being hit by the car, Harry was carried to the roadside by two men, but a second account revealed the presence of a "third man." Joined by Harry's faithful girlfriend, Anna Schmidt (Alida Valli), Holly ultimately learns that his friend faked his death to escape capture for his role in a corrupt racket that resulted in several deaths. Earning the disdain of Anna, with whom he has fallen in love,

Holly works with police to capture Harry, eventually gunning him down after a harrowing chase through the waterways of the city. (In the film's irony-tinged final scene, Holly waits for Anna to join him as they both exit Harry's second — and final — funeral. Instead, she walks past him on the road as if he isn't even there.)

Next, in a somewhat thankless role in *Beyond the Forest*, Cotten portrayed Lewis Moline, a doctor in the small mill town of Loyalton, Wisconsin, who manages to maintain a sunny disposition despite the constant griping of his discontented wife, Rosa (Bette Davis). ("Life in Loyalton is like sitting in a funeral parlor and waiting for the funeral to begin," Rosa says in one scene. "No, not sitting — lying in a coffin and waiting for them to carry you out.") In an effort to escape her dull existence, Rosa has an affair with wealthy Chicago manufacturer, Neil Latimer (David Brian), but after he announces his plan to marry a local socialite, she finds that she is carrying his child. Later, Latimer breaks his engagement to return to Rosa, who conceals her pregnancy and plans to run away with her lover, but her scheme is thwarted when Lewis' hunting buddy, Moose (Minor Watson), discovers her secret. During a hunting party, Rosa kills Moose in a shooting that is later judged accidental, but Rosa, anxious to join Latimer in Chicago, is still burdened with her burgeoning pregnancy. After throwing herself down an embankment in an attempt to induce a miscarriage, Rosa suffers peritonitis instead, and eventually dies from the disease, collapsing beside the train tracks after her final, desperate effort to leave town.

Cotten earned high marks for his understated performances in both of his 1949 noirs, particularly *The Third Man*, for which he was praised in the *Los Angeles Times* as "notably right for the American writer," and in *The New Yorker* as the "perfect embodiment [of] a man who believes in the value of his own cheap cowboy fantasies." Unfortunately, as the decade drew to an end, it became apparent that the bulk of the actor's best films and most memorable roles were behind him. He never wanted for work, however, and when his contract with Selznick expired in 1949, he signed with 20th Century–Fox, landing good parts in such well-received films as *Two Flags West* (1950), a Civil War drama starring Cotten as the leader of a band of Confederate prisoners, and *September Affair* (1950), in which he played an unhappily married man who falls in love with co-star Joan Fontaine. Not quite as popular with critics or audiences were *Peking Express* (1951), which took place aboard a train of the film's title, and *Untamed Frontier* (1952), a mediocre western with Shelley Winters and Scott Brady. The latter film was notable primarily for the ruptured disk Cotten sustained while shooting a fight with Brady.

After a small role in Orson Welles' *Othello* (1952), Cotten was back to film noir in *Niagara* (1953), co-starring Marilyn Monroe. In this rare Technicolor noir, Cotten is George Loomis, a brooding, unstable man who has been recently released from a mental institution. On vacation in Niagara Falls, George is unaware that his flashy young wife, Rose (Monroe), is having a steamy affair and that she and her lover are planning his demise. When he learns of the affair, George murders Rose and flees from police in a stolen boat, unaware that another vacationer, Polly Cutler (Jean Peters), is aboard. Caught in the churning waters of the Falls when the boat runs out of gas, George manages to help Polly to safety before he plummets over the Falls to his death.

Following the release of *Niagara*, in which he earned praise for his haunting performance of the tortured spouse, Cotten returned to his roots on the stage, starring on Broadway with Maragaret Sullavan in the hit production of *Sabrina Fair*. The following year, he made his television debut on *General Electric Theater* in "The High Green Wall," which aired on October 3, 1954. The event marked the beginning of the actor's long association with the small screen — in 1955, he hosted the 20th Century–Fox Hour, in 1956-57, he was the host and occasional lead player in *On Trial* (later changed to *The Joseph Cot-*

ten Show), and for the next two decades he would appear on such popular series as *Zane Grey Theater*, *Producers' Showcase*, *The Barbara Stanwyck Show*, *Alfred Hitchcock Presents*, *Wagon Train*, *The Virginian*, *Cimarron Strip*, *It Takes a Thief*, *The Rockford Files*, *The Streets of San Francisco*, and *The Hardy Boys/Nancy Drew* Mysteries.

Meanwhile, Cotten returned to the silver screen in 1956, continuing his sojourn in the shadowy dominion of noir with *The Killer Is Loose* (1956), his fifth feature from the era. Here, Cotten portrayed Sam Wagner, a police detective who accidentally shoots and kills the spouse of a bank robber, Leon Poole (chillingly played by Wendell Corey). Vowing revenge on Wagner, Poole later escapes from prison, bent on vindicating his wife's death by killing Wagner's spouse (Rhonda Fleming). Artfully avoiding the dragnet that surrounds the area, Poole makes his way to Wagner's home, where he nearly succeeds in exacting his revenge before being gunned down by police.

Although *The Killer is Loose* is a taut, well-acted feature, it was trashed by critics, including Bosley Crowther of the *New York Times*, who bitingly wrote that "the only thing remarkable about this picture is that is could be so absolutely dull with Mr. Cotten and Mr. Corey in it. That must have taken genius on the part of them." Cotten's follow-up to this film was better received — in *The Bottom of the Bottle* (1956), he turned in a first-rate performance as a prominent attorney whose prosperous life is disrupted when his estranged brother escapes from prison and turns up at his door.

Cotten finished out the decade with *The Halliday Brand* (1957), a top-notch western with Betsy Blair and Viveca Lindfors; *From the Earth to the Moon* (1958), a tiresome science-fiction feature; and a role that amounted little more than a cameo appearance in *Touch of Evil* (1958), an outstanding film noir written and directed by his old friend Orson Welles.

For his next film, *The Angel Wore Red* (1960), co-starring Ava Gardner and Dirk

Bogarde, Cotten traveled with his wife, Lenore, for on-location shooting in Rome. But while he was there, tragedy struck — on Christmas Day in 1959, Lenore fell ill and checked into the Salvator Mundi International Hospital. Newspapers reported that she was suffering from a condition diagnosed as pernicious anemia and plans were made to return her to the United States, but on January 7, 1960, Lenore died of leukemia. She was only 53 years old.

Just 10 months later, in October 1960, Cotten was in the news again when he announced that he was planning another trip down the aisle — wife number two was 37-year-old, British-born actress Patricia Medina, with whom Cotten had been friends for several years. A few weeks after the announcement hit the newspapers, the two were married in a small ceremony at the Beverly Hills home of producer David O. Selznick, who gave the bride away.

In addition to his continued work in film — including *The Last Sunset* (1961) with Rock Hudson and Kirk Douglas— and television (in 1963, Cotten hosted a weekly television series, *Hollywood and the Stars*), the actor began appearing on stage with his new wife. Their first production together was a 56-city road tour of *Prescription Murder*, followed by 222 Broadway performances of *Calculated Risk*, directed by Robert Montgomery. Over the next two decades, the couple would appear in several more plays together, as well as such feature films as *Timber Tramps* (1973).

"I'd like to contradict the opinion that husbands and wives should not work together," Cotten told a reporter in 1965. "I consider the chance to appear with [Patricia] the best kind of luck I could have."

As Cotten continued to accept film roles, the quality of the features steadily diminished. There were notable exceptions, however, including such box-office winners as *Hush … Hush, Sweet Charlotte* (1964), with Bette Davis in the title role; *The Oscar* (1966), another Bette Davis starrer; the quirky horror film, *The Abominable Dr. Phibes* (1971); and *Twilight's Last Gleaming* (1977), a star-studded

political thriller with a cast that included Burt Lancaster, Richard Widmark, Charles Durning, and Melvyn Douglas. These profit-makers aside, most of Cotten's appearances during this period were in films like *Jack of Diamonds* (1967), an insipid thriller starring George Hamilton, and *Doomsday Voyage* (1972), in which Cotten played a ship's captain whose daughter is raped by a political assassin. He also starred in a string of low-budget European productions, and was seen in a series of commercials for Bufferin aspirin. Of the latter job, Cotten contended that the "money was too good and it would have been disrespectful to turn it down."

"I went through a period where friends and a thoughtful agent urged me to be 'selective'— to hold out for only the best. I did, and I didn't work for over a year," Cotten said once. "I am frankly aware of the fact that I do a number of films and even television shows that may not win Oscars or other awards … but there's little satisfaction in sitting home and looking at your awards while the other fellow is working. The ideal existence for an actor is to keep working and to be associated with as little junk as possible."

Cotten made his last film appearances in the notorious box office flop *Heaven's Gate* (1980), starring Kris Kristofferson and Christopher Walken, and *The Survivor* (1981), a fairly good supernatural drama that was produced in Australia and never released in U.S. theaters. Shortly after the release of *The Survivor*, Cotten was felled by a massive stroke that left him unable to speak. After several months of therapy, however, he regained some of his speech ability.

The actor was out of the public eye for most of the 1980s, until his autobiography, *Vanity Will Get You Somewhere*, was published in 1987. The book was hailed by critics— the reviewer for *Publisher's Weekly* termed it "engagingly humorous and touching," and Herb Caen of the *San Francisco Chronicle* gushed: "A great actor simply has no right to write so good."

But just three years after the triumphant release of his book, Cotten faced another health crisis when cancer of the larynx forced him to undergo surgery for the removal of his voice box. Veteran columnist Army Archerd shared the news with his readers in *Variety* by reporting that "the inimitable romantic voice of Joseph Cotten will be stilled forever today."

"His ever-attentive and beautiful wife Pat Medina tearfully said he is being 'terribly brave — and is only worrying about me,'" Archerd wrote. "Cotten has taken up sculpting and told Pat, 'If I can't speak and I can't act, I can be a sculptor.'" Less than four months later, Cotten was able to communicate by using an electronic voice box and, Archerd announced, "[did] not sound like other friends who underwent similar surgery and use earlier, older devices that give the voice a mechanical robot-like sound. Cotten's immediate self-application to the change is a tribute to his perseverance, his actor's training — and the devotion of his dear wife."

Sadly, just four years later, at the age of 88, Cotten contracted pneumonia and died on February 6, 1994. His wife, Patricia, was at his side.

With a career that encompassed radio, television, film, and the stage, included acting and writing, and spanned nearly a half-century, Joseph Cotten left behind a legacy with which to be reckoned. While the fact remains that most of his memorable films were produced in the early part of his screen career, there is no denying that an examination of his cinematic contributions reveals a body of work that is impressive as well as appreciated. Perhaps it was writer Charles Champlin who best encapsulated Joseph Cotten's lasting appeal:

"The persisting core of Cotten's work has been an elegant and unobtrusive craftsmanship which emphasized the role that Cotten was playing rather than the fact that Cotten was playing it," Champlin said. "Not often has an important Hollywood personality of Cotten's generation been so deferential to the material itself."

Film Noir Filmography

Journey Into Fear. Director: Norman Foster (and Orson Welles, uncredited). Producer: Orson Welles. Running time: 71 minutes. Released by RKO, March 18, 1943. Cast: Joseph Cotten, Dolores Del Rio, Orson Welles, Ruth Warrick, Agnes Moorehead, Everett Sloane, Jack Moss, Jack Durant, Eustace Wyatt, Frank Readick, Edgar Barrier, Stefan Schanbel, Hans Conreid, Robert Meltzer, Richard Bennett, Shifra Haran, Herbert Drake, Bill Roberts.

Shadow of a Doubt. Director: Alfred Hitchcock. Producer: Jack H. Skirball. Running time: 108 minutes. Released by Universal, January 12, 1943. Cast: Teresa Wright, Joseph Cotten, Macdonald Carey, Henry Travers, Patricia Collinge, Hume Cronyn, Edna Mae Wonacott, Wallace Ford, Irving Bacon, Charles Bates, Clarence Muse, Janet Shaw, Estelle Jewell, Minverva Urecal, Isabel Randolph, Earle S. Dewey. Awards: Academy Award nomination for Best Original Story (Gordon McDonell).

The Third Man. Director: Carol Reed. Producer: Alexander Korda. Running time: 104 minutes. Released by London Films, 1949. Cast: Joseph Cotten, Orson Welles, Alida Valli, Trevor Howard, Paul Hoerbiger, Ernst Deutsch, Erich Ponto, Siegfried Breuer, Bernard Lee, Geoffrey Keen, Hedwig Bleibtreu, Annie Rosar, Herbert Halbik, Alexis Chesnakov, Wilfrid Hyde-White, Paul Hardtmuth, Nelly Arno, Jenny Werner, Leo Bieber, Frederick Schreicher, Paul Smith, Martin Boddey. Awards: Academy Award for Best Black and White Cinematography (Robert Krasker). Academy Award nominations for Best Director (Carol Reed), Best Film Editing (Oswald Hafenrichter).

Niagara. Director: Henry Hathaway. Producer: Charles Brackett. Running time: 92 minutes. Released by 20th Century-Fox, January 21, 1953. Cast: Marilyn Monroe, Joseph Cotten, Jean Peters, Casey Adams, Dennis O'Dea, Richard Allan, Don Wilson, Lurene Tuttle, Russell Collins, Will Wright.

The Killer Is Loose. Director: Budd Boetticher. Producer: Robert L. Jacks. Running time: 73 minutes. Released by United Artists, March 2, 1956. Cast: Joseph Cotten, Rhonda Fleming, Wendell Corey, Alan Hale, Jr., Michael Pate, Virginia Christine, John Larch, John Beradino, Paul Bryar, Dee J. Thompson.

Touch of Evil. Director: Orson Welles. Producer: Albert Zugsmith. Running time: 95 minutes. Released by Universal-International, May 21, 1958. Cast: Charlton Heston, Janet Leigh, Orson Welles, Joseph Calleia, Akim Tamiroff, Joanna Moore, Marlene Dietrich, Ray Collins, Dennis Weaver, Victor Millan, Lalo Rios, Valentin de Vargas, Mort Mills, Mercedes McCambridge, Wayne Taylor, Ken Miller, Raymond Rodriguez, Michael Sargent, Zsa Zsa Gabor, Keenan Wynn, Joseph Cotten, Phil Harvey, Joi Lansing, Harry Shannon, Rusty Wescoatt, Arlene McQuade, Domenick Delgarde, Joe Basulto, Jennie Dias, Yolanda Bojorquez, Eleanor Corado.

References

Alpert, Don. "Joseph Cotten — He'll Gladly Meet Fame and Fortune Half Way." *Los Angeles Times*, June 13, 1965.

Ames, Walter. "Cotten, Sullavan to Be Reunited in Big Tver; Bing Crosby Salute Set." *Los Angeles Times*, September 21, 1954.

Archerd, Army. "Just for Variety." *Variety*, January 10, 1990.

Bacon, James. "Joseph Cotten." *Los Angeles Herald-Examiner*, December 6, 1971.

Bamoel, Lois. "Joseph Cotten's Career in Films Launched by 'Citizen Kane' Role." *Boxoffice*, September 29, 1975.

Biography of Joseph Cotten. Alexander Korda Films, circa 1941.

Biography of Joseph Cotten. Paramount Pictures, January 24, 1946.

Biography of Joseph Cotten. Vanguard Films, October 1943.

Canfield, Alyce. "King Cotten." *Liberty*, October 26, 1946.

Champlin, Charles. "A Solvent Serf in the Land of Cotten." *Los Angeles Times*, April 25, 1980.

_____. "Joseph Cotten: Courtly Competence at the Core." *Los Angeles Times*, May 3, 1987.

_____. "Joseph Cotten: The Film Actor and the Gentleman." *Los Angeles Times*, February 8, 1994.

Cook, Bruce. "Dependable Joseph Cotten Proves Himself Again." *Los Angeles Daily News*, May 24, 1987.

Cotten, Joseph. "Orson and Me." *Los Angeles Magazine*, September 1985.

"Cotten Prefers Acting to 'Other Things.'" *Long Beach Press-Telegram*, March 18, 1977.

Crump, Constance. "Joseph Cotten." *Cinegram*, circa 1977.

Deere, Dorothy. "Cotten Tale." Publication Unsourced, circa 1945.

Flint, Peter B. "Joseph Cotten, 88, Is Dead; Actor on Stage and in Films." *New York Times*, February 7, 1994.

Galligan, David. "His Career Is a History of Film." *Drama-Logue*, December 17 — 23, 1987.

Gautschy, Dean. "Cotten Defends Co-Stars." *Los Angeles Herald-Examiner*, April 3, 1965.

Hare, William. "Joseph Cotten: Superstar of the Film Classics." *Hollywood Studio Magazine*, March 1980.

"'Holding Out for Best' Can Prove a Disaster." *Hollywood Citizen-News*, September 11, 1967.

Hopper, Hedda. "Joseph Cotten and Patricia Medina to Wed." *Los Angeles Times*, October 8, 1960.

_____. "Joe Cotten — Nice Guy." *Chicago Sunday Tribune*, September 5, 1948.

Humphrey, Hal. "Joseph Cotten: His Accent's on Acting." *Los Angeles Times*, July 18, 1968.

"Joe Cotten." *Chicago Tribune*, circa 1941.

"Joe Cotten, Frau Teamed in Pic." *Variety*, July 20, 1972.

"Joseph Cotten Dies at Age 88." *The Hollywood Reporter*, February 7, 1994.

"Joseph Cotten to be Host-Narrator of 'Hollywood and the Stars.'" NBC Television Network News, July 9, 1963.

Kahn, Alexander. "Joe Cotten's Not Really So Decrepit." *Hollywood Citizen-News*, August 3, 1942.

"Leukemia Fatal to Wife of Star Joseph Cotten." *Los Angeles Mirror*, January 7, 1960.

Manners, Dorothy. "Cotten: Low-Key, Reputable Professional." *Los Angeles Herald-Examiner*, September 3, 1971.

Natale, Richard. "'Kane' Star Cotten Dies." *Variety*, February 7, 1994.

Obituary. *Variety*, February 14, 1994.

Oliver, Myrna. "Debonair Actor Joseph Cotten Dies at 88." *Los Angeles Times*, February 7, 1994.

Parsons, Louella O. "Joseph Cotten Hurt in Film Fight with Scott Brady." *Los Angeles Examiner*, December 20, 1951.

"Patricia Medina and Joseph Cotten." *Los Angeles Times Home Magazine*, January 21, 1979.

"Rome Rites Planned for Mrs. Cotten." *Los Angeles Examiner*, January 8, 1960.

Skolsky, Sidney. "Tintypes: Joseph Cotten." *Hollywood Citizen-News*, September 6, 1945.

Steele, Joseph Henry. "Portrait in Cotten." *Photoplay*, February 1945.

"The Elegant Ex-Potato Salad Salesman." *TV Guide*, March 14–20, 1964.

Thompson, Howard. "Scanning Cotten's Territory." *New York Times*, November 23, 1952.

"Vanity Will Get You Somewhere" (Book Review). *Variety*, May 26, 1987.

JAMES CRAIG

"This is all nice and friendly. You can give me the dough now. Don't you want to be friendly? Or you want us to drop by the hospital and see your wife and kid?"— James Craig in *Side Street* (1949)

Towering and brawny, with distinctive features and an appealing acting style, James Craig had what it took — on the surface, at least — to achieve cinematic fortune and fame. Despite appearances in more than 60 feature films, however, it was Craig's life off-screen that garnered most of the headlines. Frequently accused of heavy drinking and spousal abuse, the actor found himself all-too-often embroiled in domestic incidents that overshadowed his efforts on the silver screen and made for lively copy for the publications of the 1940s and 1950s. Still, while he never reached the heights of fame he may have sought, Craig was shown to good advantage in such films as *The Devil and Daniel Webster* (1941) and *The Human Comedy* (1943), and was featured in four films noirs: *Side Street* (1949), *A Lady Without Passport* (1950), *The Strip* (1951), and *While the City Sleeps* (1956).

Craig — who was compared throughout his career to Clark Gable — was born James Henry Meador on February 4, 1912, the second of three children of Bertha and Olen Walter Meador. A building contractor, Olen Meador frequently moved his family from town to town, and during his childhood, young James lived at various times in Kansas, Florida, New York, and Virginia. After graduating in 1929 from Austin Peay Normal Junior College in Clarksville, Tennessee, James hitchhiked to Houston, Texas, where he enrolled at Rice Institute and planned to pursue a medical career. By the time of his graduation, however, the young man had decided that further medical studies were too demanding — instead, he found work in the oil fields of Huntsville, Texas, and later at the General Motors factory in Houston. During a break from the latter, James traveled to Hollywood, where the idea of becoming an actor first took hold.

"I was out there on a vacation and looking around and I saw a lot of people making a lot of money," he later recalled. "If they can do it, why couldn't I?"

While in California, James sought out a casting agent, who advised him to seek experience in little theater groups and take a course in diction that would tone down his thick Texas accent. Returning to Texas, James studied speech and drama with actor Cyril Delavanti, joined a local theater group, and soon began landing small roles in such productions as *The Petrified Forest* and *The Last Mile*, billed as James Meade. Later, while starring in the play *Craig's Wife*, he decided to change his last name to Craig.

In 1937, the newly christened James Craig returned to Hollywood. According to his studio biography, the would-be screen actor tracked down Paramount talent executive Oliver Hinsdell, showed him his photograph and press clippings, and managed to earn a screen test. Another source, however, states that Craig bluffed his way into the studio by only *claiming* to know Hinsdell, who was on vacation at the time. Regardless of the method he used, Craig was rewarded with a studio contract, and later that year appeared in his first film, *Sophie Goes West* (1937), as a waiter in restaurant scene. This was followed by such features as *Thunder Trail* (1937), a western starring Gilbert Roland and Marsha Hunt; *The Buccaneer* (1938), a big-budget adventure with Fredric March, Walter Brennan, and Margot Grahame; and *Pride of the West* (1938), starring William Boyd as Hopalong Cassidy.

Frustrated by the lack of progress in his film career, Craig abruptly returned to the stage, landing a role in the September 1938 Broadway production of *Missouri Legend*. The play closed after only 48 performances —

despite a first-rate cast that included Karl Malden, Dan Duryea, Jose Ferrer, and Dorothy Gish — but Craig's performance attracted the notice of a Columbia Studios scout and the actor inked an agreement with the studio. In contrast to his anticipated improvement in screen assignments, however, Craig was disappointed to find himself cast in a variety of programmers and serials, such as *Blondie Meets the Boss* (1938), *North of Shanghai* (1939), and *Flying G-Men* (1939).

With his film career at a virtual standstill, Craig was at least faring better off screen. On April 15, 1939, he married Mary June Ray, at that time a rising young starlet with David O. Selznick Productions. Mary abandoned her acting career and two years later, the couple's first child, James, Jr. was born.

Meanwhile, when his Columbia contract ended, Craig switched over to Universal Studios, where he was seen as a drunken college student in *Enemy Agent* (1940); a reporter in *Black Friday* (1940), which featured Boris Karloff and Bela Lugosi; a murder victim in the Johnny Mack Brown starrer *Law and Order* (1940); and an ensign in *Seven Sinners* (1940), the first of three films starring Marlene Dietrich and John Wayne. But just when it appeared that the actor would spend the rest of his film career as a virtual unknown, he got the break for which he had been waiting — the role of a struggling young doctor who woos the title character in *Kitty Foyle* (1940). Produced by RKO, the film, along with its principal actors, received a spate of favorable notices (Ginger Rogers, as Kitty, won her only Academy Award for the role), and RKO executives bought out the remainder of Craig's contract from Universal. He was next cast in *Unexpected Uncle* (1941), a box-office bomb starring Anne Shirley and Charles Coburn, and *All That Money Can Buy* (1941). For his performance in the latter film, which was renamed *The Devil and Daniel Webster*, Craig was singled out in *Variety* as a "quite capable young actor," but the film earned a disappointing reception from moviegoers. The following year, Craig starred in *Valley of the Sun* (1942), playing opposite Lucille Ball in a role

that had been turned down — with good reason — by Joel McCrea.

Despite the lackluster film roles that Craig was racking up, he was courted by MGM and signed a seven-year contract with the studio. After first starring in back-to-back "B" westerns — *The Omaha Trail* (1942), with Dean Jagger and Chill Wills, and *Northwest Rangers* (1942), a loose reworking of *Manhattan Melodrama* (1934) — Craig landed the romantic lead in The *Human Comedy* (1943). Starring Mickey Rooney, Marsha Hunt, and Fay Bainter, the film was a solid hit with the public and Craig's luck appeared to be turning.

Although he next appeared with William Powell and Hedy Lamarr in a so-so comedy, *The Heavenly Body* (1943), Craig received a second-place nod in the annual Motion Picture Herald "Stars of Tomorrow" poll of film exhibitors. He was in fine company — other actors named that year included Barry Fitzgerald, June Allyson, Sydney Greenstreet, and Roddy McDowall. Unfortunately, the designation did little to raise the level of films to which Craig was assigned. Over the next six years, he appeared with Marlene Dietrich and Ronald Colman in *Kismet* (1944), a big-budget, moderately entertaining Arabian Nights extravaganza; *Marriage Is a Private Affair* (1944), where he was part of a love triangle involving Lana Turner and John Hodiak; *Gentle Annie* (1944), an offbeat western that suffered when director W.S. Van Dyke fell ill and was replaced halfway through filming; and *Dark Delusion* (1947), featuring Craig as Dr. Kildare in the 15th and final entry in the MGM series. He was also loaned out for two westerns — *Man from Texas* (1948) and *Northwest Stampede* (1948) — to Eagle-Lion Studios, which was a sure sign that Craig's tenure at MGM was coming to an end. His best-received film during this period was *Our Vines Have Tender Grapes* (1945), which starred Edward G. Robinson as a Norwegian farmer.

After the Eagle-Lion loanouts, Craig was cast in the first of his four films noirs, *Side Street* (1948), starring Farley Granger as Joe Norson, a young married letter carrier who finds himself in over his head when he impulsively steals a cache of money from a crooked attorney, Victor Backett (Edmon Ryan). When Norson tries to return the money, Backett feigns ignorance, suspecting that Norson is an agent of the police — instead, he dispatches his partner, George Garsell (Craig), to retrieve the cash. The ruthless Garsell is more than up to the task; he first viciously beats Norson in the back seat of a taxicab, and later kills his own former lover, Harriet Sinton (Jean Hagen), after she is contacted by Norson. Along with his sidekick, taxicab driver Larry Giff (Harry Bellaver), Garsell abducts Norson in the film's climax, leading a chase through the city with police close behind. Giff later tries to abandon his murderous pal and Garsell shoots him in the back, but his deadly deeds finally come to an end when detectives catch up to him and gun him down.

As the vicious gangster, Craig turned in a fine performance and, along with co-stars Paul Kelly and Edmon Ryan, was noted by one critic as "stand out[s] as assorted thugs and cops." The reviewer for the *Los Angeles Times* offered a rather backhanded compliment, however, writing that "even if you are persuaded by his performance ... you are hardly likely to put much credence in the behavior of James Craig as one of the blackmailers. He's just too killing for words." Craig followed this film with two more noir entries, *A Lady Without Passport* (1950) and *The Strip* (1951). The former — and the weaker of the two — featured Craig as an immigration officer who works with undercover agent Pete Karczag (John Hodiak) to shut down an illegal alien smuggling operation. Craig had little to do here, besides barking orders at Karczag over the telephone, and despite fair performances from co-stars Hodiak and George Macready, audiences stayed away in droves. However, Craig's next venture into film noir, *The Strip*, was somewhat better. In this feature, he portrayed Delwyn "Sonny" Johnson, a hard-hearted Hollywood bookmaker who is characterized by his fondness for plants and his tendency to silence his girlfriend's ramblings with an annoyed, "Please!" The film's

other principal players were Stanley Maxton (Mickey Rooney), a jazz drummer and former employee of Johnson's, and Jane Tafford (Sally Forrest), a would-be actress who uses Stanley's affections in an effort to further her career. When Johnson puts the moves on Jane, promising to set up a screen test, she gladly leaves Stanley behind, but the drummer warns her of Johnson's intentions and earns a beating for his troubles. Ultimately, however, Johnson gets his just desserts when Jane accidentally kills him during an argument — and is herself fatally wounded during the struggle. While *The Strip* did slightly better than *Passport* at the box office, critics were impressed more with the film's musical offerings than the performances of the players — in the *Los Angeles Times*, Philip K. Scheuer wrote that "the thin plot ... is relieved at intervals by musical specialists like Monica Lewis and Vic Damone," and the *Los Angeles Examiner*'s Lynn Bowers judged that "there is a lot of entertainment offered on a tour of the Sunset Strip to bolster up a story that somehow doesn't go with the implied gaiety of this famous belt." As for Craig, his portrayal of the cold-hearted hood was dismissed in *Variety* as "the type which repetition has hackneyed." *The Strip* was Craig's last film under his MGM contract.

On the home front, Craig's wife, Mary, had given birth to their second son, Robert, in 1944, and a daughter, Diane, in 1946. Sadly, Robert suffered kidney failure and died on April 19, 1948. Two years later, the first of a staggering series of news articles on the personal life of the Craig family began to appear. In September 1950, newspapers reported that Mary Craig had been found wandering the street near the couple's ranch in North Hollywood, her nightgown ripped and her face and body bruised. After a neighbor discovered her and rushed her to the hospital, investigating officers reported that she "apparently had been beaten and ran into the street." Famed attorney Jerry Giesler promptly arrived on the scene, and Mary later announced to police officers and the press: "I do not want to prosecute my husband."

When contacted for his version of the events, Craig stated that "there was a disagreement" and his wife ran out of the house. "In her condition, she might have run into a tree," Craig said. "I never laid a hand on my wife. This is embarrassing, humiliating." Craig was never charged. Four years later, claiming mental cruelty, Mary Craig filed for divorce, but the couple reconciled and in 1956, another son, Michael was born. But the marriage could not be salvaged. In July 1958, Mary again filed for divorce, requesting an order to keep Craig from "molesting" her, and seeking a share of their $500,000 in community property, which included their prosperous North Hollywood chicken ranch and a liquor store. The divorce was granted a year later.

Meanwhile, after the end of his association with MGM, Craig found that his film career was on the downslope. There were a few exceptions, however, including RKO's *Drums in the Deep South* (1951), a lavish and convincing Civil War drama that found Craig portraying the leader of a band of rebel soldiers. Another bright spot was Craig's final film noir, *While the City Sleeps* (1956), an engrossing tale focusing on three morally bankrupt employees of a news enterprise (Craig, Dana Andrews, and George Sanders), who will stop at nothing to crack a murder case and win a coveted management post at the publication. As "Honest" Harry Kritzer, Craig portrayed the photo service editor who endeavors to use his influence with the publisher's wife, Dorothy (Rhonda Fleming)— with whom he is having a dalliance — to land the job. By the film's end, however, Harry confesses the affair, choosing his relationship with Dorothy over his ambition, and the job is given to the company's upstanding newspaper editor, played by Thomas Mitchell.

As Craig's career continued its descent, it was matched by his personal life. In August 1959, just a month after his divorce from Mary, he enthusiastically announced plans to marry starlet Jil Jarmyn, who was best known for what Hollywood insiders termed "Up in Barry's Room." The label referred to

a headline-making incident in 1955 when Jarmyn protested to police that she had been assaulted by Susan Hayward when Jarmyn walked into the bedroom of actor Don "Red" Barry, whom she claimed to be her finance, and found Hayward there in her pajamas. ("I could say I was in the dining room at the time," Hayward had told the press, "but I wasn't. I was in the bedroom.") Craig and Jarmyn wed in Las Vegas on August 22, 1959, but the couple separated just two months later, and in February 1962, Jarmyn obtained an annulment, citing Craig's refusal to have children and charging that on one occasion the actor "threatened my life and threatened to take his own life."

Just four months later, *Los Angeles Herald-Examiner* columnist Harrison Carroll reported that Craig and his first wife, Mary, had remarried in Las Vegas. Carroll wrote: "'We couldn't be happier,' James called to tell me, 'and so are our children.'" But the second time around wasn't the charm for the couple, and the following year, on March 17, 1963, Craig married again, this time to a former model, Jane Valentine, who had a young son by a previous marriage. "My wife is a redhead and is a wonderful woman," Craig told Carroll. "I have never been so happy in my life."

His happiness, however, was short-lived. The couple separated after three months, Jane Craig sued for divorce, and in October of that year, Craig was slapped with a felony wife-beating charge. According to newspaper accounts, Jane Craig told police that the actor had "beaten her about the face and body with his fists." Several weeks later, during a court hearing, Jane charged that Craig had sawed a chain lock, split a door, and threatened to burn the apartment house where she lived "in order to gain access to my residence." Still, as she left the courtroom, Jane told reporters: "I really don't want a divorce. I still love him. He's a wonderful man when he's not drinking. He needs help and he knows it."

The battle escalated to even more bizarre levels when Craig failed to show up for a November 1963 court date, and later explained his absence by claiming that Jane "locked up" most of his clothing and "wouldn't let [me] have proper attire for a court appearance." Jane countered with a claim that Craig had "destroyed $500 worth of her clothing," prohibiting her ability to seek employment.

Finally, in March 1964, the Craigs' divorce was granted. Craig stated in court that he did not oppose the divorce, but he did protest the charge of cruelty. "I think this young lady should have a divorce," he said, "but I also think that two of the cruelest things you can say about a man are that he beats his wife and that he drinks to excess." (Sadly, this was not the last chapter in the saga of Jane Craig. On May 29, 1967, in a motel in Oceanside, California, she fatally shot her 11-year-old son and then turned the gun on herself. The bodies were found by the motel owner, who entered the room after hearing a barking dog. Jane left a note to her parents, in which she stated that she was despondent over marital difficulties and "didn't want her son to grow up and suffer for her mistakes." The note also gave detailed instructions on who was to receive and care for the dog. Craig was never mentioned by name, and did not comment publicly on the tragic incident.)

Beginning in the late 1950s, Craig had made frequent appearances on various television programs, including *Ford Theater, Broken Arrow, Have Gun Will Travel,* and *The Virginian.* His big-screen efforts in later years were in a series of inauspicious films whose titles alone indicate their bargain basement quality: *Doomsday Machine* (1967), *If He Hollers, Let Him Go!* (1968), and *Bigfoot* (1970). His last film appearance was in *The Tormentors* in 1971. With his film career all but over, Craig turned to another avocation — real estate. He obtained a license, took a job with a realty company in Huntington Beach, California, and managed to eke out a successful living.

In the mid 1980s, after complaining of feeling ill, James Craig was diagnosed with lung cancer. Three weeks later, he was admitted to the Western Medical Center in Santa Ana, where he died on June 28, 1985. He was survived by his three children and four grandchildren.

Sadly, James Craig is an actor whose professional triumphs in such films as *Kitty Foyle* and *Our Vines Have Tender Grapes* were overshadowed by his personal setbacks that ranged from the death of his son to the murder-suicide involving his third wife. One can only speculate on the effect that these events had on his career, and on the demons that he surely battled as he watched his life story played out in the daily press.

Film Noir Filmography

Side Street. Director: Anthony Mann. Producer: Sam Zimbalist. Running time: 83 minutes. Released by MGM, March 23, 1950. Cast: Farley Granger, Cathy O'Donnell, James Craig, Paul Kelly, Edmon Ryan, Paul Harvey, Jean Hagen, Charles McGraw, Ed Max, Adele Jergens, Harry Bellaver, Whit Bissell, John Gallaudet, Esther Somers, Harry Antrim, George Tyne, Kathryn Givney, King Donovan, Norman Leavitt, Sid Tomack.

A Lady Without Passport. Director: Joseph H. Lewis. Producer: Samuel Marx. Running time: 72 minutes. Released by MGM, August 3, 1950. Cast: Hedy Lamarr, John Hodiak, James Craig, George Macready, Steven Geray, Bruce Cowling, Nedrick

Young, Steven Hill, Robert Osterloh, Trevor Bardette, Charles Wagenheim, Renzo Cesana, Esther Zeitlin, Carlo Tricoli, Marta Metrovitch, Don Garner, Richard Crane, Nita Bieber.

The Strip. Director: Leslie Kardos. Producer: Joe Pasternak. Running time: 84 minutes. Released by MGM, August 1951. Cast: Mickey Rooney, Sally Forrest, William Demarest, James Craig, Kay Brown, Louis Armstrong and Band, Tommy Rettig, Tom Powers, Jonathan Cott, Tommy Farrell, Myrna Dell, Jacqueline Fontaine, Vic Damone, Monica Lewis.

While the City Sleeps. Director: Fritz Lang. Producer: Bert Friedlob. Running time: 99 minutes. Released by RKO, May 16, 1956. Cast: Dana Andrews, Rhonda Fleming, George Sanders, Howard Duff, Thomas Mitchell, Vincent Price, John Barrymore, Jr., James Craig, Ida Lupino, Robert Warwick, Ralph Peters, Vladimir Sokoloff, Mae Marsh, Sandy White.

References

"Actor a Determined Husband, Says Bride." *Los Angeles Herald-Examiner*, October 21, 1963.

"Actor Craig's Wife Beaten." *Los Angeles Examiner*, September 27, 1950.

"Actor's Ex Kills Son and Herself." *New York Daily News*, May 30, 1967.

Bentley, Janet. "Big Jim." *Photoplay*, July 1944.

Biography of James Craig. Paramount Studios, July 14, 1937.

Biography of James Craig. Paramount Studios, March 1952.

Biography of James Craig. Paramount Studios, February 1967.

Biography of James Craig, Warner Brothers Studios, November 1956.

Carroll, Harrison. "James Craig Re-Weds Ex-Wife in Las Vegas." *Los Angeles Herald-Examiner*, June 4, 1962.

Coons, Robbin. "Others Make Money, So Jim Does It, Too." *Toledo Blade*, November 28, 1941.

"'Had No Clothes for Court Appearance'— Actor Craig." *Los Angeles Herald Examiner*, November 21, 1963.

"James Craig, Actor, 74, Dies; Once Called Gable Successor." *New York Times*, July 10, 1985.

"James Craig Awarded Divorce." *Los Angeles Mirror News*, July 31, 1959.

"James Craig Charged in Wife Row." *Hollywood Citizen-News*, October 17, 1963.

"James Craig, Hollywood Lead Of '40s And '50s, Dead At 73." *Variety*, July 10, 1985.

"James Craig, Once Billed as 2nd Gable, Dies." *Los Angeles Times*, July 9, 1985.

"James Craig Sued by Wife." *Los Angeles Examiner*, September 4, 1954.

"James Craig Takes New Wife — No. 3." *Los Angeles Herald-Examiner*, March 18, 1963.

"James Craig to Wed TV's Jul Jarmyn." *New York Post*, August 16, 1959.

"James Craig Wife Shoots Son, Self." *Hollywood Citizen-News*, May 29, 1967.

"Jil Jarmyn Marriage Voided." *Los Angeles Herald Examiner*, February 2, 1962.

"Jim Craig Finds Success." *Richmond (Virginia) News Leader*, December 11, 1941.

"Mrs. James Craig Given $475 a Month Alimony." *Los Angeles Times*, November 4, 1954.

Parsons, Louella O. "Craig to Marry Jill Jarmyn." *Los Angeles Examiner*, August 15, 1959.

Roberts, Barrie. "James Craig: In Gable's Shadow." *Classic Images*, August 1996.

"She Wins Divorce From James Craig." *Los Angeles Herald-Examiner*, circa March 1964.

"Wife Hid Clothes, Actor Craig Explains to Court." *Los Angeles Herald-Examiner*, November 21, 1963.

"Wife of 19 Years Sues James Craig." *Los Angeles Examiner*, July 16, 1958.

"Woman Kills Son, Self." *Los Angeles Herald-Examiner*, May 29, 1967.

—— BRODERICK CRAWFORD ——

"I'd fit into your gang perfectly. I could maim and disfigure people for you, and shoot up the ones you don't like." — Broderick Crawford in *The Mob* (1951)

Broderick Crawford's voice was once likened to a cross between "the love call of a caribou and the horn of a diesel streamliner." A versatile actor of the screen, television, stage, and radio, Crawford used his memorable voice and considerable performing talents most notably in such films as *All the King's Men* (1949) and *Born Yesterday* (1950), and the popular television series *Highway Patrol*. Although his promising career was hampered by a longtime battle with alcoholism and frequent skirmishes with the law, Crawford was nonetheless a prominent figure in film noir, with widely varying roles in six features from the era: *Black Angel* (1946), *Convicted* (1950), *The Mob* (1951), *Scandal Sheet* (1952), *Human Desire* (1954), and *New York Confidential* (1955).

Born William Broderick Crawford in Philadelphia, Pennsylvania, on December 9, 1911, the hulking actor had show business in his blood; his maternal grandparents, William Broderick and Emma Kraus, were popular opera singers; his father, Lester Crawford, enjoyed a long career in vaudeville; and his mother, Helen Broderick, was a well-known star of Broadway and the screen. Before he was even able to walk — at the age of eight months — Crawford was introduced to show biz when he was carried onto the stage by his parents during a vaudeville performance. Seven years later, the lad was paid a dollar by actor Harry Breen to run across the stage during his act shouting, "Tag, you're it!" This initial brush with fame was apparently all the youngster needed to set his course for the future. After the performance, he reportedly informed his parents, "I don't want to go back to school — I want to be an actor."

Crawford later attended Dean Academy in Franklin, Massachusetts, where he played baseball and football — during a game for the latter sport, he suffered a broken nose (the first of six). Upon his graduation in 1928, Crawford joined his parents in a vaudeville company touring the country, playing minor parts in several sketches, including an abbreviated version of *The Trial of Mary Dugan*. When the tour ended the following year, Crawford caved in to pressure from his parents and enrolled at Harvard University, but after only three weeks, he left the school and signed on as a longshoreman in New York City, earning $18.50 a month. He later landed a post as a seaman on a tanker, remaining in the maritime service for nearly a year before returning to New York and appearing on a series of radio programs, including *Twenty*

Thousand Years in Sing Sing. During his stint on radio, he also worked for 13 weeks playing a "stooge" on the Marx Brothers show.

It wasn't until 1934 that Crawford landed his first role in a legitimate stage production, the London production of *She Loves Me Not*, in which he was seen as a football player. The play closed after only three weeks, but during his stay in London, the actor was noticed by playwright Noel Coward, who cast him in his Broadway production *Point Valaine*, starring Alfred Lunt and Lynn Fontanne. Following this well-received play, Crawford appeared in *Punches and Judy* and *Sweet Mystery of Life*, but neither was successful. He spent the next few years honing his craft in a variety of stock companies and summer theaters, then signed with producer Sam Goldwyn for his film debut, playing a comic butler in *Woman Chases Man* (1937).

"I wasn't able to make a living at acting on a full-time basis until 1938," Crawford once recalled. "Acting was in my blood, and besides, it sure as hell beat working for a living."

After his appearance in *Woman Chases Man*, Crawford returned to New York to audition for the role of Lennie in *Of Mice and Men*, delivering such a "definitely authentic" reading that director George Kaufman hired him on the spot. Crawford was a sensation in the play and was praised for his "meticulous and affectionately modulated" portrayal of the dim-witted Lennie. Despite Crawford's outstanding performance, however, the role of Lennie in the 1939 screen version went to Lon Chaney, Jr., and Crawford returned to Hollywood for such forgettable "B" features as *Sudden Money* (1939), a lightweight comedy about a salesman who wins a sweepstakes; *Ambush* (1939), a mediocre crime drama; *Undercover Doctor* (1939), a standard programmer starring Lloyd Nolan; and *I Can't Give You Anything but Love, Baby* (1940), a slightly ludicrous musical comedy which found the actor portraying a gangster who longs to be a songwriter. He then signed a contract with Universal and was cast in a series of westerns, including *When the Daltons Rode* (1940), earning praise for playing his role with "proper vigor"; *Badlands of Dakota* (1941), *Sin Town* (1942), and *North to the Klondike* (1942).

With the onset of World War II, Crawford enlisted in the Army Air Corps, where he served as a sergeant for the next four years. One of the actor's first films upon his release from the service, *Black Angel* (1946), marked his foray into the world of film noir. Here, Crawford played Capt. Flood, a soft-spoken, no-nonsense detective investigating the strangulation murder of a popular singer, Marvis Marlowe (Constance Dowling). Flood quickly arrests Kirk Bennett (John Phillips), a married man who was being blackmailed by Marlowe. But Bennett's loyal wife, Catherine (June Vincent), refuses to believe that her husband is capable of murder, and teams with Marlowe's alcoholic ex-husband, Martin Blair (Dan Duryea), in an attempt to unearth the real killer. Ultimately, the two prove unsuccessful, but just before Bennett's scheduled execution, Blair realizes that *he* committed the murder during an alcoholic binge, and turns himself in.

Although *Black Angel* was dismissed in the *New York Times* as "a ragged and jumbled affair which no self-respecting armchair sleuth would put up with for long," Crawford was singled out by several reviewers for his restrained performance; John L. Scott wrote in the *Los Angeles Times* that he "run[s] through [his] paces satisfactorily," and the critic for the *New York Times* cited Crawford, along with co-stars Peter Lorre and Wallace Ford, for his "expert" performance.

These favorable notices notwithstanding, Crawford was dropped by Universal soon after the film's release — along with the studio's other contract players — when the studio was bought by William Goetz. On his own, Crawford spent the next few years freelancing in such features as *Slave Girl* (1947), described by one critic as a "harem-scarum farce"; *The Time of Your Life* (1948), in which he earned praise for his portrayal as a policeman who "grows skeptical of his calling"; and *Anna Lucasta* (1949), starring Paulette Goddard in the title role.

But the actor's best-remembered screen role was just ahead — he was cast by director-producer Robert Rossen to star in Columbia's *All the King's Men* (1949). For his portrayal of ruthless political boss Willie Stark, Crawford was universally hailed; in a typical notice, the reviewer for the *New York World-Telegram* wrote: "For once the full force of this magnetic and dominant actor is allowed to sweep unchecked and the result is a memorable performance." His portrayal earned Crawford an Academy Award for Best Actor, beating out Kirk Douglas in *Champion* (1949), Gregory Peck in *12 O'Clock High* (1949), Richard Todd in *The Hasty Heart* (1949), and John Wayne in *The Sands of Iwo Jima* (1949). He also earned similar honors from the New York Film Critics, the San Francisco Critics' Circle, the Hollywood Foreign Correspondents Association, the New York Foreign Language Press, and *Look* Magazine.

"When I won the Academy Award ... I did just what Willie did in the picture: I discarded a prepared speech and ad-libbed," Crawford told *The Saturday Evening Post* in 1950. "The big difference was that I didn't do it deliberately. I just couldn't remember what

I had planned to say, so I blurted out, 'Paul Douglas said we weren't to thank anybody. But I thank everybody, and especially, thank God.' It wasn't much of a speech, but it certainly reflected my feelings about the role. Way back when I first read the novel, I thought, 'The actor who plays the part of Willie Stark will be a very lucky guy.' I didn't dream then that I'd be the lucky guy."

Signing with Columbia after his success in *All the King's Men*, Crawford scored another hit the following year when he starred with Judy Holliday and William Holden in the hilarious and often touching comedy *Born Yesterday* (1950). Although most of the lauds went to the Academy Award–winning performance of Holliday, Crawford was noticed by several critics for his memorable portrayal of a blustering profiteer who hires a reporter to "smarten up" his ditzy girlfriend. Also that year, the actor was seen in his second film noir, *Convicted* (1950), playing a sympathetic district attorney, George Knowland, who reluctantly prosecutes Joe Hufford (Glenn Ford), a luckless brokerage firm employee accused in the accidental death of a man during a barroom brawl ("You got a good war record, no previous arrests, but I'm still on the job where I have to prosecute you," Knowland tells the man. "There's a man dead—accident or no accident, you knocked him down and killed him…. Once we get into court, I can't give you any breaks, do you understand that?") Several years later, Knowland is appointed as warden of the prison where Hufford has been sentenced, and attempts to make amends by employing him as his chauffeur. When Hufford refuses to implicate his cellmate (Millard Mitchell) in the murder of a prison stoolie, Knowland is forced to place him in solitary confinement, but after the real killer confesses his guilt, the warden later uses his influence to gain Hufford's parole. While *Convicted* was only a mediocre offering from the film noir era, Crawford managed to rise above the material, and was mentioned in *Variety* for his "good performance."

During the years that Crawford's star was rising on the screen, the actor was busy mak-

ing news off-camera, as well. In November 1940, he was married to movie and radio actress Kay Griffith, who announced to the press that she planned to relinquish her career because "we don't want this to be a Hollywood marriage—we want it to last." The couple adopted a son, William Christopher (known as Kim), in 1947, and happily revealed in 1951 that Griffith was pregnant. But just one month after releasing this news, Griffith filed for divorce, charging the actor with cruelty and seeking custody of both Kim and the couple's unborn child. Although Crawford and Griffith reconciled before the birth of their son, Kelly, the marriage remained a rocky one and reached the point of no return in 1955 when rumors surfaced about a romance between Crawford and a young actress, Lisa Ferraday. Crawford's marriage finally ended in 1956 after a contentious divorce battle that was characterized by a virtual tug-of-war over the family Jaguar, attempts by Crawford to gain custody of the children, and accusations by Griffith that the actor was an unfit father. Although it was later announced that Crawford would marry Ferraday, the actress vehemently denied the rumor in a 1958 interview with famed columnist Louella Parsons.

"I am very sorry that Broderick gave out such a story," Ferraday said. "This is most embarrassing to me, because I am much in love with someone else and I hope to marry him later."

As if Crawford's rocky love life wasn't enough fodder for the Hollywood press, the actor began cropping up in the news for his increased drinking and frequent brushes with the law. In June 1947, he was arrested for drunk driving after police found him asleep in his car in a residential area of Van Nuys, California. Authorities said the actor's car had jumped the curbing and smashed into a guardrail. Five years later, in November 1952, Crawford was again arrested for drunk driving, this time after he crashed his vehicle into two parked cars on Sunset Boulevard. The actor, who told police he had been celebrating the completion of his latest film, pleaded guilty and was fined $250. And in December

1954, Crawford racked up his third drunk driving arrest after leaving an "all-night party" with actor Myron McCormick and actress Abigail Adams, the on-again, off-again fiancée of comedian George Jessel. After pleading guilty and paying another $250 fine, Crawford was lambasted by presiding judge Leo Freund, who termed it "a shame that a man who can win an Academy Award and who make such a success of himself as an actor should turn out to be such a drunken bum."

"You think more of drinking and getting drunk than you do of your career," the judge told Crawford. "When you are a great actor, you belong to the people, anything you do, anything you act or anything you say becomes a matter of importance to those people. And when you get out of character and become a drunken bum — and that is exactly what you are — then it is a shame because you are hurting yourself. I assure you that if you are arrested again you will go to jail."

Throughout the 1950s, Crawford also became notorious for verbal altercations and public brawls; in two separate fights, the actor suffered a broken nose, but in a 1956 interview in *Pageant* magazine, he offered a rationale for the incidents.

"A guy like me, with a fairly well-known face, goes into a bar late at night with a couple of friends ... and pretty soon some unknown character weaves up and says, 'So you're Brod Crawford, the big movie tough guy. Well I don't think you're so tough,'" Crawford said. "And you've got to move fast, because this skinny little monkey is already throwing a punch, for the entertainment of his friends, and sometimes you don't move fast enough and he clips you and you might just be impatient enough to clip him back, before you think it over, and then all his friends are screaming, and it's pretty hard for newspapers to get a true story."

Due in large part to the actor's escalating bouts with alcohol, the quality of Crawford's films declined during the 1950s — his long-time agent, Al Melnick, once said that Crawford "could have been the greatest, but the one problem that always did him in was the bot-

tle. Brod was a two-bottle-a-day guy." During this period, the actor was seen in several mediocre features, including Columbia's *The Last of the Comanches* (1952), a cliche-ridden western featuring the actor as a cavalry sergeant, and *The Last Posse* (1953), which was overly complicated by a series of flashbacks and flash-forwards, and a loan-out to Warner Bros. for *Stop, You're Killing Me* (1953), a remake of the superior 1938 Edward G. Robinson feature, *A Slight Case of Murder*. He was seen to better advantage, however, in *Lone Star* (1951), starring Clark Gable and Ava Gardner; *Down Three Dark Streets* (1954), a fast-paced crime drama; and his remaining films noirs, *The Mob* (1951), *Scandal Sheet* (1952), *Human Desire* (1954), and *New York Confidential* (1955).

In *The Mob*, Crawford starred as Johnny Damico, a cop who goes undercover to infiltrate an organized waterfront crime ring. After rising in the ranks of the gang, Damico learns that he is not the only undercover officer on the case — fellow dock worker, Tom Clancy (Richard Kiley), whom Damico was investigating, is actually a special investigator working on a phony insurance swindle. ("Why don't they tell us these things?" Damico asks after learning Clancy's true line of work. "We go around gumshoeing after each other.... I've had a guy tailing you for two days.") With Clancy's help, Damico discovers that the leader of the mob has been right under his nose — the bartender of the local tavern, known as Smoothie (Matt Crowley). When Smoothie has Damico's fiancée, Mary (Betty Buehler), abducted and beaten, the detective is forced to shed his undercover role, but although he wounds the mob boss in a shootout, Smoothie manages to escape. Later, while Damico is visiting Mary in the hospital, Smoothie resurfaces, planning to kill them both, but before he can carry out his scheme, he is gunned down by police snipers.

The following year, in *Scandal Sheet*, Crawford portrayed a hard-hitting newspaper editor, Mark Chapman, who accidentally kills his shrewish wife, Charlotte (Rosemary DeCamp, in a rare departure from her maternal screen persona) during an argument. Disposing of any clues that would point to his involvement, Chapman later encourages one of his reporters, Steve McCleary (John Derek), to investigate the crime, but he is forced to kill again when a former writer for the paper (Henry O'Neill) discovers Chapman's guilt. Working with a fellow reporter (Donna Reed), McCleary ultimately identifies his boss as the killer. Rather than surrender to police, however, Chapman pulls a gun and fires a harmless shot, prompting them to shoot him. "You remember I told you that someday you were going to have a really big story?" Chapman says to Steve before he dies. "Well, this one ought to do it."

In Crawford's third consecutive noir, *Human Desire*, the actor played Carl Buckley, whose hair-trigger temper results in his dismissal as an assistant yard master at the local railroad. At Carl's insistence, his sultry wife, Vicki (Gloria Grahame), convinces wealthy shipper John Owens (Grandon Rhodes) to restore Carl's position, but Carl suspects Vicki's methods of persuasion and murders the shipper in a jealous rage. Meanwhile, Vicki begins an affair with railroad engineer Jeff Warren (Glenn Ford), and urges him to kill her husband, telling him that Carl possesses a note incriminating her as Owens' killer. Jeff manages to retrieve the letter, but is unable to commit the murder and ends his relationship with Vicki. When Carl later discovers Vicki's plans to leave him, he begs her to stay, but Vicki only mocks him, cruelly admitting that she'd had an affair with the shipper: "Owens did have something to do with me," she tells him. "But it was because *I* wanted him to. I wanted that big house he lived in. I wanted him to get rid of that wife of his. But he wasn't quite the fool *you* are. He knew what I was after. And you know what? I admired him for it. If I'd been a man, I'd have behaved exactly as he did." Enraged by Vicki's words of ridicule and contempt, Carl strangles her to death in the final reel.

Next, Crawford starred as syndicate boss Charlie Lupo in *New York Confidential*, whose focus is explained in the opening narration:

"Here, in a city of millions of decent, industrious people is a handful of men who form the top echelon of organized crime. Hoodlums? Yes. But now clothed in respectability to form a cartel known as The Syndicate." Hard-hitting, grim, and unusually violent, the film details the organization's corrupt activities and stringent set of rules, characterized by the murder of a government lobbyist; the suicide of Lupo's daughter (Anne Bancroft), who loathes her father's criminal involvement ("I love him as a father — I detest him as a man," she says); and the organization's plot to force Lupo to take the rap for a high-profile killing. Despite the long-standing rule that "the syndicate comes first," Lupo is enraged by the decision of the "high court" to tap him as the fall guy: "Lousy ingrates!" he tells his right-hand man, Nick Magellan (Richard Conte). "After all I've done for the organization. I *am* the organization!" Rather than take the fall, Lupo plans to expose the inner-workings of the organization to authorities, but before he has a chance to testify, he is gunned down by Magellan, who is himself shot and killed by an unseen assailant at the film's end.

Crawford was singled out for praise in each of his final film noir appearances, earning his best reviews for *The Mob*; for his performance in this feature, the actor was labeled "excellent" in the *Hollywood Citizen-News*, the *Los Angeles Examiner*'s reviewer hailed "the authority always found in his characterizations," and the critic for the *New York Times* raved: "Crawford slouches through the film with gusty savour, playing the melodramatic highspots for all they are worth, and extracts as much tension and suspense as possible from an unpolished script."

After *New York Confidential*, Crawford turned his sights to the medium of television, taking on the role of police chief Dan Mathews in *Highway Patrol*. Typically, Mathews would be seen encountering a highway crime scene, eventually solving the case by cracking an alibi and trapping the suspect after a climactic car chase. The popular series, in which Crawford introduced the term "10-4" into the public vernacular, ran for four years.

The role was not without its drawbacks, however; Crawford insisted on doing most of his own stunts and incurred a number of injuries during the run of the show, including a broken arm and a fractured skull. Years later, he joked that fellow actor Clark Gable had initially tried to talk him out of accepting the role.

"I was making *Lone Star* with Clark Gable and Ava Gardner. When the film was finished, I told Gable, 'I think I'll go into TV.' Clark says, 'I think you are out of your mind,'" Crawford recalled in a 1982 article. "Then, I was on *Highway Patrol*, and I bumped into Clark one day and he says, 'Tell me, Crawford, how the hell do I get into television?'"

While starring on *Highway Patrol*, Crawford continued to appear sporadically in feature films, including *The Fastest Gun Alive* (1956), a well-received western starring Glenn Ford; *Between Heaven and Hell* (1956), a war drama featuring Crawford as a psychopathic commanding officer; and *The Decks Ran Red* (1958), a profitable sea thriller with James Mason and Dorothy Dandridge. Beginning in the late 1950s and for the next two decades, the actor also guested on such television series as *Bat Masterson*, *The Man from U.N.C.L.E.*, *Love, American Style*, *Get Smart*, *It Takes a Thief*, *Alias Smith and Jones*, *Night Gallery*, *Banacek*, *Harry O*, *CHiPs*, *Simon and Simon*, and *Fantasy Island*. He also made two more attempts at series television, but both shows, *King of Diamonds* in 1961, and *The Interns* in 1970, were short-lived.

After *Highway Patrol* left the air in 1959, Crawford moved to England and appeared in such dreadful foreign productions as *Goliath and the Dragon* (1960) and *The Last of the Vikings* (1961). Far better was the grim and powerful *Square of Violence* (1962), filmed in Yugoslavia, in which Crawford portrayed a member of the resistance in a Nazi-occupied town during the war. Back in the United States, Crawford was seen in succession of time-wasters, including *A House Is Not a Home* (1964), a biopic based on the life of 1920s Broadway bordello madam Polly Adler; *The Oscar* (1966), a laughable drama starring

Stephen Boyd and Elke Sommer; and *The Vulture* (1966), a horror feature about a deadly bird with a human head. His best film during this period was *Red Tomahawk* (1967), a western featuring such screen veterans as Wendell Corey, Scott Brady, and Richard Arlen.

Meanwhile, Crawford had taken another trip down the aisle in 1962 when he married 28-year-old actress Joan Tabor. But this union, too, was destined for failure, and in 1965, Tabor filed for divorce. In her lawsuit, Tabor charged that the actor "strikes me and abuses me," and that he used "abusive language to such an extent that [I] developed stomach ulcers." The divorce was finalized in 1967. (Tabor remarried a short time later, but in December 1968, she was found dead of an accidental overdose of drugs.) In 1973, the actor would remarry again, this time to Mary Alice Michel, a 49-year-old widow who had appeared in television soap operas. For Crawford, the third time would be the charm; he and Michel would remain married until the actor's death.

Career-wise, the onset of the 1970s saw a decline in Crawford's film offers and he was seen in such forgettable features as *Hell's Bloody Devils* (1970), a violent, low-budget actioner; *Terror in the Wax Museum* (1973), notable only for the appearance of such old-time stars as Ray Milland, Elsa Lanchester, Maurice Evans, and John Carradine; and *Won Ton Ton, the Dog That Saved Hollywood* (1973), an unfunny comedy featuring a star-studded cast of Hollywood vets. Between these big-screen assignments, Crawford returned to his roots on the stage, appearing in 1973 in a revival of *Born Yesterday* at the Barn Dinner Theatre in St. Louis, Missouri, and the following year in an East coast tour of *That Championship Season*. He also served for a time as the raspy voice of the pink S.O.S. scouring pad in television commercials. Later in the decade, the actor made a cinematic comeback of sorts, earning praise for his title performance in the big-screen feature *The Private Files of J. Edgar Hoover* (1977), and making a cameo appearance in a charming

Broderick Crawford and Gloria Grahame in *Human Desire* (1954).

barbershop. Hollywood's been good to me and I've been good to Hollywood. But it used to be a lot more fun to be an actor."

Crawford made only three more feature films—*There Goes the Bride* (1979), a humorless comedy starring Tommy Smothers and Twiggy; *Harlequin* (1980), a drama filmed in Australia; and *Liar's Moon* (1982), a love story starring Matt Dillon. The latter would mark the actor's last big-screen appearance. On New Year's Eve 1984, during a party at his home, Crawford suffered a major stroke that affected his speech and left him with a slight impediment in his right leg. Over the next year, he suffered a series of minor strokes, and was admitted to the Eisenhower Medical Center in Rancho Mirage, California, on April 5, 1986. Several weeks later, on April 26, 1986, Crawford succumbed to complications from the strokes. His wife, Mary Alice, sons Christopher and Kelly, and his first wife, Kay Griffith, were at the hospital when the 74-year-old actor died.

romantic comedy, *A Little Romance* (1979). Still, the actor bemoaned the changes that had taken place in Hollywood, stating that he no longer spent much of his time in the film capital.

"What do I need with this town?" Crawford said in a 1977 interview. "Around here you stagnate, breathe in the smog, and listen to actors cry over the lack of work. At every party I go to, somebody wanders over to me to say, 'I saw your last picture.' And he always says it with a look that tells me he hopes I won't make anymore. Camaraderie is gone. There are more guys hoping you'll fall on your face than guys cheering you on. The moguls who invented this town knew what the public wanted. They had great taste. These new boy wonders ... if you mention the cutting room, they think you're talking about the

Although Broderick Crawford's potential as an actor was certainly hampered by his battle with alcoholism, his performances in his film noir features, as well as his portrayals in *All the King's Men* and *Born Yesterday*, have left behind an indelible representation of his notable impact during Hollywood's golden age. And despite the disappointments and unfulfilled successes that the actor experienced during his 50-year career, Crawford himself once declared that he never had any regrets.

"If I had it to do over again, I'd make the same damn mistakes," he said. "Because that's the way people are. And I'm proud to be a part of an industry that has brought so much happiness to so many people. And that's all I've got to say."

Film Noir Filmography

Black Angel. Director: Roy William Neill. Producers: Tom McKnight, Roy William Neill. Running time: 83 minutes. Released by Universal, August 2, 1946. Cast: Dan Duryea, June Vincent, Peter Lorre, Broderick Crawford, Constance Dowling, Wallace Ford, Hobart Cavanaugh, Freddie Steele, Ben Bard, John Phillips, Junius Matthews, Maurice St. Clair, Vilova, Pat Starling.

Convicted. Director: Harry Levin. Producer: Jerry Bresler. Running time: 91 minutes. Released by Columbia, August 1950. Cast: Glenn Ford, Broderick Crawford, Millard Mitchell, Dorothy Malone, Carl Benton Reid, Frank Faylen, Will Geer, Martha Stewart, Henry O'Neill, Douglas Kennedy, Ronald Winters, Ed Begley, Frank Cady, John Doucette, Ilka Gruning, John A. Butler, Peter Virgo, Whit Bissell.

The Mob. Director: Robert Parrish. Producer: Jerry Bresler. Running time: 87 minutes. Released by Columbia, October 17, 1951. Cast: Broderick Crawford, Betty Buehler, Richard Kiley, Otto Hulett, Matt Crowley, Neville Brand, Ernest Borgnine, Walter Klavun, Lynne Baggett, Jean Alexander, Ralph Dumke, John Marley, Frank De Kova, Jay Adler, Duke Watson, Emile Meyer, Carleton Young.

Scandal Sheet. Director: Phil Karlson. Producer: Edward Small. Running time: 82 minutes. Released by Columbia, January 16, 1952. Cast: John Derek, Donna Reed, Broderick Crawford, Rosemary DeCamp, Henry O'Neill, Henry Morgan, James Millican, Griff Barnett, Jonathan Hale, Pierre Watkin, Ida Moore, Ralph Reed, Luther Crockett, Charles Cane, Jay Adler, Don Beddoe.

Human Desire. Director: Fritz Lang. Producer: Lewis J. Rachmil. Running time: 90 minutes. Released by Columbia, August 6, 1954. Cast: Glenn Ford, Gloria Grahame, Broderick Crawford, Edgar Buchanan, Kathleen Case, Diane DeLaire, Grandon Rhodes, Dan Seymour, John Pickard, Paul Brinegar, Dan Riss, Victor Hugo Greene, John Zaremba, Carl Lee, Olan Soule.

New York Confidential. Director: Russell Rouse. Producer: Clarence Greene. Running time: 87 minutes. Released by Warner Brothers, February 18, 1955. Cast: Broderick Crawford, Richard Conte, Marilyn Maxwell, Anne Bancroft, J. Carrol Naish, Onslow Stevens, Barry Kelley, Mike Mazurki, Celia Lovsky, Herbert Heyes, Steven Geray.

References

"Actor Brod Crawford Marries." *Los Angeles Examiner*, January 5, 1962.

"Actor Broderick Crawford Recovering from Stroke." *Los Angeles Herald-Examiner*, January 5, 1985.

"Actor Seized in Auto Crash." *Hollywood Citizen-News*, June 23, 1947.

Biography of Broderick Crawford. Columbia Studios, December 1953.

Biography of Broderick Crawford. Universal Studios, June 1940.

"Born to the Stage, This Actor Found Odds Against Him." *New York Herald Tribune*, January 14, 1940.

"Brod Crawford, Actress Drunk, Police Charge." *Los Angeles Times*, December 13, 1954.

"Brod Crawford Called 'Drunken Bum' by Judge." *Los Angeles Times*, December 4, 1954.

"Brod Crawford Granted Custody of Sports Car." *Los Angeles Examiner*, March 10, 1956.

"Brod Crawford Sued for Divorce.' *Los Angeles Times*, December 30, 1965.

"Brod Crawford to Marry Again." *Newark News*, July 11, 1958.

"Broderick Crawford Divorced." *Los Angeles Times*, April 27, 1967.

"Broderick Crawford Is Father of Boy." *Los Angeles Evening Herald-Express*, July 27, 1951.

"Broderick Crawford, Oscar-Winning Tough, Dies." *New York Times*, April 28, 1986.

"Broderick Crawfords Battle Over $5000 Car." *Los Angeles Examiner*, March 10, 1956.

"Broderick Crawford, 2 Pals Arrested on Drunk Charges." *Los Angeles Examiner*, December 13, 1954.

"Broderick Crawford Weds Widow." *Los Angeles Times*, August 9, 1973.

Cohen, Jerry. "Broderick Crawford, Oscar Winner in 1949, Dies at 74." *Los Angeles Times*, April 27, 1986.

Crawford, Broderick, as told to Bill Kelly. "Broderick Crawford, As He Sees It!" *Hollywood Studio Magazine*, April 1982.

Crawford, Broderick. "The Role I Liked Best." *The Saturday Evening Post*, June 3, 1950.

"Crawford Fined in Drunk Driving." *Los Angeles Examiner*, November 8, 1952.

Cuskelly, Richard. "Crawford Wasn't Born Yesterday." *Los Angeles Herald-Examiner*, June 5, 1977.

Fink, Mitchell. "Broderick Crawford Dead at 74." *Los Angeles Herald-Examiner*, April 27, 1986.

"Former Wife of Actor Dies of Overdose." *Hollywood Citizen-News*, December 19, 1968.

Hopper, Hedda. "Like Mother, Like Son." *Chicago Sunday Tribune*, March 12, 1950.

"'King's Man' Jailed as a Drunk Driver." *Los Angeles Mirror*, November 7, 1952.

McCarthy, Todd. "Broderick Crawford Dies; Rites Pending." *Variety*, April 28, 1986.

Page, Don. "Brod Crawford Comes in Clear." *Los Angeles Times*, October 30, 1970.

Parsons, Louella O. "Broderick Crawford." *Los Angeles Examiner*, March 26, 1950.

_____. "Lisa Says She Won't Wed Brod." *Los Angeles Examiner*, July 11, 1958.

_____. "Broderick Crawfords Expect Baby in July." *Los Angeles Examiner*, January 24, 1951.

_____. "Mr. and Mrs. Broderick Crawford and Kim." *Los Angeles Examiner*, April 20, 1952.

"Players File Nuptial Notice." *Hollywood Citizen-News*, November 14, 1940.

"Screen Couple to Be Wed Next Thanksgiving Day." *Los Angeles Times*, November 15, 1940.

Walker, Turnley. "Broderick Crawford: 'It's a Helluva Life.'" *Pageant*, December 1956.

Whitney, Dwight. "I Have a Jaundiced Eye but a Young Mind." *TV Guide*, March 6, 1971.

"Wife Calls Crawford Unfit for Sons' Custody." *Los Angeles Times*, January 26, 1956.

"Wife Seeks Separation from Broderick Crawford." *Los Angeles Times*, February 15, 1951.

JOHN DALL

"Shooting's what I'm good at. It's the only thing I like. It's what I want to do when I grow up…. I like shooting 'em, Judge. I don't know why, but I feel good when I'm shooting them. I feel awful good inside, like I'm somebody." — John Dall in *Gun Crazy* (1950)

John Dall was once described as possessing "Jimmy Stewart's forelock, Gary Cooper's ranginess, nice brown eyes, talent, exuberance, and more energy than a 2200-horsepower Cyclone engine"— but his name is rarely recognized by today's audiences. And with good reason: he was seen in only eight films during a span of 16 years. Nonetheless, during his sparse film career, Dall was seen in such acclaimed films as *The Corn Is Green* (1945), Alfred Hitchcock's *Rope* (1948), and *Spartacus* (1960), as well as one of the quintessential examples of the film noir era — *Gun Crazy* (1950).

Dall was born John Jenner Thompson in New York City on May 26, 1918, the second son of Charles Jenner Thompson, a civil engineer, and his wife, the curiously named Henry Worthington Thompson. John became interested in acting at the young age of seven, when he and a cousin began producing plays for their neighborhood playmates. His mother often took him to the local movie theater, but she would hide his eyes when the films depicted violence or sex, leaving the youngster with an insatiable curiosity about the world of movies.

When John was 10, his father's work took the family to Panama, where Charles Thompson worked as an engineer on the airport being constructed there. In Panama, the youngster reportedly "developed a knack" for sneaking out to the movies, including climbing out of windows or borrowing the price of a ticket. After several years in Panama, John landed a job as a handyman for a local theater company, memorizing the actors' lines as he worked. One night, an elderly actor in the company's play, *Yes Means No*, became ill shortly before the curtain was scheduled to open, and the 13-year-old, six-foot-one inch John convinced the director to allow him to take the actor's place. It was his "professional" stage debut.

When John's family returned to New York City, the boy attended Horace Mann High School, then briefly enrolled at Columbia University where he intended to follow in his father's footsteps by pursuing a degree in engineering. But during his freshman year, he realized that his true love was the stage and left Columbia, enrolling instead at the Irvine School for acting. He later changed his name to John Dall and joined Clare Tree Major's famed children's theater, with whom he toured in *Robin Hood*. When the tour ended, Dall honed his acting skills in six years of stock, during which he made ends meet by securing such jobs as selling pajamas at Macy's Department store, carrying trays in Schrafft's Restaurant, working as an elevator operator, and writing pulp stories for confessional magazines.

Dall finally got his first break in 1943 when he landed a walk-on in the hit Broadway production of *Janie*, produced by Brock Pemberton, directed by Antoinette Perry (after whom the theater's "Tony Award" is named), and starring Janie Colburn and Herbert Evers. He was next cast as the vacation replacement for the lead in the Broadway production of *The Eve of St. Mark*—and was spotted by a talent agent from Warner Bros. In rapid fashion, Dall signed a contract with Warners, moved to California and, for his film debut, was cast opposite Bette Davis in *The Corn Is Green* (1945). Dall was hailed for his performance as a Welsh coal miner, and was rewarded for his efforts with an Academy Award nomination for best supporting actor. Although he lost to James Dunn in *A Tree Grows in Brooklyn* (1945), Dall's introduction to Hollywood couldn't have been more impressive.

After this triumphant debut, Dall was promptly cast in *Dear Ruth* on Broadway, co-starring Virginia Gilmore and Lenore Lonergan, then returned to Hollywood for *Something in the Wind* (1947), a comedy-musical starring Deanna Durbin; *Another Part of the Forest* (1948), the "prequel" to the Bette Davis starrer, *The Little Foxes* (1941); and the underrated *Rope* (1948), directed by Alfred Hitchcock. Based on the famed 1924 murder by rich Chicago youths Nathan Leopold and Richard Loeb, *Rope* is notable primarily for Hitchcock's experiment in filming the scenes in uncut, 10-minute intervals. Although audiences were unimpressed with the film, Dall's performance was singled out by reviewers—the critic for *Variety* wrote that "Dall stands out as the egocentric who masterminds the killing and ghoulish wake," and in the *New York Times*, Bosley Crowther wrote that Dall "does a hard, aggressive job of making this unpleasant fellow supremely contemptible."

Of landing the starring role in *Rope*, Dall later said, "Hitchcock not only didn't know about me; he didn't want me. I found out where he ate dinner, I stayed there every night and I talked to him as often as I could. He was pleasant, but he always said no. You know, I wore him down. I ran up a check for $1000 worth of food and martinis, but I wore him down. He gave in and gave me the part."

After *Rope*, Dall stepped into the realm of film noir in *Gun Crazy* (1950), starring as gun-obsessed Bart Tare. The film starts out showing Bart as a lad, breaking into a store to steal a gun and being sent to reform school. When he returns to his hometown years later, Bart meets and falls in love with Annie Laurie Starr (Peggy Cummins), a carnival sharpshooter. Bart joins the carnival, but he and Annie are fired when the carnival's owner (Berry Kroeger)—who is himself enamored with Annie—learns of their affair. The two marry, but when their meager funds run out, Annie urges her spouse to join her in a series of bank robberies. Bart agrees, but his reluctance is palpable: "It's just that everything's going so fast," he tells Laurie. "It's all in such high gear, and sometimes it doesn't feel like me…. I wake up sometimes. It's as if none of it really happened, as if nothing were real anymore." When Annie's trigger-happy behavior results in several deaths, the couple goes on the run from the law, finally seeking refuge in Bart's hometown. As police close in, Bart and Annie flee into the nearby mountains, but Bart kills Annie as she prepares to fire at the approaching officers, and is himself gunned down moments later. The bandit lovers die in a swampy marsh, in a final embrace. Hailed upon its release as "dramatic and compelling," *Gun Crazy* earned rave reviews for Dall, with the critic from *The Hollywood Reporter* terming him "excellent indeed."

By now, rumors were beginning to circulate around Hollywood regarding John Dall's sexuality. Dall had had a short-lived, seldom-discussed marriage in the early 1940s. Although the actor was once quoted in a fan magazine as claiming that "you're not whole till you find the right girl," the director of

Dall's film debut, Irving Rapper, claimed that the actor was "sexually ambiguous, which was not permitted at the time." In addition, Joseph Lewis, who helmed *Gun Crazy*, claimed that the actor's sexuality was a significant factor in his being cast in the film.

"I wanted someone with a weakness," Lewis said in 1991. "Dall was a homosexual and I knew he'd be trying to keep that secret all through the film."

Dall followed *Gun Crazy* with his second and last film noir, *The Man Who Cheated Himself* (1950). Here, the actor played Andy Cullen, a young San Francisco detective who is partnered on the force with his seasoned older brother, Ed (Lee J. Cobb). Assigned to a case involving a man found murdered at the local airport, Andy grows increasingly suspicious as clues begin to point to his own brother's entanglement in the crime. As it turns out, the dead man was killed by his wife (Jane Wyatt, in a rare "bad girl" role), with whom Ed is having an affair. Despite his reluctance to pursue his sibling, Andy's sense of duty wins out. ("Look — you're my brother, Ed," he says in one scene. "I'd hate to send other guys after you.") Although Ed knocks

Andy unconscious and flees with his lover, Andy later tracks the couple to an abandoned fort at the base of the Golden Gate bridge, where they are captured by police. For his role as the conflicted brother, Dall earned mostly good reviews; while the critic for the *New York Times* found him "serious but callow," Wylie Williams wrote in *Hollywood Citizen-News* that the actor "comes through well in the climactic scenes," and the *Los Angeles Times*' Philip K. Scheuer reported that Dall "emerges most believably as the rookie brother."

Reportedly tiring of the roles in which he was being cast — particularly such "sociopaths" as the character he portrayed in *Gun Crazy* — Dall left Hollywood after *The Man Who Cheated Himself* and returned to the stage, appearing in such productions as *The Heiress* with Basil Rathbone and Edna Best, *Red Gloves* with Charles Boyer, *The Hasty Heart*, and *Champagne Complex*. In between stage performances, Dall turned to other performing mediums — in 1953, he starred with Diana Lynn and Jessie Royce Landis in "A Quiet Wedding," which aired on radio's *United States Steel Hour*, and he appeared on a variety of television programs, including several episodes on the popular courtroom drama *Perry Mason*.

In 1960, Dall made a brief big screen comeback, portraying Marcus Publius Glabrus in the big budget blockbuster *Spartacus*, whose all-star cast included Kirk Douglas, Laurence Olivier, Tony Curtis, Jean Simmons, and Peter Ustinov. But Dall didn't fare as well with his follow-up film, *Atlantis, the Lost Continent* (1961), which was panned in *Variety* as a "tired, shopworn melodrama." Dall's depiction of the evil Zaren in this film would be his last role on the silver screen. He focused his energies instead on his stage and television roles, but just a decade later, on January 15, 1971, he died of a heart attack in Hollywood. He was 51 years old.

While Dall's contribution to feature films is certainly limited, his performances in such films as *The Corn is Green* and *Gun Crazy* effectively illuminate his talents, and his range of roles demonstrate his versatility. He never approached stardom, but he did manage to score successes in film and television as well as the stage and radio. Perhaps it was his philosophical approach to life that kept him going not only through the whispers about his personal life, but also despite the disappointments he may have experienced professionally.

"I believe we were put here for a purpose — that we go to prep school here for 70 years or so," Dall said in a 1945 interview. "There has to be some point to the business of building up a life. I figure anything you don't solve now, you have to work out later. So I try to make the best possible thing out of each opportunity, take advantage of each chance that comes along. I won't be told anything is impossible. I want to find out for myself.

"I have a feeling maybe nothing is impossible."

Film Noir Filmography

Gun Crazy. Director: Joseph H. Lewis. Producer: Frank and Maurice King. Running time: 87 minutes. Released by United Artists, as Deadly Is The Female on January 26, 1950; re-released as Gun Crazy on August 24, 1950. Cast: Peggy Cummins, John Dall, Berry Kroeger, Morris Carnovsky, Anabel Shaw, Harry Lewis, Nedrick Young, Trevor Bardette, Mickey Little, Rusty Tamblyn,

Paul Frison, Dave Bair, Stanley Prager, Virginia Farmer, Anne O'Neal, Frances Irwin, Don Beddoe, Robert Osterloh, Shimen Ruskin, Harry Hayden.

The Man Who Cheated Himself. Director: Felix E. Feist. Producer: Jack M. Warner. Running time: 81 minutes. Released by 20th Century-Fox, February 8, 1951. Cast: Lee J. Cobb, John Dall, Jane Wyatt, Lisa Howard, Alan Wells, Harlan Warde, Tito Vuolo, Mimi Aguglia, Charles Arnt, Marjorie Bennett, Bud Wolfe, Morgan Farley, Howard Negley.

References

Biography of John Dall. Margaret Ettinger and Company, April 1948.
Biography of John Dall. Warner Bros. Pictures, circa 1945.
Cooke, Marion. "Career Crasher." *Motion Picture Magazine*, August 1945.
"Film News." *The Village Voice*, May 21, 1991.
"Film Star John Dall Dies at 50." *Los Angeles Herald-Examiner*, January 18, 1971.
"John Dall, 50, Dies; Stage, Screen Actor." *Los Angeles Times*, January 15, 1971.
Obituary. *The Hollywood Reporter*, January 19, 1971.
Obituary. *Variety*, January 18, 1971.
Redelings, Lowell. "The Hollywood Scene." *Hollywood Citizen-News*, May 22, 1950.
Squire, N.W. "Johnny Come Lately." *Modern Screen*, circa 1947.
Smith, Darr. "John Dall." *Los Angeles Daily News*, June 5, 1950.
Stafford, Muriel. "Script Reveals More Than Face." *Los Angeles Daily News*, March 1, 1951.

HOWARD DA SILVA

"Don't you tell me what to do. You ask me if I wanna do it." — Howard Da Silva in *They Live By Night* (1948)

Howard Da Silva wore many hats. Once described as possessing "a voice as sweet as molasses and as mellow as rum," the beefy character actor enjoyed a distinguished career not only as an actor, but as a director, producer, and author as well. Although his name was sullied and his career temporary stalled by accusations of Communism, Da Silva man-

aged to earn acclaim in film, radio, television, and the stage, and was memorable in four films noirs from the 1940s and 1950s: *The Blue Dahlia* (1946), *They Live By Night* (1948), *Border Incident* (1949), and *M* (1951).

Da Silva was born Howard Silverblatt on May 4, 1909, in Cleveland, Ohio. When the actor was a small boy, his parents— Benjamin

Silverblatt, a dress cutter, and his wife, Bertha, a women's rights activist — moved to the Bronx, New York, where young Howard attended P.S. 40 and Stuyvesant High School. His introduction to performing came during his matriculation at the latter institution, where he appeared in a number of student productions. During summers, however, Howard indulged his love for the outdoors by working as a harvest hand in rural New York, and for a time toyed with the idea of becoming a farmer. Lacking the funds to buy a farm after his high school graduation, he set his sights on an acting career, moving to Pittsburgh and working in the local steel mills to finance his tuition at the Carnegie Tech School of the Drama.

Following his studies at Carnegie Tech, the budding thespian changed his surname to Da Silva and headed for New York, where he was hired as an apprentice with the Eva Le Gallienne acting group. After a year's time, Da Silva was made a full member of the group and appeared during the next four years in nearly 40 productions.

"I was paid about 15 bucks a week," Da Silva recalled several years later. "The maximum salary you could expect in those days was about equal to today's minimum rehearsal pay. But before that, when I started out, there wasn't any rehearsal pay at all. How we escaped starving in those days, I can't understand now."

With his popularity on the rise, Da Silva accepted an offer in the late 1920s to become a director and actor at the Cleveland Playhouse in Ohio, where his productions included such successes as *Rain from Heaven* and *Between Two Worlds*. While in Cleveland, Da Silva caught the eye of a Paramount talent scout, who gave him a small role in the Ben Hecht–Charles MacArthur feature *Once in a Blue Moon* (1936), filmed at Paramount's New York studio.

A short time after his film debut, Da Silva was lured back to New York by a local radio station, WMCA, which hired him as director for their on-air programs. While there, he became associated with Orson Welles, who

cast Da Silva in the leading role of his stage play, *The Cradle Will Rock*. Da Silva also joined the famed Group Theater, for which he starred in *Golden Boy*, *Waiting for Lefty*, and *Casey Jones*, and appeared in the Broadway productions of *Alice in Wonderland*, *Two on an Island*, and *Abe Lincoln in Illinois*. After his appearance in the latter play, Da Silva was beckoned by the silver screen again, this time to reprise his role for the film version of *Abe Lincoln in Illinois* (1940). He was also featured that year in RKO's *I'm Still Alive* (1940), a weak comedy starring Robert Taylor, and in a Warner Bros. short, *The Dog in the Orchard* (1940), after which he signed a contract with the studio.

Da Silva was kept busy the following year with appearances in a whopping 10 films, the best of which were *The Sea Wolf* (1941), starring Edward G. Robinson as a tyrannical ship's captain, and *Sergeant York* (1941), which featured Gary Cooper in the Academy Award–winning title role of the World War I hero. Despite his frenetic schedule, however, Da Silva found time for romance — on January 10, 1941, he married actress Jane Taylor in Yuma, Arizona, and the two later had a son, Peter. But after seven years, the marriage would end bitterly, with both filing suit against the other for "extreme cruelty." In court, Jane would testify that although she had to rise early each morning to care for their baby, "I still tried to wait up for my husband, but he kept coming in later and later, and would only say he had been 'out' when I asked him where he'd been." Da Silva would marry twice again, and father four more children, Daniel, Rachel, Judith, and Margaret.

Career-wise, Da Silva was seen eight fairly forgettable films in 1942, including *Juke Girl*, a dreary melodrama starring Ronald Reagan and Ann Sheridan, and *Bullet Scars*, a programmer featuring Regis Toomey as a doctor kidnapped by gangsters. He fared better, however, when his Warners contract ended and he signed with MGM, appearing in the big-budget Joan Crawford vehicle, *Reunion in France*.

The actor's back-to-back screen appearances came to a screeching halt in 1943 — after appearing in the war drama *Tonight We Raid Calais*, he returned to New York to originate the role of Jud in the Broadway production of *Oklahoma*. After 500 performances in the successful play, Da Silva was back to Hollywood for one of his most acclaimed roles, portraying Nat the bartender in the harrowing feature, *The Lost Weekend* (1945). Da Silva apparently made quite an impact in the film — after his death, most of his obituaries falsely claimed that he had earned an Academy Award nomination for his portrayal. Da Silva was similarly credited — and just as inaccurately — for his acclaimed performance in *Two Years Before the Mast* (1946), where he played a sadistic ship's captain whose tyranny even extends to murder.

In his second film of 1946, Da Silva entered the realm of film noir with a showy role in *The Blue Dahlia*, which provided the third on-screen teaming of Alan Ladd and Veronica Lake. Among the film's cast of interesting characters were Johnny Morrison (Ladd), a war veteran accused of murdering his playgirl spouse, Helen (Doris Dowling); Eddie Harwood (Da Silva), an oily nightclub owner who was romantically involved with Helen; Harwood's estranged wife, Joyce (Lake); and Johnny's buddy, Buzz Wanchek (William Bendix), who suffers from bouts of amnesia due to a war injury. While police question several suspects, Johnny zeroes in on Harwood, tracking him to an abandoned house, but the nightclub owner reacts with unflappable calm when he is accused of shooting Helen: "In a hotel bungalow?" he asks Johnny in an amused tone. "With a .45? I could've arranged things better than that." Shortly after this declaration of innocence, Harwood is accidentally shot while his partner is struggling with Johnny, and Johnny learns that the real killer was a hotel detective who was not only blackmailing Harwood, but Johnny's wife as well.

After *The Blue Dahlia*, which was hailed by one critic as "tremendously effective," Da Silva was featured in the box office hit *Blaze of Noon* (1947), with William Holden and Sterling Hayden; portrayed himself in Para-

mount's big-budget musical jamboree, *Variety Girl* (1947); then returned to the dark side of the screen in the best of his four film noir features, *They Live by Night* (1948). In this Depression-era film, Da Silva portrayed Chickamaw, a hardened, one-eyed convict who escapes from jail along with two fellow inmates, Arthur "Bowie" Bowers (Farley Granger) and T-Dub (Jay C. Flippen). Chickamaw and T-Dub talk the naive Bowie into committing a local bank robbery, but the heist goes awry — Bowie is injured in a car accident during the getaway and Chickamaw shoots and kills a police officer. Nursed back to health by Chickamaw's niece, Keechie (beautifully played by Cathy O'Donnell), Bowie falls for and marries the young girl, and the two go on the run, seeking refuge at a motel run by T-Dub's sister, Mattie (Helen

Craig). T-Dub, meanwhile, is killed during another heist, and Chickamaw meets his demise when he is shot trying to break into a liquor store. At the film's end, Bowie himself is gunned down by police when Mattie turns him in, leaving the now-pregnant Keechie to face her future alone.

Described as a man who "lives for trouble," Chickamaw was Da Silva's most outstanding noir character, noted for his heavy drinking and his desire for notoriety. In an early scene, he complains about the press coverage of the men's prison break, stating, "They didn't print a very big piece about us. In a few days, they'll really have something to print about us. Three boys like us, we can charge any bank in the country — any bank." And later, after Bowie is prominently featured in newspaper accounts of the men's ill-fated robbery attempt, he grouses, "It rips my guts out. Bowie the Kid.... All the newspapers print about is you — you and that two-bit girl of yours. Makes me look like a penny in a slot machine." For his memorable performance, the actor earned well-deserved praise from critics; in a typical notice, the reviewer from *Variety* remarked that the actor "clicks as a ruthless, one-eyed bank robber." The same critic also lauded the production itself, calling it "a moving, somber story of hopeless young love. There's no attempt at sugarcoating a happy ending, and [the] yarn moves towards inevitable, tragic climax without compromise."

Da Silva's next film appearance was in the Alan Ladd starrer *The Great Gatsby* (1949), followed by his third film noir, *Border Incident* (1949). In this dark tale of Mexican farmworkers smuggled over the U.S. border, Da Silva starred as crooked rancher Owen Parkson. Parkson's lucrative operation involves hiring out the illegal aliens in the United States, then bringing them back toward the boarder, where they are robbed and murdered. The successful scheme is threatened, however, when Parkson's gang is infiltrated by two undercover agents, one from the United States (George Murphy), the other from Mexico (Ricardo Montalban). The American

agent, Jack Bearnes, meets a gruesome end at Parkson's hand when the rancher learns his true identity — after Parkson directs his henchman to "make it look like an accident," Bearnes is run over by a tractor. In the film's climax, however, Parkson himself dies when his henchman turns on him, shooting him and watching him expire in a pool of quicksand. Although *Border Incident* is viewed today as a striking example of film noir, the feature earned mixed reviews from critics. Lynn Bowers of the *Los Angeles Examiner* labeled the feature a "tense, tough-fisted story," and the *Los Angeles Times*' Philip K. Scheuer praised it as "one of the year's top-drawer thrillers; if comparisons are in order, it is at least as nerve-racking as *Treasure of the Sierra Madre*." But Bosley Crowther vehemently disagreed, writing in the *New York Times*, "The whole story smacks of illogic, contrivance and unreality." Da Silva was nearly universally praised, however — Crowther rather grudgingly noted his "adequately villainous" performance, and in *Motion Picture Herald*, Charles J. Lazarus wrote, "Howard Da Silva makes the part of the rancher who hires the slave labor stand out."

Following a rare comedic appearance in *Three Husbands* (1950) and a role as the henchman for a corrupt railway official in *Wyoming Mail* (1950), Da Silva starred in his final film noir, *M* (1951). On the right side of the law for a change, Da Silva played Inspector Carney, a diligent cop frustrated in his efforts to find a serial child-killer (David Wayne) who is terrorizing the city: "The ordinary murder, you're looking for a dame or a bankbook. Got a victim with known enemies," Carney says. "What are we looking for? A man with a twisted mind. Could be anybody." As police continue their fruitless investigation, a local mob leader by the name of Marshall (Martin Gabel) undertakes his own probe, seeking to favorably alter the outcome of an upcoming grand inquiry into his criminal activities. Carney and his partner (Steve Brodie) ultimately identify the killer, but Marshall's network of underlings finds him first and the psychologically damaged murderer is nearly killed by a vicious mob of citizens before police arrive to take him away.

Although most critics focused their reviews on Wayne's frightening portrait of the child-killer, Da Silva was singled out in several notices, with Philip K. Scheuer of the *Los Angeles Times* including the actor in his mention of "others [in the cast] who score in varying degrees," and the *New York Times'* critic writing that the actor "contributed competently" to the production. At this point, however, Da Silva cinematic contributions faded in significance when he found himself caught up in the anti–Communism fever that had swept the Hollywood community, courtesy of the House Un-American Activities Committee (HUAC).

The committee had been investigating Communism in the motion picture industry since 1947, and Da Silva was named before the committee by popular actor Robert Taylor, who testified: "I can name a few who seem to sort of disrupt things once in a while. Whether or not they are Communists I don't know. One chap we have currently, I think, is Howard Da Silva. He always seems to have something to say at the wrong time." Called before the committee, Da Silva refused to answer questions and was subsequently blacklisted — he would not appear in a feature film for nearly a decade. In addition, Da Silva was cut from the movie *Slaughter Trail* (1951), and all of the scenes in which he had appeared — about 2,000 feet of film — were reshot with actor Brian Donlevy instead.

In the years to come, Da Silva would rarely discuss his experience with the blacklist, but in 1976, he did admit feeling a degree of compassion for some of his colleagues who "named names."

"But there are some people, who will remain forever nameless, that I will not forgive," Da Silva said. "Never."

Unable to find work in Hollywood, Da Silva returned to New York and the stage — among his more successful productions were *The World of Sholem Aleichem* in 1953, in which he starred, as well as co-produced and directed; and *Fiorello!* in 1959. In July 1960,

along with three other cast members of *Fiorello*, Da Silva was scheduled to appear in *The Great American Game*, a live broadcast on WNBC-TV, which would have ended the actor's banishment from television. But days before the airdate, *New York Journal-American* writer Jack O'Brian penned a column in which he attacked Da Silva for his "communist sympathies," and the program never aired.

"It was incredible — the blacklist in 1960!" recalled WNBC producer Gordon Hyatt. "The broadcasters caved in and announced that the program had to be 'preempted' for a news special. I had to call Howard and tell him we were cancelled. He was heartsick — as were we all."

Da Silva rebounded from this disappointment, however, when he directed the highly successful stage play *Purlie Victorious* in 1961.

"I love this play and I love directing it," Da Silva said in *Cue* Magazine. "It has such joy and warmth and loving in it." During his interview with the magazine, Da Silva also mentioned his desire to return to the big screen, cryptically telling the reporter that there were "good chances" that he would soon resume his film career. And indeed he did. After 11 years, Da Silva played the acclaimed role of psychiatrist Dr. Swinford in *David and Lisa* (1962), earning a nomination from the British Academy Award of Film and Television Arts (BAFTA). He also began appearing on such television series as *The Outer Limits* and *The Man from U.N.C.L.E.*

Throughout the remainder of the 1960s and into the 1970s, Da Silva continued his work on the stage, on screen, and in television, both in front of the camera and behind the scenes. He co-wrote *The Zulu and the Zaya*, a musical play about prejudice and Apartheid that opened on November 10, 1965, at the Cort Theatre in New York and ran for 179 performances; played a recurring role on the William Shatner television series *For the People* (1965); portrayed a work camp warden in the Steve McQueen starrer *Nevada Smith* (1966); starred on Broadway in 1970 as Benjamin Franklin in the hit play *1776*, then reprised his role for the big screen two years later; appeared in the remake of *The Great Gatsby* (1974), 25 years after his featured role in the original; portrayed Soviet Premier Nikita Khrushchev in the highly-rated television drama *The Missiles of October* (1974); provided voiceovers for the popular British cult science fiction series *Dr. Who*; and was seen in *Hollywood on Trial* (1976), a compelling documentary about the HUAC investigations.

Now past 70, Da Silva continued to work in television and feature films—he won an Emmy Award for his performance in the television movie *Verna: U.S.O. Girl*, and made a memorable impact as MGM head Louis B. Mayer in the unintentionally hilarious *Mommie Dearest* (1981). In his last film appearance, he was seen as photographer Angelo Dokakis in *Garbo Talks* (1984), starring Anne Bancroft and Ron Silver.

On February 16, 1986, Howard Da Silva died of lymphoma at his home in Ossining, New York. He was 76 years old and left behind his wife, Nancy, and five children—Peter, Rachel, Judith, Daniel, and Margaret. He also left a legacy of excellence and of determination under fire; despite the setbacks he experienced because of the HUAC "witch-hunts," Da Silva maintained a "never say die" demeanor that sustained his career in spite of an 11-year absence from movies and television. Still, notwithstanding the accolades he received throughout his lengthy career, Da Silva was never one to rest on his laurels—he seemed always to be striving for perfection:

"When you think you have it, and are happy about it, there arises the problem of keeping what you've found as fresh as at the instant you found it," Da Silva once said. "How are you going to do it? You are pretending and you're sure your pretending is right. There's the difficulty to keep the pretending always new and spontaneous, to give the audience something alive and true each time."

Film Noir Filmography

The Blue Dahlia. Director: George Marshall. Producer: John Houseman. Running time: 98 minutes. Released by Paramount, April 19, 1946. Cast: Alan Ladd, Veronica Lake, William Bendix, Howard Da Silva, Doris Dowling, Tom Powers, Hugh Beaumont, Howard Freeman, Don Costello, Will Wright, Frank Faylen, Walter Sande. Awards: Academy Award nomination for Best Original Screenplay (Raymond Chandler).

They Live by Night. Director: Nicholas Ray. Producer: John Houseman. Running time: 95 minutes. Released by RKO, June 28, 1948. Cast: Cathy O'Donnell, Farley Granger, Howard Da Silva, Jay C. Flippen, Helen Craig, Will Wright, Marie Bryant, Ian Wolfe, William Phipps, Harry Harvey.

Border Incident. Director: Anthony Mann. Producer: Nicholas Nayfack. Running time: 96 minutes. Released by MGM, November 19, 1949. Cast: Ricardo Montalban, George Murphy, Howard Da Silva, James Mitchell, Arnold Moss, Alfonso Bedoya, Teresa Celli, Charles McGraw, Jose Torvay, John Ridgely, Arthur Hunnicutt, Sig Ruman, Otto Waldis, Harry Antrim, Tony Barr, Rozene Jones, John McGuire, Jack Lambert, Nedrich Young, Fred Graham, Lynn Whitney.

M. Director: Joseph Losey. Producer: Seymour Nebenzal. Running time 87 minutes. Released by Columbia, June 10, 1951. Cast: David Wayne, Howard Da Silva, Martin Gabel, Luther Adler, Steve Brodie, Glenn Anders, Norman Lloyd, Walter Burke, Raymond Burr.

References

"Actor Da Silva Plans to Wed Marjorie Nelson." *Los Angeles Times*, July 4, 1950.

Biography of Howard Da Silva. Paramount Studios, circa 1943.

"Blacklist-Era Show Set by CBS." *Variety*, October 13, 1976.

Brown, James. "Today's Face of Franklin." *Los Angeles Times*, June 29, 1976.

"Da Silva and Actress Get Marriage License." *New York Times*, circa August 1950.

"Da Silva Cut Out of Film." *Los Angeles Times*, May 5, 1951.

Dennis, Landt. "From 20th-Century Stage Star to 18th-Century Sage." *The Christian Science Monitor*, June 30, 1969.

Finnegan, Les. "Star Shines as Unionist." *Public Employee Press*, May 2, 1969.

Grover, William. "That's Ben Franklin, the Broadway Star." *Los Angeles Herald-Examiner*, June 22, 1969.

Hammel, Faye. "Director in Love." *Cue*, September 23, 1961.

"Howard Da Silva, 76, Actor-Director, Dies." *Los Angeles Herald-Examiner*, February 18, 1986.

"Howard Da Silva, 76, Longtime Actor, Director." *South Jersey Courier-Post*, February 18, 1986.

"Howard Da Silva Dies at 76; Actor, Director and Author." *New York Times*, February 18, 1986.

"Jane Da Silva: How Marriage to Actor Failed, Told Court." *New York Herald-Express*, July 28, 1948.

Obituary. *Variety*, February 19, 1986.

Pollock, Arthur. "H. Da Silva, Man in Love with His Work." *The Sunday Compass*, October 22, 1950.

"Star of Broadway's '1776' Dies of Lymphoma at Age 76." *New York Daily News*, February 18, 1986.

Raidy, William A. "A Man for All Roles, He's Suited for Ben." *Staten Island Sunday Advance*, August 23, 1970.

Wahls, Robert. "Footlights: Backstage with Ben." *New York Daily News*, June 29, 1969.

"Wife Sues Da Silva, Actor, for Divorce." *New York Herald Express*, June 17, 1948.

TED DE CORSIA

"If you're smart, you can be a hero. If you're dumb, you can be dead." — Ted De Corsia in *The Enforcer* (1951)

Graced with one of screendom's most menacing visages, Ted De Corsia was a natural for the gritty, realistic characters that were a staple of the film noir era. A performer from an early age, the actor also possessed a deep voice and gruff manner that transferred well over the airwaves and he was a prominent figure in New York radio for a number of years. In addition to roles in more than 60 feature films and appearances in some of television's highest rated series, De Corsia was seen in a total of nine films noirs: *The Naked City* (1948), *The Lady From Shanghai* (1948), *The Enforcer* (1951), *The Turning Point* (1952), *Crime Wave* (1954), *The Big Combo* (1955), *Slightly Scarlet* (1956), *The Killing* (1956), and *Baby Face Nelson* (1957).

Edward Gildea De Corsia was born on September 29, 1903 (some sources state 1904 or 1905), in Brooklyn, New York, the only child of vaudeville performers Edward De Corsia and Helen Le Sage. Because his parents' career took them from town to town, De Corsia attended schools in cities all over the country. He also inherited his parents' affinity for the stage — his first experience as a performer reportedly came at the age of 6, when he appeared in a play written by his father called *Red Ike*.

An enterprising young man, De Corsia attended night school at New York Evening High School and New York University, earning money during the daylight hours as a plumber, electrician, and salesman. He also worked for a time as a short-order cook, which led De Corsia to open his own restaurant in Brooklyn — the venture was "an artistic success but a financial flop," the actor later said.

With his failed restaurant attempt behind him, De Corsia decided in 1924 to try his hand in the relatively new medium of radio, and found that he was an instant success — he not only possessed a distinctive voice quality, but he was able to mimic more than 50 different dialects, which made him a popular addition to a wide range of programs. He would continue his radio career for nearly three decades, playing on thousands of network shows, including *Mr. President, Family Theater, Lux Radio Theater, This Is Your FBI, Joe and Mabel, Pursuit, Escape, The Six-Shooter*, and *Ellery Queen*. He was also the narrator on the long-running series *The March of Time*. De Corsia's versatility in radio was the stuff of legend — on one occasion, he was scheduled to perform in a two-man dramatic program, but before the show went on the air it was learned that the other actor could not make it to the station. So De Corsia went on alone — playing both parts.

At one point, De Corsia was a member of Orson Welles' famed Mercury Players — which would figure significantly in his later career — and eventually, the actor formed his own company, The Monticello Players. As De Corsia's radio career continued to flourish, he took time out to appear on Broadway in *The Father Returns*, which closed shortly after its May 1929 opening, and the 1930 production of *Scarlet Sister Mary*, starring Ethel Barrymore, whom De Corsia labeled "the greatest actress in America and the most interesting person I have ever met."

But the actor's life was not completely focused on his career. He married a woman named Mary Robertson — in the early 1930s, it is believed — but the two were divorced in 1935. Several years later, in 1939, he wed Rachel Thurber, with whom he had two daughters, Carey and Deidre.

In the late 1940s, De Corsia's old pal from the Mercury Theater days, Orson Welles, asked him to come to Hollywood — Welles had gone west several years earlier with a number of the performers from his radio company and had made his mark on the silver screen in such films as *Citizen Kane* (1941) and *The Magnificent Ambersons* (1942). De Corsia readily agreed, and traveled to Hollywood to accept a featured role in Welles' production of *The Lady from Shanghai* (1948). After filming on *Shanghai* was complete, De Corsia returned to New York for his second film — *The Naked City* (1948), which was released several months before *Shanghai* and became the actor's film debut.

Shot entirely on location in New York, this gritty film noir focuses on the murder of local playgirl Jean Dexter and the efforts of two police detectives— portrayed by Barry Fitzgerald and Don Taylor — to catch the killer. They soon zero in on Frank Niles (Howard Duff) and learn that he was part of a jewel theft ring, along with the dead girl and a former wrestler named Willie Garzah (De Corsia). It turns out that the crafty and physically imposing Garzah not only killed Jean, but also another hood, Pete Backalis (Walter Burke), who helped to commit the robberies. Cornered by one of the detectives, Garzah overpowers him and holds him at gunpoint: "I'll prove I'm smart, copper, you know how?"

Garzah asks. "You're scared right now I'm gonna rub you out, but I ain't, 'cause I'm smart. Rub out a cop and you'll really get the chair. All I need to do is put you to sleep. Then I'm off. Try and find me. This is a great, big, beautiful city. Just try and find me." Garzah does indeed manage to escape, but police track him through the crowded streets of New York and onto the top of the Williamsburg Bridge, where he is ultimately gunned down. Hailed upon its release as "what might have been just another crime story, but isn't," *The Naked City* was a hit with audiences and critics alike, and De Corsia was singled out in the *New York Times* as "especially good ... as an athletic thug."

Next, in the actor's second film noir, *The Lady from Shanghai*, De Corsia portrays Sidney Broom, a private detective hired by crippled attorney Arthur Bannister (Everett Sloane) to spy on his beautiful but amoral wife, Elsa, played by Rita Hayworth. Boasting a plot even more complex and convoluted than the average noir, *The Lady from Shanghai* also starred Orson Welles as Michael O'Hara, a hapless Irish seaman who falls in love with Elsa and finds himself caught up in an elaborate conspiracy that results in his arrest for two murders. (One of those allegedly killed by the seaman is Broom, who was actually shot by Bannister's partner, George Grisby [Glenn Anders], who was, in turn, murdered by Elsa.) In the midst of his court trial, O'Hara manages to escape, and in the film's oft-seen climax, Elsa and her husband face off in shootout inside a House of Mirrors at a shuttered amusement park.

Although De Corsia's role in *Shanghai* was a relatively minor one, he was a notable presence, particularly in the scene where he confronts Grisby, essaying a blackmail scheme that ultimately leads to his death: "I wonder am I the only one that's on to you and [Elsa]. Nobody else seems to guess you're sweet on her. That oughta be worth a little extra. But I'll throw it in for the same price," he says. "You see, I'm a snoopy kind of guy. I find things out. I get around." After his appearance in the film (which was described by one critic as a "frequently illogical story that spins so dizzily it's almost impossible to follow"), De Corsia began shuttling between New York, where he continued his successful radio career, and California, appearing in a series of films over the next several years. The best of these were *The Life of Riley* (1949), starring William Bendix as the bumbling patriarch; *It Happens Every Spring* (1949), an amusing tale of a scientist who uses an invention to lead a baseball team to victory; *Three Secrets*, directed by Robert Wise and starring Patricia Neal and Ruth Roman; *A Place in the Sun* (1951), the George Stevens–directed classic, in which De Corsia portrayed a judge; *Inside the Walls of Folsom Prison* (1951), where the actor portrayed one of his favorite roles as a sadistic guard; and *The Enforcer* (1951), his third film noir.

Here, in one of his most unforgettable roles, De Corsia played gang leader Joseph Rico, who, as the story begins, is being held in protective custody, expected to testify the following day against his much-feared boss, Albert Mendoza (Everett Sloane). Despite Mendoza's incarceration, Rico is terrified of the repercussions that are likely to result from his testimony: "Stop tellin' me to sit down — 'Take it easy, Rico, relax, Rico,'" he tells Assistant D.A. Martin Ferguson (Humphrey Bogart). "Well, it's my neck — he tried once in the farm, once in the jail, and once in the hotel. He's gonna get me!" Rico's fear leads him to attempt an escape from authorities, but he falls from a building ledge to his death, and Ferguson begins a painstaking review of Rico's taped confession in an attempt to unearth evidence that will result in Mendoza's conviction. After several hours, the prosecutor succeeds in finding a previously overlooked clue and locates a young woman who had witnessed a murder Mendoza had committed years earlier. For his standout role as Rico, De Corsia was hailed by numerous critics, including Edwin Schallert of the *Los Angeles Times*, who wrote that the actor was "right up for top honors," and the *Los Angeles Examiner*'s Ruth Waterbury, who raved, "Ted De Corsia, as the law's only witness, who dies rather than 'sing,' etches a portrait of naked terror that is goosebump-making of the first order."

After a small part as a mobster in another film noir, *The Turning Point* (1952), De Corsia was seen in a series of films of varying quality, from *Captain Pirate* (1952), a run-of-the-mill swashbuckler, to *Ride Vaquero* (1953), a box-office smash with Robert Taylor and Ava Gardner, and the top-notch Disney science fictioner *20,000 Leagues Under the Sea* (1954). He also added another film noir to his dark side repertoire, *Crime Wave* (1954), starring Sterling Hayden and Gene Nelson. In this feature, De Corsia portrayed ex-convict Doc Penny, who makes life miserable for a former fellow inmate, Steve Lacey (Nelson). Since his release, Lacey has turned his life around, settling down with wife Ellen (Phyllis Kirk) and landing a steady job as an airplane mechanic. But his straight-and-narrow life takes a curve when Penny shows up with another ex-con, Ben Hastings (Charles Buchinsky, before changing his last name to Bronson). The hard-boiled Penny abducts Steve and Ellen, planning to force Steve into taking part in a bank heist, but he is being trailed by a local detective (Hayden). In the midst of the robbery, police converge on the scene, Penny is gunned down, and in the final reel, Steve and Ellen return home to resume their life of normalcy. Directed on a low budget by Andre deToth (ex-husband of "Peekaboo Blonde" Veronica Lake), *Crime Wave* was a well-done feature that was described in the *Los Angeles Daily News* as a "much better-than-average presentation." Although former dancer Gene Nelson garnered most of the attention from reviewers, however, De Corsia was singled out by Bosley Crowther of the *New York Times*, who noted his "effective" performance.

After *Crime Wave*, De Corsia was seen the following year in another hard-hitting noir, *The Big Combo* (1955), which centered on the obsessive efforts of a cop, Leonard Diamond (Cornel Wilde), to nab a vicious mobster known as Mr. Brown (Richard Conte). Diamond's relentless pursuit of Brown

ultimately leads him to Bettini (De Corsia), a shipman who is able to tie Brown to the disappearance of his wife (Helen Walker). When Diamond first turns up at his run-down apartment, however, Bettini is certain that he has been sent by Mr. Brown: "I've been waiting for you a long time," he says with an air of resignation. "You look like such a nice young feller. That Brown sure knows how to pick 'em. I'd never have suspected. Can I lie down? Make it easier? Come closer— one shot ought to do it."

While De Corsia's 10th billed role in *The Big Combo* was limited to a single scene, he earned mention in the *New York Times* as "dandy." But by now, having fashioned a solid career in radio and film, De Corsia began expanding his performing horizons to include the budding medium of television. During the remainder of the 1950s and throughout the following decade, he would be seen in countless programs, including *Frontier, The Adventures of Jim Bowie, Have Gun Will Travel, Maverick, The Rifleman, The Twilight Zone, The Untouchables, Bat Masterson, Rawhide, Alfred Hitchcock Presents, Gunsmoke, The Outer Limits, The Man from U.N.C.L.E.,*

Daniel Boone, and *The Wild, Wild West,* and such comedies as *Get Smart, I Dream of Jeannie, Green Acres,* and *The Monkees.* He also starred as Mike Hammer, one of his few "good guy" roles, in the series, *The Mickey Spillane Mysteries.*

Between television appearances, De Corsia didn't slow down his film career. In 1956, in addition to *The Steel Jungle,* a low-budget crime drama with newcomers Perry Lopez and Beverly Garland, and *The Kettles in the Ozarks,* the eighth in the "Ma and Pa Kettle" series, the actor was featured in two more films noirs—*Slightly Scarlet* and *The Killing.*

In *Slightly Scarlet,* one of the few noirs filmed in Technicolor, De Corsia was a stand-out as Sol Caspar, a powerful crime boss who is contemptuously described by one character as "a low-grade moron with delusions of grandeur." Despite his wide-reaching web of influence, which includes local politicians and police officials, Caspar finds his kingdom in jeopardy after he humiliates one of his underlings, Ben Grace (John Payne), in front of the rest of his gang. When Grace exposes his role in the murder of a prominent newspaperman, Caspar flees the country and Grace assumes command of his operations. Caspar later returns, however, luring Grace to his beachhouse with plans to exact a deadly revenge. After notifying a local detective to meet him at the beach house at a prearranged time, Grace shows up and goads Sol into firing at him. ("You got me zeroed in and you still can't do it yourself," Grace taunts. "No dirty hands, no guts. No guts. Oh, I forgot— you work on the brain level now. Too important to the organization. Solly Caspar—gutless wonder.") Taking the bait, Caspar grabs a gun and starts shooting, riddling Grace's body with bullets, just in time for police to arrive and nab him with the gun in his hand.

Upon its release, *Slightly Scarlet* saw only moderate business at the box-office, and was dismissed by one reviewer who said that the picture's producer, writer, and director should "get three Technicolored black marks." De Corsia fared far better, however, in his second noir of the year, *The Killing,* portraying

Rhonda Fleming with Ted De Corsia and Arlene Dahl in *Slightly Scarlet* (1956).

a corrupt cop, Randy Kennan, who is in debt to local mobsters. An absorbing, first-rate film directed by Stanley Kubrick, *The Killing* centers on a motley crew of men — including Kennan — who band together to execute the near-flawless robbery of a racetrack. Despite the intricate planning, however, the scheme unravels, and each of the men wind up dead or, in the case of the gang's mastermind, in the hands of police. Unlike *Slightly Scarlet*, *The Killing* was praised by critics, including A.H. Weiler of the *New York Times*, who called it a "fairly diverting melodrama." For his efforts, De Corsia was labeled "interesting" by one critic, but he also received praise decades later from co-star Coleen Gray, who said in 2001 that she found De Corsia to be a "solid performer."

Also in 1956, De Corsia was featured in *The Conqueror*, branded in at least one book as one of the 50 worst films of all time. Starring John Wayne as Genghis Khan and Susan Hayward as the daughter of a Tartar king, the picture was saddled with atrocious dialog and terrible casting. More notable than these failures, however, was the fact that a number of the scenes from the movie were filmed near Yucca Flat, Nevada, where extensive atomic bomb testing had taken place. Over the next several years, nearly half of those who worked on the film — including Wayne, Hayward, Agnes Moorehead, Pedro Armendariz, and Dick Powell — would contract various forms of cancer. The link between the diseases and the shooting of the film would not be discovered until decades later.

Meanwhile, with the debacle of *The Conqueror* behind him, De Corsia was seen the following year in a string of box-office hits, including *The Joker is Wild* (1957), starring Frank Sinatra as singer Joe E. Lewis; *The Midnight Story* (1957), a first-rate whodunit featuring Tony Curtis and Gilbert Roland; and *Gunfight at the O.K. Corral* (1957), the acclaimed retelling of the battle between Wyatt Earp and his friend Doc Holliday against the nefarious Clanton brothers. Also that year, De Corsia was featured in his final film noir, *Baby Face Nelson* (1957), starring Mickey Rooney in the title role. Here, De Corsia portrayed Rocca, a 1930s-era mobster who arranges for the prison release of a small-time hood named Lester M. Gillis, who would later be known as Baby Face Nelson (Rooney). As it turns out, the purpose for Rocca's benevolence was to frame Nelson for the murder of a local union organizer. When Nelson is arrested for the crime, he manages to escape with the help of his longtime girlfriend, Sue (Carolyn Jones), and promptly goes gunning for Rocca, killing him and two of his gang. Nelson goes on to a notorious life of crime, teaming up at one point with renowned gangster John Dillinger (Leo Gordon), and taking over his gang when Dillinger is killed by police in Chicago. After committing several heists and leaving behind a string of dead bodies, however, Nelson is finally nabbed by lawmen and dies in a graveyard by a country road. After the film's release, most reviewers focused on the snarling performance turned in by Rooney, but De Corsia was singled out in a number of notices; in his best review, the critic for the *Hollywood Citizen-News* wrote that De Corsia and several other supporting players were "expertly cast — and expert in their performances."

De Corsia was seen in a handful of mostly forgettable films during the rest of the decade, including the poorly conceived remake of *The Buccaneer* (1958), starring Yul Brynner, and *Handle with Care* (1958), a tiresome drama about city hall corruption. But he was back to the blockbusters in 1960 with a small role in the big-budget epic *Spartacus*, starring Kirk Douglas, Jean Simmons, and Laurence Olivier.

By now, De Corsia spent most of his time on his television appearances, but he did find time for minor parts in such films as the Jerry Lewis slapstick comedy *It's Only Money* (1962); *Blood on the Arrow* (1964), a routine cowboys-and-Indians feature; and *The King's Pirate* (1967), a mediocre remake of Errol Flynn's 1952 hit, *Against All Flags*. His best films during this period included *Nevada Smith* (1966), a violent Steve McQueen vehicle in which De Corsia portrayed a bartender, and *Five Card Stud* (1968), a western starring Robert Mitchum and Dean Martin that flopped at the box office, but deserves a second look.

With both his television and film careers now winding down, De Corsia took on only a few roles in the early 1970s, including *The Delta Factor* (1971), an action film based on a Mickey Spillane novel, and *The Outside Man* (1973), an offbeat crime drama. The latter film — in which De Corsia, fittingly, played a mob boss — marked the actor's last big-screen appearance. On April 12, 1973, Ted De Corsia was found dead in his home in Encino. It was ruled that he died of natural causes.

Although Ted De Corsia was never one of Hollywood's household names, he was a gifted character actor who found success in radio, television, and film. Along with his talent for expertly depicting a variety of dialects, and his commanding screen presence, De Corsia was, at his best, one of film noir's meanest personages and most outstanding performers.

Film Noir Filmography

The Naked City. Director: Jules Dassin. Producer: Mark Hellinger. Running time: 96 minutes. Released by Universal-International, March 4, 1948. Cast: Barry Fitzgerald, Howard Duff, Dorothy Hart, Don Taylor, Ted De Corsia, House Jameson, Anne Sargent, Adelaide Klein, Grover Burgess, Tom Pedi, Enid Markey, Frank Conroy, Mark Hellinger.

The Lady from Shanghai. Director and Producer: Orson Welles. Running time: 86 minutes. Released by Columbia, June 10, 1948. Cast: Rita Hayworth, Orson Welles, Everett Sloane, Glenn

Anders, Ted De Corsia, Erskine Sanford, Gus Schilling, Carl Frank, Louis Merrill, Evelyn Ellis, Harry Shannon, Wong Show, Sam Nelson.

The Enforcer. Director: Bretaigne Windust. Producer: Milton Sperling. Running time: 88 minutes. Released by Warner Brothers, February 24, 1951. Cast: Humphrey Bogart, Zero Mostel, Ted De Corsia, Everett Sloane, Roy Roberts, Lawrence Tolan, King Donovan, Robert Steele, Patricia Joiner, Don Beddoe, Tito Vuolo, John Kellogg, Jack Lambert, Adelaide Klein, Susan Cabot, Mario Siletti.

The Turning Point. Director: William Dietele. Producer: Irving Asher. Running time: 85 minutes. Released by Paramount, November 14, 1952. Cast: William Holden, Edmond O'Brien, Alexis Smith, Tom Tully, Ed Begley, Dan Dayton, Adele Longmire, Ray Teal, Ted De Corsia, Don Porter, Howard Freeman, Neville Brand.

Crime Wave. Director: Andre DeToth. Producer: Bryan Foy. Running time: 73 minutes. Released by Warner Bros., January 12, 1954. Cast: Gene Nelson, Phyllis Kirk, Sterling Hayden, James Bell, Ted De Corsia, Charles Buchinsky, Ned Young, Jay Novello, Walter Dub Taylor, Richard Benjamin, Mack Chandler, Gayle Kellogg, James Hayward, Timothy Carey.

The Big Combo. Director: Joseph Lewis. Producer: Sidney Harmon. Running time: 89 minutes. Released by Allied Artists, February 13, 1955. Cast: Cornel Wilde, Richard Conte, Brian Donlevy, Jean Wallace, Robert Middleton, Lee Van Cleef, Earl Holliman, Helen Walker, Jay Adler, John Hoyt, Ted De Corsia, Helen Stanton, Roy Gordon, Whit Bissell, Steve Mitchell, Baynes Barron, James McCallion, Tony Michaels, Brian O'Hara, Rita Gould, Bruce Sharpe, Michael Mark, Philip Van Zandt, Donna Drew.

Slightly Scarlet. Director: Allan Dwan. Producer: Benedict Bogueaus. Running time: 99 minutes. Released by RKO, February 1956. Cast: John Payne, Arlene Dahl, Rhonda Fleming, Kent Taylor, Ted De Corsia, Lance Fuller, Buddy Baer, Frank Gerstle, Ellen Corby.

The Killing. Director: Stanley Kramer. Producer: James B. Harris. Running time: 84 minutes. Released by United Artists, May 20, 1956. Cast: Sterling Hayden, Coleen Gray, Vince Edwards, Jay C. Flippen, Marie Windsor, Ted De Corsia, Elisha Cook, Jr., Joe Sawyer, Timothy Carey, Jay Adler, Kola Kwarian, Joseph Turkell, James Edwards.

Baby Face Nelson. Director: Don Siegel. Producer: Al Zimbalist. Running time: 85 minutes. Released by United Artists, November 1957. Cast: Mickey Rooney, Carolyn Jones, Sir Cedric Hardwicke, Leo Gordon, Ted De Corsia, Anthony Caruso, Jack Elam, Chris Dark, Emile Meyer, Dan Terranova, Dabbs Greer, Bob Osterloh, Dick Crocett, Paul Baxley, Thayer David, Ken Patterson, Sol Gorse, Gil Perkins, Tom Fadden, Lisa Davis, John Hoyt, Elisha Cook, Jr., Murray Alper, George E. Stone, Hubie Kerns, Paul and Richard Donnelly.

References

Biography of Ted De Corsia. Warner Brothers Studios, circa 1950.
"T. De Corsia, Character Actor, Dies." *Los Angeles Times*, April 12, 1973.
"'Tough Guy' Ted De Corsia of Movies, TV, Dies." *Los Angeles Herald Examiner*, April 13, 1973.
Obituary. *Variety*, April 16, 1973.

ALBERT DEKKER

"A minute ago we were talkin' about reputations. Well, you got quite a reputation yourself. You're supposed to be a troublemaker. Okay. Make some." — Albert Dekker in *The Killers* (1946)

Albert Dekker was a brilliant, intense actor, with such memorable stage roles to his credit as Willy Loman in *Death of a Salesman*, and appearances in more than 60 films, including *Dr. Cyclops* (1940), *Gentleman's Agreement* (1947), *East of Eden* (1955), and *The Wild Bunch* (1969). Unfortunately, Dekker's impressive body of work is frequently overshadowed by his bizarre death, the circumstances which remain a mystery to this day. The actor's tragic end notwithstanding, Dekker was known among friends and family for his kind and sensitive nature, and among movie fans for his first-rate character performances, which included roles in six films noirs: *Among the Living* (1941), *Suspense* (1946), *The Killers*

(1946), *The Pretender* (1947), *Destination Murder* (1950), and *Kiss Me Deadly* (1955).

Thomas Albert Ecke Van Dekker was born on December 20, 1905, in Brooklyn, New York, the only child of Albert and Grace Ecke Van Dekker. The future actor, who was 6 feet tall by the age of 13, attended Richmond Hill High School, where he was seen in such productions as *Othello*, *Hamlet*, and *Macbeth*. Later, at Bowdoin College in Maine, Dekker majored in pre-med with plans to become a doctor, but after appearing in several school plays, he was encouraged by a school friend to pursue a career in the theater.

"I guess I had no total conviction until a letter to Alfred Lunt got me a job in the Stuart Walker stock company," Dekker recalled in a 1962 interview. "I got [good] notices and Lunt hired me for Broadway the next season. Maybe I should have been a doctor, who knows?"

At the age of 21, Dekker (still using his given name of Van Dekker) debuted on Broadway in the Theatre Guild production of *Marco's Millions*, which starred Lunt in the title role. In the play, Dekker impressed audiences with his portrayal of four separate roles, a Chinese man at ages 40 and 60, a 50-year-old Persian, and an 80-year-old Italian priest. During the run of the play, Dekker met actress Esther Theresa Guerini, and the two were married in 1929. They would go on to have three children, Jan, John, and Benjamin, but after more than 30 years of marriage, the couple would divorce in the early 1960s.

Meanwhile, Dekker was earning a favorable reputation on Broadway with acclaimed appearances in such productions as *Volpone*, starring Sydney Greenstreet; *Lysistrata* with Fay Bainter; *Grand Hotel*, in which he played the role performed by John Barrymore in the film version; *Brittle Heaven*, opposite Dorothy Gish; *R.U.R.*, where he played Radius, a robot that destroys the world; and *Conflict*, in a cast that included Spencer Tracy, Edward Arnold, and Frank McHugh. In the late 1930s, while performing in a festival in Ann Arbor, Michigan, Dekker was spotted by a Hollywood agent and was promptly cast in his film

debut, portraying a fencer in the Warner Bros. comedy *The Great Garrick* (1937). Dekker followed this entertaining, James Whale–directed feature with small roles in *She Married an Artist* (1938), in which he was billed as Albert Van Dekker; *The Last Warning* (1938); *Extortion* (1938), an altogether forgettable whodunit; *Marie Antoinette* (1938), starring the always captivating Norma Shearer in the title role; and *Never Say Die* (1939), a popular Bob Hope vehicle.

After portraying a Cossack officer in Paramount's *Hotel Imperial* (1939), Dekker was signed to a contract with the studio and began appearing in such first-rate features as *Beau Geste* (1939), a superb adventure yarn starring Gary Cooper; *The Man in the Iron Mask* (1939), in which he played Louis XIII; *Strange Cargo* (1940), a mystical tale featuring Clark Gable and Joan Crawford; and *Seven Sinners* (1940), the first of three films starring Marlene Dietrich and John Wayne. Dekker was then cast in his first starring role, and the film for which he is perhaps best remembered, *Dr. Cyclops* (1940). With a bald head and sporting thick spectacles, Dekker offered an eerie portrayal of a demented scientist in the Amazon who reduces unwary travelers to doll size.

In a series of supporting parts, Dekker was next seen in films of such varying quality as *You're the One* (1941), a contrived musical-comedy featuring Edward Everett Horton, and *Honky Tonk* (1941), a box-office smash starring Clark Gable and Lana Turner. He then returned to top billing for a dual role in *Among the Living* (1941), his first film noir. Here, Dekker portrayed John Raden, a southern millionaire who is believed to be responsible for a series of murders that were actually committed by his mentally deranged, identical twin brother, Paul, who was thought to have died as a child. When Paul attacks the flirtatious daughter (Susan Hayward) of a boarding house owner, he is shot by police, but he manages to flee. Instead, an enraged mob of townspeople mistakes John for his brother and prepare to lynch him. Chased by the bloodthirsty crowd, John is saved only when he trips over the dead body of Paul.

After earning praise for his distinct portrayals of the twin brothers in *Among the Living*, Dekker entered the busiest year of his career, portraying a gangster in the musical comedy *Yokel Boy* (1942); a hard-boiled civilian construction boss in *Wake Island* (1942); an American spy in *Once Upon a Honeymoon* (1942); a police lieutenant in *A Night in New Orleans* (1942); and a dishonest gunman in *In Old California* (1942). He also appeared as himself in *Star-Spangled Rhythm*, Paramount's star-studded tribute to the war effort, joining a cast that included Bob Hope, Ray Milland, Alan Ladd, Susan Hayward, Paulette Goddard, Veronica Lake, Dorothy Lamour, Bing Crosby, Fred MacMurray, and Dick Powell. Ending his association with Paramount, he slowed down considerably in 1943, appearing in only three westerns: *The Kansan* and *Buckskin Frontier*, both starring Richard Dix, and *In Old Oklahoma*, with John Wayne and Martha Scott.

Dekker switched vocational gears in 1944, running for state assemblyman for the 57th district which, at that time, included parts of Hollywood. The actor won a landslide victory, and spent the next two years serving in the assembly, championing such liberal causes as support for unwed mothers and indigent children. During his tenure in the legislature, Dekker was seen in several films, including *Incendiary Blonde* (1945), an entertaining musical starring Betty Hutton, and *Salome, Where She Danced* (1945), a vehicle for Yvonne DeCarlo that was panned by critics but attracted moviegoers in droves. Dekker returned to films on a full-time basis in 1946, however, claiming that the trips to the capital in Sacramento had interfered with his movie career.

"Politics would be all right if I were a bad actor," Dekker said. "But I'm not. I'm a good actor and I like the job of acting."

Back in Hollywood, Dekker returned to the dark world of film noir with featured roles in two features from the era, *Suspense* (1946) and *The Killers* (1946). In *Suspense*, Dekker portrayed Frank Leonard, a fastidiously eccentric owner of a Los Angeles ice show ("I never shake hands," he remarks in one scene,

"It's unsanitary"), which stars his wife, Roberta Elba (Belita). After hiring former promoter Joe Morgan (Barry Sullivan) to sell peanuts at the show, Frank quickly elevates him to the show's ringmaster, but he later learns that Joe has become romantically involved with Roberta. During a vacation to his remote mountain lodge, Frank is believed killed in an avalanche, but Roberta is haunted by the memory of her spouse and is reluctant to continue her relationship with Joe. Later, Frank reappears and Joe kills him, incinerating his body in a rolltop desk. Joe admits his crime to Roberta, claiming self-defense, but when she insists that he turn himself into police, Joe plans to kill her during a performance, changing his mind just seconds before carrying out the deed. Leaving the ice show behind, Joe leaves the stadium, only to be gunned down by a jilted ex-lover (Bonita Granville). Praised upon its release as "a gripping drama from start to finish," *Suspense* turned a tidy profit at the box office, and although he was off-screen for much of the film, Dekker was singled out for his "effective" performance by Lloyd L. Sloan in the *Hollywood Citizen-News*.

Dekker's second noir of the year, *The Killers*, begins with the chilling, execution-style murder of a former boxer known as "the Swede" (Burt Lancaster) by two hit men. In a series of flashbacks, the remainder of the film centers on the events that led up to the Swede's death and introduces a mélange of memorable characters, including his duplicitous girlfriend, Kitty (Ava Gardner), a Philadelphia detective (Sam Levene), and a New Jersey maid to whom the Swede bequeathed his meager life insurance policy. As gangleader Big Jim Colfax, Dekker provided the key to the mystery — after a chance encounter with the Swede at his gas station, it was Big Jim who had ordered the Swede's murder — but he meets an ignominious end, gunned down by one of the members of his own gang. In a cast of standout performances, Dekker was labeled "excellent" in *Motion Picture Herald*, and Thalia Bell of *Motion Picture Daily* wrote that the actor "as always, is assured and competent in his characterization."

After appearing in a pair of box-office hits, *Gentleman's Agreement* (1947), a powerful indictment of anti–Semitism, and *Cass Timberlane* (1947), starring Spencer Tracy and Lana Turner, Dekker starred in his fourth film noir, *The Pretender* (1947). Here, the actor portrayed Kenneth Holden, an investment broker who schemes to marry a wealthy client, Claire Worthington (Catherine Craig), after embezzling funds from her estate. When Claire rejects Kenneth's proposal because of her engagement to local doctor Leonard Koster (Charles Drake), Dekker arranges for Koster's murder, telling the hitman, Fingers Murdock (Tom Kennedy) that the doctor's photograph will appear in an engagement announcement in the newspaper. The tables are turned, however, when Claire abruptly ends her engagement and agrees to marry Kenneth, whose picture is placed in the paper instead. Fearing for his life and consumed by paranoia, Kenneth exhibits increasingly bizarre behavior, confining himself to his room, wearing dark sunglasses, and eating only canned goods. Finally, seeing a man lurking outside his window, Kenneth shoots at him

and drives off into the night, followed by two cars. When his car careens off a cliff, Kenneth is killed, never knowing that he was being followed by a bodyguard hired by his wife to protect him, and by Fingers Murdock — who was trying to return Kenneth's fee for the cancelled hit. Although this Republic Pictures production received little attention (the critic for the *New York Times* dismissed it as "much too long and too boring a time"), *The Pretender* is highlighted by the ironic twist at the end, and Dekker turns in a well-done portrait of the neurotic embezzler doomed by his unwarranted paranoia.

During the remainder of the decade, Dekker's films were a mostly forgettable lot, including *Lulu Belle* (1948), a tepid musical-drama starring Dorothy Lamour; *Tarzan's Magic Fountain* (1949), notable only as the first Tarzan film with Lex Barker in the title role; and *Bride of Vengeance* (1949), an elaborate costume drama about the feud between Basare Borgia and Duke of Ferrara. Infinitely more watchable, however, was *Fury at Furnace Creek* (1948), in which Dekker was featured as a dastardly silver tycoon. After appearing in a slow-moving Audie Murphy western, *The Kid from Texas* (1950), and *The Furies* (1950), starring Walter Huston in his last role before his death, Dekker was seen in his fifth film noir, *Destination Murder* (1950). In this feature, Dekker portrayed Armitage, a sadistic nightclub owner whose quirky personality includes his habit of referring to himself in the third person and a penchant for carrying out beatings while listening to classical music. When a wealthy local man is murdered, his daughter, Laura Mansfield (Joyce MacKenzie), suspects Armitage and gets a job as a cigarette girl in his nightclub, where she becomes involved with Armitage's manager, Stretch Norton (Hurd Hatfield). As it turns out, Stretch is the actual brains behind the outfit and is using Armitage as a front; Stretch later kills his underling, planning to frame him for the murder of Laura's father, but a crafty lawman (James Flavin) figures out the scheme and Stretch is gunned down by police in the film's climax.

A box-office bomb, *Destination Murder* was panned by critics and, perhaps tiring of his string of hit-or-miss film assignments, Dekker returned to Broadway after its release for *Death of a Salesman*, taking over the role of Willy Loman from Gene Lockhart. Dekker told the press that it took a part like Willy Loman to lure him back to the stage.

"When you have been away from the theater for 12 long years enjoying the luxury of a family in Hollywood and the pleasant living in that colony, you don't up and leave it do any old play unless you are plain crazy," Dekker said.

Back in Hollywood, Dekker had a small role in *As Young as You Feel* (1951), a pleasant comedy starring Monty Woolley, and was fourth-billed in *Wait 'Til the Sun Shines, Nellie* (1952), a moving turn-of-the-century drama featuring David Wayne and Jean Peters. But these well-received films would mark Dekker's last screen appearances for three years. The actor, who had maintained an interest in politics since his years in the California assembly, had made no secret of his disdain for Sen. Joseph McCarthy, and his ongoing Communist "witchhunts." Dekker verbally attacked the senator in the press, and on one occasion called him "insane." As a result, Dekker found himself "gray-listed" and unable to find work at any studio in Hollywood. To make ends meet, Dekker toured with actress Edith Atwater in poetry readings in New York and London, and was booked for speaking engagements for colleges and literary groups.

"It was a hard, hard time," Dekker's daughter, Jan, said in a 1999 television documentary.

In 1955, however, Dekker signed a contract with Warner Bros. and was back on screen in *Illegal* (1955), playing a notorious racketeer; *East of Eden* (1955), which featured the impressive screen debut of James Dean; and *Kiss Me Deadly* (1955), his final film noir. Starring Ralph Meeker as two-fisted private detective Mike Hammer, this complicated noir introduces a motley crew of unconventional characters including Christina (Cloris Leachman), who is first seen running down a highway in her bare feet, and whose death by torture sets the wheels of the complicated plot in motion; Carl Evello (Paul Stewart), a ruthless but refined mobster; Velda (Maxine Cooper), Hammer's besotted "Girl Friday"; Lily Carver (Gaby Rodgers), Christine's soft-voiced, treacherous roommate; Nick (Nick Dennis), a garage mechanic pal of Hammer's who punctuates his conversations with such enthusiastic utterances as "Vavoom!" and "Pow!"; and Dr. Soberin (Dekker), an imperturbable physician. Focusing on the characters' search for a leather-bound box referred to only as "the great whatsit," the film reaches an explosive climax when the box is opened, setting off a fiery, apocalyptic blaze. For his small but pivotal role, Dekker was described as "up to standard" by the *Los Angeles Examiner*'s Sara Hamilton, who stressed the film's "impregnable" plot and wrote: "After a real lulu of an opening, the tale becomes entangled in its own web, with too many crisscross threads obscuring the pattern. And then, quite suddenly, it straightens out for a smasheroo finish."

With his film career back on track, Dekker also began to accept several stage roles and was on tour in one such production when tragedy struck. After concluding his performance in a play in Palm Beach, Florida, the actor was told that his 16-year-old son, John, was dead. According to news accounts, John was found by his mother at the family home in Hastings-on-Hudson, New York. He died from a single shot from a 22-caliber rifle, which had pierced his right eye. With no understudy available, Dekker finished his engagement and returned home two days later, telling reporters that his son had been experimenting during the last year on constructing a rifle silencer. The shooting was ruled an accident.

"I think, for [my parents], it was absolutely devastating," said Dekker's youngest son, Benjamin, in 1999. "And for my father, specifically, I think that he must have felt a tremendous guilt."

In an effort to assuage his grief, Dekker

continued to perform, starring in 1958 opposite Mari Blanchard in *Machete*, and the following year in several films, including *The
Sound and the Fury* (1959), a weighty melodrama starring Yul Brynner; *Middle of the
Night* (1959), featuring Fredric March as a
clothing manufacturer who falls for a woman
30 years his junior; and *Suddenly, Last Summer* (1959), a box-office success despite a
rather bizarre story that combined the twin
themes of homosexuality and cannibalism.

Dekker returned to Broadway in 1960
for a starring role in *The Andersonville Trial*,
earning raves from critics, including Brooks
Atkinson of the *New York Times*, who described his performance as "thunderous."
Despite his success on the stage, however,
Dekker told the press that the theater was "a
horrible place in which to make a living."

"They sit you on a shelf for years. They
take you off and brush you off and later you
have to find your way back to that shelf," he
told critic Ward Morehouse. "The theater
hasn't been rough or tough for me, but it's
saddening to see capable people discarded or
ignored." As Dekker himself admitted, however, he had "never been really out of work,"
and after the close of *Andersonville*, he went
on to appear in the Broadway production of
Face of a Hero, starring Jack Lemmon; portrayed Henry VIII in a Canadian production
of *Royal Gambit* in 1961; directed the off-
Broadway production of *The Angels of Ana-
darko* in 1962; and starred on Broadway in *A
Man for All Seasons* in 1964. He also helmed
a production of the latter play for the Paper
Mill Playhouse in 1965.

While appearing in *A Man for All Seasons*, Dekker met former fashion model Jeraldine Saunders (who would go on to write *The
Love Boats*, on which the popular, long-running television series would be based). The
two began dating and eventually, according to
Saunders, planned to marry. However, it was
around this time that Dekker's personal life
began to nosedive. Like many celebrities in
the 1950s and 1960s, Dekker became a client
of Dr. Max Jacobson, a New York physician
known as "Dr. Feelgood" for administering

"vitamin cocktails" that were later discovered
to be laced with amphetamines.

"It just gave him a tremendous boost of
energy ... [he] would tell me that he was able
to stay up for 24, 36, 40 hours at a time," said
Dekker's son, Benjamin, in a 1999 documentary. "I think [in] the long term, [the drugs]
were very detrimental to his health. And I
think that was the beginning of his, somewhat, demise."

Meanwhile, after an absence of six years,
Dekker was back on the big screen in 1965,
starring in *Gamera, the Invincible*, a rather
dreadful, Japanese-made science fictioner
about a gigantic flying, fire-spitting turtle.
Having debuted on the small screen in 1951,
Dekker was also seen during this period on
a number of television series, including *Rawhide* and *Mission: Impossible*, as well as two
teleplays, Tennessee Williams' *Ten Blocks
Along the Camino Real*, and *Death of a Salesman* (although the role he played on Broadway, Willy Loman, was portrayed here by Lee
J. Cobb, who had originated the stage role).

With Dekker's performing ability perhaps impaired by his growing dependence on
the drugs being administered by Max Jacobson, the actor was seen in only a few productions during the next few years. In 1967, he
co-starred with Troy Donahue in *Come Spy
with Me*, an amateurish thriller, and guested
the following year on the popular television
series *I Spy*. Also in 1968, Dekker was cast as
a tough railroad detective in *The Wild Bunch*
(1969), appearing alongside veteran actors
William Holden, Ernest Borgnine, and Robert Ryan. During the on-location filming in
Mexico, Dekker was reportedly "the life of
the set with his endless fund of dialect stories." Sadly, he would not live to see the film's
release.

Shortly after returning to Hollywood
from Mexico in May 1968, Dekker and Jeraldine Saunders took in a play, *The Latent
Heterosexual*, at the Huntington-Hartford
Theater. Afterward, Dekker returned to the
apartment in which he had been living, with
a promise to call Saunders the following day.
It was the last time she would see the actor

alive. Several days later, on May 5, 1968, concerned that she had not heard from Dekker, Saunders requested that the building manager open the apartment door. Dekker's body was found inside.

"It was so horrible that when I saw the body, I simply passed out," Saunders recalled in a 1979 *Los Angeles Herald-Examiner* article.

The 62-year-old actor was found naked, kneeling in the bathtub, with a hypodermic needle sticking out of each arm. A noose was tied around his neck, and in his mouth was a rubber ball with a metal wire passed through it, like a horse's bit. Metal chains attached to the wire were tied tightly around his head. Leather belts were girded around his neck and chest, attached to a rope that ran the length of his body and tied his ankles together. Handcuffs were around both wrists, and in red lipstick on his chest, abdomen, and buttocks were written words like "whip" and "slave."

Authorities determined that Dekker died from asphyxiation and initially ruled the death a suicide, but it was later judged to be accidental.

"We have no information that this individual planned to take his own life, so it will be listed as an accidental death," Deputy Coroner Herbert McRoy told reporters. "This is certainly a strange death. But just because there was a rope around his neck does not mean that he committed suicide."

Dekker's shocking death invited numerous theories and countless reactions. Paul Lukas, an old friend of Dekker's who appeared with him in *Strange Cargo* (1940) and *Experiment Perilous* (1944) refused to accept the coroner's ruling.

"Al never would leave the world in such a terrible shambles," Lukas told the press. "He was a man of culture and breeding."

Similarly, Jeraldine Saunders questioned the verdict, expressing the belief that Dekker's death had involved a robbery. According to Saunders, a large amount of cash and the actor's expensive camera equipment were missing from the apartment.

"I can't say who took it, but foul play based on theft of the money seems to me the answer," Saunders maintained. "I think it was someone he knew and let into the apartment."

But Dekker's son, Benjamin, offered another scenario.

"His death was the result of an accident that was between or occurred during a relationship of two consenting adults," Benjamin said in 1999. "There are some things that are private. One of those things is a person's private life. As long as what they do does not affect, in a pejorative fashion, the lives of others, they have a right to be able to do whatever they wish to do. It's that simple."

The circumstances surrounding Albert Dekker's death will, in all likelihood, remain a mystery; a greater crime, however, would be to allow the manner in which he died to overshadow the way in which he lived. Dekker not only left behind an impressive body of stage, screen, and television performances but, by all accounts, he was a generous and compassionate man who was much beloved by his family and friends.

"Al has a fine mind," actor Alfred Lunt once said, "and a soul in which unkindness is wholly absent."

Film Noir Filmography

Among the Living. Director: Stuart Heisler. Producer: Sol C. Siegel. Running time: 67 minutes. Released by Paramount, September 1941. Cast: Albert Dekker, Susan Hayward, Harry Carey, Frances Farmer, Gordon Jones, Jean Phillips, Ernest Whitman, Maude Eburne, Frank M. Thomas, Harlan Brigges, Archie Twitchell, Dorothy Sebastian, William Stack.

Suspense. Director: Frank Tuttle. Producers: Maurice and Frank King. Running time: 101 minutes. Released by Monogram, June 15, 1946. Cast: Belita, Barry Sullivan, Albert Dekker, Eugene Pallette, Bonita Granville, Edith Angold, George Stone.

The Killers. Director: Robert Siodmak. Producer: Mark Hellinger. Running time: 105 minutes. Released by Universal, August 28, 1946. Cast: Edmond O'Brien, Ava Gardner, Albert Dekker, Sam Levene, John Miljan, Virginia Christine, Vince Barnett, Burt Lancaster, Charles D. Brown, Donald MacBride, Phil Brown, Charles McGraw, William Conrad, Queenie Smith, Garry Owen, Harry Hayden, Bill Walker, Jack Lambert, Jeff Corey, Wally Scott, Gabrielle Windsor, Rex Dale. Awards: Academy Award nominations for Best Director (Robert Siodmak), Best Film Editing (Arthur Hilton), Best Score/Drama or Comedy (Miklos Rozsa), Best Screenplay (Anthony Veiller).

The Pretender. Director and Producer: W. Lee Wilder. Running time: 69 minutes. Released by Republic, August 13, 1947. Cast: Albert Dekker, Catherine Craig, Charles Drake, Alan Carney, Linda Stirling, Tom Kennedy, Selmer Jackson, Charles Middleton, Ernie Adams, Ben Welden, John Bagni, Stanley Ross, Forrest Taylor, Greta Clement, Peggy Wynne, Eula Guy, Cay Forrester, Peter Michael, Michael Mark, Dorothy Scott.

Destination Murder. Director: Edward L. Cahn. Producers: Edward L. Cahn and Maurie M. Suess. Running time: 72 minutes. Released by RKO, June 8, 1950. Cast: Joyce MacKenzie, Stanley Clements, Hurd Hatfield, Albert Dekker, Myrna Dell, James Flavin, John Dehner, Richard Emory, Norma Vance, Suzette Harbin, Buddy Swan, Bert Wenland, Franklyn Farnum.

Kiss Me Deadly. Director and Producer: Robert Aldrich. Running time: 105 minutes. Released by United Artists, May 18, 1955. Cast: Ralph Meeker, Albert Dekker, Paul Stewart, Maxine Cooper, Gaby Rodgers, Wesley Addy, Juano Hernandez, Nick Dennis, Cloris Leachman, Marian Carr, Jack Lambert, Jack Elam, Jerry Zinneman, Percy Helton, Fortunio Bonanova, Silvio Minciotti, Leigh Snowden, Madi Comfort, James Seay, Mara McAffee, Robert Cornthwaite, James McCallian, Jesslyn Fax, Mort Marshall, Strother Martin, Marjorie Bennett, Art Loggins, Bob Sherman, Keith McConnell, Paul Richards, Eddie Beal.

References

"Actor Albert Dekker Dies; Known for Character Roles." *Box Office*, May 13, 1968.

"Actor Albert Dekker Found Hanged Here." *Los Angeles Herald Examiner*, May 6, 1968.

"Actor Dekker Death Called Accidental." *Los Angeles Times*, May 9, 1968.

"Albert Dekker, Actor, Dead at 62." *New York Times*, May 7, 1968.

"Autopsy Performed on Actor Albert Dekker." *Los Angeles Times*, May 7, 1968.

Biography of Albert Dekker. Paramount Studios, August 1944.

Bongard, Dale. "Original Script to Bow in Tonight—'The Great Man' at the Century Theater." *Los Angeles Daily News*, circa 1960.

"Dekker Died Accidentally—Coroner." *New York Post*, May 9, 1968.

"Noted Actor Albert Dekker Dies Hanging." *Hollywood Citizen-News*, May 6, 1968.

Obituary. *Newsweek*, May 20, 1968.

"Rule Out Foul Play in Dekker Suicide." *Variety*, May 7, 1968.

"Son of Actor Albert Dekker Shot to Death." *Los Angeles Times*, April 19, 1957.

Stump, Al. "The Beautiful and the Deal ... Hollywood's Unsolved Mysteries." *Los Angeles Herald-Examiner*, December 16, 1979.

Wahls, Robert. "Offstage Character." Publication Unsourced, February 25, 1962.

Documentary

"Mysteries and Scandals: Albert Dekker." E! Entertainment Television. Copyright 1999.

BRAD DEXTER

"Half-drunk, I got better wits than most people. And more nerve."— Brad Dexter in *The Asphalt Jungle* (1950)

Square-jawed, broad-shouldered, and menacingly handsome, Brad Dexter made a name for himself as a reliable screen heavy.

"I love playing heavies," Dexter once said. "Literary-wise, it's the best-written character. The hero is always bland. Most people are larcenous and they pull for the heavy."

After appearing in 30 films over a span of three decades, however, Dexter all but abandoned his acting career, earning a measure of fame as the producer of such features as *Lady Sings the Blues* (1972). On screen, however, the actor appeared in such classic Hollywood fare as *The Magnificent Seven* (1960) and *Shampoo* (1972), and was featured in five offerings from the era of film noir: *The Asphalt Jungle*

(1950), *The Las Vegas Story* (1952), *Macao* (1952), *99 River Street* (1953), and *House of Bamboo* (1955).

The actor once labeled as the "sweetest meanie to ever slug a hero or tussle with a lady" was born Boris Milanovich on April 9, 1917, in the mining town of Goldfield, Nevada. Brought to Los Angeles by his Yugoslavia-born parents while still an infant, Dexter graduated from Belmont High School and enrolled at the University of Southern California, where he appeared in a number of campus productions and distinguished himself as a member of the boxing team. After later becoming a Golden Gloves light heavyweight, Dexter reportedly refused several offers to turn pro, choosing instead to pursue his interest in acting and winning a scholarship to the Pasadena Playhouse.

Following his apprenticeship with the Pasadena Players, Dexter decided to try his luck in New York and swiftly landed a role in the Elia Kazan–directed production of *Café Crown*. His budding career was interrupted, however, by World War II, and he enlisted in the Army Air Forces; during two of his four years in the service, he toured in Moss Hart's production of *Winged Victory*, and reprised his role in the 1944 screen version, along with fellow servicemen Edmond O'Brien and Lee J. Cobb. Following his discharge, Dexter immediately returned to Broadway, appearing opposite Ilka Chase in *Laughter From a Cloud*, Jessie Royce Landis in *Magnolia Alley*, and with Mae West in *Diamond Lil*. Between productions, the actor found success on the radio in a variety of soap operas and such programs as *Gangbusters*, *Mr. District Attorney*, and *Cavalcade*, and was seen in minor roles in two feature films, *Heldorado* (1946), a Roy Rogers western, and *Sinbad the Sailor* (1947), starring Douglas Fairbanks, Jr., in the title role.

Then, with the onset of the 1950s, Dexter hit pay dirt — when director John Huston was seeking cast members for an upcoming crime feature, he recalled Dexter's Broadway performance in *Magnolia Alley* and tapped him for a role in what would become the

actor's first film noir, *The Asphalt Jungle* (1950). One of the era's quintessential offerings, this film centers on an elaborately designed jewel heist executed by a group of men assembled by veteran criminal Doc Riedenschneider (Sam Jaffe). Although the gang succeeds in nabbing the valuable loot, their plan begins to unravel when they are double-crossed by an unprincipled attorney Alonzo Emmerich (Louis Calhern), and, ultimately, each of the men involved in the caper are captured by police or killed. As Bob Brannom, Dexter played the brief but pivotal role of a hard-boiled private detective hired by Emmerich to assist in his plan to keep the entire cache of jewels for himself. Despite appearances in only two scenes, Dexter made the most of his time on screen and was singled out by the critic for *Variety* for "lend[ing] capable assistance to the well-rounded characters in the script."

Signing a contract with RKO, Dexter returned to the world of film noir in 1952 with "heavy" performances in two additional features from the era, *The Las Vegas Story* and *Macao*. In the first, he portrayed Tom Hubler, a private detective representing an insurance company that holds a policy on a valuable necklace owned by former singer, Linda Rollins (Jane Russell). Seeking to acquire the necklace for himself, Hubler trails Linda and her businessman husband, Lloyd (Vincent Price), to Las Vegas, where Lloyd attempts to raise a large sum of money in order to cover his role in an embezzlement scheme. When Lloyd gives the necklace to a casino owner in exchange for $10,000, Hubler kills the proprietor and abducts Linda, leading to a spectacular helicopter chase with police that ends when he is gunned down in the tower of an abandoned airfield.

Next, in *Macao*— set on "a fabulous speck on the Earth's surface just off the coast of China"— Dexter was featured as gambling house owner Vincent Halloran, a notorious hood who is wanted by authorities in America. By remaining within the safe borders of the colony, Halloran has managed to avoid arrest and has already disposed of three detectives who attempted to capture him. When he hears another lawman is in town, Halloran puts the finger on newly arrived Nick Cochran (Robert Mitchum), not knowing that Cochran is actually an ex–GI who has arrived in Macao to escape imprisonment for a minor offense in the States. The real detective, Lawrence Trumble (William Bendix), is accidentally killed during the attempt on Cochran's life, but before dying, Trumble enlists Cochran's aid in luring Halloran outside of Macao. With help from Halloran's mistress (Gloria Grahame), Cochran manages to trap the gambling house owner aboard his own boat and drives him beyond the colony's borders, where he is snagged by police.

Although Dexter enjoyed significant screen time in both of his 1952 noirs, neither made much of an impression on audiences or critics, although the critic for *Variety* conceded that "the only real thrill point in the plot [of *The Las Vegas Story*] is the helicopter chase after Dexter and the kidnapped Miss Russell. It's 10 minutes of exciting footage that enlivens an otherwise rather dull 87 minutes." As for *Macao*, *Variety*'s reviewer found that Dexter was "okay as the heavy," but in the *New York Times*, Bosley Crowther opined that the

roles played by stars Russell and Mitchum were designed to "ornament the motif, which is simply s-e-x, and beside them Mr. Bendix, Thomas Gomez, Gloria Grahame, and Brad Dexter are in the shade."

With regard to quality — if not the reaction of critics— Dexter fared better in his next film noir, *99 River Street*, his sole screen appearance of 1953. Here, Dexter turned in a fine performance as Victor Rawlins, a ruthless hood who is embroiled in an affair with Pauline Driscoll (Peggie Castle), the wife of cab driver and former boxer Ernie Driscoll (John Payne). After stealing $50,000 in diamonds, Rawlins plans to flee the country with Pauline, but when the jewel fence, Mr. Christopher (Jay Adler), strenuously objects to Pauline's involvement and refuses to purchase the diamonds, Rawlins kills her. He later returns to Christopher and forces him to pay him for the jewels, telling the fence, "You said you didn't want to deal with Pauline — so I got rid of her. I think you were right about women in business— they're not dependable." Meanwhile, Rawlins places Pauline's dead body in the back seat of Ernie's cab, and the taxi driver launches a desperate search for the killer, accompanied by local actress Linda James (Evelyn Keyes). At the same time, Christopher and two of his henchmen set out after Rawlins to retrieve the $50,000, and all of the parties converge at a waterfront bar located at 99 River Street. When Rawlins emerges from the bar, the gangsters follow in their car, but they crash into a steel barrier following a shoot-out and the chase is continued by Ernie, who uses his prowess as a former boxer to subdue Rawlins until police arrive.

Despite Dexter's standout portrayal of the vicious killer in *99 River Street*, the film was panned by critics, including the *New York Times*' Bosley Crowther, who described it as "one of those tasteless melodramas peopled with unpleasant hoods, two-timing blondes, and lots of sequences of what purports to be everyday life in the underworld." This characterization notwithstanding, the film stands up today as a creditable entry in the era of film noir and is well worth viewing for the performances of Dexter, Payne, Castle, and Adler.

Around this time, Dexter was making news for reasons other than his cinematic offerings; on January 4, 1953, the actor married popular singer Peggy Lee in a lavish garden ceremony that featured 350 guests including Bing Crosby, Bob Hope, Jane Russell, Victor Mature, and Dan Dailey. But the hoopla over the union was short-lived, and just nine months later, Lee sued for divorce.

"I doubt if I'll ever get married again," the actor said in a 1965 interview in the *Los Angeles Times*. "I can't put up with 'What are you doing?' and 'Where are you going?' and 'Where have you been?'" Despite his convictions, Dexter would take two more trips down the aisle — in 1992 to Mary Bogdonovich and, after her death, in 1994 to June Deyer, with whom he remained until his passing in 2002.

Career-wise, after being absent from the big screen in 1954, Dexter appeared in three features the following year, *Untamed* (1955), a big-budget costumer set in Africa and starring Tyrone Power; *Violent Saturday* (1955), which centered on three hoods who arrive in a small town to rob a bank; and *House of Bamboo* (1955), his final film noir. In this feature, the actor played the rather thankless role of Capt. Hanson, an American military officer stationed in Japan who assigns agent Eddie Kenner (Robert Stack) to infiltrate a local gang operated by Sandy Dawson (Robert Ryan). Eddie is successful in his mission, but after a planned heist is thwarted, his identity is discovered and Dawson cooks up a scheme designed to result in Eddie's death at the hands of police. When authorities are contacted, Dawson engages in a shootout with police at an amusement park, but the gangster is finally gunned down by Eddie on a revolving attraction at a department store.

Aside from a mention in one review as a member of *House of Bamboo*'s cast, Dexter's performance in the film went virtually unnoticed, but the feature itself earned a number of good reviews; although the critic for the *Hollywood Citizen-News* termed it an "all-too familiar tale," Kay Proctor of the *Los Angeles Examiner* found that the film was "jam-packed with action plus other solid entertainment values," and the *New York Times*' Bosley Crowther hailed it as "a fast and intriguing melodrama."

During the next five years, Dexter was seen in only seven features; the best of these were *The Oklahoman* (1957), where he played a villainous cattle baron who loses his life in a gunfight with Joel McCrea; *Run Silent, Run Deep* (1958), a first-rate wartime drama starring Burt Lancaster and Clark Gable; and *Last Train from Gun Hill* (1959), a stylish western featuring a superb cast that included Kirk Douglas, Anthony Quinn, Carolyn Jones, and Earl Holliman. The actor also scored a hit with his appearance in his best-remembered film, *The Magnificent Seven* (1960), where he played one of seven gunmen assembled to defend the residents of a small Mexican village against a gang of bandits. In addition to Dexter, the film's outstanding cast included Steve McQueen, Horst Bucholz, Eli Wallach, Charles Bronson, James Coburn, Robert Vaughn, and Yul Brynner.

"The reason why the movie was such a hit was because of the chemistry that existed between the actors," Dexter said in a 1997 interview in *The Big Reel*. "You really cared about those guys. It's something that's missing from many of today's films."

During production of the film, Dexter developed an especially close friendship with co-star Yul Brynner and served as best man at the actor's wedding, which took place on the set of the movie. Dexter and Brynner went on to make three more movies together, *Taras Bulba* (1962), with Brynner playing the title role of a 16th century Cossack leader; *Kings of the Sun* (1963), an historical drama set in Mexico; and *Invitation to a Gunfighter* (1964), an offbeat western centering on a half–Black, half–Creole gunman. Also during this period, Dexter was seen in such features as the disappointing biopic *The George Raft Story* (1961), portraying notorious gangster "Bugsy"

Siegel; *Twenty Plus Two* (1961), where he played a movie star who murders his secretary; and *Johnny Cool* (1963), in which he was seen as a Hollywood gangster who is killed after a bomb is planted in his house.

Between films, Dexter was frequently seen on the small screen, appearing in such series as *Wagon Train, Have Gun Will Travel, 77 Sunset Strip, Bat Masterson, Wanted: Dead or Alive, Cimarron City, Hawaiian Eye*, and *The Investigators*. In the early 1960s, however, the actor began refusing television offers, saying that "even the worst picture is better than the best television show."

"The only way you can create a worldwide image is a good role in a good movie," Dexter said in a 1965 interview with *Los Angeles Times* reporter Don Alpert. "Television doesn't provide this. Television is really the low rung of the entertainment ladder. It doesn't create a Julie Andrews or an Audrey Hepburn or a Tony Quinn. That's why I've stopped doing television." The actor would later reverse his stance to a degree, accepting roles in handful of TV's top-rated shows, including *Mannix, Kojak, S.W.A.T.*, and *The Incredible Hulk*.

Away from performing, Dexter enjoyed friendships with such stars as Anthony Quinn and Frank Sinatra, and he reportedly saved the latter from drowning while vacationing in Hawaii. The actor modestly said later that he didn't "like to discuss it," insisting he "would have done the same for anyone else."

"I consider Frank one of my closest friends," Dexter said. "He's a fighter and an unorthodox guy. I walk into a room with him and you've got the biggest people there, and they all accept the fact that he's the leader. They bow to him. He is a magical guy."

Soon after the incident in Hawaii, Dexter was featured in two Frank Sinatra starrers, *Von Ryan's Express* (1965) and *None but the Brave* (1965), and in 1966 was named vice-president in charge of all motion picture activities for Sinatra Enterprises. In his first film for the company, Dexter served as producer for *The Naked Runner*, a spy drama in which Sinatra starred. The experience was a dismal one, however, characterized by Sinatra reportedly walking off the set and later firing Dexter when he tried to complete the picture. Further, according to some sources, Dexter never received his final payment for his production duties.

Despite his less-than-pleasant initial outing as a producer, Dexter went on to sign a three-picture production deal with Paramount Studios, earning plaudits for his producing duties on *The Lawyer* (1970), with Barry Newman; *Little Fauss and Big Halsy* (1970), featuring Robert Redford and Michael J. Pollard; and *Lady Sings the Blues* (1972), a box-office smash starring Diana Ross as singer Billie Holiday.

After a seven-year absence, Dexter returned to the big screen in 1972 for *Jory*, a mediocre western where he was seen in another role as a villain, then essayed a rare comedic performance three years later in *Shampoo* (1975), with Warren Beatty and Julie Christie. The actor continued to appear sporadically in feature films during the remainder of the decade in such pictures as *The Private Files of J. Edgar Hoover* (1977), starring Broderick Crawford in the title role, and his last U.S. film, *Winter Kills* (1979), a first-rate comedy-thriller. Although he remained out of the limelight during the next two decades, Dexter was seen in 2000 in the television documentary *Guns for Hire: The Making of "The Magnificent Seven,"* where he was interviewed regarding his filming experience on the classic western. Two years after his appearance in the documentary, on December 12, 2002, Dexter died of emphysema in a Rancho Mirage, California, hospital. He was 85 years old.

Although typecast throughout most of his career as the villain, Brad Dexter embraced the screen persona, turning in a variety of memorable performances in nearly 40 films. And whatever the role the actor portrayed, Dexter approached his performances with a commitment to give it all he had.

"I was told that it's better to amuse your audience for five minutes than bore them for two hours," Dexter once said. "If I can amuse them for five minutes, that's the role I want to do."

Film Noir Filmography

The Asphalt Jungle. Director: John Huston. Producer: Arthur Hornblow, Jr. Running time: 112 minutes. Released by MGM, June 8, 1950. Cast: Sterling Hayden, Louis Calhern, Jean Hagen, James Whitmore, Sam Jaffe, John McIntire, Marc Lawrence, Barry Kelley, Anthony Caruso, Terese Calli, Marilyn Monroe, William Davis, Dorothy Tree, Brad Dexter, Alex Gerry, Thomas Browne Henry, James Seay, Don Haggerty, Henry Rowland, Helene Stanley, Raymond Roe, Charles Courtney. Awards: Academy Award nominations for Best Director (John Huston), Best Supporting Actor (Sam Jaffe), Best Black and White Cinematography (Harold Rosson), Best Screenplay (Ben Maddow, John Huston).

The Las Vegas Story. Director: Robert Stevenson. Producer: Robert Sparks. Running time: 87 minutes. Released by RKO, January 1952. Cast: Jane Russell, Victor Mature, Vincent Price, Hoagy Carmichael, Brad Dexter, Jay C. Flippen, Gordon Oliver, Will Wright, Bill Welsh, Ray Montgomery, Colleen Miller, Bob Wilke.

Macao. Director: Josef von Sternberg. Producer: Alex Gottlieb. Running time: 81 minutes. Released by RKO, April 30, 1952. Cast: Robert Mitchum, Jane Russell, William Bendix, Thomas Gomez, Gloria Grahame, Brad Dexter, Edward Ashley, Philip Ahn, Vladimir Sokoloff, Don Zelaya.

99 River Street. Director: Phil Karlson. Producer: Edward Small. Running time: 83 minutes. Released by United Artists, October 3, 1953. Cast: John Payne, Evelyn Keyes, Brad Dexter, Frank Faylen, Peggie Castle, Jay Adler, Jack Lambert, Eddy Waller, Glen Langan, John Day, Ian Wolfe, Peter Leeds, William Tannen, Gene Reynolds.

House of Bamboo. Director: Samuel Fuller.

Producer: Buddy Adler. Running time: 105 minutes. Released by 20th Century-Fox, July 1, 1955. Cast: Robert Ryan, Robert Stack, Shirley Yamaguchi, Cameron Mitchell, Brad Dexter, Sessue Hayakawa, Biff Elliot, Sandro Giglio, Elko Hanabusa, Harry Carey, Peter Gray, Robert Quarry, DeForest Kelley, John Doucette.

References

Alpert, Don. "Brad Dexter: Trained on the Stage but Sold on the Movies." *Los Angeles Times*, May 30, 1965.

Biography of Brad Dexter. 20th Century-Fox Studios, circa 1952.

Biography of Brad Dexter. Universal Studios, April 18, 1964.

"Brad Dexter." *Films and Filming*, June 1976.

"Brad Dexter Former Boxer." *Hollywood Citizen-News*, June 20, 1963.

"Brad Dexter Heads All Sinatra Film Activities." *The Hollywood Reporter*, April 5, 1966.

Gautschy, Dean. "Brad Dexter Plans to Meet His Clan." *Los Angeles Herald-Examiner*, July 23, 1954.

"Hollywood Wedding." *Los Angeles Daily News*, January 5, 1953.

Johns, Howard. "The Magnificent Seven Magnificent for Dexter." *The Big Reel*, September 1997.

"Magnolia Alley." *Playbill*, April 19, 1949.

McClay, Howard. "Brad Dexter." *Los Angeles Daily News*, May 7, 1952.

"Peggy Lee Files Suit for Divorce." *Hollywood Citizen-News*, September 30, 1953.

Scott, Vernon. "Grateful." *Newark Evening News*, November 3, 1964.

"Singer Peggy Lee Wed to Actor Brad Dexter." *Los Angeles Times*, January 5, 1953.

"Singer Weds Actor." *Saturday Evening Post*, January 1953.

"Thesp Brad Dexter Takes on Executive Role, Too." *Film Daily*, September 9, 1965.

BRIAN DONLEVY

"Doing the right thing never works out. In this world, you turn the other cheek and you get hit with a lug wrench." — Brian Donlevy in *Impact* (1949)

It was once said that Brian Donlevy was so frequently cast as a gambling house proprietor that "when you meet him on the street, you expect to see him picking his teeth with

a pair of dice." Although the Ireland-born actor became known for portraying the tough guy with the heart of gold, however, he distinguished himself with appearances in nearly

100 films during a 40-year career, including such classics as *Union Pacific* (1939) and *Beau Geste* (1939). During the late 1940s, his respected career was somewhat overshadowed by a messy, highly publicized divorce and custody battle, but the actor's body of film earned him a solid place in film history and in the annals of film noir, with five features to his credit: *The Glass Key* (1942), *Kiss of Death* (1947), *Impact* (1949), *Shakedown* (1950), and *The Big Combo* (1955).

The son of an Irish whiskey distiller, Waldo Brian Donlevy was born on February 9, 1901 (some sources say 1903), in what is now Portadown, Craigavon District, in Northern Ireland. When Donlevy was 10 months old, his family moved to the United States and settled in Sheboygan, Wisconsin, where his father changed vocations and went into the wool business.

Donlevy's early life was as exciting as any movie script, but it is difficult to discern fact from fabrication. According to most accounts, Donlevy ran away from home at the age of 14 and lied about his age so that he could join General John J. Pershing's pursuit of Mexican revolutionary Pancho Villa. After nine months, the young man was returned home and his parents enrolled him in St. John's Military Academy in Delafield, Wisconsin, but Donlevy later ran away again, reportedly to serve in World War I. Some versions also claim that Donlevy served during the war as a pilot with the Lafayette Escadrille, was promoted to sergeant, and was wounded on two separate occasions. (Exactly where the young man learned to fly is a bit of a mystery.) At some point during these years, Donlevy developed a love for poetry-writing, which remained a favorite pastime for the rest of his life.

"I was lucky because I came out all right, my wounds not serious, but many boys didn't," Donlevy was quoted in a 1938 magazine article. "But at the time, of course, I thought enlisting was a good idea, and because I was so young and harebrained, I didn't realize then that it was a mistake."

After the war, Donlevy was accepted into the U.S. Naval Academy at Annapolis, but he left two years later after developing an interest in the theater. He moved to New York, hoping to find fame and fortune on the stage, but was forced to make ends meet by attempting to sell his poetry and other writings, and posing for magazine advertisements. He was also seen in bit parts in several New York-based silent films, including *Jamestown* (1923), *Damaged Hearts* (1924), and *Monsieur Beaucaire* (1924). His years of struggle paid off in 1924 when he landed a role in the Broadway hit, *What Price Glory?*, but after the two-year run of the play, Donlevy found it difficult to find a good stage role. He later claimed that he was hampered during this period because he appeared to be shorter than he really was.

"This physical phenomena nearly nipped my career," Donlevy said. "I was pretty much at a stalemate until I ran across what seemed a real break. Bill Harris was to produce *Three in One* and interviewed me for one of the leading roles. After days of negotiations, Harris called me into his office to break the sad news." The producer informed Donlevy that he couldn't use him in the play because he needed an actor who was six feet tall. "I walked over to the wall, backed against it and chalked off a mark just above my head. Harris measured the distance, found it a shade over the required six feet, and gave me the job."

Following *Three in One*, Donlevy was cast in such Broadway productions as *Up Pops the Devil*, *Hit the Deck*, *Life Begins at 8:40*, and *Three Cornered Moon*. He also appeared in a bit part in his first talkie, *Gentlemen of the Press* (1929), which starred Walter Huston and Kay Francis, and was later seen in *A Modern Cinderella* (1932), a comedy-musical short starring Ruth Etting. Then, in 1934, after scoring a hit in the Broadway play, *The Milky Way*, Donlevy was asked to come to Hollywood to reprise the role in a film version, but once in Tinseltown, the actor discovered that the production had been delayed. (The film would ultimately be made in 1936, with William Gargan playing the role Donlevy had been slated to portray.) With no further prospects in California, Donlevy was preparing to return to New York when he was tapped by producer Sam Goldwyn for a supporting role in his upcoming film, *Barbary Coast* (1935). An action packed drama set in 1850s San Francisco, *Barbary Coast* featured Donlevy as Knuckles Jacobi, the black-shirted bodyguard of a ruthless casino owner (played with gusto by Edward G. Robinson). The film was a hit, and Donlevy was on his way.

"I was prepared for the screen because I knew the business of acting," Donlevy once said. "I understood how to put over a characterization. I don't doubt that it was also a help to get such an actor-proof role as the one I played in *Barbary Coast.*"

The following year, Donlevy signed a contract with 20th Century–Fox and appeared in a whopping eight films, including *Human Cargo* (1936), a crime drama co-starring Rita Cansino (soon to be transformed into Rita Hayworth); *High Tension* (1936), an entertaining comedy featuring Donlevy as a deep-sea diver who falls for a writer; and *Half Angel* (1936), a comedy-mystery co-starring Frances Dee. The actor continued to work steadily during the next several years, making a series of solid but fairly standard features until 1939, when he was seen in four smash hits: *Union Pacific*, a lavish epic produced and directed by Cecil B. DeMille; *Jesse James*, starring Tyrone Power in the title role; *Destry Rides Again*, a first-rate western that successfully combined action, romance, and suspense; and *Beau Geste*, an adventure tale in which Donlevy's snarling, scene-stealing portrayal of a Foreign Legion sergeant earned the actor an Academy Award nomination for Best Supporting Actor (he lost, however, to Thomas Mitchell for *Stagecoach*).

"During my first year or so in pictures, I was rather proud of being the big, bad man who scared little children," Donlevy in 1940. "Kids along the street would give me side glances, and shudder — and I'd leer at them and giggle inwardly. Then, the novelty wore off, and in the past four years I have been fighting desperately against heavies. What I want to do is make 'em laugh."

Donlevy got his wish when he signed with Paramount Studios and was cast in the starring role of *The Great McGinty* (1940), a well-received Preston Sturges satire in which the actor played a down-and-out loner who is transformed into a polished politician. But he was back on the wrong side of the law in such features as *Two Yanks in Trinidad* (1942), co-starring Pat O'Brien; *Nightmare* (1942), a mediocre spy thriller; and *The Glass Key* (1942), his first film noir.

In this well-done feature, Donlevy portrayed Paul Madvig, a crude political boss who falls for Janet Henry (Veronica Lake), the daughter of a local senator. The story, adapted from a Dashiell Hammett novel, contains a variety of quirky characters and complex plot twists, including the murder of Janet's brother, who was having an affair with the sister of Madvig, the chief suspect in the crime. By the time this labyrinthine yarn reaches its end, it is revealed that the senator accidentally killed his son during a fight, and Madvig, a witness, agreed to take the blame.

As the boorish Paul Madvig, Donlevy

offered a fascinating portrayal of a complex character noted for a two-fisted style of behavior, an unending loyalty to his friends, and a sentimentality that was effectively masked by his gruff exterior. The latter quality was best illustrated in the film's final scene, in which Madvig gives his blessing to Janet and his chief aide, Ed Beaumont (Alan Ladd), after acknowledging that they "got it bad for each other." Earning praise in *Variety* for "mak[ing] the most of his role" in *The Glass Key*, Donlevy next offered acclaimed performances in *Wake Island* (1942), a rousing war picture, and *Two Yanks in Trinidad* (1942), a comedy directed by former actor Gregory Ratoff. The following year, however, Donlevy was suspended by Paramount for refusing to appear opposite Betty Hutton in *Incendiary Blonde* (1943), forcing the actor to remain idle until the completion of the film. During the next several years, he was seen in films of varying quality, including *The Miracle of Morgan's Creek* (1944), a first-rate comedy helmed by Preston Sturges, in which Donlevy reprised his role as Governor McGinty; *Our Hearts Were Growing Up* (1946), the somewhat disappointing sequel to the popular *Our Hearts Were Young and Gay* (1944); *Two Years Before the Mast* (1946), in which he played a seaman gathering material for an exposé on the harsh treatment of sailors; and *Canyon Passage* (1946), a well-done western co-starring Dana Andrews and Susan Hayward.

By now, Donlevy had been seen in more than 40 features, and was in the middle of a four-year contract with MGM, an association the actor described as a "sentimental connection."

"My first film for this studio was *Billy the Kid*, and I was then in what they call the 'feature players' dressing room building. But next to my building was another called the 'stars' dressing room building–where such big stars as Robert Taylor, Clark Gable, Robert Montgomery and others dressed. I used to look over there and wonder what it was like in the stars' dressing room building. I know now, because I'm in that building myself."

But if Donlevy's screen career was moving along at a steady, successful pace, the same could not be said of his off-screen life. While the actor was building his cinematic repertoire, he had also led a busy private life — in 1928, he married Yvonne Grey, whom he divorced in 1936 to marry actress and nightclub singer Marjorie Lane. In February 1943, Donlevy and Lane became parents of a baby girl, Judith Ann, but by 1946, accusations of cruelty and infidelity were edging the union to the breaking point. The final straw came in December 1946, when Donlevy, along with several friends and police detectives, broke into a New York hotel room occupied by Lane and local socialite James Hannan. Photographers engaged by Donlevy recorded the scene, and three days later, the actor filed for divorce. During the February 1947 court hearing, however, the New York hotel incident was never mentioned.

An interlocutory divorce decree was granted, with Donlevy agreeing to give Lane $33,000 in securities, $750 a month for two years, $400 for three years, $250 for five years, and $50 thereafter. In addition, Donlevy was awarded primary custody of the couple's daughter. But the story didn't end there. In September 1947, Marjorie Lane filed a motion seeking to have the divorce decree set aside, claiming that Donlevy used "threats and intimidation and high-handed pressure" to ensure that she agreed to the divorce settlement.

"I was told by my husband that if I refused these terms I would get nothing in the way of property and that every asset which stood in my name would be taken from me and that the custody of my child or the opportunity to ever to see her would be taken from me," Lane charged.

Donlevy swiftly launched a counter-attack, filing a total of 10 affidavits, and a half-dozen photographs, revealing the details of the incident involving Lane and the New York socialite, charging that his ex-wife was "an unfit mother to raise our baby." When news of the incident hit the press, Lane stated that she had been "entrapped" by Donlevy, claiming that the actor had encouraged her to date other men, and had used the hotel break-in to "coerce her into signing away her child and her property rights." Lane also charged that for more than a month before the divorce was granted, Donlevy had hidden their child from her and refused to indulge the child's whereabouts. Donlevy ultimately admitted that he had, indeed, concealed their daughter's location ("On the advice of my doctor," he vaguely explained), but he insisted that Lane had "entrapped herself" regarding the New York hotel incident.

"I deny that I or anyone else with my knowledge and consent laid a trap for Mrs. Donlevy," the actor said. "Photographs taken at the time ... reflect the disgraceful scene. I was outraged, the sanctity of my home was violated, and our little child's moral welfare was affected."

On September 30, 1947, Superior Court Judge Allen W. Ashburn granted Lane's motion to set aside the divorce decree, ruling that Donlevy had forced his wife by "undue influence, coercion, duress and fraud" to submit to the initial agreement. The judge further ruled that Donlevy had held their daughter "as hostage" to compel Lane to agree to his terms. After the ruling, Lane sued for divorce, and although she claimed that she would "not stoop to the sordid vilification which has been used against me," she promptly leveled more sensational charges against Donlevy, claiming that he had verbally harassed her, had once attempted to run over her with his automobile, and had threatened her with a gun. The entire seamy episode was finally resolved in December 1947, when Donlevy agreed to pay Lane $50,000 outright, $25,000 in a year, and $10,000 each year for five years, provided she did not remarry. Custody of 4-year-old Judith was split evenly, with each parent slated to have her six months out of the year. (It would be nearly 20 years before Donlevy found love again; in 1966, he married Lillian Lugosi, the widow of horror film veteran Bela Lugosi. The two remained together until Donlevy's death.)

Although Donlevy's film plots could scarcely compare with the drama of his personal life, he managed to turn in well-received performances in several features in 1947, including *Killer McCoy*, in which he played a villainous gambler; *Heaven Only Knows*, a pleasant western-fantasy co-starring Robert Cummings; and *The Beginning or the End*, which focused on the development of the atomic bomb. Also in 1947, Donlevy returned to the realm of film noir with his second entry from the era, *Kiss of Death*.

Here, Donlevy played D'Angelo, an assistant district attorney whose determination to crack down on crime leads him to career lawbreaker Nick Bianco (Victor Mature). In his first encounter with the hardened criminal, D'Angelo is frustrated by Bianco's refusal to provide information in exchange for a prison release: "You've got that good old hoodlum complex — no squealing," D'Angelo tells him. "Desert your kids. Let 'em starve. Let your home go to pot. But don't squeal on some no-good hoodlums who wouldn't turn a finger for you. I hate crooks." Several years later, when Bianco's two young children are committed to an orphanage following their mother's suicide, Bianco alters his stance and D'Angelo succeeds in putting a number of hoods away. But when one of the criminals, the homicidal Tommy Udo (Richard Widmark), is acquitted for murder, Bianco fears for the lives of his daughters and his new wife (Coleen Gray) and devises an elaborate scheme to trap Udo. In carrying out his plan, Bianco is severely wounded by Udo, but the psychotic killer is, in turn, gunned down by police. After its release, *Kiss of Death* was hailed in *Motion Picture Herald* as "among the all-time best of its kind" and, despite the showier roles performances essayed by Mature and Widmark, Donlevy was hailed by several critics, including the reviewer for *Variety*, who wrote, "Brian Donlevy and Coleen Gray justify their star billing."

After Donlevy's sensational 1947 divorce, his screen appearances slowed down dramatically. With appearances in only two films a year for the next several years, his best features during this period were *A Southern Yankee* (1948), a Red Skelton starrer, and

Command Decision (1948), in which he co-starred with Clark Gable as a tough Air Force general. He was also seen in two more films noirs, *Impact* (1949) and *Shakedown* (1950).

In the first, Donlevy starred as successful San Francisco businessman Walt Williams, whose wife, Irene (Helen Walker), teams with her lover in an attempt to kill him. Instead, the lover, Jim Torrance (Tony Barrett), is killed in a fiery auto accident, his charred remains are identified as Walt, and Helen is accused of her husband's murder. Walt, meanwhile, establishes a new life for himself as a service station mechanic in Idaho, where he finds himself attracted to the station's appealing owner, Marsha Peters (Ella Raines). After revealing his past to Marsha, however, Walt refuses to consider her suggestion that he return to San Francisco to clear Helen's name: "Wild horses couldn't drag me back," he says bitterly. "She deserves everything she's getting.... I'll never think of our moments together without nausea." After a change of heart, Walt follows Marsha's advice, only to find himself charged with the murder of Torrance, but Marsha works with a crafty police detective (Charles Coburn) to unearth evidence of Walt's innocence, and they wind up together in the final reel.

In his second consecutive noir with a San Francisco setting, Donlevy was featured in *Shakedown*, which centered on the exploits of an unscrupulous newspaper photographer, Jack Early (Howard Duff). In his drive for fame and fortune, Early cozies up to a camera-shy mobster, Nick Palmer (Donlevy), shamelessly encouraging him to pose for a picture by playing on his ego: "You know, Mr. Palmer, if you keep on acting the way you do, the public will get an impression that you're a crook," Early says. "After all, you're a businessman. Hiding behind your fedora like that, who's going to have confidence in your perfectly respectable enterprises? Now, why not do it my way? Just give me a couple of seconds and tomorrow morning, you'll be delivered with the milk looking like George Washington." Impressed by Early's audacity, Palmer allows the coveted picture, and later

invites the photographer into his inner-circle, providing Early with information that allows him to snap a rival gangster, Harry Coulton (Lawrence Tierney), in the process of a robbery. When Coulton learns of Palmer's betrayal, he plants a bomb in his car, providing Early with yet another photo opportunity, but the shutterbug's unprincipled acts finally catch up with him when he is shot and killed by Coulton.

Donlevy's latest two noirs met with varying reactions from critics; in the *Los Angeles Times*, Grace Kingsley wrote that *Impact* "grips emotionally," and praised the film's "top-notch cast," but the *Los Angeles Daily News*' Darr Smith concluded that director Arthur Lubin "apparently was looking the other way when his actors were on stage." Smith was equally disparaging toward *Shakedown*, saying "there was a good idea there somewhere along the line," but Margaret Harford of the *Hollywood Citizen-News* praised Donlevy's "convincing" performance, and the critic for the *Los Angeles Evening Herald Examiner* labeled the feature "good thrill stuff."

As the 1950s unfolded, Donlevy was seen in a handful of run-of-the-mill films, including *Kansas Raiders* (1950), and *The Woman They Almost Lynched* (1953) (he played Civil War–era outlaw William Quantrill in both); *Hoodlum Empire* (1952), in which he portrayed a crusading senator; and *Ride the Man Down* (1953), a western co-starring Rod Cameron and Ella Raines. He fared better, however, in his last film noir, *The Big Combo* (1955). A typically complex offering from the era, this feature depicted a medley of shady characters, including Mr. Brown (Richard Conte), a sadistic mobster; Susan Lowell (Jean Wallace), his weak-willed socialite lover; Joe McClure (Donlevy), who used to be Mr. Brown's boss and is now his underling; and Leonard Diamond (Cornel Wilde), a police detective obsessed with exposing Brown's criminal activities. After a series of violent episodes, including Diamond's savage beating and torture, Diamond and Susan team up to finally bring Brown to justice.

As an aging mobster with a hearing impediment, Donlevy essayed his most intriguing and memorable noir character; the "Rodney Dangerfield" of his organization, McClure garnered no respect. This characterization is clearly illustrated in scene after scene — in one, McClure objects when one of the gang's hoods charges him a fee for the privilege of working Diamond over. "Didn't Mr. Brown pay you?" McClure asks. And the hood responds, "You're not Mr. Brown. For Mr. Brown, I'd snatch a judge from a Superior Court for a chocolate soda." Later, Brown himself berates McClure after he kills a potential witness, telling him, "You — get upstairs. Go to bed. Stay there. You been sick, understand — sick. And if they take you to police headquarters, shoot yourself in the head. It'll make everything a lot simpler." And in the final ignominy of McClure's life, he attempts to take over Brown's organization, only to have Brown's two henchmen gun him down instead. (As a last "favor" to the doomed McClure, Brown removes his hearing device so that "you won't hear the bullets.") Although Donlevy was mentioned in the *New York Times* for "do[ing] his level best as a quiet henchman," *The Big Combo* earned mixed reviews — in the *New York Times*, the critic panned the film's "open-throttle monotonous serving of mayhem," but the reviewer for *Variety* praised its "bare-knuckle direction" and "hard-hitting melodramatics."

The Big Combo would be one of the last of Donlevy's first-rate films. He was seen, however, in *A Cry in the Night* (1956), a dark melodrama about a psychotic kidnaper, and two well-received British science fiction films, *The Quatermass Experiment* (1955) and *Quatermass II* (1957), in which he starred as a gruff, slightly menacing scientist. He also appeared in small roles in *Cowboy* (1958), starring Glenn Ford and Jack Lemmon; *Escape from Red Rock* (1958), where he played the leader of a group of outlaws; and *Juke Box Rhythm* (1959), a cutesy rock-and-roll musical starring Jo Morrow.

In addition to his big-screen work, Don-levy co-produced the television adventure series *Dangerous Assignment* in 1952. Based on the radio program of the same name, the series was canceled after 39 episodes. He was also seen throughout the 1950s and 1960s in guest spots on such television programs as *Lux Video Theater* (where he played an abbreviated version of *The Great McGinty*), *Motorola TV Theater*, *Rawhide*, *Wagon Train*, *Hotel de Paree*, *Zane Grey Theater*, *Perry Mason*, and *Family Affair*.

Meanwhile, Donlevy was beginning to make news more for his off-screen adventures than his roles as a performer; in 1950, his single-engine plane lost its propeller and crashed into a pasture in Solvang, California. Donlevy, who was flying the plane, and his co-pilot were on a flight from Santa Ynez to Hollywood when the incident occurred. Both men escaped serious injury and were able to walk to a nearby ranch for help. A few years later, in 1953, Donlevy's television production company was sued by a man named Rudolf Beiser, who objected to the rerunning of one of the *Dangerous Assignments* episodes. Seeking $100,000 for invasion of privacy, Beiser charged that a character on the program, with the same name, age, and physical characteristics as his own, was depicted as a "criminal possessed of evil character and guilty of criminal conduct." As a result, Beiser claimed, he received numerous inquiries as to whether the episode was based on his own life, and the program had "destroyed his privacy, humiliating, annoying and disgracing him, and exposing him to public contempt and ridicule." The case was later dismissed, but Donlevy was in court again in 1955 when his new convertible jumped a curb, rolled into a parking lot, and hit another car–across the street from the Beverly Hills police station. After a bench trial, Donlevy was found guilty of drunk driving and put on summary probation, provided that he pay a fine of $150, stop drinking liquor for one year, and refrain from driving for 90 days except from home to work and back. Then, in 1957, Donlevy was again the subject of a lawsuit when Carthay Productions sued him for $39,000, charging that he had breached a contract to play the leading role in their stage play *King of Hearts* in October 1955. The matter was later settled out of court.

Professionally, the actor returned to his roots on the stage in the early 1960s in *The Andersonville Trial*, which was presented as part of the Topeka (Kansas) Broadway Theater Series. He was absent from the big screen for several years, however, having decided to indulge in what he termed a "self-imposed professional exile" in Palm Springs, California.

"I sort of quit for a while," Donlevy said in a 1964 interview. "But I got tired of the grass and jack-rabbits and came back to town where it's civilized. All of a sudden I woke up and found I was getting lazy. To waste your time is the biggest sin in the world. Who wants to take pills to stay young? I haven't fallen apart yet."

Unfortunately, Donlevy's return to feature films was characterized by a series of timewasters, including *How to Stuff a Wild Bikini* (1965), *Gamera the Invincible* (1965), *Curse of the Fly* (1965), and *The Fat Spy* (1966), notable only as the screen debut of Phyllis Diller. He fared slightly better with *Five Golden Dragons* (1967) and *Arizona* (1968), but these were of interest primarily because of their casts of veteran screen actors; the first featured small roles from Dan Duryea, Christopher Lee, and George Raft, while the latter included appearances from John Ireland, Barton MacLane, and James Craig.

In 1969, Donlevy was top-billed in *Pit Stop*, a low-budget race car saga co-starring a young Ellen Burstyn (then known as Ellen McRae). Now approaching his 70s, the actor decided after this film that it was time to retire. Moving with wife, Lillian, to Palm Springs, Donlevy focused his energies on writing short stories and reaping the benefits from a prosperous tungsten mine he had purchased in the late 1930s. But just a few years later, in 1971, Donlevy's idyllic retirement was clouded by the news that he had been diagnosed with throat cancer. The actor underwent surgery later that year, but he died on April 6, 1972, at the Motion Picture Country Hospital in Woodland Hills, California.

Known as "Old Marble Puss," Brian Donlevy excelled at portraying characters that audiences not only "loved to hate," but also "hated to love." During his prolific career, the actor showed his ability to play varied roles in such features as *The Great McGinty*, but he will be best remembered for his villainous turns in films including *Barbary Coast* and *Beau Geste*. His persona as a screen heavy notwithstanding, Donlevy himself once noted that he had a softer side.

"If my fans could have seen me working for months to bring out a new violet," Donlevy said, "I'd probably be washed up as a tough guy on the screen."

Film Noir Filmography

The Glass Key. Director: Stuart Heisler. Producer: B.G. DeSylva. Running time: 85 minutes. Released by Paramount, October 15, 1942. Cast: Brian Donlevy, Veronica Lake, Alan Ladd, Bonita Graville, Joseph Calleia, Richard Denning, Moroni Olsen, William Bendix, Margaret Hayes, Arthur Loft, George Meader, Eddie Marr, Frances Gifford, Joe McGuinn, Frank Hagney, Joseph King.

Kiss of Death. Director: Henry Hathaway. Producer: Fred Kohlmar. Running time: 98 minutes. Released by 20th Century-Fox, August 27, 1947. Cast: Victor Mature, Brian Donlevy, Coleen Gray, Richard Widmark, Karl Malden, Taylor Holmes, Howard Smith, Anthony Ross, Mildred Dunnock, Millard Mitchell, Temple Texas. Awards: Academy Award nomination for Best Supporting Actor (Richard Widmark), Best Original Story (Eleazar Lipsky).

Shakedown. Director: Joe Pevney. Producer: Ted Richmond. Running time: 80 minutes. Released by Universal-International, September 23, 1950. Cast: Howard Duff, Brian Donlevy, Peggy Dow, Lawrence Tierney, Bruce Bennett, Anne Vernon, Stapleton Kent, Peter Virgo, Charles Sherlock.

Impact. Director: Arthur Lubin. Producer: Leo C. Popkin. Running time: 108 minutes. Released by United Artists, April 1949. Cast: Brian Donlevy, Ella Raines, Charles Coburn, Helen Walker, Anna May Wong, Mae Marsh, Tony Barrett, William Wright, Robert Warwick, Philip Ahn, Art Baker, Erskine Sanford.

The Big Combo. Director: Joseph Lewis. Producer: Sidney Harmon. Running time: 89 minutes. Released by Allied Artists, February 13, 1955. Cast: Cornel Wilde, Richard Conte, Brian Donlevy, Jean Wallace, Robert Middleton, Lee Van Cleef, Earl Holliman, Helen Walker, Jay Adler, John Hoyt, Ted De Corsia, Helen Stanton, Roy Gordon, Whit Bissell, Steve Mitchell, Baynes Barron, James McCallion, Tony Michaels, Brian O'Hara, Rita Gould, Bruce Sharpe, Michael Mark, Philip Van Zandt, Donna Drew.

References

"Actor Has Lively Interest in Topeka. *Topeka Daily Capital*, October 22, 1960.

Biography of Brian Donlevy. Universal Studios, circa 1946.

"Brian Donlevy Back to Work; on 'Show of the Week' April 5." *New York Morning Telegraph*, April 3, 1964.

"Brian Donlevy Convicted of Drunk Driving Charge." *Los Angeles Times*, April 3, 1955.

"Brian Donlevy Denies Breach of Film Contract." *Los Angeles Examiner*, June 14, 1957.

"Brian Donlevy in Crash; Booked as Drunk Driver." *Los Angeles Times*, March 13, 1955.

"'Dangerous' Telepic Sullied His Good Name, Suit Charges." *Variety*, December 17, 1953.

"Donlevy Divorce." *Los Angeles Herald-Express*, October 1, 1947.

"Donlevy Files New Writ Plea." *Los Angeles Examiner*, October 3, 1947.

"Donlevy Loses New Court Tilt." *Los Angeles Herald Express*, October 7, 1947.

"Donlevy Tells of Raid on Former Wife's Room." *Los Angeles Times*, September 23, 1947.

"Donlevy Will Get New, More Costly Decree." *Los Angeles Daily News*, circa 1947.

Gilbert, Douglas. "Trend to Good Film Acting Pleases Donlevy." *New York World Telegraph*, June 19, 1947.

Green, Alice. "Fighting Irishman." *Film Weekly*, January 9, 1937.

Hyatt, Jack. "Tough Mr. Donlevy Who Couldn't Date His Wife." *The American Weekly*, February 6, 1947.

Johaneson, Blaud. "Portrays Villain Better Than Hero." *New York Daily Mirror*, December 19, 1937.

Keavy, Hubard. "Actor Goes Out to Get Self Married." *Tampa Tribune*, July 16, 1936.

Kistler, Robert. 'Tough Guy' Actor Brian Donlevy Dies." *Los Angeles Times*, April 6, 1972.

"Mrs. Donlevy Gets $50,000." *Los Angeles Times*, December 27, 1947.

"Mrs. Donlevy Fires New Salvo in Divorce Battle." *Los Angeles Times*, September 26, 1947.

"Mrs. Donlevy Wins in Court." *Los Angeles Examiner*, September 30, 1947.

"Paid 'Private Eve' $20,000 to Trail Wife, Says Donlevy." *Los Angeles Herald Express*, November 13, 1947.

Parsons, Louella O. "Brian Donlevy Case Settled." *Los Angeles Examiner*, December 22, 1947.

_____. "Mrs. Donlevy to Ask Divorce." *Los Angeles Examiner*, December 18, 1944.

"Propeller Lost; Brian Donlevy in Plane Crash." *Los Angeles Times*, circa January 1950.

Roberts, John. "Brian Donlevy: Irish Tough Guy Becomes Hollywood Star." *Classic Images*, November 1990.

Thirer, Irene. "Exhibitor-Star Confabs Extolled by Donlevy." *New York Post*, July 17, 1940.

"Truck 'Treed' Brian Donlevy." *New York Morning Telegraph*, December 24, 1940.

Wallace, Inez. "Brian Donlevy, Star, Finds Gold in 'Them Thar Hills.'" *Cleveland Plain Dealer*, August 27, 1944.

Weiler, A. H. "Donlevy, the Miner." *New York Times*, August 20, 1944.

KIRK DOUGLAS

"You butcher one more patient and, law or no law, I'll find you. I'll put a bullet in the back of your head and dump your body in the East River. And I'll go home and I'll sleep sweetly." — Kirk Douglas in *Detective Story* (1951)

Take one distinctive cleft chin, sculptured features, and a powerful physique. Toss in an acting talent capable of depicting every emotion from heart-melting tenderness to volcanic wrath. Mix in generous amounts of professional determination, personal integrity, and family devotion. Finish with a dollop of unflagging fortitude and admiration-provoking longevity — and you get Kirk Douglas.

One of Hollywood's most respected and enduring stars, Kirk Douglas has always seemed to operate with a "never-say-die" outlook — even in the face of such personal setbacks as a near-fatal helicopter crash and a disabling stroke — and has exceeded his abilities as an on-screen performer to include acclaimed talents as a director, producer, and author. In addition to his standout portrayals in such cinema classics as *The Bad and the Beautiful* (1952), *Lust for Life* (1956), *Gunfight at the O.K. Corral* (1957), and *Spartacus* (1960), Douglas was also a memorable contributor to film noir, starring in six superb offerings from the era: *The Strange Love of Martha Ivers* (1946), *Out of the Past* (1947), *I Walk Alone* (1948), *Champion* (1949), *The Big Carnival* (1951), and *Detective Story* (1951).

One of seven children of Russian-Jewish immigrants Hershel and Bryna Danielovich, Kirk Douglas entered this world as Issur Danielovich on December 9, 1916, a native of Amsterdam, New York. Along with his six sisters, young Issy — as he was know to his family and friends — endured a childhood of poverty.

"Unless you've been hungry-poor, you don't know what poor means," the actor once said. "Whatever we had to eat, we ate every scrap. That habit has lasted all my life. I seldom leave anything on my plate."

To supplement his father's meager income as a peddler of food, wood, and rags, Issy worked a variety of jobs while growing up in Amsterdam, including delivering newspapers and selling pop and candy to the workers at the local carpet mill. He was bitten by the acting bug at an early age, however, with his recitation of a poem during a first grade production, and frequently involved his siblings in his theatrical exploits.

"We'd play theater all the time — that's the way we played," the actor's sister, Fritzi Becker, recalled in a 1988 interview on the ABC-TV news magazine *20/20*. "Kirk made us dance and we really had to practice the routine, and do it well. Sometimes, we could've killed him. He would really take it seriously — he was like the director."

Douglas was a popular student at Amsterdam's Wilbur Lynch High School. His acting ability was nurtured by a teacher, Louise Livingston, and he honed his budding talent through participation in a series of oratorical contests and school plays. Following his graduation, he worked for a year as a department store clerk, then took his savings of $163 and hitch-hiked with a friend to St. Lawrence University in Canton, New York.

"Our last ride was on a truckload of fertilizer," the actor wrote in his 1988 autobiography, *The Ragman's Son*. "We crouched on top of the flapping canvas, our heads bowed against the whipping wind as we sped away from Amsterdam, toward the unknown — college — with that strong odor that I knew so well."

Despite his meager cache of funds for tuition, and reeking with the lingering aroma from his hitch-hiking trek, Douglas made a favorable impression on the school's dean and enrolled at St. Lawrence in 1935. During the next four years, he made ends meet by working as a gardener, janitor, and waiter; joined the wrestling team, earning a distinguished record as the school's undefeated champion and winner of the Intercollegiate Wrestling Championship; became the school's first non-fraternity member to be elected student body president; and furthered his acting pursuits by appearing in several college productions and serving as president as the school's drama club, The Mummers. Demonstrating the indefatigable sense of resourcefulness and determination with which he seemed to be born, the future star earned extra cash during one summer break by competing in wrestling competitions at a local carnival, and frequently managed to eke out his meals with the aid of classmates who would each donate a portion from their own plates.

After graduating with honors from St. Lawrence in 1939, Douglas won a scholarship to New York's American Academy of Dramatic Arts, where he studied for the next two years. During summers, he performed in local stock theaters and served as a drama coach at the Greenwich House Settlement, then made his Broadway debut in 1941, portraying a singing Western Union messenger in *Spring Again*. Later that year, he was cast in his second Broadway production, *The Three Sisters*, in which had a brief walk-on and played an off-stage echo.

Douglas' budding stage career was interrupted by World War II; trained as a naval officer at the Notre Dame Midshipman School, he served in the Navy for two years before an injury during a training activity earned him an honorable discharge. By this time, Douglas had married model-turned-actress Diana Dill, a former classmate from the American Academy of Dramatic Arts. In 1944, the couple had their first child, Michael (who would grow up to earn fame as one of Hollywood's biggest stars), and three years later would have a second son, Joel. (Although the union of Douglas and Dill ultimately ended in divorce in 1951, the parting was, by accounts, an amiable one, and the actor would later cast Dill in the 1955 feature *The Indian Fighter*, the first film produced by his independent company.)

Professionally, Douglas lost little time in resuming his Broadway career following his discharge from the Navy. He was first seen in *Kiss and Tell*, taking over the role played by Richard Widmark, followed by parts in *Trio*, *Star in the Window*, and *The Wind Is Ninety*, for which he was singled out by critic Howard Barnes, who wrote in the *New York Herald Tribune*: "Although he plays the impossible role of the Unknown Soldier, he plays it with a jaunty grace that endows it with dignity and feeling."

At this point, fate — in the form of actress Lauren Bacall — stepped in to change the direction of Douglas' career. A friend of the actor's since their days as students at the American Academy, Bacall recommended Douglas to producer Hal Wallis for a role in his upcoming film.

"I said to Hal, 'there's a marvelous actor in a play in New York, and you've got to go see it,'" Bacall said in a 1997 documentary on Douglas' life. "And he went to see it and he

brought Kirk out to California for a screen test and cast him in a part."

The film would mark not only Douglas' screen debut, but also his entry into the world of noir — *The Strange Love of Martha Ivers* (1946). This riveting feature starred Barbara Stanwyck in the title role of a wealthy small-town businesswoman characterized by her passion for spinning a web of control and power over all those who came within her sphere. Among Martha's hapless victims was her weak-willed, alcoholic husband, Walter (excellently played by Douglas), who had existed in Martha's shadow since childhood. When another chum from their past, gambler Sam Masterson (Van Heflin), returns to town, it sets in motion a chain of events that includes Martha's affair with Sam, her unsuccessful attempt to convince Sam to murder her husband, and the ultimate murder-suicide of the married couple at the film's end.

Douglas' performance in his screen debut was cheered by critics; William Hawkins of the *New York World-Telegram* reported that the actor "gives the weakling Walter a convincingly sustained color"; *Variety*'s critic found that Douglas "show[s] up strongly among the more experienced players"; and the reviewer for *Film Daily* wrote: "The cast is an almost perfect one, every role being played for all its worth, with Heflin and Douglas stealing most of the honors." After a return to Broadway for the short-lived *Woman Bites Dog* in the summer of 1946, Douglas followed his triumphant initiation to the screen with his second film noir, *Out of the Past* (1947).

Here, playing the virtual opposite of his first noir character, Douglas was seen as Whit Sterling, a powerful mobster whose amiable facade masks a sadistic sense of steely resolve. Told mostly in flashback, the film's story focuses primarily on a triangle of love and murder involving Whit, private detective Jeff Bailey (Robert Mitchum), and Whit's girlfriend, Kathie Moffett (Jane Greer), for whom Jeff forms an irrevocable and, ultimately, fatal attraction. By the conclusion of this typically complex noir, the duplicitous Kathie causes the deaths of no less than three characters— including both Whit and Jeff— before she herself meets the same fate. Considered today as the quintessential film noir, *Out of the Past* earned raves upon its release, with one critic describing it as a "flashy addition to the tough-guy film archives," and another calling it "a hard-boiled melodrama strong on characterization, considerable production polish, effective direction, and compelling mood." For his portrayal of Whit, Douglas earned similar accolades; the reviewer for *Motion Picture Herald* praised his "believable" portrayal, *Variety*'s critic singled him out for his "impressive trouping," and in *The Hollywood Reporter*, he was applauded for "manag[ing] to convey the fanatacism of the big league operator without overstretching things."

In as many years, Douglas added two more features to his noir repertoire — the first was *I Walk Alone* (1948), which also marked the first of his seven pictures with lifelong friend Burt Lancaster. In this feature, Douglas portrayed Noll "Dink" Turner, a nightclub owner whose wealth resulted, in part, from his betrayal of former partner Frankie Madison (Lancaster), recently released from

prison after a 14-year stretch for bootlegging. Refusing to honor the profit-sharing agreement he made with Frankie before his imprisonment ("How can you collect on a race when you don't hold a ticket?" he asks), the unscrupulous Dink has added insult to injury by employing Frankie's brother, Dave (Wendell Corey) as his accountant. Later, when Dave stands up to his boss, Dink has him killed, but he gets paid back in full when he is forced to confess to the crime by Frankie, and is gunned down by police while trying to escape.

After earning mention for his "fairly effective" performance in *I Walk Alone*, Douglas was seen in *My Dear Secretary* (1948), co-starring Laraine Day, and *A Letter to Three Wives* (1948), a first-rate drama helmed by Joseph Mankiewicz. He was then offered two projects simultaneously: *The Great Sinner* (1948), a big-budget MGM costumer starring Ava Gardner, Gregory Peck, and Ethel Barrymore, and an independent feature produced by Stanley Kramer, *Champion* (1948).

"I insisted on doing *Champion*," Douglas said in a 2001 interview in *The Hollywood Reporter*. "They thought I was a crazy New York actor. It was the first really physical role I had to play. It did well for me. Incidentally, *The Great Sinner* was a flop."

In *Champion*, Douglas' fourth film noir, the actor played Midge Kelly, a boxer who uses his talent and determination to fight his way to the top — managing, along the way, to alienate nearly all of those close to him, including his crippled brother, Connie (Arthur Kennedy), his long-suffering wife, Emma (Ruth Roman), and his loyal manager, Tommy Haley (Paul Stewart). In the film's climactic fight scene, Midge is mercilessly battered by his opponent, but summons the will for a final triumphant comeback. Although he is declared the winner, however, Midge has been severely injured, and later dies from a brain hemorrhage in his locker room, imagining that he is again striving for the championship bout. Douglas' outstanding performance catapulted him into stardom and *Champion* was a commercial and critical success; in one of Douglas' best notices, Alton Cook of the *New York World-Telegram* labeled him one of Hollywood's "most accomplished actors, full of the charm that can become an obvious veneer when he chooses, with a few slight gestures, to hint at the depths of a seething deviltry that lies just beneath." His memorable portrayal of Midge also earned Douglas his first Academy Award nomination for Best Actor (he lost to Broderick Crawford for *All the King's Men*), and a lucrative long-term contract with Warner Bros. studios.

In his first film for Warners, Douglas learned to play the trumpet for a starring role opposite his old friend Lauren Bacall in *Young Man with a Horn* (1950), garnering praise in the *New York Times* for "mak[ing] a pathetic and interesting person out of the sensitive genius." He followed this feature with starring roles in *The Glass Menagerie* (1950), based on the award-winning Tennessee Williams play, and *Along the Great Divide* (1951), his first western, then returned to the world of the film noir with back-to-back features, *The Big Carnival* (1951) and *Detective Story* (1951).

Titled *Ace in the Hole* in its initial release, *The Big Carnival* tells the story of Charles Tatum (Douglas), an unethical reporter whose view of his profession is expressed early in the film: "I didn't go to any college, but I know what makes a good story," he says. "Bad news sells best. Good news is no news." Determined to work his way back to the "big time" after being fired from 11 newspapers, Tatum is finally presented with the ideal opportunity — while working on a small New Mexico publication, he happens upon Leo Minosa (Richard Benedict), a curio shop merchant trapped in an old Indian cavern. After learning that rescuers can free Minosa within a day's time, Tatum works in concert with the corrupt local sheriff (Ray Teal) to effect an operation that will take at least a week, providing him the chance to write a daily series of widely read articles. Although the merchant's slovenly wife, Lorraine (Jan Sterling), planned to use the accident as a chance to leave her spouse, Tatum convinces her to stay, using her status as a "grieving spouse" to spice up his acclaimed stories. As time wears on, the rescue site takes on a circus-like atmosphere (hence, the title), Minosa contracts pneumonia and dies inside the cavern, and Lorraine stabs Tatum with a pair of scissors during a struggle. At the film's end, the conscious-stricken reporter plans to reveal his hoax in an article, but he dies from the stab wound before the story can be written.

Next, Douglas' sixth and final noir, *Detective Story*, focused on a 24-hour period in a New York police station and introduced a series of memorable characters, with Douglas' detective Jim McLeod, serving as the fulcrum. Characterized by an inflexible, highly principled disposition, McLeod's persona is revealed early on when he refuses to dismiss a minor embezzlement charge committed by Arthur Kindred (Craig Hill), a first-time offender: "When you're dealing with the criminal mind, softness is dangerous," McLeod cautions the man's employer. "It's never a first offense, it's just the first time they get caught." As the plot unfurls, the passage of a normal workday in McLeod's life is shattered when he discovers that his wife, Mary (Eleanor Parker), underwent an abortion several years before their marriage. Despite a sincere effort, McLeod's rigid sense of morality renders him incapable of forgiving Mary's misdeed ("I thought you were everything good and pure," he tells her); later, devastated by Mary's decision to leave him, McLeod recklessly places himself in the path of danger when a local hood grabs an officer's gun during an escape attempt. Mortally wounded by the gunman, McLeod experiences a final change of heart and orders the release of Kindred, reciting the Acts of Contrition as his co-workers look on in sorrow and pity.

Douglas received well-deserved acclaim for his final two films noirs; although audiences were perhaps put off by *The Big Carnival*'s unremittingly grim story, the critic for *Motion Picture Herald* wrote that Douglas "enacts the heel reporter ably, giving it color to balance its unsympathetic character," and in the *New York Times*, Bosley Crowther described the actor as "full of the arrogance and the cruelty of the desperately insecure." Similarly, following the release of *Detective Story*— one of the most highly praised films of the year — Douglas was labeled "superb" in the *New York Times* and "never before so convincing" by the critic for *The New Yorker*.

In 1951, Douglas broke his contract with Warner Bros. ("I like to stay free," he told a reporter), and appeared during the next several years in such features as RKO's *The Big Sky* (1952), an interesting western directed by Howard Hawks; MGM's *The Bad and the Beautiful* (1952), which earned the actor his second Academy Award nomination for Best Actor (he lost this time to Gary Cooper in *High Noon*); MGM's *The Story of Three Loves* (1953), for which he mastered and performed his own stunts as a trapeze artist; Columbia's *The Juggler* (1953), a top-notch drama directed by Edward Dmytryk and produced by Stanley Kramer; and Disney's *20,000 Leagues Under the Sea* (1954), a popular action-adventure saga co-starring James Mason, Paul Lukas, and Peter Lorre.

While he was becoming one of Hollywood's top stars, Douglas managed to find time for romance, but although he was linked with a variety of women, from stars to starlets, the actor later admitted that the years following his 1951 divorce were unhappy ones.

"What a waste! A different girl every night, a different night club. I can't begin to remember the names," Douglas said in a 1957 interview. "You show me a guy who runs around like that and I'll show you an unhappy one who's trying to prove something. These lotharios are pitiful and I was a shining example."

Douglas' days as a "lothario" were about to end, however. After a brief engagement to Pier Angeli — his co-star in *The Story of Three Loves*— Douglas began dating German-born Anne Buydens, who had served as the actor's publicist in Paris on his 1953 feature *Act of Love*. The two were married on May 29, 1954, and went on to add two more sons to Douglas' clan, Peter in 1955 and Eric in 1958. Nearly

a half-century later, the union remains one of Hollywood's most successful.

Meanwhile, Douglas was about to begin another chapter in his profession; in 1955, the actor started his own production company, named Bryna Productions after his mother.

"My mother used to say, 'Oh my son, he has his name in lights,'" Douglas said in a 1974 interview. "And I'd say, just wait mom, I'll put *your* name in lights.'"

During the next three decades, Douglas would produce a variety of films under the Bryna banner, beginning with his first release in 1955, *The Indian Fighter*, and including such features as *Paths of Glory* (1957), a gritty World War I drama directed by Stanley Kubrick; *The Vikings* (1958), a lavish Nordic saga co-starring Tony Curtis and Ernest Borgnine; *Strangers When We Meet* (1960), which focused on adultery among middle-class suburbanites; *Scalawag* (1973), a box-office flop that marked the actor's debut as a director; *Posse* (1975), Douglas' second and final directorial effort; and *Tough Guys* (1986), which featured Douglas and Burt Lancaster as a pair of aging crooks. His most notable Bryna production, however, was the 1960 epic *Spartacus*, which starred Douglas in the title role of the courageous gladiator. The film not only offered an impressive depiction of ancient Rome, but in hiring — and giving screen credit to— blacklisted writer Dalton Trumbo, Douglas played a significant role in ending the anti–Communism blacklist that had gripped Hollywood since the House Un-American Activities Committee hearings of the late 1940s.

"Dalton Trumbo wrote the script under the name 'Sam Jackson,'" Douglas explained in a 2001 interview in *The Hollywood Reporter*. "I got so annoyed with the hypocrisy of the studio. They knew he was writing it, but they looked the other way. They said, 'Don't have him come to the studio.' What was that? I said, 'To hell with it.' I called the gate and left a pass in the name of Dalton Trumbo. I'll never forget it. He came on the lot with tears in his eyes, and he said, 'Thanks for giving me my name back.' Later on, I took some heat for what we did.... But when you talk about lifetime achievements, that's what I am most proud of."

In addition to those produced by Bryna, one of Douglas' most acclaimed films was his 1956 feature *Lust for Life*, in which he portrayed the gifted but tortured artist Vincent Van Gogh. For his memorable portrayal, the actor earned a third Academy Award nomination for Best Actor; although the Oscar was won by Yul Brynner for *The King and I*, Douglas received a Golden Globe Award and the New York Film Critics Circle Award for his performance, and racked up widespread acclaim, including praise from co-star Anthony Quinn, who played French painter Paul Gauguin.

"I thought I was going to be lost in that picture because I didn't think anybody could compete with [Douglas'] performance — it was absolutely magnetic to see him working," Quinn said in a 1997 documentary. "I used to spend a lot of hours walking all over the hills and trying to find Gauguin for myself, and find the same dedication to Gauguin that he had for Vincent Van Gogh." (Ironically, Quinn, too, was nominated for an Academy Award for his performance in the picture — and won.)

During the 1960s and 1970s, Douglas continued to appear in several films a year, but by now, their quality had started to decline; his best features during this period included *Lonely Are the Brave* (1962), produced under the actor's Joel Productions banner (an offshoot of Bryna Productions), and considered by Douglas to be his favorite film; *Seven Days in May* (1964), another Joel Production, co-starring Hollywood veterans Burt Lancaster, Fredric March, Ava Gardner, and Edmond O'Brien; and *The War Wagon* (1967), a first-rate western with John Wayne, Howard Keel, and Robert Walker. He was less successful, however, in such pictures as *For Love or Money* (1963), a rare comedy effort in which he co-starred with Gig Young and Thelma Ritter; *The Arrangement* (1969), an Elia Kazan-directed flop that was notable primarily for the nude scenes of co-star Deborah Kerr;

Catch Me a Spy (1971), a colorless tale of espionage; and *Once is Not Enough* (1975), a turgid melodrama described by one critic as "a lot of people spending good money trying to be serious and making fools of themselves."

Between films, Douglas focused much of his efforts as a performer on the small screen, appearing in such made-for-television features as *Dr. Jekyll and Mr. Hyde* (1973), *The Moneychangers* (1976), *Victory at Entebbe* (1976), *Holocaust 2000* (1977), *Remembrance of Love* (1982), *Queenie* (1987), and *Inherit the Wind* (1988). He also earned Emmy nominations for three of his performances, a starring role in the made-for-television film, *Amos* (1986), and guest spots in two series, *Tales from the Crypt* (1992), and *Touched by an Angel* (2000).

To complement his film and television work, Douglas also returned to his roots on the stage, producing and starring in the 1963 Broadway production of *One Flew Over the Cuckoo's Nest*. Following the play's brief run, Douglas purchased the rights to the Ken Kesey novel on which it was based, but was unable to interest a studio in filming it. Ironically, more than a decade later, Douglas' son Michael proved to be successful in securing financing for the feature, but at age 59, Douglas was judged too old to play the lead character of McMurphy. The film went on to earn five Academy Awards, including Best Picture and Best Actor for Jack Nicholson, who played the part originally performed by Douglas.

"It was a very, very difficult moment, for myself and for Dad," Michael Douglas said later. "I think he understood it logically, but emotionally, it was a difficult one to accept."

In 1988, Douglas further expanded his realm of talent when he wrote his autobiography, *The Ragman's Son*. The candid and highly acclaimed best-seller would be only the first of a series of well-received non-fiction and fiction books authored by the actor, including *Dance with the Devil* (1990), *The Gift* (1992), *Climbing the Mountain: My Search for Meaning* (2000), *My Stroke of Luck* (2002), and two children's books. Amazingly, Douglas also found time for pursuits that were completely outside of the creative realm; in the early 1960s, the actor served as a self-financed goodwill ambassador on behalf of the United States Information Agency service and the State Department, traveling throughout Europe, South America, the Middle East, the Far East, and the USSR, and in 1982, at the request of Pakistan President Zia-ul Haq, the actor visited Red Cross hospitals and Afghan refugee camps. In addition, in recent years, Douglas and his wife, Anne, through their Douglas Foundation, rebuilt and re-equipped nearly 200 of the 450 playgrounds in the widespread Los Angeles Unified School District, personally attending the dedication of the new facilities. The Douglas Foundation has also built playgrounds and parks in Israel (with one of the most elaborate located in the Arab quarter of the Old City); funded an Alzheimer's wing at the Motion Picture House and Hospital, called "Harry's Haven"; and created the Anne Douglas Shelter for homeless women in downtown Los Angeles. Among their latest projects is the Kirk Douglas Theatre in Culver City, which will open in 2004.

For both his humanitarian and his creative efforts, Douglas has accumulated a wide variety of awards and honors, including the Presidential Medal of Freedom (awarded by President Jimmy Carter in 1981); the George Washington Carver Award for outstanding contributions to the arts, humanities, and betterment of racial relations; the Bill of Rights Award from the American Civil Liberties Union for his contribution toward breaking the blacklist; the Jefferson Award from the American Institute for Public Service; the Life Achievement Award from the American Film Institute; the Cecil B. DeMille Award from the Hollywood Foreign Press Association; an honorary Oscar for Lifetime Achievement from the Academy of Motion Picture Arts and Sciences; the Screen Actors Guild Award for Lifetime Achievement; a Kennedy Center honor; the Legion d'Honneur for services to France; the United Nations Ralph Bunche Award; and the 2001 Golden Bear Award at the Berlin Film Festival. He also received the

Presidential Medal of the Arts in April 2002, and has been cited on three occasions in the United States Congressional Record, for service to his country as a goodwill ambassador, for an article he wrote on discrimination, and for a *New York Times* article on abuse of the elderly.

Despite Kirk Douglas' phenomenal triumphs, both professional and personal, the actor's life has not been free from struggles, setbacks, and near-tragedies. In 1991, Douglas was involved in a life-threatening accident that resulted after the helicopter he was in collided in mid-air with a light plane shortly after take-off. Two other passengers were killed in the crash and Douglas sustained severe back injuries. Five years later, the actor suffered a stroke that initially rendered him unable to speak; with his typical fortitude — and the loving support of his wife, Anne — he underwent extensive rehabilitation and in 1999, appeared in his first feature film in five years, *Diamonds*, co-starring Dan Aykroyd and Lauren Bacall. The following year, Douglas was Emmy-nominated for his role in an episode of TV's *Touched by an Angel* entitled "The Bar Mitzvah" (which was penned by one of the rabbis with whom the actor had studied for his own second Bar Mitzvah at the age of 83).

Notwithstanding his triumphant "comeback" after his stroke, Douglas spoke frankly during a January 2002 promotional tour for his latest autobiography, *My Stroke of Luck*, sharing the realities of his health-related challenges and their frightening aftermath.

"When I first had my stroke, I went through suicidal impulses. An actor who can't talk! What would I do?" Douglas said. "I think almost everybody with a stroke has thoughts of suicide. It seemed hopeless with me at that age. At that time I was thinking I would never be able to talk and act."

In dealing with his stroke, Douglas developed an "Operator's Manual" for living life — his six recommendations include, "When things go bad, always remember it could be worse"; "Never lose your sense of humor. Laugh yourself, laugh with others";

and "Stem depression by thinking of, reaching out to, and helping others." As he celebrates life by following these "rules," Douglas continues to soar — in 2003, he was seen in *It Runs in the Family*, a dramatization of a dysfunctional family that co-starred his real-life son, Michael, and the third generation of acting Douglases, his grandson, Cameron. (In addition, Michael's mother, Diana, appears in the film as Douglas' wife.) And in 2004, the actor plans to renew his wedding vows with Anne on their 50th anniversary. Beyond these momentous events, only time will tell.

"It seems as if only now I really know who I am," Douglas said recently. "My strengths, my weaknesses, my jealousies— it's as if all of it has been boiling in a pot for all these years, and as it boils, it evaporates into steam, and all that's left in the pot in the end is your essence, the stuff you started out with in the very beginning."

Film Noir Filmography

The Strange Love of Martha Ivers. Director: Lewis Milestone. Producer: Hal B. Wallis. Running time: 115 minutes. Released by Paramount, July 24, 1946. Cast: Barbara Stanwyck, Van Heflin, Lizabeth Scott, Kirk Douglas, Judith Anderson, Roman Bohnen, Darryl Hickman, Janis Wilson, Ann Doran, Frank Orth, James Flavin, Mickey Kuhn, Charles D. Brown. Awards: Academy Award nomination for Best Original Screenplay (Jack Patrick).

Out of the Past. Director: Jacques Tourneur. Producer: Warren Duff. Running time: 96 minutes. Released by RKO, November 25, 1947. Cast: Robert Mitchum, Jane Greer, Kirk Douglas, Rhonda Fleming, Richard Webb, Steve Brodie, Virginia Huston, Paul Valentine, Dickie Moore, Ken Niles.

I Walk Alone. Director: Byron Haskin. Producer: Hal B. Wallis. Running time: 98 minutes. Released by Paramount, January 22, 1948. Cast: Burt Lancaster, Lizabeth Scott, Kirk Douglas, Wendell Corey, Kristine Miller, George Rigaud, Marc Lawrence, Mike Mazurki, Mickey Knox, Roger Neury.

Champion. Director: Mark Robson. Producer: Stanley Kramer. Running time: 99 minutes. Released by United Artists, January 1949. Cast: Kirk Douglas, Marilyn Maxwell, Arthur Kennedy, Paul Stewart, Ruth Roman, Lola Albright, Luis Van Rooten, John Day, Harry Shannon. Awards: Academy Award for Best Film Editing (Harry Gerstad). Academy Award nominations for: Best Actor (Kirk Douglas), Best Supporting Actor (Arthur Kennedy), Best Black and White Cinematography (Frank Planer), Best Score (Dimitri Tiomkin), Best Screenplay (Carl Foreman).

The Big Carnival. Director and Producer: Billy Wilder. Running time: 119 minutes. Released by Paramount, June 29, 1951. Cast: Kirk Douglas, Jan Sterling, Robert Arthur, Porter Hall, Frank Cady, Richard Benedict, Ray Teal, Lewis Martin, John Berkes, Frances Dominguez, Gene Evans, Frank Jacquet, Harry Harvey, Bob Bumps, Geraldine Hall, Richard Gaines, Paul D. Merrill, Stewart Kirk Clawson. Awards: Academy Award nomination for Best Original Screenplay (Lesser Samuels, Walter Newman).

Detective Story. Director and Producer: William Wyler. Running time: 105 minutes. Released by Paramount, November 6, 1951. Cast: Kirk Douglas, Eleanor Parker, William Bendix, Cathy O'Donnell, George Macready, Horace McMahon, Gladys George, Joseph Wiseman, Lee Grant, Gerald Mohr, Frank Faylen, Craig Hill, Michael Strong, Luis Van Rooten, Bert Freed, Warner Anderson, Grandon Rhodes, William "Bill" Phillips, Russell Evans. Awards: Academy Award nominations for Best Actress (Eleanor Parker), Best Supporting Actress (Lee Grant), Best Director (William Wyler), Best Original Screenplay (Philip Yordan, Robert Wyler).

References

"Actor Kirk Douglas' Wife Sues for Divorce." *Los Angeles Times*, January 6, 1950.
Ardmore, Jane. "Kirk Douglas— Actor, Communicator." *San Antonio Light*, September 12, 1982.
Berg, Louis. "Doubling in Brash." *Los Angeles Times*, July 12, 1953.
Biography of Kirk Douglas. 20th Century-Fox Studios, circa 1948.
Carter, Kelly. "Kirk Douglas, at 85, Feeling Lucky and in Love." *USA Today*, January 3, 2002.
"Douglas Gets U.S. Olympic Post, Sparks Fund Drive." *The Hollywood Reporter*, August 7, 1967.
Douglas, Kirk. *The Ragman's Son: An Autobiography*. New York, NY: Simon and Schuster, 1988.
Downey, Mike. "Riches from a Ragpicker's Son." *Los Angeles Times*, May 28, 2000.
Ebert, Roger. "Kirk Douglas at Large." *Esquire*, February 1970.
"Film Star Enters Spangler Inquiry." *Los Angeles Times*, October 14, 1949.
"Film Star Views Misery of Reds." *Hollywood Citizen-News*, May 13, 1966.

Fleming, Michael. "'Smack' Dab for Son, Dad." *Variety*, November 13, 2001.

Hopper, Hedda. "World Travels Add Polish to an Already-Bright Kirk." *Los Angeles Times*, May 30, 1954.

Hyams, Joe. "Kirk Douglas Learns the Hard Way." *New York Herald Tribune*, August 15, 1957.

"Iron Curtain Descends on Provocative Subjects, Kirk Douglas Found on Trek." *Variety*, May 13, 1966.

"Kirk Douglas Divorced; Wife Blames Rudeness." *Los Angeles Times*, February 9, 1950.

"Kirk Douglas' Father Dies." *Los Angeles Times*, April 13, 1954.

"Kirk Douglas Hits Back at Reds on Radio." *Los Angeles Mirror*, August 27, 1954.

"Kirk Douglas, Housing Aide to Speak at College." *Los Angeles Times*, March 26, 1967.

"Kirk Douglas Marries Parisienne at Las Vegas." *Los Angeles Times*, May 31, 1954.

"Kirk Douglas to Be Juror at Moscow Film Festival." *Boxoffice*, March 27, 1967.

"Kirk Douglas Sued by Wife After Long 'Marital Vacation.'" *Los Angeles Examiner*, January 6, 1950.

"Kirk Douglas to Direct Olympics Fundraising." *Variety*, August 7, 1967.

Knickerbocker, Cholly. "Is It Love for Irene and Kirk?" *Los Angeles Examiner*, May 26, 1950.

"Lifetime Achievement: Kirk Douglas." *The Hollywood Reporter*, February 6, 2001.

Mann, Roderick. "Kirk Douglas and the Privileges of Stardom." *Los Angeles Times*, April 18, 1982.

Maynard, John. "Man on a Mountaintop." *Motion Picture*, May 1957.

_____. "What Can Money Buy?" *Photoplay*, November 1956.

"Memories of the Blacklist." *Variety*, February 5, 2001.

Mosby, Aline. "Comes Home to House He Never Saw Before." *Hollywood Citizen-News*, March 22, 1954.

"Movie Star Hits Slurs, Russ Lies." *Beverly Hills Newslife*, August 26, 1954.

"Nine Are Honored for Public Service." *The New York Times*, July 20, 1983.

Oppenheimer, Peer J. "Kirk Douglas: Has Message, Will Travel." *Hollywood Citizen-News*, September 11, 1966.

Parsons, Louella O. "Kirk Douglas." *Los Angeles Examiner*, November 2, 1952.

_____. "Kirk Douglas and Wife Part; Actor Moves to Apartment." *Los Angeles Examiner*, February 8, 1949.

_____. "Kirk Douglas Wed to Anne Buydens in Las Vegas Rites." *Los Angeles Examiner*, May 31, 1954.

Pollock, Louis. "A Young Man's Fancy." *Redbook*, July 1950.

Sager, Mike. "What I've Learned: Kirk Douglas." *Esquire*, April 2001.

Sloan, Lloyd L. "Kirk Douglas Has Split Personality Problems." *Hollywood Citizen-News*, February 18, 1949.

Thomas, Bob. "Douglas Conquers Despair in 'Stroke of Luck' Memoir." *Chicago Sun-Times*, January 3, 2002.

Thomas, Tony. *The Films of Kirk Douglas*. New York, NY: Carol Publishing Group, 1991.

Thompson, Howard. "Kirk Douglas Reflects on Rough Road to Success Both Here and Abroad." *The New York Times*, circa February 1954.

Trachtenbert, J.A. "Kirk Douglas: TV Is Where the Action Is." *W*, December 31, 1982.

Williams, Jeannie. "3 Generations of Douglases get 'Few Good Years' Together. *Chicago Sun-Times*, May 13, 2002.

Documentary

"Kirk Douglas: A Lust for Life." Produced by ABC News Productions for A&E Network. Copyright 1997.

HOWARD DUFF

"I can't even look at my own kid anymore. I can't look in the mirror without gagging."— Howard Duff in *Private Hell 36* (1954)

Ruggedly handsome with an appealing smile, a devilish glint in his eye, and bushy, expressive brows, Howard Duff enjoyed a successful and steady career in films and television, but never quite reached the ranks of stardom. More often than not, his life in front of the camera was overshadowed by his stormy marriage to film star Ida Lupino and his highly publicized romances with a string of actresses including Yvonne DeCarlo and Ava

Gardner. His personal life aside, Duff was seen to good advantage in five notable examples of the film noir era: *Brute Force* (1947), *The Naked City* (1948), *Shakedown* (1950), *Private Hell 36* (1954), and *While the City Sleeps* (1956).

Howard Duff was born in Bremerton, Washington, on November 24, 1913, a day he once described as "so foggy that even the birds were walking." His family moved to nearby Seattle when Duff was a child, and the young man's initial interest in acting was sparked while attending Roosevelt High School there. After taking a drama course because he "thought it would require little study," Duff was encouraged by a teacher to continue acting, and he appeared in a number of school productions, including the lead in *Trelawney of the Wells*. Following his graduation, Duff joined the Seattle Repertory Company, performing there three nights a week for five years.

"The Seattle Repertory Company was my college education," Duff said in a 1978 interview. "I was very lucky to have been a part of it, because wherever our director led, we followed, and he led us into some pretty serious drama."

To make ends meet while working with the repertory company, Duff got a job as an assistant window trimmer at the Bon Marche Department Store, but he was fired when he refused to give up his theater activities to work nights at the store. Instead, he signed on as staff announcer at radio station KOMO, which permitted him to continue performing with the Seattle Repertory Players. During this time, he also worked with the Washington State Theater and appeared in plays without salary on a small local radio station each Sunday.

In the late 1930s, Duff moved to San Francisco, where he landed the starring role in a popular children's radio series, *The Phantom Pilot*. He remained with the program for two years, then was drafted into the United States Army to serve in World War II. (At the induction center, Duff met the man who would become his lifelong friend and agent, Mike Meshekoff.) Attached to the Armed Forces

Radio Service, Duff served time in Iwo Jima, Saipan, and Guam, and was discharged as a staff sergeant five years later. Heading for Hollywood after his release, he performed with a number of radio serials before landing the title role in *The Adventures of Sam Spade*. The series first aired as a summer replacement show in July 1946 and Duff remained in the popular starring role until 1950. According to the show's producer Bill Spier, Duff was cast in the part because he possessed all of the characteristics attributed to the hard-boiled detective.

"We didn't want our man to be an armchair detective. He had to be a real guy; and the less he sounded like an actor, the better. Sam, being human, was subject to making many mistakes. But he had to have an honest integrity as well as candor," Spier told columnist Hedda Hopper. "That was the way we conceived the character, and Howard seemed to have all those qualifications. He's completely without affectation. The air of reality which he brings ... makes him seem like anybody's son or husband. I think that's the reason for his wide appeal."

In 1946, between appearances on *Sam Spade*, Duff landed his first professional stage role in *Birthday*, directed by Jules Dassin. Later that year, when Dassin was tapped by producer Mark Hellinger to direct his upcoming Universal feature, *Brute Force*, Duff was cast in a featured role, marking his film debut and his entry into the world of film noir.

A brutally realistic drama, *Brute Force* is set in a men's prison where the inmates are endlessly brutalized by a sadistic guard, Capt. Munsey (Hume Cronyn), and plan a prison break to escape their inhumane treatment. Focusing on the five inmates of one cell, the film shows the reminisces of each man, including Soldier (Duff), who dreams of returning to the small town in Italy where he met his wife, Gina, played by Yvonne DeCarlo. (A flashback reveals that Soldier is the inmate who is least deserving of his imprisonment; during the war, Soldier was hunted down by military police while smuggling food to Gina and her father. When Gina's father refused to

cover for Soldier, Gina shot and killed him, and Soldier took the blame, resulting in his lengthy jail term and his permanent estrangement from his beloved.) When Munsey learns of the planned break, the inmates revolt and the guard meets a brutal end when he is thrown from a tower into a swarm of hate-filled inmates. Hailed as "tremendously vivid" after its release, *Brute Force* earned mostly good reviews for Duff; although Harrison Carroll wrote in the *Los Angeles Evening Herald Express* that the actor "doesn't have enough to do here really to prove himself," the *Los Angeles Times*' Philip K. Scheuer included Duff in his praise of several actors who provided "striking individual support," and he was singled out by Jack D. Grant of *The Hollywood Reporter*, who wrote: "Howard Duff, of *Sam Spade* radio fame, does a sharp job of a sensitive lad."

During the shooting of *Brute Force*, Duff became involved in a highly publicized relationship with his on-screen wife, DeCarlo, and by the end of production, the two were engaged. But in her 1987 autobiography, De-Carlo wrote: "All was well, except that with

the little diamond ring on the third finger I began to get that old trapped feeling. When the press pressured me about the marriage date, I hedged as best I could." Before long, the relationship came to an unceremonious end.

Meanwhile, signing a contract with Universal, Duff was next seen in *All My Sons* (1948), a riveting story about a small-town arms manufacturer who knowingly sends defective parts to the Army Air Force, and Mark Hellinger's *The Naked City* (1948), the actor's second film noir. Narrated by Hellinger in his last film before his unexpected death, this feature focuses on a police investigation of the murder of a young woman; Duff portrayed Frank Niles, a friend of the victim who baffles detectives when he offers a series of easily exposed lies to explain his whereabouts: "Mr. Niles, I've been 38 years on the force," says the chief detective, Dan Muldoon (Barry Fitzgerald), "but in a lifetime of interrogating and investigating, you are probably the biggest and most willing liar I ever met." It is later revealed that Niles and the dead girl were part of a jewel theft ring, along with former wrestler Willie Garzah (Ted De Corsia), who turns out to be the killer. After a harrowing chase across New York's Williamsburg bridge, Garzah is shot by police and falls from a tower to his death. In his second-billed role as the mendacious brains of the gang, Duff turned in a well-received performance, and was noticed by several reviewers, including the *New York Times*' Bosley Crowther, who wrote: "Several [of the actors] do pretty good jobs of playing 'types,' especially Howard Duff as a 'con' man."

After such features as *Johnny Stool Pigeon* (1949), where he played a fearless federal agent, and *Red Canyon* (1949), his first western, Duff returned to the realm of film noir in what was arguably his best feature from the era, *Shakedown* (1950). Here, Duff played newspaper photographer Jack Early, described by a critic as "one of the season's most thorough-going heels," whose ambition leads him to such unprincipled acts as instructing an accident victim to stick his head out the window of a sinking car so that Early can shoot his photograph. ("I have a way of just happening to pass by at important moments and taking pictures," Early later explains.) After befriending mobster Nick Palmer (Brian Donlevy), Early garners information about an upcoming bank heist masterminded by Palmer's nemesis, Harry Coulton (Lawrence Tierney), and takes a series of incriminating shots. Early blackmails Coulton with the negative, and when Coulton exacts revenge on Palmer by blowing up his car, Early is once again on the scene, earning nationwide fame with a picture of the mobster's death. After falling for Palmer's widow, Early uses photos of the mobster rigging Palmer's car to force Coulton into aiding him in a heist at a charity ball where he is slated to serve as the official photographer. Coulton reluctantly agrees, but reveals Early's prior knowledge of Palmer's death to his widow, who confronts the photographer at gunpoint at the ball. Early tries to flee, but he is gunned down by Coulton and, as his last act before he dies, he snaps a photo of his killer. In the final scene, as his editor prepares to run Early's final photograph, a reporter remarks, "It's a great picture. And I'll bet for the first time, he really just happened to be passing by."

Although Darr Smith of the *Los Angeles Daily News* opined that Duff "doesn't seem to be thoroughly happy with or at home in what he is asked to do in *Shakedown*," the actor earned mostly good reviews for his nefarious role; in the *Hollywood Citizen-News*, Margaret Harford termed him "thoroughly despicable," and the critic for the *Los Angeles Evening Herald Examiner* wrote: "Duff makes an attractive and relatively understandable personality out of this sinister hero, fitting his rugged screen appeal to the type and getting in some interesting touches where the speed of the action permits."

Off-screen, Duff's personal escapades were by now becoming popular fodder for the press, with newspapers frequently accounting his romances with such actresses as Piper Laurie, Ava Gardner, and Marta Toren, who later described the actor as "the most natural man I've ever gone with ... who's not interested in impressing anyone." And in April 1949, Duff was in the news following an altercation that took place while he was on a date with Gardner at Ciro's nightclub on the Sunset Strip. According to Duff's agent, Mike Meshekoff, the dinner check had just been paid when a stranger "let fly with a haymaker at Howard and then ran like a turkey."

"Duff and I can't figure out what he had in mind," Meshekoff told reporters. "Haven't seen him since."

The actor's professional and personal lives merged in 1950, when he starred opposite Ida Lupino in the well-done thriller, *Woman in Hiding.* (Duff wasn't the first choice for the role of the ex-soldier Keith Ramsey — the part was originally intended for actor Ronald Reagan, who broke his leg in a charity baseball game and was unable to appear in the film.) Upon their initial meeting, Lupino claimed that she "couldn't stand" Duff, who rejoined that the strong-willed actress "scared" him. Before long, however, the two were an item, despite the fact that Lupino was married at the time to Columbia Studios executive Collier Young. On October 20, 1951, Duff and Lupino were married, just one day following her divorce from Young. Six months later, on April 23, 1952, Lupino gave birth to the couple's only child, Bridget Mirella, with Collier Young and his soon-to-be wife, Joan Fontaine, serving as the child's godparents.

Meanwhile, also in 1950, Duff's budding career reached a stumbling block when he found himself embroiled in the Communism hunt that was sweeping Hollywood. Several years earlier, Duff had signed a "friend of the court" petition for the 10 directors and screenwriters known as the Hollywood Ten, who were jailed for contempt of Congress for refusing to answer questions about Communism in the motion picture industry. Because of this demonstration of support, Duff found himself included in the publication *Red Channels*, which identified more than 100 writers, directors, and performers who were suspected of Communist affiliations.

"We didn't take [*Red Channels*] very

seriously when it came out. That shows you how silly we were. The networks took it very seriously. It destroyed — really destroyed — a lot of people," Duff said in the early 1980s. "It was crazy. I was never a Communist or anything like that. I was sort of a half-assed liberal. The only thing I could have been cited for was lack of intelligence."

After the release of *Red Channels*, Duff was removed from the cast of *Sam Spade* and replaced by Steve Dunne. He was unable to find work in radio for the next two years, and his screen appearances dwindled to a handful of pictures, including *The Lady From Texas* (1951), in which he portrayed a drifter who saves the ranch of a Civil War widow, and *Models, Inc.* (1952), a bland drama where he was third-billed as a steel mill worker. Following the latter film, Duff requested a release from his Universal contract.

"There are two kinds of careers in Hollywood. One is the type where you do everything you are asked to do by the studio," Duff told *Los Angeles Daily News* columnist Darr Smih. "The other is sort of the Monty Clift type career where you only do what you want to do. Independent."

As a freelancer, Duff was seen in a series of run-of-the-mill features, including *Spaceways* (1953), a British science fictioner; *Roar of the Crowd* (1953), in which he starred as a race car driver; *Jennifer* (1953), a gloomy crime drama co-starring wife Ida Lupino; and *Tanganyika* (1954), a jungle adventure focusing on a manhunt for an escaped killer. The best of his features during this period came in the form of *Private Hell 36* (1954), his fourth film noir. In this film, which reteamed Duff with Lupino, the actor played Jack Farnham, an upstanding policeman and family man who, along with his partner, Cal Bruner (Steve Cochran), finds a cache of stolen money inside a wrecked automobile. Although Bruner comes up with a scheme to keep a portion of the money, Farnham wants to turn it over to their superior, telling his partner, "Sure, I thought of what I could do with all that dough. But wanting it and taking it are two different things." Bruner ultimately persuades Farnham

to pocket the cash by noting the benefits the money could provide for his wife and small child, but later, when a mysterious caller demands the money's return, Farnham overrides his partner and insists on heeding the man's request. In the film's climax, when the two officers show up at the planned meeting place, Bruner shoots Farnham in the back and is, in turn, plugged by police, who knew all along of their crime. Although his role was less showy than that of co-star Cochran, Duff earned mention in *Variety* for his "suitable performance."

Away from the camera, Duff's domestic life was on shaky ground. In July 1953, he and Ida Lupino split for the first time, with the actress telling reporters that she was "just fed up ... I stood on my head to make this marriage work, and it was just no good. I don't believe Howard likes being married." The couple reconciled a month later, but they separated again in November 1954; Hollywood insiders speculated that the couple's conflict stemmed from Lupino's burgeoning career as a film director.

"We didn't have any fight," Lupino told columnist Louella Parsons. "Howard has been acting very strange lately. He just told me that marriage wasn't for him and I'm afraid this is final. I tried everything but it doesn't seem any use."

Despite the finality of Lupino's words, the couple once again reunited, and Duff's screen career continued with appearances in *The Broken Star* (1955), in which he was featured as a deputy marshal who crosses over to the wrong side of the law; *Women's Prison* (1955), where he starred with Lupino as the caring doctor of a women's institution; *Blackjack Ketchum, Desperado* (1956), with Duff in the title role of a reformed gunslinger; and *While the City Sleeps* (1956), the last of his films noirs. This interesting, multifaceted feature focused on the efforts of four employees of a media conglomerate to track down a criminal known as "The Lipstick Killer," thereby winning the newly created position of executive director of the corporation. Among those vying for the post are newspaper editor

John Day Griffith (Thomas Mitchell), television anchor Edward Mobley (Dana Andrews), and local reporter Mildred Donner (Ida Lupino). Using his fiancée as bait, Edward eventually catches the killer, but gives the scoop to Griffith, who is awarded the coveted job. As Lt. Burt Kaufman, a police detective investigating the case, Duff had relatively little to do here, and was overlooked by most critics. The film was a hit at the box office, however, and earned widespread praise, with the reviewer from *Variety* writing: "The old-fashioned 'stop the presses' newspaper yarn has been updated with intelligence and considerable authenticity, and further brightened with crisp dialog from the pen of Casey Robinson."

In 1957, Duff and Lupino appeared together on the small screen on an episode of *The Lucy-Desi Comedy Hour*, and later that year they starred in their own television series, *Mr. Adams and Eve*, produced by Lupino's ex-husband, Collier Young. The comedy series mirrored the couple's real life, focusing on husband and wife film stars who battle studios, agents, and each other. After 68 episodes, the series was cancelled, but following appearances in guest spots on such programs as *Target*, *Bonanza*, and *The Twilight Zone*, Duff returned to series television in 1960 for *Dante*, in which he played the title role of an ex-gambler who runs a San Francisco nightspot. The pilot episode of the adventure series was directed by Lupino, and Duff later stated that he would "just as soon she didn't direct any more of his shows."

"Not that she isn't a good director," Duff told *Los Angeles Examiner* columnist Charles Denton. "She's really great. And we worked all right together, too. We didn't have any problems, but I want to keep it that way. I think a man and wife blow up a little quicker at each other than a couple of people who don't know each other so well, don't you?"

Dante was cancelled after one season and during the next several years, Duff divided his time between such feature films as *Boys' Night Out* (1962), a comedy starring Kim Novak and James Garner, and a series of television appearances on shows including *Com-*

bat!, *The Virginian*, *The Rogues*, *I Spy*, and *Batman*, in which he appeared with Lupino. (Soon after their performance on the campy comic book series, Duff and Lupino separated again. This time, the split was for good, but the couple would not divorce until nearly 20 years later, in 1983.) Duff also went behind the camera, serving as director for the half-hour comedy series, *Camp Runamuck*, which depicted the lively hijinks at a pair of summer camps.

"What a shattering experience," Duff said in a 1981 *TV Guide* interview. "I did it in the middle of a heat wave, knocking myself out trying to get something out of those kids. Not to mention a lot of grown-up kids."

After the cancellation of *Camp Runamuck* in 1966, Duff landed the role of Detective Sam Stone in *Felony Squad*, a popular television crime drama that remained on the air until January 1969. During the run of the show, Duff made a rare screen appearance in *Panic in the City* (1967), a tiresome thriller in which he played a federal agent investigating the murder of a nuclear scientist. After *Felony Squad* left the air, the actor continued to focus most of his energies on the small screen, appearing in such television movies as *In Search of America* (1970), *A Little Game* (1971), *The Heist* (1972), *Snatched* (1973), *In the Glitter Palace* (1977), *Ski Lift to Death* (1978), and *Battered* (1978). He was also seen in several summer stock productions, including *Under the Yum Yum Tree* and *Come Blow Your Horn*, and was a frequent guest on some of television's most highly rated series, including *Alias Smith and Jones*, *Medical Center*, *Kung Fu*, *The Streets of San Francisco*, and *The Rockford Files*.

After an absence from the big screen of nearly a decade, Duff returned to feature films for a small part in *The Late Show* (1977), starring Art Carney and Lily Tomlin. The following year, he portrayed an alcoholic doctor in Robert Altman's *The Wedding* (1978), joining a huge cast that included Lillian Gish, Carol Burnett, Viveca Lindfors, Dennis Franz, Lauren Hutton, Geraldine Chaplin, Paul Dooley, Mia Farrow, and Desi Arnaz, Jr. Next, he earned praise for his portrayal of Dustin Hoffman's pragmatic attorney in the Academy Award–winning drama *Kramer vs. Kramer* (1979).

"Now that I'm older, I'm getting the more interesting parts," Duff said in 1980. "That's the only virtue I can see in getting a little older. I love those roles. I've been kind of lucky lately."

Relishing his "second" career as a character actor, Duff starred during the 1981-82 television season in *Flamingo Road*, based on the 1949 film of the same title. In the series, Duff played Sheriff Titus Semple (portrayed in the screen version by Sydney Greenstreet). Throughout the remainder of the decade, he was a frequent presence on the small screen, appearing in the popular miniseries *East of Eden* (1981) and *War and Remembrance* (1989); in such television movies as *This Girl for Hire* (1983), *Love on the Run* (1985), *Roses are for the Rich* (1987), and *Settle the Score* (1989); in recurring roles on the popular nighttime soapers *Knots Landing* and *Dallas*; and in guest spots on series including *Charlie's Angels, St. Elsewhere, Murder, She Wrote, Scarecrow and Mrs. King, Simon and Simon*, and *The Golden Girls*. On the silver screen, he found time to appear in *No Way Out* (1987), a stylish thriller that was a remake of the 1948 film noir, *The Big Clock*; and *Monster in the Closet* (1987), a fairly amusing parody of the horror and science fiction features of the 1950s.

Away from his prolific performing projects, Duff had finally managed to achieve an even keel in his personal life. Shortly after his 1983 divorce from Ida Lupino, the actor married Judy Jenkinson, an aspiring stage producer he met while playing summer stock in Connecticut. The couple remained together until Duff's death, which came on July 8, 1990, following a heart attack at his Santa Barbara home. His death, at age 76, came just a day after Duff took part in a local telethon to raise money for victims of a devastating fire in Santa Barbara. The following year, *Too Much Sun* (1991), Duff's final feature film, was released. In it, he played a dying billionaire.

Talented and dependable, Howard Duff always loved the career of acting, and never lost his enthusiasm for his chosen profession. His dedication toward performing was best summed up by his longtime friend and agent, Mike Meshekoff.

"Howard's whole world," Meshekoff once said, "centers around one thing — his tremendous compulsion to act."

Film Noir Filmography

Brute Force. Director: Director: Jules Dassin. Producer: Mark Hellinger. Running time: 95 minutes. Released by Universal-International, June 6, 1947. Cast: Burt Lancaster, Hume Cronyn, Charles Bickford, Yvonne DeCarlo, Ann Blyth, Ella Raines, Anita Colby, Sam Levene, Howard Duff, Art Smith, Roman Bohnen, John Hoyt, Richard Gaines, Frank Puglia, Jeff Corey, Vince Barnett, James Bell, Jack Overman, Whit Bissell, Sir Lancelot, Ray Teal, Jay C. Flippen, James O'Rear, Howland Chamberlain, Kenneth Patterson, Crane Whitley, Charles McGraw, John Harmon, Gene Stutenroth, Wally Rose, Carl Rhodes, Guy Beach, Edmund Cobb, Tom Steele.

The Naked City. Director: Jules Dassin. Producer: Mark Hellinger. Running time: 96 minutes. Released by Universal-International, March 4, 1948. Cast: Barry Fitzgerald, Howard Duff, Dorothy Hart, Don Taylor, Ted De Corsia, House Jameson, Anne Sargent, Adelaide Klein, Grover Burgess, Tom Pedi, Enid Markey, Frank Conroy, Mark Hellinger. Awards: Academy Awards for Best Black and White Cinematography (William H. Daniels), Best Film Editing (Paul Weatherwax). Academy Award nomination for Best Motion Picture Story (Malvin Wald).

Shakedown. Director: Joe Pevney. Producer: Ted Richmond. Running time: 80 minutes. Released by Universal-International, September 23, 1950. Cast: Howard Duff, Brian Donlevy, Peggy Dow, Lawrence Tierney, Bruce Bennett, Anne Vernon, Stapleton Kent, Peter Virgo, Charles Sherlock.

Private Hell 36. Director: Don Siegel. Producer: Collier Young. Running time: 81 minutes. Released by Filmmakers, September 3, 1954. Cast: Ida Lupino, Steve Cochran, Howard Duff, Dean Jagger, Dorothy Malone, Bridget Duff.

While the City Sleeps. Director: Fritz Lang. Producer: Bert Friedlob. Running time: 99 minutes. Released by RKO, May 16, 1956. Cast: Dana Andrews, Rhonda Fleming, George Sanders, Howard Duff, Thomas Mitchell, Vincent Price, Sally

Forrest, John Barrymore, Jr., James Craig, Ida Lupino, Robert Warwick, Ralph Peters, Vladimir Sokoloff, Mae Marsh, Sandy White.

References

"Actor Howard Duff, Radio's Sam Spade." *Newsday*, July 10, 1990.

Anderson, Nancy. "Actor Duff Laxes Villain Role." *The (Warren, Ohio) Tribune Chronicle*, March 17, 1978.

Bender, Harold. "Gambling for Ratings." *New York Journal-American*, August 21, 1960.

Buck, Jerry. "The Evil One." *Los Angeles Herald Examiner TV Weekly*, September 7, 1980.

Denton, Charles. "Duff Sore About Actors' Anxieties." *Los Angeles Examiner*, October 3, 1960.

"Duff Service." *Variety*, July 12, 1990.

Folkart, Burt A. "Howard Duff; Starred in Radio, TV, Films." *Los Angeles Times*, July 10, 1990.

Hopper, Hedda. "Everybody Likes Duff!" *Chicago Sunday Tribune*, April 1, 1951.

"Howard Duff: 'Adventures of Sam Spade.'" CBS Biographical Service, Columbia Broadcasting System, October 25, 1946.

"Howard Duff Obtains His Release From U-I." *The Hollywood Reporter*, circa 1952.

"Howard Duff, 76; Hard-Boiled Actor In Movies and TV." *New York Times*, July 10, 1990.

Humphrey, Hal. "Duff's Latest Role Classified a Felony." *Los Angeles Times*, January 3, 1967.

"Ida, Howard Back Tomorrow." *Hollywood Citizen-News*, October 22, 1951.

"Ida Lupino Becomes Bride of Howard Duff." *Los Angeles Times*, October 22, 1951.

"Ida Lupino, Duff Through, She Asserts." *Los Angeles Examiner*, November 26, 1953.

"Ida Lupino, Howard Duff, Living Apart." *Los Angeles Times*, November 24, 1953.

Lewis, Dan. "Duff Chose His Best Bad Guy Part." *Los Angeles Daily News TV Weekly*, February 8–14, 1981.

Meshekoff, Mike. "I Live with the Lug." *Motion Picture Magazine*, June 1951.

Minoff, Philip. "Non-Private Lives?" *Cue*, January 1957.

O'Hallaren, Bill. "How Bad Can He Get?" *TV Guide*, September 5, 1981.

Parsons, Louella O. "Ida Lupino Becomes Bride of Actor Howard Duff." *Los Angeles Examiner*, October 22, 1951.

_____. "'This Time He Means It,' Says Actress." *Los Angeles Times*, July 29, 1953.

Raddatz, Leslie. "The Howard Duff Syndrome." *TV Guide*, June 3, 1967.

Sloan, Lloyd L. "Sam Spade Horrified by Duff's Screen Capers." *Hollywood Citizen-News*, circa 1950.

Smith, Cecil. "Howard Duff Discovers Villainy." *Los Angeles Times*, June 1, 1981.

Smith, Darr. "Howard Duff." *Los Angeles Daily News*, November 28, 1952.

"Stranger Aims 'Sunday' Punch at Howard Duff." *Los Angeles Times*, April 12, 1949.

Van Horne, Harriet. "'Lucy's Vacation' Takes Believing." *New York World Telegram*, June 9, 1954.

DAN DURYEA

"You're not talkin' to a cluck, Charlie. You're talkin' to a guy who knows all the angles. I got everything all planned out. Very, very carefully." — Dan Duryea in *Manhandled* (1949)

When he wasn't on the big screen, Dan Duryea was the diametric opposite of his celluloid image. Although he played the consummate cinema "stinker" to perfection, in reality, the actor was educated at an Ivy League university, remained married for 35 years to the same woman, was active in the PTA at his sons' school, and spent his free time not planning the ideal caper or knocking around flashy dames, but creating oil paintings, cultivating his garden, or building sailboats in the backyard.

"I make a great effort to be extra pleasant the first time I meet anybody," Duryea once said. "People approach an introduction to me with their mental dukes up. If I'm lucky, I can overcome the aversion they've already built up."

The shifty-eyed actor with the slicked back hair and the fiendish smirk was featured in such Hollywood classics as *The Little Foxes* (1941), *Pride of the Yankees* (1942), and *None but the Lonely Heart* (1944), and later found a successful second career on the small screen, but it was in the era of film noir that Duryea truly made his memorable mark, with starring turns in a total of 10 features: *The Woman in the Window* (1945), *Ministry of Fear* (1945), *Scarlet Street* (1945), *Black Angel* (1946), *Criss Cross* (1949), *Manhandled* (1949), *Too Late for Tears* (1949), *World for Ransom* (1954), *Storm Fear* (1956), and *The Burglar* (1957).

The only son of Mabel Hoffman and textile salesman Richard Hewlett Duryea, Daniel Edwin Duryea was born on January 23, 1907, in the New York suburb of White Plains. He first showed an affinity for acting while participating in the drama club at White Plains High School, and later, at Cornell University where, as an English major, he succeeded fellow thespian Franchot Tone as president of the Dramatic Club. Despite his leaning towards the arts, however, Duryea allowed his persuasive parents to steer him toward a career in advertising.

"It was pointed out to me that the average income of an Equity actor in New York was less than $400 a year," Duryea said. "Even the most unsuccessful ad salesman made twice that much, so the choice was easy."

Duryea landed a job selling advertising space in small daily and weekly newspapers for N.W. Ayer, commuting daily from his White Plains home to the company's office in New York City. During one day's commute, he was offered a ride from the station by a fellow passenger who was being picked up his daughter, Helen Bryan. When Duryea met the young woman, it was virtually love at first sight — the two were married on April 15, 1932, and later had two sons, Peter Lane in 1939, and Richard William in 1942. They would remain together until Helen's death in 1967.

Although it appeared that Duryea was building a solid career in the advertising field, fate stepped in when he suffered a mild heart attack in 1934 while playing basketball at a picnic. Encouraged by doctors to choose a less stressful job, Duryea immediately hit upon the perfect profession — acting. While his wife worked for $5 a day in a local dress shop, Duryea found small roles in summer stock and made his Broadway debut in 1935 in *Dead End*, written by a former Cornell classmate, Sidney Kingsley. For 85 weeks, Duryea was seen in several walk-ons in the successful production, but toward the end of the run, he was given the lead role of Gimpty, an unemployed architect.

After the close of *Dead End*, Duryea returned to work in summer stock, but he wouldn't be there for long. While performing in *Ned McCobb's Daughter* in Westport, Connecticut, he caught the eye of Elizabeth Ginty, who had recently written a comedy about Jesse James, titled *Missouri Legend*. Ginty urged the play's producer to cast Duryea in the production and the actor joined a stellar company that included Dean Jagger, Dorothy Gish, Jose Ferrer, Karl Malden, and Mildred Natwick. Although the play ran for only six weeks, Duryea's performance led to his first big break — when *Missouri Legend* closed, the actor was promptly hired for the part of Leo Hubbard in Lillian Hellman's *The Little Foxes*, starring Tallulah Bankhead. Duryea was a sensation as the dim-witted, devilishly lazy Leo, remaining with the production throughout its two-year Broadway run and nationwide tour. When producer Sam Goldwyn bought the rights to the screen version of the film, Duryea was hired to reprise his role and made his big-screen debut in the feature in 1941. Later that year, Goldwyn cast Duryea in another hit film, the Barbara Stanwyck starrer *Ball of Fire* (1941), in which he played a gangster with the colorful name of Duke Pastrami.

During the next few years, Duryea was seen portraying a cynical sportswriter in Goldwyn's blockbuster *Pride of the Yankees* (1942), which starred Gary Cooper as baseball legend Lou Gehrig; a jealous fiancé in 20th Century-Fox's romantic comedy, *The Other Woman* (1942); a member of Humphrey Bogart's tank crew in Columbia's rousing wartime adventure, *Sahara* (1943); a lowly outcast on London's East End in *None but the Lonely Heart*

(1944); and a spoiled, third-generation member of an elite New York clan in *Mrs. Parkington* (1944). He also entered the realm of film noir during this period, with featured roles in three Fritz Lang-directed features, *The Woman in the Window* (1945), *Ministry of Fear* (1945), and *Scarlet Street* (1945).

Duryea's first noir, *The Woman in the Window*, begins with a chance encounter between stodgy college professor Richard Wanley (Edward G. Robinson) and a beautiful dark-haired woman, Alice (Joan Bennett), whose portrait he'd admired in an art gallery window. Invited to Alice's home for a drink, Wanley's pleasant evening is shattered with the arrival of the woman's wealthy financier boyfriend and, after a scuffle, Wanley fatally stabs the man with a pair of scissors. The financier's bodyguard, Heidt (Duryea), soon enters the picture, attempting to extort money from the pair and, unable to face the scandal, Wanley plans to commit suicide. Meanwhile, Heidt dies in a shootout with police, who find the financier's gold watch on his body and assume that he is the killer. Alice telephones Wanley to share this latest development, but the professor has swallowed poison and is unable to answer the call. Finally, in one of the biggest letdowns in film noir, the feature concludes with Wanley being awakened by an employee of his men's club and his realization that the entire incident was only a dream. After the film's release, Duryea was labeled "outstanding" by the critic for *Variety*, and was singled out by Thomas Pryor, who wrote in the *New York Times* that Duryea's performance was "so good you feel like hissing him."

The actor's second noir of the year, *Ministry of Fear*, was set in World War II London and centered on the interconnecting lives of a variety of characters, including Stephen Neale (Ray Milland), recently released from prison after the mercy killing of his wife; Carla Hilfe (Marjorie Reynolds), an Austrian refugee who falls in love with Stephen; Carla's duplicitous brother, Willi (Carl Esmond); Mr. Rennit (Erskine Sanford), a liquor-swilling private detective; and Dr. Forrester (Alan Napier), a mysterious psychiatrist. During the course of the complex and often confusing plot, Neale becomes inadvertently involved with a Nazi espionage ring, finds himself the chief suspect in the murder of the private detective and, with Carla's aid, ultimately identifies Dr. Forrester and Willi Hilfe as high-ranking members of the spy ring. As Travers, Duryea played the small but pivotal role of Forrester's tailor, who uses his tailored clothing to transport valuable documents to the spies. For his performance, Duryea was singled out by one reviewer as "appropriately malevolent," but the film earned mixed reactions from critics; while *Variety*'s reviewer found that the film "starts out to be a humdinger, but ... becomes drawn out and elementary," Bosley Crowther of the *New York Times* wrote that it was "as eerie a package as has come along in quite a pretty while."

After playing a third-rate vaudevillian in *The Great Flamarion* (1945) and a quick-on-the-draw gunman in the comedy western *Along Came Jones* (1945), Duryea signed a lucrative contract with Universal Studios and was reunited with his *Woman in the Window* co-stars for his third Fritz Lang–directed film noir of the year, *Scarlet Street* (1945). Here, Duryea played Johnny Prince, a callous conman who becomes involved in a lethal triangle involving his indolent girlfriend, Kitty March (Bennett) and Christopher Cross (Robinson), a mild-mannered cashier and amateur painter who first encounters the couple when he stops Johnny from beating Kitty on a deserted street. Believing that Cross is a wealthy artist, Johnny encourages Kitty's relationship with him, finds a market for Cross' offbeat paintings, and passes Kitty off as the artist, earning her sudden acclaim. When Cross learns of Kitty's deception, he forgives her, but after she scoffs at his proposal of marriage, he becomes unglued and savagely stabs her to death with an ice pick. Ironically, it is Johnny who is accused and convicted of Kitty's murder, and Cross spends the rest of his days in madness, unsuccessfully trying to convince the authorities of his guilt.

One of Fritz Lang's most riveting offer-

ings from the film noir period, *Scarlet Street* was a commercial and critical success, with one reviewer describing it as "peopled with some of the most repulsive, reprehensible, and revolting characters who ever stalked through a movie; so evil they are doubly fascinating." Duryea also earned raves for his performance as the nefarious con-man; in the *New York Times*, Bosley Crowther wrote, "Only Dan Duryea hits a proper and credible stride, making a vicious and serpentine creature out of a cheap, chiseling tinhorn off the streets," and the critic for *The Hollywood Review* gushed: "Dan Duryea creates a priceless portrait of an absolute scoundrel. There is variety and infinite color to his work and he shades it like a master artist with Lang's skillful guidance. There is much to admire in his sharp sketching of this most unadmirable character and it stands unequalled as one of the year's greatest supporting roles."

The following year, Duryea made an attempt at changing his image in the 1946 comedy *White Tie and Tails*, with Ella Raines and William Bendix, but the actor later called it "a dismal failure." He fared far better with a return to the dark side in his fifth film noir,

Black Angel (1946). The fascinating opening shot of this feature begins as Duryea's character, Martin Blair, stands on the street, staring up at a high rise building. Panning upward, the camera eventually selects a single apartment window, takes the audience inside, and finally settles on the glittering glass of a crystal chandelier. The resident of the apartment is one Mavis Marlowe (Constance Dowling), a beautiful but shrewish singer — and Martin's ex-wife. Soon after Marlowe sends word to the lobby that she does not want to see Martin "tonight or ever," she is found strangled to death on the floor of her bedroom. Martin, an alcoholic songwriter, is cleared of suspicion; instead, police arrest Kirk Bennett (John Phillips), a married man who was being blackmailed by the singer after ending their affair. When Kirk is convicted and sentenced to death for the crime, his loyal wife, Catherine (June Vincent) joins forces with Martin to unearth the real killer, focusing on a shady nightclub owner known as Mr. Marko (Peter Lorre). Marko ultimately is proven innocent and, with Kirk's execution approaching, Martin reveals his growing feelings for Catherine. She rejects him, however, and later, during an alcoholic binge, Martin realizes that he was the real killer. He confesses his guilt ("Don't be unhappy, Cathy," he tells her; "I'm not"), saving Kirk from the chair in the nick of time.

After earning praise in the *New York Times* for his portrayal of "a rather sympathetic character, for a change," Duryea was seen in a series of villainous parts, including a violent outlaw in *Black Bart* (1948), in which he played the title role, and a ruthless gangster in *Larceny* (1948). Also, in *Another Part of the Forest* (1948), the "prequel" to *The Little Foxes* (1941), he played the weak-willed Oscar Hubbard, the father of the character of Leo he portrayed in the earlier film. He followed these features with three more dastardly roles in his next three films noirs, all filmed in 1949: *Criss Cross*, *Manhandled*, and *Too Late for Tears*.

In the first, acclaimed for its "breathless suspense and nerve-jarring tension," Duryea played Slim Dundee, a ruthless gambler with underworld connections. When Slim discovers his wife, Anna (Yvonne DeCarlo), alone with her ex-husband, Steve Thompson (Burt Lancaster), the latter hastily concocts a story to mask their affair, explaining that he wants Slim's help in carrying out a heist of the armored car company where he works. In exchange for half of the profits, Slim agrees, but during the robbery, three men are killed and Anna disappears with the stolen cash. Later, Steve bribes one of Slim's hoods to take him to a cottage where Anna is waiting, but she realizes the man will inform Slim of their whereabouts and prepares to leave, taking the money with her. Before she can flee, Slim arrives, calmly telling Steve, "You always wanted her, didn't you, Thompson? You really loved her. You know I did, too? But you won out, Thompson. You've got her. She's all yours now. Hold her. Hold her tight." Slim shoots them both, and Anna and Steve die in each other's arms, with the sound of approaching police sirens wailing in the background.

After the release of *Criss Cross*, Duryea was hailed by one critic as "just as mean and dangerous as an audience could wish him to be." He wasn't as fortunate in his second noir of the year, however. By far the weakest of the actor's film noir offerings, *Manhandled* begins as writer Alton Bennett (Alan Napier) describes to his psychiatrist, Dr. Redman (Harold Vermilyea), a recurring dream in which he bludgeons his wife to death with a perfume bottle. When his wife is found dead a short time later, Bennett is immediately suspected by police, but their investigation quickly turns to Dr. Redman's secretary, Merl Kramer (Dorothy Lamour), who had access to the psychiatrist's files on Bennett. As it turns out, the actual killer was Dr. Redman, who stole the woman's jewels and was, in turn, killed by private detective Karl Benson (Duryea), Merl's would-be boyfriend. When Merl realizes that Karl is the killer, the crooked detective plants damaging evidence in her apartment and plans to toss her from the roof of her building, disguising the act as a suicide. In the nick of time, police intervene, charging

Karl with Mrs. Bennett's murder; in an ironic twist, Karl insists that it was the psychiatrist who killed the wealthy woman, but realizes, too late, that the murdered psychiatrist cannot corroborate his story. A disappointment at the box office, *Manhandled* was slammed by critics, including the reviewer for the *New York Times*, who called it "a cheap, sensational hodgepodge of incredible melodramatics."

But the actor bounced back with his third noir of 1949, *Too Late for Tears*, starring Lizabeth Scott and Don DeFore. As this feature opens, a suitcase filled with money is mistakenly tossed into the car of Jane Palmer (Scott) and her husband, Alan (Arthur Kennedy), who insists on turning in the cash to police. But the money-grubbing Jane has other plans, and when the rightful owner, Danny Fuller (Duryea), shows up to claim the money, Jane kills Alan, threatening to frame Danny if he doesn't help her dispose of the body. (Even Danny is impressed by Jane's gumption: "You know, honey? You've got quite a flair. I like you," he tells her. "Too bad you're a chiseler.") After arranging to split the $60,000 cache with Danny, Jane murders him instead, fleeing to Mexico with the money, where she enjoys a brief spell living the high life. Jane's scheme is ultimately thwarted, however, when she is tracked down by the brother (DeFore) of her first husband, whom she had driven to suicide. While trying to escape, Jane trips and falls from a balcony to her death, with the precious bills fluttering around her body. Once again, Duryea earned kudos for his performance; in *Motion Picture Digest*, Charles J. Lazarus labeled him "a standout," and the *New York Times'* reviewer wrote that Duryea "adds another excellent and familiar portrait to his gallery of tough muggs."

By now, Duryea's reputation as an oily, self-serving screen heavy was a solid one. But while the actor made a few conscious attempts at transforming his screen image, he ultimately resigned himself to the bad-guy persona that moviegoers had come to expect, explaining that "these roles not only pay well, but it seems, fortunately or not, that the audience remembers the killer a lot longer than the hero. I've hit more than a dozen [actresses] and the parts keep rolling in. My fan mail goes up every time I tee off on a girl." Duryea also revealed that he used his past experiences to motivate him in carrying out his villainous portrayals.

"I thought about some of the people I hated in my early as well as later life," Duryea told columnist Hedda Hopper in 1950. "Like the school bully who used to try and beat the hell out of me at least once a week … little incidents with trade people who enjoyed acting superior because they owned their business, overcharging you. Then, the one I used when I had to slap a woman around was easy! I was slapping the overbearing teachers who would fail you in their 'holier-than-thou' class and enjoy it!"

With the onset of the 1950s, Duryea was seen with James Stewart in *Winchester '73* (1950), portraying Waco Johnny Dean, the Kansas Kid; *The Underworld Story* (1950), in which he played an unethical journalist who uncovers corruption in a New England town; and *One Way Street* (1950), where the actor starred as a gangster who vows revenge after losing his girl to a doctor. After the latter film, which ended Duryea's contract with Universal, the actor starred in *Chicago Calling* (1951), playing a down-and-out photographer who awaits word about his wife and son after learning that they were in an automobile crash. The film was a disappointment at the box office, but Duryea later considered it to be his favorite role.

"I took no salary but just a percentage of any profits. There weren't any, but I have no regrets," he said in a 1965 interview. "The role made my wife cry, and [that] was a tremendous compliment from one whose judgment I revere."

In 1952, Duryea turned his considerable talents to the medium of television, taking on the starring role in *The Adventures of China Smith*. The popular half-hour series about a Far East soldier-of-fortune ran for 26 episodes, and Duryea reprised the role in another 26 shows two years later in *The New Adventures of China Smith*. During the next 15 years,

the actor would appear in guest spots in more than 70 television programs, including *The United States Steel Hour*, *Zane Grey Theater*, *Adventure Theater*, *Wagon Train*, *Cimarron City*, *Laramie*, *The Twilight Zone*, *Route 66*, *Rawhide*, *Combat!*, and *The Virginian*.

On the big screen, Duryea played a pair of rare non-villainous parts in *Thunder Bay* (1953), his second western with James Stewart, and *This Is My Love* (1954), in which he portrayed the invalid husband of Linda Darnell.

"It's the most sympathetic, yet dramatic, part I've played," Duryea said of the latter role. "It's mentioned early in the picture that I was a dancer before I become an invalid, so I do my entire part, except for a dream sequence, either in a wheelchair or in bed."

Also in 1954, Duryea was seen in his first — and last — role as a film noir hero in *World for Ransom*. Set in Singapore, this Robert Aldrich–directed feature centers on Mike Callahan (Duryea), a private investigator who finds himself thrust into an investigation of the kidnapping of noted nuclear physicist Sean O'Connor (Arthur Shields). One of the men involved in the crime is Julian March (Patric Knowles), whose wife, Frennessey (Marian Carr), is Mike's former lover. With the promise of leaving her spouse and reuniting with Mike, Fren convinces him to extricate Julian from his illegal activities with Alexis Pedras (Gene Lockhart), the black marketeer who is behind the kidnapping. With the help of a British intelligence agent (Reginald Denny), Mike finds Julian at the jungle hideout where O'Connor is being held, but during his rescue of the scientist, Mike is forced to kill Julian in self-defense. He returns to resume his relationship with Fren, only to discover that she was merely using him to save her husband.

After earning mention, along with his co-stars, for "making the story live" in *World for Ransom*, Duryea was kept busy in a series of westerns, including *Silver Lode* (1954), in which he played a sheriff who tries to railroad an innocent man; *Ride Clear of Diablo* (1954), starring Audie Murphy; *Rails Into Laramie*, where he was featured as a crooked barkeep; and *The Marauders* (1955), which starred Duryea as a greedy cattle rancher. These fairly entertaining features were followed by the actor's final descent into film noir in back-to-back features, *Storm Fear* (1956) and *The Burglar* (1957).

In the first, Duryea played an unsuccessful writer by the name of Fred, whose ill-health has forced him to live in a remote mountain cabin with his wife, Elizabeth (Jean Wallace), and his 12-year-old son, David (David Stollery). The story heats up with the arrival of Fred's no-good brother, Charlie (Cornel Wilde), and two members of his gang, Benjie (Stephen Hill), a violent sociopath, and Edna (Lee Grant), an amiable moll characterized by her fondness for her mink coat. Charlie — who is Elizabeth's ex-lover and the actual father of David — reveals that he has been shot in the leg during a robbery heist, and he persuades David to lead his gang over the snow-covered mountains to the state highway. Attempting to thwart his brother's plans by notifying police, Fred is later found dead in the snow, but Charlie is stopped by the family's hired man, Hank (Dennis Weaver), shortly before he is able to reach the highway. Although Duryea was saddled with the least showy of the film's roles, it is his character who engenders the most sympathy; during the group's 24-hour sojourn in the cabin, he is beaten on two occasions by the volatile Benjie, receives a notice in the mail that his latest manuscripts have been rejected, and learns that Elizabeth (whom he married after she was impregnated and abandoned by Charlie) will never love him. "I thought I was being noble when I married you, but I was only thinking of myself," Fred tells his wife. "I thought you would forget Charlie and love me. I want you to love me the way you love Charlie."

Duryea's final film noir, *The Burglar*, was a highly stylized feature with a cast of offbeat characters including Nat Harbin (Duryea), the career thief of the film's title; Baylock (Peter Capell), a member of Nat's gang who fantasizes about retiring to Central America;

and Gladden (Jayne Mansfield, in a surprisingly good performance), who was raised with Nat by her kind but larcenous father. The film's complex plot includes the gang's theft of an expensive necklace and the efforts of a crooked cop named Charlie (Stewart Bradley) and his moll, Della (Martha Vickers), to gain possession of the stolen jewel. Ultimately, the cop succeeds in his mission and kills Nat, claiming to fellow officers that he shot in self-defense, but Della arrives to contradict his story and Charlie is arrested for his crimes.

As Duryea continued to build his career on a foundation of despicable characters, he expressed concerns that his on-screen characterizations would adversely affect the lives of his two young sons. As a result, the actor was determined to overcompensate in his off-screen life for his performances in film.

"You know, other kids at school often say to my boys, 'I know your daddy. He's a bad man,'" Duryea said. "It bothered me a lot.... Everyone thought of me as a villain or degenerate, depending on which movie they had seen me in. My wife and I actually over-did it to correct things. We joined the PTA, Boy Scouts, worked at neighborhood improvement, playing all sorts of benefits in order to let people know I was only an actor, not a true-to-life no-good."

The next few years saw Duryea in a number of films of varying quality, including *Slaughter on Tenth Avenue* (1957), a hard-hitting melodrama focusing on corruption on the New York waterfront; *Kathy O'* (1958), a box-office success which featured the actor as a desperate public relations man; *Platinum High School* (1958), a tiresome melodrama co-starring Mickey Rooney and Terry Moore; and *Six Black Horses* (1962), a cliché-ridden western. In 1963, Duryea planned to return to his roots on Broadway in *A Case of Libel*, but after a dispute with director Sam Wanamaker during the first week of rehearsals, Duryea left the cast. A short time later, he revealed that his reasons for accepting the stage role were purely financial.

"I suppose a lot of people will want to kill me for saying it, but I wanted to use

Broadway so I could make more money in the movies," the actor said. "Some actors act for art's sake and starve. That's not for me. I can't afford it. My reputation as an actor is a good one, but I've no illusions about it being the world's greatest. A Broadway success would have given it a boost."

Back in Hollywood, Duryea appeared with his oldest son, Peter, in a pair of westerns, *Taggart* (1965) and *Bounty Killer* (1965). (Peter would go on to appear in such popular television programs as *Bewitched*, *Star Trek*, *I Spy*, and *Family Affair*, while Duryea's younger son, Richard, went into the entertainment management business and at one time worked as the road manager for the Beach Boys singing group.) The actor also traveled to Italy to star as the hero in *Un Fiume Di Dollari* (1966), which was released in the United States as *The Hills Run Red*.

In January 1967, tragedy struck Duryea's life when Helen, his wife of 35 years, suffered a fatal heart attack at the age of 56. Later that year, Duryea underwent surgery for a tumor that turned out to be benign, according to doctors. After recovering from the operation, the actor signed on as the villainous Eddie Jacks on the popular television series *Peyton Place*, and also appeared in the small screen remake of his 1950 feature film, *Winchester '73*, this time playing the smaller role of the hero's uncle. The following year, Duryea starred in a dreadful science-fiction thriller, *The Bamboo Saucer* (1968), portraying an American Intelligence officer hunting down a flying saucer in Red China. The film would be Duryea's last. On the morning of June 7, 1968, while in the bathroom of his Mulholland Drive home, Duryea collapsed and died. It was later revealed that the actor was suffering from cancer. He was 61 years old.

Dan Duryea was never a matinee star, but he managed to turn his penchant for villainy into a stable and enduring Hollywood career. While he demonstrated his versatility as an actor in such films as *None but the Lonely Heart* and *Chicago Calling*, it was as one of the screen's premier scoundrels that Duryea will best be remembered. And unlike most typecast actors, the role was one that Duryea relished and cultivated.

"When I decided to become an actor ... I looked in the mirror and knew with my 'puss' and 155-pound weakling body, I couldn't pass for a leading man, and I had to be different," the actor once said. "So I chose to be the meanest SOB in the movies ... here, indeed, was a market for my talents."

Film Noir Filmography

The Woman in the Window. Director: Fritz Lang. Producer: Nunnally Johnson. Running time: 99 minutes. Released by RKO, January 25, 1945. Cast: Edward G. Robinson, Joan Bennett, Raymond Massey, Edmond Breon, Dan Duryea, Thomas E. Jackson, Arthur Loft, Dorothy Peterson, Frank Dawson, Carol Cameron, Bobby Blake. Awards: Academy Award nomination for Best Score/Drama or Comedy (Hugo Friedhofer, Arthur Lange).

Ministry of Fear. Director: Fritz Lang. Producer: Seton I. Miller. Running time: 86 minutes. Released by Paramount, February 7, 1945. Cast: Ray Milland, Marjorie Reynolds, Carl Esmond, Hillary Brooke, Percy Waram, Dan Duryea, Alan Napier, Erskine Sanford, Thomas Louden, Aminta Dyne, Eustace Wyatt, Mary Field, Byron Foulger, Lester Matthews.

Scarlet Street. Director: Fritz Lang. Producer: Walter Wanger. Running time: 102 minutes. Released by Universal, December 28, 1945. Cast: Edward G. Robinson, Joan Bennett, Dan Duryea, Jess Barker, Margaret Lindsay, Rosalind Ivan, Samuel S. Hinds, Arthur Loft, Vladimir Sokoloff, Charles Kemper, Russell Hicks, Anita Bolster, Cyrus W. Kendall, Fred Essler, Edgar Dearing, Tom Dillon, Chuck Hamilton, Gus Glassmire, Ralph Littlefield, Sherry Hall, Howard Mitchell, Jack Staham, Rodney Bell.

Black Angel. Director: Roy William Neill. Producers: Tom McKnight, Roy William Neill. Running time: 83 minutes. Released by Universal, August 2, 1946. Cast: Dan Duryea, June Vincent, Peter Lorre, Broderick Crawford, Constance Dowling, Wallace Ford, Hobart Cavanaugh, Freddie Steele, Ben Bard, John Phillips, Junius Matthews, Maurice St. Clair, Vilova, Pat Starling.

Criss Cross. Director: Robert Siodmak. Producer: Michel Kraike. Running time: 88 minutes. Released by Universal-International, January 12, 1949. Cast: Burt Lancaster, Yvonne DeCarlo, Dan Duryea, Stephen McNally, Richard Long, Esy Morales, Tom Pedi, Percy Helton, Alan Napier, Griff Barnett, Meg Randall, Joan Miller, Edna M.

Holland, John Doucette, Marc Krath, James O'Rear, John Skins Miller, Robert Osterloh, Vincent Renno, Charles Wagenheim.

Manhandled. Director: Lewis R. Foster. Producers: William H. Pine and William C. Thomas. Running time: 97 minutes. Released by Paramount, May 25, 1949. Cast: Dorothy Lamour, Dan Duryea, Sterling Hayden, Irene Hervey, Philip Reed, Harold Vermilyea, Alan Napier, Art Smith, Irving Bacon.

Too Late for Tears. Director: Byron Haskin. Producer: Hunt Stromberg. Running time: 98 minutes. Released by United Artists, August 14, 1949. Cast: Lizabeth Scott, Don DeFore, Dan Duryea, Arthur Kennedy, Kristine Miller, Barry Kelley.

World for Ransom. Director: Robert Aldrich. Producers: Robert Aldrich and Bernard Tabakin. Running time: 82 minutes. Released by Allied Artists, January 27, 1954. Cast: Dan Duryea, Gene Lockhart, Patric Knowles, Reginald Denny, Nigel Bruce, Marian Carr, Douglas Dumbrille, Keye Luke, Clarence Lung, Lou Nova, Arthur Shields.

Storm Fear. Director and Producer: Cornel Wilde. Running time: 88 minutes. Released by United Artists, February 1, 1956. Cast: Cornel Wilde, Jean Wallace, Dan Duryea, Lee Grant, David Stollery, Dennis Weaver, Steven Hill, Keith Britton.

The Burglar. Director: Paul Wendkos. Producer: Louis W. Kellman. Running time: 90 minutes. Released by Columbia, June 1957. Cast: Dan Duryea, Jayne Mansfield, Martha Vickers, Peter Capell, Mickey Shaughnessy, Wendell Phillips, Phoebe Mackay, Stewart Bradley, John Facenda, Frank Hall, Bob Wilson, Steve Allison, Richard Emery, Andrea McLaughlin, Frank Orrison, Sam Elber, Ned Carey, John Boyd, Michael Rich, George Kane, Sam Cresson, Ruth Burnat.

References

Champlin, Charles. "Rewards of Villainy." *Los Angeles Times*, October 13, 1965.

"Character Roles to Chew On." *Los Angeles Herald-Examiner*, April 23, 1967.

Churchill, Reba and Bonnie. "Script Reforms Screen Meanie." *Beverly Hills Newslife*, April 7, 1954.

"Dan Duryea, Actor, Dies at 61; Played Unsavory Characters." *New York Times*, June 8, 1968.

"Dan Duryea Dabbling." *Variety*, July 1, 1965.

"Dan Duryea Dies of Cancer at 61." *Variety*, June 10, 1968.

"Dan Duryea, Movie Star, Dead at 61." *San Francisco Chronicle*, June 8, 1968.

"Dan Duryea's Wife Dies." *Los Angeles Times*, January 22, 1967.

Dolven, Frank. "Dan Duryea: Charming Villain." *Classic Images*, April 1996.

"Duryea's Will Filed." *Los Angeles Herald-Examiner*, June 21, 1968.

"Frightful Father." *American Magazine*, June 1946.

Greenberg, Abe. "Dan Duryea on Good vs. Bad." *Hollywood Citizen-News*, May 11, 1965.

_____. "Rome Films Make Most Boom-Booms." *Hollywood Citizen-News*, April 18, 1966.

Houser, John G. "Dan Duryea." *Los Angeles Herald-Examiner*, January 11, 1965.

Johnson, David. "Dan Duryea: Had Sense Enough to Recognize His Limitations." *Films in Review*, circa 1975.

"Like Dan, Like Son." *Los Angeles Herald-Examiner*, October 3, 1965.

Malnic, Eric. "Dan Duryea, Tough Guy of Movies, Dies." *Los Angeles Times*, June 8, 1968.

Martin, Pete. "The Screen's No. 1 Heel." *The Saturday Evening Post*, March 13, 1948.

Pitts, Michael R. "Dan Duryea." *Classic Images*, March 1981.

Sloan, Lloyd L. "Such a Tough Life This Duryea Leads!" *Hollywood Citizen-News*, January 30, 1940.

"Today's Film Stars Aren't Temperamental: Duryea." *Los Angeles Herald-Examiner*, November 28, 1965.

"You Can Have Good Old Days—Duryea." *Film Daily*, February 8, 1967.

JAY C. FLIPPEN

"Don't ask me no favors — I can't be bribed, see. Besides, you ain't got enough money to bribe me." — Jay C. Flippen in *Brute Force* (1947)

It was once said that Jay C. Flippen had "the face of ill-assembled grandeur — as if Mount Rushmore had been taken apart stone by stone and put back together again by a well meaning idiot." This colorful description notwithstanding, the burly character actor was a man of fortitude and determination — a veteran of vaudeville, radio, theater, screen, and television, Flippen continued to appear in feature films and television shows even after his leg was amputated late in his career. With performances in nearly 60 films, alongside such stars as Spencer Tracy, Joseph Cotten, and James Stewart, Flippen was also a contributor to five films noirs: *Brute Force* (1947), *They Live by Night* (1949), *The People Against O'Hara* (1951), *The Las Vegas Story* (1952), and *The Killing* (1956).

Flippen ("Yes, that's my real name," he said once. "Who would change their name to Jay C. Flippen?") was born in Little Rock, Arkansas, on March 6, 1899 (some sources say 1900). Possessing an affinity for performing from an early age, Flippen gained experience in local talent shows produced by his mother, who also taught ballroom dancing. By the time he reached his teens, he was substituting for acts that failed to appear for their engagements at the town's Majestic Theater.

"Whenever someone on the bill got sick, the manager called in my mother and she put the finger on me," Flippen once recalled. "A format? Material? Who needed them? There were a million jokes around."

At the age of 16, while performing in blackface in a local minstrel show, Flippen's antics caught the eye of the proprietor of the traveling Al G. Fields Minstrel Show. Fields hired Flippen as an understudy, and after a year, he was a regular performer with the act. Later, Flippen worked with famed comedian Al Jolson, then moved on to burlesque.

"We did 14 shows a week, a matinee, and an evening performance daily, with a new show every week," Flippen said. "Because of this, they were a great training school for an acting career."

In 1920, Bert Williams, a famous black comedian of the era, got Flippen his first New York stage role in *Broadway Brevities*. Before long, Flippen was signed by the famed theatrical producers, the Shuberts, and by the mid-1920s, he had achieved star status, appearing in 1926 alongside Jack Benny, Arthur Treacher, and Hazel Dawn in *The Great Temptations*, and the following year with Texas Guinan and Lillian Roth in *Padlocks of 1927*.

Over the next few years, Flippen would also work with such greats as Fanny Brice, Sophie Tucker, and Elsie Janis.

Flippen expanded his performing repertoire to include radio in 1930, utilizing his comedic talents on his own show, *The Flippen-Cies*, which established him as a top emcee. He was also heard on such broadcasts as *Col. Flippen's Amateur Hour*, *Earn Your Vacation*, *Battle of the Sexes*, and *Correction Please*, and — in his spare time — took up broadcasting New York Yankee baseball games. In years to come, Flippen would utilize his talents as a toastmaster to host four Birthday Balls for President Franklin D. Roosevelt and the "roasting" of Milton Berle at Hollywood's Masquers' Club, as well as serving as Abbot of the New York Friars Club.

In 1934, Flippen turned to the big screen, appearing in small roles in Universal's *Million Dollar Ransom*, with Edward Arnold and Phillips Holmes, and Fox's *Marie Galante*, starring Spencer Tracy. He promptly returned to New York, however, resuming his busy career on radio and on the stage. During the war years, as a leading personality in the American Guild of Variety Artists, Flippen headed several cross-country tours to raise money for the Red Cross. He did not return to films until more than a decade later when, in 1947, friend and producer Mark Hellinger cast him as a prison guard in *Brute Force*, his entry into film noir.

Hailed as a "powerful, action-packed story," *Brute Force* focused on a planned escape break headed by the inmates of a single cell in a men's prison. Among the film's numerous memorable characters are Joe Collins (Burt Lancaster), the determined mastermind of the plot; Capt. Muncie (Hume Cronyn), the sadistic and brutal head guard; Louie Miller (Sam Levene), a reporter on the prison newspaper who is savagely beaten by Muncie when he refuses to expose the plan; Freshman (Jeff Corey), whose duplicity leads to the failure of the escape; and Doc Walters (Art Smith), the prison's alcoholic but compassionate physician, whose rueful commentary ends the picture: "Nobody escapes. Nobody ever escapes." Flippen's minor role as a guard was overlooked by critics, but the film was lauded upon its release; in a typical notice, the reviewer for *Newsweek* called it "a forceful, even sadistic melodrama with moments of terrifying action and a climax that will raise the hackles on your neck."

With his first role in a major film behind him, Flippen decided to settle in Hollywood — but not only because of his prospects on the silver screen. Shortly after the release of *Brute Force*, a writer for MGM by the name of Ruth Brooks was searching for the lyrics to an old vaudeville tune, and was reportedly told, "Get in touch with Jay C. Flippen. If he doesn't know 'em, no one does." Brooks followed the advice, and a few months later, she and Flippen were married. Their marriage would last until Flippen's death in 1971, and Ruth Brooks Flippen would later become a well-known television comedy writer, penning episodes for such shows as *Bewitched*, *The Brady Bunch*, *My World and Welcome to It*, and *Gidget*. (The couple would never have children, but they did have two beloved basset hounds named Grand and Glorious — last name: Technicolor.)

Meanwhile, Flippen was next seen in *Intrigue* (1947), a cliché-ridden adventure starring George Raft; *Oh, You Beautiful Doll* (1949), a pleasant musical biography of songwriter Fred Fisher; *A Woman's Secret* (1949), a drama that was confusing and mundane despite direction from Nicholas Ray and a first-rate cast that included Melvyn Douglas, Gloria Grahame, and Maureen O'Hara; *Down to the Sea in Ships* (1949), a rousing, 19th-century sea adventure; and *They Live by Night* (1949), Flippen's second film noir.

Here, Flippen played a featured role as T-Dub, a hardened criminal who escapes from prison with two fellow inmates, Chickamaw (Howard Da Silva) and Arthur "Bowie" Bowers (Farley Granger). After planning and executing a successful heist, the three men separate, with Bowie marrying and settling down with Chickamaw's good-hearted niece, Keechie (Cathy O'Donnell). But later, when Chickamaw and T-Dub find themselves in

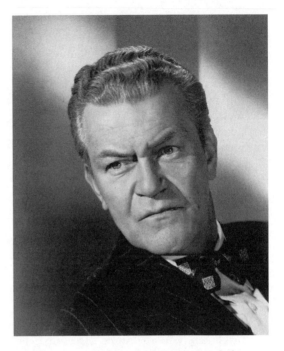

need of more cash, they force Bowie into helping out with one more job: "'Listen, you — we took you outta that prison camp when it was plenty others we coulda took," T-Dub tells the reluctant Bowie. "So to speak, you're an investment. And you're gonna pay off. You hear me?" The robbery is all ill-fated one, however; during the attempt, T-Dub is killed, Chickamaw is later shot while trying to break into a liquor store, and Bowie finds himself the focus of a nationwide manhunt. In the film's fast-moving and touching finale, T-Dub's sister (Helen Craig) contacts authorities while Bowie and Keechie are hiding out at her motel, and Bowie is gunned down by police.

They Live by Night opened to raves from audiences and critics alike; the reviewer in *Motion Picture Herald* termed it "terrific stuff ... combining shrewd writing and forceful direction with superb acting," and Flippen was singled out by *Variety* for his "top-notch ... delineation of a criminal." Interestingly, Flippen recalled years later that he was not the first choice for the role of T-Dub.

"[Director Nicholas Ray] had a helluva time talking [RKO head] Dore Schary into it," Flippen told *TV Guide* in 1962. "'Flippen? Nah!

He's a comic, everybody knows that,' Schary argued. 'Assuming he can act — which I seriously doubt — he certainly couldn't play the scene where he has to slap Farley Granger around.' Anyway, I tested — with Farley. I told him, 'Kid, you don't mind if I beat the socks off you, do you?' Well, the picture was a big smash ... but for years, I couldn't get a comedy part. 'Flippen? Nah!' they told my agent. 'I saw him slap Farley Granger around.'"

After this superb film, Flippen was seen in a series of well-received features, including *Winchester '73* (1950), a superior western in which he portrayed a calvary sergeant; *Two Flags West* (1950), another western, this one starring Joseph Cotten and Linda Darnell; and *Flying Leathernecks* (1951), a wartime drama starring John Wayne and Robert Ryan. In the latter film, Flippen was featured prominently in a running gag as an army sergeant who steals from other companies to ensure that his own outfit is well-equipped. Also during this period, Flippen added two more noirs to his repertoire, *The People Against O'Hara* (1951), and *The Las Vegas Story* (1952).

The People Against O'Hara tells the story of James Curtayne (Spencer Tracy), a former defense attorney who was forced out of practice because of a drinking problem, but is lured back to defend a boy accused in a fatal shooting. In a small but pivotal role, Flippen played Sven Norson, a Swedish seaman who was a witness to the crime and collects a payoff from both Curtayne and the district attorney (John Hodiak) in exchange for his testimony. Curtayne ultimately volunteers to be used as bait to lure the real killer, but the plan works too well and the attorney loses his life in the process. For his portrayal of the duplicitous sailor, Flippen was noted in several reviews, with the *Los Angeles Times*' Philip K. Scheuer calling him "effortlessly expert," and W.E. Oliver of the *Los Angeles Evening Herald Examiner* including the actor in his praise of the "good roles" played by the film's supporting actors.

Flippen's next noir, *The Las Vegas Story*, includes a plethora of intertwined plot elements, including a wealthy man desperate to raise cash to cover his role in an embezzlement scheme; the murder of a casino owner; a reignited affair between a police lieutenant and his former lover; and a private detective chasing a $10,000 diamond necklace. The various facets reach a neat conclusion when the embezzler (Vincent Price) is jailed for his crimes, the private detective (Brad Dexter) is revealed as the murderer and is killed following a helicopter chase, and the embezzler's wife (Jane Russell) winds up in the arms of the lieutenant (Victor Mature). In the midst of these characters is the local sheriff portrayed by Flippen, who is characterized by his fondness for trout fishing and his over-inflated sense of self-importance ("You know the Strip better than anybody," he tells his lieutenant in one scene, "except me"). His rather comical performance was noticed by one reviewer who said he was "adequate to demands," but the picture, a box office disappointment, was trashed by critics, with the reviewer for *Variety* writing: "Principal point against film is the obscure motivations of plot principals. A little more light on the subject would have helped, but scripters and direction apparently prefer to keep both audience and players in the dark."

During the next several years, Flippen appeared in films of varying quality. Some were outstanding, including *Bend of the River* (1952), a well-done western with James Stewart and Arthur Kennedy; *The Wild One* (1953), the classic rebellious biker film starring Marlon Brando; *Man Without a Star* (1955), a tautly written and directed western featuring Kirk Douglas; and *Oklahoma!* (1955), the popular musical starring Gordon MacRae, Gloria Grahame, and Gene Nelson. Others ranged from mediocre to downright lousy, including *Thunder Bay* (1953), which flopped at the box office despite its filming in the new wide screen process and three-speaker stereophonic sound; *East of Sumatra* (1953), a tiresome bit of escapism starring Jeff Chandler; *Devil's Canyon* (1953), a dull jail-break melodrama filmed in 3-D; and *The King and*

Four Queens (1956), a weak western starring Clark Gable. But Flippen rebounded from these forgettable features with his final film noir, *The Killing* (1956).

This superb offering focuses on an intricate race track heist planned by ex-con Johnny Clay (Sterling Hayden) with the assistance of a variety of characters, including Randy Kennan (Ted De Corsia), a cop with a sizable mob debt hanging over his head; George Peatty (Elisha Cook, Jr.), a mild-mannered race track cashier with a contemptuous, gold-digging wife; and Marvin Unger (Flippen), a bookkeeper with an unusual affection for Johnny, who puts up the front money for the operation. Set in motion by George's wife, Sherry (Marie Windsor) and her lover (Vince Edwards), the plan ultimately goes awry, with Marvin the only member of the gang to escape unscathed. Although Flippen was noted only for portraying an "interesting but not new type" by one reviewer, *The Killing* remains, arguably, the best of his five noirs, and was deservedly praised in *Variety* for its "tense and suspenseful vein which carries through to an unexpected and ironic windup."

Few of Flippen's films during the remainder of the 1950s were memorable; notable exceptions included *Run of the Arrow* (1957), a violent western in which he portrayed a Sioux Indian named Walking Coyote; *The Midnight Story* (1957), a first-rate whodunit starring Tony Curtis; and *The Halliday Brand* (1957), a gripping western drama featuring Flippen as the father of a half-breed Indian boy. In addition to his feature film work during this period, Flippen was seen on a number of television series, including *Goodyear Television Playhouse*, *Rawhide*, *The Untouchables*, *Stagecoach West*, *The Dick Van Dyke Show*, *Johnny Ringo*, *Wanted: Dead or Alive*, and *Gunsmoke*. He also starred as the cantankerous captain Homer Nelson on the military sitcom *Ensign O'Toole*, which ran from 1962 to 1963 on NBC-TV.

On the big screen, Flippen was cast in a string of westerns during the early 1960s— *Wild River* (1960), starring Montgomery Clift and directed by Elia Kazan; *The Plunderers* (1960), featuring Jeff Chandler as a one-armed Civil War hero; *How the West Was Won* (1962), a sweeping drama with an all-star cast that included James Stewart, Karl Malden, Debbie Reynolds, Henry Fonda, John Wayne, Richard Widmark, Lee J. Cobb, Thelma Ritter, Walter Brennan, and Gregory Peck; and *Cat Ballou* (1965), a western spoof starring Jane Fonda and Lee Marvin in a dual role.

In 1963, during filming on the latter feature, Flippen suffered an experience that threatened to end his lengthy and successful career. After injuring his right leg while opening a car door, Flippen developed a sore that would not heal. The actor tried to treat it with home remedies, but an infection set in and the leg became gangrenous. Upon completing his role for the film, Flippen was hospitalized for 10 weeks.

"The doctor told me I could stay in the hospital and be a parsnip, or I could lose my leg," Flippen said. "So I lost my leg."

The actor remained in the hospital until March 1965, during which his weight dropped from 195 pounds to 105. He later admitted that he feared he would never act again.

"My wife gave me my key line," he said. "I said, after the operation, wallowing in self-pity, 'How am I going to act with one leg?' She looked at me and said, 'Jay, you don't act with one leg.' That gave me buoyancy."

Following his release from the hospital, Flippen practiced walking daily at home with his prosthetic limb and underwent training three times a week at UCLA. A year later, he was seen in his first acting role since the amputation, a guest spot on *The Virginian*, playing his part from a wheelchair. He followed this appearance with a made-for-television movie, *Fame is the Name of the Game*, starring Anthony Franciosa and Jill St. John.

"After I did my first scene, I looked around. Everybody was crowding around the set trying to see the old boy working again," Flippen said in a 1966 interview. "And when the director called 'cut,' a great big hand went up for this old-timer. I've had some pretty good receptions at the old Palace Theater, but this spontaneous ovation on the sound stage really got me — right here."

During the next few years, Flippen continued to act in a number of television movies, including *The Sound of Anger* (1968), *The Old Man Who Cried Wolf* (1970), and *Sam Hill: Who Killed Mr. Foster?* (1971), as well as such feature films as *The Spirit Is Willing* (1967), a haunted house comedy starring Sid Caesar; *Firecreek* (1968), a James Stewart vehicle that was vaguely reminiscent of *High Noon* (1952); *Hellfighters* (1968), based on the life of oil firefighter "Red" Adair; and *The Seven Minutes* (1971), a talky drama about a movie star who is brought to trial for writing an allegedly pornographic novel. It would be Flippen's last film.

On February 2, 1971, just days after receiving a "clean ticket" by his doctor, Flippen suffered a brain aneurysm while watching television at home. He died the following day at Cedars of Lebanon Hospital in Hollywood, a month before his 72nd birthday. The eulogy for his memorial service was conducted by comedian and longtime friend, Milton Berle.

With his roots in vaudeville and burlesque, and his successful conquering of every medium of entertainment, Jay C. Flippen truly enjoyed one of Hollywood's most colorful careers. Known for his humor and wit, Flippen's contribution to the annals of film is outmatched only by his courage and determination following his potentially career-ending amputation and his determination to resume his livelihood. With typical modesty, Flippen always credited his wife, Ruth, with supplying him with the fortitude to forge ahead.

"All that time," Flippen said once, "she never let me forget that I'm an actor first — and a man somewhere down the line."

Film Noir Filmography

Brute Force. Director: Jules Dassin. Producer: Mark Hellinger. Running time: 95 minutes. Released by Universal-International, June 6, 1947.

Cast: Burt Lancaster, Hume Cronyn, Charles Bickford, Yvonne DeCarlo, Ann Blyth, Ella Raines, Anita Colby, Sam Levene, Howard Duff, Art Smith, Roman Bohnen, John Hoyt, Richard Gaines, Frank Puglia, Jeff Corey, Vince Barnett, James Bell, Jack Overman, Whit Bissell, Sir Lancelot, Ray Teal, Jay C. Flippen, James O'Rear, Howland Chamberlain, Kenneth Patterson, Crane Whitley, Charles McGraw, John Harmon, Gene Stutenroth, Wally Rose, Carl Rhodes, Guy Beach, Edmund Cobb, Tom Steele.

They Live by Night. Director: Nicholas Ray. Producer: John Houseman. Running time: 95 minutes. Released by RKO, June 28, 1948. Cast: Cathy O'Donnell, Farley Granger, Howard Da Silva, Jay C. Flippen, Helen Craig, Will Wright, Marie Bryant, Ian Wolfe, William Phipps, Harry Harvey.

The People Against O'Hara. Director: John Sturges. Producer: William H. Wright. Running time: 102 minutes. Released by MGM, September 5, 1951. Cast: Spencer Tracy, Pat O'Brien, Diana Lynn, John Hodiak, Eduardo Ciannelli, James Arness, Yvette Duguay, Jay C. Flippen, William Campbell, Richard Anderson, Henry O'Neill, Arthur Shields, Louise Lorimer, Ann Doran, Emile Meyer, Regis Toomey, Katherine Warren, Paul Bryar, Peter Mamakos, Perdita Chandler, Frank Fergusson, Don Dillaway, C. Anthony Hughes, Lee Phelps, Lawrence Tolan, Jack Lee, Tony Barr.

The Las Vegas Story. Director: Robert Stevenson. Producer: Robert Sparks. Running time: 87 minutes. Released by RKO, January 1952. Cast: Jane Russell, Victor Mature, Vincent Price, Hoagy Carmichael, Brad Dexter, Jay C. Flippen, Gordon Oliver, Will Wright, Bill Welsh, Ray Montgomery, Colleen Miller, Bob Wilke.

The Killing. Director: Stanley Kramer. Producer: James B. Harris. Running time: 84 minutes. Released by United Artists, May 20, 1956. Cast: Sterling Hayden, Coleen Gray, Vince Edwards, Jay C. Flippen, Marie Windsor, Ted De Corsia, Elisha Cook, Jr., Joe Sawyer, Timothy Carey, Jay Adler, Kola Kwarian, Joseph Turkell, James Edwards.

References

"Actor Jay C. Flippen Services Set for Today." *Los Angeles Times*, February 5, 1971.

Biography of Jay C. Flippen. NBC Radio, August 16, 1943.

Biography of Jay C. Flippen. RKO Radio Studios, circa 1953.

Flippen, Jay C. "Were the Good Old Days So Good?" *The Hollywood Reporter*, November 12, 1954.

Heffernan, Harold. "Jay C. Flippen Gets Biggest Hand." *Hollywood Citizen-News*, August 1, 1966.

"Jay C. Flippen, 71, Dies of Aneurysm." *Variety*, February 4, 1971.

"Jay C. Flippen, Actor, Dies at 70; Was Entertainer for 50 Years." *New York Times*, February 5, 1971.

"Jay C. Flippen Death Reported." *The Hollywood Reporter*, February 4, 1971.

"Jay C. Flippen." *Variety*, February 3, 1971.

"Jay C. Flippen Is Dead at 71." *New York Daily News*, February 5, 1971.

"Jay C. Flippen, 70." *New York Post*, February 5, 1971.

"Look Who's in the Navy." *TV Guide*, December 15–21, 1962.

"Teller's Shubert." *Brooklyn Daily Times*, April 14, 1925.

Smith, Darr. "Jay C. Flippen." *Los Angeles Daily News*, February 8, 1950.

GLENN FORD

"You have no idea how faithful and obedient I can be — for a nice salary." — Glenn Ford in *Gilda* (1946)

For Glenn Ford, acting was a means to an end.

"It was a way to help his mom and dad with expenses," said Ford's son, Peter. "He loved acting, but it was really just a job. He never desired to be a movie star — just an actor — but hard work and good fortune had other plans for him."

Those plans had a fortuitous outcome for the actor's legion of admirers as well — over the course of seven decades, Ford appeared in more than 100 films, including such memorable features as *Blackboard Jungle* (1955) and *The Rounders* (1965), and he excelled in seven examples from the film noir era: *Gilda* (1946), *Framed* (1947), *The Undercover Man* (1949), *Convicted* (1950), *Affair in Trinidad* (1952), *The Big Heat* (1953), and *Human Desire* (1954).

The only child of Hannah and Newton Ford, a conductor with the Canadian Pacific Railroad, Gwyllyn Samuel Newton Ford was born in Sainte-Christine, Quebec, Canada, on May 1, 1916. But with a dash of the drama that the acclaimed actor would later embrace in his career, Ford almost didn't make it into the world — approximately three weeks before Hannah was due to give birth, a fire broke out in the store over which the Fords made their home. Newton was rescued without incident, but as a fireman was carrying Hannah down a ladder, the rungs of the ladder broke, and both fell two stories to the ground.

"They all survived," Peter Ford said, "but there was some question as to whether [the baby] would live." Ford recovered from his traumatic pre-birth adventure, however, and enjoyed an uneventful childhood in Quebec, until his family moved to Santa Monica, California, because of Newton's health, which thrived in the area's warm climate.

It was while he was a student at Santa Monica High School that young Ford was first exposed to acting — he played the lead in his first production, *The Thirteenth Chair*, just before his graduation from the school in 1934. Years later, Ford recalled that his parents never objected to his theatrical ambitions, but his father insisted that he learn to work with his hands, in case his acting career did not pan out.

"Learning to work with my hands has given me a way of life most actors don't have," Ford told the *Saturday Evening Post* in 1958. "It tided me over during the years I was trying to crash the theater."

After graduation, Ford joined a local group, the Santa Monica Players, and performed in a variety of plays, including *When's Your Birthday?*, *The Royal Family*, *Death Takes a Holiday*, *Parnell*, and *Room Service*. He also served dual roles as stage manager and actor for *Golden Boy*, starring Francis Lederer, and *The Children's Hour* at the Biltmore Theater in downtown Los Angeles. Then, in 1938, he appeared in a production of *Soliloquy* that first played Santa Barbara, then San Diego, and wound up on Broadway. Once it reached New York, however, the play quickly folded, and Ford was forced to borrow train fare to return to Los Angeles. A short time later, after managing to find work in only a few minor productions, Ford finally got the break for which he'd been waiting when he was contacted by Tom Moore, a 20th Century-Fox talent agent who'd been following Ford's stage career.

"Tom took him to Fox, and he did a screen test, and they ended up putting him in his first film," said Peter Ford. "They didn't hold high hopes for him, however. They deemed him too skinny and not very good looking, but they sensed a 'presence' and took a chance."

The film, *Heaven with a Barbed Wire Fence* (1939), co-starring Jean Rogers and Richard Conte, was a mild success at the box office. After its release, Ford hired Zeppo Marx as his agent and signed a long-term contract with Columbia Studios, for whom he would work for the next 14 years.

Ford's first film for Columbia was *My Son Is Guilty* (1940), a grim programmer starring Bruce Cabot, followed by such features as *Men Without Souls* (1940), a prison drama with John Litel and Barton MacLane (1940), and *The Lady in Question* (1940), the first of five pictures that Ford would make with actress Rita Hayworth. (Their teaming on this film led to a lifelong friendship — at one point, the two lived next door to each other in Beverly Hills, Hayworth was a guest at the wedding of Ford's son, and Ford served as a pallbearer at Hayworth's 1987 funeral.) Ford also earned rave reviews for his performance as a young Jewish man in *So Ends Our Night* (1941); co-starred in *Texas* (1941) with William Holden, who would become his closest friend; and appeared in an aviation picture, *Flight Lieutenant* (1942), that was notable primarily because Ford's co-star on the film, Pat O'Brien, introduced the actor to renowned tap dancer and actress Eleanor Powell.

"Pat thought they were both real whole-some, nice people," Peter Ford said, "and that they'd be perfect for each other."

By the end of the year, Ford and Powell were engaged, and they married on October 23, 1943, in the house that Powell rented at 727 North Bedford Drive in Beverly Hills. Meanwhile, Ford had enlisted in the United States Marines, and after the couple's brief honeymoon in San Francisco, the actor returned to service, where he would eventually rise to the rank of sergeant. Stationed at nearby Camp Pendleton, Ford was allowed to make frequent visits to his new bride, and the couple's only child, Peter Newton, was born on February 5, 1945.

When the war ended, Ford returned home to few prospects on screen, but it wasn't long before his career was up and running again — while having lunch with a friend at the Warner Bros. studio, he caught the attention of actress Bette Davis, who later tapped him as her co-star in a film she was producing, *A Stolen Life* (1946).

"It was a pivotal film for him," Peter Ford said, "because Bette Davis was a giant star, and he was just coming along. Bette was instrumental in giving him the break he needed."

After the release of this popular film, Ford entered the realm of film noir with one of the era's best-known features, *Gilda* (1946). Here, the actor portrayed Johnny Farrell, a two-bit gambler who is involved in a triangle of passion and deceit with a powerful casino owner, Ballin Mundson (George Macready) and his wife, Gilda (Rita Hayworth), with whom Johnny was romantically involved years before. When Ballin appears to have perished in an airplane crash, Johnny finds himself both drawn to and repulsed by Gilda, and although he later marries her, he tortures her with cruel indifference. ("You've had such a full life up to now," Johnny sarcastically tells Gilda in one scene. "I thought a little peace and quiet would do you good. Give you time to think.") They later reconcile, but Mundson — who faked his death — resurfaces with plans to murder the couple, and is shot and killed by the casino's washroom attendant, leaving Johnny and Gilda free to face their future together.

A hit with moviegoers, *Gilda* was slammed by critics upon its release, but Ford's performance was singled out for praise — in the *New York Herald Tribune*, Howard Barnes labeled Ford's portrayal "excellent," and the critic for *Variety* said that Ford was a "far better actor than the tale permits." Of all the films in which Glenn Ford appeared during his lengthy career, *Gilda* remains his favorite.

"It's because he was in it with Rita. Still, to this day, he carries a torch for her," Peter said of his father. "When she lived next door, she used to come to the house and sit by the pool — they'd look at the stars and talk about the old days. They had a very tender, lifelong affection, and he still talks about her in the fondest way. To this day, he keeps a special photo Rita inscribed to him on the end table next to his bed."

After starring as real-life aviation pioneer James Montgomery in the bio-pic *Gallant Journey* (1946), Ford returned to noir in *Framed* (1947), playing Mike Lambert, an out-of-work mining engineer. In typical noir fashion, Mike becomes involved with a scheming femme, Paula Craig (Janis Carter), who teams with her lover to embezzle $250,000 from the bank where he works and frame Mike for the crime. Instead, Paula kills her partner and convinces Mike that he was responsible for his death. ("We can't go to the police — it wasn't that kind of an accident. You killed him, Mike. Don't you remember?" Paula says smoothly. "If you go the police, you'll hang. You came into this town a drifter, and they'll never believe that you didn't mean to kill him. I'll hang, too. I helped to cover for you. To make it look like an accident.") After an innocent man is arrested for the killing, Mike uncovers the truth and notifies the police, who nab Paula after she collects the stolen cache of money from the bank. At the film's end, a bank security guard congratulates Mike for his role in the woman's arrest, assuring him that he will receive a reward. "You keep it," Mike laconically replies.

After earning praise for his "usual rugged

screen charm" in *Framed*, Ford appeared in four mostly forgettable films in 1948, although *The Loves of Carmen*, in which he co-starred with Rita Hayworth, was a box-office hit. Still, Ford reportedly was dissatisfied with the film and called his role as Don Jose "the most ludicrous casting in the history of motion pictures. When it comes on television now, I pull the plugs out of all the sets."

Returning to film noir, Ford next starred in *The Undercover Man* (1949) as Frank Warren, an IRS tax agent who is investigating a notorious mob boss known as the "big fellow." During his six-month pursuit, Warren is beaten by henchmen of the "big fellow," but he continues his quest, eventually persuading a local informant, Salvatore Rocco (Anthony Caruso), to turn over valuable evidence. But when Rocco turns up dead and Warren's wife is threatened by a high-powered mob attorney (Barry Kelley), the agent decides to resign from the agency. His decision is protested, however, by Rocco's Italian immigrant mother, who begs him not to abandon the case: "Grandmother says this is the same as when people see evil and run away," the woman's granddaughter translates. "When people will not speak out against evil." When the woman turns over a ledger found in her son's belongings, Warren finally finds the evidence needed to indict the "big fellow" and send him to prison. Like the film itself, Ford earned mixed reviews for his performance — he was praised by Fred Hift in *Motion Picture Herald* for his "restrained yet very effective performance," but Bosley Crowther wrote in the *New York Times* that Ford, "in a battered gray hat and a baggy suit, makes a pretty case for higher salaries to civil servants, but a not very impressive sleuth."

Ford followed this film with *Mr. Soft Touch* (1949), his sixth film with fellow Columbia star Evelyn Keyes; *Lust for Gold* (1950), where he played a miner driven mad by greed; *The Flying Missile* (1950), in which he starred as a submarine commander; *The Redhead and the Cowboy* (1950), co-starring titian-haired Rhonda Fleming; and his fourth film noir, *Convicted* (1950).

Here, Ford portrayed Joe Hufford, an ill-fated brokerage firm worker whose fistfight in a bar results in the accidental death of an influential local boy. Sent to prison for the crime, Joe is later befriended by the prison's new warden, George Knowland (Broderick Crawford), who, as a district attorney, was the reluctant prosecutor of Joe's case. Although Knowland tries to make amends by appointing Joe as his chauffeur, the warden is forced to place Joe in solitary confinement when he refuses to implicate his cellmate, Malloby (Millard Mitchell), in the murder of a prison stoolie. Suspected of committing the crime himself, Joe continues to maintain his silence, even as he is taunted by a sadistic guard, Capt. Douglas (Carl Benton Reid), but Malloby stabs Capt. Douglas in the film's climax and confesses to the stoolie's murder before he is gunned down by guards. During the course of these events, Joe has fallen for the warden's daughter, Kay (Dorothy Malone), and when Knowland later uses his influence to secure Joe's parole, he is free to start a new life with Kay. The film was not a blockbuster at the box office, but Ford was singled out for his "good" performance, and the critic for

Variety wrote that the "romance angle between Ford and Dorothy Malone ... is kept within believable bounds."

Never at a loss for film assignments, Ford turned in a memorable performance as real-life golfer Ben Hogan in *Follow the Sun* (1951), and demonstrated a previously untapped comedic flair in *Young Man with Ideas* (1951), co-starring Ruth Roman and Nina Foch. He was also re-teamed with Rita Hayworth in *Affair in Trinidad* (1952), his fifth film noir.

More than faintly reminiscent of *Gilda* in tone and plot, *Affair in Trinidad* tells the story of Steve Emery (Ford), an American who travels to Trinidad to visit his brother, Neil, only to be told on his arrival that Neil has committed suicide. Steve initially reacts with hostility toward his brother's widow, Chris (Hayworth), telling her, "I just have to look at you to know what happened. I can see how Neil fell for a dame like you, and I know what kind of time you gave him. It's too bad I got here a few days too late." Before long, however, Steve manages to warm up to Chris and, after learning that Neil was murdered, the two combine forces with the local inspector (Torin Thatcher) to trap the suspected killer, local gangleader Max Fabian (Alexander Scourby). By the film's end, proof of Fabian's guilt is unearthed, Steve kills the gangster in a gun battle, and Chris and Steve return to America together.

Although *Affair in Trinidad* was popular with moviegoers, it was panned by critics as "trite" and "unwittingly comic," and Ford's performance was dismissed by the reviewer for *Variety*, who wrote: "Ford gives his role the old college try, but succeeds mainly in effecting a belligerent air." The actor fared far better, however, with a starring role in his sixth and — arguably — his best film noir, *The Big Heat* (1953).

In this gripping film, Ford portrayed Dave Bannion, a conscientious and tenacious cop who is investigating the suicide of a fellow police officer. After Bannion finds evidence that may link the officer to a local gangster, Mike Lagana (Alexander Scourby), a bomb is planted in his car, killing his wife

Left to right: Valerie Bettis, Steven Geray, Karel Stepanek, Alexander Scourby, Glenn Ford, and Rita Hayworth in *Affair in Trinidad* (1952).

(Jocelyn Brando). Devastated by his wife's death and embittered by the inaction of his superiors, Bannion quits the force and focuses on finding her killer, ignoring the sympathetic advice of a former co-worker. ("You're on a hate binge," the officer warns. "You've decided people are all scared rabbits. And you spit on 'em. No man's an island, Dave. You can't set yourself against the world and get away with it.") Bannion centers his investigation on Lagana's top henchman, Vince Stone (Lee Marvin), but it is Vince's girlfriend (Gloria Grahame) who provides the missing link and causes "the big heat" to fall, ultimately resulting in the capture of Vince and Lagana. Hailed by one reviewer as "a sizzling nest of vipers melodrama," *The Big Heat* was a critical and financial success, and Ford earned raves for his effective, low-key perfor-

mance; in a typical review, the critic for *Variety* wrote that his "portrayal of the homicide sergeant is honest and packs much wallop."

Around this time, Ford's contract with Columbia — now in its second seven-year stretch — was rewritten to allow him to freelance in films for Warner Brothers, Universal, and RKO. He was seen in a number of films for these studios, including RKO's *Appointment in Honduras* (1953), but in 1954, in his sole film of the year, he was back at Columbia to co-star with Gloria Grahame in *Human Desire*, his final film noir. Brimming with typically flawed noir characters, *Human Desire* focused on the illicit affair between train engineer Jeff Warren (Ford), and Vicki Warren (Grahame), whose husband, Carl (Broderick Crawford), is unable to keep a job due to his violent temper. When Carl murders

Gloria Grahame and Glenn Ford in *The Big Heat* (1954).

a man he suspects of having an affair with his sultry spouse, he uses blackmail to keep his straying wife at his side by threatening to reveal a letter that incriminates her for the deed. Vicki uses her wanton wiles to urge Jeff to retrieve the letter and get rid of her husband, allowing them to be together, but Jeff is ultimately unable to go through with the deed and ends the relationship. ("It's all wrong," he tells her. "The whole thing's been wrong from the beginning. And I feel dirty.... I'd have done anything for you — except that.") In the final reel, Vicki leaves her husband, but not soon enough — he catches up with her and strangles her to death aboard a train.

Inexplicably, *Human Desire* was a disappointment at the box office, despite good performances from Ford, Grahame, and Craw-

ford, and critics were unimpressed as well — the reviewer for *Variety* dismissed the production, saying that it lacked "any genuine suspense or excitement and the players down the line impart light conviction to their parts." The following year, however, Ford rebounded with one of the best-remembered films of his career, *Blackboard Jungle* (1955), where he was a standout as a beleaguered inner-city school teacher who refuses to give up on his class of juvenile delinquents. The film was a box office hit and Ford was universally praised by critics, including William K. Zinsser, who wrote in the *New York Herald Tribune* that "Ford's performance is excellent. There is something about him that is immensely appealing." Also in 1955, Ford starred with Frank Lovejoy and Cesar Romero in *The Americano*, a western set in Brazil.

This feature was notable as the first film role of Ford's son, Peter, and the first of several films in which father and son would appear together, including *Gazebo* (1959), *Fate Is the Hunter* (1964), and *Day of the Evil Gun* (1968).

"It was a great opportunity for us to be together," Peter said. "I also worked as dialog director on many other films with him. I would rehearse his lines with him by portraying the other actors and reading their parts. If my dad were in a scene with a lot of other actors, and for whatever reason they weren't there, I would read their lines."

Ford was in a series of top-notch films throughout the remainder of the decade, including *Trial* (1955), a gripping courtroom drama co-starring Arthur Kennedy; *Interrupted Melody* (1955), produced by MGM, with whom the actor signed a long-term contract after the film's release; *The Teahouse of the August Moon* (1956), one of MGM's top money-makers of the year; *Ransom* (1956), a tautly directed suspenser starring Ford as a father unwilling to yield to the demands of his son's kidnappers; *3:10 to Yuma* (1957), a western reminiscent of *High Noon* (1952); *Don't Go Near the Water* (1957), for which he was praised for his "sly and adept" comedic abilities; and *Gazebo* (1959), a black comedy with Debbie Reynolds.

By now, Ford had become one of the country's most popular actors, and in 1958 earned the label of "Number One Box Office Star in America" in the annual exhibitors poll conducted by *Motion Picture Herald*. Off-screen, however, he wasn't quite so fortunate; in 1959 Ford was divorced from his wife of 16 years, Eleanor Powell. Ford would marry on three more occasions—in 1966, he wed actress Kathryn Hays—best known for her long-running role on the television soap opera *As the World Turns*—but the marriage ended two years later. On September 10, 1977, Ford walked down the aisle again, this time with Cynthia Louise McCabe, who played a small role in a 1974 television movie starring Ford, *Punch and Jody*. This union, too, was unsuccessful, ending in the late 1980s. Ford's final marriage was a short-lived affair with Jeanie Bauss, a local nurse. The two were married in March 1993, but the union lasted only 49 days.

Career-wise, the advent of the 1960s saw Ford in a series of box-office disappointments, including *Cimarron* (1960), a western about the great Oklahoma land rush in 1889; *Four Horsemen of the Apocalypse* (1961)—a career boon for Rudolph Valentino in 1924—which was a $6 million flop; and *Pocketful of Miracles* (1961), Frank Capra's last film and a remake of his earlier success *Lady for A Day* (1933). Ford rebounded in 1963, however, with a starring role in one of his most popular films, *The Courtship of Eddie's Father*, later made into a successful television series featuring Bill Bixby. He was also seen to good advantage in *Fate Is the Hunter* (1964), with Nancy Kwan and Rod Taylor; *The Rounders* (1964), a comedy with a western locale; and *The Last Challenge* (1967), another western, this one helmed by veteran director Richard Thorpe.

Around this time, the actor took time off from his big-screen battles to serve in a real-life conflict—in 1967, as a commander in the Naval Reserves, he volunteered for five secret missions in Vietnam, and was attached to the Marines as a Lt. Colonel. In an interview in *Classic Images* magazine, Ford's commanding officer during the missions said that the actor was nearly killed on several occasions.

"He's one of the bravest men I've ever met," said retired Col. James Williams. "Time after time the star risked his neck for his country.... One of the Marines joked, 'Hey, Mr. Ford, sir, this ain't no movie. Them's real bullets out there.' Glenn just smiled at him."

Back home after his service in Vietnam, Ford appeared in a handful of feature films throughout the 1970s, including the box office smash, *Superman* (1978), but he focused most of his energies on television projects—in addition to such made-for-television movies as *Jarrett* (1973), *The Disappearance of Flight 412* (1974), and *The Gift* (1979), he also starred in two series, *Cade's County*, which ran in 1971 on CBS and co-starred his son, Peter, and *The*

Family Holvak, an NBC drama set in the 1930s, in which he portrayed a minister and family man. Of his role in the latter series, Ford told a *TV Guide* reporter that he was "essentially playing myself."

"I suppose I'm like the Reverend Holvak," he said. "I don't speak unless I have something to say. I think actors talk too much anyhow."

Ford's career began to wind down in the 1980s and 1990s and he appeared in only a handful of films, including *Happy Birthday to Me* (1981), a slasher movie in which he played a cameo role as a psychiatrist; *Casablanca Express* (1988), a World War II feature notable primarily because it starred the sons of veteran actors Anthony Quinn and Sean Connery; and *Raw Nerve* (1991), a crime drama featuring Jan-Michael Vincent. Ford's last big screen appearance was in a documentary, *Our Hollywood Education* (1992), which consisted of interviews with such industry insiders as director/actor Spike Lee, producer/director Oliver Stone, and actress Sally Kirkland. On television, Ford was featured in 1989 on an episode of the popular series, *Lifestyles of the Rich and Famous*, and played his final television role in *Final Verdict* (1991), as the father of co-star Treat Williams.

Amazingly, despite his superb performances in countless feature films, Ford was never nominated for the industry's highest honor, an oversight that is particularly felt by his son, Peter.

"He's never been one who sought glory for his career in any way," Peter said, "but when you look at the totality of his career — the film noir, the westerns, the comedies, the socio-dramas, and he did a lot of military films, too — he is an incredibly talented actor. Very sadly for me, he's never really been honored in any way by his peers for his tremendous career."

Peter states that he hopes his father will consent to appear in a film during the 2000s, which would represent eight decades of filmmaking. He adds, however, that Glenn Ford is more content to remain out of the limelight.

"He cannot walk unassisted, but he looks tremendous, and he's as healthy as an ox," Peter said in 2001. "He still gets a tremendous amount of fan mail — every day he hears from fans from around the world. There is even an Internet site developed in his honor. I think it would be great for him to be embraced by those people personally, and I'm working to get him more engaged publicly. For the moment, though, he chooses to let people remember him as this virile cowboy or holding Rita Hayworth in his arms.

"As always, he doesn't want to disappoint those who mean the most to him — his fans."

Film Noir Filmography

Gilda. Director: Charles Vidor. Producer: Virginia Van Upp. Running time: 110 minutes. Released by Columbia, May 15, 1946. Cast: Rita Hayworth, Glenn Ford, George Macready, Joseph Calleia, Steven Geray, Joe Sawyer, Gerald Mohr, Robert Scott, Lionel Royce, S.Z. Martel.

Framed. Director: Richard Wallace. Producer: Jules Schermer. Running time: 82 minutes. Released by Columbia, May 25, 1947. Cast: Glenn Ford, Janis Carter, Barry Sullivan, Edgar Buchanan, Karen Morely, Jim Bannon, Sid Tomack, Barbara Wooddell, Paul Burns.

The Undercover Man. Director: Joseph H. Lewis. Producer: Robert Rossen. Running time: 85 minutes. Released by Columbia, April 20, 1949. Cast: Glenn Ford, Nina Foch, James Whitmore, Barry Kelley, David Wolfe, Frank Tweddell, Howard St. John, John F. Hamilton, Leo Penn, Joan Lazer, Esther Minciotti, Angela Clarke, Anthony Caruso, Robert Osterloh, Kay Medford, Patricia White, Peter Brocco, Everett Glass, Joe Mantell, Michael Cisney, Marcella Cisney, Sidney Dubin, William Vedder.

Convicted. Director: Harry Levin. Producer: Jerry Bresler. Running time: 91 minutes. Released by Columbia, August 1950. Cast: Glenn Ford, Broderick Crawford, Millard Mitchell, Dorothy Malone, Carl Benton Reid, Frank Faylen, Will Geer, Martha Stewart, Henry O'Neill, Douglas Kennedy, Ronald Winters, Ed Begley, Frank Cady, John Doucette, Ilka Gruning, John A. Butler, Peter Virgo, Whit Bissell.

Affair in Trinidad. Director and Producer: Vincent Sherman. Running time: 98 minutes. Released by Columbia, 1952. Cast: Rita Hayworth, Glenn Ford, Alexander Scourby, Valerie Bettis, Torin Thatcher, Howard Wendell, Juanita Moore.

The Big Heat. Director: Fritz Lang. Producer: Robert Arthur. Running time: 90 minutes. Released by Columbia, October 14, 1953. Cast: Glenn Ford, Gloria Grahame, Jocelyn Brando, Alexander Scourby, Lee Marvin, Jeanette Nolan, Peter Whitney, Willis Bouchey, Robert Burton, Adam Williams, Howard Wendell, Chris Alcaide, Michael Granger, Dorothy Green, Carolyn Jones, Ric Roman, Dan Seymour, Edith Evanson.

Human Desire. Director: Fritz Lang. Producer: Lewis J. Rachmil. Running time: 90 minutes. Released by Columbia, August 6, 1954. Cast: Glenn Ford, Gloria Grahame, Broderick Crawford, Edgar Buchanan, Kathleen Case, Diane DeLaire, Grandon Rhodes, Dan Seymour, John Pickard, Paul Brinegar, Dan Riss, Victor Hugo Greene, John Zaremba, Carl Lee, Olan Soule.

References

Canfield, Alyce. "Where Do They Get That Stuff?" *Motion Picture Magazine*, circa 1949.

Cummings, Mitzi. Order of the Wedding Day. *Photoplay*, January 1944.

Curreri, Joe. Glenn Ford — America's Real-Life Hero. *Classic Images*, August 1993.

Ford, Glenn. "How We Rediscovered Sunday." *Guideposts*, April 1956.

Ford, Glenn, as told to Jane Kesner Ardmore. "I Can Always Escape." *The Saturday Evening Post*, circa 1957.

Galligan, David. "Glenn Ford." Publication Unsourced, circa 1984.

Hoover, Eleanor. "Couples." *People*, August 21, 1978.

Hopper, Hedda. "He Says What He Thinks!" Publication Unsourced, circa 1953.

_____. "The Neighborly Fords." *Chicago Sunday Tribune*, circa 1951.

Itria, Helen. "The Movie Star and the Bucket of Paint." *Los Angeles Examiner*, August 11, 1957.

MacKenzie, Bob. "Now Just … Just a Darned Minute." *TV Guide*, October 11, 1975.

Oppenheimer, Peer J. "Glenn Ford Proves: Actors Don't Have to Be Kooks." *Family Weekly*, February 27, 1966.

Parsons, Louella O. "Glenn Ford." *Los Angeles Examiner*, November 14, 1948.

_____. "They Find Happiness in Helping Youth." *Los Angeles Examiner*, April 10, 1955.

"The Woman Glenn Ford Loved in Vietnam." *Movie Stars*, August 1967.

Wilson, Liza. "Always Out on a Limb." *Los Angeles Examiner*, November 18, 1956.

——— WALLACE FORD ———

"All you guys, all the same. You talk big, how honest you are. You walk away when you see something like me coming. Then when you get in a jam, you're just like any anybody else. A chiseler." — Wallace Ford in *The Breaking Point* (1950)

Wallace Ford's life was stranger than fiction.

He was raised in an orphanage and a series of foster homes. He lived the life of a hobo as a teenager and adopted his stage name from a fellow tramp. His early training as a performer took place in dance halls and vaudeville troupes. He was 38 years old before he learned the identity of his parents. And he reportedly never attended a day of school in his life, but became one of Hollywood's most dependable actors, with roles in more than 100 movies.

During his prolific screen career, Ford was seen opposite a variety of leading ladies including Joan Crawford, Jean Harlow, and Loretta Young, and he was featured in such popular features as *The Informer* (1935), *Spellbound* (1945), and *The Rainmaker* (1956). But the movies that were, arguably, the best of the actor's career were his eight film noir entries: *Shadow of a Doubt* (1943), *Black Angel* (1946), *Crack-Up* (1946), *Dead Reckoning* (1947), *T-Men* (1948), *The Set-Up* (1949), *The Breaking Point* (1950), and *He Ran All the Way* (1951).

The star of stage and screen was born Samuel Jones in Bolton, Lancashire, England, on February 12, 1898, but the early circumstances of his life are somewhat sketchy. According to one account, the youngster's father,

Samuel Jones, Sr., was killed in India while fighting the British. Still a toddler at the time of his father's death, young Samuel became "accidentally" separated from his mother. Another version claims that Samuel's mother was led to believe that her baby died at birth and the infant was placed in an orphanage by a relative. The details of his beginnings notwithstanding, it is known that Samuel lived for several years in London's Bernardo Foundling Home, and was later transferred to the institution's Canadian branch, from which he was farmed out to 17 foster homes before the age of 11. Samuel ran away from the 17th placement — with a farmer in Manitoba — and joined a vaudeville troupe known as the Winnipeg Kiddies.

Leaving the troupe in 1914, Samuel made his way to Philadelphia, Pennsylvania, where he earned money selling newspapers and performing in local saloons and pool halls. In one such pool hall, Samuel met a tramp by the name of Wallace Ford. The two became fast friends and, impressed with Samuel's dancing ability and amusing impersonations of Charlie Chaplin and Theodore Roosevelt, Ford arranged for the talented young man to perform in various vaudeville houses they encountered while "hoboing" across the country. With the entry of the United States in World War I in 1917, Samuel and Ford planned to enlist, but Ford first wanted to return to his hometown in Sioux City, Iowa, to bid farewell to his mother. The men never made it. Ford was killed in a freight train accident and, in homage to his friend, Samuel adopted his name.

The newly christened Wallace Ford served during the war with the U.S. Calvary at Fort Riley, Kansas, and after his release, he signed on with a stock company in Grand Island, Nebraska. The company was known for performing "pirated" plays, by which they paid a man in Chicago to attend the opening nights of new plays, write down the dialogue and directions in shorthand, type the notes, and ship them off to Grand Island. Ford appeared in several of these productions, including *Her Legal Prisoner*, *Sappho*, and *Human Hearts*. Later, the actor joined Stuart Walker's stock company in Indianapolis, and in 1919 appeared in the company's hit production of *Seventeen*, which ran for nine months in Chicago and received a rousing reception on Broadway.

For the next decade, Ford was seen in a variety of Broadway productions, including *Abraham Lincoln*, *Pigs*, *Bad Girl*, *Young Sinners*, *Gypsy*, and *Abie's Irish Rose*. In the cast of the latter production, in which he played the title role, Ford met a young actress named Martha Haworth. The two were married on November 27, 1922, welcomed a baby girl, Patricia Ann, five years later, and would go on to enjoy one of Hollywood's longest marriages.

Meanwhile, Ford's entry into films was just ahead. In 1930, the actor appeared in two Warner Bros. shorts, *Fore* and *Absent Minded*, then got his big screen break when he was cast as Joan Crawford's husband in MGM's *Possessed* (1931). During the next four years, the actor was seen in an average of eight films a year, including such features as *Freaks* (1932), the cult classic Tod Browning film that utilized actual circus "freaks"; *The Beast of the City* (1932), where he was a weak-willed cop who falls for a gangster's moll played by Jean Harlow; *Three Cornered Moon* (1933), a hilarious screwball comedy starring Claudette Colbert; *Employees Entrance* (1933), starring Ford as the ambitious husband of Loretta Young; *Men in White* (1934), a Clark Gable-Myrna Loy starrer; *The Whole Town's Talking* (1935), a first-rate comedy directed by John Ford and starring Edward G. Robinson and Jean Arthur; and *The Informer* (1935), which earned Academy Awards for Best Actor (Victor McLaglen), Best Director (John Ford), and Best Screenplay (Dudley Nichols).

In 1936, Ford took a break from his frenetic shooting schedule after receiving a letter from a woman claiming to be his aunt. The letter informed Ford that his mother was alive and residing in England, but there was no further information. Ford returned to his homeland to institute a search, and when the London press printed articles about Ford's quest, the actor was contacted by dozens of women claiming to be his long-lost relative. Finally, in January 1937, Ford found his 56-year-mother living in an automobile trailer with her husband, a blind match-seller. His mother declined Ford's offer to move to the United States, but happily accepted his gift of a "cozy rose-covered" cottage in Manchester.

Later that year, Ford returned to his stage roots when he originated the role of George in John Steinbeck's celebrated play *Of Mice and Men*. Playing opposite Broderick Crawford as the simple-minded Lennie, Ford earned rave reviews for his performance, and was hailed for his "brilliant projection." Back in Hollywood after his triumphant run in the play, Ford was seen in a spate of mostly forgettable films, including *Back Door to Heaven* (1939), a docudrama starring Ford as a gangster; *Isle of Destiny* (1940), a laughable jungle epic; *Murder by Invitation* (1941), a run-of-the-mill whodunit; *A Man Betrayed* (1941), starring John Wayne; *Seven Days' Leave* (1942), a comedy-drama that flopped despite a cast headed by Victor Mature and Lucille Ball; and *The Marines Come Through* (1943), a low-budget war drama. The actor did appear in a handful of well-received films during this period, however, most notably *Blues in the Night* (1941), which focused on the lives of itinerant jazz musicians; *All Through the Night* (1942), a spy thriller starring Humphrey Bogart and Conrad Veidt; and *Shadow of a Doubt* (1943), Ford's first film noir.

Here, Ford played the supporting role of Fred Saunders, a detective who travels with his partner, Jack Graham (Macdonald Carey), to the town of Santa Rosa, California, seeking the killer of several wealthy widows. The detectives' prime suspect is Charlie Oakley (Joseph Cotten), in town visiting the family of his sister, Emma (Patricia Collinge). Saunders and Graham focus their investigation on Oakley's niece and namesake, Charlie Newton (Teresa Wright), who gradually comes to believe that her uncle is guilty. Before the detectives can close in on Oakley, another suspect in the "Merry Widow" murders is killed while fleeing police and the case is officially

closed. But when Oakley abruptly decides to leave town, he tries to kill his still-suspicious niece by throwing her from a moving train; the tenacious girl hangs on to a door frame, and Oakley falls to his death instead.

Although Ford's relatively minor part was overlooked by critics, the Alfred Hitchcock-directed *Shadow of a Doubt* received mostly favorable notices upon its release, although the *New York Times'* Bosley Crowther complained that the feature "becomes a bit too specious in making a moralistic show of the warmth of an American community toward an unsuspected rascal in its midst." Crowther did, however, find that there was "sufficient sheer excitement and refreshing atmosphere in the film to compensate in large measure for its few disappointing faults," and the critic for *Variety* wrote that "the suspenseful tenor of dramatics associated with director Alfred Hitchcock is utilized here to good advantage."

In 1945, two years after *Shadow of a Doubt*, Ford was seen in a small role in another Alfred Hitchcock feature, *Spellbound*, playing a hotel masher. Also that year, he appeared in *The Great John L.*, a biopic about the rise and fall of heavyweight boxing champion John L. Sullivan, and *Blood on the Sun*, a James Cagney starrer that was a box-office smash, followed by supporting roles in four consecutive films noirs: *Black Angel* (1946), *Crack Up* (1946), *Dead Reckoning* (1947), and *T-Men* (1948).

In the first, *Black Angel*, Ford was seen as Joe, the closest friend of alcoholic songwriter Martin Blair (Dan Duryea), whose shrewish ex-wife Marvis Marlowe (Constance Dowling), is found strangled to death in her bedroom. Although he'd tried unsuccessfully to visit Marvis on the night of her murder, Blair is provided with an airtight alibi by Joe, who'd locked him in his room because "he was on a bender." When another man, Kirk Bennett (John Phillips) is convicted and sentenced to death for the crime, his loyal wife, Catherine (June Vincent), teams with Martin to find the real killer. Catherine and Martin ultimately come up short in their efforts,

film's "competent performances," he predicted that audiences would be "overwhelmed by its inadequacies." In *Motion Picture Herald*, however, Ray Lanning described the film as "a surprisingly suspenseful melodrama that will often chill audiences to their seats," assuring his readers that *Crack-Up* "should disappoint no one."

Barely noticed by critics for his performance in *Crack-Up*, Ford earned his best notices to date in his next film noir outing, *Dead Reckoning*, starring Humphrey Bogart as former paratrooper Rip Murdock, and Lizabeth Scott as Coral Chandler, the beautiful but deadly singer with whom he falls in love. Investigating the disappearance — and, later, the mysterious death — of his war buddy Johnny Drake (William Prince), Rip learns from Coral that she accidentally killed her first husband, a crime of which Johnny was accused before the war, and that a local gangster named Martinelli (Morris Carnovsky) possesses the gun that can prove her involvement. Contacting McGee (Ford), a "crackerjack safecracker," Rip is given an extensive lesson on how to break into Martinelli's safe, but when he attempts to retrieve the evidence, he is informed by the gangster that Coral murdered her husband for his money, and that he and Coral have been secretly married for years. When Rip reveals his plans to turn Coral in to police, she shoots him, causing a car crash that results in her death. This time around, Ford's supporting role earned praise from several reviewers, including the critic for *Variety*, who said that he "makes a real portrait out of a safecracker bit," and Jack D. Grant of *The Hollywood Reporter*, who labeled the actor "terrific."

In Ford's fifth offering from the era, *T-Men*, he enjoyed his juiciest role yet — an oily hood who is part of a widespread network of counterfeiters operating in Detroit and Los Angeles. The action in the story focuses on two treasury agents — the "T-Men" of the film's title — who go undercover to infiltrate the gang. One of the agents, Dennis O'Brien (Dennis O'Keefe), goes on the hunt for a man in Los Angeles known as Schemer (Ford),

but shortly before Bennett's death sentence is carried out, Martin realizes that he committed the murder while in an alcohol-induced stupor and reveals his guilt in time to save Bennett's life. Despite Ford's brief appearance in the film, he was singled out in the *New York Times*, whose critic wrote: "Generally, the supporting cast conducts itself expertly, especially ... Wallace Ford as a seedy clerk of a hole-in-the-wall hotel."

Next, in *Crack-Up*, Ford portrayed Lt. Cochrane, one of two officials investigating the case of an art forgery expert, George Steele (Pat O'Brien), who breaks into a museum and tells a wild tale about being involved in a train wreck. Informed by Cochrane that there was no train wreck, Steele determines to unravel the mystery and soon unearths a plot to substitute valuable museum artwork with forgeries. Before he can contact authorities, Steele is abducted and taken to the home of Dr. Lowell (Ray Collins), the brains behind the operation, but Steele is saved from certain death when Cochrane arrives on the scene and guns Lowell down. *Crack-Up* earned widely varying reviews upon its release; although the *New York Times* critic praised the who reportedly smokes cigars, chews Chinese health herbs, frequents Turkish baths—and has a source that can produce top-quality counterfeit paper. O'Brien and his partner, Tony Genaro (Alfred Ryder)—who has infiltrated the Detroit faction — succeed in tracking down the elusive Schemer, who harbors fears that he is being targeted by the Midwest boys. Schemer's suspicions turn out to be correct, but in a last-ditch effort to save himself, he tells a Detroit hood named Moxie (Charles McGraw) that he believes Genaro is an undercover agent. The plot is unsuccessful, and Schemer meets a horrifying end when Moxie keeps him locked in a steam room until he dies. Meanwhile, Genaro unearths valuable information about the operation that was among Schemer's possessions, but he is later killed by the hoods as O'Brien is forced to look on in silence. O'Brien's cover is subsequently blown as well and he is shot in the back by Moxie, but a series of police raids finally shuts down the lucrative network and O'Brien ultimately recovers from his injuries.

In the midst of filming his series of noir features, Ford found himself in trouble with the law. In January 1947, the actor was arrested after his car struck another vehicle and landed in a ditch. Ford originally claimed that he had not been driving the car but that, instead, one of his employees had been at the wheel and had disappeared after the crash. This alibi was later abandoned by the actor, however, who stood trial on charges of felony drunk driving. But after two movie cronies testified that Ford had been sober after joining them for dinner, the actor was acquitted of the charges.

Back on screen after dodging this bullet, Ford starred opposite June Vincent in a mediocre crime drama, *Shed No Tears* (1948); portrayed a detective in the Warner Bros. drama *Embraceable You* (1948); and was featured in a trio of westerns, *Coroner Creek* (1948), starring Randolph Scott; *Man from Texas* (1948), a timewaster with James Craig and Lynn Bari; and *Red Stallion in the Rockies* (1949), a fairly entertaining tale about a wild stallion that finds protection from local ranchers. He then returned to the dark side of the screen for three films noirs in as many years, *The Set-Up* (1949), *The Breaking Point* (1950), and *He Ran all the Way* (1951). *The Set-Up*, which ranks among the best fight films ever produced, focused on a single bout in the career of an aging boxer, Stoker Thompson (Robert Ryan). One of the memorable highlights of this gritty and atmospheric film was its depiction of a series of individuals seated in the audience for the night's action, including a blind man who has the fights described to him, an obese fan who sits eating popcorn as if he's a kid at the circus, and a woman who complains that she will be unable to watch but later views the battles in a frenzy of excitement and even screams at one point, "Quit stalling—let's have some action!" Ford played Gus, the wise, compassionate dressing-room attendant where Stoker is preparing for his bout, unaware that his manager (George Tobias) has accepted $50 from a gangster known as Little Boy (Alan Baxter) to ensure Stoker's defeat. In the midst of the fight, Stoker is informed of the deal, but he refuses to take a dive and emerges the winner. He later pays for his victory, however, when he is cornered after the fight by Little Boy and his hoods, who beat him severely and break his hand, ending his career forever.

After earning mention in *Motion Picture Herald* for "contribut[ing] nicely" to the cast of *The Set-Up*, Ford was back on the wrong side of the law in *The Breaking Point*, playing sleazy, cigar-chomping attorney F.P. Duncan, who convinces a cash-strapped charter boat owner to smuggle a group of Chinese refugees from Mexico to the United States. During the trip, the boat captain, Harry Morgan (John Garfield), is forced to shoot in self-defense the refugees' representative, Mr. Sing (Victor Sen Yung), dumping his body overboard. Duncan later approaches Harry for another job, this time to provide an escape for a quartet of hoods after their successful heist at a local race track. As a reward for his efforts as a go-between, Duncan is gunned before the hoods join Harry, who realizes that he will be killed by the men once they reach their destination. One by one, Harry manages to kill his nefarious passengers, but he is severely wounded and is convinced by his tearful wife (Phyllis Thaxter) in the film's final scene to allow his arm to be amputated, thereby saving his life and allowing him to face a brighter future. After the release of the film, which was labeled "hard-driving" and "realistic," Ford was singled out for notice in the *Los Angeles Times*, whose critic wrote that he "scores as a despicable, weak-kneed shyster."

The following year, Ford was again featured with John Garfield in the final film noir of his career, *He Ran All the Way* (1951). Here, the actor played Mr. Dobbs, a genial family man who lives with his wife (Selena Royle) and two children, Peg (Shelley Winters) and Tommy (Bobby Hyatt). Dobbs' contented world is shattered, however, when Peg comes home with Nick Robey (Garfield), a young man she met at the local swimming pool. Unbeknownst to Peg, Nick has just been involved in a payroll robbery that resulted in the shooting of a police officer, and he holds the family hostage for the next three days as he desperately searches for a means of escape. When Nick secures a car and plans to flee with Peg, Mr. Dobbs shoots at him ("You're not taking my baby!" he shouts), but Nick's ultimate downfall comes at the hands of Peg, who guns him down in the street. Once again, Ford earned praise for his performance, with the critic for *Variety* writing: "Support is unusually good. Wallace Ford, as the helpless father; Selena Royle, as the tortured mother, and Bobby Hyatt, as the kid brother, keep the performance level high."

Throughout the remainder of the 1950s, Ford was seen primarily in a series of westerns, including *Rodeo* (1952), in which he played an aging bronco buster named Barbecue Jones; *The Nebraskan* (1953), a cowboys-and-Indians saga filmed in 3-D; *Wichita* (1955), where he was featured in a good role as a small-town newspaper editor; *The Man from Laramie* (1955), starring James Stewart and Arthur Kennedy; *Stagecoach to Fury* (1956), which centered on a group of stagecoach passengers held hostage by Mexican bandits; and *The Maverick Queen* (1956), where Barbara Stanwyck was featured as a saloon owner. But his best films of this period were two non-oaters—*The Rainmaker* (1956), starring Burt Lancaster as a charismatic con man, and *The Matchmaker* (1958), with Shirley Booth in the title role. Between films, the actor appeared in guest spots on such television series as including *Goodyear Television Playhouse* and *Trackdown*, and was seen in a recurring role as Marshal Herb Lamson in the first season of *The Deputy*, a western series that ran from 1959 to 1961.

At this point in his career, Ford's feature film and television appearances dropped off dramatically. Now in his 60s, Ford was seen in such small screen series as *The Wide Country* and *The Andy Griffith Show*, and in only two more films, *Tess of the Storm Country* (1961), an interesting period piece starring Diane Baker, and *A Patch of Blue* (1965), in which he played the good-natured, alcoholic father of Shelley Winters. In February 1966, Martha Haworth, his wife of more than 40 years, died after a long illness. Just four months later, on June 11, 1966, Ford suffered a heart attack and died while hospitalized at the Motion Picture Country House and Hospital in Woodland Hills, California. Friends surmised that the actor's grief over his wife's death had hastened his own demise.

Several days after his death, Ford was honored at a memorial service in Brentwood, California; reading like a list of "who's who" of the screen, the actor had more than 60 honorary pallbearers, including such luminaries as John Ford, Pat O'Brien, Spencer Tracy, Lee Tracy, Lloyd Nolan, Bing Crosby, Ralph Bellamy, Ed Begley, William Talman, Alan Hale, J. Carroll Naish, Frank McHugh, Alan Mowbray, Otto Kruger, Keenan Wynn, Leon Ames, Vincent Price, Clarence Muse, and Arthur O'Connell. Although the "histrionic hobo" started his life in an orphanage and honed his craft in saloons and pool rooms, Ford rose above his circumstances and managed to become one of the most respected and beloved performers of his time.

Film Noir Filmography

Shadow of a Doubt. Director: Alfred Hitchcock. Producer: Jack H. Skirball. Running time: 108 minutes. Released by Universal, January 12, 1943. Cast: Teresa Wright, Joseph Cotten, Macdonald Carey, Henry Travers, Patricia Collinge, Hume Cronyn, Edna Mae Wonacott, Wallace Ford, Irving Bacon, Charles Bates, Clarence Muse, Janet Shaw, Estelle Jewell, Minverva Urecal, Isabel Randolph, Earle S. Dewey. Awards: Academy Award nomination for Best Original Story (Gordon McDonell).

Black Angel. Director: Roy William Neill. Producers: Tom McKnight, Roy William Neill. Running time: 83 minutes. Released by Universal, August 2, 1946. Cast: Dan Duryea, June Vincent, Peter Lorre, Broderick Crawford, Constance Dowling, Wallace Ford, Hobart Cavanaugh, Freddie Steele, Ben Bard, John Phillips, Junius Matthews, Maurice St. Clair, Vilova, Pat Starling.

Crack-Up. Director: Irving Reis. Producer: Jack J. Gross. Running time: 93 minutes. Released by RKO, October 6, 1946. Cast: Pat O'Brien, Claire Trevor, Herbert Marshall, Ray Collins, Wallace Ford, Dean Harens, Damian O'Flynn, Erskine Sanford, Mary Ware.

Dead Reckoning. Director: John Cromwell. Producer: Sidney Biddell. Running time: 100 minutes. Released by Columbia, January 22, 1947. Cast: Humphrey Bogart, Lizabeth Scott, Morris Carnovsky, Charles Cane, William Prince, Marvin Miller, Wallace Ford, James Bell, George Chandler, William Forrest, Ruby Dandridge.

T-Men. Director: Anthony Mann. Producer: Aubrey Schenck. Running time: 92 minutes. Released by Eagle-Lion Films, January 22, 1948. Cast: Dennis O'Keefe, Alfred Ryder, May Meade, Wallace Ford, June Lockhart, Charles McGraw, Jane Randolph, Art Smith, Herbert Heyes, Jack Overman, John Wengraf, Jim Bannon, William Malten. Awards: Academy Award nomination for Best Sound Recording (Sound Services, Inc.).

The Set-Up. Director: Robert Wise. Producer: Richard Goldstone. Running time: 72 minutes. Released by RKO, March 29, 1949. Cast: Robert Ryan, Audrey Totter, George Tobias, Alan Baxter, Wallace Ford, Percy Helton, Hal Fieberling, Darryl Hickman, Kenny O'Morrison, James Edwards, David Clarke, Phillip Pine, Edwin Max.

The Breaking Point. Director: Michael Curtiz. Producer: Jerry Wald. Running time: 97 minutes. Released by Warner Bros., September 30, 1950. Cast: John Garfield, Patricia Neal, Phyllis Thaxter, Juano Hernandez, Wallace Ford, Edmon Ryan, Ralph Dumke, Guy Thomajan, William Campbell, Sherry Jackson, Donna Jo Boyce, Victor Sen Yung, Peter Brocco, John Doucette, James Griffith.

He Ran All the Way. Director: John Berry. Producer: Bob Roberts. Running time: 77 minutes. Released by United Artists, July 13, 1951. Cast: John Garfield, Shelley Winters, Wallace Ford, Selena Royle, Bobby Hyatt, Gladys George, Norman Lloyd.

References

"Actor Back After Reunion." *Los Angeles Examiner*, July 27, 1937.

"Actor's Mother Gains Her Wish." *Los Angeles Times*, December 24, 1936.

Biography of Wallace Ford. Columbia Studios, March 1958.

Biography of Wallace Ford. Paramount Studios, July 1936.

Biography of Wallace Ford. Universal Studios, 1943.

"Court Clears Wallace Ford." *Los Angeles Examiner*, May 2, 1947.

"Final Rites Conducted for Actor Wallace Ford." *Los Angeles Times*, June 16, 1966.

"Ford Was Sober, Say Two Movie Cronies of Actor." *Los Angeles Daily News*, April 17, 1947.

"Histrionic Ex-Hobo." *New York Times*, September 22, 1946.

"Parent of Ford in England." *Los Angeles Examiner*, January 11, 1937.

"Peddler Who Found Actor Stepson Dies." *Hollywood Citizen-News*, January 12, 1937.

"Wallace Ford Appears for Trial Wearing Beard." *Los Angeles Times*, April 16, 1947.

"Wallace Ford Final Honors Today." *Hollywood Citizen-News*, June 15, 1966.

"Wallace Ford Goes on Trial." *Los Angeles Examiner*, April 16, 1947.

"Wallace Ford Is Dead at 68; Acted in More Than 200 Films." *New York Times*, June 12, 1966.

"Wallace Ford Rites Tomorrow." *New York Times*, June 14, 1966.

"W. Ford, Actor, 68." *Newark Evening News*, June 11, 1966.

DOUGLAS FOWLEY

"You don't scare me, Walt. And I don't like doing business with guys that push me around."— Douglas Fowley in *Desperate* (1947)

Douglas Fowley was primarily recognized in the Hollywood community for two characteristics: his versatility as an actor and his apparent fondness for the institution of marriage. In more than 200 films during a 46-year screen career, he depicted everything from hard-boiled gangsters to weary cowpokes, and in one feature, *Barabbas* (1962), he played eight separate roles, including a blind man, a gladiator, and a hunchback. He also used his multifaceted talents to good advantage on the small screen, with numerous guest spots on a variety of programs and a regular role as Doc Holliday on the popular series, *The Life and Legend of Wyatt Earp*. While he wasn't performing, however, Fowley seemed to spend most of his time walking down the aisle, marrying six times between 1935 and 1954.

In addition to *Barabbas*, the most prominent among Fowley's many feature films included *Dodge City* (1939), *Singin' in the Rain* (1952), *The High and the Mighty* (1954), and *Walking Tall* (1973), and he appeared during his career alongside such top stars as Clark Gable, Ava Gardner, Gene Kelly and Frank Sinatra. Fowley was also a featured player in five examples from the era of film noir: *Fall Guy* (1947), *Desperate* (1947), *Behind Locked Doors* (1948), *Edge of Doom* (1950), and *Armored Car Robbery* (1950).

Born in Greenwich Village, New York, on May 30, 1911, Daniel Vincent Fowley came by his creativity naturally — his mother, Anna O'Conner, was a singer, and his father, John, was a painter, sculptor, writer, and linguist who was educated at Trinity College in Dublin. He first became interested in acting at the age of nine, while studying at the St. Francis Xavier Military Academy and, already preparing for his future career, reportedly changed his name to Douglas a short time later.

Following his schooling, Fowley joined the Walter Hampden Theatre, playing the title role in *Julius Caesar*, and was seen in productions with a variety of stock companies, including the Perruschi Players in Sarasota, Florida. He later traveled west, attending Los Angeles City College; while there, Fowley continued to pursue his acting career and his performance in a stock production of *Sailor, Beware* earned the actor a small role in his screen debut, *The Mad Game* (1933), starring Spencer Tracy and Claire Trevor.

Signing a contract with Universal (and later switching over to Fox), Fowley began a phenomenal string of film appearances, averaging nine pictures a year between 1934 and 1954. His performances encompassed a variety of roles, including gangsters, reporters, cowboys, taxi drivers, cops, soldiers, and bartenders. Remarkably, during his first six years in Hollywood, Fowley also took time out to work the vaudeville and nightclub circuits as a comedian, master of ceremonies, singer, and dancer.

The quality of the films in which Fowley appeared were as wide-ranging as his roles. During the 1930s, he was seen in such fare as *Gift of Gab* (1934), a musical that flopped at the box office despite a talented cast that included Alice White, Ethel Waters, and Ruth Etting; *Straight from the Heart* (1935), a tearjerker starring Mary Astor; *Sing, Baby Sing* (1936), an entertaining musical with Alice Faye and Adolphe Menjou; *36 Hours to Kill* (1936), where Fowley was featured as a top-level gangster; *On the Avenue* (1937), another popular musical, this time starring Dick Powell as a Broadway producer; *Submarine Patrol* (1938), a sea adventure directed by John Ford; *Arizona Wildcat* (1938), a western comedy featuring child star Jane Withers; and *Dodge City* (1939), a box-office hit starring Errol Flynn and Olivia deHavilland in the fifth of their 12 films together.

Away from the big screen, Fowley had embarked on what would be a continuous series of marriages. He got off on the wrong foot with his initial trip to the altar, however, eloping in July 1935 with actress Marjorie Reid and causing what one reporter described as "thunderheads of parental displeasure."

"Marjorie has known the man but six weeks," the bride's parents were quoted in a *Los Angeles Examiner* article. "We are bitterly opposed to this union. We don't know what's to be done."

The young woman's parents didn't have long to wait — the couple stayed married less than two years, and in 1938, Fowley wed wife number two, socialite Shelby Payne. This marriage lasted until 1943, when Payne filed for divorce, claiming that she had been physically abused by Fowley.

"He struck me several times ... once right on the jaw," Payne testified. "He told me he didn't love me, and when he left, he said, 'This should have happened four or five years ago.'"

A year later, while Fowley was serving in the U.S. Navy, he married Mary Hunter, a civilian employee at the San Diego naval station, but in 1947, this union, too, ended in divorce. That same year, following a whirlwind courtship, Fowley wed Vivian Chambers, described as a "non-professional," followed by wife number five, Joy Torstup, in 1950. And the list increased to six in 1954 with Fowley's marriage to secretary Mary Ann Walsh, who was 20 years his junior. Fowley and Walsh lived together for less than a year before separating, and during their divorce hearing, Walsh claimed that her spouse was extremely jealous, preventing her from leaving the house without his permission, and even refusing to allow her to see her family "without a big fight about it."

"It all made me feel terrible," Walsh said. "I lost weight and was a nervous wreck."

Between matrimonial entanglements, Fowley continued his non-stop film schedule, appearing in such well-received features as *Somewhere I'll Find You* (1942), starring Clark Gable and Lana Turner; *Pittsburgh* (1942),

which reunited Marlene Dietrich, John Wayne, and Randolph Scott following their earlier hit, *The Spoilers* (1942); *The Story of Dr. Wassell* (1944), with Gary Cooper in the title role of the real-life missionary doctor; *See Here, Private Hargrove* (1944), an entertaining wartime comedy in which Fowley was seen as an Army captain; *The Glass Alibi* (1946), which starred Fowley as a reporter who plots the murder of his wealthy wife; *Coroner Creek* (1948), a Randolph Scott western; *Flaxy Martin* (1949), a gangster melodrama where Fowley played a detective; and *Battleground* (1949), a first-rate war feature directed by William Wellman and starring Van Johnson, John Hodiak, and Ricardo Montalban. (Fowley's performance in the latter production was one of his most memorable; he played the role of Kipp Kippton, a toothless soldier with ill-fitting dentures. The role was made to order for Fowley — during his service as a first-class Navy seaman in World War II, the actor had been involved in an accidental explosion in which he suffered a broken jaw and lost most of his teeth.)

Also during the 1940s, Fowley made his foray onto the shadowy side of the screen — among the 19 films in which he appeared in 1947 were his first two films noirs, *Fall Guy* and *Desperate*. In the first, based on a short story, "Cocaine," by Cornell Woolrich, Fowley played Inspector Shannon, who heads up the investigation of a man found unconscious in the street with a bloody knife beside him. When he regains consciousness in a hospital, the man, Tom Cochrane (Clifford Penn), is questioned in rapid-fire fashion by Shannon. ("Who did you kill? Where did that knife come from? Who did you kill?") Unable to remember the circumstances that led to his capture by police, Cochrane escapes from the hospital and determines to find out the truth, aided by his girlfriend, Lois Walter (Teala Loring), and a police friend, Mac McLaine (Robert Armstrong). Cochrane remembers blacking out at a party and finding the dead body of a woman in a closet, but it isn't revealed until the film's climax that the dead woman was the mistress of Lois' uncle, who killed the woman and attempted to frame Tom for the murder.

Fowley's second film noir of 1947, *Desperate*, begins as truck driver Steven Randall (Steve Brodie) is enticed into hauling a shipment of perishables by an old neighborhood pal, Walt Radak (Raymond Burr), only to find that the cargo actually contains stolen goods. When Randall tries to back out of the deal by hailing a passing cop, a gun battle breaks out, resulting in the death of the policeman and the arrest of Walt's kid brother, Al (Larry Nunn), for murder. Managing to escape from Walt and his hoods, Randall goes on the lam with his pregnant wife (Audrey Long); to track him down, Walt hires Pete Lavitch (Fowley), described by one character as "a pretty good private dick 'til he lost his license." Lavitch succeeds in identifying Randall's whereabouts, but he refuses to follow him until Walt forks over more money: "The farm is in Minnesota," Lavitch says. "I gotta take a train. I like riding cushions, Walt. That costs dough." After tracking Randall to the farm, Lavitch returns to Walt, but when police show up a short time later, Walt blames Lavitch for leading them there and kills him. Meanwhile, Walt catches up to Randall shortly before his brother's planned execution and holds him hostage, planning to shoot him at the moment of Al's death. Fleeing from Walt, Randall turns the tables on the vengeful hood and finally guns him down after stalking him through the winding staircases of an apartment building.

Fowley continued his streak of film noir features in 1948 with a third-billed role in *Behind Locked Doors* (1948). Here, clean-shaven and bespectacled, the actor was nearly unrecognizable as Larson, a sadistic guard in a sanitarium where a corrupt judge has taken refuge from the authorities who are hunting him. After reporter Kathy Lawrence (Lucille Bremer, in her last role) learns of the judge's whereabouts, she hires a private detective, Ross Stewart (Richard Carlson), to infiltrate the sanitarium and gain proof that the law-breaking lawman is inside. Arranging to have himself committed to the sanitarium, Stewart ultimately locates the elusive judge, but he nearly loses his life when Larson discovers his real identity and locks him in a cell with a deranged inmate known as "The Champ" (Tor Johnson). Fearing that Stewart is in danger, Kathy gains entry to the sanitarium by disguising herself as the judge's girlfriend and succeeds in preventing Stewart's murder. Meanwhile, "The Champ" manages to escape from his cell and attacks Larson, but police show up in time to gun down the former wrestler and arrest the lot of bad guys. For Fowley's creepy performance as the guard, one critic noted that he showed "intelligent restraint," while another singled him out as "fine."

Throughout the 1950s, Fowley was seen in such varied roles as a detective in *Bunco Squad* (1950), a quickie crime drama; a cab driver in *Angels in the Outfield* (1951), an enjoyable fantasy-comedy featuring Paul Douglas; an ice man in *Room for One More* (1952), a Cary Grant starrer; a beleaguered movie director in *Singin' in the Rain* (1952), a hit musical comedy starring Gene Kelly and Debbie Reynolds; an auctioneer in *The Band Wagon* (1953), another popular musical, this one starring Fred Astaire; a bartender in *The Lone Gun* (1954), a well-done western with George Montgomery and Dorothy Malone; a sheriff in *Raiders in Old California* (1957), a Republic Pictures western starring Jim Davis; and a Korean War soldier in *The Geisha Boy* (1957), a Jerry Lewis comedy. He was also seen on opposite sides of the law in his final two films noirs, playing a luckless hood in *Armored Car Robbery* (1950), and a hard-boiled detective in *Edge of Doom* (1950).

In *Armored Car Robbery*, Fowley played Benny McBride, who joins in the planned heist of an armored car in the hopes of regaining the affections of his money-grubbing wife, Yvonne LeDoux (Adele Jergens). The estranged couple's relationship is illuminated during an early exchange when Yvonne tells Benny that their relationship is over. "What would you say," Benny asks, "if I told you I was about to hit the big time?" And Yvonne nonchalantly rejoins, "I wouldn't know what to say — it'd be such a shock." The elaborately designed robbery, masterminded by a cold-blooded hood, Dave Purvis (William Talman), is nearly foiled when cops arrive on the scene, leaving one of the officers dead and Benny severely wounded. The quartet of robbers— which includes Al Mapes (Steve Brodie) and Ace Foster (Gene Evans)— manages to get away with the money, but Dave refuses Benny's repeated pleas for medical attention. Benny is killed by Dave after confronting the gangleader at gunpoint, and the group's number continues to dwindle when Al is arrested and Ace is shot by police. Finally, arriving at a local airport with Yvonne, with whom he has been having an affair, Dave meets an unexpected end when he is struck and killed by a departing airplane. For his well-done performance as Benny, Fowley was labeled "expert" by the critic for *Variety*, who termed the film a "tough meller" and wrote that it "plays off at a good pace."

Fowley's final film noir, *Edge of Doom*, focused on Martin Lynn (Farley Granger) and his role in the murder of a local priest who refused to provide a "fine funeral" for Lynn's recently deceased mother. Fowley was featured as the tough detective who first arrests Martin, suspecting him of robbing a movie house cashier. After he successfully provides an alibi on the robbery charge, Martin tries to conceal his involvement in priest's death, but he is worn down by his conscience and the increasing suspicions of the new parish priest, Father Roth (Dana Andrews). Finally, after Martin confesses his guilt while visiting his mother's dead body in the chapel, he turns to Roth for help and ultimately surrenders. Upon its release, *Edge of Doom* earned mixed reviews from critics, with Wylie Williams of the *Hollywood Citizen-News* calling the feature "an adult film with a believable message," and the *New York Times* reviewer judging that it followed "a rather conventional melodramatic course." Fowley, however, was singled out for mention by *Los Angeles Times* critic Philip K. Scheuer, who included the actor in his praise of the film's "skillful supporting cast."

Between appearances in nearly 60 feature films during the 1950s, Fowley also began making a name for himself on the small screen. In addition to his role as Doc Holliday on *The Life and Legend of Wyatt Earp*, which ran on ABC from 1955 to 1961, Fowley was a cast member of *Pistols 'n' Petticoats*, a half-hour CBS comedy-western from the 1966-67 season, and *Detective School*, a short-lived ABC sitcom that aired from July to November 1979. He was also seen in such made-for-television movies as *Guns of Diablo* (1964), *Arthur Hailey's The Moneychangers* (1976), and *Sunshine Christmas* (1977), and guested on dozens of series, including *Richard Diamond, Private Detective*; *Wanted: Dead or Alive*; *The Adventures of Rin Tin Tin*; *Death Valley Days*; *Perry Mason*; *Bonanza*; *Daniel Boone*; *Gomer Pyle, U.S.M.C.*; *Mayberry R.F.D.*; *Gunsmoke*; *Kung Fu*; *The Streets of San Francisco*, *Marcus Welby, M.D.*; *CHiPs*; *Father Murphy*, and *The Rockford Files*.

In 1960, Fowley expanded his list of performing credits to include duties as producer and director on *Macumba*, a low-budget programmer shot in Brazil, but after this poorly received feature, he remained in front of the camera. Although his big-screen appearances began to decrease during this period, Fowley continued accepting feature film assignments in a number of films, including *Who's Been Sleeping in My Bed?* (1963), a bedroom farce starring Dean Martin; *Seven Faces of Dr. Lao* (1964), where his World War II accident served him in good stead in his role as a toothless cowboy; *Walking Tall* (1973), a wildly popular drama in which he portrayed a judge; *From Noon 'Til Three* (1976), a passable western starring Charles Bronson; and *The North Avenue Irregulars* (1979), an entertaining Disney comedy. The latter film was Fowley's last — at the age of 68, with hundreds of screen and television roles behind him, the actor retired from performing.

On May 21, 1998, Douglas Fowley died of natural causes at the Motion Picture and Television Country House and Hospital in Woodland Hills, California. The 86-year-old actor was survived by his five children — and the last of his numerous wives, Jean. (One of his children, Kim — son of the actor's second wife, Shelby Payne — had become involved in such creative outlets as acting, composing, and record producing and, most significantly, served as music producer for the hit 1973 film *American Graffiti*.)

Today, neither the name nor the countenance of Douglas Fowley is likely to be recognized by modern audiences. In his heyday, however, the actor was one of Hollywood's busiest performers, demonstrating a talent for comedy and drama alike, and earning a reputation for dependability and versatility. In many of his early features, and in such films as *Desperate* (1947) and *Armored Car Robbery* (1950), Fowley exhibited a flair for villainy that unquestionably earned him a slot in the Hollywood history books.

Film Noir Filmography

Fall Guy. Director: Reginald LeBorg. Producer: Walter Mirisch. Running time: 64 minutes. Released by Monogram, March 15, 1947. Cast: Clifford Penn, Teala Loring, Robert Armstrong, Virginia Dale, Elisha Cook, Jr., Douglas Fowley, Charles Arnt, Harry Strang.

Desperate. Director: Anthony Mann. Producer: Michel Kraike. Running time: 73 minutes. Released by RKO, May 20, 1947. Cast: Steve Brodie, Audrey Long, Raymond Burr, Douglas Fowley, William Challee, Jason Robards, Sr., Freddie Steele, Lee Frederick, Paul E. Burns, Ilka Gruning.

Behind Locked Doors. Director: Oscar [Budd] Boetticher, Jr. Producer: Eugene Ling. Running time: 62 minutes. Released by: Eagle-Lion, November 1, 1948. Cast: Lucille Bremer, Richard Carlson, Douglas Fowley, Thomas Browne Henry, Herbert Heyes, Ralf Harolde, Gwen Donovan, Morgan Farley, Trevor Bardette, Dickie Moore.

Edge of Doom. Director: Mark Robson. Producer: Samuel Goldwyn. Running time: 99 minutes. Released by RKO, September 27, 1950. Cast: Dana Andrews, Farley Granger, Joan Evans, Robert Keith, Paul Stewart, Mala Powers, Adele Jergens, Harold Vermilyea, John Ridgeley, Douglas Fowley, Mabel Paige, Howland Chamberlain, Houseley Stevenson, Sr., Jean Innes, Ellen Corby, Ray Teal, Mary Field, Virginia Brissac, Frances Morris.

Armored Car Robbery. Director: Richard Fleischer. Producer: Herman Schlom. Running time: 67 minutes. Released by RKO, June 8, 1950. Cast: Charles McGraw, Adele Jergens, William Talman, Douglas Fowley, Steve Brodie, Don McGuire, Don Haggerty, James Flavin, Gene Evans.

References

"Actor Beat Her, Says Wife, Freed." *Los Angeles Examiner*, August 12, 1943.

Biography of Douglas Fowley. MGM Studios, June 15, 1949.

Biography of Douglas Fowley. Paramount Pictures, August 20, 1940.

Biography of Douglas Fowley. RKO Radio Pictures, circa 1947.

"Douglas Fowley Wed in San Diego." *Los Angeles Examiner*, September 28, 1944.

"Douglas V. Fowley, 86, Versatile Character Actor." *New York Times*, May 29, 1998.

"Featured Actor Weds Vivian Chambers." *Los Angeles Herald-Express*, May 29, 1947.

"Fowley Divorced by Mate." *Los Angeles Herald Express*, circa 1955.

"Fowley, Miss Payne, Admit Divorce Due." *Los Angeles Herald-Express*, June 17, 1943.

"Pertinent and Impertinent." *Los Angeles Times*, June 19, 1934.

Obituary. *Variety*, June 22, 1998.

"Sixth Wife Sues Screen Actor." *Los Angeles Times*, February 24, 1955.

"Socialite Actress Elopes." *Los Angeles Examiner*, July 23, 1935.

"Versatile Actor Plays Eight Roles." *Newark Evening News*, December 30, 1961.

"Wife Divorces Actor 20 Years Her Senior." *Los Angeles Times*, June 23, 1956.

JOHN GARFIELD

"You don't love me. You never loved me. Nobody loves anyone."— John Garfield in *He Ran All the Way* (1950)

One of filmdom's most talented and most underrated actors, John Garfield died before reaching the age of 40 and left behind a film legacy that, sadly, was often overshadowed by his reported link with Communism. This tarnish on his memory notwithstanding, Garfield's was a true "Cinderella" story — born and raised on the lower East side of New York City, he was rescued from a life of truancy and misbehavior by a benevolent educator and eventually found stardom on Broadway and in Hollywood. With only 31 films over a 12-year-period to his credit, Garfield nonetheless demonstrated a natural acting talent in such classics as *Gentleman's Agreement* (1947), and was featured in six exceptional offerings from the film noir era: *The Postman Always Rings Twice* (1946), *Nobody Lives Forever* (1946), *Body and Soul* (1947), *Force of Evil* (1948), *The Breaking Point* (1950), and *He Ran All the Way* (1951).

The actor who was, in his words, "born to be a mug or a gangster if ever a guy was," entered the world as Jacob Julius Garfinkle on March 4, 1913, the oldest of two boys born to David Garfinkle, a Jewish tailor, and his wife, Hannah. Julie, as he was called by his family and friends, suffered his first tragedy at the early age of seven when his mother died, leaving their father to raise two small boys alone. His mother's death had a significant impact on Julie's upbringing — in a 1946 magazine article, the actor said: "Not having a mother, I could stay out late, I didn't have to eat regularly or drink my milk at 4 o'clock; I could sleep out and run away, which I did a lot of."

Julie was shuffled around to various relatives in the Bronx, Brooklyn, and Queens until the age of 10, when his father remarried and the family was reunited. Still, in an effort to garner the "attention I missed at home," the actor said that he became the leader of a local gang.

"[But] it wasn't a bad gang ... we never robbed at the point of a gun," he later revealed. "Just potatoes we'd steal from a grocery store, or crackers."

Julie contracted scarlet fever when he was 12 (which led to the heart damage that would plague him throughout his life), and after his recovery he enrolled at P.S. 45, described by the press as a school for "problem children" and "juvenile delinquents." The actor later insisted, however, that the school was just "full of tough kids because it was in a poor neighborhood."

The principal of P.S. 45 was Angelo Patri, a renowned educator whom the actor credited with setting him on the right path. The school offered a variety of activities for students, including athletics, carpentry, orchestra, printing, and dramatics. Encouraged by Patri, Julie took up boxing, eventually becoming a semi-finalist in a local Golden Gloves tournament. Patri also steered the boy toward the field of acting.

"I always wanted to be in the limelight and I found I could get it by being on the stage," the actor said. "That was the beginning of everything for me."

Patri later arranged for Julie to attend Roosevelt High School and was instrumental in securing a scholarship for the boy to the Heckscher Foundation dramatic school, where he appeared in several productions,

including *A Midsummer Night's Dream*. Later, after being loaned the tuition by Patri, Julie studied under Madame Maria Ouspenskaya at the American Laboratory Theatre, and went on to land a job with the Eva Le Gaillienne Civic Repertory Theater. He made his Broadway debut in 1932 in *Lost Boy*, and later that year appeared in *Counsellor at Law* with Paul Muni. He then joined the famed Group Theatre, which, the actor said later, "taught me an entirely new approach, an entirely new technique. I didn't learn anything about acting until I joined the Group Theatre." As part of the Group Theatre, the actor—who had by now changed his name to Jules Garfield—racked up experience in a number of productions, including *Johnny Johnson*, *Waiting for Lefty*, and *Awake and Sing*. Meanwhile, in 1934, Garfield married his high school sweetheart, Roberta Seidman, whom the actor later described as "the most important single element in my life." At the end of the decade, the couple would have their first child, a daughter they named Katherine.

Garfield won his first Broadway lead in 1937, in *Having Wonderful Time*, but he left the $300-a-week role later that year to accept a small part in Clifford Odets' Group Theatre

production of *Golden Boy*. It was the first— but not the last—instance of Garfield forsaking money for art's sake. The act proved to be a fortuitous one, however; the actor was seen in *Golden Boy* by a talent scout from Warner Bros., and was offered a seven-year contract. The soon-to-be-star signed—on the condition that he be allowed to take time out each year to return to the stage—and changed his name again, to John Garfield.

In his screen debut, *Four Daughters* (1938), starring Claude Rains and the Lane sisters, Priscilla, Rosemary, and Lola, Garfield was a sensation—one reviewer wrote that he "stopped the show" in his first scene in the movie and that "nobody before on the screen had ever smoked a cigarette the way he did.... He had individuality plus a peculiar menace." Audiences and critics alike were bowled over the actor's soulful eyes and boyish grin, and Garfield was nominated for a Best Supporting Actor Oscar (he lost to Walter Brennan in *Kentucky*).

Garfield followed this triumph in 1939 with *They Made Me a Criminal*, a top-notch Warners feature in which he portrayed a cynical, hard-drinking boxer whose life is transformed when it is believed that he murdered a reporter and was killed in a car crash. Also that year—the busiest of his career—he appeared in *Juarez*, with Bette Davis and Paul Muni; *Blackwell's Island*, in which he played a crusading reporter; *Dust Be My Destiny*, which told the well-worn tale of a slum kid imprisoned for a crime he didn't commit; and the sequel to *Four Daughters*, entitled *Daughters Courageous*.

In 1940, Garfield exercised his contractual right to return to the stage, starring in the Broadway production of *Heavenly Express* with Aline MacMahon and Art Smith, but the play was a flop. "When I got back to the studio, some folks gave me that 'I told you so,'" Garfield told a *New York Times* reporter. "But I did it and I didn't regret it a bit." On screen that year, Garfield was seen in a quartet of fairly forgettable films—*The Castle on the Hudson* (1940), where he played a jewel thief in prison for a 25-year stretch; *Saturday's*

Children (1940) co-starring Anne Shirley; *Flowing Gold* (1940), an oil-town saga with Frances Farmer (with whom the actor reportedly had a torrid affair); and *East of the River* (1940), which was reminiscent of the more superior MGM feature, *Manhattan Melodrama* (1934). He fared better the following year, however, scoring a meaty role alongside Edward G. Robinson and Ida Lupino in *The Sea Wolf*. Having become disenchanted with the recent films he was being assigned to by Warners, Garfield had actively campaigned for the role and, after winning it, successfully lobbied the screenwriter, Robert Rossen, to rewrite it to better suit his personality. The result was an outstanding film, one of Garfield's best and most memorable.

Garfield turned in another top-notch performance in *Out of the Fog* (1941), portraying a menacing racketeer, then was loaned to MGM for *Tortilla Flat* (1942), a superb adaptation of the John Steinbeck novel co-starring Spencer Tracy and Hedy Lamarr. Although the latter film was well-received by critics, audiences weren't nearly as enthusiastic. And back at Warners', the actor was placed on one of a series of suspensions for refusing to play the roles he was assigned. ("Don't blame the studio," he said several years later, "but that's the trouble with studios, they spend money building you up and when you're a hot investment, naturally they want to keep coining in on you regardless of whether they have the right script.") However, the actor was reportedly forced to acquiesce when his funds began running low, and he accepted the starring role in a spy thriller, *Dangerously They Live* (1942), with Nancy Coleman and Raymond Massey, followed by *Thank Your Lucky Stars* (1943), a musical showcasing a host of stars from the Warner Bros. roster, in which Garfield was seen half-talking, half-singing "Blues in the Night."

After this bit of fluff, Garfield's cinematic fortunes began to look up — he played a wise-cracking sailor in the blockbuster *Destination Tokyo* (1943), and was praised by critics for his superior portrayal of a bomber plane crew member in the World War II propaganda movie *Air Force* (1943), and his "engrossing characterization" in *The Fallen Sparrow* (1943), as a tortured veteran of the Spanish Civil War. And in 1945, he turned in what one reviewer termed "the best performance of his career" in *Pride of the Marines*, portraying Al Schmidt, a real-life veteran who was blinded during the war. Garfield himself later considered the role of Schmidt as his favorite.

"In order to live the character honestly and with understanding, I stayed at Al Schmidt's house for a month," the actor told the *Saturday Evening Post*. "After I got to know Al well, I felt it was … an honor to impersonate him on the screen."

Off screen, Garfield and his wife welcomed their second child, David Patton, on July 25, 1943, and the following year the actor did his part for the war effort by participating in an eight-week entertainment tour of the front lines in Italy.

"The heroes of this war are the G.I. foot soldiers," he said upon his return, stressing that it was "every actor's duty" to visit troops overseas. "You get a proud feeling to know the kind of tough guys out there fighting for us."

But tragedy struck the actor's personal life the year following his successful tour to Italy when his six-year-old daughter, Katherine, died suddenly, on March 18, 1945. Newspaper accounts reported that the child had left her home on the previous day with Hilda Wane, Garfield's secretary, to spend the weekend with her grandparents in nearby Vista, California. After Katherine had complained of a sore throat on Saturday night and again on Sunday morning, Ms. Wane rushed her back to her home, but she died there about 10 minutes after her arrival. It was later determined that Katherine died from an allergic reaction to something she had eaten and, as a result, her throat closed in and she was asphyxiated.

Garfield and his wife, Roberta, were reportedly "prostrate with grief" over the child's unexpected death, and the actor began suffering from "insomnia and a general depression," consumed with guilt over not being at his daughter's side during her last moments. Years later, director Vincent Sherman, who directed Garfield in *Saturday's Children*, recalled encountering Garfield shortly after Katherine's death.

"I stopped off to tell Julie how sorry I was. He was walking alone," Sherman told the *Los Angeles Times* in 1983. "He said [that] maybe God was paying him back for being so successful so quickly. He said, 'Maybe I didn't behave right.' You can understand his guilt feelings about his child."

The actor's sorrow and guilt may have been somewhat lessened, however, when he and Roberta had a third child, a girl they named Julie Roberta, on January 10, 1946. Garfield, who was shooting a film on the Warner Brothers lot at the time, reportedly rushed from the studio to Cedars of Lebanon Hospital just in time to greet his new daughter on her arrival. Both of Garfield's surviving children, David and Julie, became involved in the motion picture industry as adults. David, who was sometimes billed as John Garfield, Jr., appeared in such pictures as *The Swimmer* (1968), *The Other Side of the Mountain* (1975), and *The Rose* (1979). He then moved into the field of film editing, editing a total of 14 films, including *All the Right Moves* (1983) and *The Karate Kid, Part II* (1986). Sadly, like his father, he would die of a heart attack at a young age, on November 24, 1994. Julie Garfield would go on to appear in films including *Love Story* (1970), *Ishtar* (1987), and *Goodfellas* (1990).

Professionally, in 1946, Garfield entered the realm of film noir with one of his most memorable movies—*The Postman Always Rings Twice*. Garfield starred as Frank Chambers, a drifter with "itchy feet" who happens upon a roadside diner owned by Nick Smith (Cecil Kellaway) and his wife, Cora (Lana Turner). Before long, Frank and Cora become embroiled in a heated affair and wind up murdering Nick so that they can be together. Their guilt in the crime is soon suspected, and Frank is tricked by the district attorney into

signing a complaint against Cora, who later receives only a suspended sentence for manslaughter. The couple later marry, but Cora remains embittered over Frank's betrayal, and the two reconcile only after Cora discovers that she is pregnant. Ironically, during a drive down the coast highway, the couple is involved in an auto accident that results in Cora's death. Despite his innocence, Frank is accused of Cora's murder, found guilty, and sentenced to die. He accepts his fate philosophically, realizing that both he and Cora had to pay with their own lives for the murder of her husband: "You know there's something about this which is like expecting a letter you're just crazy to get, and you hang around the front door for fear you might not hear him ring," Frank tells the district attorney. "You never realize that he always rings twice. He rang twice for Cora. And now he's ringing twice for me, isn't he?"

Garfield's performance as Frank Chambers was lauded by critics; in a typical review, the *New York Times'* Bosley Crowther noted his "extraordinarily honest" portrayal, stating that Garfield "reflects to the life the crude and confused young hobo who stumbles aimlessly into a fatal trap." As his follow-up to *Postman*, Garfield remained in the dark world of noir with his second film from the era, *Nobody Lives Forever* (1946). Here, he played Nick Blake, a notorious gambler who returns home from the war to find that his girlfriend has stolen his $50,000 in savings and used it to start a nightclub with her new lover. ("Look—I know all about you, King," Nick tells the man. "You can always get a bankroll if there's some dumb dame around—that's okay with me. Just so long as it's not my dough.") Nick later moves to Los Angeles, joining forces with an old friend, Pop Gruber (Walter Brennan) and a local hood, Doc Hanson (George Coulouris), to swindle money from a wealthy widow (Geraldine Fitzgerald). Instead, Nick falls for the widow, and tries to back out of the scheme, planning to pay off Doc Hanson with his own money. Doc rejects his offer and kidnaps the widow, but is killed—along with Pop Gruber—during a gun battle when Nick shows up to the rescue.

Although the film itself was given only passable notices, Garfield was singled out for his performance; the *New York Times'* Crowther wrote that he turned in an acting job that was "worthy of better material," and the critic for the *Motion Picture Herald* found that Garfield's performance was "excellent."

Nobody Lives Forever was followed by three of Garfield's most memorable movies. In the first, he starred opposite Joan Crawford in *Humoresque* (1946), portraying a sensitive violin virtuoso who has an ill-fated affair with a rich society patroness. (Many movie magazines noted that Garfield had spent several months learning to master violin technique for the film. Other sources, however,

John Garfield (center) in *Body and Soul* (1947).

claim that a real violinist's arm was passed through a hole in Garfield's coat so the fingering would be authentic, and that a second violinist hid behind Garfield and took care of the bow work.)

After this box-office hit, Garfield's contract with Warner Bros. expired and, despite offers from several studios, he decided to remain independent.

"I wouldn't mind signing with [a studio] for a single picture a year," Garfield told the *Los Angeles Times* in 1947. "But I don't want to get tied up completely with any studio. I want to be free to pick stories that I think fit me." Instead, Garfield formed a partnership with Bob Roberts, his former business manager, and screenwriter/director Abraham Polonsky, to create the independent production

company Enterprise Productions. The arrangement allowed Garfield to earn a portion of the profits and select his own stories—the first was *Body and Soul* (1947), his third film noir.

In this gripping feature, Garfield portrayed Charlie Davis, who is determined to earn money for his family through the professional boxing game. He gradually works his way up to the top of his field, but at a price — he is forced to fork over a large percentage of his earnings to a local gangster (Lloyd Goff), his relationship with his long-time sweetheart (Lilli Palmer) is imperiled when he has an affair, and he becomes entangled in boxing corruption when he is ordered to throw an important fight. At the film's powerful conclusion, Davis is able to summon a lingering shred of self-respect and refuses to lose the match, knocking his opponent unconscious. Knowing that this act has endangered his life, he nonetheless boldly tells the thugs who confront him: "So—what are you going to do? Kill me? Everybody dies!" For his multifaceted performance, Garfield was nominated for an Academy Award for Best Actor, but lost to Ronald Colman in *A Double Life* (1947). Still, he earned some of the finest reviews of his career for *Body and Soul*; in the *Los Angeles Daily News*, Virginia Wright declared that Garfield "plays the fighter with compelling simplicity and a solid sincerity that makes this his best work on the screen," Bosley Crowther wrote in the *New York Times* that the actor gave "a rattling good performance," and in the *Hollywood Citizen-News*, Lowell E. Redelings claimed that Garfield "is never better than in his fight scenes, although his entire performance is magnificent."

Later that year, Garfield played a small role in another blockbuster, *Gentleman's Agreement* (1947), the first major Hollywood film to address anti–Semitism. A powerful and, for the time, controversial film, *Gentleman's Agreement* starred Gregory Peck as a magazine writer who pretends to be Jewish in order to write a series of articles on anti–Semitism. Garfield, appearing in only a few scenes, portrayed Peck's Jewish best friend who encounters prejudice despite his status as a hero of World War II.

"It's not the lead," Garfield told the *New York Times* before filming began on the movie. "But it's a character with guts." The film was a critical and financial success, and went on to win Academy Awards for Best Picture, Best Supporting Actress (Celeste Holm), and Best Director (Elia Kazan).

After *Gentleman's Agreement*, Garfield returned to the stage, accepting a salary of $80 a week to star in *Skipper Next to God*, a drama about a cargo steamer captain who tries to deliver a boatload of displaced Jews to sympathetic soil. Despite his meager pay for the part, Garfield told the *Los Angeles Times* that he had "definite reasons" for signing on with the play.

"In the first place, I'm a stage craftsman. I need practice at my craft to keep a firm hold on any ability I enjoy in my trade," he said in January 1948. "But the legitimate stage has to have encouragement in every branch if it is to prosper. Above other considerations, I hope I'm proving to actors fortunate enough to be in well-placed financial brackets that they can do more than lip service if they will come to New York and appear in experimental plays." His performance in the play earned the actor a Tony Award.

When his stint with *Skipper* ended, Garfield returned to films—and film noir—with *Force of Evil* (1948), co-starring Thomas Gomez, Beatrice Pearson, and Marie Windsor. Here, Garfield is Joe Morse, a slick, self-absorbed attorney hired to carry out a syndicate king's plan to "legalize" a large-scale numbers racket by forcing the smaller bookies out of commission. Joe's estranged brother, Leo (Thomas Gomez), is one of the bookies who would be affected by the scheme, so Joe puts him in charge of the new organization ("Everything I touch turns to gold," Joe loftily proclaims). But later, when Joe finds he can no longer control the rapidly developing events, he tries unsuccessfully to extricate himself and his brother from the organization. Leo is murdered and Joe metes out a deadly punishment to those responsible, but he ultimately decides to expose the syndicate and its entire operation to the authorities.

Force of Evil—Garfield's second venture with Bob Roberts and Enterprise—met with wildly varying reviews upon its release. Bosley Crowther raved in the *New York Times* that the film was "a dynamic crime-and-punishment drama, brilliantly and broadly realized." He also praised Garfield's performance, calling him a "tough guy to the life. Sentient, underneath a steel shell, taut, articulate—he is all good men gone wrong." But the reviewer for *Motion Picture Herald* was not nearly as impressed, condemning the film's script as "cluttered with muddled and confused dialogue presumably designed to be worldly and philosophical with something allegedly bearing on the poetic added." The critic from

Variety agreed, claiming that the film "fails to develop the excitement hinted at in the title," but he found Garfield's appearance worthy of applause, writing that "as to be expected, [he] comes through with a performance that gets everything out of the material furnished."

Garfield's next few films were mostly mediocre; *We Were Strangers* (1949), directed by John Huston, was pulled from theaters shortly after its release because of its poor showing at the box office; *Jigsaw* (1949) was a crime drama financed by Franchot Tone and notable primarily for its numerous celebrity cameos that included Garfield as a street loiterer, Henry Fonda as a waiter, Marlene Dietrich as a nightclub patron, and Burgess Meredith as a bartender; and *Under My Skin* (1950) was a so-so drama that featured the actor as a crooked jockey who flees to France with his young son after being barred from racing in the United States. He took a break from these pictures, though, to star on Broadway opposite Nancy Kelly in *The Big Knife* in 1949.

During this time, Garfield suffered the first of a series of health scares—in early 1949 he suffered a heart attack while playing tennis in Beverly Hills and was carried from the tennis court in a state of semi-consciousness. The filming of *Under My Skin* was postponed for nearly a month while he recovered. Then, in September 1949, newspapers reported that the actor was admitted to Cedars of Lebanon hospital after complaining of dizziness. According to friends of the actor, he was advised by his physicians to avoid overexertion at all times.

Garfield's physical ailments didn't keep him off of the screen, however, and he was next seen in back-to-back films noirs; in the first, *The Breaking Point* (1950), he portrayed Harry Morgan, the financially strapped owner of a charter boat who finds himself in a series of circumstances beyond his control after he is hired by a sports fisherman and his girlfriend for a trip to Mexico. When the fisherman leaves town without paying, Harry reluctantly accepts an offer from a shady lawyer, F.P. Duncan (Wallace Ford), and a mysteri-

ous Asian gentleman, Mr. Sing (Victor Sen Yung), to smuggle a group of refugees into the United States. Once again stiffed on his payment, Harry gets into a scuffle with Mr. Sing and shoots him in self-defense. Desperate to earn money to support his wife and two young daughters, Harry again joins forces with Duncan, this time to provide an escape for a quartet of hoods after their successful heist at a local race track. Realizing that the men will kill him once they reach their destination, Harry guns them down one by one, but is severely injured himself during the shootout. In the film's final scene, his tearful wife (Phyllis Thaxter) convinces Harry to allow his arm to be amputated, thereby saving his life and leaving him free to face a new future.

The second film version of *To Have and Have Not* by Ernest Hemingway, *The Breaking Point* was a hit with audiences and earned excellent notices, with John L. Scott of the *Los Angeles Times* labeling it "a taut, hard-driving melodrama," and Bosley Crowther writing in the *New York Times* that the film contained "all of the character, color, and cynicism of Mr. Hemingway's lean and hungry tale." Crowther was equally complimentary towards Garfield's performance, claiming that he was "tops in the principal role."

Garfield followed *The Breaking Point* with *He Ran All the Way* (1951), an engrossing noir entry in which he portrayed Nick Robey, a petty hood who is sought for murder when a payroll robbery scheme goes wrong and he shoots a policeman. Desperate and paranoid, he meets a young woman, Peg Dobbs (Shelley Winters), at a local swimming pool, escorts her home, and holds her family hostage when he mistakenly believes that her parents know of his crime: "All I ever asked you people was just for a place to hole up for a couple of days, that's all," Nick says. "Something you'd give an alley cat." Over the course of the next few days, Nick comes to believe that Peg has fallen for him and plans for the two to flee together, but in the final reel, Peg shoots him as he attempts his escape and he dies in the gutter.

Garfield delivered another outstanding portrayal in *He Ran All the Way*—he was praised by the *New York Times'* Bosley Crowther for a "stark performance" that was "full of startling glints from start to end," and hailed as "excellent" and "highly effective" in *Variety*. Sadly, it would be his last screen role—Garfield's life was about to veer into a direction from which the actor would never return.

On April 23, 1951, just over a month after filming was completed on *He Ran All the Way*, Garfield was called to testify before the House Un-American Activities Committee (HUAC). The committee had been investigating Communism in the motion picture industry since 1947, and in the fall of that year, Garfield was among a large contingent of Hollywood notables who traveled to Washington, D.C., to offer their support to the writers, directors, and actors who were being targeted by the committee.

The committee revealed to the press that Garfield had been involved in such Communist Party–related activities as signing an appeal to lift the embargo on the shipment of arms to the Communist Group in Spain, speaking at the Conference of American-Soviet Friendship, and issuing a statement in support of the USSR in the periodical *Soviet Russia Today*. Still, Garfield insisted during his testimony that he had never been a member of the Communist Party: "I am no Red," he said. "I am no pink, I am no fellow traveler." When questioned about the organizations with which his name had been linked, he told the committee that his name had been used without his authority: "I'd like to point out what a situation a guy like me is in. I get a million requests to appear, some of them are all right, some of them are not."

Despite his insistence that he was not involved with the Communist Party, and his disavowal of the Party as "subversive, a dictatorship, and against democracy," Garfield suddenly found himself blacklisted in Hollywood. In addition, several members of the committee reportedly were not convinced by Garfield's testimony, and turned it over to the Department of Justice for investigation. According to his daughter, Julie, the events had a profound effect on the actor.

"His passion was acting," Julie said in a 1999 documentary on the actor's life. "It was all he wanted to do in his life, and when that was taken away from him, he was devastated, and he was in a deep depression. He was trying to figure out some way to clear his name."

Garfield's life continued its downhill slide when in January 1952, he ended his association with Enterprise Productions, claiming that he had not been paid the salary that had been due to him by producer Bob Roberts. Around this time, he also separated from his wife, Roberta, and moved into a New York hotel. Unable to find work in Hollywood, Garfield managed to land the starring role in a production of *Golden Boy*, which ran for nine weeks at the American National Theater and Academy in New York. After the play closed, he was slated to star in a television production of the play on CBS-TV with actress Kim Stanley, but before filming could begin, the network abruptly cancelled the production. Then, in March 1952, Garfield bought the rights to the play *Fragile Fox*, and announced his plans to star and direct. But the actor's directorial debut would not come to pass. Just two months later, on May 21, 1952, Garfield was found dead of a heart attack in the Gramercy Park apartment of Iris Whitney, a 36-year-old actress and dancer.

Whitney told reporters that she and Garfield had dined together at Luchow's Restaurant on the night before his death. Returning to her apartment later that evening, Whitney said Garfield complained of feeling ill, but declined her offer to call a doctor.

"He said he was feeling awful," Whitney said. "He was too ill to leave. We decided he should stay overnight."

Garfield went to bed—while she slept on the couch, Whitney noted—and the following morning, unable to awaken him, she contacted Garfield's physician, who pronounced the actor dead. Whitney also said that she had only known the actor for two months, and flatly denied any romantic attachment between the two.

Just one day after the actor's death, a *New York Daily Mirror* columnist, Victor Riesel, wrote that he had spoken to Garfield shortly before his death and that the actor had prepared a "full statement" revealing the "whole truth" about his involvement with the Communist Party. According to Reisel, the actor planned to modify his previous HUAC testimony and admit that he'd worked closely with Reds and carried out their orders.

"We talked just a few hours before he died," the column read. "He told me he'd hold nothing back. He'd tell the whole truth despite the Communist pressure and traditional torture."

Reisel further claimed that Garfield told him, "Actors are emotional, Vic. The Commies would come to us and say 'sign here, everybody's doing it for civil liberties.' Or they would say, 'sign here and save the bread and butter of children of writers and actors banned from the studios because of political beliefs.' So I would sign."

In response to the news that Garfield had planned to recant his HUAC testimony, one of the members of the committee, Rep. Donald L. Jackson of California, told reporters: "The case is now before a higher tribunal than that of man. His reported decision before his death to clarify his past activities is welcome news to all who have been concerned with the Garfield case. Death prevented that appearance, but it is good to learn that John Garfield had made a great and difficult decision." Despite these comments, Garfield's attorney, Louis Nizer, denied that the actor had any intention of revisiting his HUAC testimony, telling reporters that "Garfield was frank and told all he knew when he went before the committee."

The actor's widow, Roberta Garfield, who collapsed upon hearing the news of her husband's death, commented little on Garfield's alleged intention to alter his previous testimony, except to deny reports that these plans were the cause of their separation. She was left Garfield's entire $221,000 estate, and in September 1954, she married Sidney E. Cohen, a 46-year-old attorney.

Garfield's funeral was held in New York on the day following his death, and a near-riot resulted when more than 10,000 people showed up to pay their last respects. After about 500 fans filed passed his casket at the Riverside Memorial Chapel on 76th Street, Garfield's family closed the chapel to outsiders. According to press accounts, "an unruly, squealing mob of bobby soxers and grown women elbowed one another and police for a final glimpse" of the actor's body until the family relented and allowed the doors to be reopened. Approximately 50 police officers were called in to contain the crowd, which jammed the street, crowded front stoops, and leaned out of the windows of nearby houses.

With a stellar career that paved the way for such later toughs as James Dean and Marlon Brando, it is a tragic reality that Garfield is seldom remembered today. He wasn't forgotten by his friends and family, however. In September 1983, a group of his pals gathered at the Rivera Country Club in Los Angeles to honor his memory and launch the John Garfield Foundation, a non-profit venture set up by the actor's brother to offer aspiring actors, writers, and directors an opportunity to work on stage with professionals. Among the guests was former Dead-End Kid Huntz Hall, who appeared with Garfield in the film *They Made Me a Criminal.* Prior to the event, Hall recalled that Garfield had served as a mentor to him and his fellow Dead-Enders, and expressed regret over his treatment at the hands of the HUAC.

"The committee was a terrible thing. John was persecuted. I know this, John loved the American people like I do," Huntz told the *Los Angeles Times.* "I'm glad they're doing this [tribute]. I want to see him remembered. He's been too long in the background."

In films that included *The Postman Always Rings Twice, Body and Soul,* and *Pride of the Marines,* John Garfield proved that he not only possessed star quality, but also a genuine and versatile talent. While he left behind controversy and mystery in his private life, on screen he will forever live as an actor of fascinating, undeniable, and infinitely watchable ability.

"He came like a meteor," it was fittingly proclaimed at his memorial service, "and like a meteor he departed."

Film Noir Filmography

The Postman Always Rings Twice. Director: Tay Garnett. Producer: Carey Wilson. Released by MGM, May 2, 1946. Running time: 113 minutes. Cast: Lana Turner, John Garfield, Cecil Kellaway, Hume Cronyn, Leon Ames, Audrey Totter, Alan Reed.

Nobody Lives Forever. Director: Jean Negulesco. Producer: Robert Buckner. Running time: 100 minutes. Released by Warner Bros., November 1, 1946. Cast: John Garfield, Geraldine Fitzgerald, Walter Brennan, Faye Emerson, George Coulouris, George Tobias, Robert Shayne, Richard Gaines, Dick Erdman, James Flavin, Ralph Peters.

Body and Soul. Director: Robert Rossen. Producer: Bob Roberts. Running time: 105 minutes. Released by United Artists, August 22, 1947. Cast: John Garfield, Lilli Palmer, Hazel Brooks, Anne Revere, William Conrad, Joseph Pevney, Canada Lee, Lloyd Goff, Art Smith, James Burke, Virginia Gregg, Peter Virgo, Joe Devlin, Shirmin Rushkin, Mary Currier, Milton Kibbie, Tim Ryan, Artie Dorrell, Cy Ring, Glen Lee, John Indrisano, Dan Tobey. Awards: Academy Award for Best Film Editing (Francis Lyon, Robert Parrish). Academy Award nominations for Best Actor (John Garfield), Best Original Screenplay (Abraham Polonsky).

Force of Evil. Director: Abraham Polonsky. Producer: Bob Roberts. Running time: 88 minutes. Released by Enterprise Studio and MGM, December 26, 1948. Cast: John Garfield, Beatrice Pearson, Thomas Gomez, Howland Chamberlain, Roy Roberts, Marie Windsor, Paul McVey, Tim Ryan, Sid Tomack, Georgia Backus, Jan Dennis, Stanley Prager.

The Breaking Point. Director: Michael Curtiz. Producer: Jerry Wald. Running time: 97 minutes. Released by Warner Bros., September 30, 1950. Cast: John Garfield, Patricia Neal, Phyllis Thaxter, Juano Hernandez, Wallace Ford, Edmon Ryan, Ralph Dumke, Guy Thomajan, William Campbell, Sherry Jackson, Donna Jo Boyce, Victor Sen Yung, Peter Brocco, John Doucette, James Griffith.

He Ran All the Way. Director: John Berry. Producer: Bob Roberts. Running time: 77 minutes. Released by United Artists, July 13, 1951. Cast: John Garfield, Shelley Winters, Wallace Ford, Selena Royle, Bobby Hyatt, Gladys George, Norman Lloyd.

References

"10,000 Fans Jam Street for Garfield's Funeral." *Los Angeles Times*, May 24, 1952.
"Actor John Garfield's Estate Willed Wife." *Los Angeles Mirror-News*, March 10, 1959.
Cooper, Marion. "Once Was Enough!" *Silver Screen*, May 1940.
Downing, Hyatt. "The Secret of Happiness." *Motion Picture Magazine*, December 1950.
"Every Actor's Duty to Go Overseas, Says Garfield." *Variety*, April 13, 1944.
"Film Red 'Plants' Bared by Inside Garfield Story." *Los Angeles Examiner*, May 23, 1952.
Foley, Thomas J. "John Garfield Red Disavowal Being Probed." *Los Angeles Examiner*, May 19, 1951.
"Garfield Admitted: 'I Was Dupe of Reds.'" *Los Angeles Mirror News*, May 22, 1952.
"Garfield Buys Play to Stage, Star." *Variety*, March 5, 1952.
"Garfield Dies in Home of Actress." *Los Angeles Daily News*, May 21, 1952.
"Garfield Record." *Los Angeles Herald Express*, April 24, 1951.
"Garfield Rites Today." *Variety*, May 23, 1952.
Garfield, John. "Speaking of Garfield." *Photoplay*, May 1943.
_____. "The Role I Liked Best." *Saturday Evening Post*, January 12, 1946.
_____, as told to Dena Reed. "My Life Is Different Because." *Today's Woman*, July 1947.
"Garfield's Film Life." *Los Angeles Herald Express*, May 21, 1952.
"Garfield's Plans Told." *Los Angeles Herald-Express*, May 23, 1952.
"Garfield's Political Past Probed." *Hollywood Citizen-News*, May 22, 1952.
Gelman, Howard. "John Garfield: Blacklist Victim." *Close-Ups: The Movie Star Book*, Edited by Danny Peary, 1978.
Graham, Nancy. "Friends to Honor Late Actor Garfield." *Los Angeles Times*, September 22, 1983.
"Heart Attack Fatal; Girl Bars Police." *Los Angeles Herald Express*, May 21, 1952.
Hopper, Hedda. "Own Film Ideas Tried by Garfield." *Los Angeles Times*, February 23, 1947.
"John Garfield, Actor, Dies of Heart Attack." *Los Angeles Mirror-News*, May 21, 1952.
"John Garfield Back from Italy with Nazi Gun." *Los Angeles Times*, April 12, 1944.
"John Garfield Daughter Dies." *Los Angeles Examiner*, March 19, 1945.

"John Garfield's Daughter Dies." *Los Angeles Times*, March 19, 1945.

"John Garfield Death Bares Secret Confession on Reds." *Los Angeles Examiner*, May 22, 1952.

"John Garfield Delighted Over 'Peer Gynt' Role." *Los Angeles Times*, December 17, 1950.

"John Garfield Dies at Home of Friend." *New York Times*, May 22, 1952.

"John Garfield Dies in N.Y. Home of Actress." *Los Angeles Times*, May 22, 1952.

"John Garfield Dies of Cardiac Trouble." *The Hollywood Reporter*, May 22, 1952.

"John Garfield's Widow to be Wed." *Los Angeles Times*, September 25, 1954.

"John Garfield to be Buried Tomorrow." *Los Angeles Daily News*, May 22,1952.

"John Garfield Widow Willed Entire Estate." *Los Angeles Times*, June 10, 1952.

Kirsch, Robert. "John Garfield: Antihero's Rise, Fall." *Los Angeles Times*, May 16, 1975.

Locke, Charles. "In the Shadow of a Legend." *Los Angeles Herald-Examiner*, July 5, 1986.

Moler, Murray M. "Garfield Not So 'Tough' in Real Life." *Hollywood Citizen-News*, June 23, 1945.

Morris, Mary. "Zing, Spit, Fire!" *PM*, May 5, 1946.

O'Brian, Jack. "John Garfield Doing Role on Stage for $80 Weekly." *Los Angeles Times*, February 1, 1948.

"Order Autopsy in Death of Actor's Daughter." *Los Angeles Herald Express*, March 19, 1945.

Parsons, Louella O. "John Garfield." *Los Angeles Examiner*, September 28, 1947.

Riesel, Victor. "Garfield Leaves Red Expose." *Hollywood Citizen-News*, May 24, 1952.

_____. "Garfield's Days of Torment Told." *Los Angeles Examiner*, May 23, 1952.

_____. "Garfield's Story Coming Out." *Hollywood Citizen-News*, June 2, 1952.

Scheuer, Philip K. "John Garfield Likes 'Flexible' Career." *Los Angeles Times*, April 16, 1950.

"Stage, Screen Star Stricken in N.Y. Apt." *Los Angeles Herald Express*, May 21, 1952.

Stincic, Jim. "John Garfield on Broadway." *World of Yesterday*, May 19, 1980.

Strauss, Theodore. "Dialogue Ad-Libbed from a Dentist's Chair." *New York Times*, September 26, 1943.

Taplinger, Robert S. Biography of John Garfield. Warner Brothers Studios, circa 1938.

"Teen-Agers, Fans Create Disorder at Garfield Rites." *Hollywood Citizen-News*, May 23, 1952.

"The Happy Worrier." *Los Angeles Times, This Week Magazine*, February 15, 1948.

"Thousands at Funeral of Garfield." *Los Angeles Daily News*, May 24, 1952.

"'Tough Guy' of Movies Stricken by Heart Attack." *Los Angeles Daily News*, May 21, 1952.

"Unruly Mob Struggles to Pass Garfield's Bier." *Los Angeles Times*, May 23, 1952.

Waterbury, Ruth. "Close-Up of John Garfield." *Liberty*, July 1, 1939.

Weiler, A.H. "Garfield Plans Film Here — On the Life of Jane Froman and Other Matters." *New York Times*, October 1, 1950.

Wilson, Earl. "Writer Hears Million Dollar Dialog When Actor Meets Pug." *Los Angeles Daily News*, circa May 1947.

Documentary

"Mysteries and Scandals: John Garfield." E! Entertainment Television. Copyright 1999.

THOMAS GOMEZ

"You'll discover as you grow older that sometimes a man does things he'd prefer not to do." — Thomas Gomez in *Force of Evil* (1948)

From the wealthy King Croesus to Blackbeard, from gangsters to detectives, and from clergymen to cowpokes, Thomas Gomez essayed a wide variety of characters throughout his impressive career, and he always delivered. The veteran of nearly 60 feature films, as well as countless credits on television, radio, and Broadway, Gomez was also a significant presence in six film noirs: *Phantom Lady* (1944), *Johnny O'Clock* (1947), *Ride the Pink Horse* (1947), *Key Largo* (1948), *Force of Evil* (1948), and *Macao* (1952).

The talented and respected character actor was born Sabatino Tomas Gomez on July 10, 1905, in Long Island, New York. His family hailed from around the globe — his paternal grandfather came to the United States in 1842 from Santander, Spain; his paternal grandmother was a native of Gibraltar; his maternal grandfather arrived in the United

States from Strasbourg in the Alsace; and his maternal grandmother was born in New Market, Ireland.

After attending P.S. 77 in Long Island and graduating from Jamaica High School, Gomez entered an oratory contest in New York City, reading 20 lines of a Falstaff speech from Shakespeare's *King Henry IV*. The 18-year-old future actor came away with first prize — a scholarship to a local drama school. Fortuitously, the vice-president of the school was famed Shakespearean actor Walter Hampden, who noted Gomez's talent and invited him to join his repertory company. As a member of Hampden's group, Gomez made his professional debut in 1924 in *Cyrano de-Bergerac*. He later appeared in *Caesar and Cleopatra* with Helen Hayes and in *Hamlet* with Hampden and Ethel Barrymore.

After seven years with Hampden's company, Gomez joined the Cleveland Playhouse, playing an estimated 40 roles in three years. From there, he further honed his skills as part of the prestigious troupe of stage veterans Alfred Lunt and Lynn Fontanne, appearing in such productions as *The Taming of the Shrew*, *Idiot's Delight*, and *There Shall Be No Light*. Also during this period, Gomez made a pioneering appearance in the early days of television with a featured role on *Lux Video Theater* in a playlet called "A Game of Chess."

When he was singled out by critics for his performance in the 1942 production of *Flowers of Virtue*, Gomez caught the attention of Hollywood and he was signed to a contract with Universal Studios. He made his film debut later that year, portraying a megalomaniacal Nazi spy in *Sherlock Homes and the Voice of Terror*, the first of the 12-episode series starring Basil Rathbone as the pipe-smoking detective. Also in 1942, Gomez was seen in *Who Done It?*, an amusing Abbott and Costello comedy; *Pittsburgh*, which reteamed Marlene Dietrich, John Wayne, and Randolph Scott after their successful outing in *The Spoilers* (also in 1942); and *Arabian Nights*, an action-packed adventure tale which saw Gomez featured as Hakim, the slave trader.

Gomez played the first of his many villains in 1943 when he appeared in the entertaining, if somewhat silly, *White Savage*, with Jon Hall and Maria Montez, followed by a series of films of varying quality, including *Corvette K-225* (1943), a well-received feature in which actress Ella Raines made her screen debut; *Dead Man's Eyes*, a mediocre mystery starring Lon Chaney, (1944); *The Climax* (1944), a horror film with Boris Karloff and Susanna Foster; *Can't Help Singing* (1944), Deanna Durbin's first color musical; and his first film noir — *Phantom Lady* (1944).

A top-notch offering from the era, *Phantom Lady* focuses on the murder conviction of an innocent man, Scott Henderson (Alan Curtis), and the efforts of his secretary, Carol (Ella Raines), to unearth the real culprit. Gomez portrayed Inspector Burgess, a conscientious cop who teams up with the secretary in a frantic search for the "phantom lady," a mysterious woman who can provide Henderson with the alibi he needs to clear his name. Ultimately, Burgess and Carol learn that the killer is Henderson's best friend, Jack Marlow (Franchot Tone), who had been having an affair with Henderson's wife and killed her in a fit of rage. ("She laughed at me," Jack confesses. "I had to stop her laughing.")

After earning good reviews for his portrayal of the wily inspector in *Phantom Lady*, Gomez appeared in a slew of mostly forgettable films in 1945, including the low-budget *Frisco Sal*, starring Susanna Foster and Turhan Bey. The following year, he was in only one feature, opting instead to return to Broadway as Claudius in *Hamlet*. Upon his return to Hollywood, Gomez resumed his busy filming schedule, appearing in *Singapore* (1947), starring Ava Gardner and Fred MacMurray; *Captain from Castile* (1947), which marked the successful screen debut of Jean Peters; and back-to-back films noirs, *Johnny O'Clock* (1947) and *Ride the Pink Horse* (1947.)

In *Johnny O'Clock*, Gomez played Guido Marchettis, who operates a casino with the Johnny of the film's title (Dick Powell). When a hatcheck girl from the casino is found murdered, Johnny is suspected — although he later learns that Marchettis is responsible. As if that weren't enough, Johnny is also being bedeviled by overtures from Marchettis' wife, Nelle (Ellen Drew), with whom he'd been romantically involved years before. In one of the film's most memorable scenes, Marchettis realizes that his wife is still in love with Johnny and nearly strangles her to death: "I oughta kill you. I could so easy, too," he says. "Just like this—on that white throat of yours. That pretty white throat of yours. This is Guido Marchettis saying this—your husband. The greaseball. That's what you thought all the time, didn't you?" Marchettis decides to spare Nelle's life, but when Johnny plans to leave town, Marchettis confronts his partner, planning to kill him. Instead, Johnny guns Marchettis down in self-defense, only to find himself accused of murder by his ex-lover when he rejects Nelle's plans to reunite. Trapped inside the casino, Johnny intends to blast his way out and make a break for it, but after the plaintive pleas of girlfriend Nancy (Evelyn Keyes), he turns himself in.

Gomez's second film noir of the year was the outstanding *Ride the Pink Horse*, which takes its name from a pink horse on a merry-go-round operated by Gomez's character, Pancho. The film's action focuses on Lucky Gaugin (played by Robert Montgomery, who also directed), an ex–GI who travels to a small Mexican town to avenge the murder of his pal, Shorty, ordered by racketeer Frank Hugo (Fred Clark). Gaugin is aided in his quest by a mysterious Mexican girl, Pila (Wanda Hendrix), and the jovial carousel operator, who is brutally stabbed in one scene by local hoods looking for Gaugin. (Pancho takes the injury in stride, however, telling Gaugin, "Knife is good. It's more easy to fix. I got knifed three times. When you're young, everybody sticks knife in you.") By the film's end, Lucky corners the hearing-impaired mobster, leading to his capture by police.

Gomez was hailed for his performances in both of his 1947 films noirs, but he was particularly acclaimed for his superb portrait of Pancho; in *Motion Picture Herald*, he was praised for his "sparkling performance," and the *Los Angeles Examiner*'s Dorothy Manners

wrote: "Another outstanding character is the proprietor of the Mexican merry-go-round." His first-rate portrayal also earned Gomez an Academy Award nomination for Best Supporting Actor, but he lost to Edmund Gwenn for *Miracle on 34th Street*.

The following year, Gomez recreated his Oscar-nominated role on the *Lux Radio Theater*, starring with Robert Montgomery, Wanda Hendrix, and Alan Reed. He was also seen in *Casbah* (1948), described as "*Algiers* (1938) with music"; *Angel in Exile* (1948), starring John Carroll and helmed by veteran director Allan Dwan; and two highly acclaimed examples of film noir —*Key Largo* (1948) and *Force of Evil* (1948).

Gomez is memorable in *Key Largo*, managing to make his character, "Curly" Hoff, a standout among a spate of top-notch performances. Gomez's Curly is a member of a gang run by Johnny Rocco (Edward G. Robinson), who takes over a hotel in Key Largo and uses it as his headquarters while waiting to sell a batch of counterfeit bills to an associate. The cast of characters held prisoner inside the hotel includes owner James Temple (Lionel Barrymore), his daughter-in-law, Nora (Lauren Bacall), a war buddy of Nora's deceased husband, Frank McCloud (Humphrey Bogart), and Gaye Dawn (Claire Trevor), Johnny Rocco's boozy girlfriend. After collecting the money for the counterfeit cash, Johnny forces Frank to pilot a boat for the gang's escape to Cuba, but during the voyage, Frank manages to systematically pick off each one of the gang, and return triumphantly to the hotel. The film was a top money maker for Warner Bros. upon its release, and was lauded by one reviewer as "a sweeping, exciting narrative that carries the spectator along in a fascinated manner from its provocative opening to its suspenseful conclusion."

Force of Evil, Gomez' second film noir of 1948, tells the story of crooked attorney Joe Morse (John Garfield), who is hired to carry out a scheme to "legalize" a large-scale numbers racket by putting the squeeze on smaller bookies, including his estranged brother, Leo (Gomez). Joe taps his sibling to head up the

jumbo," and the reviewer for *Variety* wrote: "Makers apparently couldn't decide on the best way to present an expose of the numbers racket, winding up with neither fish nor fowl."

During the next several years, Gomez appeared in a string of successful films, including *Come to the Stable* (1949), a popular feature about two French nuns who are determined to build a children's hospital in New England; *The Furies* (1950), a moody western starring Barbara Stanwyck and Walter Huston (in his last role); *Anne of the Indies* (1951), which starred Jean Peters as the captain of the Spanish Main; and *The Harlem Globetrotters* (1951), a bit of fluff that provided an entertaining look at the popular basketball team. Gomez was also featured during this period in his final film noir, *Macao* (1952), starring Robert Mitchum and Jane Russell.

Here, Gomez portrayed Lt. Jose Sebastian, a crooked police detective in Macao, the "quaint and bizarre" Chinese colony of the film's title. (Sebastian's disingenuous nature is revealed in an early scene; after secretly taking a photo of a newly arrived visitor, he smarmily tells the man, "It is our fond hope that all visitors to Macao should feel as untroubled here as Adam in the Garden of Eden.") Also in Macao are out-of-towners Nick Cochran (Robert Mitchum), an ex–GI wanted for a minor offense in the United States; Julie Benton (Jane Russell), a nightclub singer; and Lawrence Trumble (William Bendix), a New York detective posing as a salesman. After a series of plot entanglements and unexpected murders, the film concludes with Nick's capture of a notorious gambling house owner (Brad Dexter) — and a clinch with Julie in the final reel. Despite its high-powered cast, *Macao* was a flop at the box office and was panned by critics, including Bosley Crowther of the *New York Times*, who labeled it "flimflam and no more," and the reviewer for *Variety*, who called it "a routine formula pic," adding: "Thomas Gomez, a fine actor, is wasted in the role of a corrupt police official."

newly formed organization, but Leo initially balks at the offer. ("Joe's here now — I won't have to steal pennies anymore," Leo says. "I'll have big crooks to steal dollars for me.") Ultimately, Leo reluctantly accepts the post, but the well-designed plan goes awry, resulting in Leo's murder. Joe later avenges his brother's death and the film's end finds him determined to expose the organization to authorities.

As Leo, Gomez offered a memorable, well-drawn character of a man struggling with his conscience and torn between love and bitterness toward his younger brother. In one revealing scene, Leo tells Joe, "I wanted to be the lawyer, and I could've been the lawyer, if I'd thrown you out of the house when our parents died. But, no— I worked for you, like a fool. For you — and I gave you everything." Although *Force of Evil* is viewed today as a first-rate offering from the noir era, it earned widely varying reviews from critics; it was lauded in the *New York Times* as "a dynamic crime-and-punishment drama, brilliantly and broadly realized," but Red Kann of *Motion Picture Herald* dismissed it as "excessively talky and ... loaded down with mumbo

After this disappointment, Gomez was

tapped to portray Pasquale on *Life with Luigi*, a CBS-TV series based on the popular radio program of the late 1940s and early 1950s. But the sitcom, which starred J. Carroll Naish as an Italian immigrant working as an antiques dealer in Chicago, was short-lived, reportedly due to the program's racial stereotypes and problems obtaining sponsorship. Gomez did find success on the small screen, however — he made numerous appearances in some of the medium's most popular programs; from the mid-1950s through the last 1960s, he was seen on such series as *Gunsmoke, Playhouse 90, The Rifleman, The Twilight Zone, Route 66, The Virginian, Laredo, Mister Ed, Bewitched, The F.B.I*, and *It Takes a Thief*. He also appeared in a number of made-for-television movies, including *The Power and the Glory* (1961) and *Shadow Over Elveron* (1968).

In addition to his television work, Gomez remained active on both the stage and the big screen throughout the remainder of the 1950s and the 1960s — his stage work included acclaimed performances in *Cat on a Hot Tin Roof* and *A Man for All Seasons*, but most of his films were fairly forgettable and, more so than in previous years, Gomez was cast in a series of ethnic roles, including Don Homero Calderon in *Sombrero* (1953), Osman Aga in *The Adventures of Hajji Baba* (1954), Al "Gimpy" Sirago in *Las Vegas Shakedown* (1955), Wang Khan in *The Conqueror* (1956), Demetrios Bacos in *But Not for Me* (1959), and Papa Zacharias in *Summer and Smoke* (1961). And in 1968, after a seven-year absence from feature films, Gomez portrayed the provincial Navajo grandfather of Elvis Presley in *Stay Away, Joe*. Two years after this film, Gomez was seen in *Beneath the Planet of the Apes* (1970), the first sequel to the popular *Planet of the Apes* (1968). It would be his last film.

In late May 1971, Gomez was involved in an automobile accident and fell into a coma. He never recovered, dying at St. John's Hospital in Santa Monica, California, on June 18, 1971. He was 65 years old.

Although Thomas Gomez was often cast in the role of the heavy, he once stated that he preferred to play characters with "some rascality, warmth and dimension." His versatility in playing these characters was evidenced in such parts as the courageous and compassionate carousel operator in *Ride the Pink Horse* and the determined inspector in *Phantom Lady*. For these standout performances, and many others, he should be remembered.

Film Noir Filmography

Phantom Lady. Director: Robert Siodmak, Producer: Joan Harrison. Running time: 87 minutes. Released by Universal, February 17, 1944. Cast: Franchot Tone, Ella Raines, Alan Curtis, Thomas Gomez, Fay Helm, Elisha Cook, Jr., Andrew Tombes, Jr., Regis Toomey, Virginia Brissac, Milburn Stone.

Johnny O'Clock. Director: Robert Rossen. Producer: Edward G. Nealis. Running time: 95 minutes. Released by Columbia, March 27, 1947. Cast: Dick Powell, Evelyn Keyes, Lee J. Cobb, Ellen Drew, Nina Foch, Thomas Gomez, John Kellogg, Jim Bannon, Mabel Paige, Phil Brown, Jeff Chandler, Kit Guard.

Ride the Pink Horse. Director: Robert Montgomery. Producer: Joan Harrison. Running time: 101 minutes. Released by Universal-International, October 8, 1947. Cast: Robert Montgomery, Thomas Gomez, Rita Conde, Iris Flores, Wanda Hendrix, Grandon Rhodes, Tito Renaldo, Richard Gaines, Andrea King, Art Smith, Martin Garralaga, Edward Earle, Harold Goodwin, Maria Cortez, Fred Clark.

Key Largo. Director: John Huston. Producer: Jerry Wald. Running time: 100 minutes. Released by Warner Brothers, July 16, 1948. Cast: Humphrey Bogart, Edward G. Robinson, Lauren Bacall, Lionel Barrymore, Claire Trevor, Thomas Gomez, Harry Lewis, John Rodney, Marc Lawrence, Don Seymour, Monte Blue, Jay Silver Heels, Rodric Redwing. Awards: Academy Award for Best Supporting Actress (Claire Trevor).

Force of Evil. Director: Abraham Polonsky. Producer: Bob Roberts. Running time: 88 minutes. Released by Enterprise Studio and MGM, December 26, 1948. Cast: John Garfield, Beatrice Pearson, Thomas Gomez, Howland Chamberlain, Roy Roberts, Marie Windsor, Paul McVey, Tim Ryan, Sid Tomack, Georgia Backus, Sheldon Leonard, Jan Dennis, Stanley Prager.

Macao. Director: Josef von Sternberg. Producer: Alex Gottlieb. Running time: 81 minutes. Released by RKO, April 30, 1952. Cast: Robert Mitchum,

Jane Russell, William Bendix, Thomas Gomez, Gloria Grahame, Brad Dexter, Edward Ashley, Philip Ahn, Vladimir Sokoloff, Don Zelaya.

References

Biography of Thomas Gomez. MGM Studios, October 1955.

Biography of Thomas Gomez. Paramount Studios, August 1949.

Biography of Thomas Gomez. Universal Studios, August 14, 1947.

"Gomez's 45th Anni." *The Hollywood Reporter*, May 13, 1969.

Obituary. *The Hollywood Reporter*, June 23, 1971.

Obituary. *Variety*, June 22, 1971.

"Thomas Gomez, Actor, 65, Dies." *New York Times*, June 20, 1971.

"Thomas Gomez as 'Grandpa Lightcloud.'" *Red Rock News*, November 9, 1967.

"Thomas Gomez, Veteran Actor, Dies at 65 After Brief Illness." *Los Angeles Times*, June 21, 1971.

"Veteran Character Actor Thomas Gomez Dies at 65." *Los Angeles Examiner*, June 21, 1971.

FARLEY GRANGER

"I've done something horrible…. I know it was wrong, crazy wrong. I must've known that. I had this stupid notion that a couple hundred dollars could cure everything."
— Farley Granger in *Side Street* (1950)

With his handsome visage, captivating on-screen presence, and considerable acting talents, Farley Granger appeared to be a natural for big-screen stardom. But Hollywood wasn't exactly Granger's kind of town.

"I didn't like all the fuss over movie stars—I just didn't," Granger said in 2001. "I didn't feel I was really accomplishing something."

This viewpoint notwithstanding, during his 12-year stay in Hollywood during the 1940s and 1950s, Granger managed to turn in standout performances in such films as *The Purple Heart* (1944), *Rope* (1948), *O. Henry's Full House* (1952), *Hans Christian Andersen* (1952), and *The Story of Three Loves* (1953). He also starred in a total of four films noirs, including two of the era's finest offerings, *They Live by Night* (1949) and *Strangers on a Train* (1951).

Born Farley Earl Granger, II, on July 1, 1925, the future actor gained his first performing experience at the tender age of five, when he stepped onto the stage of the private school he attended in his home town of San Jose, California.

"They put on Christmas plays—I was Santa Claus' elf," Granger recalled. "I was in the first and the third acts, but on the night of the performance, one of the boys in the second act couldn't make it. I took his place. Luckily he only had a few lines, but I was the big hero of the Christmas play."

Not long after his memorable performing debut, however, the Granger family was hit hard by the effects of the Great Depression. Granger's father, a prosperous automobile distributor, lost his job and the family's savings.

"My childhood was very good until my father lost all his money," Granger said. "Then we moved to Studio City and he just worked at various jobs. My whole life changed, but I survived somehow."

During his senior year at North Hollywood High School, Granger indulged his long-time interest in acting by appearing at a local little theater in his first production, an English play called *The Wookie*. It turned out to be more than just Granger's professional debut — it was his proverbial "big break."

"A casting director for Sam Goldwyn saw me in it, and had me go to the studio to read. Then they said 'thank you, we'll call you,'" Granger recalled. "I said, 'Oh boy, they're going to call me!' About three weeks later, they called back again."

At his second reading, Granger appeared before Goldwyn, director Lewis Milestone, and writer Lillian Hellman, who were collaborating on a wartime feature, *The North Star* (1943). Granger was given a new scene to read, and an hour to prepare. Upon his return, he was directed to the office of Benno Snyder, a drama coach from New York.

"Benno told me what the scene was about, and I read it," Granger said. "There was a pause, he looked at me, and then he said, 'You're the boy.'"

Granger's impromptu delivery earned him a small role in *The North Star*, and a personal contract with Goldwyn, who wasted no time in loaning the young actor to 20th Century-Fox for a featured part in another World War II film, *The Purple Heart* (1944), starring Dana Andrews and Richard Conte. But the actor's blossoming career was interrupted after the film's release when he enlisted in the Navy, where he was stationed in Hawaii until the war's end.

In his first film after the war, Granger was seen starring opposite John Dall in Alfred Hitchcock's experimental "stunt," *Rope* (1948), notable for being shot in what appears to be one continuous take, followed by *Enchantment* (1948), a sweeping love story co-starring David Niven, Teresa Wright, and Evelyn Keyes, and *Roseanna McCoy* (1949), a box-office disappointment about the famed feud between the Hatfields and the McCoys. Granger recalled the film's ludicrous on-location shooting as typical of his experience in Hollywood.

"We went up to the Sierra Madre mountains with a complete cast. And no script. The sets were built, the houses were all around. And no script," Granger said. "I rode my horse from left to right. Right to left. Up the hill. Down the hill. That's what we did for two weeks. Months later, we went up again. We'd get up at four in the morning and drive up higher in the mountains, and then I'd sit in a car all day in the pouring rain. I nearly went mad, I really did. We'd wait from 6 A.M. to 5 P.M., because the sun might come out. And you could see it wasn't going to come

out because it was pouring rain. That's just stupid. It was an obscene waste of time, of money, of everything."

Granger rebounded from his unpleasant experience on *Roseanna McCoy* with a starring role in his first film noir, RKO's *They Live by Night* (1949), directed by Nicholas Ray.

"Nick Ray had seen me at a party," Granger recalled. "He called me and said he wanted me to take a test. He asked if there was anyone I'd like to work with, and I said Cathy O'Donnell. We did the test, and they wanted us, but most people didn't want to get involved with Goldwyn because he was such a pain in the neck. Dore Schary — the head of RKO — said, 'We have all these young guys under contract here, I don't want to go and borrow someone from Goldwyn.' But [producer John] Houseman and Ray insisted and they got us. Nick was just a joy to work with — he was a wonderful director."

In this outstanding feature, Granger is Arthur "Bowie" Bowers, an impressionable young convict who escapes from prison with two hardened comrades, Chickamaw (Howard Da Silva) and T-Dub (Jay C. Flippen). Hiding out at the home of Chickamaw's brother, Mobley, Bowie meets and falls for Mobley's daughter, Keechie (O'Donnell), with whom he shares his plans to seek a pardon and "get myself squared around." Later, the two get married, but their idyllic life in the mountains comes to a halt when they are found by Chickamaw and T-Dub, who force the reluctant Bowie into joining them in one last heist. The plan goes awry, however, when T-Dub is fatally shot during the robbery, Chickamaw is later killed trying to break into a liquor store, and Bowie — labeled "Bowie the Kid" — becomes the focus of a nationwide manhunt. Bowie and his now-pregnant wife go on the lam, seeking refuge with T-Dub's sister, Mattie (Helen Craig). But Mattie double-crosses the young couple, notifies police, and Bowie is gunned down as his horrified wife looks on.

For their memorable and touching performances as the luckless lovers, Granger and O'Donnell earned glowing reviews — the critic

from *Variety* labeled them "a gifted team of young players," and the review in *Motion Picture Herald* noted their "exceptional skill." But the film received a less enthusiastic reception from moviegoers, which Granger attributed to a two-year delay in its release.

"Dore Schary left RKO to go to MGM, and Howard Hughes came," Granger said. "He saw the film and hated it. Hated it. Because it had no tits and ass in it. He shelved it, and it sat there for two years. Finally, it opened in a little theater in London and got terrific reviews. That just shows you how things can get screwed up in [Hollywood]."

Granger remained in the realm of noir with his next two film appearances, *Edge of Doom* (1950) and *Side Street* (1950). In the first, Granger is Martin Lynn, a young man living with his sickly mother and trying to survive by working as a delivery man for a neighborhood florist. When his mother dies, Martin is determined that she be given "a fine funeral," and pays a visit to the parish priest, Father Kirkman (Harold Vermilyea), who'd refused to bury Martin's father in consecrated ground when he committed suicide years earlier. When the priest denies his latest request, Martin kills him with a single blow from a heavy crucifix and flees the church shortly before the body is found by Kirkman's assistant, Father Roth (Dana Andrews). As the days pass, Martin faces the increasing suspicions of police and Father Roth, while still endeavoring in vain to acquire expensive floral arrangements and other costly accoutrements for his mother's service. Finally, alone with his mother's body in the chapel, the emotionally spent youth confesses his crime: "Father Roth knows ..." Martin says. "I was angry but I didn't mean him any harm. It was just that nobody cared. It made no difference to anybody what was happening to us ... I was trying to tell that to Father Kirkman. I wanted him to look at me like he cared.... That's all I wanted." Martin's confession is overheard by Father Roth, who offers him support in his plans to turn himself in to authorities.

Edge of Doom earned lackluster reviews upon its release — in a typical notice, the critic from the *New York Times* singled out Granger for his "competent performance," but labeled the film "contrived." Granger went a step further, saying he "thought it was awful."

"I never saw the edited version that they did because I was so angry," Granger said. "I thought the book was awful, and they kept rewriting the script because it wasn't working. It was supposed to be my first starring role for Goldwyn and they gave me this mess."

The actor took a more favorable view of his next film noir, *Side Street*, in which he was re-teamed with Cathy O'Donnell. Here, the duo portrayed newlyweds, Joe and Ellen Norson, who are expecting their first baby and struggling to make ends meet on Joe's meager salary as a part-time letter carrier. During a delivery to the office of Attorney Victor Backett (Edmon Ryan), Joe pilfers a folder containing what he thinks is $200 in cash, but is stunned to find that it's actually filled with bills totaling $30,000. Unaware that the money is a blackmail payoff involving the murder of a local "B" girl, Lucky Colner (Adele Jergens), Joe stashes the money with a friend, Nick (Edwin Max), and returns to Backett's office, telling him that he is acting as a "go-between" for the person who stole the money. ("He thought maybe if you knew how it happened, you could see you way clear to giving him another chance," Joe says. "He never got off base before — you can check his record.") Suspecting that Joe has been sent by police to trap him, Backett pretends to know nothing of the theft, and instead sends his partner, George Garsell (James Craig), to retrieve the cash. Meanwhile, when Nick turns up dead, Joe finds himself sought by police for the deaths of both Nick and Lucky, and his luck takes another turn for the worse when he is abducted and beaten by Garsell and his sidekick, Giff (Harry Bellaver). Joe's nightmare finally comes to an end during a high-speed chase and a shootout with police; Garsell and Giff are killed and Joe is injured, but he is reunited with Ellen in the final reel.

Overall, critics were only mildly impressed with *Side Street,* but Granger's portrayal of Joe was noted by several reviewers, including Bosley Crowther, who wrote in the *New York Times* that the actor "makes a vividly terrorized lad." Years later, Granger recalled the making of the film as one of his more pleasant filmmaking experiences.

"It was nice. I enjoyed it," Granger said. "It was the first time we went to New York to do locations in real places, and that was fun because I loved New York and eventually wanted to live here. And I eventually did."

Next, Granger was seen in *Our Very Own* (1950), a sentimental soaper co-starring Ann Blyth; *I Want You* (1951), a first-rate Korean War drama that was virtually ignored by moviegoers; and *Behave Yourself!* (1951), a comedy in which Granger was teamed with actress Shelley Winters, with whom he'd had an on-again, off-again romance for two years. The couple's often volatile relationship was frequently covered in the movie magazines of the day, and the two were even engaged for a time.

"Luckily, I decided not to do it," Granger said. "And to spite me, she married Vittorio Gassman. She said, 'If you're not going to marry me, I've met this very nice Italian guy

and I'm going to marry him.' And she did. She was crazy. She was certifiable."

Career-wise, Granger was becoming increasingly dissatisfied with the direction of his film career and the nature of his roles. On several occasions, he was reprimanded by Goldwyn for refusing to accept his assignments ("I just kept turning things down and I was on suspension all the time," he said). But he hit the jackpot with his final film noir appearance, and the movie for which he is perhaps most closely associated — Alfred Hitchcock's *Strangers on a Train* (1951).

"I loved *Strangers on a Train* because I became very close with Alfred Hitchcock and [his wife] Alma, and [his daughter], Pat. He was a genius," Granger said. "I just loved the movie, and working with [Robert] Walker. I thought it was a terrific script."

Strangers begins with the seemingly accidental meeting of tennis pro Guy Haines (Granger) and Bruno Antony (Robert Walker), a self-professed fan, aboard a train bound for New York City. Bruno engages the unhappily married Guy in conversation, ultimately entertaining him with his theory for the perfect murder: "Two fellows meet accidentally, like you and me ... each has somebody that he'd like to get rid of. So they swap murders ... for example your wife, my father!" When Guy's wife later turns up dead, he is not only suspected of her murder, but also finds himself being stalked by Bruno, who insists that Guy complete his end of the "deal." When Guy refuses to kill Bruno's father, he learns that Bruno plans to plant evidence at a small-town amusement park to implicate Guy in the murder of his wife. With police close behind, Guy follows Bruno to the park and confronts him on a merry-go-round, but when an accident causes the ride to spin out of control, Bruno is fatally injured. With his last breath, he insists that Guy is the killer, but as he dies, his clenched fist opens, revealing Guy's cigarette lighter — which he'd planned to leave behind to point to Guy's guilt.

Surprisingly, the release of *Strangers on a Train* provoked mixed reviews; the critic

Robert Walker and Farley Granger in *Strangers on a Train* (1951).

from *Variety* praised the film and labeled Granger's performance as "excellent," but Bosley Crowther, of the *New York Times*, dismissed the feature as "thin and ... utterly unconvincing," and wrote that Granger "plays the terrified catspaw as though he were constantly swallowing his tongue." Today, however, the film stands up as a riveting thriller and is one of Hitchcock's best.

Granger followed *Strangers* with a role in the "Gift of the Magi" segment of *O. Henry's Full House* (1952); portrayed Niels in the Danny Kaye vehicle *Hans Christian Andersen* (1952); played a millionaire playboy opposite Jane Powell in *Small Town Girl* (1953); and appeared alongside Ethel Barrymore and Leslie Caron in *The Story of Three Loves* (1953), one of his favorite films. The actor was next tapped for the starring role in the big-budget biblical saga *The Egyptian* (1954), but he declined the part.

"It was a terrible script — Marlon Brando had just turned it down," Granger recalled. "It was just a big, dumb epic." Instead, frustrated by years of lackluster film assignments, the actor bought out of his contract.

"[Goldwyn] loaned me out for 101 things that were crap — he just wanted to make money off of me, he didn't know how to work with a young actor," Granger said. "And it just got impossible, that's all. I gave him all the money I had."

Eager to work in the New York theater, Granger moved east, but was promptly approached by his agent, Charlie Feldman, for a starring role in an Italian film, *Senso* (1954). Granger was reluctant to take the part, but his agent offered a convincing argument.

"Charlie said, 'you gotta get one thing straight — you don't have any money,'" Granger laughingly recalled. "'You gave it all back to

Goldwyn, you idiot.' So I thought I'd better do it."

For the next year, Granger worked in Italy on *Senso*, which co-starred Alida Valli and was helmed by famed director Luchino Visconti.

"It was a marvelous experience," Granger said. "When it was first completed, the government of Italy objected to certain things in it and it disappeared for a while. Then it came back, and was reviewed as one of Visconti's first great pictures. It's a classic now."

After briefly returning to Hollywood for *The Girl in the Red Velvet Swing* (1955) and *The Naked Street* (1955), Granger concentrated most of his energies on the stage, appearing over the next three decades in a wide variety of productions, including *The Heiress, The Carefree Tree, Advise and Consent, The Warm Peninsula, First Impressions, The Seagull, The Crucible, Hedda Gabler, Ring Round the Moon, Lilliom, A Month in the Country, Brigadoon, The Sound of Music, Private Lives,* and *Talley and Son*, for which he won a Best Actor Obie, an annual award given to off–Broadway plays and performers. His numerous stage performances evoked in Granger a solid respect for the theater, but also served to heighten his disdain for his experience in Hollywood.

"I find making a film difficult because of the way it's shot — with a play you go from the beginning to the end. With a movie, God knows how you go — from the middle to the end to the beginning, to whatever," Granger said. "And in the movies, some of the directors were stupid. They were really stupid. Many of the lesser directors I worked with would come in and grab the cameraman, and say, 'What are we doing today, Charlie?' A lot of them were totally unprepared. But the theater — that's where I really learned to act."

After leaving Hollywood, Granger also appeared in a number of television programs — in addition to recurring roles on two daytime series, *As the World Turns* in 1956 and *One Life to Live* in 1968, the actor was seen in *Playhouse 90, Wagon Train, The United States Steel Hour, Get Smart, Matt Helm, Ellery Queen, The Love Boat, Tales from the Darkside,* and *Murder, She Wrote*. In addition, during the 1970s, Granger lived for several years in Italy, where he was seen in such local fare as *La Rossa dalla pelle che scotta* (1972), *Lo chiamavano Trinita* (1972), and *La Polizia chiede aiuto* (1974).

"They asked me to do some films, and I just thought it would be fun," Granger said of the Italian features. "They didn't give me an enormous salary, but I like the Italians and I like the country. It was just sort of a lark."

In the early 1970s, Granger returned to Hollywood in *Arnold* (1973), a weak comedy starring Stella Stevens and Roddy McDowall, and was later seen in such productions as *The Prowler* (1981), *Deathmask* (1984), *Very Close Quarters* (1986), and *The Imagemaker* (1986). The actor's most recent big-screen appearances were in the documentary *The Celluloid Closet* (1996), a fascinating examination of the portrayal of gays in film, and *The Next Big Thing* (2002), an independent film where he played an opportunistic art dealer.

Although he continued to appear in stage productions into the late 1990s, Granger's acting career ran into a snag while rehearsing for a play in London. The play called for Granger's character to be shot, and during a fall, he injured his knee and was forced to pull out of the production. Since that incident, the actor has indulged himself in one of his favorite pastimes — traveling.

"I love travel," he said. "It started when I was young — ever since *Edge of Doom*. After the disastrous premiere, I thought, 'I'm getting out of town!'"

Looking back on his successful career, Granger stated that, if he could do it over again, he would have started in the theater, where he feels that he made a greater impact as a performer.

"I felt I accomplished something in the theater," Granger said. "I believe in taking chances and I'm glad I did. It's easy to play it safe. If you fail, you fail. No one is going to kill you."

Film Noir Filmography

Edge of Doom. Director: Mark Robson (with additional scenes by King Vidor). Producer: Samuel Goldwyn. Running time: 99 minutes. Released by RKO, September 27, 1950. Cast: Dana Andrews, Farley Granger, Joan Evans, Robert Keith, Paul Stewart, Mala Powers, Adele Jergens, Harold Vermilyea, John Ridgeley, Douglas Fowley, Mabel Paige, Howland Chamberlain, Houseley Stevenson, Sr., Jean Innes, Ellen Corby, Ray Teal, Mary Field, Virginia Brissac, Frances Morris.

They Live by Night. Director: Nicholas Ray. Producer: John Houseman. Running time: 95 minutes. Released by RKO, June 28, 1948. Cast: Cathy O'Donnell, Farley Granger, Howard Da Silva, Jay C. Flippen, Helen Craig, Will Wright, Marie Bryant, Ian Wolfe, William Phipps, Harry Harvey.

Side Street. Director: Anthony Mann. Producer: Sam Zimbalist. Running time: 83 minutes. Released by MGM, March 23, 1950. Cast: Farley Granger, Cathy O'Donnell, James Craig, Paul Kelly, Edmon Ryan, Paul Harvey, Jean Hagen, Charles McGraw, Ed Max, Adele Jergens, Harry Bellaver, Whit Bissell, John Gallaudet, Esther Somers, Harry Antrim, George Tyne, Kathryn Givney, King Donovan, Norman Leavitt, Sid Tomack.

Strangers on a Train. Director and Producer: Alfred Hitchcock. Running time: 101 minutes. Released by Warner Bros., June 30, 1951. Cast: Farley Granger, Ruth Roman, Robert Walker, Leo G. Carroll, Patricia Hitchcock, Laura Elliott, Marion Lorne, Jonathan Hale, Howard St. John, John Brown, Norma Varden, Robert Gist, John Doucette. Awards: Academy Award nomination for Best Black and White Cinematography (Robert Burks).

References

Beier, Carol. "Glitter of Hollywood Didn't Blind Granger." Theater Column of the New York Public Library, circa 1979.

Biography of Farley Granger. Susan Bloch and Co., circa 1980.

Biography of Farley Granger. 20th Century-Fox Studios, circa 1944.

Burden, Martin. "Those Hollywood Types." *New York Post*, March 17, 1981.

Granger, Farley. (as told to Ira Bilowit). "I Couldn't Just Act in Movies." *Backstage*, December 23, 1988.

"Granger: Old Movie Moguls Had Class." *New York Daily News*, February 26, 1982.

"It's Now or Never." *Modern Screen*, November 1951.

Pela, Robert L. "Goldenboy." *The Advocate*, August 20, 1996.

Shea, Sandra. "Finding Out About Farley." *Photoplay*, October 1944.

SYDNEY GREENSTREET

"I distrust a close-mouthed man. He generally picks the wrong time to talk and says the wrong things." — Sydney Greenstreet in *The Maltese Falcon* (1941)

Once labeled "the greatest unstarred star on the stage," Sydney Greenstreet was a Hollywood oddity — an overnight cinematic sensation at the age of 61. Debuting as the "Fat Man" in the film noir classic *The Maltese Falcon* (1941), Greenstreet was acclaimed by critics, applauded by audiences, and rewarded with an Academy Award nomination. Although his screen career spanned less than a decade, the corpulent English actor was a memorable presence in such features as *Casablanca* (1942) and *Between Two Worlds* (1944) and, in addition to *The Maltese Falcon*, was featured in the film noir features *The Mask*

of Dimitrios (1944), *Conflict* (1945), and *The Velvet Touch* (1948).

Sydney Hughes Greenstreet was born in Sandwich, Kent, England on December 27, 1879, one of eight children of John Jack Greenstreet, a leather merchant, and his wife, Ann Baker. At the Dane Hill Preparatory School in Margete, England, Greenstreet appeared in several amateur stage productions and excelled in sports, including tennis and soccer. At the age of 19, he landed a job as a tea planter in Ceylon (now known as Sri Lanka), but returned to England two years later when a drought destroyed the tea crops, and worked for the next year for an agency that handled the Watneys, Coombes and Reed's Brewery. It wasn't until 1902 that Greenstreet turned his sights toward the theater — with his mother's blessings and despite his father's misgivings, he signed on with the Ben Greet Academy of Acting, making his debut as a murderer in *Sherlock Holmes*. In 1903, Greenstreet toured England in *The Eternal City* and in a variety of roles in Shakespearean stock productions, including Bottom in *A Midsummer Night's Dream* and Casca in *Julius Caesar*. He made his first trip to the United States in 1904 with a company of Shakespearean performers that included famed actors Fritz Leiber and Sybil Thorndike, and debuted on Broadway the following year, portraying "Good Fellowship" in the morality play *Everyman*.

For the next several years, Greenstreet toured throughout the world, appearing in Shakespearean plays in Canada, South America, India, Italy, France, and North Africa, taking time out in 1918 to marry Dorothy Marie Ogden, a non-professional. The two later had a son, John Ogden, and remained married until Greenstreet's death.

Meanwhile, during the 1920s and 1930s, Greenstreet was seen in a variety of productions, including *Lady Windemere's Fan*, *The Student Prince*, *Marco's Millions*, *Lysistrata*, *The Good Earth*, and *Roberta*, a hit 1933 musical that co-starred Bob Hope, George Murphy, and Fred MacMurray. A short time after his triumphant appearance in *Roberta*, Greenstreet joined the famed acting team of Alfred Lunt and Lynn Fontanne, starring for six years in such hit plays as *Idiot's Delight*, *Amphtryon 38*, and *There Shall Be No Night*. While touring in Los Angeles in the latter production, Greenstreet caught the attention of fledgling director John Huston, who convinced the portly thespian to accept the role of Kaspar "The Fat Man" Gutman in *The Maltese Falcon* (1941).

This classic feature, Greenstreet's first venture into the world of film noir, offered a complex, sometimes confusing, but always riveting story with such unforgettable characters as a no-nonsense private detective,

Sam Spade (Humphrey Bogart); the beautiful but pathologically deceitful Brigid O'Shaughnessy (Mary Astor); the mild-mannered and steel-willed Kasper Gutman (Greenstreet); Gutman's inept gunman, Wilmer Cook (Elisha Cook, Jr.); and the foppishly meticulous Joel Cairo (Peter Lorre). After the principal characters cross and double-cross each other in a desperate attempt to locate the bejeweled figurine of the title, the film ends with the bird still missing and Gutman vowing to continue the search ("Well, sir, what do you suggest? We stand here and shed tears and call each other names, or shall we go to Istanbul?" he proposes), while Spade fingers Brigid as a murderer and ships her off to jail.

The release of *The Maltese Falcon* elicited a shower of praise from critics; in a typical review, the *New York Times*' Bosley Crowther wrote: "It's the slickest exercise in cerebration that has hit the screen in many months, and it is also one of the most compelling nervous-laughter provokers yet." Crowther was equally impressed with Greenstreet's standout performance, labeling him "magnificent as a cultivated English crook," and the actor earned similar praise from the reviewer for

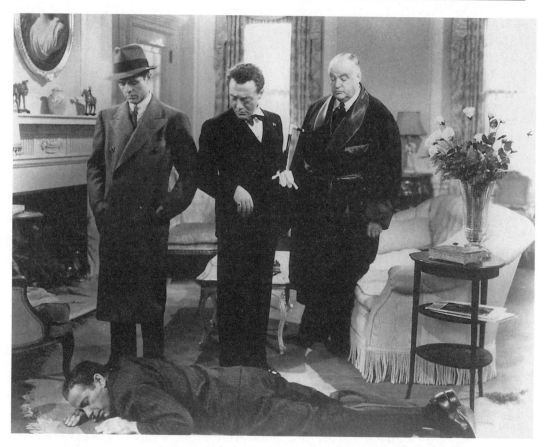

Elisha Cook, Jr., Peter Lorre, and Sydney Greenstreet as "The Fat Man" Gutman look upon the body of Humphrey Bogart in *The Maltese Falcon* (1941).

Newsweek, who wrote that the actor offered an "unctuous and sinister impersonation of a criminal master mind. Mr. Greenstreet brings to Hollywood a talent for comedy and villainy that should keep him here indefinitely." Greenstreet's portrayal earned him an Academy Award nomination for Best Supporting Actor, but he would lose to Donald Crisp for *How Green Was My Valley*. Despite his accolades, however, Greenstreet would later say that he was stunned by his initial appearance on the screen.

"The first time I saw myself I was embarrassed," he told columnist Hedda Hopper in 1944. "I got the shock of my life. I wanted to die. I knew I was pretty bad, but there I was on the screen — a horror."

By now, Greenstreet's voluminous physique — with a weight ranging from 275 to 320 — was becoming the stuff of legend. Once described as "almost as broad as he is tall," the actor reveled in retelling a variety of tales that emphasized his girth. According to one story, Greenstreet was appearing in an outdoor performance of *As You Like It* when the platform on which he was standing collapsed beneath him. Always the professional, Greenstreet reportedly crawled from the hole in the wooden structure in time to pick up his cue and deliver his next line: "'True is't we have seen better days." Another anecdote claimed that, while crossing a New York street, Greenstreet had been hit by a runaway horse pulling a heavy cart. The actor emerged from the incident unharmed, the legend states, but the impact killed the unfortunate horse. Still, while Greenstreet often encouraged the spread of such stories, he lamented his image in *The*

Maltese Falcon, saying that the camera "helped me achieve the effect of fatness."

"To be sure, I'm not exactly a flyweight; I weighed 285 at the time," he said in an interview in the *Saturday Evening Post*. "But by bringing the camera near the floor and shooting up, they made me weigh about 350!"

After *The Maltese Falcon*, Greenstreet was seen in a small but showy role as a general in *They Died With Their Boots On* (1941), followed by a cameo in John Huston's *In This Our Life* (1942), along with several of his *Maltese Falcon* co-stars, including Peter Lorre, Elisha Cook, Jr., and Barton MacLane. He was reunited with Huston, Humphrey Bogart, and Mary Astor later that year in *Across the Pacific* (1942), for which he was praised by Bosley Crowther in the *New York Times* as "entirely an enigma — malefic yet dignified, urbane and full of enviable refinement, yet hard and unpredictable beneath."

In Greenstreet's third film of 1942, *Casablanca*, he was seen in the small but memorable role of Senor Ferrari, the head of the Black Market, followed by *Background to Danger* (1943), a spy melodrama that marked the actor's fourth screen appearance with Peter Lorre. In 1944, the busiest year of Greenstreet's screen career, the actor appeared in *Passage to Marseille*, a somewhat confusing but highly entertaining actioner starring Humphrey Bogart and Claude Rains; *The Conspirators*, a mediocre spy saga that endeavored to recreate the success of *Casablanca* by reteaming Greenstreet with Paul Henreid and Peter Lorre; and *Between Two Worlds*, an atmospheric film that focused on passengers on an ocean liner who learn that have died and are bound for the hereafter. Although the latter film was only a modest success, Greenstreet's portrayal of "The Examiner," who decides the ultimate destinations of the passengers, was singled out in the *Los Angeles Examiner*, whose critic wrote that Greenstreet "gives the most natural performance we've seen on the screen in years." Also that year, Greenstreet made an appearance as himself in *Hollywood Canteen*, Warner Bros.' star-studded salute to the war effort,

then returned to the dark realm of film noir in *The Mask of Dimitrios*.

Here, Greenstreet starred as Mr. Peters, an ex-convict who is obsessed with finding Dimitrios Makropoulos (Zachary Scott, in his film debut), whose betrayal involving a jewel smuggling ring resulted in Peters' imprisonment. In his quest to locate the notorious criminal, Peters meets with detective story writer Cornelius Leyden (Peter Lorre), who has developed an interest in Dimitrios' fascinating criminal past. When Peters finally catches up to his prey, he barely manages to mask his hatred, telling Dimitrios, "You haven't changed at all ... always impetuous, always a little unkind. After all these years, no word of greeting, no word of regret for all the unhappiness you've caused me." Having learned that Dimitrios now holds an important position in the financial community, Peters blackmails him for one million francs, but Dimitiros double-crosses him, shooting Peters after turning over the money. As Dimitrios struggles with Leyden, Peters shoots and kills him, then surrenders to police, telling Leyden, "I've done what I had to do."

After earning praise for playing his role in *Dimitrios* with "archly pontifical style," Greenstreet assessed his film career to date, admitting that he found stage acting to be easier than emoting on the screen.

"Pictures are much harder.... On the stage you have the drive and momentum of your role, but here you enter a scene cold-bloodedly," Greenstreet told Hedda Hopper. "On the stage the audience is remote from you. In the movies you are placed on an operating table and told to be artistic. You're at the mercy of camera angles and the piecemeal pieces. You have to be on edge all day, because you don't know which portion of the film will be used. A performance on the screen is like 40 New York opening nights."

Despite his misgivings about the pressures of screen acting, however, Greenstreet continued to demonstrate his versatility in such films as *Pillow to Post* (1945), a lightweight comedy with Ida Lupino; *Christmas in Connecticut* (1945), an amusing holiday

Esther Howard, Rosalind Russell, and Sydney Greenstreet (foreground) in *The Velvet Touch* (1948).

farce co-starring Barbara Stanwyck; and *Conflict* (1945), his third film noir.

In this thriller, Greenstreet made his sixth and final appearance with Humphrey Bogart, playing a shrewd psychologist, Mark Hamilton. After a family friend turns up missing, Hamilton suspects that she has been murdered by her husband, Richard Mason (Bogart), and sets about planting evidence and staging illusions to entrap him. Constantly playing on Mason's increasing paranoia, Hamilton craftily tells him in one scene, "A murderer's whole safety depends on a complication of lies—that he had no motive, no access, that his alibi is perfect. Even if he feels no remorse, think of the strain he endures in knowing that one error will be his undoing. That if he is forgetful enough to contradict one of his statements, if his act of innocence is

unconvincing in any detail, if he so much as talks in his sleep." Finally, convinced that that his wife is still alive, Mason returns to the remote wooded area where he concealed her corpse, and is met there by Hamilton — and police. Earning mixed reviews from critics, *Conflict* was labeled "a convincing study" in *Variety*, but the *New York Times*' Bosley Crowther claimed that it was "all very obvious from the start." Greenstreet was favorably mentioned in most notices, however, with *Variety*'s critic terming him "creditably restrained."

Having expressed a desire to play "anything with edge and authority to it … human and significant," Greenstreet followed *Conflict* with a series of well-done features, including *Devotion* (1946), a highly fictionalized biography of the Bronte sisters; *Three Strangers*

(1946), a riveting drama in which he was paired as a shady lawyer alongside Peter Lorre, who portrayed a small-time hood; *The Verdict* (1946), a first-rate mystery and the last of Greenstreet's 10 features with Lorre; *The Hucksters* (1947), a big-budget hit starring Clark Gable and Deborah Kerr; *The Woman in White* (1948), where he played an unscrupulous count; *Ruthless* (1948), which featured Greenstreet in a small role as a scripture-quoting utilities magnate; and *The Velvet Touch* (1948), his final film noir.

In this feature, Greenstreet portrayed Captain Danbury, a shrewd homicide detective investigating the murder of famed Broadway producer Gordon Dunning (Leon Ames). Although all signs point to Dunning's former lover, Marion Webster (Claire Trevor), Danbury seems have reserved a modicum of suspicion for the producer's biggest star, comedienne Valerie Stanton (Rosalind Russell). After Webster commits suicide, however, Danbury announces that the case has been closed, but the real killer — Stanton — is tortured by her conscience, and confesses to Danbury after her opening night performance in a new dramatic play.

As Danbury, Greenstreet depicted a lawman who hid his crafty instincts beneath a mask of geniality and self-deprecating humor. Frequently mocking his "considerable bulk," Danbury in one scene encounters a group of reporters, one of whom asks if the Dunning murder will be a "big case." Danbury feigns outrage — snapping, "Don't be personal!" — before bursting into laughter. For his performance, he was lauded in *Variety* as "a mighty crowd-pleaser," and the critic for *The Hollywood Reporter* wrote that "he scores decisively as the police inspector."

Greenstreet enjoyed one of his last good roles in 1949, playing a malevolent sheriff in the Joan Crawford starrer *Flamingo Road*, but after his next picture, *Malaya* (1950), a wartime adventure with James Stewart and Spencer Tracy, the actor retired from the screen. The following year, he told the press, "I was a character comedian on the stage for 41 years, but not one single comedy role has come my way in Hollywood. So I'll keep turning down sinister parts and take it easy until something worthwhile comes along, but it will have to be good." The part never came — Greenstreet died on January 19, 1954, a few weeks after his 74th birthday. He had been suffering for several years from diabetes and Bright's Disease, a condition characterized by an inflammation of the kidneys.

Forever to be remembered for his best-known role, The Fat Man, in *The Maltese Falcon*, Sydney Greenstreet illustrated in a variety of stage and screen performances that he possessed a talent of depth, versatility, and dedication. In a review of Greenstreet's performance in a 1940 stage play, a critic offered a description that provides an apt synopsis of the actor's abilities as a thespian throughout his career.

"Something very special must be said about Sydney Greenstreet," wrote George Freedley in the *New York Morning Telegraph*. "His is a rich portrayal which is many layers deep in his thought and performance.... He is an extremely satisfying actor."

Film Noir Filmography

The Maltese Falcon. Director: John Huston. Producer: Hal B. Wallis. Running time: 100 minutes. Released by Warner Brothers, October 3, 1941. Cast: Humphrey Bogart, Mary Astor, Gladys George, Peter Lorre, Barton MacLane, Sydney Greenstreet, Ward Bond, Jerome Cowan, Elisha Cook, Jr., James Burke, Murray Alper, John Hamilton, Emory Parnell. Awards: Academy Award nominations for Best Picture, Best Supporting Actor (Sydney Greenstreet), Best Screenplay (John Huston).

The Mask of Dimitrios. Director: Jean Negulesco. Producer: Henry Blanke. Running time: 95 minutes. Released by Warner Brothers, June 23, 1944. Cast: Sydney Greenstreet, Zachary Scott, Faye Emerson, Peter Lorre, Victor Francen, Steve Geray, Florence Bates, Eduardo Ciannelli, Kurt Katch, Marjorie Hoshelle, Georges Metaxa, John Abbott, Monte Blue, David Hoffman.

Conflict. Director: Curtis Bernhardt. Producer: William Jacobs. Running time: 86 minutes. Released by Warner Brothers, June 15, 1945. Cast: Humphrey Bogart, Alexis Smith, Sydney Greenstreet, Rose Hobart, Charles Drake, Grant Mitchell,

Patrick O'Moore, Ann Shoemaker, Frank Wilcox, James Flavin, Edwin Stanley, Mary Servoss.

The Velvet Touch. Director: John Gage. Producer: Frederick Brisson. Running time: 97 minutes. Released by RKO, 1948. Cast: Rosalind Russell, Sydney Greenstreet, Leo Genn, Claire Trevor, Leon Ames, Frank McHugh, Walter Kingsford, Dan Tobin, Lex Barker, Nydia Westman, Theresa Harris, Irving Bacon, Esther Howard, Harry Hayden, Walter Erwin, Martha Hyer, Michael St. Angel, Louis Mason, James Flavin, Charles McAvoy, Dan Foster, Bess Flowers, Jim Drum, Allan Ray, Bill Wallace, Russell Hicks, James Todd, Joyce Arling, Ida Schumaker, Phillip Barnes, Bessie Wade.

References

"Apes His God in Musical Heavens." *New York Sun*, August 5, 1940.

Dickens, Homer. "Sydney Greenstreet." *Screen Facts*, circa 1964.

Deutsch, Helen. "An Actor Here, Another There, and Soon It's a Regular Troupe." *New York Herald-Tribune*, February 13, 1938.

Freedley, George. "'There Shall Be No Night' Still Holds Its Own, Six Months After Opening." *New York Morning Telegraph*, September 22, 1940.

Goodman, Ezra. "Milwaukee Knows This Plump Man." *Milwaukee Journal*, November 22, 1942.

Hopper, Hedda. "They Liked 'Fat Man.'" *Baltimore Sun*, September 10, 1944.

"'Idiot's Delight' Cast." *New York Herald-Tribune*, February 24, 1936.

Jones, Carlisle. "Unstarred Star of British Stage a Hit in Films." *New York Herald-Tribune*, September 28, 1941.

Obituary. *New York Daily News*, January 20, 1954.

Pitts, Michael R. "Sydney Greenstreet." *Classic Images*, November 1981.

Pickard, Roy. "Sydney Greenstreet." *Films in Review*, August/September 1972.

"Shakespeare and Greenstreet Got to Be Chums in Ceylon." *Brooklyn Daily Eagle*, October 16, 1932.

"S.H. Greenstreet, 'The Fat Man,' Dies." *New York Times*, January 20, 1954.

STERLING HAYDEN

"All right, sister. That's a mighty pretty head you've got on your shoulders. Do you want to keep it there, or do you want to start carrying it around in your hands?" — Sterling Hayden in *The Killing* (1956)

Unconventional, outspoken, and often controversial, Sterling Hayden's life reads like the story for a fascinating, if improbable, screenplay. He was a seafaring adventurer as a teenager, married one of his famed leading ladies, named fellow actors in the Communist witch-hunt of the 1950s, waged a bitter battle over his children, became a successful writer, battled alcoholism for years, publicly embraced the virtues of marijuana — and continued his acting career while making no secret of his disdain for the profession and for Hollywood. Despite his frequent deprecation of his acting abilities ("I never knew what the damn hell I was doing," he once said), Hayden turned in first-rate performances in such films as *Dr. Strangelove* (1964), *The Godfather* (1972), and *The Long Goodbye* (1973) and was a standout in six features from the

film noir era: *Manhandled* (1949), *The Asphalt Jungle* (1950), *Crime Wave* (1954), *Suddenly* (1954), *The Killing* (1956), and *Crime of Passion* (1957).

The actor once labeled "The Beautiful Blond Viking God" was born Sterling Relyea Walter in Montclair, New Jersey, on March 26, 1916, to George Walter, an advertising salesman for the *New York Journal*, and his wife, Frances. As the only child in a well-to-do family, Sterling enjoyed a happy childhood, but his carefree life changed at the age of nine when his father died. To make ends meet, Sterling's mother took a job at *Good Housekeeping* magazine in Manhattan, leaving her son in the care of her parents — the actor later recalled the effect of his mother's absence: "Night after night I would kneel on the chair in our dining room, looking out the window

... watching for the lights of my mother's car, terrified that she wouldn't come home."

Four years after her husband's death, Sterling's mother married James Watson Hayden, whose last name the boy adopted. Described in one news account as a "pleasant-enough character who lived on borrowed money," James Hayden frequently moved his new family from town to town, resulting in a spotty education for the future actor. At the age of 16, Sterling Hayden abandoned his school altogether; by now, he had discovered something far more worthy of his time — the sea.

"The glow inside me turned to a dancing flame," Hayden said of his first sailing experience in Boothbay Harbor, Maine. "I had been hanging around in public libraries, reading sea stories by Melville, Stevenson, Villers, Dana, and London. Finally, I just decided the hell with it."

Seeking a more adventurous experience that could be provided in books, Hayden landed a post as a seaman aboard the schooner *Puritan*, which sailed from New London, Connecticut, to San Pedro, California. During the next several years, he took on similar jobs — at the age of 20, he was first mate on a round-the-world voyage aboard the *Yankee*, and two years later, he served as skipper of an 89-foot ship, the *Florence B. Robinson*, sailing from Gloucester, Massachusetts to Tahiti. It was after this voyage that Hayden's life changed course, headed straight for Tinsel Town.

Several versions exist regarding Hayden's entry into films. According to one, he took on a few modeling jobs to earn extra money and was spotted by executives from Paramount Studios. In another account, Hayden's voyage aboard the *Robinson* was written up in local newspapers and he was offered a screen test. Another claimed that Paramount execs convinced Hayden to take a screen test after spying his photograph in a travel magazine, where he appeared in a layout on sailing. And still another version claims that a crewmate on the *Robinson* took note of Hayden's towering physique and movie-star good looks, wrote letters to nearly every studio in Hollywood, and finally hit pay dirt when the correspondence reached film producer E.H. Griffith. One news account also quotes Griffith's reaction when he first saw Hayden's photograph: "I had a hunch he was the man I needed."

Regardless of the path Hayden took to Hollywood, his film debut came in 1941, when he was cast as the second lead in *Virginia*, starring Madeleine Carroll and Fred MacMurray. Billed as "Stirling" Hayden, the actor was hailed in one review as "a Viking god over whom the females swooned," but Hayden himself later downplayed his performance in the film ("I was plain awful," he said.).

Paramount wasted no time casting Hayden as the star in *Bahama Passage* (1941), in which he was re-teamed with Madeleine Carroll. A tiresome drama set on an exotic island, the film was slammed by critics, who were far less kind to Hayden his second time around — Bosley Crowther of the *New York Times* wrote that the actor "just stands straight as a mainmast and speaks his lines in a truculent monotone."

Years later, Hayden recalled his early impressions of Hollywood following his brief foray into filmmaking: "The way Hollywood used to be structured, if you were brought into a 'stable,' they just went to work on you," he told a reporter from *Newsday* in 1977. "It was a lot like a sawmill. They took you in as a tree, and if they wanted a two-by-two, you came out a two-by-two, and if they wanted a two-by-six, you came out that way." The actor's disillusionment with his newfound profession became apparent in November 1941 when he announced to the press that he was abandoning his career because he was "fed up" and "did not wish to be tied to Hollywood."

Ever the sea-lover, Hayden turned up a month later aboard a ship in Iceland, but his abrupt departure from Hollywood didn't signal the end of his life in the public eye — he made news again in July 1942 when he revealed that he and the co-star of his first two films, Madeleine Carroll, had secretly married three months earlier.

"Madeleine and I got together for a lot of reasons," Hayden explained later. "One of them was that we both had a lot of skepticism about Hollywood." But Hayden and his new bride had little time to be together — shortly after revealing the marriage, the actor joined the Marines and was transferred to the Office of Strategic Services (O.S.S.).

Because of the publicity surrounding his enlistment, and seeking to further distance himself from his acting career, Hayden went to court in 1943 to legally change his name to John Hamilton. As Capt. Hamilton, he distinguished himself during World War II, operating a small fishing boat along the Dalmatian and Albanian coasts as head of the O.S.S. air rescue team. Part of his duties included helping Allied flyers to escape to Italy, carrying supplies to O.S.S. agents in Yugoslavia and Greece, and aiding Marshal Tito's partisans in guerrilla warfare against the Germans. For his efforts, Hayden (or Hamilton) was awarded the Silver Star and was cited by Tito's government following the war.

But Hayden emerged from the war to bachelorhood. "The wartime separations and other stresses had ended the marriage to Madeleine," he wrote in his 1963 autobiography, *Wanderer*. "We met one last time in Paris, in 1946, and we knew, without knowing why, without much discussion, that the marriage had dissolved." The couple was divorced later that year.

Unable to raise the funds needed to return to the sea, Hayden made his way back to Hollywood. Paramount executives gleefully announced to the press that the actor had returned to the fold, ensuring the public that his first assignment would be "an important one." He was first seen playing himself (with his name now correctly spelled) in the studio's star-studded musical extravaganza, *Variety Girl* (1947), then portrayed a flying circus family member in *Blaze of Noon* (1947); although both films were box-office hits, they didn't quite offer Hayden the stellar roles he'd been assured. But by now, the actor was making headlines for reasons other than his return to the big screen — on April 25, 1947, he married Betty DeNoon, a socialite and designer from Pasadena, California. The couple made their home aboard Hayden's 50-foot schooner, *Brigadoon*, and within three years, they had three children, Christian Winslow, born in August 1948, Dana Morgan in June 1949, and Gretchen Louise in September 1950.

Meanwhile, after being off screen during 1948, Hayden was back to business in two films the following year — the first was *El Paso* (1949), a mediocre western starring John Payne and Gail Russell, and the next was his entry into the realm of film noir —*Manhandled* (1949). Here, Hayden portrayed insurance investigator Joe Cooper, who finds his work cut out for him when he tries to locate the person behind the murder and jewel robbery of a wealthy socialite (Irene Hervey). Initially, the woman's husband, Alton Bennett (Alan Napier), is the chief suspect — shortly before the incident, Bennett had described a recurring dream to his psychiatrist in which he bludgeoned his wife to death with a perfume bottle. Cooper soon learns that he is on the wrong track; as it turns out, the woman was killed and robbed by her husband's psychiatrist who was, in turn, murdered by a corrupt private detective, Karl Benson (Dan Duryea). When his neighbor and would-be girlfriend, Merl Kramer (Dorothy Lamour) realizes that Benson is the killer, the private detective plants damaging evidence in her apartment, planning to kill her and disguise her death as a suicide. He is nabbed before he can carry out his plan, however, and — ironically — charged with the murder of Mrs. Bennett.

Audiences stayed away from *Manhandled* in droves and the film was panned by critics; in a particularly disparaging review, the *New York Times* critic wrote: "Irene Hervey was the luckiest member of the cast, for she got herself killed fairly early in the proceedings. Miss Lamour, Mr. Duryea, and Sterling Hayden were less fortunate."

By now, Hayden's dissatisfaction with his career was creeping back, along with his longing for the sea — "I had the post war jitters," he told a reporter. "Mostly I wanted a boat and some relaxation." After his somewhat average performances in his previous three films, he was dropped from his Paramount contract and "I just sat for a long time," the actor said. "I never called my agent. I had a few bucks in the bank. I waited and waited."

The actor's next film was worth waiting for — in his sole feature of 1950, Hayden starred in one of the best films of his career, and one of noir's best entries — MGM's *The Asphalt Jungle*. As Dix Handley, Hayden portrayed a member of a motley crew assembled to pull a jewel heist, masterminded by an aging criminal (Sam Jaffe) who has been recently released from prison. Despite the intricate planning, the scheme begins to unravel when one of the hoods (Anthony Caruso) is accidentally shot during the robbery, the crooked attorney engaged to fence the jewels attempts to double-cross the group, and the leader of the gang is captured by police while trying to flee. As for Dix, whose dream is only to return to his home in Kentucky, he is mortally wounded when he confronts the attorney, but he is determined to make it back to the South, accompanied by his faithful girlfriend, Doll (superbly played

by Jean Hagen). He manages to reach a farm field, but he dies there, surrounded by the horses he loved.

Almost universally hailed by critics, *Asphalt Jungle* was a hit at the box office, and Hayden was singled out for his understated performance — Bosley Crowther wrote in the *New York Times* that the actor was "sure-fire as a brazen hoodlum who just wants to go back home," and the critic for *Variety* declared that the character of Dix was Hayden's "best chance to date and he makes the most of it."

After the acclaim earned by *The Asphalt Jungle,* Hayden expected to be offered a series of first-rate roles, but the much-awaited calls never came. "I thought that would crack everything wide open," he said. "I'd just sit back and be turning down offers. Well, I got a few, but none good." Finally, the actor returned to Paramount. "I ... made a clean breast of everything," he said. "I said I knew I was an offbeat guy and had acted foolishly. I grew up slow, living in a never-never land that suited me. Now I realize that you can't be an escapist all your life."

A short time later, in October 1950, Paramount signed the actor to a long-term contract, announcing plans to groom him as an action star, but he was immediately loaned out to Fox for *Journey into Light* (1951), in which he played a minister who abandons his church after the suicide of his alcoholic wife. Back at Paramount, he next starred in a so-so oater, *The Flaming Feather* (1951), as a rancher who helps to rescue a girl captured by Indians. After this feature, Paramount intended to loan Hayden to Republic Studios for a war-time actioner, *Wings Across the Pacific*, but Hayden balked at the plan and asked to be released from his contract, less than six months after signing. He told the press that he was seeking roles with "real depth." "I can't see myself as having a future simply in action pictures," he said. "How can you run up and down on a horse constantly and look yourself in the face?"

While struggling to find his niche in pictures, however, Hayden discovered that he had more urgent matters to face. In April 1951, he was called as a "cooperative witness" before the House Un-American Activities Committee, which had been investigating Communism in Hollywood since the late 1940s, and had led to the blacklisting of numerous actors, writers, and directors in the film industry. Appearing before the committee, Hayden testified that he was urged to join the Communist Party by a woman named Bea Winters, who worked as a stenographer for Horizon Pictures. The actor also admitted that he joined the Party in 1946, "because I felt I wanted to do something for a better world," but that he renounced his membership seven months later.

"It was the stupidest, most ignorant thing I ever did in my life," he said.

In addition to acknowledging his own membership, Hayden also named a number of his fellow actors who he claimed were involved in Communist activities, including screenwriters Abraham Polonsky, author of the noir classics *Body and Soul* (1947) and *Force of Evil* (1948), and Robert Lees, who penned such features as *Abbott and Costello Meet Frankenstein* (1948). Blacklisted as a result of the HUAC investigation, Polonsky would not have a screenwriting credit for nearly 20 years, and Lees never wrote another screenplay after 1952. And Bea Winters, the stenographer named by Hayden, was told by her employer on the day following Hayden's testimony, "not to come to work until this thing is cleared up."

Hayden's testimony before HUAC was praised by actor Ronald Reagan, then president of the AFL Screen Actors Guild, who stated: "The guild congratulates Sterling Hayden on his honesty and frankness in his testimony which confirms the fact that the guild, with the full support of 98% of the Hollywood actors, defeated the Communist Party's attempts to use the guild for Communist causes." But Hayden came to genuinely regret his actions—calling it his "one-shot stoolie show"—and detailed his contrition years later in his autobiography: "I was a real daddy longlegs of a worm when it came to crawling," he

wrote. "Not often does a man find himself eulogized for having behaved in a manner that he himself despises."

With this distasteful episode behind him, Hayden returned to his screen career, becoming the first actor subpoenaed by HUAC to land a major acting assignment — he starred with Edmond O'Brien and Dean Jagger in Paramount's *Denver and Rio Grande* (1952), a western about rival railroad builders. But the actor's life behind the screen was far from smooth. On December 28, 1951, he filed for divorce from his wife of four years, charging that she was "guilty of extreme cruelty, treating him in a cruel and inhuman manner that caused him to suffer great humiliation, anguish, and embarrassment." But less than a month later, Hayden asked the Santa Monica Superior Court to dismiss the suit, and later that year, in the summer of 1952, the couple's fourth child, Matthew, was born.

Just four months after the birth of their son, Hayden's wife, Betty, filed a suit of her own — she testified in court that Hayden became "cool and indifferent ... and refused to explain frequent absences from home. When he came home after long absences, he would say it was none of my business where he had been." An interlocutory divorce was granted in April 1953, but the couple remained together until 1954, when they separated. The following year, in August 1955, Hayden won a final divorce from his wife. In his court testimony, he stated that Betty "began trying to dominate me and dictate who our friends should be and how my profession should be handled." Although the court maintained jurisdiction over the couple's four children, they continued to live with their father.

Career-wise, Hayden appeared in a series of films of varying quality during the next several years— the best of these were *The Star* (1952), featuring Bette Davis as onetime Oscar winner whose career is on the downswing; *Flat Top* (1952), a war-time actioner in which Hayden played the tough commander of an aircraft carrier; *So Big* (1953), the third and best film version of Edna Ferber's famed novel of a teacher in a country school; and *Johnny Guitar* (1954), an existential western co-starring Joan Crawford and Mercedes McCambridge. He also starred in two films noirs in 1954 — *Crime Wave* and *Suddenly*.

Crime Wave, directed by Andre DeToth, tells the story of Steve Lacey (dancer Gene Nelson), an ex-con whose efforts to straighten out his life are stymied when a former fellow inmate shows up at his door. Suffering from a gunshot wound after taking part in a gas station stick-up, the man later dies, and before long, Steve is visited by two more hoods from his past, Doc Penny (Ted De Corsia) and Ben Hastings (played by Charles Buchinsky, before his name change to Bronson). Abducting Steve and his wife, Ellen (Phyllis Kirk), Doc outlines his plan to force Steve into participating in a bank heist. Meanwhile, the men's actions are being closely followed by Detective Sgt. Sims (Hayden), a tough-talking, toothpick-chewing cop who shows up in time to thwart the bank robbery and capture the bad guys. At the film's end, Sims reveals the heart of gold behind his gruff manner when he tells Steve and Ellen, "Next time, Lacey, call me but quick. A cop's job is to protect the citizens.... Now, beat it outta here before I run ya in."

In *Suddenly*, Hayden's second film noir of the year, the actor portrayed Tod Shaw, a small-town sheriff determined to stop the planned assassination of the president of the United States. The man behind the scheme is John Baron (Frank Sinatra), a psychopathic killer who takes over a house overlooking a small-town railway depot, intending to gun down the president as his motorcade leaves the station. Along with the residents of the house — Shaw's would-be girlfriend, Ellen (Nancy Gates), her father-in-law (James Gleason), and her young son (Kim Charney) — the sheriff conspires to outsmart Baron and his gang, endeavoring on numerous occasions to push the unstable killer over the edge. ("You know, Baron, you got the yard look. You look yardbird to me," Shaw taunts the war veteran at one point. "Come on, tell me — where were you court-martialed? What was

it for — rape? Nah, nah, not rape. Killing — that's what you like, killing. Maybe shooting down unarmed PWs.... You know, I knew guys like you. Killing was sweet. Rather kill a man than love a girl.") Ultimately, the combined efforts of the hostages prove successful, and after Baron is shot by Ellen, Shaw finishes him off. Hayden earned mixed reviews for the first of his 1954 noirs; while Philip K. Scheuer of the *Los Angeles Times* applauded his "real characterization as a time-worn stereotype," the actor was dismissed as "a little too laconic" in the *Los Angeles Daily News*, and the critic for the *New York Times* seemed completely baffled by his performance, writing that "Mr. Hayden's paradoxical behavior strikes and sustains a disturbing note of righteous sadism. His snarling allergy to 'any ex-con' and his bland bullying of the open-faced couple make Mr. Hayden a peculiar paragon of justice indeed." The actor received a better reaction, however, for his portrayal of the courageous sheriff in *Suddenly* (which, incidentally, was the name of the small-town where the film's action takes place, so named, according to one character, because "that's the way things used to happen here — suddenly"). Although most of the accolades were showered on the standout performance offered by Sinatra, Hayden was singled out in *Variety* for his "authoritative handl[ing]" of his role, and by Wylie Williams of the *Hollywood Citizen-News*, who wrote: "[Hayden's] calm virility and poise are perfect counterpoint to the spitfire cop-hating venom of the tightly strung Sinatra."

Although Hayden continued his non-stop film schedule, most of his films were fairly forgettable — *Timberjack* (1955) was a dull tale of two feuding families in Montana, and *Battle Taxi* (1955) told the humdrum story of a helicopter rescue group during the Korean War — but the actor fared better with such features as *The Last Command* (1955), in which he portrayed Jim Bowie, the famed knife-fighting adventurer who died at the Alamo. Also of note was the actor's return to film noir in *The Killing* (1956).

Much like Hayden's earlier *The Asphalt*

Jungle, this superb contribution to the film noir era, centers on a crime — this time, a race-track heist — carefully planned and executed by a mixed bag of criminals and would-be criminals, including ex-con Johnny Clay (Hayden), a cop (Ted De Corsia) who owes money to the mob; a meek race track cashier (Elisha Cook, Jr.), who is goaded by his gold-digging wife into taking part in the robbery; and a bartender (Joe Sawyer) supporting his invalid wife. As in *The Asphalt Jungle*, the group's best-laid plans are usurped by unforeseen circumstances, most notably an attempted double-cross by the wife of the cashier (Marie Windsor) and her lover (Vince Edwards) — which goes horribly wrong. In the film's final, gripping scene, Johnny and his childhood sweetheart (Coleen Gray) are seen at the bus station, attempting to escape with a suitcase filled with cash. Ironically, the bulging bag falls from a luggage cart and breaks open, and Johnny watches helplessly as the cash scatters in the wind and waits with resignation for the police to arrest him. For his performance, Hayden earned well-deserved praise from reviewers, including A.H. Weiler, who wrote in the *New York Times* that he "makes a restrained but hard and efficient leader."

The following year, Hayden made his final appearance in film noir, starring opposite Barbara Stanwyck in *Crime of Passion* (1957). Here, Hayden played police lieutenant Bill Doyle, whose wife, Kathy (Stanwyck), abandons her successful career as a newspaper reporter following her marriage. Quickly bored with the life of a housewife, Kathy focuses her energies into furthering her husband's career, and cozies up to his boss, Inspector Tony Pope (Raymond Burr), in hopes of encouraging her spouse's promotion. Kathy even submits to a one-night stand with Pope upon learning of his imminent retirement, but when she discovers that Pope plans to appoint another man as his replacement, she shoots him in the film title's "crime of passion." Determined to find the inspector's killer, Bill is dismayed to finally unearth his wife's culpability, but in the film's final reel,

he is seen putting his duty before his love for Kathy and escorting her to justice. After the film's release, Hayden was singled out by the reviewer for the *New York Times*, who said that he "does what he can as the dumbest detective-husband on record" — the same critic dismissed the movie as "the most curiously misguided missile to hit town in some time," but it stands up today as a interesting entry in the film noir realm.

Hayden continued to star in a series of mostly mediocre films — a notable exception was *Terror in a Texas Town* (1958), a stylishly offbeat western helmed by Joseph Lewis — but his life was about to take a turn far more dramatic than any movie script could offer. For several years, the actor had entertained the notion of taking a year-long sailing trip in order to make a "television adventure film" that would "show truthfully the vigors and pleasures of a voyage to the South Seas." He also planned for his four children to accompany him on the journey. But Hayden hadn't reckoned on his ex-wife.

In August 1958, Betty deNoon filed an affidavit in Superior Court, seeking to block Hayden from taking the children on the trip. She also sought to gain custody of the youngsters, who had continued to live with Hayden since the divorce. "Sterling and his attorneys have made it clear that if I go to court and oppose this trip, they will attack me viciously. If I don't, my children might well die on this voyage," Betty stated in the affidavit.

Hayden countered with the revelation that he'd had Betty investigated in early 1955, prior to their divorce, and learned that she had "engaged in intimacies with approximately six men." After this discovery, Hayden claimed, Betty "implored" him not to expose her, and had signed an agreement giving him custody of their children. Calling Hayden and his attorneys "bullies," Betty struck back with another affidavit, which read in part: "I made every possible effort to make our marriage a happy and successful one. I bore Mr. Hayden four children out of love. I was a devoted and faithful wife and mother. If he had devoted the attention to our lives that he did to hating his first wife, and his mother, and women generally, maybe we could have had a successful marriage."

On January 15, 1959, following a 20-day hearing, Superior Judge Emil Gumpert issued a lengthy opinion in which he held that Betty was "not a fit and proper person to have the care and custody of the children.... The uncontradicted evidence impels the court to express the wish that all children might be blessed with a love and devotion, a concern and care, equal to that which this father has bestowed upon his off-spring." Despite this glowing testament to Hayden's parenting skills, however, the judge also ruled that the actor's 60-year-old sailing vessel was unsafe, and that he would not be allowed to take the children on the planned cruise.

But the judge's ruling did not end the case. A little over a week later, Betty deNoon was back in court, expressing her fears that Hayden had "kidnapped" their children — the actor had sailed with the children for what was purported to be a three-day trip from San Francisco to Santa Barbara, but after six days, they had not been spotted. Moreover, Betty claimed, it was learned that the actor's 98-foot schooner, the *Wanderer*, was equipped with 100 pounds of meat, nearly 30 gallons of milk, and 50 gallons of water, and was also carrying 15 other passengers, including a doctor and a teacher.

The case, which was being reported on daily, took on an even wilder spin when, on January 24, 1959, the families of the *Wanderer* crew received a letter from Hayden that read: "When and if you read this, we will be on our way with the oft-postponed voyage in spite of a certain ruling of the court. I regret that such action is required but the reasons are so obvious as to require no comment ... Hail and farewell."

After learning of the letter, Betty filed an affidavit charging Hayden with contempt of court, telling the press, "He's gone out of his mind. He'll kill them on that ship." But others had a less vituperative reaction. "He's probably headed for Shangri-La," said Hayden's agent, William Shiffrin. "This man was

born in the wrong century. He should have been a sea captain in the 1800s." Equally dismissive was Judge Roger Alton Pfaff, who ruled that the matter was out of his hands. "I could find him in contempt today, and tomorrow he could be back at the moorings saying he had not been beyond our territorial limits."

Refusing to back down, Betty obtained an arrest warrant for her ex-husband, but no word was heard from the actor until nearly two months later when, on March 6, 1959, Hayden and his children arrived in Papeete, Tahiti. In a brief cable sent by the actor, he explained that his motivation for the voyage was simple: "An ounce of freedom is worth a ton of gold." Betty fired back with still another complaint in court, this time charging the actor with conspiracy to commit a number of offenses, including child theft. And, in an attempt to cut off Hayden's source of supplies, Betty filed suit against Time, Inc., Edward Small Productions, and Libra Productions, Inc., which she identified as the financial backers of Hayden's filmmaking venture. She also filed suit seeking custody of the four children, claiming that Hayden took the children to use "as actors in a television series, thereby endangering their lives for the sake of monetary gain."

Still, it wasn't until November 1959 — and only because his "money ran out" — that Hayden finally announced that he was returning home with his children to face the music. Frankly detailing his adventure to the press, Hayden said that the trip was a "search for truth."

"I want to live life not as people say it ought to be done, but the way I want to do it," he said. "It's damn hard trying to go against the grain. But I'm sorry for nothing. It was wonderful for the kids. They haven't seen TV in a year, haven't listened to the radio in six months. What did they do in Tahiti? They played."

Upon the actor's arrival in California, the District Attorney announced that all charges — including conspiracy and child stealing — would be dismissed against Hayden if he returned to Los Angeles to face the contempt charges. The actor agreed, and in January 1960, entered a plea of guilty on charges that he defied the court order that prohibited him from taking the trip with the children. However, he explained to Superior Judge Emil Gumpert that he "had to make a ... choice between being in contempt of court or becoming in contempt of the children's best interests. [The trip] seemed the lesser of two evils."

Judge Gumpert ordered Hayden to serve five days in county jail and pay a fine of $500, then suspended the sentence on the condition that the actor not remove the children from the state without his ex-wife's written consent. Incredibly, in making his ruling, the judge harshly condemned Betty deNoon, stating that for the last four years, she had "almost continuously harassed and bedeviled [Hayden] by a mass of repetitious and unsuccessful court proceedings. This unremitting activity has constituted an enormous drain on Hayden's time, finances, and ... emotional resources. This court accepts that [Hayden] meant no disrespect to the court or for the law [and] accepts his sincere apology. The court is not blind to forces which control human behavior under emotionally charged circumstances. The court is convinced that the ends of justice will best be served by not now punishing [Hayden's] behavior." After the judge's decision, Betty deNoon was reportedly heard in the courtroom murmuring, "I can't believe it."

After his astonishing adventure, Hayden revealed to the press that he had no plans to return to Hollywood and, instead, intended to continue writing an autobiography that he had started during his journey. "I was never really an actor. I was essentially more of a personality," he told reporters. "Los Angeles epitomizes all that's wrong. You sell out there. Lots of people fit very well in Hollywood, but I never did. I always hated acting, but I kept on acting ... a commuter on a tinsel train. It was an easy way to make money. It was an escape. They give you a check for doing nothing. I have no one but myself to blame for not getting away from it sooner."

After the storm died down following Hayden's legal battles, the actor took another trip down the aisle — wife number three was Catherine Denise McConnell, whom he had met a year earlier. The couple later had two children, both boys, but in his typical unconventional style, the actor spent half of each year with his wife and children in Wilton, Connecticut, and the other half living alone on a Dutch canal barge in France, called the *Who Knows*.

In 1963, Hayden completed the autobiography he had started several years before — entitled *Wanderer*, it was received with universal acclaim. In *Book Week*, Joe Hyams said that Hayden wrote "beautifully and with compassion," and Joseph Wershba raved in the *New York Post*: "This is a superb piece of writing. It ranks with the best of modern self-examination.... It is literate and literary, in and out, rebellious and beatnik — and thoroughly American Gothic. Everything is here, with echoes from Poe and Melville to Steinbeck and Mailer. But it's all of one piece, a work of fascination on every level."

The year after his book's release, Hayden returned to the big screen as the cigar-chomping General Jack D. Ripper in *Dr. Strangelove or: How I Learned to Stop Worrying and Love the Bomb* (1964), earning praise for his "gritty realism" and for keeping the film on a "sharp satirical edge." His next appearance in feature films came five years later, in *Sweet Hunters* (1969), where he played the patriarch of a family living on a remote tropical island, and *Hard Contract* (1969), a fast-paced thriller starring James Coburn and Lee Remick. By now, Hayden was also seen on a variety of television shows — since the late 1950s, he had appeared on such programs as *DuPont Show of the Month*, *Playhouse 90*, *Zane Grey Theater*, and *Schlitz Playhouse of Stars*, as well as a number of made-for-television movies including *Ethan Frome* (1960) and *Carol for Another Christmas* (1964).

As the 1970s dawned, Hayden continued to accept small roles in such box-office hits as *The Godfather* (1972), where he played the corrupt police captain who is shot in the head by Michael Corleone (Al Pacino), and *The Long Goodbye* (1973), in which he was seen as an alcoholic writer. Years later, Hayden would call the latter role his favorite. "When I meet my maker, and he says, 'Sterling, forgive my impertinence, but if you had one piece of film you wanted to leave behind, what would it be?' Hell, I'd say, 'Just give 'em *The Long Goodbye*. That wasn't acting. That was me.'" During the next several years, he also appeared in *The Last Days of Man on Earth* (1975), a fairly silly science fiction feature; *1900* (1976), an epic tale of the hostilities between landowners and peasants in turn-of-the-century Italy; *King of the Gypsies* (1978), with Susan Sarandon and Shelley Winters; *Winter Kills* (1979), a first-rate, political black comedy; and *9 to 5* (1980), a hit comedy starring Lily Tomlin, Jane Fonda, and Dolly Parton. When he wasn't acting, Hayden was busy writing — in 1976, he published *Voyage*, a 700-page epic novel of the sea. As with his first book, *Voyage* earned widespread plaudits — Judson Hand, of the *New York Daily News*, wrote that the book was "never boring or false," and in *Time*, John Skow called the novel a "somber study of the human condition."

But despite the success of his book and his well-received film and television performances, all was not well with Hayden. A longtime heavy drinker, in 1972 the actor had suffered what he termed "a complete breakdown," and although he spent six weeks in a hospital for rehabilitation, his struggles with alcohol continued. Always surprisingly candid about his personal life, Hayden told a reporter in 1978 that he was still drinking.

"I drink a lot," he told Roderick Mann of the *Los Angeles Times*. "Yes, I do. Trouble is, when I get on a run, oh man, I drink. I went to Stockholm this year on a book thing. I got there a little drunk and got drunker."

But two years later, Hayden announced that he was winning the battle with the bottle and revealed that he was achieving it through a new method; during an interview with Ron Base of the *Toronto Sun*, Hayden extolled the virtues of marijuana and hashish, and even offered some to the reporter.

"The main thing right now is to bring the booze under control," Hayden said. "I'm absolutely fascinated by booze. It's one of the great common denominators. [But] grass is all I do now. Grass and hash. Grass came into me and said take it easy. That's why I love it so much." The actor also admitted that he had been under the influence of drugs during several of his recent film performances, including *The Long Goodbye* and *The Godfather* — on the latter film, he said, just before he got out of the police car and cuffed Al Pacino across the head, he took a "long draw on his hash pipe."

"As you can tell, I don't take it very seriously," Hayden said. "I've worked slightly stoned on camera for the past 10 years."

Eight months after that interview, on April 16, 1981, Hayden was arrested at the Toronto International Airport after customs officials discovered more than an ounce of hashish in the actor's luggage. The prosecutor for the case sought a conviction and a fine, but Judge Kenneth Langdon later dismissed the possession charge, stating, "The severity of the consequences might outweigh the nature of the offense. The court does not single out an individual because the press has done so."

In 1982, Hayden made his final television appearance, portraying John Brown in the popular mini-series *The Blue and the Gray*. In the mini-series, the actor was still sporting the wild, gray beard he had worn since the late 1970s; on several occasions, he'd been asked to shave the beard for a role, but — in true Sterling Hayden fashion — he refused.

"Sounds silly, huh? But I like being bearded," he told Mann in the *Los Angeles Times*. "If I take it off, it reminds me of those old Hollywood days when I was a male starlet. And I don't care to remember them."

Hayden also told Mann that he was "straight" while playing the role of John Brown.

"I wasn't stoned, and I wasn't drinking when I did it," he said. "I have too much reverence for that man John Brown. Also, for the first time, I find I have a modicum of confidence about my acting. Remember, I never knew what the damn hell I was doing as an actor. I knew I wasn't good; I knew I didn't know my craft. It wasn't that I disliked acting, although I used to say that. It was that I was permanently embarrassed."

Also in 1982, Hayden was featured in *Venom*, a horror film about a deadly snake, starring Klaus Kinski and Oliver Reed, and the following year, he was the subject of an acclaimed documentary, *Pharos of Chaos*, which showed his life aboard the *Who Knows* in Paris. The documentary on Hayden's life was his last appearance on screen. On May 23, 1986, at the age of 70, the actor died following a lengthy battle with cancer — his son-in-law, George Rickert, told reporters that it was "a quiet passing. He more or less went in his sleep." The actor was survived by his wife, Catherine, and his six children.

One of noir's archetypal performers, Sterling Hayden offered a series of often understated, but never unnoticed, performances that serve as a testament to his talent as an actor. While he led a fascinating life that often overshadowed his screen accomplishments, Sterling Hayden possessed a genuine acting ability that only increased with age. Perhaps the best summation of Hayden the performer and Hayden the man was provided by writer Howard Skiles, who wrote of the actor in 1976: "He was always somehow larger than life. You just couldn't imagine all that strength and energy failing to do anything it set out to do. He was like a force of nature; an element. That he could also act — really act, bring a true character to life on the screen — was sort of like putting a few stray diamonds on top of a solid-gold Cadillac."

Film Noir Filmography

Manhandled. Director: Lewis R. Foster. Producers: William H. Pine and William C. Thomas. Running time: 97 minutes. Released by Paramount, May 25, 1949. Cast: Dorothy Lamour, Dan Duryea, Sterling Hayden, Irene Hervey, Philip Reed, Harold Vermilyea, Alan Napier, Art Smith, Irving Bacon.

The Asphalt Jungle. Director: John Huston. Producer: Arthur Hornblow, Jr. Running time: 112 minutes. Released by MGM, June 8, 1950. Cast: Sterling Hayden, Louis Calhern, Jean Hagen, James Whitmore, Sam Jaffe, John McIntire, Marc Lawrence, Barry Kelley, Anthony Caruso, Terese Calli, Marilyn Monroe, William Davis, Dorothy Tree, Brad Dexter, Alex Gerry, Thomas Browne Henry, James Seay, Don Haggerty, Henry Rowland, Helene Stanley, Raymond Roe, Charles Courtney. Awards: Academy Award nominations for Best Director (John Huston), Best Supporting Actor (Sam Jaffe), Best Black and White Cinematography (Harold Rosson), Best Screenplay (Ben Maddow, John Huston).

Crime Wave. Director: Andre DeToth. Producer: Bryan Foy. Running time: 73 minutes. Released by Warner Bros., January 12, 1954. Cast: Gene Nelson, Phyllis Kirk, Sterling Hayden, James Bell, Ted De Corsia, Charles Buchinsky, Ned Young, Jay Novello, Walter Dub Taylor, Richard Benjamin, Mack Chandler, Gayle Kellogg, James Hayward, Timothy Carey.

Suddenly. Director: Lewis Allen. Producer: Robert Bassler. Running time: 77 minutes. Released by United Artists, October 7, 1954. Cast: Frank Sinatra, Sterling Hayden, James Gleason, Nancy Gates, Kim Charney, Paul Frees, Christopher Dark, Willis Bouchey, Paul Wexler, Jim Lilburn, Charles Smith, Ken Dibbs, Clark Howatt, Dan White, Richard Collier.

The Killing. Director: Stanley Kramer. Producer: James B. Harris. Running time: 84 minutes. Released by United Artists, May 20, 1956. Cast: Sterling Hayden, Coleen Gray, Vince Edwards, Jay C. Flippen, Marie Windsor, Ted De Corsia, Elisha Cook, Jr., Joe Sawyer, Timothy Carey, Jay Adler, Kola Kwarian, Joseph Turkell, James Edwards.

Crime of Passion. Director: Gerd Oswald. Producer: Herman Cohen. Running time: 85 minutes. Released by United Artists, January 9, 1957. Cast: Barbara Stanwyck, Sterling Hayden, Raymond Burr, Fay Wray, Royal Dano, Virginia Grey, Dennis Cross, Robert Griffin, Jay Adler, Malcolm Atterbury, John S. Launer, Brad Trumbull, Skipper McNally, Jean Howell, Peg La Centra, Nancy Reynolds, Marjorie Owens, Robert Quarry, Joe Conley, Stuart Whitman.

References

"Actor Divorces Wife Who Divorced Him." *Los Angeles Mirror-News*, August 27, 1955.
"Actor Hayden Asks to Drop Divorce Suit." *Los Angeles Times*, January 22, 1952.

"Actor Hayden Back on Job." *Los Angeles Examiner*, May 29, 1951.

"Actor Hayden Files Suit for Divorce." *Los Angeles Times*, December 19, 1951.

"Actor Hayden Has Second Son for Crew." *Los Angeles Times*, July 1, 1949.

"Actor Hayden Hates Movies, Loves the Sea." *Los Angeles Times*, November 21, 1959.

"Actor Hayden May Marry Pasadena Girl." *Los Angeles Times*, March 10, 1947.

"Actor Hayden Presented with Baby Son." *Los Angeles Times*, circa August 1948.

"Actor Hayden Says He Will Ask Divorce." *Hollywood Citizen-News*, January 31, 1946.

"Actor Hayden's Ex-Wife Blocks Sea Trip Plans." *Los Angeles Times*, August 25, 1958.

"Actor Hayden Takes Pasadenan as His Bride." *Los Angeles Times*, April 26, 1947.

"Actor Hayden to Be Called in Red Probe." *Los Angeles Times*, April 7, 1951.

"Actor Hayden Wins Children's Custody." *Los Angeles Mirror-News*, January 16, 1959.

"Actor's Sloop Towed In." *Los Angeles Times*, December 19, 1951.

"Actor Sterling Hayden Charges Misconduct." *Los Angeles Times*, October 30, 1958.

"Actor Sterling Hayden Divorced." *Los Angeles Examiner*, April 24, 1953.

"Actor Sterling Hayden to Keep Four Children." *Los Angeles Times*, January 16, 1959.

"Actor Sterling Hayden Weds Pasadena Society Woman." *Los Angeles Examiner*, April 26, 1947.

"Actor Who Got 'Lost' With Madeleine Carroll 'Quits.'" *Los Angeles Times*, November 14, 1941.

Base, Ron. "Sterling Hayden Kicks Mash for Hash and Grass." *Toronto Sun*, August 31, 1980.

Biography of Sterling Hayden. Paramount Studios, circa 1940.

Biography of Sterling Hayden. Paramount Studios, August 1941.

Black, Eleanor Garner. "Hayden Tells Judge Why He Defied Order." *Los Angeles Examiner*, January 6, 1960.

_____. "Judge Blasts Wife's Harassing of Hayden." *Los Angeles Examiner*, January 8, 1960.

"Contempt Charge on Hayden Denied." *Los Angeles Times*, January 27, 1959.

"Daughter Born to Hayden's Wife." *Hollywood Citizen-News*, September 18, 1950.

"Delay Given on Hayden's Contempt Case." *Los Angeles Times*, February 3, 1959.

"Due at Tahiti in March, Hayden Message Says." *Los Angeles Times*, February 24, 1959.

"Ex-Red, Film Star Sues for Divorce." *Los Angeles Herald-Express*, December 28, 1951.

"Ex-Wife Again Sues Hayden." *Los Angeles Examiner*, December 18, 1959.

"Ex-Wife Balks Cruise for Hayden, Children." *Los Angeles Times*, September 17, 1958.

"Ex-Wife Fears Hayden 'Kidnapped' Children." *Los Angeles Times*, January 23, 1959.

"Ex-Wife Gets Warrant for Hayden Arrest." *Los Angeles Times*, January 30, 1959.

"Guilty Plea Scheduled by Hayden." *Hollywood Citizen-News*, December 3, 1959.

"Hayden Accuses Ex-Wife." *Los Angeles Examiner*, October 30, 1958.

"Hayden Arrest Warrant Signed." *Hollywood Citizen-News*, January 29, 1959.

"Hayden Charges Intimacies." *Los Angeles Mirror-News*, October 29, 1958.

"Hayden Cleared on Hashish Charge." *Los Angeles Herald-Examiner*, April 28, 1981.

"Hayden Confirms Reports of Marriage to Miss Carroll." *Los Angeles Times*, July 1, 1942.

"Hayden Cruise Case Postponed by Judge. " *Hollywood Citizen-News*, September 17, 1958.

"Hayden Defies Court, Sails for Tahiti with Children." *Los Angeles Times*, January 25, 1959.

"Hayden 1st Ex-Red Set by Major Co." *Variety*, May 28, 1951.

"Hayden Gets Off Contempt 'Hook.'" *Hollywood Citizen-News*, January 7, 1960.

"Hayden Gets Suspended Sentence for Voyage." *Los Angeles Times*, January 8, 1960.

"Hayden Given Custody of 4." *Hollywood Citizen-News*, January 16, 1959.

"Hayden Halted in Effort to Sail with Children." *Hollywood Citizen-News*, September 24, 1958.

"Hayden Home; Faces Court Appearance." *Beverly Hills Citizen*, November 16, 1959.

"Hayden in Hot Water Atty Says." *Hollywood Citizen-News*, January 24, 1959.

"Hayden Pleads Guilty in Defying Court Order." *Los Angeles Times*, January 6, 1960.

"Hayden Returns; Must Face Court." *Los Angeles Examiner*, November 15, 1959.

"Hayden Sailing Home to Face Court Charge." *Los Angeles Times*, October 9, 1959.

"Hayden Says He Joined Party After War Service." *New York Post*, April 10, 1951.

"Hayden Ship in Tahiti." *Los Angeles Examiner*, March 6, 1959.

"Hayden's Ex Asks Custody of Children." *Hollywood Citizen-News*, October 29, 1959.

"Hayden's Ex-Wife Blocks Sea Voyage." *Los Angeles Examiner*, September 16, 1958.

"Haydens Fight Over Children." *Los Angeles Mirror-News*, September 16, 1958.

"Hayden Signed by Paramount." *Paramount News*, October 16, 1950.

"Hayden Sues Miss Carroll for Divorce." *Los Angeles Times*, March 15, 1946.

"Haydens Will Share Their Children's Yule." *Los Angeles Times*, December 22, 1959.

"Hayden Tentative for Role in 'Sang.'" *Variety*, October 23, 1985.

"Hayden to Appear on New Restraint Order." *Los Angeles Times*, December 18, 1959.

"Hayden Will Freelance." *Los Angeles Times*, February 21, 1951.

"Hayden Won't Be Fired, Film Producer Says." *Los Angeles Times*, April 11, 1951.

"Madeleine Carroll Bride of Hayden." *Los Angeles Herald*, July 1, 1942.

"Madeleine Carroll, in Paris, Divorces Sterling Hayden." *Los Angeles Examiner*, May 9, 1946.

Mann, Roderick. "Sterling Hayden Talks on Beards, Barges and Booze." *Los Angeles Times*, November 14, 1982.

_____. "Sterling Hayden: The Beard Must Remain." *Los Angeles Times*, December 26, 1978.

McCarthy, Todd. "Sterling Hayden, 70, Dies at Sausalito Home After Bout with Cancer." *Variety*, May 27, 1986.

"Mrs. Hayden Agrees to Let Actor Sail Canal." *Los Angeles Times*, May 14, 1959.

"Mrs. Hayden Hurls New 'Epithets.'" *Hollywood Citizen-News*, December 18, 1959.

"Mrs. Hayden Seeks to Block Actor's Funds." *Los Angeles Times*, April 22, 1959.

Othman, Frederick C. "Handsome Sailor Hayden Got Razzed Into Movies." *Hollywood Citizen-News*, November 15, 1940.

Parsons, Louella O. "Actor Hayden Plans to Wed." *Los Angeles Examiner*, March 10, 1947.

Quigg, Jack. "Wanderlust Gone, Sailor Now Acts." *Buffalo Courier Express*, January 14, 1951.

"Screen Actress Carroll Freed from War Hero." *Los Angeles Times*, May 9, 1946.

"Spice Likely at Hayden Court Tiff." *Los Angeles Mirror-News*, August 25, 1958.

Spiro, J.D. "The Sailor Home from the Sea." *The Milwaukee Journal*, April 20, 1941.

"Sterling Hayden and 4 Children Vanish on Ship." *Los Angeles Times*, January 24, 1959.

"Sterling Hayden and Schooner in Legal Storm." *Hollywood Citizen-News*, January 26, 1959.

"Sterling Hayden Arrives in Marquesas Islands." *Hollywood Citizen-News*, February 21,1959.

"Sterling Hayden Divorced from 'Dominating Wife.'" *Los Angeles Mirror-News*, August 26, 1955.

"Sterling Hayden Fine, Sentence Is Suspended." *Beverly Hills Citizen*, January 7, 1960.

"Sterling Hayden Hates Women, Ex-Wife Says." *Los Angeles Times*, November 4, 1958.

"Sterling Hayden on Iceland Duty." *Hollywood Citizen-News*, December 17, 1941.

"Sterling Hayden Quits Hollywood to Live Own Life." *Los Angeles Herald*, November 4, 1941.

"Sterling Hayden Seeking Divorce; Tells 'Humiliation.'" *Los Angeles Examiner*, December 29, 1951.

"Sterling Hayden's Daring Air Rescue War Feats Disclosed." *Los Angeles Times*, November 27, 1945.

"Sterling Haydens Have Daughter." *Los Angeles Times*, September 19, 1950.

"Sterling Hayden 'Vanishes' with Kids on High Seas; Ex-Wife Pondering Suit." *Variety*, January 24, 1959.

"Sterling Hayden Wins Custody of Children." *Los Angeles Examiner*, January 16, 1959.

"Stirling Hayden Leaves to Face House Red Quiz." *Los Angeles Times*, April 10, 1951.

Thackrey, Ted Jr.. "Actor Sterling Hayden Dies at 70." *Los Angeles Times*, May 24, 1986.

"Trip Legal, Says Aide to Hayden." *Hollywood Citizen-News*, February 3, 1959.

"Wife of Actor to Get 55 Pct. of Earnings." *Los Angeles Herald Express*, April 23, 1953.

VAN HEFLIN

"So I'm no good. Well, I'm no worse than anybody else…. Whatever I did, I did for you."— Van Heflin in *The Prowler* (1951)

Van Heflin was, by all accounts, an "actor's actor."

"I have to be," he once said. "Because I'm neither a 'personality' nor one endowed with good looks. If I'm to get by at all, it has to be on talent."

Once described as "attractively homely," Heflin earned respect on the screen, stage, and television for his versatility and his ability to completely consume a character and make it his own. Heflin, winner of an Academy Award for Best Supporting Actor, played throughout his career alongside Hollywood's top stars, including Robert Taylor, Barbara Stanwyck, Joan Crawford, Alan Ladd, and Lionel Barrymore. With such memorable features to his credit as *Madame Bovary* (1949), *Shane* (1953), and *Airport* (1970), Heflin was also seen in five films noirs: *Johnny Eager* (1942), *The Strange Love of Martha Ivers* (1946), *Possessed* (1947), *Act of Violence* (1949), and *The Prowler* (1951).

Emmet Evan Heflin, Jr., was born on December 13, 1910, in Walters, Oklahoma, the son of a dentist. The Heflins moved to nearby Oklahoma City when the future actor was a year old, and he attended school there until the seventh grade, when his parents separated. After the split, his mother moved to Long Beach, California, taking Heflin, his older brother, and his infant sister, Frances (who would later find fame as Mona Kane on the popular daytime soap opera *All My Children*). It was there that the youngster developed a lifelong fascination with the ocean, and decided to make seafaring his career. During vacations from Long Beach Polytechnic High School, Heflin spent his time sailing on schooners bound for Mexico, Hawaii, and South America, and after his graduation, he landed a job on a tramp steamer headed for England.

Heflin worked for several years as a seaman — during which his fellow sailors dubbed him "Van"— then yielded to the wishes of his parents (who had by now reunited) and enrolled at the University of Oklahoma. Following his sophomore year, however, the "call of the running tide" beckoned to Heflin again, and he signed on with a cargo boat headed for New York. At this point, numerous stories abound as to the course of Heflin's life, including two different versions told by the actor himself. In one scenario, Heflin claimed that, after serving as third mate on the cargo ship, he "got the idea I'd like a fling at acting," and decided to pay a visit to famed producer Channing Pollock. While waiting in the outer office of Pollock's agency, Heflin said, he offered his seat to an elderly man.

"We got to talking. I told him I was going to play a role in Pollock's new play," Heflin recalled. "The elderly man looked surprised. Then he said, 'Well, maybe you better come on into my office and talk to me about it!' And that was how Pollock gave me a letter of introduction to his director Richard Boleslawski."

Years later, however, Heflin stated that he was on an inter-coastal freighter bound for New York when he met and struck up a friendship with Boleslawski.

"[He] insisted that I had launched myself on the wrong career and cast me in a role in his play," Heflin said in a 1970 interview.

According to the most widespread version, Heflin decided to visit a distant relative during a stop in New York, and found himself in the midst of a "cocktail party of smart people going full blast." Several of the party-goers, noting Heflin's unique attire — which included a Stetson hat and cowboy boots— mentioned Channing Pollock's new play and suggested that Heflin try out for a role. Heflin reportedly visited the producer, armed with a list of phony plays in which he had appeared and Pollock, amused by the young man's mettle, decided to give him an audition.

Regardless of the questionable path that led Heflin to his first stage role, it is a fact that he first appeared on Broadway in the late 1920s in *Mr. Moneypenny*. The play, however, was a failure, and Heflin became quickly disillusioned.

"[The stage] is like Hawaii," he once said.

"You dream you can reach up and pick mangoes or beautiful babes out of the trees. You find it's just another place."

Turning his back on his brief acting career, Heflin sailed to the Orient, South America, and Alaska, even entertaining the notion of becoming a maritime lawyer. But after three years on the seas, a fateful brush with the law changed his course for good.

"I had enough service to get my third mate's license," Heflin told *TV Guide* in 1964. "Then one night in San Francisco I went to a speakeasy. The next thing I knew, I was being shoved into a paddy wagon. Somebody had given me knockout drops, taken my money, and thrown me in an alley. Afterwards I said to myself, 'You started out to be a lawyer, but you're ending up a bum!' I decided to go back to college."

After graduating from the University of Oklahoma in 1931, Heflin decided to give acting another try and joined the Hedgerow Theatre in Pennsylvania. He followed this stint with a year at the Baker Workshop of the drama school at Yale University, then honed his acting skills in a summer stock company in Denver and appearances throughout the East in "a series of bad plays, short runs, and failures." In one of these productions, the Broadway play, *The Bride of Totozko*, Heflin's performance was panned by *New York Herald Tribune* critic as "unreasonably bad." The actor reportedly carried the review with him for the rest of his career.

"Whenever I get a little cocky," the actor said years later, "I pull out that review and read it again."

During this period, Heflin's time wasn't completely devoted to acting; after a brief romance, he married actress Esther Shaw on July 20, 1934. But the union was a rocky one, and short-lived. The couple lived together less than six months and divorced in 1936, with Heflin charging that his wife "insisted on accompanying her friends to Greenwich Village parties and came home intoxicated at least four mornings a week between 2 and 5 A.M." Afterward, the actor spoke of his first marriage in only the briefest of terms.

Professionally, after several years of flops, Heflin got his big break when he was cast opposite Ina Claire in the Broadway production of *End of Summer*. He not only earned good reviews, but his performance caught the notice of screen actress Katharine Hepburn, who asked her home studio, RKO, to sign the actor for her new picture, *A Woman Rebels* (1936). Inking a seven-year contract with RKO, Heflin headed for Hollywood for his film debut, but the movie was a flop and lost an estimated quarter of a million dollars. The following year, Heflin was seen in four films for the studio, including a routine western, *The Outcasts of Poker Flat* (1937), starring Preston Foster, and *Annapolis Salute* (1937), a profitable but rather dull tale set at a naval academy. Although Heflin fared better with *Flight from Glory* (1937), in which he played a weak-willed pilot, he was disappointed by the studio's choice of film assignments and asked for a release from his contract.

"What I thought of them is exactly what they thought of me," Heflin said later. "I felt like a failure and, come to think of it, I was."

Heflin returned to New York, but his absence from the stage had resulted in a dearth of offers from Broadway. Instead, he landed a job on a radio soap opera, eventually logging nearly 2,000 performances. After two years on the radio, Broadway beckoned again when he was tapped to star with Katharine Hepburn in *The Philadelphia Story*, portraying a magazine reporter that playwright Philip Barry had reportedly written with Heflin in mind. He earned raves for his performance, with a typical review offered by *New York Times* critic Brooks Atkinson, who wrote: "It would be hard to improve upon Van Heflin's honest and solid description of a tough-minded writer." When MGM produced the film version of the play in 1940, James Stewart was cast in the role played by Heflin; throughout his two-year run with the stage production, Heflin refused to see the feature film, fearing that his portrayal would be unconsciously influenced.

"The night the play closed, I went to see the movie, and I was amazed," Heflin said later. "The picture was so very much better than the play that I decided Hollywood was for me. I headed west. [But] the movies weren't overwhelming me with offers. I was trying to overwhelm the movies. I was banging on their door."

Heflin first landed a small role as a villain in the Warner Bros. western *Santa Fe Trail* (1940), then contacted MGM casting director Billy Grady and requested a screen test. After the successful test (made with Donna Reed, who also signed with the studio), Heflin was cast in *The Feminine Touch* (1941), a witty comedy starring Rosalind Russell; *H.M. Pulham, Esq.* (1941), a well-done drama where he was featured as a cynical advertising man; *Tennessee Johnson* (1942), in which he earned raves for his "tremendous intensity" in the title role; *Seven Sweethearts* (1942), Heflin's first romantic lead, which was panned by one critic as "unconscionably quaint"; and *Johnny Eager* (1942), his first film noir.

This feature starred Robert Taylor as the title character, a mob leader and ex-convict who covers his illegal activities by posing as a cab driver. Along with his alcoholic sidekick, Jeff Hartnett (Heflin), Johnny plans to open a new dog-racing track, but finds his efforts stymied by district attorney John Benson Farrell (Edward Arnold). Meanwhile, Johnny encounters Farrell's attractive young stepdaughter, Lisbeth Bard (Lana Turner), and implicates her in a staged murder, planning to use the scheme to blackmail Farrell into lifting the injunction he has imposed on the dog track. With Hartnett serving as the voice of his conscience, Johnny later tells Lisbeth the truth, even risking his life to prove it to her, and after nobly turning her over to her former fiancé, the gangster is gunned down in the street by rival mobsters and police. In the final reel, Harnett cradles his friend as he dies, tearfully telling a police officer, "This guy could've climbed the highest mountain in the world, if he'd just started up the right one."

Heflin earned universal raves for his picture-stealing performance as the moraliz-

ing lush; *Variety*'s reviewer proclaimed that he "is an actor certain to be much in demand," and the critic for *The Hollywood Reporter* wrote: "Van Heflin can date his rise to screen prominence with his performance of Jeff.... Admittedly, Jeff is a grand role, but Heflin does it proud." For his standout performances, Heflin won an Academy Award for Best Supporting Actor, beating out such formidable competition as William Bendix, Walter Huston, Frank Morgan, and Henry Travers.

Shortly after his triumph at the Academy Awards, Heflin gave marriage a second try, marrying actress Frances Neal, whom he had met at the home of MGM producer Joseph Pasternak six months earlier. The couple went on to have two daughters, Vana, born on June 20, 1943, and Cathleen, on July 13, 1946; and a son, Tracy, on July 8, 1954. Several months after his May 1942 wedding, Heflin enlisted as a second lieutenant in the U.S. Army Air Corps, spending the next three years as a combat photographer. Heflin's first picture upon his release was a return to film noir in one of the best features of his career, Paramount's *The Strange Love of Martha Ivers* (1946).

"I chose the script and the role of Sam Masterson, the hero, because both help me escape specialization," Heflin said. "Sam is a typical guy. He's been around and knows the score. You meet somebody like Sam every day. The character of Sam spells variety for an actor. That's for me."

A riveting example of film noir, this feature centers on a quartet of distinctive characters, Heflin's Masterson, a professional gambler who finds more than he bargains for when he returns to his boyhood town; the wealthy and powerful Martha Ivers (Barbara Stanwyck); Martha's weak-willed husband, Walter O'Neill (Kirk Douglas); and Toni Marachek (Lizabeth Scott), a down-on-her-luck drifter whom Sam befriends. As the story unfolds, the lives of the four principal players intertwine in a dramatic and deadly fashion, with the core of the conflict focusing on Martha's childhood murder of her hated aunt, Walter's complicity in denying her role

Van Heflin with Barbara Stanwyck looking down the staircase at the figure of Kirk Douglas in *The Strange Love of Martha Ivers* (1946).

in the crime, and the mistaken belief held by both Martha and Walter that Sam witnessed the incident. By the film's end, Sam has been beaten by thugs hired by Walter and tempted — however briefly — to succumb to Martha's scheme to murder her husband, but the final reel shows him heading out of town with Toni at his side, cautioning her not to look back.

Described by one reviewer as "a forthright, uncompromising presentation of evil, greedy people, and human weaknesses,"

Martha Ivers was a hit with both audiences and critics, and Heflin's performance earned universal raves. In *The Hollywood Reporter*, Jack D. Grant praised the actor's "smashing piece of work"; the critic for *Time* applauded his "excellent" portrayal of the no-nonsense gambler; and the *New York Times* reviewer wrote: "It is Van Heflin who has the meatiest role, and he makes the most of it.... He brings to it that quality of rugged integrity and certainty of action that is characteristic of Spencer Tracy's acting."

After roles in *Till the Clouds Roll By* (1947), which dramatized the life of songwriter Jerome Kern, and *Green Dolphin Street* (1947), an overblown but popular drama starring Lana Turner and Donna Reed, Heflin was loaned to Warner Bros. for his third film noir, *Possessed* (1947). Here, Heflin portrayed David Sutton, an engineer who ends his affair with local nurse Louise Howell (Joan Crawford) when her love for him begins to border on obsession. ("Everyone wants to be loved," David says, "but no one wants to be smothered.") After the death of the invalid in her charge, Louise marries the woman's widower, Dean Graham (Raymond Massey), but she begins to hallucinate that she caused the woman's death. Her psychosis deepens when David becomes involved with Dean's daughter (Geraldine Brooks), and she becomes increasingly unable to distinguish reality from fantasy. Finally, after learning that David plans to marry, Louise pulls a gun on him, but David views her threat with sarcastic amusement: "Go ahead and shoot," he tells her. "Mathematically, the chances of you hitting me are slight. And as far as killing me, well — I don't think you're that good a shot." Unfortunately for David, his assessment was inaccurate — Louise shoots him dead and is later found wandering the streets of the city in a state of near-catatonia, repeatedly calling David's name.

Despite the showier role portrayed by Crawford (which earned her an Academy Award nomination), Heflin was singled out by numerous reporters for his performance in *Possessed*; Virginia Wright, of the *Los An-*

geles Daily News, hailed his "fine, straightforward account"; *The Hollywood Reporter*'s Jack D. Grant stated that Heflin "capitalizes upon a devil-may-care attitude that is just what his role demanded"; and the reviewer for *Variety* wrote: "By sheer power of personal wit ... Heflin infuses his role with charm and degree of credibility." Following this triumph, Heflin was seen in a mixed bag of features, including *B.F.'s Daughter* (1947), a box-office disappointment despite a cast that included Barbara Stanwyck, Keenan Wynn, and Charles Coburn; *Tap Roots* (1948), a sprawling, tiresome Civil War epic that Heflin filmed on loan to Universal; *The Three Musketeers* (1948), a smash hit starring Lana Turner, Gene Kelly, and June Allyson; and *Madame Bovary* (1949), a lavishly mounted period piece featuring Heflin as a small-town doctor. Also during this period, Heflin returned to his roots in radio, originating the title role in *The Adventures of Philip Marlowe*, and as the decade came to an end, he starred with Robert Ryan and Janet Leigh in his fourth film noir, *Act of Violence* (1949).

In this tautly directed feature, Heflin starred as Frank Enley, a successful businessman with a wife and a baby, whose seemingly ideal existence is shattered when he finds that he is being stalked by a vengeful ex-war buddy, Joe Parkson (Robert Ryan). Although Frank earns the viewer's initial sympathy, it is revealed that Parkson is intent on killing Frank as retribution for being a "stool pigeon for the Nazis" during their term in a wartime prison camp. Seeking solace in the bottle, Frank shares his dilemma with a local barfly, Pat (Mary Astor), who introduces him to "a private policeman ... someone who can handle himself." The man, known only as Johnny (Berry Kroeger), shrewdly convinces Frank to hire him to kill Parkson; it isn't until he sobers up that Frank realizes what he has done and goes after Johnny in an effort to thwart the crime. Encountering Johnny and Parkson at the local train station, Frank steps in front of the bullet intended for Parkson, then causes Johnny's car to crash as he tries to flee. Frank's wounds are fatal, however, and he dies in the final reel as his former comrade looks on. After its release, *Act of Violence* earned mostly good reviews, with one critic terming it a "killer-diller in the documentary style," and another praising its "tightly woven, splendidly directed bit of suspense-building." The *New York Times'* Bosley Crowther disagreed, however, writing that the film "touches all the bases in its circuit chase. But it is as though it were doing it on the strength of a long, foul ball." Following this feature, Heflin ended his contract with MGM and turned instead to freelancing.

"This way I can play the roles I like and also, if I make a mistake, I want it to be my own," Heflin said. "Studios must use contract players and I feel that if, over that necessary expense, they still engage me and pay my high salary, then the part is really for me. Probably some of my movies were so bad that only my mother would look at them but still, I like it this way."

Off-screen the following year, Heflin made his television debut in 1950 on *Robert Montgomery Presents*, in an episode entitled "Arrowsmith." This appearance notwithstanding, Heflin for many years was seldom seen on the small screen and publicly eschewed its impact on the careers of feature film performers.

"Actors should stick to selling their own commodity, not someone else's, especially movie actors," he said. "I've said it before, and I'll say it again; a film star who deposits himself weekly in the living rooms of the nation is just destroying his power to draw at the box office. Free and casual entertainment is fine, but how many video fans will stir from their easy chairs, load up the family vehicle, trek to a theater, and part with three, four, or five dollars to see a guy — or a gal — they've been looking at 39 weeks for free?"

Meanwhile, Heflin's first outings as a freelancer were two features for Universal, *Weekend with Father* (1951), a charming romantic comedy co-starring Patricia Neal, and *Tomahawk* (1951), a mediocre, cliché-ridden western. These were followed by Heflin's final foray into film noir, United Artists' *The Prowler* (1951). In this well-done feature, Heflin portrayed Webb Garwood, a cop who becomes involved in a torrid affair with housewife Susan Gilvray (Evelyn Keyes), after investigating a complaint of a prowler at her home. Later, while responding to another call at Susan's home, Webb mortally wounds her husband, but the shooting is ruled justifiable homicide and the two marry. When Webb discovers that Susan is four months pregnant, he insists that they relocate to a remote cabin in the desert, fearing that this evidence of their prior involvement will serve as an indication of his guilt. Webb's murderous bent comes to light after the baby is delivered, however, when Susan learns that he not only murdered her husband, but also plans to kill the doctor who delivered their child. Susan tips off the doctor, who escapes with the baby, but when Webb tries to follow him, he is killed by police. For his performance, Heflin earned mixed reviews — *Variety*'s critic found him "a little out-of-place in portraying an unsavory character," while the reviewer for the *New York Times* wrote that "credit must be given to Van Heflin in essaying an unsympathetic assignment" — but *The Prowler* stands up today as one of film noir's frequently overlooked gems.

Between films, Heflin enrolled in the Theater Arts school at the University of California at Los Angeles, because, he said, "if a cutter leaves me on the cutting room floor now, I can tell him where he is wrong." But his studies were interrupted when the actor accepted producer Kermit Bloomgarden's offer to star in the road version of his successful stage play, *The Shrike*, which starred Jose Ferrer on Broadway.

"I felt that months, if not years might pass before I could get a part and a play as good," Heflin said in 1952. "Fine roles, as many Hollywood actors will attest, are few and far between. I needed a career change of pace, and I was anxious to go back on the stage. Scores of film people have that yen to return; it's knowing *when* that can spell the difference between success and disaster."

But although Heflin earned favorable notices for his portrayal of a mild-mannered man driven to madness by his manipulative wife, the play closed after seven months when Heflin abruptly left the show, reportedly in order to accept a role in Universal's *Wings of the Hawk* (1953). After this fairly interesting western, filmed in 3D, Heflin landed a role in one of his best-remembered films, *Shane* (1953), co-starring Alan Ladd and Jean Arthur. For Heflin, however, the film was memorable for more than its rave reviews and overflowing box office receipts; during a day off from the on-location shooting in Jackson, Wyoming, the actor was involved in a boating accident on the Snake River in the Teton mountains. Along with four other men, including Paramount publicity director Jerry Smith, Heflin departed Moose, Wyoming, for an all-day fishing excursion, only to find a short time later that the motor on the rubber boat had stopped working. The men had been drifting on the river for three hours when the craft struck a submerged tree and capsized, forcing them to swim through the turbulent rapids to safety. All five men suffered from cold and exposure, and Heflin also sustained numerous bruises and facial cuts. Still, the actor later seemed more concerned with the aborted fishing expedition than his own safety.

"We had our limit of fish," he wryly told reporters, "and lost them when the boat went over."

Of Heflin's five films in 1954, the best was *Woman's World*, an insightful glimpse into the world of big business, the men who run it, and the influence held by the women in their lives. In a stellar cast that included Lauren Bacall, Cornel Wilde, and Clifton Webb, Heflin portrayed a district manager who possessed the ability, but not the drive, to get ahead. In concert with his appearance in the film, Heflin placed his hand and footprints in the forecourt at Grauman's (now Mann's) Chinese Theater in Hollywood.

The following year, Heflin returned to Broadway after a 15-year absence, starring in Arthur Miller's *A View From the Bridge*,

spending $125,000 of his own money as a co-investor in the production. After the play's eight-month run, Heflin was seen during the remainder of the decade in several box-office hits, including *Battle Cry* (1955), an $8 million winner for Warner Bros.; *Patterns* (1956), a first-rate drama about the conflicts among corporation executives; and *3:10 to Yuma* (1957), an engrossing western in which he starred as a peace-loving rancher who is forced to stand up to a ruthless lawbreaker. Between screen performances, Heflin reversed his previous opinion about the small screen, appearing on *Playhouse 90* in "The Dark Side of the Earth" in 1957 and "The Rank and File" in 1959. The actor told the press that he revised his stance when movie studios began selling feature films to television studios.

"You can't be loyal to an industry which isn't loyal to you in return," Heflin said in 1957. "To me, the most convincing thing happened when the studios dumped their old product on the TV market, a move I thought was foolish of the industry. It was almost like liquidating the industry, or the first move toward that. From now on I will give TV offers a more receptive reaction. An actor's no good unless he's acting. The quality of film scripts submitted me has been awful. I rejected 100 in the last two years. I'd rather do a good TV show than a bad picture."

With the onset of the 1960s, however, the quality of Heflin's screen offers continued to deteriorate. Like many performers, he briefly sampled the foreign market, appearing in two Italian-made features, *Under Ten Flags* (1960), a box-office disappointment co-starring Charles Laughton, and *The Wastrel* (1961), a humdrum melodrama with a mostly Italian cast. Heflin returned to the small screen in 1963, signing on as narrator of *The Great Adventure*, an anthology series produced by John Houseman. He left the series after a year, however, to star in the Broadway production of *A Case of Libel*, earning acclaim for his "ingratiating, wily, affable, humorous, and keen-witted" portrayal of a crusading attorney.

"It's a good way to chip off the rust that

you get working in films, whether for the big screen or the small TV screen," Heflin said of his return to Broadway. "You develop bad habits, you know that if you make a mistake, you can do it again. If you make a mistake on stage, that's it."

After a cameo in the sweeping 1963 biblical epic *The Greatest Story Ever Told* ("If you sneeze or yawn during the picture, you'll miss me," Heflin quipped), the actor was seen in his first MGM production in nearly 20 years, *Once a Thief* (1965), a fairly interesting crime drama co-starring Alain Delon and Ann-Margret. He followed this feature with *Stagecoach* (1966), an inferior remake of the 1939 John Ford classic; *The Ruthless Four* (1966), another Italian production; and *The Man Outside* (1968), in which he played a former CIA agent framed for murder. Despite the decline in the number and quantity of offers he was receiving, Heflin showed no signs of calling an end to his career.

"I've seriously thought of retiring," he said, "but I've also thought, what would I do with myself? When I'm not on a film or planning a trip for fishing or Europe or whatnot, I get up in the morning and it settles down into the most maddening routine. What would I do with myself? My supreme interest has always been acting."

But around this time, Heflin's career faded in significance and his personal life took center stage when, in a move that stunned the Hollywood community, the actor's 25-year marriage came to an end. In filing for divorce, Frances Heflin charged that her husband was subject to "outbursts of uncontrollable temper"—on one occasion, she stated, the actor struck her and knocked her down, and on another, he "physically assaulted her and forced her to flee in front of her daughter, Cathleen." Frances, who was represented by famed attorney Marvin Mitchelson, was awarded custody of the couple's 13-year-old son, Tracy, along with 15 percent of Heflin's gross earnings as alimony, $400 a month in child support, and half of their $1 million community property, including the family home in Brentwood, California.

Later, Heflin candidly discussed the impact of the divorce on his life.

"Frances and I and the three children had many years of happiness, a very few years of unhappiness. That's the way I remember our marriage — as a happy one," he told *Los Angeles Herald-Examiner* columnist Dorothy Manners in 1968. "I'm really not yet adjusted to being unmarried. Every working day around six P.M., I get that old tug of realizing with surprise that no one is waiting for me at home.... Since our divorce, I've thought, 'My God, I don't know what to do with myself.' Divorce isn't all the carefree bachelorhood most people suspect. But then the phone rings and it's your agent with another interesting job — and you're busy again. Which helps a lot. So, you think another little prayer, 'Thank God for work.'"

Heflin's vehicles for keeping his thoughts away from his home life included two made-for-television movies, *Certain Honorable Men* (1968), and *A Case of Libel* (1968), for which he reprised his acclaimed stage role. He was also seen on the big screen in *The Big Bounce* (1969), a trashy soaper notable only as the film debut of Ryan O'Neal, and *Airport* (1970), a box-office smash with a star-studded cast that included Helen Hayes, Burt Lancaster, Maureen Stapleton, Lloyd Nolan, Dean Martin, and Jean Seberg. The latter would be his last feature film.

On June 6, 1971, Heflin suffered a massive heart attack while swimming in the pool of his Hollywood apartment, and was found by the building handyman, clinging to a rung of the pool ladder with his head barely above water. Placed in intensive care at Cedars of Lebanon Hospital, Heflin never regained consciousness and, after nearly seven weeks in a coma, the actor died on July 23, 1971. In accordance with Heflin's wishes, his body was cremated and the ashes were scattered over the Pacific Ocean. (Four months after his death, Heflin was seen on television in his final performance in the well-done futuristic drama, *The Last Child* [1971], in which he played a United States senator.)

Once aptly described as possessing the

ability to dissect a character the way a surgeon works with a scalpel, Van Heflin was one of the greatest character actors in the annals of film. In addition to his appearances in numerous box-office hits, he was also able to transcend his material, when necessary, nearly always turning in first-rate performances. In an interview several years before Heflin's death, actor Robert Stack succinctly and appropriately described the actor's great talent.

"Van is pliable, imaginative, and goes to work on his own initiative, blocking in a characterization until it is created into a real-life personality," Stack said. "He stayed in your mind long after you'd left the theater...."

Film Noir Filmography

Johnny Eager. Director: Mervyn LeRoy. Producer: John W. Considine, Jr. Running time: 102 minutes. Released by MGM, February 19, 1942. Cast: Robert Taylor, Lana Turner, Edward Arnold, Van Heflin, Robert Sterling, Patricia Dane, Glenda Farrell, Barry Nelson, Henry O'Neil, Charles Dingle, Cy Kendall, Don Costello, Paul Stewart. Awards: Academy Award for Best Supporting Actor (Van Heflin).

The Strange Love of Martha Ivers. Director: Lewis Milestone. Producer: Hal B. Wallis. Running time: 115 minutes. Released by Paramount, July 24, 1946. Cast: Barbara Stanwyck, Van Heflin, Lizabeth Scott, Kirk Douglas, Judith Anderson, Roman Bohnen, Darryl Hickman, Janis Wilson, Ann Doran, Frank Orth, James Flavin, Mickey Kuhn, Charles D. Brown. Awards: Academy Award nomination for Best Original Story (Jack Patrick).

Possessed. Director: Curtis Bernhardt. Producer: Jerry Wald. Running time: 108 minutes. Released by Warner Brothers, May 29, 1947. Cast: Joan Crawford, Van Heflin, Raymond Massey, Geraldine Brooks, Stanley Ridges, John Ridgely, Moroni Olsen, Erskine Sanford, Gerald Perreau, Isabel Withers, Lisa Golsm, Douglas Kennedy, Monte Blue, Don McGuire, Rory Mallinson, Clifton Young, Griff Barnett. Awards: Academy Award nomination for Best Actress (Joan Crawford).

Act of Violence. Director: Fred Zinnemann. Producer: William H. Wright. Running time: 81 minutes. Released by MGM, January 23, 1949. Cast: Van Heflin, Robert Ryan, Janet Leigh, Mary Astor, Phyllis Thaxter, Berry Kroeger, Nicholas Joy, Harry Antrim, Connie Gilchrist, Will Wright.

The Prowler. Director: Joseph Losey. Producer: Sam Spiegel. Running time: 92 minutes. Released by United Artists, July 2, 1951. Cast: Van Heflin, Evelyn Keyes, John Maxwell, Katharine Warren, Emerson Tracy, Madge Blake, Wheaton Chambers, Louise Lorimer, Robert Osterloh, Sherry Hall.

References

"Alimony 'Terrified' Actor — He Must Pay." *New York Daily News*, May 5, 1936.

Alpert, Don. "Van Heflin Plays It for Keeps." *Los Angeles Times*, October 10, 1965.

Bacon, James. "Van Heflin: Returned to the Ocean He Roamed in His Boyhood Days." *Los Angeles Herald-Examiner*, July 25, 1971.

Biography of Van Heflin. 20th Century-Fox Studios, circa 1964.

Carroll, Harrison. "Actor Van Heflin Sued for Divorce." *Los Angeles Herald-Examiner*, February 20, 1967.

Chapman, John. "Van Heflin Wins Praise in 'Case of Libel' Drama." *Los Angeles Times*, October 18, 1963.

"Film World Mourns Van Heflin Death." *Los Angeles Herald-Examiner*, July 24, 1971.

Graham, Sheilah. "Heflin Speaks Up." *New York Journal-American*, January 5, 1964.

Greenberg, Abe. "Van Heflin Scoffs at Outlandish Star Salaries." *Hollywood Citizen-News*, October 31, 1969.

"Heflin Pic Deal Forcing Fold of 'Shrike' March 21." *Variety*, March 4, 1953.

"Heflin Pulled from Pool." *Variety*, June 6, 1971.

"Heflin Risking 'All,' Invests in New Play." *Los Angeles Times*, May 22, 1955.

"Heflin's Acting Gets in Way of His Studies." *Variety*, February 4, 1953.

Hopper, Hedda. "Frustrated Sailor." *Rocky Mountain Empire Magazine*, January 23, 1949.

_____. "Quite a Man — This Van!" *Chicago Tribune Magazine*, August 15, 1954.

Humphrey, Hal. "Van and Video? It's No Sale." *Los Angeles Times*, July 12, 1963.

Jennings, Betty. "Van Heflin: Still Misty-Eyed About the Sea." *Picture Show*, January 9, 1960.

Keating, John. "Heflin at the Bar." *New York Times*, January 19, 1964.

"Long Fight Lost: Van Heflin Is Dead." *Los Herald-Examiner*, July 23, 1971.

Manners, Dorothy. "Reminiscing with Van Heflin." *Los Angeles Herald-Examiner*, October 20, 1968.

_____. "Van Finds Self Target in Revolt." *Los Angeles Examiner*, June 29, 1952.

_____. "Van Heflin Wears Father's Day Ties — and Likes 'Em." *Los Angeles Examiner*, June 20, 1954.

_____. "Van Heflin: Trouble Trouble Everywhere." *Los Angeles Herald-Examiner*, May 17, 1970.

McClay, Howard. "Heflin Against Too Much TV." *Los Angeles Daily News*, October 5, 1953.

Mosby, Aline. "Van Heflin Buys Part of Broadway Play; Going East." *Hollywood Citizen-News*, May 14, 1955.

Othman, Frederick C. "Stage Actor Finds Films Preferable." *Hollywood Citizen-News*, February 28, 1942.

Raddatz, Leslie. "'…And Then His Symmetricals Began to Slip.'" *TV Guide*, December 28, 1963.

Scott, John L. "Heflin Can Pick His Roles." *Los Angeles Times*, March 20, 1960.

_____. "Van Heflin, Back for 3D, to Limit Stage Appearances." *Los Angeles Times*, April 19, 1953.

"Screen Starlet Becomes Bride of Rising Young Film Actor." *Los Angeles Times*, May 17, 1942.

Shaw, David "Van Heflin, Oscar Winner, Dies at 60." *Los Angeles Times*, July 24, 1971.

_____. "Van Heflin Stricken in Pool; Condition 'Extremely Critical.'" *Los Angeles Times*, June 7, 1971.

Smith, Cecil. "Van Heflin to Star in Playhouse 90." *Los Angeles Times*, May 24, 1959.

Taylor, Tim. "A View of Van Heflin." *Cue*, September 24, 1955.

"Telecast of His Old Pix Puts New Life Into Career, Feels Van Heflin." *Variety*, January 15, 1968.

"Van Heflin, Actor, Dead at 60; Won Fame in Film and on Stage." *New York Times*, July 24, 1971.

"Van Heflin Braves Death in Boat Upset." *Los Angeles Times*, August 28, 1951.

"Van Heflin Dies After 6 Weeks in Coma." *Variety*, July 26, 1971.

"Van Heflin Dies Here at 60." *The Hollywood Reporter*, July 26, 1971.

"Van Heflin Divorced." *Los Angeles Herald-Examiner*, August 4, 1967.

"Van Heflin Faces Court Fees Suit." *Los Angeles Herald-Examiner*, March 9, 1967.

"Van Heflin Gets Split Lip as Boat Hits Tree, Turns Over." *Los Angeles Evening Herald and Express*, August 28, 1951.

"Van Heflin Footprinting Set for 2:30 P.M. Today." *The Hollywood Reporter*, October 8, 1954.

"Van Heflin Plays the Field." *New York Times*, January 8, 1950.

"Van Heflin Makes Second Film Debut." *Paramount News of Hollywood*, December 3, 1945.

"Van Heflin's Condition Unchanged." *Los Angeles Times*, June 23, 1971.

"Van Heflin's Latest Movie to Be on ABC-TV October 5." *Box Office*, September 27, 1971.

"Van Heflin Starts Army Duty Today." *Los Angeles Times*, November 19, 1942.

Wallace, Inez. "Van Heflin Strives to Hold Public, Win Young Friends." *Cleveland Plain Dealer*, October 28, 1951.

JOHN HODIAK

"Do you know what it's like to be alone in the world? Really alone in the whole world? A billion people — every one of them a stranger. Or what's worse, not a stranger. Somebody, maybe, who knows you. Hates you. Wants you to die." — John Hodiak in *Somewhere in the Night* (1946)

According to John Hodiak, his film career was sheer luck.

"I've always been a firm believer in the Fates," he once said.

But luck was not on his side when Hodiak, hailed near the start of his career as "another Gable," went from leading man to supporting player in a matter of years and, later, was felled by a fatal heart attack at the age of 41. Despite his unfulfilled potential as an actor, Hodiak did appear in a number of well-received films, including *Lifeboat* (1944), *A Bell for Adano* (1945), and *The Harvey Girls* (1946). He was also featured in four films from the era of noir: *Somewhere in the Night* (1946), *The Bribe* (1949), *A Lady Without Passport* (1950), and *The People Against O'Hara* (1951).

The man who was frequently described as quiet-spoken and likeable was born in Pittsburgh, Pennsylvania, on April 16, 1914, the oldest son of Ukranian immigrants Walter and Anna Pogorzeliec Hodiak. When young Hodiak was eight years old, his family moved to Hamtramck, Michigan, a suburb of Detroit with a large immigrant population. There, his father took a job at an automobile factory, and Hodiak began performing in Ukranian and Russian plays presented twice monthly by members of the local parish. His father, himself an amateur actor, sometimes appeared in these productions as well.

Hodiak attended Holbrook Elementary School and Hamtramck High School, where he appeared in most of the school productions. After high school, the young man reportedly won a scholarship to Northwestern University in Evanston, Illinois, but turned it down in favor of pursuing an appointment at the prestigious military institution, West Point. He was not successful.

"It was a shattering disappointment," Hodiak said years later. "It shaped my whole philosophy. I was never going to break my heart again, trying for something I wasn't intended to have."

Throughout Hodiak's career, it was also widely reported that he turned down a major baseball contract from the St. Louis Cardinals that was offered while he was still in high school. But in a 1954 interview with then-newspaper columnist Ed Sullivan, Hodiak dismissed this claim.

"That's for the birds," he said. "I was one of some 200 Hamtramck school baseball players surveyed by scouts. Steve Gromek [pitcher for the Cleveland Indians and the Detroit Tigers] was the one who made the big league grade from our area."

After high school, Hodiak tried for a job at a local Detroit radio station, but was shot down by the station's program manager who "told me to forget the whole thing — my diction was lousy," Hodiak recalled.

Instead of the desired radio gig, Hodiak found employment as a caddy at a nearby country club, but the job would be a fortuitous one. Among the golfers was a Chevrolet Motor Company executive, who offered Hodiak an office job there.

"A large part of the job consisted of reading figures aloud and, automatically, the necessity of reading those figures clearly improved my diction," Hodiak said. "After about three years, I went back to the radio station, a humble and chastened young man, and asked if they might be able to use me. They took me on as a bit player, at no salary. But

that was all right. I had a daytime job that paid off. I wasn't in any danger of starving."

Over time, Hodiak began getting larger parts at the radio station and in 1935, moved to Chicago, where he found work playing a variety of roles, including the original Lil' Abner. Hodiak's years on the radio finally paid off in 1942, when MGM talent scout Marvin Schenck heard the actor on a broadcast and arranged for Hodiak to make a screen test, along with another performer under consideration, Canada Lee.

Years later, Hodiak admitted to Ed Sullivan that he wasn't at all daunted by the possible career-altering test.

"For the sake of the story, I'd like to tell you I was nervous," Hodiak said, "but I wasn't. I've never been nervous about anything. I've always sat back and waited for things to happen. I've always felt that if I were the guy to do something, I'd be sought out to do it. Otherwise, I'd be far happier right where I was."

Hodiak's performance in the test earned him a seven-year contract with MGM, but he promptly shot down the studio's intentions to change his name, insisting that it "sounds like I look." The actor also cited the sense of obligation he felt toward his fellow Ukranians.

"There are many reasons why I want to arrive," he said in a 1944 interview. "I want other Ukranians to feel that they have a chance. Maybe not in this field, but in any other. I receive a lot of mail ... from Ukranians who thank me because I haven't changed my own name and because I don't pretend to be either Polish or Russian."

For the next year, the actor languished in a series of minor roles in such films as *Swing Shift Maisie* (1943), in which he was unbilled; *Song of Russia* (1943), where he portrayed a Russian peasant farmer; and *I Dood It* (1943), a popular Red Skelton vehicle. He fared better in 1944, however, playing a soldier opposite Lana Turner in *Marriage Is a Private Affair*, followed by his breakout role as a Nazi-hating seaman in Alfred Hitchcock's *Lifeboat*. True to his

ter was a former socialite and the granddaughter of famed architect Frank Lloyd Wright), the two married on July 7, 1946. Nearly five years later to the day, on July 9, 1951, their only child, Katrina, was born and, for a while at least, they appeared to be one of Hollywood's happiest and most successful couples.

Meanwhile, in Hodiak's sole film of 1945, the actor portrayed his favorite role, Major Joppolo in *A Bell for Adano* (1945), a touching World War II story about an American soldier determined to restore a church bell in a small Italian town. (In real life, incidentally, the actor was unable to serve in the war due to hypertension.) Hodiak's performance earned nearly universal accolades, including praise from *New York Times* critic Bosley Crowther, who wrote that the actor was "excellent as Joppolo, firm and unquestionably sincere with just the right shades of emotion in his response to human problems."

Off screen, the family-minded Hodiak purchased a six-room house in late 1945 and moved his entire clan there—including his parents, three siblings, and their families.

"I've been so absorbed … now it's time to think of my family," the actor said. "Happiness starts in the family and sort of ripples out of the community to the world at large. I shall never have money. There are too many things that need to be done with it." In addition to spending his salary on his loved ones, Hodiak quietly contributed to a number of causes, including the creation of "kid's club centers" in his hometown of Hamtramck.

"A lot of people claim to have discovered me, and a lot of people have helped me," he said. "Frankly every one of them is right, and I'm one actor who is plenty grateful."

Hodiak followed his triumphant appearance in *Adano* with a starring role opposite Lucille Ball in the forgettable feature, *Two Smart People* (1946), but he rebounded with his next two films—*The Harvey Girls* (1946), a lightweight musical co-starring Judy Garland, and *Somewhere in the Night* (1946), his initial foray into the realm of film noir. As this feature opens, Hodiak's character awakens in

insistence that his career success was based on luck, Hodiak was reportedly chosen for *Lifeboat* after Hitchcock, looking for a black actor to play the steward in the film, viewed the screen test that featured Hodiak with Canada Lee. After tapping Lee for the role, Hitchcock gave Hodiak a second look and, ultimately, hired him as well. Although the part was Hodiak's first starring turn, he relied on his instincts to bring the hot-tempered character to life.

"I never had a dramatic lesson," he would tell columnist Hedda Hopper in 1947, "never formally studied diction, never had anybody to teach me timing. I just picked it all up as I went along. It's my belief that acting's essentially a quality within a person and not a mere bag of tricks and mannerisms to be exhibited externally."

Also that year, Hodiak starred with 21-year-old Anne Baxter in *Sunday Night for a Soldier* (1944), a sweet film about a family scrimping their meager resources to invite a soldier for a chicken dinner. Hodiak and his leading lady began dating and, despite reported opposition from Baxter's mother and the vast differences in their backgrounds (Baxa military hospital to discover that he does not know who he is. He is called "George Taylor" by hospital personnel, however, and finds a disturbing note in his wallet: "These are my last words to you ... I despise you now, and the memory of you. I'm ashamed for having loved you. And I shall pray as long as I live for someone or something to hurt and destroy you. Make you want to die, as you have me." Traveling to Los Angeles, Taylor learns that he has been left $5,000 — and a gun — by a man named Larry Cravat, and he determines to find him, certain that he holds the key to Taylor's past. Instead, Taylor meets a series of individuals, each of whom have some connection to Cravat, including Christy Smith (Nancy Guild), a nightclub singer whose best friend was jilted by Cravat; Christy's boss, Mel Phillips (Richard Conte), who offers to help Taylor find the missing man; and Lt. Donald Kendall (Lloyd Nolan), a crafty detective who reveals that Cravat disappeared with $2 million several years before. Ultimately, Taylor realizes that *he* is actually Larry Cravat — and that Mel Phillips is his former partner, from whom he took the $2 million. When Phillips demands the return of the cash, Taylor/Cravat leads him to a deserted dock area, but before Phillips can locate the money and finish off his old buddy, Lt. Kendall shows up and guns Phillips down.

Despite a complicated and often confusing plot, *Somewhere in the Night* earned good reviews upon its release, with one critic lauding it as "a well-written, gripping mystery, a little on the tough side, as is the current trend, that skips most of the standard gimmicks (such as bodies falling out of closets) and will hold your undivided attention from the opening frame." Hodiak was praised for his performance as well; the *New York Times'* Bosley Crowther said that he "plays the blanked-out veteran darkly and desperately," and in the *Los Angeles Examiner*, James O'Farrell wrote: "Hodiak probably has here his best opportunity to date to act. His role is difficult, because it calls for the interpretation of a dogged personality who wants to find where he came from and who he was — with few clues

and little promise of his ability to cope with the destructive forces quite evidently lined up against him."

Unfortunately, with the return from World War II of such matinee stars as Clark Gable and Robert Taylor, Hodiak's promising career began a gradual downward spiral around this time, in terms of both the quality of his films and the size of his roles. During the next two years, he was seen in such vehicles as *Desert Fury* (1947), which was panned in the *New York Times* as a "beaut of a Technicolor mistake from beginning to end"; *Love from a Stranger* (1947), a tiresome drama with Sylvia Sidney; and *Homecoming* (1948), notable primarily for its teaming of Clark Gable and Lana Turner, and Hodiak's supporting role opposite his real-life wife, Anne Baxter. His best films during this period were *Ambush* (1949), a fast-moving western starring Robert Taylor, and *Command Decision* (1948), a wartime feature with Clark Gable, Walter Pidgeon, and Van Johnson. But Hodiak was becoming increasingly frustrated with the direction in which his career was headed, and openly discussed his concerns in the press.

"So far as the actor is concerned, the attitude of producers seems to be this: 'You're getting parts and you're getting paid, so what are you beefing about?'" Hodiak said. "But there are such things as honesty and integrity to be preserved. If you keep betraying these qualities, you'll eventually lose them. This I do not want."

Shortly after this interview, Hodiak returned to the dark world of film noir, appearing in three features in as many years: *The Bribe* (1949), *A Lady Without Passport* (1950), and *The People Against O'Hara* (1951). In the first, set in an island off the coast of Central America, Hodiak played the supporting role of Tugwell Hintten, a former U.S. Air Force pilot who is part of an illegal war surplus racket run by a man named Carwood (Vincent Price). The action heats up with the arrival of a federal agent, Rigby (Robert Taylor), who falls for Hintten's wife, Elizabeth (Ava Gardner), but their romantic plans are put on hold when Hintten is bedridden by a heart condition. Confronted by Carwood, Hintten threatens to contact the authorities when the racketeer reveals that he has involved Elizabeth in the scheme: "I sold her down the river, but only part way," Hintten says. "I let her be used to keep Rigby where we could watch him. But that was all. She wasn't to know about the deal. She wasn't to know about me." But Hintten's threat turns out to be his undoing — moments later, Carwood smothers him to death with a pillow. Tracked down by Rigby, Carwood and the federal agent engage in a chase during a crowded carnival celebration, and after they exchange gunfire during a sensational fireworks display, Rigby ultimately emerges the victor.

Next, in *A Lady Without Passport*, Hodiak returned to leading man status, starring as special agent Pete Karczag, who poses as a Hungarian immigrant in an effort to break up an illegal alien smuggling ring in Cuba. During his assignment, Karczag becomes romantically involved with a refugee, Marianne Lorress (Hedy Lamarr), who is trying to gain entry into the United States. Karczag also locates the brains behind the operation, Palinov (George Macready), but his cover is later blown and Palinov flees the country with Marianne and a group of immigrants. With Karczag hot on his trail, Palinov's plane crashlands in the Florida everglades, where he plans to escape in a waiting boat. But Karczag manages to empty most of the fuel in the craft, then allows Palinov to escape, assuring Marianne, "He isn't going as far as he thinks he is."

Hodiak's fourth and final noir, *The People Against O'Hara*, starred Spencer Tracy as a former criminal attorney, James Curtayne, whose battle with alcoholism forced him to abandon his career. When Johnny O'Hara (James Arness), the son of a family friend, is accused of murder, Curtayne reluctantly takes the case, going up against the politically ambitious, cold-as-ice assistant district attorney, Louis Barra (Hodiak). Plagued with self-doubt, Curtayne turns to the bottle and, in

desperation, gives a $500 payoff to a man (Jay C. Flippen) who witnessed the shooting and promises to testify on Johnny's behalf. On the stand, however, the man reneges on his offer, and Johnny is found guilty. After the verdict, Curtayne manages to unearth evidence that will prove his client's innocence and volunteers to be used as bait to lure the real killer; following the attorney in a police van, Barra realizes that Curtayne's life is in jeopardy, but it is too late — after a shootout, police converge in time to catch the killers, but Curtayne loses his life in the process.

Of Hodiak's three back-to-back noirs, the actor earned his best notices for his role in *The People Against O'Hara*, with W.E. Oliver of the *Los Angeles Evening Herald-Express* praising his "clean, clipped" performance, and Margaret Harford writing in the *Hollywood Citizen-News* that the actor "handles himself well as the ambitious prosecutor." The following year, he was again cast as an attorney, this time in *The Sellout* (1952), the last film under his MGM contract. After this feature, Hodiak turned his sights eastward, making his Broadway debut in *The Chase*, which was directed and produced by actor Jose Ferrer.

"Regarding the professional stage, the biggest hurdle was Mr. Ferrer and the author, Horton Foote, deciding to cast me," Hodiak said. "I'm a pretty good listener, and I can adapt myself pretty easily. Anyway, my problems were minimized because I have so great respect for Jo[se] and his talent. But I'm finding out what a challenge it is."

Although Hodiak was hailed for his portrayal of a small-town sheriff in the production, and received the Donaldson Award for his performance, the play closed after a short run and the actor returned to Hollywood to star in a string of fairly forgettable wartime features — *Battle Zone* (1952), co-starring Linda Christian; *Mission Over Korea* (1953), with John Derek and Audrey Totter; and *Dragonfly Squadron* (1953), opposite Barbara Britton. He was also seen in two mediocre westerns, *Conquest of Cochise* (1953), in which the actor was miscast as the famed Apache chief, and *Ambush at Tomahawk Gap* (1953), where he was teamed with John Derek, Ray Teal, and David Brian as a group of ex-cons searching for their stolen money.

But by now, Hodiak had more serious concerns than his disappointing film career. In December 1952, Anne Baxter filed for divorce from her husband of six years, and the couple released a statement to the press that read in part: "We have tried very hard to avoid the finality of the word divorce.... We have no other interests and no career problems. We feel heartsick and defeated that in spite of all our hopes and efforts at understanding, basic incompatibilities have made our life together impossible." Baxter was less tactful a month later, however. During her court testimony, she tearfully described Hodiak as rude and insulting, and claimed that she had found it difficult to work due to "such tension and strain."

"For months we had been trying to work out our problems at mealtime after a day's work. He would imitate me and more or less mock me, in an insulting tone," Baxter testified. "I'd say, 'But John, I don't understand.' And in a shrill, high voice, he would imitate me by repeating, 'But John, I don't understand.' Finally it would get so bad that I'd have to take my plate upstairs to finish the meal in peace." The couple's divorce was finalized in January 1953, and Hodiak eventually moved into his parents' house in Tarzana. Although he would later date such starlets as Janis Paige and Eva Gabor, none of the relationships lasted and a friend of Hodiak's stated that the actor "was not interested in marrying again — he had been hurt once."

Career-wise, Hodiak had decided to take his acting in a new direction.

"The picture business was going stale for me and I was for it," the actor said. "I just wasn't cut out to play the star's brother all the time. I was getting second fiddle roles. It began to be obvious to me that I wasn't in line to become a Gary Cooper, a John Wayne, or a Bing Crosby. Oh, I had good parts. But not top star roles."

Returning to New York, the actor took on the role of Lt. Stephen Maryk in *The Caine Mutiny Courtmartial*, which opened on Broadway to rave reviews in January 1954. Critics were unanimous in their praise of the production, and Hodiak was singled out by several reviewers, including Brooks Atkinson of the *New York Times*, who wrote that Hodiak's performance "had strength, charm, candor, and the stamp of a human being. Every stroke in it is genuine and pertinent." By now, Hodiak had also made several well-received appearances on the small screen as well, in such series as *Your Show of Shows*, *Hollywood Playhouse*, and *Ford Theater*.

After several months with *Caine Mutiny*— which the actor termed "the most wonderful experience of my life"— Hodiak went back to the big screen and his former studio for a featured role in MGM's *Trial* (1955), a powerful courtroom drama starring Glenn Ford and Arthur Kennedy. Prior to the release of this film, Hodiak began work on *On the Threshold of Space* (1956), a drama about aviators testing supersonic aircraft. Playing an Air Force surgeon who specializes in rocket sled experiments, Hodiak was required to perform a variety of taxing maneuvers, some of them inside the jets. He completed the bulk of his role on October 18, 1955, but reportedly flubbed his lines on several occasions.

"I can't understand why I'm forgetting them," Hodiak was later quoted by crew members. "I've never done this before."

The following day (which, ironically, marked the nationwide opening of Hodiak's film, *Trial)* would be the actor's last. In the early morning hours, he complained of gas pains to his mother and sister and, later, while shaving, he collapsed in the bathroom, dying instantly of a coronary thrombosis. He was only 41 years old.

Hodiak's death was a shock to the Hollywood community, which had also recently suffered the untimely departures of Carmen Miranda, James Dean, Suzan Ball, and Robert Francis (who starred in *The Caine Mutiny* [1954], the screen version of Hodiak's last play). Although Hodiak had no history of heart problems, however, he had suffered for several years from hypertension, the condition that prevented his service in World War II, and a number of friends and co-workers suggested that the actor's moodiness and sensitivity had also contributed to his sudden death.

"He was the most sensitive person," said his ex-wife, Anne Baxter. "He was hurt inside, many times, and that probably did it."

Actor Lloyd Nolan, who appeared with Hodiak in *Somewhere in the Night* and *Caine Mutiny Courtmartial,* offered a similar assessment.

"He had ultra-sensitiveness," said Nolan, who was among the active pallbearers at Hodiak's funeral service on October 22, 1955. "He was very sincere about acting, and very serious about it. He also was terribly nervous at times. Even at parties in New York, he'd get butterflies in his stomach, like a child."

These characteristics notwithstanding, John Hodiak was far more likely to be touted as soft-spoken, well-liked, and loyal to a fault. And although he appeared to be forever striving for an undefined goal ("I keep looking for something that I've never found," he once said), he offered memorable performances in a number of films and can best be remembered for his admirable rise from the caddy with "lousy diction" to one of the stars of the silver screen.

"He had been in every medium and conquered them all," Anne Baxter said after Hodiak's death. "He did it all himself. Nobody ever helped John."

Film Noir Filmography

Somewhere in the Night. Director: Joseph L. Mankiewicz. Producer: Anderson Lawler. Running time: 110 minutes. Released by 20th Century-Fox, June 12, 1946. Cast: John Hodiak, Nancy Guild, Lloyd Nolan, Richard Conte, Josephine Hutchinson, Fritz Kortner, Margo Woode, Sheldon Leonard, Lou Nova, John Russell, Houseley Stevenson, Charles Arnt, Al Sparlis, Jeff Corey, Henry Morgan.

The Bribe. Director: Robert Z. Leonard. Producer: Pandro S. Berman. Running time: 98 min-

utes. Released by MGM, February 3, 1949. Cast: Robert Taylor, Ava Gardner, Charles Laughton, Vincent Price, John Hodiak, Samuel S. Hinds, John Hoyt, Tito Renaldo.

A Lady Without Passport. Director: Joseph H. Lewis. Producer: Samuel Marx. Running time: 72 minutes. Released by MGM, August 3, 1950. Cast: Hedy Lamarr, John Hodiak, James Craig, George Macready, Steven Geray, Bruce Cowling, Nedrick Young, Steven Hill, Robert Osterloh, Trevor Bardette, Charles Wagenheim, Renzo Cesana, Esther Zeitlin, Carlo Tricoli, Marta Mitrovitch, Don Garner, Richard Crane, Nita Bieber.

The People Against O'Hara. Director: John Sturges. Producer: William H. Wright. Running time: 102 minutes. Released by MGM, September 5, 1951. Cast: Spencer Tracy, Pat O'Brien, Diana Lynn, John Hodiak, Eduardo Ciannelli, James Arness, Yvette Duguay, Jay C. Flippen, William Campbell, Richard Anderson, Henry O'Neill, Arthur Shields, Louise Lorimer, Ann Doran, Emile Meyer, Regis Toomey, Katherine Warren, Paul Bryar, Peter Mamakos, Perdita Chandler, Frank Fergusson, Don Dillaway, C. Anthony Hughes, Lee Phelps, Lawrence Tolan, Jack Lee, Tony Barr.

References

"Anne Baxter Cuts John Hodiak Ties." *Los Angeles Times,* January 28, 1953.

"Anne Baxter and Hodiak Expect Baby in Fall." *Los Angeles Times,* February 28, 1951.

"Anne Baxter Gives Birth to Daughter." *Los Angeles Examiner,* July 10, 1951.

"Anne Baxter, Hodiak Part." *Hollywood Citizen-News,* December 22, 1952.

"Anne Baxter Sues for Divorce." *Los Angeles Examiner,* December 23, 1952.

Arvad, Inga. "Hodiak's Old Folks Come West." *The Baltimore Sun,* November 19, 1944.

Biography of John Hodiak. MGM Studios, March 1946.

Biography of John Hodiak. MGM Studios, July 24, 1951.

Biography of John Hodiak. 20th Century-Fox Studios, September 13, 1943.

"Family Reunion Marks Fulfillment of Pledge." *Los Angeles Times,* October 15, 1944.

Gebhart, Myrtle. "Biggest Film Fight Ever." *Boston Post,* May 10, 1945.

Hall, Prunella. "Screen Gossip." *Boston Post,* March 27, 1950.

Hawkins, William. "Hodiak Bets 'The Chase' Makes Good." *New York World-Telegram and Sun,* April 15, 1952.

"Hodiak-Baxter Wedding Today." *Hollywood Citizen-News,* July 6, 1946.

Hodiak, John. "The Role I Liked Best." *The Saturday Evening Post*, June 28, 1947.

"Hodiak 'Mimicry' Wins Anne Baxter Divorce." *Los Angeles Examiner*, January 28, 1953.

Hopper, Hedda. "John Is No Hodiakcident." *Chicago Sunday Tribune*, January 12, 1947.

"Hustlin' Along with Hodiak." *Motion Picture*, circa 1946.

"John Hodiak Dies on Day of New Film." *Hollywood Citizen-News*, October 19, 1955.

"John Hodiak Service Set." *Los Angeles Examiner*, October 21, 1955.

"John Hodiak Sued for Divorce by Anne Baxter." *Los Angeles Herald-Express*, December 22, 1952.

Manners, Dorothy. "Snappy Stories: John Hodiak." *Los Angeles Examiner*, January 30, 1949.

Mosby, Aline. "John Hodiak Easily Hurt, Says Anne Baxter." *Hollywood Citizen-News*, October 20, 1955.

Obituary. *Time*, October 31, 1955.

Parsons, Louella O. "John Hodiak, Film Star, Succumbs to Heart Attack." *Los Angeles Examiner*, October 20, 1955.

"Screen Stars to Separate." *New York Daily News*, December 22, 1952.

Shaffer, Rosalind. "Stars Made John Hodiak Star." *Boston Post*, March 12, 1944.

"Simplicity Marks John Hodiak Rites." *Los Angeles Times*, October 23, 1955.

Skolsky, Sidney. "Meticulous Dishwasher." *New York Post Weekend Magazine*, July 26, 1947.

"Star John Hodiak Dies." *Los Angeles Mirror-News*, October 19, 1955.

Sullivan, Ed. "Behind the Scenes." *New York Daily News*, August 4, 1954.

_____. "Broadway at 42d." *New York Daily News*, October 21, 1955.

Van Neste, Dan. "John Hodiak: The Hero from Hamtramck." *Classic Images*, August 1998.

Wahls, Robert. "At Last Hodiak Feels Like Legitimate Actor." *New York Daily News*, August 8, 1954.

Weiler, A.H. "Journey to a Star." *New York Times*, July 8, 1945.

White, Bob. "John Hodiak's Rise from Coal Pits to Renown Saga of Family Loyalty." *Los Angeles Times*, September 2, 1945.

Wilson, Earl. "This Hodiak's No Scene Stealer." *Los Angeles Daily News*, April 10, 1954.

WILLIAM HOLDEN

"It was all very queer, but queerer things were yet to come." — William Holden in *Sunset Boulevard* (1950)

Who was William Holden?

For much of his career, the strikingly handsome actor portrayed the proverbial boy next door, the "Smiling Jim" who could take it on the chin and still maintain a sunny outlook. But off screen, he demonstrated an adventurous nature that bordered on dangerous recklessness. In films, he was self-possessed and in control, but behind the scenes, he relied on alcohol to bolster his courage. His acting talent earned him three Academy Award nominations during an illustrious career that spanned six decades but, by all accounts, he never took his profession seriously and, according to a friend, "never really respected himself."

With nearly 80 features to his credit, Holden turned in standout performances in some of Hollywood's most admired films, including *Golden Boy* (1939), *Our Town* (1940), *Born Yesterday* (1950), *Stalag 17* (1953), *The Country Girl* (1954), *Picnic* (1955), *The Bridge on the River Kwai* (1957), *The Wild Bunch* (1969), and *Network* (1976). Although he seldom portrayed the heavy, he was nonetheless a prominent contributor to film noir, with starring roles in four first-rate examples of the era: *The Dark Past* (1948), *Union Station* (1950), *Sunset Boulevard* (1950), and *The Turning Point* (1952).

The oldest of three boys, the future star of the screen was born William Franklin Beedle, Jr., on April 17, 1918, in O'Fallon, Illinois, a small town situated approximately 20 miles east of St. Louis. His parents, a chemist and a school teacher, moved the family to Monrovia, California, in 1922, where William, Sr., took on a job in the chemical analysis business and later became head of the George W. Gooch Laboratories. Growing up in Monrovia, young William became known for his daredevil stunts; one of his favorite antics was walking on his hands on the outer ledge of a structure in town known as Suicide Bridge.

After graduating from South Pasadena High School in 1936, William enrolled as a chemistry major at South Pasadena Junior College, with plans to follow in his father's footsteps. While there, he became an amateur boxer, participating in the Golden Gloves tournament and, after taking a course in radio drama, acted in several plays on local station KECA. In 1938, William landed the role of an 80-year-old man in a college production called *Manya*, which was performed at the Pasadena Workshop Theatre. His opening night performance caught the attention of Paramount talent scout Milton Lewis, who arranged for the actor to appear in a test opposite another screen hopeful by the name of Rebecca Wasson. The test led to a contract with the studio, where executives promptly set about changing the actor's name. The head of the publicity department, Terry De Lapp, hit on a proper moniker while speaking one day to a local newspaper editor by the name of William Holden. He asked the editor if he could use his name, and when the editor agreed, William Holden, actor, was born. Although he had a new name, however, Holden was idle for most of the first six months of his contract, appearing only in bit parts as an inmate in *Prison Farm* (1938), and as a school graduate in *Million Dollar Legs* (1939).

"In *Million Dollar Legs*, I said two words: 'thank you'," Holden later recalled.

But the actor's big break was just around the corner. Over at Columbia, a massive casting search was underway for the role of Joe Bonaparte, a violinist-turned-boxer in the studio's upcoming film, *Golden Boy* (1939). The film's producer, William Perlberg, asked to see a copy of the screen test featuring actress Rebecca Wasson, who was being considered for a role. Instead, it was Holden's performance that caught his eye.

Holden tested for the role — becoming the 66th actor to do so — and clinched the part, joining a cast that included Barbara Stanwyck, Adolphe Menjou, and Lee J. Cobb. *Golden Boy* began production on April 17, 1939 — the actor's 21st birthday — but Holden's excitement over landing the coveted role was overshadowed by self-doubt. When the actor's shaky performance threatened to result in his dismissal from the picture, Stanwyck stepped in, reading lines with him every night and offering valuable coaching tips. (As an expression of his gratitude, Holden sent the veteran actress two dozen red roses and a white gardenia each year on the anniversary of the film's starting date. He carried on the tradition until his death in 1981.) Holden also took violin and boxing lessons in order to increase his preparation for the part.

"After I'd finished my day's work in the picture, I went to my dressing room and Julian Brodetsky tried to teach me how to finger the instrument. Then I had a light supper and went over to the Hollywood Athletic Club and had a boxing workout for an hour and a half," the actor told *Saturday Evening Post* writer Pete Martin in 1954. "But I didn't mind those lessons as much as I did that curl in my hair. To keep it curly, I had to get up at five-thirty in the morning and go to the hairdresser."

Despite the grueling lessons and the assistance provided by his leading lady, however, Holden still seemed to lack the confidence he needed. According to Holden's biographer, Bob Thomas, the actor discovered another means of bolstering his courage.

"He would need a shot or two of whiskey in the morning to face this huge challenge of playing a leading role opposite Barbara Stanwyck," Thomas said in a 2000 documentary on the actor's life. The reliance on alcohol that was initiated during the filming of *Golden Boy* would later mushroom into a problem that would plague Holden for the rest of his life.

After Holden's performance in *Golden Boy*, Harry Cohn struck a unique deal with Paramount to purchase half of the actor's contract, an agreement that remained in effect for the next 14 years. He was promptly loaned to Warner Bros. for a minor part in *Each Dawn I Die* (1940), starring James Cagney, and a role as the younger brother of George Raft in *Invisible Stripes* (1940). While on the Warners lot, Holden fell for contract player Brenda Marshall, and the two were married the following year, with actor Brian Donlevy serving as best man. The union got off to a rocky start, however. Holden chartered a plane to Las Vegas for the ceremony, but when the couple reached Nevada, they found that the regular airfield was closed. Forced to land on an unpaved airstrip being prepared for the Army, Holden and Marshall had to walk a mile to the air terminal, and by the time they reached the church, it was closed. They finally managed to locate the pastor, who married the couple at 4 o'clock in the morning in a hotel room (but not the bridal suite, which had been given to another couple). Holden and Marshall's troubles didn't end there. The night after their wedding, Holden was felled by an attack of appendicitis. While he recovered, Marshall headed out for a three-week location shot in Canada, and upon her return, it was discovered that she, too, had contracted appendicitis.

"To sum it up," Holden later recalled, "we were married in July 1941, but it was two and a half months before we were able to look at each other as man and wife."

Professionally, Holden earned mostly good reviews for his performance in *Our Town* (1940) — he was praised by the *New York Times'* Bosley Crowther for his "clean and refreshing youthfulness," but the critic for the *New York Herald-Tribune* wrote that Holden was "the only player I found wanting, and he doesn't seriously hurt any scene." During this time, Holden also began portraying roles that fell into what he referred to as his "Smiling Jim" phase.

"[Smiling Jim] didn't have a powerful personality. On the other hand, he wasn't a killer type," Holden once explained. "If he got into a tough spot, he smiled his way out of it. If a stranger got mad at him in traffic and yelled and cursed, old Smiling Jim just

kept on smiling and before long the stranger was smiling too."

Holden portrayed "Smiling Jim" roles in such lightweight features as *The Fleet's In* (1942), notable as the film debut of Betty Hutton; *The Remarkable Andrew* (1942), where he played a bookkeeper accused of misappropriating funds; *Meet the Stewarts* (1942), a marital farce with Frances Dee; and *Young and Willing* (1942), a low-budget, all-but-forgotten comedy gem co-starring Susan Hayward, Eddie Bracken, and Robert Benchley.

In late 1942, Holden's career was interrupted when he enlisted as a private in the Air Force during World War II. The actor entered Officers Candidate School in Florida and was graduated a second lieutenant, spending the remainder of the war performing public relations and entertainment duties and appearing in training films. His first child, Peter Westfield, was born on November 18, 1943, while Holden was still in the service, and wife Brenda was expecting their second son when the actor was discharged in December 1945. Scott Porter Holden was born to the couple on May 2, 1946. The actor's return to Hollywood, however, was not a happy one.

"I was short-tempered, moody, and depressed," Holden said. "I avoided all my friends. I saw every movie I had missed. I read every available script at Paramount. I worked around the house. Finally I felt that everything had ended. Naturally, after the Army, I had expected there would be some adjustment requiring about a month at the most. Well for 10 months I was a fugitive from a psychoanalyst."

Holden's first screen appearance after the war finally came in *Blaze of Noon* (1947), which focused on the early efforts to carry mail by air. This was followed by the film that catapulted the actor into stardom — *Dear Ruth* (1947), co-starring Joan Caulfield. After the release of this amusing comedy, Holden was singled out by a number of critics, including John Thompson of the *New York Mirror*, who called Holden "one of the most

engaging light comedians in the business," and the reviewer for the *New York Times*, who noted that "there is an easy naturalness about William Holden's performance that was not apparent in his previous acting." In response to the film's popularity, Holden and Caulfield recreated their *Dear Ruth* roles on *Lux Radio Theater* in April 1948 and December 1949.

In a trio of rather thankless roles, Holden was next seen in *Rachel and the Stranger* (1948), playing a frontiersman who nearly loses his wife (Loretta Young) to a mysterious drifter (Robert Mitchum); *The Man from Colorado* (1948), where he portrayed the steadfast friend of a sadistic Civil War veteran-turned-judge (Glenn Ford); and *Apartment for Peggy* (1948), in which co-star Edmund Gwenn practically stole the movie. Holden rebounded from these lackluster parts, however, with a starring role in his first film noir, *The Dark Past* (1948).

Most of this tense feature is told in flashback, as police psychiatrist Andrew Collins (Lee J. Cobb) shares a personal experience with a co-worker in an effort to demonstrate the value of criminal psychiatric treatment. Three years earlier, while he was vacationing

with his wife, son, and a group of friends, Collins' lakeside cabin was taken over by ruthless killer Al Walker (Holden), a recent prison escapee. As Walker and his gang await the arrival of a boat, Collins learns that Walker suffers from recurring nightmares and an inexplicably paralyzed hand. During the night-long ordeal, Walker gradually opens up to the understanding doctor and ultimately reveals that, as a child, he had been indirectly responsible for the shooting death of his father. Having uncovered the root of his nightmares, Walker's recollection of the event renders him unable to kill again, and when police later surround the cabin, he peaceably surrenders.

Although Holden was praised for his portrayal of the psychopathic gangster, he followed *The Dark Past* with another series of the dreaded "Smiling Jim" roles in *Dear Wife* (1949), the somewhat disappointing sequel to *Dear Ruth*; *Miss Grant Takes Richmond* (1949) co-starring Lucille Ball; and *Father Is a Bachelor* (1950), an unfunny comedy panned by critics as "saccharine" and "paper-thin."

"I got into the rut of playing all kinds of nice-guy, meaningless roles in meaningless movies ... in which I found neither interest nor enjoyment," Holden said once. "I had appeared in 11 movies that, for me, added up to one big static blur. Then in 1950, I played the part of Joe Gillis, the opportunistic, caddish writer in *Sunset Boulevard*. It was a turning point for me."

Sunset Boulevard, Holden's second excursion into the murky realm of noir, was indeed a turning point for the actor. Far from the "Smiling Jim" parts that had so frequently been assigned to him, Holden's role in *Sunset Boulevard* represented a stark contrast, a man of irresponsibility and uncertainty who was not above using others for his own gain. As this top-notch feature begins, Holden's character, Joe Gillis, is seen floating dead in a swimming pool: "Poor dope," Joe's voice intones. "He always wanted a pool. Well, in the end he got himself a pool. Only the price turned out to be a little high." Shown in flashback, the film centers on the relationship between Gillis, a young, unemployed writer, and aging silent movie star Norma Desmond (Gloria Swanson). Following a chance encounter with the eccentric actress, Joe finds himself saddled with the role of her ghostwriter, lover, and constant companion. Despite the financial benefits of the arrangement, however, Joe ultimately finds that the oppressive affection of Miss Desmond is too much to bear. After a series of secret meetings with another writer (Nancy Olson) leads to love, Joe tries to leave Norma but, instead, loses his life at her hand. It was one of the best roles of Holden's career.

"He understood Joe's desperation, his fright, his weakness," Olson said in a 2000 documentary on the actor's life. "*Sunset Boulevard* would not be the film that it is without Bill Holden. He *is* that character."

Holden rightfully earned raves for his performance; he was labeled "exceptionally fine" in *Variety*, and the critic for the *New York Times* proclaimed that Holden had done "the finest acting of his career. His range and control of emotions never falters and he engenders a full measure of compassion for a character who is somewhat less than admirable." Holden's efforts earned him his first Academy Award nomination for Best Actor, but he lost to Jose Ferrer in *Cyrano deBergerac*.

Holden followed *Sunset Boulevard* with another first-rate film, the hilarious and often touching comedy *Born Yesterday* (1950), portraying an intellectual reporter hired to tutor a chorus girl (Judy Holliday) in life's finer things. Also that year, he was reteamed with Nancy Olson for his third film noir, *Union Station* (1950).

Here, Holden starred as William Calhoun, a Union Station police lieutenant who works feverishly to locate a wealthy blind girl (Allene Roberts) kidnapped by a trio of ruthless hoods. After a harrowing chase in the bowels of the city's municipal tunnel, Calhoun locates the girl, shoots her captor, and safely returns her to her grateful father.

As Calhoun, Holden portrayed a tough, no-nonsense character whose complete control over of the station under his command was clearly demonstrated early in the film — during a single stroll through the station's main terminal, Calhoun wordlessly nabs a small-time hood trying to steal a traveler's suitcase, stops a station employee from flirting with a passerby, and orders the arrest of a pair of con men in the act of fleecing a small-town hick. For his performance, Holden earned praise in the *New York Times*, whose reviewer wrote: "Although he seems a mite young to head the police force of this undesignated city's terminal, William Holden is a serious, alert dick, who can spot a con man or a masher, if not kidnapper, before you can say Grand Central."

Despite Holden's superb performances, and the favorable box office receipts that were generated by his films, the actor continued to be cast in less than stellar vehicles, including *Force of Arms* (1951), his third film with Nancy Olson, in which he played a world-weary lieutenant stationed in World War II Italy; *Boots Malone* (1952), a so-so sports drama; and *Submarine Command* (1952), again with Nancy Olson, where he was seen as a tormented ship's officer. He was also seen in 1952 in his final film noir, *The Turning Point*.

Inspired by the Estes Kefauver congressional investigations of organized crime, *The Turning Point* starred Holden as Jerry McKibbon, a jaded newspaper columnist who is described by one character as "a detached, cynical observer, faintly amused by the follies of other humans." Jerry's tainted view of life is further revealed when his boyhood chum, John Conroy (Edmond O'Brien), is appointed as special prosecutor to break up a local crime syndicate: "You're a man who wants to do good," Jerry says. "Sure, you always wanted to do good. I don't say that's wrong, I say that's the way you are." Jerry experiences a change of heart, however, when the syndicate's actions result in a spate of murders, including John's policeman father and several residents of an apartment building. But Jerry's newfound sense of justice turns out to be his undoing — after writing a series of exposés on the syndicate, and locating a key witness, he is targeted for death and ultimately loses his life after a tense chase scene in a crowded boxing arena. For his performance in this modest box-office success, Holden was included in the praise of *Los Angeles Times* critic Philip K. Scheuer, who wrote that the film's "acting is generally of a high order."

Although the actor in 1951 received an award from the Hollywood Women's Press Club for the screen's "most cooperative actor," Holden was becoming increasingly frustrated with the direction of his career, and went on suspensions following both *Sunset Boulevard* and *Submarine Command* when he refused to accept film assignments that he considered to be below par.

"It's necessary to capture the fancy of the public," he once said, "but also to stimulate their thinking." Holden's cinematic fortunes changed in 1953, however, with his starring role in *Stalag 17*, a superb comedy-drama set in a German POW camp. For his portrayal of Sefton, a sarcastic and cynical prisoner of war, Holden was heaped with praise, with *Life* magazine calling the role "the most memorable character to come out of Hollywood this year," and the reviewer for the *Christian Science Monitor* labeling the actor "excellently hard-eyed and taciturn as the shrewdly opportunistic Sefton." Holden's outstanding efforts earned him his second Best Actor Academy Award nomination, and this time the actor took home the prize, beating out Marlon Brando in *Julius Caesar* (1953), Richard Burton in *The Robe* (1953), and Montgomery Clift and Burt Lancaster in *From Here to Eternity* (1953).

After Holden's triumph at the Oscar ceremony, he was rewarded by Paramount with a revised 14-year contract, paying him an annual salary of $250,000 for two pictures a year, and allowing him to make one picture each year outside the studio. (The lucrative deal prompted a noted producer to proclaim: "In the movie business, Holden's contract is called security with a built-in tax disposal.") During the next three years, Holden starred in some of the most memorable films of his career. In 1954, he was seen in *The Country*

Girl, portraying a hard-nosed director who is determined to be the force behind the comeback of an alcoholic has-been (excellently played by Bing Crosby); *Executive Suite*, where he was teamed with his *Golden Boy* co-star Barbara Stanwyck as an idealistic but practical young executive; *The Bridges at Toko-Ri*, where he was seen as a Korean war lieutenant torn by his duty for his country and his resentment at the war's effects on his personal life; and *Sabrina*, in which he vied with his screen sibling Humphrey Bogart for the affections of chauffeur's daughter Audrey Hepburn. Later in the decade, Holden was a standout in *Picnic* (1955), earning high praise for his portrayal of a braggart drifter; *Love is a Many Splendored Thing* (1955), a box-office smash featuring Holden as a married war correspondent who falls in love with a Eurasian doctor in Hong Kong; and *Bridge on the River Kwai* (1957), a stirring wartime drama that earned seven Academy Awards including Best Picture and Best Director (David Lean). Also during this period, Holden formed his own company, Toluca Productions, and produced his first and last film, *Toward the Unknown*, in 1956.

"I made *Toward the Unknown* as an actor by day and, by night, a caster, a cutter, and a producer," Holden said. "I'll never do anything like that again!"

Throughout the mid- to late 1950s, Holden was heaped with a variety of accolades—in 1957, the *Motion Picture Herald* poll of exhibitors proclaimed him the nation's top box-office attraction, and an article in *The Saturday Evening Post* declared him "as hot as flaming napalm." His screen successes also translated into a financial boon, with the actor commanding as much as $750,000 per role, and inking a lucrative deal for *Bridge on the River Kwai* in which he accepted only a nominal salary but received a hefty percentage of the gross. Holden's earnings allowed him to indulge his newfound fascination with African safaris, and he entered a partnership with two associates to create the Mount Kenya Safari Club in Nairobi, today one of the most popular attractions for wealthy tourists in East Africa.

But with the onset of the 1960s, Holden's luck began to change. Having moved his family to Switzerland in the late 1950s for tax purposes, the actor was seen in a series of overseas features, including *The Key* (1958), with Sophia Loren, and *The Lion* (1962). Not only did the films flop at the box office, but Holden was criticized by industry guilds and even several U.S. congressmen, who blasted the actor for taking away jobs from American craftsmen by forcing producers to hire overseas crews. Holden didn't hesitate in responding to these critics.

"It seems to me that Americans have always been noted for moving around, for being unafraid of new challenges and new frontiers," Holden said. "Now certain people are trying to tell us to stay home and not work abroad. It's a form of isolationism."

The downward slide in Holden's career was also reflected by increasing turmoil in his personal life. Despite his marital status, the actor reportedly engaged in affairs with several of his leading ladies over the years, including Grace Kelly, Audrey Hepburn, and Capucine, his co-star in *The Lion*. In 1963, Brenda Marshall separated from the actor and, although Holden told reporters that he "just wanted to be on my own for a while to think things out," the couple would divorce a decade later. Meanwhile, Holden's penchant for alcohol had continued to increase, and in 1966, he made headlines in Italy when was involved in an automobile accident while driving in his sports car between Florence and Pisa with two women from New York. The driver of the other vehicle was killed, and the actor was charged with manslaughter. The following year, he received an eight-month suspended sentence, paid $80,000 to the dead driver's widow, and was banned from driving in Italy for nearly a year.

"He managed to evade any prison time, but it was a great blow to his reputation," biographer Bob Thomas said in a 2000 documentary. "He started drinking as much as ever before."

Professionally, Holden continued to appear in one box office bomb after another until 1969, when his career was briefly revived with his role as an aging outlaw in Sam Peckinpah's classic western *The Wild Bunch*. Although many reviewers objected to the film's extreme violence, Holden's performance was praised as his best in years. But after this triumphant comeback, the actor was seen in only a handful of features, including *Wild Rovers* (1971), a mediocre western co-starring Ryan O'Neal, and *The Towering Inferno* (1974), a big-budget, star-studded disaster film helmed by Irwin Allen. Also during this period, the actor made a rare television appearance in a well-received four-part miniseries, *The Blue Knight* (1973), playing a soon-to-retire police officer. Holden's portrayal of the demanding role — he was never off-camera — earned him an Emmy Award for Best Lead Actor in a Limited Series. And in 1976, Holden took on what some considered to be his last memorable role, playing an aging newsman in the blockbuster feature film, *Network*. Praised for his "outstanding" performance, Holden earned his third Academy Award nomination for Best Actor, but lost this time around to his co-star in the film, Peter Finch, who was awarded the Oscar posthumously.

Off screen, Holden's life appeared to be on the upswing; he became a passionate advocate for the preservation of wildlife in Africa, and since 1974, he had been involved in a seemingly solid relationship with actress Stefanie Powers. As the years passed, however, Holden's drinking escalated, despite his efforts to quit.

"He would go to AA meetings," said Bob Thomas, "but his periods of abstinence did not last very long and often he would fall off the wagon with a sickening thud."

Still, the actor continued to sporadically appear in feature films, including *Ashanti* (1979), a tiresome chase movie set in the Middle East; *The Earthling* (1980), starring Holden as a terminally ill man who befriends a recently orphaned youngster; and *S.O.B.* (1981), a biting black comedy co-starring Julie

Andrews and Loretta Swit. The latter feature, directed by Blake Edwards, would offer Holden's last screen performance. On November 16, 1981, newspapers nationwide carried the shocking news that the actor had been found in his Santa Monica apartment, where he had lain dead for four days after falling and striking his head on a table. Evidence revealed that the actor had tried to stem the bleeding from his head wound with tissues, but had lost consciousness after a half-hour and bled to death. The Los Angeles County Coroner, Thomas Noguchi, reported that at the time of his death, the actor had a blood alcohol level of .22 percent, twice the legal limit.

"This may be one of the reasons why the bleeding never did stop. Alcohol interferes with the clotting mechanism," Noguchi said in a 2000 documentary. "There was a blood stain on the top of the telephone, but there was no indication that the telephone receiver was picked up. If he was able to call, he would be still alive."

After Holden's death, actress Stefanie Powers established the William Holden Wildlife Foundation, a 15-acre education center on the slopes of Mt. Kenya that houses a youth hostel, lecture hall and library, llama compound, fish farms, tree nursery, and solar energy installations. The center focuses on the wildlife issues to which Holden was so dedicated, and also teaches environmental studies and conservation methods.

Despite the problems that plagued him off screen, and the sudden, tragic manner in which he died, William Holden is seen today as one of the finest actors of his time. In numerous outstanding roles in classic, beloved films, his talent shines through and offers a beacon that eclipses the darker side of his life.

"You always were rooting for him," a Holden co-star once remarked. "And he never let you down."

Film Noir Filmography

The Dark Past. Director: Rudolph Mate. Producer: Buddy Adler. Running time: 74 minutes. Released by Columbia, December 22, 1948. Cast: William Holden, Nina Foch, Lee J. Cobb, Adele Jergens, Stephen Dunne, Lois Maxwell, Barry Kroeger, Steven Geray, Wilton Graff, Robert Osterloh, Kathryn Card, Bobby Hyatt, Ellen Corby, Charles Cane, Robert B. Williams.

Union Station. Director: Rudolph Mate. Producer: Jules Schermer. Running time: 80 minutes. Released by Paramount, October 4, 1950. Cast: William Holden, Nancy Olson, Barry Fitzgerald, Lyle Bettger, Jan Sterling, Allene Roberts, Herbert Heyes, Don Dunning, Fred Graff, James Seay.

Sunset Boulevard. Director: Billy Wilder. Producer: Charles Brackett. Running time: 115 minutes. Released by Paramount, August 10, 1950. Cast: William Holden, Gloria Swanson, Erich von Stroheim, Nancy Olson, Fred Clark, Lloyd Gough, Jack Webb, Cecil B. DeMille, Hedda Hopper, Buster Keaton, Anna Q. Nilsson, H.B. Warner, Franklyn Farnum, Sidney Skolsky, Ray Evans, Jay Livingston. Awards: Academy Awards for Best Art Direction/Set Direction (Hans Dreier, John Meehan, Sam Comer, Ray Moyer), Best Score/Drama or Comedy (Franz Waxman), Best Story and Screenplay (Charles Brackett, Billy Wilder, D.M. Marshman, Jr.). Academy Award nominations for Best Picture, Best Director (Billy Wilder), Best Actor (William Holden), Best Actress (Gloria Swanson), Best Supporting Actor (Erich von Stroheim), Best Supporting Actress (Nancy Olson), Best B/W Cinematography (John F. Seitz), Best Film Editing (Arthur Schmidt, Doane Harrison).

The Turning Point. Director: William Dietele. Producer: Irving Asher. Running time: 85 minutes. Released by Paramount, November 14, 1952. Cast: William Holden, Edmond O'Brien, Alexis Smith, Tom Tully, Ed Begley, Dan Dayton, Adele Longmire, Ray Teal, Ted De Corsia, Don Porter, Howard Freeman, Neville Brand.

References

"Actor Holden Convicted in Italian Traffic Death." *Los Angeles Times*, October 27, 1967.

Bacon, James. "Holden at Home in the Jungle." *Los Angeles Herald-Examiner*, May 7, 1976.

_____. "William Holden, 'Golden Boy' of Films, Dead at 63." *Los Angeles Herald-Examiner*, November 17, 1981.

Batchelor, Ruth. "A Charming Anti-Socialite Talks About Oscar Chances." *Detroit Free Press*, January 21, 1977.

Biography of William Holden. Paramount Pictures, July 1941.

Carroll, Harrison. "William Holdens Separated." *Los Angeles Herald Express*, August 28, 1963.

Charlton, Linda. "William Holden Dead at 63; Won Oscar for 'Stalag 17.'" *New York Times*, November 17, 1981.

Doherty, Thomas. "Golden Boy." *American Movie Classics Magazine*, July 1990.

Hopper, Hedda. "Golden Boy Holden." *Chicago Sunday Tribune*, February 12, 1950.

Hyams, Joe. "Hollywood's Busiest Leading Man." *Cue*, April 24, 1954.

Jones, Jack and Graham, Nancy. "Holden Died from Blood Loss." *Los Angeles Times*, November 18, 1981.

Klein, Doris. "William Holden, Actor, Is Now Conservationist William Holden." *The Hollywood Reporter*, October 30, 1967.

Lamb, David. "Holden's Star Still Shines Bright in Kenya." *Los Angeles Times*, December 13, 1991.

Love, Keith and Pollock, Dale. "Manner of Holden's Death Troubles Friends, Fans." *Los Angeles Times*, November 19, 1981.

Mann, Roderick. "Holden Makes a Detour to Avoid Hollywood Jungle." *Los Angeles Times*, January 27, 1980.

_____. "William Holden: In Full Bloom in Desert." *Los Angeles Times*, October 30, 1980.

Marill, A.H. "William Holden." *Films in Review*, October 1973.

Martin, Pete. "Hollywood's Most Improbable Star." *The Saturday Evening Post*, August 28, 1954.

McCarthy, Todd. "Bill Holden, 63, Found Dead in His Santa Monica Home." *Variety*, November 17, 1981.

"Official: Star Died in Drunken Fall." *New York Post*, November 18, 1981.

Oppenheimer, Peer J. "The Many Worlds of Bill Holden." *Family Weekly*, June 5, 1960.

Robb, David. "William Holden Found Dead in Santa Monica Apartment." *The Hollywood Reporter*, November 17, 1981.

Scott, John L. "Bill Holdens a Hit Both in Film and Family Roles." *Los Angeles Times*, January 16, 1949.

"Screen Couple Flies to Las Vegas." *Los Angeles Times*, July 13, 1941.

Swanson, Pauline. "Mr. Dynamite." *Photoplay*, January 1952.

"William Holden." *Architectural Digest*, April 1992.

Wilson, Earl. "It Happened Last Night." *New York Post*, January 29, 1958.

_____. "Bill Holden Still Acting, Staying Dry." *Los Angeles Herald-Examiner*, March 8, 1976.

Documentaries

"William Holden: An Untamed Spirit." Produced by Van Ness Films in Association with Foxstar Productions, Fox Television Studios, and A&E Networks. Twentieth Century-Fox Film Corporation. Copyright 1999.

"Mysteries and Scandals: William Holden." E! Entertainment Television. Copyright 2000.

JOHN HOYT

"Don't disappoint me and turn out to be honest." — John Hoyt in *Loan Shark* (1952)

Typed throughout his screen career as a sinister Nazi or a stern-faced heavy, John Hoyt enjoyed a colorful professional life that took him from the Ziegfeld Follies to a featured role on the long-running 1980s television sitcom *Gimme a Break*. During a span of five decades, Hoyt was seen alongside such film stars as Alan Ladd, Burt Lancaster, Bette Davis, and Glenn Ford, and appeared in a number of blockbusters, including *When Worlds Collide* (1951), *Blackboard Jungle* (1955), *Spartacus* (1960), and *Cleopatra* (1963). He was also featured in five films from the era of noir: *Brute Force* (1947), *The Bribe* (1949), *Loan Shark* (1952), *The Big Combo* (1955), and *Baby Face Nelson* (1957).

The versatile actor of stage, screen, and television was born John Hoysradt in New York City, on October 5, 1905, the son of an investment broker. The president of his high school drama club, Hoysradt earned his bachelor's and master's degrees from Yale University, where he participated in such school productions as ... *And for Yale*, co-starring his classmate and future film actor, Sonny Tufts. Despite his interest in the theater, Hoysradt turned to the field of education after leaving Yale, serving as a history instructor at the Groton School in Massachusetts; his pupils there included the sons of future president Franklin D. Roosevelt, Elliot and Franklin, Jr.

After two years at Groton, Hoysradt heeded the call of the stage, joining a summer theater in Southampton, New York, under the direction of actor Monty Woolley, and performing in Stuart Walker's repertory company in Cincinnati. At the latter company, he met actress Ann Revere, who was responsible for introducing the actor to his first wife, Marion Burns. (The couple had a son, David, but the marriage ended in divorce. Remarrying years later, the actor remained wed to his second wife, Dorothy, until his 1994 death.)

Hoysradt made his Broadway debut in 1931 in *Overture*, in which he played a German officer. He later recalled that the Nazi-themed production was "ahead of its time."

"Nazism was so new at the time that we didn't even know the word 'swastika,'" the actor said. "There was such a profusion of accents on the stage that no one knew who was who. I was a Wehrmacht officer who condemned [co-star] Colin Clive to death and led him to the stake. Clive died bravely — and so did the play."

In the coming years, Hoysradt formed a fortuitous association with Broadway star Katherine Cornell, serving as her offstage "ghost" pianist in her role as a concert musician in *Alien Corn*, and later joining her in *Candida*, *The Barretts of Wimpole Street*, and *Romeo and Juliet*, which featured Basil Rathbone and a young Orson Welles. He was also seen during this period in such Broadway productions as *Springtime for Henry*, *Storm Over Patsy*, and *The Masque of Kings*, and appeared with Bob Hope, Josephine Baker, and Fanny Brice in *The Ziegfeld Follies of 1936*. The year after his appearance in the *Follies*, Hoysradt joined Orson Welles' Mercury Theater, performing in the company's highly successful production of *Julius Caesar*.

"I was first cast as [Decius] Brutus, but I played him for only a short while," the actor recalled. "Welles insisted on using a real knife for the assassination scenes, and one night the actor playing Caesar yelped a bit too realistically. We soon discovered, to our horror, that the stain on the stage was blood, not catsup.

The poor man lost two quarts — and I was assigned his role."

Hoysradt continued to hone his skills in a variety of venues, including appearing on stage with Monty Woolley in *The Man Who Came to Dinner* and Tallulah Bankhead in *Private Lives*; joining stage actress Gertrude Lawrence in a USO tour of the South Pacific; and performing as a stand-up comedian at New York's famed Rainbow Room and the Dorcester House in London. By the mid-1940s, his versatility had attracted the attention of Hollywood talent scouts, and he was signed to a contract by Paramount Studios. Shortening his last name to Hoyt, the actor debuted on screen as a sophisticated Nazi general in *O.S.S.* (1946), starring Alan Ladd.

"That was the beginning of my career in the German Army," Hoyt said in a 1986 interview in *Fangoria* magazine. "When I came to Hollywood, they put me in a Nazi uniform and a hanging judge's robes and I didn't get any more comedy until *Gimme a Break*."

After a loan-out to Warner Bros. for *The Unfaithful* (1947) — a remake of *The Letter* (1941) — Hoyt entered the realm of film noir, playing a hard-boiled convict in *Brute Force* (1947). This feature focused on a group of cellmates who plan and execute a prison break, driven primarily by their desire to escape the tortuous treatment of a sadistic guard, Capt. Munsey (Hume Cronyn). As the cellmate named Spencer, Hoyt was particularly steely; in one of the film's most memorable scenes, a group of prisoners converge on a fellow inmate who has been tagged as a stool pigeon. It is Spencer who takes the lead in driving the man to a grisly death by threatening him with a blowtorch until he is crushed between the jaws of a huge piece of machinery. Despite the careful planning, Munsey learns of the plot, and the would-be escapees are killed by waiting guards. In a poetic twist, however, Munsey loses his life as well when the leader of the plot, Joe Collins (Burt Lancaster), tosses him from a burning tower into a sea of inmates waiting below.

Among a cast of outstanding performances, Hoyt was singled out by several critics for his menacing, stone-faced portrayal, including Philip K. Scheuer, who wrote in the *Los Angeles Times* that he offered "striking individual support" to star Burt Lancaster. In addition, Jack D. Grant of *The Hollywood Reporter* included Hoyt in his praise of the "others of merit" in the cast, and the critic for *Newsweek* wrote, "Much of the film's interest arises from the fact that the convicts kept in sharpest focus are distinct and believable characters. In particular, there are Burt Lancaster, Charles Bickford, Sam Levene, John Hoyt, and Art Smith."

During the next two years, Hoyt was fourth-billed as a friend of spinster Bette Davis in *Winter Meeting* (1948); played a suspected Nazi general in *Sealed Verdict* (1948); starred with Lloyd Nolan as a government agent in *Trapped* (1949); provided psychiatric support for Barbara Stanwyck in *The Lady Gambles* (1949); and was seen in a small role in his second film noir, *The Bribe* (1949). Here, Hoyt played Gibbs, a federal official who sends Agent Rigby (Robert Taylor) to a small island off the coast of Central America to break up a war surplus racket. During his assignment, Rigby falls for Elizabeth Hintten (Ava Gardner), the sultry wife of a man suspected of being a member of the smuggling ring, and eventually comes to believe that Elizabeth herself is involved in the criminal activities. It turns out, however, that the mastermind is a mining engineer by the name of Carwood (Vincent Price), who murders Elizabeth's husband before being shot down by the agent in the midst of a carnival celebration.

Although Hoyt's role in *The Bribe* was a relatively thankless one, he rebounded in 1951 with one of his most memorable parts, playing a crippled millionaire in the Academy Award–winning science fictioner, *When Worlds Collide*. Also during this period, Hoyt began what would become a highly prolific career on the small screen; beginning in the early 1950s with an appearance on *Philco Television Playhouse*, he went on to perform in more than 100 television series over the next

40 years. Among these were some of the most top-rated programs on the air, including *Gunsmoke*, *Leave it to Beaver*, *The Rifleman*, *The Untouchables*, *Perry Mason*, *The Twilight Zone*, *Petticoat Junction*, *The Big Valley*, *Hogan's Heroes*, *Ironside*, *It Takes a Thief*, *Police Woman*, and *Battlestar Gallactica*. He was also seen on the short-lived program, *Tom, Dick and Mary* in 1964, and held the distinction of appearing in the original 1966 pilot for the long-running series *Star Trek*, portraying Dr. Philip Boyce. The pilot was rejected by NBC, however, and when it was remade, Hoyt — along with most of the original cast — was not asked to return.

"I saw the pilot before it aired ... and it was *really* a dog," Hoyt said in 1986. "People at the screening departed in silence afterwards, and no one thought *Star Trek* would come to anything. And *look* what happened."

Meanwhile, on the big screen, Hoyt returned to the world of the dark for his third film noir, *Loan Shark* (1952), starring George Raft and Dorothy Hart. Here, the actor was featured as Vince Phillips, the apparent "Mr. Big" of a lucrative loan sharking racket that has ensnared a number of employees at a local tire factory. When the brother-in-law of factory worker Joe Cargen (Raft) is killed, he infiltrates the loan sharking gang — it is Phillips who brings Cargen into the organization, telling an underling, "He's one of those hard apples who likes money better than he does relatives." As Cargen rises in the ranks of the organization, however, he grows suspicious of Phillips' claim that he is the leader of the illegal operation. As it turns out, Cargen was on target — the gang is actually run by an unassuming accountant, Walter Karr (Larry Dobkin), and during a gun battle, Joe shoots both Phillips and Karr, bringing the deadly racket to an end. While *Loan Shark* was labeled an "okay melodrama" by one critic, Hoyt's portrayal of the venomous gang member was singled out in several notices following the film's release — the reviewer for *Variety* judged that the actor and several of his co-stars "put over their respective chores as members of the racket," and the *New York*

Times critic wrote, "Paul Stewart, Helen Westcott, John Hoyt, and Henry Slate, on both sides of the law, contribute some telling punches of their own."

During the next several years, Hoyt was seen in a widely varying series of features, including *The Black Castle* (1952), a horror film where he portrayed a German character known as Herr Stricken; *Androcles and the Lion* (1952), a mediocre costumer starring Victor Mature and Jean Simmons; *Julius Caesar* (1953), a first-rate film version of the Shakespearian drama, directed by Joseph Mankiewicz and produced by John Houseman; *The Student Prince* (1954), a big-budget box-office disappointment starring Edmund Purdom; *Trial* (1955), an acclaimed drama featuring Glenn Ford as an attorney who defends a Mexican youth accused of murder; *Blackboard Jungle* (1955), the classic tale of juvenile delinquents in an inner-city high school, in which Hoyt played the school principal; and his fourth film noir, *The Big Combo* (1955).

This excellent example from the noir era starred Richard Conte as a vicious gangster known only as Mr. Brown, and Cornel Wilde

as Leonard Diamond, the police detective who is determined to find positive proof of Brown's various misdeeds. After unsuccessfully essaying a number of methods in his efforts to nab Brown, Diamond finally learns that the gangster murdered his former boss, Grazzi, depositing his body at the bottom of the sea. Diamond's search for the captain of the boat that carried Grazzi leads him to Nils Dreyer (Hoyt), who has been set up in business by Brown as an antiques dealer. In his single scene in the film, Hoyt is a standout; his Dreyer is cool under pressure, refusing to divulge any information about Brown and declining Diamond's offer of protection against Brown's repercussions. Just minutes after Diamond's departure, however, Dreyer is gunned down outside his antiques store by Brown's men. After failing to ferret out the truth from Dreyer, Diamond manages to track down Brown's presumed-dead wife, Alicia (Helen Walker), whom Brown has hidden away in a mental institution. Alicia reluctantly provides the detective with the evidence he needs, and Diamond finally gets his man as he tries to flee the country.

In his brief appearance on screen, Hoyt managed to deliver a well-drawn portrait of the hard-boiled antiques dealer. Dreyer initially makes light of Diamond's visit to his store, punctuating his comments with a staccato laugh that indicates his appreciation for his own wry humor. "I have complete books," he tells Diamond. "Every dollar is there in black and white. Unless it goes in the red. Ha ha." And later, he acknowledges to Diamond that he'd recently dined with Brown: "Because I have lunch with him, that is not a crime. I have lunch with anybody — I'm democratic. I'll even have lunch with *you*. Ha ha."

After earning praise in the *New York Times* for his "dandy" performance in *The Big Combo*, Hoyt finished out the decade in such features as *The Conqueror* (1956), the notoriously bad epic starring John Wayne as Genghis Khan; *The Come On* (1956), in which he played a man who fakes his death in an effort to frame his wife and her lover; *God Is My Partner* (1957), an overly preachy film about a retired surgeon who tries to donate $50,000 to a religious cause; *The Beast of Budapest* (1957), a tiresome re-telling of the Hungarian Revolution of 1956; *Attack of the Puppet People* (1958), a science fictioner in which Hoyt starred as a lonely dollmaker who discovers a way to shrink humans to doll-size; and *Riot in Juvenile Prison* (1959), where he played a sadistic warden. The actor's sole bright spots during this period were *Never So Few* (1959), a war drama starring Frank Sinatra and Steve McQueen, and *Baby Face Nelson* (1957), his final film noir.

This feature starred Mickey Rooney in the title role of the 1930s gangster, following his release from prison, his frame-up by a mob boss and his later revenge, his association with fellow criminal John Dillinger (Leo Gordon) and his subsequent takeover of Dillinger's gang, and his ultimate liquidation on a Wisconsin highway after a tension-filled auto chase. In a supporting role, Hoyt played Samuel Parker, a shrewd FBI man who heads up the hunt for Nelson and finally zeroes in on one of his associates, blueprint company owner Fatso Nagel (Jack Elam). Despite Fatso's reluctance, Parker forces him to aid in the gangster's setup: "Fatso, you've been in San Francisco," Parker says in a mild tone. "You've seen that big rock out in the bay? You wouldn't want to spend the rest of your life there. So you figure out a way to make him hold still and listen." For his portrayal of the determined lawman, Hoyt earned mention in the *Hollywood Citizen-News* for being "expertly cast—and expert in [his] performance," and the film itself earned mostly good reviews, with John L. Scott of the *Los Angeles Times* labeling it "a hard-hitting story," and the critic for the *Hollywood Citizen-News* praising it as "top-notch." The *New York Times'* reviewer disagreed, however, calling the feature "a thoroughly standard, pointless, and even old-fashioned gangster picture, the kind that began going out along with the old-time sedans."

During the early 1960s, Hoyt was seen in a pair of classic Hollywood features, playing Caius in *Spartacus* (1960), and Cassius in

Cleopatra (1963), as well as back-to-back science fiction hits, *X—The Man with the X-Ray Eyes* (1963), starring Ray Milland in the title role, and *The Time Travelers* (1964), which focused on a group of scientists who are transported into the future. Also during this period, Hoyt made a brief attempt to expand his moviemaking horizons, serving as writer, producer, and star of *The Glass Cage* (1964). Years later, however, he recalled that his behind-the-scenes experience was less than pleasant.

"An unscrupulous distributor stole the film from right under our noses and left us with the creditors," Hoyt told *Fangoria* magazine. "I raised most of the money by doing things like going back to my college reunion and bleeding all my classmates. Of course, they lost everything they put into it. That was my last venture into independent production. I never did any screenwriting after that—once burned, twice shy."

By now, Hoyt's energies were primarily focused on his busy television career, but he found time to stage a one-man show in 1969 at the New Hope Inn in Los Angeles, and continued to accept assignments in a number of big screen features including *Two on a Guillotine* (1965), a horror film written and directed by actor William Conrad; *Duel at Diablo* (1966), a violent western starring James Garner and Sidney Poitier; *Panic in the City* (1968), a mediocre thriller about a Communist conspiracy; and *Flesh Gordon* (1972), a *Flash Gordon* spoof that was rife with sexual innuendos and featured characters with such names as Emperor Wang the Perverted and Dr. Flexi Jerkoff.

"I didn't know how pornographic it was going to be when I first learned about it," Hoyt said in his 1986 *Fangoria* interview. "As a matter of fact, I think *Flesh Gordon* turned out not to be porno or to be funny enough. It didn't get anyplace. My wife was so horrified when she saw it that she wanted to divorce me! It was terrible."

In addition to his television series work, Hoyt was seen in several made-for-television movies, including *Winchester '73* (1967),

Welcome Home, Johnny Bristol (1972), *The Turning Point of Jim Malloy* (1975), and *The Winds of Kitty Hawk* (1978). And he hit the jackpot in 1982 when he joined the cast of the NBC series *Gimme a Break*, starring Nell Carter as the housekeeper for a widowed police chief and his three daughters. In this popular sitcom, Hoyt played Grandpa Kanisky, the cantankerous but lovable father of the chief, remaining with the show until it left the air in 1987.

After the cancellation of *Gimme a Break*, Hoyt retired from performing and faded from the limelight. Then, in the early 1990s, he was diagnosed with lung cancer, succumbing to the disease on September 15, 1991. (At least one of the actor's obituaries noted that he was one of numerous cast members of the 1956 film *The Conqueror* to suffer from cancer; decades after the release of the film, a possible connection was made between these high incidents of cancer and the location where much of the film was shot, which took place less than 200 miles from a site where extensive atomic bomb testing had been conducted a year earlier. Other members of the cast who contracted the disease included John Wayne, Susan Hayward, Agnes Moorehead, Dick Powell, and Pedro Armendariz.)

With a face that is almost instantly recognizable, John Hoyt enjoyed an impressive career as a character actor in motion pictures, and an even greater success on the small screen. And despite the fact that he was typecast throughout much of his screen career, Hoyt viewed his experience with a measure of appreciation and good humor.

"You have to accept typecasting up to a point," the actor said late in his career, "because it's your daily bread."

Film Noir Filmography

Brute Force. Director: Jules Dassin. Producer: Mark Hellinger. Running time: 95 minutes. Released by Universal-International, June 6, 1947. Cast: Burt Lancaster, Hume Cronyn, Charles Bickford, Yvonne DeCarlo, Ann Blyth, Ella Raines, Anita Colby, Sam Levene, Howard Duff, Art Smith, Roman Bohnen, John Hoyt, Richard Gaines, Frank Puglia, Jeff Corey, Vince Barnett, James Bell, Jack Overman, Whit Bissell, Sir Lancelot, Ray Teal, Jay C. Flippen, James O'Rear, Howland Chamberlain, Kenneth Patterson, Crane Whitley, Charles McGraw, John Harmon, Gene Stutenroth, Wally Rose, Carl Rhodes, Guy Beach, Edmund Cobb, Tom Steele.

The Bribe. Director: Robert Z. Leonard. Producer: Pandro S. Berman. Running time: 98 minutes. Released by MGM, February 3, 1949. Cast: Robert Taylor, Ava Gardner, Charles Laughton, Vincent Price, John Hodiak, Samuel S. Hinds, John Hoyt, Tito Renaldo.

Loan Shark. Director: Seymour Friedman. Producer: Bernard Luber. Running time: 79 minutes. Released by Lippert, May 23, 1952. Cast: George Raft, Dorothy Hart, Paul Stewart, Helen Westcott, John Hoyt, Henry Slate, William Phipps, Russell Johnson, Benny Baker, Larry Dobkin, Charles Meredith, Harlan Warde, Spring Mitchell, Margie Dean, Ross Elliott, Robert Bice, Robert Williams, Michael Ragan, Virginia Caroll.

The Big Combo. Director: Joseph Lewis. Producer: Sidney Harmon. Running time: 89 minutes. Released by Allied Artists, February 13, 1955. Cast: Cornel Wilde, Richard Conte, Brian Donlevy, Jean Wallace, Robert Middleton, Lee Van Cleef, Earl Holliman, Helen Walker, Jay Adler, John Hoyt, Ted De Corsia, Helen Stanton, Roy Gordon, Whit Bissell, Steve Mitchell, Baynes Barron, James McCallion, Tony Michaels, Brian O'Hara, Rita Gould, Bruce Sharpe, Michael Mark, Philip Van Zandt, Donna Drew.

Baby Face Nelson. Director: Don Siegel. Producer: Al Zimbalist. Running time: 85 minutes. Released by United Artists, November 1957. Cast: Mickey Rooney, Carolyn Jones, Sir Cedric Hardwicke, Leo Gordon, Ted DeCorsia, Anthony Caruso, Jack Elam, Chris Dark, Emile Meyer, Dan Terranova, Dabbs Greer, Bob Osterloh, Dick Crocett, Paul Baxley, Thayer David, Ken Patterson, Sol Gorse, Gil Perkins, Tom Fadden, Lisa Davis, John Hoyt, Elisha Cook, Jr., Murray Alper, George E. Stone, Hubie Kerns, Paul and Richard Donnelly.

References

Biography of John Hoyt. Paramount Studios, January 1948.

Folkhart, Burt. "John Hoyt; Versatile Actor of Stage, Films." *Los Angeles Times*, September 21, 1991.

"John Hoyt Is Dead; Actor, 86, Played in Films and on TV." *New York Times*, September 21, 1991.

"John Hoyt: 1904—1991." *Starlog*, January 1992.
Obituary. *The Hollywood Reporter*, September 27, 1991.
Obituary. *Variety*, September 23, 1991.

Smith, Darr. "John Hoyt." *Los Angeles Daily News*, February 16, 1950.
Timpone, Anthony. "Puppet Master Speaks!" *Fangoria*, January 1986.

JOHN IRELAND

"Let them get me, let them do what they like. I don't care if they get me. I don't care if I live or die."— John Ireland in *The Gangster* (1947)

John Ireland was not your standard movie actor — his background, his looks, his Hollywood career, and his life behind the screen all represented an individual who was outside the realm of the norm. During Ireland's heyday in Tinseltown, he was seen in such classic fare as *My Darling Clementine* (1946) and *Red River* (1948), and earned an Academy Award nomination for his role in *All the King's Me*n (1949). But the actor's tenure near the top of the Hollywood heap was brief; he spent the bulk of his career in a series of westerns and foreign films, and in the late 1980s, he was compelled to place a newspaper advertisement proclaiming his desire for work. Despite his unfulfilled potential, however, Ireland was highly respected for his unquestionable talent, which he showed to good advantage in his four film noir appearances: *The Gangster* (1947), *Railroaded* (1947), *Raw Deal* (1948), and *Party Girl* (1958).

A native of Victoria, British Columbia, John Benjamin Ireland was born on January 30, 1914. When Ireland was still a child, his parents—a horse breeder and a school teacher — moved the family first to San Francisco, and later to Harlem in New York City, where they struggled to make ends meet. Never a top student, Ireland recalled in later years that he first left school in the seventh grade.

"It bored me," he said. "I wanted to go to work. But I was kept in school until I was 17. The only subject I was interested in was English literature. I flunked everything else, mainly because I carried around English books and read them in my other classes."

While attending summer camps during his teen years, Ireland became a promising swimmer, and honed his skill in New York's East River. On one occasion, Ireland competed with future Olympian and actor Johnny Weismuller, and on another, he participated in a grueling 15-mile marathon. After leaving high school, he used his aquatic prowess to perform underwater stunts at a local carnival, where he also worked as a barker.

Ireland's entry in the acting world came strictly by chance when he went inside the Davenport Free Theater in Manhattan one day, thinking he would take in a free show. Instead, he found that the company offered free acting training, along with room and board, and a dollar per day. Financially strapped and lacking a direction for his future, the young man signed up with the theater, where he ultimately appeared in a variety of productions, including plays by Ibsen, Shaw, and Shakespeare.

After a year at the Davenport Theater, Ireland moved on to apprenticeships at companies in Martha's Vineyard and Arden, Delaware; toured for six months with the James Hendrickson Shakespearian Company in Delaware; appeared in dramas with the Irish Repertory Players; and toured the country in *Peter Pan* with Clare Tree Major's Children's Theater. Back in New York, Ireland made his Broadway debut in the 1941 production of *Macbeth*, starring Maurice Evans and Judith Anderson, and over the next several years, appeared in a succession of Broadway plays, including *A Highland Fling, Doctors Disagree, Richard III*, and *A New Life*. He also toured the Atlantic coast with Sylvia Sidney in *Jane Eyre* and portrayed the miner in the road company of *The Moon is Down*.

Ireland's prolific performing schedule left little time for a personal life, but the actor did find time during the early 1940s to marry fellow actress Elaine Ruth Rosen, with whom he later had two sons, John Anthony and Peter Ray. The marriage didn't last, however, and in 1948 the couple divorced, with Elaine charging that Ireland "associated with other women [and] kept late hours without explanation." (Several years later, in 1952, Elaine sued Ireland for more than $30,000 in unpaid alimony and child support. A Superior Court judge ruled that the couple's original settlement agreement was "vague and uncertain," ordering the actor to pay only $2,207, at the rate of $25 a month.)

Meanwhile, Ireland's successes on the stage had by now caught the attention of Hollywood, and the actor was cast in 1945 in his first film, 20th Century-Fox's *A Walk in the Sun*, in which he was third billed as a letter-writing soldier named Windy. Prior to beginning work in the film, however, Ireland was reportedly encouraged by studio executives to have cosmetic surgery on his rather prominent nose. The actor refused, later revealing that his female fans were attracted to his "king-sized" proboscis.

"A woman in Phoenix wanted me to send her an impression of my nose. I presume she meant in plaster," Ireland once said. "Almost every letter mentions my 'virile' nose and most women ask for profile photographs. I've been puzzled by this.... Maybe it all started with Cyrano DeBergerac. He had a legend of being quite a guy with the ladies."

Signing a short-term contract with Fox, Ireland was seen in four features for the studio in 1946, including *My Darling Clementine*, a first-rate retelling of the conflict between Wyatt Earp and the infamous Clanton clan. The following year, he was seen in back-to-back film noir features for independent companies: Allied Artists' *The Gangster* (1947) and Eagle-Lion's *Railroaded* (1947).

The first was a bleak tale depicting a collection of quirky characters, including Shubunka (Barry Sullivan), a refined but neurotic mobster; Nick Jammey (Akim Tamiroff), an ice cream parlor owner and Shubunka's nervous right-hand man; and Karty (Ireland), described by one character as "once a first-class public accountant, only the racing bug got him. He's a goner." Although the feature centers on an attempt by a rival hood (Sheldon Leonard) to take over Shubunka's territory, a series of intertwining stories are presented, including Karty's gambling addiction and his increasing desperation that ultimately drives him to murder. Seen today, the film is fascinating in its depiction of the various characters and separate storylines, but it was panned by critics upon its release; Philip K. Scheuer of the *Los Angeles Times* found that the feature "glows fitfully but does not coalesce," the *Los Angeles Daily News*' Virginia Wright complained about the "choppy, excessively wordy script," and the reviewer for the *New York Times* wrote: "*The Gangster* is a shoddy example of picture making. Several of the characters talk so deep down inside their throats that at times their speech is incoherent."

Ireland fared better with his next film noir, the Anthony Mann-directed *Railroaded*. Here, the actor starred as Duke Martin, a vicious and thoroughly conscienceless hood who is characterized by his violent disdain of women and his penchant for perfuming the bullets of his gun. The film's action involves Duke's murder of a policeman during a holdup, his subsequent framing of an innocent local boy (Ed Kelly), and the efforts of the boy's sister (Sheila Ryan) to prove his innocence. After committing a string of murders, including his alcoholic girlfriend (Jane Randolph) and Chubb (Clancy Cooper), the mobster he works for, Duke is hunted down by a persistent cop (Hugh Beaumont) and dies in a shoot-out.

As the sadistic gunman, Ireland offered a vivid portrayal; he is especially memorable in a scene where he asks Chubb in a conversational tone, "Did I ever tell you about the guy I killed in Detroit? Worked for him.

Didn't treat me right. We were just talking like this, like you and me are. You know?" Without another word, Duke shoots his boss, unceremoniously shoves his body to the floor, and steals his cache of money. After the release of *Railroaded*, Ireland was praised by one reviewer for his "convincing performance," and the film was hailed by the critic for *Motion Picture Herald*, who described it as "a story produced on a modest budget ... which has emerged with a format as smooth as any similar picture in its category."

The following year, Ireland signed a contract with famed director Howard Hawks, and was cast in the role of Cherry Valance in the epic western *Red River* (1948), starring John Wayne and Montgomery Clift. Although Ireland's character was initially a significant part of the story, however, the role was later reduced; some sources maintained that Hawks cut the part as a result of Ireland's drinking on the set. But Ireland's son, John, later refuted this theory, stating that the actor quit the picture following a dispute with his agent Charlie Feldman.

"He felt he had been lied to and cheated out of money by his agent ... who, as it turned out, was partnered with Hawks in the company making the film. Hawks was furious when my dad said he wanted out and Hawks told [John] Wayne, 'that son of a bitch should do the part for nothing,'" Ireland's son said in a 1997 letter to the *Los Angeles Times*. "The only reason Cherry was around at the end of the film is that those scenes were shot before my dad's falling out with his agent and Hawks."

Ireland's conflict with Hawks abruptly ended his association with the director, and he followed *Red River* with his third film noir, *Raw Deal* (1948). Helmed by Anthony Mann, this feature starred Dennis O'Keefe as Joe Sullivan, a gangster imprisoned for a crime committed by his underworld boss Rick Coyle (Raymond Burr). Although Coyle craftily aids Joe's jailbreak, expecting him to be caught by authorities, Joe manages to slip through the extensive police dragnet, accompanied by Pat Regan (Claire Trevor), his faith-

ful moll, and Ann (Marsha Hunt), a social worker he abducts and later falls for. Meanwhile, having promised to meet with Joe to provide him with $50,000, Coyle instead sends his gunman, Fantail (Ireland), to kill him. At the deserted beachfront meeting place, Fantail holds Joe at gunpoint — directing him outside where "the sand is soft — you won't hurt yourself when you fall" — but Joe disarms Fantail and during a struggle, Ann shoots and kills him. Going after Coyle, Joe ultimately wreaks his revenge, but he is later gunned down in the street, where he dies in Ann's arms.

After earning mention for his "sharp portrayal" in *Raw Deal*, Ireland signed a seven-year contract with Columbia, and was cast in supporting roles in such features as *The Walking Hills* (1949), a low-budget, well-crafted western starring Randolph Scott; *Mr. Soft Touch* (1949), a rather unconvincing drama with Glenn Ford and Evelyn Keyes; *The Doolins of Oklahoma* (1949), an above-average Randolph Scott starrer; and *Anna Lucasta* (1949), based on the Broadway play by Philip Yordan. He also appeared in two stage plays in LaJolla, California, over the objections of studio executives (who reportedly told the actor, "What do you think we want you to turn into — a ham?")

During this period, Ireland was also loaned to other studios for several films, including *Joan of Arc* (1949), RKO's superb account of the life of the French peasant girl who became a Catholic saint; and Lippert's *I Shot Jesse James* (1949), which featured Ireland as Bob Ford, the "I" of the film's title. But his best film of this period — and, arguably, the best of Ireland's career — was Columbia's *All the King's Men* (1949). Playing a newspaper reporter who recounts the rise and fall of a powerful and ruthless politician (excellently portrayed by Oscar winner Broderick Crawford), Ireland earned an Academy Award nomination for Best Supporting Actor. Although he lost to Dean Jagger in *12 O'Clock High* (1949), Ireland's performance in the film and his subsequent accolades were viewed as the beginning of

his rise to cinematic stardom. Instead, the actor found himself promptly cast in a relatively insignificant role in *Convicted* (1950), starring Broderick Crawford and Glenn Ford. Outraged by what he termed the studio's "virtual servitude," Ireland balked at the role and was placed on suspension. A Columbia representative claimed that Ireland had "previously informed the studio that he would report for work but would not perform, and that he intended to cost the studio a lot of money." According to Ireland's attorney, however, the actor had reported to the set as instructed and was "put out of the picture."

"They told me I was being just another temperamental actor, that I should be ashamed of myself," Ireland told *Los Angeles Daily News* columnist Darr Smith. "Of course this refers to the fact that the studio owns us, body, soul, and temperament." Charging that the studio was "maliciously conspiring" to deprive him of the opportunity to become a star, Ireland petitioned the Superior Court to release him from his contract, and later agreed to give the studio 25 percent of his gross earnings for the next five years.

Meanwhile, although his appearance in *All the King's Men* did not result in better

screen roles for Ireland, his association with the film did have an immediate impact on his personal life. During shooting of the feature, Ireland began dating co-star Joanne Dru, whom he had first met when both appeared in *Red River*. Following a whirlwind romance, the couple married on August 7, 1949 (just weeks after Dru's former husband, crooner Dick Haymes, wed the ex-spouse of Errol Flynn). The wedding took place in the Valencia Hotel in LaJolla, with director John Ford's daughter, Barbara, serving as maid of honor, and actors Gregory Peck and Mel Ferrer standing up for Ireland.

During the next several years, Ireland was seen in a string of westerns, including *Vengeance Valley* (1951), starring Burt Lancaster and Robert Walker; *Red Mountain* (1951), where he portrayed the notorious real-life Confederate captain William Clarke Quantrill; *Little Big Horn* (1951), which centered on a group of calvarymen trying to warn General George Custer of a Sioux ambush; and *The Bushwackers* (1952), in which Ireland was top-billed as an ex–Civil War soldier. The actor didn't object to his frequent appearances in these oaters, however, and offered a philosophical view of his roles in the films.

"In New York, it was mostly Shakespeare; here it's mostly westerns," Ireland said in 1953. "And in these things I feel like I'm not acting at all; just wandering around in clothes I like to wear, feeling comfortable."

This stance notwithstanding, Ireland also proclaimed that "an actor's career is limited," and in 1953 teamed with cinematographer Lee Garmes to co-direct and co-produce *Hannah Lee* (also known as *Outlaw Territory*), believed to be the first western shot in 3-D. Along with stars MacDonald Carey and Joanne Dru, the actor's younger son, Peter, also had a small role in the film.

"In the main, the career of an actor is short. And not always so sweet as the fan magazines would have it," Ireland told *Los Angeles Daily News* columnist Howard Mc-Clay. "My thinking about a career as a director is based on the fact [that] there's a better future in it. Acting's fine, but directing's better when it comes to having a confidential credit talk with your banker."

But Ireland's initial outing behind the camera was a disappointment; several decades later, MacDonald Carey told *The Big Reel* newspaper that the film's limited production values led to its poor showing at the box office.

"[John] played the hero, I played the heavy. We'd get together at night, write a scene, and do it the next day," Carey said in a 1992 interview. "Unfortunately, it didn't do well because the 3-D optics were off and everyone left the theater rubbing their eyes."

The following year, Ireland directed his second feature, *The Fast and the Furious* (1954), in which he starred as a man on the lam after being framed for murder. The low-budget film was only moderately successful and would be the actor's last directorial effort, but by now, Ireland had more pressing matters with which to contend. Having appeared since the early 1950s on such television programs as *Philco Television Playhouse*, Ireland was tapped for the starring role in the small screen series *The Adventures of Ellery Queen*. Shortly before shooting was to begin, however, Ireland was discharged from the show. The actor promptly filed a $1.7 million breach of contract and slander lawsuit against the program's producers, Norvin Productions, alleging that the dismissal was based on what the company termed Ireland's "supposed disloyalty to the United States of America."

"I am an actor and a director," Ireland said. "I don't know anything about politics. I am frank to admit it. My one political activity has been to vote on election day just like any other American."

Norvin countered that Ireland had been dismissed because he had recently entered into an agreement to endorse a tobacco product in competition with one of the show's sponsors. Despite this initial stance, the production company settled the suit out of court two months later for a "substantial" sum, and issued a statement that Ireland was "a loyal American citizen who has never committed any act which would reflect unfavorably upon his character or patriotism."

Professionally, Ireland resumed his screen career with such films as *Southwest Passage* (1954), in which he was again teamed with wife Joanne Dru; *The Good Die Young* (1954), a gripping crime thriller starring Laurence Harvey (with whom Ireland developed a life-long friendship); *Queen Bee* (1955), starring Joan Crawford as the manipulative, dominating woman of the film's title; *The Glass Cage* (1955), a fairly interesting mystery set in a carnival; and *The Gunslinger* (1956), an off-beat western produced and directed by Roger Corman.

Soon after the release of *The Gunslinger*, Ireland's personal life exploded into the press again, this time as a result of an incident between the actor and his wife following a Fourth of July celebration at the home of actor Mark Stevens. Initial press reports claimed that during an altercation after the party, Ireland broke his wife's nose and blackened both of her eyes. Later, Ireland reportedly visited Dru's beside at Cedars of Lebanon Hospital, and swallowed a handful of sleeping pills.

"He came into the hospital room asking for a reconciliation," an unnamed source said in the *New York Daily Mirror*. "He yanked out the bottle of sleeping pills and threatened to swallow them if she didn't forgive him. He swallowed the pills. The nurse screamed and grappled with him." Ireland's stomach was pumped and he was admitted to the hospital along with his wife.

After the couple's release from the hospital, however, Dru insisted that she had been hurt as a result of a minor car accident, and Ireland claimed that he'd inadvertently taken too many sleeping pills during an airplane flight earlier on the day of the incident. Despite these assertions, Dru announced less than a week later that she and Ireland had separated.

"We feel we can work out our problems better if we are away from each other for a few weeks," Dru told *New York Daily News* columnist Florabel Muir. "And I need absolute rest for a few days to pull myself together." According to Dru, however, the trial separation "only served to convince her that their marriage was a failure," and in November 1956, the actress filed for divorce. (Three years later, in 1959, Ireland made headlines again when he became embroiled in a widely publicized affair with then 16-year-old actress Tuesday Weld. The 45-year-old actor told the press that he would ask Weld to marry him "if there wasn't such a difference in our ages ... that and her mother are the only things that stop me." Ireland was later linked with several other starlets, including Natalie Wood, but in 1962, the actor settled down for a third try at marriage. Wife number three was 26-year-old Daphne Cameron, the ex-wife of oil millionaire George Cameron — and mother of a 6-year-old son named Cameron Cameron. The couple remained together until Ireland's death.)

During the next several years, Ireland's screen career witnessed a steady decline, but he was seen in a handful of memorable features, including *Gunfight at the O.K. Corral* (1957), in which he turned in a fine performance as outlaw Johnny Ringo, and *Spartacus* (1960), a sweeping epic about the slave rebellion that swept Rome in 73 B.C. Ireland was also seen during this period in the last of his film noir features, *Party Girl* (1958). Here, Ireland was fourth-billed as Louis Canetto, a gunman for big-shot mobster Rico Angelo (Lee J. Cobb). Set in Chicago during the 1930s, the story focused on Thomas Farrell (Robert Taylor), a corrupt mob lawyer who is determined to extricate himself from his lifestyle after falling for a showgirl (Cyd Charisse). Farrell eventually succeeds — but only after Rico accidentally douses himself with acid and is shot by police. As Rico's sleazy henchman, Ireland had little to do, but he was particularly memorable in a scene in which he tries to seduce Farrell's girl and gets beaten with a hairbrush for his troubles. His performance in the film earned only lukewarm reviews, however; although the *Los Angeles Times'* Philip K. Scheuer included Ireland in his mention of the "good cast," another critic referred to the actor's "routine" portrayal of the gangster, and he was merely labeled "adequate" in the *New York Times*.

With the onset of the 1960s, Ireland was seen in a series of foreign productions, including *No Time to Kill* (1961) in Sweden; *The Ceremony* (1963) in Spain; *Hate for Hate* (1967) in Italy; and *Dirty Heroes* (1967) in France. He also appeared in such thrillers as *I Saw What You Did* (1965), which reteamed him with his *Queen Bee* co-star, Joan Crawford, and introduced a new catchphrase into the popular culture.

"It became a little fad for everybody to call up somebody [and say 'I saw what you did']," Ireland said in a 1992 interview in *Classic Images*. "Even women will call up married men and ask, 'Well, was it good for you, too?' and hang up. If the wife would happen to pick up the other phone and overhear this, there was hell to pay."

In addition to his screen work during the 1960s, Ireland landed regular roles on two television series, *The Cheaters* and *Rawhide*, and was seen in guest spots on such programs as *Alfred Hitchcock Presents*, *Branded*, *The Man Who Never Was*, *Gunsmoke*, and *The Iron Horse*. The next two decades would see him in a variety of television movies, including *The Girl on the Late, Late Show* (1974), *The Millionaire* (1978), *The Courage of Kavik, the Wolf Dog* (1980), and *Marilyn: The Untold Story* (1980), in which he portrayed veteran Hollywood director John Huston. Ireland was also part of the cast of the short-lived series *Cassie and Company* in 1982; continued appearing in numerous foreign productions; and was seen in such forgettable American features as *The House of Seven Corpses* (1974) and *Satan's Cheerleaders* (1977), both cheapie horror films co-starring John Carradine; *Delta Fox* (1979), a humdrum crime drama; *The Shape of Things to Come* (1979), an unsuccessful remake of the 1936 science fiction classic *Things to Come*; and *Thunder Run* (1986), a horrid actioner notable only as the final screen appearance of actor Forrest Tucker. The sole bright spot during this part of Ireland's cinematic career came with his appearance in *Farewell, My Lovely* (1975), a well-done adaptation of the Raymond Chandler novel, starring Robert Mitchum and Charlotte Rampling.

By the late 1980s, Ireland was desperate for work. Although he continued to sporadically guest in such television series as the *Fall Guy* and *Airwolf*, the actor was seeking "real" jobs.

"I don't consider that acting," he said of the television spots. "That has no guts. You just go on, and that's it."

In a last-ditch effort to jump-start his flagging career, Ireland in March 1987 placed a full-page, two-color advertisement on the back page of *The Hollywood Reporter*. Setting the actor back nearly $2,000, the ad simply read: "I'm an actor. PLEASE ... let me act."

"It was part humorous and part serious," the 73-year-old actor said in the *Los Angeles Times*. "I was watching *A Chorus Line* the other day and there's a song in which a character says, 'I wanna dance for you.' Well, I wanna act for you, and I'm just not getting the opportunities. I felt it was time to do something about it."

After placing the advertisement, Ireland reported that his "phone hasn't stopped ringing," and a short time later was cast in *Bonanza: The Next Generation* (1988), playing Captain Cartwright, the brother of Ben Cartwright. (Actor Lorne Greene, who originated the role of Ben in the popular TV series *Bonanza*, was signed for the TV movie, but died shortly before production commenced.) The movie was intended to serve as the pilot for a weekly syndicated series, but the program never materialized. Ireland was also sent the script for the Kathleen Turner–Burt Reynolds comedy *Switching Channels* (1988); was told there was a possible role for him in a feature film, *Collision Course* (1989), with Jay Leno and Pat Morita; and was considered for a regular role as a U.S. marshal on a Canadian series, *Bordertown*, which ran from 1988 to 1991.

Ultimately, Ireland would not be involved with any of these projects. Instead, he appeared in such television features as *Perry Mason: The Case of the Lady in the Lake* (1988), and on the big screen in *Sundown: The Vampire in Retreat* (1989), a serio-comic horror story, and *Waxwork II: Lost in Time* (1992), a fantasy-horror film in which Ireland played King Arthur. But Ireland's search for quality acting parts abruptly ended when, after a brief illness, the actor died of leukemia at the Santa Barbara Cottage Hospital. He was 78 years old.

While well-respected and extensive, John Ireland's career was also unusual and often frustrating, consisting primarily of supporting roles in major films, or leading roles in run-of-the-mill, low-budget features. This conundrum notwithstanding, Ireland managed to distinguish himself in numerous films, demonstrating an unquestionable talent and far-reaching versatility in such features as *Railroaded*, *The Bushwackers* and, of course, *All the King's Men*. Possessing an unwavering devotion to his craft, Ireland continued to perform until his health prevented him from doing so; an anecdote told by John Sturges, who directed Ireland in two features, provided a fitting illustration of Ireland's determination to act. According to Sturges, he was in the process of casting the 1949 western, *The Walking Hills*, when he encountered Ireland.

"I saw him walking on the sidewalk and he said, 'I'm starving — I need a job,' and I said, 'You've got it!' because I knew what he could do," Sturges said in a *Big Reel* interview shortly after the actor's death. "Likeable guy. And a very good actor. I'll miss him."

Film Noir Filmography

The Gangster. Director: Gordon Wiles. Producers: Maurice and Frank King. Running time: 84 minutes. Released by Allied Artists, October 1947. Cast: Barry Sullivan, Belita, Joan Lorring, Akim Tamiroff, Henry Morgan, John Ireland, Fifi D'Orsay, Virginia Christine, Sheldon Leonard, Leif Erickson, Charles McGraw, John Kellogg, Elisha Cook, Jr., Ted Hecht, Jeff Corey.

Railroaded. Director: Anthony Mann. Producer: Charles F. Riesner. Running time: 71 minutes. Released by Eagle-Lion, October 30, 1947. Cast: John Ireland, Sheila Ryan, Hugh Beaumont, Jane Randolph, Ed Kelly, Charles D. Brown, Clancy

Cooper, Peggy Converse, Hermine Sterler, Keefe Brasselle, Roy Gordon.

Raw Deal. Director: Anthony Mann. Producer: Edward Small. Running time: 79 minutes. Released by Eagle-Lion, July 8, 1948. Cast: Dennis O'Keefe, Claire Trevor, Marsha Hunt, John Ireland, Raymond Burr, Curt Conway, Chili Williams, Richard Fraser, Whit Bissell.

Party Girl. Director: Nicholas Ray. Producer: Joe Pasternak. Running time: 99 minutes. Released by MGM, October 28, 1958. Cast: Robert Taylor, Cyd Charisse, Lee J. Cobb, John Ireland, Kent Smith, Claire Kelly, Corey Allen, Lewis Charles, David Opatoshu, Kem Dibbs, Patrick McVey, Barbara Lang, Myrna Hansen, Betty Utey, Jack Lambert.

References

"Actor Ireland's Suit Closed by Settlement." *Los Angeles Times*, May 22, 1954.

"Actor John Ireland Files $1,756,000 Slander Suit." *Los Angeles Times*, March 3, 1954.

"Actor John Ireland's Alimony Row Tangled." *Los Angeles Examiner*, June 19, 1952.

"Actor John Ireland Suspended by Studio." *Los Angeles Times*, December 21, 1949.

"Actor John Ireland Will Marry." *Los Angeles Herald-Examiner*, July 21, 1962.

Biography of John Ireland. Paramount Pictures, February 1967.

Biography of John Ireland. 20th Century-Fox Studio, circa 1945.

Carroll, Harrison. "Actor John Ireland to Marry" *Los Angeles Herald-Examiner*, July 22, 1962.

Ireland, John Jr. "Duking It Out" (Letter to the Editor). *Los Angeles Times*, April 27, 1997.

"Ireland Ordered to Pay Alimony, Child Support." *Los Angeles Examiner*, June 24, 1952.

"John Ireland Agrees to Settling of Suit." *New York Times*, May 22, 1954.

"John Ireland Escapes Court Contempt Fine." *Hollywood Citizen-News*, June 24, 1952.

"John Ireland in Blue Knight." *Los Angeles Times*, September 22, 1976.

"John Ireland in 'I Saw What You Did.'" *Classic Images*, December 1992.

"John Ireland, 78; Acted in 200 Movies." *Chicago Sun-Times*, March 26, 1992.

"John Ireland, 78, Dies of Leukemia." *Santa Barbara Metro*, March 26, 1992.

"John Ireland Sued for Back Alimony." *Hollywood Citizen-News*, March 22, 1952.

Lambert, Bruce. "John Ireland, 78, Longtime Actor with Role in 'All the King's Men.'" *New York Times*, March 23, 1997.

"'Marriage Failure'—Joanne Dru." *Los Angeles Examiner*, November 6, 1956.

McClay, Howard. "Ireland Looks to the Future." *Los Angeles Daily News*, August 28, 1953.

"Miss Dru Has Shiner; John Denies Rift." *Hollywood Citizen-News*, July 6, 1956.

Mosby, Aline. "The Great Profile Is Not Dead." *Los Angeles Daily News*, circa 1945.

Muir, Florabel. "Joanne, John Cool Off—Apart." *New York Daily News*, July 11, 1956.

"Norvin TV Firm in Statement on Ireland Suit." *Hollywood Citizen-News*, March 4, 1954.

Obituary. *The London Times*, March 24, 1992.

Parsons, Louella O. "Joanne Dru, Ireland Wed." *Los Angeles Examiner*, August 8, 1949.

"Pills Fell John Ireland After Row with Joanne." *New York Mirror*, July 7, 1956.

"Remembering Ireland." *New York Daily News*, March 24, 1992.

Scheuer, Philip K. "In Debut, John Ireland Directs 2D, 3D, Color and Wide Screen Western." *Los Angeles Times*, June 21, 1953.

Smith, Darr. "John Ireland." *Los Angeles Daily News*, March 31, 1949.

_____. "John Ireland." *Los Angeles Daily News*, February 21, 1950.

Spiller, Nancy. "Help Wanted." *Los Angeles Herald Examiner*, March 27, 1987.

"The Luck of the Ireland." *Los Angeles Times*, April 5, 1987.

"The Passing Scene." *The Big Reel*, May 1992.

PAUL KELLY

"If you weren't Lil's brother, I'd push your lyin' face out through the back of your head."— Paul Kelly in *Fear in the Night* (1947)

Paul Kelly's life was replete with hills and valleys. Once the darling of Broadway, he spent time in prison for manslaughter. Enabled after many years to marry his true love, he lost her in a tragic automobile accident. And shunned by Hollywood after his conviction, he ended up making one of the most significant comebacks in the history of Tinseltown. Along the way, Kelly appeared in an estimated 80 stage plays and — by his own estimation — more than 400 films, including four offerings from the era of film noir: *Fear in the Night* (1947), *Crossfire* (1947), *The File on Thelma Jordon* (1949), and *Side Street* (1950).

Born in the Flatbush section of Brooklyn, New York, Paul Michael Kelly entered the world on August 9, 1899, the ninth of ten children. Kelly was attracted to performing from an early age; the family home was located near the old Vitagraph Studios and, as a child, he often watched the production of silent films from a perch atop a stepladder.

The youngster made his stage debut at the age of seven in the David Belasco production of *The Grand Army Man*, in a cast that included David Warfield, Jane Cowl, and Antoinette Perry (for whom the "Tony" stage award would later be named). Kelly landed the job through his sister, Doris, a dancer in the show, who learned that the producer was seeking a boy who could whistle. According to one account, when Doris brought her little brother with her to rehearsal, Kelly "couldn't whistle worth a hoot," but he looked "picturesque" carrying a drum, and was hired for the part. Most sources say, however, that Kelly's ability to blow shrilly through his teeth earned him the job. Regardless of the circumstances, Kelly performed in the play six nights and two matinees a week.

The story of Kelly's entry into the cinematic world is even more colorful than the rationale behind his stage debut. Because of the family's proximity to the Vitagraph studios, producers frequently borrowed furniture from Kelly's mother, who reportedly suggested one fateful day that they "borrow" her son as well. In addition to appearing in countless one-reel pictures for the studio, Kelly gained further experience on his first stage tour at the age of nine.

"We did a Shakespearean repertoire that included most of the famous plays," Kelly recalled years later. "If that doesn't teach a youngster something about acting, nothing will."

As one of the first of Vitagraph's juvenile performers to receive a stage credit, Kelly became known as "the Vitagraph boy," and went on to appear in one of the first two-reelers ever filmed, *Billy's Burglar*, in 1912. Despite his busy schedule of acting assignments, Kelly managed to eke out a sketchy education, but by the age of 17, his energies were completely focused on his career. During the next several years, the actor divided his time between the stage and the screen, appearing with a young Helen Hayes in *Penrod*, playing the lead in Stuart Walker's *Seventeen*, and earning acclaim for his "fervor and conviction" in Owen Davis' *Up the Ladder*. He was also seen in numerous silent features, including *Knights of the Square Table* (1917), *Anne of Green Gables* (1919) (opposite Mary Miles Minter), *Uncle Sam of Freedom Ridge* (1920), *The Old Oaken Bucket* (1921), and *The Great Adventure* (1921).

"[They] used to call us nickel actors," Kelly said in a 1949 interview, "because most of the gang worked legitimate theater nights, and took a subway ride for a nickel out to Vitagraph for daytime jobs."

In the late 1920s, Kelly earned acclaim for his performance in the Broadway production of *Bad Girl*, opposite Sylvia Sidney, then went to Hollywood where he was seen in *The New Klondike* (1926), directed by Lewis Milestone; *Slide, Kelly, Slide* (1927), starring William Haines and Sally O'Neil; and *Special Delivery* (1927), a comedy helmed by actor Roscoe "Fatty" Arbuckle. But at this point, as Kelly teetered on the brink of stardom, fate stepped in to turn his life upside down.

Since arriving in Tinseltown, Kelly had become involved with actress Dorothy Mackaye, the wife of musical comedy star Ray Raymond and mother of a young girl, Valeria. After several months, the love triangle reached a climax when Raymond suffered fatal injuries following a fist fight with Kelly on April 27, 1927. In a statement to police, Kelly stated that he had informed Raymond two months earlier that he was in love with his wife and "since that time, there had been ill feelings between the two." The animosity between Kelly and Raymond culminated with the latter's return to California from the road production of *Castles in the Air*.

"I heard he was making wisecracks about me and his wife, and was saying he would get me if he knew where I was," Kelly said. "I called him on the phone and he asked me to come over to his place.... One thing led to another and finally I slapped him. Then we started fighting. I knocked him down and when he wouldn't get up I left the house." The altercation was witnessed by the Raymond's housekeeper, who told police that her employer made no attempt to defend himself.

Raymond's wife, Dorothy Mackaye, reportedly returned home later that evening to find her husband in bed, but when she awoke the following morning, Raymond was on the floor, struggling to breathe. The actor was rushed to the hospital, but he slipped into a coma a short time later and died of a brain hemorrhage induced by the blows he sustained during the fight. After Raymond's death, Mackaye revealed that she had suffered physical abuse from her husband, saying "he wasn't very kind to me."

"He was always accusing me of terrible things, of being too friendly with Paul and other people," Mackaye said in a statement to authorities. "My relationship with Paul was always a noble thing. I didn't want to give it up just because Ray acted so silly."

Kelly was arrested on suspicion of murder and Mackaye, along with a doctor who attended Raymond shortly before his death, was charged with compounding a felony in seeking to conceal circumstances surrounding Raymond's death. The charges against the doctor were later dropped, but after separate trials in the spring of 1927, both Kelly and Mackaye were convicted. Kelly was sentenced to a term of one to ten years in San Quentin prison for manslaughter, and Mackaye was ordered to serve one to three years in the same institution for conspiracy. According to press reports, Kelly gamely announced, "I can whip this," before beginning his sentence.

"I'm going to work and study and fight my way back," Kelly said. "I don't care how long it takes."

Assigned to the prison's jute mill (where plant fibers were used to make products such as sacking, cordage and backing materials for carpet and linoleum), Kelly served two years and one month of his sentence before earning his parole. Mackaye, meanwhile, was released from the prison after 10 months; upon leaving San Quentin, she told reporters, "If you ever hear of me falling in love again you'll know I've lost my mind." She and Kelly never mentioned each other, and it was assumed by the public that the romance between the two was permanently over.

According to the terms of his release, Kelly was prohibited from marrying for 18 months, and was required to take a job as a clerk at $30 a week. After a few weeks working as a clerk, however, Kelly appealed to his parole officer to allow his return to acting and he promptly landed a role in a Broadway production, *The Nine-Fifteen Revue*— at the required $30 weekly salary. Upon the expiration of his parole term, Kelly's salary was immediately increased to $125 a week and he exercised his right to marry — on February 10, 1931, Kelly and Dorothy Mackaye became man and wife.

"I'll never act again," Mackaye said. "I don't want a career. I just want to be a good wife and mother."

Kelly and Mackaye bought a 45-acre ranch in Tarzana, California, Kelly adopted his wife's daughter Valeria (later known as Mimi), and for several years, the couple lived in apparent bliss. But tragedy struck again less than a decade later when Mackaye, driving home from Los Angeles, swerved to avoid an oncoming car and was pinned when the automobile turned over in a ditch. She died from internal injuries a few hours later, on January 5, 1940. (Kelly married actress Mardelle Zwicker the following year — the couple remained together until the actor's death.)

Professionally, Kelly tried to return to his screen career after his parole, but found that the doors in Hollywood were closed to him. Undaunted, he continued his work on the stage, appearing in one hit after another, including *Hobo*, *Adam Had Two Sons*, *The Great Magoo*, and *Angel*. Kelly's success on the stage once again brought Hollywood running, and while touring in the latter production, he was signed to a contract by 20th Century-Fox executives Darryl F. Zanuck and Joseph Schenck, who promptly cast him in *Broadway Through a Keyhole* (1933).

"We have signed Paul Kelly on the dotted line on a long-term contract," Zanuck announced. "There may be some reaction, but we believe the boy is entitled to his chance."

Before long, Kelly was seen in a string of films for Fox and in loanouts to other studios, including *Death on the Diamond* (1934), a sports drama for Metro; *Side Streets* (1934), a Warner Bros. production co-starring Aline MacMahon; *Blind Date* (1934), a cliché-ridden drama produced by Columbia; and RKO's *Star of Midnight* (1935), starring William Powell and Jean Arthur. During the next decade, Kelly appeared in a whopping 55 movies; although he became known as "The King of the Bs," he was seen during this period in such memorable features as *The Roaring Twenties* (1939), a first-rate Warner Bros. gangster film starring James Cagney and Humphrey Bogart; *Flight Command* (1940), an action-packed war drama; *Ziegfield Girl* (1941), an MGM extravaganza featuring Hedy Lamarr, Lana Turner, and Judy Garland; *Flying Tigers* (1942), in which he played a weary wartime pilot with failing eyesight; and *The Story of Dr. Wassell* (1944), with Gary Cooper in the title role of the real-life missionary doctor. Also, in 1942, Kelly starred in the 15-episode Columbia serial, *The Secret Code*, playing a police lieutenant working against enemy agents, and he returned to the stage in 1945 for *Beggars Are Coming to Town*.

Then in 1947, Kelly stepped into the dark world of noir, with featured roles in two films from the era, *Fear in the Night* and *Crossfire*. The first, adapted from a short story by Cornell Woolrich, begins as a man's voice describes a frightening dream sequence: "At first, all I could see was this face coming to-

ward me. Then I saw the room. A queer, mirrored room. And somehow, I was inside it. There was danger there, I knew that. I wanted to turn and run, but I couldn't. It seemed as if my brain was handcuffed. And I had to do what I'd come to do." In the hazy dream, a man comes upon a couple breaking into a safe inside the "queer" room. A struggle ensues and, in self-defense, the narrator kills the man, hides his body inside a closet in the room, and pockets the key. As it turns out, the dream is a real-life nightmare for Vince Grayson (DeForrest Kelley), who soon realizes that he actually committed the murder. Vince turns to his detective brother-in-law Cliff Herlihy (Kelly) for help, but Cliff initially dismisses the wild tale. When Cliff later learns that Vince was involved with the killing, he is furious, accusing him of concocting the entire story to mask his guilt: "You came to me for help, but you didn't have guts enough to come clean," he says. "No—you had to cook up a dream. I can respect a guy no matter how rotten a crime he's committed who'll own up to it. I can understand a guy who'll deny it flatly. But a guy that'll come to someone, trading on the fact he's married to his sister, abuse his common sense, and make a fool out of him like you did to me — I got no use for." Despite his anger, the crafty cop suspects there is more to the story, and after investigating the case on his own, Cliff discovers that Vince was hypnotized into committing the murder by a neighbor, Lewis Belnap (Robert Emmett Keane). Working with Vince, Cliff sets a trap that nearly backfires when Belnap hypnotizes Vince into attempting suicide in a nearby lake, but Cliff arrives in time to save Vince from drowning, and Belnap is killed in a car crash while trying to flee.

After earning mention for his "believable" performance in *Fear in the Night*, Kelly was seen in his second film noir, *Crossfire*, which starred Robert Ryan as a violent racist who murders a Jewish war veteran, and Robert Young as the determined detective who solves the case. In a relatively minor role, Kelly was billed merely as "the Man," portraying a mentally unbalanced fellow who seeks out a world-weary bar girl, Ginny (Gloria Grahame, in an Academy Award-nominated role). In Kelly's only scene, his character shows up at the girl's apartment, but he finds an ex-serviceman (George Cooper) there instead and tells him that he is Ginny's husband: "She was a tramp when I married her. I didn't know it at first, but I knew it before we were married.... But I still want her. I still love her." The man then changes his story — more than once — telling the former GI, "I met her the same as you did, at the joint. I can't keep away from her. I want to marry her, and she won't have me. Do you believe that? Well, that's a lie, too. I don't love her and I don't want to marry her. She makes good money there. You got any money on you?"

By now, two decades after the death of Ray Raymond and Kelly's subsequent imprisonment, Hollywood seemed to have forgotten all about the crime. Kelly's press releases included no mention of the incident, and feature stories in newspapers and magazines effortlessly glossed over the years between 1927 and 1931, preferring to focus on

such matters as the actor's polo playing prowess and his fondness for the Brooklyn Dodgers baseball team. Even as early as 1934, just a few years after Kelly's release from prison, he was identified in a popular movie magazine merely as "a smiling Irish lad with a friendly manner and a firm handclasp."

"Everyone on the set likes Paul Kelly," the photo caption stated. "Everyone off the set does, too."

Kelly's professional comeback reached new heights of success shortly after he completed his work on *Crossfire*, when he was contacted by famed Broadway producer Kermit Bloomgarden regarding his upcoming play, *Command Decision*. Based on the novel by William Wister Haines, *Command Decision* focused on a group of air force generals during World War II and their struggle to balance effectiveness and morality while making life-and-death decisions. Kelly was offered the plum role of Brig. Gen. K.C. Dennis.

"It didn't take me long to answer him.... In my bones, I felt that my hour had struck," Kelly wrote in a 1948 article. "During the rehearsals ... neither Bloomgarden nor Haines made any comment on my performance. It wasn't until the last night in Baltimore, on the eve of the opening [on Broadway], that Bloomgarden came up to me and said, 'Paul, you'll be great. You can't miss.' Just before the curtain on the second night, Bloomgarden came into my dressing room and sat down. 'What do you think of the notices?' he asked. Before I could reply he continued, 'Paul ... your name will be up in lights tomorrow night.' I tried to voice my thanks, but I blew my lines. Had I started to say anything I would have blubbered like a child."

Kelly's portrayal of the tough but compassionate general earned him universal accolades, including the Variety Critics Award, the Donaldson Award, and the Tony Award. The actor performed in the play for 52 weeks on Broadway, then another 20 weeks on the road. Although Kelly was disappointed when the starring role in the 1948 screen version of the play went to Clark Gable, he acknowledged that the play was the most gratifying experience of his career.

"A phantom I had pursued for 40 years had become a reality," Kelly once said.

After the close of *Command Decision*, Kelly returned to films, appearing in his two final noirs, *The File on Thelma Jordon* (1949) and *Side Street* (1950). The former focuses on the title character, ably portrayed by Barbara Stanwyck, who murders her wealthy aunt and suckers the district attorney, Cleve Marshall (Wendell Corey), into believing that she is innocent. But chief investigator Miles Scott (Kelly), convinced of her guilt from the outset, is unmoved by her air of imperious innocence during questioning. (At one point, Thelma even chastises Scott for his techniques: "In your dealings with me — your questioning — your suspicion — don't be sarcastic. I'm not a criminal, don't treat me so." Without missing a beat, Scott wryly rejoins, "You almost have me apologizing. But I'll control myself.") In prosecuting Thelma for the killing, Cleve purposely bungles her court case, resulting in her acquittal. He soon learns, however, that Thelma is not only a murderer, but that she is married and planned the crime with her husband, Tony Laredo (Richard Rober). Thelma later leaves town with Laredo, but she has a last-minute change of heart and causes their car to crash, surviving long enough to confess her crimes to police and tell Cleve: "I couldn't go on with him. You did that for me."

Although one critic complained that Kelly "never really gets a chance to stretch his legs and show just what he is capable of," the actor was praised as "particularly good" in the *Los Angeles Times* and singled out for his "intelligent performance" in the *Los Angeles Examiner*. The *Examiner* critic also offered high praise for the film, writing: "If *Thelma Jordon* is the harbinger of the kind of pictures we may expect from Hollywood in 1950, we're all in for a whale of a year of moviegoing. Expertly produced, directed, and enacted from a tightly written and somewhat offbeat thriller screenplay, *Thelma Jordon* is the kind of modern melodrama which sends you from the theater with that not-too-common reaction of 'That one certainly was worth the money!'"

In *Side Street*, the last noir of Kelly's career, the actor was once again on the right side of the law, portraying a police detective investigating the murder of a local "B" girl known as "Lucky" Colner (Adele Jergens). The case becomes more complex when part-time letter carrier Joe Norson (Farley Granger) steals a cache of money from an office, not knowing that it is actually a blackmail payoff involving Lucky's murder. Joe — who is married with a baby on the way —finds himself in even more trouble when he unsuccessfully tries to return the money, leaves the cash with a friend, and later finds that the friend has been murdered and the money is gone. Hounded by local hoods for the cash, Joe is abducted and taken on a high-speed chase through the streets of New York, with police close behind. After a shoot-out, Joe's abductors are killed and he is injured, but he is reunited with his wife by the film's end and the narrator informs the viewer that "he's going to be all right."

Following *Side Street*— in which he was noted in the *Los Angeles Times* for "appear-[ing] to advantage"— Kelly returned once again to Broadway, starring in *The Country Girl* as a washed-up, alcoholic actor who is given one last chance at resurrecting his career. Co-starring Uta Hagen, the play earned rave reviews; the screen version was made in 1954 by Columbia, with Bing Crosby portraying the role originated by Kelly on the stage, and co-starring William Holden and Grace Kelly.

Back in Hollywood, Kelly was seen in a pair of westerns, *Springfield Rifle* (1952), with Gary Cooper, and *Gunsmoke* (1953), an Audie Murphy starrer. He also starred in *The Painted Hills* (1951), notable primarily as the last MGM film featuring the popular collie, Lassie, and a taut thriller, *Split Second* (1953), the first feature directed by actor Dick Powell. But Kelly's performing scheduled was halted in early 1953, when he suffered a major heart attack and was hospitalized in critical condition at St. John's Hospital in Santa Monica. (Perhaps assuming Kelly's imminent demise, most newspaper accounts focused less on his hospitalization than on raking up the lurid details of his manslaughter conviction and imprisonment.) The actor later recovered, however, and wasted little time in returning to the big screen in such features as *The High and the Mighty* (1954), a well-done disaster film starring John Wayne and Claire Trevor; *Duffy of San Quentin* (1954), with Kelly in the title role of the renowned prison reformer; and *Storm Center* (1956), starring Bette Davis as a librarian accused of communism.

Despite Kelly's continued film appearances, the actor had been in guarded health since his 1953 heart attack, and in August 1956, he was hospitalized following a mild stroke. The actor recovered sufficiently to complete filming on a picture, but three months later, on November 6, 1956, Kelly suffered a massive heart attack and died before doctors could reach his home. He was 57 years old. (After the actor's death, his two final films were released: *Curfew Breakers* [1957], in which Kelly portrayed a community leader investigating a murder by a drug-crazed youth; and *Bailout at 43,000* [1957], a routine drama focusing on the development of a special ejection seat for fighter planes.)

Although Kelly's impressive stage and screen career is often viewed in the context of his incredible comeback from his manslaughter conviction and imprisonment, the actor possessed an undeniable talent that served him well throughout his career. Kelly was never considered a major star, but he was certainly respected throughout the Hollywood community for the versatility that allowed him to perform with equal aplomb in dramas and comedies alike. A 1936 *Boston Post* feature on the actor perhaps came closest to describing his unique talent:

"Nobody has ever doubted his talents as an actor," wrote Edith Dietz. "In a place of personalities, such as Hollywood, his gifts have been at various times overlooked, but in the end he is bound to win, for his is a distinct genius for getting into the skin of another man and making him convincing, real, and vital."

Film Noir Filmography

Fear in the Night. Director: Maxwell Shane. Producers: William H. Pine, William C. Thomas. Running time: 71 minutes. Released by Paramount, April 18, 1947. Cast: Paul Kelly, DeForrest Kelley, Ann Doran, Kay Scott, Robert Emmett Keane, Jeff York, Charles Victor, Janet Warren, Michael Harvey, John Harmon, Gladys Blake, Stanley Farrar, Julia Faye, Dick Keane, Joey Ray, Chris Drake, Loyette Thomson, Jack Collins, Leander de Cordoba.

Crossfire. Director: Edward Dmytryk. Producer: Adrian Scott. Running time: 85 minutes. Released by RKO, July 22, 1947. Cast: Robert Young, Robert Mitchum, Robert Ryan, Gloria Grahame, Paul Kelly, Sam Levene, Jacqueline White, Steve Brodie, George Cooper, Richard Benedict, Richard Powers, William Phipps, Lex Barker, Marlo Dwyer. Awards: Academy Award nominations for Best Picture, Best Director (Edward Dmytryk), Best Supporting Actor (Robert Ryan), Best Supporting Actress (Gloria Grahame), Best Screenplay (John Paxton).

The File on Thelma Jordon. Director: Robert Siodmak. Producer: Hal B. Wallis. Running time: 100 minutes. Released by Paramount, January 18, 1950. Cast: Barbara Stanwyck, Wendell Corey, Paul Kelly, Joan Tetzel, Stanley Ridges, Richard Rober, Minor Watson, Barry Kelley, Laura Elliott, Basil Ruysdael, Jane Novak, Gertrude W. Hoffman, Harry Antrim, Kate Lawson, Theresa Harris, Byron Barr, Geraldine Wall, Jonathan Corey, Robin Corey.

Side Street. Director: Anthony Mann. Producer: Sam Zimbalist. Running time: 83 minutes. Released by MGM, March 23, 1950. Cast: Farley Granger, Cathy O'Donnell, James Craig, Paul Kelly, Edmon Ryan, Paul Harvey, Jean Hagen, Charles McGraw, Ed Max, Adele Jergens, Harry Bellaver, Whit Bissell, John Gallaudet, Esther Somers, Harry Antrim, George Tyne, Kathryn Givney, King Donovan, Norman Leavitt, Sid Tomack.

References

"Actor Paul Kelly Dies at 57; Life Was 'Comeback' Story." *Hollywood Citizen-News*, November 7, 1956.

Allison, Gordon. "Paul Kelly Loses Ramrod After 43 Years." *New York Herald Tribune*, December 17, 1950.

Biography of Paul Kelly. MGM Studios, August 1950.

Biography of Paul Kelly. Paramount Pictures, January 23, 1940.

Biography of Paul Kelly. Paramount Pictures, circa 1947.

Coughlin, G. "Of the Stage." *The American Weekly*, September 12, 1948.

Dietz, Edith. "Pennies to Polo." *Boston Post*, February 3, 1936.

"Good Material Declared Basis of Good Playing." *Los Angeles Times*, January 17, 1935.

"Heart Attack Kills Paul Kelly." *Los Angeles Examiner*, November 7, 1956.

"He Makes Mr. Raft Respectable, for Even Villainy Is Relative." New York Herald Tribune, January 14, 1940.

Kelly, Paul. "How Playing a General Put Name in Lights." *New York Journal-American*, July 12, 1948.

Neill, Frank. "Kelly Thankful for Gray Locks." *New York Journal-American*, June 18, 1949.

Obituary. *Time*, November 9, 1956.

"Old Scandal of Love and Liquor Echoes as Paul Kelly Near Death." *Los Angeles Herald Express*, March 14, 1953.

"Paul Kelly, Actor on Stage, Screen." *New York Times*, November 7, 1956.

"Paul Kelly Critically Ill in Hospital." *Los Angeles Examiner*, March 14, 1953.

"Paul Kelly, 57, Dies; Acted in 400 Movies." *New York Post*, November 7, 1956.

"Paul Kelly Leaves Estate to Wife." *Los Angeles Examiner*, November 20, 1956.

"Paul Kelly Weds Dorothy Mackaye." *New York Times*, February 11, 1931.

"Paul Kelly Will Filed." *Beverly Hills Citizen*, November 20, 1956.

"Ray Raymond Killed in Fight Over His Wife." *Boston Post*, April 20, 1927.

Rice, Vernon. "Actor Plays an Alcoholic Actor." *New York Post*, November 10, 1950.

Roosevelt, Edith. "Kelly Prefers Native Irish." *New York Morning Telegraph*, November 24, 1952.

Wahls, Robert. "Once Set in Stage Role, Kelly Likes a Long Run." *New York Times*, April 8, 1951.

ARTHUR KENNEDY

"You stink! You stink from corruption! You're worse than a murderer — you're a grave robber!" — Arthur Kennedy in *Champion* (1949)

Arthur Kennedy was once described as "one of the subtlest American supporting actors, never more so than when revealing the malice or weakness in an ostensibly friendly man." The five-time Academy Award nominee who appeared in nearly 100 movies over a span of six decades brought this description to life in a variety of screen gems, including *Bright Victory* (1951), *Trial* (1951), *Peyton Place* (1957), and *Elmer Gantry* (1960). Kennedy was also a significant presence in the film noir era, with five features to his credit: *High Sierra* (1941), *The Window* (1949), *Champion* (1949), *Too Late for Tears* (1949), and *Chicago Deadline* (1949).

John Arthur Kennedy was born in Worcester, Massachusetts, on February 17, 1914, the only child of dentist John Timothy Kennedy and his wife. After receiving his secondary and preparatory education in Worcester at South High School and Worcester Academy, Kennedy studied drama at the Carnegie Institute of Technology (now Carnegie Mellon University) in Pittsburgh, Pennsylvania. In 1936, after his graduation from Carnegie, Kennedy headed for New York, where he lived in a brownstone with several actors, including David Wayne and Ben Yaffee.

"Half of us slept on cots. We'd pound at Shubert Alley doors during the day and then try to whip together enough to eat for supper," Kennedy recalled in a 1952 interview. "With a dollar, Yaffee could somehow bring back half a delicatessen. When things were really rough, Wayne used to cook griddle cakes like crazy — when I think of the stuff I've put in my stomach!"

After 10 months in the Big Apple,

Kennedy landed a job with the Globe Theatre traveling repertory company, which performed abridged versions of Shakespearean plays at fairs throughout the Midwest. Appearing in as many as seven shows on weekdays, eight on weekends, and nine on holidays, Kennedy considered his tenure with the Globe to be invaluable, despite the often unusual atmosphere in which he performed.

"The experience I gained more than made up for such minor irritations as low pay and the barker across the midway proclaiming the wonders of a wax museum and yelling, 'Why see Julius Caesar knocked off for 40 cents when you can see Bruno Hauptmann burn for a dime?'" Kennedy once recalled.

After a year with the Globe Theatre, Kennedy joined Maurice Evans' Shakespearean company, making his Broadway debut in 1937 as Bushy in *King Richard II*. Initially billed as John Kennedy, the actor later changed his stage name to J. Arthur Kennedy because there was already a John Kennedy on the rolls of Actors Equity. After a few years, he dropped the first initial, saying that he considered it "unnecessarily pretentious."

With his professional stage career underway, Kennedy took time out in 1938 to marry actress Mary Cheffey, whom he had met while both were students at the Carnegie Institute. The couple went on to have two children, Terence Gordon, born in 1943, and Laurie Ewing (who later became an actress herself) in 1945. Kennedy and Mary remained together until her death in 1975.

In 1939, Kennedy again performed with Evans' troupe, this time in *King Henry IV, Part I,* then appeared in *Life and Death of an American*, presented by the Federal Theatre Project, a component of Franklin D. Roosevelt's Works Progress Administration (WPA). Although he earned praise for his "winning honesty" for his role as Jerry, Kennedy did not view his experience with the Federal Theatre as a happy one.

"The red-tape was awful. One night before the opening of the play, we were in desperate shape and were rehearsing in the ladies'

lounge of the theater. An old man came down and told us that we couldn't rehearse there and he'd have to turn in a report," Kennedy recalled. "Months later — the play had closed and I was in Hollywood — a letter reached me from the head of the WPA. It said, 'It has come to my attention that you have been rehearsing in the ladies' lounge. This is an infraction of the rules. Any further infraction and you will be dismissed.'"

Kennedy was next seen as a dancing cab driver in *Madam, Will You Walk*, starring George M. Cohan, who termed the actor "the most brilliant actor on Broadway." But Kennedy was about to leave the bright lights of New York — while performing in *Life and Death of an American*, he had been spotted by a talent scout from Warner Bros., who recommended him for the role of James Cagney's younger brother in *City for Conquest* (1940). After a screen test, Kennedy won the role and a contract with the studio.

In the year following his well-received screen debut, Kennedy appeared in five features, including starring roles as an honest cop framed for a crime he didn't commit in *Strange Alibi* (1941); a cocky boxer whose fame interferes with his marriage in *Knockout* (1941); and a criminal on the lam in *Highway West* (1941). Also that year, Kennedy appeared as a supporting player in his first film noir, *High Sierra* (1941), starring Humphrey Bogart and Ida Lupino.

Here, Kennedy portrayed Red, a minor-league hood who joins forces with notorious ex-convict "Mad Dog" Roy Earle (Bogart) to rob a California resort hotel. (Upon his first meeting with Earle shortly after his release from prison, Red is practically star-struck, telling the veteran criminal, "With you on the job, we feel like we're traveling in fast company. I sure heard a lot about ya.") Along with Earle and Red, the heist is carried out by Babe (Alan Curtis), Mendoza (Cornel Wilde), the "inside man" at the hotel, and Earle's girl, Marie (Lupino), who serves as the lookout. Despite the careful planning, however, the scheme goes awry — Earle is forced to shoot a guard, Babe and Red die in a fiery auto crash, and Earle flees into the nearby Sierra Mountains, where he is gunned down by police.

After earning praise for his "effective" portrayal of Red, Kennedy was seen in the box-office hit *They Died With Their Boots On* (1942), starring Errol Flynn as the ill-fated George Armstrong Custer, followed by two wartime dramas, *Desperate Journey* (1942), again starring Flynn, and *Air Force* (1943), one of the best aviation films of the era. Following the release of the latter film, Kennedy himself joined the Army Air Forces, where he traveled the country in the same unit as such stars as William Holden, Ronald Reagan and Robert Young, making a series of training films that included *How to Fly the B-17* and *Resisting Enemy Interrogation*.

The actor's first feature after the war was *Devotion* (1946), which had been shelved for three years. Kennedy later admitted that the film, a fanciful biography of authors Charlotte, Emily, and Anne Bronte, "impressed neither the critics nor the movie-going public," but he counted his role as Branwell Bronte among his favorites.

"Like the picture, Branwell was a failure," Kennedy said. "However, the role was tremendously interesting … and I'd far rather play the part of an interesting failure than a so-called successful role in a successful picture that has been written strictly according to formula."

After the traditional horse-opera *Cheyenne* (1947), Kennedy's final film under his Warner's contract, the actor appeared as a freelancer in *Boomerang!*, helmed by actor-turned-director, Elia Kazan, with whom Kennedy had appeared in *City for Conquest*. (Years later, the famed director hailed Kennedy as "an exceptionally honest, fine actor, and an exceptionally nice person.") Kennedy then made a triumphant return to Broadway in *All My Sons* (1947), portraying a war veteran who discovers that his father (Ed Begley) was responsible for selling defective airplane parts to the government. For his performance, the actor was applauded by Brooks Atkinson, who wrote in the *New York Times* that Kennedy gave "a superb performance with

great power for the climax and with insight into the progress of the character."

Back in Hollywood, Kennedy entered his biggest year for film noir—in 1949, he appeared in a whopping four features from the era: *The Window, Champion, Too Late for Tears*, and *Chicago Deadline*.

In *The Window*, Kennedy played Ed Woodry, a hard-working family man who is constantly bedeviled by the overactive imagination and fanciful stories told by his son, Tommy (Bobby Driscoll). When Tommy witnesses a murder committed in the tenement building where the family lives, he finds that he is a victim of the boy-who-cried-wolf syndrome, as no one believes his story: "You don't ever want me to be ashamed of you, do you?" Woodry asks his son. "Well, don't you see that might happen if you keep this up? People are going to say that Ed Woodry's son doesn't know the difference between what's real and what isn't. Why, they may even say that you're—a liar." When Tommy's mother forces him to apologize the couple he accused of the killing, the little boy finds himself in mortal danger; stalked by the couple, Joe and Jean Kellerson (Paul Stewart and Ruth

Roman), Tommy manages to escape, fleeing to a nearby abandoned building. After a tension-filled chase, Joe Kellerson falls to his death, Jean is arrested, and Tommy is rescued from a precarious perch by officials. Although co-stars Driscoll, Stewart, and Roman were seen in showier roles, Kennedy was singled out in reviews for his "believable" and "altogether natural" performance.

Next, in *Champion*, Kennedy turned in a first-rate performance as Connie Kelly, the crippled brother of boxer Midge (Kirk Douglas), who will stop at nothing to fight his way to the top. Along the way, the morally bereft boxer alienates those closest to him, including his brother and his wife, Emma (Ruth Roman), who decides to obtain a divorce to marry Connie. Although Midge initially appears to approve of the relationship between his brother and his estranged wife, he later seduces Emma, leading to a stormy confrontation with Connie: "Emma's gone, Midge," Connie tells him. "You know why. You're no different, you're only worse — your blood has turned cold. My number finally came up, too, didn't it? And Emma. Once wasn't enough for you. You couldn't let her live and be happy, could you? Why did you do it? Because you were bored, did you have to prove to yourself that you're really the champion?" In the film's memorable climax, Midge is severely beaten during a bout and dies from his injuries; afterward, when Connie is asked to give a statement to the press, he chooses to uphold his brother's reputation, telling reporters, "He went out like a champion — he was a credit to the fight game 'til the very end." In a film rife with outstanding performances, Kennedy was a standout, and was rewarded for his portrayal with an Oscar nomination for Best Supporting Actor. He lost, however, to Dean Jagger in *12 O'Clock High*.

Kennedy followed this first-rate noir with *Too Late for Tears*, appearing in the minor role of Alan Palmer, whose wife, Jane (Lizabeth Scott), is frustrated by the couple's inability to "keep up with the Joneses." When a satchel full of money is inexplicably tossed into their car, the upstanding Alan insists that they turn it in: "We've got as much right to that money as if we went into a bank and lifted a bag full off the counter," he tells his spouse. Jane's plans for the money are further complicated when the rightful owner, Danny Fuller (Dan Duryea), appears at her door and demands its return. Teaming with Danny, Jane kills her hapless husband, then poisons Danny and flees to Mexico with the coveted cash. She doesn't enjoy the fruits of her lethal labors for long, however — a short time later, she is confronted in her hotel room by the brother (Don DeFore) of her first husband, whom she had driving to suicide. While trying to escape, Jane accidentally falls from the balcony of her room to the ground below, with the stolen bills fluttering around her body as she dies.

Noted for his "smooth" portrayal in *Tears*, Kennedy next appeared in his final noir, *Chicago Deadline*, portraying Tommy Ditman, whose sister, Rosita (Donna Reed), is found dead in a dilapidated boarding house. When newspaper reporter Ed Adams (Alan Ladd) finds Rosita's address book, he contacts Tommy, learning that the two grew up on a Texas farm, and that Rosita later moved to San Francisco, was married and widowed, and wound up in Chicago, where Tommy lost track of his sister. Determined to piece together the puzzle of Rosita's past, Adams continues to use her address book as a guide, ultimately uncovering two murders and finally putting the finger on a local mobster known as Solly Wellman (Berry Kroeger), who he guns down during a shootout in the film's climax. Upon its release, this fast-paced feature earned mostly good notices (although the *New York Times*' Bosley Crowther found it to be "a mish-mosh of two-penny-fiction clichés, recklessly thrown together in an almost unfathomable plot."). For his small but memorable role as the dead girl's mournful sibling, Kennedy was praised as "top-caliber" in the *Los Angeles Examiner*, along with co-stars Ladd, Kroeger, and Reed.

Between his noir appearances in 1949, Kennedy found time to accept the role of Biff in the Broadway production of *Death of a*

Salesman. For his portrayal of the disappointing son of Willy Loman, Kennedy was universally lauded by critics and won the Tony Award for Best Supporting Actor. (When the play was made into a film by Columbia in 1951, however, Kennedy's role was given to newcomer Kevin McCarthy.)

During the next decade, Kennedy turned in outstanding performances in such films as *The Glass Menagerie* (1950), where he played a poetic son yearning to escape his claustrophobic family, and *Bright Victory* (1951), in which he starred as a World War II veteran who was blinded in the war. His superb performance in the latter film earned him the Actor of the Year award from the New York Film Critics and an Academy Award nomination for Best Actor (he lost to Humphrey Bogart for *The African Queen*). To prepare for the difficult role, Kennedy worked with real-life blind veterans and wore opaque contact lenses over his eyes.

"You can't see very well through them, but that, of course, was the idea, and they helped me in the part," Kennedy said in a 1952 interview with *Los Angeles Times* reporter Philip K. Scheuer. "You do things instinctively with them on that you wouldn't without them. More importantly, you think differently."

Other top-notch vehicles in which Kennedy appeared during the 1950s were *Rancho Notorious* (1952), an absorbing western where he starred opposite Marlene Dietrich; *Trial* (1955), which saw Kennedy nominated for his third Academy Award (this time losing to Jack Lemmon in *Mister Roberts*); *The Desperate Hours* (1955), starring Humphrey Bogart as an escaped convict who holds a family hostage in their home; *The Man from Laramie* (1955), where Kennedy starred as the adopted son of a megalomaniac rancher; *Peyton Place* (1957), in which Kennedy's exceptional portrayal of an alcoholic who rapes his stepdaughter landed him yet another Oscar nod (he lost to Red Buttons in *Sayonara*); and *Some Came Running* (1958), where he earned his final Academy Award nomination portraying a rigid businessman who is

having an affair with his assistant (he lost this time to Burl Ives in *The Big Country*).

Despite his numerous screen appearances, Kennedy managed to find opportunities to continue his involvement in the theater. In 1951, he formed a theatrical group known as the Theater Workshop (later renamed the Stage Society), which was designed to provide local actors with a forum for honing their craft.

"It's not a showcase for talent, nor a professional school. We charge $20 a month, enough to rent the theater," Kennedy told columnist Hedda Hopper. "Actors need this. Painters paint alone, musicians play or sing alone, but what can an actor do when he isn't working?"

Kennedy also went back to Broadway during this period, starring in 1953 in Arthur Miller's *The Crucible*, in 1956 in *Time Limit* and *The Loud Red Patrick* (which co-starred his former griddle cake–cooking roommate, David Wayne), and in 1960 in *Becket*. In the latter, Kennedy took over the title role from Laurence Olivier, who had assumed the role of King Henry II in the play after it was vacated by Anthony Quinn. *New York Post* critic Richard Watts, Jr., reported that the juggled casting made *Becket* "an even finer play … and Mr. Kennedy's sensitive characterization contributes importantly to its power."

The quality of Kennedy's films began to diminish with the onset of the 1960s, but he still appeared in several memorable features, including *Elmer Gantry* (1960), starring Burt Lancaster in the title role of the charismatic con man; *Lawrence of Arabia* (1962), in which Kennedy played a character based on journalist and commentator Lowell Thomas; *Barabbas* (1962), where Kennedy was singled out by critics for his standout portrayal of Pontius Pilate; and *Fantastic Voyage* (1966), an inventive science fictioner about a team of doctors who are miniaturized and injected in a man's body. More often, however, Kennedy was stuck in a series of duds, including *Claudelle Inglish* (1961), a trite drama about a farm girl who goes to pieces when she is abandoned by her soldier boyfriend, and such foreign-made films as *Murieta* (1965), a tedious drama based on the true story of a Mexican immigrant turned bandit, and *Anzio* (1968), which flopped at the box office despite a first-rate cast that included Robert Mitchum, Robert Ryan, and Peter Falk.

"You have to make a dog once in a while to keep up with the economic situation," Kennedy said once.

Having made his television debut on *Ford Theater* in 1954, Kennedy was infrequently seen on the small screen, but he did appear on such dramatic series as *Alcoa Premiere, Zane Grey Theater, Playhouse 90*, and *Kaleidoscope*. He also served as host and narrator for *F.D.R.*, a series of 27 half-hour documentaries on the life of the late president; co-starred in a short-lived crime drama called *Nakia*, which ran from September to December 1974; and appeared in such made-for-television movies as *The Movie Murderer* (1970), *Crawlspace* (1971), and *The President's Plane Is Missing* (1973). The actor also returned to Broadway in 1968 for *The Price*, his fourth and final play written by Arthur Miller, and in 1973 for *Veronica's Room*.

On the big screen, Kennedy continued to appear almost exclusively in foreign films (he later labeled these movies "stinkers" and termed his appearance in them "a major career mistake"). A notable exception was *The Sentinel* (1977), a repulsive horror film that boasted a cast of such Hollywood veterans as Jose Ferrer, Ava Gardner, Burgess Meredith, John Carradine, and Eli Wallach. After the death of his wife, Mary, in 1975, Kennedy's interest in acting began to wane, and he "threw in the towel" after a series of medical maladies during the late 1970s, including thyroid cancer and corneal transplants to regain his sight after a battle with cataracts. The actor also stopped drinking during this period, following an on-again, off-again battle with alcohol that had lasted for several decades.

"The doctor told me if I didn't stop drinking, I'd soon be dead, so I stopped," Kennedy said in a 1989 interview in the *New York Times*. "My only regret is that more than a few of my brain cells have been a bit singed by alcohol."

But after a 10-year absence from film, Kennedy returned in 1989 for *Signs of Life*, playing a curmudgeonly shipbuilder who fights to prevent the closing of the boatyard that bears his father's name. Kennedy learned of the role through the agent of his daughter, Laurie, a New York-based actress.

"I didn't give it much thought, but true to his word, [the agent] called back and set up a meeting with the producer and director," Kennedy said. "I read the script and was mighty impressed. The dialogue, the rhythms, had real quality. What began to seep through my troubled brain was that I needed a good part and here it was."

Shortly after the release of *Signs of Life*, Kennedy was diagnosed with a brain tumor. He was admitted to the Connecticut Hospital in Branford, Connecticut, in October 1989, and he died three months later, on January 5, 1990. He was 75 years old.

While often underrated, Arthur Kennedy was truly one of Hollywood's finest acting talents. In his five Oscar-nominated performances, as well as numerous others, he demonstrated a brilliant ability to adapt himself to any character and make him come alive. Director Mark Robson, who helmed two of Kennedy's finest films, once offered a fitting testament to the imagination, integrity, and perspective that Kennedy brought to his roles, as well as the esteem in which he was held by his peers.

"On Broadway they told me Arthur Kennedy was an actor's actor," Robson said. "There exists a certain reverence among stage people for him that is not unlike the way they consider Alfred Lunt or Laurence Olivier. After directing Art in *Champion* and *Bright Victory*, I'd say he's a director's actor also. He knows instinctively what you wish him to convey on the screen and has a profound sense of real-life drama."

Film Noir Filmography

High Sierra. Director: Raoul Walsh. Producer: Hal B. Wallis. Running time: 100 minutes. Released by Warner Bros., January 4, 1941. Cast: Humphrey Bogart, Ida Lupino, Alan Curtis, Arthur Kennedy, Joan Leslie, Henry Hull, Barton MacLane, Henry Travers, Elisabeth Risdon, Cornel Wilde, Minna Gombell, Paul Harvey, Donald MacBride, Jerome Cowan, John Eldredge, Isabel Jewell, Willie Best, Arthur Aylsworth, Robert Strange, Wade Boteler, Sam Hayes.

The Window. Director: Ted Tetzlaff. Producer: Frederic Ullman, Jr. Running time: 73 minutes. Released by RKO, August 1949. Cast: Barbara Hale, Bobby Driscoll, Arthur Kennedy, Paul Stewart, Ruth Roman. Awards: Academy Award nomination for Best Film Editing (Frederic Knudtson).

Champion. Director: Mark Robson. Producer: Stanley Kramer. Running time: 99 minutes. Released by United Artists, January 1949. Cast: Kirk Douglas, Marilyn Maxwell, Arthur Kennedy, Paul Stewart, Ruth Roman, Lola Albright, Luis Van Rooten, Harry Shannon, John Day, Erskine Sanford, Esther Howard. Awards: Academy Award for Best Film Editing (Harry Gerstad). Academy Award nominations for Best Actor (Kirk Douglas), Best Supporting Actor (Arthur Kennedy), Best Black and White Cinematography (Frank Planer), Best Score (Dimitri Tiomkin), Best Screenplay (Carl Foreman).

Too Late for Tears. Director: Byron Haskin. Producer: Hunt Stromberg. Running time: 98 minutes. Released by United Artists, August 14, 1949. Cast: Lizabeth Scott, Don DeFore, Dan Duryea, Arthur Kennedy, Kristine Miller, Barry Kelley.

Chicago Deadline. Director: Lewis Allen. Producer: Robert Fellows. Running time: 87 minutes. Released by Paramount, November 2, 1949. Cast: Alan Ladd, Donna Reed, June Havoc, Irene Hervey, Arthur Kennedy, Berry Kroeger, Harold Vermilyea, Shepperd Strudwick, John Beal, Tom Powers, Gavin Muir, Dave Willock, Paul Lees.

References

Alpert, Don. "Art of Acting in U.S." *Los Angeles Times*, June 21, 1964.
"Arthur Kennedy Called Best Technical Actor." *Los Angeles Times*, December 3, 1950.
"Arthur Kennedy Forms Legit Theatre Workshop." *The Hollywood Reporter*, June 1, 1951.
"Arthur Kennedy in 'Signs.'" *Variety*, February 8, 1989.
Collins, Glenn. "Arthur Kennedy: Comeback for a Curmudgeon." *New York Times*, April 30, 1989.
Fleming, Charles. "Legendary Arthur." *Los Angeles Herald-Examiner*, May 5, 1989.
Greenberg, Abe. "Arthur Kennedy Deserts Broadway for Hollywood." *Hollywood Citizen-News*, May 8, 1969.
Hopper, Hedda. "Bright Victory for Arthur!" *Chicago Sunday Tribune*, circa 1951.
Kennedy, Arthur. "The Role I Liked Best." *Saturday Evening Post*, June 14, 1952.
"Kennedy Comeback." *Los Angeles Times*, February 18, 1989.
McKinley, James C. Jr. "Arthur Kennedy, Actor, 75, Dies; Was Versatile in Supporting Roles." *New York Times*, January 7, 1990.
Obituary. *People*, January 22, 1990.
Obituary. *Time*, January 15, 1990.
Marill, Alvin H. "Arthur Kennedy." *Films in Review*, March 1974.
Mitgang, Herbert. "Man of Many Parts." *New York Times*, March 23, 1952.
Moss, Morton. "He Knows the Secret." *Los Angeles Herald-Examiner*, November 6, 1969.
Linet, Beverly. "One of the Best." *Photoplay*, April 1952.
Parsons, Louella O. "Arthur Kennedy." *Los Angeles Examiner*, September 17, 1950.
Peck, Seymour. "Growth — and Growing Pains — of an Actor." *New York Times Magazine*, February 15, 1953.
Ramos, George. "Arthur Kennedy; Actor, 5-Time Oscar Nominee." *Los Angeles Times*, January 7, 1990.
Scheuer, Philip K. "Kin Roles Haunt Arthur Kennedy." *Los Angeles Times*, October 8, 1950.

BERRY KROEGER

"I'm a businessman. Me and you are gonna do a little business."— Berry Kroeger in *Act of Violence* (1949)

Before turning his sights to the big screen, character actor Berry Kroeger made a name for himself on the stage and in radio, appearing on Broadway opposite such luminaries as

Ingrid Bergman and Helen Hayes, and holding down roles on a variety of popular radio programs including *Superman* and *The Thin Man*. During his 36 years in Tinseltown, he was seen in only 31 features— nearly a third of which were horror films released toward the end of his career — but he used his intimidating manner and penetrating gaze to turn in a series of memorable performances during the film noir era. In only a two-year period, Kroeger was prominently featured in five films noirs: *Cry of the City* (1948), *The Dark Past* (1948), *Chicago Deadline* (1948), *Act of Violence* (1949), and *Gun Crazy* (1950).

Berry (sometimes spelled "Barry") Kroeger was born on October 16, 1912, in San Antonio, Texas. As a youngster he showed talent as a pianist, but he was encouraged to pursue acting after winning a state-wide dramatic contest at the age of 15. Following his high school graduation, he enrolled at the University of California at Berkeley, then returned to Texas a year later to study as an apprentice with the San Antonio Little Theater Group. During his tenure with the theater group, Kroeger not only gained valuable experience on the stage, but he also performed a variety of other duties, including writing and directing plays, and building scenery.

Before long, Kroeger began acting professionally on the radio, eventually using his versatility to serve as chief announcer, continuity writer, and program director for San Antonio's largest station. In 1940, having saved $150, Kroeger traveled to California for a vacation, but wound up staying for the next two years after landing a job on a Hollywood radio station. While there, he was heard on a number of programs, most significantly as the narrator of *The Louella Parsons Show*. He also made his film debut in a bit part in an amusing Ginger Rogers comedy, *Tom, Dick, and Harry* (1941), and began honing his skills as an actor at the famed Pasadena Playhouse and with the Max Reinhardt Workshop.

Kroeger relocated to New York in 1942, parlaying his resonant voice and acting talent into what one columnist called an "om-

nipresence" on the radio. For the next several years, he was heard on nearly every major show or network serial on the airwaves, including *Big Sister*, *Grand Central Station*, *Young Dr. Malone*, *Inner Sanctum*, *Light of the World*, *The Thin Man*, *The Voice of the Army*, *The Son of Man*, *Superman*, *Perry Mason*, and *Salute to Youth*. He was also one of several actors to play the title role in *The Falcon*; guested on such dramatic anthology series as *Lux Radio Theater*, *CBS Radio Workshop*, *The First Nighter Program*, *Mystery Theater*, and Orson Welles' *Mercury Theater of the Air*; and narrated *The Big Story*, which presented dramatizations of reportorial exploits. In a bit of an understatement, a friend of Kroeger's remarked years later, "He had a good voice for radio."

The actor didn't spend all of his time on radio sound stages, however. In 1943, he debuted on Broadway in the short-lived Nunnally Johnson comedy *The World's Full of Girls*. He followed this production with such plays as *Therese* with Eva LeGallienne; *The Tempest* with Helen Hayes; and *Joan of Lorraine* opposite Ingrid Bergman. During the 199 performances of the latter production, Kroeger caught the eye of Hollywood director William Wellman, who tapped him for a part in his upcoming spy drama, *The Iron Curtain* (1948), starring Dana Andrews and Gene Tierney. After earning several good notices for his supporting role, Kroeger was seen in the first of his five consecutive films noirs, *Cry of the City* (1948). In this feature, Kroeger played an oily attorney, Niles, who is first seen trying to exact a murder-jewel heist confession from small-time hood Martin Rome (Richard Conte) as he lay in the hospital. Martin, who was shot during a foiled restaurant hold-up that left a policeman dead, denies his involvement, but Niles approaches him again during his recovery from surgery, offering him $10,000 to take the rap. ("Be practical, friend," Niles tells him. "You're going to the chair anyway. You killed a cop — you can't beat that.") After Niles threatens to implicate Martin's innocent girlfriend, Teena (Debra Paget) in the crime, Martin escapes from the hospital, discovers that it is actually Niles who was behind the jewel robbery, and forces him to hand over the stolen goods. When Niles tries to shoot Martin, he stabs the attorney and flees, hunted by a detective, Lt. Vittorio Candella (Victor Mature). Ultimately, Candella catches up with Martin at a local church, where he has gone to meet Teena. After Candella reveals Martin's true nature to his girlfriend, Teena backs out of her plans to leave the country with Martin, and the hood is gunned down in the street outside the church as he tries to run.

Next, in *The Dark Past* (1948) — a remake of 1939's *Blind Alley* — Kroeger played Mike, a henchman of escaped convict Al Walker (William Holden). After his prison break, Walker and his gang await the arrival of a getaway boat at a lakeside cabin occupied by police psychiatrist Andrew Collins (Lee J. Cobb), his wife and son, and several weekend guests. During the tense hostage situation, Collins learns that the violent, psychologically damaged Walker suffers from recurring nightmares and eventually induces the criminal's recollection of a traumatic childhood incident that serves as the source of the dream. Later, when police surround the house, Walker finds that this revelation has rendered him incapable of committing further violence, and he surrenders without incident.

Kroeger's third film noir, *Act of Violence* (1949), centered on a successful businessman, Frank Enley (Van Heflin), who finds his comfortable life forever altered when he becomes the subject of a vendetta by ex–war buddy Joe Parkson (Robert Ryan). As it turns out, during the war, the seemingly upstanding Enley reported a planned prison break to his Nazi captors, resulting in the deaths of nearly a dozen of his fellow P.O.W.s. Overcome with shame and fear, Enley goes on a drinking binge and encounters a thug known as Johnny (Kroeger), who offers to kill Parkson for $10,000. Enley is initially horrified by the suggestion, but Johnny works to convince him: "Take it easy, friend. You ain't thinkin' right," Johnny says soothingly. "This joker's gonna give it to you. You got a wife. A kid.

You want them to stand around cryin' when they put you down in that big hole? Just 'cause you ain't got what it takes? Come on, sucker — I'm tellin' you. It's your only way out." Enley eventually agrees and Johnny arranges to meet Parkson at the local train station the following evening, but after sobering up, Enley shows up at the station to warn his former friend. Spotting Johnny as he aims at Parkson, Enley steps in front of the bullet, then attacks Johnny as he speeds away, causing his car to crash and ignite into flames.

Later that same year, Kroeger was seen in *Chicago Deadline*, which centered on the death of a young woman, Rosita Jean d'Ur (Donna Reed), and the efforts of reporter Ed Adams (Alan Ladd) to uncover the circumstances of her past. Using Rosita's address book to guide him, Adams contacts a series of individuals who knew the woman, including Blacky Franchot (Shepperd Strudwick), a small-time hood with whom she was once in love, and Solly Wellman (Kroeger), a powerful local mobster. During his first encounter with Adams, Solly denies that he knew Rosita. ("I never heard of her," he says. "If I were you, you didn't either.") As Adams grows closer to the truth, Solly determines to kill the reporter. During a confrontation in a parking garage, Solly and Adams engage in a gun battle, but the reporter craftily pretends to run out of ammunition and, when he steps out from hiding to surrender, he plugs Solly with his last remaining bullet.

In the final film noir of his career, Kroeger was seen in the cult classic *Gun Crazy*, which focused on the doomed relationship between gun-obsessed Bart Tare (John Dall) and trigger-happy Annie Laurie Starr (Peggy Cummins). At a traveling carnival owned by Packett (Kroeger), the two meet by chance during Annie's performance as a sharp shooter. When Bart demonstrates a similar talent during a competition, Annie urges Packett to hire him, and before long, the two are embroiled in an affair, much to Packett's dismay: "I saw the two of you — the way you were looking at each other tonight," Packett tells Annie. "Like a couple of wild animals."

portrait of [a] scoundrel" in *Act of Violence*; and he was noted for his "unobtrusive but neat characterization" in *The Dark Past* by the *New York Times'* A.H. Weiler. His best notices, however, were for *Cry of the City* and *Gun Crazy*; of his performance in the former, George H. Spires of *Motion Picture Herald* opined that the actor's "characterization of the unscrupulous and criminally inclined lawyer is a highlight of the picture," while the *Los Angeles Examiner's* Kay Proctor raved, "Standout, too [is] the performance of Berry Kroeger (ugh, but he's the nasty one!)." And for *Gun Crazy*, the critic for *The Hollywood Reporter* wrote that Kroeger made "an impression with his splendid performance as a carnival barker."

Between his film noir appearances, Kroeger was also seen in such features as *Fighting Man of the Plains* (1949), a Randolph Scott western; *Down to the Sea in Ships* (1949), a well-done sea saga with Richard Widmark and Lionel Barrymore; and *Black Magic* (1949), an Orson Welles starrer that tanked at the box office. Although he appeared in a total of 10 features between 1948 and 1950, however, he was seen in only half that number during the entire decade that followed, including *The Sword of Monte Cristo* (1951), where he played an evil minister in the court of Napoleon III, and *Blood Alley* (1955), a John Wayne actioner in which Kroeger was seen as an elderly Chinese villager. Also during this period, Kroeger expanded his repertoire to include the medium of television, guesting during the next two decades on such programs as *Suspense, Perry Mason, Mr. Lucky, The Rifleman, Bonanza, Hawaiian Eye, Get Smart, It Takes a Thief, The F.B.I., Longstreet,* and *WKRP in Cincinnati.* In addition, Kroeger returned to the Broadway stage in the 1956 musical comedy *Shangri-La*, but despite a cast that included Jack Cassidy, Alice Ghostley, and Carol Lawrence, the play closed after just 21 performances. He showed his dependability on the stage the following year when he briefly substituted for actor Thayer David in a production of *Oscar Wilde*. After David fell and injured his arm while exiting a train,

Despite Packett's drunken pleas, Annie rejects him, and when he tries to force his affections on her, Bart shows up and shoots at him, leading Packett to fire them both. Bart and Annie marry, but when their money runs out, they stage a series of holdups that result in several deaths. On the run from the law, the couple wind up near Bart's boyhood home, where they are pursued into the mountains. As police approach, Annie prepares to fire at them, but Bart kills her before she has the opportunity to shoot. Hearing the report of the gun, the cops open fire, resulting in the deaths of both outlaws.

Kroeger was lauded by reviewers for each of his noir performances—all of which depicted characters on the wrong side of the law. For his role in *Chicago Deadline*, he was cited in *Hollywood Citizen-News* as a "thoroughly believable heavy"; Bosley Crowther of the *New York Times* praised his "squalid

Kroeger was called in as a last-minute replacement and, according to one reviewer, "played the part with the script in hand."

When he wasn't accepting guest spots on the small screen, Kroeger continued to appear sporadically in feature films, including *Seven Thieves* (1960), a well-done caper where Kroeger played an expert wheel man, and *Atlantis, the Lost Continent* (1961), an adventure-fantasy about the mythical "eighth continent." Unfortunately, the latter part of his film career was comprised mostly of a series of schlocky horror films, including *Chamber of Horrors* (1966), a gory feature set in 18th century Baltimore; *Nightmare in Wax* (1969), an amateurish clone of the Vincent Price thriller, *House of Wax* (1953); *The Mephisto Waltz* (1971), which bore more than a passing resemblance to the popular *Rosemary's Baby* (1969); *The Incredible 2-Headed Transplant* (1971), a dreadful flick with a cast that included Bruce Dern and Casey Kasem; and *Pets* (1974), an offensive timewaster about a sadistic man who keeps women as pets. He fared slightly better, however, with his final feature film, *Demon Seed* (1977), a science-fiction thriller starring Fritz Weaver and Julie Christie.

After the latter feature, Kroeger retired from performing, citing health reasons, and faded from the public eye. Nearly 15 years later, on January 4, 1991, the actor died from kidney failure at Cedars-Sinai Medical Center in Los Angeles. Survived by his wife, Mary Agnes, the actor was 78 years old.

Interestingly, with only supporting roles in five films noirs to his credit, Berry Kroeger managed to secure a solid place in the annals of the era, turning in memorable performances of a series of thoroughly despicable characters. Logging little screen time in comparison with his better-known co-stars, Kroeger possessed a menacing screen presence that rendered him unforgettable.

Film Noir Filmography

The Dark Past. Director: Rudolph Mate. Producer: Buddy Adler. Running time: 74 minutes. Released by Columbia, December 22, 1948. Cast: William Holden, Nina Foch, Lee J. Cobb, Adele Jergens, Stephen Dunne, Lois Maxwell, Barry Kroeger, Steven Geray, Wilton Graff, Robert Osterloh, Kathryn Card, Bobby Hyatt, Ellen Corby, Charles Cane, Robert B. Williams.

Cry of the City. Director: Robert Siodmak. Producer: Sol Siegel. Running time: 96 minutes. Released by 20th Century–Fox, September 29, 1948. Cast: Victor Mature, Richard Conte, Fred Clark, Shelley Winters, Betty Garde, Berry Kroeger, Tommy Cook, Debra Paget, Hope Emerson, Roland Winters, Walter Baldwin, June Storey, Tito Vuolo, Mimi Aguglia, Konstantin Shayne, Howard Freeman.

Chicago Deadline. Director: Lewis Allen. Producer: Robert Fellows. Running time: 87 minutes. Released by Paramount, November 2, 1949. Cast: Alan Ladd, Donna Reed, June Havoc, Irene Hervey, Arthur Kennedy, Berry Kroeger, Harold Vermilyea, Shepperd Strudwick, John Beal, Tom Powers, Gavin Muir, Dave Willock, Paul Lees.

Act of Violence. Director: Fred Zinnemann. Producer: William H. Wright. Running time: 81 minutes. Released by MGM, January 23, 1949. Cast: Van Heflin, Robert Ryan, Janet Leigh, Mary Astor, Phyllis Thaxter, Berry Kroeger, Nicholas Joy, Harry Antrim, Connie Gilchrist, Will Wright.

Gun Crazy. Director: Joseph H. Lewis. Producer: Frank and Maurice King. Running time: 87 minutes. Released by United Artists, as Deadly Is The Female on January 26, 1950; re-released as Gun Crazy on August 24, 1950. Cast: Peggy Cummins, John Dall, Berry Kroeger, Morris Carnovsky, Anabel Shaw, Harry Lewis, Nedrick Young, Trevor Bardette, Mickey Little, Rusty Tamblyn, Paul Frison, Dave Bair, Stanley Prager, Virginia Farmer, Anne O'Neal, Frances Irwin, Don Beddoe, Robert Osterloh, Shimen Ruskin, Harry Hayden.

References

"Berry Plays Oscar." *New York Herald Tribune*, April 25, 1957.
Biography of Berry Kroeger. NBC Radio, April 16, 1947.
Fraser, C. Gerald. "Berry Kroeger, 78, An Actor in Radio, Theater and Films." *New York Times*, January 12, 1991.
"Joan of Lorraine." *Playbill*, November 18, 1946.
Obituary. *Variety*, January 14, 1991.
"The Son of Man." *Variety*, April 9, 1947.
"The Tempest." *Playbill*, January 25, 1945.
"The World's Full of Girls." *Playbill*, December 6, 1943.

ALAN LADD

"I know you think you're too beautiful to hit. You've always counted on that with guys, haven't you? Even when you've been shooting them down in cold blood."— Alan Ladd in *Calcutta* (1947)

Alan Ladd's life was a paradox.

One of the biggest movie stars of his time, he was never nominated for an Academy Award and only a handful of his films are remembered today. He was larger than life on the silver screen, but he was short in stature in real life and to achieve his cinema height, he often wore shoe lifts or stood on platforms. In films, he exuded confidence, poise, and stamina; behind the scenes, he was overly sensitive, filled with self-doubt, and developed an increasing reliance on alcohol. He seemed to have it all — polished good looks, a dedicated wife, successful children, wealth, and fame — but he died alone, the victim of a lethal combination of drugs and alcohol.

"I feel every day as if it's all a dream," Ladd said once. "That I'm going to wake up and find myself pushing scenery around again."

While Ladd was seldom touted for his abilities as an actor, he unquestionably made his biggest cinematic impact during the film noir era, with appearances in some of the period's most memorable offerings: *This Gun for Hire* (1942), *The Glass Key* (1942), *The Blue Dahlia* (1946), *Calcutta* (1947), *Chicago Deadline* (1949), and *Appointment with Danger* (1951).

An only child, Alan Walbridge Ladd, Jr., was born on September 3, 1913, in Hot Springs, Arkansas. When young Alan was just four years old, his accountant father suffered a fatal heart attack ("I don't remember anything about him," Ladd once said, "and my mother never spoke of him"). The year after his father's death, Ladd and his mother, Ina, moved to Oklahoma City, where she met and married husband number two, a house painter by the name of Jim Beavers.

Rather frail and undersized as a child, Ladd was teased unmercifully by his school-

mates, so he doubtlessly felt a sense of relief when his mother and stepfather decided in the early 1920s to move to California. But the 1,000-mile trek was more than the youngster had bargained for; traveling in Beavers' run-down Model T Ford, it took the trio four months to arrive at their destination. And the family's circumstances weren't much better in sunny California.

"Those were the rough days. I used to hike six miles to school from the combination garage-house we built," Ladd recalled years later. "We got potato soup and cheap mutton week after week at home. I still turn green when lamb is served."

In school, Ladd once again encountered trouble from his classmates— his small stature led to the hated nickname of "Tiny," and the actor once admitted that the harassment inflamed his "lousy temper."

"The first day, some kid pushed my head into the fountain," Ladd told the *Saturday Evening Post* in a 1957 interview. "I started to punch him and found out he was twins, but I licked them both."

An average student, Ladd graduated from elementary school in 1930 and enrolled in North Hollywood High School, where he discovered an affinity for sports. During the next several years, he played varsity football, held the 1931 San Fernando Valley shot-put record, won the 50-yard freestyle interscholastic swimming championship, and was a top diver in the area. His swimming ability was so outstanding, in fact, that Ladd aspired to compete in the 1932 Olympics on the swim team from the United States, but these hopes were dashed when he hit his head on a diving board during a freak accident.

"I lost my nerve. I hit my head once and knocked myself cold," Ladd recalled. "From then on I found that every time I went to make a dive, I was worrying more about whether I would hit my head again than I was about my form.... When I couldn't concentrate on that anymore, I knew I'd never be any good — so I quit."

Between classes and his sports activities, Ladd served as head of the school's World Friendship Club, captain of the swimming, track, and football teams, and president of the student body. He also found time to hold down a series of odd jobs, including selling newspapers, pumping gas, and delivering potato chips by bicycle. But it wasn't until his senior year at North Hollywood that he developed an interest in acting, after being convinced by an English teacher to participate in the school's drama activities. Following small roles in several school productions, Ladd was cast in the Gilbert and Sullivan musical, *The Mikado*, earning rave reviews for his portrayal of Ko-Ko, the Lord High Executioner. After his high school graduation, Ladd landed a spot in a stock company of young actors and actresses put together by Universal Studios. Despite his initial excitement at being selected for the group, Ladd lasted four months before being dropped (along with most of his fellow performers, including a young Tyrone Power). Abruptly forced into the "real world," Ladd went to work at a local newspaper, the *San Fernando Valley Sun-Record*, working his way from copy boy to advertising manager.

Leaving the paper after two years, Ladd opened his own hot dog stand, naming it — ironically — "Tiny's Patio." He also worked as a salesman for National Cash Register, reported the radio news for an oil company, and — still harboring his ambition to become an actor — hired on as a grip for Warner Bros. Studios.

"They put me to work rigging scaffoldings and readying sets for use," Ladd said. "My work would be finished by the time the actors and camera moved. Then I'd go to another set. In two years, I never saw them shoot a single scene."

While Ladd was struggling to find his way professionally, his personal life was not neglected. In 1936, he married Marjorie Jane

"Midge" Harrold, a local girl he'd met several years earlier while working as a movie theater usher. The following year, the couple had a son, Alan Ladd, Jr. (who would grow up to become president of 20th Century-Fox Studios, Chairman and CEO of Pathe Entertainment, and head of his own company, The Ladd Company). Ladd's domestic bliss was shattered in 1937, however, when, a year after the sudden death of his stepfather, Ladd's mother, Ina, committed suicide by ingesting ant paste. (Ladd's grief over his mother's death was exacerbated by his overwhelming guilt — following an argument with Ina, he had given her money, unaware of her intent to purchase the lethal insecticide.)

Meanwhile, determined to give acting another try, Ladd pooled his meager savings and enrolled in the Ben Bard School of Acting, supporting his family by making transcription records for radio and playing bit parts in such films as *All Over Town* (1937), *Hold 'Em Navy* (1937), and *Freshman Year* (1938). But it was his increasingly frequent appearances on Los Angeles radio station KFWB that led to Ladd's first big break. With roles on up to 20 shows each week, Ladd was heard one fateful day by actress-turned-agent Sue Carol, who invited the actor to her office.

"He came in wearing a long, white trench coat," Carol recalled years later. "His blond hair was bleached by the sun. He looked like a young Greek god, and he was unforgettable…. I thought he was great. I never doubted he'd be a star."

Ladd signed with Carol's agency and soon found himself in a series of minor roles in a variety of films including *Rulers of the Sea* (1939), starring Douglas Fairbanks, Jr.; *Hitler, Beast of Berlin* (1939), in which he was credited as "Allan" Ladd; *The Light of Western Stars* (1940), where he played a saloon cowhand; *Captain Caution* (1940), an action-adventure featuring Victor Mature; *Her First Romance* (1940), directed by Edward Dmytryk; *Great Guns* (1941), a Laurel and Hardy comedy in which Ladd had only one line; *They Met in Bombay* (1941), with Clark Gable and Rosalind Russell; and *Cadet Girl* (1941), a Carole Landis starrer. Ladd was also cast in an unbilled role in the Orson Welles' classic, *Citizen Kane* (1941); he can be briefly spotted in the shadows of one scene, wearing a porkpie hat.

"I tried for better roles over and over again," Ladd said once, "but directors or producers just kept saying I was too young or too old, too slight or too blond. Or else my name lacked prestige for the part. It was always something."

But Ladd's days of futilely searching for significant movie roles were nearing an end. After attracting notice in a small but showy role as an ill-fated British flier in RKO's *Joan of Paris* (1942), Ladd learned that director Frank Tuttle was looking for an unknown to star as a ruthless killer in his upcoming feature for Paramount, *This Gun for Hire* (1942).

"Alan and I went over to see Frank, who said that Alan looked like someone who would say, 'Tennis, anyone?'" Sue Carol later recalled. "Luckily, I'd brought along some mood stills of Alan — you know, with him looking sinister, smoking a cigarette with smoke curling out of his nose. They were quite effective. Alan photographed beautifully. Frank Tuttle studied the stills for a few minutes. Then he looked up at us and didn't say anything for what seemed like ages. Finally, he said, 'Let me test him.'"

Ladd won the role — and a contract with Paramount — and entered the realm noir in the first of his six characterizations from the era, an icy killer named Raven whose violent background is revealed early in the film: "Every night I dream … I dream about a woman," he says. "She used to beat me. 'Whip the bad blood outta me,' she said. My old man was hanged. My mother died right after that and I went to live with that woman. My aunt. She beat me from the time I was three 'til I was 14. One day she caught me reaching for a piece of chocolate. She was saving it for a cake. Crummy piece of chocolate. She hit me with a red-hot flat iron. Crushed my wrist with it. I got the knife. I let her have it. In the throat. They stuck a label on me — killer. Shoved me in a reform school and they beat me there, too. But I'm glad I killed her." As the story opens, Raven is hired for murder by Willard Gates (Laird Cregar), the agent of a company that sells chemical formulas to the Nazis. Double-crossed by Gates, who pays him off in "hot" money, Raven is determined to exact his revenge, and tracks him to Los Angeles. On the way, he encounters Ellen Graham (Veronica Lake), who is working as a spy for the federal government in an effort to unravel a plot to sell poisonous gas to the enemy. Infiltrating the headquarters of Gates' boss, Alvin Brewster (Tully Marshall), Raven kills his betrayer and forces Brewster to sign a confession, but before he can escape, he is gunned down by Ellen's lawman boyfriend.

The release of *This Gun for Hire* transformed Ladd into an overnight sensation and his portrayal of the baby-faced assassin was met with rave reviews; the critic for *The Hollywood Reporter* wrote that his performance was "fascinating in its brutality, a study of terrific power," and *Variety*'s reviewer gushed: "Young Ladd … looms as one of the most promising of the screen's newcomers in a long time. He handles his role with a still ferocity, with an un-actorish intensity and a display of skill adequate for every little or major demand."

Ladd's sudden catapult into cinematic fame was accompanied by dramatic upheavals off screen as well. During the two years of his association with Sue Carol, Ladd and his agent had become increasingly close, despite the fact that both were married. And Ladd's wife, Midge, according to her sister, was not "a fighter."

"Besides, [Midge] was too young, too guileless to cope with a woman of Sue's experience," Barbara Harrold Grether said in Beverly Linet's 1979 book, *Ladd*. "Sue had money, though not a great fortune. But what she really had was power. She had a way of getting what she wanted."

Undoubtedly, what Sue Carol wanted was Alan Ladd, and in July 1941, Ladd's marriage ended in divorce. Carol was granted a divorce from her third husband the following March, and a week later, Ladd and his agent, who was 10 years his senior, were quietly married in Tijuana, Mexico. The couple later had two children, Alana Sue in 1943, and David Alan in 1947 (who grew up to marry — and later, divorce — actress Cheryl Ladd, of *Charlie's Angels* fame, and attain success as a television and film producer).

"When Sue became my wife," Ladd told reporters after their wedding, "I realized that at last I had everything in life that I wanted."

Meanwhile, Paramount, wanting to capitalize on the success of *This Gun for Hire*, quickly reteamed Ladd and Veronica Lake in the actor's second film noir, *The Glass Key* (1942). This feature centered on a hodgepodge of characters with intertwined lives; Ladd portrayed Ed Beaumont, chief aide to political boss Paul Madvig (Brian Donlevy), who is engaged to Janet Henry (Lake), daughter of local reform candidate, Senator Henry (Moroni Olsen), whose son, Taylor (Richard Denning), is having an affair with Madvig's sister, Opal (Bonita Granville). When Taylor is found murdered, Madvig is implicated in the crime, but Beaumont ultimately guesses the killer's real identity and in the film's climax, has police arrest Janet for the crime,

forcing the senator to admit that it was he who accidentally killed his son.

As in their first outing, Ladd and Lake demonstrated considerable chemistry in *The Glass Key*, although the first meeting of their characters was rife with tension — after observing Janet's subtle mockery of the loutish Madvig during a dinner party, Beaumont manages to take her down a peg with a few chosen words and a chilly smile: "I think you've had enough laughs from the wrong side of tracks for one evening. There *are* people that don't laugh at Paul," he tells her. "I get along very well with Paul because he's on the dead up-and-up. Why don't you try it sometime?" By the final reel, however, the two acknowledge their mutual attraction and are given the blessing of Madvig, who tells them they "got it bad for each other." After scoring another hit with *The Glass Key*, Ladd next starred opposite Helen Walker in *Lucky Jordan* (1942), followed by a cameo in Paramount's star-studded musical tribute to the war effort, *Star Spangled Rhythm* (1942), and *China* (1943), a popular wartime adventure with Loretta Young and William Bendix. In January 1943, before the release of *China*, Ladd enlisted in the Army Air Forces, but before the year was out, the actor was given an honorable medical discharge for what was termed a "double hernia."

During Ladd's service in the armed forces, his popularity had continued to climb; in the 12-month period between January and December 1943, he was featured in 16 articles in one fan magazine alone, he was named "Man of the Year" by another, and his weekly fan mail numbered in the tens of thousands. And by all accounts, Ladd was devoted to his fans as well.

"I think any movie star who refuses autographs has a hell of a nerve," the actor once said. "It seems to me that as long as my pictures go into theaters and we ask people to pay to see what I do on the screen, I should not object if customers want to know what kind of man I am, how I live, what I do with my spare time."

Although his next film, *And Now To-*

morrow (1944) was panned by *New York Times* critic Bosley Crowther as "a very stupid little movie," Ladd had yet another hit on his hands. And this box-office success was followed by a series of pictures that, while disdained by reviewers, attracted moviegoers in droves, including *Salty O'Rourke* (1945), in which Ladd played the title role of a slick gambler; *Duffy's Tavern* (1945), a comedy musical with a star-packed cast including Barry Sullivan, Paulette Goddard, Brian Donlevy, and Veronica Lake; *Two Years Before the Mast* (1946), featuring Ladd as a seaman who leads a ship's mutiny; and *The Blue Dahlia* (1946), his third film noir. Here, Ladd portrayed Johnny Morrison, a war veteran who returns from service to discover that his wife, Helen (Doris Dowling), is romantically involved with nightclub owner Eddie Harwood (Howard Da Silva). When Helen is murdered, Johnny is suspected of the crime and determines to find the real killer, meeting up with the nightclub owner's estranged wife, Joyce (Veronica Lake): "They're looking for me," Johnny tells her. "And if they catch me, they're not going to worry about trying to pin it on somebody else.... Even if we weren't happy, Helen was my wife. And the man who killed her isn't going to get away with it. He just thinks he is." Although police focus on several other suspects in addition to Johnny, it is revealed in the film's climax that the murder was committed by a hotel detective who was blackmailing Helen. *The Blue Dahlia* was well received by both audiences and critics; the reviewer for *Variety* wrote that the actor did "a bang-up job"; Jack D. Grant of *The Hollywood Reporter* found Ladd "in fine form"; and in the *Los Angeles Examiner*, Ruth Waterbury raved, "When you see the blockbusting job Alan does here — the power, the charm, and persuasion he generates, the mystery grows as to why Paramount doesn't give him a production built in lavish style."

Shortly after he completed filming on *The Blue Dahlia*, Ladd was suspended by Paramount after refusing to report to work on the film *California* (later made with Ray Milland). According to *The Hollywood Reporter*, Ladd contended that he "should be paid a salary commensurate with his high box-office position," and after a four-month layoff, the actor inked an agreement with the studio that guaranteed him $75,000 per film.

"I still don't know what my next picture will be," Ladd said after the suspension was lifted. "All I hope is it's a good one."

In his first film after the suspension, Ladd starred opposite Geraldine Fitzgerald in *O.S.S.* (1946), a well-done spy drama, followed by *Wild Harvest* (1947), a rural drama with Dorothy Lamour and Robert Preston, and *Calcutta* (1947), Ladd's fourth entry in the realm of film noir. Set in India, this feature focused on three commercial pilots, Neale Gordon (Ladd), Pedro Blake (William Bendix), and Bill Cunningham (John Whitney). When Bill is found murdered, Neale initially suspects the man's fiancée, Virginia Moore (Gail Russell), but is soon attracted by her demeanor of innocent vulnerability. As it turns out, Bill's first impressions were on target; Virginia is revealed as a member of a jewel smuggling ring who was indirectly responsible for Bill's death and murdered another man involved with the lucrative scheme. Despite his feelings for Virginia ("You're pretty hard to resist — you really got under my skin," Neale says), the pilot beats a confession out of her and at the film's end, turns her over to police. Although fans once again flocked to see Ladd on the big screen, *Calcutta* was viewed with less favor by critics; the reviewer for the *New York Times* found that Ladd turned in a "competent" performance, but panned the film as "a sorry mess indeed," and in *Motion Picture Herald*, Ray Lanning wrote: "Though filled with the basic essentials of romance, mystery, and adventure, *Calcutta* does not fully capitalize on them, does not get all the suspense out of them."

During the next two years, Ladd continued his successful run on the big screen, with features such as *Whispering Smith* (1948), his first western and his first film in Technicolor; *Saigon* (1948), his final teaming with Veronica Lake; *Beyond Glory* (1948),

Howard Da Silva and Alan Ladd in *The Blue Dahlia* (1946).

where he starred as a West Point cadet; and *The Great Gatsby* (1949), the second of three screen versions of the F. Scott Fitzgerald novel. Although reviews of Ladd's performance in the latter film were lukewarm at best (with *Time* magazine's critic saying he looked "as comfortable as a gunman at a garden party"), his characterization of the ill-fated bootlegger is today viewed as one of the better portrayals of his career.

Also during this period, Ladd returned to the dark side of the screen, starring with Donna Reed and Arthur Kennedy in *Chicago Deadline* (1949), his fifth film noir. Here, as Ed Adams, Ladd portrayed a persistent newspaper reporter who is determined to uncover the events leading to the death of a woman (Donna Reed) found in a dilapidated hotel room ("Little dark-haired girl who looked so

sweet," Ed muses in one scene. "How did you ever come to this? I wonder what kind of a girl she really was?"). Using the dead woman's address book, Ed encounters a variety of characters, including G.G. Temple (Gavin Muir), a wealthy industrialist with whom the woman had an affair, and a small-time hood, Blacky Franchot (Shepperd Strudwick). After Franchot is murdered, Ed fingers mobster Solly Wellman (Berry Kroeger) as the killer and fatally wounds him during a shootout in a parking garage. In the film's last scene, at the woman's memorial service, Ed burns the address book, satisfied that he has done justice to her memory.

Although this well-done feature was a box-office success, critics were mixed in their opinions. Lynn Bowers of the *Los Angeles Examiner* praised Ladd's "brilliant" performance and termed the film "as exciting a story as you're likely to see hereabouts," but Ann Helming wrote in the *Hollywood Citizen-News* that "the performances are on a par with the vehicle itself, meaning average." And Bosley Crowther wrote a particularly savage review in the *New York Times*, referring to Ladd's "ridiculous posturing as a brilliant newspaper man-sleuth," and his "tight-lipped and nonchalant style that those people who cherish the illusion will no doubt idolatrously admire."

With the dawn of the 1950s, Ladd continued to ride on a wave of public adoration, and his fans continued to show up in large numbers for such mediocre features as *Captain Carey, U.S.A.* (1950), notable primarily for introducing the popular Nat King Cole hit "Mona Lisa"; *Branded* (1950), dismissed by the *New York Times*' Crowther as "a pretty dull lot of stuff"; and *Red Mountain* (1951), in which Ladd portrayed a Confederate officer during the Civil War. Despite his spate of box-office successes, Ladd was by now becoming increasingly disillusioned with his screen assignments, but it appeared that his luck had changed when *The Hollywood Reporter* broke the news that he was slated to star in the screen version of the Pulitzer Prize–winning play *Detective Story*. Unfortunately, the publication's pronouncement was premature; the coveted role of the brash, inflexible detective was ultimately given to Kirk Douglas and Ladd was cast, instead, in *Appointment With Danger* (1951), the last of his six films noirs. In this feature, Ladd portrayed Al Goddard, a U.S. postal inspector noted for his implacable — and typically noir — nature outside of the office: "You've been chasing hoodlums for so long, you don't know how to treat ordinary people," his superior tells him. "That badge and a few law books have turned you into a nut. You don't like anybody, you don't believe anybody, you don't trust anybody. You think everybody has a pitch." Although Goddard himself reveals his outlook that a love affair is "what goes on between a man and a .45 pistol that won't jam," his skills on the job are without peer, and he utilizes them to investigate the murder of a fellow inspec-

tor. Aided by a nun (Phyllis Calvert) who is able to identify the killers, Goddard poses as a crooked government agent and infiltrates a local gang run by Earl Boettiger (Paul Stewart), but he finds his life in jeopardy when the nun is kidnapped by the gang and accidentally blows his cover. During a gun battle with the mobsters, police arrive in the nick of time and Boettiger is gunned down just as he prepares to shoot Goddard.

Termed by one critic as a "good cops-and-robbers actioner [with] ... a tough flavor, interesting plot, and tight pace," *Appointment with Danger* represented another profitable picture for the actor, but with his Paramount contract nearing expiration, Ladd decided that the time had come to bid farewell to the studio that had been his home for the last decade. After agreeing to make two more pictures for Paramount at a salary of $100,000 each, Ladd signed a six-picture deal with Warner Bros., in which he was guaranteed $150,000 per picture and 10 percent of the gross. He was also granted story approval and the right to make outside pictures. In 1952, Ladd starred in his first feature for Warners, *The Iron Mistress*, portraying the inventor of the Bowie knife, then returned to Paramount for what would turn out to be the best-remembered film of his screen career —*Shane* (1953). In his sensitive portrayal of the mysterious stranger who helps defend a family against ruthless cattle barons, Ladd earned well-deserved acclaim; in a typical review, the critic from *Variety* wrote, "Alan Ladd's performance takes on dimensions not heretofore noticeable in his screen work." Ladd earned similar praise from the film's director, George Stevens, who said Ladd "seems to have decency on the screen even in violent roles like this one. He always seems to have a large measure of reserve and dignity." And, answering critics who referred to Ladd's tendency to project a single expression on the screen, Stevens replied, "Give me an actor with one good expression and I'll be happy." Unfortunately, while Oscar nominations were doled out to co-stars Brandon DeWilde and Jack Palance, Ladd was overlooked by the Academy; some say that because of Ladd's imminent defection from Paramount, studio heads declined the opportunity to lobby for a nomination on his behalf. Still, the film serves as a lasting testament to Ladd's talent and remains one of the finest westerns ever made.

After *Shane*, Ladd's career began a downhill slide from which he would never recover. In the second of his two films under his Paramount contract, he starred in *Botany Bay* (1953), an 18th-century sea saga that, like most of his features, failed to impress critics but struck gold at the box office. Ladd's continued popularity was once again evidenced when he was named in 1954, along with Marilyn Monroe, as *Photoplay* magazine's "most popular star," and he made his television drama debut that year on *General Electric Theater*, in an episode entitled "Committed." But on screen, Ladd continued to star in such run-of-the-mill features as *Desert Legion* (1953), panned by one critic as "an impossibly dull type of ephemera"; *Saskatchewan* (1954), where he portrayed a Canadian mountie; and a series of forgettable productions filmed in England, including *Hell Below Zero* (1954) and *The Black Knight* (1954).

Upon Ladd's return from England, the actor announced the creation of his own company, Jaguar Productions, and starred as a member of the U.S. Calvary in the first film under the Jaguar banner, *Drum Beat* (1954). This was followed by *Hell on Frisco Bay* (1955), another Jaguar film, and *The McConnell Story* (1955), a biopic about real-life Korean War hero Joseph McConnell (who was killed while testing a Sabre jet just weeks before filming began). During filming of the latter feature, rumors flew that Ladd was having an affair with his co-star, June Allyson, wife of actor-director Dick Powell. (According to Beverly Linet's book, *Ladd*, Sue Carol called Powell to inform him that her husband was in love with Allyson, to which Powell reportedly replied, "Isn't everyone?") After filming, Ladd and Carol briefly separated, but they reunited a short time later, with Carol telling columnist Louella Parsons that "everything is all right."

"There isn't a chance of our marriage, which has been so perfect for fourteen years, coming to an end," Carol said. "I love Alan and he loves me. What was a temporary and personal problem between us—and will remain that—could have easily been solved in privacy and would have been forgotten by both of us now, if it had come at a different time. We had a quarrel when both of us were nervous wrecks ... we both acted impulsively, each of us guilty of feeding the gossips."

While life on the home front had seemingly returned to an even keel, the decline in Ladd's career was hastened when he turned down the role of Jett Rink in George Stevens' *Giant* (1956). Ladd was reportedly torn between the desire to work again with Stevens, who had directed him in *Shane*, and a reluctance to accept the secondary role, but most sources say that Ladd ultimately rejected the part upon the advice of his wife. The role went, instead, to James Dean, who was killed in an automobile accident just days after filming ended, and was posthumously nominated for an Academy Award for Best Supporting Actor. Years later, Sue Carol would tell *The Hollywood Reporter* that the decision to reject the part was "as much my fault as Alan's."

"I was used to his being top banana," Carol said, "and we both felt the Jimmy Dean role was a secondary part. It didn't turn out that way. But no matter."

Instead of *Giant*, Ladd was next seen in *Santiago* (1956), a lively action-adventure tale co-starring Lloyd Nolan, and several Jaguar Productions, including *The Big Land* (1957), a sprawling western which marked the film debut of Ladd's son, David, and was termed by one reviewer as "downright synthetic." Ladd also traveled to Greece to co-star with Sophia Loren in *Boy on a Dolphin* (1957), but his experience on this feature was far from idyllic.

"I like Sophia. If she dislikes me, I'm sorry," Ladd told the *New York Herald Tribune* in 1961. "All that happened during *Boy on a Dolphin* was that the director, Jean Negulesco, fell in love with her, with the result that she got all the good close-ups. All you ever saw of me in most scenes was the back of my neck. Sophia's a big girl and I'm a little guy, and I got fed up with it."

Ladd rebounded the following year with *The Proud Rebel* (1958), a well-received Civil War drama that again featured his son, David, but as he neared his mid-40s, the actor's handsome looks had started to fade, aided by what many viewed as an escalating drinking problem. More than one reviewer made a point to comment on the change in Ladd's appearance; after *Boy on a Dolphin*, columnist Sheilah Graham sniped, "Won't Alan Ladd have to go on a diet if he wants to continue playing lover-boy roles?" And Ladd's role in the mediocre 1960 Western *Guns of the Timberland* (also featuring his daughter, Alana) prompted a similar comment from Dorothy Kilgallen, who wrote: "Audiences viewing *Guns of the Timberland* express surprise at Alan Ladd's initial appearance; he's gained so much weight he looks quite different from the actor they remember as the star of other films."

In an effort to jump-start his career, Ladd turned to the small screen, announcing plans to enter the arena of television production. But Ladd's high hopes were dashed when his two television pilots, *Box 13* and *Ivy League*, were rejected by all of the major networks. He experienced even worse luck on the big screen; of his performance in *One Foot in Hell* (1960), one critic wrote that he "mumbled through his role with one [foot] in his mouth," and his appearance in *All the Young Men* (1960) was panned in *Time* magazine, whose reviewer noted that the film's co-star, real-life heavyweight boxer Ingemar Johansson, had bested Ladd in the acting department because the fighter "used two basic expressions— faintly amused and faintly serious— and beat actor Ladd's range by one." By now, Ladd's drinking was getting out of control, he had started adding sleeping pills to his alcohol intake, and rumors flew that his behavior had deemed him nearly unemployable.

Professionally, it appeared that Ladd's troubles couldn't get much worse, but his cinematic descent was hastened with the 1961 Italian production, *Duel of Champions* (also known as *Horatio*). The problems began during filming — after working for 11 weeks without pay, Ladd walked off the picture, returning only after another production company stepped in to rescue the picture. They needn't have bothered; eventually trimmed from three hours to only 71 minutes, the film was released three years later and was dismissed by one reviewer as "a thoroughly indifferent spectacle."

Ladd's life seemed to be spiraling out of control by November 1962, when the foreman of his ranch in Hidden Valley, California, found the actor in his pajamas, semi-conscious, with a bullet wound in his chest. Although the bullet had passed through one lung, Ladd made a speedy recovery, and later explained to reporters that, thinking he heard a prowler, he had picked up his gun and "stumbled over something in the dark." When he hit the floor, Ladd said, the gun went off.

"I reached for the phone and called Sue. 'Migosh,' I told her, 'I think I've been shot!'" Ladd told *Modern Screen* writer Kirtley Baskett. "Then I passed out, with the receiver still off the hook. Now wasn't that a damn fool performance?"

Following this incident, Ladd was tapped for a featured role in *The Carpetbaggers* (1964), based on the trashy best-seller by Harold Robbins— but the film would be his last. Although he remained sober throughout filming, Ladd reportedly began drinking after the end of the production, and on January 29, 1964, he was found dead in bed at his Palm Springs home. His death was ruled an accident, due to a reaction of chemical depressants and a "high level of alcohol." Ladd was 50 years old.

One of Hollywood's true stars, Alan Ladd is more often lauded more for his screen persona than for his acting ability, but in a handful of films, especially *Shane*, he evinced the ability to stretch beyond his cinematic image and display a talent capable of genuine depth. In a 1998 documentary on the actor's life, Paramount executive A.C. Lyles offered an explanation for Ladd's phenomenal appeal.

"I think every big star has a certain individual quality," Lyles said. "Alan Ladd had his own, very distinct qualities. He had that very stone face at times, and he had a voice that just went with it. And he had such a command on screen.

"The camera fell in love with him."

Film Noir Filmography

This Gun for Hire. Director: Frank Tuttle. Producer: Richard M. Blumenthal. Running time: 80 minutes. Released by Paramount, May 13, 1942. Cast: Alan Ladd, Veronica Lake, Robert Preston, Laird Cregar, Tully Marshall.

The Glass Key. Director: Stuart Heisler. Producer: B.G. DeSylva. Running time: 85 minutes. Released by Paramount, October 15, 1942. Cast: Brian Donlevy, Veronica Lake, Alan Ladd, Bonita Graville, Joseph Calleia, Richard Denning, Moroni Olsen, William Bendix, Margaret Hayes, Arthur Loft, George Meader, Eddie Marr, Frances Gifford, Joe McGuinn, Frank Hagney, Joseph King.

The Blue Dahlia. Director: George Marshall. Producer: John Houseman. Running time: 98 minutes. Released by Paramount, April 19, 1946. Cast: Alan Ladd, Veronica Lake, William Bendix, Howard Da Silva, Doris Dowling, Tom Powers, Hugh Beaumont, Howard Freeman, Don Costello, Will Wright, Frank Faylen, Walter Sande. Awards: Academy Award nomination for Best Original Screenplay (Raymond Chandler).

Calcutta. Director: John Farrow. Producer: Seton I. Miller. Running time: 83 minutes. Released by Paramount, May 30, 1947. Cast: Alan Ladd, Gail Russell, William Bendix, June Duprez, Lowell Gilmore, Edith King, Paul Singh, Gavin Muir, John Whitney, Benson Fong.

Chicago Deadline. Director: Lewis Allen. Producer: Robert Fellows. Running time: 87 minutes. Released by Paramount, November 2, 1949. Cast: Alan Ladd, Donna Reed, June Havoc, Irene Hervey, Arthur Kennedy, Berry Kroeger, Harold Vermilyea, Shepperd Strudwick, John Beal, Tom Powers, Gavin Muir, Dave Willock, Paul Lees.

Appointment with Danger. Director: Lewis Allen. Producer: Robert Fellows. Running time: 89 minutes. Released by Paramount, May 9, 1951. Cast: Alan Ladd, Phyllis Calvert, Paul Stewart, Jan Sterling, Jack Webb, Stacy Harris, Henry Morgan, David Wolfe, Dan Riss, Harry Antrim, Paul Lees.

References

"Alan Ladd, Actor." *Newark Evening News*, January 29, 1964.

"Alan Ladd, Actor, Dies at 50; Appeared in 150 Movie Roles." *New York Times*, January 30, 1964.

"Alan Ladd Dead at 50; Two-Fisted Film Star." *New York Herald Tribune*, January 30, 1964.

"Alan Ladd Dies in Calif. at Age 50." *Newsday*, January 30, 1964.

"Alan Ladd's Death Ruled 'Accidental.'" *New York Post*, February 4, 1964.

"Alan Ladd's Death Still a Mystery." *New York Daily News*, February 1, 1964.

Berg, A. Scott. "At Home with Alan Ladd." *Architectural Digest*, April 1994.

"Cause of Alan Ladd's Death to Be Determined by Tests." *New York Times*, February 1, 1964.

"'Dream' Is Over for Alan Ladd, 50." *New York Journal-American*, January 30, 1964.

Fagen, Herb. "Hollywood's Forgotten Ladd — The Lost Legacy of Alan Ladd. *Classic Images*, October 1992.

"Final Curtain for Alan Ladd." *Los Angeles Herald-Examiner*, January 30, 1964.

Graham, Lee. "The Legacy of Ladd — Romantic Tough Guy." *Hollywood Studio Magazine*, August 1978.

Hubler, Richard G. "Hollywood's Unlikely Hero." *Saturday Evening Post*, February 9, 1957.

Koven, Stan. "Autopsy Due in Death of Alan Ladd, 50." *New York Post*, January 30, 1964.

Linet, Beverly. *Ladd: A Hollywood Tragedy*. New York: Berkley Publishing Corporation, 1979.

"Long and Short of It All." *New York Post*, March 8, 1979.

Lucas, William D. "Alan Ladd: This Gun for Hire." *Classic Images*, September 1984.

Parsons, Harriet. *Keyhole Portraits: Alan Ladd and Veronica Lake*. Hollywood Studio Magazine, August 1979.

"Rites on Sat. for Alan Ladd." *New York Morning Telegraph*, January 31, 1964.

Roman, Robert C. "Alan Ladd." *Films in Review*, April 1964.

"'Short' Ladd Was Made to Look Tall Enough." *New York Post*, March 29, 1979.

St. Johns, Adela Rogers. "What You Don't Know About Alan Ladd's Marriage." *Photoplay*, July 1943.

Worthington, Rogers. "The Unhappy Fate of a Gun for Hire." *San Francisco Examiner*, April 15, 1979.

Documentary

"Alan Ladd: The True Quiet Man." A Wombat Production. Produced in Association with Janson Associates. Copyright 1998.

JACK LAMBERT

"Spill it, punk. Or I'll splash your brains out."— Jack Lambert in *99 River Street* (1946)

Despite roles in more than 50 feature films and numerous television appearances throughout the 1950s and 1960s to his credit, Jack Lambert falls into the category of an actor whose face is familiar, but whose name you can't place. He landed parts in a number of box-office hits— including *The Harvey Girls* (1946), *Abilene Town* (1946), *Scared Stiff* (1953), and *How the West Was Won* (1962)— but his specialty was utilizing his squinty-eyed, dour demeanor to portray a series of hoods who grew up on the other side of the tracks and wound up on the wrong side of the law. He played these roles to perfection in six examples from the film noir era: *The Killers* (1946), *The Unsuspected* (1947), *Border Incident* (1949), *The Enforcer* (1951), *99 River Street* (1953), and *Kiss Me Deadly* (1955).

Once labeled as "the man with the meanest eyes in Hollywood," John Taylor Lambert II was born on April 13, 1920, in Yonkers, New York. After attending elementary and secondary schools there, Lambert enrolled in Colorado College, where he majored in English and planned to teach English and drama. Instead, after graduating, he turned to the theater, working as a prop man and assistant director in several local companies back home in Yonkers. Before long, Lambert was appearing in small acting roles, and his career path was set. But the road was not smooth. While performing in his first road tour, he was fired from the play, and the manager of the production reportedly told him with some sarcasm, "You ought to go to New York."

"So I took his advice and went," Lambert later recalled.

In New York, Lambert wasted no time landing a role in a Theater Guild production of *The Fifth Column*, and a short time later, made his Broadway debut playing a brakeman in *Heavenly Express*. He was also seen portraying a gangster in *Blind Alley* and won his

first leading role in *Brother Cain*, playing a miner. Ironically, despite his academic expertise in the English language, Lambert found himself continually cast as men with less than lofty educational backgrounds.

"Of course, it isn't exactly what I've been wanting, but I guess I'll just have to wait," Lambert told the *New York Post* in 1941. "Besides, this is a leading role in *Brother Cain*, so I shouldn't complain too much. I'm still hoping, though, and my teachers at Colorado will bear with me, I guess— and hope, too."

Lambert later was seen in roles in the stage productions of *Hangtails* and *Johnny 2 x 4*, and when the latter play closed, the actor decided to try his luck in Hollywood, traveling west in January 1943 with $200 and a return ticket to New York. After four weeks of making the rounds at the Hollywood studios, Lambert won his first film role, playing a hood named Lefty Moran in MGM's *Lost Angel* (1943), starring Pat O'Brien. Later that year, he was also seen in small parts in *The Cross of Lorraine* (1943), an all-male war drama with Sir Cedric Hardwicke and Gene Kelly, and *Hostages* (1943), starring William Bendix. During the next few years— after taking time out to marry Frances Dalton in May 1945 — he played a series of undistinguished roles in all-but-forgotten features, including *The Hidden Eye* (1945), a dull programmer with Edward Arnold and Frances Rafferty. He was seen in more noticeable parts, however, in *Abilene Town* (1946), a well-done Randolph Scott western; *The Harvey Girls* (1946), a big-budget musical starring Judy Garland and Angela Lansbury; and *The Killers* (1946), Lambert's entry into the world of film noir.

In this first-rate offering, Lambert played Dum Dum, a vicious but slightly dull-witted member of a gang responsible for a large payroll heist. The other members of the motley group of hoods included gangleader Big Jim

Colfax (Albert Dekker), Blinky (Jeff Corey), and "the Swede" (Burt Lancaster), who falls for Big Jim's girl, Kitty (Ava Gardner), and plans to double cross the crew, take the money, and get the girl. Instead, the Swede finds himself duped by Big Jim, and winds up with no cash and no Kitty. As the years go by, the Swede makes a new life for himself at a gas station attendant in Brentwood, California, but when Big Jim learns of his whereabouts by happenstance, he has the Swede killed by the two assassins of the film's title. The Swede's killing sets off a chain of events that includes Dum Dum's search for the missing heist money, his murder of former partner Blinky, and his ultimate confrontation with Big Jim, which leads to both their deaths. The feature was hailed by critics upon its release, with the critic from *Variety* writing that "every character has its moment to shine and does," and William R. Weaver declaring in *Motion Picture Herald*: "The production is an elaborate and cunningly wrought expansion of the Ernest Hemingway short story ... with a masterly screenplay by Anthony Veiller [and] powerfully directed by Robert Siodmak."

After a minor role as a German lieutenant in *O.S.S.* (1946) and another small part in a passable western, *The Vigilantes Return* (1947), Lambert returned to film noir in *The Unsuspected* (1947), starring Claude Rains and Joan Caulfield. In this complex but riveting feature, Rains played Victor Grandison, a popular radio personality and, as it turns out, multiple murderer. In his quest to gain control of the fortune of his wealthy ward, Mathilda (Caulfield), Grandison's first victim is his secretary (Barbara Woodell), followed by his trampy niece (Audrey Totter) and her alcoholic husband (Hurd Hatfield). Before Grandison can succeed in adding Mathilda and her boyfriend, Steven Howard (Michael North), to the pile of bodies, he is fingered by authorities, and begins his final radio broadcast as he watches police arrive to arrest him.

As Mr. Press in *The Unsuspected*, Lambert played the pivotal role of a killer who confesses his crime to Grandison and is then blackmailed by the radio star to help in his nefarious murder plot. It is Mr. Press who, on Grandison's orders, attacks Steven, places his body in a trunk, and drives him to a nearby city dump, where he is nearly incinerated before police arrive in the nick of time. Although he turned in a good performance as the frightening killer, however, Lambert was overlooked by critics, most of whom panned the film; the reviewer for *Variety* found it "loaded with thrills and suspense," but John McCarten of the *New Yorker* dismissed it as "a seedy mystery," and *Motion Picture Herald*'s William R. Weaver labeled it "a bit too complicated for its own good."

During the remainder of the decade, Lambert kept busy in such films as *Dick Tracy's Dilemma* (1947), where he camped it up as "The Claw"; *Belle Starr's Daughter* (1948), the tiresome sequel to the earlier *Belle Starr* (1941); *The Great Gatsby* (1949), starring Alan Ladd in the title role; *Big Jack* (1949), notable chiefly as the last film in Wallace Beery's prolific career; and *Border Incident* (1949), his third film noir. Directed by Anthony Mann, this feature focused on an illegal alien smuggling ring operated by rancher Owen Parkson (Howard Da Silva). In a small but memorable role, Lambert played one of Parkson's hench-men, Chuck, who meets a violent end when he is confronted and killed by an undercover immigration agent (Ricardo Montalban). As the 1950s dawned, Lambert was seen in *North of the Great Divide* (1950), a Roy Rogers west-ern; *Dakota Lil* (1950), another western, this one starring George Montgomery and Marie Windsor; *Stars in My Crown* (1950), an easy-going drama featuring Joel McCrea as a coun-try parson; and his fourth film noir, *The En-forcer* (1951).

Once again cast as a ruthless hood, Lam-bert here portrays Philadelphia Tom Zaca, described by one character as a guy who "wasn't all there — but nobody ever said that when he was around." This hard-hitting fea-ture follows the efforts of district attorney Martin Ferguson (Humphrey Bogart) to nail an elusive gang leader who is the brains be-hind a powerful murder-for-hire syndicate. After the key witness against the gang leader falls to his death while trying to escape police custody, the film demonstrates, in a series of flashbacks, Ferguson's meticulous review of every detail of the case. By the film's end, he successfully identifies a clue that had been pre-viously overlooked and obtains the evidence he needs. Although critics once again failed to mention Lambert's performance, *The En-forcer* earned rave reviews, with Ruth Water-bury of the *Los Angeles Examiner* predicting that it would give audiences "a shuddery, tense couple of hours — and that ain't bad."

The following year, Lambert was back in the realm of film noir in *99 River Street* (1952), this time portraying Mickey, the vi-cious henchman of a jewel fence known as Christopher (Jay Adler). When a local gang-ster, Victor Rawlins (Brad Dexter) steals $50,000 from the fence, Christopher pursues him to a New Jersey bar (located at 99 River Street). Meanwhile, Rawlins is also being sought by cab driver Ernie Driscoll (John Payne), whose wife Rawlins murdered and placed in Ernie's cab. (Mistaking Driscoll for Rawlins' partner, Mickey attacks the luckless cabbie in Rawlins' apartment, but Driscoll soon turns the tables, using his skills as an

ex-boxer to pummel Mickey into submission. Amusingly, when the battered and bruised gunman returns to his boss, he tells Christo-pher he was beaten by *two* hoods.) After a shootout, Christopher's car is involved in a crash, but Ernie continues to pursue his prey, ultimately capturing him and holding him until police arrive. Although *99 River Street* was trashed by critics (Bosley Crowther wrote in the *New York Times* that "to say that this film is offensive would be kind"), Lambert turned in another well-done performance, depicting a particularly savage and memo-rable criminal.

Perhaps in an effort to distance himself, however briefly, from his spate of roles as a vicious hood, Lambert took on a brief job in 1954, performing in a musical comedy revue at Top's in San Diego, California. The actor had reportedly participated in concert sing-ing as a teenager ("until his voice changed," according to press reports), and he called on this experience during his live stage show, earning good reviews in *Variety*, whose critic reported that Lambert "proves himself an-other actor with surprisingly pleasant pipes."

Meanwhile, never at a loss for on-screen work, Lambert was seen in a number of well-received films during the next two years, in-cluding *Vera Cruz* (1954), starring Burt Lan-caster and Gary Cooper; *The Warriors* (1955), an Errol Flynn swashbuckler; *Three Cases of Murder* (1955), which presented a trio of sep-arate murder mysteries; and *Run for Cover* (1955), a James Cagney western directed by Nicholas Ray. Also in 1955 — the busiest year of his career — Lambert was featured in his sixth film noir, the classic *Kiss Me Deadly*.

Directed by Robert Aldrich, this feature starred Ralph Meeker as two-fisted private eye Mike Hammer, who becomes embroiled in a quest for a mysterious leather-bound satchel after a hitchhiker he picked up is sav-agely tortured and killed. Hammer's involve-ment leads him to such shady characters as Lily Carver (Gaby Rodgers), the gun-toting roommate of the dead girl, and Carl Evello (Paul Stewart), a lethal but refined gangster. As Sugar, one of Evello's henchmen, Lambert has little to do here — within moments of his first appearance on screen, his character is knocked unconscious by Hammer, and in his second encounter with Hammer, Sugar meets with a swift, unceremonious, and deadly end.

As the 1950s wound down, Lambert continued his busy shooting schedule, but the quality of his films were mediocre at best, including *The Little Hut* (1957), a disappointing bedroom farce starring Ava Gardner and Stewart Granger, and *Hot Car Girl* (1958), a violent juvenile delinquent drama starring a cast of youthful unknowns. His best feature during this period was also his final foray into the realm of film noir — *Party Girl* (1958). But in this rare color noir focusing on a corrupt mob lawyer (Robert Taylor) and his ultimate effort to extricate himself from the gangster for whom he works, Lambert's role as a bartender amounted to little more than a bit part.

Although he continued to play small roles in feature films, Lambert had by now turned his attention to the small screen — since 1954, and throughout the remainder of the decade, he was seen in numerous guest spots in such series as *The Adventures of Rin Tin Tin*, *Alfred Hitchcock Presents*, *Gunsmoke*, *Wagon Train*, *The Rifleman*, *Bat Masterson*, *The Californians*, and *Frontier Doctor*. And in 1959, he was cast as Joshua in NBC-TV's *Riverboat*, an hour-long adventure series starring Darren McGavin as a 1940s riverboat captain. The series ran until January 1961.

During the early 1960s, Lambert was seen in such big-screen productions as *Freckles* (1960), the fourth screen version of the 1901 Gene Stratton-Porter novel; *The George Raft Story* (1961), starring Ray Danton in the title role; and *How the West was Won* (1962), a sweeping, first-rate western with an all-star cast. But by now, after more than two decades in film, essentially playing the same psychopathic hood in a variety of incarnations, Lambert decided that he'd had enough. After a minor role in an entertaining Frank Sinatra–Dean Martin western, *Four for Texas* in 1963, the actor retired from the big screen. He continued to accept roles in such television series as *Frontier Circus*, *The Virginian*, *Get Smart*, and *Branded*, but in the mid-1960s, he left his acting career behind him, and has since been out of the public eye.

Although Jack Lambert was never seen in a starring role, and was frequently disappointed by his inability to break out of the "heavy" mold with which he'd been saddled since his days on Broadway, the actor nonetheless left behind a number of memorable performances that proved his on-screen worth. Perhaps it was Jeff Corey, his co-star in the film noir classic, *The Killers*, who best summed up Lambert's experience, when he labeled him as a "gentle man."

"He wouldn't swat a fly," Corey said in an interview in 2000. "But his career was typecasting at its best."

Film Noir Filmography

The Killers. Director: Robert Siodmak. Producer: Mark Hellinger. Running time: 105 minutes. Released by Universal, August 28, 1946. Cast: Edmond O'Brien, Ava Gardner, Albert Dekker, Sam Levene, John Miljan, Virginia Christine, Vince Barnett, Burt Lancaster, Charles D. Brown, Donald MacBride, Phil Brown, Charles McGraw, William Conrad, Queenie Smith, Garry Owen, Harry Hayden, Bill Walker, Jack Lambert, Jeff Corey, Wally Scott, Gabrielle Windsor, Rex Dale. Awards: Academy Award Nominations for Best Director (Robert Siodmak), Best Film Editing (Arthur Hilton), Best Score/Drama or Comedy (Miklos Rozsa), Best Screenplay (Anthony Veiller).

The Unsuspected. Director: Michael Curtiz. Producer: Charles Hoffman. Running time: 103 minutes. Released by Warner Brothers, October 3, 1947. Cast: Joan Caulfield, Claude Rains, Audrey Totter, Constance Bennett, Hurd Hatfield, Michael North, Fred Clark, Harry Lewis, Jack Lambert, Ray Walker, Nana Bryant, Walter Baldwin.

Border Incident. Director: Anthony Mann. Producer: Nicholas Nayfack. Running time: 96 minutes. Released by MGM, November 19, 1949. Cast: Ricardo Montalban, George Murphy, Howard Da Silva, James Mitchell, Arnold Moss, Alfonso Bedoya, Teresa Celli, Charles McGraw, Jose Torvay, John Ridgely, Arthur Hunnicutt, Sig Ruman, Otto Waldis, Harry Antrim, Tony Barr, Rozene Jones, John McGuire, Jack Lambert, Nedrich Young, Fred Graham, Lynn Whitney.

The Enforcer. Director: Bretaigne Windust. Producer: Milton Sperling. Running time: 88

minutes. Released by Warner Bros., February 24, 1951. Cast: Humphrey Bogart, Zero Mostel, Ted De Corsia, Everett Sloane, Roy Roberts, Lawrence Tolan, King Donovan, Robert Steele, Patricia Joiner, Don Beddoe, Tito Vuolo, John Kellogg, Jack Lambert, Adelaide Klein, Susan Cabot, Mario Siletti.

99 River Street. Director: Phil Karlson. Producer: Edward Small. Running time: 83 minutes. Released by United Artists, October 3, 1953. Cast: John Payne, Evelyn Keyes, Brad Dexter, Frank Faylen, Peggie Castle, Jay Adler, Jack Lambert, Eddy Waller, Glen Langan, John Day, Ian Wolfe, Peter Leeds, William Tannen, Gene Reynolds.

Kiss Me Deadly. Director and Producer: Robert Aldrich. Running time: 105 minutes. Released by United Artists, May 18, 1955. Cast: Ralph Meeker, Albert Dekker, Paul Stewart, Maxine Cooper, Gaby Rodgers, Wesley Addy, Juano Hernandez, Nick Dennis, Cloris Leachman, Marian Carr, Jack Lambert, Jack Elam, Jerry Zinneman, Percy Helton, Fortunio Bonanova, Silvio Minciotti, Leigh Snowden, Madi Comfort, James Seay, Mara Mc-Affee, Robert Cornthwaite, James McCallian, Jess-lyn Fax, Mort Marshall, Strother Martin, Marjorie Bennett, Art Loggins, Bob Sherman, Keith McConnell, Paul Richards, Eddie Beal.

Party Girl. Director: Nicholas Ray. Producer: Joe Pasternak. Running time: 99 minutes. Released by MGM, October 28, 1958. Cast: Robert Taylor, Cyd Charisse, Lee J. Cobb, John Ireland, Kent Smith, Claire Kelly, Corey Allen, Lewis Charles, David Opatoshu, Kem Dibbs, Patrick McVey, Barbara Lang, Myrna Hansen, Betty Utey, Jack Lambert.

References

Biography of Jack Lambert. RKO Radio Pictures, Inc., circa 1947.

"Jack Lambert." *Variety*, April 7, 1954.

"Lambert is Typed in 'Cain.'" *New York Post*, August 1941.

"Brother Cain." *Playbill*, September 12, 1941.

"What Price Education? Actor Asks." *New York Times*, September 8, 1945.

— BURT LANCASTER —

"You can't live on dreams forever. Waiting only weakens you and your dream. My motto is if you want something, get it now." — Burt Lancaster in *Sorry, Wrong Number* (1948)

Burt Lancaster was larger than life.

He began his career as a circus acrobat, became an Academy Award–winning performer of the silver screen, and helped to launch one of the most successful independent production companies of his time. Intensely private in his personal life, the Burt Lancaster of the cinema offered an undeniable presence — a combination of striking good looks, brawny physique, and superior acting ability that earned him the justified title of "star."

"Any time Burt was in a film, you wanted to go see it. Any time he was on television you wanted to watch it," actress Rhonda Fleming once said. "That's the magic and the magnetism that he had."

During his 43-year career, Lancaster starred in such Hollywood treasures as *From Here to Eternity* (1953), *The Rainmaker* (1956), *Gunfight at the O.K. Corral* (1957), and *Elmer Gantry* (1960), and made his mark in the realm of film noir with roles in seven features: *The Killers* (1946), *Brute Force* (1947), *I Walk Alone* (1948), *Sorry, Wrong Number* (1948), *Kiss the Blood Off My Hands* (1948), *Criss Cross* (1949), and *Sweet Smell of Success* (1957).

Once labeled "Mr. Muscles and Teeth," Burton Stephen Lancaster was born on November 2, 1913, one of five children of postal clerk James H. Lancaster and his wife, Lizzie. A native of a poor section of New York City where, he later recalled, "the kids used to carry knives," Lancaster attended P.S. 83 and De-Witt Clinton High School, managing to steer clear of a path of juvenile delinquency by spending much of his time at the public library and the Union Settlement House, a local youth club and sports center.

"We wore castoff clothes, but we were lucky," Lancaster once said. "We always had food on the table."

While participating in the activities offered at the Union Settlement House, Lancaster and his closest friend, Nick Cravat, were introduced to Australian acrobat Curley Brent, who taught the boys acrobatics and gymnastics. After his high school graduation, Lancaster enrolled at New York University on a basketball scholarship, planning to become a physical education teacher, but he abruptly changed his vocational course during one fateful school day in 1931: "I walked out of that class and never went back," he said years later.

Lancaster teamed with his boyhood chum to form an act known as Lang and Cravat, and the pair joined the Kay Brothers Circus in Petersburg, Virginia, earning $3 a week, plus board. After 30 weeks with Kay Brothers, the two young men signed on with a bigger company, and for the next seven years, they performed throughout the United States in a variety of tent shows, vaudeville, and even a stint with the Ringling Brothers Circus.

"It was a great life," Lancaster said in a 1988 interview. "Doing an act in front of people … feeling like a million dollars, strong enough to lift a building, and hearing the plaudits of the people, such as they were, for a little cockamamie act. But it didn't make any difference. For us, it was a very glamorous life, traveling all over the country."

Lancaster didn't spend all of his time under the big top, however. In 1935, he married circus aerialist June Ernst, but the union was short-lived and the actor seldom mentioned his first wife in later years, except to commend her talent as "the only woman in America who could do horizontal bar tricks." He also took a leave from the act in the late 1930s to join New York's Federal Theatre Project, a government-funded initiative that provided work for unemployed actors.

Although Lancaster returned to his acrobatic act following his tenure with the Federal Theatre Project, fate soon stepped in to change his course again. While performing in St. Louis, he suffered an injury to his right hand that later became infected; doctors gave him a choice between possible amputation or quitting the act, which spelled the end of Lang and Cravat. (A decade later, after Lancaster had achieved screen fame, he again joined with Nick Cravat, performing for the Cole Brothers Circus—this time around, the act commanded the significantly higher sum of $11,000 a week.)

At loose ends after the abrupt end of his career as an acrobat, Lancaster was taken in by a circus family in Chicago, where he spent the next three years earning a living in such varied posts as engineer for a meatpacking firm, salesman of furniture and men's haberdashery, and floorwalker in the lingerie department at Marshall Field's department store. In 1942, he was hired as a promoter for the Community Concerts Bureau in New York, but he was drafted into the armed services a short time later, spending the bulk of his time entertaining troops in North Africa, Sicily, Italy, and Austria, and performing in a military revue called *Stars and Gripes*. During his tour of Italy, Lancaster met a USO performer named Norma Anderson; the two went on to marry in December 1946 and later had four children, William, Susan, Joanna, and Sighle. (In 1969, after a 22-year union, Lancaster and Anderson divorced, and the actor wed again in 1989; this marriage, to Susan Martin, lasted until Lancaster's 1994 death.)

After the war, Lancaster returned to New York City, where Norma had landed a job as secretary to a radio producer. According to legend, fate intervened once again when Lancaster arrived at the RCA building one day to take Norma to lunch—on the elevator, he found that he was being intensely observed by a fellow passenger, who turned out to be an associate of Broadway producer Irving Jacobs. Impressed by former acrobat's bearing and good looks, the man suggested that Lancaster audition for the role of an American soldier in Jacobs' upcoming play, *A Sound of Hunting*. To his surprise, Lancaster won the role and debuted on Broadway on November 21, 1945.

"I wasn't nervous at all," Lancaster later recalled. "'What can happen to me?' I said to myself. 'I can miss a line, but I can't get hurt.'"

Although the production closed after only 23 performances, Lancaster caught the attention of critics, including the reviewer for *PM*, who noted his "attractive" performance, and Robert Garland of the *New York Journal-American*, who wrote: "Burton Lancaster, as Mooney, is the non-com every private prays for." Upon the recommendation of co-star Sam Levene, Lancaster engaged the services of an agent, Harold Hecht, and a short time later signed a long-term, two-picture-a-year deal with Hollywood producer Hal B. Wallis. (Wallis, incidentally, wanted to change the actor's name to Stuart Chase; fortunately, Lancaster refused.)

Within the span of a year, Lancaster filmed four features—the first picture into release also marked his entry in the world of the film noir: *The Killers* (1946). Featuring taut direction and a top-notch cast, this film begins as Lancaster's character, Pete Lund—better known as "the Swede"—is shot and killed by the gunmen of the title. Although he is warned of the killers' impending arrival, however, the Swede seems resigned to his fate, telling a friend, "Once I did something wrong." In a series of flashbacks, the feature shows the circumstances that led to the Swede's murder, centering on his involvement in a payroll robbery and his obsession with a beautiful but double-crossing dame, Kitty Collins (Ava Gardner). By the final reel, a slew of corpses have joined that of the Swede, including the two men who gunned him down (William Conrad and Charles McGraw), and the three other members of the gang who carried out the heist, Dum Dum (Jack Lambert), Blinky (Jeff Corey), and the group's mastermind, "Big Jim" Colfax (Albert Dekker). The only principal player of the gang left standing is Kitty, who is last seen begging her dying spouse, Colfax, to clear her name.

"In *The Killers* I was a big, dumb Swede," Lancaster said years later. "I could be very simple in the part; there was no need to be highly ostentatious or theatrical. For a new actor, this is much easier than something histrionic. There's no question about the good fortune of being ushered into films in that kind of role."

Lancaster's association with the film was indeed teeming with good fortune—he became an overnight star and critics hailed his performance; the reviewer for *Variety* applauded his "strong" portrayal of the central character, William R. Weaver of *Motion Picture Herald* announced that he "plays the murder victim with conviction," and in *Motion Picture Daily*, Thalia Bell wrote: "Burt Lancaster, as the Swede, makes an auspicious screen debut."

The following year, Lancaster was top-billed in his second film noir, *Brute Force* (1947), where he portrayed prison inmate Joe Collins. Spurred both by the dehumanizing treatment of a sadistic guard, Capt. Munsey (Hume Cronyn), and his desire to return to his wheelchair-bound girlfriend (Ann Blyth), Joe joins with his cellmates to plan an intricate prison break. ("Nothing's okay," he grimly tells his fellow prisoners. "It never was and it never will be. Not 'til we're out. You get that? Out.") Munsey ultimately learns of the plan, however, and the film culminates in the violent deaths of the inmates involved in the break, as well as Munsey himself, who is tossed by Joe from a tower into a swarming sea of convicts. After the film's release, Lancaster earned mostly good reviews—although one critic termed him "an overplaying ham," Lloyd L. Sloan praised his "fine" performance in the *Hollywood Citizen-News*, and Harrison Carroll of the *Los Angeles Evening Herald Express* applauded Lancaster for his "angry, forceful performance that will boost him up another notch in his screen career."

In his third film noir in as many years, Lancaster next appeared in *I Walk Alone* (1948), co-starring Lizabeth Scott and Kirk Douglas. (Lancaster and Douglas went on to make five more feature films together and develop an often-contentious but lifelong friendship: "Kirk's a very dear friend of mine

... and we have a lot of controversy and conflict when we work, because he's very much like me," Lancaster once said of his relationship with Douglas. "He's conceited — he tries to tell me how to act, I try to tell him how to act ... and strangely enough, out of this kind of feuding and fighting and fussing has come a great respect and mutual love.")

I Walk Alone centered on bootlegger Frankie Madison (Lancaster), who emerges from a 14-year prison stretch to learn that his former partner, Noll "Dink" Turner (Douglas), is now the successful owner of a swank nightclub. In an early scene, Frankie bitterly reveals that he was all but abandoned by Dink during his imprisonment: "My pal, Dink — he sent me a carton of cigarettes a month," he says. "Never a visit, never even a letter. I was 63 minutes away by the new parkway — he never drove it once." Frankie's rancor increases when it becomes obvious that Dink plans to renege on the profit-sharing agreement that the pair made before Frankie was jailed, and that Frankie's own brother, Dave (Wendell Corey), is in Dink's employ. When Dave tries to extricate himself from Dink's underhanded machinations, he is murdered by the refined thug, but Frankie later forces a confession from his former partner, who is gunned down by police while trying to escape.

The least impressive of Lancaster's seven noirs, *I Walk Alone* was completely dismissed by the reviewer for *Commonweal*, who wrote: "If by any chance you're in the market for a nightclub, you better see this picture. I can't think of any other reason for bothering about it." Critics were also less than kind toward Lancaster's performance this time around; the reviewer for *Newsweek* opined that the actor "is tougher than he is convincing," and in the *New York Times*, Bosley Crowther wrote that Lancaster played "the would-be 'muscler' with the blank-faced aplomb of Tarzan."

In an effort to break out of the "tough guy" mold that had formed his early career, Lancaster fought for and won the role of Chris Keller in *All My Sons* (1948), based on the stage play by Arthur Miller and co-star-

ring Edward G. Robinson and Mady Christians. Although one critic complained that the film "depends too much on obvious dramatic contrivances," Lancaster's portrayal of the naive son of a war profiteer earned fine notices, with the critic from *Newsweek* terming him "surprisingly good," and *Time*'s reviewer including Lancaster in his praise of the "unusually well-acted" performances of the film's stars.

After *All My Sons*, Lancaster starred opposite Barbara Stanwyck in his fourth film noir, *Sorry, Wrong Number* (1948). Here, the actor played Henry Stephenson, whose domineering wife, Leona (Stanwyck), uses her heart condition to keep him ensconced in a meaningless job at her father's pharmaceutical company. The bedridden Leona, who keeps constant contact with the outside world via telephone, overhears a conversation one night in which two men are discussing the murder of a woman. Through a series of calls, Leona not only discovers that Henry is involved in the crime-to-be, but that *she* is the intended victim. As it turns out, Henry had been supplementing his income by stealing drugs from the pharmaceutical company, but was blackmailed by a former partner for $200,000 and planned Leona's demise in order to obtain the needed funds. At the last minute, Henry experiences a change of heart and warns his wife to escape, but it is too late; in horror, he listens on the telephone to Leona's screams as the killer enters her bedroom. When Henry calls back minutes later, a man picks up the phone and laconically states, "Sorry, wrong number."

As the cuckolded Henry Stephenson, Lancaster turned in a fine performance of a man torn between love for his wife and frustration over his inability to fulfill his own dreams: "I don't belong to your father's organization," he tells Leona in one scene. "Sure, I married his daughter — so I'm a vice-president now. I have a nice office, my name on the door. Even a secretary. But what do I do? Nothing…. Working for your father is like running in a dream — no matter how hard you try, you know you'll never get anywhere." Although most of the accolades from critics were reserved for Stanwyck's Academy Award–nominated performance, Lancaster earned his share of applause, with the reviewer from *Look* claiming that he "continues his steady advance from muscle-man to accomplished actor" and Harold Barnes of the *New York Herald-Tribune* terming him "grimly persuasive." Once again, however, Lancaster was slammed in the *New York Times* by the acerbic Bosley Crowther, who dismissed his performance as "painfully obtuse."

At this point, Lancaster decided to take the direction of his professional career into his own hands. Along with his agent, the actor formed Hecht-Norma Productions (named after Lancaster's wife and his agent, Harold Hecht). Of his decision to create the independent production company, Lancaster joked years later, "Here were a couple of bums without a quarter between us discussing producing our own pictures."

The maiden offering of Hecht-Norma Productions was the outstanding feature, *Kiss the Blood Off My Hands* (1948), Lancaster's fifth film noir. As the picture opens, the narrator intones, "The aftermath of war is rubble — the rubble of cities and of men…. The cities can be rebuilt, but the wounds of men, whether of the mind or of the body, heal slowly." The story of *Kiss the Blood* focuses on one such man, Bill Saunders (Lancaster), whose luckless existence in post-war London spirals downhill when he accidentally kills a bartender in a local pub. Bill begins to turn his life around, however, after seeking sanctuary in the apartment of a young woman, Jane Wharton (Joan Fontaine). Bound by their mutual loneliness, Bill and Jane grow closer over time, but Bill's bliss is shattered when he is blackmailed by Harry Carter (Robert Newton), a pub patron who knows of the circumstances surrounding the bartender's death. When the oily blackmailer pays a visit to Jane, she stabs him with a pair of scissors; although the wound is not fatal, Carter later dies during a scuffle with Bill. Planning to flee the country with Jane, Bill is dismayed when she insists that the two turn themselves in to authorities and, in the somewhat disappointing finale, Bill ultimately agrees: "If we go back and stick together," he says, "maybe somebody will give us a break."

Kiss the Blood Off My Hands was universally applauded by critics — the reviewer for *Commonweal* termed it "an exceptionally well made Hollywood production," and the feature was praised in the *Rotarian* for its "imaginative direction, intelligent performances, and a camera that explores the foggy London setting for all it's worth." Lancaster earned accolades for his performance as well, with the *New York Times* critic proclaiming that he "walks off with the acting honors even with stiff competition from Joan Fontaine."

The following year saw Lancaster's appearance in his sixth film noir, *Criss Cross* (1949), with Yvonne DeCarlo and Dan Duryea. In this well-done example from the era, Lancaster portrayed Steve Thompson, who finds himself caught in a triangle of passion and murder involving his ex-wife, Anna (DeCarlo), and her new spouse Slim Dundee (Duryea), a gambler with underworld connections. Returning to his hometown after a year's absence, Steve is swiftly lured by Anna's charms: "A man eats an apple, gets a piece of the core stuck between his teeth," he explains. "He tries to work it out with some cellophane off a cigarette pack — what happens? The cellophane gets stuck in there too. Anna — what was the use? I knew one way or the other, somehow I'd wind up seeing her that night." After becoming involved with Anna again, Steve tries to cover their affair by suggesting to Slim that they team up for a payroll heist, but the scheme ultimately ends in disaster — Anna disappears with the stolen loot and Steve manages to find her, only to learn that she plans to flee without him ("How far could I get with you?" Anna asks bluntly. "You have to watch out for yourself. That's the way it is.") Before Anna can carry out her plans, however, Slim catches up to the pair, shoots them both, and they die in each other's arms. Although Lancaster was dismissed in the *New York Times* for playing "the same old tough guy of yore," he was praised in *Motion Picture Herald* for his "fine performance as a man driven to crime," and the critic for *Variety* wrote: "Lancaster's role is a made-to-order part of a two-fisted square-shooter who gets fouled up in a jam through no fault of his own."

Around this time, Lancaster inked a deal with Warner Bros. for six pictures, three of which would be films produced by the actor's company. In the first of these, Lancaster starred in *The Flame and the Arrow* (1950), an entertaining swashbuckler in which he earned praise from one critic for his "amazing feats of derring-do in the manner of those celebrated by Douglas Fairbanks, Sr." (The cast of *The Flame and the Arrow* also included Nick Cravat, Lancaster's boyhood chum and former circus partner; over the next two decades, Cravat would appear in a number of Lancaster's films, including *Run Silent, Run Deep* [1958], *Airport* [1970], and *Valdez Is Coming* [1971].)

In addition to his highly physical performance in *The Flame and the Arrow*, Lancaster displayed his athleticism in such features as *Jim Thorpe — All American* (1951), where he played the real-life Native American football

star and gold medal-winning Olympian; *Ten Tall Men* (1951), a Foreign Legion actioner; and *The Crimson Pirate* (1952), a Hecht-Norma production that was enthusiastically described in *Newsweek* as "a wonderful bedlam of skyscraping bravura and seafaring skullduggery that needs no explanation beyond its physical impact … It's wonderful, really." Despite the success of these features, however, Lancaster was determined to demonstrate that his capabilities as a performer extended beyond the physical.

"I'll go on making swashbucklers for my own company," he said. "But in my outside pictures, I want to do things that will help me as an actor against the time when I have to give up all this jumping around." In one such feature, Lancaster starred opposite Shirley Booth in *Come Back, Little Sheba* (1952), a first-rate drama in which he played a middle-aged, recovering alcoholic. For his performance, the actor was once again showered with praise from critics — in a typical notice, the reviewer for *The Hollywood Reporter* raved that Lancaster's portrayal of Doc Delaney was "a complete switch from anything he has ever done and easily the outstanding effort of his career. His surprise casting results in a dramatic bombshell!"

Throughout the remainder of the 1950s, Lancaster continued to demonstrate his versatility in such blockbusters as *From Here to Eternity* (1953), for which he received his first of four Academy Award nominations for Best Actor (he lost to William Holden in *Stalag 17*, but he won the New York Film Critics Award); *The Rose Tattoo* (1955), where he played an Italian truck driver; *The Rainmaker* (1956), an outstanding drama co-starring Katharine Hepburn that was praised in *Time* as "one of the most warmly appealing romantic comedies of the year"; *Gunfight at the O.K. Corral* (1957), in which he played Wyatt Earp to Kirk Douglas' Doc Holliday; and *Sweet Smell of Success* (1957), his final film noir.

In *Sweet Smell*, Lancaster played one of the most venomous roles of his career, powerful Broadway gossip columnist J.J. Hunsecker, who is described by one character as possessing "the scruples of a guinea pig and the morals of a gangster." The story here centers on Hunsecker's abnormal possessiveness toward his kid sister, Susan (Susan Harrison), and his obsession with ending her engagement to local musician Steve Dallas (Martin Milner). Hunsecker engages a self-serving press agent, Sidney Falco (Tony Curtis), to break up the romance, and Sidney rises to the occasion, arranging for the musician's arrest on drug possession charges and initiating a smear campaign that hints at his affiliation with the Communist Party. Ultimately, however, Hunsecker's plan backfires—he savagely beats Sidney after mistakenly suspecting him of putting the moves on his sister; Sidney lets it slip that Hunsecker was behind the scheme to thwart Susan's relationship; and Susan flees to join her lover, leaving Hunsecker alone in his penthouse overlooking the city.

Replete with unsavory, unredeemable characters, *Sweet Smell of Success* earned mostly rave reviews from critics; Sara Hamilton of the *Los Angeles Herald Examiner* judged that "the production as a whole was well-handled"; the *New York Times*' A.H. Weiler praised the film's "pulsating dialogue, brisk direction, [and] good performances"; and Philip K. Scheuer wrote in the *Los Angeles Times*: "*Sweet Smell* may be unfair to columnists, but it will be relished by all those who seek confirmation of, and take vicarious delight in, the depravity of others. And that includes an awful lot of us." Lancaster earned similar acclaim for his portrayal of the venal columnist, with Weiler judging that he gave the part "its proper modicum of callousness," and the critic for *Variety* describing his role as "cunningly played." And Scheuer viewed the actor's performance in context with his entire career when he opined: "Burt Lancaster is an actor who will not be typecast and will play anything to prove that he isn't. In *Sweet Smell of Success*, he plays a man who, in a quite different and thoroughly hair-raising way, will not stop at anything either."

Throughout the decade, Lancaster continued to increase his output of films through his production company (which, in the early 1950s underwent a name change to Hecht-Lancaster, and later still was altered to incorporate new partner James Hill, becoming Hecht-Hill-Lancaster). The films varied in quality; the best of these included *Vera Cruz* (1954), a western co-starring Gary Cooper and Denise Darcel; *Marty* (1955), a surprise hit that won the Academy Award for Best Picture (and was one of the company's few films in which Lancaster did not appear); *Trapeze* (1956), which gave Lancaster a prime opportunity to demonstrate his still-outstanding acrobatic prowess; *Run Silent, Run Deep* (1958), hailed in the *New York Times* as "a submarine picture, every tense, exciting moment of the way"; *The Bachelor Party* (1957), another feature whose cast did not include Lancaster; and *Separate Tables* (1958), which featured Oscar-winning performances by David Niven and Wendy Hiller. Lancaster was less successful, however with such films as *Apache* (1954), in which he portrayed an Indian warrior, and *The Devil's Disciple* (1959), a dull costumer set in New England during the 1700s. Lancaster also struck out in his sole effort as a director, *The Kentuckian* (1955), which was panned by the critic for *Newsweek*, who wrote: "Fringed buckskins and shaggy neck hair are now being sported by Burt Lancaster. Other frontiersmen have little to worry about, however, unless Lancaster gets better movies than this one to wear them in." Lancaster himself acknowledged the latter film's lack of quality, placing the blame firmly on his own shoulders.

"Long ago, I learned it's no trick to be a director. The tough job is being a good director," Lancaster said. "I probably will never again act in a picture I also direct."

Now entering the mid-century of his life, Lancaster continued to turn in first-rate performances in a number of films, including *Elmer Gantry* (1960), where his portrayal of a charismatic con-man earned him an Academy Award for Best Actor and his second New York Film Critics Award; *Judgment at Nuremberg* (1961), which was hailed in the *Saturday Review* as "the most important

American picture of the year"; *Birdman of Alcatraz* (1962), which earned Lancaster a third Academy Award nod (he lost this time to Gregory Peck in *To Kill a Mockingbird*); *A Child is Waiting* (1963), which prompted *Time*'s critic to proclaim that Lancaster "has never been better"; *The Leopard* (1963), in which the actor turned in what he called "some of my best work"; *Seven Days in May* (1964), described by one critic as "an almost perfect thriller"; *The Professionals* (1966), a top-notch western with Lee Marvin, Robert Ryan, and Woody Strode; *The Scalphunters* (1968), a comedy-western for which Lancaster was lauded in the *New York Times* for acting his role with "gusto"; and *The Swimmer* (1968), an offbeat feature in which Lancaster played a disillusioned suburbanite who makes his way home after a party via the backyard pools of his neighbors.

By now, Lancaster had dissolved his partnership with Harold Hecht and James Hill — although it had produced some of the most memorable features of the era, the actor explained that the company had become too costly to maintain.

"We had built up an organization that was too big for the things we wanted to do," Lancaster said. "We had taken on some of the overhead-aches of a major studio and could no longer afford to operate the way we wanted to. You can't spend two or three years preparing for a film that will have limited appeal when your overhead is the size of ours."

Despite his busy film schedule, Lancaster found time for exercising other passions — a strong supporter of the civil rights movement of the 1960s, the actor participated in the famed March on Washington helmed by Dr. Martin Luther King; gathered 2,000 signatures on a petition in support of civil rights to present to Dr. King; and served a term as President of the American Civil Liberties Union. Also during this period, Lancaster expanded his performing realm, returning to the stage for the first time in nearly three decades for *Knickerbocker Holiday* (1971), and making his television debut later that year as host of the PBS-TV special *An Amer-*

ican Christmas. Although his appearances on the small screen were rare, Lancaster was later seen in such varied programs as the popular, long-running children's program *Sesame Street* (1972), on which he recited the alphabet; *Moses the Lawgiver* (1976), a miniseries in which he played the title role; *Victory at Entebbe* (1976), a popular made-for-TV movie; *Night of 100 Stars* (1982), the centennial celebration for the Actors Fund of America; *Marco Polo* (1982), a 10-hour miniseries in which he was seen as Pope Gregory X; *Barnum* (1986), where he portrayed the famed circus impresario; and *Legacy of the Hollywood Blacklist* (1987), for which he served as host.

Lancaster also continued to average one movie each year on the big screen, including the blockbuster hit *Airport* (1970), which the actor characterized as "at best, a cockamamie film"; *Ulzana's Raid* (1972), a well-done western helmed by Robert Aldrich; *The Midnight Man* (1974), which the actor co-produced and co-directed with Roland Kibbee; *Buffalo Bill and the Indians* (1976), co-starring Paul Newman in the title role; *The Island of Dr. Moreau* (1977), a science fiction-horror film described by one reviewer as "creepily good"; *Atlantic City* (1981), for which the actor earned his fourth and final Oscar nomination (he lost this time to fellow Hollywood veteran Henry Fonda for *On Golden Pond*); *Tough Guys* (1986), Lancaster's final screen teaming with Kirk Douglas, in which they played a pair of aging criminals; and *Field of Dreams* (1989), a highly acclaimed baseball fantasy where Lancaster was featured as ex-ballplayer "Doc" Graham.

"I really wanted a movie star for this part," said Chris Alden Robinson, the writer-director of the latter film. "Someone who became famous in another era and sill has that magic about him. Burt Lancaster certainly fills those requirements. He is one of the great movie actors of all time."

Sadly, *Field of Dreams* would contain Lancaster's final appearance on the silver screen. The following year, while visiting a friend in the hospital, the actor suffered a massive cerebral stroke, after which his body slowly deteriorated over the next four years. He died on October 20, 1994, after succumbing to a fatal heart attack. He was 80 years old.

With his incredible presence, magnificent acting talent, and outstanding body of cinematic work, Burt Lancaster was a star of the screen whose light has not diminished with time. Perhaps it was the actor himself who best described his contribution to the annals of film and the impact that he still has today.

"We're all forgotten sooner or later," Lancaster once said. "But not the films. That's all the memorial we should need or hope for."

Film Noir Filmography

The Killers. Director: Robert Siodmak. Producer: Mark Hellinger. Running time: 105 minutes. Released by Universal, August 28, 1946. Cast: Edmond O'Brien, Ava Gardner, Albert Dekker, Sam Levene, John Miljan, Virginia Christine, Vince Barnett, Burt Lancaster, Charles D. Brown, Donald MacBride, Phil Brown, Charles McGraw, William Conrad, Queenie Smith, Garry Owen, Harry Hayden, Bill Walker, Jack Lambert, Jeff Corey, Wally Scott, Gabrielle Windsor, Rex Dale. Awards: Academy Award nominations for Best Director (Robert Siodmak), Best Film Editing (Arthur Hilton), Best Score/Drama or Comedy (Miklos Rozsa), Best Screenplay (Anthony Veiller).

Brute Force. Director: Jules Dassin. Producer: Mark Hellinger. Running time: 95 minutes. Released by Universal-International, June 6, 1947. Cast: Burt Lancaster, Hume Cronyn, Charles Bickford, Yvonne DeCarlo, Ann Blyth, Ella Raines, Anita Colby, Sam Levene, Howard Duff, Art Smith, Roman Bohnen, John Hoyt, Richard Gaines, Frank Puglia, Jeff Corey, Vince Barnett, James Bell, Jack Overman, Whit Bissell, Sir Lancelot, Ray Teal, Jay C. Flippen, James O'Rear, Howland Chamberlain, Kenneth Patterson, Crane Whitley, Charles McGraw, John Harmon, Gene Stutenroth, Wally Rose, Carl Rhodes, Guy Beach, Edmund Cobb, Tom Steele.

I Walk Alone. Director: Byron Haskin. Producer: Hal B. Wallis. Running time: 98 minutes. Released by Paramount, January 22, 1948. Cast: Burt Lancaster, Lizabeth Scott, Kirk Douglas, Wendell Corey, Kristine Miller, George Rigaud, Marc Lawrence, Mike Mazurki, Mickey Knox, Roger Neury.

Sorry, Wrong Number. Director: Anatole Litvak. Producers: Hal B. Wallis, Anatole Litvak. Running time: 98 minutes. Released by Paramount, September 1, 1948. Cast: Barbara Stanwyck, Burt Lancaster, Ann Richards, Wendell Corey, Harold Vermilyea, Ed Begley, Leif Erickson, William Conrad, John Bromfield, Jimmy Hunt, Dorothy Neumann, Paul Fierro. Awards: Academy Award nomination for Best Actress (Barbara Stanwyck).

Kiss the Blood Off My Hands. Director: Norman Foster. Producer: Harold Hecht. Running time: 79 minutes. Released by Universal-International, October 29, 1948. Cast: Joan Fontaine, Burt Lancaster, Robert Newton, Lewis L. Russell, Aminta Dyne, Grizelda Hervey, Jay Novello, Colin Keith-Johnston, Reginald Sheffield, Campbell Copelin, Leland Hodgson, Peter Hobbes.

Criss Cross. Director: Robert Siodmak. Producer: Michel Kraike. Running time: 88 minutes. Released by Universal-International, January 12, 1949. Cast: Burt Lancaster, Yvonne DeCarlo, Dan Duryea, Stephen McNally, Richard Long, Esy Morales, Tom Pedi, Percy Helton, Alan Napier, Griff Barnett, Meg Randall, Joan Miller, Edna M. Holland, John Doucette, Marc Krath, James O'Rear, John Skins Miller, Robert Osterloh, Vincent Renno, Charles Wagenheim.

Sweet Smell of Success. Director: Alexander MacKendrick. Producer: James Hill. Running time: 96 minutes. Released by United Artists, June 27, 1957. Cast: Burt Lancaster, Tony Curtis, Susan Harrison, Martin Milner, Sam Levene, Barbara Nichols, Jeff Donnell, Joseph Leon, Edith Atwater, Emile Meyer, Joe Frisco, David White, Lawrence Dobkin, Lurene Tuttle, Queenie Smith, Autumn Russell, Jay Adler, Lewis Charles.

References

"Actor Called 'Angry Man.'" Los Angeles Times, October 8, 1946.

Biography of Burt Lancaster. Hecht-Hill-Lancaster Companies, March 21, 1957.

Bray, Christopher. "Beauty and the Beef." The (London) Sunday Times, July 16, 2000.

Buford, Kate. "Burt Lancaster." Architectural Digest, April 1998.

Canby, Vincent. "Of Time and Talent: The Growth of Burt Lancaster." New York Times, May 24, 1981.

Corliss, Richard. "His Own Man." *Time*, October 31, 1994.

DeVine, Lawrence. "The Movies: A Grand Lancaster Gesture." *Los Angeles Herald-Examiner*, circa 1968.

Dodson, Marcida. "Lancaster Stricken, Is Hospitalized." *Los Angeles Times*, December 1, 1990.

French, Phillip. "Leopard Who Never Changed Spots." *The London Observer*, October 23, 1994.

Fury, David. *The Cinema History of Burt Lancaster*. Minneapolis, MN: Artists's Press, 1989.

Gomez, James M. "Lancaster Stable After Moderate Stroke." *Los Angeles Times*, December 2, 1990.

Gussow, Mel. "From Acrobat to Actor, Embracing Risks All the Way. *New York Times*, April 6, 2000.

"Healing Lancaster." *The Hollywood Reporter*, December 12, 1990.

Hopper, Hedda. "Big Burt Makes Good!" *Chicago Tribune Magazine*, May 22, 1955.

_____. "The Lancaster Lad." *Chicago Sunday Tribune*, June 13, 1948.

"Lancaster Resting After Stroke; Side Is Weak, Speech Slurred." *The Hollywood Reporter*, December 3, 1990.

"Lancaster's Wife Wins Divorce Suit." *Los Angeles Herald-Examiner*, June 18, 1969.

"Lancaster Undergoes Paralysis Therapy." *Variety*, December 12, 1990.

Lax, Eric. "A Man in Full." *Los Angeles Times*, March 26, 2000.

Mallon, Thomas. "Mr. Muscles and Teeth." *GQ*, March 2000.

Martin, Pete. "Burt Lancaster." *The Saturday Evening Post*, June 24, 1961.

Natale, Richard. "H'w'd Remembers Lancaster." *Variety*, October 24, 1994.

Oppenheimer, Peer J. "Burt Lancaster: The Star Nobody Knows." *Family Weekly*, March 18, 1962.

"Oscar Winner Burt Lancaster Dies at 80." *Los Angeles Times*, October 22, 1994.

Parsons, Louella O. "Burt Lancaster, Film Actor, to Wed Girl 'From Back Home.'" *Los Angeles Examiner*, November 9, 1946.

Roberts, Ovid. "He'd Rather Take a Chance." *Parade*, November 6, 1988.

Schuster, Mel. "Burt Lancaster." *Films in Review*, July 1969.

Skolsky, Sidney. "Tintypes: Burt Lancaster." *Hollywood Citizen-News*, June 28, 1968.

Thomson, David. "Poet's Look, Killer's Poise." *The [London] Independent on Sunday*, October 23, 1994.

Wilson, Elizabeth. "Big Guy." *Liberty*, January 1949.

Wilson, Jeff. "Burt Lancaster." *The [Palm Springs] Desert Sun*, October 22, 1994.

Wilson, Liza. "They Say He's Not an Actor." *Los Angeles Examiner*, July 4, 1954.

Documentary

"Burt Lancaster: Daring to Reach." A Wombat Production. A Division of the CineMasters Group, in association with Cinemax. Copyright 1991.

SHELDON LEONARD

"Try something funny and I'll run you right out of town. Double-cross me and I'll get you back here and kick your fat stomach off." — Sheldon Leonard in *The Gangster* (1947)

Portraying screen characters with such monikers as Blackie, Swifty, Lucky, Smacksie, and Pretty Willie, Sheldon Leonard was once one of Hollywood's most reliable bad guys.

"Leonard was the architect of some of the more sinister hoodlum scenes in motion picture annals," a critic once wrote. "He was so realistic that legitimate gangsters started emulating him."

But after more than two decades in Tinseltown, Leonard abandoned his vocation as a cinematic gunsel and launched a second, even more successful career on the small screen. As a creator, writer, director, and producer, Leonard applied his considerable talents toward such television gems as *The Dick Van Dyke Show*, *The Andy Griffith Show*, *Lassie*, and *I Spy*. Along the way, he was nominated for 18 Emmy Awards, won three, was inducted into the Television Hall of Fame, and was feted by such groups as the Directors Guild of America, the American Society of Cinematographers, and the Pacific Pioneer Broadcasters. Of his screen roles, Leonard is perhaps best remembered by today's audiences as the bartender who tossed George Bailey on his ear in the perennial holiday favorite *It's a Wonderful Life* (1946), but the actor also made a notable contribution in his appearances in four films noirs: *Street of Chance* (1942), *Somewhere in the Night* (1946), *Decoy* (1946), and *The Gangster* (1947).

The actor who was once called the "pinup boy of the Mafia" was born Sheldon Leonard Bershad on February 22, 1907, in New York City, the oldest of two boys. When Leonard was 12 years old, his salesman father, Frank Bershad, moved the family to Belleville, New Jersey, where they became the only Jewish family in town. The actor would later recall the "traumatic" experiences he encountered there with anti–Semitism.

"It colored years of my life," Leonard said in a 1964 *TV Guide* interview. "Pugnacity answered my prestige needs. I won the next best thing to friendship: respect and fear. I went out looking for fights. But I still had no friends. All I had were sycophants and enemies. I was alone and miserable."

Two years later, the family returned to New York and Leonard attended Stuyvesant High School, where he joined the school's dramatic society and participated in several student productions. Despite this brush with acting, however, Leonard was more interested in the business end of the stage and later studied theater management at Syracuse University.

"I stepped right into the Depression when I got out of college," Leonard once recalled. "I was whirling like a log-roller, trying to keep from drowning."

While hunting for a position in his chosen field, Leonard took on a series of odd jobs, including working as a longshoreman, lifeguard, and printing salesman. Finally, in 1931, he landed a post as manager of the Eastman Theater in Rochester, New York, and later served as house manager of the Paramount Theater on Broadway.

"But I wasn't making enough money to suit me," Leonard said, "so I went into the millinery business. That was awful — so I decided to try acting." With the help of a former Syracuse classmate, Leonard was cast in his first film, a low-budget drama originally entitled *Drums in the Night*.

"[My friend] said he knew a man who needed some actors … he made a phone call. Later that day, I walked out of an office, and in my pocket was a contract for 350 smackers a week," Leonard said. "I was a 'movie' actor sailing the next day for the West Indies, all expenses paid. Let me tell you, I thought a lot of things that afternoon, but the one thing I remember thinking was: 'Baby, this is the career for me.'"

Leonard's introduction to the silver screen was not quite the idyll he'd anticipated, however. The on-location filming took place in a jungle in Jamaica and the actor later recalled that during the production, "I lost 18 pounds, got delirious, kept offering $100 bills to the monkeys." The film, written, directed, and produced by George Terwilliger (later a writer for D.W. Griffith) was not released until three years later, as *Ouanga* (1936).

Disillusioned by his first screen experience, Leonard turned to the stage, debuting on Broadway in 1934 in *Hotel Alimony*, which he labeled "a terrible flop." He fared little better in his second stage production, *The Night Remembers*, but the following year, Leonard scored a hit with *Fly Away Home* and *Three Men on a Horse*, touring in the latter production for 64 weeks. He was later seen in *Kiss the Boys Goodbye*, *Having Wonderful Time*, and *Margin for Error*, and between engagements worked as a play reader for famed theater producers George S. Kaufman and George Abbott. The actor also found time for romance; in 1931, he married his high school sweetheart, Frances Babor, with he had two children, Andrea in February 1939 and Stephen in October 1942. The couple remained together until Leonard's death more than 65 years later.

Meanwhile, by 1939, box office receipts on Broadway were in decline and Leonard decided to give Hollywood a try, landing a small role in *Another Thin Man* (1939), the third entry in the popular series starring William Powell and Myrna Loy. During the next few years, Leonard was kept busy in numerous features, including *Weekend in Havana* (1941), an Alice Faye musical; *Rise and Shine* (1941), in which he played a gangster by the name of Menace; *Married Bachelor* (1941), an entertaining comedy starring Robert Young; *Tortilla Flat* (1942), MGM's first-rate adaptation of the John Steinbeck novel; and Paramount's *Street of Chance* (1942), his first film noir.

Leonard was featured here as Joe Marucci, a detective on the trail of a man, Frank Thompson (Burgess Meredith), who is knocked unconscious by a falling piece of wood from a building under construction. When Thompson comes to, he is confused to find himself in an unfamiliar section of town with personal items in his possession containing the initials D.N., and when he returns home to his wife, Virginia (Louise Platt), Thompson learns that he has been missing for more than a year. Determined to uncover his "missing" past, Thompson returns to the scene of the accident, where he is spotted by Ruth Dillon (Claire Trevor), who calls him "Dan Nearing" and hides him in her apartment. While there, he learns that, as Nearing, he is wanted for the murder and robbery of the wealthy landowner for whom Ruth worked as a maid. Meanwhile, Marucci catches up with Ruth, trying to bait her into exposing Thompson's whereabouts by revealing the existence of the man's wife, Virginia. When Ruth refuses to believe the detective's story of her lover's second life, Marucci sarcastically replies, "Oh no—rats like Danny Nearing never cheat. They may carve up helpless old men and steal their dough, but they never, never know any Virginias when they're going around with dames named Ruth." Against Ruth's objections, Thompson insists on returning to the landowner's mansion, and by developing a system of communication with the dead man's paralyzed mother (Adeline de Walt Reynolds), Thompson discovers that the real killer was Ruth. When Thompson reveals the truth about his "real life" to Ruth, she pulls a gun, but Thompson's life is spared

with the arrival of the ever-present Marucci, who fatally shoots her.

After being singled out in the *New York Times* as "sufficient in [a] secondary role," Leonard followed *Street of Chance* with a series of mostly forgettable pictures—one notable exception was the hit Humphrey Bogart–Lauren Bacall drama, *To Have and To Have Not* (1944), in which he was seventh-billed as a police lieutenant. Also during this period, Leonard expanded his performing repertoire to include radio, writing several plays for the medium and appearing regularly on *The Jack Benny Show*, *Lineup*, and *Duffy's Tavern*.

Leonard enjoyed the busiest year of his screen career in 1946, appearing in eight features, including perhaps his best-known film, *It's a Wonderful Life*, starring James Stewart and Donna Reed. He also returned that year to film noir, with featured roles in back-to-back offerings, *Somewhere in the Night* and *Decoy*. The first starred John Hodiak as amnesia victim George Taylor, who tries to unearth the secret of his past with only a handful of clues, including $5,000 in cash left to him by a man named Larry

Cravat, and a note from a woman proclaiming her hatred for him. Determined to find Cravat, Taylor encounters nightclub singer Christy Smith (Nancy Guild), whose best friend was the author of the note; Christy's boss, Mel Phillips (Richard Conte), who is recruited by Christy to help Taylor with his quest; Lt. Donald Kendall (Lloyd Nolan), a detective who is searching for Cravat in connection with the theft of $2 million; a mysterious woman, Phyllis (Margo Woode), who is also trying to find the elusive Cravat; and Phyllis' jealous spouse, Sam (Leonard). By the film's end, Taylor learns that *he* is actually Cravat, and that he stole the $2 million from his former associate, Phillips, who demands its return. Forced at gunpoint to retrieve the cash, Taylor/Cravat leads Phillips to a deserted dock area, but before Phillips can make good on his threat to kill his ex-partner, Lt. Kendall appears on the scene and shoots Phillips. Upon its release, *Somewhere in the Night* earned mixed reviews from critics; while James O'Farrell of the *Los Angeles Examiner* described the film as a "well-written, gripping mystery," the *New York Times*' Bosley Crowther admitted that he was "completely baffled" by the plot, asking, "Who was who, and who got shot?" As for Leonard, his performance was mostly overlooked by reviewers, but he was singled out for praise by O'Farrell, who wrote, "Some of the smaller parts are well worth noting, particularly the role of ... a distrusting husband, [played] by Sheldon Leonard."

The actor enjoyed a meatier role, however, in his second film noir of the year, *Decoy*, in which he played Sgt. Joe Portugal, who encounters a woman, Margot Shelby (Jean Gillie), as she lies dying in her apartment, the victim of a gunshot wound. As Margot reveals the circumstances of her demise to Portugal, an extensive flashback depicts her association with a trio of lovers including one, Frankie Olins (Robert Armstrong), who stole $400,000 and hid the money prior to his execution for the murder of a policeman. Immediately after Frankie's death in the gas chamber, Margot arranges to abduct

his body and he is revived by a doctor, Lloyd Craig (Herbert Rudley), whom Margot has seduced into a life of crime. A short time later, however, the third member of the gang, Jim Vincent (Edward Norris), shoots Frankie after he draws a map indicating the hiding place of the stolen loot. The ruthless Margot later runs a car over Vincent and shoots the doctor after the map leads them to the buried money box, but Craig manages to make his way to Margot's home, where he guns her down in revenge. With her dying breath, Margot laughs at Portugal, who opens the coveted money box to find a only a single dollar bill inside. Described by one critic as a "double-cross ... played out with unrelenting viciousness," this low-budget Monogram feature did only modest business at the box office, but Leonard once again earned mention, with Bosley Crowther of the *New York Times* noting his "competent" performance.

After appearing in *Sinbad the Sailor* (1947) as an auctioneer, and *Violence* (1947), a crime drama starring Nancy Coleman, Leonard was seen in his final film noir, *The Gangster* (1947). Here, in his best noir role, the actor portrayed Cornell, a refined but ruthless hood who is characterized by his culinary prowess — in one scene, while meeting in a restaurant with his henchmen, Cornell discusses his plans to defeat a rival gangster, all the while preparing an elaborate salad dressing. The rival in question is the powerful Shubunka (Barry Sullivan), who finds his territory in jeopardy when Cornell decides to take over. Although Shubunka tells his nemesis that he "hasn't seen the day when you can throw me out on the junk pile," Cornell chips away at Shubunka's base of power, first by securing the loyalty of his right-hand man, Nick Jammey (Akim Tamiroff). Assuring Shubunka that he will be "dead in 20 minutes" if Jammey is harmed, Cornell finishes off the gangster through his longtime girlfriend, Nancy (Belita), a nightclub performer who double-crosses her lover when Cornell promises her a part in a show. Meanwhile, Jammey is killed by a desperate gambler (John Ireland) seeking money to pay off a debt; remembering Cornell's threat, Shubunka flees through the streets during a driving rainstorm, but a short time later he is gunned down by an unseen assailant and dies in the gutter. Rife with interesting characterizations, but featuring an atmospheric and sometimes confusing plot, *The Gangster* was mostly panned by reviewers. Although Virginia Wright of the *Los Angeles Daily News* judged that the film's producers displayed "commendable intentions," she found that the script was "overwritten," and "a great deal of extraneous matter clutters the scene." And similarly, in the *Los Angeles Times*, Philip K. Scheuer wrote that "much of [the script] rings with truth and integrity, [but] some of it is merely cryptic.... It is comparatively honest — but there is a tortured, arty quality in the writing and direction that imparts a kind of nightmarish unreality to the whole."

Throughout the remainder of the decade, Leonard continued to portray a series of characters from the other side of the tracks in such films as *Madonna of the Desert* (1948), *Jinx Money* (1948), starring the Bowery Boys, and *Daughter of the Jungle* (1949). But he also showed his versatility in a number of comedies, including *If You Knew Susie* (1948), starring and produced by Eddie Cantor, and *Alias a Gentleman* (1948), a vehicle for Wallace Beery.

The onset of the 1950s brought more gangster roles in films including *Behave Yourself* (1951), where Leonard played a bad guy known as Shortwave Bert; *Come Fill the Cup* (1951), a James Cagney starrer in which Leonard was seen as a sadistic mobster; *Stop, You're Killing Me* (1952), in which he was featured as an ex-hood named Lefty; and *Here Come The Nelsons* (1952), an Ozzie and Harriet Nelson comedy co-starring Leonard as a robber who steals the proceeds from a local rodeo. Despite Leonard's frequent appearances as a cinematic hood, however, he never objected, accepting the typecasting with good humor.

"I never complained about that," he once said. "It was inevitable.... The only thing is, if you're typecast as an ancient Eskimo for instance, I hate to think of how little you'd work in a year."

But by now, Leonard's sights were turned toward the small screen. In 1950, he sold his first television script and in 1953, he joined the series *Make Room for Daddy*, starring Danny Thomas. In the first year of the popular sitcom, later renamed *The Danny Thomas Show*, Leonard served as director; he was later named executive producer and appeared on the program as Thomas' agent. As director, Leonard went on to win two Emmy Awards, in 1956 and in 1961. The show would be one of the most successful sitcoms of its time, running from 1953 to 1964.

"I don't want to sound egotistical, but nobody can tell me what to do in this business — nobody knows more than I do," Leonard once said of his performance as a fledgling director and producer. "The truth is, nobody knows very much. We can't learn anything from anybody, because we're doing it right now. We have to discover how because it hasn't been done before. We make lots of mistakes, but don't forget, we're writing the book."

Pooling their creative and financial resources, Leonard and Thomas formed T & L Productions in 1961, and developed several television sitcoms, including *The Real McCoys*, *The Andy Griffith Show* (a spinoff from an episode of *The Danny Thomas Show*) and *Gomer Pyle U.S.M.C.*, many episodes of which were directed or written by Leonard. Also in 1961, Leonard and Thomas joined with actors Dick Van Dyke and Carl Reiner to create one of the best-loved sitcoms in television history, *The Dick Van Dyke Show*. The four owners of the series formed a legal partnership entitled Calvada Productions, creating the name out of parts of the names of each ("CA" for Carl Reiner, "L" for Sheldon Leonard, "VA" for Van Dyke, and "DA" for Danny Thomas). During the run of the show, the company's name would be included in various episodes as an inside joke; in one, Leonard appeared in the series as a gangster named Big Max Calvada.

Co-creator Carl Reiner would later recall that Leonard not only lent his creative abilities to *The Dick Van Dyke Show*, but also demonstrated a sense of activism by hiring writers who had been blacklisted because of suspected ties with Communism.

"The guy who took the stand very early was Sheldon Leonard," Reiner told the *New York Times* in 1997. "Sheldon was one of the guys who said, 'This is stupid and ridiculous.' Sheldon very quietly decided to use people who were good writers and who had been shamelessly torn out of their jobs. In terms of the blacklist, he was courageous. He just did what he thought was right."

And in a 2002 interview, Leonard's daughter, Andrea Bershad, stated that her father's decision to become involved in hiring the blacklisted writers ranked among his most meaningful achievements.

"My father was apolitical, but he thought the blacklist was a horrible thing — there was such a fear that permeated the industry," Bershad said. "He was really happy to have the opportunity to give jobs to the writers. And until he died, there were many who remained personal friends and were overwhelmingly grateful. He always felt that it was a privilege to be able to give them work."

While labeled by many as a "genius," however, Leonard also suffered mild rebukes from critics who faulted his comedies for their bland, sugar-coated views of life. Never one to mince words, Leonard responded to such claims by insisting that "it's time we stopped apologizing for television's shortcomings and started taking pride in its accomplishments."

"I get very tired of the apologists for television. I don't see any articles in the Sunday book review sections complaining about the overall mediocrity of literature, in spite of the fact that 90 percent of the stuff that's put between hard covers is not worth reading," Leonard said in a 1961 *TV Guide* article. "In all other creative areas, it is taken for granted that the commonplace will outnumber the exceptional, but television is always being stoned because you can't view a masterpiece every time you twist the dial. Any-

one who aspires to a high place must believe in himself — in his taste, his judgment. If you try to please everyone, you wind up pleasing no one. Ultimately, the only man you must please is the one you look at when you're shaving every morning."

As he was building his reputation on the small screen, Leonard continued to make periodic appearances in such films as *Guys and Dolls* (1955), a hit MGM musical with Marlon Brando and Frank Sinatra, and *Pocketful of Miracles* (1961), starring Bette Davis as a fruit vendor named Apple Annie. But most of Leonard's efforts throughout the 1950s and 1960s were centered on his television career; in addition to packaging and producing shows for T & L Productions, he directed episodes of *Lassie*, *General Electric Theater*, *The Jimmy Durante Show*, *Damon Runyon Theater*, and *The Bill Dana Show*. And in 1965, Leonard parted company with Danny Thomas and formed Sheldon Leonard Enterprises, making television history by casting a black actor, Bill Cosby, in a lead role in the hour-long espionage series *I Spy*. Also starring Robert Culp, *I Spy* was nominated for an Emmy for Outstanding Dramatic Series during each year of its three-year run, and Leonard earned an Emmy nomination for directing in 1966.

"He liked all of his shows, but he was especially proud of *I Spy*," Andrea Bershad said. "It turned out that it was a milestone for providing an opportunity for a black man to co-star in a television series. I don't know that he anticipated that — he just went in thinking that Bill was the best person for the job, and he was right. Bill remained unbelievably appreciative, and my dad viewed him like a son."

Leonard added another hit to his string of successes in 1969 when he created *My World and Welcome To It*, an imaginative comedy based on the stories of James Thurber and featuring animated versions of Thurber's cartoons. The critically acclaimed NBC-TV series, which starred William Windom, won an Emmy for Best Comedy Series in 1970, but it was abruptly yanked after just one season, causing Leonard to declare that he was "canceling NBC!"

"The only thing they ever did for me was put *I Spy* on the air. Then they killed it," Leonard told the *Los Angeles Times* in 1970. "I never had trouble with networks. Once CBS had the five top shows and four of them were mine ... but NBC, I'm canceling!"

After producing two short-lived series in the early 1970s—*Shirley's World*, starring Shirley MacLaine, and *The Don Rickles Show*—Leonard stepped back from his producing duties, explaining that "the packaging business has stopped being fun. First, the congestion is too great. Second, the chances for survival are poor. Third, the chances for profit are poor." Instead, Leonard concentrated mainly on his new responsibilities as secretary-treasurer of the Director's Guild of America, a position he would hold until his death. But he wasn't idle for long; in 1975, Leonard returned to television, starring opposite Sheree North in the title role of *Big Eddie* for CBS.

"I couldn't sit around doing nothing," Leonard said. "Recreation doesn't appeal to me. I'd get no excitement making a hole in one in Palm Springs. I don't see myself standing around and looking at the Pyramids. There's just no substitute to me for putting a show together, although I never thought I'd do one again."

But the series, in which Leonard played — what else?—an ex-gangster, was canceled after just three months and Leonard wasn't seen on the small screen again until 1978, when he appeared in two made-for-television movies, playing a mobster in *The Islander*, starring Dennis Weaver and Sharon Gless, and appearing with Bill Cosby in *Top Secret*, for which he also served as executive producer. In addition, Leonard returned to feature films that year, portraying FBI director J. Edgar Hoover in *The Brinks Job*, starring Peter Falk and Peter Boyle. It would be his final big screen appearance. Instead, during the next several years, Leonard limited his activities to guest spots on such television series as *Sanford and Son*; *The Cosby Show*; *The Facts of Life*; *Murder, She Wrote*; *Matlock*; and *Cheers*, for which he received an Emmy nomination for Outstanding Guest Actor in a Comedy Series.

In 1993, at the age of 86, Leonard was recruited by actor Bill Cosby to serve as executive producer on the made-for-television movie, *I Spy Returns*, which reunited Cosby with his former co-star, Robert Culp. And three years later, Leonard was honored at a gala presented by the Directors Guild of America, titled "Sheldon Leonard, This Is Your Wonderful Life." During the event, Leonard was showered with accolades from such notables as Culp, Sid Caesar, Carl Reiner, and Ron Howard, who starred in Leonard's *The Andy Griffith Show* and went on to become an Oscar-winning Hollywood director.

"You have had a critical and very obvious impact on my life," Howard wrote in a letter read during the event. "The hours I was allowed to spend listening to you ... proved to be an invaluable eight-year tutorial on character development, editing, entertainment value, and good, solid storytelling."

Just four months following the Director's Guild celebration, Sheldon Leonard died of natural causes at his Beverly Hills home on January 10, 1997, leaving behind not only a collection of memorable screen roles, but a legacy of work in television that earned him the apt label of "a Renaissance man of the entertainment industry." And although Leonard viewed his success with both frankness and modesty, his daughter remembered him as "a bigger-than-life person."

"He was so intelligent and well-read, with a strong set of values that he implemented in his life. I think he was so well-respected because he hung in there for the things he believed," Andrea Bershad said. "He had a really good life — one step just led to another, kind of effortlessly. He never had a plan, yet he experienced so many facets of the entertainment industry.

"His career was just magical."

Film Noir Filmography

Street of Chance. Director: Jack Hively. Producer: Sam Spiegel. Running time: 74 minutes. Released by Paramount, November 18, 1942. Cast: Burgess Meredith, Claire Trevor, Louise Platt, Sheldon Leonard, Frieda Inescort, Jerome Cowan, Adeline de Walt Reynolds, Arthur Loft, Clancy Cooper, Paul Phillips, Keith Richards, Ann Doran, Cliff Clark, Edwin Maxwell.

Somewhere in the Night. Director: Joseph L. Mankiewicz. Producer: Anderson Lawler. Running time: 110 minutes. Released by 20th Century-Fox, June 12, 1946. Cast: John Hodiak, Nancy Guild, Lloyd Nolan, Richard Conte, Josephine Hutchinson, Fritz Kortner, Margo Woode, Sheldon Leonard, Lou Nova, John Russell, Houseley Stevenson, Charles Arnt, Al Sparlis.

Decoy. Director: Jack Bernhard. Producers: Jack Bernhard, Bernard Brandt. Running time: 76 minutes. Released by Mongram, September 14, 1946. Cast: Jean Gillie, Edward Norris, Herbert Rudley, Robert Armstrong, Sheldon Leonard, Marjorie Woodworth, Philip Van Zandt, John Shay.

The Gangster. Director: Gordon Wiles. Producers: Maurice and Frank King. Running time: 84 minutes. Released by Allied Artists, October 1947. Cast: Barry Sullivan, Belita, Joan Lorring, Akim Tamiroff, Henry Morgan, John Ireland, Fifi D'Orsay, Virginia Christine, Sheldon Leonard, Leif Erickson, Charles McGraw, John Kellogg, Elisha Cook, Jr., Ted Hecht, Jeff Corey.

References

"Actor Wins Movie Pact After 1st Role." *New York Morning Telegraph*, December 27, 1940.
Barthel, Joan. "What a TV Producer Produces." *New York Times Magazine*, November 21, 1965.
Biography of Sheldon Leonard. CBS Television Network, July 1995.
Bruni, Frank. "Sheldon Leonard, Film Actor and TV Producer, Dies at 89." *New York Times*, January 13, 1997.
Cool, Judy. "The Man with the Eloquent Face." *Los Angeles Herald-Examiner*, September 10, 1967.
Davies, Jonathan. "Admirers Spy Leonard As He Nears 90." *The Hollywood Reporter*, September 30, 1996.
DGA Honors Activist Leonard. *Variety*, February 21, 1995.
"'Ex-Hood' Sheldon Leonard Now a Big-Time Producer." *New York Morning Telegraph*, July 9, 1963.
Frymer, Murry. "When He Deals, It's Straight from the Top." *Newsday*, September 14, 1967.
Gardella, Kay. "Producer Insists Imitation Is Hazard to TV's Future." *New York Daily News*, August 11, 1967.
Hano, Arnold. "Sometimes Right, Sometimes Wrong, But Never in Doubt." *TV Guide*, August 15, 1964.
"He Lifted Foot Off Brass Rail to Be an Actor." *New York Herald Tribune*, January 22, 1939.
Hellman, Jack. "Pacific Pioneer B'Casters Won't Soon Forget Leonard's Tribute." *Variety*, March 18, 1974.
Hickok, Stephen S. "Update on Sheldon Leonard." *Variety*, November 13, 1974.
Jampel, Dave. "Sheldon Leonard in Tokyo Recalls Trick Dialog, Menacing Kisser Days." *Variety*, May 22, 1963.
Johnson, T. "'Godfather' Leonard Honored by the DGA." *Variety*, September 30, 1996.
Lavin, Cheryl. "The Small Screen Became His Big Picture." *Chicago Tribune*, October 18, 1990.
Leonard, Sheldon. "In Russia, 'I Spy' Was Out in the Cold." *New York Times*, May 12, 1968.
_____. Why Do You Laugh? *TV Guide*, February 11, 1961.
"Manager Into an Actor." *Brooklyn Daily Eagle*, January 30, 1938.
"'Man of the Year' Award to Sheldon Leonard." *The Hollywood Reporter*, August 18, 1966.
Minoff, Philip. "TV's Triple Threat." *Cue*, June 19, 1954.
Moss, Morton. "Brief Retirement a Bore, So Sheldon Leonard Is Big Eddie." *Los Angeles Herald-Examiner*, August 6, 1975.
Obituary. *Variety*, January 20, 1997.
Page, Don. "Moviedom's Mobster Who Got Ahead of the Racket in TV." *Los Angeles Times*, September 3, 1966.
Robb, David. "Writers Banned from Film Helped Craft Golden Era." *The Hollywood Reporter*, November 14, 1997.
Salmaggi, Bob. "Sheldon Leonard: Talk with a Tough Guy." *New York Herald Tribune*, June 13, 1959.
Scheuer, Steven H. "Sheldon Leonard States His Views on Television." *Brooklyn Eagle*, May 11, 1954.
"Sheldon Leonard, 89; Emmy Winner Produced 'Andy Griffith,' 'I Spy.'" *Chicago Sun-Times*, January 12, 1997.
"Sheldon Leonard Returns to Features." *The Hollywood Reporter*, February 23, 1968.
Smith, Cecil. "Sheldon Leonard Cancels a Network." *Los Angeles Times*, July 13, 1970.

Stein, Herb. "Leonard Spreads Comedic Know-how." *New York Morning Telegraph*, April 21, 1961.
_____. "Sheldon Leonard — Man of Many Talents." *New York Morning Telegraph*, April 20, 1961.

Thomas, Bob. "Hey, Bud — Sheldon's Back." *Los Angeles Times*, May 2, 1975.
Williams, Bob. "Leonard Bets on New Show." *New York Post*, August 5, 1975.

SAM LEVENE

"Don't ask a dying man to lie his soul into hell." — Sam Levene in *The Killers* (1946)

Sam Levene was nothing if not candid. "An actor is not very important. If I had invented penicillin or if I had found a way to make a person live to be 200, I think maybe that would be important," Levene said once. "[Acting] is not glamour, it's goddamn hard work — getting a part, getting yourself up for the performance night after night, keeping your concentration — and when it's over, they forget you. I'm in the business for two reasons — it's the only thing I know how to do, and it pays money."

Despite his cynicism, however, Levene was praised for his acting ability throughout his impressive career, which included roles in *Guys and Dolls* and *The Sunshine Boys* on the stage, and such films as *Golden Boy* (1939), *Action in the North Atlantic* (1943), and *Slaughter on Tenth Avenue* (1957). He was also a strong contributor to five films noirs: *The Killers* (1946), *Crossfire* (1947), *Brute Force* (1947), *Guilty Bystander* (1950), and *Sweet Smell of Success* (1957).

The veteran character actor was born Samuel Levine in Russia on August 28, 1905, the youngest of five children of a synagogue cantor, Harry Levine, and his wife, Beth Weiner. (He would later alter the spelling of his surname when he learned there was already a "Samuel Levine" registered with Actor's Equity.) When young Levene was two years old, his family moved to New York's Lower East Side, where he attended P.S. 64 and Stuyvesant High School. Despite his aspirations of becoming a doctor, Levene went to work after his high school graduation, running errands for a dressmaking company

owned by his brother, Joseph. After two years, his brother made Levene a partner in the business and, in an effort to rid himself of his accent and enhance his professionalism, Levene enrolled in night courses for poise, diction, and manners in the nearby Academy of Dramatic Arts. To his surprise, the head of the academy offered him a scholarship as a day student and urged him to pursue a career in the theater.

"I gave up the shop, the whole works — Joe wouldn't talk to me for two years," Levene said in a 1959 interview. "I was so flattered this man thought I was good enough to go to school regularly. I thought I was entering a wonderful world of make-believe and glamour."

After Levene's graduation from the academy in 1927, he debuted on Broadway, landing a five-line role as a district attorney in *Wall Street*. But his ease in finding work was not a harbinger of good fortune for Levene — during the next several years he appeared in a series of successive flops. His luck began to change in 1932, however, when he appeared in the George Kaufman–Edna Ferber production of *Dinner at Eight*, co-starring Jane Wyatt and Constance Collier. A year later, he was favorably reviewed for his roles in Sidney Howard's *Yellow Jack* and the George Abbott–John Cecil Holm hit *Three Men on a Horse*. Of Levene's performance as a small-time gambler in the latter production, the reviewer from the *New York Times* wrote: "Still looking like a man whose eyes have been allocated the wrong size eyelids ... Mr. Levene is great. No one in the world plays

Mr. Levene as he does." In 1934, Levene made his film debut, reprising his role in *Three Men on a Horse* when the screen rights to the film were purchased by Warner Bros.

During the remainder of the decade, Levene was seen in supporting roles in such films as *After the Thin Man* (1936), second in the popular series starring William Powell and Myrna Loy; *The Shopworn Angel* (1938), a touching melodrama with Margaret Sullavan and James Stewart; *Yellow Jack* (1938), the film version of Levene's earlier Broadway success; *The Mad Miss Manton* (1938), a crime-comedy featuring Henry Fonda and Barbara Stanwyck; and *Golden Boy* (1939), a critical and popular smash starring Stanwyck and William Holden. Between film assignments, Levene continued to accept roles in such stage productions as *Room Service* in the 1936-37 season, *Margin for Error* in 1939, and *A Sound of Hunting* in 1945 (which featured the stage debut of future star Burt Lancaster).

On screen, Levene was seen in a series of light comedies, including another entry in the Thin Man series, *The Shadow of the Thin Man* (1941); *Married Bachelor*, starring Robert Young and Ruth Hussey; and the popular Red Skelton vehicle *I Dood It* (1943), as well as such rousing wartime fare as *Gung Ho* (1943), with Randolph Scott; *Action in the North Atlantic* (1943), starring Humphrey Bogart and Raymond Massey; and *The Purple Heart* (1944), a box-office hit with a strong anti-Japanese sentiment. Levene also made his descent into the world of film noir, co-starring with Burt Lancaster and Edmond O'Brien in *The Killers* (1946).

Through the use of flashback, *The Killers* tells the fateful story of "the Swede" (Lancaster), an ex–prize fighter who is murdered in the first few minutes of the film, leaving behind only a small life insurance policy as a clue to his past. Levene was featured as Sam Lubinsky, a police lieutenant and boyhood chum of the Swede, who witnessed first-hand the Swede's gradual moral decline after he meets local party girl Kitty Collins (Ava Gardner) and falls hard. ("I joined the [police] department, he started fighting ... I saw his

first fight and I saw his last," Lubinsky says.) Working with insurance investigator Jim Reardon (O'Brien), Lubinsky becomes an integral part of the quest to uncover the events that led to the Swede's murder, and steps in to save Reardon's life when he is nearly gunned down by the same deadly duo who brought the Swede's life to an end. For his well-done role, Levene was singled out by William R. Weaver of *Motion Picture Herald* and Thalia Bell of *Motion Picture Daily* —both wrote that the actor had "one of the best roles of his career."

The following year, Levene co-starred with Burt Lancaster, Howard Duff, and Hume Cronyn in his second film noir, *Brute Force* (1947). This gripping, often brutal feature focused on a men's prison and the mélange of characters within its walls, including Capt. Munsey (Cronyn), a sadistic guard; Dr. Walters (Art Smith), a boozy prison doctor with a heart of gold; Joe Collins (Lancaster), a steel-willed convict who plans an intricate prison break; and Louie (Levene), who aids in the prison break by serving as a message courier. When Munsey learns of the planned escape, he savagely tortures Louie, but the stoic convict refuses to rat on his pals and nearly dies as a result. ("You can hit me. You can keep on hitting me. I don't know what you want," he tells Munsey.) The film's violent climax sees the death not only of each of the men involved in the planned escape, but of Munsey as well, who is tossed from a burning tower into a swarm of inmates. Although most of the notices for the film focused on the performances of Lancaster and Cronyn, Levene was mentioned by several critics, including the reviewer for *Newsweek*, who included the actor in his praise of the film's "distinct and believable characters," and Virginia Wright of the *Los Angeles Daily News*, who wrote that Levene gave a "good sketch" as the courageous inmate.

Later in 1947, Levene was seen in his third film noir, *Crossfire*, portraying Jewish war veteran Joseph Samuels, who is found murdered in his apartment. Headed by police detective Finlay (Robert Young), an investigation reveals that Samuels met a rowdy bunch of ex-soldiers in a bar on the night of his death, including Arthur Mitchell (George Cooper), Floyd Bowers (Steve Brodie) and Montgomery (Robert Ryan). During questioning, the blustering Montgomery reveals a seething core of racism, but insists that he'd last seen Samuels at his apartment with Mitchell, who becomes the prime suspect in the case. Aided by Mitchell's roommate (Robert Mitchum), Finlay discovers that Montgomery and Bowers were responsible for the beating death of Samuels, and that Montgomery later killed Bowers in order to ensure his silence. In the film's final reel, while attempting to flee from police, Montgomery is gunned down in the street.

As Joseph Samuels, Levene's role was a relatively small, but pivotal one; in the actor's best scene, his character displays a demeanor of kindness and sensitivity during an encounter with the emotionally war-damaged Mitchell: "It's worse at night, isn't it?" Samuels says. "I think maybe it's suddenly not having a lot of enemies to hate any more…. Now we start looking at each other again. We don't know what we're supposed to do, we don't know what's supposed to happen. We're too used to fighting. But we just don't know what to fight. You can feel the tension in the air. A whole lot of fight and hate that doesn't know where to go." Although Robert Ryan's portrait of the sneering racist landed most of the accolades after the release of *Crossfire*, the critic for *Variety* hailed the film's "gripping portraitures" and labeled it "a frank spotlight on anti–Semitism [that] … pulls no punches."

After a triumphant return to Broadway as an egotistic producer in Moss Hart's *Light Up the Sky* in 1948–49, Levene was seen in such varied cinematic fare as *Boomerang* (1947), a semi-documentary style dramatization of the 1920s murder of a Brooklyn priest; *The Babe Ruth Story* (1948), an overly sentimental biopic starring William Bendix in the title role; and *Dial 1119* (1950), a taut thriller about a police psychiatrist being stalked by an escapee from a mental institu-

tion. During this period, Levene was also seen in his fourth film noir, *Guilty Bystander* (1950), in which he played the hard-nosed but sympathetic former boss of Max Thursday (Zachary Scott), an alcoholic ex-cop. Thrown off the force for his boozing, Thursday now works as house detective in a seedy waterfront hotel, but finds himself thrust into a desperate search for his kidnapped son. During his quest, Thursday encounters a shady doctor and a gang of gem smugglers, but he ultimately learns that the kidnapping was engineered by Smitty (Mary Boland), the proprietess of the hotel where he works. For his performance in the feature, Levene was singled out in *Variety* for instilling his role with the "proper meller flavor," and in the *New York Times*, where Bosley Crowther noted his "capable performance."

Continuing to divide his time and talents between Hollywood and Broadway, Levene scored the biggest stage success of his career in 1950 when he landed the role of Nathan Detroit in the smash hit *Guys and Dolls*. In the *New York Daily News*, critic John Chapman wrote: "What makes [Levene] so funny is the complete sincerity with which he plays. He does Nathan Detroit as though it were Richard II." The entertaining musical was also significant for personal reasons; during its year-long run, Levene married Constance Kane, and the couple later had a son, Joseph. After fewer than 10 years, however, the union ended.

Levene was also seen throughout the 1950s in such stage productions as *Fair Game*, *Make a Million* (in which his comic ability was hailed by one reviewer as "one of the joys of the American theater … wonderful to behold"), and *The Matchmaker*. He left the latter production, a rousing success in London, for the chance to direct his first play, *The Hot Corner*.

"I couldn't resist. Nobody had ever offered to let me direct before. I had to direct," Levene recalled. Unfortunately, while *The Matchmaker* went on to run for 488 performances at the Royale Theater on Broadway, *The Hot Corner*, playing next door at

the Golden Theater, closed after only five. "I'd look up at that sign on the Royale every time I came out of the Golden and die," Levene said.

Although the actor was, at this point, primarily focusing on his stage career, Levene made a number of appearances on such television shows as *Studio One, The U.S. Steel Hour,* and *The Untouchables,* and made-for-television movies including *The World of Sholom Aleichem* (1959). The actor also appeared in a handful of feature films during this period, including *Three Sailors and a Girl* (1953), an entertaining musical starring Jane Powell and Gordon MacRae; *The Opposite Sex* (1956), a mediocre remake of *The Women* (1939); and his final film noir, *Sweet Smell of Success* (1957). Here, Levene is Frank D'Angelo, the uncle of sleazy press agent Sidney Falco (Tony Curtis, in one of the best performances of his career), whose overarching ambition centers on getting his clients noticed by powerful newspaper columnist J.J. Hunsecker (Burt Lancaster). The unprincipled Sidney stoops to new lows when he becomes involved in Hunsecker's efforts to end the relationship between his sister, Susan (Susan

Harrison) and her musician boyfriend, Steve Dallas (Martin Milner). Although Sidney nearly succeeds in his mission, the scheme unravels when Hunsecker suspects Sidney of molesting his sister and turns him over to a crooked cop (Emile Meyer). Although the film stands up today as a fascinating entry in the realm of noir, *Sweet Smell* was a disappointment at the box office, with audiences turned off by its unredeemable characters and relentless cynicism. It was deservedly hailed by critics, however; the reviewer for *Variety* wrote that the film "captures the feel of Broadway and environs after dark," and in the *Los Angeles Examiner,* Sara Hamilton opined: "The acrid odor of the film ... permeates the nostrils long after the final reel has been unwound. It's that pungent." Hamilton also singled out Levene in her praise of the characters who "roam the unpleasant atmosphere doing good jobs in the awful world in which they find themselves."

By now, Levene had become known as an outspoken, straightforward, and somewhat acerbic member of the acting community. Labeled by one newspaper columnist as "one of the Last Angry Men," Levene particularly seemed to enjoy espousing his views on the field of acting, complaining primarily about its "lack of continuity."

"The theater is an elusive thing — a constant fight to survive," Levene said in a 1957 interview. "Always closing, always opening. Even with a hit, an actor says to himself, 'What am I going to do next year?' Always groping for something. My advice is to go back to the dress business. I wish I had."

But Levene's apparent disdain for his chosen career had little effect on his non-stop working schedule. During the next two decades, he continued his frenetic performance docket, appearing in feature films including *Act One* (1963), a biopic about playwright Moss Hart; *Such Good Friends* (1971), a poorly received comedy/drama directed by Otto Preminger; and *And Justice for All* (1979), starring Al Pacino; such stage productions as *Seidman and Son, Goodnight Grandpa, The Sunshine Boys,* co-starring Jack Albertson,

and *The Devil's Advocate*, for which he earned
a Tony nomination for Best Dramatic Actor;
and television dramas including *The Royal
Family* (1977), based on the play of the same
name, in which Levene had appeared in a
1975-76 Broadway revival.

In March 1980, Levene appeared opposite actress Esther Rolle in the Broadway production of *Horowitz and Mrs. Washington* and,
in typical Levene fashion, the actor demonstrated his notoriously cantankerous demeanor when asked by a reporter to describe
the character he portrayed in the play.

"This guy's an old Jew who's crippled,"
Levene said. "I never played an old Jew who's
crippled before. What else do you want me
to say?"

Despite the chemistry between Levene
and Rolle, and guidance from veteran director Joshua Logan, the play quickly closed, although it was taken on a road tour later in
the year. On December 26, 1980, shortly returning to New York after an appearance in
the play in Toronto, Canada, Sam Levene
suffered a fatal heart attack in his apartment
in the St. Moritz Hotel. His body was found
by his son, Joseph. He was 75 years old.

Levene's protestations to the contrary,
the actor was a talented artist who obviously
enjoyed his craft.

"Isn't it kind of silly," he once said, "for
a big grown man to come to a dressing room
and put paint on his face. I feel kind of foolish doing [it]. But when I go out on stage and
the audiences cries ... or laughs ... it's very
rewarding, and quite fulfilling."

Film Noir Filmography

The Killers. Director: Robert Siodmak. Pro-
ducer: Mark Hellinger. Running time: 105 min-
utes. Released by Universal, August 28, 1946. Cast:
Edmond O'Brien, Ava Gardner, Albert Dekker,
Sam Levene, John Miljan, Virginia Christine,
Vince Barnett, Burt Lancaster, Charles D. Brown,
Donald MacBride, Phil Brown, Charles McGraw,
William Conrad, Queenie Smith, Garry Owen,
Harry Hayden, Bill Walker, Jack Lambert, Jeff
Corey, Wally Scott, Gabrielle Windsor, Rex Dale.
Awards: Academy Award nominations for Best

Director (Robert Siodmak), Best Film Editing
(Arthur Hilton), Best Score/Drama or Comedy
(Miklos Rozsa), Best Screenplay (Anthony Veil-
ler).

Brute Force. Director: Director: Jules Dassin.
Producer: Mark Hellinger. Running time: 95
minutes. Released by Universal-International,
June 6, 1947. Cast: Burt Lancaster, Hume Cronyn,
Charles Bickford, Yvonne DeCarlo, Ann Blyth,
Ella Raines, Anita Colby, Sam Levene, Howard
Duff, Art Smith, Roman Bohnen, John Hoyt,
Richard Gaines, Frank Puglia, Jeff Corey, Vince
Barnett, James Bell, Jack Overman, Whit Bissell,
Sir Lancelot, Ray Teal, Jay C. Flippen, James
O'Rear, Howland Chamberlain, Kenneth Patter-
son, Crane Whitley, Charles McGraw, John Har-
mon, Gene Stutenroth, Wally Rose, Carl Rhodes,
Guy Beach, Edmund Cobb, Tom Steele.

Crossfire. Director: Edward Dmytryk. Pro-
ducer: Adrian Scott. Running time: 85 minutes.
Released by RKO, July 22, 1947. Cast: Robert
Young, Robert Mitchum, Robert Ryan, Gloria
Grahame, Paul Kelly, Sam Levene, Jacqueline
White, Steve Brodie, George Cooper, Richard
Benedict, Richard Powers, William Phipps, Lex
Barker, Marlo Dwyer. Awards: Academy Award
nominations for Best Picture, Best Director (Ed-
ward Dmytryk), Best Supporting Actor (Robert
Ryan), Best Supporting Actress (Gloria Grahame),
Best Screenplay (John Paxton).

Guilty Bystander. Director: Joseph Lerner. Pro-
ducer: Rex Carlton. Running time: 92 minutes.
Released by Film Classics, April 21, 1950. Cast:
Zachary Scott, Faye Emerson, Mary Boland, Sam
Levene, J. Edward Bromberg, Kay Medford, Jed
Prouty, Harry Landers, Dennis Harrison, Elliot
Sullivan, Garney Wilson, Ray Julian.

Sweet Smell of Success. Director: Alexander
MacKendrick. Producer: James Hill. Running
time: 96 minutes. Released by United Artists, Jun
27, 1957. Cast: Burt Lancaster, Tony Curtis, Susan
Harrison, Martin Milner, Sam Levene, Barbara
Nichols, Jeff Donnell, Joseph Leon, Edith Atwater,
Emile Meyer, Joe Frisco, David White, Lawrence
Dobkin, Lurene Tuttle, Queenie Smith, Autumn
Russell, Jay Adler, Lewis Charles.

References

"Actor Sam Levene Found Dead by Son." *New
York Post*, December 29, 1980.
"Actor Sam Levene, 75, Dies." *Los Angeles Her-
ald-Examiner*, December 29, 1980.
Albelli, Alfred. "Sam Levene, Comic and Wife
Star as the Triangle Players." *New York Daily
News*, May 14, 1963.

Barbanel, Josh. "Sam Levene, Comic Stage and Screen Actor, Dies at 75." *New York Times*, December 29, 1980.

Beckley, Paul V. "A Familiar Routine for Sam Levene." *New York Herald Tribune*, December 29, 1957.

Beaufort, John. "Meet a Broadway 'Sunshine Boy.'" *Christian Science Monitor*, January 25, 1973.

Biography of Sam Levene. Hecht-Hill-Lancaster Companies, December 13, 1956.

Biography of Sam Levene. RKO Radio Studios, circa 1944.

Biography of Sam Levene. United Artists Corporation, circa 1979.

Blau, Eleanor. "Sam Levene, Crusty Old Softie." *New York Times*, March 24, 1980.

Crisler, B.R. "Of Pictures and People." *New York Times*, June 19, 1938.

"Funeral Today for Sam Levene." *New York Times*, December 30, 1980.

Glover, William. "Master Laughmaker's Humor in 8 Worlds." *Baltimore Sun*, February 22, 1959.

_____. "Levene's Ethnic Roles." *Los Angeles Herald Examiner*, June 4, 1967.

Griffin, Alice. "A Theatre Portrait: Sam Levene." *The Theatre*, May 1961.

McMorrow, Tom. "Sacred Cows Slaughtered by Sam." *New York Sunday News*, April 18, 1976.

Millstein, Gilbert. "'Acting? My Aching Back!'" *Theatre Arts*, June 1959.

Mockridge, Norton. "Those 40 Impossible Years." *New York World Journal Tribune*, April 6, 1967.

Obituary. *Newsweek*, January 12, 1981.

Raidy, William A. "Sam Wouldn't Play It Again." *Los Angeles Times*, January 20, 1974.

Rhodes, Russell. "Roles as Typical New Yorker Fit Sam Levene Into New Play." *New York Herald Tribune*, December 26, 1948.

Rose, Robert L. "Sam Levene: 'I'm a very limited actor [but] what I do, I do well.'" *Sunday Star-Ledger*, August 25, 1974.

"Sam Levene Dead; Stage & Film Star." *Variety*, December 31, 1980.

"Sam Levene Dies at 75; Veteran Actor Was in More Than 100 Movies, Plays." *Los Angeles Times*, December 30, 1988.

"Sam Levene Named March of Dimes Chairman." *New York March of Dimes*, October 18, 1966.

Sardi, Vincent. "Funny Things Happen." *Vis a Vis*, July 1987.

"Son Finds Body of Sam Levene, 75." *Variety*, December 30, 1980.

"The Leavin' Mr. Levene." *New York Times*, October 23, 1938.

Wershba, Joseph. "Daily Closeup: Sam Levene." *New York Post*, October 30, 1959.

GENE LOCKHART

"My old man always said, 'Liquor doesn't drown your troubles — just teaches 'em how to swim.'" — Gene Lockhart in *Red Light* (1950)

Gene Lockhart was an artistic jack-of-all-trades; during his 50-year career, he was known, alternately, as an actor, director, producer, composer, lyricist, writer, teacher, lecturer, and coach.

"My parents were most ambitious — they were convinced I was a genius," the stocky performer once said. "But they were continually debating the specific line of endeavor I should follow. So it happened that I was exposed to almost every form of learning, every art form."

With appearances in more than 100 films, Lockhart performed with such stars as Cary Grant in *His Girl Friday* (1940), Errol Flynn in *They Died with Their Boots On* (1941), and Edward G. Robinson in *The Sea Wolf* (1941).

An Academy Award nominee for *Algiers* (1938), Lockhart was also featured in four films from the noir era: *The House on 92nd Street* (1945), *Leave Her to Heaven* (1945), *Red Light* (1950), and *World for Ransom* (1954).

Edward Eugene Lockhart was born in London, Ontario, Canada, on July 18, 1891, one of three children of singer John Coates Lockhart and his wife, Ellen Mary. One of Lockhart's earliest brushes with performing came at the age of four, when he danced the Highland fling in a concert given by the 48th Highlander's regimental band (later to gain fame as the Canadian Kilties Band). Lockhart received his education at St. Michael's School and DeLaSalle Institute in Toronto, and despite his portly appearance in subsequent years, the future actor was quite athletic — he played halfback for the Toronto Argonauts football team, managed the hockey team at DeLaSalle, and in 1909, swam Toronto Bay to win the country's one-mile championship — setting a record that stood for many years.

After studying at the Brompton Oratory School in London, England, Lockhart took a business course, worked for a while in a railroad ticket office, then landed a job as a typist with the Underwood Typewriter company in Toronto, where he exercised his budding artistic talent by writing all the material for the company's annual musical revue. By the time he reached the age of 22, Lockhart had decided to try his hand on Broadway.

"[I was] armed with the injunction from my mother to 'see that nice man, George M. Cohan, and tell him how you'll astound New York.' I didn't," Lockhart recalled in a 1952 interview. "In a week, I was broke and hungry. I got on my knees and prayed. An hour later I had a filing job. While working, I took singing lessons at Carnegie Hall."

Lockhart's first professional performing appearance in America was on a Chautauqua circuit (large traveling tent shows that brought entertainment, education, and culture to audiences nationwide). In September 1917, after a season with the Chautauqua, Lockhart won a part in his first Broadway play, *The Riviera Girl*. Later, he performed in several Gilbert and Sullivan productions with a light opera company in Boston; wrote the book and music for *The Pierrot Players* and toured Canada with the production; and wrote the lyrics for *Heigho-Ho*, a musical fantasy that had a short run but introduced what would become a widely popular ballad, "The World is Waiting for the Sunrise."

The actor saw his first success as a dramatic actor in 1923, when he portrayed a mountaineer moonshiner in *Sun Up*, an American folk play that started out in a Greenwich Village little theater and wound up with a two-year run in a larger venue in New York. The following year, during the run of the play, Lockhart married English actress Kathleen Arthur — the couple had been intro-

duced two years earlier by famed inventor Thomas Edison while they were participating in a promotional tour. The husband-and-wife team went on to collaborate on numerous productions together, including hosting two weekly radio shows, touring the United States in *Recital-Revue* programs from 1927 to 1931, and appearing in 16 feature films. The year after their wedding, the couple had a daughter, June, who later achieved fame as an actress in her own right on such television programs as *Lassie*, *Petticoat Junction*, *Lost in Space*, and *General Hospital*, and in films including *All This and Heaven, Too* (1940), *Meet Me in St. Louis* (1944), and *The Yearling* (1946). She also appeared along with her parents in her debut film, *A Christmas Carol* (1938). (Years later, an adult June Lockhart would say, "I gathered my grandchildren around the television to watch *A Christmas Carol*. How many people can say, 'There's your great-grandparents and your grandmother at age 12 up there on the screen?'")

Throughout the 1930s, Lockhart continued to expand his artistic experiences. He wrote a series of articles for a theatrical magazine, coached members of New York's Junior League in dramatics, taught a class on dramatic technique at the Juilliard School of Music, authored numerous scripts for radio programs and revues, directed a revival of *The Warrior's Husband*, and portrayed Uncle Sid in the Theater Guild production of *Ah, Wilderness!*, starring George M. Cohan. Lockhart's performance in the latter play led to a contract offer from RKO Studios for his film debut, *By Your Leave* (1935), an appealing comedy starring Frank Morgan and Genevieve Tobin.

Once on screen, Lockhart seemed to be a permanent fixture — during the next 10 years, he was seen in a whopping 72 films. Among these were a number of well-remembered successes, including *Blondie* (1938); *The Story of Alexander Graham Bell* (1939); *Blackmail* (1939), for which the actor won the British Film Award for Best Feature Performance; *His Girl Friday* (1940); *The Sea Wolf* (1941); *Meet John Doe* (1941); *The Gay Sisters*

(1942); *Mission to Moscow* (1944); and *Going My Way* (1944). He also earned an Academy Award nomination for Best Supporting Actor for his performance of an informer in *Algiers* (1938), but lost to Walter Brennan in *Kentucky* (1938). During this period, the actor signed a long-term contract with Warner Bros., but terminated the relationship two years later, telling a reporter that "the character actor has a better chance as a free lance."

"He can choose his roles and avoids being cast in unsuitable parts because he is on the salary roll of one company," Lockhart said. And the actor went on to demonstrate his knack for selecting interesting roles when he entered the world of film noir in 1945 with back-to-back features, *The House on 92nd Street* and *Leave Her to Heaven*.

Based on actual F.B.I. files and shot on location in New York and Washington, D.C., *The House on 92nd Street* tells the documentary-style story of a young college senior, William Dietrich (William Eythe), who is recruited by Nazis to serve as a spy for the Germans. Notifying federal agents, Dietrich goes to work for the F.B.I. as an undercover agent, ultimately exposing a scheme by the Germans to steal the United States' secret atomic bomb formula. As Charles Ogden Roper, Lockhart plays a scientist who utilizes his photographic recall to memorize parts of the formula for the Germans, not knowing that they plan to "liquidate him upon completion of his mission." His life is spared, however, when federal agents unearth the plan and he is arrested for his role in the scheme. By the film's end, the German spies are captured or killed, and the film's narrator assures the audience that "not one single act of enemy-directed sabotage was perpetuated within the United States. Nor was one major war secret stolen." The film was universally praised by critics upon its release, and Lockhart was singled out for his performance in *Motion Picture Herald*, where he was labeled "first-rate," and *The Hollywood Reporter*, whose reviewer wrote that Lockhart and co-star Renee Carson "make a neat Nazi gang that smacks of the genuine."

Lockhart's second noir of the year, *Leave Her to Heaven*, centered on a pathologically possessive woman, Ellen Berent (Gene Tierney), whose all-consuming love for her husband leads her to engineer the drowning of her invalid brother-in-law (Darryl Hickman), deliberately cause the death of her unborn child, and even commit suicide in order to throw the suspicion of murder on her sister, with whom her husband has fallen in love. Lockhart played Dr. Saunders, a sympathetic but plain-speaking doctor who attended Ellen during her pregnancy and subsequent miscarriage. A key to the doctor's personality was provided during a house call at Ellen's home — when she complains that the baby is restricting her actions and "making a prisoner" out of her, Dr. Saunders snappily rejoins, "Then what are you having it for then?" (It is the doctor, however, who unwittingly gives Ellen an idea for escaping her "prison" — shortly after Dr. Saunders warns her to "stay away from shrimps and stairs," Ellen throws herself down a staircase, causing her miscarriage.) For his performance, Lockhart was lauded along with several other performers in the film as "highly effective," and the film, labeled an "arresting picturization" in the *Hollywood Citizen-News*, was a box-office hit.

After his initial film noir features, Lockhart and his wife returned to Broadway, starring in 1945 as the Reverend Homer Whatcoat and his spouse, Martha, in *Happily Ever After*. Although *New York Herald Tribune* critic Howard Barnes compared the comedy to a "collapsed souffle," he credited the Lockharts with giving the play "a recurring life of sharp characterization and pungent pantomime." Also that year, the Lockharts were heard as regular performers on the radio comedy series *The Nebbs*.

On screen, Lockhart was seen in such top-notch offerings as *The Shocking Miss Pilgrim* (1947), an entertaining turn-of-the-century musical vehicle for Betty Grable; *Miracle on 34th Street* (1947), the perennial holiday favorite starring John Payne and Maureen O'Hara, in which he played the judge;

Apartment for Peggy (1948), a sweet comedy featuring William Holden and Jeanne Crain as young marrieds; *That Wonderful Urge* (1948), starring 20th Century-Fox favorites Tyrone Power and Gene Tierney; and *The Inspector General* (1949), with the zany Danny Kaye in the title role. Less successful were *The Foxes of Harrow* (1947), a mediocre treatment of Frank Yerby's bestselling novel; *Cynthia* (1947), a sub-par vehicle for a young Elizabeth Taylor; and *I, Jane Doe* (1948), a so-so drama for Republic Studios. Lockhart fared better, however, with his return to film noir in *Red Light* (1950), co-starring George Raft and Virginia Mayo.

This film, rife with religious undertones, focuses on the mysterious murder of Army chaplain Jess Torno (Arthur Franz), and the efforts of his brother, John (Raft), to hunt down the killer. Shot in a hotel room, Jess cryptically tells his brother before he dies that the key to solving his murder is "written in the bible," leading Torno on a dogged search for the hotel room's missing bible. Ultimately, he learns that his brother's death was engineered by Nick Cherney (Raymond Burr), the former bookkeeper for Torno's freight company, whom Torno had pinched years earlier for embezzling.

As Warni Hazard, Torno's dependable right hand, Lockhart portrayed a "mother-hen" type, constantly worrying over the mental and physical health of his employer. (At one point, Torno snaps, "Run my business, but not my life." Undaunted, Hazard replies, "What are *you* trying to do—wreck both of them?") His mothering instincts aside, Hazard is also at the center of the film's most harrowing scene — stalked by Cherney through a deserted freight yard, Hazard hides beneath a truck trailer, but meets a grisly end when Cherney kicks the jack holding the trailer aloft, crushing Hazard beneath.

After the release of *Red Light*, Lockhart returned to Broadway, replacing Lee J. Cobb as Willy Loman in the long-running *Death of a Salesman*. Of his portrayal of the luckless merchant, Richard Watts, Jr., wrote in the *New York Post* that Lockhart was "more con-

vincingly pathetic" than his "dynamic predecessor." Back in Hollywood after leaving the cast of *Salesman*, Lockhart continued his frenetic shooting schedule, appearing in such features as *Riding High* (1950), directed by Frank Capra; *Rhubarb* (1951), which featured the actor as the eccentric millionaire owner of the alley cat of the film's title; *I'd Climb the Highest Mountain* (1951), with Susan Hayward, William Lundigan, and Lockhart's wife, Kathleen; and his final film noir, *World for Ransom* (1954).

In this tautly directed feature, Lockhart portrays Alexis Pederas, a formidable black marketeer who orders the kidnapping of Sean O'Connor (Arthur Shields), a noted nuclear physicist, and ransoms him to the highest bidder. The film's quirky cast of characters includes one of Pedras's underlings, Julian March (Patric Knowles), who poses as a British officer to carry out the abduction; Julian's wife, Frennessey (Marian Carr), who is concerned about her spouse's activities; and Frennessey's former lover, Mike Callahan (Dan Duryea), a World War II veteran turned private eye. With the promise of leaving her husband and reuniting with Mike, Fren convinces him to extricate Julian from his illegal association with Pedras. On the lam from authorities, who suspect him of murdering a local photographer, Mike finds Julian at the jungle hideout where O'Connor is being held. With the help of a British intelligence agent, Mike rescues the scientist, but is forced to kill Julian in self-defense. Returning to Fren, Mike is dismayed to learn that she was only using him to save her spouse, to whom her heart truly belonged.

After *World for Ransom*, Lockhart was seen in the title role of a short-lived television series, *His Honor, Homer Bell*, then returned to the big screen for a trio of box-office hits: *Carousel* (1956), a beautifully filmed version of the Rogers and Hammerstein musical; *The Man in the Gray Flannel Suit* (1956), starring Gregory Peck as a suburban family man struggling to cope with the after-effects of World War II on his life and career; and *Jeanne Eagles* (1957), a biography of the ill-fated Broadway actress.

Jeanne Eagles would be Lockhart's last film. On March 30, 1957, just hours after appearing in a television play for 20th Century Fox Studios, the actor suffered a heart attack. Rushed to St. John's Hospital in Santa Monica, Lockhart died the following day, with his wife, Kathleen, and daughter, June, at his bedside. He was 66 years old.

Although he was often cast as less-than-upstanding characters (the weasily traitor in *Algiers* and the self-absorbed judge in *Miracle on 34th Street*, among many others), Gene Lockhart managed to avoid being typed as a villain and demonstrated his versatility throughout his film and stage career. In so doing, he successfully carved for himself a solid niche in the annals of Hollywood, and will be remembered as one of the screen's most talented and prolific character performers.

Film Noir Filmography

House on 92nd Street. Director: Henry Hathaway. Producer: Louis de Rochemont. Running time: 89 minutes. Released by 20th Century-Fox, September 26, 1945. Cast: William Eythe, Lloyd Nolan, Signe Hasso, Gene Lockhart, Leo G. Carroll, Lydia St. Clair, William Post, Jr., Harry Bellaver, Bruno Wick, Harro Meller, Charles Wagenheim, Alfred Linder, Renee Carson, John McKee, Edwin Jerome, Elisabeth Newmann, George Shelton, Alfred Zeisler, Reed Hadley.

Leave Her to Heaven. Director: John M. Stahl. Producer: William A. Bacher. Running time: 110 minutes. Released by 20th Century-Fox, December 25, 1945. Cast: Gene Tierney, Cornel Wilde, Jeanne Crain, Vincent Price, Mary Phillips, Ray Collins, Gene Lockhart, Reed Hadley, Darryl Hickman, Chill Wills, Paul Everton, Olive Blakeney, Addison Richards, Harry Depp, Grant Mitchell, Milton Parsons. Awards: Academy Award for Best Color Cinematography (Leon Shamroy). Academy Award Nominations for Best Actress (Gene Tierney), Best Sound Recording (Thomas T. Moulton), Best Interior Decoration/Color (Lyle Wheeler, Maurice Ransford, Thomas Little).

Red Light. Director: Roy Del Ruth. Producer: Roy Del Ruth. Running time: 84 minutes. Released by United Artists, January 15, 1950. Cast: George Raft, Virginia Mayo, Gene Lockhart, Barton MacLane, Henry Morgan, Raymond Burr, Arthur Franz, Arthur Shields, Frank Orth, Philip Pine, Movita Castenada, Paul Frees, Claire Carleton, Soledad Jiminez.

World for Ransom. Director: Robert Aldrich. Producers: Robert Aldrich and Bernard Tabakin. Running time: 82 minutes. Released by Allied Artists, January 27, 1954. Cast: Dan Duryea, Gene Lockhart, Patric Knowles, Reginald Denny, Nigel Bruce, Marian Carr, Douglas Dumbrille, Keye Luke, Clarence Lung, Lou Nova, Arthur Shields.

References

Biography of Gene Lockhart. National Artists Corporation, circa 1955.

Biography of Gene Lockhart. Paramount Pictures, circa 1937.

Biography of Gene Lockhart. RKO Radio Pictures, Inc., circa 1941.

"Death Claims Veteran Actor Gene Lockhart." Publication Unsourced, April 4, 1957.

Fields, Sidney. "Only Human." *New York Daily Mirror*, September 30, 1952.

"Gene Lockhart, Actor 60 Years, Dies Suddenly." *Los Angeles Examiner*, April 1, 1957.

Hall, Prunella. "Screen Gossip." *Boston Post*, January 1, 1952.

Lockhart, Gene. "A Doting Father and His Talented Daughter." *New York Herald Tribune*, July 21, 1940.

McPherson, Jim. "Genial Gene, One of Ours." *TV6*, February 14, 1988.

"Papa Is Only Villain in Acting Household." *New York Morning Telegraph*, November 13, 1941.

PETER LORRE

"You, you imbecile! You bloated idiot! You stupid fathead!"— Peter Lorre in *The Maltese Falcon* (1941)

Pudgy, nasal-voiced, and moon-faced, with a chilling, often-imitated voice and eyes that he himself likened to "soft-boiled eggs," Peter Lorre had a career that ran the gamut from terrifying homicidal maniac to comic caricature. But behind the facade of the psychotic criminal was a man of sensitivity and gentle wit who became a beloved and highly respected member of the film community. And although the actor is most closely identified with films of the horror genre, Peter Lorre was a standout in six examples from the film noir era: *Stranger on the Third Floor* (1940), *The Maltese Falcon* (1941), *The Mask of Dimitrios* (1944), *Black Angel* (1946), *The Chase* (1946), and *Quicksand* (1950).

Lorre, the oldest of four boys, was born Laszlo (some sources say Ladislav) Loewenstein on June 26, 1904, in Rosenberg, Hungary, a village in a remote section of the country's Carpathian mountains. When the future actor was six years old, his mother, Elvira, died, and his father, Alois, later moved his family to Vienna, where he worked for the Steyr automobile company.

Although he had never seen a theatrical production, young Laszlo ran away from home at the age of 17 to seek a career in the theater. For the next three years, he eked out a meager existence by performing a variety of odd jobs, including working as a bank clerk (until he was fired) and a "clapper" (a person planted in an audience to applaud), and giving one-man performances in the Stegreif-theater (Theater of Improvisations) in Vienna. It was the head of the Stegrief-theater, Jacob Moreno, who gave the young man the stage moniker of Peter Lorre.

In 1924, Lorre landed a position with a stock theater company in Breslau, Germany, and spent the rest of the decade appearing in plays in Zurich, Vienna, and the Volksbuehne

(People's Theater) in Berlin. While in Zurich, however, Lorre underwent surgery to correct the chronic gallbladder problem that had plagued him for years, and was administered morphine to help him cope with the lingering pain. The actor reportedly became addicted to the drug, and would be in and out of sanitariums for the rest of his life.

Meanwhile, at the People's Theater, while playing in *Awakening of Spring*, Lorre was spotted by veteran director Fritz Lang, who later offered the actor the role of a psychopathic child-killer in his first sound film, *M* (1931). Lorre's frightening depiction of a man driven to murder was a world-wide sensation — of his performance, one critic wrote that "the modern psychopath, through Lorre's acting, attains the dignity of tragic hero."

After *M*, Lorre appeared in a string of rather forgettable German-language pictures, including *Mann ist Mann* (1931), *Die Koffer des Herrn O.F.* (1931), *F.P.1 Antwortet Nicht* (1932), and *Du Haut En Bas* (1933). His career was revived, however, when he was tapped by director Alfred Hitchcock for a role in his upcoming film, *The Man Who Knew Too Much* (1934)— despite the fact that the Lorre spoke no English.

"At the time, the only English I knew was 'yes' and 'no,'" Lorre recalled later. "Hitch talked, and I leaned forward looking intelligent but not understanding a word. Naturally I couldn't say 'no' because I'd have had to elaborate on it. So I just kept saying 'yes' to Hitch and roaring at his jokes, although I didn't understand a word of them. I got the role and it was two weeks before Hitch found out I didn't speak any English. I must say he got a big kick out of it."

Lorre learned English as the production progressed; his accent changed so notably, in fact, that his scenes had to later be reshot.

After the filming ended, Lorre married actress Celia Lovsky, whom he had known since his acting days in Berlin, and who played a bit part as a Russian aristocrat in *The Man Who Knew Too Much*. (Although the couple divorced 11 years later, they remained close friends until Lorre's death.)

Following the favorable reception of *The Man Who Knew Too Much* by critics as well as audiences, Lorre signed a contract with Columbia Pictures and moved to Hollywood, where he was promptly loaned to MGM for *Mad Love* (1935). After his eerie performance of a doctor driven mad by his unrequited lust for an actress, Lorre starred with Edward Arnold in Columbia's *Crime and Punishment* (1935), then traveled to England to play a bald, demented professional killer in Alfred Hitchcock's *Secret Agent* (1936).

Upon the completion of the latter film, Lorre signed on with 20th Century–Fox, which starred him in an offbeat comedy, *The Crack-Up* (1937), with Brian Donlevy; a spy drama co-starring George Sanders, *Lancer Spy* (1937); and a kidnapping story, *Nancy Steele Is Missing* (1937). The actor was then cast as Mr. Moto, a quiet but deadly Japanese detective — "Instead of committing murders, I'll be solving them," Lorre joked. During the next two years, Lorre made eight films for the series, then entered the dark realm of film noir with *The Stranger on the Third Floor* (1940).

Described by one critic as "two arty for average audiences," this feature begins as the court testimony of "star reporter" Michael Ward (John McGuire) results in a murder conviction for a hapless taxi driver who insists that he is innocent. The cabbie, Joe Briggs (Elisha Cook, Jr.), was spotted by Michael fleeing the scene seconds after the owner of a diner was found with his throat slashed, but Michael's girlfriend, Jane (Margaret Tallichet), believes that Briggs is innocent. As Michael himself begins to doubt Briggs' guilt, he spies a suspicious character in a white scarf (Lorre) lurking around his building and a short time later notices that he no longer hears the incessant snoring from the apartment of

his neighbor, Meng (Charles Halton). Worrying that the white-scarfed "stranger on the third floor" might have done away with Meng, Michael falls asleep and experiences a horrifying nightmare in which he is tried and convicted for his neighbor's murder. Michael awakens to discover that Meng's throat has been slashed and deduces that Meng's killer was the same man who murdered the proprietor of the diner, but when he reports his suspicions to police, he is arrested for the crimes instead. Meanwhile, Jane recognizes the mysterious stranger in the street, and he ultimately reveals to her that he is the killer, but Jane flees when he tries to attack her and he is struck by a truck and killed.

A low-budget "B" picture, *Stranger on the Third Floor* was overlooked by most critics, and the reviewer for *Variety* noted that Lorre's character, though pivotal, goes unseen for the first two reels: "It is only in the final footage that he has much of anything to do," the critic observed. "By that time, the picture has lost its momentum." Despite its lack of impact upon its release, however, the feature is considered today as "the first true film noir," and is characterized by a distinctive style that merits it a significant standing in the era.

Leaving 20th Century–Fox in 1940, Lorre appeared in a series of features that ranged from first-rate — such as *Strange Cargo* (1940), starring Joan Crawford and Clark Gable — to downright lousy, including *The Island of Doomed Men* (1940), and *Mr. District Attorney* (1941), with Dennis O'Keefe. But it wasn't long before the actor received a much-needed career boost with his casting as the effeminate Joel Cairo in his second film noir, *The Maltese Falcon* (1941). As Cairo, Lorre is one of a trio of individuals who would stop at nothing to locate the valuable black bird of the film's title; along with the compulsively deceitful Brigid O'Shaughnessy (Mary Astor) and the deceptively convivial Kaspar Gutman (Sydney Greenstreet), Cairo seeks the aid of private detective Sam Spade (Humphrey Bogart) in securing the falcon. Even before he first appears on screen, Cairo makes an impression; when he pays a visit to Spade's office, he is preceded by his business card which, according to Spade, smells of gardenias. And just minutes after meeting Spade, Cairo pulls a gun on the detective, politely telling him, "You will please clasp your hands together at the back of your neck. I intend to search your offices." By the film's end, Cairo has been knocked around by both Spade and O'Shaughnessy, and nearly used as the fall guy for a pair of murders, but the black bird remains at large and the final reel sees the entire group rounded up and taken to jail.

After his success in *The Maltese Falcon*, for which he was singled out for praise by several critics, Lorre inked an agreement with Warner Bros. and was immediately reunited with Bogart and Greenstreet in *Casablanca* (1942), the wildly successful wartime drama that earned eight Academy Award nominations and won Oscars for Best Picture, Best Screenplay, and Best Director. (A renowned wit, Lorre — who remained with Warners for several years— once joked that he'd only met Jack Warner on one occasion: while the studio head was getting a massage. Asked how he liked Warner, Lorre would shrug and say, "What can you tell from a fanny? I never saw the rest of him.")

Lorre followed the top-notch *Casablanca* with a return to the horror movie genre, appearing with Boris Karloff in *The Boogie Man Will Get You* (1942), followed by a cameo role in the John Huston–directed *In This Our Life*, starring Bette Davis and Olivia deHavilland. (As an inside gag, Huston assembled several cast members from the recently-filmed *The Maltese Falcon*— Lorre, Humphrey Bogart, Mary Astor, Elisha Cook, Jr., Sydney Greenstreet, Ward Bond, and Barton MacLane — and filmed them seated at a bar, being served by "bartender" Walter Huston.) Other roles played by Lorre during the early 1940s included a spy in yet another Bogart starrer, *All Through the Night* (1942), and a vicious Nazi sergeant in *The Cross of Lorraine* (1943). He was also seen during this period in three of his eight film pairings with Sydney Greenstreet, *Background to Danger* (1943), a fast-

paced spy drama; *Passage to Marseilles* (1944), a wartime actioner; and *The Mask of Dimitrios* (1944), his third film noir.

Here, Lorre portrayed detective story writer Cornelius Leyden (although "not very effectively," according to one critic), who becomes intrigued with the background of a notorious criminal, Dimitrios Makropoulos (Zachary Scott), whose body washes up on an Istanbul shore. ("What an evil genius that man was, but fascinating," Leyden says. "What is it about a man like that? There is so much I don't know —for instance, why does anybody trust him in the first place?") Determined to reconstruct the man's life, Leyden encounters a series of individuals who knew Dimitrios, including his former girlfriend, Irana Preveza (Faye Emerson), and a man double-crossed by Dimitrios after they teamed up to steal government secrets. Leyden also discovers that he is being trailed by Mr. Peters (Sydney Greenstreet), who spent time in prison after Dimitrios betrayed him in connection with a jewel smuggling ring. Contending that Dimitrios faked his death and is still alive, Peters reveals his plan to gain revenge on the criminal by blackmailing him for one million francs. Although Dimitrios delivers the money as ordered, he then tries to kill Peters, who is forced to shoot his nemesis in self-defense — as he surrenders to police in the final reel, Peters matter-of-factly tells Leyden, "I've done what I had to do."

Also that year — the busiest of his career — Lorre appeared in the patriotic comedy-musical *Hollywood Canteen* (1944), with a star-studded cast that included Bette Davis, Joan Crawford, the Andrews Sisters, John Garfield, Sydney Greenstreet, Ida Lupino, and Barbara Stanwyck; *The Conspirators* (1944), a spy yarn in which Lorre was again reteamed with Greenstreet; and *Arsenic and Old Lace* (1944), a hit comedy about a pair of spinster sisters who kill their gentlemen callers with poisoned elderberry wine.

The actor slowed down his film schedule in 1945, appearing in only two features—both spy dramas—*Hotel Berlin*, with Raymond Massey, and *Confidential Agent*, starring Charles Boyer and Lauren Bacall. He was perhaps more occupied that year with his personal life; in March 1945, Lorre divorced his first wife, Celia Lovsky, and three months later, he married actress Karen Verne, whom he had met three years earlier when they appeared together in *All Through the Night*.

On the big screen in 1946, Lorre was seen in such well-received — if typical — fare as *The Beast with Five Fingers*, which he once termed as the only "horror" film he ever made ("I have played in 'terror' movies— I prefer the word 'terror' to 'horror'" he said), and his final two films with Sydney Greenstreet, *Three Strangers* and *The Verdict*. ("We broke up the team ourselves," Lorre said later. "We didn't want to become the dramatic Abbott and Costello.") The actor was also seen that year in back-to-back films noirs, *The Black Angel* (1946) and *The Chase* (1946).

In *The Black Angel*, Lorre is Mr. Marko, a nightclub owner who hires a new act, Carver and Martin, comprised of singer Catherine Bennett (June Vincent) and alcoholic pianist Martin Blair (Dan Duryea), not knowing that they suspect him of the murder of Blair's ex-wife, Marvis (Constance Dowling). The two are working against time to identify the

real killer, as Katherine's husband Kirk (John Phillips) has been convicted of the crime and is awaiting execution. The sleuthing duo are certain that they've found their man when Katherine discovers that Marvis was blackmailing Mr. Marko, threatening to thwart his daughter's marriage to a prominent young man by exposing his prison record. It turns out, though, that Marko is innocent and later, in the throes of an alcoholic stupor after his advances are rejected by Katherine, Blair realizes that he is the real killer. With just hours to spare before Kirk's execution, Blair admits his guilt, telling Katherine that they had a good team "while it lasted." For his performance as Marko, Lorre was singled out by the *Los Angeles Times*' John L. Scott, who judged that the actor and several other co-stars "[ran] through their paces satisfactorily," and Bosley Crowther of the *New York Times*, who wrote, "Generally, the supporting cast conducts itself expertly, especially ... Peter Lorre as a nightclub owner with criminal tendencies."

Next, in *The Chase*, Lorre portrayed Gino, the henchman and confidante of Miami mobster Eddie Roman (Steve Cochran), whose character is defined not only by his sadism, but also by his unique limousine which is rigged to allow him to control the car's speed from the back seat. Ostensibly a businessman, Roman's facade is exposed early on, when he orders Gino to kill a business rival, Emmerick Johnson (Lloyd Corrigan), in the cellar of his mansion. Also on hand in the cavernous dwelling are Roman's unhappy wife, Lorna (Michele Morgan), and his chauffeur, Chuck Scott (Robert Cummings), who is hired by Roman as a reward for returning his lost wallet. (A key to the relationship between the sadistic crook and his wife is provided when Johnson invites the couple to his home in Havana, Cuba, but Roman informs him that Lorna doesn't travel much. Johnson asks, "Oh — doctor's orders?" and Roman bluntly rejoins, "No. Mine.") Before long, Scott becomes romantically involved with Lorna and the two plan to flee to Cuba, but before they depart, Scott falls ill. In his feverish state, he dreams that Lorna is stabbed to death after their arrival in Cuba and that he is sought for her murder — he also learns that Gino is the real killer, only to be killed himself. Recovering from this vivid nightmare, Scott continues to carry out his plan to meet Lorna at the local dock, but Roman has learned of the rendezvous and heads out in his limousine, with Gino at the wheel, to stop the couple. On the way, however, Gino tries to cross in front of a speeding train, which hits the car, killing the two instantly and leaving Scott and Lorna free to begin a new life together. Based on the novel *The Black Path of Fear* by Cornell Woolrich, this somewhat offbeat feature was praised as "exciting" and "suspenseful" in the *Los Angeles Times*, whose critic noted that Lorre "aided materially" in his role as the mysterious Gino.

Appearing in only two films in as many years — he played a killer in the popular Bob Hope comedy-mystery, *My Favorite Brunette* (1947), and was a standout in the rather weak remake of *Algiers*, *Casbah* (1948) — Lorre instead focused on expanding his performing repertoire. Returning to his roots on the stage, he toured during 1947 in a road production of Edgar Allen Poe's *The Tell-Tale Heart*, and in July of that year, he started his own radio series on NBC, *Mystery in the Air*. (Lorre's program was replaced in September of that year by *The Bob Hawks Quiz Show*, prompting the actor to quip, "They tell me Mr. Hawks doesn't murder anyone, he just quizzes them. Well, to each his own.")

After reuniting with *Casablanca* co-stars Paul Henreid and Claude Rains in *Rope of Sand* (1949), and starring in a low-budget crime drama, *Double Confession* (1950), Lorre was seen in his final film noir, *Quicksand* (1950). Here, Lorre portrays Nick Dramoshag, the owner of a penny arcade who becomes involved in a set of nightmarish circumstances experienced by local garage mechanic Dan Brady (Mickey Rooney). When Brady falls for the charms of diner cashier Vera Novak (Jeanne Cagney) — who also happens to be Nick's ex-girlfriend — Brady "borrows" $20 from his work cash register to pay

for their first date. From that initial, relatively innocuous act, Brady escalates to a series of increasingly illegal and immoral deeds, including robbing a drunken bar patron to pay off a watch he hocked in order to replace the original $20. Nick enters the story at this point, learning of Brady's role in the robbery and forcing him to steal a new car from his job as payoff for his silence, but Brady's boss, Mr. Mackie (Art Smith), later tells him that he was spotted committing the crime and demands full payment for the vehicle. Brady continued to sink even further when he breaks into Nick's arcade and steals a cache of money, strangles Mackie when he pulls a gun and threatens to phone police, and finally abducts a motorist, planning to force him to drive him to Mexico. Although he is eventually captured by police, all ends relatively well for the hapless mechanic — it turns out that Mackie survived the choking that Brady dispensed, and Brady's faithful former girlfriend, Helen (Barbara Bates), will be waiting for him after he serves a prison stretch of 1–10 years. As the oily Nick, Lorre was hailed by several critics, including the reviewer for the *Los Angeles Times*, who dubbed him "duly sinister," *Variety*'s critic, who wrote that he "acquits himself with his usual nastiness," and Darr Smith of the *Hollywood Citizen-News*, who opined, "Peter Lorre, Taylor Holmes, and Art Smith have meaty roles and they romp through them, chomping all the way."

Quicksand was slated to be the first of a three-film collaboration between Lorre and Rooney — Rooney's independent company would produce, and Lorre would direct. It was later announced, however, that while Lorre would star in all three films, Rooney would serve as both producer and director. Ultimately, *Quicksand* was the only film to be made.

Disappointed with the collapse of his arrangement with Rooney, plagued by financial problems that had forced him to file bankruptcy in 1949, and "fed up with making faces" on screen, Lorre returned to Europe in 1950, where he wrote, directed, produced, and starred in *Der Verlorene* (*The Lost One*), a World War II psychological drama. Although Lorre won awards in Germany for Best Actor, Best Director, and Best Script, the film was a financial flop, and a short time later the actor became seriously ill, gaining nearly 100 pounds. When he recovered, Lorre returned to the United States, declaring that he "[could not] stand living in Europe."

"I like Hollywood," Lorre told reporters. "It is not a crazy, nervous place. An actor is less bothered here than anywhere else. You can live your life as you please and nobody cares."

But Lorre's private life continued to intrude on his public persona. Separated from wife Karen Verne since 1950, Lorre was charged by his estranged spouse with desertion and failure to provide support. Verne claimed that she had given up her career in order to "mollify" Lorre, and that she was forced after his departure to sell most of her wardrobe and find work as a salesgirl. While she was struggling in this manner, Verne claimed, Lorre was "feasting on the finest foods in expensive restaurants." The couple divorced in June 1953, but the acrimonious union seemed to have little effect on Lorre's marital leanings. Just a month after his final split from Verne, Lorre took a third trip down the aisle, marrying 27-year-old Annemarie Stoldt, who had provided publicity services for Lorre's film in Germany. A few months after their Hamburg, Germany, wedding, Lorre's only child, Katherine, was born.

Career-wise, Lorre returned to the silver screen in 1954 for his first American movie in four years, Disney's *20,000 Leagues Under the Sea*, followed by *Beat the Devil*, a subtly humorous crime spoof written by Truman Capote, directed by John Huston, and starring Humphrey Bogart. Throughout the remainder of the decade, Lorre was seen in small roles in such films as the Elvis Presley starrer *Viva Las Vegas* (1956), *Around the World in 80 Days* (1956), *The Story of Mankind* (1957), and *The Buster Keaton Story* (1957). Also during this period, he was seen in such television series as *Playhouse 90*, *Alfred Hitchcock Presents*, and *Wagon Train*, as

well as a number of made-for-television movies, including *Fifth Wheel* (1955) and *Arsenic and Old Lace* (1955).

In May 1959, during filming of the "Smell-O-Vision" feature *Scent of Mystery* (1960), in Granada, Spain, the press reported that the 58-year-old actor suffered a heart attack, brought on by overwork and sun exposure. Lorre later disavowed the experience.

"Heart attack — bah," he said in January 1960. "I had a sunstroke. I was back at work in three days. Under that glaring sun, with reflectors and arc lights on me, it was fierce heat. I was all right. But afterwards, they treated me like I was a vet of the Spanish-American War."

With the dawn of the new decade, Lorre's cinematic prospects were few in number and varying in quality — *Voyage to the Bottom of the Sea* (1961), for instance, was a well-received science fictioner that launched a long-running television series, but *Five Weeks in a Balloon* (1962), with Red Buttons and Barbara Eden, offered a mediocre adaptation of Jules Verne's first novel. It was Lorre's life off screen, however, that often garnered the most interest.

In July 1963, Lorre objected to the request made by a 29-year-old, would-be actor to change his name to Peter Lorie (different spelling, same pronunciation). Eugene Weingand, a German-born real estate salesman residing in North Hollywood, filed a petition for the name change; according to the man's attorney, "his friends think he looks like Peter Lorre so they call him that. Because of this, he's taken to using the name." Three months later, Superior Court Judge Burnett Wolfson denied the petition, ruling that Weingand was "attempting to cash in on the reputation of Peter Lorre, the actor."

"I don't question the man's right to change his name, but why out of 111 million names did he choose this one? Why does a man look for trouble?" Judge Wolfson asked. "It would be a gross injustice to grant him the request because it does not ring with the spirit of fairness."

Meanwhile, although Lorre was able to

salvage his name, his wife was trying to shed hers. In the midst of the court battle with Weingand, Anne-Marie Lorre had filed for a divorce, charging that her husband was a "spendthrift" who "spends all he earns." The complaint, filed on August 15, 1963, claimed that Lorre's earnings were "rarely less than $70,000 a year, all of which he has irresponsibly wasted and squandered."

Lorre continued to act in a handful of movies, but most of his roles by now were self-parodies— with renowned horror film actors Vincent Price and Boris Karloff he formed "The Great Triumvirate of Terror," starring in the highly successful horror spoof, *The Raven* (1963), and *The Comedy of Terrors* (1963). He also played a character known as Mr. Strangdour in *Muscle Beach Party* (1964), one of a series of mindless but entertaining beach movies starring Frankie Avalon and Annette Funicello, and was seen in Jerry Lewis' *The Patsy* (1964) alongside such fellow Hollywood veterans as Everett Sloane, Phil Silvers, Keenan Wynn, and John Carradine (who had appeared 25 years earlier in one of Lorre's Mr. Moto films, *Mr. Moto's Last Warning*).

The Patsy would be Peter Lorre's cinematic swan song. On Monday, March 23, 1964, the actor was felled by a stroke and was found in his apartment by his housekeeper. Ironically, Lorre's estranged wife, Anne-Marie, was due in court on the day of the actor's death, to obtain a default divorce decree. Lorre was 59 years old.

After his death, an outpouring of tributes from the film community served as a testament to Peter Lorre's on-screen talent and off-screen affability — director John Huston described the actor as "one of the finest actors in Hollywood," and comedian Red Skelton told reporters, "We have lost a great actor, a man of great depth. I loved him and loved to watch him work." Lorre's memorial service was attended by numerous Hollywood notables, including Edward G. Robinson, Howard Duff, Jerry Lewis, Morey Amsterdam, Gilbert Roland, Sebastian Cabot, Francis Lederer, Everett Sloane, and Vincent Price, whose touching eulogy provided a fitting tribute to the actor and the man.

"Peter had no illusions about our profession. He loved to entertain, to be a face maker, as he said so often of our kind," Price said. "But his was a face that registered the thoughts of his inquisitive mind and his receptive heart, and the audience, which was his world, loved him for glimpses he gave them of that heart and mind. Peter held back nothing of himself. He shared his wit, his curiosity, and yet he always seemed to be exploring you. The aura of devotion that surrounded him made all men glad to be his friend, to feed him and be fed by him in turn."

Film Noir Filmography

Stranger on the Third Floor. Director: Boris Ingster. Producer: Lee Marcus. Running time: 64 minutes. Released by RKO, September 1, 1940. Cast: Peter Lorre, John McGuire, Margaret Tallichet, Charles Waldron, Elisha Cook, Jr., Charles Halton, Ethel Griffies, Cliff Clark, Oscar O'Shea, Alec Craig, Otto Hoffman.

The Maltese Falcon. Director: John Huston. Producer: Hal B. Wallis. Running time: 100 minutes. Released by Warner Brothers, October 3, 1941. Cast: Humphrey Bogart, Mary Astor, Gladys George, Peter Lorre, Barton MacLane, Sydney Greenstreet, Ward Bond, Jerome Cowan, Elisha Cook, Jr., James Burke, Murray Alper, John Hamilton, Emory Parnell. Awards: Academy Award nomination for Best Picture, Best Supporting Actor (Sidney Greenstreet), Best Screenplay (John Huston).

The Mask of Dimitrios. Director: Jean Negulesco. Producer: Henry Blanke. Running time: 95 minutes. Released by Warner Brothers, June 23, 1944. Cast: Sydney Greenstreet, Zachary Scott, Faye Emerson, Peter Lorre, Victor Francen, Steve Geray, Florence Bates, Eduardo Ciannelli, Kurt Katch, Marjorie Hoshelle, Georges Metaxa, John Abbott, Monte Blue, David Hoffman.

Black Angel. Director: Roy William Neill. Producers: Tom McKnight, Roy William Neill. Running time: 83 minutes. Released by Universal, August 2, 1946. Cast: Dan Duryea, June Vincent, Peter Lorre, Broderick Crawford, Constance Dowling, Wallace Ford, Hobart Cavanaugh, Freddie Steele, Ben Bard, John Phillips, Junius Matthews, Maurice St. Clair, Vilova, Pat Starling.

The Chase. Director: Arthur Ripley. Producer: Seymour Nebenzal. Running time: 86 minutes.

Released by United Artists, November 22, 1946. Cast: Michele Morgan, Robert Cummings, Steve Cochran, Lloyd Corrigan, Jack Holt, Don Wilson, Alexis Minotis, Nina Koschetz, Peter Lorre, Yolanda Lacca, James Westerfield, Jimmy Ames, Shirley O'Hara.

Quicksand. Director: Irving Pichel. Producers: Mickey Rooney and Peter Lorre. Running time: 79 minutes. Released by United Artists, 1950. Cast: Mickey Rooney, Jeanne Cagney, Barbara Bates, Peter Lorre, Taylor Holmes, Art Smith, Wally Cassell, Richard Lane, Patsy O'Connor, John Gallaudet, Minerva Urecal, Sid Marion, Jimmy Dodd, Lester Dorr.

References

"Actor Peter Lorre Dies; Played Sinister Roles." *Boxoffice*, March 30, 1964.

"A Great Actor's Tribute to a Great Actor." *American International Pictures Magazine*, April 1964.

Alpert, Don. "Lorre Laughs When It Hurts." *Los Angeles Times*, January 20, 1963.

Biography of Peter Lorre. 20th Century-Fox Studios, March 17, 1937.

Boynoff, Sara. "Not Much — But Something About Peter Lorre." *Los Angeles Daily News*, June 14, 1937.

Burgess, Jim. "Peter Lorre." *Classic Images*, June 1986.

Calanquin, Leon V. "Saga of Peter Lorre." *Classic Images*, December 1988.

Corneau, Ernest N. "Peter Lorre — Master of the Unusual." *Classic Film Collector*, Winter 1975.

Di Castri, Daphne. "Peter Lorre: When He Was Bad — He Was Very Good." *Hollywood Studio Magazine*, November 1981.

"Divorce Asked by Wife of Actor Peter Lorre." *Los Angeles Times*, August 16, 1963.

Frazier, George. "Peter Lorre: 'I Got to Go Make Faces.'" *True*, July 1947.

George, Manfred. "Peter Lorre Returns to the German Cinema." *New York Times*, September 23, 1951.

"'Had Crumbs,' Charges Wife." *Los Angeles Herald Express*, December 16, 1952.

"He's Only Human." *TV Guide*, November 2, 1957.

"Ingeborg Lorre Divorces Mate." *Los Angeles Examiner*, June 21, 1953.

"Lorre Denies He Had Heart Attack." *Los Angeles Mirror-News*, January 27, 1960.

"Lorre Estate Put in Hands of Widow." *Hollywood Citizen-News*, May 7, 1964.

"Lorre Prefers Role of Villain." *Detroit Free-Press*, January 4, 1937.

"Lorre's Fabulous Career." *Los Angeles Herald-Examiner*, March 24, 1964.

Luft, Herbert G. "Peter Lorre." *Films in Review*, May 1960.

Obituary. *Newsweek*, April 6, 1964.

Obituary. *The Hollywood Reporter*, March 24, 1964.

Obituary. *Variety*, March 25, 1964.

"One (1) Peter Lorre, The Judge Rules." *Los Angeles Herald-Examiner*, October 3, 1963.

"Peter Lorre Eulogized as Face Maker." *Los Angeles Times*, March 27, 1964.

"Peter Lorre Has Heart Attack." *Los Angeles Times*, May 13, 1959.

"Peter Lorre Likes His Name, Wants to Keep It for Himself." *Los Angeles Times*, July 24, 1963.

"Peter Lorre Rites Slated Thursday." *Hollywood Citizen-News*, March 24, 1964.

"Peter Lorre to Hollywood." *Variety*, June 6, 1954.

"Peter Lorre Weds Again." *Los Angeles Examiner*, July 24, 1953.

Sheridan, Michael. "Merchant of Menace." *Modern Screen*, February 1945.

Soter, Tom. "Lorre: A Melodrama." *Video*, October 1985.

Trimborn, Harry. "Peter Lorre, Famed Movie Villain, Dies at 59 in His Hollywood Home." *Los Angeles Times*, March 24, 1964.

Weiler, A.H. "Mild Mannered Villain." *New York Times*, June 24, 1944.

"Wife Divorces Peter Lorre." *Los Angeles Times*, June 21, 1953.

"Wife Seeking Divorce from Peter Lorre." *Hollywood Citizen-News*, August 16, 1963.

Yeaman, Elizabeth. "Peter Lorre's Patience Pays as Cinema Horror Identity Thing of Past." *Hollywood Citizen-News*, November 27, 1937.

FRANK LOVEJOY

"I've never been in trouble before. I don't know what to do." — Frank Lovejoy in *Try and Get Me* (1951)

Although his film career, remarkably, spanned only a decade, Frank Lovejoy not only managed to make a name for himself on the silver screen, but he also successfully conquered the stage, radio, and television as well. A pleasantly handsome man, Lovejoy was frequently typecast as the "nice guy," but he made his mark in the dark world of film noir, starring in four features from the era: *In a Lonely Place* (1950), *Try and Get Me* (1951), *I Was a Communist for the FBI* (1951), and *The Hitch-Hiker* (1953).

The actor with the hazel eyes and earnest face was born on March 28, 1914, in the Bronx, New York, the only child of Frank Andrew Lovejoy, Sr., a salesman for Pathe Films, and his wife, Dora Garvey. When Lovejoy was a boy, his family moved to Woodridge, New Jersey, where he attended school and showed an early initiative by selling newspapers. By the age of 15, he was working as a runner for a Wall Street brokerage firm, but that vocation came to an abrupt end as a result of the stock market crash of 1929. Years later, Lovejoy said that he used his observations during that time in his career as an actor.

"I was down there when the crash came," he said in 1950. "I saw an awful lot of naked emotion, and I learned how people react, what shows on their faces and what doesn't."

Although some sources state that Lovejoy studied banking and finance at New York University for two years, the actor never mentioned it in interviews. Instead, he contended, he was always interested in acting.

"I was born ... a few blocks from the old Biograph Studios and my dad was a film salesman for Pathé," Lovejoy told columnist Hedda Hopper in 1951. "It's all I ever knew, all I ever heard."

After the stock market crash, Lovejoy served an apprenticeship with the Theatre Mart in Brooklyn, and acted in small roles in local little theater companies. By 1933, he found the need to subsidize the meager income he was earning on the stage, and he turned to radio, quickly becoming one of the busiest actors on the air. The following year, Lovejoy made his debut on Broadway — he spoke a single line in *Judgment Day*, which starred actor-turned-director Vincent Sherman. During the 1935-36 season, he was seen at the Barter Theater in Virginia, performing in *The Pursuit of Happiness*, and later toured with the play. When the production closed in Cincinnati, Lovejoy applied for a job at a local radio station there, WLW, becoming part of the station's staff. After building a following in Cincinnati, Lovejoy returned to radio in New York, starring in such productions as *Gangbusters*, *This Is Your FBI*, *Mr. District Attorney*, and *Philo Vance*. The actor would later estimate that during his career, he performed on nearly 5,000 shows.

Despite his busy radio schedule, Lovejoy managed to find time for a personal life. On June 30, 1939, he married Frances Williams, a Broadway star who had appeared in several editions of *George White's Scandals* and was credited with introducing the Charleston to the general public. Eleven years Lovejoy's senior, and a three-time divorcee, Williams gleefully announced to the press on her wedding day: "This is my last try." But Williams was mistaken — less than a year later, on February 23, 1940, she was granted an uncontested divorce from Lovejoy, on the grounds that his "cruelty" interfered with her acting.

Lovejoy, however, was not single for long. In January 1940, he joined the cast of the radio program *This Day Is Ours*, which starred a striking, 21-year-old actress named Joan Banks. The attraction between the two performers was mutual and instantaneous — they were married in Norwalk, Connecticut, in June of that year, and later had two children, Judith in 1945, and Stephen in 1948.

Career-wise, Lovejoy continued his busy radio schedule and later returned to Broadway in several plays, including *A Sound of Hunting* and *Woman Bites Dog* (the casts of which also featured two future film stars, Burt Lancaster and Kirk Douglas, respectively). Neither production lasted long, and Lovejoy would later admit that he had never performed in a successful stage play.

"In *Woman Bites Dog* ... you could almost hear that one closing as we did the third act," he told *Los Angeles Times* writer Philip Scheuer in 1950. "It lasted two nights."

But two nights was long enough for Lovejoy to be spotted by Hollywood producer Stanley Kramer, who had recently become a partner in a new production company, Story Productions. In 1946, Kramer signed Lovejoy to an exclusive contract for a film entitled *This Side of Innocence*, excluding him from all other film work for a year. Lovejoy moved with Joan to Hollywood, but the film was never made.

"That first year wasn't the hardest," Lovejoy later recalled, "but it certainly was the dullest. I sat around doing nothing except one weekly radio show, *The Amazing Mr. Malone*."

Instead of making his debut for Stanley Kramer, Lovejoy was first seen on screen in 1948, when Kramer loaned him to Universal for *Black Bart*, a western starring Dan Duryea and Yvonne DeCarlo. Lovejoy would later say that the experience was one he "prefers to disremember."

"[I played] a Wells Fargo agent," Lovejoy said. "I thought my career had ended before it started."

But things began to look up when Kramer left Story Productions to form his own company—Screen Plays—and tapped Lovejoy for a featured role in his new film, *Home of the Brave* (1949). In this daring film about racial prejudice among World War II soldiers, Lovejoy was a standout as a hardboiled sergeant.

After next appearing in Universal's *South Sea Sinner*, Lovejoy portrayed a newspaper reporter in Warner Bros.' *Three Secrets* (1950), an engrossing tale of a rescue attempt of a young boy involved in a plane crash, and the three women who each believe that he is her son. Following Lovejoy's well-received performance in this film, he was signed to a long-term contract by the studio.

In his first film under his new contract, Lovejoy played another sergeant, this time in *Breakthrough* (1950), with David Brian and John Agar. (The actor later joked that he "must have the kind of face they figure has got to belong to a sergeant. Is that good or bad?") Next, the actor entered the realm of film noir with back-to-back features, a loan-out to United Artists for *Try and Get Me* (1950) and Warners' *In A Lonely Place* (1950). In the first, Lovejoy starred as Howard Tyler, an unemployed, down-on-his-luck war veteran. Frustrated by his inability to support his wife and young son, Howard is pulled into a life of petty crime by an acquaintance, Jerry Slocum (Lloyd Bridges), and even goes along with Slocum's scheme to kidnap a wealthy local man, Donald Miller (Carl Kent). When Jerry needlessly kills their kidnap victim, Howard becomes increasingly unglued, finally admitting the murder to a galpal of Jerry's girlfriend ("Why did he have to kill him?" Howard drunkenly asks. "All he said was he was going to hold him until we got the money. He never said he was going to kill him. Why did he have to kill him?"). After the woman reports the duo to police, Howard and Jerry are jailed, but before they can be brought to trial, a vicious mob forms, breaks into the jail and, in a shocking conclusion, kills both men. Although the film stands up today as a first-rate example of film noir, as well as a stark warning against mob violence, critics were not impressed—Bosley Crowther of the *New York Times*, in particular, argued that the film's director failed to offer any "demonstration of correction or even hope."

Lovejoy had better luck with his next venture into film noir—in *In A Lonely Place*, he played Brub Nicolai, a police detective whose friend, Dixon Steele (Humphrey Bogart), is a talented screenwriter with a volatile temper. When a local hatcheck girl is found murdered hours after being in Dix's company, the screenwriter is suspected of the crime, and is released from police custody only after being provided with an alibi from his neighbor, Laurel Gray (Gloria Grahame, in a top-notch performance). Before long, Dix and Laurel are an item and plan to marry, but Dix's increasingly aggressive behavior cause even Laurel to doubt his innocence in the hatcheck girl's death. Her fears and growing suspicions finally lead Laurel to leave Dix — it is only after this decision (and Dix's frighteningly violent reaction) that Laurel receives a telephone call informing her that the real killer has been captured.

As Brub, Lovejoy played a character whose loyalty to his friend remained solid, even in the face of mounting evidence that pointed toward the screenwriter's guilt. In one scene, after Dix reveals his graphic theory of the murder, Brub's wife (Jeff Donnell) labels him as "a sick man," but Brub continues to defend him: "I didn't go to college, but I know Dix better than you do," he heatedly tells her. "There's nothing the matter with his mind except that it's superior." For his performance, Lovejoy was singled out in *Variety*, whose critic wrote that he "heads the supporting cast convincingly," and the film was unanimously hailed by reviewers who praised its "forceful" screenplay and "intelligent" editing.

Lovejoy's five films in 1951 included his first role as a romantic lead, in *Goodbye, My Fancy*, opposite Joan Crawford. The always-candid actor viewed his new status with amusement.

"If you think of [a leading man] as wearing tails, holding a cup of tea and remarking, 'Isn't that the duke's yacht in the harbor?' — then I suppose I'm a character actor," Lovejoy said. "But if the public looks up at the screen and says, 'I like that gal and I like that guy' — why, then I guess I'll get by as a leading man."

Also that year, Lovejoy appeared in Warner Bros. star-studded tribute to the war,

Starlift, in a cast that included Doris Day, James Cagney, Virginia Mayo, Randolph Scott, Ruth Roman, Gary Cooper, and famed columnist Louella Parsons. He followed this bit of fluff with a starring role in his third film noir, *I Was a Communist for the FBI*.

In this blatant and often too simplistic condemnation of Communism, Lovejoy portrayed Matt Cvetic, a real-life Pittsburgh steelworker who conducts a nine-year investigation of the Communist Party by infiltrating its ranks under the guise of membership. In the course of his quest to fight "a dark and dangerous force," Matt loses the respect of his son and the support of his brothers, all of whom believe that he is truly a Communist. It is only after Matt kills two thugs while coming to the aid of a Communist Party defector (Dorothy Hart), and later testifies before the House Un-American Activities Committee, that he is reunited with his family. (After learning the truth, Matt's son asks for his forgiveness, and Matt replies: "Even when you hated me, I loved you for it.") Upon its release, the film was a hit with moviegoers, but received mixed reviews from critics — the reviewer from *Variety* applauded the film's "excitement and suspense," but in the *New*

Frank Lovejoy and Dorothy Hart in *I Was a Communist for the FBI* (1951).

York Times, Bosley Crowther characterized it as "an erratic amalgam of exciting journalistic report, conventional 'chase' melodrama, patriotic chest-thumping, and reckless 'red' smears." Still, Lovejoy's performance was universally hailed, with one critic writing that he "clicks strongly in his role."

After featured roles in such popular fare as *I'll See You in My Dreams* (1952), starring Danny Thomas as songwriter Gus Kahn, and *The Winning Team* (1952), in which Ronald Reagan portrayed baseball legend Grover Cleveland Alexander, Lovejoy was back to the shadowy world of film noir in *The Hitch-Hiker* (1953).

In this feature, superbly directed by Ida Lupino, Lovejoy stars as Gilbert Bowen, a family man on a fishing trip with pal Roy Collins (Edmond O'Brien), who makes the mistake of offering a lift to a hitch-hiker. The man turns out to be Emmet Myers (William Talman), a psychotic killer on the run from the law, who forces the men to drive him to Mexico. Throughout the suspenseful film, Myers sadistically amuses himself with his captives—in one particularly tense scene, the killer forces Collins to hold a can while Bowen tries to shoot it out of his hand. Despite his nervousness, Bowen ultimately succeeds, after which Myers sardonically remarks, "You guys worked up quite a sweat." During the journey to the border, the level-headed Bowen manages to leave his wedding ring in a spot where it is later discovered by police, resulting in an important clue that aids in the lawmen's search. Although Bowen and Collins come close to death on more than one occasion, Myers is ultimately tracked down and captured, and in the final reel Bowen tells his friend, "It's all right now." Once again, Lovejoy racked up raves for his solid portrayal, with critics lauding his "expert" and "impressive" performance.

By now, Lovejoy had ventured onto the small screen, appearing on a number of programs including *The United States Steel Hour* and *Four-Star Playhouse*. But although he had also continued his radio work — he played newspaperman Randy Stone in *Night Beat* for several years — the actor revealed that he had no interest in returning to the stage.

"Memories of your days on the stage are like memories of the ol' swimming hole. You tend to remember only the better and more pleasant things and shut out from your memory the disagreeable things," Lovejoy said, noting the "dirty, smelly" dressing rooms and uncomfortable road tours. "A lot has been said about acting in front of an audience, how heartwarming it is to hear the applause and all that. All I have to say is that ego-satisfaction isn't enough to make up for the rest of it. New York is a wonderful place, but you'll notice the trains and planes going west are always filled with actors."

Around this time, Lovejoy became the first actor to appear in two features filmed in the new 3D process — the first-rate horror classic *House of Wax* (1953) and *The Charge at Feather River* (1953). In an interview with *Los Angeles Times* reporter John Scott, Lovejoy appeared to be cautiously excited about the "new medium."

"No one at this early time can say which actors and actresses will shine in 3D," he said. "[But] anything that creates interest in motion pictures is good for our profession. A good, solid performer should adapt himself to the new medium after studying it and listening to his director and photographer."

Lovejoy continued his non-stop filming schedule during the next two years, appearing in nine features, including *Men of the Fighting Lady* (1954), in which he earned acclaim for his portrayal of a commander on an aircraft carrier; *Strategic Air Command* (1955), a box-office hit starring James Stewart and June Allyson; *Mad at the World* (1955), a campy teenage exploitation picture co-starring Keefe Brasselle; and *The Crooked Web* (1955), which suffered from the wildly implausible plot of a wealthy father trying to bring to justice the man who killed his soldier son eight years earlier in Berlin. As the killer in the latter film, Lovejoy was seen in one of the few "bad guy" roles of his career. He later admitted that audiences had come to expect his "hero" status.

"I'm the ordinary man on the street and when I get in a jam, everyone in the audience is rooting for me," he told columnist Joe Hyams in 1955. "In a form of typecasting, I'm a bargain. Audiences see me and know right away that I'm a nice guy.... It is written in my face."

In 1956, Lovejoy was in only one feature film — *Julie*, a weak suspense film co-starring Doris Day and Louis Jourdan — but, as was typical of the actor throughout his career, he was not idle. In July of that year, he took on the starring role of Mike Barnett in NBC-TV's *Man Against Crime*, a summer replacement for the popular *Loretta Young Show*. The following summer, he landed the title role in a half-hour NBC-TV crime drama, *Meet McGraw* (later changed to *The Adventures of McGraw*). Portraying the detective with no first name, Lovejoy opened each episode with the pronouncement, "This is McGraw, just McGraw. It's enough of a name for a man like McGraw."

Lovejoy expressed anticipation and excitement over the new series, which he called "fun to play."

"McGraw is what every Walter Mitty would like to be — if his wife would let him. He's a wanderer, a child of fortune. He'll do anything for a fast buck, provided it leads to interesting action," Lovejoy told actress-turned-columnist/talk show host Faye Emerson. And he confessed to another writer that the timing for the show was "perfect."

"I don't think I'm being over-confident, but I'm not in the least nervous about this series," he said. "Two years ago, when we first had the idea for the show, we couldn't give it away. But this is the year for the adult Western series, and I'm convinced it's the year for the adult mystery series, too."

Filming the show was not all fun, however. In December 1957, while diving out of a window for a scene, Lovejoy broke his leg and had to be rushed to the Sherwood-Trimble Clinic in Venice, California. He was in a cast for four weeks.

"We did the rehearsal for the scene perfectly five times," Lovejoy told Louella Parsons. "Then when the camera started turning for the first official 'take,' I have to go and break a leg."

McGraw lasted only one season, but Lovejoy stayed busy with TV guest shots on *Zane Grey Theater* and *Wichita Town*, and in such feature films as *Three Brave Men* (1957), starring Ernest Borgnine, and *Cole Younger, Gunfighter* (1958), a mediocre western in which he played the title role. The latter picture would be the last of his career.

With few film offers coming his way, Lovejoy continued his television work and later contradicted his earlier dismissal of stage work, returning to Broadway in 1960 to star as a bigoted political candidate in *The Best Man*. The actor received rave reviews for his performance, and later went on tour with the production, but the next time he made the newspapers, it was not because of his acting skills.

On January 20, 1962, newspapers across the country announced that the "15-year marriage" of Lovejoy and his wife had ended in divorce in the third civil court of Juarez, Mexico. The papers carried the false information that Lovejoy's real name was Franklin M. Doolittle, and at least one publication wrote that Lovejoy was 38 years old, that his wife's name was Veronica, that the couple was married on May 27, 1947, and that they had no children. Two days later, Lovejoy angrily denied the reports.

"I've been appearing eight times a week in a play in Washington," Lovejoy said. "It would be absolutely impossible for me to be in Juarez. I have not filed for divorce." No explanation for the mysterious report was ever given.

Sadly, just eight months later, Lovejoy was in the news again — in the early morning hours of October 2, 1962, the 50-year-old actor was found dead in New York's Hotel Warwick on West 54th Street. According to Joan Lovejoy, the couple, who had been appearing in the road production of *The Best Man* in nearby Paramus, New Jersey, had watched a baseball game on television the night before, and Lovejoy had retired early, complaining of fatigue. It was later determined that Lovejoy had suffered a heart attack.

Despite the shock of Lovejoy's sudden death, cutting short his still-promising career, his contribution to film, television, stage, and radio is irrefutable. Particularly in films such as *Home of the Brave*, *The Hitch-Hiker*, *Try and Get Me*, and *Men of the Fighting Lady*, he demonstrated a versatility that was first-rate, as well as an appeal that seemed to shine through whatever persona he assumed. And the impact of his passing can be somewhat assuaged by the fact that Lovejoy seemed to genuinely enjoy what he did — his was not a career filled with complaints, regrets, run-ins with the law, or problems with substance abuse. Simply, Lovejoy was content with every aspect of his life.

"The work is interesting, full of variety. I've played a different type of character in each film, so far. And besides, working in the pictures gives you a chance to have a permanent home," Lovejoy said in 1952. "I'm a middle-class square. I like to coach the Little League games. I like baseball and television. We have a nice, comfortable house ... we usually take a vacation, and we save pennies for the day they don't pick up the option.

"This is good living and we've no complaints."

Film Noir Filmography

In a Lonely Place. Director: Nicholas Ray. Producer: Robert Lord. Running time: 94 minutes. Released by Columbia, May 17, 1950. Cast: Humphrey Bogart, Gloria Grahame, Frank Lovejoy, Carl Benton Reid, Art Smith, Jeff Donnell, Martha Stewart, Robert Warwick, Morris Ankrum, William

Ching, Steven Geray, Hadda Brooks, Alice Talton, Jack Reynolds, Ruth Warren, Ruth Gillette, Guy Beach, Lewis Howard.

Try and Get Me. Director: Cyril Endfield. Producer: Seton I. Miller. Running time: 90 minutes. Released by United Artists, December 12, 1950. Cast: Frank Lovejoy, Kathleen Ryan, Richard Carlson, Lloyd Bridges, Katherine Locke, Adele Jergens, Art Smith, Renzo Cesana, Irene Vernon, Lynn Gray, Cliff Clark, Dabbs Greer, Mack Williams, Jane Easton, John Pelletti, Mary Lawrence, Donald Smelick.

I Was a Communist for the FBI. Director: Gordon Douglas. Producer: Bryan Foy. Running time: 84 minutes. Released by Warner Bros., May 2, 1951. Cast: Frank Lovejoy, Dorothy Hart, Philip Carey, Dick Webb, James Millican, Ron Hagerthy, Paul Picerni, Frank Gerstle, Russ Conway, Hope Kramer, Kasia Orzazekski, Eddie Norris, Ann Morrison, Konstantin Shayne, Roy Roberts. Awards: Academy Award for Best Documentary Feature.

The Hitch-Hiker. Director: Ida Lupino. Producer: Collier Young. Running time: 71 minutes. Released by RKO, April 29, 1953. Cast: Edmond O'Brien, Frank Lovejoy, William Talman, Jose Torvay, Sam Hayes, Wendell Niles, Jean Del Val, Clark Howat, Natividad Vacio, Rodney Bell, Nacho Galindo, Martin Garralaga, Tony Roux, Jerry Lawrence, Felipe Turich, Joe Dominguez, Rose Turich, Orlando Veltran, George Navarro, Jun Dinneen, Al Ferrara, Henry Escalante, Taylor Flaniken, Wade Crosby, Kathy Riggins, Gordon Barnes, Ed Hinton, Larry Hudson.

References

"4th Marital Plunge for Aquacade Star." Publication Unsourced, July 1, 1939.

"Actor Frank Lovejoy Denies Divorce Suit." *Los Angeles Times*, January 22, 1962.

"Actor Frank Lovejoy Gets Mexico Divorce." *Los Angeles Herald-Examiner*, January 20, 1962.

Best, William. "Actor Decries Film Versions of Reporters." *Los Angeles Daily News*, September 7, 1951.

Biography of Frank Lovejoy. NBC-TV, June 22, 1956.

Biography of Frank Lovejoy. Twentieth Century-Fox Studios, circa 1957.

Biography of Frank Lovejoy. Warner Bros. Studio, circa 1952.

Emerson, Faye. "This Guy McGraw's a Versatile Hero." *New York World Telegram*, July 2, 1957.

"Frances Williams Wins Her Fourth Divorce." *New York Sun*, February 24, 1940.

"Frank Lovejoy, Actor, Is Dead; Appeared on Stage, Screen, TV." *New York Times*, October 3, 1962.

"Frank Lovejoy Is Dead; Broadway and TV Star." *New York Daily News*, October 3, 1962.

"Frank Lovejoy of 'Grand Central Station' Marries CBS Actress Joan Banks." Columbia Broadcasting System, June 18, 1940.

"Frank Lovejoy Surprised at Romantic Lead with Joan Crawford." *New York Herald Tribune*, December 4, 1950.

"Frank Lovejoy Testifies as Hit-Run Case Witness." *Los Angeles Times*, April 23, 1955.

"Frank's Not Nervous." *New York Daily News*, July 31, 1957.

Fuller, Tyra. "Frank Lovejoy: He Likes to Play a Variety of Roles." *Worcester Sunday Telegram*, August 24, 1952.

Greenletter, Horace. "He Likes It Here." *Los Angeles Daily News*, August 28, 1952.

Hall, Prunella. "Screen Gossip." *Boston Post*, January 31, 1950.

Hopper, Hedda. "Lovejoy's Name Tells His Outlook." *Los Angeles Times*, September 23, 1951.

Hyams, Joe. "This Is Hollywood." *New York Herald Tribune*, December 9, 1955.

McManus, Margaret. "Meet Lovejoy." *The Pittsburgh Press*, July 28, 1957.

"Meet Lovejoy of 'Meet McGraw.'" *TV Guide*, August 24, 1957.

"Mexican Parting." *New York Daily News*, January 20 1962.

Obituary. *Variety*, October 3, 1962.

Parsons, Louella O. "TV Hero Lovejoy Breaks Leg in Window Dive." Publication Unsourced, December 19, 1957.

Scheuer, Philip K. "Frank Lovejoy Takes Promotion to Leading Parts 'In Character.'" *Los Angeles Times*, December 3, 1950.

Scott, John L. "Lovejoy's a Veteran with Two 3D Movies." *Los Angeles Times*, April 5, 1953.

Sher, Jack. "Romance on the Run." *Radio and Television Mirror*, February 1942.

Spinrad, Leonard. "Frank Look at Lovejoy." *New York Times*, November 12, 1950.

BARTON MACLANE

"Don't be a sap, Earle — Mac's dead and we're rich." — Barton MacLane in *High Sierra* (1941)

Perhaps best known to modern audiences as the blustering General Peterson on the hit television comedy *I Dream of Jeannie*, Barton MacLane was better recognized in his heyday as one of the screen's most enduring heavies. In a film career that spanned decades, Mac-Lane was seen alongside such cinematic legends as Humphrey Bogart, James Cagney, Errol Flynn, and Paul Muni, and was featured in a number of classic screen gems, including *The Treasure of the Sierra Madre* (1948). As adept at comedy as he was at heavy drama, the versatile character actor also appeared in four films noirs: *High Sierra* (1941), *The Maltese Falcon* (1941), *Red Light* (1949), and *Kiss Tomorrow Goodbye* (1950).

MacLane was born in Columbia, South Carolina, on Christmas Day, 1902, the son of the superintendent of a Columbia mental hospital. When MacLane was seven, his family — which included four siblings — moved to Cromwell, Connecticut, where he attended elementary and secondary school. After high school, MacLane enrolled as an English major at Wesleyan University in Middletown, Connecticut, where he was captain of the basketball team and a star of the football team. MacLane's athleticism proved to serve as his introduction to the world of the cinema when, in a football game against Massachusetts State University during his senior year, he returned a kickoff for 100 yards, a touchdown, a season record — and nationwide attention.

"It was good for quite a bit of publicity," MacLane modestly recalled years later.

Among those who took note of Mac-Lane's feat was actor Richard Dix, who was in nearby Long Island, New York, preparing for a new film, *The Quarterback*. After seeing a newspaper article on MacLane, Dix sent for him, casting the young man in a bit part as a football player. The exposure to the cel-luloid atmosphere of the movies was all it took to change MacLane's career direction from writing to performing.

After graduating from Wesleyan, Mac-Lane studied for a year at the American Academy of Dramatic Arts and began appearing with a stock company in Brooklyn. He made his Broadway debut in the late 1920s with a walk-on in *The Trial of Mary Dugan*, and later appeared in such productions as *Steel, The Tree*, the long-running *Subway Express, Yellow Jack*, and *Hangman's Whip*. During his appearance in the latter play, MacLane was spotted by a talent scout from Paramount Studios, signed to a standard contract, and began appearing in minor roles in such films as the Marx Brothers feature *The Cocoanuts* (1929); *His Woman* (1931), starring Gary Cooper and Claudette Colbert; and *Tillie and Gus* (1933), a W.C. Fields vehicle.

In the summer of 1932, MacLane wrote his own play, *Rendezvous*, which he sold to producer Arthur Hopkins, obtaining a contract to play the lead. The production earned favorable notices, including one from *New York Times* critic Brooks Atkinson, who wrote that MacLane "has written [*Rendezvous*] in a glow of youthful exaltation. Although it is realistic in form and told in the resilient argot of the streets, it is more properly a fantasy of what might happen if a courageous bruiser set about reforming the world at the point of a pistol."

When his contract with Paramount expired, MacLane was picked up by Warner Bros., where he earned a reputation for portraying gangsters, convicts, or desperadoes in such films as *'G' Men* (1935), *Black Fury* (1935), and *Bullets or Ballots* (1936). But Mac-Lane wasn't always a villain — in a rare departure from his "heavy" mantle, he played an animal tamer in *The Bengal Tiger* (1936) and was lauded by one of the film's professional animal handlers for his "utter confidence and courage." He also turned in a top-notch performance as a prize fighter in *The Kid Comes Back* (1938); in a typical notice, *New York Times* reviewer Frank S. Nugent wrote: "[MacLane], who has been in so many Warner Class B's that he has begun to buzz when he talks, has found a solid role at last. His Gunner Malone is the stout fighting heart of [the movie] ... keeping the prize-ring melodrama on its cinematic feet long after the scriptwriters have grown too weary to punch out another line or jab a new situation." Also during this period, MacLane appeared on the right side of the law as Lt. Steve McBride in the *Torchy Blane* series, opposite Glenda Farrell.

With his film career in full gear, MacLane also found time for romance. In the early 1930s, he married a non-professional named Martha Stewart, with whom he had two children, William and Marlane. (His daughter would make headlines in 1953 after revealing that she had worked for the FBI as an undercover agent in the Communist Party.) Before the end of the decade, however, the union was over, and in 1939 MacLane married actress Charlotte Wynters, an actress who would be seen in bit roles in such films as *The Women* (1939), *The Great Lie* (1941), and *Now, Voyager* (1942). The couple would remain married until the actor's death three decades later.

Career-wise, MacLane made his first film noir appearances in 1941, with featured roles in two of the finest examples of the era, *High Sierra* and *The Maltese Falcon*. The first, *High Sierra*, starred Humphrey Bogart as "Mad Dog" Roy Earle, a veteran criminal who, after an eight-year stretch in prison, emerges to plan the heist of a resort hotel. With the help of two henchmen, Red (Arthur Kennedy) and Babe (Alan Curtis), Roy pulls off the job, but Babe and Red are killed in a car crash and Roy is ultimately cornered and gunned down by police in the High Sierra mountains.

As Jake Kranmer, MacLane played a double-crossing hood who plans to steal Roy's take from the heist after the death of their boss, Big Mac (Donald MacBride)—"I can get a fence to handle this stuff," Kranmer initially tells Earle. "Dontcha see it? We're rich. Use your head, man—this is the chance of a lifetime." But when Earle insists on following Big Mac's written instructions, Kranmer tries to take the jewels at gunpoint; he manages to wound Earle, but he gets killed for his efforts. Although the showier roles played by Bogart and co-stars Ida Lupino and Joan Leslie garnered most of the attention from critics, the film was hailed as "truly magnificent, that's all," by the *New York Times'* Bosley Crowther.

Next, in *The Maltese Falcon*, MacLane was on the right side of the law, portraying Lt. Detective Dundy, a tough, uncompromising cop who suspects private eye Philip Marlowe (Humphrey Bogart) of murder. The principal focus of the film centers on the quest for a bejeweled figurine known as the Maltese Falcon, and the ruthless deeds that are committed by those in search of it. Among these are Brigid O'Shaughnessy (Mary Astor), a beautiful but deadly woman who becomes romantically involved with Marlowe; Kasper "The Fat Man" Gutman (Sydney Greenstreet), a portly English gentleman; and Joel Cairo (Peter Lorre), Gutman's foppish partner. By the end, the valuable bird is still not found, Gutman good-naturedly continues his search, and Marlowe turns his lover in to police for murder. The film was released to rave reviews, with one critic labeling it "packed with blistering dialogue and suspenseful motivation, and direction that never falters for a moment," and *Hollywood Citizen-News* reviewer James Francis Crow writing that MacLane, Ward Bond (who portrayed his partner), and several other supporting players were "all at advantage under Huston's directorial guidance."

Never at a loss for film assignments, MacLane was seen throughout the 1940s in a wide variety of features, including horror films (*The Mummy's Ghost* [1944], *Cry of the Werewolf* [1944]), westerns (*Santa Fe Uprising* [1946]) war-themed offerings (*Secret Command* [1944], *Marine Raiders* [1944]), prison

pictures (*San Quentin* [1946]), and even two entries in the Tarzan series (*Tarzan and the Amazons* [1945] and *Tarzan and the Huntress* [1947]). Also during this period, MacLane was seen in the well-received Humphrey Bogart starrer, The *Treasure of the Sierra Madre* (1948); wrote his second play, *Black John*, which was produced in 1948 in Dallas and Los Angeles; and appeared in two more films noirs, *Red Light* (1948) and *Kiss Tomorrow Goodbye* (1950).

The first, a mediocre offering with strong religious overtones, starred George Raft as Johnny Torno, a trucking magnate who is bent on avenging the shooting death of his chaplain brother. In a fairly good-sized role, MacLane portrayed a cop, Strecker, who investigates the murder; ultimately, it is learned that the man behind the killing is Torno's former employee, Nick Cherney (Raymond Burr), who was sent to prison after embezzling from the company. In the film's action-packed conclusion, Torno corners Nick on the top of his trucking headquarters during a driving rainstorm; although Torno's conscience prevents him from shooting, Nick dies seconds later when he steps on a wire

and is electrocuted. As he surveys the scene, Torno is joined by Strecker, who delivers the film's last line: "Well, Johnny — your brother believed that somebody else was on the job. Looks like he was right."

After earning praise from critics for his "outstanding" performance in *Red Light*, MacLane played yet another cop in his final film noir, *Kiss Tomorrow Goodbye*, starring James Cagney as a ruthless hood who breaks out of prison as the film opens. Settling in a small town, Cagney's character, Ralph Cotter, continues his criminal activities — stealing a grocery store payroll, killing the owner, and blackmailing two crooked cops — Inspector Charles Weber (Ward Bond) and Lt. John Reece (MacLane) — who try to seize his loot. Also involved in the film's illegal goings-on are such characters as Holiday (Barbara Payton), Ralph's girlfriend, and Cherokee Mandon (Luther Adler), a corrupt attorney. By the film's end, all of the crooks wind up on trial, with the exception of the catalyst, Cotter, who is shot and killed by his jealous moll.

As in *The Maltese Falcon* nearly a decade earlier, MacLane was partnered as a lawman with Ward Bond, this time playing the less assertive and less intelligent of the two. For his performance as the conniving cop, MacLane was once again praised by reviewers, including Edwin Schallert of the *Los Angeles Times*, who labeled him "tops."

During the 1950s, MacLane played supporting roles in such box office successes as *The Glenn Miller Story* (1954), an entertaining biopic of the big band leader with James Stewart in the title role. But he was more often to be seen in a spate of westerns that included *Best of the Badmen* (1951), *The Half-Breed* (1952), *Jack Slade* (1953), *Kansas Pacific* (1953), *Rails Into Laramie* (1954), *Jubilee Trail* (1954), *Hell's Outpost* (1954), *Foxfire* (1955) — one of five films in which MacLane appeared with his wife — *Treasure of Ruby Hills* (1955), *The Silver Star* (1955), *Last of the Desperados* (1955), *Sierra Stranger* (1957), *Hell's Crossroads* (1957), and *Frontier Gun* (1958). MacLane also busied himself during this period with guest spots on such television series as

Four Star Playhouse, Cheyenne, Lux Video Theater, Fireside Theater, Crossroads, Black Saddle, Texas John Slaughter, Overland Trail, and *Gunsmoke.*

MacLane departed from his typical bad guy persona in 1960, when he took on the part of U.S. Marshal Frank Caine in the NBC-TV series *The Outlaws.* The change was a welcome one for the actor, who admitted that felt uncomfortable portraying the villain.

"I've never liked playing heavies," the actor told *TV Guide* in 1961. "In fact I hated 'em. But that's what they wanted. And that's what they got. Well, eventually old heavies mellow. TV is giving me something I have seldom had before — a chance to play the fine fellow. It's a good feeling."

After one season on the program, MacLane — along with most of the series' regulars — was cut from the cast of *The Outlaws,* but the actor continued to stay busy both on the small screen and in feature films. His television work included appearances on *Perry Mason* and *Laramie,* and he was seen on the big screen in *Pocketful of Miracles* (1961), Frank Capra's final directing effort; *Law of the Lawless* (1964), a mildly diverting western with Dale Robertson and Yvonne DeCarlo; *Town Tamer* (1965), starring Dana Andrews; and *The Rounders* (1965), an amusing comedy-western featuring Glenn Ford and Henry Fonda.

Also in the mid-1960s, MacLane landed a recurring role on the hit situation comedy series *I Dream of Jeannie,* portraying General Martin Peterson, a no-nonsense Air Force official. During the course of the five-year series, MacLane took time out to return to feature films, playing a country doctor in *Buckskin* (1968) and a sheriff in *Arizona Bushwackers* (1968). But the latter would be his final screen appearance. Shortly after filming an episode for *I Dream of Jeannie,* MacLane was admitted to St. John's Hospital in Santa Monica, California, suffering from double pneumonia. Two weeks later, on January 1, 1969, the 66-year-old actor succumbed to the illness.

Typically cast throughout his career in a series of roles calling for ruthless outlaws, hard-edged convicts, venal cops, or bullying gangsters, MacLane nonetheless managed to bring a special something to his performances, creating memorable portraits out of cardboard-cutout characters. With his trademark scowl and raspy voice, MacLane demonstrated that he was— as labeled by one writer —"as fine a heavy … as ever shot his way down the movie pike."

Film Noir Filmography

High Sierra. Director: Raoul Walsh. Producer: Hal B. Wallis. Running time: 100 minutes. Released by Warner Bros., January 4, 1941. Cast: Humphrey Bogart, Ida Lupino, Alan Curtis, Arthur Kennedy, Joan Leslie, Henry Hull, Barton MacLane, Henry Travers, Elisabeth Risdon, Cornel Wilde, Minna Gombell, Paul Harvey, Donald MacBride, Jerome Cowan, John Eldredge, Isabel Jewell, Willie Best, Arthur Aylsworth, Robert Strange, Wade Boteler, Sam Hayes.

The Maltese Falcon. Director: John Huston. Producer: Hal B. Wallis. Running time: 100 minutes. Released by Warner Brothers, October 3, 1941. Cast: Humphrey Bogart, Mary Astor, Gladys George, Peter Lorre, Barton MacLane, Sydney Greenstreet, Ward Bond, Jerome Cowan, Elisha Cook, Jr., James Burke, Murray Alper, John Hamilton, Emory Parnell. Awards: Academy Award nominations for Best Picture, Best Supporting Actor (Sidney Greenstreet), Best Screenplay (John Huston).

Red Light. Director and Producer: Roy Del Ruth. Running time: 84 minutes. Released by United Artists, January 15, 1950. Cast: George Raft, Virginia Mayo, Gene Lockhart, Barton MacLane, Henry Morgan, Raymond Burr, Arthur Franz, Arthur Shields, Frank Orth, Philip Pine, Movita Castenada, Paul Frees, Claire Carleton, Soledad Jiminez.

Kiss Tomorrow Goodbye. Director: Gordon Douglas. Producer: William Cagney. Running time: 102 minutes. Released by Warner Bros., August 4, 1950. Cast: James Cagney, Barbara Payton, Helena Carter, Ward Bond, Luther Adler, Barton MacLane, Steve Brodie, Rhys Williams, Herbert Heyes, John Litel, William Frawley, Robert Karnes, Kenneth Tobey, Dan Riss, Frank Reicher, John Halloran, Neville Brand.

References

"Barton MacLane's Daughter Reveals Spy Role for FBI." *Los Angeles Times,* December 2, 1953.

"Barton MacLane, Veteran Film Actor, 66, Dies of Pneumonia." *Los Angeles Times*, January 2, 1969.
"Barton MacLane, Villain in a Host of Films, Dies." *New York Times*, January 2, 1969.
Biography of Barton MacLane. Paramount Studios, November 1944.
Biography of Barton MacLane. Publication Unsourced, circa 1955.

Dembart, Lee. Barton MacLane Dies— He Was a Good Bad Guy." *New York Post*, January 2, 1969.
"Film 'Tough Guy' MacLane Dies, 66." *Los Angeles Herald-Examiner*, January 2, 1969.
Obituary. *New York Daily News*, January 2, 1969.
Obituary. *Variety*, January 8, 1969.
"What Happens to Old Heavies?" *TV Guide*, April 15, 1961.

FRED MACMURRAY

"Yes, I killed him. I killed him for money and for a woman. I didn't get the money and I didn't get the woman. Pretty, isn't it?"— Fred MacMurray in *Double Indemnity* (1944)

Once one of Hollywood's highest paid actors, Fred MacMurray insisted that his cinematic success was sheer luck.

"I never planned to be an actor," he said. "I'm one by accident."

Serendipity aside, MacMurray was seen in more than 80 films during a career that spanned six decades, and in his heyday, starred opposite some of Hollywood's top actresses, including Claudette Colbert, Katharine Hepburn, Carole Lombard, Marlene Dietrich, Barbara Stanwyck, Alice Faye, Jean Arthur, and Susan Hayward. Best known to modern audiences as the patient, loving father on the long-running sitcom *My Three Sons*, MacMurray specialized on the big screen in light comedies but left an indelible mark on film noir in one of his two features from the era, the classic *Double Indemnity* (1944).

A native of Kankakee, Illinois, Frederick Martin MacMurray was born on August 30, 1908, the only child of Frederick MacMurray, a concert violinist, and his wife, Maleta Martin. From an early age, MacMurray was taught the violin and made his debut when he was five years old, playing a duet with his father. But his initial performance was not a favorable experience for the youngster.

"I trembled. I shook. I had trouble fingering the strings," MacMurray recalled in a 1962 interview in *The Saturday Evening Post*. "I loathed every second of it, but I did it."

A few years after this inauspicious debut,

MacMurray's parents divorced and Maleta MacMurray moved with her son to Madison, Wisconsin, where she took a job as a stenographer. His father died a short time later and, as an adult, MacMurray would admit that he "hardly remember[ed] him." Meanwhile, the future actor's first taste of stage fright had turned out to be an enduring malady. Throughout his elementary school years, he suffered during required recitations, and was unable to complete a speech he was slated to give at his eighth grade graduation ceremony.

"My first two lines were, 'In a dingy garret in the lonely city of London lay a dying man. His legs were clothed in long, military boots,'" MacMurray said. "That's as far as I got. I sat down and shut my mouth."

But MacMurray did not let his performance anxiety stop him from pursuing a career in music. After spending a year at a military academy in Quincy, Illinois, MacMurray settled with his mother in Beaver Dam, Wisconsin, where the teenager attended the local high school and played the baritone saxophone in the American Legion band. Before long, he had formed his own orchestra, Mac's Melody Boys, with whom he also began to sing a few songs.

"I made myself stand up and sing with a megaphone, but it was soul wrenching," MacMurray said. "Then I got so I could sing without the megaphone, but I had to lean on a piano, propping myself up with one hand.

My other hand was shoved in my jacket pocket so convulsively that I couldn't get it out even to make gestures."

After graduating from Beaver Dam High School, MacMurray enrolled at Carroll College in Waukesha, Wisconsin, where he spent most of his time playing football or warbling on his trusty saxophone six nights a week in a local nightclub. Realizing that his extra-curricular activities left little time for studying, MacMurray left school and moved to Chicago.

"My aunt knew Maurie Sherman, who had an orchestra in a room called The College Inn. It was a showcase for bands," MacMurray recalled in 1962. "When I met him I had my sax. I also had the shakes. Sherman put a piece of music in front of me. I was so nervous I couldn't read it. He said, 'Fake it, kid.' I did. He said, 'Fine, boy, fine,' and listed me with a booking office. The result was that I got a job playing with a combo from Loyola University."

MacMurray played several engagements with the Loyola University band, known as The Royal Purples, which led to a booking at a lake resort in Wisconsin in the summer of 1928. When his summer gig came to an end, MacMurray met with the first of a series of fortuitous circumstances that would culminate in his screen stardom.

"My grandmother was in California," MacMurray recalled. "My mother and my aunt wanted to go to the coast. Neither of them could drive. I drove. I took my sax with me."

Once in California, however, MacMurray was prevented from using his saxophone to earn a living because of a union regulation that required musicians to be residents of the state for six months before being allowed to work. Instead, the industrious young man turned to the movies.

"To be a movie extra, you had to be registered with the Central Casting Agency, but at the time they were taking virtually no registrations," MacMurray said. "However, sound was coming in, so they began registering a few people who could sing. I had sung a little, so they registered me."

The following year, MacMurray was seen in bit parts in a Fox comedy, *Girls Gone Wild* (1929), starring Sue Carol, and Warner Bros.' *Tiger Rose* (1929), with Lupe Velez and Monte Blue. Still determined to pursue a career in music, MacMurray recorded two singles with a local band led by George Olsen, "After a Million Dreams" and "I'm in the Market for You." A short time later, he signed on with a specialty band known as The California Collegians, and performed with the group in the long-running Broadway musical revue *Three's a Crowd*, starring Libby Holman, Fred Allen, and Clifton Webb.

"For one scene, I wore a sailor suit and stood close to Libby," MacMurray said. "She sang 'Something to Remember You By' and, when she finished the song, she threw her arms around me. I was stiff with fright.... I was so self-conscious that I wanted to break away and stumble off the stage."

After the close of *Three's a Crowd*, MacMurray continued to perform with The Collegians at local nightclubs and vaudeville houses, then was seen with the group in another popular Broadway production, *Roberta*, starring newcomer Bob Hope. After traveling in a road version of the play, MacMurray returned to New York where he was awaited by another "lucky" happenstance. Picking up his mail one day from a booking office located in the Paramount Building, MacMurray encountered a young man by the name of Dave Jonas, who asked him, "Why don't you go into the movies?"

"Oscar Serlin, who was head of Paramount's talent department, had his office upstairs," MacMurray recalled. "Serlin ... set up a screen test. When they sent my test to the Paramount Studio on the coast, word came back, 'Send him out.'"

With that, MacMurray signed a seven-year contract with the studio, and he was on his way to Tinseltown. Once in Hollywood, however, the would-be actor was idle, doing little more than soaking up the California sun and drawing a paycheck of $250 a week. Finally, after six months, MacMurray received his first film assignment — a loan-out to RKO Studios for *Grand Old Girl* (1935), in which he played a truck driver who falls for the daughter of a high school principal. MacMurray's scenes as the film's male lead included a sequence where he is seen concentrating on eating a bag of popcorn at a school football games. The actor's on-screen munching served him well when Paramount execs began a search for a star for the studio's upcoming film, *The Gilded Lily* (1935), with Claudette Colbert.

"*The Gilded Lily* called for a lot of popcorn eating, so when they stared looking around for a popcorn eater, I got the job," MacMurray said. "Kissing Claudette before the crew, the props, and the electricians had me so embarrassed I didn't know what I was doing. It was worse than standing there reacting while Libby Holman sang to me. Claudette rumpled my hair and kidded me, and finally I made it."

MacMurray's performance as a sloppy newspaper reporter in *The Gilded Lily* turned the newcomer into an overnight star. He was next starred in such box-office winners as *Alice Adams* (1935), opposite Katharine Hepburn, *The Princess Comes Across* (1936), co-

starring Carole Lombard, *The Bride Comes Home* (1936), with Claudette Colbert, and *The Trail of the Lonesome Pine* (1935), with Sylvia Sidney. With his popularity on the rise, MacMurray took out time to marry actress Lillian Lamont, whom he had met several years earlier while both were appearing on Broadway in *Roberta*. The couple later adopted two children (Susan in 1942 and Robert in 1945), but Lamont would be in ill health for several years, dating from an attack of influenza she contracted during their 1936 honeymoon voyage to Hawaii.

Meanwhile, MacMurray continued his steady road to fame. In 1937, he portrayed the fiancé of Frances Farmer in *Exclusive*; got a chance to display his musical prowess in *Swing High, Swing Low*, opposite Carole Lombard; and was teamed again with Lombard in *True Confession*, portraying a struggling lawyer. He hit a rare sour note, however, in *Maid of Salem* (1937), with a miscast role as an Irish adventurer who falls in love with a New England girl (Claudette Colbert) accused of witchcraft.

"I can remember one review after the picture came out that said, 'At any minute we expected Fred MacMurray to take a saxophone out from under his cape,'" the actor once recalled with amusement.

Throughout the remainder of the decade, MacMurray was kept busy in such features as *Men With Wings* (1938), a box-office disappointment that saw the actor vying with Ray Milland for the affections of Louise Campbell; *Sing You Sinners* (1938), an entertaining musical comedy featuring Bing Crosby and Donald O'Connor; *Cocoanut Grove* (1938), in which MacMurray portrayed a bandleader opposite Harriet Hilliard; *Invitation to Happiness* (1939), co-starring Irene Dunne; and *Café Society* (1939), a popular comedy with Madeleine Carroll. The actor continued his non-stop film schedule with the onset of the 1940s, beginning with in *Remember the Night* (1940), co-starring Barbara Stanwyck. After this first-rate comedy, however, the actor appeared in a series of duds, including *Little Old New York* (1940), for which he was loaned to 20th Century-Fox (his first loan-out in five years); Columbia's *Too Many Husbands* (1940), a mediocre comedy with Jean Arthur and Melvyn Douglas; *Rangers of Fortune* (1940), a tiresome tale about three adventurers who befriend a little girl and her grandfather; *One Night in Lisbon* (1941), a dismal blend of comedy, drama, and romance; *Take a Letter, Darling* (1942), a flimsy comedy directed by Mitchell Leisen and co-starring Rosalind Russell; and *Above Suspicion* (1943), an improbable spy farce with Joan Crawford. MacMurray fared better, however, with the witty comedy *No Time for Love* (1943), his fourth of seven teamings with Claudette Colbert. Between film assignments, MacMurray—who, now in his early 30s, was judged too old for active service in World War II—found time to serve as an air raid warden and entertain soldiers at the Hollywood Canteen.

Up to now, MacMurray had built his popularity in a string of mostly lightweight comedies and romances, but his career took a startling turn in 1944 when he was cast in the role of a murderous insurance agent in the first of his two films noirs, *Double Indemnity*. But according to the film's director, Billy Wilder, MacMurray was far from the first choice for the plum role.

"I went around from leading man to leading man. I even asked George Raft to play the part. He turned me down," Wilder said in a 1983 interview. "I stumbled on the idea of Fred MacMurray ... I pleaded with [him], 'Look, the time has come for you to do something that will be more serious, more demanding.' He said, 'I'm only a saxophone player. I can do a little comedy and I get away with it. Don't shove me. Don't ruin my career.' I was persuasive enough to make him do it."

As insurance salesman Walter Neff in *Double Indemnity*, MacMurray portrayed a man driven to murder because of his passion for the sultry Phyllis Dietrichson (Barbara Stanwyck). After first encountering Phyllis during a routine call, Walter soon discovers that she is an unhappily married housewife, but he balks when she subtly reveals a desire

to kill her husband (Tom Powers): "Whaddya think I was anyway? A guy that walks into a good-looking dame's front parlor and says, 'Good afternoon. I sell accident insurance on husbands. Have you got one that's been around too long? One you'd like to turn into a little hard cash? Just give me a smile and I'll help you collect?' Boy, what a dope you must think I am!" Despite his vehement reaction, Walter soon finds himself planning a detailed scheme to murder Phyllis' spouse and collect the money from his accident insurance, but the plot derails when Walter's relentless boss, Barton Keyes (Edward G. Robinson), grows suspicious. The relationship between the killers further erodes when Walter discovers that Phyllis is having an affair with Nino Zachette (Byron Barr), the boyfriend of Phyllis' hated stepdaughter, Lola (Jean Heather). Ultimately, the murderous lovers turn on each other as a result of their mutual mistrust and paranoia, and their declared intention of sticking together "straight down the line" is fatally shattered.

In sharp contrast to his customary screen persona, MacMurray created a character in *Double Indemnity* who was at once shrewd, cold-blooded, and deadly. These qualities were clearly illustrated in a riveting scene toward the film's end, in which Walter confronts Phyllis with murderous intent: "You got me to take care of your husband for you," he says coolly. "Then you get Zachette to take care of Lola. Maybe take care of me, too. Then somebody else would've come along to take care of Zachette for you. That's the way you operate, isn't it, baby?" For his standout portrayal in this smash-hit, MacMurray was singled out by numerous critics, including James Agee of *The Nation*, who labeled him "perceptive," and the reviewer for *Variety* who raved, "MacMurray has seldom given a better performance. It is somewhat different from his usually light roles, but is always plausible and played with considerable restraint." Despite his initial misgivings about playing the part, MacMurray would later consider both the role and the film as his favorites.

Barbara Stanwyck and Fred MacMurray in *Double Indemnity* (1944).

"There seems to be a Hollywood myth about me," he said in 1962. "It goes this way: If you take the Wilshire Boulevard bus from Westlake near downtown Los Angeles to Santa Monica, you'll always have a piece of MacMurray-owned real estate in view, no matter which side of the bus you sit on. I don't know how that all started."

After his Paramount contract expired, MacMurray promptly signed with 20th Century-Fox, but his first Fox feature, *Where Do We Go From Here?* (1945), was an offbeat musical fantasy that flopped with audiences and critics alike. He rebounded somewhat with his next film for the studio, *Captain Eddie* (1945), in which he played the title role of real-life World War I flying ace Eddie Rickenbacker, followed by his first and last film as a producer, *Pardon My Past* (1946). Released by Columbia Studios and directed by Leslie Fenton, the film featured MacMurray in the dual role of a debt-ridden playboy and an ex–GI who is mistaken for the wastrel gadabout, but it was a disappointment at the box office.

By this time, MacMurray had become known throughout Hollywood as one of the screen's wealthiest stars. (As a testament to MacMurray's success, it is widely held that the actor served as the inspiration for the popular comic book hero Captain Marvel.) In addition to earning upward of $430,000 from his 1944 film appearances alone, it was reported that MacMurray held investments in a golf and tennis club, a knitting mill, an oil company, California orange groves and, according to a 1945 *Saturday Evening Post* article, "one of the finest herds of milking shorthorns on the Pacific Coast." MacMurray downplayed the stories of his vast holdings, laughingly dismissing them as "preposterous."

During the remainder of the 1940s, MacMurray continued to appear in an average of three films per year, but most were such forgettable fare as *Suddenly, It's Spring* (1946), co-starring Paulette Goddard; *Singapore* (1947), an adventure story set in the Orient; and *An Innocent Affair* (1948), a bland drama notable only as MacMurray's fifth and final teaming with Madeleine Carroll. His more successful features during this period included *The Egg and I* (1947), a popular comedy co-starring Claudette Colbert, and *Father Was a Fullback* (1949), in which MacMurray excelled as a troubled football coach.

Although both the quality and the quantity of MacMurray's cinematic offerings began to decline during the 1950s, the actor scored a trio of hits in 1954, *The Caine Mutiny*, where he was a standout as a Navy lieutenant who encourages the uprising of the film's title but disavows his responsibility during the resulting military trial; *Woman's World*, in which he portrayed one of three cutthroat executives striving for a top-level position; and *Pushover*, his second and final film noir.

Reminiscent in many ways of *Double Indemnity*, *Pushover* starred MacMurray as police detective Paul Sheridan, who falls for a bank robber's attractive girlfriend, Lona McLane (Kim Novak). Like Walter Neff, Paul is initially reluctant when his lover proposes that they kill her beau and pocket his stolen bankroll, but he later devises a detailed plot that begins to unravel when he is forced to kill a fellow officer. Paul desperately tries to flee police by taking a hostage (Dorothy Malone), but he is later gunned down in the street and remarks to Lona with a touch of plaintive irony, "We didn't really need that money, did we?" Although the film suffered in comparison with the clearly superior *Double Indemnity*, MacMurray earned good reviews, with the critic from *Variety* praising his "low-key, moody delineation in keeping with the character of the role."

While most of his films during the 1950s were fairly standard fare, MacMurray did begin a relationship late in the decade that would last for the next several years. In 1959, the actor marked his return to comedy, starring in the Disney feature, *The Shaggy Dog*, as a befuddled father whose son is transformed into a sheep dog. The successful comedy led to a string of Disney appearances for MacMurray, including *The Absent-Minded Professor* (1961), *Bon Voyage* (1962), *Son of Flubber* (1963), *Follow Me Boys* (1966), *The Happiest Millionaire* (1967), and *Charley and the Angel* (1973). While the features were popular with moviegoers, however, critics were often unimpressed; one reviewer characterized *Follow Me Boys* as a film that "represents the depths of boobery and the heights of gooey," and another panned *The Happiest Millionaire* as "a contender for the worst Hollywood film of the year."

With his film career moving along at a steady clip, MacMurray was experiencing both highs and lows in his personal life. In 1953, after years of frail health, his wife of 17 years, Lillian Lamont, died, plunging the actor into a deep depression. Finally, in May 1954, he was convinced by friends Walter and Madeleine Lang to attend a party honoring John Wayne's birthday.

"When dinner was served, I sat with the Langs when this agent Harold Rose came over, took my plate and said, 'Come on over here,' and sat me down next to June Haver," MacMurray recalled. "We later danced and I took her home."

The 45-year-old actor and the 28-year-old Haver, who had worked together previously in the 1945 feature, *Where Do We Go From Here?*, soon became an item, and after a whirlwind romance, they were married on June 28, 1954. By all accounts, the union was a happy one (MacMurray once said of his wife, "People who know June know why I like to come home at night"), and the couple would later adopt two children, twin girls named Katie and Laurie. Years after the adoption, MacMurray recalled with amusement that fatherhood a second time around was not precisely what he'd planned.

"After June and I had been married awhile and had no children, she asked, 'Can't we adopt one?' I didn't go along with the idea.... So I told her, 'I hope you understand. I don't want to be selfish, but that's it,'" MacMurray told *The Saturday Evening Post*. "The next thing I knew I was sitting in a golf club after a game and was called to the phone. It was [obstetrician] Dr. Prucher, and he said, 'Sit down, Fred.' I asked why. He said, 'Well, Fred, you're a father again. I said, 'Wonderful, what is it?' Then he told me, 'It isn't one. It's two. You've got twin girls.' When I tell this story, I usually end by saying, 'Then I fainted,' but I don't really mean that. I was very happy, and once again very lucky, too. Someday I must ask June how the whole thing happened."

Professionally, most of MacMurray's films during this period were lightweight Disney comedies, but in 1960 he took on one of his best roles, playing an adulterous cad in the outstanding Billy Wilder feature *The Apartment*. The film was a blockbuster at the box office and MacMurray was singled out in several reviews, along with stars Jack Lemmon and Shirley MacLaine, for his performance. But while MacMurray wowed the critics, some of his fans were less than appreciative of his portrayal. Visiting Disneyland with Haver and his twin daughters on the day after *The Apartment* was released, MacMurray encountered one such fan.

"This woman came up to me and said how she'd always liked my pictures, but that she'd taken her children to see *The Apartment* the evening before and 'Now I hate you,' and hit me right on the head with her purse," MacMurray said. "It was a totally mad situation."

Having guested on the small screen since the late 1950s in such shows as *The Lucy-Desi Comedy Hour*, *The Twentieth Century–Fox Show*, and *The George Gobel Show*, MacMurray in 1960 took on the role with which he is best associated, the patient and understanding father in *My Three Sons*. Initially, however, however, the actor was reluctant to take on the part.

"When [producer] Don Fedderson approached me ... I just kept saying that I didn't want to work that hard. A lot of people enjoy working until their rumps drag. I don't," MacMurray later recalled. But Fedderson persisted, ultimately developing a partnership deal for the actor and an arrangement for him to work only a few months out of the year. "I thought, 'If I only have to work three months a year for that kind of money plus a partnership percentage, I'd be a chowder head to duck it.' I said, 'O.K.' and I've never regretted it. *My Three Sons* is work, but no more wearying than

shooting a movie. I just change my ties, shirts, and suits faster."

After the premiere of the series in September 1960, *My Three Sons* was hailed by critics, including Jack O'Brian of the *New York Journal-American*, who wrote that it was "an amazingly unexpected television program, an intelligent domestic situation comedy." For the next 12 years, MacMurray played widowed patriarch Steven Douglas, and viewers tuned in faithfully to watch as his television sons grew up and Douglas became a grandfather to triplets, remarried, and adopted his second wife's daughter.

When *My Three Sons* ended its long run in 1972, MacMurray was seen in several made-for-television movies, including *The Chadwick Family* (1974), *Beyond the Bermuda Triangle* (1975), and *Joys* (1976), appeared in guest spots on such programs as *The Dinah Shore Show* and *The Tony Orlando and Dawn Show*, and served as a television pitchman in a series of commercials for the Greyhound bus company. In 1978, after a six-year absence from the big screen, MacMurray appeared in *The Swarm* alongside such Hollywood veterans as Richard Widmark, Olivia deHavilland, Jose Ferrer, and Lee Grant. Despite this high-powered cast, the Irwin Allen–directed movie about a swarm of killer African bees was a box-office disaster and marked the actor's last feature film appearance.

In the 1980s, MacMurray took on only a few roles, but he was seen in the American Film Institute tributes to Frank Capra in 1982 and Billy Wilder in 1985. The latter, who directed MacMurray in two of his best films, *Double Indemnity* and *The Apartment*, once described the actor as "everybody's nice fellow. He gives people the feeling that he's kind to dogs, children, mothers, and widows." A few years after the Wilder tribute, MacMurray contracted pneumonia and died on November 5, 1991. He was 83 years old.

While Fred MacMurray was labeled throughout his career with such descriptors as "a typical American," "big and awkward and cheerful and happy," and "as down to earth as applesauce," it is his portrayals of dastardly villains in *Double Indemnity*, *The Caine Mutiny*, and *The Apartment* that stand out as the actor's finest screen moments. Mac-Murray himself once provided a key to his success in these memorable roles.

"I'd say I'm a switch-hitter as an actor. If I'm playing a heavy, I don't play it that way from the beginning of a film, the way a Brando or a Sir Alec Guinness would. That's the way a *real* actor would do it," MacMurray said. "Whether I play a heavy or a comedian, I'm always the same fellow when I start out. If I play a heavy, there comes a spot in the film when the audience gets the message that I'm really a heel. I start out Smiley MacMurray, 'a decent Rotarian type.' Then I do or say something, and people know I'm a bastard."

Film Noir Filmography

Double Indemnity. Director: Billy Wilder. Producer: B.G. DeSylva. Running time: 106 minutes. Released by Paramount, September 7, 1944. Cast: Fred MacMurray, Barbara Stanwyck, Edward G. Robinson, Porter Hall, Jean Heather, Tom Powers, Byron Barr, Richard Gaines, Fortunio Bonanova, John Pilliber. Awards: Academy Award nominations for Best Picture, Best Actress (Barbara Stanwyck), Best Director (Billy Wilder), Best Sound Recording (Loren Ryder), Best B/W Cinematography (John Seitz), Best Score/Drama or Comedy (Miklos Rozsa), Best Screenplay (Raymond Chandler, Billy Wilder).

Pushover. Director: Richard Quine. Producer: Jules Schermer. Running time: 88 minutes. Released by Columbia, July 30, 1954. Cast: Fred MacMurray, Kim Novak, Phil Carey, Dorothy Malone, E.G. Marshall, Allen Mourse, Phil Chambers, Alan Dexter, Robert Forrest, Don Harvey, Paul Richards, Ann Morris.

References

Amory, Cleveland. "Hollywood's Ho-Hum Boy." *The Saturday Evening Post*, March 3, 1945.

Biography of Fred MacMurray. Paramount Studios, March 1940.

Clary, Patricia. "F. MacMurray Says Acting for Movies Is a 'Soft Job.'" *Pittsburgh Press*, August 26, 1945.

Coons, Robbin. "MacMurray Is a Horizontal Star." *20th Century-Fox News*, circa June 1945.

Corneau, Ernest. "That Most Likeable Guy." *Classic Film Collector*, circa 1973.

Dawes, Amy. "Versatile, Durable Fred MacMurray Dies." *Variety*, November 6, 1991.

"Film Success Still Amazes 'Wallflower' MacMurray." *Dayton [Ohio] Daily News*, October 15, 1944.

Flint, Peter B. "Fred MacMurray, Film and TV Actor, Is Dead at 83." *New York Times*, November 6, 1991.

Folkart, Burt A. "Movie and TV Actor Fred MacMurray Dies." *Los Angeles Times*, November 6, 1991.

"Fred MacMurray." In J.R. Parish and D.E. Stanke, *The All Americans*. New Jersey: Rainbow Books, 1977.

"Fred MacMurray, Star of Films, Buys Rivera Citrus Ranch." *Los Angeles Times*, March 31, 1940.

"Fred M'Murray Weds Model in Las Vegas." *Los Angeles Herald*, June 20, 1936.

Heffernan, Harold. "Fred Is Shy Guy of Long Standing." *Detroit News*, October 11, 1944.

Hopper, Hedda. "Fred Is Boss at Home!" *Chicago Tribune Sunday Magazine*, December 9, 1956.

_____. "Fred MacMurray: Plain American." *Youngstown [Ohio] Vindicator*, March 25, 1945.

_____. "MacMurray: The All-America Millionaire?" *Los Angeles Times*, February 7, 1960.

MacMurray, Fred, as told to Pete Martin. "I've Been Lucky." *Saturday Evening Post*, February 24, 1962.

MacMurray, Haver Nuptial Move Denied. *Los Angeles Daily News*, March 1, 1954.

MacMurray, June Haver, as told to Carl Schroeder. "The Magic of a Good Marriage." *Good Housekeeping*, October 1971.

Miller, Arthur. "'I Just Talk Lines' Says MacMurray." *Los Angeles Times*, July 22, 1945.

"Model and Star Elope." *Los Angeles Times*, June 20, 1936.

Mosby, Aline. "M'Murray Tells Marriage Delay." *Los Angeles Daily News*, April 29, 1954.

Neal, Jim. "Fred MacMurray Dies." *Comic Buyer's Guide*, November 29, 1991.

Nielsen, Ray. "Billy Wilder and Double Indemnity." *Classic Images*, December 1983.

Obituary. *The [London] Times*, November 7, 1991.

"$1,068,857 Left by Wife of Fred MacMurray. *Hollywood Citizen-News*, November 1, 1954.

Parsons, Louella O. "A Real Hollywood Love Story." *Los Angeles Examiner*, December 13, 1953.

Penton, Edgar. "'My Three Sons' Lures Holdout Fred MacMurray." *Showtime*, September 24–25, 1960.

Scott, Vernon. "Millionaire 'Bum' Takes a Job." *New York World Telegram and Sun*, April 23, 1960.

Skolsky, Sidney. "Tintypes: Fred MacMurray." *Hollywood Citizen-News*, July 27, 1962.

Thomas, Bob. "Homecoming Week for a Guy Named Fred at Paramount." *Hollywood Citizen-News*, March 4, 1946.
"Top Salaries to Cooper, Cagney, Ford, Wallis, Zanuck, Crosby." *Motion Picture Herald*, August 9, 1941.
"Twin Infants Adopted by Fred MacMurrays." *Los Angeles Times*, December 5, 1956.

Waterbury, Ruth. "The Saga of Frederick and Lilly." *Photoplay*, May 1945.

Documentary

"Fred MacMurray: The Guy Next Door." A Wombat Production. A Division of The CineMasters Group. Produced in association with Janson Associates and A&E Network. Copyright 1996.

GEORGE MACREADY

"I make my own luck."— George Macready in *Gilda* (1946)

One of screendom's most menacing character actors, George Macready was also one of its busiest — during a career that spanned four decades, he was seen in more than 60 films, 100 stage productions, and 250 television shows, including TV's *Peyton Place*, on which he portrayed partriarch Martin Peyton. Despite being typically cast as a bad guy, however, Macready did manage to snag a number of roles that showed him in a good light, including his portrayal of a crusading newspaper editor in *The Man Who Dared* (1946) and a minister in *Alias Nick Beal* (1949). But his cold, implacable veneer, along with the scar that marred his right cheek, lent itself ideally to the darker roles in which he excelled, and he was a memorable contributor to six films noirs: *My Name is Julia Ross* (1945), *Gilda* (1946), *The Big Clock* (1948), *Knock on Any Door* (1949), *A Lady Without Passport* (1950), and *Detective Story* (1951).

A descendant of Shakespearean actor William Charles Macready, George Macready was born on August 29, 1908, in Providence, Rhode Island, where his father worked as the manager of a shoe factory. After being educated in the public schools of Providence, Macready enrolled in Brown University, where he made his first attempt at exploring his long-time interest in performing. His effort was less than successful, however.

"My freshman year I tried out for the dramatic club. I have been interested in the theater ever since I can remember," Macready recalled in a 1936 interview. "I worked diligently over 'Friends, Romans, Countrymen …' and when it was my turn to try out for the club, I got to my feet and began Antony's lines. After I finished, the president of the organization turned to another member, and I heard him ask, 'What in the world was he saying?' My name did not appear on the list of dramatic club fledglings the next morning when I hopefully went to look for it."

Stymied in his initial audition, Macready turned instead to other extracurricular activities, including managing the school's football team. But during his second year at the school, the actor was involved in an accident that left him with the distinctive scar on his cheek which served him so well in later years.

"He was riding with six of his frat brothers in a Model T Ford and they hit an icy road, hit a telephone pole, and he went through the windshield," Macready's son, Michael, said in a 2001 interview. "The only doctor for miles around was a veterinarian, who sewed him up, but he woke up with scarlet fever because the guy hadn't washed his hands properly."

Despite this near-tragic incident, Macready later graduated from Brown and, determined not to work in his father's factory, he headed for New York to try his luck on Broadway. But he was no more successful in the New York theater than he had been with his college efforts and, instead, he found work in the traffic department of the *New York Daily News*.

"A year later, I was traffic manager — and bored silly," Macready said in 1954. "I was amusing myself by taking singing and piano lessons at night, and somewhere along the line I met a chap who was affiliated with a wonderful theater group of that time."

The "wonderful theater group" was the American Laboratory Theater, founded by veteran performers Richard Boleslawski and Maria Ouspenskaya. Macready made his stage debut with the company playing the duke in *Twelfth Night*, and remained under Boleslavsky's tutelage for the next three years. He left the company when he was given the opportunity to play in Gordon Craig's production of *Macbeth*, starring Florence Reid and Lyn Harding.

"I was asked to read 'Malcolm,'" Macready recalled. "Fortunately, this time, after it was over, no one turned and asked, 'What in the world was he saying?' I toured and played for one year. [But] you know how the theater is. Stock companies followed."

While playing in a "straw hat" theater in Detroit, Macready got an unexpected break when the production's leading lady forgot her lines.

"I managed, somehow, to give her lines and my own, too," Macready said. "Then came the finale when a rope, manipulated by pulleys and concealed from the audience, was to assist me into 'heaven.' It darned near did — it broke. I wasn't hurt, fortunately, but a very famous stock company manager was in the audience — Jessie Bonstelle. She came backstage and said, in substance, that any young actor who could play both leading man and leading lady in the same play at the same time, and make such an abrupt descent from heaven with such good grace, ought to be good enough for her company."

For the next three years, Macready appeared in countless productions for Bonstelle, playing in everything from Broadway hits to Shakespeare and Ibsen — "You name it," he said. During this period, he met actress Elizabeth Dana, another member of Bonstelle's company; the couple married and later had three children, Michael in 1932, Marcia in 1934, and Elizabeth in 1938, but the marriage ended in divorce in 1942.

After leaving Detroit, Macready landed parts in such Broadway productions as *Lucrece* with Brian Aherne, *Romeo and Juliet* with Katherine Cornell and Orson Welles, and *Victoria Regina* with Helen Hayes and Vincent Price. (In 1943, Macready, Price, and artist Howard Warshaw would open a Los Angeles art gallery named The Little Gallery. It closed after only a year, however, because "it turned mostly into a coffee klatch for artists — people came to talk and gossip and nobody bought any pictures," Michael Macready said.)

By now, Hollywood had taken notice of the tall, distinguished actor, and Macready made his film debut in 1942, playing a small role as a school teacher in Columbia's *The Commandos Strike at Dawn*, starring Paul Muni and directed by John Farrow. Signing a long-term contract with the studio, Macready became one of the busiest actors in Hollywood, appearing in such features as *The Story of Dr. Wassell* (1944), starring Gary Cooper in the title role of the real-life missionary doctor; *The Seventh Cross* (1944), a World War II drama with a top-notch cast that included Spencer Tracy, Hume Cronyn, Jessica Tandy, and Agnes Moorehead; *Follow the Boys* (1944), an entertaining, star-studded musical tribute to the war effort; *A Song to Remember* (1945), a biopic of composer Frederic Chopin; and *My Name is Julia Ross* (1945), the actor's initial foray into the shadowy domain of film noir.

In this tense, stylish thriller, Macready played the psychotic Ralph Hughes, who kidnaps his mother's live-in secretary, Julia Ross (Nina Foch), passing her off as his dead wife. To her horror, Julia soon learns that Ralph has murdered the real Marion Hughes Ross and, along with his mother (Dame May Whitty), plans to kill Julia, make her death appear a suicide, and profit from Marion's sizable estate. Before Ralph and his nefarious mother can successfully carry out their plan,

Julia's fiancé arrives with police and Ralph is shot and killed while trying to escape.

As Hughes, Macready turned in a frightening performance of a man unable to suppress his deadly madness, despite the unflagging efforts of his mother to shield him. Hughes' persona, and his relationship with his mother, are revealed early in the film, when he is seen intently and methodically ripping a lace garment. "Put that knife away," his mother admonishes him. "Try to remember — if it weren't for your temper, we wouldn't be in this awful trouble today."

After earning a spate of good reviews for his portrayal, Macready was seen in his second film noir, *Gilda* (1946), playing Ballin Mundson, a Buenos Aires casino owner and head of a Nazi-controlled cartel. One of noir's best-known features, the film focuses on the relationship between Mundson, his beautiful but unfaithful wife, Gilda (Rita Hayworth), and Johnny Farrell (Glenn Ford), a two-bit gambler whom Mundson hires as his casino manager. As it turns out, Johnny and Gilda were lovers years before, and after a series of plot twists and turns, Mundson is killed by the casino's washroom attendant moments before he plans to shoot the couple.

Macready's Mundson was the actor's most memorable noir character, a powerful, deadly, and possessive man, noted chiefly for his unyielding will and his constant companion — a cane with a retractable blade. ("It is a most faithful, obedient friend," Mundson says of the cane. "It is silent when I wish to be silent. It talks when I wish to talk.") Macready's portrayal brought rave reviews for the actor, with critics nearly running out of adjectives to praise his performance. The *Los Angeles Times'* Edwin Schallert noted his "first-line work," Ruth Waterbury of the *Los Angeles Examiner* labeled him "superlative," and Thalia Bell declared in *Motion Picture Daily* that he "brings the advantage of native talent and long experience." And in his best review, Macready was applauded by the critic for the *Hollywood Review*, who wrote: "George Macready is in command of every scene in which he appears, no matter who shares it with him. He is superb as the man of mystery."

During the remainder of the decade, Macready continued his busy film schedule, playing villains in such features as *The Swordsman* (1948), a swashbuckler starring Larry Parks; *The Black Arrow* (1948), a romantic adventure based on Robert Louis Stevenson's novel; and *Coroner Creek* (1948), a Randolph Scott western. He also played featured roles in two additional films noirs, *The Big Clock* (1948) and *Knock on Any Door* (1949).

In the first, Macready portrayed Steve Hagen, an employee of a mammoth media enterprise who becomes a furtive accomplice when his boss, Earl Janoth (Charles Laughton), confesses to him that he murdered his mistress ("I just killed someone," Janoth says laconically). When magazine editor George Stroud (Ray Milland) unearths a set of circumstantial clues indicating that Steve is the killer, and Janoth gravely promises to "use every resource at our disposal" to defend him, Steve reveals the truth. Janoth promptly shoots Steve and attempts to flee, but seconds later falls down an elevator shaft to his death.

In this feature, Macready offered a perfect balance between loyal employee and sardonic observer — in a telling exchange with Janoth after the publisher admits his crime, Steve first exhibits a sense of righteousness on his boss's behalf, telling him that his mistress "has been asking for it for a long time." But when Janoth then defends the woman's honor, Steve calmly asks, "Then why did you kill her?" For his role in this nail-biter, Macready was praised by critics, who labeled his performance "sleek" and "top-notch."

Next, in *Knock on Any Door*, Macready played District Attorney Kerman — described as "a vicious, contemptible gent" — who prosecutes a "pretty boy hoodlum," Nick Romano (John Derek), for the murder of a police officer. Romano is passionately defended by attorney Andrew Morton (Humphrey Bogart), but Kerman is equally passionate. In one scene, he threatens his own witness, a local hood who changes his testimony on the stand: "You lied all the way didn't you?" Kerman asks. "You're lying this very moment, aren't you? You'll be arrested before you leave this building. I'm going to send you up for this." But it is Kerman's cross-examination of the luckless defendant that provides the turning point in the trial — his vehement, relentless questioning finally causes the boy to confess to the crime. Although critics disagreed in their views of the film (Frank Eng labeled it "forthright and engrossing" in the *Los Angeles Daily News*, and Bosley Crowther dismissed it in the *New York Times* as "hokum from the start"), they were in accord about Macready's performance; in a typical appraisal, Eng wrote: "As the actual 'heavy,' Macready makes expertly brutal use of his material."

As the new decade began, Macready continued to maintain his busy work schedule — his five films in 1950 included *The Nevadan*, a fast-paced western with Randolph Scott and Dorothy Malone; *The Desert Hawk*, an Arabian Nights adventure that saw the actor portraying an evil despot opposite Yvonne DeCarlo; and his fifth film noir, *A Lady Without Passport*. In this box-office disappointment, Macready was cast as Palinov, the mastermind of a scheme to smuggle illegal aliens from Cuba into the United States. When his plot is discovered by undercover agent Pete Karczag (John Hodiak), Palinov flies to America with a group of aliens that include a young immigrant, Marianne Lorress (Hedy Lamarr), with whom Karczag has fallen in love. With the agent hot on his trail, Palinov crashlands in the Florida Everglades and prepares to flee in a waiting boat, planning to take Marianne along. When he is confronted by Karczag, however, Palinov uses Marianne as a means of escape: "We both have something the other wants," he says. "If you try to keep me here, you'll only take one of us alive. It won't be the one you want." After secretly emptying the boat of most of its fuel, Karczag allows Palinov to board the craft, assuring Marianne that he will be caught.

The weakest of Macready's five films noirs, *A Lady Without Passport* was justifiably panned by several critics, including the reviewer for the *New York Times*, who dismissed it as "unimpressive," and Lowell E. Redelings of the *Hollywood Citizen-News*, who wrote: "[The film] is not very well cast, acted, directed, or screen-written. The main drawback is an unbelievable script. The situations are neither novel or interesting." The feature fared better with the *Los Angeles Times* critic, however, who concluded that "any excitement-thirsty fan will be able to take in whole gulps of thrills," and praised Macready as "all that could be desired in the way of the sinister foreigner."

Ever the scoundrel, Macready was next featured as a gunrunner in *Tarzan's Peril* (1951), one of the better entries in the *Tarzan* series. He followed this with a portrayal of Gen. Fritz Bayerlein in the outstanding James Mason starrer *The Desert Fox* (1951), and a standout role as an unscrupulous doctor in his final film noir, *Detective Story* (1951). This tautly directed film starred Kirk Douglas as Jim McLeod, a morally inflexible New York detective who encounters, during a single day, a variety of characters including a befuddled shoplifter (Lee Grant), a young executive (Craig Hill), who steals in an effort to impress his would-be girlfriend, and Karl Schneider (Macready), a reprehensible abortionist who, McLeod learns, performed a procedure on his wife years before. It is Schneider who serves as the catalyst for the film's climax — after the detective finds out about his wife's relationship with Schneider, he is unable to forgive her. Overcome with despair when she leaves him, he recklessly endangers his life to stop a gun-crazy hoodlum and dies in the final reel. Along with the film's other principals, Macready was hailed for his performance, and the feature was applauded in the *New York Times* as "hard-grained entertainment, not revealing, but bruisingly real."

As the 1950s continued, Macready expanded his performing repertoire to include the medium of television. Over the next two decades, he would be seen in a variety of programs including *The United States Steel Hour, Alfred Hitchcock Presents, Goodyear Television Playhouse, Gunsmoke, Perry Mason, Wanted: Dead or Alive, The Rebel, The Rifleman, The Twilight Zone*, and *The Man from U.N.C.L.E.* He also starred for five years in the 20th Century-Fox television series *Peyton Place*, in the role of town patriarch Martin Peyton. As in films, Macready continued his tendency toward villainous characterizations on the small screen, but the actor seemed to relish the roles.

"Just finished one … A *Four Star Playhouse* thing called House for Sale," he said in a 1954 interview. "I play a mad — a maniacal — killer. Fun." Despite the enjoyment Macready gained from such roles, however, he was also "an excellent comedian," according to his son, Michael.

"People didn't know that," Michael said. "He did a lot of comedy parts when he was in the theater, but there was only one picture he played in where he got to show his talents in that regard."

On the big screen, Macready's most memorable films during the 1950s and 1960s included *Julius Caesar* (1953), a star-studded hit whose cast included Marlon Brando, John Gielgud, Louis Calhern, Deborah Kerr, Greer Garson, and Edmond O'Brien; *Vera Cruz* (1954), an action-packed western starring Gary Cooper and Burt Lancaster; *A Kiss Before Dying* (1956), a thriller featuring Robert Wagner; *Paths of Glory* (1958), an epic anti-war film where he played a contemptible French general; *Seven Days in May* (1964), a political thriller penned by Rod Serling, of *Twilight Zone* fame; and *The Great Race* (1965), a fun-filled romp starring Jack Lemmon, Tony Curtis, Natalie Wood, and Peter Falk. Less successful were *Plunderers of Painted Flats* (1959), notable only as the last western produced by Republic Studios; *The Alligator People* (1959), which starred Macready as a doctor in the Louisiana bayou country who discovers a serum from alligators that enables humans to regenerate lost limbs; and *The Human Duplicators* (1965), a low-budget science fictioner featuring Richard Kiel as an alien sent to Earth to duplicate its leaders. Macready's final two films, *Count Yorga, Vampire* (1970) and *The Return of Count Yorga* (1971), were produced by his son, Michael. The former, for which Macready provided the narration, was a surprise hit, and in the sequel, he was seen in a cameo role as a professor.

"It was interesting having my father in my films," Michael said, "but it was sad in a way. The last picture he ever did was a picture that I produced, and he was very ill at the time. We brought the whole crew to his house and shot the scene in his garden." Two years after this appearance, on July 2, 1973, Macready died of emphysema at UCLA Medical Center. He was 63 years old.

Although Macready's performances consisted mostly of characters who were deceitful at best and manically homicidal at worst, he managed to bring a special spark to every role. In such films as *My Name is Julia Ross, Gilda*, and *Detective Story*, he demonstrated a noteworthy knack for creating multifaceted characters that remained in the memory long after the images left the screen. In any event, the actor himself once noted that he enjoyed these roles "purely in an academic way.

"At heart," he said, "I am a kind man."

Film Noir Filmography

My Name Is Julia Ross. Director: Joseph H. Lewis. Producer: Wallace MacDonald. Running time: 64 minutes. Released by Columbia, November 8, 1945. Cast: Nina Foch, Dame May Whitty, George Macready, Roland Varno, Anita Bolster, Doris Lloyd, Leonard Mudie, Joy Harrington, Queenie Leonard, Harry Hays Morgan, Ottola Nesmith, Olaf Hytten, Evan Thomas.

Gilda. Director: Charles Vidor. Producer: Virginia Van Upp. Running time: 110 minutes. Released by Columbia, May 15, 1946. Cast: Rita Hayworth, Glenn Ford, George Macready, Joseph Calleia, Steven Geray, Joe Sawyer, Gerald Mohr, Robert Scott, Lionel Royce, S.Z. Martel.

The Big Clock. Director: John Farrow. Producer: Richard Maibaum. Running time: 93 minutes. Released by Paramount, April 9, 1948. Cast: Ray Milland, Charles Laughton, Maureen O'Sullivan, George Macready, Rita Johnson, Elsa Lanchester, Harold Vermilyea, Dan Tobin, Henry Morgan, Richard Webb, Tad Van Brunt, Elaine Riley, Luis Van Rooten, Lloyd Corrigan, Margaret Field, Philip Van Zandt, Henri Letondal, Douglas Spencer.

Knock on Any Door. Director: Nicholas Ray. Producer: Robert Lord. Running time: 100 minutes. Released by Columbia, February 22, 1949. Cast: Humphrey Bogart, John Derek, George Macready, Allene Roberts, Susan Perry, Mickey Knox, Barry Kelley, Cooley Wilson, Cara Williams, Jimmy Conlin, Sumner Williams, Sid Melton, Pepe Hern, Dewey Martin, Robert A. Davis, Houseley Stevenson, Vince Barnett, Thomas Sully, Florence Auer, Pierre Watkins, Gordon Nelson, Argentina Brunetti, Dick Sinatra, Carol Coombs, Joan Baxter.

A Lady Without Passport. Director: Joseph H. Lewis. Producer: Samuel Marx. Running time: 72 minutes. Released by MGM, August 3, 1950. Cast: Hedy Lamarr, John Hodiak, James Craig, George Macready, Steven Geray, Bruce Cowling, Nedrick Young, Steven Hill, Robert Osterloh, Trevor Bardette, Charles Wagenheim, Renzo Cesana, Esther Zeitlin, Carlo Tricoli, Marta Mitrovitch, Don Garner, Richard Crane, Nita Bieber.

Detective Story. Director: William Wyler. Producer: William Wyler. Running time: 105 minutes. Released by Paramount, November 6, 1951. Cast: Kirk Douglas, Eleanor Parker, William Bendix, Cathy O'Donnell, George Macready, Horace McMahon, Gladys George, Joseph Wiseman, Lee Grant, Gerald Mohr, Frank Faylen, Craig Hill, Michael Strong, Luis Van Rooten, Bert Freed, Warner Anderson, Grandon Rhodes, William "Bill" Phillips, Russell Evans. Awards: Academy Award nominations for Best Director (William Wyler), Best Actress (Eleanor Parker), Best Supporting Actress (Lee Grant), Best Screenplay (Philip Yordan, Robert Wyler).

References

"Actor George Macready, 63; Movie Villain." *Los Angeles Times*, July 4, 1973.

"Actor Swears Off Beards." *New York Morning Telegraph*, September 28, 1944.

"Additions to Guild Cast." *New York Herald Tribune*, October 9, 1933.

Biography of George Macready. RKO Radio Studios, circa 1951.

Biography of George Macready. 20th Century–Fox Studios, circa 1970.

Biography of George Macready. Columbia Studios, May 26, 1946.

Chapman, John. "Julie Harris and 'The Lark' Co. Repeat Rave Show in the West." *New York Times*, August 6, 1956.

Cini, Zelda. "George Macready Gave Up Broadway for a Movie Career." *Hollywood Studio Magazine*, circa 1975.

"Civilians to Do 'Middle Watch.'" *Detroit Times*, June 22, 1930.

"George Macready, the 'Villain' in Many Plays and Films, Dies." *New York Times*, July 4, 1973.

"Heidelberg Via Jersey City." *New York Herald Tribune*, October 25, 1936.

Leavitt, Martha. "From College to Stage Career." *New York Herald Tribune*, May 17, 1936.

"Macready Still Storm Trooping." *New York Post*, June 1, 1939.

Obituary. *New York Daily News*, July 4, 1973.

Obituary. *Variety*, July 5, 1973.

HERBERT MARSHALL

"Remember, any accusation you make against me will be ridiculed — the ravings of a
pitiful lunatic. There's no possible way you can prove I killed your wife." — Herbert Marshall in *The High Wall* (1947)

On the big screen, Herbert Marshall was the epitome of the debonair, gracious, and cultured English gentleman — but behind the scenes, the actor's real-life romantic entanglements were nearly as numerous and as scandalous as his celluloid relationships. Married five times, and once embroiled in a public affair with film star Gloria Swanson, Marshall managed to keep his personal and professional lives separate, and appeared in nearly 80 silent and sound films over a span of 50 years. The actor, who — unknown to audiences of the day — lost his right leg while serving in World War I, was most popular in drawing-room dramas or witty comedies, but he was also right at home in four features from the film noir era, *The Letter* (1940), *Crack-Up* (1946), *The High Wall* (1947), and *Angel Face* (1955).

Herbert Brough Falcon Marshall was born in London on May 23, 1890, the son of actor Percy F. Marshall and actress Ethel May Turner. After graduating from St. Mary's College in Harlow, England, Marshall rebelled at following in his parents' footsteps and took a position, instead, as a clerk at an accounting firm in London's financial district.

"I am the only member of my family who did not want to go on the stage," Marshall once said. "My father and mother were both in the theater and I thought their choice of profession very mundane. You see, I wanted to do something glamorous when I grew up."

But the field of accounting didn't offer the glamour Marshall sought and before long, he left the firm and signed on with an acting company in Bruxton as a stage manager's assistant. In 1911, he made his first stage appearance, a walk-on in *The Adventures of Lady Ursula*, and two years later he debuted in London in *Brewster's Millions*. After roles in a number of local plays, Marshall landed

a role in *Grumpy*, which toured in the United States and Canada in 1915. That same year, the actor entered into the first of his five marriages, although the existing details of the union are sketchy. Most sources agree that his first wife was Mollie Maitland, a popular actress on the British stage, but one source identifies her as a model, and another states that Marshall's first wife was named Hilda Lloyd.

The name and occupation of his spouse notwithstanding, both the budding thespian's career and marriage were interrupted in 1916 when he enlisted in the British Army and served with the British Expeditionary Forces. During a battle at Arras, Marshall was severely wounded, which resulted in the amputation of his right leg and a 13-month stay in an army hospital. But the actor was determined that the loss of his limb would not lead to the end of his career.

"Only his close friends knew it, but his victory over this handicap was a monument to courage and perseverance," columnist John McClain wrote in the *New York Journal American* after Marshall's death. "He soon realized that his career as an actor depended upon his ability to walk about without any apparent hindrance and he laboriously learned how to maneuver the artificial limb so that people who were unaware of his misfortune never suspected it."

After the war, Marshall resumed his acting career and honed his skills at the Lyric Opera House Company in Hammersmith.

"I studied the methods of the stars ... and learned, not how to *act*, but how *not* to act, which was a beginning, anyway," Marshall said.

During the next decade, Marshall appeared in such London productions as *Make Believe, The Merchant of Venice, Windows,*

Lavender Ladies, Abraham, and *As You Like It*, and several Broadway plays, including *The Voice from the Minaret, These Charming People*, and *This Marriage*, with Tallulah Bankhead. In 1927, the actor was seen in his screen debut, a British silent film, *Mumsie*. This was followed by a series of British features that included *Dawn* (1928); *The Letter* (1929), his first talking picture; and *Murder* (1930), directed by Alfred Hitchcock. After signing a contract with Paramount Studios, Marshall appeared in his first American film, *Secrets of a Secretary* (1931), starring Claudette Colbert and helmed by famed Broadway director George Abbott.

While his film career was on the rise, Marshall's personal life was heating up as well. In 1925, he met British stage actress Edna Best, who later gained fame in such popular American films as Hitchcock's *The Man Who Knew Too Much* (1934), *Intermezzo* (1939), and *The Ghost and Mrs. Muir* (1947). At the time, Best was married to fellow stage performer William Seymour Beard, with whom she had twin sons. But the marital status of Marshall and Best did not stop them from falling in love, and in 1928, they divorced their respective spouses and married in Jersey City, New Jersey. The two went on to appear in a number of stage productions together, including *The Swan, Michael and Mary*, and *There's Always Juliet*.

But the happy early years of Marshall's marriage to Best would not last. In 1932, Best learned that she was expecting the couple's first child and returned to her home in England to await the baby's birth. During her absence, rumors abounded that Marshall had become involved with screen star Gloria Swanson, but the speculation ceased when Marshall traveled to England for the birth of his daughter, Sarah, in May 1933 (Sarah later followed in her parents' footsteps, appearing in such films as *The Long Hot Summer* [1958], *Dave* [1993], and *Dangerous Minds* [1995], as well as a variety of television series and made-for-TV movies). Later that year, the couple returned to Hollywood, leaving Sarah behind. ("We didn't want her to make the long jour-

ney," Marshall was quoted.) But the stories about Marshall and Swanson refused to die — one newspaper claimed that "on a specially hired yacht, [Marshall and Swanson] weekend off Santa Catalina islands, and Miss Swanson wears dark glasses to disguise herself when she goes for a stroll on the Isle." Still, Marshall dismissed the growing rumors of his plans to divorce Best and marry Swanson.

"Such a thing is absurd," he told reporters. "There is no thought of such a thing on the part of either of us." Before long, however, Best returned to London — alone.

With talk of Marshall's suspected dalliance still swirling about, the actor found himself in the news again in September 1934. While attending a party at the home of director Ernst Lubitsch, Marshall was knocked to the floor during a "one-blow fight" with novelist John Monk Saunders who, at the time, was married to actress Fay Wray. According to accounts, Marshall — accompanied to the party by Swanson — "began a tirade" against the novelist after Saunders mentioned some photographs he'd spotted in a fan magazine that compared the beauty of Swanson and Edna Best.

"I thought it was a gag, and paid no attention to the remarks," Saunders said. "Finally he called me a name. I looked to see if he were smiling, but he was not."

Saunders promptly knocked Marshall to the floor, and the two actresses lifted him and placed him in a chair. Marshall later refuted Saunders' account.

"I can only say that Mr. Monk Saunders' statement is the best proof to date that he is a writer of melodramatic fiction," Marshall said. "The only active part I played in his melodrama was to resent his insulting behavior to a lady at my table."

Marshall's life finally seemed to settle back into normalcy over the next year, and in 1936, he joined his wife in London, after which the couple enjoyed a second honeymoon. But it was the beginning of the end, as Marshall was again besieged with charges of infidelity — in April 1938, he was named in a $250,000 alienation suit by singer Eddy

The couple had a daughter, Ann, in 1942, and for a time, Marshall's personal life possessed a veneer of placid contentment.

Meanwhile, as Marshall's off-screen concerns were being chronicled in the media, the actor's stardom on-screen had continued to rise, and he starred throughout the 1930s opposite some of Hollywood's most popular leading ladies, including Kay Francis and Miriam Hopkins in *Trouble in Paradise* (1932), Marlene Dietrich in *Blonde Venus* (1932), Norma Shearer in *Riptide* (1934), Greta Garbo in *The Painted Veil* (1934), Constance Bennett in *Outcast Lady* (1934), Margaret Sullavan in *The Good Fairy* (1935), Ann Harding in *The Flame Within*, Katharine Hepburn in *A Woman Rebels* (1936), Jean Arthur in *If You Could Only Cook*, Barbara Stanwyck in *Breakfast for Two* (1937), Marlene Dietrich in *Angel* (1937), and Deanna Durbin in *Mad About Music* (1938). In addition, his films were helmed by such top directors as Josef von Sternberg, Ernst Lubitsch, Cecil B. DeMille, William Wyler, and George Cukor. While most of his films were lightweight fare, however, the actor wandered onto the dark side of the screen when he starred opposite Bette Davis in his first film noir, *The Letter* (1940).

One of the earliest entries of the noir era, *The Letter* begins with the shocking shooting death of a Malaysian plantation overseer by his lover, Leslie Crosbie (Bette Davis). After the murder, Leslie concocts a fantastic tale to cover the crime, thoroughly convincing her faithful spouse, Robert (Marshall), who tells her, "You did what every woman would have done in your place. Only nine-tenths of them wouldn't have had the courage." When an incriminating letter surfaces that would reveal the adulterous relationship between Leslie and the dead man, Robert — without knowing its precise contents — authorizes its purchase, and Leslie is later cleared in court. But when Robert insists on knowing the contents of the letter, Leslie not only admits her guilt, but also her inability to continue with their marriage ("With all my heart, I still love the man I killed!" she cries).

Brandt, who claimed that the actor was responsible for his November 1937 divorce from actress and one-time department store model, Lee Russell.

"We had been on the coast. I returned to New York, leaving her there, as she wanted to do some movie work. I received many letters from her, telling me how lonely she was," Brandt told reporters. "Then suddenly came a letter saying she had attended a party at Edgar Selwyn's and had met Herbert Marshall. Three weeks later another letter came. She wrote that she had believed I was the only man in the world for her, but now the situation was changed. She said she was not coming back and that there was no use in my coming out."

The lawsuit was ultimately dropped, but Brandt later insisted that the matter had been settled out of court for $10,000. Marshall denied that any payment had been made by him.

Newspaper accounts claimed that Edna Best "was not greatly perturbed" over her husband's new romance — in 1940, she obtained a Nevada divorce in Reno, and promptly married agent Nat Wolfe. Several weeks later, Marshall made Lee Russell wife number three.

Herbert Marshall and Bette Davis in *The Letter* (1940).

Despite her acquittal, however, Leslie does pay for her crime — in the film's atmospheric final reel, she is murdered by her dead lover's Eurasian spouse (Gale Sondergaard). Hailed after its released for its direction and superb cast, *The Letter* also earned good notices for Marshall; the reviewer for *Variety* wrote that he "never falters."

By now, Marshall's popularity as a leading man had begun to wane, and he moved into more character roles. Still, he was seen in a number of box office hits, and earned good reviews for his role in *Foreign Correspondent* (1940), a spy thriller directed by Alfred Hitchcock; *The Little Foxes* (1941), where he portrayed an invalid who dies at the hand of his mercenary spouse; and *Duel in the Sun* (1946), starring Gregory Peck and Jennifer Jones. Marshall didn't fare as well with critics,

however, for his performances in *Flight for Freedom* (1943), based on the life of aviatrix Amelia Earhart, and *The Enchanted Cottage* (1945), a sensitive film about two social outcasts who find love in a magical cottage. In the first film, Marshall's performance was dismissed as "wan," and in the latter, he was labeled "uncomfortably unctuous." But the actor rebounded from these criticisms with a role as a Scotland Yard inspector in his second film noir, *Crack-Up* (1946).

Praised as a "surprisingly suspenseful melodrama," *Crack-Up* starred Pat O'Brien as George Steele, an expert on art forgeries who stumbles on a devious plot to substitute museum artwork with high-quality imitations. After a colleague is murdered, Steele becomes the chief suspect, but he later tracks down the actual killer, the art-loving Dr.

Lowell (Ray Collins). Marshall was seen in the significant role of Traybin, a Scotland Yard art expert who was working undercover to locate a pair of original paintings that had been replaced in the museum. His undercover status notwithstanding, Traybin gives a mild clue to his real vocation early in the film when he admonishes Steele and his girlfriend, Terry Cordeau (Claire Trevor), about their contentious dealings with the local authorities: "It's strange, but you Americans are always fighting an undeclared war against your police — why is it? You hire them to do a job, then you dare them to do it, then you almost resent it if they succeed. It may be an impertinent suggestion — as, after all, I'm only a visitor — why don't you meet them half way? Cops are only human. They might respond to a little respect and affection."

A year after earning praise for his "competent" performance in *Crack-Up*, Marshall was cast in his third noir, *The High Wall* (1947), in which he memorably played one of the few villains of his career. This feature centers on Steven Kenet (Robert Taylor), a former pilot who is committed to a psychiatric hospital after admitting that he has strangled his wife (Dorothy Patrick) but cannot remember the circumstances. Administered a dose of sodium pentathol, Kenet is eventually able to piece together the events and realizes that his wife was killed by her employer, Willard Whitcombe (Marshall), an ambitious publishing company executive with whom she was having an affair. As it turns out, Whitcombe not only murdered his mistress, but also Henry Cronner (Vince Barnett), a hapless janitor who attempted to blackmail the publisher by threatening to provide valuable information for Kenet's defense. ("Cronner, the janitor — you haven't heard? He can't testify for you," Whitcombe later tells Kenet. "Poor fellow met with a tragic end. Fell down the elevator shaft, from my floor to the basement.") As the dastardly, deadly Whitcombe, Marshall turned in a chilling performance, and the film was praised after its release as "a likely lot of terrors, morbid and socially cynical."

By now, Marshall's personal life had cropped up in the news once again. In January 1947, after seven years of marriage, Lee Russell divorced Marshall on the grounds of incompatibility.

"I will never say anything against [Marshall]," Russell told columnist Louella Parsons. "He is one of the most charming people I have known. [He] just returned from New York and it was after that we decided upon the break. I suppose you had better call it 'incompatibility,' although actually, nobody could say that he was incompatible. I really don't want to discuss the reason."

But Hollywood insiders suspected that the reason for the divorce was Boots Mallory, with whom Marshall had been seen publicly on numerous occasions. A former Ziegfeld Follies performer and Wampas Baby Star of 1932, Mallory had recently divorced her husband, William Cagney, brother of actor James Cagney. Sure enough, on August 4, 1947, the 55-year-old Marshall and the 34-year-old Mallory were wed. By all accounts, Marshall's fourth marriage appeared to be a happy one; sadly, in December 1958, after a 16-month illness, Boots Mallory would die of a chronic throat ailment at the age of 45.

Career-wise, Marshall was seen in a dwindling number of films of varying quality during the late 1940s and 1950s, including *The Secret Garden* (1949), a delightful feature in which he played the irascible uncle of Margaret O'Brien; *Black Jack* (1950), a forgettable crime drama; *Riders to the Stars* (1954), a tiresome science fiction saga; *The Virgin Queen* (1955), highlighted by Bette Davis' portrayal of the title role; and *The Fly* (1958), a horror film that has become a cult classic of the genre. One of his best films during this period was his final film noir, *Angel Face* (1953).

Here, Marshall portrayed financially-strapped novelist Charles Tremayne, devoted father of the beautiful but mentally disturbed Diane (Jean Simmons) and husband to Diane's wealthy but hated stepmother, Katherine (Barbara O'Neil). Tremayne's attachment to his daughter and his financial reliance upon his wife are clearly illustrated in an early scene, in which he confesses to Katherine that he has used her credit card for a recent purchase: "I'm terribly sorry, darling, but the moment I saw that dress, I knew there was only one person in the world who could wear it — my own dearly beloved and horribly spoiled Diane... It was $300 plus sales tax. I have just enough for the tax." Jealous of Katherine's relationship with her father, and frustrated by her own monetary restrictions, Diane makes an unsuccessful attempt to kill her stepmother by turning on the gas in her room. Later, Diane tries another method — rigging the family car to drive in reverse over a cliff with her stepmother inside — but this time, her plan succeeds too well when her father, a last-minute passenger, is killed along with Katherine. In the film's climax, Diane deliberately meets the same fate, along with her husband, Frank Jessup (Robert Mitchum), who'd planned to leave her after discovering her guilt. For his performance of the devoted father, Marshall was singled out by Bosley Crowther, who said in the *New York Times* that the actor "does well in his role," but the film earned mixed reviews; while the critic for the *Hollywood Citizen-News* praised its "good suspense," the *Los Angeles Daily News*' Howard McClay panned it as "a rather messy movie melodrama."

In addition to his screen work, Marshall also began appearing on various television programs during the 1950s— in 1952, he was the host of *The Unexpected*, a half-hour suspense anthology series, and during the remainder of the decade, he guested on such series as *Alfred Hitchcock Presents, Adventures in Paradise*, and *Zane Grey Theater*. The actor also kept busy portraying intelligence agent Ken Thurston on the CBS radio series *The Man Called X*, which ran from 1947 to 1952.

Marshall gave marriage one more try in 1960, when he married Dee Anne Kahmann, a 38-year-old department store buyer in Los Angeles. That same year, the actor shared with the press his frustrations concerning the decline of his career, and his search for more "rugged" roles.

"Not that I want to go jumping into a western right away, but I would like a chance to be as rough and tough as the next fellow," Marshall said. "I've done it on the stage in years gone by and there's no reason why I can't do that type of role now. I'm accused of being poised and cultured, only some of which I subscribe to. It's been 20 years since I've done a play. And I should very much like to do another."

But Marshall appeared in only a handful of films during the remainder of his career. Most were such forgettable offerings as *College Confidential* (1960), a laughable exposé of campus life; *A Fever in the Blood* (1961), a political comedy in which he portrayed a governor; and *The Caretakers* (1963), an over-the-top melodrama set in a mental hospital. The actor fared a little better, however, with *The List of Adrian Messenger* (1963), a somewhat confusing but engrossing drama directed by John Huston, and his final film, *The Third Day* (1965), a fairly good suspenser starring George Peppard and Elizabeth Ashley.

After filming his role for *The Third Day*, Marshall, in failing health for several years, was admitted to the Motion Picture Country Home and Hospital. After a two-month stay, he was released, but 18 days later, on January 22, 1966, the actor died of a heart attack at his Beverly Hills home. He was 75.

Although his infinitely fascinating romantic exploits often garnered more attention for Herbert Marshall than did his screen roles, the actor demonstrated his versatility in films that varied from drawing room comedies to science fiction, pirate adventures to costume dramas, and detective thrillers to sweeping romances. Although frequently typecast due to his clipped accent and self-described "poise," the actor was a standout in roles that broke out of this mold, most notably his trusting, long-suffering spouse in *The Letter*, and his ill-fated Horace Giddens in *The Little Foxes*.

To both friends and fans, the actor remained, always, the polished and urbane gentleman that he so ably portrayed on screen, as well as a man of mettle, whose fortitude and perseverance served to overcome a handicap that could have ended his career. These qualities were touchingly noted in a letter written by actor Reginald Denham, who played alongside Marshall in the London cast of *Abraham Lincoln* in 1919.

"In most of his obituary notices, he seems to be remembered as having been a superb exponent of elegant 'perfect gentleman' parts, which indeed he was," Denham wrote in *Variety*. "However, my own main memory of him is as a young eagle, a wounded eagle, with indomitable courage."

Film Noir Filmography

The Letter. Director: William Wyler. Producer: Hal B. Wallis. Running time: 95 minutes. Released by Warner Bros., November 22, 1940. Cast: Bette Davis, Herbert Marshall, James Stephenson, Frieda Inescort, Gale Sondergaard, Bruce Lester, Elizabeth Earl, Cecil Kellaway, Sen Yung, Willie Fung, Doris Lloyd, Tetsu Komai. Awards: Academy Award nominations for Best Picture, Best Director (William Wyler), Best Actress (Bette Davis), Best Supporting Actor (James Stephenson), Best B/W Cinematography (Gaetano Gaudio), Best Film Editing (Warren Low), Best Original Score (Max Steiner).

Crack-Up. Director: Irving Reis. Producer: Jack J. Gross. Running time: 93 minutes. Released by RKO, October 6, 1946. Cast: Pat O'Brien, Claire Trevor, Herbert Marshall, Ray Collins, Wallace Ford, Dean Harens, Damian O'Flynn, Erskine Sanford, Mary Ware.

The High Wall. Director: Curtis Bernhardt. Producer: Robert Lord. Running time: 100 minutes. Released by MGM, December 25, 1947. Cast: Robert Taylor, Audrey Totter, Herbert Marshall, Dorothy Patrick, H.B. Warner, Warner Anderson, Moroni Olsen, John Ridgeley, Morris Ankrum, Elisabeth Risdon, Vince Barnett, Jonathan Hale, Charles Arnt, Ray Mayer, Dick Wessell, Robert Emmet O'Connor, Celia Travers, Mary Servoss, Bobby Hyatt, Eula Guy, Jack Davis, Tom Quinn.

Angel Face. Director and Producer: Otto Preminger. Released by RKO, February 2, 1953. Running time: 91 minutes. Cast: Robert Mitchum, Jean Simmons, Mona Freeman, Herbert Marshall, Leon Ames, Barbara O'Neil, Kenneth Tobey, Raymond Greenleaf, Griff Barnett, Robert Gist, Morgan Farley, Jim Backus.

References

"Actor Herbert Marshall, 75." *New York Journal-American*, January 22, 1966.

"Actor Set to Marry Fifth Time." *Los Angeles Times*, April 26, 1960.

"Boots Mallory, Ex-Actress, Dies." *Los Angeles Examiner*, December 2, 1958.

Denham, Reginald. "Recalls Bart Marshall As Young London Actor After First World War." *Variety* (Letter to the Editor), February 23, 1966.

"Disconcerting Charm." *The American Weekly*, June 1, 1947.

Dudley, Fredda. "Marshall: Miracle of Modesty." *Fan Fare*, September 4, 1942.

"Film Notables in Fist Fight at Gay Party." *New York Daily News*, September 25, 1934.

Finnigan, Joe. "Marshall No 'Type.'" *Newark Evening News*, March 3, 1960.

"Herbert Marshall." *New York Sunday News*, October 12, 1941.

"Herbert Marshall, Actor, Dies at 75." *New York World-Telegraph and Sun*. January 22, 1966.

"Herbert Marshall-Edna Best Marital Rift Confirmed." *Los Angeles Times*, November 19, 1939.

"Herbert Marshall Is Called Wife Stealer." *New York Daily News*, April 15, 1938.

"Herbert Marshall Is Dead at 75; Actor with a Sympathetic Air." *New York Times*, January 23, 1966.

"Herbert Marshall — Suave Star, 75." *New York Journal-American*, January 23, 1966.

McClain, J. "Gallant Man's Final Curtain." *New York Journal-American*, January 25, 1966.

Obituary. *Time*, January 28, 1966.

Parsons, Louella O. "H. Marshall, Wife Separate." *Los Angeles Examiner*, December 9, 1945.

"Rites Thursday for Wife of Herbert Marshall." *The Hollywood Reporter*, December 2, 1958.

"Two New Hollywood Divorces." *Los Angeles Examiner*, January 13, 1947.

VICTOR MATURE

"Go ahead. Call my bluff." — Victor Mature in *Cry of the City* (1948)

Early in his career, handsome, curly-locked actor Victor Mature was tagged with such labels as "Glamour Boy," "Beautiful Hunk of a Man," "King of Beefcake," and "A Face That Would Melt in Your Mouth." But the monikers didn't faze Mature a bit.

"I don't mind being called 'Glamour Boy' so long as that check comes in on Friday," he once said. "I won't say I like it. Because of the moronic opinion people seem to have of Glamour Boys. But that's a demonstrable error. So it's all right with me. As I say, if properly compensated I can stomach anything."

Although the attention to his good looks and massive physique often overshadowed his acting ability, Mature was seen to good advantage in some of Hollywood's most memorable Biblical epics, including *Samson and Delilah* (1949) and *The Robe* (1953), as well as such features as *My Darling Clementine* (1946), in which he gave one of the best performances of his career. Mature was also a significant presence in five examples of film noir: *The Shanghai Gesture* (1941), *I Wake Up Screaming* (1942), *Kiss of Death* (1947), *Cry of the City* (1948), and *The Las Vegas Story* (1952).

Victor John Mature was born on January 19, 1915 (numerous sources state his birth year as 1913 or 1916), in Louisville, Kentucky, the youngest of three children born to Marcellus George Mature and his wife, Clara. (Mature's two siblings, a brother and a sister, both died at a young age.) An Austrian immigrant, Mature's father began his life in America as a scissors grinder, eventually finding success in the commercial refrigeration business.

By all accounts, young Victor was somewhat less than an ideal child. On his first day at the George H. Tingley school, he was sent home for biting his teacher, and he later at-

tended such schools as St. Xavier where, Mature once said, his mother was summoned so often that the other students thought she worked there. In newspaper and magazine reports of Mature's childhood, he was saddled with a number of negative references, including "the terror of the neighborhood," and the actor himself once admitted that he was "a stubborn kid."

"I'd cut school all the time and when exams came along, I'd answer one question after another, right down the line, by writing a big zero for each one," Mature said. "I was kicked out of a couple before I finally quit."

At the age of 15, Mature got a job as a salesman with a wholesale candy house, and a short time later began his own enterprise as a candy jobber. (He also reportedly worked for a time at the Brown Hotel, until he was fired for dancing on the roof garden while on duty.) A few years later, the industrious young man opened his own restaurant in Louisville. But the youthful businessman encountered more than he'd bargained for.

"The first month I lost $300 and from the looks of it, I'd have been in the hole even more the second [month]," Mature said in a 1953 interview. "The help was stealing me blind, and I didn't have sense enough to know it. Finally I contacted the manager of the famous Childs Restaurant. He was going on a two weeks vacation, but I told him I'd pay double his salary if he'd spend one week helping me at the restaurant." The manager agreed, and two months later, Mature broke even and sold the restaurant.

On a whim, Mature decided to "do something different" and, announcing his plans to become an actor, he set out for California, armed with a supply of canned goods and a stock of candy. Once there, he sold enough candy to afford the rent on a partly burned-out garage, which he made his home. But his sudden lifestyle change didn't set well with the family back home.

"Dad didn't disapprove but he just didn't feel that acting was practical," Mature recalled. "And so I had to go it on my own. When I got to Hollywood, I had 11 cents left after paying $8 rent.... I wired Dad saying all I had was 11 cents and he wired back saying that was six cents more than he had when he came over from Austria, and furthermore, he couldn't speak English, but I could."

On the advice of a friend, Mature auditioned for the drama school of the Pasadena Community Playhouse. Landing a spot at the school, Mature was given his first role in the play *Paths of Glory*, which debuted at the theater on November 16, 1936. He went on to appear in roles in more than 100 plays over the next several years, including *Autumn Crocus*, in which he played his first lead. To help pay for his tuition and other expenses, Mature worked a series of odd jobs, including cleaning wallpaper, mowing lawns, washing dishes, and waxing floors in the local YMCA. He also maintained an average food budget of forty-six cents a day. To save on rent money, the budding actor fashioned a makeshift tent and moved into the backyard of the Pasadena Playhouse (or into the backyard of a friend's house, depending on which story is to be believed).

On January 20, 1938, Mature married Frances Evans, another member of the Pasadena Playhouse. The union was an impulsive one, however, and Mature reportedly continued to reside in his tent while Frances lived in the girls dormitory. Destined for failure from the start, the marriage would end three years later.

Meanwhile, Mature's big break was close at hand. But the manner in which it arrived is a bit of a mystery. One version claims that a local newspaper reporter wrote a human interest story in 1939 about Mature's living situation and his acting ambitions, describing him as a "struggling derelict actor." The article was allegedly spotted by producer Hal Roach, who took pity on the homeless young man and promptly signed him to a movie contract. Contrary to this fanciful tale, however, most sources report that Mature was playing the lead in the Playhouse production of *To Quito and Back* when Roach (or his vice-president, Frank Ross) spotted the virile young actor, recognized in him the potential for movie stardom, and signed him up.

Despite the ambiguity of the route that led Mature to the Hal Roach studios, it is a fact that in 1939, Roach cast the young man as a lovesick gangster named Lefty in his film debut, *The Housekeeper's Daughter*, starring Joan Bennett. Mature was on screen only a short time, but his brief appearance incited an avalanche of fan mail and led Roach to award Mature with his first starring role, playing opposite Carole Landis in *One Million B.C.* (1940). The money-making caveman epic turned Mature into an overnight star. Mature was rushed into two more movies, *Captain Caution* (1940), a sea saga set during the war of 1812, and *No, No Nanette* (1940), starring Anna Neagle. The latter film was a loanout to RKO Studios, and after its release, RKO purchased half of Mature's contract from Hal Roach.

Meanwhile, with his fame suddenly on the rise, Mature began to display what one reporter called a "natural talent for self-promotion." The actor's efforts to cultivate press coverage were an overwhelming success, leading to countless articles and photo opportunities, as well as his acquisition of a slew of descriptors, including "Mr. Beautiful" and "Irresistible Male."

"I know, that glamour boy stuff makes me look like a drip," Mature candidly acknowledged in a 1941 interview. "But you know what that build-up did for me? It made me somebody. Supposing no one had paid any attention to me, hadn't written or said a thing about me? Where would I be now — back in a tent, perhaps, living on 50 cents a day. I'd rather be where I am today, and be regarded as a jerk, than to have been ignored."

Still, Mature was savvy enough to realize that he could not sustain a successful film career on a reputation as a "glamour boy."

So, following his first four screen appearances, he turned his sights toward Broadway.

"One of the reasons I was anxious to get away from Hollywood was to slay, while it was still in the process of growing, the legend that I was just a glamour boy with a lucky streak," Mature said later. "I convinced Roach, too, that his investment in me might be worth more if the public were to learn that I was more serious about my acting than I was supposed to be about nightclubs, glamour girls, and just playing around. He agreed with me." Offered his choice of four roles, Mature chose the lead in Moss Hart's "play with music," *Lady in the Dark*, co-starring Gertrude Lawrence and Danny Kaye. The production was a smash hit and Mature earned raves for his performance; in a typical review, Sidney B. Whipple of the *New York World-Telegram* wrote that Mature acted "with an engaging manner, simply, directly, and effectively."

Mature's tenure in New York wasn't all business, however. While there, he met 22-year-old Martha Stephenson Kemp, a former John Powers model and widow of band leader Hal Kemp, who was killed in an automobile crash in December 1940. After a whirlwind romance, the two were wed on June 17, 1941, but the union was a rocky one from the start, and Mature and Kemp separated in less than a year.

Professionally, Mature returned in triumph to Hollywood, where he was loaned to producer Arnold Pressburger for his first film noir, *The Shanghai Gesture* (1941). Released by United Artists, this exotic noir takes primarily in an immense casino operated by the mysterious Mother Gin Sling (Ona Munson). The feature's complex story involves a diversity of quirky characters, including Dr. Omar (Mature), who describes himself as "a doctor of nothing — it sounds important and hurts no one," Poppy (Gene Tierney), a flighty socialite enticed by the casino's seedy decadence, and Sir Guy Charteris (Walter Huston), a highly-respected financier who is determined to close the gambling hall. As the plot unfolds, it is revealed that, unknown to Poppy, Gin Sling and Charteris are her par-

ents, and this disclosure ultimately leads to Poppy's death at her mother's hand.

Recognized today as a stylish early example from the film noir era, *The Shanghai Gesture* was almost universally panned by critics upon its release and was a disappointment at the box office. Mature fared only slightly better in his next noir — another loan-out, this time to 20th Century-Fox for *I Wake Up Screaming* (1942). Here, Mature starred as promoter Frankie Christopher, who is suspected of murdering Vicky Lynn (Carole Landis), a model and would-be actress he discovered working as a waitress. Although little evidence exists that can link Frankie to the crime, he is pursued by a relentless detective, Ed Cornell (Laird Cregar), who tells him in one scene, "I could arrest you today, but you might get some smart mouthpiece and get off with life instead of the chair. I won't be satisfied until I'm sure it's the chair." When Cornell shows up to arrest him, Frankie goes on the lam, intent on finding the killer, who turns out to be Harry Williams (Elisha Cook, Jr.), the switchboard operator in Vicky's apartment building. The twist at the end comes with the disclosure that Cornell knew of Williams' guilt, but kept quiet because of his obsessive love for the actress and his jealousy over her relationship with Frankie. ("I lost Vicky long before Williams killed her," Cornell says. "You were the one who took her away from me, not him.") Like Mature's first noir, this feature was not well-received by critics, including Bosley Crowther of the *New York Times*, who termed it "a pretty obvious whodunnit and a strangely unmoving affair." Crowther also included Mature in his sweeping distaste of the film, writing that "three of the principal roles are played with virtually no distinction." Despite such criticism, however, the film was a modest box office success, adding to Mature's growing popularity with moviegoers.

At this point in Mature's burgeoning career, 20th Century-Fox took over his contract from Hal Roach for the reported sum of $80,000, which included a multiple loanout provision to RKO and gave the actor an increase in salary from $450 to $1,200 a week. The following year, three of Mature's four features were 20th Century-Fox musicals, *Footlight Serenade* (1942) and *Song of the Islands*, both co-starring Betty Grable, and *My Gal Sal* (1942), with Rita Hayworth. During filming of the latter production, Mature fell in love with his beautiful co-star and, although he was still married to Martha, he and Hayworth were expected to become man and wife.

But the union of the titian-haired beauty and the Glamour Boy wasn't meant to be. World War II proved to be the first obstacle — on July 2, 1942, Mature signed up with the Coast Guard Temporary Reserve, and that fall enlisted in the regular Coast Guard. After five months in San Pedro, Mature was transferred to Boston, where he spent the next 14 months aboard a Coast Guard cutter in the North Atlantic patrol. Meanwhile, rumors were rampant throughout Hollywood that Mature's wife was refusing to divorce him — the talk was so widespread, in fact, that Martha Mature penned an article in *Photoplay* magazine, telling readers, "I feel I must tell my side."

"Ever since Victor and I separated, friends and acquaintances — and I might add strangers, too — have been asking me, 'Why do you persist in standing in the way of Vic's happiness when you know he loves another woman?'" the January 1943 article read. "Please believe me, I am not refusing Vic a divorce. I am eager and anxious to be free and to give him his freedom to marry the woman he loves."

One month after the article appeared, Mature and Martha were divorced, but by now, a third obstacle had cropped up in the form of actor-director Orson Welles, who had used Hayworth as part of his USO magic show. After dating Welles for several months, Hayworth married him on September 7, 1943.

"Apparently, the way to a woman's heart is to saw her in half," Mature quipped after news of the Welles-Hayworth marriage broke. Despite this jocular response, however, the actor was obviously wounded, and later told columnist Louella Parsons, "Rita Hayworth is the only girl I ever felt I truly loved."

At least Mature had the war to keep his mind off of his troubled love life. In 1944, he returned to shore duty to appear in *Tars and Spars*, an all–Coast Guard musical revue that played in film and vaudeville houses nationwide. Mature also participated in coast-to-coast war bond tours and, near the end of the war in Europe, served aboard a troop transport, the U.S.S. *Admiral Mayo*. He was honorably discharged in November 1945 with the rank of chief boatswain's mate.

Returning to 20th Century-Fox after the war, Mature was promptly cast alongside Henry Fonda and Linda Darnell in the John Ford–directed story of the shootout at the O.K. Corral, *My Darling Clementine* (1946). In one of his best performances, Mature was a standout as Doc Holliday, and earned praise from such critics as Eileen Creelman of the *New York Sun*, who wrote that Mature "forgets about his good looks and actually does some acting.... It's a good part and a good performance."

The following year, Mature demonstrated his versatility by playing a well-bred

Englishman in *Moss Rose* (1947), a turn-of-the-century mystery, then returned to the world of the film noir in *Kiss of Death* (1947). In this first-rate offering, Mature played Nick Bianco, a luckless, small-time hood who becomes a reluctant stool-pigeon in order to earn his release from prison and reclaim his two small daughters. After marrying a sweet local girl (Coleen Gray), Nick's life of normalcy is disrupted after the murder acquittal of psychotic killer Tommy Udo (Richard Widmark), against whom Nick had testified. When Udo later threatens the lives of Nick's wife and children, the now-reformed hood decides to take matters into his own hands: "You had a perfect case and he beat you on it," Nick tells the assistant district attorney (Brian Donlevy). "You couldn't even keep a tail on him. He's nuts, and he's smarter than *you* are. I'm through trusting you, the police, or anybody but me. There's only one way to get Udo. And that's *my* way." Devising an intricate scheme to trap Udo, Nick is severely wounded when the killer fires on him at point-blank range, but he ultimately achieves his goal when Udo is gunned down in the street while trying to flee police.

Mature's performance of the determined hood-turned-family man was universally hailed after the release of *Kiss of Death*; Thomas Pryor of the *New York Times* found that there was a "depth and mobility" to the actor's portrayal that "was not hitherto noticeable," and in the *New York Herald Tribune*, Howard Barnes wrote: "Mature has been growing in acting stature so immensely that it is no surprise to find him playing ... with persuasion and finesse." Mature himself viewed the role of Nick Bianco as one of his favorites, announcing that "such roles got me out of the 'jerk' department, and I'm going to stay out of it from now on."

Years later, the actor's *Kiss of Death* co-star, Coleen Gray, recalled her experiences on the film with Mature, saying, "He was fun — we had fun."

"I remember that he was a womanizer, and he kind of made a pass at me, and I said, 'Please, I'm happily married,' and we got over

that alright, and we were friends. [*Kiss of Death*] was his best picture, and he had this pretty boy image ... Victor claimed that he wasn't an actor — he deprecated his talent — but I was very pleased for him that in his career he had *Kiss of Death* to point to."

Making good on his vow to distance himself from the "jerk department," Mature remained in the realm of noir the following year, starring with Richard Conte in *Cry of the City* (1948). In this fast-paced feature, the actor portrayed Lt. Vittorio Candella, a New York cop doggedly pursuing murder suspect Martin Rome (Richard Conte). As Rome uses a series of individuals to secure and maintain his freedom, Candella stalks him with single-minded determination, even disallowing a bullet wound to keep him from staying one step behind the small-time killer. In the film's finale, Candella finally catches up to Rome at a local church, where he plans to meet with his naïve girlfriend, Teena (Debra Paget), and flee the country with her. Determined to prevent Rome from ruining yet another life, Candella exposes the killer's true nature to Teena: "She knows that you killed two men. But does she know about the others?" Candella says. "You forgot all about them, didn't you? No, he didn't forget them. He didn't even think about them. He used them and brushed them aside, just like he's used everybody he's ever known." When these revelations cause Teena to abandon Rome, the killer flees the church, but he is shot and killed by Candella and dies in the street. For his powerful, understated portrayal of the relentless cop, Mature was labeled "excellent" in the *Los Angeles Examiner* and the *New York Times* reviewer wrote: "Victor Mature, an actor once suspected of limited talents, turns in a thoroughly satisfying job as the sincere and kindly cop, who not only knows his business but the kind of people he is tracking down."

Also in 1948, Mature gave marriage another try, but the third time wouldn't be the charm. On February 28, 1948, he wed Dorothy Stanford Berry, but after just a year of marriage, Berry would file for divorce. The couple later reconciled, but would experience a series of break-ups over the next several years before finally splitting for good in November 1955.

On screen, Mature was loaned to Paramount for the first of his biblical epics, *Samson and Delilah* (1949), co-starring Hedy Lamarr. During filming, director Cecil B. DeMille reportedly wanted Mature to wrestle with a tame, aging lion for a crucial action scene, but Mature refused. DeMille tried to persuade the star, telling him that the old lion had no teeth.

"Yeah?" Mature responded in a now-famous quote. "Well, I don't want to be gummed to death, either." DeMille managed to shoot the scene using a lion skin, and upon its release, *Samson and Delilah* was a smash hit, raking in $12 million in domestic box office alone. (The popular film also gave rise to an oft-repeated wisecrack from comedian Groucho Marx, who announced: "I don't like any movie where the leading man's chest is bigger than the leading lady's!")

Mature followed this hit with two musicals, *Red, Hot and Blue* (1949), starring Betty Hutton, and *Wabash Avenue* (1950), with Betty Grable, before returning to the dark world of noir for his final film from the era, *The Las Vegas Story* (1952). In this feature, the weakest of his five noirs, Mature played David Andrews, a lieutenant with the Las Vegas sheriff's department. Encountering his former lover, Linda (Jane Russell), who is now married to wealthy businessman Lloyd Rollins (Vincent Price), David is initially filled with bitterness, telling the woman, "You've got everything you've always wanted. And whatever you came to Vegas for, find it quick and get out. I have to live in this town." Later, however, after rekindling his relationship with Linda, David finds himself in the midst of a case involving the murder of a casino owner and a plot to steal Linda's $10,000 necklace. After a spectacular helicopter chase, David kills the private detective (Brad Dexter) responsible for the crimes and prepares to begin a new life with Linda when her luckless spouse is arrested for embezzlement.

Although Mature was mentioned in one review as "tak[ing] advantage of an occasional bright piece of dialogue tossed [his] way," *The Las Vegas Story* was a box office flop and was dismissed in *Variety* as "only a fair amount of melodrama entertainment." Mature bounced back the following year, however, when he appeared in the blockbuster biblical saga, *The Robe* (1953), starring Richard Burton and Jean Simmons. The first film shot in Cinemascope, *The Robe* earned a total of $17.5 million, and offered Mature one of his best roles as the gladiator, Demetrius, who becomes a follower of Christ. He reprised the role in 1954 as the star of *Demetrius and the Gladiators* (1954), opposite Susan Hayward, and filmed his fourth bible-themed feature later that year, *The Egyptian* (1954).

Mature's appearance in *The Egyptian* marked the end of his lucrative 20th Century-Fox contact and the beginning of a decline in his career. During the remainder of the decade, he was seen in few films of real quality; the best were *Betrayed* (1954), a wartime Clark Gable-Lana Turner starrer, in which Mature played a traitorous agent known as The Scarf; *Violent Saturday* (1955), an interesting crime drama directed by Richard Fleischer; *China Doll* (1958), a rather touching tale of the romance between a tough Air Corps captain and his Chinese housekeeper; and *The Big Circus* (1959), a rare non-disaster feature from producer Irwin Allen.

Away from the big screen and his faltering career, Mature was gearing up for another walk down the aisle. Despite being a three-time loser in the matrimonial sweepstakes, Mature maintained an optimistic view, insisting in a 1957 interview that marriage was "too good a thing to get soured on."

"It has to be more than getting taken for loot, for me to be soured on marriage," Mature told columnist Sheilah Graham. "Marriage is great when it goes well." Proving his point, in 1959 Mature married wife number four, Adrianne Joy Urwick, the daughter of an English physician, but this union, too, did not last. It was not until 1974, when he married former opera singer Loretta "Lorey"

Sebena, that Mature found true happiness in love. Mature and Lorey not only remained together until his death nearly 25 years later, but in 1975, the couple welcomed Mature's first and only child, Victoria.

Professionally, Mature announced plans in 1961 to retire from pictures and concentrate on his business investments which, at the time, included a meatball canning business in San Francisco and a television store in Los Angeles.

"It's a gold mine sure, but it's much more than that to me," Mature said of the store. "I've met a lot of people in our industry that I probably would never meet otherwise.... It seems that whenever anyone wants a television set, he says, 'Guess I'll call that jerk actor, Vic Mature.'"

After five years, however, Mature was lured back to the big screen for a role in the Peter Sellers comedy *After the Fox* (1966), in which he offered an hilarious self-parody, playing an aging movie star. He made only rare appearances after this comeback, however, including *Head* (1968), a surprisingly entertaining romp featuring the musical group known as The Monkees, and co-produced and co-written by Jack Nicholson; *Every Little Crook and Nanny* (1968), starring Lynn Redgrave; and *Won Ton Ton, the Dog That Saved Hollywood* (1976), a notoriously unfunny comedy notable only for its cameo appearances by such veterans as Virginia Mayo, Andy Devine, Joan Blondell, Broderick Crawford, Yvonne DeCarlo, Rhonda Fleming, and Stepin Fetchit. His last big screen appearance was a minor role in *Firepower* (1979), a ludicrous thriller starring Sophia Loren and James Coburn. Mature also made a rare television appearance several years later, making his small screen debut in *Samson and Delilah* (1985), where he played Samson's father. When asked by reporters how he felt about playing the patriarch of the character he'd portrayed nearly 40 years earlier, Mature responded with typical good humor.

"Heck," he said. "I'd play Samson's mother!"

In his later years, Mature lived mostly out of the spotlight, raising his daughter and spending a great deal of time playing golf, often with his closest friend, actor Jim Backus. On August 4, 1999, after battling leukemia for three years, Mature died at his home in Rancho Santa Fe, California, at the age of 86. His wife, Lorey, and daughter, Victoria, were at his side.

Throughout his successful Hollywood career, Victor Mature battled his own image, striving to demonstrate the real talent that existed behind the brawn. Sometimes he was successful, sometimes not, but he always viewed his career with a sense of amused realism, ever appreciative of his good fortune.

"I'm identified in print as a 'lush Lothario,' 'Technicolor Tarzan,' and 'overripe Romeo,'" Mature once said. "Directors who make pictures for the ages and actors who make pictures with one eye cocked on the Academy Award dismiss me as ham — uncured and uncurable.... Little guys are forever yearning to cut me down to their size. Even scripters who get paid out of the same till as I do find it hard to resist the temptation to take a poke at me by writing cute little scenes in which I am supposed to cavort as a strong boy of sorts.

"But don't get me wrong, whatever you do. I picked this racket, and I love it."

Film Noir Filmography

The Shanghai Gesture. Director: Josef von Sternberg. Producer: Arnold Pressburger. Running time: 106 minutes. Released by United Artists, December 26, 1941. Cast: Gene Tierney, Walter Huston, Victor Mature, Ona Munson, Phyllis Brooks, Albert Basserman, Maria Ouspenskaya, Eric Blore, Ivan Lebedeff, Mike Mazurki, Clyde Fillmore, Rex Evans, Grayce Hampton, Michael Delmatoff, Marcel Dalio, Mikhail Rasumni, John Abbott.

I Wake Up Screaming. Director: H. Bruce Humberstone. Producer: Milton Sperling. Running time: 82 minutes. Released by 20th Century-Fox, January 16, 1942. Cast: Betty Grable, Victor Mature, Carole Landis, Laird Cregar, William Gargan, Alan Mowbray, Allyn Joslyn, Elisha Cook, Jr., Chick Chandler, Morris Ankrum, May Beatty.

Kiss of Death. Director: Henry Hathaway. Producer: Fred Kohlmar. Running time: 98 minutes. Released by 20th Century-Fox, August 27, 1947. Cast: Victor Mature, Brian Donlevy, Coleen Gray, Richard Widmark, Karl Malden, Taylor Holmes, Howard Smith, Anthony Ross, Mildred Dunnock, Millard Mitchell, Temple Texas. Awards: Academy Award nominations for Best Supporting Actor (Richard Widmark), Best Original Story (Eleazar Lipsky).

Cry of the City. Director: Robert Siodmak. Producer: Sol Siegel. Running time: 96 minutes. Released by 20th Century-Fox, September 29, 1948. Cast: Victor Mature, Richard Conte, Fred Clark, Shelley Winters, Betty Garde, Berry Kroeger, Tommy Cook, Debra Paget, Hope Emerson, Roland Winters, Walter Baldwin, June Storey, Tito Vuolo, Mimi Aguglia, Konstantin Shayne, Howard Freeman.

The Las Vegas Story. Director: Robert Stevenson. Producer: Robert Sparks. Running time: 87 minutes. Released by RKO, January 1952. Cast: Jane Russell, Victor Mature, Vincent Price, Hoagy Carmichael, Brad Dexter, Jay C. Flippen, Gordon Oliver, Will Wright, Bill Welsh, Ray Montgomery, Colleen Miller, Bob Wilke.

References

Arvad, Inga. "Vic Mature Evades an Interview." *Newark Evening News*, November 3, 1943.

"Film Star Victor Mature, 86." *Chicago Tribune*, August 10, 1999.

Gordon, Gordon. "V. Mature, Artful Zany." *The Sunday Compass*, October 16, 1949.

Graham, Sheilah. "Home from Long War Service Mature Deserves a He-Man Title." *Buffalo Evening News*, circa 1946.

_____. "Mature Approach to Marriage." *New York Mirror*, October 6, 1957.

Heffernan, Harold. "Filmdom More Colorful Since Mature Returned." *The Baltimore Sun*, January 20, 1946.

"Hollywood Star Victor Mature Dies." *Chicago Sun-Times*, August 10, 1999.

Irwin, Virginia. "From Cave Man to Glamour Boy." *St. Louis Dispatch*, March 9, 1941.

Kemp, Martha. "Why I'm Not Divorcing Victor Mature." *Photoplay*, January 1943.

Kirkley, Donald. "'Beautiful Hunk of Junk' Winner by Being Jilted." *The Baltimore Sun*, August 13, 1944.

_____. "Film Notes." *The Baltimore Sun*, March 14, 1942.

"Mature's 3d Wife Also Wants Out." *New York Daily News*, August 14, 1954.

Niderost, Eric. "Victor Mature." *Classic Images*, March 1995.

Nisbet, Fairfax. "Hit in Stage Play Put Him Over Hurdle." *Dallas Morning News*, November 9, 1941.

"The Poor Vanquished Victor. *The American Weekly*, October 24, 1943.

Thirer, Irene. "Glamour Boy—Admits It." *New York Post*, December 18, 1940.

"Vic Mature Knew What He Wanted—Now He's Not Sure." *New York Morning Telegraph*, August 5, 1941.

"Young Man in the Bed." *The New Yorker*, March 1, 1941.

——— MIKE MAZURKI ———

"You shouldn't have done that. You shouldn't have hit me."—Mike Mazurki in *Murder, My Sweet* (1944)

Beefy, brawny, and once characterized as a "lovable gargoyle," Mike Mazurki's looks were deceiving. He was typecast throughout his film career as a sort of dimwitted giant, but he was a college man who graduated at the top of his class. A popular wrestler who battled opponents for many years under the moniker of "Iron Mike," he was described as "extraordinarily gentle" outside the ring. And in his more than 80 screen appearances, Mazurki rarely got the girl, but he wasn't soon forgotten by her—who wouldn't remember an encounter with a colossus named Lunk, Flat Mouth, Mountain Ox, or Rhino?

During his career, Mazurki could hardly be considered a leading man, but he appeared in such blockbusters as *Samson and Delilah (1949), Some Like it Hot* (1959) and *It's a Mad*

Mad Mad Mad World (1963), and was seen in no less than eight films noirs: *The Shanghai Gesture* (1941), *Murder, My Sweet* (1944), *Nightmare Alley* (1947), *I Walk Alone* (1948), *Abandoned* (1949), *Night and the City* (1950), *Dark City* (1950), and *New York Confidential* (1950).

Michail Mazuruski (some sources say Mazurkiewicz) was born on December 25, 1909, in Tarnopol, Austria-Hungary (now Ukraine). Determined to have their only child educated in the United States, the future actor's parents migrated to America in 1913, settling in Cohoes, New York, near Albany, and "Americanized" his name to Mike Mazurki. After grammar school in Cohoes, the boy attended LaSalle Institute, a Christian Brothers military academy in Troy, New York, and received athletic and academic scholarships to Manhattan College. With a 6-foot, 4-inch frame, and weighing in at nearly 250 pounds, Mazurki was a natural for athletics and was quickly tagged for the school's football team.

"I'd never seen a football game until I was in one," he recalled in a 1971 interview. "It was against Rutgers and I was a tackle. All the coach told me was to get in the line and not let anyone get by me. I did what he said."

After graduating with honors in 1930, Mazurki found work as an auditor with a Wall Street firm and attended law school in the evenings. After a year of this grueling schedule, Mazurki was attracted by a new opportunity by a friend who played basketball for a team called the Brooklyn Visitations.

"He told me that one of their forwards was hurt and they needed another player," Mazurki later said. "So I tried out, made the team, and they paid me $50 a game with two games per week. So I was making a hundred dollars a week there compared to the $25 or $30 I was making on Wall Street."

A short time later, Mazurki also began playing professional football with a franchise in Staten Island, New York, and quickly determined that he was "wasting my time on Wall Street and in law school." From basket-ball and football, Mazurki graduated to professional wrestling, winning his first match in five minutes and earning $500.

"Before I knew it, I was wrestling all around the East, and finally all over the country," Mazurki said.

It is believed that Mazurki also made his film debut around this time — a few sources claim that he appeared in the Mae West vehicle *It Ain't No Sin* (1933), while several others contend that he was first seen on screen in another West starrer, *Belle of the Nineties* (1934). Mazurki himself later credited the buxom comic actress with starting his career in movies, explaining that West had an affinity for boxers and wrestlers — her father had been a fighter — and that she often found odd jobs around the studio for them.

"I used to pick up $25 a day that way," Mazurki said in a 1945 *Los Angeles Times* interview. "Mae West is a real lover of sports."

Mazurki's first "real" screen role, however, came in 1941, after a fateful encounter with famed director Josef von Sternberg. While appearing in a wrestling match at the Olympic Theater in Los Angeles, Mazurki was spotted by the director, who was in the process of casting "foreign types" for his upcoming feature, *The Shanghai Gesture*. After being tapped for the role, however, Mazurki recalled that his resemblance to the film's star, Victor Mature, almost lost him the part before shooting began.

"Apparently, at that time, I looked enough like Victor Mature to be his brother," Mazurki said in 1982. "They decided they didn't want me ... Walter Huston suggested they shave my head, and I got the part. So I owe my career in motion pictures to Walter Huston."

The Shanghai Gesture (1941), Mazurki's entry into the world of film noir, was based on a highly successful Broadway play by John Coulton. Set in a cavernous gambling den, the feature focuses primarily on the relationship between Poppy (Gene Tierney), a young, impressionable woman who is seduced by the decadent atmosphere; Mother Gin Sling (Ona Munson), the casino's enigmatic owner; and Sir Guy Charteris (Huston), a wealthy financier who is determined to close down the establishment. As Coolie, a close-mouthed rickshaw driver, Mazurki was on the perimeter of the main action of the film, which culminates with Gin Sling's revelation that Poppy is the daughter that Charteris had abandoned years before; when Poppy hysterically rejects them both, Gin Sling kills her. Although the film was panned upon its release (Tierney later recalled that critics found it "hollow and absurd"), this early entry from the noir era is today considered a stylish and fascinating offering.

Mazurki continued to accept small roles in a spate of films— including the Errol Flynn starrer *Gentleman Jim* (1942); an Abbott and Costello comedy, *It Ain't Hay* (1943); and an all-star musical, *Thank Your Lucky Stars* (1943)— but it wasn't until 1944 that he got the nod for his first featured role, in the film noir classic *Murder, My Sweet*.

According to Mazurki, winning the pivotal role of Moose Malloy in *Murder, My Sweet* was pure luck. He was spotted in the RKO commissary one day by then-studio head Charlie Koerner, who recommended him for the role, but the film's director, Edward Dmytryk, wasn't convinced.

"He kept telling me that I just didn't fit it," Mazurki said. "He told me, 'Sure, you're an actor — on the [wrestling] mat.' Fortunately for me, he was overruled by Charlie Koerner."

This typically complex feature begins as Mazurki's Moose hires private detective Philip Marlowe (Dick Powell) to locate his missing girl, Velma Valento. ("Eight years since I seen her. Six she didn't write," Moose tells the detective. "But she'll have a reason.") During his search, Marlowe encounters such offbeat personages as Lindsay Marriott (Douglas Walton), an ill-fated gigolo; Amthor (Otto Kruger), a sadistic, self-described "quack" psychologist; Mr. Grayle (Miles Mander), an aging millionaire; Mrs. Grayle (Claire Trevor), his duplicitous young wife; and Ann (Anne Shirley), her hated stepdaughter. After a plethora of plot twists, it is disclosed that Mrs. Grayle is Moose's long, lost girl; Moose—

along with half the cast, it seems— winds up dead; and Marlowe winds up in a final clinch with the sharp-witted, strong-willed Ann.

Based on the novel *Farewell, My Lovely*, by Raymond Chandler, *Murder, My Sweet* opened to rave reviews, with Otis L. Guernsey, Jr., of the *New York Herald Tribune* labeling it "top-notch thriller fare," and the reviewer from *Time* favorably comparing it with *Double Indemnity* (1944), released a few months earlier: "In some ways, it is even more likable, for though it is far less tidy, it is more vigorous and less slick, more resourcefully photographed, and even more successfully cast." For his performance of the "gigantic imbecile," Mazurki earned applause as well; the critic from the *New York Times* called his role "exceptionally well-played," and in the *Los Angeles Times*, Edwin Schallert found Mazurki's performance "definitely compelling."

By now, World War II was in full force, but Mazurki's numerous injuries as a wrestler — including three cracked ribs, a broken shoulder, and a twisted vertebra —classified him as 4-F, and he was rejected by three of the major branches of the armed services. In a 1945 interview with *Los Angeles Times* reviewer Philip K. Scheuer, Mazurki expressed his regret at being unable to serve and his discomfort when fellow civilians challenged his patriotism.

"Little men always want to fight," Mazurki said. "They come up [in barrooms] and say, 'You're not so tough,' and then you say, 'Go 'way' and give them a little push, and presently you look up and they are back with a chair or a bottle."

His encounters with inebriated patriots aside, Mazurki's life off screen was—for a while, at least — seemingly ideal; on June 30, 1945, he married Jeannette Briggs, a society woman and newspaper reporter from Glendale, California. The two later had two daughters, Manette and Michelle. But after just five years, the couple divorced, and Mazurki claimed he had been "bamboozled" into marriage.

"Newspaper reporters got a knack that

way," Mazurki said years later. "We were married, but I kept traveling a lot, and while I was away she threw parties all the time. She was a boozer."

Meanwhile, soon after his marriage to Jeannette, Mazurki announced that he was abandoning his vocation as a wrestler.

"It's like this— wrestling is a bloodthirsty business," Mazurki said in 1945. "You've got to get out and break an arm or a leg to convince 'em it isn't a fake; and the women are more bloodthirsty than the men. It isn't worth it. I quit."

Instead, the actor continued to rack up screen credits— he was seen as "Splitface" in *Dick Tracy* (1945), appeared with John Wayne and Walter Brennan in a fast-paced oater, *Dakota* (1945), played Yusuf in *Sinbad the Sailor* (1947), and was featured as Bruno, the carny show strongman, in his third film noir, *Nightmare Alley* (1947). This dark and moody offering starred Tyrone Power as Stanton Carlisle, a wily, charismatic carnival barker who stops at nothing to achieve fame and fortune as a renowned "mentalist." Along the way, he steals trade secrets, causes the death of an alcoholic carny worker, and uses confidential information from a sexy psychologist (Helen Walker) to dupe her wealthy patients. When Stanton's hoax is exposed by his reluctant wife, Molly (Coleen Gray), his fall from grace is swift, and he winds up as the carnival "geek," where his chief job is biting the heads off of live chickens.

As Bruno, Mazurki was mostly overlooked in reviews, but he was memorable as the dim-witted but morally righteous strongman who forces Stanton to marry Molly after he realizes they have spent the night together. Years later, Coleen Gray recalled Mazurki as "strong and quiet."

"He was a nice guy," Gray said in 2001, "but he could be menacing without saying anything. Just his presence and his sinister look."

Gray wasn't the only cast member of *Nightmare Alley* who found Mazurki to be menacing. Several decades after the release of the film, Mazurki related an amusing anec-

dote about co-star Tyrone Power. During one scene, Mazurki explained, he had to grab Power, but the other actor kept breaking away — which wasn't in the script.

"Finally the director says, 'Mazurki, you big stoop, you're a wrestler and you can't hold Tyrone Power?' I'm embarrassed as hell," Mazurki recalled in 1982 interview with *American Classic Screen* magazine. "So the next time I grab him, I grab hair, skin and all. This time he stays put." When Mazurki was berated by the film's producer, George Jessel, for his rough treatment, Power explained that he'd been trying to "show this big bastard up" by breaking Mazurki's hold. "After that we became the best of friends," Mazurki said.

The following year saw Mazurki's appearance in only three films— the best of these was his fourth noir, *I Walk Alone* (1948), starring Burt Lancaster and Kirk Douglas. Here, Mazurki played Dan, the formidable doorman of a successful nightclub run by Noll "Dink" Turner (Douglas). When Dink's former partner, Frankie Madison (Lancaster), is released from prison, he clashes with Dink, who refuses to honor a profit-sharing deal they made before Frankie's arrest. In Mazurki's biggest scene, he makes mincemeat out of

Lancaster's character but solicitously warns him, "Take it easy, Frankie. The way I got you, if you fight against it, your windpipe will be crushed." But Mazurki made little impact on critics, who were equally unimpressed with the film — obviously put off by the feature's surfeit of unlikable characters, Bosley Crowther wrote in the *New York Times*: "It's a mighty low class of people that you will meet in Paramount's *I Walk Alone*—and a mighty low grade of melodrama, if you want the honest truth."

Mazurki stepped up his filming schedule in 1949 — his five screen credits that year included *Come to the Stable*, starring Loretta Young and Celeste Holm, and the big-budget epic *Samson and Delilah*, in which he played a Philistine leader. Also that year, he returned to the realm of film noir, this time in *Abandoned*. But in this mediocre offering, which focused on a baby-selling racket, Mazurki had little to do besides crack his knuckles and look intimidating. He was noticed by one reviewer, however, who included him in a mention of the film's various "ringleaders or stooges."

Of Mazurki's three films in 1950, two were films noirs—*Dark City* and *Night and the City*. In the first, he played Sidney Winant, the psychotic brother of a guileless salesman who commits suicide after losing $5,000 in a crooked poker game. Determined to avenge his brother's death, Sidney stalks and kills nearly every one of the players in the game, before being trapped and gunned down by police.

Next, in *Night and the City*, Mazurki is seen in another standout role — here, he portrays a wrestler known as the Strangler, who is hired by a would-be sports promoter, Harry Fabian (Richard Widmark), to fight the protégé of a legendary Greco-Roman wrestler, Gregorious (Stanislaus Zbyszko). Before the contracts for the money-making event can be signed, the Strangler and Gregorious engage in an impromptu fight ("Gregorious the Great … wrestling joke!" the Strangler taunts him), and the older fighter suffers a fatal heart attack. Harry goes on the run, with a price

on his head offered by Gregorious' son, but his luck runs out when the Strangler catches up to him, kills him, and unceremoniously tosses his body in the river.

In both *Dark City* and *Night and the City*, Mazurki played characters that represented a dramatic departure from the hulking, two-fisted moron that he depicted in previous noirs. As the mentally unbalanced Sidney, Mazurki is a serial killer whose eerie, shadowy presence sets the downbeat tone of the entire film. And in his role as the Strangler, Mazurki offers an even more distasteful characterization — with his drunken brawling and his sneering derision of the Greco-Roman wrestlers, he is at once frightening, unlikable, and invincible.

Meanwhile, life imitated art when, despite Mazurki's declaration several years earlier that he was giving up wrestling, the actor began to resume his personal appearances in wrestling bouts— his promotional material played on his acting career to entice arena owners: "Mike Mazurki will be in your city soon.... No wrestler is better known to the amusement crowd ... 80% of the people in your city have seen him in the movies.... Jam your arena with Mike Mazurki!" After appearing in six films in 1951— including the popular Bob Hope comedy *My Favorite Spy* and *Ten Tall Men*, an action-comedy starring Burt Lancaster — Mazurki was not seen on screen for another three years.

"I just happen to be a big guy, but that doesn't keep me from being able to count to five," Mazurki told a United Press reporter in 1952. "If I can make good money acting like a dope in Hollywood and make more throwing guys around, why shouldn't I?" When he wasn't tossing his opponents around the ring, Mazurki took time out for his stage debut in the hit production of *Guys and Dolls*, replacing former boxer "Slapsie" Maxie Rosenbloom as "Big Jule."

Back on screen, Mazurki's sole appearance in 1954 was as the Death House Foreman in *The Egyptian* (1954), a big-budget biblical epic starring Victor Mature and Jean Simmons. He was next seen the following year in such moneymakers as *Blood Alley* (1955), with John Wayne and Lauren Bacall, and *Davy Crockett, King of the Wild Frontier* (1955), the big-screen version of the popular Disney television series. Also in 1955, Mazurki appeared in his final film noir, *New York Confidential* (1955). This hard-hitting feature focused on an organized crime syndicate and boasted a first-rate cast, including Broderick Crawford as the powerful head of the organization, Richard Conte as a fast-rising triggerman, and Anne Bancroft as Crawford's conflicted daughter who ultimately commits suicide. As Arnie Wendler, Mazurki played the pivotal role of a gunman who is marked for death by the organization after his successful hit on a high-powered government official. In an effort to save his life, Arnie offers to turn state's evidence on the syndicate, setting in motion a chain of events that leads to the eventual murder of the top man in the racket. Upon its release, the film was hailed in the *New York Times* as "quite the smoothest such exposé to come along in many a moon," and Mazurki garnered mention for his role as a henchman by several critics, including S.A. Desick of the *Los Angeles Examiner*, who termed him a "persuasive performer."

Throughout the remainder of the decade, Mazurki was seen in a handful of mostly routine films—two notable exceptions were his cameo appearance in the star-studded *Around the World in Eighty Days* (1956), and his portrayal of a dull-witted hood in the hilarious *Some Like it Hot* (1959). Mazurki's film choices improved during the 1960s, however, with his appearance in a string of such high quality films as the entertaining comedy *It's a Mad Mad Mad Mad World* (1963); a fast-paced action-comedy, *Donovan's Reef* (1963), starring John Wayne and Lee Marvin; and *7 Women* (1966), the final film helmed by legendary director John Ford.

"Ford had a way of deflating you to bring out your best," Mazurki recalled later. "At first I didn't know what to make of it ... Ford believed that if he got you all riled up he would get the best scenes out of you. Those

directors in the old days, all those great men, took the time and patience to work with you."

By now, Mazurki had begun to appear frequently on the small screen—beginning in the mid-1950s and continuing through the next two decades, he appeared on such top-rated television series as *Gunsmoke, Wagon Train, Perry Mason, The Untouchables, Bonanza, Gilligan's Island, Batman, I Dream of Jeannie, Adam-12, The Beverly Hillbillies, The Munsters, Mannix,* and *Charlie's Angels.* He was also a recurring cast member in two series, *It's About Time,* which aired from 1966 to 1967, and in 1971, *Chicago Teddy Bears,* described by Mazurki as "a kind of *Untouchables* ... without the violence."

"I like the idea of my role," the actor said during the production of the latter series. "I get to play a good guy for a change."

Between movie and television appearances, Mazurki had managed to find time in 1968 for a second walk down the aisle—with his longtime agent, Sylvia Weinblatt.

"Syl helped raise [my daughters] since they were little," Mazurki recalled. "When I finally got a divorce, the kids said, 'Dad, you're gonna marry Sylvia and we're gonna give you away.' We went up to Las Vegas and sure enough, they gave me away." Mazurki and Sylvia remained married until the actor's death.

During the 1970s, Mazurki made few feature film appearances, but hc did appear in the first starring role of his career, portraying a mad trapper on the run from North Alaskan police in *Challenge to Be Free* (1976). He later considered the role as his favorite.

"We were in Nome [Alaska] six weeks, working in 80-below-zero weather," Mazurki recalled. "I'd walk from here to the door, outside—I had a beard—and it was covered with icicles by the time I reached the door. But I would have done that picture for nothing. It was a great film."

After *Challenge to Be Free,* Mazurki's big-screen jobs dwindled to only scattered appearances; in 1978, he was seen in a small role in the all-but-unknown Jack Palance starrer *The One Man Jury* (1978), and two years later, he played himself in an amusing detective spoof, *The Man with Bogart's Face* (1980). He spent most of his time in commercial work and on various television series, but he admitted in a 1982 interview that he was often frustrated when encountering casting agents for the small screen.

"Lots of time I go for an audition and I go into a room with four guys, 25 to 39 years old. The head guy says ... 'what have you done Mr. Mazurki?' Then on top of this, they want you to read," Mazurki told Bill Kelly in *American Classic Screen* magazine. "I hate cold reading. [They say] 'Oh, you have to read so we can get an idea what you sound like.' I say, 'I'm talking to you—can't you get an idea what I sound like?' I'm not knocking these kids, I'm just saying it's a new generation, that's all. But they should do their homework."

When he wasn't being put through his paces at casting offices, one of Mazurki's favorite pastimes was serving as president of the Cauliflower Alley Club, an organization for retired boxers and wrestlers.

"It's a place of pure affection," Mazurki said. "Some will shout, 'I love ya, baby.' Others tell their old cronies, 'I still think I can lick ya, ya big bum!'" The organization is still going strong, holds annual conventions, and has an international membership.

After being off screen for five years, Mazurki returned for a small role in an unfunny comedy, *Doin' Time* (1985), in a cast that included Richard Mulligan, Muhammad Ali, and Jimmie Walker. Then, following another five-year screen absence, he appeared in the big-budget, star-studded *Dick Tracy* (1990), the remake of the film in which he had appeared as Splitface 45 years earlier. This time, Mazurki was seen in a cameo role as an old man at a hotel. It was his last film.

Shortly after the release of *Dick Tracy*, on December 9, 1990, Mazurki died in Glendale Adentist Medical Center. A spokesman for the hospital revealed that Mazurki had been ill for some time, and listed the cause of death as heart failure.

With a face once described as "an eroded slag heap ... traversed by gullies," Mike Mazurki was pigeon-holed throughout his career in a series of roles that he himself categorized as either "a comedy moron [or] a killer." But in such films as *Murder, My Sweet* and *Night and the City*, Mazurki demonstrated that, while typecast as these characters, he excelled at bringing them to life.

Film Noir Filmography

The Shanghai Gesture. Director: Josef von Sternberg. Producer: Arnold Pressburger. Running time: 106 minutes. Released by United Artists, December 26, 1941. Cast: Gene Tierney, Walter Huston, Victor Mature, Ona Munson, Phyllis Brooks, Albert Basserman, Maria Ouspenskaya, Eric Blore, Ivan Lebedeff, Mike Mazurki, Clyde Fillmore, Rex Evans, Grayce Hampton, Michael Delmatoff, Marcel Dalio, Mikhail Rasumni, John Abbott. Awards: Academy Award nominations for Best Interior Decoration/Black and White (Boris Leven), Best Score/Drama or Comedy (Richard Hageman).

Murder, My Sweet. Director: Edward Dmytryk. Producer: Adrian Scott. Running time: 95 minutes. Released by RKO, December 18, 1944. Cast: Dick Powell, Claire Trevor, Anne Shirley, Otto Kruger, Mike Mazurki, Miles Mander, Douglas Walton, Don Douglas, Ralf Harolde, Esther Howard.

Nightmare Alley. Director: Edmund Goulding. Producer: George Jessel. Running time: 110 minutes. Released by 20th Century-Fox, October 9, 1947. Cast: Tyrone Power, Joan Blondell, Coleen Gray, Helen Walker, Taylor Holmes, Mike Mazurki, Ian Keith, Julia Dean, James Flavin, Roy Roberts, James Burke.

I Walk Alone. Director: Byron Haskin. Producer: Hal B. Wallis. Running time: 98 minutes. Released by Paramount, January 22, 1948. Cast: Burt Lancaster, Lizabeth Scott, Kirk Douglas, Wendell Corey, Kristine Miller, George Rigaud, Marc Lawrence, Mike Mazurki, Mickey Knox, Roger Neury.

Abandoned. Director: Joseph M. Newman. Producer: Jerry Bresler. Running time: 78 minutes. Released by Universal-International, October 28, 1949. Cast: Dennis O'Keefe, Gale Storm, Jeff Chandler, Meg Randall, Raymond Burr, Marjorie Rambeau, Jeanette Nolan, Mike Mazurki, Will Kuluva, David Clarke, William Page, Sid Tomack, Perc Launders, Steve Darnell, Clifton Young, Ruth Sanderson.

Night and the City. Director: Jules Dassin. Producer: Samuel G. Engel. Running time: 95 minutes. Released by 20th Century-Fox, June 9, 1950. Cast: Richard Widmark, Gene Tierney, Googie Withers, Hugh Marlowe, Francis L. Sullivan, Herbert Lom, Stanislaus Zbyszko, Mike Mazurki, Charles Farrell, Ada Reeve, Ken Richmond.

Dark City. Director: William Dieterle. Producer: Hal Wallis. Running time: 98 minutes. Released by Paramount, October 18, 1950. Cast: Charlton Heston, Lizabeth Scott, Viveca Lindfors, Dean Jagger, Don DeFore, Jack Webb, Ed Begley, Henry Morgan, Walter Sande, Mark Keuning, Mike Mazurki, Stanley Prager, Walter Burke.

New York Confidential. Director: Russell Rouse. Producer: Clarence Greene. Running time: 87 minutes. Released by Warner Brothers, February 18, 1955. Cast: Broderick Crawford, Richard Conte, Marilyn Maxwell, Anne Bancroft, J. Carrol Naish, Onslow Stevens, Barry Kelley, Mike Mazurki, Celia Lovsky, Herbert Heyes, Steven Geray.

References

"Actor Mike Mazurki Dies at 82." *The Hollywood Reporter*, December 11, 1990.
Biography of Mike Mazurki. RKO Studios, circa 1947.
Biography of Mike Mazurki. 20th Century–Fox Studios, May 19, 1950.
Canty, Tim. "Stage Bug Has Mike Mazurki." *New York Morning Telegraph*, July 17, 1952.

Folkart, Burt A. "Mike Mazurki Dies; Acted as the Heavy in Films." *Los Angeles Times*, December 11, 1990.
Freedgood, Mort. "'Iron' Mike Mazurki: Keeps in Trim for Movie Roles by Wrestling." *New York Times*, April 23, 1950.
Hare, William. "Mike Mazurki: The Man of a Thousand Roles." *Hollywood Studio Magazine*, April 1977.
Kelly, Bill. "Mike Mazurki: Hollywood's Favorite Tough Guy." *American Classic Screen*, 1982.
Mesmer, Marie. "Mike Mazurki Points Out Some Nifty 'Holds.'" *Los Angeles Daily News*, July 20, 1953.
"Mike Mazurki." Internet Resource: http://www.echonyc.com/~hwdarch/MikeMazurki1.html.
"Mike Mazurki Fete Planned." *Los Angeles Times*, March 4, 1983.
"Mike Replaces Maxie." *Chicago Sun-Times*, June 1, 1952.
Obituary. *The London Times*, December 28, 1990.
Obituary. *Los Angeles Times*, December 14, 1990.
Obituary. *Variety*, December 17, 1990.
Scheuer, Philip K. "Former Matman Likes Hollywood Atmosphere." *Los Angeles Times*, April 15, 1945.
Scott, Vernon. "Mazurki Is a 'Teddy Bear.'" *Los Angeles Herald-Examiner*, September 15, 1971.
Teal, Scott. "Wrestling Legends." Internet Resource: http://www.1wrestlinglegends.com.
"Wrestler's Wife Granted Support in Divorce Plea." *Los Angeles Times*, July 22, 1950.

CHARLES MCGRAW

"You fouled us up good, didn't you? You're always so smart, so careful. The mastermind nobody could touch. Brother, when you flop, you flop good."— Charles McGraw in *Border Incident* (1949)

With his jutting jaw, twice-broken nose, and hard-as-granite gaze, Charles McGraw was no Prince Charming. He appeared in a variety of roles— often cast as the heavy — in nearly 80 films, but he never quite became the household name that his talent surely warranted. Still, McGraw made much of his opportunities and was one of the quintessential actors of the film noir era, with appearances in 12 films noirs. Of these, the actor was seen in featured roles in *The Killers* (1946), *T-Men* (1948), *Border Incident* (1949), *Armored*

Car Robbery (1950), *Roadblock* (1951), *His Kind of Woman* (1951), *The Narrow Margin* (1952), and *Loophole* (1954).

Like a great number of Hollywood stars, the details of Charles McGraw's early life are somewhat sketchy. While his 1966 Paramount studio biography states that he was born in County Meath, Ireland, nearly every obituary printed after his 1980 death claimed that he was born in the Far East. Most sources, however, agree that the future tough guy was born Charles Butters in New York City on May 10,

1914. When Charles was five years old, his family moved to Akron, Ohio, where he attended school until the age of 17, then returned to New York and secured a job as a deck boy aboard a freighter bound for India. He traveled in this fashion for the next two years, seeing countries around the world—"much of it through portholes," the actor said later.

When his sea duty ended, Charles returned to Ohio and, mostly to appease his parents, enrolled at the University of Akron. But after his many adventures on the sea, Charles found that the academic life paled in comparison, and he left school after only a year. Returning to New York, Charles made ends meet by whatever means he could, including working as a waiter, bartender, bus boy, taxi driver, and even a dancer in a nightclub. Having always been a first-rate athlete, Charles also tried his hand at boxing, and eventually fought 19 amateur and 20 professional fights as a middleweight. He didn't escape his stint as a boxer unscathed, however—Charles wound up having his nose broken on two separate occasions.

According to legend, Charles was rooming with a student from New York's American Academy of Dramatic Arts when the course of his life changed forever. At the time, Charles was between jobs and, having nothing better to do, tagged along when his friend asked him to accompany him on an interview for a role in the play *The Jazz Age*.

"I was waiting for my friend," the actor later recalled. "When the director ushered him to the door, he saw me sitting there and said, 'I think you might do—you *look* like a heavy!' So, suddenly I'm an actor."

Although the play closed after only a week, Charles—who had, by now, changed his name to McGraw—promptly landed a role in the road company of *Boy Meets Girl*, which toured the country for 80 weeks. Upon his return, he found work in productions including *Dead End*, *Brother Rat*, and *Golden Boy*, in which he played a leading role and served as understudy for actor-turned-director Elia Kazan. When the road version of the latter play traveled to London, Charles met and fell in love with Freda Choy, described in news accounts as a Parisian hat designer of Chinese descent. On October 12, 1938, the two were married, and three years later, their daughter, Jill, was born.

In 1939, shortly after the onset of World War II, the struggling actor returned to America with his new wife, only to find that acting jobs were scarce. For a while, McGraw worked as a soda jerk, then signed on as a performer with the "Railroads on Parade" exhibit at the 1939 New York World's Fair. Earning $30 a week for four shows a day, seven days a week, McGraw was seen alongside such future Hollywood personalities as Betty Garrett, John Lund, and Don DeFore.

McGraw's appearance at the World's Fair led to a featured role in Orson Welles' 1941 Broadway production of *Native Son*, starring Canada Lee. When the play closed after more than 100 performances, the actor moved his family to Hollywood, where he made his rather inauspicious film debut in a bit part as a carriage driver in Fox's *The Undying Monster* (1942). He followed this with small roles in a spy drama, *They Came To Blow Up America* (1943), and another horror film, *The Mad Ghoul* (1943). Neither did much to enhance the actor's bid for fame.

After three more movies in 1943—including a bit part in the box office hit *Corvette K-225*—McGraw enlisted in the U.S. Army, serving in the field artillery. When the war ended in 1945, McGraw returned with his family to New York, only to find that he was unable to find work.

"Most of my old contacts were gone or had long since stopped thinking of me when a part came up," he said. "So, like a lot of other new vets, I had to start all over again."

At this point in McGraw's life story, the details grow sketchy again. According to one source, McGraw was working as a bartender in New York when he was spotted by producer Mark Hellinger, who offered him a film role on the spot. But a more colorful variation of this account states that McGraw walked into a neighborhood bar in May 1946 and was asked by the bartender if he had played the "heavy" in the stage version of *Golden Boy*. When McGraw answered in the affirmative, the bartender shared a recently published newspaper column which announced that film producer Mark Hellinger was seeking the actor who'd played in *Golden Boy* nine years before. He had a role for the actor in his upcoming film.

McGraw — so the story continues — promptly called Hellinger at Universal Studios in Hollywood, who wired the actor $500 and directed him to catch the next plane to Hollywood.

"My wife had gone through the months of uncertainty and in security without a complaint," McGraw was quoted. "But when I came home and showed her the $500, I think her first thought was that I'd robbed a bank."

Regardless of the circumstances, the role that McGraw landed was a meaty one — he played a ruthless gunman in his entry into film noir, *The Killers* (1946). As Al, one of the two "killers" of the film's title, McGraw opened the film with a chilling exchange with fellow gunman Max (William Conrad), as the two wait in a small-town diner for the arrival of their intended victim, "the Swede" (Burt Lancaster). After harassing the owner of the diner by repeatedly referring to him as "bright boy," and insisting that he guess the purpose for their visit, Al and Max locate the Swede at his apartment and riddle him with bullets. The remainder of this fast-paced feature centers on insurance investigator Jim Reardon (Edmond O'Brien) as he seeks to discover the circumstances that led to the Swede's murder. During his quest, Reardon encounters a variety of characters who played a part in the Swede's past, including his double-crossing girlfriend, Kitty (Ava Gardner); Big Jim Colfax (Albert Dekker), the leader of a gang of which the Swede was once a part; and Sam Lubinsky (Sam Levene), the Swede's longtime pal-turned-cop, who aids Reardon in the investigation. As Reardon gets closer to unearthing the truth, Al and Max re-enter the picture, planning to murder the insurance investigator on orders from Big Jim, but Lu-

binsky is lying in wait for them and guns them down. After Big Jim is fatally wounded by one of his former underlings, it is not only revealed that he was responsible for the hit on the Swede, but also that he is married to Kitty, and the film ends as Kitty begs in vain for her spouse to clear her name. A box-office hit, *The Killers* earned widespread raves from reviewers, with *Variety*'s critic praising "the handpicked cast that troupes to the hilt," and Thalia Bell describing the feature in *Motion Picture Daily* as "absorbing" and "ingenious."

After appearances in a mediocre western, *On the Old Spanish Trail* (1947), and *The Long Night* (1947), a wartime drama that flopped at the box office, McGraw returned to familiar film noir ground, appearing briefly as a hood in *The Gangster* (1947), which featured Barry Sullivan and John Ireland, and in the prison noir *Brute Force* (1947), where he was seen as an inmate who equips a group of would-be escapees with a cache of makeshift firebombs. The following year — the busiest year of his film career — McGraw was seen in a larger role in yet another film noir, *T-Men* (1948), where he was a standout as a member of a widespread counterfeiting ring.

In an effort to break up the gang, two treasury agents, Dennis O'Brien (Dennis O'Keefe) and Tony Genaro (Alfred Ryder), work undercover to infiltrate factions in Detroit and Los Angeles, using a wily hood named Schemer (Wallace Ford) as the key to cracking the case. As Moxie, McGraw portrayed a particularly vicious character; in one scene, suspecting that Schemer plans to expose the operation, Moxie murders him by locking him in a steam bath and coolly watching through the window as the man begs for his life. Later, Moxie murders Genaro after discovering his real identity and shoots O'Brien in the back during a gun battle, but O'Brien manages to turn the tables on the hood and finally guns him down in the film's climax. A low-budget sleeper, *T-Men* was a hit at the box office and critics hailed its hard-hitting reality; the reviewer for the *Los Angeles Times* judged that it was "intelligently conceived, and at the same time offers pulse-pounding action," and the *New York Times*' Bosley Crowther described the feature as "a cops-and-robbers film in this new 'semi-documentary' format which, for action, is one of the best."

By now, having proven his effectiveness as a villain in his noir features and such films as *The Big Fix* (1947), *Roses are Red* (1947), and *The Threat* (1949), McGraw was tiring of being typecast as the heavy, and told the press that he planned to increase his asking price for roles and become more selective about those he accepted.

"One reason I'm going shopping [for roles] from now on is that in some of my pictures I've been such a *heavy* heavy that I couldn't let my own kid go see them," he told *L.A. Daily News* columnist Darr Smith. "I've got a product to sell and it's perishable. I want to get all I can out of it before it disintegrates. If people want me, they are going to have to pay for me."

One chance to distance himself from his frequent "bad boy" roles came when McGraw was cast as Lt. Brooks in the radio series *The Amazing Mr. Malone*, a mystery/detective drama focusing on a crime-solving attorney. He also showed his versatility in a featured role opposite Dick Powell in a radio version of the hit play, *The Front Page*.

Meanwhile, McGraw chalked up appearances in two more films noirs, playing a bit part as an Army colonel in the post–World War II *Berlin Express* (1949), and a featured role in *Border Incident* (1949), which centered on an illegal smuggling operation headed by rancher Owen Parkson (Howard Da Silva). Parkson's profitable racket of secreting Mexican farmworkers over the U.S. border is threatened when his operation is infiltrated by two undercover agents, one from Mexico, Pablo Rodriguez (Ricardo Montalban), and the other, Jack Bearnes (George Murphy), from the United States. Bearnes' cover is blown, however, and Parkson's hard-boiled foreman, Jack Amboy (McGraw) murders him in a memorably gruesome fashion, running him down with a tractor as Pablo looks on helplessly. Later, as the operation begins to crumble, Amboy turns on his boss and kills him, but he is shot by Rodriguez and the gang is ultimately destroyed. Although one critic found that *Border Incident* "smacks of illogic, contrivance and unreality," and another labeled it a "top-drawer thriller," there was no disagreement on McGraw's performance, with Bosley Crowther singling him out in the *New York Times* as "vicious," and the *Los Angeles Times*' Philip K. Scheuer noting his "general fiendishness."

After minor roles in the dreadful drama *I Was A Shoplifter* (1950) and a passable Donald O'Connor musical, *Double Crossbones* (1950), McGraw parodied his gangster image, playing "Shotgun Mike" Munger in *Ma and Pa Kettle Go to Town* (1950), the second in the series about the folksy parents of 15 children. But he returned to the real thing that year with back-to-back film noir features, *Armored Car Robbery* (1950), and *Side Street* (1950). In the first, McGraw played Lt. Jim Cordell, a cop bent on avenging the death of his partner (James Flavin), who was killed during the holdup of an armored car. With single-minded determination, Cordell tracks down the hoods responsible for the heist, killing one at the gang's waterfront hideout, trapping another in a movie theater, and catching up with the gang's mastermind, Dave Purvis (William Talman), at the local airport. As Purvis tries to flee with the cache of money, Cordell shoots him on the runway, and the gangleader is struck and killed by a departing airplane, with the bills floating around his dead body. A tense, attention-holding thriller, *Armored Car Robbery* received only a lukewarm reception from critics, but McGraw's intense performance was noted by a number of critics, including the reviewer for *Variety*, who stated that he did "very well" in his portrayal.

In his next film noir, *Side Street* (1950), McGraw portrayed Detective Stan Simon, who is investigating the murder of a local "B" girl known as "Lucky" Colner (Adele Jergens). Before long, Simon and his fellow detectives center their probe on Joe Norson (Farley Granger), a part-time mail carrier, and Lucky's boyfriend, attorney Victor Backett (Edmon Ryan). As it turns out, Norson had impulsively stolen a file folder from Backett's offices, not knowing that it contained $30,000 in blackmail money that Lucky had received from a former lover. When he learns of the folder's contents, Norson tries to return the money, but Backett denies any knowledge of the cash, suspecting that Joe has been sent by police. Instead, Backett tries to retrieve the money through his accomplice, George Garsell (James Craig), who beats and abducts the hapless mailman. Police manage to track down Garsell's whereabouts, however, and after an early morning chase through the empty streets of the city, Garsell is killed. Although McGraw's minor role was mostly overlooked by critics, the film earned fairly respectable reviews upon its release; a typical assessment was offered by Bosley Crowther of the *New York Times*, who labeled the feature "a fair enough crime picture ... it can only be fully recommended to those who have a deep and morbid interest in crime."

By now, McGraw had developed a reputation in Hollywood as being excessively aggressive with directors, with a frequently lackadaisical approach to acting. Although

he could be counted on to arrive at the studio promptly with his lines memorized, McGraw was also known for heavy drinking and a penchant for becoming involved in brawls. It is believed that these qualities contributed to the demise of the actor's career or, at the very least, helped to impede his ascent to stardom. Indeed, in 1951, McGraw appeared in only two films (a far cry from the eight features he made just four years earlier), both of which were entries in the film noir era.

In the first of McGraw's 1951 features, *Roadblock*—which is reminiscent in theme to *Double Indemnity* (1944)—the actor played insurance investigator Joe Peters, who falls for a beautiful brunette (Joan Dixon) in search of a man with more material worth than Joe can offer. Motivated by his desire for the woman, Joe becomes involved in an organized crime theft of $1 million, but when a postal worker is killed, the carefully arranged scheme begins to unravel and Joe is forced to go on the run. Ultimately, the police catch up with him, and after a suspenseful car chase through the riverbeds of Los Angeles, Joe is gunned down.

Next, in McGraw's second film of 1951, *His Kind of Woman*, he provided the opening voice-over narration, explaining that the story begins "in one of those big, quiet, peaceful villas overlooking the bay" in Naples, Italy. After this introduction, it is revealed that McGraw's character, Thompson, is a henchman for gang leader Nick Ferraro (Raymond Burr), who has been exiled to Italy from the United States and is scheming to return. In order to effect his plan, Ferraro lures gambler Dan Milner (Robert Mitchum) to an isolated Mexican resort with the promise of $50,000, planning to murder him and assume his identity. After killing a federal agent (Tim Holt) who has discovered the mobster's plan, Thompson tries to force Milner aboard Ferraro's nearby yacht, but Milner escapes and swims to shore. With Thompson and his fellow hoods in hot pursuit, Milner finds an ally in Mark Cardigan (Vincent Price), a ham movie actor who is vacationing at the resort. Viewing the conflict as a scene from a film,

Cardigan guns down two of Thompson's sidekicks, then wounds Thompson himself, turning him over to police. Milner, meanwhile, has returned to the yacht in an effort to capture Ferraro, but he is subdued and is seconds from death when Cardigan storms the boat with a crew of assorted hotel guests and local police. In the ensuing confusion, Milner finds a gun and finally kills Ferraro. Today, *His Kind of Woman* stands up as a time-worthy and — due to Price's hilarious performance — somewhat campy addition to the noir era, but it was panned by reviewers of the day, with the *New York Times* critic admitting that he was "still wondering what it was all about."

McGraw remained in realm of film noir the following year, starring opposite Marie Windsor in one of his best features from the era, *The Narrow Margin* (1952). Here, McGraw portrayed Walter Brown, a detective assigned to escort a murdered racketeer's widow by train from Chicago to Los Angeles, where she is slated to testify before a grand jury regarding her late husband's "payoff list." Before leaving Chicago, Brown's partner is gunned down by the dead gangster's associates, who are determined to ensure that the widow, Mrs. Neil (Marie Windsor), never reaches her destination, and once aboard the train, Brown is approached by two gangsters who try unsuccessfully to bribe him into turning the widow over to them. When a third gangster boards the train, Mrs. Neil is shot and killed in her cabin, and it is only then that Brown learns that the woman he was escorting was actually a policewoman planted to ensure the safety of the real Mrs. Neil (Jacqueline White), who is traveling on the train with her young son. Before the train pulls into Los Angeles, Brown has succeeded in nabbing the murderous hoods and he later escorts the woman to the Hall of Justice. In this taut feature, Graw does a fine job exhibiting every emotion from sorrow and guilt when his partner is murdered, to frustration with the "witness" he is protecting, to brief but palpable indecision when he is offered the bribe in exchange for the widows' life.

Critics agreed, with the reviewer in *Variety* labeling his performance "excellent" and the *New York Times* critic declaring him "splendidly incisive." For its imaginative plot, *The Narrow Margin* received an Academy Award nomination for Best Motion Picture Story, but lost to *The Greatest Show on Earth* (1952).

Shortly after the release of *The Narrow Margin*, McGraw was in the news again, once more complaining to the press about his screen image. This time, his grievances included the dearth of romantic roles he was offered because "Hollywood feels the pretty boy types make the best lovers."

"Women have always liked the rough, tough guy," McGraw told Edith Kermit Roosevelt, a correspondent for United Press International. "Hollywood doesn't understand this. They think all American women are only looking for sons to mother." While admitting that he was pleased with the finished product of *The Narrow Margin*, McGraw also groused that many of Hollywood's screenwriters did not have the experience to write characters that were rooted in reality.

"I don't mind playing the bum and the tough guy in pictures if it's real," McGraw explained. "But some of those long-haired script writers kick it in the head because they seldom go outside a studio or college library. I really blow my top when they try and foist on me some foreign-born writer's idea of the New York or Chicago gangster world."

McGraw's discontent probably increased with his roles in his next two films, both westerns. The first, *War Paint* (1953), was a mediocre oater starring Robert Stack, and the second, *Thunder Over the Plains* (1953), with Randolph Scott and Lex Barker, was only slightly better. But he fared better when he returned to the dark side of the screen with his final feature of the noir era, *Loophole* (1954). In this film, McGraw played Gus Slavin, a sadistic private detective for a bonding company who is obsessed with proving that bank teller Michael Donovan (Barry Sullivan) is guilty of a $50,000 theft. Although police are convinced of Donovan's innocence, he is fired from his job when the bonding company cancels his policy, and Slavin continues to harass him, causing him to lose four successive jobs and his home. ("What he needs is a case of the rubber hose," Slavin says. "I'll use any way I can to break this guy down.") Meanwhile, Donovan tracks down the real thief, a bank teller named Herman Tate (Don Beddoe), but before he can capture him, Slavin shows up to thwart his efforts. Ultimately, Donovan catches up to Tate and his money-grubbing girlfriend Vera (Mary Beth Hughes) at a local beach house; although Vera shoots Donovan, he manages to subdue them both until police arrive and in the final reel, the narrator informs the audience, "Well, it's over. Everything ends sooner or later. Even the bad things. Everything is rosy now." Described by one critic as a "mighty respectable little melodrama," *Loophole* did brisk business at the box office and McGraw was singled out in *Variety*, whose critic noted his "acceptable job," and in the *New York Times*, whose reviewer praised McGraw and his co-stars for their "good performances."

Also that year, McGraw earned favorable notices for his performance as a tough commander in the blockbuster war film, *The Bridges at Toko-Ri* (1954), starring William Holden and Grace Kelly, and his career prospects continued to look bright when he broke into the medium of television in 1955 with the series *Casablanca*. Based on the hit 1942 movie, the television series starred McGraw as Rick Blaine—the character portrayed by Humphrey Bogart in the film—and also featured Clarence Muse as Sam and French actor Marcel Dalio as Capt. Renaud. The series was short-lived, but later in 1955, McGraw landed the title role on a second series, *The Adventures of Falcon*, which ran for 39 episodes.

Back on screen, McGraw appeared in 11 films over the next four years; most were such well-received films as *Toward the Unknown* (1956), which was notable for its exciting aerial shots; *Slaughter on Tenth Avenue* (1957), an absorbing waterfront drama starring Richard Egan and Jan Sterling; and *The Defiant Ones* (1958), a first-rate film focusing on the relationship that develops between two escaped convicts, one black (Sidney Poitier) and one white (Tony Curtis). During these years, McGraw did appear in a few clunkers, however—*Twilight for the Gods* (1958), which starred Rock Hudson as a court-martialed ship's captain, was tedious and lacked suspense, and *The Man in the Net* (1959), an Alan Ladd starrer, suffered from an implausible story and unfocused direction.

During the next decade, McGraw divided his time between feature films and increased television appearances. In guest spots, he was seen on some of network television's most popular programs, including *Gunsmoke, Bonanza, The Alfred Hitchcock Hour, The Virginian, Voyage to the Bottom of the Sea, The Man from U.N.C.L.E., Mission Impossible, The Untouchables, Wagon Train, The Wild, Wild West*, and *Emergency!*. His feature film appearances included roles in a number of box-office hits, such as *Spartacus* (1960), where he portrayed Marcellus, a loathesome Roman who meets his demise by being drowned in a vat of soup; *The Birds* (1963), Alfred Hitchcock's classic horror film about nature run amuck; *It's a Mad Mad Mad Mad World* (1963), Stanley Kramer's big-budget, all-star comedy; *Hang 'Em High* (1963), one of Clint Eastwood's popular westerns; *In Cold Blood* (1967), based on the bestseller by Truman Capote; and *Tell Them Willie Boy Is Here* (1969), a gripping drama starring Robert Redford and Katherine Ross.

McGraw focused most of his energies during the 1970s on television, continuing his series guest spots and appearing in a number of made-for-television movies, including *The Night Stalker* (1972), *The Longest Night* (1972), *A Boy and His Dog* (1975), *The Killer Inside Me* (1976), and *Perilous Voyage* (1976). In his last feature film appearance, McGraw portrayed a member of the U.S. president's Joint Chiefs of Staff in *Twilight's Last Gleaming* (1977), a fast-paced political thriller starring Burt Lancaster and Richard Widmark.

After this film, McGraw faded from public view. Then, in August 1980, newspapers throughout the country reported that the actor had died in a bizarre freak accident in his home. Most accounts stated that McGraw was "taking a shower when he fell through a glass shower door, suffering extensive cuts." Paramedics who arrived on the scene were unable to stop the bleeding, and the actor died a few hours later. He was 66 years old. Several days after the incident, one newspaper, the *Los Angeles Times*, reported that the actor had suffered from a "degenerative hip condition that had curtailed his work in recent years," implying that the fall had been a result of this condition. But in recent years, it has been stated that the accident occurred because McGraw was in a state of "extreme intoxication."

The curious circumstances of McGraw's sudden death notwithstanding, the actor left behind an impressive body of film and television work, and a collection of performances that never fail to capture and maintain viewers' attention. Although often typed as a "bad guy," he proved in numerous performances that his talent extended beyond a fedora and a gun. Still, it is as the "heavy" that McGraw will always be best remembered, and it certainly cannot be denied that he excelled in these roles. Just a few moments' viewing of his stone-faced gunman in *The Killers* or his maniacal henchman in *His Kind of Woman* is proof enough of that.

Film Noir Filmography

The Killers. Director: Robert Siodmak. Producer: Mark Hellinger. Running time: 105 minutes. Released by Universal, August 28, 1946. Cast: Edmond O'Brien, Ava Gardner, Albert Dekker, Sam Levene, John Miljan, Virginia Christine, Vince Barnett, Burt Lancaster, Charles D. Brown, Donald MacBride, Phil Brown, Charles McGraw, William Conrad, Queenie Smith, Garry Owen, Harry Hayden, Bill Walker, Jack Lambert, Jeff Corey, Wally Scott, Gabrielle Windsor, Rex Dale. Awards: Academy Award nominations for Best Director (Robert Siodmak), Best Original Screenplay (Anthony Veiller), Best Editing (Arthur Hilton), Best Score (Miklos Rozsa).

Brute Force. Director: Jules Dassin. Producer: Mark Hellinger. Running time: 95 minutes. Released by Universal-International, June 6, 1947. Cast: Burt Lancaster, Hume Cronyn, Charles Bickford, Yvonne DeCarlo, Ann Blyth, Ella Raines, Anita Colby, Sam Levene, Howard Duff, Art Smith, Roman Bohnen, John Hoyt, Richard Gaines, Frank Puglia, Jeff Corey, Vince Barnett, James Bell, Jack Overman, Whit Bissell, Sir Lancelot, Ray Teal, Jay C. Flippen, James O'Rear, Howland Chamberlain, Kenneth Patterson, Crane Whitley, Charles McGraw, John Harmon, Gene Stutenroth, Wally Rose, Carl Rhodes, Guy Beach, Edmund Cobb, Tom Steele.

The Gangster. Director: Gordon Wiles. Producers: Maurice and Frank King. Running time: 84 minutes. Released by Allied Artists, October 1947. Cast: Barry Sullivan, Belita, Joan Lorring, Akim Tamiroff, Henry Morgan, John Ireland, Fifi D'Orsay, Virginia Christine, Sheldon Leonard, Leif Erickson, Charles McGraw, John Kellogg, Elisha Cook, Jr., Ted Hecht, Jeff Corey.

T-Men. Director: Anthony Mann. Producer: Aubrey Schenck. Running time: 92 minutes. Released by Eagle-Lion Films, January 22, 1948. Cast: Dennis O'Keefe, Alfred Ryder, May Meade, Wallace Ford, June Lockhart, Charles McGraw, Jane Randolph, Art Smith, Herbert Heyes, Jack Overman, John Wengraf, Jim Bannon, William Malten. Awards: Academy Award nomination for Best Sound Recording (Sound Services, Inc.).

Berlin Express. Director: Jacques Tourneur. Producer: Bert Granet. Running time: 86 minutes. Released by RKO, May 1, 1948. Cast: Merle Oberon, Robert Ryan, Charles Korvin, Paul Lukas, Robert Coote, Reinhold Schunzel, Roman Toporow, Peter Von Zerneck, Otto Waldis, Fritz Kortner, Michael Harvey, Richard Powers, Charles McGraw.

Border Incident. Director: Anthony Mann. Producer: Nicholas Nayfack. Running time: 96 minutes. Released by MGM, November 19, 1949. Cast: Ricardo Montalban, George Murphy, Howard Da Silva, James Mitchell, Arnold Moss, Alfonso Bedoya, Teresa Celli, Charles McGraw, Jose Torvay, John Ridgely, Arthur Hunnicutt, Sig Ruman, Otto Waldis, Harry Antrim, Tony Barr, Rozene Jones, John McGuire, Jack Lambert, Nedrich Young, Fred Graham, Lynn Whitney.

Side Street. Director: Anthony Mann. Producer: Sam Zimbalist. Running time: 83 minutes. Released by MGM, March 23, 1950. Cast: Farley Granger, Cathy O'Donnell, James Craig, Paul Kelly, Edmon Ryan, Paul Harvey, Jean Hagen, Charles McGraw, Ed Max, Adele Jergens, Harry Bellaver, Whit Bissell, John Gallaudet, Esther Somers, Harry Antrim, George Tyne, Kathryn Givney, King Donovan, Norman Leavitt, Sid Tomack.

Armored Car Robbery. Director: Richard Fleischer. Producer: Herman Schlom. Running time: 67 minutes. Released by RKO, June 8, 1950. Cast: Charles McGraw, Adele Jergens, William Talman, Douglas Fowley, Steve Brodie, Don McGuire, Don Haggerty, James Flavin, Gene Evans.

Roadblock. Director: Harold Daniels. Producer: Lewis J. Rachmil. Running time: 73 minutes. Released by RKO, September 17, 1951. Cast: Charles McGraw, Joan Dixon, Lowell Gillmore, Louis Jean Heydt, Milburn Stone, Joseph Crehan.

His Kind of Woman. Director: John Farrow. Producer: Robert Sparks. Running time: 120 minutes. Released by RKO, August 1951. Cast: Robert Mitchum, Jane Russell, Vincent Price, Tim Holt, Charles McGraw, Marjorie Reynolds, Raymond Burr, Leslye Banning, Jim Backus, Philip Van Zandt, John Mylong, Carleton G. Young, Erno Verebes, Dan White, Richard Bergren, Stacy Harris, Robert Cornthwaite.

The Narrow Margin. Director: Richard Fleischer. Producer: Stanley Rubin. Running time: 71 minutes. Released by RKO, May 4, 1952. Cast: Charles McGraw, Marie Windsor, Jacqueline White, Gordon Gebert, Queenie Leonard, David Clarke, Peter Virgo, Don Beddoe, Pal Maxey, Harry Harvey. Awards: Academy Award nomination for Best Original Screenplay (Martin Goldsmith, Jack Leonard).

Loophole. Director: Harold Schuster. Producer: Lindsley Parsons. Running time: 79 minutes. Released by Allied Artists, March 12, 1954. Cast: Barry Sullivan, Charles McGraw, Dorothy Malone, Don Haggerty, Mary Beth Hughes, Don Beddoe, Dayton Lummis, Joanne Jordan, John Eldredge, Richard Reeves.

References

"Actor Charles McGraw, 66, Dies in Accident at Home." *Variety*, August 1, 1980.
"Actor Charles McGraw Dies at 66." *Los Angeles Herald-Examiner*, August 2, 1980.
Biography of Charles McGraw. Paramount Studios, November 1966.
Biography of Charles McGraw. United Artists Studio, June 18, 1958.
Biography of Charles McGraw. Universal Studios, June 28, 1956.
"Charles McGraw, Actor, Dies in Fall at His Home." *New York Times*, August 2, 1980.
Dolven, Frank. "Charles McGraw." *The Big Reel*, August 1995.
_____. "The Saga of Tough Guy Charles McGraw." *Classic Images*, August 1992.
"Film Bad Guy Charles McGraw in Fatal Mishap." *New York Post*, August 2, 1980.
"Home Accident Fatal to Character Actor Charles McGraw, 66." *Dallas News*, August 2, 1980.
Malnic, Eric. "'Tough' Image Meant Work if Not Fame." *Los Angeles Times*, August 4, 1980.
Obituary. *New York Daily News*, August 2, 1980.
Roosevelt, Edith K. "Fans Want More Love, Actor Says." *Los Angeles Daily News*, June 7, 1952.
Smith, Darr. "Charles McGraw." *Los Angeles Daily News*, November 1, 1949.

RALPH MEEKER

"I should've thrown you off that cliff back there. I might still do it."— Ralph Meeker in *Kiss Me Deadly* (1955)

Known for his gritty portrayals of mean-spirited villains, ruthless tough guys, and psychotic ex-soldiers, Ralph Meeker was perhaps most celebrated during his heyday for his acclaimed roles in the stage productions of *Picnic* and *A Streetcar Named Desire*, in which he ably replaced star Marlon Brando. With appearances in less than 50 movies, Meeker's name and face are not today instantly recognizable, but he possesses a firm standing in the annals of film noir for his memorable performance in one of the classics of the era, the gripping and tawdry *Kiss Me Deadly* (1955).

The man once described as "a rough kid who became an actor" was born Ralph Rathgeber on November 21, 1920, in Minneapolis, Minnesota, the son of Ralph and Magnhild Senovia Haavig Meeker Rathgeber. When he was three years old, Rathgeber's family moved to Chicago, where he attended four different elementary schools, Austin High School, Leelanau Academy in Glen Arbor, Michigan, and Northwestern University in Evanston, Illinois. While at the latter institution, Rathgeber starred in numerous University Dramatic Club productions, frequently appearing with two of his classmates, future actresses Patricia Neal and Jean Hagen.

With the onset of World War II, Rathgeber enlisted in the Navy, but after one year, he received a medical discharge following a shipboard accident in which he injured his neck. Heading for New York to launch his acting career, he appeared in more than 70 productions for local stock companies, then adopted his mother's maiden name of Meeker and, in 1943, was seen in the national company of *Doughgirls*. Later, the actor traveled to Italy with the USO production of *Ten Little Indians*, appeared with Jose Ferrer in *Strange Fruit* and *Design for Living*, and was featured in *Mister Roberts*, the Broadway hit of 1948.

In 1949, when Marlon Brando left the Broadway production of *A Streetcar Named Desire*, Meeker got the nod as his replacement, although he later admitted that it was "terrible" following Brando.

"Now there's a sensational talent!" Meeker said of Brando in a 1953 interview. "He was so great that even though I purposely avoided doing the role the way he did, the part was so strong that everybody said I was just like him."

Despite Meeker's misgivings, his performance in *Streetcar* not only attracted the notice of critics and audiences—it also led to his debut on the big screen in MGM's *Teresa* (1951), a moving drama about an Italian GI bride that also launched the careers of Pier Angeli and Rod Steiger. Meeker next starred in the Swiss-made *Die Vier im Jeep* (*Four in a Jeep*) (1951), then signed a contract with MGM and returned to Hollywood for *Shadow in the Sky* (1952), in which he offered a vivid portrayal of a shell-shocked war veteran. In 1953, Meeker was seen in such vehicles as *Jeopardy*, a suspenseful thriller where he played a criminal on the lam; *Code Two*, a forgettable drama about a motorcycle cop in training; and *The Naked Spur*, an action-packed oater featuring Meeker as a vicious fugitive. Later that year, Meeker was back on Broadway for his biggest stage success, portraying the role of Hal Carter in the original production of *Picnic*, which ran for 477 performances (actor Paul Newman made his Broadway debut in a supporting role in the production and also served as Meeker's un-

derstudy). For his outstanding turn as the luckless drifter, Meeker was awarded the New York Critic's Circle Award, but three years later, when Columbia Studios turned the play into a feature film, the role of Hal Carter was given to actor William Holden. Meeker would later say that he had been offered the role, but turned it down because of Columbia's insistence that he sign a long-term contract.

Instead, the actor obtained a release from his MGM contract, telling reporters that he "hate[d] being tied down." Back on screen as a freelancer, Meeker starred in *Big House U.S.A.* (1955), a hard-hitting crime drama in which he portrayed yet another villain, this time the scheming kidnapper of a young boy. This tense film was followed by the screen role for which Meeker is best remembered — private detective Mike Hammer in his sole film noir, *Kiss Me Deadly* (1955). Complex, often confusing, but always fascinating, this feature opens with the startling image of a barefoot, trenchcoat-clad woman (Cloris Leachman) running down a highway, trying to flag down passing cars. Finally, the woman, Christine, stops directly in front of the sporty convertible driven by Hammer, forcing him into a ditch. (Hammer provides a pithy clue to his character when, rather than demonstrate concern for the woman, he mutters in disgust, "You almost wrecked my car.") Hammer consents to take her to a bus stop, but before long, the two are ambushed by several men and, in a particularly harrowing scene, Christine is next heard screaming in agony — the audience sees only her feet dangling above the floor and a man holding a pair of pliers. Seconds later, she dies, and the remainder of the film involves the detective's unflagging efforts to find Christine's killer. Along the way, he encounters a motley crew of memorable characters, including Lily Carver (Gaby Rodgers), the dead woman's roommate, who first greets Hammer with a gun in her hand; Carl Evello (Paul Stewart), a suavely frightening mobster; and Dr. Soberin (Albert Dekker), a soft-spoken physician with a lethal bedside manner. Ultimately, Hammer learns that Christine's death is tied to the search for "the great whatsit," a leather-bound box that he is told contains radioactive material. The film's heart-pounding, action-packed climax ends with a literal bang as Hammer and his faithful secretary, Velda (Maxine Cooper), escape from a fiery beach house set ablaze after the mysterious box is opened.

Described by one reviewer as "not for children, not for the squeamish, and certain not for those seeking pleasant diversion," *Kiss Me Deadly* remains one of film noir's most widely admired and comprehensively dissected offerings. Among the many appealing aspects of the film, including its labyrinthine plot, diverting dialogue, and unforgettably repellent characters, a highlight is the portrayal by Meeker of the callous, brash detective. For his performance, Meeker was praised in numerous notices, including the review from the *Los Angeles Examiner*'s Sara Hamilton, who wrote: "Ralph Meeker does a good job as Hammer. His good looks and physical appeal are reinforced with a believable kind of toughness that defies extermination. His ability to survive the bloodiest kind of punishment goes unquestioned. Beat him, maul him, throw him over steep cliffs— pooh, nothing!"

After *Kiss Me Deadly*, Meeker returned to the stage for a brief run in *Top Man*, co-starring Polly Bergen and Lee Remick, then returned to Hollywood for *A Woman's Devotion* (1956), portraying a mentally unstable ex-soldier who is suspected of murder. Other films during the remainder of the decade included *Run of the Arrow* (1957), an offbeat but fascinating western starring Rod Steiger and Brian Keith; *Paths of Glory* (1957), a wartime epic helmed by veteran director Stanley Kubrick; and *The Fuzzy Pink Nightgown* (1957), a time-wasting farce starring Jane Russell as a movie star who is kidnapped by Meeker and co-star Keenan Wynn. Off screen for the next three years, Meeker was seen in the Broadway production of *Cloud 7* with Martha Scott, John McGiver, and Anne Helm. He also focused his energies on his television career, which had begun in 1951 with his appearance on NBC's *Kraft Television Theatre*. For the next two decades, he would be seen on a wide variety of programs, including guest shots on *Toast of the Town* (on which he guest hosted for Ed Sullivan), *Studio One*, *Alfred Hitchcock Presents*, *Studio 57*, *Jane Wyman Theatre*, *Alcoa Hour*, *Zane Grey Theatre*, *The 20th Century-Fox Hour*, *Wagon Train*, *The Loretta Young Show*, *Schlitz Playhouse of Stars*, *Wanted: Dead or Alive*, *The Texan*, *The Lawbreakers*, *Route 66*, *The U.S. Steel Hour*, *The Outer Limits*, *The Defenders*, *The Nurses*, *The F.B.I.*, *Green Hornet*, *The High Chaparral*, *The Name of the Game*, *Ironside*, *The Night Stalker*, *Room 222*, *Police Story*, *Toma*, *Cannon*, *The Rookies*, *Harry O*, *Police Woman*, and *The Eddie Capra Mysteries*. He also starred in the syndicated series *Not for Hire*, which ran for one season, from 1959 to 1960. Here, Meeker portrayed U.S. Army Sergeant Steve Dekker, described by the actor as "a guy with a sense of humor, but everything he does is wrong."

With his frequent television appearances, Meeker had little time for feature films but still managed to appear in several films during the 1960s and 1970s, including *Ada* (1961), a turgid drama starring Dean Martin and Susan Hayward; *The Dirty Dozen* (1967), the smash-hit war movie whose all-star cast included Lee Marvin, Charles Bronson, Telly Savalas, Robert Ryan, and Ernest Borgnine; *The St. Valentine's Day Massacre* (1967), the violent re-telling of the gangland conflict between Al Capone and Bugs Moran, memorably played by Meeker; *The Anderson Tapes* (1971), a well-done surveillance caper directed by Sidney Lumet; *The Happiness Cage* (1972), a confusing drama about Army mind-control experiments; *Brannigan* (1975), a passable crime drama starring John Wayne; *Food of the Gods* (1976), an unintentionally hilarious science-fiction film about a remote island inhabited by giant chickens, rats, and wasps; *My Boys are Good Boys* (1978), for which Meeker served as executive producer; and *Winter Kills* (1979), a first-rate black comedy starring Jeff Bridges and John Huston.

Despite his busy career, the prolific actor also found the opportunity for a personal life — in 1964, he married movie and television actress Salome Jens, but by 1966, the marriage had ended. He fared better the second time around; his second wife, Colleen, appeared with him in his 1972 film, *The Happiness Cage*, was a co-producer on *My Boys are Good Boys*, and went on to serve as associate producer on such features as *Hollywood Hot Tubs* (1984) and *Party Camp* (1986). Their union lasted until Meeker's death.

Never one to remain idle, Meeker continued to take on stage work during this period, starring in such productions as *After the Fall* and *But For Whom Charlie*, both directed by Elia Kazan and co-starring Jason Robards; *Mrs. Dally*, with Arlene Francis; and *The House of Blue Leaves*, co-starring John Glover and Georgia Engel (who would later gain fame as Georgette, the ditzy girlfriend of anchorman Ted Baxter on *The Mary Tyler Moore Show*).

Meeker's final performance came in the 1980 film *Without Warning*, a lame horror/science fiction feature notable primarily for its cameo appearances from such Hollywood veterans as Neville Brand, Jack Palance, Cameron Mitchell, and Martin Landau. After suffering a series of strokes over a period of several years, the actor was admitted in 1987 to the Motion Picture and Television Hospital in Woodland Hills, California, where, on August 5, 1988, he suffered a fatal heart attack. He was 67 years old.

One of the screen's best "bad guys," and a deserving star of the stage, Ralph Meeker may not be a household name, but a viewing of his performances in such films as *Jeopardy*, *A Woman's Devotion*, and *Kiss Me Deadly* clearly illustrates his dynamic talent. It was famed columnist James Bacon who, after Meeker's death, most eloquently summarized his impact when he called him "an actor's actor."

"He was one of the better actors in the movies," Bacon said, "but he was strictly a journeyman actor and he never received the stardom he deserved."

Film Noir Filmography

Kiss Me Deadly. Director and Producer: Robert Aldrich. Running time: 105 minutes. Released by United Artists, May 18, 1955. Cast: Ralph Meeker, Albert Dekker, Paul Stewart, Maxine Cooper, Gaby Rodgers, Wesley Addy, Juano Hernandez, Nick Dennis, Cloris Leachman, Marian Carr, Jack Lambert, Jack Elam, Jerry Zinneman, Percy Helton, Fortunio Bonanova, Silvio Minciotti, Leigh Snowden, Madi Comfort, James Seay, Mara McAffee, Robert Cornthwaite, James McCallian, Jesslyn Fax, Mort Marshall, Strother Martin, Marjorie Bennett, Art Loggins, Bob Sherman, Keith McConnell, Paul Richards, Eddie Beal.

References

"Actor Ralph Meeker, 67." *Newsday*, August 6, 1988.

Biography of Ralph Meeker. Paramount Studios, November 1951.

Biography of Ralph Meeker. 20th Century-Fox Studios, December 1, 1967.

Folkart, Burt A. "Ralph Meeker; Stage, Screen, TV Actor." *Los Angeles Times*, August 6, 1988.

Masters, Dorothy. "Meeker Scores Women of Wit in First Place." *New York Daily News*, December 14, 1952.

Meeker, Ralph. "I'm Tired of Peeling!" *Screen Fan*, July 1953.

Obituary. *Variety*, August 8, 1988.

Peper, William. "Ralph Meeker Takes a Chance." *New York World Telegram*, February 11, 1955.

Pollock, Arthur. "Ralph Meeker, Who Always Seems to Play Sergeants." *The Daily Compass*, June 8, 1951.

"Ralph Meeker, Stage and TV Actor, Dies." *The Hollywood Reporter*, August 8, 1988.

"Ralph Meeker Studies Characters He Portrays in His Stage Roles." Nat Dorfman-Irvin Dorfman Press Representatives, circa 1955.

"The Meeker Museum Collection." Internet Resource: http://www.neosoft.com/~meeker/biograph.html.

ROBERT MITCHUM

"I don't like playing games when I'm the fall guy."— Robert Mitchum in *Out of the Past* (1947)

Barrel-chested and cleft-chinned, Robert Mitchum possessed an insolent gaze and a veneer that could cause even the most fearless screen hood to think twice. Off screen, the multi-talented actor boasted a colorful life that included time on a Georgia chain gang and a highly publicized arrest for marijuana possession, but he was also known for his penchant for weaving tall tales.

"They're all true—booze, brawls, broads—all true," Mitchum once said. "Make up some more if you want to."

During a screen career that spanned six decades, Mitchum was nominated for an Academy Award and starred in such memorable feature films as *Night of the Hunter* (1955), *Heaven Knows, Mr. Allison* (1957), and *Cape Fear* (1962), and the top-rated television miniseries *The Winds of War* (1983). But it was as an icon of the film noir era that Mitchum is perhaps best remembered, lending his take-no-prisoners countenance to 10 examples from the period: *When Strangers Marry* (1944), *Undercurrent* (1946), *The Locket* (1947), *Crossfire* (1947), *Out of the Past* (1947), *Where Danger Lives* (1950), *His Kind of Woman* (1951), *The Racket* (1951), *Macao* (1952), and *Angel Face* (1953).

The man once touted as "one of the finest instinctive actors in the business" was born Robert Charles Durman Mitchum in Bridgeport, Connecticut, on August 6, 1917. When Mitchum—the second of three children—was 18 months old, his railroad switchman father was killed in a freight yard accident and his mother, Ann, supported the family for several years as a photographer's assistant and a linotype operator for the *Bridgeport Post*. In 1927, Ann married Hugh Cunningham-Morris, a British World War I veteran and an editor at the *Post*, but the establishment of this outwardly stable familial structure had little effect on the roguish young Mitchum, who once admitted that his was a childhood of "broken windows and bloody noses."

For a time, Mitchum and his siblings lived on their grandmother's farm in Delaware, where the future star attended Felton High School and developed the antithetical reputation as one of the smartest students in his class and one of its most rebellious. After his alleged participation in a school prank got him expelled from Felton, Mitchum moved with his family to the Hell's Kitchen neighborhood in New York, where his older sister, Annette, had established a career as a vaudeville performer. But at the age of 14, after only a brief stint at Haaren High School, Mitchum decided that he'd had enough.

"There wasn't much to hang around home for," he said.

For the next several years, Mitchum hitchhiked and rode freight trains from one end of the country to the other, sometimes making ends meet by such means as dish-washing, fruit picking, or ditch-digging, and on other occasions through methods that were less legitimate.

"When I got to California, I lay on the beach and rolled drunks," the actor once recalled. "I didn't know any better."

In the early 1930s, Mitchum found himself in trouble with the law when he was picked up for vagrancy in Savannah, Georgia, and sentenced to hard labor on a Chatham County chain gang. The actor ultimately spent six grueling days on the chain gang, but Mitchum himself offered more than one version of the manner in which he left his imprisonment; in a 1949 account, Mitchum stated that he was released after his mother notified Georgia authorities that he was younger than he had originally claimed, but years later, he maintained that he escaped.

"I saw no particular future in [working on a chain gang]," he wryly commented in a 1991 documentary. "So I ambled off."

The circumstances of his departure notwithstanding, Mitchum's chain gang experience left him with a badly infected injury that nearly resulted in the loss of his leg. After recuperating at his family's new residence in Delaware, Mitchum worked for six months with the federally funded Civilian Conservation Corps, then relocated once again, following his sister, Annette, to Long Beach, California. During the remainder of the decade, Mitchum worked at a number of widely varying jobs, from such manual vocations as stevedoring and truck-loading, to more creative pursuits, including writing children's plays, editing lecture presentations for famed astrologist Carroll Righter, and performing, at the urging of his sister, in several productions with the Long Beach Players Guild. Mitchum also spent a brief stint during this period as a boxer, but abruptly quit after a bout left him with a broken nose.

In March 1940, Mitchum married Dorothy Spence, whom he had first met when she was a 13-year-old high school student: "Her serene, tall beauty instantly hooked me

... she was it and that was that," the actor once said. The union produced three children, James in 1941, Christopher in 1943, and Petrine in 1952, and although the marriage suffered two separations and the actor's numerous purported affairs with such notables as Shirley MacLaine and Ava Gardner, Mitchum and Dorothy remained married until the actor's 1993 death.

"Whatever he does," Dorothy was once quoted, "he always comes back to his family."

Mitchum's status as a married man required him to find steady employment and he went to work as a shaper operator at the Lockheed aircraft plant in Burbank, California (where one of his co-workers was future star Marilyn Monroe). But his tenure at the plant was short-lived.

"I was running some horrible monster of an infernal machine and I was afraid of it," Mitchum recalled. "I couldn't eat or sleep and I was finally living on No-Doz, and chewing tobacco with hot sauce sprinkled on it to keep me awake."

Finally, when the stress of the job began to affect his eyesight, Mitchum left Lockheed behind, briefly clerking in a shoe store before following the suggestion of his mother and setting his sights on a career in the movies. Before long, Mitchum had hired an agent and, after first appearing as a model in the 1942 documentary *The Magic of Makeup*, he was cast as an outlaw in his acting debut, *Border Patrol* (1943), starring William Boyd as Hopalong Cassidy. Also that year — the busiest of his career — Mitchum appeared in six more "Hopalong Cassidy" films, including *Hoppy Serves a Writ* (1943), *False Colors* (1943), and *Riders of the Deadline* (1943), as well as such features as Universal's *The Dancing Masters* (1943), a Laurel and Hardy comedy; *Doughboys in Ireland* (1943), a Columbia musical; *The Human Comedy* (1943), a well-received MGM picture starring Mickey Rooney; and *Corvette K-225* (1943), a wartime hit produced by Howard Hawks and featuring Ella Raines in her screen debut. Although the work was steady, allowing the actor and his family to move to a bungalow court in West Hollywood, Mitchum downplayed the impact of his new vocation, later maintaining that "movies bore me — especially my own."

"It's a job," the actor said late in his career. "One of the greatest movie stars that ever lived was Rin Tin Tin and that was a mother dog, so there couldn't be that much of a trick to it. You get up in the morning and go to work, and they paint a face on you or glue a moustache on, and they tell you what jokes to say, and you say them and that's it. And then you turn around and come home at night."

Despite his professed indifference, however, Mitchum was continuing to grow as a performer with each successive screen appearance, and in 1944 made an impact in MGM's *Thirty Seconds Over Tokyo* (1944). Mitchum's portrayal of a crewman in the film attracted the notice of RKO studio executives, who signed the actor to a long-term contract, a portion of which was purchased by famed producer David O. Selznick. Shortly after inking this agreement, Mitchum completed filming on a one-week quickie at Monogram Studios that served as his entry into the world of film noir — *When Strangers Marry* (1944).

Also known as *Betrayed*, this low-budget feature begins with the murder of a drunken Philadelphia conventioneer after he recklessly boasts at a hotel bar that he is toting a bankroll of $10,000. Although the man's assailant is unseen, all signs point to an unemployed salesman (Dean Jagger), whose mysterious behavior arouses the concern of his bride, Millie (Kim Hunter). Fueling Millie's growing suspicions is Fred Graham (Mitchum), a former boyfriend from her Ohio hometown who happens to turn up at the New York hotel where Millie has arranged to meet her husband. Despite Fred's solicitous manner, Millie later realizes that he is the killer, and Fred exposes his guilt in the film's climax when a crafty detective (Neil Hamilton) discovers him trying to mail the stolen $10,000 to his house in Ohio.

After his appearance in *When Strangers*

Marry— which was praised by the critic for *The Nation*, who wrote, "I have seldom for years now seen one hour so energetically and sensibly used"— Mitchum was drafted into the Army for service in World War II. His assignment was deferred, however, so that he could appear in the film that would catapult him into the nation's consciousness, *The Story of G.I. Joe* (1945). The actor earned raves for his portrayal of a beloved infantry captain and was rewarded with what would be his only Academy Award nomination; although he lost the Best Supporting Actor honor to James Dunn for *A Tree Grows in Brooklyn* (1945), Mitchum had demonstrated a depth of talent that was incontrovertible.

"In *The Story of G.I. Joe*, Mitchum played the tired captain, writing letters to mothers of kids who'd been killed," the film's director William Wellman recalled years later. "In this one scene, I saw one of the few instances in my whole career something so wonderful, so completely compelling. He was nominated for the Academy Award that year and I think he should have won it. There is something about Mitchum that just thrills me to death. I think he is one of the finest, most solid, real actors that we have in the world today."

After filming his role for *G.I. Joe*, Mitchum served in the real-life Army for eight months before receiving a hardship discharge because of his six dependents (which, in addition to his wife and two children, consisted of his mother, stepfather, and half-sister, Carol). He immediately returned to the big screen and the world of film noir, appearing in four features from the era during the next two years: *Undercurrent* (1946), *The Locket* (1947), *Crossfire* (1947), and *Out of the Past* (1947).

Undercurrent, the weakest of the actor's films noirs, starred Katharine Hepburn and Robert Taylor as newlyweds Ann and Alan Garroway, who are both revealed to possess an unnatural fixation on Alan's long-missing brother, Michael (Mitchum). A wealthy inventor and businessman, Alan's obsession stems from his belief that Michael was their mother's "favorite," and his contention that Michael disappeared after he was discovered stealing funds from the family business. As for Ann, she becomes fascinated with Michael after talking to several of his closest friends and forming an image of him as a sensitive and kind soul who may have met a violent end at the hands of his brother. When Michael resurfaces, it is revealed that Alan gained his fame and fortune after murdering an engineer and stealing his plans for a new invention; after Michael threatens to expose this truth to Ann, Alan realizes that his wife no longer loves him and tries to kill her during a horseback ride through the woods. Ann is injured after being thrown to the ground and Alan prepares to finish her off by bludgeoning her to death with a rock, but before he can carry out the deed, he is trampled to death by his own horse.

Although Mitchum's role in *Undercurrent* was secondary to those portrayed by Taylor and Hepburn, the actor was singled out by several reviewers, including Lloyd L. Sloan of the *Hollywood Citizen-News*, who said that he "does a capable job," and the *New York Times*' Bosley Crowther, who wrote: "You may also find Robert Mitchum fairly appealing in a crumpled, modest way as the culturally oriented brother, even though he appears in only a couple of scenes." Interestingly, in the years following Mitchum's appearance in the film, an anecdote was widely circulated regarding the purported hostility between the actor and Katharine Hepburn. According to the story, the acclaimed actress resented Mitchum's bawdy humor and on-the-set pranks, and told him one day, "You know you can't act, and if you hadn't been good looking you would never have gotten a picture. I'm tired of playing with people who have nothing to offer." In a 1996 interview for the Turner Classic Movies cable channel, however, Mitchum vehemently denied that the incident took place.

"That is not true," Mitchum told interviewer Robert Osborne. "Believe me, I would have remembered that. Believe me."

Next, in the first of his 1947 noirs, Mitchum was seen in *The Locket*, which used the unique method of flashbacks framed within flashbacks to illustrate the psychotic decline of a young woman named Nancy Blair (Laraine Day). On the day of Nancy's wedding, her first husband, psychiatrist Harry Blair (Brian Aherne), visits her fiancé in order to reveal that Nancy is a "hopelessly twisted personality" with a history of kleptomania. Her illness, according to the doctor, stemmed from a childhood trauma in which she was falsely accused of stealing a locket by the wealthy matron for whom her mother worked as a housekeeper. Blair also explains that he first learned of Nancy's affliction from her former boyfriend, artist Norman Clyde (Mitchum), who sought the doctor's help in saving the life of a wrongly convicted man. As it turns out, Nancy was responsible for a series of jewel thefts, even committing murder to obtain the coveted items, but Blair refused to believe Clyde's tale, the innocent man was executed, and Norman was so tormented by the chain of events that he committed suicide. But just as Blair initially doubted Clyde, Nancy's fiancé, John Willis (Gene Raymond), is unable to accept the doctor's story and the wedding proceeds as planned. As Nancy is preparing for the processional, however, she is given a gift of a locket by John's mother — the same woman who had accused Nancy of stealing the necklace when she was a child. Walking down the aisle, Nancy is tormented by her memories of the past and suffers a complete breakdown, collapsing as she reaches John. In the film's final scene, Blair explains that she has reverted to the days of her childhood and has no recollection of any of the events since then, but John insists on accompanying her as she is led away to a mental hospital.

An excellent offering from the noir era, *The Locket* was a critical and financial success, and Mitchum earned mostly good reviews for his performance, with Lowell E. Redelings of the *Hollywood Citizen-News* terming him "very credible," and the *Los Angeles Daily News'* Virginia Wright writing that he "makes the cynical, sarcastic painter a character of some force." In the *New York Times*, however, Bosley Crowther vehemently disagreed with these assessments, opining that "in the central role as the one man who fathoms her mental problems, Robert Mitchum gives a completely monotonous and inexpressive performance. There is not the slightest hint about this rigid face of the temperament of an artist, even granting that the fellow he is representing is a moody sort."

Crossfire, Mitchum's second noir of the year, centered on the murder of Jewish war veteran Joseph Samuels (Sam Levene) and the unflagging efforts of a detective, Lt. Finlay (Robert Young), to find the killer. Finlay is aided in his quest by an ex-serviceman, Keeley (Mitchum), whose roommate, Arthur Mitchell (George Cooper), was one of four soldiers who met Samuels at a bar on the evening of his death. When the police investigation centers on Mitchell, Keeley helps to hide his friend until the true killer can be found and, ultimately, it is discovered that the murder was committed by two of the soldiers, Bowers (Steve Brodie) and Montgomery (Robert Ryan), a blustering braggart characterized by an invective anti–Semitic stance. When Montgomery later kills Bowers to ensure his silence, he is confronted by Finlay,

who guns him down in the street as he tries to escape.

After earning mention from one critic for portraying "the 'right' sort of cynical G.I." in *Crossfire*, Mitchum was seen in a starring role in his best-known film noir, *Out of the Past*. This first-rate, quintessential noir offering opens as gas station owner Jeff Bailey (Mitchum) is revealing his past to his girlfriend, Ann (Virginia Huston). By utilizing a flashback structure that lasts until the mid-point of the film, it is revealed that, as a private detective years before, Jeff had been hired by mobster Whit Sterling (Kirk Douglas) to find his girlfriend, Kathie Moffett (Jane Greer), who'd shot him and stolen $40,000. Tracking her to Mexico City, Jeff falls in love with Kathie, believing her denial that she stole the money from Whit. Kathie's true colors are later revealed, however, when she fatally shoots Jeff's partner, Jack Fisher (Steve Brodie), who had been hired by Whit to find the pair, and Jeff discovers that Kathie actually was guilty of stealing the money from Whit. Disillusioned by Kathie's duplicity, Jeff started a new life in Bridgeport, California, but his past returns to haunt him when he is summoned by Whit again and learns that Kathie has returned to him. Blackmailing Jeff regarding Fisher's murder, Whit forces Jeff to obtain a set of potentially damaging tax records from a turncoat accountant, but after the accountant turns up dead, Jeff realizes too late that Whit plans to frame him for the killing. Confronted by Jeff, Whit later agrees to expose Kathie for Fisher's murder, but before he can effect his plan, he is killed by Kathie, who then convinces Jeff to flee the country with her. Jeff agrees, but secretly contacts police; when they later encounter a roadblock, Kathie shoots Jeff before being riddled with bullets by police, and they both perish.

Based on the Geoffrey Holmes novel *Build My Gallows High*, *Out of the Past* was a box-office smash that was recently described as "one of those films that gets better every year." The critics of the day were similarly impressed, with Ann Helming of the *Holly-*

wood *Citizen-News* terming the film a "taut and suspenseful melodrama," and the critic for *Variety* hailing it as "a flashy addition to the tough-guy film archives." Mitchum was lauded for his performance as well; the critic for *Variety* wrote that he "gives out with one of his forceful he-man characterizations"; *Film Daily*'s reviewer found that the film "gives Robert Mitchum [an] opportunity to capably render a new sort of role"; and the critic for *The Hollywood Reporter* raved: "Robert Mitchum is at his very best in the role of the plain-speaking sleuth, a role tailored to his measure and consequently played to the hilt."

On the heels of his triumph in *Out of the Past*, Mitchum continued to enhance his on-screen reputation with a starring role in *Blood on the Moon* (1948), a first-rate western directed by Robert Wise. But Mitchum's burgeoning status as a film star faded in significance in the summer of 1948 when he was involved in an incident that would forever be an integral part of the actor's lore. On the evening of August 31, 1948, Mitchum was house-hunting with real-estate agent Robin Ford when he reluctantly agreed to Ford's suggestion to stop at the house of actress Lila Leeds. Upon his arrival, Mitchum said, Leeds handed him a marijuana cigarette and seconds later, "there was a loud crash and two men burst into the room."

"Without bothering to drop the cigarette, I crouched to throw the small table before me at the men, thinking it was a holdup, and at the same instant one of the men shouted, 'police officers,' and moved toward me," Mitchum stated in a detailed account that ran in the February 17, 1949, issue of the *Los Angeles Herald-Express*. "Realizing that I had burnt my fingers, I released the cigarette and rubbed my sore fingers on the couch. Sergeant Barr retrieved the cigarette and moved across the room to Miss Leeds…. I observed a partial package of cigarettes in a crumpled Phillip Morris wrapper on the table, and pushed them over toward Barr, who was crossing back toward me. After an interval, he attempted to thrust the package

into my hands, and said: 'These are yours.' I replied that they were not. He said, 'Look, don't give me any business and we'll get along fine.'"

Despite his insistence that he "did not have any marijuana when I entered the house, nor did I know or believe that anyone else there would have any marijuana available," Mitchum was convicted of drug possession and sentenced to a two-year probation, with 60 days to be served in the county jail. After 50 days at an honor farm — during which the actor was seen in a famous newspaper photograph swabbing floors with a mop — Mitchum was released, telling the press in one of his best-known quotes, that "jail is like Palm Springs without the riffraff. A great place to get in shape, only you meet a better class of people." Two years later, in January 1951, the case was reviewed and following an investigation, the conviction was overturned and expunged from the record.

"What people forget is that the whole thing was thrown out," Mitchum said in a 1991 documentary. "And it was stricken from the record because it was not a true case."

Although Mitchum's conviction provoked dire preditions that his career was over, RKO head Howard Hughes continued to support the actor, maintaining his studio contract, loaning him money for attorney fees, and immediately casting him upon his release in the 1949 feature *The Big Steal*. ("Any other studio chief would have hung me out to dry," Mitchum later said.)

Disproving the statements from numerous columnists regarding the negative impact of the incident on Mitchum's career, audiences turned *The Big Steal* into a box-office success, and Mitchum went on to appear in *The Red Pony* (1949) opposite Myrna Loy; *Holiday Affair* (1949) with Janet Leigh, and *Where Danger Lives* (1950), his sixth film noir. In this feature, Mitchum portrayed Jeff Cameron, a compassionate doctor who falls in love with a mysterious beauty named Margo Lannington (Faith Domergue) after she is admitted to the hospital following a suicide attempt. During a surprise visit to her house, Jeff is disgusted to learn that Margo is married, but he comes to her rescue when she claims that she has been attacked by her husband. When Lannington (Claude Rains) strikes Jeff in the head with a poker, the doctor knocks him out cold, then leaves the room to get water, instructing Margo to put a pillow under Lannington's head. Minutes later, however, Margo informs Jeff that her husband is dead and, ignoring his plans to contact the police, convinces him to flee with her to Mexico. On the way, Jeff realizes that he has suffered a concussion and warns Margo that he is likely to become paralyzed and wind up in a coma. The couple stop off in a small Arizona town to get married, but radio news accounts not only reveal that Lannington died after being smothered by a pillow, but that his wife had previously undergone "extensive psychiatric treatment." By the time Jeff realizes that Margo killed her husband, however, the left side of his body has become paralyzed and he is unable to fight when Margo knocks him down and smothers him with a pillow. Margo flees, planning to hitch a ride across the border to Mexico, but when Jeff comes to and staggers after her, she shoots him before being gunned down herself by police.

Although Bosley Crowther in the *New York Times* singled out Mitchum's performance as "fairly credible," and famed columnist Louella Parsons found that he "has seldom appeared to better advantage," most reviewers overlooked the actor in favor of his co-star Domergue, a highly touted discovery of Howard Hughes. But the film itself was less favorably viewed, with Lowell E. Redelings of the *Hollywood Citizen-News* calling it a "far-fetched yarn," and Darr Smith dismissing it in the *Los Angeles Daily News* as "static, talky, and muggy." Despite its rather campy nature, however, the film stands up today as a worthwhile example of the era that holds the interest from beginning to end.

The following year, Mitchum remained in the realm of film noir with starring roles in back-to-back features, *His Kind of Woman* (1951) and *The Racket* (1951). In the first, Mitchum was Dan Milner, a professional gambler and ex-con who is offered $50,000 to leave the United States for a year. Accepting the proposal, Milner travels to Mexico to await further instructions, unaware that an exiled syndicate boss, Nick Ferraro (Raymond Burr), plans to kill him and assume his identity. Tipped off by a federal agent, Milner learns of Ferraro's plot, but the agent later turns up dead and Milner is forced aboard the mobster's nearby yacht. As an associate of Ferraro's prepares to inject Milner with an anesthetic that will result in his death, the gambler gets help from an unlikely source — Mark Cardigan (Vincent Price), a visiting film star, learns of Milner's plight, gathers a posse of hotel guests and local police, and storms the boat. After Cardigan shoots several of the men on board, Milner is able to break free from his captors and kill Ferraro.

While *His Kind of Woman* was panned in the *New York Times* for depicting "the crudest, cheapest kind of sensationalized violence," Mitchum fared better in his second noir of the year, *The Racket*, portraying Capt. Tom McQuigg, an honest cop whose persona is clearly illustrated when he addresses his men during his first day in a new district: "I will not stand for laxity, slovenliness, or second best," McQuigg says. "You do your jobs right or you'll hear from me. As for dishonesty or shady stuff— one time and you're out. There's no excuse for it." McQuigg's chief nemesis is a middle-level gangster named Nick Scanlon (Robert Ryan), who was responsible for the murder of a police informant, and has used his connections with crooked city officials to arrange for McQuigg's transfers from district to district. In his quest to nab Scanlon, McQuigg enlists the help of one of his brightest officers, Johnson (William Talman), but Scanlon has a bomb planted at McQuigg's home and later kills Johnson during a scuffle. Ultimately, it is Scanlon's own mob that brings him down; after his superiors object to the mobster's out-of-control violence, he is gunned down by a corrupt state inspector. This remake of a 1928 film of the same name did brisk business at the box office, and Mitchum was hailed for his portrayal of

McQuigg; in a typical review, the critic for *Variety* wrote that both Mitchum and Ryan "dominate the picture with forceful, credible performances that add a lot of interest."

After appearances in a pair of clunkers, *My Forbidden Past* (1951), a dull soaper set in New Orleans in the 1890s, and *One Minute to Zero* (1952), a cliché-ridden war saga, Mitchum hit pay dirt with *The Lusty Men* (1952), turning in a fine performance as a former rodeo star. He also starred during this period in his final two films noirs, *Macao* (1952) and *Angel Face* (1953).

Macao saw the actor reteamed with his *His Kind of Woman* co-star Jane Russell, this time playing an ex–G.I., Nick Cochran, who flees to the title colony to escape prosecution for a minor criminal offense in the United States. Also arriving in Macao are singer Julie Benton (Russell) and Lawrence Trumble (William Bendix), an undercover New York detective whose assignment centers on the arrest of gambling house owner Vincent Halloran (Brad Dexter). When Halloran mistakes Nick for a detective, he orders him killed but, ironically, Halloran's underlings murder Trumble instead. Before he dies, the detective reveals to Nick the reason for his presence in Macao and, soliciting Julie's aid, Nick traps the gambling house owner aboard his own boat and drives him outside the colony's borders, where he is captured.

Next, in his final film noir, Mitchum was once again seen portraying a man whose attraction for a femme turns out to be a fatal one. In *Angel Face*, he portrayed Frank Jessup, an ambulance driver who is captivated by a young woman, Diane Tremayne (Jean Simmons), whom he first meets when her stepmother (Barbara O'Neil) is "accidentally" overcome by escaping gas. It is soon revealed that the "accident" was actually caused by Diane, and a short time later, Frank reveals his intention to end their relationship: "How stupid do you think I am?" he asks. "You hate that woman and some day you're going to hate her enough to kill her. It's been in the back of your mind all along." Swayed by Diane's considerable charms, Frank decides to stay,

but his prediction comes true when Diane makes another attempt to do away with her stepmother and rigs the family car. Her plan works too well, however, and her beloved father (Herbert Marshall) is killed as well. Both Diane and Frank are indicted for the couple's murder, but after they are urged to marry in an effort to sway the jury, they are found not guilty. Despite this exoneration, Frank realizes that his "angel face" is a cold-blooded killer and prepares to leave her. Diane, however, has other ideas— offering to drive Frank to the bus station, she deliberately throws the car into reverse, sending them both careening over a cliff to their deaths.

Mitchum's final two films noirs were met with mixed reviews from critics; the reviewer for *Variety* found that he was "passable" in *Macao*, but the *New York Times*' Bosley Crowther offered faint praise at best, writing that "Mr. Mitchum, who plays an 'operator,' drifting hither and yon like the wind, does manage to look more than slumberous in a couple of muscle-wrenching scenes." As for *Angel Face*, while the critic for the *New York Times* observed that "Mr. Mitchum's laconic utterances may or may not be perfectly in keeping with the chain of events," Lowell E. Redelings wrote in the *Hollywood Citizen-News* that the actor was "nicely cast," and the *Los Angeles Herald-Express* critic opined: "He handles the acting windfull in good style, relaxing his way through character touches of a likable fellow with a weakness for an easy set up and a strong sense of maleness."

During the next two decades, Mitchum was seen in a number of films of varying quality. On the plus side were such features as *River of No Return* (1954), an Otto Preminger–directed western that teamed Mitchum with his old friend from Lockheed aircraft, Marilyn Monroe; *Night of the Hunter* (1955), where Mitchum turned in a memorable role as a psychotic preacher with the words "LOVE" and "HATE" tattooed on his hands; *Heaven Knows, Mr. Allison* (1957), helmed by John Huston, who later called Mitchum "the most talented actor he had ever directed"; *The*

Jane Russell and Robert Mitchum team up in *Macao* (1952).

Enemy Below (1957), a well-done wartime film, not to be confused with the actor's *Fire Down Below*, released the same year; *Thunder Road* (1958), an interesting crime feature co-starring Mitchum's oldest son, Jim, and which Mitchum not only wrote and produced, but also wrote the theme song for; *The Sundowners* (1960), where he portrayed an Australian sheep farmer; *Home from the Hill* (1960), after which he was voted the year's best actor by the National Board of Review of Motion Pictures' Committee on Exceptional Films; *Cape Fear* (1962), in which he essayed a frightening performance as a vengeful ex-con; *The Longest Day* (1962), an epic war film featuring an all-star cast including John Wayne, Henry Fonda, and Rod Steiger; *El Dorado* (1967), where he played a drunken sheriff; and *Five Card Stud* (1968), an underrated western featuring Mitchum as a mur-derous preacher who hides his gun inside his bible.

With the onset of the 1970s, Mitchum's roles began to decrease in both quality and quantity, but he did offer memorable performances in *Ryan's Daughter* (1970), later earning praise from the film's director, David Lean, who said, "Mitchum can, simply by being there, make almost any other actor look like a hole in the screen"; *The Friends of Eddie Coyle* (1973), in which Mitchum played the title role of a petty crook; *Farewell, My Lovely* (1975), where he was seen in the made-to-order role of world-weary private detective Philip Marlowe; and *The Last Tycoon* (1976), which featured him as a conniving studio executive. As the actor entered the sixth decade of his life, most of his best roles were behind him, but Mitchum showed no signs of permanently throwing in the cinematic towel.

"Retire? I retire every morning," he once said.

With his feature film offers at a minimum, Mitchum began spending more of his acting energies on the small screen, earning a new generation of fans with his standout portrayal of Victor "Pug" Henry in the World War II miniseries *The Winds of War* (1983). (He reprised the role in the 1988 sequel, *War and Remembrance*, but this 34-hour production, which ran in seven parts in November 1989 and five in May 1989, was a ratings disappointment.) Mitchum also appeared in such television projects as *North and South* (1985), another successful miniseries, this one focusing on the Civil War; *Promises to Keep* (1985), notable primarily because it featured performances by Mitchum, his youngest son, Christopher, and his grandson, Bentley; and *The Hearst and Davies Affair* (1985), where he played media mogul William Randolph Hearst opposite Virginia Madsen's Marion Davies.

By now, Mitchum had developed a reputation as a hard drinker, and was frequently known to imbibe on the sets of his films. In a 2000 documentary, actor George Hamilton, who co-starred with the actor in *Home from the Hill* (1960), recalled that Mitchum frequently ate oranges during the production that had been injected with alcohol, and that he kept a water cooler in his dressing room filled with vodka. By the mid-1980s, however, Mitchum's decades-long dependence on alcohol had caught up with him, and he entered the renowned Betty Ford Center in Rancho Mirage, California, for treatment. After his brief stay, Mitchum emerged to resume his old habits.

"I stayed there until they were through with me," he told reporters. "I don't know if it 'worked.' I don't understand that."

Aside from an appearance as a police lieutenant in the 1991 remake of Mitchum's earlier film *Cape Fear*, the actor was seen in only a handful of productions during his later years, few of which were worthy of his talent. On television, he played recurring roles in two short-lived series, *A Family for Joe*, a 1990 sitcom where he was seen as the surrogate grandfather for four orphaned children, and *African Skies*, a cable series starring Catherine Bach. He also provided the narration for the feature film *Tombstone* (1993), a hit retelling of Wyatt Earp's conflict with the Clancy boys, and also lent his distinctive voice to a number of television commercials, including a series for The American Beef Council, in which he told audiences, "Beef— it's what's for dinner."

In the 1990s, Mitchum's health began to decline and after years of heavy smoking, it was learned that he was suffering from emphysema. In spring 1997, the actor was diagnosed with lung cancer and on July 1, 1997, he died from the disease. He was 79 years old.

Throughout Mitchum's prolific career, his understated performances were often overlooked or dismissed, but he possessed an undeniable presence that infused any scene in which he appeared and transformed him into one of the screen's best loved stars. The essence of what he brought to his roles seems to be an indefinable quality, but whether it was his gravelly, instantly recognizable voice, his devil-may-care air, his ruggedly handsome visage, or his unique way of putting over a line, Robert Mitchum had what it took to become a lasting icon of the silver screen.

"I don't know how to analyze what Mitchum's appeal is," said director Sidney Pollack, who helmed the actor's 1975 film, *The Yakuza*. "It's there. It's immediate. You can feel it. It's palpable."

Film Noir Filmography

When Strangers Marry. Director: William Castle. Producer: Franklin King. Running time: 67 minutes. Released by Monogram, August 21, 1944. Cast: Dean Jagger, Kim Hunter, Robert Mitchum, Neil Hamilton, Lou Lubin, Milt Kibbee, Dewey Robinson, Claire Whitney, Edward Keane, Virginia Sale, Dick Elliot, Lee "Lasses" White.

Undercurrent. Director: Vincente Minnelli. Producer: Pandro S. Berman. Running time: 114 minutes. Released by MGM, November 28, 1946. Cast: Katharine Hepburn, Robert Taylor, Robert Mitchum, Edmund Gwenn, Marjorie Main, Jayne Cotter, Clinton Sundberg, Dan Tobin, Kathryn

Card, Leigh Whipper, Charles Trowbridge, James Westerfield, Billy McLain.

The Locket. Director: John Brahm. Producer: Bert Granet. Running time: 85 minutes. Released by RKO, March 19, 1947. Cast: Laraine Day, Brian Aherne, Robert Mitchum, Gene Raymond, Sharyn Moffett, Ricardo Cortez, Henry Stephenson, Katherine Emery, Reginald Denny, Fay Helm, Helene Thimig, Nella Walker, Queenie Leonard, Lilian Fontaine, Myrna Dell, Johnny Clark.

Crossfire. Director: Edward Dmytryk. Producer: Adrian Scott. Running time: 85 minutes. Released by RKO, July 22, 1947. Cast: Robert Young, Robert Mitchum, Robert Ryan, Gloria Grahame, Paul Kelly, Sam Levene, Jacqueline White, Steve Brodie, George Cooper, Richard Benedict, Richard Powers, William Phipps, Lex Barker, Marlo Dwyer. Awards: Academy Award nomination for Best Picture, Best Director (Edward Dmytryk), Best Supporting Actor (Robert Ryan), Best Supporting Actress (Gloria Grahame), Best Original Screenplay (John Paxton).

Out of the Past. Director: Jacques Tourneur. Producer: Warren Duff. Running time: 96 minutes. Released by RKO, November 25, 1947. Cast: Robert Mitchum, Jane Greer, Kirk Douglas, Rhonda Fleming, Richard Webb, Steve Brodie, Virginia Huston, Paul Valentine, Dickie Moore, Ken Niles.

Where Danger Lives. Director: John Farrow. Producer: Irving Cummings, Jr. Running time: 82 minutes. Released by RKO, July 14, 1950. Cast: Robert Mitchum, Faith Domergue, Claude Rains, Maureen O'Sullivan, Charles Kemper, Ralph Dumke, Billy House, Harry Shannon, Philip Van Zandt, Jack Kelly.

His Kind of Woman. Director: John Farrow. Producer: Robert Sparks. Running time: 120 minutes. Released by RKO, August 1951. Cast: Robert Mitchum, Jane Russell, Vincent Price, Tim Holt, Charles McGraw, Marjorie Reynolds, Raymond Burr, Leslye Banning, Jim Backus, Philip Van Zandt, John Mylong, Carleton G. Young, Erno Verebes, Dan White, Richard Bergren, Stacy Harris, Robert Cornthwaite.

The Racket. Director: John Cromwell. Producer: Edmund Grainger. Running time: 88 minutes. Released by RKO, December 12, 1951. Cast: Robert Mitchum, Lizabeth Scott, Robert Ryan, William Talman, Ray Collins, Joyce MacKenzie, Robert Hutton, Virginia Huston, William Conrad, Walter Sande, Les Tremayne, Don Porter, Walter Baldwin, Brett King, Richard Karlan, Tito Vuolo.

Macao. Director: Josef von Sternberg. Producer: Alex Gottlieb. Running time: 81 minutes. Released by RKO, April 30, 1952. Cast: Robert Mitchum, Jane Russell, William Bendix, Thomas Gomez, Gloria Grahame, Brad Dexter, Edward Ashley, Philip Ahn, Vladimir Sokoloff, Don Zelaya.

Angel Face. Director and Producer: Otto Preminger. Released by RKO, February 2, 1953. Running time: 91 minutes. Cast: Robert Mitchum, Jean Simmons, Mona Freeman, Herbert Marshall, Leon Ames, Barbara O'Neil, Kenneth Tobey, Raymond Greenleaf, Griff Barnett, Robert Gist, Morgan Farley, Jim Backus.

References

"Bob Mitchum." *Modern Screen*, December 1965.

"Break Up Party in Home of Lila Leeds." *Los Angeles Herald-Express*, September 1, 1948.

Carroll, Harrison. "Bob Wants Dorothy to Reconcile, Join Him on Mexican Location." *Los Angeles Herald-Express*, March 19, 1953.

Curreri, Joe. "In Memory of Mitchum." *The Big Reel*, August 1997.

Hale, Wanda. "Mitchum of Maryland." *New York Daily News*, April 26, 1965.

Hirshberg, Jack. "Hollywood Hearsay." Publication Unsourced, circa 1949.

Hopper, Hedda. "He Says What He Thinks!" *Chicago Sunday Tribune*, June 28, 1953.

Hyams, Joe. "Angler Robert Mitchum vs. Work." *New York Herald Tribune*, April 30, 1959.

Mann, Roderick. "I Gave Up Being Serious." *New York World-Telegram*, August 15, 1959.

Mitchell, Charles P. "The Robert Mitchum Drug Case." *Films of the Golden Age*, Fall 1997.

"Mitchum's Career Safe Despite Jail." *Los Angeles Times*, February 10, 1949.

"Mitchum Story Tells Hard Road to Fame." *Los Angeles Herald-Express*, February 17, 1949.

"Mitchum, Three Others Indicted on Two Counts." *Los Angeles Examiner*, September 8, 1948.

Muir, Florabel. "What Now for Mitchum?" *Photoplay*, April 1949.

Parsons, Louella O. "Hollywood's Determined Rebel." Publication Unsourced, circa 1955.

Ringgold, Gene. "Robert Mitchum." *Films in Review*, May 1964.

Ruark, Robert C. "Mitchum's Sins." *Los Angeles Times*, September 9, 1948.

Scott, Vernon. "Mitchum Doesn't Pull His Punches." *Hollywood Citizen-News*, April 10, 1965.

"Series Debut for Mitchum." *Los Angeles Times*, November 21, 1989.

Waterbury, Ruth. "He's Murder." *Photoplay*, April 1948.

Winsten, Archer. "Rages and Outrages." *New York Post*, April 5, 1965.

Documentaries

"Mysteries and Scandals: Robert Mitchum." E! Entertainment Television. Copyright 2000.
"Private Screenings: Jane Russell and Robert Mitchum." Turner Classic Movies. Copyright 1996.
"Robert Mitchum: The Reluctant Star." A Wombat Production, in association with Cinemax. Copyright 1991.

HARRY MORGAN

"One thing about me, I never stick my nose into business that don't concern me. It don't pay."— Harry Morgan in *The Gangster* (1947)

Harry Morgan is best known to modern audiences as the irascible Col. Sherman Potter on TV's *M*A*S*H*, or as Officer Bill Gannon, the erstwhile partner of Joe Friday on the classic cop show *Dragnet*. But in his Hollywood heyday, the slightly built actor appeared in a spate of big-screen gems, including *The Ox-Bow Incident* (1943), *All My Sons* (1948), *Madame Bovary* (1949), *What Price Glory?* (1952), *High Noon* (1952), and *About Mrs. Leslie* (1954). A veteran of more than 100 films over a span of six decades, Morgan was also a prolific contributor to the noir era, with featured roles in seven films noirs: *The Gangster* (1947), *Appointment with Danger* (1951), *The Big Clock* (1948), *Moonrise* (1949), *Red Light* (1950), *Dark City* (1950), and *Scandal Sheet* (1952).

Morgan was born Harry Bratsburg in Detroit, Michigan, on April 10, 1915, the son of an automobile worker who hailed from Scandinavia. At the age of four, Harry's family moved to nearby Muskegon, where the youngster attended elementary and high school before enrolling at the University of Chicago as a pre-law student.

"I wasn't in Chicago long, just a few months, thinking about being a lawyer. I wanted to be Clarence Darrow," the actor said in a 1986 interview. "But it was the middle of the Depression and a tough time to be in school."

Forced by lack of finances to drop out of college after his first year, Harry made his way to Washington, D.C., where he landed a job selling desks for an office supply company. Before long, however, he found that he was "a lousy salesman and ... very lonely."

"I read an article about tryouts at the new Civic Theater," the actor later recalled. I figured it sounded easy, so I went to one."

The Civic Theater director cast Harry as Duke Mantee in *The Petrified Forest*, and later tapped the young man to reprise the role at the Westchester Playhouse in Mt. Kisco, New York. At Mt. Kisco, Harry was cast opposite budding actress Frances Farmer; his association with the talented (and, ultimately, tragic) actress turned out to be a fortuitous one. Farmer introduced Harry to her understudy, Eileen Detchon—the two were married the following year and would go on to have four sons, Chris, Charles, and twins Paul and Daniel. The union would last for more than 40 years, until Eileen's death from heart failure in 1985.

Harry benefited professionally, as well, from his friendship with Farmer. When the actress was wooed by the famed Group Theater for its Broadway production of *Golden Boy*, Farmer suggested Harry for the play and he was cast by director Elia Kazan as Pepper White, a punch-drunk ex-fighter. For his debut on the Great White Way, the actor changed his name, appearing in *Golden Boy* as Henry Morgan. After the close of the long-running play, Morgan was seen in numerous Broadway productions, including *Gentle People*, *My Heart's in the Highlands*, *Night Music*, and *Heavenly Express*. But his experience in New York was not always easy.

"Another old friend from Mt. Kisco,

Henry Fonda, was also in New York," Morgan told *TV Guide* in 1984. "He got me an agent and pushed me for a bunch of roles. But overall, after the dust cleared, I was better off hustling desks. I remember one year in New York when I was in three plays on Broadway.... And I made less than $1,000 for that whole year. The most I ever made in New York was 75 bucks a week. It was exciting, until the kids started coming and we needed to eat."

In 1941, Morgan moved his family to Hollywood, where he got a helping hand from Frances Farmer, who had already begun to establish herself in films.

"She fed us, lent us money, introduced us around," Morgan recalled.

While performing in a one-act play in David O. Selznick's summer stock company, Morgan was spotted by talent scouts from 20th Century-Fox, who signed him to a contract and cast him in *To the Shores of Tripoli* (1942), a rousing wartime drama starring John Payne and Maureen O'Hara. He was next seen in small roles in *Orchestra Wives* (1942), a behind-the-scenes look at a swing band; *The Omaha Trail* (1942), a passable western starring James Craig; *The Loves of Edgar Allan Poe* (1942), starring Shepperd Strudwick (credited as John Shepperd) in the title role; and, what he considered the best film of his career—*The Ox-Bow Incident* (1943).

"Hank Fonda helped me again out here as well," Morgan later said. "He got me into *Ox-Bow*—we rode into the film together."

After *The Ox-Bow Incident*, Morgan appeared in a number of such high-quality films as *State Fair* (1945), a delightful musical with Jeanne Crain and Dana Andrews; *A Bell for Adano* (1945), a touching depiction of World War I soldiers in Italy; and *Dragonwyck* (1946), an atmospheric gothic tale starring Vincent Price and Gene Tierney. Less successful were *Roger Touhy, Gangster* (1944), an all-but-forgotten crime drama starring Preston Foster, and *Avalanche* (1946), a tiresome, low-budget mystery whose main attraction was a trained raven who picked up bar glasses in its

beak. Also during this period, Morgan entered the realm of film noir, playing a bit part as a bathhouse attendance in *Somewhere in the Night* (1946), and a featured role the following year in *The Gangster* (1947), starring Barry Sullivan and Belita. In this unusual entry from the noir era, Sullivan portrayed a neurotic gangster known as Shubunka, who finds his world turned upside down when his territory is threatened by a rival (Sheldon Leonard). In a film rife with offbeat characters, Morgan was no different; he portrayed Shorty, an employee of the ice cream parlor frequented by Shubunka. A self-proclaimed "ladies' man," Shorty's primary function in the film centered on his alleged romantic prowess and his ultimately fruitless pursuit of a flirtatious widow: "One thing about me, whenever I go out on a date, I always dress immaculate," Shorty boasts in one scene. "I take 'em out in style. Treat 'em like a queen. Chop suey for dinner, see a show. Oh, sure — psychology. Puts 'em in a frame of mind where they naturally feel obligated, dontcha know." Although Morgan earned brief mention in a handful of reviews, the film was panned by reviewers, including Virginia Wright of the *Los Angeles Daily News*, who faulted *The Gangster*'s "choppy, excessively wordy script."

During the next two years, Morgan was seen in a series of top-notch features, including *Yellow Sky* (1948), which won the Writers Guild award for Best Written American Western of the year; *All My Sons* (1948), a riveting drama with Edward G. Robinson and Burt Lancaster; *Madame Bovary* (1949), a period piece with Jennifer Jones in the title role; and *Down to the Sea in Ships* (1949), an sea saga featuring Richard Widmark and Lionel Barrymore. He was also seen during this period in two more films noirs: *The Big Clock* (1948) and *Moonrise* (1949).

In the first, *The Big Clock*, Morgan was featured as Bill Womack, a taciturn but deadly masseuse who works for publishing mogul Earl Janoth (Charles Laughton). When Janoth kills his lover (Rita Johnson), he craftily directs his crime magazine staff— headed by

editor George Stroud (Ray Milland)—to un-earth the killer. As it turns out, the staff stum-bles on a series of clues that point to Stroud, who had been out on the town with the dead woman on the night of her murder. As Stroud desperately tries to identify the real killer, he is stalked by Womack, acting on orders from Janoth. Stroud ultimately exposes Janoth, but when the publisher tries to escape, he plunges down an elevator shaft to his death.

Morgan's next noir, *Moonrise*, was set in a small Southern town and focused on the life of Danny Hawkins (Dane Clark), who suffered years of physical and emotional tor-ture after his father was hanged for murder during his childhood. As an adult, Danny kills one of his chief tormentors, Jerry Sykes (Lloyd Bridges), during a fight, and buries his body in a nearby marsh. Although Danny is befriended by local schoolteacher Gilly Johnson (Gail Russell), he grows increasingly paranoid after Jerry's body is found, and nearly strangles a deaf-mute man, Billy Scrip-ture (Morgan), who finds a switchblade that can tie Danny to the murder. After finally confessing his crimes to Gilly, Danny makes plans to flee the town, but he first stops at the home of his grandmother (Ethel Barrymore), who helps him come to terms with his past,

and he later returns to the town to face his future.

Interestingly, although Morgan played pivotal roles in both *The Big Clock* and *Moon-rise*, he did not have a single line of dialogue in either. His performances were mostly over-looked by critics, but of the two features, *The Big Clock* earned the best reviews, with Bos-ley Crowther labeling it "a seventeen-jewel entertainment guaranteed to give a good — if not perfect time," and Lowell E. Redelings assuring readers of the *Hollywood Citizen-News* that the film "will completely satisfy most moviegoers." Critics were less impressed with *Moonrise*, however; the reviewer for *Va-riety* described it as "heavy melodrama, well made, but too drab," and the *New York Times'* critic dismissed the film "a clouded tale filled largely with pallid people."

With the onset of the 1950s, Morgan continued his non-stop film schedule with appearances in *The Showdown* (1950), a Re-public Studios western starring Bill Elliot; *The Blue Veil* (1951), an episodic drama star-ring Jane Wyman; *The Well* (1951), which ex-amined racial tensions in a small town; *What Price Glory?* (1952), a wartime feature directed by John Ford; and *High Noon* (1952), the ac-claimed western starring Gary Cooper and Grace Kelly. The early 1950s also saw Mor-gan's final run of films noirs: *Red Light* (1950), *Dark City* (1950), *Appointment with Danger* (1951), and *Scandal Sheet* (1952).

In *Red Light*, Morgan enjoyed his showi-est noir role to date, portraying Rocky, an ex-convict who is dispatched by a prison pal to commit a murder of revenge. An unusual noir entry with a heavy religious undertone, *Red Light* centered on the quest of a truck-ing company owner, Johnny Torno (George Raft), to find the killer of his Army chaplain brother (Arthur Franz). Torno's search even-tually leads him to Nick Cherney (Raymond Burr), a former accountant for the trucking firm who was imprisoned after Torno caught him embezzling from the company. Torno also sets a trap to nab Rocky, shooting him as he flees his run-down apartment and after this encounter, Rocky tells Nick he is no longer working for him: "I'm through. I ain't no clay pigeon. All I'm gettin' outta this is a lot of bad health. You gotta get another boy. I'm retirin'— on full pay." For his troubles, Rocky gets pushed from a moving train — and later, shot — by Nick, but he survives long enough to point the finger at the man who hired him, who dies a short time later while fleeing police. Upon the release of this feature, Morgan earned good reviews from critics, including Lloyd L. Sloan of the *Hollywood Citizen-News*, who included the actor in his praise of the film's supporting cast: "Most credit goes to Henry Morgan, Arthur Franz, Arthur Shields, Frank Oth, Philip Pine and Paul Frees for their realistic bits."

Years after the release of *Red Light*, Morgan admitted that he enjoyed playing characters on the wrong side of the law.

"I didn't get to be a heavy very often," the actor said, "but when I did, it was fun. I did three pictures with George Raft, worked with Raymond Burr in two. We pushed people around, snarled. I tell you, we were *bad*. We had a helluva time."

Morgan's second noir of 1950, *Dark City*, centered on a trio of con men whose fleecing of traveling salesman Arthur Winant (Don DeFore) during a poker game leads to the man's suicide. Morgan played a "punchy" ex-boxer named Soldier, who chastises the men for their role in the salesman's death, and he willingly gives out the address of their hangout when an anonymous call comes in: "I was hoping it was the cops," Soldier tells the men. "'Cause I wish somebody would come down and kill the whole murderin' lot of you. The lieutenant was a good guy! You didn't have to right to cheat him." As it turns out, the anonymous caller was the salesman's psychotic brother, Sidney (Mike Mazurki), who proceeds to stalk the con men, killing two of them and trailing the third, Danny Haley (Charlton Heston, in his film debut), as he tries to find the murderer before becoming his next victim. Finally, after first eschewing the help of local authorities, Danny turns to police for help and acts as a decoy for Sidney, nearly losing his life before police gun down

the killer. For his performance in this feature, Morgan received little notice, but he was singled out by the critic for *Variety*, who wrote: "Others adding to the generally okay story telling include Jack Webb, Ed Begley, Henry Morgan and Mike Mazurki."

Morgan's sixth noir, *Appointment with Danger*, starred Alan Ladd as U.S. postal inspector Al Goddard, who is investigating the murder of his co-worker. Goddard soon discovers that a local nun, Sister Augustine (Phyllis Calvert), can identify the gang members responsible for the killing, Joe Regas (Jack Webb) and George Soderquist (Morgan). After Soderquist barely manages to escape from a policeman who is tailing him, Regas and the leader of their gang, Earl Boettiger (Paul Stewart), insist that he leave town. Soderquist balks, however, and his partner in crime proceeds to beat him to death with a bronze baby shoe. (Ironically, only moments before, Soderquist had shared with Regas and Boettiger that the baby shoe belonged to his son: "You know it was terrible how his mother took him away. She just up and left one night and I didn't see him since. But I still had a picture. And the baby shoes, the way they fix 'em up with bronze for a keepsake.") Meanwhile, Goddard infiltrates the mob, but his cover is blown by Sister Augustine, who has been kidnapped by Regas. During a shootout, Goddard is nearly killed by Boettiger, but police arrive, gunning down the gang leader in the nick of time.

After earning mention for his "capable" and "competent" work in *Appointment with Danger*, Morgan made his final film noir appearance in the Broderick Crawford starrer, *Scandal Sheet*. In this well-done feature, Morgan played Biddle, a hard-boiled newspaper photographer whose outlook toward his profession is revealed early on when he shows up at the scene where a woman has been murdered: "You know, that wasn't a bad-lookin' dame," he remarks. "Too bad the guy used an ax on her head — spoiled some pretty pictures for me." In addition to Biddle, *Scandal Sheet* featured a core of intriguing characters, including ambitious newspaper editor Mark

Chapman (Crawford); his bitter, long-estranged wife (Rosemary DeCamp); the newspaper's star reporter, Steve Cleary (John Derek); and Charlie Barnes (Henry O'Neill), a one-time Pulitzer Prize–winning reporter whose career ended because of his alcoholism. The film's story focuses on Chapman, who accidentally kills his wife during an argument and desperately tries to conceal his role in the crime, even as Cleary works to land a scoop for the newspaper by finding the killer. As he continues to cover his tracks, Chapman is forced to kill again — this time, the victim is Barnes, who discovered Chapman's guilt. Ultimately, Cleary succeeds in fingering Chapman for both killings, and the editor is shot to death in his newspaper office after pulling a gun on police.

During the remainder of the decade, Morgan was seen in such features as *The Forty-Niners* (1954), a low-budget western in which he portrayed a crooked gambler; *About Mrs. Leslie* (1954), a memorable tearjerker starring Shirley Booth in the title role; *The Glenn Miller Story* (1954), the hit biopic about the famed bandleader; *Not As a Stranger* (1955), starring Robert Mitchum and Frank Sinatra; and *The Teahouse of the August Moon* (1956), an amusing comedy starring Marlon Brando. Also during this period, Morgan started what would become a successful career on the small screen, beginning with a featured role in the television sitcom *December Bride*.

"You go where the jobs are," Morgan said once. "Not always by preference."

On *December Bride*, which starred screen veteran Spring Byington, Morgan portrayed Pete Porter, neighbor of the title character and the henpecked spouse of his never-seen wife, Gladys. When he accepted the role, Morgan changed his name again, this time returning to his given name of Harry, to avoid confusion with the Henry Morgan who was at that time a regular on the popular game show *What's My Line?* With his new moniker, Morgan remained with the popular CBS series until 1959.

"It was very pleasant—five years went by like one," Morgan told *TV Guide* in 1967.

His experience on the show wasn't all fun and games, however; after four years on the show, Morgan recalled, he had to fight for a raise in salary. "I said, 'If I don't get it, I'm leaving,' They said, 'You'll never work again.' I said, 'I don't give a damn. I'll go back to Michigan where I was born and be a toolmaker like my old man.' And I would have."

In 1960, after *December Bride* ended its five-year run, Morgan reprised his role as Pete Porter in *Pete and Gladys*, one of television's first spin-offs. For this series, Pete's wife was brought to life by actress Cara Williams, who became known for her temperamental behavior.

"Let's just say I wasn't sorry to see it end," Morgan later said of the two-year series.

After the cancellation of *Pete and Gladys*, Morgan wasted no time in signing on as one of 11 repertory players on *The Richard Boone Show* (1963), a drama series that presented a play each week. The following year, Morgan was cast as a regular in *Kentucky Jones* (1964), a comedy-drama starring Dennis Weaver in the title role. Like *The Richard Boone Show*, *Kentucky Jones* was canceled after one season.

Morgan didn't lack employment, however. Since his 1954 television debut, the actor had continued to appear in feature films, including such hits as *Inherit the Wind* (1960), a top-notch courtroom drama starring Spencer Tracy as lawyer Henry Drummond and Fredric March as fundamentalist Matthew Harrison Brady, and *How the West Was Won* (1962), a big-budget western with a star-studded cast that included Lee J. Cobb, Henry Fonda, Gregory Peck, Debbie Reynolds, James Stewart, Richard Widmark, John Wayne, and Thelma Ritter. But Morgan also appeared in a series of duds: *John Goldfarb, Please Come Home* (1965), a rather silly football farce; *What Did You Do in the War, Daddy?* (1966), a lame wartime comedy, directed by Blake Edwards and written by William Peter Blatty (later to gain fame as author of *The Exorcist*); and *Frankie and Johnny* (1966), a mediocre Elvis Presley vehicle. The actor rebounded from these box-office disappointments, however, when he returned to series television for one of his best-remembered roles— Officer Bill Gannon in *Dragnet*.

Along with Jack Webb, who starred as the laconic Sgt. Joe Friday, Morgan was seen on the enormously popular cop series for the next four years. He also reprised his role on a made-for-TV movie of the same name in 1969. When *Dragnet* ended its run in 1970, Morgan focused most of his energies on the small screen, appearing as Doc Coogan in the series *Hec Ramsey*, and in such TV movies as *But I Don't Want to Get Married!* (1970), *The Feminist and the Fuzz* (1971), *The Last Day* (1975), *Murder at the Mardi Gras* (1977), and *Maneaters Are Loose!* (1978). He was also seen in two well-received mini-series, *Backstairs at the White House* (1979) and *Roots: The Next Generations* (1979), and worked as director on several episodes of such series as *Adam-12* and *The D.A.* But Morgan's longest-running and, perhaps, most beloved role came in 1975 when he was cast in the popular television series *M*A*S*H*.

"I didn't come [to the cast] until the fourth year," Morgan said in a 1992 interview in *Parade* magazine, "and I don't know just why they called me, to be perfectly frank. In the third year, I played a sort of crazy general in one episode, and they liked me. Then, six or seven months later, McLean Stevenson was leaving, and they needed a replacement— not precisely for him, but a new character— and they called me."

Morgan remained with the show until the end of its run in 1983, and later recalled the experience as "totally wonderful … the most rewarding thing I've ever done."

"People forget your movies," the actor said. "But it's funny. I still get reactions from people for four [television] shows. Some people remember *December Bride* and when they see me they say, 'Hi, Pete!' You'd think they'd never seen *M*A*S*H*! Other people remember the same character from *Pete and Gladys*. Others remember me from *Dragnet*. And then, of course, there is *M*A*S*H*… . Nothing I have done compared in overall quality to *M*A*S*H*."

When *M*A*S*H* ended, Morgan signed on with co-stars Jamie Farr and Bill Christopher for *AfterMASH*, which reunited three of the characters from the original series in a Midwestern hospital. Although the series debuted as the top show of the 1983-84 season, its ratings later plummeted and it was cancelled after only a year.

"After *AfterMASH*, I quit," Morgan said in 1984. "I'm not gonna produce or direct or write or roam the globe. I'll spend a lot of time with my wife, our four sons and their wives, and my seven grandchildren."

Still, throughout the 1970s and 1980s, Morgan continued his appearances in both television movies and feature films, including *The Apple Dumpling Gang* (1975), a Disney comedy starring Don Knotts, and its sequel *The Apple Dumpling Gang Rides Again* (1979); *The Shootist* (1976), John Wayne's final movie; and *Dragnet* (1987), a comedy spoof of the television series, starring Dan Aykroyd and Tom Hanks. In the latter, Morgan was seen in a cameo role as Bill Gannon, now promoted to captain.

"The movie's played for comedy, but it's a reverent treatment," Morgan said of the *Dragnet* film.

Morgan gave series television another try in 1986 when he starred with Hal Linden in *Blacke's Magic*, which focused on a magician and his con-man father who solve mysteries using a combination of sleight of hand and con games. The show's premise was an interesting one, but viewers failed to tune in and the series was canceled after its first year.

With the onset of the 1990s, Morgan entered his sixth decade of performing; he guested on such television series as *The Simpsons* and *3rd Rock from the Sun*, and portrayed the role of Judge Stoddard Bell in three made-for-television movies, *The Incident* (1990), *Against Her Will: An Incident in Baltimore* (1992), and *Incident in a Small Town* (1994).

Now in his 80s, Morgan seemed to show no signs of winding down his acting career, but in the mid-1990s, the actor was making news for more than his longevity in the entertainment industry. A year after the 1985 death of his first wife, Eileen, Morgan had remarried; wife number two was Barbara Quine, the daughter of silent screen star Francis X. Bushman. Shortly after midnight on July 2, 1996, police arrived at Morgan's Brentwood home in response to a 911 call placed by his 70-year-old wife. Officers reportedly heard a woman's screams as they approached the house; inside they found Barbara Morgan with an injured left foot, a small cut near her right eye, and a bruised arm. Barbara told police that the couple had argued at a dinner party earlier that evening, and their disagreement turned violent when they returned home. Morgan was arrested and charged with misdemeanor spousal battery. His attorney, Harland Braun, later told the press that the incident was not the first time that the couple had battled, adding that they had engaged in mutual incidents of violence throughout their nine-year marriage.

"Harry admits he was being verbally abusive, but he didn't hit her. He was trying to stop her from throwing things around the house when something fell on her foot and injured her," Braun said. "Mr. and Mrs. Morgan will go to joint counseling. They are both going in to learn how to get along. They will be able to vent their feelings."

Morgan pleaded not guilty to the battery charge and a jury trial was set, but the charges were dropped in June 1997 after the actor completed a six-month counseling program for domestic violence and anger management.

On the silver screen, Morgan's most recent appearance to date was in *Family Plan* (1997), a comedy starring Leslie Nielsen. He has remained out of the public eye since his participation in a 2002 *M*A*S*H* documentary, but he continues to delight a new generation of fans who enjoy reruns of *Dragnet* or *M*A*S*H*, or catch Morgan's performance in one of his nearly 60 feature films. Morgan's long-reaching impact on *M*A*S*H* was demonstrated in 1998, when a poll of *TV Guide* viewers indicated that viewers' favorite TV boss was Morgan's Col. Potter, who beat out such beloved characters as

Sheriff Andy Taylor on *The Andy Griffith Show* and Lou Grant on *The Mary Tyler Moore Show*. As for Morgan, he views his long and prolific career with philosophical appreciation.

"I look back on my life and I know that it could have been better, it could have been worse," the actor said once. "I think it's winding up real well, which is the best way to go…. We had some rough times, my family and I…. But when I think back on those years, I don't remember the bad times. I remember all the good things that have happened to us, all the wonderful people we've met, all the work we've done."

Film Noir Filmography

Somewhere in the Night. Director: Joseph L. Mankiewicz. Producer: Anderson Lawler. Running time: 110 minutes. Released by 20th Century–Fox, June 12, 1946. Cast: John Hodiak, Nancy Guild, Lloyd Nolan, Richard Conte, Josephine Hutchinson, Fritz Kortner, Margo Woode, Sheldon Leonard, Lou Nova, John Russell, Houseley Stevenson, Charles Arnt, Al Sparlis, Jeff Corey, Henry Morgan.

The Gangster. Director: Gordon Wiles. Producers: Maurice and Frank King. Running time: 84 minutes. Released by Allied Artists, October 1947. Cast: Barry Sullivan, Belita, Joan Lorring, Akim Tamiroff, Henry Morgan, John Ireland, Fifi D'Orsay, Virginia Christine, Sheldon Leonard, Leif Erickson, Charles McGraw, John Kellogg, Elisha Cook, Jr., Ted Hecht, Jeff Corey.

Appointment with Danger. Director: Lewis Allen. Producer: Robert Fellows. Running time: 89 minutes. Released by Paramount, May 9, 1951. Cast: Alan Ladd, Phyllis Calvert, Paul Stewart, Jan Sterling, Jack Webb, Stacy Harris, Henry Morgan, David Wolfe, Dan Riss, Harry Antrim, Paul Lees.

The Big Clock. Director: John Farrow. Producer: Richard Maibaum. Running time: 93 minutes. Released by Paramount, April 9, 1948. Cast: Ray Milland, Charles Laughton, Maureen O'Sullivan, George Macready, Rita Johnson, Elsa Lanchester, Harold Vermilyea, Dan Tobin, Henry Morgan, Richard Webb, Tad Van Brunt, Elaine Riley, Luis Van Rooten, Lloyd Corrigan, Margaret Field, Philip Van Zandt, Henri Letondal, Douglas Spencer.

Moonrise. Director: Frank Borzage. Producer: Charles Haas. Running time: 90 minutes. Released by Republic Pictures, March 6, 1949. Cast: Dane Clark, Gail Russell, Ethel Barrymore, Allyn Joslyn,

Rex Ingram, Henry Morgan, David Street, Selena Royle, Harry Carey, Jr., Irving Bacon, Lloyd Bridges, Houseley Stevenson, Phil Brown, Harry V. Cheshire, Lila Leeds. Awards: Academy Award nomination for Best Sound Recording (Republic Sound Department).

Red Light. Director: Roy Del Ruth. Producer: Roy Del Ruth. Running time: 84 minutes. Released by United Artists, January 15, 1950. Cast: George Raft, Virginia Mayo, Gene Lockhart, Barton MacLane, Henry Morgan, Raymond Burr, Arthur Franz, Arthur Shields, Frank Orth, Philip Pine, Movita Castenada, Paul Frees, Claire Carleton, Soledad Jiminez.

Dark City. Director: William Dieterle. Producer: Hal Wallis. Running time: 98 minutes. Released by Paramount, October 18, 1950. Cast: Charlton Heston, Lizabeth Scott, Viveca Lindfors, Dean Jagger, Don DeFore, Jack Webb, Ed Begley, Henry Morgan, Walter Sande, Mark Keuning, Mike Mazurki, Stanley Prager, Walter Burke.

Scandal Sheet. Director: Phil Karlson. Producer: Edward Small. Running time: 82 minutes. Released by Columbia, January 16, 1952. Cast: John Derek, Donna Reed, Broderick Crawford, Rosemary DeCamp, Henry O'Neill, Henry Morgan, James Millican, Griff Barnett, Jonathan Hale, Pierre Watkin, Ida Moore, Ralph Reed, Luther Crockett, Charles Cane, Jay Adler, Don Beddoe.

References

"Actor Harry Morgan Accused of Beating Wife." *Los Angeles Times*, July 11, 1996.

"All the Best of CBS." *TV Guide*, May 16, 1998.

Brady, James. "In Step with Harry Morgan." *Parade* Magazine, June 7, 1992.

Daley, Steve. "Harry Morgan: Proof Positive He's a Man of Versatility." *L.A. Life, Daily News*, March 3, 1986.

DuBrow, Rick. "From Officer to Colonel to Captain." *Los Angeles Herald-Examiner*, June 26, 1987.

Fessier, Mike Jr. "You Ought to See What They've Got Harry Doing Now." *TV Guide*, May 6, 1967.

Herz, Peggy. "A Smashing Career Peak." *American Way*, June 1982.

Hicks, Jack. "He Rode with Henry Fonda, Snarled with George Raft, Drank with Jack Webb." *TV Guide*, April 28, 1984.

"MASH Star's Domestic Abuse Case Dropped." *Los Angeles Times*, June 26, 1997.

"Morgan Plea Entered." *Los Angeles Times*, July 24, 1996.

"No Small Incidents." *Los Angeles Times*, January 23, 1984.

TOM NEAL

"Thumbing rides may save you bus fare. But it's dangerous. You never know what's in store for you when you hear the squeal of brakes." — Tom Neal in *Detour* (1945)

Tom Neal's life was like a movie — a tragic one. He was born with the proverbial "silver spoon," received a quality education at the nation's finest schools — he was the All-American boy. When he decided to pursue an acting career, he had little trouble getting started, and while his films were not usually of top-notch caliber, he at least never wanted for assignments. But his career was cut short due to a romantic entanglement and a volatile temper, he was faced with calamitous circumstances when trying to turn his life around, and he finally wound up imprisoned for killing his wife. Not exactly the stuff of which dreams are made.

Neal is one of only two actors in this publication who boasted a single noir appearance — but his starring role in the noir cult classic *Detour* (1945) earns him a rightful place here.

The luckless actor with the rugged good looks was born on January 18, 1914, in Evanston, Illinois, the first of two children of Mary Martin Neal and her wealthy banker husband, Thomas C. Neal. He attended Lincoln School, Lake Forest Academy, and Northwestern University before graduating in 1934 from Harvard University. While at college he excelled at track, golf, tennis, skiing, and boxing, and made All-American on the football team. Neal's interest in acting was first demonstrated through his performances in college plays, and after his graduation, he did summer theater in the Catskills, toured in the play *The Old Maid*, and appeared in a number of short-lived productions, including *Spring Dance* starring Jose Ferrer, and *Summer Nights* with Louis Calhern. While playing a featured role in *Love Is Not Simple*, he attracted the notice of MGM talent scout Martin Stein, who arranged for a screen test and promptly signed the 24-year-old to a contract.

Neal made his screen debut in *Out West with the Hardys* (1938), the fourth in the long-running *Andy Hardy* series, followed by *Burn 'Em Up O'Connor* (1938), starring Dennis O'Keefe and Cecilia Parker. The following year, he appeared in nearly a dozen films, mostly forgettable, including *Four Girls in White* (1939), a so-so hospital drama, and *They All Come Out* (1939), which started out as a short in the *Crime Does Not Pay* series and was expanded to a full-length feature. His best performance that year came in *Within the Law* (1939), for which the critic in *Variety* wrote: "Tom Neal, displaying a rugged and vigorous personality similar to John Garfield, gets his first crack at a lead and puts it over most competently."

By now, Neal had established himself as a reliable member of the MGM family, and his efforts were rewarded when he was cast in the big-budget Joan Crawford–Clark Gable starrer *Strange Cargo* (1940). Instead of capitalizing on his big break, however, Neal made the first of many mistakes. Before filming began, Neal made an unwelcome pass at Crawford, who reported the incident to MGM chief Louis B. Mayer. Neal was unceremoniously removed from the film, replaced by actor John Aldridge, and as additional punishment, was loaned out to RKO for *Courageous Dr. Christian* (1940), starring Jean Hersholt. Although Neal received good notices for his performance, he was dropped by MGM after small roles in just three more pictures.

Before long, Neal was picked up by Columbia Studios, and in his first film there, *Under Age* (1941), he earned praise in *Variety* for his "life-like character" portrayal. This film was followed by another series of mediocre features including *Jungle Girl* (1941), a Republic serial; *Bowery at Midnight* (1942), an often-confusing but appropriately scary film starring Bela Lugosi; and *There's Something About a Soldier* (1943), in which he starred opposite Evelyn Keyes. Although Neal was still not on his way to star status, he was nonetheless kept busy, and also appeared in a number of films featuring such Hollywood elite as John Wayne in *Flying Tigers* (1942), Gary Cooper in *Pride of the Yankees* (1942), Gene Tierney in *China Girl* (1942), John Garfield in *Air Force* (1943), and Claudette Colbert and Fred MacMurray in *No Time for Love* (1943).

Another big break appeared to come Neal's way in 1943 when he was cast in RKO's *Behind the Rising Sun*, in an interesting cast that included Margo, J. Carroll Naish, Robert Ryan, and Mike Mazurki. Termed by one reviewer as an anti-war feature focusing on how the "Japanese military machine ... can turn an upright and honorable man into a snarling and killing cur," this film was a huge box-office success and earned Neal some of the best notices of his career. He followed it up, however, with starring roles in a series of duds, including *Klondike Kate* (1943), *The Racket Man* (1944), and *Two-Man Submarine* (1944).

But the highlight of Neal's film performances was just ahead. In 1945, he starred opposite Ann Savage in his sole film noir, *Detour*, a grim story about a hard-luck everyman who makes wrong choices and finds himself caught up in circumstances beyond his control — not unlike Neal himself. As the film begins, Neal's Al Roberts, a New York piano player, decides to follow his fiancée, Sue (Claudia Drake), to Hollywood, where she plans to seek fame and fortune as a singer. But his trip to the coast turns out to be more than Al bargained for. After he hitches a ride, the car's driver, Charles Haskell, Jr. (Edmund MacDonald), inexplicably dies and Al, fearing he will be blamed for the death, hides the body and intends to assume the man's identity. But a monkey wrench is thrown into his plan when he picks up a woman, Vera (Ann Savage), who just happens to be an acquaintance of the dead man. Vera learns that Haskell was the heir of a dying millionaire and blackmails Al into continuing his impersonation in order to collect the money, but while holed up in a dilapidated Los Angeles apartment, Al and Vera quarrel and he accidentally strangles her with a telephone cord. Without ever seeing the fiancée whom he'd originally intended to join, Al flees to Reno, where the film's end finds him sitting morosely in a diner: "I keep trying to forget what happened, and wonder what my life might've been like if that car of Haskell's hadn't stopped. But one thing I don't have to wonder about. I know. Some day a car will stop to pick me up that I never thumbed." As Al speaks these words in the final reel, he is seen climbing in the back of a highway patrol car.

A low-budget feature that cost only about $20,000 to make, *Detour* turned out to be one of the sleepers of the year, and decades later, ranks among film noir's most famous entries. Upon its release, the film was labeled "one of the most poignant and disturbing stories to reach the screen in any year," and Neal was singled out for praise in numerous reviews; the critic for *Variety* said he "does well with a difficult role that rates him a break in something better," and the *Los Angeles Times* reviewer wrote: "Tom Neal grips you with every move and facial expression."

However, as much as *Detour* was the highlight of Neal's career, it also marked the turning point. He continued his spate of non-stop filming, but the only picture of note was *First Yank Into Tokyo* (1945), the first American film to depict the atomic attack on Japan. After this picture, Neal returned to his roots on the stage, touring during the summer of 1945 with Miriam Hopkins in *Laura*, portraying the role popularized by Dana Andrews in the 1944 film. Back in Hollywood after the tour ended, Neal was signed to a contract by Universal, starring opposite Martha O'Driscoll in a silly whodunit, *Blonde Alibi* (1946), and in *The Brute Man* (1946), with disfigured

character actor Rondo Hattan, who died before the film was released. During the shooting of this gruesome feature, Universal merged with International Pictures and, along with most of the studio's contract players, Neal was dropped. He spent the next several years playing lackluster roles in mediocre films for such poverty row studios as Monogram, PRC, and Lippert, which signed him to a contract. His only features for major studios during this era were Paramount's *Beyond Glory* (1948), a passable drama starring Alan Ladd and Donna Reed, and *Bruce Gentry, Daredevil of the Skies* (1949), a Columbia serial in which Neal portrayed the title role.

Off screen, Neal married for the first time in 1948, to actress Vicki Lane, whose best screen role was probably her portrayal of a half-ape, half-woman in Universal's *The Jungle Captive* (1945). The couple divorced in 1950. The following year, Neal was introduced to actress Barbara Payton at a party — the meeting would signal the onset of a drastic descent in the actor's personal life. Payton, a buxom, attractive blonde, was well on her way to a promising screen career, having starred opposite James Cagney in *Kiss Tomorrow Goodbye* (1950) and with Gregory Peck in *Only the Valiant* (1951). At the time of their meeting, Payton was involved with actor Franchot Tone, but she and Neal plunged headlong into a whirlwind romance and after just a few weeks, Payton ended her relationship with Tone by announcing to the press that she and Neal were engaged. The actress then changed her mind and again became involved with Tone, only to once more reverse her affections two months later and return to Neal. The couple told the press that they would marry on September 14, 1951.

On the night before the wedding was to take place, Neal learned that Payton was on a date with Tone, and he waited at Payton's home for their return. According to newspaper accounts, Payton and Tone arrived at her house in the pre-dawn hours and Neal confronted them on the front lawn. An argument ensued and, while there was dispute about who threw the first punch, the facts are plain

that Neal's battering left Tone with a brain concussion, a broken nose, and fractured cheekbones. The enraged actor struck Payton as well.

Neal was arrested and charged with "using his fists as a weapon." In addition, Tone sued him for $150,000. Although Payton visited the ailing Tone in the hospital and tearfully declared her love for him to the press, newspapers reported just days after the incident that she was once again seeing Neal on the sly. Still, following Tone's release from the hospital, he and Payton were married on September 28, 1951. Afterward, Hedda Hopper commented on the union in her column, saying, "Thank God, now we can all relax." But the story didn't end there.

Just seven weeks later, Payton and Tone separated and were divorced the following May. Meanwhile, after Neal served eight months in the Los Angeles County Prison for the incident, and was ordered to pay Tone $100,000 in damages, he and Payton resumed their volatile relationship. But the scandal had taken its toll on both their careers. Barbara was fired from a Walter Wanger production in which she'd been scheduled to star, *Lady in the Iron Mask* (1952), and was re-

placed by Patricia Medina. Instead, she was loaned out by Warner Bros. for a low-budget horror flick, *Bride of the Gorilla* (1951). Neal found the doors in Hollywood closed to him as well. With only one more picture left on his contract with Lippert, the studio craftily attempted to capitalize on Neal and Payton's notoriety by casting them together in a quickie western, *The Great Jesse James Raid* (1953). It would be Neal's last film appearance. The couple also toured Detroit, Chicago, and Pittsburgh in a production of *The Postman Always Rings Twice*, billed as "The Tempestuous Colorful Hollywood Stars."

In 1953, Neal accompanied Payton to London where she was scheduled to star in an English feature. Neal hoped to make Payton his wife, telling the press of his plans to "marry her and have five or six children," but Payton was less enthusiastic. "Marry Tom?" she was quoted in one article. "I just don't know. My career is so important." During their stay in London, Neal and Payton fought constantly, and Neal ultimately returned to Hollywood alone, finally signaling the end of their turbulent union. (Payton would appear in only three more films. In later years, she was arrested for passing bad checks, turned to alcohol and prostitution, and died in San Diego at the home of her parents in 1967. She was 38 years old.)

As for Neal, after the demise of his relationship with Payton, he moved to Chicago, where he appeared on a local soaper, *A Time to Live*. The following year, he returned to Hollywood but, unable to find work, he moved to Palm Springs, where he worked as night manager in a restaurant.

At this point in Neal's stormy life, things finally began to look up. Having had an interest in gardening since his childhood, he obtained a license for landscape architecture and started a successful landscaping business. "It was tough work at first under the broiling desert sun, but it was worth it," Neal told United Press writer Vernon Scott in 1957. "I really found myself—the first time in my life." Neal also began studying the Christian Science faith and remarried, this time to

Patricia Fenton, a local girl, with whom he had a son, Thomas, Jr. "I'm a very fortunate man," he told Scott. "I wouldn't go back to acting for anything. I've found religion, a good wife and work I can be proud of."

But Neal's happiness wouldn't last. In 1958, Patricia died of cancer, their young son was sent to live with Neal's sister in Evanston, Illinois, and the former actor's life began another downward slide. He began drinking heavily, and in 1961 married Gale Bennett, a former hostess in a tennis club, but the stormy marriage was doomed from the start. His business later failed, and he was forced to file for bankruptcy. Then, in 1965, while Neal was visiting his son in Evanston, his wife filed for divorce. It was upon Neal's return to Palm Springs that things truly took a turn for the worse. On April 2, 1965, newspaper headlines screamed the news that the body of Gail Neal had been found on the living room sofa in the couple's home. She had been shot in the head. Neal was charged with murder.

According to Neal, his wife was accidentally shot while they struggled for a gun that she had pulled on him, angered because of Neal's accusations of infidelity. During Neal's subsequent trial, however, witnesses told a different story. One, the co-owner of a local restaurant, said that Neal had come to his establishment on the night of the shooting and told him: "I shot her. She was napping."

In November 1965, Neal was convicted of involuntary manslaughter and sentenced by Superior Court Judge Hilton H. McCabe to 1 to 10 years at Soledad State Prison. "Even God has to answer to McCabe, I guess," Neal told reporters after the sentencing. "This is his vengeance." The former actor served part of his sentence there, then was assigned to the work-furlough program at the state's Institution for Men in Chino, California, where he was paroled in December 1971.

Following his six-year imprisonment, Neal, now appearing far older than his years, returned to Hollywood, where he took up residence with his then-15-year-old son. He told reporters that he planned to join an Encino-based television firm, but it wasn't

to be. Just eight months after his parole, on August 7, 1972, Neal was found dead in his bed by his son. An autopsy later determined that he died of heart failure.

Ironically, almost two decades after his father's death, Tom Neal, Jr., starred in a remake of his father's best-remembered film, *Detour*, playing the same role of the hapless musician that his father had portrayed in the mid-1940s. The remake, unfortunately, failed to live up to the original and after playing in limited theatrical release in 1992, was finally released to video in 1998.

There are few Hollywood stories as grim and relentless as the life of Tom Neal. Like the character he played in his famed film noir, he often seemed caught up in circumstances beyond his control. In a description of the character his father played, Tom Neal, Jr., seemed to accurately typify his father's fate as well: "[He wasn't] a loser in the classic sense — he's a guy in a jam. And once he gets there, there's no getting out."

Film Noir Filmography

Detour. Director: Edgar G. Ulmer. Producer: Leon Fromkess. Running time: 68 minutes. Released by PRC, November 30, 1945. Cast: Tom Neal, Ann Savage, Claudia Drake, Edmund MacDonald, Tim Ryan, Roger Clark, Pat Gleason.

References

"10-Year Term Asked for Neal." *New York Daily News*, January 15, 1966.
"Actor Tom Neal; Fight Killed Career." *Newark Evening News*, August 8, 1972.
"Actor Tom Neal Guilty of Manslaughter in Wife Shooting." *New York Journal-American*, November 19, 1965.
Broeske, Pat H. " The Son Also Takes a 'Detour.'" *Los Angeles Times*, September 25, 1988.
Dolven, Frank. "Tom Neal: The Life and Times of a Rogue Actor." *The Big Reel*, March 1996.
"Ex-Actor Neal Held in Wife's Slaying." *New York World-Telegram and Sun*, April 2, 1965.
"Ex-Actor Tom Neal, Survivor of Famous Love Triangle, Dies." *Los Angeles Times*, August 8, 1972.

"Franchot Tone Asks Action Against Neal." *New York Herald Tribune*, September 25, 1951.

"Franchot Tone Tells Police About Fight." *New York Herald Tribune*, September 17, 1951.

"Neal Charged with Murder." *New York Daily News*, April 6, 1965.

"Neal Gets 1 to 15 Yrs. As Wife Killer." *New York Daily News*, circa November 1965.

"Neal Loves Babs, She Loves Job." *New York Journal-American*, circa 1953.

Obituary. *Variety*, August 8, 1972.

Roberts, Barrie. "Tom Neal: Unlucky in Love." *Classic Images*, March 1995.

"Rumor Payton-Tone Affair Palls As She Dates Neal." *New York Morning Telegraph*, September 22, 1951.

Scott, Vernon. "Tom Neal Cultivates New Life." *New York World Telegram*, November 15, 1957.

"Tom Neal, Actor, Beat Franchot Tone." *New York Times*, August 8, 1972.

"Tom Neal Dies; Actor Paroled in '71." *Philadelphia Daily News*, August 6, 1972.

"Tom Neal Dies in the Shade." *New York Daily News*, August 8, 1972.

"Tom Neal Is Convicted in the Killing of His Wife." *New York Times*, November 19, 1965.

"Tom Neal's Death Ends Violent Life." *Los Angeles Herald-Examiner*, August 7, 1972.

LLOYD NOLAN

"I'll be a good cop. After tonight."— Lloyd Nolan in *Lady in the Lake* (1947)

With appearances in nearly 100 films, most of which are scarcely remembered today, Lloyd Nolan was known as the actor who gave "A" performances in "B" films. However, the respected character actor was not only seen in such notable features as *Guadalcanal Diary* (1943), *A Tree Grows in Brooklyn* (1945), and *Peyton Place* (1957), he also appeared in the popular, groundbreaking television series, *Julia*, and won an Emmy for his portrayal of Captain Queeg in the televised drama, *The Caine Mutiny Court-Martial*. Still, the actor's energies were not strictly focused on his prolific career; late in his life, the father of two turned a secret family tragedy into outspoken advocacy after revealing that his son was one of the nation's first children to be diagnosed with autism.

Unlike most noir actors, Nolan rarely played the heavy; he holds the distinction, in fact, of being the only actor from the period to portray a featured role as an officer of the law in each of his film appearances. But although he played smart, unyielding, and dogged cops in three of his films noirs— *The House on 92nd Street* (1945), *Somewhere in the Night* (1946), and *The Street with No Name* (1948) — in the fourth, *Lady in the Lake* (1947), Nolan offered a memorable portrait of a deadly detective that was a dramatic departure from his more upstanding noir roles.

Once labeled "Hollywood's most popular forgotten man," Lloyd Benedict Nolan was born in San Francisco, California, on August 11, 1902, the son of a shoe manufacturer. The great San Francisco earthquake hit the city when Nolan was just four years old — "At that age, I thought it was fun," he once recalled.

After five years at Santa Clara Preparatory School, Nolan enrolled at Stanford University, where he appeared in his first production, *The Hottentot*. According to most accounts, Nolan was more focused on college dramatics than he was on his school work.

"I always wanted to act. My father was in the shoe business and he wanted me to go in with him, but I worked at the store in the summertime and found it very distasteful," Nolan said in a 1969 article. "At Stanford, all I did was dramatics, but they didn't give any credit for that. Finally, the president and I had a little chat about my grades. 'Why don't you act?' he said. 'That's what you want to do most.'"

Nolan promptly left Stanford and signed on with the Pasadena Playhouse, appearing during the next year alongside such seasoned performers as Victor Jory and Helen Brooks, then joined the road company of *The Front Page* for a 32-week engagement in Chicago. When this stint was over, Nolan took a job as a stagehand at the Dennis Theater in Cape Cod, Massachusetts.

"I got my first break in a musical called *Cape Cod Follies*," Nolan recalled. "I was painting scenery and stage handling, but I had the best tan of the lot, so I was cast as a pirate. The Shuberts took it to Broadway, but it lasted only a few weeks there. It had youth and vigor and not much else."

During the next few years, the actor appeared in the road company of *High Hat* and a revival of *The Blue and the Grey, or War Is Hell* in Hoboken, New Jersey, and was in stock productions in Cleveland with Helen Hayes and Pat O'Brien. He was also in the Broadway productions of *Reunion in Vienna*, starring Alfred Lunt and Lynn Fontanne, a musical called *Americana*, and a drama entitled *Sweet Stranger*. While playing an office boy in the latter production, Nolan fell in love with Mary Mell Elfird, who portrayed a stenographer in the play.

"Mell and I were in the first and third acts of that show," Nolan once said, "and it gave us the second act to romance in." Nolan and Mell married two years later and went on to have a daughter, Mellinda Joyce, in November 1940, and a son, Jay Benedict, in 1943. The couple remained together for 47 years, until Mell's 1981 death from cancer.

Meanwhile, after the close of *Sweet Stranger*, Nolan landed a role as a small-town bully in the long-running Broadway production of *One Sunday Afternoon*. (Three film versions of the play would be made in subsequent years but, as Nolan noted in 1957, "never with me in it.")

"I was a hit in that show," Nolan said in 1954. "If I could have followed it up with another good part, I think I would have been made."

Instead, the actor followed this success with such short-lived shows as *Raggedy Army*, which closed after two days; *Gentlewoman*, which lasted two weeks; and *The Third Ameri-*

cana Revue, notable only for introducing the hit song "Brother, Can You Spare a Dime?" Finally, Nolan turned his sights to the west.

"I decided, what the hell, I had to eat, so I went to Hollywood," Nolan later recalled.

Armed with his reputation from *One Sunday Afternoon* as "a rough guy no doll could resist," the actor was quickly tapped by Warner Bros. in 1934 to play a gangster for a role in an upcoming film, *Outrage*. As luck would have it, however, the infamous 1930 Production Code was just beginning to be rigidly enforced, imposing a variety of restrictions on what could be shown on film. Among other items, explicit limits were set on the length and manner of kisses, no explicit violence or sexuality was allowed, criminals had to be punished, and religion and the church could not be criticized. Nolan's would-be film debut was promptly cancelled — one can only guess what shocking elements the plot must have contained.

Instead, Nolan signed a contract with Paramount Studios and debuted the following year in *Stolen Harmony* (1935), a musical melodrama about an ex-convict (George Raft) who tours with a dance band and helps police capture a crime gang. Nolan portrayed a hood named Chesty Burrage, who kidnaps the entire band because he longs for a private concert. During the next two years, Nolan was kept busy playing a variety of villainous roles, including a bank robber in *One-Way Ticket* (1935); another kidnapper in *She Couldn't Take It* (1935); a gang leader (who tries to bump off star Fred MacMurray) in *Texas Rangers* (1936); a racketeer in *Exclusive* (1937); and another gangster in *Internes Can't Take Money* (1937). In a rare non-heavy role, Nolan was seen during this period in *Every Day's a Holiday* (1937), written by and starring Mae West, but years later the actor lamented the impact that the Production Code had on the film.

"As a switch, they let me play a police chief in Mae West's first film after the clean-up…. It was widely hailed by the studio as good, clean fun, something for which Mae was not noted," Nolan recalled in 1960. "Pri-

juicy melodrama starring Akim Tamiroff; *King of Alcatraz* (1938), a fast-paced thriller; *Tip-Off Girls* (1938), in which he played a federal agent investigating a series of truck hijackings; *St. Louis Blues* (1939), a Dorothy Lamour musical; and *The Magnificent Fraud* (1939), where he starred as a con man who convinces an actor to impersonate an assassinated South American dictator. Although Nolan was working non-stop in pictures, the actor joked that it took a while for him to be recognized away from the studio.

"A woman finally did, at a bar, turning to her boyfriend to say, 'Look, there's Lloyd Nolan,'" the actor recalled. "His reply I'll never forget. He said, 'Yeah, he stinks.'"

When his Paramount contract expired, Nolan signed with 20th Century-Fox; during the next two years, he appeared in 17 films, including such audience-pleasers as *Johnny Apollo* (1940), a well-acted gangster film with Tyrone Power in the title role, and *Blues in the Night* (1940), a Warner Bros. musical starring Priscilla Lane and Betty Field. Nolan also starred in *Michael Shayne, Private Detective* (1940), the first in a seven-episode series in which he portrayed a slick Irish-American sleuth. Other films in the series included *Dressed to Kill* (1941), *The Man Who Wouldn't Die* (1941), and *Just Off Broadway* (1942). Then, in 1943, making a rare step up to the "A" picture category, Nolan was cast as a Marine sergeant in *Guadalcanal Diary* (1943), a hard-hitting war drama co-starring Preston Foster, William Bendix, Richard Conte, and Anthony Quinn.

"After I signed to do the film, I found out that the producers were considering shooting some scenes on Guadalcanal itself," Nolan recalled in 1977. "The battle for the island was pretty much over, but not entirely. I thought it was good to do my bit for the country's war effort, but not for 20th Century–Fox!"

Also in 1943, Nolan was seen in MGM's *Bataan*, another harrowing wartime feature, this time starring Robert Taylor and Thomas Mitchell. The following year, the 40-year-old actor appeared in a military training film, *Resisting Enemy Interrogation* (1944), and in

vately, I heard a studio executive tell her, 'One off-color line from you, and we'll close down the set.' That's how panicky Hollywood was. I remember one scene I had with Mae. She came into my office, leaned on the safe, and it popped open. That's as risqué as they'd let her be."

Finally, after two years of primarily being typed as the villain, Nolan was seen as a newspaperman hero in *King of Gamblers* (1937), starring opposite Claire Trevor. Nolan told reporters that he was pleased with the change.

"The road from heavy to hero is a long and hard one, and there are few who can succeed in making it successfully," he said in 1937. "It is very difficult to find a good villain, for there are only a few who can play 'bad' parts well enough to make screen audiences actually hate him. When a convincing bad man is discovered, casting directors keep him that way. It is only with the greatest difficulty that he can save himself from a life of crime on the screen."

Nolan continued to stay busy throughout the remainder of the decade, playing featured roles in *Dangerous to Know* (1938), a

1945, served as narrator for *War Comes to America*, the seventh episode in the series of *Why We Fight* wartime documentaries. He starred later that year in one of his finest films, *A Tree Grows in Brooklyn*, based on Betty Smith's novel of life in a working-class Brooklyn neighborhood in the early part of the century, followed by his initial foray into film noir, *The House on 92nd Street* (1945). Featuring actual F.B.I. personnel in non-lead roles, this film was based on agency files regarding a young college student, William Dietrich (William Eythe), who becomes an undercover agent to infiltrate a Nazi spy ring. The plot focuses on the Germans' efforts to acquire the United States' secret formula for the atomic bomb and Dietrich's quest to foil their plans. Ultimately, the Nazis are captured and the ringleader (Signe Hasso), mistaken by one of her co-conspirators as a federal agent, is shot and killed. Although Nolan's role as a hard-nosed F.B.I. inspector paled in comparison with the showier roles played by Hasso and fellow villains Lydia St. Clair and Gene Lockhart, he was praised in *Motion Picture Herald* as "first-rate" and in *Variety* as "stand-out," and in the *Los Angeles Examiner*, Dorothy Manners wrote: "Lloyd Nolan fits into the office of an F.B.I. inspector as though he were born there."

By now, Nolan was finally beginning to make a name for himself, with peers and critics alike. In 1946, he starred with John Hodiak and Lucille Ball in *Two Smart People* (1946), an MGM crook-chase drama; during filming, Ball told a reporter that she and Hodiak were a "mutual admiration society when it comes to Lloyd."

"He knows this movie business as few among us do," Ball said. "He almost acts too well—without that flash that attracts attention. Yet he attracts attention anyway—just by good acting. He doesn't need the flash. He knows his business from the ground up. That's why John and I watch his every move."

Following this film, Nolan was seen in three noirs in as many years: *Somewhere in the Night* (1946), *Lady in the Lake* (1947), and *The Street With No Name* (1948).

The first, *Somewhere in the Night*, centered on George Taylor (John Hodiak), an ex–Marine suffering from amnesia. Taylor's search for his true identity brings him into contact with Lt. Donald Kendall (Nolan), a crafty detective who is in the midst of his own search—for a hood named Larry Cravat, who disappeared after stealing $2 million. In one of the film's most riveting and lingo-riddled monologues, Kendall explains Cravat's past to Taylor and his associates during a Chinese restaurant lunch: "It started over in Germany when one of the Nazi hot shots saw the handwriting on the wall. He sent the $2 million over here," Kendall says between bites of egg roll. "And then before he could come over after it, he got knocked off by one of the fellow members of the lodge. And here was this big chunk of dough floatin' around loose in this country, like a pair of dice at a fireman's ball. It moved East to West—each time it moved, it left a stiff behind it with its fingers stretched out. The boys play rough with that kinda lettuce, you understand. Somehow it got to Los Angeles, somehow Cravat got mixed up with it. I don't know much more than that. Except that when Cravat blew, so did the jackpot." By the film's end, Taylor not only discovers that he and Cravat are one and the same, but that he stole the $2 million from nightclub owner Mel Phillips (Richard Conte) before disappearing several years earlier. Demanding the return of his money, Phillips plans to collect the cash and kill Taylor/Cravat once and for all—but his plan is thwarted by Kendall, who shows up at the waterfront docks in time to gun him down.

Nolan's next noir, *Lady in the Lake*, was directed by Robert Montgomery (who also starred) in the unique "first person point-of-view," where the camera served as the eyes of Montgomery's character, detective Philip Marlowe. Focusing on Marlowe's efforts to locate the missing wife of a pulp fiction publisher (Leon Ames), this complex and often confusing drama includes such characters as Adrienne Fromsett, the publisher's sexy editor (Audrey Totter); Chris Lavery, an unprincipled gigolo (Richard Simmons), and Lt.

DeGarmot (Nolan), described by one character as "a tough cop with bad manners." But DeGarmot's manners are the least of his faults; he not only attempts to frame Marlowe for drunk driving, but in the film's climax, he confronts his long-lost ex-lover (Jayne Meadows) with murder on his mind: "I never expected to find you here tonight," DeGarmot tells her after realizing that she was responsible for the deaths of both the publisher's wife and the gigolo. "I thought you were dead. I wish you were, because you're a murderess, and this time, dead's the way I'm gonna leave you." Ignoring the woman's pleas and Marlowe's advice, DeGarmot kills her, but he is shot and killed by police just seconds before he can turn his gun on the detective.

In Nolan's final noir, *The Street with No Name*, he was seen in a reprisal of his Inspector George A. Briggs role from *The House on 92nd Street*, distinguishing him as the only actor to play the same character in two films noirs. This time around, Briggs is focused on the increasing incidents of gang violence in the city: "We know gangsterism is returning," he tells agent Gene Cordell (Mark Stevens). "Since the war, at least a half a dozen gangs have sprung up in [one] area alone — the juvenile delinquents of yesterday, all of them more clever, more ruthless than the old-time mobs." In an effort to crack down on a powerful outfit run by Alec Stiles (Richard Widmark), Briggs assigns Cordell to infiltrate the gang — although the agent nearly loses his life when his cover is exposed, his mission results in unearthing a corrupt official on the police force and successfully toppling Stiles' organization.

Nolan earned mostly good notices for his appearances in these three noirs; his performance in *Somewhere in the Night* was labeled "worth noting" by James O'Farrell of the Los Angeles Examiner. But in the *New York Times*, Bosley Crowther dismissed the film as "a large-sized slice of hokum," and wrote: "Lloyd Nolan, Richard Conte, Josephine Hutchinson and several others are competent as varied pawns. Their performances are interesting; it's only too bad that they have

such turbid and inconclusive things to do." Nolan fared better with his reviews for the dastardly role he portrayed in *Lady in the Lake*, although most critics focused more on the film's unique technical aspects, and for his performance in *The Street With No Name*, the actor was singled out by the *Los Angeles Times*' critic, who praised his "brief but satisfactory account of [the] F.B.I. chief."

After following up his film noir features with such mediocre fare as *The Sun Comes Up* (1949), a three-hankie weeper starring Jeanette MacDonald, and *Bad Boy* (1949), with Jane Wyatt and Audie Murphy, Nolan decided it was time for a change.

"I went on year after year getting no place," Nolan said. "Maybe it was because the right parts didn't come along. Maybe I wasn't ambitious enough. I'd never die for a part — never lick anybody's boots. Maybe they didn't give me good parts because I didn't have a name that could help much at the box office. But I've got no crab. Life has been very good to me. Movie life is awfully well paid, even though boring."

Leaving Hollywood behind, Nolan signed on for a six-week road tour of *The Silver Whistle* for the Theatre Guild, then appeared in a musical, *Courtin' Time*, but left the cast when he lost his voice.

"I don't know how to sing," Nolan said, "and it was too much for me. My vocal cords just folded up."

Nolan's voice problems initially appeared to be a blessing in disguise; a short time later, he was offered the starring role in the popular NBC-TV series, *Martin Kane, Private Eye*, when William Gargan left the series. He was only seen on the show for one season, however, labeling it "an unfortunate experience."

"That was done live and it was no fun at all," Nolan said in 1969. "Second-rate all the way."

Back on the silver screen, Nolan played a big-time gangster in a Bob Hope comedy, *The Lemon Drop Kid* (1951), was second-billed to John Wayne in a well-done adventurer, *Island in the Sky* (1953), and appeared as narrator and co-star in *Crazylegs, All-American*

(1953), a film biography of pro-football Hall of Famer, Elroy "Crazylegs" Hirsch (who played himself in the movie). After the release of the latter film, Nolan landed the biggest break of his career when he was tapped by Broadway producer Paul Gregory to star in his new play, *The Caine Mutiny Court-martial*.

"Why I was picked I don't know," Nolan said in 1954. "He might have seen me in *The Silver Whistle*. Gregory's enthusiasm for anything is highly contagious. I took the part without even reading the script. When I did, I got so excited about it I learned my part three weeks before we went into rehearsal."

In the play, Nolan played Lt. Commander Philip Francis Queeg, a fastidious, exacting officer whose initial self-assurance disintegrates into neurotic paranoia. Before the play hit Broadway, it toured for 14 weeks in 67 cities.

"We played in everything from a theatre with a few hundred seats to a gymnasium with 8,200," Nolan said. "If it was rough, I wasn't aware of it. I was too happy being an actor again."

The show was a smash hit on Broadway, and Nolan was universally hailed by reviewers, including theater critic Walter Kerr, who wrote that, as Queeg, "Nolan holds back nothing. Yet there is no excess." The actor played the part for more than a year before taking the show to London, where he also served as director. For his efforts, the actor won the New York Critics Award and the Donaldson Award for Best Actor, as well as an Emmy Award for the 1955 television presentation of the play on *Ford Star Jubilee*. He later received high praise for his performance from co-star Barry Sullivan.

"I thought I knew a lot about acting, but Lloyd's so enormously good you can't help absorbing something from his work," Sullivan told *TV Guide* in 1969. "We both were nominated for the Emmy, and I voted for *him*. I'll bet Lloyd was a unanimous choice."

The film version of *Caine Mutiny*, starring Humphrey Bogart as Queeg, was released in 1954, but Nolan later cleared up the popular belief that he was turned down for the role on screen.

"Columbia made the movie of *The Caine Mutiny* before we did the play," Nolan said in 1970. "But the studio had released *From Here to Eternity* and it was cleaning up, and they didn't want to put out another war picture to compete with it. So they held their picture up, which gave Paul Gregory the chance to do the play. I thought I was too old to play Queeg — he should be about 31 and I was pushing 50 — but I figured if Bogie wasn't too old to play it, neither was I!"

Returning to Hollywood, Nolan was seen in two of his best films in 1957, *A Hatful of Rain*, which offered a harrowing look at heroin addiction, and *Peyton Place*, in which he played Dr. Matthew Swain, a compassionate and upstanding physician who, at the film's end, exposes the hypocrisy running rampant through the small town of the title. The latter feature was a smash at the box office and went on to earn nine Academy Award nominations. The following year, Nolan was back on series TV, starring as a federal Treasury agent in *Secret Agent 7*, but, as with *Martin Kane*, his television experience was an unpleasant one.

"I did 26 weeks and had to threaten to go to [the] law to get out," Nolan recalled.

In 1959, Nolan enthusiastically announced plans to start his own company with New York writer-producer David Yellin, saying that he had "wanted to get into the production end for a number of years." He revealed that the company had already purchased the rights to five novels, four of which were Pulitzer Prize winners. Two years later, however, the company was dissolved, and none of the properties were developed. Meanwhile, Nolan continued to divide his time between the theater, television, and the movies, including a stage production of *One More River*, which closed two weeks after it reached Broadway; guest appearances on such television series as *Bonanza, Laramie, The Outer Limits*, and *The Virginian*; and a number of films including *Portrait in Black* (1960), playing a man who is murdered by his wife's lover; *Susan Slade* (1961), a glossy soaper starring Troy Donahue and Connie Stevens; *Circus World* (1964), a sprawling big-top epic with John Wayne and Rita Hayworth; *An American Dream* (1968), a thoroughly tawdry drama about a TV commentator who accidentally causes the death of his shrewish wife; and *Ice Station Zebra* (1968), a box-office hit featuring Rock Hudson, Jim Brown, and Ernest Borgnine.

Then, in 1968, Nolan was once again lured back to series television when he was offered the role of Dr. Morton Chegley in *Julia*, a groundbreaking program that was the first to star a black woman since *Beulah* aired in the early 1950s. While the character of Beulah was a maid with a heart of gold, however, Julia (played by Diahann Carroll) was a widowed nurse, raising a young son (Marc Copage). In order to consider the role, Nolan insisted on being paid "an awful lot of money and the absolute minimum of work," his agent, Bill Robinson, told *TV Guide*. As a result, there were many episodes in which Nolan never appeared, and he was given a unique billing in the credits: "Frequently starring Lloyd Nolan."

"The pilot script was fine, exciting. And I was intrigued with the idea," Nolan said in 1968, adding that he hoped that the show's "black and white angle" would diminish as the series progressed. "It's been overstated. Diahann is a darling girl. She has great personality and it comes through in every scene. After we were 10 minutes into the filming of the pilot, I forgot she was colored."

During the three-year run of the popular series, Nolan was also seen in the blockbuster disaster hit *Airport* (1970), in a cast that included such stars as Burt Lancaster, Dean Martin, Van Heflin, and Helen Hayes. After *Julia* ended in 1971, Nolan went on to guest on such television series as *The F.B.I.*, *McMillan and Wife*, *Ellery Queen*, *The Waltons*, and *The Nancy Drew/Hardy Boys Mysteries*; appeared in several made-for-television movies including *The Abduction of Saint Anne* (1975), *The November Plan* (1976); *Flight to Holocaust* (1977); and *Fire!* (1977); and appeared in the feature films *Earthquake* (1974), another star-studded hit from the disaster movie genre; *The Private Files of J. Edgar Hoover* (1977), in which he played a minor role as an attorney; and *My Boys Are Good Boys* (1978), a fairly forgettable crime drama co-starring Ida Lupino and Ralph Meeker.

But during this period, Nolan was in the news for more than his varied performing activities; in the early 1970s, he stunned moviegoers and friends alike when he shared a painful family secret about his son, Jay. Throughout Nolan's career, numerous interviews mentioned his son in casual references, but the boy seldom appeared in photographs and a 1955 article written during the run of *Caine Mutiny* mentioned only that Nolan had received visits in New York from his wife and daughter. Later, articles that appeared in the late 1960s and early 1970s noted Jay's death at age 27, but no further information was provided; it wasn't until 1973 that Nolan revealed that Jay had been diagnosed with autism and had been institutionalized since the age of 13. His death had been caused by choking on a piece of food.

"Jay was physically perfect, a beautiful child," Nolan said in the *Los Angeles Times*. "I guess he was about two when we realized.... We used to have a photographer come out and do both children — our daughter, Mellinda, is three years older. The photographer had different tricks; he'd get the children going up the steps, then say 'Boo!' and they'd turn around and he'd get a cute little surprised picture. Jay just ignored him as if he were deaf. That's what I thought at first — that he was deaf."

After consulting with a series of doctors during the next several years, the Nolans were finally told when Jay was six that he had autism, a complex developmental disability that affects the normal development of the brain in the areas of social interaction and communication skills. At the time, the late 1940s, little was known about the condition, and no effective treatment methods had been developed. Nolan stated that Jay's behavior was characterized by day-long episodes of crying and shouting, and that he eventually had to be removed from his school. As he grew older, Nolan said, Jay's behavior became increasingly unmanageable.

"Jay's sister ... was very sweet and understanding—for a while. As she got older, it began to take a toll on her — on all of us," Nolan said. "You hesitate to bring people around because they think, 'My God, that's the most spoiled child in the world. Why don't they clobber him?' A lot of people don't understand; you can't blame them. But if you withdraw from people ... before you know it you have no friends. And that isn't good for you or the child, either."

At the age of 13, while Nolan was performing in *The Caine Mutiny Court Martial*, Jay was placed in a special school in Philadelphia, where his parents frequently visited.

"But I was never sure that he knew me," Nolan recalled. "He'd look right through me as if I wasn't there. [Or] we'd be liable to get into Philadelphia and have the school people say, 'If you don't mind, you'd better not come out. He's emotionally upset today.'"

After Jay's death, Nolan resolved to raise awareness about autism. He was named honorary chairman of the National Society for Autistic Children, and in 1977 hosted the first of eight annual telethons. Funds from the Autistic Children's Telethon, which Nolan chaired for the next several years, were used to establish a residential research center in Mission Hills, California. Originally known as the Jay Nolan Center for Autism, the center was since renamed Jay Nolan Community Services, and today serves more than 1,300 families through a variety of programs.

"When Jay was little, I don't think we knew anybody with an autistic child. We have had friends with retarded children, but that didn't help up at that time," Nolan said in 1973. "I'm sure it would have helped to have known other parents with autistic children."

Nolan suffered another blow in his personal life in 1981 when Mell, his wife of nearly 50 years, died of cancer. The actor would remarry two years later. Professionally, he continued to make sporadic appearances on television and in feature films during the 1980s, including the *Remington Steele* and *Murder, She Wrote* television series, and *Prince Jack* (1984) on the big screen, a docudrama in which he portrayed the father of John F. Kennedy. The following year, he was cast alongside Maureen O'Hara and her real-life daughter, Mia Farrow, in Woody Allen's stellar comedy *Hannah and Her Sisters* (1986). Sadly, he would not live to see the film's release. After being hospitalized at the Century City Hospital for treatment of lung cancer, Nolan died on September 27, 1985, in his Brentwood, California, home. He was 83 years old.

Although Lloyd Nolan languished throughout much of his film career in a spate of "B" movies, there was no denying his enormous talent, which was once fittingly described by columnist Hedda Hopper, who wrote that Nolan "is a thoughtful, deliberate actor. There are no happy accidents in his performances."

But Nolan's outstanding body of work is perhaps even more impressive in light of the personal pain with which he struggled because of his son's condition. His courage in revealing the details of his family's experience, as well as his commitment to educating the public and creating treatment programs, leaves an admirable legacy.

A letter written to the *Los Angeles Times* after the actor's death provides a poignant illustration of Nolan's impact in this area. The author of the letter, a resident of Hermosa Beach, wrote that her handicapped daughter was enrolled in a Jay Nolan program. The author called the Jay Nolan Community Services agency "a salvation" for parents of children with disabilities. Regretting that she had not been able to thank Lloyd Nolan and his wife personally, she extended warm thanks to their surviving family members for the legacy of the Nolan family.

Film Noir Filmography

Somewhere in the Night. Director: Joseph L. Mankiewicz. Producer: Anderson Lawler. Running time: 110 minutes. Released by 20th Century-Fox, June 12, 1946. Cast: John Hodiak, Nancy Guild, Lloyd Nolan, Richard Conte, Josephine Hutchinson, Fritz Kortner, Margo Woode, Sheldon Leonard, Lou Nova, John Russell, Houseley Stevenson, Charles Arnt, Al Sparlis, Jeff Corey, Henry Morgan.

The House on 92nd Street. Director: Henry Hathaway. Producer: Louis de Rochemont. Running time: 89 minutes. Released by 20th Century-Fox, September 26, 1945. Cast: William Eythe, Lloyd Nolan, Signe Hasso, Gene Lockhart, Leo G. Carroll, Lydia St. Clair, William Post, Jr., Harry Bellaver, Bruno Wick, Harro Meller, Charles Wagenheim, Alfred Linder, Renee Carson, John McKee, Edwin Jerome, Elisabeth Newmann, George Shelton, Alfred Zeisler, Reed Hadley. Awards: Academy Award for Best Original Screenplay (Charles G. Booth).

Lady in the Lake. Director: Robert Montgomery. Producer: George Haight. Released by MGM, January 1947. Running time: 105 minutes. Cast: Robert Montgomery, Lloyd Nolan, Audrey Totter, Tom Tully, Leon Ames, Jayne Meadows, Morris Ankrum, Lila Leeds, Richard Simmons, Ellen Ross, William Roberts, Kathleen Lockhart.

The Street with No Name. Director: William Keighley. Producer: Samuel G. Engel. Running time: 91 minutes. Released by 20th Century-Fox, July 14, 1948. Cast: Mark Stevens, Richard Widmark, Lloyd Nolan, Barbara Lawrence, Ed Begley, Donald Buka, Joseph Pevney, John McIntire, Howard Smith, Walter Greaza, Joan Chandler, Bill Mauch, Sam Edwards, Don Kohler, Robert McGee, Vincent Donahue, Phillip Pine, Buddy Wright, Larry Anzalone, Robert Karnes, Robert Patten.

References

Biography of Lloyd Nolan. 20th Century-Fox, 1941.

"Broadway's Newest Hero." *New York Evening Post*, July 29, 1933.

Camlin, Edward B. "Lloyd Nolan Tells of Tragedy in His Life: Son Who Never Spoke and Died at 27." *National Enquirer*, June 24, 1973.

deRoos, Robert. "The Unforgettable Man from Many Forgettable Movies Is Proving Unforgettable Again." *TV Guide*, December 20, 1969.

Fields, Sidney. "Lloyd Nolan: A New Pinnacle." *The Daily Mirror*, January 26, 1954.

Flynn, Hazel. "Lloyd Nolan Glad to Be Home Again." *Hollywood Citizen-News*, March 2, 1964.

Folkart, Burt A. "Lloyd Nolan, the Actor's Actor, Dies." *Los Angeles Times*, September 28, 1985.

Hopper, Hedda. "He Makes His Own Breaks!" *Chicago Sunday Tribune*, April 15, 1956.

_____. "Lloyd Nolan's Verdict on London." *Los Angeles Times*, October 28, 1962.

"It's No Use Being Your Father's Boy, Lloyd Nolan Finds." *New York Herald-Tribune*, February 19, 1933.

James, George. "Lloyd Nolan Is Dead at 83; Film, Theater and TV Actor." *New York Times*, September 29, 1985.

Johnson, Erskine. "Lloyd Nolan Recalls Era of Censorship." *Los Angeles Mirror-News*, May 26, 1960.

Kirkley, Donald. "Moonstruck and Worthy." *Baltimore Sun*, February 28, 1950.

Leamy, Edmund. "Lloyd Nolan Likes Private Eye Role." *New York World-Telegram and Sun*, September 1, 1951.

Lewis, Emory. "New Laurels for Nolan." *The New Yorker*, February 27, 1954.

Lindgren, Kris. "Lloyd Nolan Will Host Telethon to Help Autistic Children." *Los Angeles Times*, December 9, 1977.

"Lloyd Nolan; Won Emmy for 'Capt. Queeg' Role." *Chicago Tribune*, September 29, 1985.

"Longtime Film Actor Lloyd Nolan Dies." *Los Angeles Daily News*, September 29, 1985.

Millier, Arthur. "Lloyd Nolan Accents Work, Not Temperament." *Los Angeles Times*, October 7, 1945.

Moss, Morton. "A Lazy Guy Makes Good." *Los Angeles Herald-Examiner*, January 7, 1970.

"Nolan Home on TV Show." *Los Angeles Examiner*, September 9, 1962.

Page, Don. "Lloyd Nolan: The Chemistry Is Right for Julia's Boss." *TV Personality*, circa Summer 1968.

Pelswick, Rose. "Fans' Complaints Lift Lloyd Nolan from Villain to Hero." *New York Evening Journal*, June 29, 1937.

Ross, Don. "Nolan Resumes a Long-Lost Career." *New York Herald Tribune*, May 16, 1954.

Ryon, Art. "Lloyd Nolan Ready for Real Life Role." *Los Angeles Times*, September 20, 1962.

Schallert, Edwin. "Nolan to Jump Ship After 'Courtmartial.'" *Los Angeles Times*, March 6, 1955.

Scheuer, Philip K. "Nolan to Produce, Buys Five Stories." *Los Angeles Times*, January 2, 1959.

Scott, John L. "Lloyd Nolan Takes Flops, Hits with Pro's Equanimity." *Los Angeles Times*, June 19, 1960.

Smith, Cecil. "Nolan Goes from Ice Pick to Scalpel." *Los Angeles Times*, March 30, 1970.

_____. "Nolan's Star Still on Rise." *Los Angeles Times*, August 11, 1957.

Thomas, Bob. "Queeg Gives Nolan New Film Aspect." *Los Angeles Mirror-News*, January 25, 1955.

Torrez, Frank. "Lloyd Nolan at 74 — Avoiding Boredom." *Los Angeles Herald-Examiner*, March 20, 1977.

Troupe, Sheila L. "Nolan Legacy." *Los Angeles Times* (Letter to the Editor), October 9, 1985.

"TV's Newest Private Eye." *Cue*, September 22, 1951.

Vergara, John. "Quietly, the Captain Waited." *Sunday News*, December 26, 1954.

Vils, Ursula. "Lloyd Nolan Recalls Tragedy of Autism." *Los Angeles Times*, March 11, 1973.

EDMOND O'BRIEN

"One more crack like that and I'll slap your kisser off ya. Believe me?" — Edmond O'Brien in *Shield for Murder* (1954)

Although a retrospective look at the career of Edmond O'Brien leaves no doubt as to his outstanding talent as an actor, he inspired mixed reactions during the height of his popularity in Hollywood. He was labeled "great" by famed director John Ford and such peers as William Holden, but others — including O'Brien himself — felt that he lacked magnetism. Astonishingly, one reviewer once wrote that "D-U-L-L is written all over his face," and a theatrical producer went so far as to describe him as "a stony, one-note actor." Such criticisms seem today to be beyond comprehension; an Academy Award winner for *The Barefoot Contessa* (1954), O'Brien was a standout in such features as *Another Part of the Forest* (1948), *The Man Who Shot Liberty Valance* (1962), *The Longest Day* (1962), and *The Wild Bunch* (1969). He was also one of film noir's busiest actors, using his versatility to first-rate advantage in nine features from the era: *The Killers* (1946), *A Double Life* (1947), *White Heat* (1949), *D.O.A.* (1950), *711 Ocean Drive* (1950), *Between Midnight and Dawn* (1950), *The Turning Point* (1952), *The Hitch-Hiker* (1953), and *Shield for Murder* (1954).

O'Brien was born on September 10, 1915, in New York City. The very fact of his birth, according to the actor, was a stroke of fortuity.

"My father was a seventh son and I am a seventh child," O'Brien once explained. That's good luck."

As a youngster, O'Brien's initial vocational aspirations were firmly focused on a career as a magician. Harry Houdini was a neighbor and, after learning several tricks from the famed illusionist, O'Brien dubbed himself "Neirbo the Great" (O'Brien spelled backwards) and staged exhibitions for friends in the family basement. But his occupational path changed forever in his early teens when O'Brien was taken to a Broadway play by an aunt.

"From that time, I wanted to be an actor," he recalled.

After attending St. Thomas Grammar School, the actor said, he was "kicked out of four different high schools" before finally graduating from George Washington High School in 1933. O'Brien then enrolled at Fordham University, but he dropped out after a year to accept a scholarship to the Neighborhood Playhouse Dramatic School in New York, acting at night with the Columbia Laboratory Players and working at a Manhattan fruit juice hut to make ends meet. A chance meeting with a theatrical producer led to a two-week trial with a summer stock company in Westfield, Connecticut, where O'Brien's first role involved carrying a bathtub across the stage. After performing in stock in Yonkers, the budding thespian landed his first Broadway job, in *Daughters of Atreus*. This was followed by roles in John Gielgud's production of *Hamlet* (in which he played Marcellus and the second gravedigger), *Family*

Portrait, *The Star-Wagon*, *Camille*, and a road production of *Parnell*.

Around this time, O'Brien came in contact with Orson Welles, who was making a name for himself with his Mercury Players on the radio and the stage. Welles hired O'Brien for several of his radio programs, and in 1937 cast him as Marc Antony in his modern dress version of *Julius Caesar*. Two years later, while O'Brien was playing Prince Hal in Maurice Evans' *Henry IV*, Hollywood beckoned, and after a bit part as an inmate in Universal's *Prison Break* (1938), the actor was tapped by RKO director Pandro Berman for a featured role in *The Hunchback of Notre Dame* (1939).

"It was not my goal [to go into movies]," O'Brien said later. "[But] I was surprised. I liked movies immediately."

Despite his favorable experience, O'Brien returned to New York, playing Mercutio in the Laurence Olivier production of *Romeo and Juliet*, and opposite Ruth Chatterton in *Leave Her to Heaven*. The following year, however, he signed a contract with RKO, appearing in such features as *A Girl, A Guy and A Gob* (1941), co-starring Lucille Ball and directed by silent era comedian Harold Lloyd, and *Parachute Battalion* (1941), a profitable wartime melodrama. In the latter film, O'Brien co-starred with a young starlet named Nancy Kelly, who had been a family friend for many years. Although O'Brien had once insisted that their relationship was merely platonic, the two were married in the spring of 1941. But the union was a rocky one from the start, and O'Brien and Kelly separated after just a few weeks. Several reconciliations followed, but by 1942, the marriage was over.

Meanwhile, after being woefully miscast as a zany scientist in *Powder Town* (1942) and starring opposite Deanna Durbin in *The Amazing Mrs. Holliday* (1943), O'Brien joined the U.S. Army and was sent to radio operator's school. Before completing his training, he was cast in a lead role in Moss Hart's 1943 Army Air Force production of *Winged Victory*, in which he toured for the next two years. The actor was also seen in the 1944 screen version of the play, but following his release from the Army, O'Brien found it difficult to find work.

"After the war, I came back out here and they had a lot of new guys I didn't know," O'Brien said in a 1950 interview. "Nobody knew quite how to use me or gave a damn. You had to keep going around. You had to go dressed up all the time so they would look at you and think, 'Hey, there's our leading man.'"

On one fateful day, actress Ann Sheridan suggested that O'Brien pay a visit to producer Mark Hellinger, who was casting roles for his upcoming film, *The Killers* (1946). It turned out to be the break O'Brien had been seeking.

"I put my feet up on [Hellinger's] desk and ... that did it," O'Brien said. "The reason he could see me for the part was I had on an old leather jacket and scuffed pants and heavy shoes. I got the job because I looked like a bum instead of being duded up."

In *The Killers*, O'Brien's first film noir, the actor played Jim Reardon, a dogged insurance company investigator who is forced to forego a much-anticipated vacation in order to unravel a mystery surrounding the murder of a former boxer known as "the Swede" (Burt Lancaster). Reardon's quest leads him to various and sundry friends, acquaintances, and enemies of the Swede, including Big Jim Colfax (Albert Dekker), the unscrupulous leader of a gang of hoods; Kitty (Ava Gardner), the Swede's girl and, later, Jim's wife; and Sam Lubinsky (Sam Levene), the Swede's boyhood pal who grew up to be an officer of the law. After members of the gang start turning up dead, Reardon's trail leads back to Big Jim, who is gunned down in the film's climax by one of his own men, and Kitty, who desperately—and in vain—begs her dying spouse to exonerate her. Along with his stellar cast of co-stars, O'Brien was singled out by several reviewers, including the critic for *Variety*, who wrote that he "is another pivotal character who adds much to the film's acting polish," and *Motion Picture Herald*'s William R. Weaver, who predicted that *The Killers* was "likely to do for Edmond O'Brien what [*High Sierra*] did for Humphrey Bogart."

Now under contract to Universal, O'Brien next starred with William Bendix and Ella Raines in a first-rate crime drama, *The Web* (1947), then returned to film noir in *A Double Life* (1947). Using the stages of the Broadway theater as a backdrop, this feature starred Ronald Colman as Anthony John, an intense, talented actor who becomes consumed with the title character he plays in a version of *Othello*. After a local waitress (Shelley Winters) is found strangled to death, John arouses the suspicions of press agent Bill Friend (O'Brien), who devises an elaborate trap for the actor, ultimately revealing him as the killer. In the film's tension-filled climax, John fatally stabs himself during a performance, just as Bill and the authorities are preparing to move in. "Look out for the papers," John tells Bill in his last moments. "Don't let them say I was a bad actor."

Following this unusual, but often gripping noir, O'Brien enjoyed a memorable year; in 1948, he signed a contract with Warner Bros., starred in what would become one of his favorite films, *Another Part of the Forest* ("It was an actor's picture," he said); and found love with an actress-dancer by the name of Olga San Juan. According to the actor, he met San Juan after she went on a blind date with one of his brothers. After being shown a picture of the 21-year-old Latin beauty, O'Brien reportedly said, "That's for me," and wooed San Juan by quoting Shakespeare.

"Olga thought my spouting Shakespeare at her was corny," O'Brien said later, "but the tender and passionate and bitter emotions he wrote into *Romeo and Juliet* are the greatest love-making speeches ever penned — or quoted. When I fell in love with Olga, could I say it better?" O'Brien and San Juan later had three children, Bridget Ellen in 1949; Maria Mercedes (who would go to enjoy a measure of success on television and in films) in 1950; and Brandon James in 1962, but after nearly 30 years of marriage, the couple would divorce in 1976.

Professionally, O'Brien was seen in a series of well-done features for Warners, including his third film noir, *White Heat* (1949),

where he was featured as police detective Hank Fallon, who reluctantly receives an undercover assignment to pose as a prison inmate: "Look at me — college degree, lovable personality, and I spend most of my time in prison," Fallon tells his boss. "An undercover specialist — eight sentences in five years.... I joined the department to put prisoners behind bars, and here I am stir-crazy." The focus of Fallon's assignment is Cody Jarrett (James Cagney), a psychotic gangleader with an unhealthy attachment to his mother (chillingly portrayed by Margaret Wycherly). Fallon successfully earns Cody's trust while serving as his cellmate, and after Cody learns that his beloved mother has been murdered by one of his gang, Fallon joins the killer in a prison breakout. During a planned payroll heist, however, Fallon's cover is blown, and the police move in, killing most of the gang members. At the film's end, only Cody is left standing, but he perishes in a fiery explosion atop an oil refinery tank, leading Fallon to ironically remark in the final reel, "He finally got to the top of the world. And it blew right up in his face."

Despite earning good reviews for his "effective" and "fine acting" in *White Heat*, O'Brien abruptly decided to end his contract with Warners, choosing instead to freelance.

"When I was a kid actor under contract, I had no voice," the actor said in a 1964 interview. "[But] it was not considered fashionable not to be owned by a studio. I cut the natal cord before most actors. I got tired of asking for good parts. Anything that happened to me was despite the bosses, not because of them. I never became anything at the box office until I got out on my own."

Among O'Brien's choices as a freelancer during the next several years were a series of films noirs, beginning with *D.O.A.* in 1950. A riveting example of noir, this feature captures and holds the viewer's attention from the opening scene when O'Brien's character, Frank Bigelow, enters a police station and announces that he is there to report a murder. "Whose?" he is asked by a cop — to which he replies, "My own." As it turns out, Bigelow has been given a week to live after unknowingly ingesting a dose of luminous poison while visiting a local bar, and the rest of the feature focuses on his desperate efforts to unearth the responsible party. During his frenzied chase, Bigelow picks up clues from a series of notable characters, including Majak (Luther Adler), the refined but deadly purchaser of the metal; Halliday (William Ching), a suspicious-acting controller at an import-export company; and Mrs. Phillips (Lynn Baggett), Halliday's mistress, who ultimately provides the final key to the puzzle: "You knew who I was when I came here today," Bigelow tells the woman. "But you were surprised to see me alive, weren't you? But I'm not alive, Mrs. Phillips. Sure, I can stand here and talk to you. I can breathe and I can move. But I'm not alive. Because I did take that poison. And nothing can save me." Ultimately learning that the poison was administered by Halliday, Bigelow kills the man in a shootout and manages to report the entire story to police just before his life ends.

Also that year, O'Brien added two more films noirs to his repertoire, *711 Ocean Drive* and *Between Midnight and Dawn*. In the first, O'Brien starred as Mal Granger, a technology-savvy telephone repairman who changes vocations when he becomes involved with a lucrative coastal wire service operation. Before long, Granger realizes his worth and demands a percentage of the profits from the head of the operation, Vince Walters (Barry Kelley): "It was your money, but it was my brains that made you that dough," Granger tells him. "Get smart, Vince — ever since I hooked up your outfit all over the state, you've been rolling in cabbage and I know it. Your take is five times what it was. But to keep it that way, you gotta keep *me*." Granger takes over the operation when Walters is killed by a disgruntled bookie, but when the successful enterprise attracts the notice of an East Coast syndicate headed by Carl Stephans (Otto Kruger) and Larry Mason (Donald Porter), Granger's life begins to spiral out of control, characterized by his affair with Mason's wife (Joanne Dru), and his murder of

a hood he hired to kill Mason. Hunted by both police and the syndicate, Granger flees with his lover to Las Vegas, but he dies in a hail of bullets as he tries to escape across Hoover Dam.

In O'Brien's third noir of 1950, *Between Midnight and Dawn*, the actor co-starred with Mark Stevens as Dan Purvis, a big city beat cop whose jaded nature has been fostered by the variety of criminals with whom he comes in contact. Dan's cynicism is clearly illustrated in an early scene when he and his idealistic partner, Rocky Barnes (Mark Stevens), arrest a young girl for her minor role in a robbery attempt. "They're all scared the first time they're caught," Dan tells his partner. "In another year she'll be packing a shiv. Ready to stick it in somebody's gut if she has to. Maybe *your* gut." When Rocky is brutally murdered by escaped gangster Richie Garris (Donald Buka), Dan becomes obsessed with bringing the killer to justice, focusing his efforts on the man's girlfriend, Terry Romaine (Gale Robbins), whom he labels as a "dollface gutter rat." Although the woman insists that she has severed her ties with Garris, Dan continues relentlessly pursue her. ("She's just playing it cute," he says. "She's laughing at how she conned the police, waiting for a chance to make her move…. She goes home and sleeps like a cat, dreams about her bloodthirsty boyfriend.") Ultimately, Dan tracks Garris to Terry's apartment, where he is holed up with Terry and a young neighbor girl he has taken hostage. In the film's harrowing climax, Garris threatens to throw the child from an upper story window, but Dan manages to enter the apartment and, after Terry deliberately steps in front of a bullet meant for the officer, Purvis guns Garris down. By the final reel, Dan has altered his stance toward Terry, acknowledging to the press, "Maybe if she'd never met a guy like Garris, she wouldn't have become a dame like that."

O'Brien earned raves for all three of his 1950 noirs — he was labeled "exceptionally fine" in *D.O.A.* by Wylie Williams of the *Hollywood Citizen–News*; for his work in *711 Ocean Drive*, the critic for *Variety* found that he was "excellent as the hot-tempered, ambitious young syndicate chief"; and the *Los Angeles Times* reviewer noted his "appealing" performance in *Between Midnight and Dawn*.

The following year, taking a brief break from the dark world of noir, O'Brien appeared in several Paramount westerns, including *Warpath* (1951) and *Denver and Rio Grande* (1952), and was seen in an unbilled guest appearance in Cecil B. DeMille's circus epic, *The Greatest Show on Earth* (1952). Between films, he took on the title role in the radio series *Yours Truly, Johnny Dollar*, appearing from 1950 to 1952 as the hard-boiled, emotionless detective, and returned to his stage roots for *I've Got Sixpence*. In the latter, O'Brien received high praise for his portrayal of a novelist; in a typical review, *New York Times* critic Brooks Atkinson wrote that the actor played his role "with a harsh bluntness that is admirable and brings the character wholly alive in all its implications." With his popularity and visibility on the rise, it was only fitting that O'Brien was named during this period by the Young Women's League of America as having "more male magnetism than any other man in America."

"All women adore ruggedness," said the president of the national organization. "Edmond O'Brien's magnetic appearance and personality most fully stir women's imaginative impulses. We're all agreed that he has more male magnetism than any of the 60 million men in the United States today."

Shortly after receiving this honor, O'Brien put his magnetism to use in a return to the domain of noir, starring in *The Turning Point* (1952) and *The Hitch-Hiker* (1953). In *The Turning Point*, the actor portrayed John Conroy, an idealistic attorney who possesses, according to one character, "clean hands, pure heart, no political future." Hired to break up a big-city crime syndicate with the help of his boyhood friend-turned-reporter, Jerry McKibbon (William Holden), Conroy puts increasing pressure on Eichelberger (Ed Begley), the head of the syndicate, but he decides to quit after Eichelberger thwarts his case by blowing up a building con-

taining damaging evidence (killing numerous innocent residents of the building in the process). Later, when Conroy learns of a plot to murder Jerry, he valiantly tries to warn his friend, but he is too late — arriving at the crowded boxing arena where Jerry has been gunned down, Conroy ruefully remarks: "Sometimes, someone has to pay an exorbitant price to uphold the majesty of the law." Inspired by the real-life Kefauver hearings on organized crime, *The Turning Point* was released to mixed reviews; while the *Los Angeles Times*' Philip K. Scheuer praised the film's "smart and stimulating" dialogue," Margaret Harford, of the *Hollywood Citizen-News*, found that "*The Turning Point* talks itself to the boring point and adds up as just another melodrama."

Next, in the Ida Lupino–directed feature *The Hitch-Hiker*, O'Brien starred as Ray Collins, who, along with his fishing buddy, Gilbert Bowen (Frank Lovejoy), finds himself thrust into a nightmarish adventure when he picks up a hitchhiker on a roadside. The passenger turns out to be Emmett Myers (William Talman), a psychotic serial killer who forces the pair to drive him to Mexico. During the harrowing trip, Myers constantly taunts the hapless duo, frustrating their plans to escape because of a paralyzed eye that remains open even when he sleeps. Of the two captives, Collins is the more ardently vocal, telling Myers in one scene, "Sure, you'll make it to Guamos. But they'll catch up to you. And put you out of your misery. You haven't got a chance. You haven't got a thing except that gun. You better hang on to it. Because without it, you're nothing! You're finished!" Ultimately, Collins' words are prophetic; confronted by Mexican police on a local dock, Bowen knocks Myers' gun from his hands, and after a brief, futile attempt to flee, the killer is quietly placed under arrest. Along with his co-stars, O'Brien was universally hailed by critics; Lynn Bowers praised his "solid" performance in the *Los Angeles Examiner*; Lowell Redelings, of the *Hollywood Citizen-News*, found him "impressive," and the reviewer for the *New York Times* wrote: "Both Edmond O'Brien and Frank Lovejoy are experts as stalwart men gripped in a situation they never made."

With the onset of the mid-1950s, O'Brien continued choosing interesting and provocative scripts, as evidenced by his roles in such films as *Julius Caesar* (1953), a first-rate film produced by John Houseman, directed by Joseph Mankiewicz, and starring such notables as Marlon Brando and James Mason; *The Bigamist* (1953), an innovative if slightly off-center feature about a married traveling salesman living a double life; *The Barefoot Contessa* (1954), for which O'Brien earned a Golden Globe Award and an Academy Award for Best Supporting Actor; and his final film noir, *Shield for Murder* (1954), on which he made his debut as a director. This gripping, hard-hitting feature begins as police detective Barney Nolan (O'Brien) kills a small-time hood and steals his bankroll of $25,000. Although he convinces his boss (Emile Meyer) that the shooting was committed in the line of duty, Nolan is pursued by a local gangster, Packy Reed (Hugh Sanders), to whom the bankroll rightfully belonged. Meanwhile, Nolan's situation grows increasingly hopeless when he accidentally kills an elderly deaf-mute

man who'd witnessed the murder, brutally pistol-whips a pair of private detectives hired by Packy Reed, and later kills one of the detectives during a wild shootout at a crowded high school swimming pool. At the film's end, Nolan is gunned down by police in front of the suburban house he'd planned to purchase, the stolen bills fluttering around his lifeless body.

O'Brien's outstanding portrayal as the corrupt cop earned justified praise from critics, including the *Los Angeles Times* reviewer, who wrote that he "again proves himself as a master actor," and the critic for the *Hollywood Citizen-News*, who raved: "For consistency in the art of good acting, it would be hard to beat Edmond O'Brien's fine performances on screen." Shortly after the film's release, O'Brien announced plans to form his own production company, Story Tellers Presents, in partnership with his playwright brother, Liam. (The company's name was later changed to Emerald, after a baseball team managed by the boys in their youth, and later still to Tiger, after O'Brien's childhood nickname.) The siblings announced several properties that they planned to film, including *The Remarkable Mr. Pennypacker*, based on the hit Broadway play authored by Liam. (The film was eventually made in 1959, but not by the O'Brien brothers.)

"Some [actors] don't care about producing. All they're interested in is acting, and that's fine," O'Brien said in 1954. "But others, like [John] Wayne and [Burt] Lancaster have picked up enough technical knowledge and ideas on writing, directing and camera techniques to do a great job. They went out of their way to learn. So have I. My intention, eventually, is to work myself out of acting."

But during the remainder of the 1950s, O'Brien remained in front of the camera, appearing in *Pete Kelly's Blues* (1955), starring, as well as produced and directed, by Jack Webb; *1984* (1956), earning notice from the *New York Times*' Bosley Crowther, who wrote that the actor "wins genuine sympathy"; *The Girl Can't Help It* (1956), an amusing comedy in which O'Brien played the gangster boyfriend of Jayne Mansfield ("I never had more fun making a picture," the actor said following the film's release); *The Big Land* (1957), a mediocre western starring Alan Ladd; *Sing, Boy, Sing* (1958), which featured O'Brien as a pushy agent; and *Up Periscope* (1959), a wartime drama with James Garner and Alan Hale, Jr. (who would later achieve fame as the Skipper on the popular television comedy, *Gilligan's Island*). Between films, O'Brien was seen in guest spots on such television series as *Stage 7, Zane Grey Theater,* and *Laramie,* and in 1960, landed the title role of a New York private eye in the short-lived syndicated crime series, *Johnny Midnight.*

His prolific acting appearances notwithstanding, O'Brien continued to express an interest in directing, identifying the vocation as his ultimate ambition.

"But I'm too much of a hamola and I can't resist good roles," O'Brien said. "I've always dreamed of becoming a director, but acting keeps cutting in on my directing and I don't know what to do."

After directing and starring in *The Town That Slept With Its Lights On,* a teleplay written by his brother Liam, O'Brien finally got another shot at directing feature films when he helmed *Man-Trap* (1961), the sole feature produced by the actor's company. Although O'Brien earned a measure of praise for his efforts, however, the film turned out to be a rather routine melodrama and marked O'Brien's last as a director. Instead, O'Brien went on to appear in such blockbusters as *The Man Who Shot Liberty Valance* (1962), with John Wayne and James Stewart; *Birdman of Alcatraz* (1962), starring Burt Lancaster in the title role of the prison lifer who becomes a noted ornithologist; *The Longest Day* (1962), an epic wartime drama with a star-studded cast that included John Wayne, Robert Ryan, Henry Fonda, and Rod Steiger; and *Seven Days in May* (1964), in which O'Brien's portrayal of an aging, alcoholic senator earned him a Golden Globe Award and his second nomination for Best Supporting Actor. (He lost this time, however, to Peter Ustinov in *Topkapi.*)

In addition to O'Brien's feature films during this period, the actor was seen on the small screen as a colorful trial lawyer in 1962-63 on the television series *Sam Benedict.*

"If the *Sam Benedict* series hits, I don't know if I'll like it," O'Brien told *TV Guide* shortly after filming began on the series. "I really don't enjoy crowds. I think the public likes whatever they are told to like. I don't know, perhaps I'll suddenly become an idiot who'll enjoy standing there and signing autographs. I can't think of anything I'd rather do less right now."

Sam Benedict was cancelled after one season, but the actor was back on television narrating the half-hour biographical series, *Men in Crisis,* in 1965. Also that year, the actor landed the role of Will Varner on the series *The Long, Hot Summer.*

"I vowed I'd never do another [series] after *Sam Benedict,*" O'Brien said in a 1965 interview with columnist Hedda Hopper, "but [producer] Bill Self insisted and, after the fifth round, I agreed." It was reported that, as part of O'Brien's deal to star in the 20th Century-Fox Television series, the actor would produce and direct one picture per year, but the film properties never materialized and O'Brien left the show after four months. (He was replaced by Dan O'Herlihy, and the series was cancelled in June 1966).

Throughout the remainder of the decade and into the 1970s, O'Brien guested on such television series as *The Dick Powell Show, The Virginian, Mission: Impossible, It Takes a Thief, The Name of the Game, The High Chaparral, The Streets of San Francisco,* and *Cade's County,* and was seen in several made-for-television movies, including *The Doomsday Flight* (1966), *The Outsider* (1967), *The Intruders* (1970), *What's a Nice Girl Like You...?* (1971), *Jigsaw* (1972), and *Isn't It Shocking?* (1973).

On the big screen, the quality and quantity of O'Brien's roles had begun to dwindle, but the actor still managed to appear in an average of two pictures a year, most notably *Fantastic Voyage* (1966), a popular science-fictioner about a group of scientists who are miniaturized and injected into the body of a fatally ill patient; and *The Wild Bunch* (1969), Sam Peckinpah's classic western starring William Holden and Robert Ryan. Nearly unrecognizable in his role as a grizzled outlaw, O'Brien was singled out by several critics, including Vincent Canby, who wrote in the *New York Times*: "Edmond O'Brien is a special shock, looking like an evil Gabby Hayes, a foul-mouthed, cackling old man who is the only member of The Wild Bunch to survive."

Since the early 1960s, when a heart seizure forced the actor to drop out of the cast of *Lawrence of Arabia* (1962), O'Brien had been in declining health, and he was briefly hospitalized in 1971 for a "slight pulmonary condition." During this time, the actor also began to demonstrate irrational bouts of anger and had trouble remembering his lines and the names of crew members. This behavior may have surfaced as early as 1962, however, when a *TV Guide* reporter described the actor's conversation as "vague, often unfocused." But it wasn't until several years after O'Brien's last feature film, *Lucky Luciano* (1974), that he was diagnosed with Alzheimer's Disease, a progressive, degenerative brain disorder. O'Brien was ultimately placed at St. Erne's Sanitorium in Inglewood, California, where his visitors included ex-wives Nancy Kelly and Olga San Juan. The actor also received encouraging letters from such longtime friends as then-president Ronald Reagan (who, ironically, would himself be diagnosed with Alzheimer's less than a decade later). On May 9, 1985, O'Brien lost his long battle with the ravages of the disease, and died at St. Erne's at the age of 69.

Edmond O'Brien once lamented the disadvantages of being a character actor, saying that "versatility is a dangerous thing … Seldom does a producer say, 'This is an Eddie O'Brien part.'" the actor managed to parlay his talent into numerous outstanding roles over a span of a half-century, and his ability to offer equal facility to his film noir portrayals, whether cop or criminal, has made him one of the most fascinating performers of the era.

"It's me who gets a chance to do the interesting, the different, the funny," O'Brien's daughter Bridget once quoted the actor. "It's from me the audience expects the unusual. "I like it that way."

Film Noir Filmography

The Killers. Director: Robert Siodmak. Producer: Mark Hellinger. Running time: 105 minutes. Released by Universal, August 28, 1946. Cast: Edmond O'Brien, Ava Gardner, Albert Dekker, Sam Levene, John Miljan, Virginia Christine, Vince Barnett, Burt Lancaster, Charles D. Brown, Donald MacBride, Phil Brown, Charles McGraw, William Conrad, Queenie Smith, Garry Owen, Harry Hayden, Bill Walker, Jack Lambert, Jeff Corey, Wally Scott, Gabrielle Windsor, Rex Dale. Awards: Academy Award nominations for Best Director (Robert Siodmak), Best Film Editing (Arthur Hilton), Best Score/Drama or Comedy (Miklos Rozsa), Best Screenplay (Anthony Veiller).

A Double Life. Director: George Cukor. Producer: Michael Kanin. Running time: 103 minutes. Released by Universal-International, December 25, 1947. Cast: Ronald Colman, Signe Hasso, Edmond O'Brien, Shelley Winters, Ray Collins, Phillip Loeb, Millard Mitchell, Joe Sawyer, Charles La Torre, Whit Bissell, John Drew Colt, Peter Thompson, Elizabeth Dunne, Alan Edmiston, Art Smith, Sid Tomack, Wilton Graff, Harlan Briggs, Claire Carleton, Betsy Blair, Janet Warren, Marjory Woodworth. Awards: Academy Awards for Best Actor (Ronald Colman), Best Score/Drama or Comedy (Miklos Rozsa). Academy Award nominations for Best Director (George Cukor), Best Original Screenplay (Ruth Gordon, Garson Kanin).

White Heat. Director: Raoul Walsh. Producer: Lou Edelman. Running time: 114 minutes. Released by Warner Brothers, September 2, 1949. Cast: James Cagney, Virginia Mayo, Edmond O'Brien, Margaret Wycherly, Steve Cochran, John Archer, Wally Cassell, Fred Clark, Ford Rainey, Fred Coby, G. Pat Collins, Mickey Knox, Paul Guilfoyle, Robert Osterloh, Ian MacDonald, Ray Montgomery. Awards: Academy Award nomination for Best Motion Picture Story (Virginia Kellogg).

D.O.A. Director: Rudolph Mate. Producer: Harry M. Popkin. Running time: 83 minutes. Released by United Artists, April 30, 1950. Cast: Edmond O'Brien, Pamela Britton, Luther Adler, Beverly Campbell, Lynn Baggett, William Ching, Henry Hart, Neville Brand, Laurette Luez, Jess

Kirkpatrick, Cay Forrester, Virginia Lee, Michael Ross.

711 Ocean Drive. Director: Joseph M. Newman. Producer: Frank N. Seltzer. Running time: 102 minutes. Released by Columbia, July 19, 1950. Cast: Edmond O'Brien, Joanne Dru, Donald Porter, Sammy White, Dorothy Patrick, Barry Kelley, Otto Kruger, Howard St. John, Robert Osterloh, Bert Freed, Carl Milletaire, Charles La Torre, Fred Aldrich, Charles Jordan, Sidney Dubin.

Between Midnight and Dawn. Director: Gordon Douglas. Producer: Hunt Stromberg. Running time: 89 minutes. Released by Columbia, October 2, 1950. Cast: Mark Stevens, Edmond O'Brien, Gale Storm, Donald Buka, Gale Robbins, Anthony Ross, Roland Winters, Tito Vuolo, Grazia Narciso, Madge Blake, Lora Lee Michel, Jack Del Rio, Phillip Van Zandt, Cliff Bailey, Tony Barr, Peter Mamakos, Earl Brietbard, Wheaton Chambers, Frances Morris.

The Turning Point. Director: William Dietele. Producer: Irving Asher. Running time: 85 minutes. Released by Paramount, November 14, 1952. Cast: William Holden, Edmond O'Brien, Alexis Smith, Tom Tully, Ed Begley, Dan Dayton, Adele Longmire, Ray Teal, Ted De Corsia, Don Porter, Howard Freeman, Neville Brand.

The Hitch-Hiker. Director: Ida Lupino. Producer: Collier Young. Running time: 71 minutes. Released by RKO, April 29, 1953. Cast: Edmond O'Brien, Frank Lovejoy, William Talman, Jose Torvay, Sam Hayes, Wendell Niles, Jean Del Val, Clark Howat, Natividad Vacio, Rodney Bell, Nacho Galindo, Martin Garralaga, Tony Roux, Jerry Lawrence, Felipe Turich, Joe Dominguez, Rose Turich, Orlando Veltran, George Navarro, June Dinneen, Al Ferrara, Henry Escalante, Taylor Flaniken, Wade Crosby, Kathy Riggins, Gordon Barnes, Ed Hinton, Larry Hudson.

Shield for Murder. Directors: Edmond O'Brien and Howard W. Koch. Producer: Aubrey Schenck. Running time: 80 minutes. Released by United Artists, August 27, 1954. Cast: Edmond O'Brien, Marla English, John Agar, Emile Meyer, Carolyn Jones, Claude Akins, Larry Ryle, Herbert Butterfield, Hugh Sanders, William Schallert, David Hughes, Richard Cutting.

References

"Acting Experience Helps Directors, Says O'Brien." *The Hollywood Reporter*, August 5, 1954.

"Actor Edmond O'Brien Has Heart Attack." *Los Angeles Herald-Examiner*, September 1, 1971.

Cook, Maxine. "Edmond O'Brien's Here with His Long Hair." *New York World Telegram*, November 11, 1939.

"Edmond O'Brien, Actor, Dies at 69." *New York Times*, May 10, 1985.

Finnigan, Joe. "Says H'Wood Back in Stride After Period of 'Static' Films." *New York Morning Telegraph*, April 3, 1961.

"Free-Lancing Paid Off for Edmond O'Brien." *New York Morning Telegraph*, November 24, 1964.

Guernsey, Otis L., Jr. "The Playbill: 'Winged Victory' and Edmond O'Brien." *New York Herald Tribune*, December 19, 1943.

Heffernan, Harold. "Actors' Vanity Costly." *Newark Evening Post*, August 11, 1964.

Hopper, Hedda. "O'Brien Functions Best When Busy." *Los Angeles Times*, March 9, 1965.

"H'Wood's New Recruits." *Variety*, July 5, 1939.

Hyams, Joe. "This Is Hollywood." *New York Herald Tribune*, February 7, 1956.

Johnson, Erskine. "Director O'Brien Is Still an Actor." *Los Angeles Mirror*, April 1, 1961.

Manners, Dorothy. "Irish Eddie Knows His Shakespeare." *Los Angeles Examiner*, April 26, 1953.

McClay, Howard. "O'Brien Meets Shakespeare — On Film." *Los Angeles Daily Times*, August 19, 1952.

"Nancy Kelly Seeks Divorce." *New York Herald Tribune*, June 24, 1941.

O'Brien, Bridget. "The Big Night Dad Brought Home an Oscar." *Los Angeles Times*, April 10, 1988.

"O'Brien Joins Growing List of Star-Producers." *New York Morning Telegraph*, November 26, 1954.

"Olga San Juan Married to Actor Edmond O'Brien." *Los Angeles Times*, September 27, 1948.

Parsons, Louella O. "Mr. & Mrs. Edmond O'Brien and Baby Maria." *Boston Pictorial Review*, April 15, 1951.

_____. "One Oscar Made a Difference." *Pictorial TView*, March 25, 1956.

Scott, John L. "O'Brien Fell Flat in Debut." *Los Angeles Times*, December 16, 1956.

Scott, Vernon. "Film 'Toughie' Going 'Soft.'" *New York Morning Telegraph*, June 4, 1953.

Skolsky, Sidney. "Tintypes: Edmund [sic] O'Brien." *New York Post*, May 9, 1965.

Sloan, Lloyd L. "Add Movie Frustrations: O'Brien for Shakespeare." *Hollywood Citizen-News*, June 2, 1950.

_____. "A Running Report on E. O'Brien." *Hollywood Citizen-News*, June 10, 1949.

"Star O'Brien Now to Be 20th Producer-Director." *The Hollywood Reporter*, December 30, 1964.

"The Case of O'Brien vs. O'Brien." *TV Guide*, October 27, 1962.

"The Prince Hal of 'King Henry IV.'" *New York Sun*, February 25, 1939.

"'Tis a Great Day for the Irish Today So Here's an O'Brien." *Manhattan*, March 18, 1939.

MORONI OLSEN

"Being a detective is like making an automobile. You just take all the pieces and put them together one by one, and the first thing you know, you've got an automobile. Or a murderer." — Moroni Olsen in *Mildred Pierce* (1945)

Known as one of Hollywood's most dependable character actors, the mustachioed and balding Moroni Olsen frequently was seen in his films as a clergyman, doctor, or cop, but he holds a special place in cinema history for a far more unique performance — providing the voice for the Magic Mirror in the 1937 Disney classic, *Snow White and the Seven Dwarfs*. Aside from this fanciful role, Olsen was featured in nearly 100 films during his 35-year career, appearing alongside such stars as Clark Gable, Joan Crawford, and Spencer Tracy. His credits include a number of first-rate screen gems, including *The Song of Bernadette* (1943), *Notorious* (1946), and *Father of the Bride* (1950), as well as five entries from the film noir era: *The Glass Key* (1942), *Mildred Pierce* (1945), *Possessed* (1947), *The High Wall* (1947), and *Call Northside 777* (1948).

Born on June 27, 1889, in Ogden, Utah, Moroni Olsen (spelled "Maroni" at birth, according to his family's 1900 census form), was the youngest of three children born to Norwegian immigrants Edward Olsen and his wife, Martha. Although he reportedly never saw a stage play until the age of 13, Olsen was immediately captivated by the theater and determined to make his living as a performer. Shortly after playing his first stage role during his senior year of high school, Olsen organized a group known as "The Strollers," which presented one-act plays for residents of remote settlements in the area.

After his high school graduation, Olsen enrolled at the University of Utah at Salt Lake City, but spent most of his time playing bit parts in a local stock company. He eventually received his degree from the Leland Powers School of the Theater in Boston, then returned home to teach speech arts at Ogden High School. Two years later, he was tapped to direct and perform in the traveling tent

shows known as the Chautauqua Circuit. In 1920, while performing in one of the chautauquas, Olsen was spotted by director Maurice Browne and cast in his Broadway debut, playing Jason in *Medea*. Olsen went on to appear in such productions as *Joan of Arc*, *Candida*, *Iphigenia in Aulis*, and *Mr. Faust*.

Off stage, Olsen continued to share his skills and expertise with future thespians, heading the drama department at the Cornish School of Music in Seattle, organizing the Moroni Olsen Repertory Company, which toured the country for nearly eight years, and returning to his alma mater, the Leland Powers School in Boston, where he served as director. He resumed his Broadway career in 1933, earning acclaim for his portrayal of John Knox in *Mary of Scotland*, and later appearing with Katherine Cornell in *Romeo and Juliet* and *The Barretts of Wimpole Street*.

Olsen's success on the Broadway stage attracted the attention of Hollywood; in 1935, he signed a contract with RKO, debuting on the big screen as Porthos in *The Three Musketeers* (1935). Also that year he portrayed Buffalo Bill in *Annie Oakley* (1935), starring Barbara Stanwyck in the title role, and *Seven Keys to Baldpate* (1935), a mediocre comedy-mystery starring Gene Raymond.

RKO kept Olsen busy during the remainder of the decade representing a variety of vocations, including a police lieutenant in *The Witness Chair* (1936); a senator in *Gold Is Where You Find It* (1938), an attorney in *Dust Be My Destiny* (1939), and a warden in *Invisible Stripes* (1939). With the advent of the 1940s, the actor signed a contract with Warner Bros., lending his aristocratic bearing to such popular historical films as *Brigham Young — Frontiersman* (1940), with Dean Jagger in the title role; *Santa Fe Trail* (1940), where Olsen portrayed Robert E. Lee; and *One*

Foot in Heaven (1940), which was nominated for an Academy Award for Best Picture. Olsen was less successful with clunkers like *Three Sons o'Guns* (1941), a weak wartime comedy; *Ship Ahoy* (1942), a musical spy spoof with Red Skelton and Eleanor Powell; and *My Favorite Spy* (1942), a timewaster starring bandleader Kay Kyser (not to be confused with the popular 1951 Bob Hope feature of the same title). The actor fared better, however, with his first entry in the film noir era, *The Glass Key* (1942), starring Alan Ladd and Veronica Lake.

Here, Olsen portrayed Senator Ralph Henry, a political candidate whose daughter, Janet (Lake), becomes involved with the loutish but powerful Paul Madvig (Brian Donlevy) in hopes of winning his support for her father's campaign. The ambitious politician makes no bones about using Madvig for his own gain, telling his daughter, "Paul's support means the governorship for me. You must be nice to him, Janet — at least until *after* the election." When Henry's wastrel son, Taylor (Richard Denning), is murdered, suspicion is first cast on Paul, who had argued with Taylor shortly before his death. As it turns out, the real killer is the senator, who admits his guilt only when Paul's right-hand man (Alan Ladd) accuses Janet of the crime: "I'm the one you want. I killed my son," Henry confesses. "I followed Taylor and Paul after they quarreled here at the house. I caught up with them in the street. I told Taylor that he was ruining my political career. He struck me. He was going to strike again. We scuffled. Somehow, he fell. His head hit the curb. When Paul and I lifted him up, he was dead. It was an accident."

After *The Glass Key*, which earned praise from one critic as "an entertaining whodunit," Olsen appeared in *The Song of Bernadette* (1943), with Jennifer Jones playing the role of the peasant girl who sees a vision of the Virgin Mary; *Mission to Moscow* (1943), which was censured for its pro–Russian slant; *Madame Curie* (1943), starring Greer Garson; *Thirty Seconds Over Tokyo* (1944), a hit wartime drama; *Cobra Woman* (1944), a big-budget piece of escapism directed by Robert Siodmak; *Buffalo Bill* (1943), starring Joel McCrea in the title role; *Weekend at the Waldorf* (1945), a star-studded remake of *Grand Hotel* (1932); and *Pride of the Marines* (1945), a box-office smash starring John Garfield as an ex–GI blinded during the war.

Also during this period, Olsen re-entered the realm of noir, with a featured role in his second film from the era, *Mildred Pierce* (1945). In this first-rate offering, Olsen portrayed Inspector Peterson, a no-nonsense detective investigating the murder of Monte Beragon (Zachary Scott), the profligate spouse of the title character (Joan Crawford). As Peterson questions Mildred regarding her involvement, the film shows in flashback the events leading up to the crime, including Mildred's divorce from her first husband, Bert (Bruce Bennett), her marriage to Beragon, the phenomenal success of her restaurant business, and her relationship with her self-absorbed daughter, Veda (Ann Blyth). Despite Mildred's efforts to accept the blame for Monte's shooting, Peterson ultimately extracts an admission from Mildred that it was her daughter who was the real killer. Although most of the film's accolades were reserved for Crawford's Academy Award–winning performance, Olsen was singled out by several critics for his portrayal of the crafty lawman, including the reviewer for *The Hollywood Review*, who termed him "really excellent," and Red Kann of *Motion Picture Herald*, who found Olsen's performance to be "especially effective."

Following such hits as Alfred Hitchcock's *Notorious* (1946), starring Cary Grant and Ingrid Bergman, and *Life with Father* (1947), a delightful comedy featuring William Powell, Olsen was seen in a trio of films noirs, *Possessed* (1947), *The High Wall* (1947), and *Call Northside 777* (1948). The first starred Joan Crawford as Louise Howell Graham, a nurse whose obsession with her former lover, David (Van Heflin), leads her to madness and murder. Tortured by hallucinations after David ends their relationship, Louise grows increasingly delusional and finally seeks med-

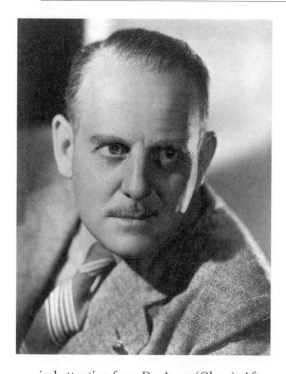

ical attention from Dr. Ames (Olsen). After examining her, Ames suggests that Louise is suffering from "neurasthenia," but assures her that she is not beyond help: "We all have dreams … bad dreams, sometimes. But we wake up, and we say, 'That was a bad dream.' Occasionally, however, we find a patient who can't wake up. He or she lacks insight, the ability to distinguish between what is real and what isn't," Ames soothingly explains. "Whatever it is that's troubling you, put an end to it. The important thing is to know that there is something the matter. Now that you know, you can do something about it." Unfortunately for David, Louise takes Ames' advice to heart; when she learns that David plans to marry another woman, Louise shoots and kills him, and is later found wandering the streets in a state of near catatonia.

Next, in *The High Wall* (1947), Olsen was again cast as a physician, this time as Dr. Philip Dunlap, the head of a psychiatric hospital where murder suspect Steven Kenet (Robert Taylor) has been admitted for treatment. Suffering from blackouts due to a subdural hematoma, Kenet is unable to recall the circumstances surrounding the strangling death of his wife, and Dunlap performs surgery on his brain in an effort to alleviate his condition. With the help of staff doctor Ann Lorrison (Audrey Totter), Kenet realizes that his wife was killed by her employer, book publisher Willard Whitcombe (Herbert Marshall), with whom she was having an affair. Unable to prove his innocence, Kenet subdues Whitcombe and Lorrison injects him with truth serum, after which the publisher admits his guilt in the crime.

Olsen's final film noir, *Call Northside 777* (1948), focused on the unflagging efforts of newspaper reporter Jim McNeal (James Stewart) to exonerate a man, Frank Wiecek (Richard Conte), who was wrongly imprisoned for the murder of a police officer 11 years before. Although McNeal manages to locate the woman who served as the primary witness in the case, however, she stubbornly refuses to admit that she was coerced by police into falsely identifying Wiecek. With time running out, McNeal stumbles upon a new police technique that helps to prove Wiecek's innocence and convinces the pardon board, headed by Olsen's character, to set the man free.

Despite his relatively minor roles in these back-to-back noir features, Olsen turned in solid performances in each, earning his best reviews for his role in *Possessed*; in the *Hollywood Citizen-News*, Lowell E. Redelings noted his "top-notch" performance, and Harrison Carroll of the *Los Angeles Herald-Express* including the actor in his praise of the film's "distinguished" supporting cast. Carroll offered similar accolades for the picture itself, terming it "a powerful film, holding a morbid fascination for the onlooker."

During the next several years, Olsen continued to appear in a number of critical and commercial successes, including *Samson and Delilah* (1949), a lavish biblical epic starring Victor Mature and Hedy Lamarr; *Task Force* (1949), a World War II drama starring Gary Cooper; *Father of the Bride* (1950) and its sequel, *Father's Little Dividend* (1951), appearing in both as the father-in-law of Elizabeth Taylor; *Lone Star* (1951), in which he portrayed Sam Houston, first president of the Republic of Texas; and *So This Is Love* (1953), an entertaining account of the life of soprano Grace Moore. Between films, the actor resumed his stage career, appearing on Broadway opposite Helen Hayes in *Mary of Scotland*, serving as co-director for Hollywood's Pilgrimage Play, and directing numerous productions for the famed Pasadena Playhouse, including *First Lady*, starring Dana Andrews, and *Merrily We Roll Along*, with Robert Preston. During the summer of 1954, he returned to his home state, directing outdoor musical pageants in Salt Lake City and Ogden that depicted the progress of Utah pioneers, and later that year was seen in the popular big screen comedy *The Long, Long Trailer* (1954), starring Lucille Ball and Desi Arnaz. Sadly, the film would be his last. On November 22, 1954, after complaining of feeling "ill and tired," Olsen was found dead in his Los Angeles apartment. The coroner's office attributed his death to natural causes, but more recent sources indicate that Olsen died after suffering a heart attack. At the time of his death, Olsen was directing rehearsals for *Trelawny of the Wells*, scheduled to open the following month at the Pasadena Playhouse. The actor, who never married, was 65 years old.

Moroni Olsen was once aptly described as possessing a "strong, rugged face, a voice of deep and powerful timbre, and a physique that takes the world in its stride." Although his name is all but forgotten by today's audiences, the character performances delivered by the actor in his impressive body of films serve as a lasting and memorable testament to his versatility, dependability, and talent.

Film Noir Filmography

The Glass Key. Director: Stuart Heisler. Producer: B.G. DeSylva. Running time: 85 minutes. Released by Paramount, October 15, 1942. Cast: Brian Donlevy, Veronica Lake, Alan Ladd, Bonita Granville, Joseph Calleia, Richard Denning, Moroni Olsen, William Bendix, Margaret Hayes, Arthur Loft, George Meader, Eddie Marr, Frances Gifford, Joe McGuinn, Frank Hagney, Joseph King.

Mildred Pierce. Director: Michael Curtiz. Producer: Jerry Wald. Running time: 113 minutes. Released by Warner Bros., September 28, 1945. Cast: Joan Crawford, Jack Carson, Zachary Scott, Eve Arden, Ann Blyth, Bruce Bennett, Lee Patrick, Moroni Olson, Jo Ann Marlowe, Barbara Brown, Charles Trowbridge, John Compton, Butterfly McQueen. Awards: Academy Award for Best Actress (Joan Crawford). Academy Award nominations for Best Picture, Best Supporting Actress (Eve Arden and Ann Blyth), Best Black and White Cinematography (Ernest Haller), Best Screenplay (Ranald MacDougall).

Possessed. Director: Curtis Bernhardt. Producer: Jerry Wald. Running time: 108 minutes. Released by Warner Brothers, May 29, 1947. Cast: Joan Crawford, Van Heflin, Raymond Massey, Geraldine Brooks, Stanley Ridges, John Ridgely, Moroni Olsen, Erskine Sanford, Gerald Perreau, Isabel Withers, Lisa Golm, Douglas Kennedy, Monte Blue, Don McGuire, Rory Mallinson, Clifton Young, Griff Barnett. Awards: Academy Award nomination for Best Actress (Joan Crawford).

The High Wall. Director: Curtis Bernhardt. Producer: Robert Lord. Running time: 100 minutes. Released by MGM, December 25, 1947. Cast: Robert Taylor, Audrey Totter, Herbert Marshall, Dorothy Patrick, H.B. Warner, Warner Anderson, Moroni Olsen, John Ridgeley, Morris Ankrum, Elisabeth Risdon, Vince Barnett, Jonathan Hale, Charles Arnt, Ray Mayer, Dick Wessell, Robert Emmet O'Connor, Celia Travers, Mary Servoss, Bobby Hyatt, Eula Guy, Jack Davis, Tom Quinn.

Call Northside 777. Director: Henry Hathaway. Producer: Otto Lang. Running time: 111 minutes. Released by 20th Century-Fox. Cast: James Stewart, Richard Conte, Lee J. Cobb, Helen Walker, Betty Garde, Kasia Orzazewski, Joanne de Bergh, Howard Smith, Moroni Olsen, John McIntire, Paul Harvey, George Tyne, Richard Bishop, Otto Waldis, Michael Chapin, E.G. Marshall, Truman Bradley.

References

"Actor-Director Moroni Olsen Taken by Death." *Los Angeles Times*, November 23, 1954.
Biography of Moroni Olsen. RKO Radio Pictures, circa 1935.
Biography of Moroni Olsen. 20th Century-Fox Studios, circa 1952.
"Character Actor Dies in Apartment." *Los Angeles Examiner*, November 23, 1954.
Dot Biography of Moroni Olsen. RKO Radio Pictures, circa 1936.

"Moroni Olsen, Actor, Found Dead in His Apartment." *Los Angeles Daily News*, November 23, 1954.

1900 Census— United States. Family of Edward A. Olsen. Ogden City, Utah, Weber County, June 1, 1900.

Obituary. *Variety*, November 24, 1954.

"Olsen Rites to Be Friday." *Hollywood Citizen-News*, November 25, 1954.

JACK PALANCE

"I've got to think fast. Got to think of a nice, foolproof little accident."— Jack Palance in *Sudden Fear* (1952)

Of Jack Palance's sculptured, high-cheek-boned visage, it was once written: "Some faces are masks, others are like architecture. Jack Palance — now there's a face! A face like the side of a cliff— a face with geography!"

And there was no dearth of explanations on how Palance's striking features came to be; according to most accounts, the actor was involved in an airplane crash during World War II that severely damaged his face and required numerous surgeries. One reporter even claimed, with considerable drama and pathos, that the accident left Palance a "shell of a man who, burned almost beyond recognition, wanted to die until psychiatrists convinced him that life still offered him something special." Palance later denied the reports, but even he essayed differing accounts, stating in 1954 that he'd undergone five operations on his nose because of numerous breaks, but claiming 30 years later that "the only plastic surgery I've ever had in my life was a 10-minute operation to open my nasal passages."

Palance's visual aspects aside, the actor became an acclaimed star of the television, stage, and screen during a career that, to date, has spanned six decades. Along the way, Palance (whose name rhymes with "balance") was seen in such screen gems as *Shane* (1953); earned an Emmy Award for his outstanding portrayal in the 1957 *Playhouse 90* presentation of "Requiem for a Heavyweight"; landed three Academy Award nominations; and won the golden statue in 1992 for his performance

in *City Slickers*. Palance was also a memorable presence in four films from the noir era: *Panic in the Streets* (1950), *Sudden Fear* (1952), *The Big Knife* (1955), and I *Died a Thousand Times* (1955).

The man with, it was once said, "the face that launched a thousand quips," was born Walter Palahnuik on February 18, 1920, in a Northeastern Pennsylvania coal mining town known as Lattimer Mines. The third of five children born to Ukranian immigrant parents, the actor once recalled his early years as pleasant ones.

"I guess it was a good childhood, like most kids think they have," Palance said in a 1954 *Saturday Evening Post* interview. "It was fine to play there, in the third-growth birch and aspen, along the sides of the slag piles, on the bright green grass that grew on the tops of the culm dumps. Baseball, mostly; when the ball was knocked into the drainage ditch, all 18 players dived after it. No ball, no game."

Interested in athletics throughout his youth, Palance demonstrated a particular talent for boxing, participating in his first match at the age of 14 when he walked seven miles to the fight and returned home with his 75-cent half of the total winnings. Palance expanded his sports activities at Hazle Township High School, playing fullback and quarterback on the school's football team and earning a spot on the All-Regional basketball team. It was also during his high school years that Palance was first bitten by the acting bug, playing the role of an attorney in his senior class play. After graduation, Palance won an athletic scholarship to the University of North Carolina, where he focused most of his energies on the school's various playing fields.

"I left in two years because I felt I couldn't stand a steady diet of football," Palance said. "The season was from August first to December. We started winter practice on January tenth. Then, we had ten weeks' spring practice. I was doing boxing, too, so it didn't leave much time for anything else."

Although his parents were unhappy with his decision to leave college ("I can still remember them standing on the porch, crying, begging me to go back and finish," the actor later recalled), Palance decided to make a career out of boxing. Billed as Rocky Palahnuik, he won 18 of 20 professional bouts, but ended his career in the ring when an opponent struck a blow to his throat that rendered him unable to speak for a week. For a brief time, Palance returned home and worked alongside his father in the coal mines, then joined the Army Air Force and began training as a bomber pilot. A year later, in November 1943, Palance took off in a B-24, but the plane's engine died and crashed shortly after take-off. Knocked unconscious by the impact, Palance spent the next two months in the hospital, but the actor denied that he underwent numerous surgeries — as so many accounts claim — because his "face was a bloody pulp." Instead, the actor said, he was kept under observation and given a succession of X-rays because "they seemed to think something was scrambled up — and maybe they were right."

"When I went out, I took the B-24 up and came in. Right before my eyes, the landing strip moved over about a hundred yards — or seemed to," Palance said in 1954. "My co-pilot took the controls. That was that."

Discharged with medical disability papers, Palance enrolled in Stanford University in 1945 under the G.I. Bill of Rights, majoring in journalism.

"I soon learned that journalism was a going concern, but I couldn't get concerned about it," Palance once said. "I switched to an English major, and concentrated on short stories." Palance also took a summer course in radio, participating in writing, announcing, producing, and acting, then renewed his interest in the stage by landing a role in a local production of *My Indian Family*. The play's star, veteran actress Aline MacMahon, encouraged Palance's theatrical aspirations and a short time later, he borrowed $100 from his roommate and headed for the bright lights of Broadway.

"I thought I would have to stretch [the money] to make it last the three years they told me would pass before I got on the stage," Palance said. "As it was, it only took me a week. I went to the audition for a play which was being directed by actor Robert Montgomery, entitled *The Big Two*. When I saw all of the other would-be actors in the waiting room, I was about to walk out when Mr. Montgomery stopped me by saying, 'I want you.' He had been looking for a Russian type and my cheekbones filled the bill."

After three weeks on Broadway and two months on the road, *The Big Two* closed, but in March 1948, Palance was cast as a circus strong man in *Temporary Island*, and earned praise for his "dynamic performance" later that year for his portrayal of Simon Peter in *The Vigil*. Both productions were flops, but the budding thespian managed to make ends meet by working a series of odd jobs, including waiter, short order cook, lifeguard, and photographer's model. He then landed a part as the understudy of actor Anthony Quinn in the road production of *A Streetcar Named Desire* (only the first of several instances where Palance would come in second to Quinn), but after four months with the play, Palance left the company and returned to New York. The experience was a disappointing one, but it did have a bright spot — while on tour, Palance fell in love with actress Virginia Baker, who understudied the role of Stella. Eight months after their first meeting, in April 1949, Palance and Baker married, and would later have three children, Holly in 1950, Brooke in 1952, and Cody in 1955.

Meanwhile, shortly after leaving the road

company of *Streetcar*, Palance was hired to understudy Marlon Brando in the Broadway version of the play and finally got a chance to appear on stage in the role of Stanley Kowalski when Brando broke his nose. (Some sources stated that it was Palance who caused the break, while sparring with the star in the boiler room of the theater.) After a week, Brando returned, and Palance moved on again, next appearing as the hero of an off–Broadway production entitled *The Silver Tassie*. During his run with the short-lived play, Palance was spotted by talent scouts from 20th Century-Fox and was signed to a contract for his screen debut — and his first film noir — *Panic in the Streets* (1950). Billed as Walter Jack Palance, the actor played Blackie, a brutish thug who is unknowingly carrying a deadly virus that could lead to a widespread plague. As Dr. Clinton Reed (Richard Widmark) of the U.S. Public Health Service tries in vain to convince his colleagues of the situation's urgency, the number of victims begins to mount. After a desperate hunt through the seedy dock section of New Orleans, Reed finally succeeds in cornering Blackie, and the near-catastrophic plague is contained.

As Blackie, Palance portrayed an especially vicious character; in one scene, he repeatedly slaps one of his partners in crime, Poldi (Guy Thomajan), even as the man lay dying from the deadly virus. And later, when Blackie and an underling, Fitch (Zero Mostel), carry Poldi down a flight of stairs on a mattress, they are confronted by Dr. Reed, who insists on examining the ailing man. To escape the doctor, Blackie tosses Poldi — mattress and all — over the railing to the ground below. For his memorable performance, Palance was hailed by critics, with Ezra Goodman writing in the *Los Angeles Daily News* that "acting honors go to towering, skeletal Walter Palance," and the *Los Angeles Times'* Philip K. Scheuer proclaiming, "In the extraordinary rogues' gallery of types, none is more fascinating than Walter (Jack) Palance, a hulking giant with a catlike grace and a caressing voice." And Palance not only caught the attention of critics with his brutal per-

formance in *Panic*— he made an impact on his fellow actors as well.

"We rehearsed a scene with a rubber gun, but unbeknownst to me, for the take, [Palance] switched to a real gun and bonged me on the head," co-star Richard Widmark recalled in a 1987 interview. "I was out for about 20 minutes. I was mad as hell when I came to, but I wasn't about to attack him. He's one tough guy, strong as a gorilla. Offstage, to get himself charged up for his scenes, he'd hammer on Zero Mostel, who played his flunky. Zero kept crying, 'Don't do that!' After a week of this, they took Zero, who was black and blue, to a hospital to soak him in Epsom pads."

After *Panic in the Streets*, Palance was rushed into *Halls of Montezuma* (1950), in which he played a former boxer by the name of Punchy. He next campaigned for the role of Eufemio in *Viva Zapata* (1952), but the part was given to Anthony Quinn and Palance reportedly walked out on his contract in frustration. Returning to New York, he was promptly cast in the Broadway production of *Darkness of Noon*, earning the designation of "most promising personality" by the Broadway stage journal, *Theatre World*. His striking portrayal of a Russian commissar also caught the eye of director George Stevens, who tapped Palance for the role of the sadistic hired gunman in *Shane* (1953), in which he offered one of the most memorable portrayals of his career.

Before *Shane* was released, however, Palance was seen in his second film noir, *Sudden Fear* (1952), playing stage actor Lester Blaine. After Blaine woos and weds wealthy playwright Myra Hudson (Joan Crawford), the blissful bride is stunned to hear a tape recording which reveals that her spouse is not only having an affair, but that he and his lover, Irene Neves (Gloria Grahame), are plotting her imminent demise: "Sometimes when I'm with her," Lester says on the tape, "it's all I can do to keep from saying, 'Wise up — love you? I never loved you. Never for one moment.' I'd like to see her face." When she recovers from the shock of this double whammy, Myra determines to get the jump on the duo, and plans an intricate scheme to murder Lester and frame Irene for the crime. At the last moment, Myra loses her nerve, but Lester has figured out her plan and tries to run her down in his car. Coincidentally, the similarly dressed Irene is on a nearby street and, mistaking her for Myra, Lester crashes into his lover, killing himself in the bargain.

The release of *Sudden Fear* brought a spate of accolades for Palance. Howard Mc-Clay, of the *Los Angeles Daily News*, praised his "exceptionally fine" performance, adding that Palance, "a guy we tabbed some time ago as star material, definitely proves his ability to handle top fare"; the critic for *The Hollywood Reporter* wrote that Palance "adds to his stature tremendously with his powerful, deadly portrayal," and the *Los Angeles Examiner*'s Ruth Waterbury, while labeling Palance "the ugliest man on the screen," nonetheless hailed the actor for his "outstanding acting ability." Palance's performance brought him a much-deserved Academy Award nomination for Best Supporting Actor, but he lost to Anthony Quinn — who else?—for *Viva Zapata*. When *Shane* was finally released the following year, Palance experienced a second wave of acclaim and his second consecutive Best Supporting Actor nomination; but he lost again, this time to Frank Sinatra in *From Here to Eternity*. His popularity was at an all-time high, however —*Look* magazine named him the Most Outstanding Newcomer of 1953, and he was receiving an average of 1,500 fan letters each week.

After his tremendous success in *Sudden Fear* and *Shane*, Palance saw his talents all but wasted in *The Silver Chalice* (1954), a disappointing biblical epic notable primarily as the film debut of 29-year-old Paul Newman; *Sign of the Pagan* (1954), a big-budget spectacle in which he chewed a considerable amount of scenery as Atilla the Hun; and *Kiss of Fire* (1955), where he was woefully miscast as Spanish nobleman known as El Tigre. Palance rebounded, however, with starring roles in back-to-back films noirs,

The Big Knife (1955) and *I Died a Thousand Times* (1955).

In the first, Palance portrayed Charlie Castle, whose transformation from an idealistic stage actor to a hard-drinking, philandering film star has led to an estrangement from his long-suffering wife, Marion (Ida Lupino). The other characters in this dark, grim tale include Charlie's sadistic studio head, Stanley Hoff (Rod Steiger); Hoff's associate, Smiley Coy (Wendell Corey); Connie Bliss (Jean Hagen), the wife of Charlie's press agent, with whom the actor had a one-night dalliance; and Dixie Evans (Shelley Winters), a local starlet who harbors a potentially damaging secret from Charlie's past. Although Charlie and Marion reconcile, the actor's life falls into an irrevocable tailspin triggered by a series of events, including the possible exposure of his involvement in a hit-and-run accident that killed a child, and the discovery by Charlie's press agent of the actor's brief affair with Connie. ("You were my friend — how could you do it?" the agent tearfully asks, then spits in Charlie's face. "That's how I resign.") Unable to cope with the pressures heaped on him, Charlie locks himself in his bathroom and slits his wrists.

Although *The Big Knife* is one of the more brutal and memorable offerings from the film noir era, it proved somewhat distasteful to critics of the day; the reviewer from *Variety* termed the film "sometimes so brittle and brutal as to prove disturbing," and in the *New York Times*, Bosley Crowther opined that the film's writers "were more disposed to extreme emotionalism than to actuality and good sense." Crowther was similarly disparaging toward Palance's hard-hitting performance, describing his character as a "big, shaggy Hollywood actor, played in a big shaggy way by Jack Palance."

Next, in *I Died a Thousand Times*, released just one day after *The Big Knife*, Palance starred as ex-convict Roy Earle, who teams with two small-time hoods to knock over a California resort hotel. Although he is attracted to Marie (Shelley Winters), the girlfriend of one of the hoods, Earle is also drawn to a local girl who suffers from a crippling clubfoot. ("Listen, I'm gonna give it to you straight," he tells Marie. "I got plans, see, personal plans, and you just don't fit into them. You could never mean much of anything to me. Nothing special, that is.") After financing an operation to correct the girl's condition, Earle is dismayed when she cruelly rejects his proposal of marriage. Meanwhile, Earle's luck continues to run out when the hotel heist goes awry, resulting in the shooting of a guard and the death of his co-conspirators in a car crash during the getaway. Accompanied by the ever-faithful Marie, Earle goes on the lam, but he is ultimately cornered and gunned down by police.

A remake of the excellent Humphrey Bogart starrer, *High Sierra* (1941), *I Died a Thousand Times* rightfully suffered in comparison with the original, with Bosley Crowther commenting in the *New York Times*, "Somehow it isn't quite as touching as it was 14 years ago." Crowther grudgingly admitted, however, that "the trouble is not wholly Mr. Palance ... [who] is a mighty fine specimen of Old World criminal. There are not many like him around these days."

After this feature, Palance continued his string of first-rate performances, playing an avenging World War II lieutenant in *Attack!* (1956), directed by Robert Aldrich; *The Lonely Man* (1957), an intriguing western co-starring Anthony Perkins, Neville Brand, and Elisha Cook, Jr.; and *House of Numbers* (1957), in which he played the dual role of twin brothers. Between films, Palance returned to the stage, appearing in the summer of 1955 in *Julius Caesar* and *The Tempest* at the first American Shakespeare Festival in Stratford, Connecticut. He also lent his talents to the small screen, starring in 1956 in the *Playhouse 90* presentation of "Requiem for a Heavyweight." For his harrowing and moving portrayal of Mountain McClintock, a broken-down boxer, Palance earned an Emmy Award for Best Single Performance by an Actor, beating out Lloyd Bridges, Red Skelton, Fredric March, and Sal Mineo.

Growing disillusioned with his Hollywood screen assignments, Palance relocated to Europe in 1958 — leaving his wife and three children behind — and appeared in a series of foreign productions over the next several years. The most notable of his features during this period included *Austerlitz* (1959), starring Rosanno Brazzi and Claudia Cardinale, and *Barabbas* (1961), with Anthony Quinn (!) portraying the title role. Palance returned to the U.S. in the early 1960s, starring as a circus boss on *The Greatest Show on Earth*, which ran on ABC-TV from September 1963 to September 1964. The actor later claimed that he agreed to do the series "against my better judgment."

"I just didn't realize how much work was required to produce a nothing," Palance said in a 1976 *TV Guide* interview. "It wrecks your day. It wrecks your week. If you don't watch out, it wrecks your life."

After the cancellation of the series, Palance was seen on the big screen in a pair of MGM productions, *Once a Thief* (1965), where he gave a chilling performance as a gangland killer, and *The Spy in the Green Hat* (1966), which featured appearances from several veterans of 1930s Warner Bros. gangster pictures, including Allen Jenkins, Eduardo

Ciannelli, and Elisha Cook, Jr. Palance followed these features with a role as a Mexican bandit in *The Professionals* (1966), a box-office hit for Columbia that starred Burt Lancaster, Lee Marvin, and Robert Ryan. The actor then switched occupational gears, making his debut as a director in the stage production of *Heaven Can Wait*, which was presented at the Melodyland Theater in Anaheim, California.

"As you get older, you realize that being a film actor is a very sedentary occupation," Palance said in a *Los Angeles Times* interview. "Working in films involves killing a lot of time waiting for someone to say, 'We're ready for you, Mr. Palance.' Directing comes as a welcome relief from all that sitting around."

The cast of *Heaven Can Wait* included Palance's wife, Virginia; in an interview conducted shortly before the two-week run of the play, the actor admitted that directing his spouse was not "a great idea."

"Things can get pretty tense," Palance said. "My wife has a laugh that could shatter glass in the lobby. I keep telling her, 'Now that will do, Miss Baker,' but it never does. Last night she told me I had said THAT once too often. I really don't know how Alfred Lunt manages it."

Ironically, less than a year after this interview, in September 1966, Palance and his wife separated, and two months later, Virginia filed a separate maintenance lawsuit, claiming that Palance was hiding more than $100,000 in property in Europe and had threatened to return to his work abroad because "I will not pay alimony to any woman." After the couple's 1968 divorce, however, Palance spoke highly of his former spouse, calling her "charming and stimulating," and attributed their split to "long absences, my work taking me away for months at a time, getting out of touch with each other, losing understanding."

While he wasn't making news because of his marital woes, Palance was in the headlines for his increasing support for the U.S. civil rights movement — his stance was typified in a 1964 letter he wrote to *Variety* stating that it was "appalling that [FBI director

J. Edgar] Hoover denounces Dr. [Martin Luther] King, a Nobel Prize winner and characterizes him as a 'liar.'" Palance also became known for his support for black performers in Hollywood and was credited for being the first white actor to hire a black stand-in, Marcello Clay, for his series, *The Greatest Show on Earth*. Shortly before the cancellation of that series, in July 1964, Palance was the inadvertent cause of a riot outside a movie theater in Tuscaloosa, Alabama, which broke out after a rumor spread that the actor had escorted a black woman to the recently integrated theater. A mob of more than 300 whites hurled bottles and stones at the movie house, dispersing only after a police force of 40 officers moved in with tear gas and high-pressure hoses. Palance, who was inside the theater with his wife and three children, later told reporters he believed he was targeted because he had "the nerve to stop on street corners and sign autographs or shake hands with Negro as well as white fans."

The frightening incident in Tuscaloosa would not be Palance's last brush with racial tensions and prejudices in the United States. Two years later, after his closing night performance in *Heaven Can Wait* in Anaheim, the actor told the audience that the "two happiest experiences of my life were escaping from Tuscaloosa and now from Anaheim." His remarks referred to local residents whom he charged with boycotting the production "because of my activities in the civil rights movement and because I put two Negroes into roles previously played by white men." A short time later, Palance announced that he was turning down a role in the upcoming MGM production of *The Dirty Dozen* (1967) because he refused to play the character of "a Negro-baiter."

"We don't need to make pictures showing how nasty the whites are to Negroes," the actor said.

Professionally, Palance was back on the big screen in 1969, starring as Fidel Castro in *Che!* He told reporters that he accepted the role because "my children are hungry."

"At this stage in my career, I don't formulate reasons why I take roles," Palance said. "The price was right."

After *Che!*, a disappointment at the box office, Palance divided his screen time during the next decade between American and foreign films, including *The McMasters* (1969), a western focusing on racial prejudices during the Civil War; *Chato's Land* (1971), filmed in Spain and starring Charles Bronson as the Apache Indian of the title; *Su Puo Fare ... Amigo* (1972), a slapstick western; *Oklahoma Crude* (1973), in which Palance played the villainous head of an oil trust; *Craze* (1973), a British horror film; *The Four Deuces* (1976), a low-budget actioner co-starring Carol Lynley; *The One Man Jury* (1978), which saw the actor portraying a brutal cop; and *The Shape of Things to Come* (1979), an inferior remake of the 1936 science-fiction classic *Things to Come*. During these years, Palance was seen in a number of television productions as well, including *Dracula* (1973), where he played the title role, and *The Last Ride of the Dalton Gang* (1979), a light-hearted depiction of the Dalton Gang's legendary raid on Coffeyville, Kansas. He also starred in his second television series, *Bronk*, playing the title role of a California police detective. The series, conceived by actor Carroll O'Connor, was cancelled in 1976 after a year-long run on CBS, and Palance later dismissed the show as "stupid."

Palance returned to series television in 1982, hosting *Ripley's Believe It Or Not* on ABC. Co-hosted by his daughter, Holly, the series ran for four years, and Palance was praised for his "enthusiastic" delivery.

"There are some actors who would have taken the hosting job, but done it offhandedly, as though they were above it," a critic for *TV Guide* wrote. "But Palance gives it everything — all his saturnine suaveness, but also real enthusiasm. He seems to be enjoying himself as he serves up a grisly item in some musty tomb — pausing pregnantly for effect before delivering the punch line, 'Believe it, or not!' with a leonine purr and a sinister smile. He is the right man for the job."

After *Believe It Or Not* left the air, Palance enjoyed a resurgence in his screen career, appearing in such films as *Young Guns* (1988), a popular western starring Emilio Estevez, Kiefer Sutherland, and Lou Diamond Phillips; *Tango and Cash* (1989), a hit buddy-cop actioner in which he played a wealthy drug dealer; *Batman* (1989), a box-office smash in which Palance was featured as a corrupt crime boss; and *City Slickers* (1991), where Palance's performance as a curmudgeonly dude ranch trail boss earned the actor an Academy Award for Best Supporting Actor. (He also won a Golden Globe award in 1992 for his portrayal.) At the March 1992 Academy Awards ceremony, where Palance beat out Tommy Lee Jones, Harvey Keitel, Ben Kingsley, and Michael Lerner, the 72-year-old actor essayed a brief acceptance speech, then demonstrated his virility by performing a series of one-arm push-ups, much to the surprise and delight of the audience. Although Palance's character died in *City Slickers*, the actor was back for the film's 1994 sequel, *City Slickers II: The Secret of Curley's Gold*, playing the trail boss's twin brother.

During the next several years, Palance was seen in such films as *Cops and Robbersons* (1994), a mediocre comedy co-starring Chevy Chase, and several television productions, including *Buffalo Girls* (1995), a CBS-TV miniseries in which he played a trapper named Bartle Bone; *Ebenezer* (1997), a wild west retelling of the Charles Dickens classic, *A Christmas Carol*; and *Sarah, Plain and Tall: Winter's End* (1999), starring Glenn Close and Christopher Walken. But the actor was spending most of his time pursuing his old love for writing, and in 1996 wrote an 87-page book of poetry, *The Forest of Love: A Love Story in Blank Verse*. The book was praised by critics, including Arlene Vigoda of *USA Today*, who wrote: "Who knew the tough guy of one-armed push-up fame could be such a romantic softie?"

Now in his 80s, Palance rarely appears in acting roles; his most recent performance was in the little-seen 2001 feature, *Prancer Returns*, starring John Corbett (best known for his roles on TV's *Northern Exposure* and *Sex in the City*.) While Palance remains one of the outstanding talents of cinema history, however, he stated late in his career that his energies were focused on more meaningful things.

"Acting is no longer important to me," Palance said. "I came to the realization that everything is so short, so temporary.... We run around for a number of years, then drop off the face of the earth as a fulfillment of that futility. The goal is to make life livable. That, finally, governs everybody."

Film Noir Filmography

Panic in the Streets. Director: Elia Kazan. Producer: Sol C. Siegel. Running time: 96 minutes. Released by 20th Century-Fox, August 4, 1950. Cast: Richard Widmark, Paul Douglas, Barbara Bel Geddes, Walter Jack Palance, Zero Mostel, Dan Riss, Alexis Minotis, Guy Thomajan, Tommy Cook. Awards: Academy Award nomination for Best Motion Picture Story (Edna and Edward Anhalt).

Sudden Fear. Director: David Miller. Producer: Joseph Kaufman. Running time: 110 minutes. Released by RKO, August 7, 1952. Cast: Joan Crawford, Jack Palance, Gloria Grahame, Bruce Bennett, Virginia Huston, Touch [Mike] Conners. Awards: Academy Award nominations for Best Actress (Joan Crawford), Best Supporting Actor (Jack Palance), Best Black and White Cinematography (Charles B. Lang, Jr.), Best Costume Design/Black and White (Sheila O'Brien).

The Big Knife. Director and Producer: Robert Aldrich. Running time: 111 minutes. Released by United Artists, November 8, 1955. Cast: Jack Palance, Ida Lupino, Wendell Corey, Jean Hagen, Rod Steiger, Shelley Winters, Ilka Chase, Everett Sloane, Wesley Addy, Paul Langton, Nick Dennis, Bill Walker, Mike Winkelman, Mel Welles, Robert Sherman, Strother Martin, Ralph Volkie, Michael Fox, Richard Boone.

I Died a Thousand Times. Director: Stuart Heisler. Producer: Willis Goldbeck. Running time: 109 minutes. Released by Warner Bros., November 9, 1955. Cast: Jack Palance, Shelley Winters, Lori Nelson, Lee Marvin, Earl Holliman, Perry Lopez, Gonzalez Gonzalez, Lon Chaney, Jr., Howard St. John, Ralph Moody, Olive Carey, Joseph Millikin, Richard Davalos, Bill Kennedy, Peggy Maley.

References

Brock, Alan. "Jack Palance: Before and After Success." *Classic Images*, July 1982.

Graham, Sheilah. "Reconciliation for Palances Foreseen." *Hollywood Citizen-News*, July 27, 1961.

Harford, Margaret. "'Heaven' Waits but Jack Can't." *Los Angeles Times*, February 8, 1966.

Hopper, Hedda. "Best of Bad Men!" *Chicago Tribune Magazine*, circa 1950.

Hubler, Richard G. "Hollywood's Frightening Lover." *The Saturday Evening Post*, November 13, 1954.

Humphrey, Hal. "Palance Joined Circus So He Could Stay Home." *Los Angeles Times*, September 15, 1962.

"Jack Palance Presence Sparks Tuscaloosa Riot." *Los Angeles Times*, July 11, 1964.

"Jack Palance Rumor Starts Riot in South." *Hollywood Citizen-News*, July 10, 1964.

Johnson, Erskine. "Realism in Rome Spurs Palance." *Los Angeles Mirror*, June 21, 1961.

Manners, Dorothy. "A Decree Does Not a Divorce Make — Palance." *Los Angeles Herald-Examiner*, April 16, 1969.

Moss, Morton. "How It Is." *Los Angeles Herald-Examiner*, March 31, 1975.

"Palance Back in H'wood for 'Good' After 5 Yrs. in Italy, Now on 'Downswing.'" *Variety*, September 11, 1962.

Palance, Jack. Letter to the Editor. *Variety*, December 4, 1964.

"Palance Plays Role of Castro." *Hollywood Citizen-News*, June 6, 1969.

"Palance Refuses to Play 'Dirty' Role for Metro." *Variety*, February 22, 1966.

"Rioters Pick Palance for Race Target." *Los Angeles Herald-Examiner*, July 10, 1964.

Stumpf, Charles. "Jack Palance — Coal Miner's Son — Part I." *Classic Images*, June 1999.

_____. "Jack Palance — Coal Miner's Son — Part II." *Classic Images*, September 1999.

Thomas, Bob. "Price Was Right for Jack Palance to Play in 'Che!'" *Los Angeles Herald-Examiner*, January 3, 1969.

Whitney, Dwight. "'In the City I Want to Scream.'" *TV Guide*, March 27, 1976.

"Wife Sues Jack Palance." *Los Angeles Herald-Examiner*, November 3, 1966.

Wilson, Earl. "Down on the Farm with Jack Palance." *Los Angeles Herald-Examiner*, May 6, 1975.

Wilson, Liza. "Gentle Killer." *The American Weekly*, July 12, 1953.

Documentary

"Jack Palance: From Grit to Grace." Produced by Van Ness Films, Inc., in Association with

Prometheus Entertainment, Foxstar Productions, Fox Television Stations and A&E Network. 20th Century-Fox Film Corporation, Copyright, 2001.

JOHN PAYNE

"All I can do is give you a gun. If you haven't got guts enough to pull the trigger, I can't help it." — John Payne in *Slightly Scarlet* (1956)

John Payne had all the makings of a movie star — he possessed a strapping physique and good looks (complete with a captivating, slightly devilish smile and an eye-catching cleft in his chin) — and to top it off, he was a versatile actor, equally at home with drama or comedy. Nonetheless, Payne never quite reached the ranks of the major performers of his day, despite being teamed during his film career with such notables as Betty Grable, Maureen O'Hara, and Alice Faye. Still, the actor is still remembered today for his starring role in the perennial holiday classic *Miracle on 34th Street* (1947), and he also made his mark in the realm of film noir,

starring in five features from that era: *The Crooked Way* (1949), *Kansas City Confidential* (1952), *99 River Street* (1953), *Hell's Island* (1955), and *Slightly Scarlet* (1956).

Payne entered the world on May 23, 1912 (some sources say May 28th), in Roanoke, Virginia, one of three boys born to George Washington Payne and his wife, Ida Hope Schaffer, who once sang minor roles with the Metropolitan Opera. A real estate and construction mogul, Payne's father kept his family in fine style — in the early 1920s, the family moved to a plantation near Salem, Virginia, and young John later attended prep school at the prestigious Mercersburg Academy in Pennsylvania. But the future actor's life changed abruptly with the stock market crash of 1929 — his father lost the bulk of his money, and died of an "apoplexy stroke" a year later.

At the time of his father's death, Payne was a student at Roanoke University, but he was forced to suspend his studies in order to help support his struggling family. In an effort to make ends meet, the young man took on a variety of jobs, including working as a male nurse to a neighboring widower's two children, and singing at local radio stations. Within a few years, Payne was able to enroll at the Pulitzer School of Journalism at Columbia University, where he paid his way by working as a pulp story writer. He also earned money as a boxer and, later, a wrestler — billed as Alexei Petroff, the Savage of the Steppes.

"When my money ran out, I ran the elevator, operated a switchboard, and took care of a pool room," Payne later recalled in an interview with famed columnist Hedda Hopper. "I'd been studying voice, so I got a job on radio. Then the Shuberts offered me a part in a road company ... I told the Shuberts I could do anything. They took me at my word for $40 a week. I ended that tour with $3.20 to my name. But show business was in my blood by then."

After his stint with the Shuberts, Payne landed a job as the understudy for actor Reginald Gardiner in a popular musical, *At Home Abroad*. The young man's role in the play turned out to be his big break. According to legend, Payne was spotted by Sam Goldwyn, who signed him to a contract and gave him a bit part in his film debut, *Dodsworth* (1936), starring Walter Huston and Ruth Chatterton. But the small role was Payne's only screen work for a year, and he was released from his contract. The following year, Payne starred opposite Stella Adler in Paramount's slapstick comedy *Love on Toast* (1937), and with Mae Clarke in a forgettable musical for Grand National, *Hats Off* (1937). Disappointed with his assignments, Payne signed with Warner Bros., where he was given the role originally intended for Dick Powell in *Garden of the Moon* (1938). Directed by Busby Berkeley, the musical was a modest success, and Payne finally seemed to be on his way. But after another four pictures—the best of which was the mildly entertaining musical comedy, *Kid Nightingale* (1939), with Jane Wyman—Payne moved on again, this time signing with 20th Century–Fox.

In his first year with Fox, Payne was seen in a whopping six films, including *Tin Pan Alley* (1940), with Alice Faye and Betty Grable; *Star Dust* (1940), which marked the debut of a young Linda Darnell; and *The Great Profile* (1940), where John Barrymore spoofed himself, playing a drunken stage ham. The handsome, six-foot, four-inch actor was a natural for the frothy musicals and lightweight comedies that were a staple at the Fox lot, and Payne found himself constantly under assignment.

"I was dropped so often by studios that I was bouncing until Twentieth put me under

contract," Payne said once. "I couldn't complain because of lack of work there. Twice I was doing two pictures simultaneously, playing in one by night and the other by day."

But by now, Payne was not only busy on screen — in 1938, after a whirlwind courtship, he married actress Anne Shirley, best known for her performance in the Barbara Stanwyck starrer *Stella Dallas* (1937). A year after their marriage, the couple had a daughter, Julie Anne. (Julie would herself later become an actress, with small roles in such popular films as *This is Spinal Tap* [1984], *Jumpin' Jack Flash* [1986], and *The Brady Bunch Movie* [1995], as well as a variety of television shows, including a recurring role as Mrs. Falcinella on the ABC-TV series *The Wonder Years*.) Despite the young couple's popularity with moviegoers, Payne and Shirley's "perfect marriage" was destined for failure, and they would divorce in 1943.

Meanwhile, Payne continued his frenetic film schedule at Fox—for the next several years, he starred in a series of box-office hits, including *Sun Valley Serenade* (1941), with popular figure skater-turned-movie star Sonja Henie, and *Remember the Day* (1941), a first-rate tearjerker that Payne called his favorite film. "There was no melodrama, no shifty triangle or furtive intrigue," Payne said in the *Saturday Evening Post*. "Just a simple, straight-forward handling of deep emotion. There was a quiet reality about it that, to me, was moving and memorable." Payne was also seen in a rousing musical with Betty Grable, *Springtime in the Rockies* (1942), and *Hello, Frisco, Hello* (1943), which featured Alice Faye singing the Oscar-winning song, "You'll Never Know." But Payne's string of hits was interrupted by the realities of life — in late 1942, he enlisted for Army pilot training and was stationed in Long Beach, California, where he served in the Army Air Corps until his discharge two years later.

Back in Hollywood, Payne's love life heated up again. Shortly after his release from the Army, Payne met actress Gloria DeHaven at a dinner party given by film star Alan Ladd and his wife, Sue. Several months later, on

Percy Helton and John Payne in *The Crooked Way* (1949).

Despite his successes, Payne had become disgruntled with his "pretty boy" image at Fox and "every week for eight months," according to the actor, he sought a release from his contract. Payne's long association with the studio was severed in 1948, and he promptly starred in two films for Universal — *The Saxon Charm* (1948) with Susan Hayward, and *Larceny* (1948), a hard-hitting crime drama — followed by his entry into the realm of film noir, United Artists' *The Crooked Way* (1949).

Opening with a shot of Letterman General Hospital in San Francisco, the film's narrator entones, "For those outside these gates, the war is over — a thing of the past. For those behind these gates, there's a grim, hard, bitter fight still going on. Take one case — the case of Eddie Rice." As Eddie, Payne portrayed a war veteran with a piece of shrapnel in his brain that has rendered him a permanent victim of amnesia. Knowing only that he enlisted in Los Angeles, Eddie returns there, quickly learning that his name is actually Eddie Riccardi and he has a lengthy police record, a bitter ex-wife, Nina (Ellen Drew), and a former partner in crime, Vince (Sonny Tufts), who is bent on paying Eddie back for a double-cross before the war. Vince nearly succeeds — he first frames Eddie for the murder of a cop and later directs his henchmen to beat Eddie to a pulp — but in the end, Eddie confronts his nemesis, kills him during a gun battle, and reunites with Nina, determined to start a new life. Upon its release, *The Crooked Way* earned mostly good reviews, with one critic labeling it "the most bloodthirsty crook melodrama in a long time." Payne's notices were only passable, however; John L. Scott of the *Los Angeles Times* referred

December 28, 1944, the two were married, and would later have three children, Kathleen, Hope, and Thomas. But after six years, this marriage, too, would end in divorce.

On screen, Payne picked up where he'd left off before the war, starring with Betty Grable and June Haver in the well-received musical *The Dolly Sisters* (1945); *Sentimental Journey* (1946), a six-hankie weeper with Maureen O'Hara; *The Razor's Edge* (1946), a post-war melodrama starring Tyrone Power; and, perhaps the highlight of Payne's career (or, at least, his best-loved film), *Miracle on 34th Street* (1947), in which he played an idealistic lawyer who helps a department store Santa Claus prove that he's the real Kris Kringle.

John Payne in *Kansas City Confidential* (1952).

to his "fair-enough portrayal," and in the *Los Angeles Daily News*, Darr Smith wrote: "Payne appears comfortably at home in the role, which requires little effort or talent in its execution."

After his freelancing experience, Payne created his own production company, Window Productions, and signed a contract for a series of action-adventure pictures for Paramount producers William Pine and William Thomas, which would include *El Paso* (1949), *Captain China* (1949), *Tripoli* (1950), *The Eagle and the Hawk* (1950), *Passage West* (1951), and *Crosswinds* (1951).

"Ever since I came to Hollywood, I wanted to make adventure films," Payne said. "It seemed like a good, healthy way to make a living."

But Payne took a break from the low-budget Pine-Thomas features in 1952 when he starred in his second film noir, *Kansas City*

Confidential, in which he portrayed Joe Rolfe, an ex-con falsely accused by police of an armored car robbery. Although Joe is later released by the cops, he is embittered by his treatment and determines to find the real culprits. His search leads him to a trio of hoods, Pete Harris (Jack Elam), Boyd Kane (Neville Brand), and Tony Romano (Lee Van Cleef), whom he suspects of involvement in the crime. He catches up to Harris in Tijuana, and after working him over, finds a plane ticket to Barbados and one half of a torn playing card. When Harris is later gunned down by police at the airport, Joe assumes his identity, meeting up with Kane and Romano in Barbados and presenting the torn card as proof that he is Harris. Once there, Joe learns that the mastermind of the scheme is Timothy Foster (Preston Foster), a disgruntled former police captain who masterminded the heist in an effort to embarrass the police department that forced him into retirement. He also falls for Foster's daughter, Helen, and after a gun battle leaves Foster mortally wounded, Joe shields her from learning of her father's role in the crime, telling police that the former captain was responsible for cracking the case. The tautly directed feature was a hit with audiences (although one critic, Bosley Crowther of the *New York Times*, found it to be an "unenlightening dossier on crime"), and years later, actress Coleen Gray, who portrayed the police captain's daughter, fondly recalled her experience on the film with Payne.

"Before I worked with him, I didn't find him appealing," Gray said in 2001. "He seemed to have a pout — I just thought he was a spoiled pretty boy. When I worked with him, I found that he had a good sense of humor — he was very nice. A gentleman. He was a much deeper person than I'd thought — interested in philosophy and all manner of things."

After several more Pine-Thomas features, none of which were very good, Payne returned to film noir, starring with Evelyn Keyes in the gritty *99 River Street* (1953). Here, Payne portrayed cab driver and ex-prize fighter Ernie Driscoll, who is constantly belittled by his money-grubbing wife, Pauline (Peggie Castle, in a small, but showy role). When his wife turns up dead in the back seat of his taxi, Ernie faces a seedy underworld to clear his name, encountering a variety of shady characters, from jewel thieves to petty hoods. He also meets actress Linda James, who joins forces with the boxer to find the killer. As it turns out, Pauline was murdered by her lover, Victor Rawlins (Brad Dexter), a sadistic criminal involved in the theft of $50,000 in diamonds— Ernie ultimately tracks Rawlins to a New Jersey bar (located at 99 River Street), and although he is wounded by the hood, he uses his boxing prowess to subdue him until police arrive. Although the film did brisk business at the box office, it was slammed by critics, including the reviewer for the *New York Times*, who dismissed it as a "one of those tasteless melodramas peopled

with unpleasant hoods, two-timing blondes, and lots of sequences of what purports to be everyday life in the underworld."

During this period, Payne decided to give marriage another try — this time, he chose a non-actress, artist Alexandra "Sandy" Crowell Curtis. For the actor, the third time was the charm — the marriage would last until his death at age 77.

"I guess I was the right one," Sandy Payne said in a 1994 interview, "because we stuck together for 37 long years."

After *99 River Street*, Payne starred in a string of westerns of varying quality —*Rails into Laramie* (1954), with Dan Duryea and Mari Blanchard, was standard fare, but Payne was seen to better advantage in *Silver Lode* (1954), also starring Duryea; *Santa Fe Passage* (1955), and *Tennessee's Partner* (1955), directed by Allan Dwan. Payne left the dusty roads and cowpokes behind, however, when he starred in back-to-back films noirs, *Hell's Island* (1955) and *Slightly Scarlet* (1956).

In *Hell's Island* (another Pine-Thomas production), Payne portrays Mike Cormack, whose drinking problem has cost him his job as district attorney. Accepting an offer of $5,000 to locate a valuable ruby assumed lost in a plane crash, he learns that his former fiancée, Janet Martin (Mary Murphy), is now married to the man suspected of causing the plane crash. When Janet is abducted and spirited off to the island of the film's title, Cormack goes to her rescue, despite the attempts of local police and assorted thugs to stymie his efforts. He later discovers, however, that Janet was responsible for the plane crash, as well as the theft of the ruby, and the film's end finds him turning her over to police.

Next, in *Slightly Scarlet*, one of the few Technicolor noirs, Payne starred as Ben Grace, a ruthless hood whose encounter with a kleptomaniac, Dorothy Lyons (Arlene Dahl), and her sister, June (Rhonda Fleming), presents him with an ideal opportunity to thwart the mayoral aspirations of June's boss and fiancé, Frank Jansen (Kent Taylor). After he is humiliated by his boss, Solly Caspar (Ted De Corsia), Ben turns on him, providing June with evidence that Caspar was responsible for the murder of Jansen's top supporter: "Mr. Jansen is a nice man," Ben tells June. "But he doesn't know how to win elections. I'm not very nice man — I know how. Takes a little dirt. I have dirt to sell." When Caspar learns of Ben's betrayal, he goes after his former underling, but Ben sets him up in a final, life-threatening scheme — after notifying police, he meets Caspar at his beachhouse, goading the gangster into shooting him just as the cops arrive to catch Caspar with the gun in his hand.

Payne's final two noirs were met with mostly disparaging comments from critics; the *New York Times* critic dismissed *Hell's Island* as "slow-moving and obvious and exasperating," and the reviewer for the *Los Angeles Times* wrote that Payne had a "propensity for making every line sound like the Declaration of Independence." *Slightly Scarlet* fared little better, with Bosley Crowther, of the *New York Times*, labeling the film "an exhausting lot of twaddle."

Payne rebounded somewhat when he starred in 1956 in a top-notch western with Ruth Roman and J. Carroll Naish, *Rebel in Town*, and *The Boss*, a hard-hitting drama set in post–World War I St. Louis. Produced and co-written by the actor, the latter film was based on the career of Tom Pendergast, who created a powerful and corrupt political machine in Kansas City during the 1920s and 1930s. Although the film was hailed by critics, however, it was condemned by the United States government as "not characteristic of the American Way" and faltered at the box office due to poor bookings.

Payne's next two films were complete timewasters—*Hidden Fear* (1957), directed by Andre deToth, was a muddled tale set in Copenhagen, and *Bailout at 43,000* (1957) was notable only as Payne's last film in his long association with Pine-Thomas. Meanwhile, with several television appearances to his credit, including *Schlitz Playhouse of Stars*, *The Best of Broadway*, and *Gunsmoke*, Payne in 1957 took on the starring role in the NBC-TV western series *The Restless Gun*. The se-

ries was popular with viewers, but after two seasons, it was cancelled.

Away from the big screen during the filming of his series, Payne returned to feature films in 1960 for a small role in *The Risk*, a so-so thriller starring Tony Britton and Virginia Maskell. Shortly after the release of this film, Payne was involved in a car accident that almost cost him his life. Struck by a car, the actor was knocked through the windshield, requiring six hours of surgery on his face. He was not seen on screen again for nearly a decade. During his time away from the camera, Payne found success in the field of real estate, purchasing property in Southern California before prices skyrocketed and buying valuable land in Montana.

In 1968, Payne was seen again on the silver screen in *They Ran for Their Lives*, a low-budget crime feature which also marked his debut as a director. A box-office bomb, the film would mark his last screen appearance. But Payne had not completely retired from acting. Several years later, in 1974, he reteamed with his former Fox co-star, Alice Faye, in a national revival tour of *Good News*.

"I just kind of lost interest in acting and I have no devouring interest in it now," Payne told a reporter from the *Los Angeles Times*. "[But] this show kept following me around for a while. I turned it down a couple of times, but then [playwright] Abe Burrows got connected with it, and then Alice was in it and I thought, 'Well, maybe I ought to come out of my shell.'"

After *Good News*, Payne concentrated on furthering his business ventures and enjoying his family, which grew to include several grandchildren. On December 6, 1989, surrounded by his wife and three children, he died at his Malibu home of heart failure.

John Payne left his mark not only in the numerous successful musicals and westerns with which he became best associated, but also in the realm of film noir, where he excelled at characterizing the world-weary everyman. Still, to Payne, acting seemed to be, more than anything else, an amusing vocation that provided the means to a comfortable and productive existence.

"I could never quite take it seriously—it was all kind of fun," Payne once said. "It was a remunerative profession. I certainly couldn't have earned that much money any other way that I can think of. Providence was very kind."

Film Noir Filmography

The Crooked Way. Director: Robert Florey. Producer: Benedict Borgeaus. Running time: 87 minutes. Released by United Artists, April 1949. Cast: John Payne, Sonny Tufts, Ellen Drew, Rhys Williams, Percy Helton, John Doucette, Charles Evans, Greta Granstedt, Harry Bronson, Hal Fieberling, Crane Whitley, John Harmon, Snub Pollard.

Kansas City Confidential. Director: Phil Karlson. Producer: Edward Small. Running time: 98 minutes. Released by United Artists, November 1952. Cast: John Payne, Coleen Gray, Preston Foster, Dona Drake, Jack Elam, Neville Brand, Lee Van Cleef, Mario Seletti, Howard Negley, Ted Ryan, George Wallace, Vivi Janiss, Helen Keeb.

99 River Street. Director: Phil Karlson. Producer: Edward Small. Running time: 83 minutes. Released by United Artists, October 3, 1953. Cast: John Payne, Evelyn Keyes, Brad Dexter, Frank Faylen, Peggie Castle, Jay Adler, Jack Lambert, Eddy Waller, Glen Langan, John Day, Ian Wolfe, Peter Leeds, William Tannen, Gene Reynolds.

Hell's Island. Director: Phil Karlson. Producer: William H. Pine, William C. Thomas. Running time: 83 minutes. Released by Paramount, May 1955. Cast: John Payne, Mary Murphy, Francis L. Sullivan, Arnold Moss, Paul Picerni, Eduardo Noriega, Walter Reed, Sandor Szabo, Robert Cabal.

Slightly Scarlet. Director: Allan Dwan. Pro-ducer: Benedict Bogueaus. Running time: 99 minutes. Released by RKO, February 1956. Cast: John Payne, Arlene Dahl, Rhonda Fleming, Kent Taylor, Ted De Corsia, Lance Fuller, Buddy Baer, Frank Gerstle, Ellen Corby.

References

"Actor's Zone Change Request Turned Down." *Los Angeles Times*, October 19, 1972.
Biography of John Payne. Paramount Studios, March 1952.
Biography of John Payne. RKO Studios, circa 1954.
Biography of John Payne. Twentieth Century-Fox Studios, circa 1943.
Biography of John Payne. Twentieth Century-Fox Studios, November 5, 1941.
Cassa, Anthony. "John Payne—The Restless Gun." *Hollywood Studio Magazine*, December 1981.
Dolven, Frank. "John Payne's Star Should Have Been Brighter!" *Classic Images*, November 1994.
Flint, Peter B. "John Payne, 77, Actor, Is Dead; Lawyer in 'Miracle on 34th Street.'" *New York Times*, December 8, 1989.
"Heart Affair." *Photoplay*, January 1943.
Hopper, Hedda. "John Payne—The Star Who Likes People." *Chicago Sunday Tribune*, circa 1952.
"John Payne, 77, Star of Movie Musicals, Remembered for 'Miracle on 34th Street.'" *Los Angeles Times*, December 7, 1989.
Payne, John. "The Role I Liked Best." *The Saturday Evening Post*, September 14, 1946.
Raidy, William A. "'Good News' with Payne." *Los Angeles Times*, September 1, 1974.
"Restless Guns." *TV & Movie Western*, December 1958.
Skolsky, Sidney. "Close-Up of John Payne—Our Cover Boy." *Motion Picture*, August 1945.
Waterbury, Ruth. "The Difference Is You." *Photoplay*, March 1945.

DICK POWELL

"Listen, I got a bullet in my gut and fire in my brain. It wouldn't take much for me to let you have it right now."— Dick Powell in *Johnny O'Clock* (1947)

Dick Powell was once called a phenomenon of show business—and rightfully so. After rising to fame as a crooner in more than 30 Warner Bros. musicals, the actor transformed his screen image from "pretty boy" to

song and dance man to hard-boiled tough guy, then switched gears again, tackling directing and producing and becoming, in the process, the head of a television empire.

"I started out with two assets," Powell

once said, "a voice that didn't drive audiences into the streets and a determination to make money. I've always worked like a dog. If you don't keep working hard in this business, you're dead."

On television, Powell made his mark as president of the company that produced such series as *Four-Star Playhouse*, *Zane Grey Theater*, *The Rifleman*, and *Robert Taylor's Detectives*, and he was credited with cultivating the early careers of a number of future stars including Robert Redford, Peter Falk, and Steve McQueen. During a span of three decades on the big screen, Powell was seen in such notable offerings as *42nd Street* (1933) and *The Bad and The Beautiful* (1952), but he made his biggest cinematic impact in his five film noir features: *Murder, My Sweet* (1944), *Cornered* (1945), *Johnny O'Clock* (1947), *Pitfall* (1948), and *Cry Danger* (1951).

Richard Ewing Powell was born on November 14, 1904, in Mountain View, Arkansas, a small town once described by the actor as "ten miles from modern conveniences." The second of three boys of Sallie and Ewing Powell, an International Harvester salesman, Powell moved to nearby Little Rock at the age of 10. There, he demonstrated a talent for singing by performing with his brothers in the church choir and for the local synagogue and Masonic Lodge.

In 1923, Powell enrolled at Little Rock College, where he headed up a popular dance band, the Peter Pan, and earned extra cash by working part-time for the telephone company. The future star also found time to get married to his college sweetheart, Mildred Maund, on May 28, 1925. A short time later, Powell dropped out of school to play a variety of club dates; during the next several years, he sang with the Royal Peacock Orchestra in Louisville, Kentucky, and the Charlie Davis Orchestra in Indianapolis, and also played vaudeville theaters for six months, adding saxophone and clarinet playing to his performing repertoire. In September 1926, he used his charisma and versatility to land a job as emcee at the Circle Theatre in Indianapolis, and a few years later became singer,

comedian, and master of ceremonies at the Stanley Theatre in Pittsburgh. During this period, Powell also hosted a weekly radio show in Pittsburgh, *The Pow Wow Club*.

"In my field, it was wonderful experience," Powell once said of his varied activities, "like playing stock is for an actor."

After several years at the Stanley, Powell was spotted by a talent scout from Warner Bros., and was invited to Hollywood. Powell's wife, who had long objected to his choice of career, declined to accompany her husband, and the union ended soon after. The termination of his marriage had little effect on Powell's performance during his Warners screen test, however, and he was promptly cast in his film debut, *Blessed Event* (1932), a musical starring Lee Tracy and Mary Brian. Years later, Brian praised Powell's performance in his initial feature film outing.

"He had all the stage presence and professional experience when he came out, although pictures were new to him," Brian said in a 1996 documentary on the actor's life. "He took to it like a duck to water."

Offered a $500 a week contract by Warners before the end of production on *Blessed Event*, Powell was seen in a series of lightweight musicals during the next few years, including *42nd Street* (1933), which, under the direction of Busby Berkeley, breathed new life into the movie musical genre; *Gold Diggers of 1933* (1933), which reteamed Powell and his *42nd Street* co-star, Ruby Keeler, for their second of seven features together; *Footlight Parade* (1933), starring James Cagney as a Broadway producer; *Wonder Bar* (1934), which featured Al Jolson, Dolores Del Rio, and Kay Francis; *Twenty Million Sweethearts* (1934), with Pat O'Brien and Ginger Rogers; *Dames* (1934), another Busby Berkeley extravaganza, which Powell later dismissed as "that corny thing"; *Flirtation Walk* (1934), which was nominated for a Best Picture Academy Award but lost to *It Happened One Night* (1934); *Gold Diggers of 1935* (1935), co-starring Adolphe Menjou and Gloria Stuart; and *Broadway Gondolier* (1935), in which Powell played a singing cab driver. During this period, Powell was also featured as a singer on the popular CBS radio series, *Hollywood Hotel*, and, in a rare non-musical screen appearance, he offered a rather awkward portrayal of Lysander in Shakespeare's *A Midsummer Night's Dream* (1935). He later admitted that he never really understood his lines, but Powell's performance in the film had little effect on his soaring popularity; in 1935, he was named among the top 10 box office stars of the year, along with such luminaries as Shirley Temple, Clark Gable, and Joan Crawford.

By now, Powell's personal life was receiving as much attention as his on-screen efforts. Romantically linked with Joan Blondell since their appearance in *Gold Diggers of 1933*, Powell married the vivacious blonde actress on September 19, 1936, aboard a luxury liner, the *Santa Paula*. A short time later, Powell adopted Blondell's young son, Norman, and in June 1938, the couple had a daughter, Ellen.

"[My mother] said she was taken with the kindness and gentleness that he exhibited toward her, and the fact that he really seemed to love me," Norman Powell said in 1996. "I think that's what attracted her to him more than any other thing I can remember."

Following his wedding, Powell returned to a spate of musicals, including such forgettable features as *Gold Diggers of 1937* (1936), the ninth of his 13 films with Joan Blondell. Several months after the release of the picture, Powell and Blondell placed their hand and footprints, in side-by-side squares, in the forecourt of Grauman's (now Mann's) Chinese Theater in Hollywood. Meanwhile, Powell followed *Gold Diggers* with *Varsity Show* (1937), where he played a Broadway producer; *Cowboy From Brooklyn* (1938), which featured Ronald Reagan in a small role; *Going Places* (1938), co-starring Anita Louise; and *Naughty But Nice* (1939), where the actor was second-billed to Ann Sheridan. But after years of such mediocre fare, Powell was growing increasingly frustrated by his casting as "the eternal juvenile" and "the filmusical glamour boy"—while undeniably lucrative, he found that the roles were no longer attractive.

"It got so I'd get a part, do my songs, and then do my best to forget all about the darned picture," Powell later said. "I made four or five of those things a year—and always the same stupid story. I just wore different clothes. Never had anything sensible to say—I looked and acted like a dope."

Rejected by studio head Jack Warner in his appeal for more varied roles, Powell abruptly left the studio in 1939, taking his wife with him. Now a freelancer, Powell starred in a delightful Preston Sturges comedy for Paramount, *Christmas in July* (1940), then teamed with Blondell for Paramount's *I Want a Divorce* (1940) and Universal's *Model Wife* (1941). In the latter, Powell earned a mention in the *New York Times*, whose reviewer found him "an altogether personable and capable actor." Powell signed a contract with Paramount in 1942, but only two of his next six features for the studio were non-musicals, *True to Life* (1943), a domestic comedy co-starring Franchot Tone, and *It Happened Tomorrow* (1944), a well-done fantasy directed by Rene Clair. Eager to change his screen image, Powell lobbied for the male lead in the studio's upcoming picture, *Double Indemnity*

(1944), but the part was given to Fred MacMurray and, instead, Powell was cast in yet another musical, *Bring on the Girls* (1945). Balking at the assignment, the actor was placed on suspension.

"This went on for 10 or 12 weeks," Powell later recalled. "One day, in an elevator, I ran into Frank Freeman, then head of Paramount's production. I said, 'Frank, this is silly. I'm not going to do that kind of picture anymore. I don't like them, and you might as well let me out [of the contract].' And he did. I then went over to RKO and told them my little tale of woe. It so happened they had just bought Raymond Chandler's *Farewell, My Lovely*. They gave me the script, I read it, and I said I'd do it. My problem was convincing the director, Edward Dmytryk. My box-office appeal was sagging and he could only see me as the singing marine. But I must have begged hard enough because he decided to take a chance on me, and it worked."

Dick Powell with Esther Howard in *Murder, My Sweet* (1945).

Renamed *Murder, My Sweet* (reportedly so that audiences would not expect another frothy Powell musical), and touting the actor "in an amazing new type of role," the 1945 film would be the beginning of a new career for the long-frustrated actor — and his initial foray into the world of film noir. Powell portrayed Philip Marlowe, a world-weary, nononsense private eye who is hired by a hulking ex-con, Moose Malloy (Mike Mazurki), to find his long-lost girlfriend, Velma. Along the way, Marlowe encounters Mrs. Grayle (Claire Trevor), a wealthy, but deadly, socialite; her hated stepdaughter, Ann (Anne Shirley); and a sinister doctor, Amthor (Otto Kruger). As Marlowe's seemingly simple case grows more complex, he becomes involved in a hunt for a stolen jade necklace, finds himself the prime suspect in a series of murders,

and ultimately discovers that Malloy's missing Velma is actually Mrs. Grayle. In the film's confrontational climax, Mrs. Grayle and Moose are both shot and killed by Grayle's millionaire husband (Miles Mander), who then turns the gun on himself.

Powell's performance in *Murder, My Sweet* was hailed by critics and audiences alike; in a typical review, Alton Cook of the *New York World-Telegram* wrote that the actor "was trying to play a subtle character, instead of adding to the glamour of his name. He did both." Author Raymond Chandler would later claim that Powell's rendition of Marlowe was his favorite, and co-star Claire Trevor laid the film's success squarely on Powell's shoulders.

"He was a revelation," Trevor said. "Up to this, he was known only as a boy singer, but now he was playing Raymond Chandler's tough private eye ... and playing it magnificently. People couldn't get over it. The film revitalized his career."

Indeed, *Murder, My Sweet* had finally given Powell the role that he had sought for so many years. But his career wasn't the only aspect of the actor's life that was undergoing a transformation. Since leaving Warner's, Powell's marriage to Joan Blondell had been increasingly strained, fostered by long absences while Blondell accepted stage roles in New York, and damaged further by rumors of her romantic involvement with producer Mike Todd. Meanwhile, while starring in the 1944 MGM musical *Meet the People*, Powell had met and fallen in love with actress June Allyson, who had an ingenue role in the film.

"He was wonderful to all of us new kids—if we had a problem, he would tell us how to do a scene or help us learn how to read a script," Allyson recalled in a 1996 documentary. "And our friendship just kind of grew." In July 1945, Powell and Blondell were divorced, and a month later the actor married Allyson; the MGM starlet was given away by studio head Louis B. Mayer. The two went on to adopt a daughter, Pamela, in 1948, and on Christmas Eve, 1950, the couple's son, Richard Keith, was born.

Professionally, after his runaway success with *Murder, My Sweet*, Powell was determined to further develop his new screen persona.

"From now on, I'm going to act," Powell wrote in a 1945 *Hollywood Citizen-News* article. "I don't care what kind of characters they hand me, just so they don't have anything to do with putting moon together with June and coming out with No. 1 on the Hit Parade."

Powell's next assignment fit the bill. In *Cornered* (1945), his second film noir, the actor portrayed Lawrence Gerard, a Canadian pilot and prisoner of war survivor bent on avenging the death of his French war bride. Informed that the guilty party is a mysterious, seldom-seen Nazi collaborator by the name of Marcel Jarnac (Luther Adler), Gerard begins a search that leads him to the devious Melchior Incza (Walter Slezak), Jarnac's mysterious wife (Micheline Cheirel), and a group of expatriates who are also on Jarnac's trail. Gerard ultimately succeeds in tracking down Jarnac, who murders Incza and plans the same fate for the flier, but during a scuffle, Gerard goes into a trance and awakens to find that he has beaten Jarnac to death. After Gerard confesses the crime to police, the film ends with one of the expatriates, Santana (Morris Carnovsky), vowing to defend him. Upon the film's release, critics once again hailed the "new" Powell; one of the best reviews was offered by Jim Henaghan of the *Los Angeles Examiner*, who wrote: "If there was any question about Dick Powell's astonishing performance in last year's *Murder, My Sweet* being due to a lucky break and a trick of miscasting, this picture will dissolve it. For in *Cornered* he plays a character equally as hard and tough, and draws a role considerably more complex and difficult to portray — and plays it to a fare-thee-well."

While cultivating the conversion of his screen image, Powell was making changes on the radio as well. No longer a charismatic crooner, the actor starred in 1945 as Richard Rogue on NBC's *Rogue's Gallery* series. He later starred as Hildy Johnson on *The Front Page*, based on the play by Ben Hecht and Charles MacArthur, and played the title role of the private eye in *Richard Diamond*.

After the expiration of his contract with RKO, Powell opted to remain a freelancer, promptly landing a starring role in his third consecutive film noir, *Johnny O'Clock* (1947), co-starring Evelyn Keyes. Here, Powell played the title character, described as the type of man who "looks at a situation, says, 'what's best for me?' and acts accordingly." Dapper and devil-may-care, Johnny finds himself suspected of murder when crooked cop Chuck Blayden (Jim Bannon) and his naïve girlfriend, Harriet Hopson (Nina Foch), both turn up dead. Also suspected is Johnny's gambling casino partner, Guido Marchettis (Thomas Gomez), whose wife, Nelle (Ellen Drew), is Johnny's one-time lover (and still carries a blazing torch). Meanwhile, when Harriet Hopson's sister Nancy (Evelyn Keyes) shows up in town, she and Johnny quickly fall for each other, but when Johnny realizes that he is marked for murder, he tries to send Nancy away: "Look, you've only known me for less than a day," he tells her after he is nearly gunned down in his car. "Make out you never met me. Make out this week only had six days in it.... With me it's trouble and grief in capital letters." Nancy insists on remaining at his side, and Johnny decides to leave town with her, stopping first at the casino to collect his share of the proceeds. While there, however, he is confronted by Marchettis, who has learned of his wife's designs on Johnny — and Johnny, in turn, realizes that Marchettis killed both Blayden and Harriet. After a shootout, Marchettis is killed and Johnny is wounded, but Nelle sees the gun battle as an opportunity to reunite with Johnny; when he rejects her, she lies to police, insisting that Johnny shot Marchettis in cold blood while trying to rob the casino. Cornered in the casino by police, Johnny plans to shoot his way out, but Nancy manages to get inside and, after an impassioned plea, she convinces Johnny to give himself up.

Even in his non-film noir features, Powell continued to play tough-guy roles; he was a narcotics investigator in *To The Ends Of The Earth* (1948), co-starring Signe Hasso; an undercover military investigator in the well-done western, *Station West* (1948); and an army intelligence agent in *Rogue's Regiment* (1948). During this period, Powell took his first step toward his future career behind the camera, forming a partnership with Samuel Bischoff and Edward Gross to create Regal Films. The company's initial effort marked Powell's fourth film noir, the underrated *Pitfall* (1948). Here, Powell starred as insurance agent Johnny Forbes, a family man discontented with his humdrum middle-class life — in an early scene, Forbes glumly asks his wife, Sue (Jane Wyatt), "Whatever happened to those two people who were going to build a boat and sail around the world?" In an amused

tone, Sue responds, "Well, I had a baby. I never did hear what happened to you." Johnny finds more excitement than he'd wished for, however, when he has a brief affair with Mona Stevens (Lizabeth Scott), the girlfriend of an imprisoned embezzler, Bill Smiley (Byron Barr), and the focus of unwanted attentions from a psychotic insurance investigator, Mack MacDonald (Raymond Burr). Goaded by Mack, Smiley goes after Forbes after his release from jail, Forbes kills him in self-defense, and Mona kills Mack when he tries to force her to run away with him. After Mona's arrest, Forbes confesses the entire story to authorities— although his killing is ruled justifiable, however, Forbes is forced to face the gravity of his actions by the district attorney, who tells him, "I'd like to hold you all right. Personally I think we've got the wrong person in the cell upstairs. But there's nothing I can do about it.... Just a little call to the police and you could have avoided all this mess. But no— you kill a man. And that's a pleasant thing to live with for the rest of your life. Or don't things like that bother you?" *Pitfall* earned mostly good notices upon its release, although Lloyd L. Sloan of the *Hollywood Citizen-News* complained of the "lack of depth which pervades the screenplay." Other reviews were more favorable, however; in the *Los Angeles Daily News*, Frank Eng praised "the thoroughly competent cast and the unobtrusively economical direction," and the *Los Angeles Times*' Philip K. Scheuer labeled *Pitfall* "a good, honest movie." Powell earned faint praise as well, with the *New York Times*' critic noting that he created "a credible character."

For Regal Films' second venture, Powell selected *Mrs. Mike* (1949), a so-so tale in which he played a Canadian mountie who marries a Boston woman (Evelyn Keyes). A disappointment at the box office, the picture would be Regal Films' last. Powell was next seen in two forgettable films with wife June Allyson, *Right Cross* (1950) and *The Reformer and the Redhead* (1950), followed by *The Tall Target* (1951), where he portrayed a detective during the Abraham Lincoln presidency, and

You Never Can Tell (1951), a silly but entertaining fantasy in which Powell played a poisoned dog who comes back to life as a man. He also starred in his final film noir, *Cry Danger* (1951), co-starring Rhonda Fleming and William Conrad. As this feature begins, Powell's character, Rocky Mulloy, is released from prison after a five-year stretch for a murder and $100,000 robbery that he did not commit. In an effort to secure the release of his friend, Danny Morgan, who was also framed for the crime, Rocky turns to a local mobster named Castro (William Conrad), who was the mastermind behind the robbery. Forcing Castro to confess, Rocky learns that Danny was actually involved in the robbery and murder, and that Danny's wife, Nancy (Rhonda Fleming)—with whom Rocky has become romantically involved—has been in possession of Danny's share of the money all along. Disregarding Nancy's declaration that "it's all worked out now," and despite his love for her, Rocky turns Nancy in to police at the film's end.

After *Cry Danger*, which was praised by one critic as "a very tidy package of fictional extravagance," Powell was cast in one of the best films of his career, *The Bad and the Beautiful* (1952). A scathing look at Hollywood behind-the-scenes, this outstanding film also starred Kirk Douglas, Lana Turner, Barry Sullivan, and Gloria Grahame (who won an Academy Award for Best Supporting Actress for her portrayal of Powell's southern belle wife). Despite the success of this feature, however, Powell was again growing frustrated with the direction of his career.

"I looked around and saw that the film business was going badly," Powell said. "All the studios were dropping their contract players. Movie theatres were closing as more and more people sat home and watched the box. I had been fascinated by television ever since we began to get network shows, mostly from New York, and I figured it was a good time to make good dramatic product in Hollywood, certainly something better than all the wrestling and the comedy shows."

Joining with actors Charles Boyer and David Niven, Powell formed Four Star Films, and created *Four-Star Playhouse*, a weekly half-hour series in which each of the three partners rotated with a different guest star. (In the second season of the five-year series, the actors invited Ida Lupino to become the show's permanent "fourth star," but she was not a stockholder in the firm, as stated in many of Powell's biographies.) With Powell as president, Four Star Films would go on to produce numerous television series over the next decade, including *Zane Grey Theatre* (which Powell hosted and occasionally starred in), *The Rifleman, Trackdown, Robert Taylor's Detectives, Wanted: Dead or Alive, Michael Shayne, Alcoa Theatre, The Dick Powell Show, The June Allyson Show, Stagecoach West, The Lloyd Bridges Show, Johnny Ringo, Peter Loves Mary, Burke's Law, The David Niven Theater*, and *The Westerner*. In its first year, the company lost $60,000, but by the 1960-61 season, the partners were raking in an estimated $40 million. More than a decade after Powell's death, a former writer for Four Star offered insight into the roots of the company's prodigious success.

"[Powell] was a man of immense self-confidence, outward ease, friendliness, warmth, and humor," Christopher Knopf wrote in a 1976 *Variety* article. "He gave approbation to everyone he employed…. If he hired you, you could do the job, or he wouldn't have hired you. His confidence in you injected confidence in yourself."

In addition to his responsibilities with Four Star, Powell had ventured behind the camera, directing his first feature film, RKO's *Split Second*, in 1953. A taut thriller starring Stephen McNally and Alexis Smith, the film earned excellent notices for Powell's directing; in one review, the critic for *The Hollywood Reporter* wrote: "Powell, who certainly must get much of the credit for the consistently excellent performances, does a masterful job of pacing, starting off in a staccato style and relentlessly building up the tension to a breathtaking climax."

The following year, Powell took his directing talents to Broadway, helming the highly acclaimed drama *The Caine Mutiny Courtmartial*, starring Lloyd Nolan and Henry Fonda. But shortly after the play opened in Santa Barbara, Powell was fired (or quit, according to the actor), and was replaced by Charles Laughton. Infuriated, Powell called the incident "an out-and-out injustice," telling reporters that it was the result of a disagreement he had with Fonda.

"Henry's a moody guy, the kind you could live with in the same house and not speak to for six months," Powell told *Cue* magazine. "Henry and I had a disagreement as to how two minor but important characters should interpret their scenes with him.... We both stuck to our guns, and since he was the star of the show and felt he was carrying the responsibility on his shoulders, he threatened to go back to New York unless the scene was changed.... I saw no reason to remain in an uncomfortable situation, so I told [the producer] I thought it would be well for me to leave."

Co-star Lloyd Nolan, however, had another take on the matter.

"Dick directed the play for laughs," Nolan said in a 1954 interview in *The New Yorker*. "But we were changing all that, and if Dick had only played along, it would have been all right. But, Queeg-like, he was stubborn."

The specific circumstances notwithstanding, Powell returned to Hollywood after leaving the play, starring opposite Debbie Reynolds in the lightweight RKO comedy *Susan Slept Here* (1954). It would be his last big screen appearance. Instead, Powell focused his attentions on his budding television empire, and on directing and producing a series of feature films—*The Conqueror* (1956), starring John Wayne as Genghis Khan; *You Can't Run Away From It* (1956), a musical remake of *It Happened One Night* (1934), with Jack Lemmon and June Allyson; *The Enemy Below* (1957), a suspenseful World War II drama that pitted Robert Mitchum against Curt Jurgens (making his American film debut); and *The Hunters* (1958), another wartime adventure, again starring Mitchum. The two latter

films were well-received by critics and audiences, but *You Can't Run Away From It* was a box-office disappointment, and *The Conqueror* was a complete flop, later appearing on lists of films considered to be the worst ever made. But the film would be more than a black spot on Powell's directing career—for two months, shooting for the feature took place in a small Utah town located just 137 miles from a site where extensive atomic bomb testing had been conducted a year earlier. Years after production ended on the film, many of those involved with *The Conqueror* would contract various forms of cancer, including Wayne, co-stars Susan Hayward, Agnes Moorehead, and Pedro Armendariz, art director Carroll Clark, makeup chief Webb Overlander—and Dick Powell. It was later determined that at least 91 of the film's 220 cast and crew suffered from the disease, but the link between these high incidences of the illness and the testing site in Nevada would not be discovered until decades later.

Meanwhile, Powell was making headlines not for his films or television work, but because of his deteriorating marriage. After reconciling with Powell following a month-long separation in 1957, June Allyson filed for divorce in 1961, citing his workaholic nature and his frequent absences from home.

"I was of the school where you should have dinner with your children—they should be part of a group, a family group. But [Dick] never got there," Allyson said in 1996. "I have to say that business was his life. He loved his family, but business was his baby."

Charging extreme mental cruelty, Allyson was granted an interlocutory divorce in January 1961, which would become final in a year. But Powell had other plans; on the day following the court hearing, Allyson said, "he was sitting at the little breakfast nook, having breakfast and reading the paper."

"And I said, 'What are you doing here? We just got a divorce,'" Allyson recalled. "He said, 'No, you didn't—you just got a paper that said you can have a divorce in a year.' And he said, 'You know, I'm never going to let you go. And you've spent all that money for no reason at all.' And went right on eating his breakfast. And we never did get the divorce. For which I'm very grateful."

Sadly, the couple's time together would be cut short; in September 1962, Powell revealed that he was undergoing treatment for malignant tumors that had been discovered in his neck and chest. After a month, Powell stepped down as president of Four Star, assuring stockholders that he was "winning the fight" against the cancer and that he was not resigning because of his health.

"I'm not a damned bit scared," he said.

But in December 1962, doctors told the press that the cancer had spread and that the actor was a "very sick man." Less than three weeks later, on January 2, 1963, surrounded by his wife, his children, and his two brothers, Dick Powell died. He was 58 years old. His passing stunned the Hollywood community, still reeling from the recent deaths of Charles Laughton, Thomas Mitchell, and Jack Carson (who died just hours before Powell), and his memorial service was attended by countless screen luminaries, including Barbara Stanwyck, James Stewart, Robert Taylor, Edward G. Robinson, Ronald Reagan, Jack Benny, Lloyd Bridges, James Cagney, George Burns, and Lloyd Nolan. During the service, the assistant rector of the All Saints Episcopal Church in Beverly Hills told the mourners that Powell "possessed qualities that make Heaven a better place because he is there."

In one of the most astounding success stories in Hollywood history, Dick Powell managed to garner acclaim in three separate careers, using his versatility and creativity to become an icon on film, radio, and television, both behind the camera and in front of it. During a span of four decades, he earned countless well-deserved accolades for his talents, but it was Powell himself who best summed up his long-lasting career:

"What counts most in this profession is survival," Powell once said. "There were lots of stars bigger than I, but I saw them come and go. Somehow, I've managed to survive, and that's what I'm proud of."

Film Noir Filmography

Murder, My Sweet. Director: Edward Dmytryk. Producer: Adrian Scott. Running time: 95 minutes. Released by RKO, December 18, 1944. Cast: Dick Powell, Claire Trevor, Anne Shirley, Otto Kruger, Mike Mazurki, Miles Mander, Douglas Walton, Don Douglas, Ralf Harolde, Esther Howard.

Cornered. Director: Edward Dmytryk. Producer: Adrian Scott. Running time: 102 minutes. Released by RKO, December 25, 1945. Cast: Dick Powell, Walter Slezak, Micheline Cheirel, Nina Vale, Morris Carnovsky, Edgar Barrier, Steven Geray, Jack La Rue, Luther Adler, Gregory Gay.

Johnny O'Clock. Director: Robert Rossen. Producer: Edward G. Nealis. Running time: 95 minutes. Released by Columbia, March 27, 1947. Cast: Dick Powell, Evelyn Keyes, Lee J. Cobb, Ellen Drew, Nina Foch, Thomas Gomez, John Kellogg, Jim Bannon, Mabel Paige, Phil Brown, Jeff Chandler, Kit Guard.

Pitfall. Director: Andre de Toth. Producer: Samuel Bischoff. Running time: 86 minutes. Released by United Artists, August 24, 1948. Cast: Dick Powell, Lizabeth Scott, Jane Wyatt, Raymond Burr, John Litel, Byron Barr, Jimmy Hunt, Ann Doran, Selmer Jackson, Margaret Wells, Dick Wassel.

Cry Danger. Director: Robert Parrish. Producers: Sam Wiesenthal and W.R. Frank. Running time: 79 minutes. Released by RKO, February 21, 1951. Cast: Dick Powell, Rhonda Fleming, Richard Erdman, William Conrad, Regis Toomey, Jean Porter, Jay Adler, Joan Banks, Gloria Saunders, Hy Averback, Renny McEvoy, Lou Lubin, Benny Burt.

References

"Actress June Allyson, Dick Powell Separate." *Beverly Hills Citizen*, February 22, 1957.

Belser, Lee. "June Allyson Plans Divorce 'Definitely.'" *Los Angeles Mirror*, January 6, 1961.

_____. "June, Dick Powell May Reconcile." *Los Angeles Mirror*, January 18, 1961.

Berman, Arthur. "Dick Powell: Sure, We're Reunited. Why?" *New York Post*, January 3, 1962.

"Better-Written Scripts Attracting More Top Stars Into Vidpix — Dick Powell." *Variety*, May 6, 1955.

Boyle, Hal. "No Drifting for Dick Powell." *Long Island Star-Journal*, August 26, 1958.

"Dick Powell and Wife Adopt Girl." *Los Angeles Times*, August 11, 1948.

"Dick Powell Asks Firm to Elect New President." *Los Angeles Times*, October 16, 1962.

"Dick Powell Cancer Patient, Keeps Busy." *Los Angeles Mirror*, September 28, 1962.

"Dick Powell Is Stricken with Cancer." *Hollywood Citizen-News*, September 28, 1962.

"Dick Powells Are Reconciled." *Los Angeles Mirror*, January 3, 1962.

"Dick Powell 'Sick' of Acting; Likes Being a Producer." *Variety*, October 1, 1957.

"Dick Powell Under Cancer Medication; Sees Full Recovery." *Variety*, September 18, 1962.

"Dick Up to His Ears in Success." *Los Angeles Daily News*, September 11, 1954.

"8-Year Marriage Ends for Powells." *Hollywood Citizen-News*, July 15, 1944.

Finnigan, Joseph. Dick Powell, Allyson May Try Again." *Hollywood Citizen-News*, August 25, 1961.

Hopper, Hedda. "Powell Wears Every Hat Well." *Los Angeles Times*, February 27, 1955.

Humphrey, Hal. "Dick Powell Isn't Retiring, but Just Relaxing His Stomach a Bit." *Los Angeles Mirror*, October 5, 1960.

"If 'Conqueror' Clicks, Powell Will Kiss-Off TV." *Variety*, November 5, 1954.

Jackovich, Karen G. and Sennet, Mark. "The Children of John Wayne, Susan Hayward and Dick Powell Fear That Fallout Killed Their Parents." *People*, November 10, 1980.

"June Allyson Divorces Powell." *Hollywood Citizen-News*, January 31, 1961.

"June Allyson, Powell Part." *Los Angeles Examiner*, January 6, 1961.

"June Allyson Rift with Dick Powell Affirmed." *Los Angeles Times*, January 6, 1961.

Knopf, Christopher. "'If My Aunt in Little Rock Doesn't Like It.'" *Variety*, October 26, 1976.

MacPherson, Virginia. "He's a Tough Guy Now—Dick Powell." *Hollywood Citizen-News*, December 1, 1944.

McClay, Howard. "Powell Back in Comedy Role." *Los Angeles Daily News*, December 30, 1963.

Morris, Mary. "The New Dick Powell." *PM*, June 3, 1945.

Mosby, Aline. "He Took a Salary Cut to Direct Film." *Los Angeles Daily News*, December 3, 1952.

"New Dick Powell Malignancy Feared." *Los Angeles Herald-Examiner*, December 19, 1962.

Parsons, Louella O. "Dick Powells Adopt Baby." *Los Angeles Examiner*, August 11, 1948.

_____. "It's a Boy (5 Lbs.) for Dick Powells." *Los Angeles Examiner*, December 25, 1950.

"Powell 'Amazed' As Gregory 'Fires' Him." *The Hollywood Reporter*, January 13, 1954.

"Powell a Reluctant Host." *Los Angeles Mirror-News*, November 6, 1956.

Powell, Dick. "The Hollywood Scene." *Hollywood Citizen-News*, August 6, 1945.

Powell, Dick, as told to Joe Hyams. "Me and the Mutiny." *Cue*, January 16, 1954.

"Powell Fighting Cancer." *The Hollywood Reporter*, September 28, 1962.

"Powell Gives June $2,500,000 Divorce." *Hollywood Citizen-News*, January 17, 1961.

"Powell's Zane Grey Theatre." *TV Westerner*, circa 1958.

Ryon, Art. "Dick Powell a 'Very Sick Man'; Doctor Fears New Complications." *Los Angeles Times*, December 19, 1962.

_____. "800 Attend Memorial Rites for Dick Powell." *Los Angeles Times*, January 5, 1963.

_____. "Winning Fight Against Cancer, Dick Powell Tells Stockholders." *Los Angeles Times*, October 17, 1962.

Schumach, Murray. "Hollywood Stirred by Death of Powell." *New York Times*, January 4, 1963.

Smith, Cecil. "June in January Is Their Song." *Los Angeles Times*, January 9, 1962.

"Stars' Cancer Deaths Linked to '53 A-Test." *Los Angeles Times*, August 6, 1979.

Taliaferro, Walt. "Dick Powell Has New Type Private Eye Show on NBC." *Los Angeles Daily News*, May 13, 1949.

"'The Happiest Pair in Town.'" *New York Post*, February 22, 1957.

Thomas, A. "Dick Powell." *Films in Review*, circa 1975.

Thomas, Tony. *The Dick Powell Story*. Burbank, California: Riverwood Press, 1993.

Documentary

"Dick Powell: Thanks a Million." Produced by Van Ness Films in Association with Foxstar Productions and A&E Network. Twentieth Century-Fox Film Corporation. Copyright 1996.

VINCENT PRICE

"Why don't you get down on all fours again, Waldo? It's the only time you've kept your mouth shut."— Vincent Price in *Laura* (1944)

Mention the name of Vincent Price today, and most moviegoers will instantly conjure an image of the macabre character roles that seemed to dominate the latter part of the actor's career. But off screen, Price was the converse of his cinema persona — known for his wit and humor, he was also an art aficionado who authored several books and once demonstrated his expertise on a popular quiz show of the 1950s. Even his roots as a performer were diametrically opposed to his later persona; he began his career as a respected leading man on Broadway, and during his Hollywood heyday, the distinctive actor was a standout in such respected films as *The House of Seven Gables* (1940), *Hudson's Bay* (1940), *The Song of Bernadette* (1943), and *Dragonwyck* (1946). Price also lent his considerable talents to six features from the era of film noir: *Laura* (1944), *Leave Her to Heaven* (1945), *The Bribe* (1949), *His Kind of Woman* (1951), *The Las Vegas Story* (1952), and *While the City Sleeps* (1956).

Vincent Leonard Price, Jr., was born on May 27, 1911, in St. Louis, Missouri, where his mother, Marguerite, worked as a school teacher and his father held the post of president of the National Candy Company. The youngest of four, Price demonstrated an early love for performing, making his acting debut at the age of four as a water sprite in a neighborhood play. In his youth, Price also exhibited a passion for the arts, and at the age of 12, purchased an original Rembrandt sketch for $37.50.

After attending the St. Louis Community School (which was co-founded by his mother), and the St. Louis Country Day School, Price enrolled at Yale University, graduating in 1933 with a Bachelor of Arts degree in English. During his college years, the future actor performed in the Yale Glee Club, continued to expand his growing art collection, and spent much of his free time at the local movie theater.

"I think I can honestly say I saw every movie, good and bad, made between the years 1930 and 1933," Price once said. "And I didn't miss many concerts, plays, or revues, either."

Briefly following in his mother's footsteps, Price taught at the Riverdale School in Yonkers, New York, also appearing in the school's production of *H.M.S. Pinafore*. After a year, Price enrolled at the Courtauld Institute in London, pursuing a master's degree in fine arts. Despite his studies, he managed to find time to indulge his budding interest in acting, reportedly seeing John Gielgud's acclaimed performance in *Hamlet* nearly a dozen times. After joining a local amateur theater company, Price landed a role as a policeman in *Chicago* at the Gate Theatre, and was later cast in the male lead in the Gate production of *Victoria Regina*. When the acclaimed play went to New York, Price went with it, debuting on Broadway opposite Helen Hayes. For his portrayal of Prince Albert, Price earned rave reviews— Brooks Atkinson wrote in the *New York Times* that he "plays [the role] beautifully enough to evoke all the romance that lay under surface of a singular royal marriage," and the *New York Herald-Tribune*'s critic proclaimed that Price added "bountifully to the appeal of *Victoria Regina*, making the role pictorial, gently dignified, and romantic."

After two years and 517 performances in *Victoria Regina*, Price was seen in a number of plays, including the short-lived Broadway production of *The Lady Has a Heart*, *The Shoemaker's Holiday* with Orson Welles' Mercury Theatre, and such stock productions as *The Wild Duck* and *Parnell*. While performing in the latter production, Price fell in love with his leading lady, Edith Barrett, and the two were wed on April 23, 1938. Two years later, in August 1940, the couple would have a son, Vincent Barrett, but the marriage would end in 1948.

Meanwhile, Price's Broadway fame had attracted the attention of Hollywood scouts and in 1938 he signed a contract with Universal Studios, appearing opposite Constance Bennett in his screen debut, *Service de Luxe* (1938). In his second cinematic outing, he was loaned to Warner Bros. for *The Private Lives of Elizabeth and Essex* (1939), starring Bette Davis and Errol Flynn, followed by Universal's *Tower of London* (1939), a gothic thriller with Boris Karloff and Basil Rathbone. After this feature, Price was back on Broadway in *Outward Bound*, and appeared on such radio programs as *Valiant Lady* and *The Chase and Sanborn Hour*, on which he reprised his *Victoria Regina* role with Helen Hayes.

In Hollywood, Price was seen in *The House of Seven Gables* (1940), with George Sanders and Margaret Lindsay; *The Invisible Man Returns* (1940), his first film in the horror genre with which he would later become so closely linked; and *Green Hell* (1940), a disastrous jungle adventure that the actor later dismissed as one of the most unintentionally funny movies ever made. ("About five of the worst pictures ever made are all in that one picture," Price said.) After this box office flop, Universal terminated Price's contract and he was quickly picked up by 20th Century-Fox, where he was cast in well-received character parts in *Brigham Young — Frontiersman* (1940), featuring Tyrone Power and Linda Darnell; *Hudson's Bay* (1940), his first of four pictures with Gene Tierney; *The Song of Bernadette* (1943), starring Jennifer Jones as the peasant girl who sees a vision of the Virgin Mary; and *The Eve of St. Mark* (1944), where he played an alcoholic Southerner that he later called his favorite role. Between pictures, Price was again lured to the Broadway stage, starring for a year in *Angel Street* and winning praise in the *New York Herald-Tribune*, where Richard Watts wrote

that the actor "has never been nearly so fine as the cold, sneering, implacable husband."

On screen, Price entered the realm of film noir with his first and — arguably — his best feature from the era, *Laura* (1944). This superb offering centered on the apparent murder of the title character (Gene Tierney), the relentless detective, Mark McPherson (Dana Andrews), who investigates the case, and the distinctively offbeat personalities that comprise the list of suspects: Laura's fiancé Shelby Carpenter (Price), a charming ne'er-do-well; Laura's aunt (Judith Anderson), who barely disguises her attraction to Shelby; and ascerbic columnist Waldo Lydecker (Clifton Webb), Laura's would-be lover. In the midst of McPherson's investigation, however, Laura turns up alive and well, and the detective soon discovers that the dead woman found in Laura's apartment was actually a local model with whom Shelby was having an affair. As Laura begins to question Shelby's possible involvement in the murder, her aunt offers a concise assessment of his persona: "I can afford him and understand him. He's no good, but he's what I want. I'm not a nice person, Laura, and neither is he. He knows I know he's just what he is. He also knows that I don't care. We belong together because we're both weak and can't seem to help it." Ultimately, McPherson pins the murder on Lydecker, who mistakenly shot the model, thinking that she was Laura. In the film's climax, the columnist returns to Laura's home to finish the job, but McPherson catches up to him and guns him down.

For his performance of the weak-willed Shelby, Price was praised as "technically brilliant" in the *Hollywood Citizen-News,* and Dorothy Manners of the *Los Angeles Examiner* noted his "fascinating portrayal." Years after the picture's release, Price himself would call it "one of the best films ever made."

"It is almost a perfect film that was brilliantly directed by Otto Preminger," Price said in a 1991 interview in *Classic Images* magazine. "With the whole cast working together, the story, the set, the cameramen, the end result was that everything about *Laura* was perfect, plus that incredible musical score which is one of the great song hits of all time."

The following year, Price was again co-starred with Gene Tierney for his second noir, a rare Technicolor example from the era, *Leave Her to Heaven* (1945). Tierney portrayed Ellen Berent, whose outward beauty masks a psychological defect that is characterized early on by her mother: "There's nothing wrong with Ellen. It's just that she loves too much. Perhaps that isn't good — it makes such outsiders of everyone else, but she can't help it." However, Ellen's penchant for "loving too much" manifests itself in a lethal manner, leading her to foster the drowning death of her young brother-in-law (Darryl Hickman), cause the miscarriage of her own child, and ultimately to kill herself in a manner that places the suspicion of homicide on her adopted sister, Ruth (Jeanne Crain), with whom her husband, Richard (Cornel Wilde), has fallen in love. Price portrayed Ellen's devoted former fiancé, Russell Quinton, a district attorney who prosecutes Ruth after receiving a letter penned by Ellen before her death: "Richard is leaving me," the letter

reads. "It was after I left the hospital that I first began to sense a change in my husband. At first, I thought it might be due to the loss of our child. And then the truth, the awful truth, began to dawn on me. The reason for the change was Ruth. Russ, they love each other and want to get rid of me." Despite Quinton's vehement and impassioned questioning during the trial, Ruth is acquitted, but after revealing his knowledge of Ellen's role in his brother's death, Richard is sentenced to two years in prison on a charge of conspiracy.

Although Price's role in *Leave Her to Heaven* was a supporting one, his performance earned the actor some of the most glowing reviews of his career. The reviewer for *Cue* opined that Price "makes his few seconds on-screen come to life"; the *Los Angeles Times'* Edwin Schallert felt that his "brilliantly sustained [performance] merits attention as contending for the Academy supporting honors"; and Lowell E. Redelings of the *Hollywood Citizen-News* wrote: "Vincent Price, as the prosecuting attorney, rises to new dramatic heights. His performance — brief as it is — shines like a beacon."

In Price's two films of 1946, the actor fostered his budding persona as a screen menace, playing a murderous psychiatrist in *Shock,* and a homicidal aristocrat in *Dragonwyck*; of his performance in the latter, Bosley Crowther wrote in the *New York Times* that Price's "moment of suave diabolism are about the best in the film." When Price's contract with Fox was not renewed in 1947, the actor returned to Universal, starring in such features as *The Web* (1947), a first-rate crime drama with Edmond O'Brien and William Bendix; *Up in Central Park* (1948), a musical in which Price was miscast as New York politician Boss Tweed; *Rogue's Regiment* (1949), a mediocre actioner starring Dick Powell; and *Bagdad* (1949), a so-so sand-and-sandals saga featuring Maureen O'Hara and Paul Christian. He was also loaned to MGM for the lavish costumer *The Three Musketeers* (1948) and his third film noir feature, *The Bribe* (1949).

This film, set on an island off the coast

of Central America, focuses on a quintet of characters: Rigby (Robert Taylor), a federal agent charged with breaking up a ring of contraband war surplus dealers; Carwood (Price), who ostensibly works as a mining engineer but is actually the head of the organization; Tug Hintten (John Hodiak), a member of the ring who suffers from a debilitating heart condition; Tug's wife, Elizabeth (Ava Gardner), who may or may not know of her husband's role in the illegal operation; and A.J. Bealer (Charles Laughton), Carwood's slovenly underling whose primary focus in life is earning enough money to pay for an operation on his feet. As Rigby grows close to breaking the case, Carwood attempts to use Elizabeth as a means of thwarting his efforts, and when her husband objects, Carwood kills him: "It'll look very natural," Carwood says. "You tried to get to your medicine. Couldn't make it. Do you really think I'd leave you around to talk? You've already talked enough. You've talked yourself to death!" Later, in the climax of this often-complicated feature, Rigby tags Carwood as the mastermind of the surplus racket, chases him through a teeming crowd gathered for a local carnival celebration, and guns him down in the midst of a spectacular fireworks display. For his performance as the murderous Carwood, Price was singled out by the *New York Times'* critic, who wrote that he "leers with diabolic glee," and the reviewer for *The Hollywood Reporter*, who judged him "excellent as the brains of the outfit."

Off screen, just 13 months after his divorce from Edith Barrett, Price took a second trip down the aisle, marrying stage and film designer Mary Grant in August 1949 (13 years later, in 1962, Price and Mary would welcome a daughter, Mary Victoria). The couple's 17-room mansion in Beverly Hills soon became a showplace for their eclectic art collection, and in 1950, Price was elected to the Board of Directors of the Los Angeles County Museum. The following year, he continued to enhance his reputation in the field of fine arts when he lectured at East Los Angeles College on "The Aesthetic Respon-

sibilities of the Citizen," and later donated 90 pieces of his personal art collection to the school. The Vincent Price Gallery is still housed at the institution in Monterey Park, California, containing artwork valued at several million dollars.

During the next several decades, Price continued to evidence his passion for fine arts through a variety of methods; he demonstrated his impressive knowledge of art on the popular quiz show, *The $64,000 Question*; opened the Modern Institute of Art in Hollywood along with such fellow art-lovers as Edward G. Robinson and Fanny Brice; worked for more than a decade as an art buyer for Sears Roebuck and Company; provided the narration for two art documentaries, *Pictura* (1952) and *The Ancient Maya* (1952); edited or authored several volumes on art, including *I Like What I Know* (1959), *Drawings of Delacroix* (1962), *The Michelangelo Bible* (1965), and *The Vincent Price Treasury of American Art* (1972); and served as a member of such art-related organizations as the Pomona College Art Historian Society, the Latin Arts and Crafts Board of the U.S. Department of the Interior, the art council of the University of California at Los Angeles, the Whitney Museum Friends of American Art, and the Fine Arts Committee of the White House. In concert with Price's love for fine arts, the actor demonstrated a zeal for the culinary arts as well, and wrote, with his wife, Mary, three books on cooking, *A Treasury of Great Recipes* (1965), *National Treasury of Cooking* (1967), and *The Come Into the Kitchen Cookbook* (1969).

Between art-related activities, Price was heard on numerous radio programs during the 1940s and 1950s, including *Lux Radio Theater, Screen Guild Players, Suspense, Theater of Romance, Cavalcade of America, Philip Morris Playhouse, Hollywood Star Time, CBS Radio Workshop,* and *Ford Theater.* He also managed to find time to continue his screen career. In 1951, he signed a non-exclusive contract with RKO, lensing his final three films noirs for the studio: *His Kind of Woman* (1951), *The Las Vegas Story* (1952), and *While the City Sleeps* (1956). The first, *His Kind of Woman*, begins as professional gambler Dan Milner (Robert Mitchum) is offered $50,000 to leave the United States for a year. Traveling to Mexico to await further instructions, Milner encounters Lenore Brent (Jane Russell), a singer posing as a wealthy heiress; Mark Cardigan (Price), a pretentious film star; and Bill Lusk (Tim Holt), an agent with the United States immigration service, who informs Milner of the real reason behind his payoff—exiled syndicate boss Nick Ferraro (Raymond Burr) plans to murder Milner and assume his identity in order to re-enter the United States. Lusk is later murdered and Milner is forced aboard Ferraro's nearby yacht, but Cardigan helps to save the day—viewing the situation as a movie plot, the actor amasses a group of local police and hotel guests to storm the ship and rescue Milner. (Offering a bit of comic relief in the film's dark plot, Cardigan dramatically browbeats a policeman who is afraid of the water: "Tell that blockhead to get aboard! There's enough wood in his head to make him float!") Although *His Kind of Woman* was labeled by one critic as "one of the worst Hollywood pictures in years," Price emerged relatively unscathed; the *New York Times*' reviewer wrote that his performance indicated that the actor was "obviously having the time of his life."

Next, in *The Las Vegas Story*, Price portrayed Lloyd Rollins, a wealthy businessman desperate to raise the funds needed to cover his role in an embezzlement scheme. Stopping in Las Vegas with his wife, Linda (Jane Russell), Lloyd gives her expensive necklace to a local casino owner in exchange for a line of gambling credit, not knowing that he is being trailed by private detective Tom Hubler (Brad Dexter). When the casino owner is found dead, Lloyd is suspected of the murder and jailed, but it turns out that the real killer is Hubler, who is chased by helicopter by David Andrews (Victor Mature), a sheriff's department lieutenant, and shot down in the tower of an abandoned airfield. As for Rollins, he is later arrested for embezzlement,

leaving the way clear for his wife to reunite with Andrews, her former lover.

Like Price's previous noir offering with Jane Russell, *The Las Vegas Story* failed to impress audiences or critics; in one of the feature's less caustic notices, the reviewer for *Variety* found that the film offered "only a fair amount of melodrama entertainment." Price fared better, however, with his final film noir, *While the City Sleeps*, which was glowingly described by one critic as an "old-fashioned 'stop the presses' newspaper yarn ... updated with intelligence and considerable authenticity, and further brightened with crisp dialog from the pen of Casey Robinson." Directed by Fritz Lang, this well-done feature begins with the death of media mogul Amos Kyne (Robert Warwick) and the takeover of his organization by his slothful son, Walter (Price). Walter promptly establishes the post of executive director ("Someone to do the actual work," he says), announcing that he will award the job to the employee who solves a series of sex murders committed by "the Lipstick Killer." Among those vying for the job are wire service manager Mark Loving (George Sanders), newspaper editor John Day Griffith (Thomas Mitchell), photo service editor Harry Kritzer (James Craig), and television anchor Edward Mobley (Dana Andrews). Each of the contenders pulls out all the stops in an effort to land the coveted post, with Kritzer asking his mistress—who also happens to be Walter's wife—to use her influence to sway the job in his favor, and Mobley setting up his girlfriend as bait for the killer. Ultimately, Mobley succeeds in catching the mentally unstable delivery boy responsible for the crimes, but he gives the scoop to Griffith, who gets the job.

His noir features notwithstanding, most of Price's films during the 1950s were fairly forgettable; there were several notable exceptions, however, including *The Ten Commandments* (1956), in which he played a sleazy Egyptian architect who meets his end at the hands of Moses. More significantly, it was during this period that Price embarked on the second phase of his career as one of the foremost masters of the macabre. He was hailed for his "splendidly clammy form" as a demented sculptor in *House of Wax* (1953), and later in the decade was seen in *The Fly* (1958), portraying the brother of a hapless scientist whose molecular constitution is intermingled with that of a housefly. But it was Price's starring role in *House on Haunted Hill* (1958), produced and directed by William Castle, that really set in motion the proverbial ball of horror. The following year, Price appeared in Castle's *The Tingler* (1959), featuring a gimmick called "Percepto," which equipped theater seats with vibrating motors that provided moviegoers with well-timed tingling sensations.

In 1960, Price teamed with American International Pictures and producer-director Roger Corman, going on to create a series of horror features, including *The Fall of the House of Usher* (1960), *The Pit and the Pendulum* (1961), *Tower of London* (1962), *Tales of Terror* (1962), *The Raven* (1963), *The Haunted Palace* (1964), *The Masque of the Red Death* (1964), and *The Tomb of Ligeia* (1965). Also for American International, Price was seen with Peter Lorre and Boris Karloff in *The Comedy of Terrors* (1963), a spoof of the horror genre; starred in *Scream and Scream Again* (1970) with Christopher Lee (another horror film icon with whom, ironically, Price shared his May 27th birthdate); portrayed the title role in *The Abominable Dr. Phibes* (1971), which was described by one reviewer as an "anachronistic period horror musical camp fantasy"; and played a demented Shakespearean actor in *Theater of Blood* (1973). (While filming the latter production in England, Price fell in love with co-star Coral Browne; their highly publicized affair led to the end of his nearly 25-year marriage to Mary Price. Price and Browne would marry on October 24, 1974, and would remain together until Browne's death from cancer in 1991.)

"I'm often asked why I make so many horror films," Price once said of his spate of frightening features. "Well, the answer is I like to eat. Katie Hepburn rang me up a while ago and asked me to play Prospero in the stage production of *The Tempest*. I'd have gotten $500 for eight weeks' work — and I just couldn't afford it."

In addition to his feature film work, Price was seen in an estimated 2,000 guest spots on the small screen, once admitting: "I made up my mind ... to go on every TV show that asked me. I go nuts when I'm not working. I'll do anything, I guess. I'm an old ham, really." Beginning in the late 1940s and continuing for the next four decades, Price appeared on such popular series as *The Red Skelton Show*, *The Steve Allen Show*, *Playhouse 90*, *Alfred Hitchcock Presents*, *Get Smart*, *Here's Lucy*, *Night Gallery*, *The Brady Bunch*, *M*A*S*H*, *The Carol Burnett Show*, *Columbo*, *The Muppet Show*, *The Sonny and Cher Show*, *The Love Boat*, *The Bionic Woman*, *Tiny Toon Adventures*, and *The Critic*. He also had a recurring role on the campy *Batman* series, playing a bald villain known as "Egghead."

"Let's face it, all the cool people were doing *Batman*, and he understood that in order to be current, you have to be current to each new generation," Price's daughter, Victoria, said in a 1997 documentary on the actor's life. "He understood that it was sort of a campy thing — the horror thing — he had fun with it. I'm not sure he would've had that much fun if he hadn't had the art to offset it. He always had that — he always had something that he could take seriously."

Price's widely varying activities also included nearly 900 appearances on *The Hollywood Squares* game show; providing the voice of Vincent VanGhoul on the *Scooby Doo* cartoon; hosting for nine years the PBS series *Mystery!*; serving as ringmaster for the 1982 *Circus of the Stars*; portraying the "spirit of the nightmare" in rocker Alice Cooper's 1975 television special, *Alice Cooper: The Nightmare*; narrating *Vincent* (1982), a short film by director-producer Tim Burton about "a little boy who is considerate and nice, but wants to be just like Vincent Price"; and providing the "rap" narration for the 1983 blockbuster song hit by Michael Jackson, *Thriller*. Never abandoning his stage roots, Price also appeared in several regional productions during the 1970s, including *Damn Yankees*, *Peter Pan*, and *Charlie's Aunt*, and essayed a tour-de-force in 1977, starring as playwright Oscar Wilde in *Diversions and Delights*. In this highly acclaimed one-man show, Price toured for five years in 800 performances throughout the United States and abroad.

In ill health as he neared his 80th year, Price continued to perform, starring with Bette Davis and Lillian Gish in the 1987 made-for-television movie, *The Whales of August*; portraying a kindly inventor in the 1990 feature film *Edward Scissorhands*, starring Johnny Depp and directed by Tim Burton; and appearing in the television movie, *The Heart of Justice* in 1992. But on October 25, 1993, suffering from Parkinson's Disease and lung cancer, Vincent Price died at the age of 82. His ashes were scattered off the California coast of Malibu — along with his favorite gardening hat.

In the annals of Hollywood, Vincent Price was nearly without peer in terms of the vastness of his capabilities, the influence of his knowledge, and the manifestations of his talent. While he is best remembered for his contribution to the horror genre, he must also be recognized for his significant gifts to the fine arts, the literary world, and the mediums of screen, stage, television, and radio. He was truly, as one columnist once termed him, "priceless."

"I think a lot of people have very fond memories of sitting around and just scaring themselves watching Vincent Price movies," Victoria Price said in 1997. "But I think the reason that those movies worked was because always underneath that, you saw this man that was having fun. And he really had fun with his life.

"It was a life well-lived."

Film Noir Filmography

Laura. Director and Producer: Otto Preminger. Running time: 88 minutes. Released by 20th Century-Fox, October 11, 1944. Cast: Gene Tierney, Dana Andrews, Clifton Webb, Vincent Price, Judith Anderson, Dorothy Adams, James Flavin, Clyde Fillmore, Ralph Dunn, Grant Mitchell, Kathleen Howard. Awards: Academy Award for Best Cinematography (Joseph LaShelle). Academy Award nominations for Best Director (Otto Preminger), Best Supporting Actor (Clifton Webb), Best Screenplay (Jay Oratler, Samuel Hoffenstein, Betty Reinhardt), Best Art Direction (Lyle Wheeler, Leland Fuller, Thomas Little).

Leave Her to Heaven. Director: John M. Stahl. Producer: William A. Bacher. Running time: 110 minutes. Released by 20th Century-Fox, December 25, 1945. Cast: Gene Tierney, Cornel Wilde, Jeanne Crain, Vincent Price, Mary Phillips, Ray Collins, Gene Lockhart, Reed Hadley, Darryl Hickman, Chill Wills, Paul Everton, Olive Blakeney, Addison Richards, Harry Depp, Grant Mitchell, Milton Parsons. Awards: Academy Award for Best Cinematography (Leon Shamroy). Academy Award nominations for Best Actress (Gene Tierney), Best Art Direction (Lyle Wheeler, Maurice Ransford, Thomas Little), Best Sound (Thomas T. Moulton).

The Bribe. Director: Robert Z. Leonard. Producer: Pandro S. Berman. Running time: 98 minutes. Released by MGM, February 3, 1949. Cast: Robert Taylor, Ava Gardner, Charles Laughton, Vincent Price, John Hodiak, Samuel S. Hinds, John Hoyt, Tito Renaldo.

His Kind of Woman. Director: John Farrow. Producer: Robert Sparks. Running time: 120 minutes. Released by RKO, August 1951. Cast: Robert Mitchum, Jane Russell, Vincent Price, Tim Holt, Charles McGraw, Marjorie Reynolds, Raymond Burr, Leslye Banning, Jim Backus, Philip Van Zandt, John Mylong, Carleton G. Young, Erno Verebes, Dan White, Richard Bergren, Stacy Harris, Robert Cornthwaite.

The Las Vegas Story. Director: Robert Stevenson. Producer: Robert Sparks. Running time: 87 minutes. Released by RKO, January 1952. Cast: Jane Russell, Victor Mature, Vincent Price, Hoagy Carmichael, Brad Dexter, Jay C. Flippen, Gordon Oliver, Will Wright, Bill Welsh, Ray Montgomery, Colleen Miller, Bob Wilke.

While the City Sleeps. Director: Fritz Lang. Producer: Bert Friedlob. Running time: 99 minutes. Released by RKO, May 16, 1956. Cast: Dana Andrews, Rhonda Fleming, George Sanders, Howard Duff, Thomas Mitchell, Vincent Price, Sally Forrest, John Barrymore, Jr., James Craig, Ida Lupino, Robert Warwick, Ralph Peters, Vladimir Sokoloff, Mae Marsh, Sandy White.

References

"Actor-Art Expert Vincent Price Biggest Buyer Since the Medici." *Los Angeles Times*, January 7, 1965.

Biography of Vincent Price. 20th Century-Fox Studios, April 19, 1958.

"But, 'Strictly Missourian' Is Vincent Price." *St. Louis Star-Times*, March 11, 1944.

Byrne, Bridget. "Vincent Price: Charming Purveyor of Camp Humor." *Los Angeles Herald-Examiner*, June 7, 1971.

Corneau, Ernest N. "Vincent Price — Menace to Madcap." Classic Film Collector, circa 1977.

Dixon, Winston Wheeler. "The Other Side of Vincent Price." *Classic Images*, June 1992.

"Film Star Price to Wed Actress." *Los Angeles Herald-Examiner*, October 25, 1974.

Hopper, Hedda. "Price of Fame." *Chicago Sunday Tribune*, November 18, 1945.

Hua, Vanessa. "Master of Horror Left an Art-Filled Legacy of Learning." *Los Angeles Times*, October 25, 1997.

Lentz, Harris III. Obituary. *Classic Images*, December 1993.

Mann, Roderick. "Top Man Among the Tombstones." *New York Times*, circa December 1965.

Marill, Alvin H. "Vincent Price." *Films in Review*, circa 1968.

Monaghan, Connie. "A Priceful Collection." *Los Angeles Weekly*, September 20, 1996.

Morris, Mary. "Leading Menace." *P.M.*, July 14, 1946.

"Mrs. Vincent Price Granted Divorce." *Hollywood Citizen-News*, June 3, 1948.

Nielsen, Ray. "Vincent Price in 'Laura.'" *Classic Images*, January 1991.

Noble, Peter. "Master of Movie Menace." *Screen International*, July 9, 1983.

Oliver, Myrna. "Veteran Actor Vincent Price Dies at 82." *Los Angeles Times*, October 26, 1993.

Pam, Jerry. "Actor Price Found Climb Upward Tough." *Beverly Hills Newslife*, March 2, 1974.

Parish, James Robert and Whitney, Steven. *Vincent Price Unmasked*. New York: Drake Publishers, 1974.

Parsons, Louella O. "Vincent Price, N.Y. Girl Wed." *Los Angeles Examiner*, October 3, 1949.

Price, Victoria. "Where Vincent Price Went to Hide." *New York Times*, June 21, 2001.

Seymour, Blackie. "The 'Price' of Hollywood." *Classic Images*, December 1993.

"The 'Compleat' Man." *Cue*, August 20, 1960.

"The Price of Success." *American Movie Classics Magazine*, May 1998.

"The Tell-Tale Heart." *People*, December 13, 1999.

Thomas, Bob. "What's So Scary About Cooking and Art?" *Long Beach Press-Telegram*, August 21, 1985.

"Vincent Price." *Drama-Logue*. June 19 — 25, 1986.

"Vincent Price." *Dramatics*, March 1981.

"Vincent Price." *The Disney Channel Magazine*, March 13 — April 23, 1988.

"Vincent Price Declares Filmmakers Must Return to 'Hoopla' of the Past." *Boxoffice*, October 11, 1971.

"Vincent Price Secretly Wed." *Hollywood Citizen-News*, October 3, 1949.

West, Dick. "Hollywood Actor Carries Culture to U.S. Capital." *Hollywood Citizen-News*, February 16, 1961.

"Wife of 'Saint' Says He Ain't." *Los Angeles Times*, June 4, 1948.

Will, Joanne. "Choice Recipes for New Adventures in Cooking." *Chicago Tribune*, June 11, 1965.

"Work by Rembrandt Opened Vincent Price's Art Love." *Hollywood Citizen-News*, August 10, 1963.

Documentary

"Vincent Price: The Versatile Villain." Produced by Van Ness Films in association with Foxstar Productions, Twentieth Television, and A&E Network. Twentieth Century Fox Film Corporation. Copyright 1997.

George Raft

"You got the brains of a two-year old. No stupid jerk like your brother is going to louse us up." — George Raft in *Rogue Cop* (1952)

Impeccably attired, with slick-backed hair and steely, coal-black eyes, George Raft was the epitome of the 1930s cinema gangster. And off screen, the actor led a life that often closely mirrored his celluloid persona.

"George was like his screen image," actress Joan Bennett once said. "An underlying toughness was forever under the finely veneered surface."

The actor who hobnobbed with such real-life hoods as Benjamin "Bugsy" Siegel and Owney Madden had a screen career that spanned seven decades— while he was never highly acclaimed for his acting ability, he was an undeniable star during the 1930s and 1940s in such vehicles as *Scarface* (1932), *Each Dawn I Die* (1939), and *They Drive By Night* (1940). He also starred in five features from the film noir era: *Johnny Angel* (1945), *Nocturne* (1946), *Red Light* (1950), *Loan Shark* (1952), and *Rogue Cop* (1954).

The actor who was self-described as "kind of a greaseball-type" was born George Ranft in New York City on September 26, 1895, one of 10 children of department store deliveryman Conrad Ranft and his wife, Eva. Growing up in the city's rough Hell's Kitchen area, the future actor (who changed his name to Raft in his late teens) frequently skipped school, spending much of his time getting involved in street brawls, hanging out on local corners, and serving for a time as mascot for the New York Highlanders baseball team.

"I played a lot of hookey in those days," Raft told biographer Lewis Yablonsky. "In fact I hardly ever saw the inside of a classroom."

At the age of 13, Raft quit school for good and left home, sleeping in subways and mission homes, and making ends meet by performing such odd jobs as shoveling snow or delivering orders for local stores. After an unsuccessful attempt at a minor-league baseball career, Raft put his street fighting prowess to good use as a professional boxer, but after fewer than 25 bouts, he hung up his gloves and switched vocational gears again. This time, Raft capitalized on his natural dancing ability, first landing a job as an instructor at the Audubon Ballroom, and later entering and winning ballroom dance contests and working as a "taxi-dancer" in local cafes. When an agent spotted him in a contest, he landed his first job on the legitimate stage, at the Union Square Theater.

"I was very nervous, but once I heard the music and began to dance, everything was okay," the actor said in his 1974 biography. "When I finished, they applauded wildly and I came back for five curtain calls. I was so excited I didn't know what happened."

Billed as "The Fastest Dancer in the World," Raft continued to enhance his status as a performer during the next several years, touring nationwide with the Orpheum and B.F. Keith vaudeville circuits, landing bookings in some of the top clubs on Broadway and in Europe, and appearing as the featured dancer at Texas Guinan's El Fey Club in New York. During this period, Raft also began to supplement his income by working for his boyhood chum, Owney Madden, who had become one of the top gangsters in New York.

"Among other things, I drove the convoy car for Madden's fleet of beer trucks," Raft told *Saturday Evening Post* writer Dean Jennings in 1957. "This was a dangerous but important assignment, and I got it after Feets Edson taught me how to drive a big car, gangland style. I had to learn how to cut corners on two wheels, turn on a dime, hold the big machine steady at high speed or take it through narrow or blocked streets where some trigger man might be waiting."

Alongside his relationship with hoods like Madden and Edson, Raft entered another relationship around this time — one that would plague him for decades to come. According to the actor, he was "tricked" into marrying Grayce Mulrooney, who had once worked as one of his ballroom dancing partners. Shortly after the ill-conceived union, Raft realized that he had "made a mistake," and the couple separated. However, Mulrooney refused to grant Raft a divorce — a stance she maintained until her death until 1970. (In 1949, Raft would sign a property settlement agreement granting Mulrooney 10 percent of his earnings, resulting in an unusual arrangement that provided "alimony" to the woman who remained his wife for more than 40 years.)

Professionally, Raft made his screen debut in 1929 when Texas Guinan offered him a role as a taxi-dancer in *Queen of the Nightclubs*, a film about her life as a famed nightclub hostess. Although the film was a disappointment at the box office, Raft remained in Hollywood, appearing in bit parts as a dancer in *Gold Diggers of Broadway* (1929) and *Side Street* (1929) before getting his first big break. While dining with friends at the Brown Derby Restaurant, Raft caught the attention of director Rowland Brown, who invited the actor to test for a role in his upcoming film, *Quick Millions* (1931). After landing the part in this Spencer Tracy starrer, Raft was seen in such films as *Hush Money* (1931), starring Joan Bennett and Myrna Loy, and *Taxi* (1931), a vehicle for James Cagney in which Raft was again seen in a minor role as a dancer. But fame and fortune were just around the corner.

Impressed by Raft's performance in *Quick Millions*, director Howard Hawks tapped the actor for a featured role in *Scarface* (1932), a thinly veiled accounting of the exploits of Chicago gangleader Al Capone. Although most of the action centered on the film's star, Paul Muni, Raft provided a menacing presence throughout and introduced what would become a trademark gesture for the actor.

"When he didn't have anything else to do, he would flip a coin," Hawks said. "It worked. From beginning to end he looked as if he'd been acting for years. Having George flip the coin made him a character. The coin represented a hidden attitude — a kind of defiance, a held-back hostility, a coolness — which hadn't been found in pictures up to that time, and it made George stand out. It probably helped make him a star."

Raft's performance in *Scarface* not only impressed critics and moviegoers; according to the actor, he also earned the approval of none other than Al Capone himself, who summoned the actor to his private office shortly after the film's Chicago release. Throughout the next several decades, Raft's film persona and his life off screen would intertwine in a similar manner, as he continued to associate with shady underworld figures, including high-profile gangster Benjamin "Bugsy" Siegel. In 1944, Raft testified on Siegel's behalf during a hearing on bookmaking charges, and three years later, *Salute* magazine printed a lengthy article on Siegel entitled "George

Raft's Gangster Friend." (In fact, on the night of Siegel's murder, in June 1947, Raft was reportedly scheduled to meet the gangster at his home, but was serendipitously delayed by a bridge game.) Raft, however, denied the rumors that frequently surfaced regarding his possible criminal activities, insisting that his relationships with the famed gangsters were far more innocuous than they were portrayed.

"To me, a Hell's Kitchen kid with no education and no special talent, the Prohibition gangsters were not criminals. They were big men, the only heroes available in my crowded, violent little sidewalk world," Raft once said. "I'm not a member of any mob, never was. Sure, I know some guys that are, but I know a lot of people. What am I supposed to do when those guys say hello to me — tell them to get lost?"

Raft's gangland connections would have a greater impact on his career in the years to come, but for now, these slightly sinister associations seemed to only add to his public appeal. Riding high following his triumph in *Scarface*, Raft signed a contract with Paramount Studios and appeared in 15 features during the next two years, including *Night After Night* (1932), Mae West's first talking picture; *The Bowery* (1933), where Raft played the real-life, Brooklyn Bridge–jumping daredevil from whom actor Steve Brodie took his name; *The Midnight Club* (1933), which showed the actor in a rare appearance on the right side of the law; *The Trumpet Blows* (1934), a clunker in which Raft was woefully miscast as a Mexican; and *Bolero* (1934), which gave the actor a chance to showcase his dancing skills opposite co-star Carole Lombard.

Although Raft was kept busy at Paramount, however, he also began wracking up suspensions from the studio for parts he refused to play. In his most highly publicized suspension, Raft turned down the male lead in *The Story of Temple Drake* (1933), a sordid tale of rape, abduction, and murder starring Miriam Hopkins in the title role. Citing the seedy nature of the character he was

newspaper reports of a "rumor[ed] hitch in settlement negotiations between George and his wife" turned out to be all too accurate, and after five years, the relationship between Raft and Pine came to an end. In later years, Raft would become involved with a number of actresses, including Norma Shearer and, most notably, Betty Grable whom, it was reported, the actor desperately wanted to marry. In a 1943 article in *Photoplay* magazine, Adela Rogers St. Johns chronicled with great pathos the romance between the two stars, writing that there was "no use saying that if he doesn't get [a divorce], the Grable-Raft romance will last. It won't. It can't. We all know that."

"George told me ... how much he and Betty want to marry," St. Johns wrote. "I don't think I ever heard more real hunger in a man's voice.... When George talked about Betty Grable, I realized that here was a love that took in the whole of love, that they were suited to each other and that George now saw in the future the home he had dreamed of and the children of his own he has always wanted." (Just months after the publication of St. Johns' article, Grable married musician Harry James, and Raft reportedly never again became involved in a long-term romance.)

On screen, Raft continued to ride high on a wave of popularity. Although reviewers often criticized his deadpan delivery and accused him of "playing George Raft," he was a hit with moviegoers in such films as *Rumba* (1935), which re-teamed him with Carole Lombard; *The Glass Key* (1935), the first screen version of the Dashiell Hammett novel (it would be remade seven years later with Alan Ladd in Raft's role); *Yours for the Asking* (1936), in which he played a streetwise hood who falls for a society beauty; and *Souls at Sea* (1937), where he gave one of his better performances as an officer on a slave ship. In 1937, however, Raft turned down a role in William Wyler's *Dead End* that would mark the start of a trend; the part of gangster Baby Face Martin was given to Humphrey Bogart, who earned acclaim for his performance. In subsequent years, Raft would turn down the starring roles in *It All Came True*

assigned to play, Raft insisted that appearing in the film would be his "screen suicide."

"If I had made a ton of money in picture and was ready to retire from the screen, it wouldn't be so bad," Raft told reporters, "but my whole career is ahead of me. The part is so repulsive to me I couldn't play it convincingly if I tried. I'm not trying to tell Paramount what kind of pictures to make, I'm merely trying to tell them that the role in *Temple Drake* probably would ruin my career." The role was subsequently assigned to Jack LaRue.

In addition to making headlines for his spats with the studio, Raft was providing juicy fodder for fan magazines and gossip columns with his romance with Chicago socialite and aspiring actress Virginia Pine, the divorced mother of a young child. In May 1934, Pine announced to columnist Louella Parsons that she and Raft would soon become man and wife, telling her, "George and I will marry the moment he is legally free. We are both very much in love and both very happy. I know that George will be good to my little daughter. She already loves him and he is devoted to her." Pine, however, hadn't reckoned on the tenacity of the current Mrs. Raft—

(1940), *High Sierra* (1941), and *The Maltese Falcon* (1941), the first two because of his determination to distance himself from his on-screen gangster persona, and the latter because he refused to work with first-time director John Huston. Each of the parts ultimately went to Bogart and, ironically, *The Maltese Falcon* would catapult both Bogart and his director into lasting fame.

In the late 1930s, after nearly 20 suspensions by Paramount execs, Raft terminated his contract with the studio and signed with Warner Bros., appearing in *Each Dawn I Die* (1939), for which one critic credited him with "stealing the entire picture" from co-star James Cagney; *Invisible Stripes* (1939), where he played the older brother of newcomer William Holden; and *They Drive By Night* (1940), one of the actor's best films, which featured a top-notch cast including Humphrey Bogart, Ann Sheridan, and Ida Lupino. Years after the latter film's release, Raft recounted a near-disaster on the set that was averted as a result of his dealings with underworld characters during his days in New York.

"I played a tough truck driver in the story, and in one scene Humphrey Bogart, Ann Sheridan and I were highballing down a long hill in an old beat-up truck," Raft said in 1957. "Halfway down, the brakes went out, and Bogart began to cuss.... Ann screamed once and turned her eyes away from the road as I fought the wheel, and I couldn't have been more scared if Machine Gun Jack McGurn himself had been on my tail. The speedometer needle was touching 80 when I saw a slash on the right bank of the road where a bulldozer had started a new road. I pulled hard on the wheel and the truck went bouncing up the embankment and finally stopped. 'Thanks, pal,' Bogart said dryly. 'Don't thank me,' I said. 'Write a letter to Owney Madden and Feets Edson.' I wonder if he knew what I meant."

By now, Raft had not only developed a reputation in the Hollywood community because of his reputed association with gangland figures, but also due to his quick temper, which often erupted in violence. Since the early 1930s, the actor had been involved in numerous incidents that were gleefully reported by the press, including a 1934 scuffle at the Brown Derby that was touted as a "near-riot" in local papers; a fist-fight with actor Wallace Beery on the set of their 1933 film, *The Bowery*; a dispute during filming of the Raft-Lombard feature *Bolero*, which the actor ended by punching the producer on the jaw; and a brawl at a Chicago nightclub that erupted after an intoxicated patron called Raft a "shitheel" for refusing to dance with his wife. And during production of the actor's 1941 feature, *Manpower*, Raft and his co-star Edward G. Robinson engaged in what one fan magazine called "one of the fieriest feuds Hollywood has enjoyed in many a moon."

"Story is that one of the boys is a camera hog and the other isn't having any of it," stated a writer for *Movie Life*. "So, being pretty pugnacious himself, he's said to have taken a poke at his co-star." (Despite their physical clashes—which at one point resulted in Robinson walking off the set—the two stars patched up their differences in later years, and shortly before his death, Robinson praised Raft as a "true actor.")

Several years after his run-in with Robinson, Raft made headlines again when he was sued by local attorney Edward Raiden in a $300,000 damage suit. Raiden claimed that he had been hired by Raft's 19-year-old former girlfriend, Betty Doss, in an effort to recover $6,000 in gifts that had reportedly been given, and later taken back, by the actor. During a December 1945 meeting to discuss the matter, Raiden charged, he was attacked by Raft and the brother of Raft's longtime bodyguard, Mack Grey.

"Raft put on kid gloves and punched away at my face, beat me about the nose, face, chest and arms [and] kicked me in the groin with his knee," Raiden claimed in his suit. Raft, however, told a different story, insisting in a deposition that the lawyer "shoved his hand into my puss—I mean face—and scratched me so bad that the blood poured out." Ultimately, in a twist worthy of any movie plot, Betty Doss told reporters that she barely knew Raiden and had never retained his services— and she praised Raft as "nothing but a gentleman — in fact, about one of the nicest I've ever met." The case was later dropped.

Between brawls, Raft managed to find time to continue his screen career, but most of his best pictures were behind him. After ending his association with Warner Bros. in 1943, the actor worked as a freelancer, starring in such features as Universal's *Follow the Boys* (1944), a star-studded salute to the war effort; 20th Century-Fox's *Nob Hill*, a likable musical set in turn-of-the-century San Francisco; and RKO's *Johnny Angel* (1945), his entry into the world of film noir. In this feature, described by one critic as "grade B melodrama and an oddly inert one at that," Raft played the title role of a ship captain investigating the mysterious death of his father and his crew. When he seeks assistance from the shipping line where he works, however, he is met with indifference from Gustafson (Marvin Miller), the head of the company, and Gustafson's secretary and former nurse, Mrs. Drumm (Margaret Wycherly). After encountering a French woman, Paulette (Signe Hasso), who was a stowaway on his father's ship, Johnny learns that his father was killed by smugglers who stole his cargo of $5 million in gold. After the smugglers removed the gold, however, they were murdered by a man that Paulette was unable to identify. Ultimately, Johnny learns that the man behind the scheme is Gustafson, who stole the gold in an effort to please his money-grubbing wife, Lilah (Claire Trevor). In the film's climax, Lilah double-crosses her husband and stabs him, but when he tries to shoot her during a confrontation at an abandoned shack, he is shot and killed by Mrs. Drumm.

A financial and critical disappointment, *Johnny Angel* earned mixed reviews at best, with the critic for *Variety* labeling the film "slow and plodding," and Bosley Crowther of the *New York Times* writing that Raft appeared "bored and indifferent." Thalia Bell

of *Motion Picture Herald* took a more favorable view of the picture, however, comparing its screenplay to *To Have and Have Not*, released a year earlier: "Indeed, if Miss Hasso were a blonde, and Raft's features less symmetrical, the pair might pass for Humphrey Bogart and Lauren Bacall. As it is, they make an interesting change."

Raft fared better the following year with his second film noir, *Nocturne* (1946), which begins with the shooting death of composer Keith Vincent (Edward Ashley) as he is in the midst of a callous break-up with an unseen woman. Although Vincent's death is originally ruled a suicide, detective Joe Warne (Raft) suspects murder and his investigation leads him to a pair of possible culprits— a bit actress, Frances Ransom (Lynn Bari), who lied about her alibi on the night of the killing, and her sister, Carol (Virginia Huston), a local nightclub singer. When Warne finds himself attracted to Frances, however, she uses her charms in an effort to sidetrack his investigation: "Isn't it better that [Vincent] is dead?" she asks during a romantic encounter with the detective. "Couldn't you drop the case? Joe — isn't it nicer like this?" Despite his growing feelings, Warne doggedly continues his pursuit of the case, but ultimately learns that it was Carol, and not Frances, who was romantically involved with the composer. Just as he is about to arrest Carol for the murder, the nightclub's pianist admits that he is Carol's husband — and the killer.

After earning praise in *Variety* for giving his portrayal in *Nocturne* "his usual, slow-paced tough touch ... to make it thoroughly effective," Raft was seen in such features as *Intrigue* (1947), where he played an ex–Army pilot falsely charged with smuggling, and *Race Street* (1948), a cliché-ridden crime drama co-starring William Bendix. He also starred during this period in the third and — arguably — the weakest of his films noirs, *Red Light* (1950). This feature, according to the foreword, depicts "one of the most unusual cases in the criminal records of San Francisco"— the murder of Army chaplain Jess Torno (Arthur Franz) in a hotel room. Just before he dies, Jess tells his older brother, Johnny (Raft), that the key to finding his killer can found "written in the bible." When he later returns to the hotel room, Johnny finds that the bible is missing and launches an exhaustive search to locate it, tracking down a list of guests who stayed in the room following his brother's murder. Johnny finally finds the elusive bible, but is dismayed to find that the name of the murderer is not written inside; instead, Jess had circled a scripture that reads, "Vengeance is mine; I will repay, saith the Lord." Meanwhile, the man responsible for the killing is revealed to be Nick Cherney (Raymond Burr), the former bookkeeper of Johnny's trucking company, who'd been sent to prison after Johnny nabbed him for embezzlement. During a gun battle atop the rain-swept roof of the trucking firm, Nick's gun runs out of bullets, offering Johnny the chance to finish him off, but he hears his brother's voice quoting the scripture from the bible and lowers his gun. Moments later, Nick is electrocuted when he steps onto a wire and falls from the roof to his death. The film's last scene shows the flashing sign from the trucking company, which now offers a deeper meaning: "24 Hour Service."

For his performance in this unusual noir entry, Raft earned widely varying reviews. Lloyd L. Sloan wrote in the *Hollywood Citizen-News* that the actor played "his usual outwardly emotional self," and the *New York Times'* Bosley Crowther judged that he was, "except for a scene or two, a singularly stony-faced citizen." But in the *Los Angeles Times*, John L. Scott opined that Raft was "convincing as the revenge-seeker," and Sara Hamilton raved in the *Los Angeles Examiner*: "George Raft merges from his emotional deep freezer to register the raging hatred of the avenging brother. It's George's best performance in a long, long time. Perhaps producer-director Roy Del Ruth has much to do with Raft's lapse into real acting but whatever the cause, Georgie should put away in mothballs forever his time-worn dead pan. He'll never need it again, so good he is."

Although Raft's screen career was now in an incontrovertible decline, he was able to land starring roles in a handful of films including *Lucky Nick Cain* (1950), a crime drama filmed in England and Italy. Raft's co-star in the film, Colleen Gray, later shared fond memories of her experience with the actor.

"Sweet guy. He taught me how to tango for that movie," Gray recalled in a 2001 interview. "He was very kind, and he gave me his raincoat — it was oiled silk, a beautiful raincoat — I still have it, and I shortened it. To this day I wear it — I have other raincoats, but that's the one I wear. He was shy, and he said he felt inferior — he knew I was a college graduate and he was almost apologetic. It didn't occur to me — I don't go around asking people, 'did you go to college?' It just didn't occur. But we got along just fine. He was delightful to work with."

Raft also starred during this period in his fourth film noir, *Loan Shark* (1952), playing ex-convict Joe Cargen, who moves in with his sister and her husband and tries to land a job at the local tire factory that employs most of the town's men. He balks when he finds out that the factory's manager actually wants to hire him to infiltrate the loan sharking gang that has ensnared many of the workers there, but when his brother-in-law is murdered by the hoods, Joe accepts the offer. As he rises in the ranks of the organization, Joe reluctantly alienates his loved ones, including his sister and his new girlfriend Ann Nelson (Dorothy Hart) — at one point, he is even forced to prove his loyalty to his bosses by "teaching a lesson" to Ann's brother. Narrowly escaping death at the hands of a gang member who discovers Joe's real objective, Joe ultimately learns that the brains behind the lucrative operation is a seemingly meek accountant, Walter Karr (Larry Dobkin). During a gun battle in an abandoned movie theater, Joe kills Karr and is later reunited with Ann. Upon its release, *Loan Shark* was praised in one notice for its "good pacing and sufficient plot punch," and Raft earned favorable reviews as well, with the critic for *Variety* claiming that he "takes easily to the tough melodramatics," and the *New York Times*' reviewer writing that "for once, Mr. Raft's tight-lipped suavity seems perfectly in order."

At this point, even Raft was forced to acknowledge that his screen career was at a near-standstill. Now in his mid-50s, the actor was receiving few offers from Hollywood, and he frankly discussed in the press the possible reasons for his fall from stardom.

"For one thing, I think I made a mistake when I stopped appearing with big names. My biggest successes were with people like Gary Cooper, Carole Lombard, Marlene Dietrich, and so forth. Maybe that made me look good; maybe I was better with them," Raft told reporter Bob Thomas in 1953. "I suppose I should have gone around with producers, directors, and writers. I could have given the big parties, as some stars did. But I was afraid to. I was afraid half of them wouldn't show up. People think I'm a tough mug, but I'm not. I bruise easily. Another mistake I made was to admit I couldn't act. I probably shouldn't have been so modest. Maybe I was better than I thought I was."

A short time after this interview, Raft's career appeared to receive a much-needed boost when he was offered the lead as a detective in the syndicated television series, *I Am the Law*. But the series was a flop and Raft took a financial hit on the project as well.

"I was supposed to get ninety thousand for doing the *Law* series," Raft was quoted in his biography. "By the time they were finished deducting expenses like office space, telephones, and stuff like that, I wound up with practically nothing. Later on they had reruns on the series, and called it *Briefcase* here and in England — but I was also cut out of those profits."

Raft took another blow later that year when he was once again tabbed in the press for his ties with organized crime figures. Although the headline in the *Los Angeles Examiner* announced "Raft Helps Free Capone," the Capone in question was the famed mobster's brother, John. According to newspaper accounts, Raft was in Capone's Beverly Hills

hotel room when police detectives "burst in to arrest the Chicagoan and a friend ... on suspicion of robbery." The *Examiner* article claimed that Raft interceded, requesting Capone's release and guaranteeing that he would "take the first plane out of here."

"As far as I knew this Capone had never done anything wrong," Raft said years later. "He was a gambler, and he used the name John Martin because he was embarrassed at the family connection. Of course Al Capone had been out of Alcatraz for some time — in fact, he was dead — but I'm sure the public thought I had brought him back to Los Angeles to start something."

Still reeling from this incident, Raft accepted a supporting role in what would be his final film noir, *Rogue Cop* (1954). Although the role depicted him in the gangster image that he'd worked so hard to erase, the actor told reporters that "the script made me change my mind about parts like this."

This well-done feature starred Robert Taylor as Christopher Kelvaney, a crooked police officer who earns money on the side by performing a variety of jobs for syndicate boss Dan Beaumonte (Raft): "[He does] a little bit of everything," Dan explains in one scene. "Keeps an eye on the bookies. Does a bit of collecting. Mostly settles beefs for us." When Kelvaney's kid brother, rookie cop Eddie (Steve Forrest), plans to identify one of Beaumonte's hoods on a murder charge, the syndicate boss tells Kelvaney to offer his brother $15,000 to change his story. Eddie refuses the offer and Beaumonte hires an out-of-town assassin named Langley (Vince Edwards) to dispose of both brothers. After Eddie is gunned down, Kelvaney questions Beaumonte's former girlfriend (Anne Francis), who is also killed by Langley, but Kelvaney manages to capture him. Beaumonte later sets a trap for Kelvaney, but he is gunned down during the shootout, along with his fellow hoods.

Raft earned universal praise for his performance as the unsavory mob boss in *Rogue Cop*; Howard McClay of the *Los Angeles Daily News* opined that the actor handled his assignment "with ease"; Wylie Williams wrote in the *Hollywood Citizen-News* that the "heartless directors of the crime syndicate are played well by [the] always menacing George Raft and Robert Simon"; and in the *Los Angeles Times*, while acknowledging that Raft was "older now [and] graying," Philip K. Scheuer labeled him as "a baddie giving a good performance."

Raft's role in *Rogue Cop* was his last part of any substance; during the next several years, he was only able to snag small roles in such films as *Around the World in 80 Days* (1956), in which he played a bouncer; *Some Like It Hot* (1959), a first-rate comedy where he spoofed his gangster image in the role of "Spats" Columbo; *Ocean's Eleven* (1960), an entertaining crime-comedy starring "Rat Pack" members Frank Sinatra, Dean Martin, and Sammy Davis, Jr.; *The Patsy* (1964), a mediocre Jerry Lewis starrer where Raft appeared in a cameo as himself; and *Five Golden Dragons* (1967), in which the actor was briefly seen as a kimono-clad gangster. Also during these years, Raft saw the release of a movie based on his life, *The George Raft Story* (1961); starring Ray Danton, the film was a dismal flop. But Raft's professional plight paled in comparison to his off-screen misfortunes.

In April 1955, Raft attempted to pay $65,000 for a two-percent interest in Las Vegas' Flamingo Hotel (formerly owned by his slain pal "Bugsy" Siegel), but his application for a gambling license was turned down by the Nevada Gaming Commission. Although commissioners refused to cite specific reasons for the denial, they issued a statement that Raft's "background doesn't warrant it," and newspapers reported that the actor's associations with John Capone and prominent gangster Mickey Cohen were factors in the decision. The Commission reversed its decision in December of that year but, ironically, the cash-strapped actor was forced to sell his interest a short time later.

Raft's luck continued to plummet; he lost money in 1959 on an investment in a Havana, Cuba, gambling casino that bore his name, and received another financial blow in the early 1960s following the bankruptcy of a chain of discount stores called Consumer Marts of America, for which he served as "public relations director." And the actor's personal life slid even further downhill in 1965 when he was indicted for income tax evasion, accused of understating his income by more than $85,000 from 1958 through 1963, and falsely claiming a capital loss of $25,000 on stock in the Havana casino. After the indictment, a host of notables reportedly wrote to the judge in the case pleading for leniency, including Bob Hope, Lucille Ball, Jimmy Durante, and Frank Sinatra, who also contacted the actor and offered to "pick up the entire tab."

Facing a possible maximum sentence of three years in prison and a $5,000 fine, Raft pleaded guilty to one count of falsifying income tax returns and was fined $2,500. According to an account that ran in the *Los Angeles Times* on September 29, 1965, the 70-year-old "former movie tough guy" was overcome with emotion during the sentencing, "clutching his grandmother's rosary and weeping unashamedly."

Despite Raft's relief over his relatively light sentence, his troubles were not behind him. Shortly after his battle with the I.R.S., the actor landed a well-paying job as manager of a posh London casino, the Colony Club. Raft was also a shareholder in the club — as was renowned gangster Meyer Lansky — and in February 1967, while Raft was in the United States for a brief stay, the British government abruptly announced that the actor was barred from returning to the country. Explaining that Raft's "continued presence in the United Kingdom would not be conducive to the public good," the British Home Office issued a statement that the actor "will be refused entry to Britain should he arrive at a British port." Raft was crushed by the unexpected action.

"They haven't accused me of anything — they've just barred me from the country without charges," Raft told the press. "Somebody must have put the finger on me. What have I got to do to clear myself? I lead a quiet life.

I don't ask for any trouble. To be barred from a country makes you feel like a spy. I don't think I've done anything wrong." A month later, Raft lost a cameo role he was to have played in the British feature film *Robbery* (1967), and the following year, the personal belongings from his Beverly Hills home were auctioned off for $63,400. Nearly 300 sightseers paid $2 each to view the actor's three-bedroom frame and stucco house. Raft had hit rock bottom.

Not long after the London debacle, Raft's anger and disappointment may have been somewhat assuaged when a host of Hollywood luminaries gathered for a special Friar's Roast in his honor. On hand to laud the actor were such screen stars as Frank Sinatra, Dean Martin, Richard Conte, Henry Fonda, Glenn Ford, Edward G. Robinson, Barry Sullivan, Jackie Cooper, George Jessel, Robert Wagner, Jack Haley, Andy Devine, and Red Buttons; singers Robert Goulet, Bobby Darin, and Johnny Rivers; and Hollywood studio execs Jack L. Warner and Richard Zanuck. Still, Raft was unable to recover professionally from the blows to his reputation, and he was seen in only six more films, including *Hammersmith Is Out* (1972), which featured Elizabeth Taylor and Richard Burton, and *Sextette* (1978), a dreadful comedy starring Mae West in her last screen role. (It is interesting to note that Raft appeared in both the first and last Mae West film, and his death came just two days after hers.)

On November 24, 1980, shortly after the release of his final film, *The Man with Bogart's Face* (1980), George Raft died. He was 85 years old.

George Raft led a personal life that often held far more excitement, peril, catastrophe, and pathos than any film in which he appeared, and he was more likely to be touted for his ties to the underworld than for his ability to emote on screen. Still, despite his brushes with the law, his gangland connections, his romantic disappointments, and his financial woes, the actor managed to make a lasting name for himself in the motion picture industry and holds a rightful place in the an-

nals of Hollywood as, perhaps not one of the screen's best actors, but certainly one of its most memorable. In an interview given shortly before his death in 1973, actor Edward G. Robinson offered a splendid commentary on Raft's acting talent and the cinematic presence that he possessed.

"George always wore this fantastic, arresting mask when he acted, yet you sensed that underneath his cool facade he was seething — boiling — writhing," Robinson said. "I've worked with many great actors both in Hollywood and on the stage. And in my opinion, no one matched George for this quality of personal power and manhood."

Film Noir Filmography

Johnny Angel. Director: Edwin L. Marin. Producer: Jack Gross. Running time: 76 minutes. Released by RKO, December 27, 1945. Cast: George Raft, Claire Trevor, Signe Hasso, Lowell Gilmore, Hoagy Carmichael, Marvin Miller, Margaret Wycherly, J. Farrell McDonald, Macy Gray.

Nocturne. Director: Edwin L. Marin. Producer: Joan Harrison. Running time: 87 minutes. Released by RKO, November 9, 1946. Cast: George Raft, Lynn Bari, Virginia Huston, Joseph Pevney, Myrna Dell, Edward Ashley, Walter Sande, Mabel Paige, Bernard Hoffman, Queenie Smith.

Red Light. Director and Producer: Roy Del Ruth. Running time: 84 minutes. Released by United Artists, January 15, 1950. Cast: George Raft, Virginia Mayo, Gene Lockhart, Barton MacLane, Henry Morgan, Raymond Burr, Arthur Franz, Arthur Shields, Frank Orth, Philip Pine, Movita Castenada, Paul Frees, Claire Carleton, Soledad Jiminez.

Loan Shark. Director: Seymour Friedman. Producer: Bernard Luber. Running time: 79 minutes. Released by Lippert, May 23, 1952. Cast: George Raft, Dorothy Hart, Paul Stewart, Helen Westcott, John Hoyt, Henry Slate, William Phipps, Russell Johnson, Benny Baker, Larry Dobkin, Charles Meredith, Harlan Warde, Spring Mitchell, Margie Dean, Ross Elliott, Robert Bice, Robert Williams, Michael Ragan, Virginia Carroll.

Rogue Cop. Director: Roy Rowland. Producer: Nicholas Nayfack. Running time: 87 minutes. Released by MGM, September 17, 1954. Cast: Robert Taylor, Janet Leigh, George Raft, Steve Forrest, Anne Francis, Robert Ellenstein, Robert F. Simon, Anthony Ross, Alan Hale, Jr., Peter Brocco, Vince Edwards, Olive Carey, Roy Bancroft, Dale Van

Sickel, Ray Teal. Awards: Academy Award nomination for Best Black and White Cinematography (John Seitz).

References

Carroll, Harrison. "Sinatra Offers Raft Help in Tax Crisis." *Los Angeles Herald-Examiner*, September 8, 1965.

Collins, Roscoe. "George Raft's Gangster Friend." *Salute*, May 1947.

"Estranged Wife Sues Raft for $43,686." *Hollywood Citizen-News*, November 16, 1960.

"Fashion Plates." *GQ*, December 1996.

Johnson, Erskine. "Raft Turns Gangster Again After 13 Years." *Los Angeles Daily News*, May 8, 1954.

"George Raft Aids Defense at Trial of Bugsy Siegel." *Los Angeles Times*, July 18, 1944.

"George Raft, at 57, Plans to Hit Road in Dancing Shoes." *Los Angeles Mirror*, May 12, 1953.

"George Raft Fined, Weeps for Joy." *Los Angeles Times*, September 29, 1965.

"George Raft Home 'Sold' for $63,400." *Hollywood Citizen-News*, May 6, 1968.

"George Raft Pleads Guilty to One Tax Charge, Innocent to 5 Others." *Los Angeles Times*, September 8, 1965.

"George Raft Returns from Cuba 'Adventure.'" *Los Angeles Times*, January 11, 1959.

"George Raft's Name Enters Divorce Battle." *Los Angeles Times*, November 20, 1946.

"George Raft Will Return to Havana." *Los Angeles Times*, January 12, 1959.

Harvey, Steve. "Only in L.A." *Los Angeles Times*, June 20, 1997.

"Lawyer in $300,000 Suit Charges Beating by Raft." *Los Angeles Times*, December 14, 1946.

"Nevada Refuses Gambling License to George Raft." *Los Angeles Times*, April 2, 1955.

"No Foolin', Raft Says He IS Tough!" *Los Angeles Daily News*, December 18, 1946.

Parsons, Louella O. "Virginia Pine Admits She'll Wed Raft Soon." *Los Angeles Examiner*, May 2, 1934.

"Raft Blames London Woe on FBI—Will See Hoover." *Los Angeles Herald-Examiner*, March 30, 1967.

Raft, George. "Me and My Job." *Film Weekly*, March 8, 1935.

Raft, George, as told to Dean Jennings. "Out of My Past." *Saturday Evening Post*, October 5, 1957.

"Raft Mixes in Battle as Companion Wallops Foe." *Los Angeles Examiner*, August 4, 1934.

"Raft Felony Writ Will Be Asked of Grand Jury Today." *Los Angeles Examiner*, December 17, 1946.

"Raft Helps Free Capone." *Los Angeles Examiner*, October 1, 1953.

"Raft Loses Role in British Film." *Los Angeles Herald-Examiner*, March 15, 1967.

"Raft's Ex-Girlfriend Jailed in Marijuana Raid." *Los Angeles Examiner*, April 28, 1950.

Sikov, Ed. "George Raft: The Gangster Star at His Hollywood Penthouse." *Architectural Digest*, April 1996.

St. Johns, Adela Rogers. "What You Don't Know About the Betty Grable-George Raft Romance." *Photoplay*, April 1943.

Toth, Robert C. "British Bar George Raft from Return to London." *Los Angeles Times*, February 25, 1967.

"Vegas Bans Raft for 'Hood' Ties." *Los Angeles Mirror*, April 2, 1955.

"What You Should Know About George Raft." *Modern Screen*, August 1932.

Wilson, Earl. "Grable Might Have Been Mrs. Raft." *The (Dayton, Ohio) Journal Herald*, July 6, 1973.

Yablonsky, Lewis. *George Raft*. New York: McGraw-Hill Book Company, 1974.

——— EDWARD G. ROBINSON ———

"Thousands of guys got guns, but there's only one Johnny Rocco."—Edward G. Robinson in *Key Largo* (1948)

Unlike the loutish, remorseless gangster with whom he is perhaps best associated, the real-life Edward G. Robinson was, as he was once described, one of Hollywood's "most gentle men." Fluent in several languages and noted for his valuable collection of French Impressionist art, Robinson viewed Hollywood society as "vapid, polite, and vaguely vulgar," and fashioned a circle of friends that included some of the most respected writers, artists, and musicians of his time. Although Robinson's screen career was nearly derailed by accusations of Communist sympathizing, the talented actor compiled a list of impressive credits that included *Little Caesar* (1930), *Five Star Final* (1931), *Barbary Coast* (1935), *The Sea Wolf* (1941), *Tales of Manhattan* (1942), *Flesh and Fantasy* (1942), *The Ten Commandments* (1956), and *The Cincinnati Kid* (1965). He also starred in some of the most highly regarded films produced during the noir era: *Double Indemnity* (1944), *The Woman in the Window* (1944), *Scarlet Street* (1945), *The Stranger* (1946), *Key Largo* (1948), *Night Has a Thousand Eyes* (1948), *House of Strangers* (1949), and *Nightmare* (1956).

One of six brothers, the talented star of the screen was born Emmanuel Goldenberg in Bucharest, Romania, on December 12, 1893. His parents, Morris and Sarah Goldenberg, sent their children to parochial school after a law was passed denying Jewish children the right to a public education. To escape the increasing persecution, the family immigrated to the United States in 1903, settling in a tenement on New York's Lower East Side.

"At Ellis Island, I was born again," the actor would later say. "Life for me began when I was 10."

Initially, young Emmanuel aspired to become a rabbi, but his career plans soon changed ("I realized I couldn't act the role of a sacrosanct gentleman 24 hours a day," he once said), and while attending Townsend Harris High School, he began to focus on the performing arts. After graduation, he studied at the City College of New York and Columbia University, where the future actor was first exposed to literature, music, and art. Developing a special affinity for the work of the French Impressionists, he reportedly purchased postcards featuring paintings by famous artists and glued them to his bedroom wall.

In October 1911, Emmanuel won a scholarship to the American Academy of Dramatic Arts, where his classmates included future co-star Joseph Schildkraut. It was around this time that the budding thespian made the decision to change his name; some sources claim that he selected Edward for the King of

England, "G" for Goldenberg, and Robinson after a character in his favorite play, *The Passerby*. Years later, however, Robinson told a reporter from United Press International: "I don't know to this day why I chose Robinson as a last name. If I had to do it over again, I'd take a shorter name. You've no idea how long it takes to write Edward G. Robinson for a flock of autograph hunters."

The path to his new designation notwithstanding, Robinson's first professional role came in 1913, in a play entitled *Paid in Full*, followed by a tour of Canada in *Kismet* and a small role in an anti-war play, *Under Fire*. He also made his first screen appearance during this period, playing a factory worker in the silent feature *Arms and the Woman* (1916), but his budding career was interrupted when he was drafted into the Navy during World War I. When the conflict ended in 1918, Robinson returned to the stage, appearing during the next several years in such plays as *First is Last* (1919), and the Theater Guild production of *Banco* (1922). After the close of the latter production, Robinson traveled to Cuba for his first major screen role in *The Bright Shawl* (1923). Despite a high-powered cast that included Richard Barthelmess, Dorothy Gish, Mary Astor, and William Powell, Robinson's experience on this silent picture was less than pleasant.

"I wasn't particularly happy with my experience because I didn't feel that I knew anything much about silent acting," Robinson said later. "I vowed never to be in a silent film again, and I kept to that vow, as a matter of fact."

Back in New York, Robinson was seen in a succession of plays for the Theater Guild, including Shaw's *Androcles and the Lion* (1925), in which he earned praise for "as usual ... round[ing] out every detail of the characterization"; *Juarez and Maximilian* (1926), co-starring Alfred Lunt and Morris Carnovsky; and *The Brothers Karamazov* (1927), where he played the epileptic brother. He also landed his first role as a gangster in *The Racket* (1927), playing a character patterned after real-life hood Al Capone. (Praised by one critic for his "masterly creation," Robinson offered such a realistic performance that the play was reportedly banned in Chicago by the city's mayor, who feared Capone's reaction.) Later, when the played toured California, Robinson recalled, "the motion picture tycoons all came."

"So the first role they ever saw me in was that of a gangster," Robinson said. "And they remembered this character and later on when they wanted me for pictures and the gangster cycle began, they thought of Eddie Robinson, the gangster."

Robinson next starred in a three-act comedy, *The Kibitzer* (1929), which he co-wrote with Jo Swerling, later the author of such screen hits as *Love Affair* (1932), *Blood and Sand* (1944), *Lifeboat* (1944), and *Leave Her to Heaven* (1945). After racking up more good reviews for this production, Robinson accepted an offer from Paramount Pictures to star opposite Claudette Colbert in his first "talkie," *The Hole in the Wall* (1929), followed by his first screen gangster performance in Universal's *Night Ride* (1930), starring his former Academy of Dramatic Arts classmate, Joseph Schildkraut. In his 1959 autobiography, *My Father and I*, Schildkraut revealed that he was responsible for Robinson's appearance in the picture.

"There was the part of a Capone-like gangster in the picture and I suggested [Robinson] for the role," Schildkraut wrote. "[Universal studio head] Carl Laemmle, Jr. had never heard of him, and it took all my persuasion to make Universal engage him. Robinson was magnificent, perfectly cast, and he 'played me right off the screen,' as the saying goes."

Robinson followed *Night Ride* with such features as Universal's *East is West* (1930), in which he played a half-caste known as The Chop Suey King of San Francisco; *A Lady to Love* (1930), a passable MGM drama co-starring Vilma Banky; and *Outside the Law* (1930), a dreadful potboiler for Universal featuring Robinson as a gangster who is killed in the film's climactic shootout. Disillusioned with these early film appearances, Robinson re-

turned to Broadway to star with Wallis Clark and Harry Redding in *Mr. Samuel*. The play turned out to be a flop, but Robinson's typically fine performance was caught by Warner Bros. producer Hal Wallis, who cast the actor in one of the best-remembered films of his career, *Little Caesar* (1931). Based on the life of Al Capone, this now-classic gangster picture chronicled the rise and fall of Rico Bandello, the Little Caesar of the title. As Rico, Robinson was a hit with critics and audiences alike, and made famous his character's dying line at the film's end, "Mother of Mercy, is this the end of Rico?" (Ironically, although he played a ruthless killer, Robinson was reportedly fearful of guns and blinked wildly each time his character was called upon to fire a gun. The problem was finally solved when director Mervyn LeRoy attached bands of transparent tape to Robinson's upper eyelids, forcing his eyes to say open.) Robinson earned raves for his knockout performance; in a typical review, the critic for the *New York Times* wrote: "Little Caesar becomes at Robinson's hands a figure out of a Greek tragedy, a cold, ignorant, merciless killer, driven on and on by an insatiable lust for power, the plaything of a force that is greater than himself."

Signing a long-term contract with Warners, Robinson played a series of hard-boiled characters during the next several years, including a ruthless newspaper editor in the excellent *Five Star Final* (1931); a barber-turned-gangster in *Smart Money* (1931), his only film with James Cagney; a convicted murderer in *Two Seconds* (1932); a Chinese assassin named Wong Low Get in *The Hatchet Man* (1932); a ruthless crime czar in 1850s San Francisco in *Barbary Coast* (1935); and a high-powered gangleader in *The Last Gangster* (1937). Contrary to Robinson's perceived screen persona, however, the actor's gangster roles actually comprised less than a third of his total film output, and during the 1930s he was also seen in such features as *Silver Dollar* (1932), delivering an excellent performance as a farmer turned silver-miner; *The Little Giant* (1933), Robinson's first comedic effort, in which he spoofed his gangster persona; *The Whole Town's Talking* (1935), an early John Ford feature starring Robinson in the dual role of a gangster and his look-alike, a timid store clerk; *Bullets or Ballots* (1936), the first of Robinson's five films with Humphrey Bogart, which saw the actor portraying a tough New York cop who infiltrates the local mob; and *Confessions of a Nazi Spy* (1939), a landmark anti–Nazi propaganda film, starring Robinson as the leader of a team of federal agents. Also during this period, Robinson starred in the popular CBS radio series, *Big Town*, where he portrayed a crusading newspaper editor. He also produced and often wrote episodes of the show, which ran for five years.

While Robinson was enhancing his reputation as one of Hollywood's top screen performers, he was busy off screen as well. In January 1927, the actor married New York actress Gladys Lloyd, and on March 19, 1933, the couple welcomed a son, Emmanuel Robinson, Jr. Purchasing a sprawling, Tudor-style home in Beverly Hills, the Robinsons became renowned for their frequent "salons," which would feature gatherings of noted musicians, artists, writers, and actors. After reportedly buying his first picture for two

dollars in 1913, the actor was also finally able to indulge his long-time interest in French Impressionism, transforming his home into an artistic showplace. Years later, Robinson would turn a badminton court at his home into a public art gallery, and in 1948, he would team with actor Vincent Price to open the Modern Institute of Art.

On screen, Robinson's career veered in a different direction with the onset of the 1940s, beginning with his outstanding portrayal of the title role in *Dr. Ehrlich's Magic Bullet* (1940), based on the real-life work of the German-Jewish scientist who discovered a cure for syphilis in the 19th century. (Still playing on Robinson's popularity as a screen gangster, the film was billed as "the war against the greatest public enemy of all.") Robinson followed this feature with another biopic, *A Dispatch from Reuters* (1940), the story of the founder of the Reuters news service; *The Sea Wolf* (1941), a first-rate sea saga in which he played a demented captain; and *Manpower* (1941), which starred Robinson and George Raft as a pair of hard-drinking power linemen vying for the affections of Marlene Dietrich. (Filming on the latter production was an unpleasant affair, characterized by Robinson's patronizing attitude and his tendency to instruct Raft on the delivery of his lines, and Raft's strenuous objection to his interference. On one occasion, the exchange between the actors escalated — several punches were thrown and Robinson walked off the set, refusing to finish the picture. Although the matter was later settled by the Screen Actors Guild, the rift between Robinson and Raft continued, not ending until several years later when the actors met on stage at a benefit performance. Robinson reportedly pointed at Raft, telling him to "get out of town," and Raft rejoined by telling his former co-star that Hollywood wasn't "big enough for both of us." The two stars then embraced and danced off the stage together. Years later, when Robinson was in the hospital, he received a telegram that read, "Get well, your pal, George Raft.")

In 1942, after starring in the gangster

spoof *Larceny, Inc.*, Robinson ended his contract with Warner Bros. As a freelancer, he was seen in such varied vehicles as Fox's *Tales of Manhattan* (1942), an interesting yarn that follows a fancy tailcoat as it affects the lives of several different wearers; Universal's *Flesh and Fantasy* (1943), a trio of stories with an all-star cast including Charles Boyer, Barbara Stanwyck, Thomas Mitchell, and Dame May Whitty; Fox's *Tampico* (1943), a box-office bomb notable only because it showed Robinson in a rare romantic light; and *Mr. Winkle Goes to War* (1944), in which Robinson portrayed a mousy, middle-aged war draftee. In the latter, another disappointment at the box office, the actor was panned by one critic as neither "meekly amusing nor properly courageous." But later that year, Robinson left the impact of this forgettable feature far behind, entering the realm of noir in *Double Indemnity* (1944).

In this first-rate example from the film noir period, Robinson portrayed insurance company investigator Barton Keyes, who possessed a crafty intuition in the form of a "little man" that facilitated his ability to expose even the most clever forms of insurance fraud. ("Every month, hundreds of claims come to this desk," Keyes tells a potential swindler. "Some of them are phonies. And I know which ones. How do I know? Because my little man tells me…. Every time one of these phonies comes along, it ties knots in my stomach. I can't eat.") In the film, Keyes' "little man" works overtime when the company is presented with a double indemnity insurance claim for a man killed after falling from a moving train. As it turns out, the man was murdered by his duplicitous wife, Phyllis Dietrichson (Barbara Stanwyck), and her lover, Walter Neff (Fred MacMurray), an insurance salesman and Keyes' closest friend. When the lovers turn on each other in suspicion and paranoia, the well-planned scheme begins to unravel, culminating when they both determine that the other must die. After killing Phyllis, the mortally wounded Walter struggles back to his office, confessing his crime on a dictating machine and concluding his

tale just as Keyes arrives. As the hard-boiled investigator with a heart of gold, Robinson was deservedly hailed by critics; in the *Hollywood Citizen-News*, Lowell E. Redelings wrote that he "fits his role perfectly and plays it for a grand slam"; Philip K. Scheuer judged in the *Los Angeles Times* that he was "slightly terrific"; and the *New York Herald Tribune*'s Howard Barnes proclaimed that Robinson played his role with "splendid authority."

Aside from a starring role as a Norwegian farmer in *Our Vines Have Tender Grapes* (1945), MGM's first-rate depiction of rural American life, Robinson's next three pictures kept him on the dark side of the screen. In the Fritz Lang–directed *The Woman in the Window* (1945), his second film noir, Robinson starred as college professor Richard Wanley, who is pleasantly surprised one evening after leaving his men's club when he meets a beautiful young woman whose portrait he'd admired in a nearby gallery window. Wanley accompanies the woman, Alice (Joan Bennett), to her home for a nightcap, but the pleasant encounter turns sour when Alice's boyfriend enters the apartment and Wanley stabs him with a pair of scissors during a struggle. After disposing of the body, Wanley learns that the dead man was a prominent financier, and the couple later find themselves being blackmailed by his bodyguard, Heidt (Dan Duryea). After a failed attempt to poison Heidt, Wanley prepares to commit suicide, but the blackmailer is later killed in a gun battle with police, who assume that he is the killer. Alice telephones Wanley to inform him of the police's findings, but he has swallowed poison and is prevented in his weakened state from answering the call. In the film's final reel, however, Wanley is awakened by an employee at his men's club and it is revealed that the entire incident was merely a dream. (In a scene reminiscent of the finale of *The Wizard of Oz*, Wanley leaves the club to find that the financier from his dream is the coat attendant, and the blackmailer, Heidt, works as the doorman.)

After being singled out in *Variety* for his "outstanding" performance in *The Woman in the Window*, Robinson reunited with Bennett and Duryea in his third film noir, *Scarlet Street* (1945). Also directed by Lang, this feature focused on a deadly triangle involving a mild-mannered cashier and amateur artist, Christopher Cross (Robinson); a beautiful but indolent woman, Kitty March (Bennett); and Kitty's abusive, con-man boyfriend, Johnny Prince (Duryea). After first meeting Kitty when he saves her from a beating from Johnny in the street, the unhappily married Chris quickly falls for her, allowing her to believe that he is a wealthy artist. Before long, Chris has established Kitty in a plush apartment that he uses as a studio, and the mercenary Johnny finds a market for Chris' unusual artwork, passing Kitty off as the artist. Blinded by love, Chris forgives Kitty when he learns of this deception, but he is driven past the point of reason when he proposes marriage and Kitty cruelly reveals that Johnny is her lover. ("How can a man be so dumb?" Kitty scoffs. "I've wanted to laugh in your face ever since I first met you. You're old and ugly and I'm sick of you!") After this rejection, Chris stabs Kitty to death with an ice pick but, ironically, it is Johnny who is arrested, tried, and ultimately executed for the crime. Driven mad by the turn of events, Chris is seen wandering the streets at the film's end, fruitlessly endeavoring to convince the authorities of his guilt. Inexplicably, Robinson's memorable performance as the hapless cashier earned mixed notices from critics of the day; while the reviewer for *Variety* found that the actor "turn[ed] in top work," and *The Hollywood Review*'s critic opined that he "is as excellent as he has ever been," the review in *The New Yorker* contained only faint praise, claiming that Robinson "conducts himself with a kind of weary competence," and Bosley Crowther wrote in the *New York Times*, "In the role of the love-blighted cashier, Edward G. Robinson performs monotonously and with little illumination of an adventurous spirit seeking air."

Next, in his fourth noir, *The Stranger* (1946), Robinson played Wilson, a member of the Allied War Crimes Commission who is determined to capture a notorious Nazi war criminal, Franz Kindler (Orson Welles). Wilson finds Kindler in Hartford, Connecticut, where he is posing as a college professor and has cemented his place in the community by marrying the daughter of a Supreme Court judge, Mary Longstreet (Loretta Young). Wilson is at first fooled by Kindler's masquerade of respectability, but after a discussion during dinner with Mary's family, his suspicions are heightened ("Who but a Nazi would deny that Karl Marx was a German because he was a Jew?" Wilson asks). Later learning that Kindler is also guilty of killing a former underling who turned up in Hartford threatening to expose him, Wilson shares his evidence with Mary, but she vehemently refuses to believe his claims. She soon is forced to face the truth, however, and during a confrontation in the town's clock tower, Mary shoots Kindler and he falls to his death, impaled on the tower's revolving mechanism. After the release of the film, Robinson was praised for his "well-restrained" performance by the *New York Times*' Bosley Crowther, and by the critic for *Variety*, who maintained that the actor and his co-stars "turn[ed] in some of their best work."

In 1946, Robinson teamed with producer Sol Lesser to form his own company, the Film Guild Corporation. The following year, they produced *The Red House* (1947), a taut thriller in which Robinson played a one-legged farmer, but although the film did brisk business at the box office, it would be the company's only product. Robinson next starred with Burt Lancaster in *All My Sons* (1948), based on the powerful play by Arthur Miller. As a small-town arms manufacturer who knowingly distributes defective materials during the war, Robinson earned well-deserved praise, with Cecilia Ager of *PM* labeling him "remarkably sincere and moving," and the critic for the *New York Times* writing that Robinson did "a superior job of showing the shades of a personality in a little tough guy who has a soft side." Robinson followed this triumph with memorable performances in three more noirs, *Key Largo*

(1948), *Night Has a Thousand Eyes* (1948), and *House of Strangers* (1949).

In the first, Robinson was a standout as exiled mobster Johnny Rocco, whose gang takes over a hotel owned by James Temple (Lionel Barrymore) and his widowed daughter-in-law, Nora (Lauren Bacall). Also on hand are ex-war hero Frank McCloud (Humphrey Bogart), and Rocco's dipsomaniac moll, Gaye Dawn (Claire Trevor, in an Academy Award-winning performance). While holding the group hostage, Rocco takes center stage, killing a local policeman, humiliating Gaye by compelling her to sing a song before he will give her a drink, and tangling with McCloud as he bemoans his eviction from the United States: "After living in the U.S.A. for more than 30 years, they called me an undesirable alien. Me. Johnny Rocco. Like I was a dirty Red or something." Following the arrival of an associate, Rocco successfully sells a stack of counterfeit bills, then forces McCloud to pilot a boat to Cuba, but he meets his end at the hands of the war veteran, who guns down Rocco's four henchmen and, finally, Rocco himself.

After earning praise for his "impressive" portrayal of the vicious gangster in *Key Largo*, Robinson starred in *Night Has a Thousand Eyes*, which centered on the relationship between a disturbed young woman, Jean Courtland (Gail Russell), and John Triton (Robinson), a mentalist who has foreseen her death. Over the objections of Jean's fiancé, Elliott Carson (John Lund), Triton moves into Jean's home in an attempt to foil the fate that awaits her. Meanwhile, suspecting Triton's motives, Carson contacts police, who also set up camp at the house. As it turns out, Triton's predictions come true when a business associate of Jean's father tries to murder her but as the mentalist is struggling with the would-be killer, the police mistake his intentions and fatally shoot him. For his performance in this unusual role, Robinson was labeled "excellent" in *Motion Picture Herald*, but the *New York Times'* Bosley Crowther was less impressed, writing that the actor "play[ed] the gent as a figure of

tragic proportions, fatefully chained to a crystal ball."

But there was no question about the caliber of Robinson's performance in his next film noir, *House of Strangers*, in which he portrayed the patriarch of an Italian family, Gino Monetti. A bank owner known for his questionable practices, Gino is the father of four boys—all of whom work in the bank for meager salaries—but he reserves his favor for only one, Max (Richard Conte). When Gino is arrested for his violations of the rules of banking, Max tries to bribe a juror but he is betrayed by his older brother, Joe (Luther Adler), and is sent to prison for seven years. Meanwhile, Gino goes free and his other three sons reopen the bank, but they refuse to allow him to resume his position and he urges Max to seek revenge upon his siblings: "You gotta make them pay," Gino says during a prison visit to Max. "They steal from me what I work my whole life for…. The bank is my life, it's my blood. They kill me, Max—they take away my blood." Initially planning to follow his father's wishes after his release from prison, Max later has a change of heart, but when his siblings try to kill him, Max barely escapes and leaves town with his faithful girlfriend (Susan Hayward) to start a new life.

Described by one critic as "dramatic, punchy, understanding, tender at times, and earthily humorous," *House of Strangers* earned high praise for Robinson's performance; he was described as "forceful" in *Newsweek*; the critic for *Motion Picture Herald* opined that he "plays a difficult part to perfection"; and Lloyd L. Sloan wrote in the *Hollywood Citizen News* that he offered "a fine and believable job." Robinson's first-rate portrayal of the self-made banker also earned him honors at the 1949 Cannes Film Festival for Best Actor.

The accolades enjoyed by Robinson for this feature, however, would be the last bright spot in the actor's life for some time to come. In 1947, when congressional hearings were convened by the House Un-American Activities Committee (HUAC) in an effort to expose Communist influences in the motion picture industry, Robinson was one of 140 actors, writers, and directors who signed a petition decrying the committee's tactics. The petition read, in part, that "any attempt to curb freedom of expression and to set arbitrary standards of Americanism is in itself disloyal to both the spirit and the letter of the Constitution." Several months later, HUAC member John Rankin read into the record a list of the signees, including "one [who] calls himself Edward G. Robinson. His real name is Emmanuel Goldenberg." (Rankin also pointed out several other actors of Jewish descent, including Danny Kaye and Melvyn Douglas, who had changed their names.)

"There are others too numerous to mention," Rankin said. "They are attacking the Committee for doing its duty to protect this country and save the American people from the horrible fate the Communists have meted out to the unfortunate Christian people of Europe."

In 1951, questions concerning Robinson's ties to Communism were again raised when HUAC instituted a second wave of hearings. Howard Rushmore, a former writer for *The Daily Worker* publication, testified: "I don't know whether or not Robinson is a Communist. But 10 years ago or more, he started joining one Communist front after another — perhaps innocently — but after 10 years, he's still doing it."

Among the organizations to which Rushmore referred was the Hollywood Anti-Nazi League, co-founded in the mid-1930s by writer Dorothy Parker and including such members as Spencer Tracy, Lucille Ball, James Cagney, Groucho Marx, and Henry Fonda. The group was later considered to be a major Communist front organization. Despite membership in these and other liberal groups, however, Robinson had long demonstrated his loyalty to the United States. On his radio show, *Big Town*, the actor often took the opportunity to champion "the American way," later earning a citation from the American Legion for his "outstanding contribution to Americanism through his stirring patriotic appeals." During World War II, Robinson donated $100,000 to the USO campaign for Army and Navy recreation facilities and was reportedly the first Hollywood star to entertain in France following the invasion of Normandy. While in Europe, he also made broadcasts of Allied propaganda in seven languages; acted the part of an American flying instructor, at the request of the British Ministry of Information, in a full-length British documentary; and served as a narrator for the *Red Cross at War*, *Moscow Strikes Back*, and *We Will Never Die* (1943), a mass memorial to the Jews who lost their lives during the Nazi regime.

Despite these varied manifestations of Robinson's staunch patriotism, the actor was included in *Red Channels*, a 1950 publication that listed 151 writers, directors, and performers who were suspected of Communist ties. With the distribution of the pamphlet, Robinson's career took an abrupt and undeniable plunge; in the next two years, he was seen only in two fairly forgettable "B" productions, *My Daughter Joy* (1950), filmed in Britain, and *Actors and Sin* (1952), co-starring Marsha Hunt (another performer whose career was tainted by the HUAC campaign). Although he insisted that the accusations against him "emanated from sick and diseased minds," Robinson was unable to escape the "guilt by association" tag with which he had been labeled.

"It's like I was accused of being a rabbit," Robinson said once. "I've never been a rabbit, but how can I prove I was not a rabbit?"

In a last-ditch effort to clear his name, Robinson requested a hearing before HUAC and appeared in three closed-door sessions before the committee. In the third, held on April 30, 1952, Robinson testified: "I now realize that some of the organizations which I permitted to use my name were, in fact, Communist fronts. I was duped, and used." Despite this revelation, which was carried in newspapers nationwide, it would be another four years before Robinson would appear in a major Hollywood production.

During this time of professional anguish, Robinson's life off screen was equally troublesome. For several years, the actor's son, called Manny by the family, had demonstrated increasingly disturbing behavior; after dropping out of school at the age of 16, he had several run-ins with the law, including arrests for passing bad checks and robbing taxi drivers. In 1956, shortly after the end of his six-year marriage to a model (which produced a daughter, Francesca), Manny attempted suicide by ingesting an overdose of sleeping pills. He recovered, but two months later, he was arrested for drunk driving after causing an accident in which a friend lost an eye. Late in the decade, Manny blamed his troubles on his parents in *My Father — My Son*, a "tell-all" book advertised as "the turbulent, passionate, emotional, and dramatic story of the son of a famous father … and his struggle to find himself."

In a 1996 documentary, Manny's daughter, Francesca Robinson-Sanchez, admitted that the elder Robinson and his wife had little time for their only son.

"I don't think they gave him the kind of love that he needed, and the devotion," Robinson-Sanchez said. "I think he felt like he was brought out, sometimes, just to be admired, patted on the head, and go back into your room." She stressed, however, that during her own childhood, it was Edward G. Robinson who furnished the parental guidance that her own father was unable to provide.

"My grandfather was the reliable one — he was the one who was always there," she said. "He went to the PTA meetings, the father-daughter dances, and I was very much part of his life … really, he was like my father."

Still, in his own memoirs, published after his death, Robinson conceded that he had failed his son.

"I am prepared to admit, in the late afternoon of my life, that I did everything wrong," Robinson wrote in *All My Yesterdays*. "Let me begin with my working hours. I'd leave the house before he was awake; I'd

usually return when he was already in bed. I'd go up and see him, awaken him, kiss him, try to prove I loved him, but he was half asleep and I was exhausted … I gave him everything but myself." (Manny later attempted a brief acting career, billing himself as Edward G. Robinson, Jr., and appearing in several television shows with his father, as well as in bit parts in a handful of films including *Some Like it Hot* [1958]. Last seen in the 1971 made-for-television movie *City Beneath the Sea*, Manny died of what the coroner termed "natural causes" at the age of 40, a year after his father's passing.)

Robinson's downward spiral during the 1950s also extended to his marriage of more than a quarter-century to Gladys Lloyd. For several years, Gladys had demonstrated wild mood swings and was finally diagnosed with manic-depression, which required extensive medical treatment and placed an increasing strain on the union. In February 1956, Gladys sued for divorce, accusing Robinson of causing the failure of her acting career and of fostering the psychiatric problems of their son. She also charged that Robinson was maintaining the residence of a dress designer, Jane Adler, at the Stanhope Hotel in New York. Although she later withdrew the latter claim, Gladys reportedly learned that Robinson planned to move their extensive art collection out of state in order to avoid California's community property laws, and insisted that the entire collection be sold. Over Robinson's objections, the valuable paintings that the couple had acquired throughout their marriage were ultimately dispensed of at a price tag of $3 million. (Robinson later managed to rebuild his collection, including 14 of his former paintings; this second collection would be sold following his death for more than $5 million.) Shortly after his 1956 divorce, Robinson married Jane Adler, with whom he remained until his death in 1973.

Meanwhile, after his testimony before HUAC, Robinson continued to appear in a series of mostly mediocre features, including *Big Leaguer* (1953), a baseball saga notable only as the first film directed by Robert

Aldrich, and *A Bullet for Joey* (1955), a muddled crime drama that reunited Robinson with his former nemesis, George Raft. In 1956, after an absence of nearly three decades, Robinson returned to Broadway, starring as a middle-aged widower in love with a younger woman in *Middle of the Night*, and earning some of the best notices of his career — in the *New York Times*, Brooks Atkinson raved: "No one could give the part more warmth or tenderness, or make an undistinguished man seem so notable.... His acting seems to be effortless."

Back in Hollywood, Robinson starred in his final film noir, *Nightmare* (1956), a remake of an earlier noir, *Fear in the Night* (1947). Here, Robinson played detective Rene Bressard, whose brother-in-law, Stan Grayson (Kevin McCarthy), experiences a horrifying dream in which he kills a man and stuffs his body in a closet behind a mirrored door. When he awakes to find thumbprints on his throat, scratches on his wrist, and a strange key in his pocket, Stan is convinced that he actually committed the crime. Stan turns to Bressard for help, but the pragmatic lawman doubts his story until evidence emerges that indicates Stan's guilt. Telling Stan that he will have to turn him in, Bressard gives his brother-in-law the chance to make a getaway; instead, Stan tries to commit suicide, leading Bressard to believe that there is more to the case than meets the eye. Conducting his own investigation, Bressard discovers that Stan had been hypnotized by a neighbor, Lewis Belnap (Gage Clark), into committing the crime. To trap the crafty hypnotist, Bressard arranges for Stan to confront Belnap and coax him into confessing, but the ploy nearly backfires when Belnap hypnotizes Stan again and coerces him into attempting suicide in a nearby lake. Bressard arrives in time to save Stan, however, and in a shootout with police, Belnap is killed. Described upon its release as "a modest melodrama with some crooked turns," *Nightmare* was overlooked by most critics, but Robinson was singled out by the reviewer for the *New York Times*, who noted his "neat performance."

By now, Robinson had added several television appearances to his performing repertoire, including guest spots on *Lux Video Theater* and such game shows as *What's My Line?* and *The $64,000 Question* (on which he matched wits with fellow art-lover Vincent Price). But it was Robinson's guest starring role on a 1956 episode of *The Martha Raye Show* that proved to be the turning point in the actor's floundering screen career. Shortly after appearing on the show, on which he spoofed his snarling "Little Caesar" image, Robinson was contacted by director Cecil B. DeMille for a role in his upcoming biblical epic, *The Ten Commandments* (1956). (A staunch conservative, DeMille reportedly told Robinson, "I've had you checked out, and you're as clean as a houndstooth.") With his memorable portrayal of Dathan, a cruel and crafty Hebrew overseer, Robinson made a triumphant return to Hollywood's "A" list, joining a cast of distinguished Hollywood veterans including Vincent Price, Judith Anderson, Anne Baxter, Nina Foch, Sir Cedric Hardwicke, and John Carradine.

Despite a pair of physical setbacks — including a massive heart attack in 1963 and a car accident in 1966 that required nine hours of surgery — Robinson continued his film and television appearances throughout the next decade, including *Grand Slam* (1968), which was filmed in such locations as Spain, France, and Rio de Janeiro; *MacKenna's Gold* (1969), a western that flopped at the box office despite a cast that included Gregory Peck, Lee J. Cobb, Keenan Wynn, and Eli Wallach; *The Old Man Who Cried Wolf* (1970), a well-done made-for-television thriller; and guest spots on such series as *Batman* and *Night Gallery*. His best role during these years came in 1965, when he starred with Steve McQueen in *The Cincinnati Kid*, playing a hard-boiled gambler named Lancey Howard.

In 1972, Robinson began work on what would be the 88th feature film of his career, *Soylent Green* (1973), an eerie science fictioner co-starring Charlton Heston and Joseph Cotten. Set in 1999, the feature depicts a bleak, arid world, and when Robinson's character, an aging researcher, learns that his government is manufacturing a food substance from human corpses, he chooses to end his life at a state-sponsored euthanasia parlor. At the time he filmed his final death scene, Robinson was already aware that he was, in real life, dying of cancer.

"He didn't go to his trailer much," Charlton Heston recalled in a 1996 documentary. "There was a comfortable chair on the set and he'd sit on the set most of the time on the days he was called…. I think he wanted to experience, to the full, what it was, one last time, to be on a movie set, because of all the people in the company, he was the only one that knew he would never be on another one."

Three months later, on January 26, 1973, Robinson died of cancer at the age of 79, leaving behind a distinguished body of film that would continue to be remembered decades later. His life served as the basis for a 1979 play, *Manny*, written by and starring Raymond Serra; a retrospective of the actor's career, including 27 of his features, was presented at the New York Museum of Modern Art in 1999; and the following year, Robinson was honored with his image on a United States postage stamp.

At the Academy Awards ceremony held the year that Robinson died, the actor was honored with a posthumous Lifetime Achievement Award for his impressive career. In presenting it to Robinson's widow, Charlton Heston shared the award's inscription, which serves as a fitting tribute to the life and career of this outstanding American:

"To Edward G. Robinson, who achieved greatness as a player, a patron of the arts, and a dedicated citizen," Heston read. "In sum, a Renaissance man."

Film Noir Filmography

Double Indemnity. Director: Billy Wilder. Producer: B.G. DeSylva. Running time: 106 minutes. Released by Paramount, September 7, 1944. Cast: Fred MacMurray, Barbara Stanwyck, Edward G. Robinson, Porter Hall, Jean Heather, Tom Powers, Byron Barr, Richard Gaines, Fortunio Bonanova, John Pilliber. Awards: Academy Award nominations for Best Picture, Best Director (Billy Wilder), Best Actress (Barbara Stanwyck), Best Cinematography (John Seitz), Best Original Screenplay (Raymond Chandler, Billy Wilder), Best Score (Miklos Rozsa), Best Sound (Loren Ryder).

Woman in the Window. Director: Fritz Lang. Producer: Nunnally Johnson. Running time: 99 minutes. Released by RKO, January 25, 1945. Cast: Edward G. Robinson, Joan Bennett, Raymond Massey, Edmond Breon, Dan Duryea, Thomas E. Jackson, Arthur Loft, Dorothy Peterson, Frank Dawson, Carol Cameron, Bobby Blake.

Scarlet Street. Director: Fritz Lang. Producer: Walter Wanger. Running time: 102 minutes. Released by Universal, December 28, 1945. Cast: Edward G. Robinson, Joan Bennett, Dan Duryea, Jess Barker, Margaret Lindsay, Rosalind Ivan, Samuel S. Hinds, Arthur Loft, Vladimir Sokoloff, Charles Kemper, Russell Hicks, Anita Bolster, Cyrus W. Kendall, Fred Essler, Edgar Dearing, Tom Dillon, Chuck Hamilton, Gus Glassmire, Ralph Littlefield, Sherry Hall, Howard Mitchell, Jack Staham, Rodney Bell.

The Stranger. Director: Orson Welles. Producer: Sam Spiegel. Running time: 95 minutes. Released by RKO, July 21, 1946. Cast: Edward G. Robinson, Loretta Young, Orson Welles, Philip Merivale, Billy House, Richard Long, Konstantin Shayne, Martha Wentworth, Byron Keith, Pietro Sosso.

Key Largo. Director: John Huston. Producer: Jerry Wald. Running time: 100 minutes. Released by Warner Brothers, July 16, 1948. Cast: Humphrey Bogart, Edward G. Robinson, Lauren Bacall, Lionel Barrymore, Claire Trevor, Thomas Gomez, Harry Lewis, John Rodney, Marc Lawrence, Don Seymour, Monte Blue, Jay Silver Heels, Rodric Redwing. Awards: Academy Award for Best Supporting Actress (Claire Trevor).

Night Has a Thousand Eyes. Director: John Farrow. Producer: Endre Bohem. Running time: 81 minutes. Released by Paramount, October 13, 1948. Cast: Edward G. Robinson, Gail Russell, John Lund, Virginia Bruce, William Demarest, Richard Webb, Jerome Cowan, Onslow Stevenson, John Alexander, Roman Bohnen, Luis Van Rooten.

House of Strangers. Director: Joseph L. Mankiewicz. Producer: Sol C. Siegel. Running time: 101 minutes. Released by 20th Century-Fox, July 1, 1949. Cast: Edward G. Robinson, Susan Hayward, Richard Conte, Luther Adler, Paul Valentine, Efrem Zimbalist, Jr., Debra Paget, Hope Emerson, Esther Minciotti, Diana Douglas, Tito Vuolo, Albert Morin, Sid Tomack, Thomas Henry

Brown, David Wolfe, John Kellogg, Ann Morrison, Dolores Parker.

Nightmare. Director: Maxwell Shane. Producers: William C. Pine, William C. Thomas. Running time: 89 minutes. Released by United Artists, May 11, 1956. Cast: Edward G. Robinson, Kevin McCarthy, Connie Russell, Virginia Christine, Rhys Williams, Gage Clark, Barry Atwater, Marian Carr, Billy May.

References

"Armand Hammer Buys Robinson's Art Collection." *Los Angeles Times*, April 4, 1973.

Biography of Edward G. Robinson. MGM Studios, November 30, 1964.

Biography of Edward G. Robinson. Paramount Pictures, May 1961.

Biography of Edward G. Robinson. Warner Bros. Studios, circa 1939.

"Edward G. Robinson A Great Actor." *The [London] Daily Telegraph*, January 29, 1973.

"Edward G. Robinson Dies Here at 79." *Los Angeles Herald-Examiner*, January 27, 1973,

"Edward G. Robinson, 79, Dies; His 'Little Caesar' Set a Style." *New York Times*, January 28, 1973.

"Edward G. Robinson Stamp." *Los Angeles Times*, October 24, 2000.

"Edward G. Robinson Swears He Is Not, Never Has Been Red." *Hollywood Citizen-News*, December 21, 1950.

Edwards, Bill. "Edward G. Robinson Hailed as 'Renaissance Man' at Funeral." *Variety*, January 29, 1973.

"Edw. G. Robinson's Wife Says Rift Is Patched Up." *Los Angeles Mirror-News*, April 15, 1955.

Eyles, Allen. "Edward G. Robinson." *Films and Filming*, January 1964.

"House Releases Robinson's Secret Red-Denial Testimony." *Variety*, January 12, 1951.

Kehr, Dave. "Always an Antihero with a Streetwise Touch of Crass." *New York Times*, March 7, 1999.

MacPherson, Virginia. "Tough Guy Turns Farmer." *Hollywood Citizen-News*, May 5, 1944.

McPhillips, William. "2,000 Say Farewell to Edward G. Robinson." *Los Angeles Times*, January 29, 1973.

"Mrs. Robinson Has 'Forgotten' Divorce Action." *Hollywood Citizen-News*, April 15, 1955.

Niderost, Eric. "Edward G. Robinson: The Classic Gangster." *Classic Images*, May 1993.

"No Mere Mummer He!" *Screen Actor*, May-June 1969.

"One of the Bumps in a Long Road." *Los Angeles Herald-Examiner*, December 16, 1962.

Othman, Frederick C. "Art Is a Tough Racket, Pal." *The Saturday Evening Post*, July 1, 1944.

Overbey, David. "Edward G. Robinson." *Take One*, May 1978.

Parsons, Louella O. "Mrs. Edward G. Robinson Sues Actor for Divorce." *Los Angeles Examiner*, February 26, 1955.

"Robinson Estate, Mainly Art Works, Put at $2.2 Mil." *Variety*, February 14, 1973.

"Robinson Jr. Denies Guilt." *Los Angeles Examiner*, April 12, 1952.

"Robinson Plans to Ignore Stage for Hollywood." *New York Herald Tribune*, May 14, 1944.

"Robinson Says He Was Duped by Reds." *Los Angeles Times*, May 1, 1952.

Schumach, Murray. "Robinson Comes Back." *New York Times*, February 5, 1956.

Skolsky, Sidney. "Tintypes: Edward G. Robinson." *Hollywood Citizen-News*, March 6, 1965.

"Son of Tough Guy Actor to Face Bad Check Trial." *Hollywood Citizen-News*, April 12, 1952.

"Strout, Dick. "Edward G. Robinson." *In Touch*, June 1974.

"The Men Mix It Up." *Collier's*, September 2, 1939.

"The Museum of Modern Art Spotlights Edward G. Robinson." Museum of Modern Art, February 1998.

Documentary

"Little Big Man: Edward G. Robinson." Produced by Peter Jones Productions for A&E Network. A&E Television Networks. Copyright 1996.

MICKEY ROONEY

"I feel like I'm being shoved into a corner and if I don't get out soon, it'll be too late. Maybe it's too late already."— Mickey Rooney in *Quicksand* (1950)

What is there to say about Mickey Rooney that hasn't already been said? The world's biggest movie star at 19, he was a has-been at 30. He has had eight wives, fathered eight children, battled drug addiction, and been forced into bankruptcy on more than one occasion.

In his best-selling autobiography, he maintained that he had affairs with such Hollywood luminaries as Lana Turner and Norma Shearer; he later claimed responsibility for discovering Sammy Davis, Jr., and Red Skelton; and he once asserted that it was his idea to change the name of Norma Jean Baker to Marilyn Monroe. Conquering nearly every performing medium, he has manifested his multifaceted talent as an actor, dancer, singer, songwriter, musician, and author. And during a career that spans an almost unimaginable nine decades, he has earned five Emmy nominations, four Academy Award nominations, and received two honorary Oscars—one for lifetime achievement.

When one speaks of Mickey Rooney, however, the shadowy realm of film noir is not exactly the first image that springs to mind. He is far more likely to be envisioned as the wholesome Andy Hardy, or dancing in a spur-of-the-moment musical number with Judy Garland at his side, than he is with a gat in his hand and his fedora cocked to one side. His most familiar screen persona notwithstanding, Rooney earned a solid place in the era of film noir with starring roles in four features from the period: *Quicksand* (1950), *The Strip* (1951), *Drive a Crooked Road* (1954), and *Baby Face Nelson* (1957).

The five-foot, three-inch actor once crowned "The King of the Movies" was born Joe Yule, Jr., on September 23, 1920, to vaudeville performers Joe Yule and his wife, Nell Carter. Young Joe was first seen on the stage at an early age; during the actor's career, more than one colorful anecdote surfaced to describe this debut. According to one account, the lad first appeared in his parents' act at the age of 15 months, portraying a midget and equipped with a tuxedo and a big rubber cigar. Another version states that Joe crawled into the orchestra pit during his parents' on-stage routine and started pounding on the drums, while a third claims that he escaped from the dressing room in a Rochester, New York theater, toddled out to the center of the stage, and stood on his head. According to Rooney himself, however, his foray into show business occurred by happenstance while he was watching his father perform at a Chicago theater. After he let out a sneeze, the spotlight focused on the two-year-old, who immediately shifted into performing mode.

"I had a harmonica I kept playing like mad," the actor said in a 1957 *McCall's* magazine article, "and I loved it out there with all those lights. It was so pretty."

Before long, the youngster was a regular part of his parents' act, but they separated when Joe was four years old and he wound up in Hollywood with his mother, where she managed a tourist home for a time. It didn't take long for Joe to pick up his budding career where he'd left off, enrolling at Daddy Mack's Dance Studio, performing in a local musical revue at the Orange Grove Theater, and making his screen debut as a midget in the 1926 silent feature, *Not to be Trusted*. Two years after his first film, Joe landed the role of Mickey "Himself" McGuire in a series of comedies released by the Standard Film Corporation, appearing in nearly 80 episodes between 1928 and 1932. During the run of the series, Joe's name was legally changed to Mickey McGuire, but it was later altered again, and Mickey Rooney was introduced to the world.

Following his stint in the Mickey McGuire films, Rooney was seen in such features as Universal's *My Pal, the King* (1932), where he played a young King Richard V; Eagle Pictures' *The Big Chance* (1933), a boxing yarn starring John Darrow; and Warner Bros.' *The World Changes* (1933), which featured Paul Muni and Mary Astor. Rooney's career really took off in 1934 when he was placed under contract by MGM, beginning an association that would last for the next 14 years. During that time, Rooney was seen in a number of Hollywood gems, including *Manhattan Melodrama* (1934), where he played Clark Gable's character, Blackie, at age 12; *A Midsummer Night's Dream* (1935), in which he turned in a memorable performance as the mischievous Puck; *Captains Courageous* (1937), starring Spencer Tracy and Freddie Bartholomew; *Boys Town* (1938), where

Rooney demonstrated his dramatic range as delinquent teen Whitey Marsh; and *National Velvet* (1944), co-starring Elizabeth Taylor. In addition to these features, Rooney appeared in 1937 in *A Family Affair*, a comedy focusing on a small-town family named Hardy. The film was an unexpected hit and led to a popular eight-year, 15-episode series starring Rooney as Andy Hardy, including *Love Finds Andy Hardy* (1938), *Andy Hardy Gets Spring Fever* (1939), *Andy Hardy's Private Secretary* (1941), *Andy Hardy's Blonde Trouble* (1944), and *Love Laughs at Andy Hardy* (1946). One of Rooney's co-stars in the series was actress Judy Garland, who portrayed Betsy Booth in three of the Andy Hardy features; following their first screen appearance in the 1937 film *Thoroughbreds Don't Cry*, Rooney and Garland would become one of Hollywood's most popular duos and appear in a total of 10 features together.

By the late 1930s, Rooney had become one of the most successful and celebrated actors in the country and in 1938 was honored, along with Deanna Durbin, with a special Academy Award for "bringing the spirit and personification of youth to the screen." The following year, the actor received his first Oscar nomination for Best Actor for his role opposite Garland in *Babes in Arms* (1939), and earned a second nomination in 1943 for his touching performance in *The Human Comedy*. Although he lost both times (the first to Robert Donat for *Goodbye, Mr. Chips*, and later to Paul Lukas in *Watch on the Rhine*), Rooney was at the height of his success, and reigned from 1939 to 1941 as the top box-office actor in Hollywood.

As a testament to Rooney's fame — as well as his versatility — the actor performed with the National Symphony Orchestra at the 1941 inaugural ceremonies for President Franklin D. Roosevelt, playing one of his own compositions, entitled "Melodante." In addition to this work, Rooney composed hundreds of songs throughout his career, including "Little Christmas Tree" and "Where I Belong," recorded by Vic Damone, and "Spoken For," made popular by Sammy Davis,

Jr. And in the late 1950s, Rooney recorded an album of his own, "Mickey Rooney Sings George M. Cohan," which included two original tunes, "I Couldn't Be More in Love" and "You Couldn't Tell the Teardrops From the Rain."

Meanwhile, Rooney had by now embarked on what he once referred to as "a lifetime of marriage." In 1942, at the age of 21, he married actress Ava Gardner, but the union lasted only 18 months. Wife number two was a 17-year-old blonde named Betty Jane Rase, a former Miss Alabama.

"I knew her two weeks, and then we got married," Rooney later recalled. The actor's first child, Mickey Rooney, Jr., was born in 1946, but the marriage ended shortly after the birth of his second son, Timothy, in 1947. Rooney wasn't unattached for long, however; shortly after his divorce, he began seeing actress Martha Vickers.

"I'd admired her so much on the screen that I tracked down her telephone number and we made a date," Rooney later recalled. "I guess we were both lonely at the time. We married fast, and stayed married for two and a half years." During that time, Rooney welcomed a third son, Theodore, born in 1950.

In 1952, a year after his divorce from Vickers, Rooney married former model Elaine Mahnken, telling one reporter, "I wish Elaine had been the first girl in my life. Things would have been a lot different." But six years later, after the actor's affair with local beauty queen Barbara Ann Thomason, this union, too, ended in divorce. A few weeks after his May 1959 divorce, Rooney and Barbara were married — and three months later, his fourth child, daughter Kelly Ann, was born. The couple would go on to have three more children, Kerry Yule, Michael Kyle, and Kimmy Sue, but this union, Rooney's longest to date, would end in tragedy.

In the mid 1960s, reportedly in retaliation for Rooney's infidelity, Barbara became involved with an aspiring actor named Milos Milosevic and Rooney filed for divorce, seeking custody of their children. He and Barbara later reconciled, but on February 1, 1966,

Milosevic shot Barbara to death in the couple's Brentwood home, then killed himself.

"I died, too," Rooney wrote in his 1991 autobiography, *Life is Too Short*. "Something like a steel band seemed to encircle my chest. And I didn't take a full breath for three years." (In later years, Rooney sued for custody of his four children with Barbara, but the court ultimately ruled that they should remain with the woman's parents.)

A year after Barbara's murder, Rooney married her closest friend, Marge Lane, but this ill-advised union ended after only 100 days, and Rooney wed wife number seven, secretary Carolyn Hockett, two years later. Rooney and Carolyn welcomed the actor's youngest child, Jonell, in January 1970, but by 1974, the marriage was over. Finally, in July 1978, Rooney took his eighth trip down the aisle — "This time for keeps," the actor has said — to Jan Chamberlin, a country-and-western singer who was nearly 20 years his junior.

"When I say 'I do,' the Justice of the Peace replies, 'I know, I know,'" Rooney once joked. "I'm the only man in the world whose marriage license reads, 'To Whom it May Concern.' But to have been married eight times is not normal. That's only half way intelligent." As of this writing, Rooney and Chamberlin are still together.

Between marriages, Rooney had seen his screen career fall as swiftly and as surely as it had risen. After serving from 1944 to 1946 in the U.S. Army, during which he entertained thousands of troops overseas, Rooney returned to Hollywood to discover that he had been dethroned as "The King of the Movies." He was first seen in *Killer McCoy* (1947), where he played a boxer who accidentally kills his mentor in the ring, followed by *Summer Holiday* (1948), a tuneful remake of Rooney's earlier hit, *Ah Wilderness!* (1935), and *Words and Music* (1948), a musical about the Broadway team of Richard Rogers and Lorenz Hart. None of the features made much of an impression on the moviegoing public, and Rooney's performance in the latter was savagely panned by critics.

After the release of *Words and Music*, Rooney severed his ties with MGM and started his own production company, a move he later called "one of the dumbest things I ever did." With few offers coming his way, Rooney was seen in a series of low-budget features, including his entry into the world of film noir, *Quicksand* (1950). Here, Rooney starred as Don Brady, a womanizing auto mechanic whose outlook toward the female sex is revealed in an early scene when he tells his pals (one of whom is Jimmy Dodd, of *The Mickey Mouse Club* fame) that he has dumped his girlfriend, Helen (Barbara Bates): "I spent four years in the Navy fighting for freedom," he says. "Why get anchored down now?" Before long, Don puts the moves on a sexy blonde cashier, Vera Novak (Jeanne Cagney), and finds himself mired in a series of misdeeds that nearly lead to his undoing, beginning with his "borrowing" of $20 from the cash register at his job in order to pay for his first date with Vera, and ending with him fleeing from authorities after strangling his boss. Although Don is ultimately shot and captured by police, the film ends on an upbeat note when the hapless mechanic learns that his boss is still alive and that his old girl-friend, Helen, will be waiting for him after he serves a stretch in prison for his varied crimes.

Although *Quicksand* is tension-filled and well-acted for most of its 79 minutes, it takes a wildly implausible turn near the end and peters out to an unsatisfying conclusion. Rooney himself wrote in *Life is Too Short*, "The less said about *Quicksand*, the better, except to note that it was aptly titled. We sank in it." The critics of the day took a more favorable view of the film, however, with Ann Helming of the *Hollywood Citizen-News* praising Rooney's "straightforward, mug-less performance," and the reviewer for *Variety* writing that he "portrays the hard-luck mechanic in convincingly somber tones without once having the chance for any comic capers."

The following year, Rooney returned to MGM for his second film noir, *The Strip* (1951), playing jazz drummer Stanley Maxton. At his new nightclub job, Stanley quickly falls for aspiring actress Jane Tafford (Sally Forrest), not knowing that she is encouraging his affections because one of his associates, Sonny Johnson (James Craig), has "connections" to the film industry. A cold-blooded racketeer who has no intentions of assisting in Jane's career, Sonny seduces the young woman, and when Stan warns Jane of Sonny's corrupt nature, he is beaten by Sonny's underlings. Meanwhile, angered by Sonny's treatment, Jane accidentally kills him during an argument, but is seriously wounded during a struggle for the gun. The ever-loyal Stan tries to shield Jane by taking the blame for Sonny's death, but Jane admits her guilt before she dies, leaving Stan to return, alone and shattered, to his job at the nightclub.

The Strip managed to turn a slight profit, but the "B" level picture was dismissed by critics, including the reviewer for *Variety*, who wrote that the "performances are generally ineffective, as characters are not real enough to be believable." The same critic acknowledged, however, that film's best moments were its musical numbers, and noted: "Rooney beats his drums solidly." Rooney was also singled out for his prowess on the drums by Philip K. Scheuer of the *Los Angeles Times*, who said the actor "really knocks himself out at the traps ... holding his own even among such fast company."

After a handful of mediocre features that included *My Brother, the Outlaw* (1952), a western in which *Variety*'s critic said he was "woefully miscast," and *All Ashore* (1953), a musical comedy with Dick Haymes, Rooney rebounded with a starring role in his third film noir, *Drive a Crooked Road* (1954). In this well-done feature, Rooney portrayed a lonely garage mechanic, Eddie Shannon, who is characterized by his talent behind the wheel as a local race car driver and his reticence toward the female sex. He overcomes the latter, however, when — to his surprise — he attracts the attentions of a gorgeous woman, Barbara Mathews (Dianne Foster), who brings her car to him for repair. Despite the chasteness of their relationship, Eddie soon falls head-over-heels for Barbara, and when he shares with her his dream to race in Europe, Barbara introduces Eddie to a friend, Steve Norris (Kevin McCarthy), who offers to help him raise the funds needed. It turns out, however, that Steve's motives are less than virtuous; in exchange for $15,000, he wants Eddie to serve as the wheel man for an intricate heist he has planned with his partner, Harold Baker (Jack Kelly). Eddie initially refuses, but he is subtly convinced by Barbara, who is actually Steve's lover and plans to flee with him after the robbery. After the successful heist, Eddie finds Barbara at Steve's beachfront house, where she reveals the entire scheme and apologizes for her deception. Fearing that Eddie will report the trio to police, Harold forces Eddie to drive to a secluded location, where he plans to kill him, but Eddie crashes the car and Harold is killed. Taking Harold's gun, Eddie manages to make his way back to the beach house and, finding Steve in a violent argument with Barbara, shoots and kills Steve. In the final scene, Eddie is seen comforting the distraught Barbara as police arrive, telling her, "Everything will be all right."

Although *Drive a Crooked Road* was a disappointment at the box office, the feature was named "Picture of the Month" by famed columnist Louella Parsons and Rooney earned raves for his performance. Margaret Harford of the *Hollywood Citizen-News* praised the actor's "earnest, sympathetic" portrayal; Philip K. Scheuer wrote in the *Los Angeles Times* that "Rooney and every one else in the cast deliver performances that scarcely could be bettered"; and in the *Los Angeles Daily News*, Roy Ringer opined: "[The film] will come as a surprise to those who can imagine Mickey Rooney only in comedy or song and dance roles. In *Drive a Crooked Road*, he switches to tragic drama and turns in a skillful and sympathetic performance."

After his triumph in *Drive a Crooked Road*, Rooney appeared to have taken the first step on the comeback trail, and a few months after the film's release he starred in his own television series, *The Mickey Rooney Show* (also known as *Hey, Mulligan*). But the half-hour sitcom, created by feature film directors Blake Edwards and Richard Quine (who directed Rooney in *Drive a Crooked Road*), was scheduled against the popular *Jackie Gleason Show* and left the air after only one season.

"Gleason beat us all to hell on the ratings," Rooney wrote in his 1991 autobiography. "While he was pulling, maybe, a forty-nine Nielsen share, we were getting a seven. I think my mother watched the show. Period."

But the actor quickly rebounded from this disappointment, turning in a well-received performance in the hit wartime drama *The Bridges at Toko-Ri* (1955), and earning an Oscar nomination for Best Supporting Actor in 1956 for *The Bold and the Brave* (he lost to Anthony Quinn in *Lust for Life*). And the following year, Rooney earned a number of favorable notices for his portrayal of the title role in his final film noir, *Baby Face Nelson* (1957). This feature — described in the prologue as a "re-creation of an era of jazz, jalopies, prohibition, and trigger-happy punks!" — depicted the transformation of ex-convict Lester M. Gillis into the violent gang-

ster known as Baby Face Nelson. Accompanied by his faithful girlfriend, Sue (Carolyn Jones), Nelson knocks off the mob boss (Ted De Corsia) who betrayed him after arranging for his prison release, teams with notorious mobster John Dillinger (Leo Gordon) and takes over his gang after he is gunned down by police, and leaves a trail of dead bodies in his wake before authorities catch up to him following a frantic car chase. In the final scene, riddled with bullets, Nelson staggers into a country graveyard and begs Sue to finish him off before he can be taken in by the cops.

Although one critic wrote that Rooney's portrayal of the infamous gangster "lacks … understanding of the lust that drove Nelson to kill," other reviewers were more impressed. John L. Scott of the *Los Angeles Times* described the film as "a hard-hitting story in which a snarling Rooney in the title role blazes a trail of murder with his machine gun," adding that "the energetic star never goes halfway in any characterization," and the critic for the *Hollywood Citizen-News* wrote, "Rooney delivers a most convincing performance as the gun-happy gangster, Baby Face."

Rooney continued to regain a measure of his former prominence during the next several years with Emmy-nominated roles in "The Comedian" on *Playhouse 90* (1958); "Eddie," a one-man melodrama on *Alcoa-Goodyear Theatre* (1959) about a small-time gambler; and "Somebody's Waiting" on *The Dick Powell Show* (1962), and exhibited a flair for character acting in such films as *The Last Mile* (1959), *Requiem for a Heavyweight* (1962), and *The Secret Invasion* (1964). Rooney also appeared in record-breaking performances during a nightclub circuit tour with Bobby Van in 1964, and in a three-week revival of *A Funny Thing Happened on the Way to the Forum* in Los Angeles, earning praise from one critic who termed his performance a "personal triumph." But although he was seen during this same period in such forgettable films as *Platinum High School* (1960), and *How to Stuff a Wild Bikini* (1965) — which was panned by one critic as "the worst film of the last two years— and maybe the next two years"— Rooney was by now facing more pressing concerns than his acting career.

In 1962, Rooney filed for bankruptcy, claiming that, while he had made more than $12 million during his career, his income had been chipped away through alimony and child support payments to his various ex-wives, his penchant for gambling, and bad business deals.

"I spent, lent, married, and I don't know how, I went through twelve million dollars," Rooney wrote in his first autobiography, *i.e.*, released in 1965. "It isn't as if my bankruptcy can be traced to any single cause, placed in any single period of years, explained with a single flip phrase. If I knew how I did it, I wouldn't have done it in the first place. Ask a drunk where the booze has gone. That's like asking me about my money." (Although Rooney eventually recovered from this financial blow, the actor filed for bankruptcy a second time in 1996, revealing that he owed the Internal Revenue Service approximately $1.75 million dating back to 1974. The action came several months after the actor was ordered to pay $72,000 to his former manager in lawyer fees for duties relating to Rooney's 1991 autobiography and a three-year cable television series.)

The 1960s also saw an escalation in Rooney's use of barbiturates, which had started during the previous decade and escalated following the 1966 murder of his fifth wife, Barbara. In his 1991 autobiography, the actor wrote that he was so "drugged out" during his subsequent marriage to Marge Lane that "I hardly remember her now."

"The pills helped me sleep at night," the actor wrote in *Life is Too Short*. "They helped get me going in the morning. Like any addiction, they took over my life, destroyed my freedom, and my sense of self. I'd make the most profoundly sincere resolutions to quit them, then be plunged into the depths of despair when, despite my good intentions, I needed to take more."

After managing to kick his addiction to pills in the early 1970s ("It wasn't easy ... [but] I looked to a Power higher than myself," Rooney recalled), the actor continued his varied professional appearances, and although the vehicles he chose were not always first-rate, the energetic actor was seldom idle. He was seen in such feature films as *Cockeyed Cowboys of Calico County* (1970), a so-so comedy western starring Dan Blocker; *Pulp* (1972), where he turned in a fine portrayal of a former movie star; and *Pete's Dragon* (1977), a run-of-the-mill Disney production about a boy who meets an animated dragon; and television programs including *The Year Without a Santa Claus* (1974), an animated holiday favorite where he provided the voice of Santa. His luck took yet another upswing late in the decade, however, when he earned an Academy Award nomination for Best Supporting Actor for his role as a former horse trainer in *The Black Stallion* (1979) (he lost to Melvyn Douglas for *Being There*); earned raves for his performance opposite Ann Miller in the three-year stage tour of *Sugar Babies* (1979); won an Emmy Award and a Golden Globe for his portrayal of a retarded man in *Bill* (1982); and received an honorary Academy Award for Lifetime Achievement (1983). In presenting the latter award to Rooney, veteran comedian Bob Hope called the actor "the kid who illuminated all our yesterdays and the man who brightens all our todays."

Now in his 80s, Mickey Rooney is still going strong. After earning a fifth Emmy nomination for *Bill: On His Own* (1983), the actor continued to accept roles in a variety of films, television shows, and stage productions, and also took time to pen his first published novel, *The Search for Sonny Skies*, in 1994. Most recently, the actor has appeared in such feature films as *Babe: Pig in the City* (1998), the sequel to the hit 1995 film, *Babe*, and *The First of May* (2000), starring Julie Harris; guested on television series including *The Simpsons* (1995) and *ER* (1998); served as television spokesperson for the Garden State Life Insurance Company; played the title role in a long-running, well-received tour of *The*

Wizard of Oz in the late 1990s; and performed in a stage show with wife Jan Chamberlin entitled *One Man— One Wife*. In December 2000, in the midst of a tour for the latter production, Rooney underwent heart bypass surgery, but was back on stage a few months later and, as of this writing, was still touring the country in the show.

Mickey Rooney—from whom, it is said, famed rodent Mickey Mouse received his name — is truly a national treasure. Essaying more comebacks than he might care to remember, and triumphing over an often rocky and sometimes tragic life off screen, Rooney demonstrated during his phenomenal career that he possessed a versatility, determination, and longevity that nearly defies description. Showing no signs of slowing down, the octogenarian recently shared his outlook that "age is experience — and some of us are more experienced than others."

"Inspire, don't retire," Rooney advised. "Life is too short to be in pain all the time or wish you could change who you are. It's being a participant in the game called life that's important."

Film Noir Filmography

Quicksand. Director: Irving Pichel. Producers: Mickey Rooney and Peter Lorre. Running time: 79 minutes. Released by United Artists, 1950. Cast: Mickey Rooney, Jeanne Cagney, Barbara Bates, Peter Lorre, Taylor Holmes, Art Smith, Wally Cassell, Richard Lane, Patsy O'Connor, John Gallaudet, Minerva Urecal, Sid Marion, Jimmy Dodd, Lester Dorr.

The Strip. Director: Leslie Kardos. Producer: Joe Pasternak. Running time: 84 minutes. Released by MGM, August 1951. Cast: Mickey Rooney, Sally Forrest, William Demarest, James Craig, Kay Brown, Louis Armstrong and Band, Tommy Rettig, Tom Powers, Jonathan Cott, Tommy Farrell, Myrna Dell, Jacqueline Fontaine, Vic Damone, Monica Lewis.

Drive a Crooked Road. Director: Richard Quine. Producer: Jonie Taps. Running time: 83 minutes. Released by Columbia, April 2, 1954. Cast: Mickey Rooney, Dianne Foster, Kevin McCarthy, Jack Kelly, Harr Landers, Jerry Paris, Paul Picerni, Dick Crockett, Mort Mills, Peggy Maley.

Baby Face Nelson. Director: Don Siegel. Producer: Al Zimbalist. Running time: 85 minutes. Released by United Artists, November 1957. Cast: Mickey Rooney, Carolyn Jones, Sir Cedric Hardwicke, Leo Gordon, Ted DeCorsia, Anthony Caruso, Jack Elam, Chris Dark, Emile Meyer, Dan Terranova, Dabbs Greer, Bob Osterloh, Dick Crocett, Paul Baxley, Thayer David, Ken Patterson, Sol Gorse, Gil Perkins, Tom Fadden, Lisa Davis, John Hoyt, Elisah Cook, JR., Murray Alper, George E. Stone, Hubie Kerns, Paul and Richard Donnelly.

References

"Author Talk." *Waldenbooks Preferred Reader Guide*, Summer 1991.

Blowen, Michael. "He's Off to Be the 'Wizard.'" *Boston Sunday Globe*, January 24, 1999.

"Calling Judge Hardy." *The Hollywood Reporter*, January 11, 1995.

Deardoff, Julie. "Mickey Rooney Sets First Novel in Hollywood, Stars Child Actor." *Long Beach Press-Telegram*, December 15, 1994.

Feld, Bruce. "Survival Is a Matter of Faith to Mickey Rooney." *Los Angeles Daily News*, June 24, 1991.

Frazier, George. "Mickey Rooney Comes of Age." *Coronet*, October 1948.

Freeman, David. "Hey, Gang, Let's Put on a Show!" *Los Angeles Times*, April 14, 1991.

Goodwin, Christopher. "Rooney Fights to Ban Animal Torture Videos." *The (London) Sunday Times*, August 29, 1999.

Harris, Eleanor. "Mickey Rooney." *McCall's*, September 1957.

Harvey, Steve. "Only in L.A." *Los Angeles Times*, January 18, 1996.

"Heard." *Time*, July 22, 1996.

Hopper, Hedda. "They Can't Keep Mickey Down." *Chicago Sunday Tribune*, circa 1958.

"Just for Variety." *Variety*, February 19, 1997.

"On the Road with Bob Dorian." *American Movie Classics Magazine*, June 1998.

Parsons, Louella O. "The Rooneys." *Pictorial Living*, October 12, 1958.

Plate, Andrea Darvi. "Life of the Rich, Famous— and Exploited." *Los Angeles Times*, April 7, 1995.

Richards, David. "He Led Eight Wives." *New York Times*, May 5, 1991.

Roberts, Jerry. "Rooney Forced to Pay $72,000 to Ex-Manager." *The Hollywood Reporter*, January 24, 1996.

"Rooney and Son." *Los Angeles Times*, December 18, 1960.

"Rooney Blasts H'Wood." *The Hollywood Reporter*, September 24, 1990.

Rooney, Mickey. *Life Is Too Short.* New York: Villard Books, 1991.

_____. "Religion and Films: They're No Longer a Match Made in Heaven." *Variety*, December 5, 1990.

_____. "Where Did the Loot Go?" *Cosmopolitan*, March 1966.

"Rooney Sued by Attorney Over Commission." *Variety*, June 24, 1992.

Rosenthal, Phil. "Reunited Wouldn't Feel So Good." *Chicago Sun-Times*, April 9, 2002.

Shales, Tom. "Rated 'R' for Rooney." *Los Angeles Times*, May 19, 1991.

Shearer, Lloyd. "Mickey Rooney Tells All." *Parade*, March 31, 1991.

Snow, Shauna. "Morning Report." *Los Angeles Times*, January 11, 1995.

"TV's Hollywood's Mickey Rooney." *TV Guide*, circa 1954.

"Walter Scott's Personality Parade." *Parade*, June 11, 2000.

Weiner, Marci. "Hollywood Beat. *Entertainment Today*, January 4, 2002.

"Where the Heart Is." *The Hollywood Reporter*, December 27, 2000.

Witchel, Alex. "At 73, Still the Star, Still the Child." *New York Times*, July 7, 1993.

ROBERT RYAN

"How do you think I got where I did? Not by being outsmarted by clucks like you."
— Robert Ryan in *The Racket* (1951)

With his intimidating stature, take-no-prisoners approach, and aura of barely suppressed ferocity, Robert Ryan was, perhaps, the quintessential film noir actor. Although the talented performer of stage and screen played a wide variety of characters during his 40-year career, it is the cold-hearted hoods, psychotic spouses, and iniquitous gangsters for which he is best remembered.

"I've played more heroes than villains," Ryan said once. "That most people have the impression that all I've played is heavies and villains leads me to believe they never saw most of my pictures. Yet, I've never stopped working, so I can't complain."

Although he appeared in numerous pictures that are now all but forgotten, Ryan starred in such well-received features as *About Mrs. Leslie* (1954), *Bad Day at Black Rock* (1955), *The Longest Day* (1962), *The Dirty Dozen* (1967), and *The Wild Bunch* (1969). He was also a powerful and salient presence in his 11 films noirs: *Crossfire* (1947), *Berlin Express* (1948), *Act of Violence* (1949), *Caught* (1949), *The Set-Up* (1949), *The Racket* (1951), *On Dangerous Ground* (1952), *Clash by Night* (1952), *Beware, My Lovely* (1952), *House of*

Bamboo (1955), and *Odds Against Tomorrow* (1959).

Robert Bushnell Ryan was born on November 11, 1909 (some sources give 1911 or 1913 as the year), in Chicago, Illinois, the first child of Timothy Ryan, a well-to-do building contractor, and his wife, Mabel. (While most articles written about the actor state that he was an only child, he actually had a younger brother, John, who died from influenza. In a rare reference to his sibling, Ryan told a *Los Angeles Times* reporter in 1972: "My brother died when he was six and I've thought about it my whole life. He never even got started.")

Schooled at Loyola Academy, a Jesuit school in Chicago, Ryan's education was supplemented by varying extracurricular pursuits. At the age of eight, he recalled, "my father arranged for me to take boxing lessons. My mother countered by fixing me up with instruction on the violin. I never became a violin virtuoso, but I did turn out to be an expert boxer." Following his 1927 graduation from Loyola, Ryan enrolled at Dartmouth College, where he edited the school newspaper, participated in track and field events, played on the football team, and became the first freshman to win the college's heavy-weight boxing championship — a title he held throughout his four years of intercollegiate competition.

Although he left Dartmouth in 1932 armed with a bachelor's degree in English, Ryan found himself at loose ends. For the next several years, he toiled at a series of jobs, including digging sewer tunnels, herding horses in Montana, working in the engine room on an ocean liner, serving as paving supervisor for the Works Progress Administration, and supervising supplies for the Chicago Board of Education. For a short time, he also worked as a bill collector for a loan company, but he quit after two weeks, unable to continue seeking money from "families who hadn't eaten in days. It was too much," the actor said.

"I just didn't know what I wanted to do," Ryan once recalled. "If times had been different, people would have called me a bum. I spent seven years of vagabonding, working at this and that and not very interested in anything I was doing."

Finally, in 1936, Ryan joined an amateur theater group in Chicago. ("Amateur is actually too strong a word — it was less than that," Ryan quipped in a 1968 interview. "But somehow I got the acting bug.") After two years with the group, Ryan set his sights on Hollywood and enrolled in the Max Reinhardt Workshop in Los Angeles. The actor would later say that "the great Reinhardt was the big influence on my career," but his association with the famed drama group also provided another perk — in 1939, he wed fellow acting student Jessica Cadwalader, with whom he would have two sons, Timothy and Cheyney, and a daughter, Lisa. The two would remain married for more than 30 years. (Jessica abandoned her acting aspirations and later became a successful writer of mystery novels and children's books.)

After making his professional stage debut in *Too Many Husbands* at the Belasco Theatre in 1940, Ryan was spotted by a Paramount talent scout and signed a $75 a week contract. (Ironically, Ryan had made a screen test for

the studio two years earlier, but was told that he was "not the right type.") In his first film, *Golden Gloves* (1940), Ryan played a bit part as a boxer, but after minor parts in four more films for the studio, his contract was not renewed. Undaunted, Ryan headed for the Eastern "straw-hat circuit," where he landed a supporting role in *A Kiss for Cinderella*, starring Luise Rainer. His favorable reviews from this production led to his casting in Clifford Odets' *Clash by Night*, featuring Tallulah Bankhead, Joseph Schildkraut, and Lee J. Cobb. Although the play closed after fewer than 50 performances, Ryan was singled out by one critic for his "manly and clearheaded" performance.

Ryan's disappointment over the brief run of *Clash by Night* was short-lived; his appearance in the play caught the attention of RKO director Pare Lorentz, who tapped the actor for the lead in his upcoming film, *Name, Age, and Occupation*. Although the Depression-era feature was later shelved, Ryan inked a $700 a week contract with RKO and was cast in such films as *Bombardier* (1943), a World War II drama starring Pat O'Brien and Randolph Scott; *Behind the Rising Sun*

Paul Douglas, Barbara Stanwyck, and Robert Ryan featured in *Clash by Night* (1952).

ing role in his first feature from the era, *Crossfire*. In this hard-hitting indictment of anti–Semitism, Ryan played Montgomery, a bigoted psychopath who kills a Jewish war veteran named Joseph Samuels (Sam Levene) while in a drunken rage. As a series of flashbacks reveals the events leading up to the murder, Montgomery's deep-seated hatred is glaringly exposed. "I don't like Jews," he proclaims in one scene. "And I don't like nobody that likes Jews." Although the investigation initially centers on a soldier, Arthur Mitchell (George Cooper), who met the Jewish veteran on the night of the killing, police later turn their sights to Montgomery, learning that he has also killed an Army pal (Steve Brodie) who was present when the murder took place. In the film's climax, Montgomery is confronted with the evidence against him and when he tries to escape, he is gunned down in the street.

Critics lauded Ryan's standout performance; Bosley Crowther of the *New York Times* labeled the actor "frighteningly real"; Alton Cook, in the *New York World-Telegram*, praised his "unusually intelligent" portrayal; and the reviewer for *Time* labeled Ryan's performance "the scariest of the season. It is gruesome to watch such a character." For his efforts, Ryan earned an Academy Award nomination for Best Supporting Actor — although he lost to Edmund Gwenn for *Miracle on 34th Street* (1947), the film provided a significant boost to the actor's rising career.

"It's a nasty, hellish part," Ryan said after the film's release, "but the picture is terrific. It also has brought me more attention than the other ... parts I have played since 1941."

(1943), which gave the actor the opportunity to display his boxing prowess; *Tender Comrade* (1943), in which he played his first romantic lead, opposite Ginger Rogers; and *Marine Raiders* (1944), where he earned raves for his portrayal of a tough Marine captain.

In 1944, Ryan enlisted in the real-life Marine Corps, serving as an infantry training instructor at Camp Pendleton in San Diego, California. After his discharge from the service, Ryan wasted no time returning to the screen, co-starring in 1947 with Randolph Scott and Anne Jeffreys in a mediocre western, *Trail Street*, and opposite Joan Bennett in a Jean Renoir–directed drama, *The Woman on the Beach*. Also that year, Ryan entered the domain of film noir with a lead-

Left to right: Roman Toporow, Merle Oberon, Robert Ryan, and Charles Korvin in *Berlin Express* (1948).

The following year, Ryan starred in his second film noir, *Berlin Express* (1948), which centered on the post-war kidnapping of a German diplomat, Dr. Bernhardt (Paul Lukas), and the efforts of four men and the man's secretary to find him. Hailing from America, France, Russia, and Britain, the men track the doctor to an abandoned brewery where he is being held by members of a Nazi underground movement, and the doctor is freed following a violent gun battle. On the train to deliver Bernhardt to an international conference, American agriculturalist Robert Lindley (Ryan) voices his suspicions about the Frenchman, Perrot (Charles Korvin), and his mistrust is confirmed when he spots Perrot strangling the German doctor through the reflection in a train window. After Lindley alerts police aboard the train, Perrot is shot

while trying to flee, and Bernhardt is safely delivered to Berlin.

An unusual noir, given its European setting, *Berlin Express* was released to mostly good notices; in a typical review, Lowell E. Redelings of the *Hollywood Citizen-News* termed it "acceptable theater fare, not outstanding but nevertheless interesting, and sometimes quite entertaining." And although the film's showier roles were portrayed by Korvin and Lukas, Ryan was singled out by Frank Eng of the *Los Angeles Daily News*, who wrote that the actor was "pleasing" and "well cast."

Of Ryan's four features in 1949, three were from the era of film noir: *Act of Violence*, *Caught*, and *The Set-Up*. In the first, Ryan starred as Joe Parkson, a disabled veteran with a mysterious and unflagging vendetta against an ex-war buddy, Frank Enley (Van Heflin). As Parkson stalks his prey from New York to Los Angeles, it is revealed that he is intent on killing Enley for a wartime betrayal that resulted in the deaths of most of the men in their prison camp. ("Did he tell you that I'm a cripple because of him?" Parkson asks Enley's wife in one scene. "Did he tell you about the men that are dead because of him? Did he tell you what happened to them before they died?... I was in the hospital, but I didn't go crazy. I kept myself sane. You know how? I kept saying to myself, 'Joe, you're the only one alive that knows what he did. You're the one that's got to find him, Joe.' I kept remembering. I kept thinking back to that prison camp.") Despite urging from his girlfriend, Ann Sturges (Phyllis Thaxter), Parkson refuses to abandon his quest; meanwhile, during a drunken night on the town, Enley hires a local hood known only as Johnny (Berry Kroeger) to kill Parkson. Later realizing what he has done, Enley rushes to warn his former pal, throwing himself in the path of the bullet as Johnny fires at Parkson.

Next, in *Caught*, Ryan played the oddly named Smith Ohrlig, a callous and self-absorbed millionaire who suffers from psychosomatic heart attacks when, according to his psychiatrist, he "doesn't get what he wants." Despite his obvious misogyny, Smith marries a local model, Leonora Eames (Barbara Bel Geddes), but drives her away with his cruel indifference, and she makes a new life for herself as the receptionist for a kind pediatrician, Larry Quinada (James Mason). Lured back to Smith by his assurances that he is a changed man, Leonora soon realizes that her husband views her only as a possession, but after she flees again, she discovers that she is pregnant. Despite her feelings for Quinada, Leonora is determined to attain security for her child and returns to Smith, who keeps her imprisoned in her room and psychologically tortures her throughout her pregnancy. In the film's climax, Leonora rebels against her husband's agonizing treatment and when he experiences a psychosomatic attack, she refuses his pleas for help. Mistakenly con-

vinced that she has killed her husband, Leonora suffers a miscarriage, but the loss leaves her free to leave her husband for good and start anew with Quinada.

In his third consecutive noir, *The Set-Up*, Ryan portrayed one of the best roles of his career, aging boxer Stoker Thompson who was, according to one description, "one punch away from being punch-drunk." Taking place on a single night at the Paradise City boxing arena, *The Set-Up* focuses on Stoker's upcoming match and his confidence that he will win, unaware that his oily manager, Tiny (George Tobias), has accepted a payoff from a local gangster to ensure Stoker's defeat. When it becomes apparent that Stoker is winning the match, Tiny orders him to take a dive, but the boxer refuses and emerges the victor. His triumph is short-lived, however; Stoker is cornered in an alley by the gangster's henchmen, who beat him and break his hand, ensuring an end to his career.

Of Ryan's three films noirs of 1949, the actor's best notices by far were for his performance as the broken down pugilist in *The Set-Up*. He was judged "excellent" by the reviewer for *Motion Picture Herald*; the *New York Times*' critic praised Ryan and his co-stars for their "crisp, believable performances"; and in the *New York Herald Tribune*, Otis L. Guernsey, Jr., wrote that the actor turned in a "first-rate acting job." Ryan himself later counted the film as one of his favorites.

"I like stories about guys who get knocked around because most people do get knocked around," Ryan said once. "It was a downbeat story, not common when the film was released. Most importantly, it was a labor of love for all those working on it."

After such features as *Born To Be Bad* (1950), co-starring Joan Fontaine; *Flying Leathernecks* (1951), a wartime saga with John Wayne; and *Best of the Badmen* (1951), in which Ryan portrayed a post–Civil war cavalry officer, the actor returned yet again to the dark world of the film noir, starring in *The Racket* (1951) and *On Dangerous Ground* (1952). *The Racket* featured Ryan as Nick Scanlon, a ruthless gangster, and Robert Mitchum

as Capt. Tom McQuigg, a no-
nonsense cop who is determined
to bring Scanlon to justice. Scanlon and McQuigg share a long
history of hostility that is best illustrated in a memorable scene
where Scanlon is confronted in
his plush apartment by the police captain: "I pay taxes. I keep
books," Scanlon says contemptuously. "For instance, my taxes
would pay the salaries of 10 guys
like you, McQuigg. Public servants." But after Scanlon engi-
neers a series of killings, including a police informant and a
young officer on the force, his
more business-minded superiors
decide that he is expendable, and
he is shot and killed by a corrupt
state inspector (William Conrad).
Upon its release, *The Racket* garnered mixed reviews from critics,
but Ryan, along with Mitchum,
was praised in *Variety* for his
"forceful, creditable" performance.

In Ryan's next noir, *On Dangerous Ground*, the actor was on
the other side of the law, portraying Sgt. Jim Wilson, a brooding
New York cop characterized by his quick
temper and violent behavior toward criminals. After a particularly vicious attack on a
murder suspect, Wilson is warned by his superior (Ed Begley) that his job is in jeopardy,
to which he sardonically responds: "Okay, so
I get thrown off the force. What kind of job
is this, anyway? Garbage — that's all we handle — garbage!" Instead of dismissal, Wilson
is assigned to a case in upstate New York,
where a young girl has been molested and
killed. Once there, Wilson encounters Mary
Malden (Ida Lupino), a blind woman who
develops a friendship with the officer and
confides that her brother, Danny (Sumner
Williams), is guilty of the crime. Wilson
promises Mary that her brother will not be
harmed, but Danny is accidentally killed while

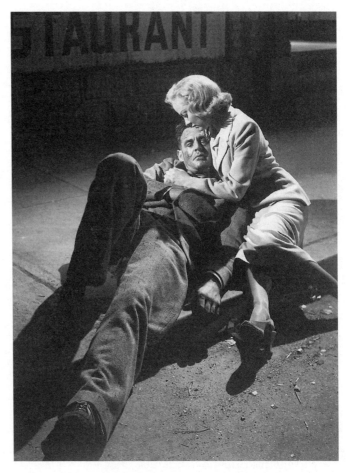

Robert Ryan and Audrey Totter in *The Set-Up* (1949).

trying to escape and Mary angrily rejects
Wilson's efforts to comfort her. He returns to
New York, but he soon realizes the transformation he has experienced because of Mary
and the film's end finds him returning to her.

On Dangerous Ground received a lukewarm reception from both audiences and
critics; the reviewer for *Newsweek* found that
it "never achieves the dramatic intensity to
match its good purposes," and although the
New York Times' Bosley Crowther noted
Ryan's "straight, cold-eyed, stout-muscled"
performance, he panned the film's "obvious
attempt to get something more than sheer
melodrama onto the screen." By now, however, Ryan's attentions were focused beyond
his career as an actor.

With his oldest son, Timothy, ready to

start school, Ryan found the local public school system to be less than adequate, and the private schools either "too snobbish" or "as overcrowded as public schools, scholastically worse off, or both." Attacking the problem with his customary determination, Ryan, his wife, Jessica, and several interested neighbors joined to form their own school. Called Oakwood, the small, private school started in the Ryans' backyard and later moved to an abandoned building with three grades, two teachers, and a handful of students.

"It took three nightmarish years to get over the hurdles," Ryan said in a 1960 interview. "Once, we were on the verge of closing the school. It's something of a miracle we survived."

All three of Ryan's children were educated at The Oakwood School, which eventually erected two new buildings and expanded to include kindergarten through 12th grade. In 2001, the school celebrated its 50-year anniversary and today remains one of the area's most highly regarded institutions.

Ryan's activism spread to other areas as well. In the decades to come, he would become involved in a variety of political and civic pursuits, including actively campaigning for Adlai Stevenson for president; co-founding the Committee for a Sane Nuclear Policy; sitting on the board of the American Civil Liberties Union; serving alongside actors Bill Cosby, Robert Culp, and Sidney Poitier as a member of AHAB (Artists Help All Blacks); and speaking out against the ultra-conservative, anti–Communist John Birch Society (which earned the actor a highly publicized bomb threat in 1962).

"The thing that baffles me about being an actor is the incredulity of some people over an actor taking an active interest in public affairs," Ryan once said. "The actor can, if he wishes, be a solid citizen and a respected member of his community. I hope I am. I try to be.... I think I have a right, as a citizen, to be as active as the butcher, the baker, or that other guy."

On screen, Ryan chalked up two more films noirs, *Clash by Night* (1952), co-starring Barbara Stanwyck and Paul Douglas, and *Beware, My Lovely* (1952), which re-teamed him with Ida Lupino. As Earl Pfeiffer in *Clash by Night*, Ryan played a cynical movie house projectionist who is attracted to Stanwyck's Mae Doyle, the world-weary wife of his best friend, Jerry (Douglas). "Jerry's the salt of the earth," he tells Mae, "but he's not the right seasoning for you.... You're like me — a dash of Tabasco or the meat tastes flat." Soon after giving birth to a baby girl, Mae begins an affair with Earl; when Jerry learns of the relationship, Earl urges his lover to run away with him, even suggesting that she leave her child behind. Ultimately, Mae chooses the simple, hard-working Jerry, and returns to her family.

Ryan's second noir of 1952, *Beware, My Lovely*, begins as an itinerant handyman, Howard Wilkins (Ryan), discovers the dead body of his employer. Unaware that he has killed her, Howard flees town and is hired by boardinghouse operator Helen Graham (Ida Lupino). Convinced that Helen is spying on him, and further provoked by her bratty niece, Howard locks the doors of the house. Holding Helen captive for the next several hours, Howard drifts in and out of reality, telling Helen at one point, "You don't know what it means like I do to find myself in the middle of a room, in the middle of a busy street, or in some house I'm working in ... and wonder where I am, and what I'm doing.... There are days when I pick up the newspaper and I see that somebody's been murdered and I wonder, could I have done that?" At one point, Howard begins to strangle Helen and she faints, awakening to find him preparing to leave, completely unaware of the day's events. The nightmarish afternoon comes to an end when a repairman arrives at the house and the mentally unbalanced Howard peaceably leaves with him.

Ryan earned good reviews for both of his latest two noirs; of his performance in *Clash by Night*, the *New York Times* reviewer wrote that he was "a natural in his depiction of a man groping for a way out of a lonely existence," and Alton Cook opined in the *New York World Telegram-Sun* that the actor "plays the interloping loner with a cunning blend of strength and weakness." And although the critic for the *Saturday Evening Post* found that there were "just too many things happening at the wrong time" in *Beware, My Lovely*, Ryan was applauded by *Commonweal*'s Philip T. Hartung, who noted his "convincingly mad and violent" portrayal, and Paul V. Beckley in the *New York Herald-Tribune*, who judged that "Mr. Ryan's acting alone warrants seeing the film."

Beware, My Lovely marked the end of Ryan's contract with RKO and the actor returned to his roots on the stage the following year, starring in the Phoenix Theatre's New York production of *Coriolanus*, a Shakespearan political tragedy. Although Ryan was praised by veteran theater critic Brooks Atkinson, his performance was panned by most critics. In a particularly savage review, George Freedley of the *New York Morning Telegraph* wrote that the actor was "as much miscast in the title role as would be — let us say — Brandon deWilde, meaning no reflection on that brilliant young actor.... It is a pity that Mr. Ryan's totally inadequate performance robs the play of the majesty which it can achieve if the title role is properly cast."

Ryan's less-than-favorable reviews for *Coriolanus* had little effect on his renewed love for the theater, however. During the rest of his career, he appeared in numerous stage productions, including *Tiger at the Gates* (1957), with John Ireland and Mary Astor; *Antony and Cleopatra* (1960), in which he starred opposite Katharine Hepburn at the American Shakespeare Festival in Stratford, Connecticut; *Othello* (1967) and *Long Day's Journey Into Night* (1967), both at the Nottingham Playhouse in England — where he reportedly became the first American actor to be invited to work with the company; *Our Town* (1968), co-starring Henry Fonda and Estelle Parsons; and the Broadway revival of *The Front Page* (1969), with Peggy Cass and Bert Convy. Ryan also co-founded the Theatre Group at the University of California at Los Angeles in 1959, with John Houseman and Sidney Harmon, and the Plumstead Playhouse Repertory Company with Henry Fonda and Martha Scott in 1968.

"Cutting room scissors have transformed many bad performances into Academy Awards, but there are no scissors on the stage," Ryan once said. "You get out there, stand there all alone, and God help you!— you act or you're done for."

During the remainder of the 1950s, Ryan was seen in some of his favorite feature films, including the poignant drama *About Mrs. Leslie* (1954), co-starring Shirley Booth; *Bad Day at Black Rock* (1955), in which he portrayed a bullying rancher; *God's Little Acre* (1958), earning praise in *Variety* for giving "the performance of his career"; and *Lonelyhearts* (1959), where he played a tortured newspaper editor. He was also seen during this period in his final films noirs, *House of Bamboo* (1955), a color remake of *The Street with No Name* (1948), and *Odds Against Tomorrow* (1959), directed by Robert Wise.

In the first, set in Japan, Ryan played Sandy Dawson, the highly intelligent but sadistic leader of a gang of thieves. Dawson has meticulously selected each of the men in his crew, all of whom have the same background — ex-convicts who were dishonorably discharged from the Army. When a young American, Eddie Spanier (Robert Stack), tries to muscle in on Dawson's "pachinko parlors" racket, Dawson investigates him and hires Eddie for his crew. Eddie quickly gains Dawson's confidence, but after a carefully planned heist goes awry, Dawson learns that his new "number-one man" is actually a military police investigator. Although Dawson sets up a scheme designed to result in Eddie's death at the hands of police, he instead becomes involved in a shootout with authorities at a local amusement park. As he flees, Dawson shoots several officers, but he is finally gunned down by Eddie, his lifeless body dangling from the revolving planet Saturn atop the Matsuma department store. Upon the release of *House of Bamboo*, critics gave more kudos to its exotic setting and color photography than its plot, but Ryan was once again hailed for his performance; in the *Los Angeles Examiner*, Kay Proctor termed the actor "softly charming and deadly as a cobra," and Bosley Crowther wrote in the *New York Times*: "Robert Ryan does a lot to give the fiction a firm and suspenseful quality. His faint hint of psychopathic tension introduces a fine uncertainty, and his skill at subdued underplaying provides a sense of dread."

Ryan's last film noir, *Odds Against Tomorrow*, centers on a carefully designed bank heist, planned by ex-cop David Burke (Ed Begley). To carry out the scheme, Burke enlists the aid of Earl Slater (Ryan), a bigoted ex-convict, and Johnny Ingram (Harry Belafonte), a black singer. The plans for the robbery proceed despite the friction between Slater and Ingram ("You didn't say nothing about the third man being a nigger," Slater tells Burke), but the plot unravels when Burke is wounded exiting the bank. With police in pursuit, Slater and Ingram flee to the top of a pair of oil storage tanks, where they turn on each other. After a shootout, the tanks explode and both men die in the ensuing blaze. The following day, with the charred bodies laid side by side, a fireman asks, "Which is which?" His partner ironically replies, "Take your pick."

Rife with desperate, hopeless, and cynical characters, *Odds Against Tomorrow* was not popular with moviegoers, but it was hailed by critics who noted its gritty realism, and Ryan was universally praised for his performance. The critic for *Time* magazine wrote that the actor was "a menace who can look bullets, and smile sulphuric acid"; the *New York Times'* Bosley Crowther labeled him "brilliant, cold and rasping"; and in *Variety*, the reviewer found that Ryan "makes the flesh crawl as the fanatical bigot."

Ryan's cinematic output during the 1960s decreased dramatically, but he was seen in three of his most popular films during the decade, *The Longest Day* (1962), a star-studded war epic with a cast that included John Wayne, Robert Mitchum, Henry Fonda, and Rod Steiger; *The Dirty Dozen* (1967), the top

moneymaker of the year, featuring Lee Marvin, Charles Bronson, and Ernest Borgnine; and *The Wild Bunch* (1969), Sam Peckinpah's highly acclaimed western about a gang of aging outlaws. Ryan's portrayal of bounty hunter Deke Thornton was labeled by one reviewer as "the performance of his career."

Between film and stage performances, Ryan also made his mark on the small screen. Having debuted on a 1955 episode of *Screen Directors Playhouse*, Ryan went on to guest on such programs as *Alcoa Theatre*, *Goodyear Theatre*, *Zane Grey Theatre*, *Playhouse 90*, and *Kraft Suspense Theatre*. He also starred in the made-for-television production of *The Snows of Kilimanjaro* in 1961 and reprised his stage role of Walter Burns in the television version of *The Front Page* in 1970.

After Ryan's appearance in *The Wild Bunch*, the actor was off screen for a year; in 1970, he was diagnosed with inoperable cancer of the lymph glands and given a 50–50 chance of survival. During his time away from feature films, Ryan underwent extensive cobalt treatments, which appeared to have arrested the disease. But two years later, in the midst of his continuing medical battle, the actor received another blow — his wife, Jessica, underwent tests in May 1972, and was diagnosed with liver cancer. She died 10 days later.

"I feel like a guy who has been slugged to the floor," Ryan said several months later. "Something very big is missing and I don't know what to put in its place."

But the indomitable actor refused to allow his personal tragedies to keep him down. He revealed his plans to spend more time with his children, and he also resumed his acting career, appearing in such feature films as *Lolly Madonna XXX* (1972), starring Rod Steiger and Jeff Bridges, and a television movie, *The Man Without a Country*, with Cliff Robertson and Beau Bridges.

"I have a whole different feeling about what are the good things," Ryan said in a September 1972 interview. "I see trees and flowers and pretty girls, I see beauty that I used to be oblivious to. I see things with a much fresher eye. And actually, life is much better enjoying it day to day."

Sadly, on July 11, 1973, less than a year after Ryan spoke those words, he succumbed to the disease that he had managed to fight for three years. His three final films, *The Outfit* (1973), *Executive Action* (1973), and *The Iceman Cometh* (1973), were released after his death. In the latter, he earned some of the best notices of his career for his portrayal of Larry Slade, a whiskey-soaked patron of the Last Chance Saloon. The reviews also offered the opportunity for critics to extend a final tribute to Robert Ryan as a man and as an actor — one of the most compelling was penned by Jay Cocks in *Time* magazine, who wrote: "The movie most securely belongs to Robert Ryan, and it is an eloquent memorial to his talent. Ryan, who died of cancer in July, was ailing while he was making *Iceman*. In the circumstances, it would be easy to sentimentalize his performance. But such a measure would diminish its greatness. With the kind of power and intensity that is seldom risked, much less realized, it has it own pride and stature."

Film Noir Filmography

Crossfire. Director: Edward Dmytryk. Producer: Adrian Scott. Running time: 85 minutes. Released by RKO, July 22, 1947. Cast: Robert Young, Robert Mitchum, Robert Ryan, Gloria Grahame, Paul Kelly, Sam Levene, Jacqueline White, Steve Brodie, George Cooper, Richard Benedict, Richard Powers, William Phipps, Lex Barker, Marlo Dwyer. Awards: Academy Award nominations for Best Picture, Best Director (Edward Dmytryk), Best Supporting Actor (Robert Ryan), Best Supporting Actress (Gloria Grahame), Best Screenplay (John Paxton).

Berlin Express. Director: Jacques Tourneur. Producer: Bert Granet. Running time: 86 minutes. Released by RKO, May 1, 1948. Cast: Merle Oberon, Robert Ryan, Charles Korvin, Paul Lukas, Robert Coote, Reinhold Schunzel, Roman Toporow, Peter Von Zerneck, Otto Waldis, Fritz Kortner, Michael Harvey, Richard Powers, Charles McGraw.

Act of Violence. Director: Fred Zinnemann. Producer: William H. Wright. Running time: 81 minutes. Released by MGM, January 23, 1949. Cast: Van Heflin, Robert Ryan, Janet Leigh, Mary Astor, Phyllis Thaxter, Berry Kroeger, Nicholas Joy, Harry Antrim, Connie Gilchrist, Will Wright.

Caught. Director: Max Ophuls. Producer: Wolfgang Reinhardt. Running time: 88 minutes. Released by MGM-Enterprise, February 17, 1949. Cast: James Mason, Barbara Bel Geddes, Robert Ryan, Ruth Brady, Curt Bois, Frank Ferguson, Natalie Schaefer, Art Smith, Sonia Darrin, Bernadene Hayes, Ann Morrison, Wilton Graff, Jim Hawkins, Vicki Raw Stiener.

The Set-Up. Director: Robert Wise. Producer: Richard Goldstone. Running time: 72 minutes. Released by RKO, March 29, 1949. Cast: Robert Ryan, Audrey Totter, George Tobias, Alan Baxter, Wallace Ford, Percy Helton, Hal Fieberling, Darryl Hickman, Kenny O'Morrison, James Edwards, David Clarke, Phillip Pine, Edwin Max.

The Racket. Director: John Cromwell. Producer: Edmund Grainger. Running time: 88 minutes. Released by RKO, December 12, 1951. Cast: Robert Mitchum, Lizabeth Scott, Robert Ryan, William Talman, Ray Collins, Joyce MacKenzie, Robert Hutton, Virginia Huston, William Conrad, Walter Sande, Les Tremayne, Don Porter, Walter Baldwin, Brett King, Richard Karlan, Tito Vuolo.

On Dangerous Ground. Director: Nicholas Ray. Producer: John Houseman. Running time: 82 minutes. Released by RKO, February 12, 1952. Cast: Ida Lupino, Robert Ryan, Ward Bond, Charles Kemper, Anthony Ross, Ed Begley, Ian Wolfe, Sumner Williams, Gus Schilling, Frank Ferguson, Cleo Moore, Olive Carey, Richard Irving, Pat Prest.

Clash by Night. Director: Fritz Lang. Producer: Harriet Parsons. Running time: 104 minutes. Released by RKO, June 18, 1952. Cast: Barbara Stanwyck, Paul Douglas, Robert Ryan, Marilyn Monroe, J. Carroll Naish, Keith Andes, Silvio Minciotti.

Beware, My Lovely. Director: Harry Horner. Producer: Collier Young. Running time: 76 minutes. Released by RKO, August 7, 1952. Cast: Ida Lupino, Robert Ryan, Taylor Holmes, Barbara Whiting, James Williams, O.Z. Whitehead, Dee Pollack.

House of Bamboo. Director: Samuel Fuller. Producer: Buddy Adler. Running time: 105 minutes. Released by 20th Century-Fox, July 1, 1955. Cast: Robert Ryan, Robert Stack, Shirley Yamaguchi, Cameron Mitchell, Brad Dexter, Sessue Hayakawa, Biff Elliot, Sandro Giglio, Elko Hanabusa, Harry Carey, Peter Gray, Robert Quarry, DeForest Kelley, John Doucette.

Odds Against Tomorrow. Director and Producer: Robert Wise. Running time: 96 minutes.

Released by United Artists, October 15, 1959. Cast: Harry Belafonte, Robert Ryan, Gloria Grahame, Shelley Winters, Ed Begley, Will Kuluva, Mae Barnes, Carmen DeLavallade, Richard Bright, Lou Gallo, Fred J. Scollay, Lois Thorne.

References

"Actor Robert Ryan, 60, Cancer Victim." *Los Angeles Herald-Examiner*, July 11, 1973.
"Actor Threatened Over Birch Show." *New York World-Telegraph and Sun*, February 5, 1962.
"A Film Hero Fights for Better Schools." *Hollywood Citizen-News*, August 7, 1960.
"Amateur Critics Lift Ryan to Stardom with 'Rave Cards.'" *New York Herald Tribune*, May 28, 1944.
Bacon, James. "Quiet Man." *Newark Evening News*, April 23, 1961.
Barnes, Aleene. "Ryan Avoids Rut to Stay in Groove." *Los Angeles Times*, March 20, 1960.
Berg, Louis. "Gentle Irishman." *Los Angeles Times, This Week Magazine*, February 4, 1951.
Biography of Robert Ryan. RKO Radio Pictures, November 18, 1946.
Bosworth, Patricia. "Robert Ryan, in Search of Action." *The New York Times*, June 1, 1969.
Cutts, John. "Robert Ryan: Villain Extraordinary." *Films and Filming*, July 1961.
Daniel, Jesse. "Big and Burly." *The Milwaukee Journal*, November 14, 1943.
Gratz, Roberta Brandes. "Robert Ryan: Softhearted Villain." *New York Post*, January 27, 1968.
Kennedy, Harold J. "Robert Ryan 1909–73." *The New York Times*, July 22, 1973.
MacPherson, Virginia. "Ryan Breaks H'Wood Tradition." *New York Morning Telegraph*, January 2, 1951.

Manners, Dorothy. "Ryan's Courage Faces Sorrow." *Los Angeles Herald-Examiner*, July 24, 1972.
McManus, Margaret. "Robert Ryan Idle, Happy." *Newark Evening News*, August 4, 1963.
Meagher, Ed. "Robert Ryan Dies of Cancer at 63." *Los Angeles Times*, July 12, 1973.
Mishkin, Leo. "Name Droppers Bemuse Ryan." *New York Morning Telegraph*, February 25, 1967.
Moss, Morton. "Buoyancy and Bounce." *Los Angeles Herald-Examiner*, January 29, 1970.
Murphy, Mary. "Robert Ryan — A New Life on Borrowed Time." *Los Angeles Times*, September 5, 1972.
"One Minute Interviews." *Hollywood Citizen-News*, November 5, 1953.
"Radio Station, Actor's Home Guarded After Bomb Threat." *Los Angeles Times*, February 6, 1962.
"Robert Ryan, 59, Dies of Cancer in N.Y. Hospital." *Variety*, July 12, 1973.
"Robert Ryan — Hero and 'Heel.'" *Coronet*, January 1960.
"Robert Ryans Greet New Son's Arrival." *Los Angeles Times*, March 11, 1948.
Schumach, Murray. "Art's Call Heard by Robert Ryan." *The New York Times*, February 5, 1960.
Scott, John L. "Good or Bad; Robert Ryan Plays Either." *Los Angeles Times*, August 10, 1947.
_____. "Ryan Lifts Self by His 'Heels.'" *Los Angeles Times*, circa 1960.
Scott, Vernon. "Ryan Works Again Despite Cancer." *Los Angeles Herald-Examiner*, August 27, 1972.
Thomas, Bob. "Tots' School Begun by Film Star Thrives." *Los Angeles Mirror-News*, July 24, 1958.
Whitman, Alden. "Robert Ryan, Actor, Dies at 63." *The New York Times*, July 12, 1973.
Zunser, Jesse. "Stratford: Ryan, Hepburn, *et al.*" *Cue*, July 30, 1960.

ZACHARY SCOTT

"Face it — if you're smart enough, you can get just about anything you want. If you can't get it one way, you can get it another." — Zachary Scott in *Danger Signal* (1945)

Smooth, suave, and sophisticated, Zachary Scott made his mark in Hollywood as "the heel with charm." In the vast majority of his nearly 40 feature films, Scott was cast as the villain who, more often than not, used his magnetic personal appeal to achieve his desired ends. Although the actor once claimed to enjoy such roles ("provided that it is vil-lainy with charm, evil with originality, and murder with music"), their frequency ultimately served to stagnate his once-promising career. As a result, while Scott displayed a genuine acting talent in a number of films, most notably in a rare departure from perfidy in *The Southerner* (1945), he is best known for his work as a cad, and played this role to the hilt in his four films noirs: *The Mask of Dimitrios* (1944), *Mildred Pierce* (1945), *Danger Signal* (1945), and *Guilty Bystander* (1950).

Entering the world with the proverbial silver spoon in his mouth, Zachary Thomson Scott, Jr., was born in Austin, Texas, on February 24, 1914, the youngest of three children and the only boy. According to the actor's studio biography, Scott got his first taste of performing at the age of three, while his prominent surgeon father was stationed during World War I in Biloxi, Mississippi. In an effort to amuse recovering soldiers, Dr. Scott invited his son to participate in an entertainment program; dressed in a sailor suit for the occasion, Scott reportedly recalled that "the sound of the applause was sweet in his ears." Another source, however, states that Scott made his debut at four years old, performing an impersonation of Charlie Chaplin at a local talent show. His early "stage work" notwithstanding, Scott was expected to follow in his father's footsteps, and after graduating from high school in 1931, he enrolled as a medical student at the University of Texas. But before long, Scott determined that the life of a doctor was not for him.

"I realized I was not emotionally qualified to do the things a doctor has to do," Scott said once. "I couldn't bear to see people burdened with anxiety or to see anyone die."

Instead, having participated in several high school drama productions, and serving in the Curtain Club at the University of Texas, Scott set his sights on an acting career. After his third year of college, he abruptly quit school and signed on as a cabin boy on a cotton freighter bound for England, where he wasted no time landing a role in his first professional stage production, *The Outsider*. To explain his southern accent, Scott claimed that he hailed from Australia.

During the next year and a half, Scott remained in London, appearing in more than 20 plays. In 1935, he returned to the United States and, on his 21st birthday, married his college sweetheart, aspiring actress Elaine Anderson. The couple spent six months pounding the boards in New York, but when

their efforts proved fruitless, they returned to Texas where their daughter, Waverly, was born later in the year. To support his small family, Scott landed a job as the director of the Austin Little Theater and he and his wife returned to college, majoring in theater arts. Between schooling and directing the little theater, Scott found time to earn extra money by working for an oil refinery and teaching advanced play-reading at the local St. Mary's Academy.

In Scott's last year of college, he got his first big break when he was introduced to stage stars Alfred Lunt and Lynn Fontanne. Impressed by glowing reports of Scott, the famed couple wrote letters of recommendation on his behalf to John Haggott and Lawrence Langner, of the Theatre Guild and the Westport Country Playhouse. After graduation, Scott packed up his family and headed for New York, and a short time later, he signed with the Westport Playhouse, appearing in such productions as *Anna Christie* and *Easy Virtue*. Three years later, Scott landed a role in his first Broadway production, *Circle of Chalk*, followed by *The Damask Cheek*, *The Rock*, and *Those Endearing Young Charms*. While appearing as a devil-may-care aviator in the latter play, Scott caught the attention of Warner Bros. studio head Jack Warner, who reportedly offered the actor a contract on the spot.

Scott's first film assignment at Warners also marked his entry into the world of film noir, playing the title role in *The Mask of Dimitrios* (1944). As this atmospheric feature begins, the body of a man identified as notorious criminal Dimitrios Makropoulos washes up on the shores of Istanbul. A local novelist, Cornelius Leyden (Peter Lorre), becomes intrigued with the man described by one character as "ruthless and primitive," and tracks down a series of offbeat characters who help him piece together Dimitrios' past. Among those Leyden encounters is a mysterious man named Mr. Peters (Sydney Greenstreet), who spent time in prison after being double-crossed by Dimitrios in connection with a jewel-smuggling ring. Mr. Peters reveals that Dimitrios faked his own death and is now working in a lucrative position in the financial world — he also divulges his intent to blackmail his nemesis for one million francs. Although Dimitrios delivers the money as directed, he shoots Peters, but during a struggle Peters manages to retrieve his gun and kill Dimitrios. ("I don't want it now. I don't want it somehow," Peters says of the money. "I've done what I had to do.")

Although *The Mask of Dimitrios* earned mixed reviews from critics, Scott was hailed for his performance; one of his best notices came from the normally acerbic *New York Times* reviewer Bosley Crowther, who wrote: "As the object of everyone's attention, Zachary Scott ... presents the rascally Dimitrios as a blue-steel American gangster type." Scott followed this triumphant debut by joining a long line of Warner Bros. stars for *Hollywood Canteen* (1944), the studio's salute to the war effort, and was next cast in the lead role in *Escape in the Desert* (1945), a remake of *The Petrified Forest* (1936), which starred Bette Davis and Leslie Howard. After several months of shooting, however, the studio determined that Scott was miscast, and replaced him with Philip Dorn. This disappointing ac-

tion would turn out to be a blessing in disguise when the actor was, instead, cast in his second film noir, *Mildred Pierce* (1945).

An outstanding example from the noir era, this feature centers on the title character (played by Joan Crawford in an Academy Award–winning performance), and her relationships with her snooty daughter, Veda (Ann Blyth); her stubborn but loyal ex-husband, Bert (Bruce Bennett); and her second spouse, the charming, dastardly Monte Beragon (Scott). As the film begins, a series of gunshots ring out and Monte falls dead, muttering only a single word, "Mildred." The remainder of the feature involves a series of flashbacks revealing the events that led to Monte's murder, including Mildred's rise from abandoned housewife to wealthy businesswoman, her marriage to Monte as part of her ongoing obsession with pleasing her daughter, and her shocking discovery that Monte and Veda are lovers. Although Mildred confesses to Monte's murder, however, it is ultimately revealed that Veda is the killer and Mildred reunites with Bert as the credits roll.

As the oily Monte Beragon, Scott played a character oozing with a surface charm that masked a shallow, mean-spirited demeanor. Beragon's true colors were unmistakably revealed, however, in a well-done scene in which he is dumped by Mildred: "I take money from you, Mildred — but not enough to make me like kitchens or cooks. They smell of grease," Monte says nastily. "I always knew that someday we'd come to this particular moment in the scheme of things. You want Veda, and your business, and a nice, quiet life, and the price of all that is me. You can go back to making your pies now, Mildred. We're through." In a cast replete with superb performances, Scott was a standout, and was hailed by reviewers, including *Variety*'s critic, who praised his "talented performance," and the *Hollywood Review* critic, who raved: "Zachary Scott is allowed to make of his assignment one of his most distinguished performances, a scoundrel so polished in his interpretation that he makes you feel pity for him. His is great acting."

Ann Blyth with Zachary Scott and Joan Crawford in *Mildred Pierce* (1945).

After his successful performance in *Mildred Pierce*, Scott starred in one of the best films of his career, *The Southerner* (1945), portraying a struggling farmer in the south. Director Jean Renoir later explained that he cast Scott in the role because, as a native of the south, the actor "contributed a kind of exterior accuracy to the film that I found to be extremely valuable." Although some reviewers were put off by the film's unrelenting realism, Scott was singled out in several publications, including the *New York Times*, whose reviewer applauded his "restrained and powerful" performance.

Next, Scott returned to his dastardly ways in his third film noir, *Danger Signal* (1945). The opening of this feature shows Scott's character, Ronald Mason, escaping from a New York apartment where a housewife lies dead of an apparent suicide. Making his way to Los Angeles, Mason becomes involved with stenographer Hilda Fenchurch (Faye Emerson), but swiftly transfers his affections to her younger sister, Anne (Mona Freeman), when he learns that the girl will inherit a significant trust fund when she marries. When she learns of his duplicity, Hilda plans an intricate scheme to poison Mason, telling him during an intimate dinner that he will be dead within the hour. (For once, Mason's confident façade is shattered as he begs Hilda to help him: "You wouldn't do such a thing, you wouldn't. You wouldn't dare," he says. "Hilda, tell me you're joking.") As it turns out, Hilda is unable to carry out the deed, but Mason meets an unceremonious end a short time later — tracked down by the husband of the New York housewife he killed, Mason runs from the man, trips over a tree root, and falls over a cliff to his death.

Although *Danger Signal* was a disappointment at the box office, Scott was once again singled out for praise; the reviewer for *Independent* wrote that his role was "well-played," and in *Motion Picture Herald*, the critic wrote: "Zachary Scott portrays with skill and a fine sense of timing the polished man of letters whose special talent is persuading his women to write suicide notes before he arranges their demise." However, with few exceptions, Scott's best films were now behind him. During the remainder of the decade, he was cast in a series of mostly forgettable features, including *Her Kind of Man* (1946), portraying what one reviewer called "another of those despicable weasel-like creatures"; *Stallion Road* (1947), in which he played a successful novelist; *Ruthless* (1948), where he was seen as an unscrupulous financier; and *Whiplash* (1948), in which he starred as the cruel, wheelchair-bound husband of Alexis Smith. He fared better, however, with *Cass Timberlane* (1947), where he was third billed as a cad who tries to steal the affections of Lana Turner from her wholesome spouse, played by Spencer Tracy; and *Flamingo Road* (1949), a tawdry Joan Crawford starrer that was a hit with moviegoers and was hailed in *Variety* as "loaded with heartbreak, romance, and stinging violence."

While Scott struggled with his on-screen career, his life away from the cameras appeared to be on a downward slide as well. In 1949, he nearly lost his life while sailing in a rubber raft on the Pacific Ocean with friend and fellow actor John Emery. When a riptide rocked the boat, Scott was thrown overboard struck his head on a rock, and was knocked unconscious. Emery rescued his drowning friend and rushed him to the hospital. Later that year, after enduring countless rumors about the state of his marriage, Scott was sued for divorce by his wife of 14 years, who charged the actor with mental cruelty. During her court appearance, Elaine Scott testified that on one occasion, while entertaining friends, Scott entered the house and threw an ashtray at the wall, adding that it was embarrassing to her and to her guests. Although

some speculated that the rift between the couple was due in part to Elaine's resentment over abandoning her budding acting career, another, more prominent rumor claimed that Elaine was having an affair with writer John Steinbeck. (The latter theory appeared to have more than a grain of validity; a year after her divorce was granted, Elaine married the writer, with whom she remained until his death in 1968.)

Professionally, Scott experienced the busiest year of his film career in 1950, appearing in a total of five features, including *Born to Be Bad*, a mediocre drama that failed to attract audiences despite direction from Nicholas Ray and a cast that included Robert Ryan and Joan Fontaine; *Shadow on the Wall*, which focused on a small child who witnesses the murder of her mother; and *Guilty Bystander*, his final film noir.

In this well-done feature, Scott was teamed for the fourth time with Faye Emerson, playing Max Thursday, an alcoholic ex-cop who is forced to rouse himself from his constant liquor-induced haze when his young son is kidnapped. (His drinking problem continues to plague Thursday, however — in one scene, he tells ex-wife, Georgia [Emerson], "All right, so I got drunk. What do you want me to do? Do you want me to stand in the corner and write, 'I won't do it again' a hundred times?") Thursday encounters a number of quirky characters during his desperate search for his son, including a mysterious doctor (Jed Prouty) and a gang of jewel smugglers but, ultimately, the winding trail of clues leads the former detective to the tawdry riverfront hotel that he calls home, where he learns that the kidnapper is none other than the establishment's proprietor, Smitty (Mary Boland).

Upon its release, *Guilty Bystander* received only lukewarm reviews, with Bosley Crowther writing in the *New York Times*: "Mind you, we aren't proclaiming *Guilty Bystander* much of a film. But for those who want cheap melodrama, it has its considerable points." Crowther viewed Scott's performance with more favor, however, saying he "plays the agonized pursuer with genuine intensity." Scott was also singled out in *Variety*, whose critic found that he "gets over the role of the drunken ex-cop capably." After this feature, Scott was seen in *Let's Make it Legal* (1951), a weak comedy co-starring Claudette Colbert; *The Secret of Convict Lake* (1951), a box office disappointment featuring Glenn Ford and Gene Tierney; and *Lightning Strikes Twice* (1951), the last film under his Warner Bros. contract.

But the actor was in the news for more than his cinematic contributions that year. While vacationing in Hawaii in July 1951, he was arrested for drunk and disorderly conduct for dancing the hula barefoot on the sidewalk outside a bar. According to the arresting officer, Scott was "belligerent" and it "took two men to arrest him." Despite this incident, the actor's personal life took an upward turn the following year when he married wife number two, actress Ruth Ford. The two went on to appear in several productions together, and Scott later legally adopted Ford's daughter, Shelley. But a few months after the wedding, in November 1952, Scott was in the headlines again; this time, he was arrested in a bar in New Orleans, Louisiana, after the actor, his wife, and several friends were seen drinking with two black patrons and charged with violating the state's segregation laws. At the night court hearing on the incident, Scott testified that he had visited the bar to find a black harmonica player by the name of "Papa" Lightfoot, and had been invited by two black customers to join them for a drink.

"[I went] to scout talent for USO shows which I and others in my profession are asked to take to the troops overseas. I'm not asked at such times to perform only for white troops or I would not go," Scott said. "I was proud to drink with them, but, of course, I would not have done so had I known it was against the law."

The charges against Scott and the others were dropped, but the presiding judge, Edwin A. Babylon, admonished them: "When you're in the South, if you do go into these kind of places, go just as spectators and don't drink."

With his run-ins with the law behind him, Scott began to refocus on his professional career. He was seen on the small screen in numerous programs throughout the decade, including *Science Fiction Theater*, *Robert Montgomery Presents*, *The United States Steel Hour*, *Viceroy Star Theater*, *General Electric Summer Originals*, and *Lux Video Theater*, on which he recreated his role as Monte Beragon in an abridged version of *Mildred Pierce*. In addition to his television work, Scott returned to the stage for a variety of productions during the 1950s, such as *Bell, Book and Candle* with Joan Bennett, *The Moon is Blue*, *Blind Alley*, *Twelfth Night*, *The Umbrella*, the London production of *Subway in the Sky*, *Requiem for a Nun* (playing opposite his wife), and *The King and I* (for which he was praised for performing his role with "assurance and individuality"). He was also seen in such feature films as *Appointment in Honduras* (1953), directed by Jacques Tourneur; *Shotgun* (1955), a routine oater starring Sterling Hayden and Yvonne DeCarlo; *Counterfeit Plan* (1957), in which he portrayed an escaped murderer; and *Violent Stranger* (1957), a crime thriller with Faith Domergue. The producer of the latter two films, Richard Gordon, later recalled with amusement his financial dealings with the actor, calling him "a very shrewd businessman."

"For *Violent Stranger*, Zach demanded a higher fee [than he did for *Counterfeit Plan*], which was not a significant amount, but his agent was not willing to negotiate the figure," Gordon told writer Dan Van Neste in a 1998 interview for *Classic Images* magazine. "I remember asking Zach after the contract was signed why he gave me such a rough time on this point. He laughed and said, 'I never work for the same person twice for the same price.'"

With the onset of the 1960s, Scott continued dividing his talents between the small screen and feature films, with appearances on such television series as *Alfred Hitchcock Presents* and *The Rogues*; made-for-television movies including *The Scarlet Pimpernel* (1960) and *Jane Eyre* (1961); and big screen features including *Natchez Trace* (1960), a low-budget, pre–Civil war western; and *La Joven* (1960), also known as *The Young One*, in which he played a bigoted game warden. Scott spoke highly of the latter film after its release, calling it "one of the two best pictures I've made," but it was a box-office disaster, hampered by poor production values and a convoluted script.

After a two-year absence, Scott was back on the big screen in 1962 for *It's Only Money* (1962), a typically silly Jerry Lewis comedy, and later starred with Mike Connors and Dina Merrill in the television movie, *The Expendables*. The following year, he starred in the stage production of *Rainy Night in Newark*, whose cast included newcomers Gene Hackman and Dody Goodman, followed by *Any Wednesday*, in which he starred opposite his wife, and a summer 1964 tour of *Mary, Mary*. During the run of the latter production, however, Scott began to complain of feeling ill. A visit to a New York hospital revealed that the actor was suffering from a malignant brain tumor. He began radiation treatments and underwent brain surgery in July 1965, but the operation revealed that the cancer had progressed too far.

In August 1965, Scott and his wife returned to his mother's home in Austin, Texas, and on October 3, 1965, he died there, at age 51. (Several years after his death, in 1971, the Zachary Scott Theatre opened in Austin; today, the center presents Broadway and off–Broadway productions, and also offers a variety of arts-related activities, including a performing arts school and a professional theater for youth. The actor continued to be remembered by his home state more than two decades after his death when, in 1988, a chair in drama was established at the University of Texas honoring Scott and his family.)

Although Zachary Scott once bemoaned the spate of villainous roles that served as the foundation and structure of his film career, it cannot be denied that when it came to sophisticated scoundrels and polished cads, he was one of the screen's best. When he was able to break out of the "heavy" mold, in such

films as *The Southerner*, and plays including *The King and I* and *Bell, Book and Candle*, the actor proved that he could offer much more. Still, in roles such as the murderous Dimitrios Makropoulos or *Mildred Pierce*'s despicable Monte Beragon, Scott left us with meaty performances that are unforgettable.

Film Noir Filmography

The Mask of Dimitrios. Director: Jean Negulesco. Producer: Henry Blanke. Running time: 95 minutes. Released by Warner Bros., June 23, 1944. Cast: Sydney Greenstreet, Zachary Scott, Faye Emerson, Peter Lorre, Victor Francen, Steven Geray, Florence Bates, Eduardo Ciannelli, Kurt Katch, Marjorie Hoshelle, Georges Metaxa, John Abbott, Monte Blue, David Hoffman.

Mildred Pierce. Director: Michael Curtiz. Producer: Jerry Wald. Running time: 113 minutes. Released by Warner Bros., September 28, 1945. Cast: Joan Crawford, Jack Carson, Zachary Scott, Eve Arden, Ann Blyth, Bruce Bennett, Lee Patrick, Moroni Olson, Jo Ann Marlowe, Barbara Brown, Charles Trowbridge, John Compton, Butterfly McQueen. Awards: Academy Award for Best Actress (Joan Crawford). Academy Award nominations for Best Picture, Best Supporting Actress (Ann Blyth), Best Supporting Actress (Eve Arden), Best Black and White Cinematography (Ernest Haller), Best Screenplay (Ranald MacDougall).

Danger Signal. Director: Robert Florey. Producer: William Jacobs. Running time: 78 minutes. Released by Warner Bros., November 14, 1945. Cast: Faye Emerson, Zachary Scott, Dick Erdman, Rosemary DeCamp, Bruce Bennett, Mona Freeman, John Ridgely, Mary Servoss, Joyce Compton, Virginia Sale.

Guilty Bystander. Director: Joseph Lerner. Producer: Rex Carlton. Running time: 92 minutes. Released by Film Classics, April 21, 1950. Cast: Zachary Scott, Faye Emerson, Mary Boland, Sam Levene, J. Edward Bromberg, Kay Medford, Jed Prouty, Harry Landers, Dennis Harrison, Elliot Sullivan, Garney Wilson, Ray Julian.

References

"Actor Scott Has Grave Brain Tumor." *Hollywood Citizen-News*, September 29, 1965.

Biography of Zachary Scott. 20th Century-Fox, circa 1951.

Biography of Zachary Scott. Warner Bros. Studios, circa 1945.

Cassa, Anthony. "Zachary Scott: Superior Scoundrel." *Hollywood Studio Magazine*, September 1982.

Chapman, John. "'King and I' Superb Revival at City Center." *New York Daily News*, April 20, 1956.

Cohn, Herbert. "Zachary Scott, a Rising Movie Idol, Might Be a Challenge to Errol Flynn." *Brooklyn Daily Eagle*, February 13, 1946.

French, Betty. "Roaring '30s Revived at Strand." *Akron Beacon Journal*, June 20, 1946.

Hall, Prunella. "Screen Gossip." *Boston Post*, August 1, 1945.

"Hula Jails Zachary Scott." Publication Unsourced, July 12, 1951.

Little, Stuart W. "Requiem for Nun Will Go on National Tour Next Fall." *New York Herald Tribune*, February 23, 1959.

Morehouse, Ward. "Scott Back in Character Role." *Long Island Star-Journal*, January 28, 1959.

"Not Every Man Can Get Away with Wearing ONE Earring." *New York Inquirer*, April 17, 1955.

Obituary. *Variety*, October 6, 1965.

Parsons, Louella O. "Zachary Scott Weds Sunday." *Los Angeles Examiner*, June 25, 1952.

"Scott on Subway Circuit." *New York Herald Tribune*, June 27, 1950.

"Scott, 10 Others Freed in Court." Publication Unsourced, circa November 1952.

Smith, Bea. "Bow to Director." *Newark Evening Post*, February 20, 1961.

Van Neste, Dan. "Zachary Scott: Scoundrel with Style." *Classic Images*, March 1998.

"Zachary Scott Divorced." *New York Times*, December 2, 1949.

"Zachary Scott, Others, Freed of Race Charges." Publication Unsourced, circa November 1952.

"Zachary Scott, Movie Tough Guy, Dies at 51." Publication Unsourced, October 4, 1965.

"Zachary Scott Signed for Starring Role in a Rainy Day in Newark." Samuel Lurie and Associates Public Relations, September 4, 1963.

"Zachary Scott, Star, Dies at 51." *Hollywood Citizen-News*, October 4, 1965.

"Zachary Scott Sued for Divorce." *New York Herald Tribune*, November 8, 1949.

"Zachary Scott Thinks His New Film Is Great." *New York World-Telegram and Sun*, January 18, 1961.

"Zachary Scott, Wife, Taken in Tavern Raid." Publication Unsourced, November 17, 1952.

"Zach Scott Dies at 51." *Variety*, October 4, 1965.

EVERETT SLOANE

"I've been gone over by experts, but you're the best. What's your name? I think I can use a guy like you. Help me up. I'll make you a rich man."—Everett Sloane in *The Enforcer* (1951)

One of the original members of Orson Welles' Mercury Theater troupe, Everett Sloane was never a renowned movie star, but he was arguably one of the finest character actors of his time. Intellectually and artistically impatient, often outspoken, and highly demanding of himself as well as others, Sloane not only tackled the silver screen, but also exhibited his considerable talents on countless productions on television, stage, and the radio. Although his film career spanned only 23 years and produced fewer than 30 features, he was a standout in such cinematic gems as *Citizen Kane* (1941) and *The Men* (1950), and was both effective and memorable in his roles in his four films from the noir era: *Journey Into Fear* (1942), *The Lady from Shanghai*

(1948), *The Enforcer* (1951), and *The Big Knife* (1955).

Sloane was born with what he termed "the urge to act." As for his more practical statistics, he entered the world on October 1, 1909, in New York City, the only child of wealthy cotton broker Nathaniel Sloane and his native Bostonian wife, Rose. His acting urge was first manifested at the age of seven, when he portrayed Puck in a production of *A Midsummer Night's Dream* at P.S. 46 in Manhattan. Throughout the rest of his grammar school experience, Sloane insisted to his friends that he would become an actor, and spent almost every Saturday at the local movie theater.

After graduating from Townsend Harris

Hall High School in New York, Sloane enrolled at the University of Pennsylvania in Philadelphia, where he signed up for the school's dramatic club. His drama club activities brought him into contact with Jasper Deeter, who operated the well-known Hedgerow Theatre in nearby Moylan, Pennsylvania, and in 1927, Sloane quit college to play a season of repertory with Deeter's company. The following year, he made his professional debut at the Cherry Lane Theatre in Greenwich Village. Sloane later admitted that he'd forgotten the name of the play, but did recall that "I wore an Inverness cape and collapsible opera hat." His performance was singled out by at least one critic, who wrote that Sloane "looked remarkably like Harpo Marx and almost as funny."

Soon after this dismal assessment, Sloane went to work as a stockbroker's runner in a New York brokerage house, at a salary of $17 a week. Within a year, he was earning $140 weekly as assistant to the managing partner. But when the stock market crash of 1929 caused his salary to be cut in half, Sloane returned to the acting profession to make ends meet, landing a small role on a local radio show, *Impossible Detective Mysteries*. He was subsequently hired for a second radio program, *40 Fathom Trawler*, and when the offers increased, Sloane quit his Wall Street job to concentrate solely on his radio engagements. Before long, he was heard on a variety of programs, including *Buck Rogers, Crime Doctor, Pretty Kitty Kelly, The Goldbergs,* and *The Shadow*, on which he played for eight years.

Sloane's personal life was on the upswing as well. In the early 1930s, he met Luba "Lovey" Herman, a student at the American Academy of Dramatic Arts. Regarding Luba's budding acting career, Sloane later told a *New York Times* reporter, "I talked her out of it in favor of marriage." The two were married in 1933, and would have two children, Nathaniel, born May 30, 1937, and Ericka, born January 21, 1944. Sloane and Luba would remain married until the actor's death in 1965.

Meanwhile, Sloane was gradually branching out from his successful radio career. In 1935, he made his Broadway debut in *Boy Meets Girl*, which ran at the Cort Theatre in New York for nearly 700 performances. He also toured with *Three Men on a Horse* in 1937, and appeared in 1938 at the Biltmore Theatre in New York in *All That Glitters*.

By now, Sloane's radio connections had led him to an association with "boy wonder" Orson Welles. "He liked me. I liked him. I was always making him laugh," Sloane told a *TV Guide* reporter in 1972. In the summer of 1938 Sloane joined Welles' troupe of radio performers, The Mercury Players, becoming a regular on the Welles-CBS radio program *Mercury Theater on the Air*. "It was one of the most exciting periods of my life," Sloane recalled. In October of that same year, Sloane was one of the cast members of Welles' famed "War of the Worlds" broadcast, which spooked radio audiences nationwide with its realistic dramatization of an invasion from Mars.

The tremendous attention fostered by the "War of the Worlds" program led to an offer by RKO Pictures for Welles to make his first film. Along with fellow Mercury Theatre performers Joseph Cotten, Ray Collins, George Coulouris, and Agnes Moorehead, Sloane was featured in Welles' 1941 cinematic masterpiece, *Citizen Kane*. "Something caught fire," Sloane said years later. "There has been nothing like it before or since."

Lauded by critics for his "splendid" performance as the title character's faithful manager, Sloane next appeared in another Welles' production, *Journey Into Fear* (1942), which marked his entry into the film noir era. This atmospheric film, which also featured Mercury Theatre regulars Cotten and Moorehead, tells the story of a munitions expert, Howard Graham (Cotten), who is caught in the middle of a Nazi conspiracy. As Kopeikin, the mysterious representative of Graham's company in Turkey (it is Kopeikin who takes Graham to an Istanbul nightclub, where he barely escapes being felled by an assassin's bullet), Sloane was overlooked in most reviews, but the film earned praise as "a terse invitation to heart failure by fright."

After *Journey Into Fear,* Sloane was absent from the screen for the next six years. Instead, he returned to Broadway for well-received performances in an adaptation of Richard Wright's *Native Son,* presented by Welles and Mercury Theatre co-founder John Houseman, and *Men in Shadow,* an English melodrama. During this period, he was also regularly appearing on several radio programs, including *You Can't Take it With You, Ellery Queen, Cavalcade of America,* and *The March of Time.* Of his prolific broadcasting career, the actor once estimated that, in his first 15 years in radio, he appeared in an average of 20 programs a week, playing approximately 15,000 roles. Having made an impression in film and theater, as well as radio, Sloane offered this assessment of the three media: "As a business proposition, radio is ... sound and occasionally satisfying," he told a *Newsweek* reporter in 1944. "The theater is ego-satisfying but otherwise unreliable; the movies are ... a lump of money."

Sloane landed one of his greatest roles in 1944, when he starred in the Broadway production of *A Bell for Adano,* which ran for 304 performances. Sloane later cited the role of the play's cynical sergeant as one of his favorites: "I suppose I like the role ... because it's closest to me," he said in 1959. "Sergeant Borth was a pretty cynical man, aware that the world is not a perfect place. But he was resigned to it and inclined to try to be a fairly nice human being in spite of the fact that other people, from time to time, are unfair and cruel." After the close of this Broadway hit, Sloane directed two New York stage productions, *The Dancer* and *Twilight Bar,* then portrayed "An Unusual Character" in Donald Ogden Stewart's *How I Wonder.*

Sloane returned to the silver screen, his association with Orson Welles, and the realm of film noir, with a prominent role in *The Lady From Shanghai* (1948), produced by Welles, and starring Welles' then-wife Rita Hayworth. Sloane portrayed Arthur Bannister, Hayworth's obsessive and manipulative attorney husband, who acts as the puppeteer in a complex murder scheme involving his sleazy law partner, George Grisby (Glenn Anders), a man he hires to spy on his wife, Sidney Broom (Ted De Corsia), and a naive Irish seaman, Michael O'Hara (Welles), who is in love with Bannister's wife, Elsa. Ultimately, when O'Hara is arrested for the murders of Grisby and Broom, it is Bannister who insists on defending him, planning to ensure that he is convicted. ("Now, lover, if your Irishman doesn't want to go to the gas chamber, he's going to have to trust me," Bannister tells Elsa before the start of the trial. "I've never lost a case, remember?") Before the morally bankrupt attorney can carry out his scheme, however, O'Hara escapes, and in the film's famed climax, Bannister and his wife confront each other in the House of Mirrors at an abandoned amusement park, shooting at their various reflections until both are dead. After the film's release, Sloane earned praise for his "credible interpretation" of the physically and psychologically impaired lawyer, and was labeled "thoroughly and satisfactorily repulsive" by the reviewer for *Cue.* The film itself, however, earned mixed reviews; *Film Daily*'s critic hailed the feature as "tense dramatic entertainment loaded with surprises and departing vividly from orthodox treatment," but the reviewer from *Variety* wrote: "Script is wordy and full of holes which need the plug of taut story-telling and more forthright action."

Over the next four years, Sloane more than made up for his previous screen scarcity, appearing in a total of 10 films, six in 1951 alone. The best of these included *Prince of Foxes* (1949), an elaborate costume epic starring Tyrone Power and Orson Welles; *The Men* (1950) — notable also as Marlon Brando's film debut — for which Sloane was praised by one reviewer for his "especially ... excellent" performance as an understanding doctor; and *The Blue Veil* (1951), a well-done soaper that garnered Oscar nominations for co-stars Jane Wyman and Joan Blondell. He was also seen in his final two film noir features, *The Enforcer* (1951) and *The Big Knife* (1955).

In The *Enforcer*, Sloane portrayed Mendoza, the head of an organized murder-for-hire racket and the focus of an intense, but futile, investigation by police. After the accidental death of one of Mendoza's underlings (Ted De Corsia) who was slated to testify against his boss, the assistant district attorney, Martin Ferguson (Humphrey Bogart), painstakingly reviews the evidence, leading to a series of flashbacks that show the manner in which the elusive mobster came to power. Ultimately, at the end of a grueling night of re-examining the case, Ferguson locates an overlooked clue regarding a murder Mendoza had committed years before. After Ferguson successfully locates the young woman who witnessed the killing, the film ends with Mendoza's fate sealed.

While Sloane's character was a strong presence throughout the film, the actor actually only appeared in a handful of scenes near the end. Still, upon the film's release, he earned praise from several critics, including Edwin Schallert of the *Los Angeles Times*, who wrote: "Sloane is, as usual, exceedingly competent."

Sloane's final noir, the grim and often morbid *The Big Knife* (1955), focused on Charlie Castle (Jack Palance), a hard-drink-ing, philandering movie star, and his relationships with his estranged wife, Marion (Ida Lupino), his sadistic studio head, Stanley Hoff (Rod Steiger), and his press agent's insatiable wife (Jean Hagen), with whom he has an affair. At the film's end, overcome by the pressures of his life — which include the threatened exposure of his involvement in a hit-and-run accident — Charlie commits suicide.

As Castle's long-time agent Nat Danziger, Sloane portrayed a man torn between his loyalty to his favorite client and his fear of the power wielded by Hoff. His stance of sympathy mixed with realism is best illustrated in an early scene when Castle objects to signing another seven-year contract with Hoff's studio: "God forbid what he would do," Nat tells him. "We've got no choice, Charlie. You know what he's got on you — that thing we don't talk about. Darling, you'll sign. Or you'll go to jail." Although *The Big Knife* was described by one critic as "sometimes so brittle and brutal as to prove disturbing," the film won third prize at the 1955 Venice Film Festival, and Sloane was singled out as "particularly touching as a kind old agent" in the *New York Herald Tribune*.

Also during this period, Sloane made his debut on the new medium of television, appearing in a brief skit with Boris Karloff on *We, the People* in 1949. However, according to a *Newsweek* article published nearly a decade later, Sloane was so appalled by this production that it took him a full year to try to television again.

"In those days, TV directors were just about six weeks away from office boy," Sloane said.

He fared better in his second television performance, the Fred Coe–Delbert Mann production of *Vincent van Gogh*, earning an Emmy nomination for Best Actor. "I think quality TV probably began with that show," he contended.

Sloane's best-received television role came in 1955, when he earned an Emmy nomination for his portrayal of a cold-blooded tycoon in the Rod Serling production of *Patterns*. He was universally hailed for his performance — in a typical review, Jack Gould of the *New York Times* raved that Sloane was "extraordinary. He made a part that easily might have been only a stereotyped 'menace' a figure of dimension, almost of stature. His interpretation of the closing confrontation speech was acting of rare insight and depth."

"After that, my fee went up three times," Sloane said later. "People began thinking about me as a cold-blooded-type heavy. I've done about a half-dozen ruthless businessmen since."

Throughout the next decade, Sloane appeared in a variety of big-screen projects, from the acclaimed *Somebody Up There Likes Me* (1956), starring Paul Newman as Rocky Graziano, to — oddly enough — two Jerry Lewis comedies, *The Patsy* (1964) and *The Disorderly Orderly* (1965). Most of his time and talents, however, were given to television appearances on what seemed to be nearly every program on the airwaves — *Gunsmoke, Bonanza, Voyage to the Bottom of the Sea, Wagon Train, Rawhide, The Virginian, The Twilight Zone, Alfred Hitchcock Presents, Zane Grey Theater, Zorro, Cimarron City, Wanted: Dead or Alive, Perry Mason*, and even the *Dick Van Dyke Show, The Andy Griffith Show*, and *Petticoat Junction*.

"Strangely enough, TV is the thing I like best," he told *Newsweek* in 1957. "Of course, nothing is perfect. In TV very often you have the problem of working on scripts you're not wild about, but I don't have to have a marvelous script as long as I have a character I can get above the cliché level."

In a bizarre twist of fate, Sloane's successful career came to an abrupt end when, on August 6, 1965, he was found dead in his Brentwood, California, home by his wife, Luba. Two notes were found — one addressed to his wife and the other to his business manager — and it was later determined that the actor had taken an overdose of barbiturates because of his fear that he was going blind. According to several newspaper accounts, Sloane was quoted as having recently told his wife: "You would be better off if I killed myself." He was 55 years old.

Everett Sloane is not a readily recognizable name today, but in his heyday, he was not only one of the most well-known actors on both the large and small screen, but one of the most well-respected as well. In countless performances in every performing medium, he solidified a deserved place as an actor of talent, discrimination, and dedication to his craft. The actor himself, however, always seemed to view his vocation with philosophical objectivity, equally accepting its failures along with its successes.

"A career," Sloane told a *Los Angeles Examiner* reporter in 1960, "has what we call, rather euphemistically, vicissitudes — sometimes known as ups and downs."

Film Noir Filmography

Journey Into Fear. Director: Norman Foster. Producer: Orson Welles. Running time: 71 minutes. Released by RKO, March 18, 1943. Cast: Joseph Cotten, Dolores Del Rio, Orson Welles, Ruth Warrick, Agnes Moorehead, Everett Sloane, Jack Moss, Jack Durant, Eustace Wyatt, Frank Readick, Edgar Barrier, Stefan Schabel, Hans Conreid, Ricard Bennett, Shifra Haran, Herbert Drake, Bill Roberts.

The Lady from Shanghai. Director and Producer: Orson Welles. Running time: 86 minutes. Released by Columbia, June 10, 1948. Cast: Rita Hayworth, Orson Welles, Everett Sloane, Glenn Anders, Ted De Corsia, Erskine Sanford, Gus Schilling, Carl Frank, Louis Merrill, Evelyn Ellis, Harry Shannon, Wong Show, Sam Nelson.

The Enforcer. Director: Bretaigne Windust. Producer: Milton Sperling. Running time: 88 minutes. Released by Warner Bros., February 24, 1951. Cast: Humphrey Bogart, Zero Mostel, Ted De Corsia, Everett Sloane, Roy Roberts, Lawrence Tolan, King Donovan, Robert Steele, Patricia Joiner, Don Beddoe, Tito Vuolo, John Kellogg, Jack Lambert, Adelaide Klein, Susan Cabot, Mario Siletti.

The Big Knife. Director and Producer: Robert Aldrich. Running time: 111 minutes. Released by United Artists, November 8, 1955. Cast: Jack Palance, Ida Lupino, Wendell Corey, Jean Hagen, Rod Steiger, Shelley Winters, Ilka Chase, Everett Sloane, Wesley Addy, Paul Langton, Nick Dennis, Bill Walker, Mike Winkelman, Mel Welles, Robert Sherman, Strother Martin, Ralph Volkie, Michael Fox, Richard Boone.

References

"Autopsy in Death of Actor Everett Sloane." *Los Angeles Herald Examiner*, August 7, 1965.
Biography of Everett Sloane. MGM Studios, June 11, 1959.
Biography of Everett Sloane, Paramount Studios, circa 1964.
Biography of Everett Sloane. RKO Radio Pictures, circa 1943.
Davis, Charles E., Jr. "Everett Sloane, Film, TV Actor, Found Dead." *Los Angeles Times*, August 7, 1965.
"Everett Sloane Dead." *Hollywood Citizen-News*, August 6, 1965.
"Everett Sloane Dead." *Los Angeles Times*, August 6, 1965.
"Everett Sloane, 55, Dies; Last Rites in Hollywood." *Boxoffice*, August 16, 1965.
Gould, J. "'Patterns' Is Hailed as a Notable Triumph." *New York Times*, January 17, 1955.
Humphrey, Hal. "He Really Isn't on TV Every Week—It Just Seems Like It." *Los Angeles Mirror*, December 26, 1961.
MacCann, Richard Dyer. "Actor Compares Two Dramas." *The Christian Science Monitor*, June 30, 1959.
"The Versatile Villain." *Newsweek*, November 18, 1957.
Whitney, Dwight. "Beacon in a Sea of Mediocrity." *TV Guide*, April 1, 1961.

MARK STEVENS

"I feel all dead inside. I'm backed up in a dark corner. And I don't know who's hitting me."—Mark Stevens in *The Dark Corner* (1946)

Mark Stevens was the movie star that wasn't. For a brief period during his screen career, it appeared that Stevens was well on his way to the highest rung of the cinematic ladder, with top-billed roles opposite such leading ladies as Joan Fontaine and Lucille Ball. But, like most actors who benefited during the war years from the absence of the studio's major actors, Stevens' ascent did not quite reach the top, and he quickly fell. He may have suffered from a lack of individuality, having once been likened to Dana Andrews, Dennis Morgan, Robert Walker, Cornel Wilde, Lew Ayres, and Alan Ladd. ("I don't see how I can look like all of them," he once said.) Still, he built a respectable career as a director and producer, earned acclaim for his appearances in such films as *Within These Walls* (1945) and *I Wonder Who's Kissing Her Now* (1947), and was featured in four films noirs: *The Dark Corner* (1946), *The Street with No Name* (1948), *Between Midnight and Dawn* (1950), and *Cry Vengeance* (1954).

The handsome actor with the appealing smile was born Richard Stevens in Cleveland, Ohio, on December 13, 1921 (some sources say 1920). The only child of Richard Morton Stevens and his wife, Willimina Morrison, young Richard was just a few months old when his parents divorced. His mother took him to Folkstone, England, where they lived with her parents, Capt. and Mrs. William Morrison. (Capt. Morrison reportedly served for many years as the official ship's captain for King George V and the Duke of Windsor.) Following the death of his grandparents three years later, Stevens and his mother returned to Cleveland for a year, then moved to Montreal, Canada, where Willimina's sister resided. When Stevens was 12, his mother married James Cooke, a top executive of the Railway and Engineering Supply Company in Montreal.

Stevens attended several Montreal schools, including Argyle High School, Westmount High School, King School, and the Beaux Arts and Sir George Williams School of Fine Arts—as one tactful reporter later put it, he was "asked to adjourn from practically every school he attended." Having long harbored an interest in acting, Stevens left school for good at age 16 and joined the Corona Barn Players in Montreal. Performing under the name Steven Richards, he was seen in several productions with the group, then auditioned for The Atterbury Players in the city and appeared in such productions as *The Drunkard, The Honest Merchant,* and *Sweeney Todd, the Demon Barber of Fleet Street.* Stevens expanded his performing experience by serving as a nightclub singer and emcee, but the low pay at these jobs spurred him to sign on at his stepfather's company. For a while, the budding actor would work from 8 A.M. to 5 P.M. at the supply company, show up for a play at 8 P.M., then leave at 11:30 P.M. and work at the nightclub until 3 A.M.

"I did everything for experience," Stevens told famed columnist Hedda Hopper in 1947. "Although I was sidetracked many times, it was an actor's career for me."

Bored with work at the supply company, Stevens decided to strike out for Hollywood, but he was struck instead with a severe attack of ptomaine poisoning before reaching his destination. Stevens recuperated in Montreal, then proceeded to bounce from job to job, including lettering posters for an engineering firm, and working as a gas station attendant and a salesman for stocking wash.

"Meanwhile, I never skipped an opportunity to do a stint in show business at night," Stevens recalled. "In 1938 I tackled Broadway and got thrown for a loss. After vainly beating the pavement for months, I landed in Central Park without a room or a thing to eat. And after a session of sleeping on park benches, I was too weak to hitchhike home. So I had to wire my father for money."

Back in Canada once again, Stevens tried to enlist in the armed services, but was rejected because of an old back injury and instead took a job managing a small general store. A year later, he left to visit relatives in Akron, Ohio, where he worked for a haberdashery and an electric razor company, and wondered whether his dreams would ever become a reality.

"When I tried out for a play, they told me, 'You'll never make an actor. But with that face, you should be in the movies,'" Stevens said.

Stevens finally decided to start small—

he got a job at a radio station WAKR in Akron, eventually working his way up to operator, engineer, and announcer. He later wrote, produced, directed, and starred in a radio drama entitled *Was I Right?*, and appeared evenings in stock productions presented by a local company, The Weatherwax Players. After a year and a half, Stevens signed on with the competition, working at station WJW as production manager and newscaster. In June 1943, armed with $1,000 he'd saved from his radio jobs, Stevens headed for Hollywood again. This time, luck was on his side. Stevens met Hollywood agents Nat and Charlie Goldstone, who arranged for him to have a screen test at Warner Bros. Warner's executives promptly signed the actor to a contract— Stevens was finally on his way.

In an unbilled role, Stevens debuted as an admiral's aide in the rousing wartime drama *Destination Tokyo* (1943), starring Cary Grant and John Garfield. He followed this film with bit parts in *Passage to Marseille* (1944), *Hollywood Canteen* (1944), and *Roaring Guns* (1944), the first film in which he received a screen credit, billed as Stephen Richards. He was cast in a larger role in *God Is My Co-Pilot* (1945), but most of his performance wound up on the proverbial cutting room floor, and he was given only one line in the highly successful John Garfield starrer, *Pride of the Marines* (1945). He fared better, however, in another war drama, *Objective, Burma!* (1945), in which the actor was billed under his new moniker, Mark Stevens.

Despite his favorable showing in *Objective, Burma!*, Warners failed to exercise the option on Stevens' contract, but he was promptly picked up by 20th Century-Fox and given a plum role in *Within These Walls* (1945), where he played a wrongfully convicted prisoner who falls in love with a judge's daughter. Next, he was loaned to RKO for a starring role opposite Joan Fontaine in *From This Day Forward* (1946), a rather sentimental love story that was a hit with moviegoers. Stevens later said that his role in the film as a returning war veteran was one of his favorites.

"Naturally I was scared and nervous, and if it hadn't been for the help of [the director], I probably would have muffed the opportunity," Stevens said in a 1950 *Saturday Evening Post* article. "As it was, I didn't try to act. I just read the lines as I myself would talk and they seemed to sound all right."

Back at Fox, Stevens was cast in another leading role, this time in his first film noir, *The Dark Corner* (1946). In this well-done feature, the actor played private investigator Bradford Galt, who moves to New York following a two-year prison stretch, only to find that he is being tailed by a mysterious man in a white suit (William Bendix). After Galt dispenses a vigorous beating, the man admits that he was hired by Tony Jardine (Kurt Kreuger), Galt's former business partner who was responsible for the frame-up that sent him to jail. As it turns out, however, "White Suit" was actually hired by wealthy art dealer Hardy Cathcart (Clifton Webb), whose wife was having an affair with Jardine. The seemingly innocuous Cathcart not only pays "White Suit" to murder Jardine and frame Galt for the crime but later, in a shocking twist, he pushes the hired killer from a skyscraper window to his death. Meanwhile, Galt manages to temporarily conceal Jardine's body and launch a frantic search for the real killer, aided by his ever-faithful secretary-turned-girlfriend, Kathleen (Lucille Ball). Finally stumbling on a clue that leads him to Cathcart, Galt finds that he is about to become victim number three, but before Cathcart can carry out his plan to kill the detective, he is riddled with bullets by his wife, who has learned of her lover's murder and knows that her husband is the guilty party.

Hailed by one critic as "tough, rugged, [and] grim in spades," *The Dark Corner* was a hit with audiences and critics alike, and Stevens earned widespread acclaim for his performance as the desperate private detective. In the *Los Angeles Examiner*, James O'Hara wrote that Stevens "will impress you more than anything else when you see the film. He's handsome, very talented, and blends a rare photogenic masculine charm with a small boy quality that should win him a lasting place in feminine hearts." The actor earned similar plaudits in the *New York Times*, whose critic claimed that Stevens "proves in *The Dark Corner* that he has a rare combination of talent and personality which, if properly developed, will place him in the forefront of leading men in short order."

Critics and audiences weren't alone in their assessment of Stevens; after only a week of shooting on *The Dark Corner*, Fox head Darryl F. Zanuck was so impressed with the actor's performance that he presented him with a large bonus check and a new contract. Despite these encouraging signs, however, Stevens frankly admitted that he was concerned that the end of the war would have a negative impact on his budding career.

"What's the use of kidding myself?" he asked reporter Bob Thomas in a 1946 interview. "After all, the major studios make about 30 big pictures a piece each year. Now that the war is over, each has about 15 leading men to choose from. That doesn't give the newcomer much hope. I know I got the breaks because men like Tyrone Power and Jimmy Stewart were away at war. Every day on *The Dark Corner* I expected a note from the boss telling me I was unsuited for the role."

But Stevens didn't have to worry — yet. He next starred opposite June Haver in *I Wonder Who's Kissing Her Now* (1947), a pleasant turn-of-the-century musical in which he played real-life vaudeville singer-songwriter Joe Howard. While his career was holding steady, however, Stevens' private life was not. In January 1945, Stevens had married Annelle Hayes, a former Miss Texas, and the two had a son, Mark, Jr., the following year. But on January 15, 1947, the couple separated, with Annelle charging that her husband was having an affair with sultry actress Hedy Lamarr, and in July of that year, she filed suit for separate maintenance. By September, the couple had reconciled, Annelle dropped her suit, and Stevens offered a contrite apology in the press.

"I was a fool to ever leave my home and Annelle and the baby," the actor told columnist Louella Parsons. "You know the trouble with those of us who have the good luck to be received in Hollywood is we believe our publicity. We get to thinking we are something very special. We get our names in the papers and we say to ourselves, 'We're pretty important.' And then — boom! All of a sudden, you realize all that's been given to you could be taken away just as fast. I'm going to try to make up to [Annelle] in every way."

Despite Stevens' intentions, however, less than six months after he returned to his family, his wife again announced that she planned to file for divorce.

"This time there will be no kiss and make up," Annelle told Louella Parsons.

Still, after a second separation, the couple would eventually reunite, and in 1951 they would have a second child, a daughter named Arrelle. But the story did not have a happy ending. In 1962, Stevens and his wife split for good, after which she married producer William Warwick.

On screen, Stevens was about to reach the pinnacle of his career, with back-to-back hits in 1948. The first, *The Snake Pit*, was a harrowing look at life inside a state mental asylum; Stevens starred as a man who is forced to commit his wife, played by Olivia deHavilland. The film was both a critical and financial smash. Next, Stevens was top-billed above Richard Widmark and Lloyd Nolan in *The Street with No Name*, his second film noir.

Based on F.B.I. files, this feature begins with a teletyped message from bureau director J. Edgar Hoover that reads, "The street on which crime flourishes is the street extending across America. It is the street with no name." Stevens portrayed federal agent Gene Cordell, who goes undercover to infiltrate a highly organized mob headed by Alec Stiles (Widmark), who prides himself on building his gang "along scientific lines." Posing as a streetwise hood, Cordell establishes himself in the neighborhood frequented by Stiles, making himself conspicuous by offering unsolicited coaching advice at a local boxing gym and needling the trainer. ("What are

you training him for, a quick dive? Why, the way he looks, he couldn't lick an ice cream cone.") Cordell's ploy works — he attracts the attention of Stiles and before long he has been recruited into his mob. But soon after Cordell tips police to an upcoming heist planned by the gang, Stiles learns of the agent's identity and marks him for murder. Rather than carry out the job himself, however, the clever gangleader has other plans: "There's only one scientific way to get rid of this stoolie — let the cops bump him off. Smart, huh?" Stiles tells Cordell. "Any minute now a squad of cops will be coming up the front way. And guess whose shadow they're gonna see on that window? And guess who they're gonna pump full of slugs, thinking they're knocking off a safecracker?" Despite his shrewd machinations, Stiles' plan goes awry, and after a lengthy chase, he is gunned down by Cordell.

After earning mention for his "sturdy, flexible job" and "pleasing assurance" in *Street*, Stevens continued to fare well with his film assignments the following year, with roles in *Oh, You Beautiful Doll* (1949), an appealing musical in which he starred opposite June Haver; *Dancing in the Dark* (1949), a witty comedy-musical co-starring William Powell; and *Sand* (1949), a passable horse story filmed in Technicolor on location in Colorado. Stevens' co-star in the latter film, Coleen Gray, would recall that the actor was "moody."

"I think he had a temper," Gray said in a 2001 interview. "I didn't experience it. He was another one who was a 'pretty boy' at Fox, who was deeper than you would think from the roles that he played. But he had a kind of pessimistic point of view."

Stevens may have had good cause for such pessimism. When his term with 20th Century-Fox expired, the studio failed to renew his contract, and the actor admitted that he had "a chip on my shoulder."

"I like Hollywood and I like making pictures," Stevens told columnist Erskine Johnson. "But nobody in Hollywood has ever said that I was a great guy. I know it. I've always incurred the wrath of people. It's because I hate pettiness and unkindness. And there's a lot of it here."

But the actor was still holding his own, career-wise, and next appeared in a romantic comedy for MGM, *Please Believe Me* (1950), with a stellar cast that included Robert Walker, Deborah Kerr, and Peter Lawford. He followed this feature with Columbia's *Between Midnight and Dawn* (1950), his third film noir.

This film centered on two police officers, the easygoing and idealistic Rocky Barnes (Stevens) and his seasoned, cynical partner, Dan Purvis (Edmond O'Brien), who have been friends for a number of years despite the differences in their personalities. ("They can't all be wrong all the way through," Rocky says of the criminals he encounters. "You gotta look inside. Maybe some of them rate a second chance.") Although both men are attracted to police dispatcher Kate Mallory (Gale Storm), it is Rocky who finally wins her over and the two make plans to marry. Meanwhile, Rocky and Dan find that their lives are in danger when a convicted killer, Richie Garris (Donald Buka), who'd threatened the officers following his sentencing,

breaks out of prison. While the officers are on patrol a short time later, Garris' car pulls alongside and, in a graphic scene, fatally shoots Rocky in the head. Dan later tracks the killer to an apartment building where he is holed up with his girlfriend and a young girl, and guns him down. Although he was killed off halfway through the film, Stevens was singled out by several reviewers for his performance, including the critic for the *Los Angeles Times*, who wrote that he "plays the dashing cop delightfully." The *Times* reviewer also praised the film's "clear and fast paced direction," and in the *New York Times*, Bosley Crowther predicted that moviegoers would "be fairly treated to a fast cops-and-robbers show."

Following his appearance in *Between Midnight and Dawn*, Stevens signed a short-term contract with Universal, but while he continued to be cast in starring roles, the quality of his films began to diminish. During the next year, he was seen in *Target Unknown* (1951), a tedious war drama co-starring Alex Nicol and Don Taylor; *Little Egypt* (1951), in which he played a con man who tries to bilk a tobacco tycoon out of a million dollars; *Reunion in Reno* (1951), a lighthearted bit of fluff featuring 10-year-old Gigi Perreau (the studio's answer to Margaret O'Brien); and *Katie Did It* (1951), a mildly entertaining comedy co-starring Ann Blyth.

Working on a freelance basis following his brief stint at Universal, Stevens' career continued to nosedive with appearances in such timewasters as *Mutiny* (1952), a predictable adventure yarn set in the 1800s, and *The Big Frame* (1952), a listless melodrama shot at the London Film Studios and featuring a cast of such virtual unknowns as Jean Kent, Garry Marsh, and John Bentley. To make matters worse, while filming a fight scene for the latter feature, Stevens was thrown against a fireplace and sustained a head injury that required two stitches.

Stevens' career saw a brief upturn in 1953 when he accepted the title role in *The New Adventures of Martin Kane*, a syndicated television series about a tough New York private detective. Stevens was the fourth actor to play the role (he was preceded by William Gargan, Lee Tracy, and Lloyd Nolan), and the show enjoyed a ratings boost after he signed on.

"When I go out and play Martin Kane on Thursday nights, actually I'm playing Mark Stevens," the actor said. "I can't be anybody else, honestly. I wear my own clothes and use my own voice and behave pretty much as I would anywhere. Then I just hope it comes off."

Unfortunately, after a year, the series was canceled. But Stevens was undaunted. He formed the Mark Stevens Production Company, through which he planned to produce both feature films and teleplays, as well as commercials. He also announced plans to build his own studio within the next two years that would cover a 12-mile radius and house eight to 10 sound stages. And when Stevens returned to the big screen, it was not only as the star of his final film noir, *Cry Vengeance* (1954), it was also in his debut as a director.

In this gripping and often moving feature, Stevens played embittered ex-cop Vic Barron, who is determined to seek revenge on the mobster he believes responsible for framing him for bribery and planting a bomb that left him disfigured and killed his wife and daughter. Released from San Quentin after a three-year sentence, Vic learns that the mobster, Tino Morelli (Douglas Kennedy), has become a respected citizen in Ketchikan, Alaska, where he lives with his young daughter, Marie (Cheryl Callaway). Unbeknownst to Vic, however, the bomb was actually planted by a hood known as Roxey (Skip Homeier), who trails Vic to Alaska, aiming to kill Morelli and frame the ex-cop once again. Meanwhile, Vic plans to abduct Morelli's daughter, but he is unexpectedly affected by the child's innocent and loving nature; in a particularly touching scene, Marie kisses Vic's scarred cheek, telling him, "I wish I could make your face well." Moved not only by his encounter with Marie, but also by his budding relationship with local bar owner Peggy Harding (Martha Hyer),Vic abruptly aban-

dons his vendetta, but he learns that Roxey has made good on his scheme to kill Morelli. Encountering Roxey at the airport, Vic engages in a car chase that ends with Roxey's death in a shootout at the town's old paper mill, and the final scene finds Vic returning alone to San Francisco. As Peggy and young Marie watch the departure of the plane, the child asks if Vic will return, and the audience is left with a glimmer of hope as Peggy replies, "I think so." Despite the rather dismal reviews earned by *Cry Vengeance*— with one critic panning it as "one slow and cheerless progression of cheap crime picture clichés"— the film stands up today as a highly watchable offering from the noir era as well as a creditable debut for Stevens' efforts behind the camera.

Later that year, Stevens returned to the small screen, starring in *Big Town*, as the managing editor of a crusading daily newspaper. After 18 episodes, Stevens also took on the duties of producing and directing the show, and managed to find time write eight scripts. The first film under the aegis of Stevens' company was *Timetable* (1956), in which he starred, as well as produced and directed. The result was a taut crime drama that suffered only from a lack of cohesive writing. After starring in a pair of oaters, *Gunsight Ridge* (1957), co-starring Joel McCrea, and *Gunsmoke in Tucson* (1958) with Forrest Tucker (1958), Stevens wrote and directed *Gun Fever* (1958), a fairly engrossing western about two brothers who set out to avenge the massacre of their parents.

Just as his production company was getting underway, however, Stevens abruptly abandoned Hollywood, moving to Majorca, Spain, and causing a minor stir in the film community. In 1960, he appeared in one feature film, a 3-D adventure tale entitled *September Storm*, but it was filmed entirely on location in Majorca. Two years after the film's release, however, a possible reason for Stevens' sudden relocation was revealed — the actor filed a bankruptcy petition, stating that he was unemployed, that he owed $439,451 in debts, and that his assets amounted to only

$500. Then, in 1964, Stevens' ex-wife, Annelle, filed a lawsuit against the actor, charging that he had failed to live up to his child support agreement. Later that year, Stevens returned to Hollywood, accepting eighth billing in *Fate is the Hunter*, starring Glenn Ford and Nancy Kwan.

The following year saw the release of a film that Stevens co-wrote, produced, directed, and starred in during his tenure in Spain: *Tierra de Fuego* (1965), followed by *Escape from Hell Island* (1965), for which he was the director and star. After the latter feature, Stevens returned to Spain where he appeared in small roles in such Spanish productions as *Vaya con Dios, gringo!* (1966), *La Lola, dicen que no vive sola* (1970), and *La Furia del Hombre Lobo* (1972).

In 1973, Stevens moved back to the United States and announced plans for a comeback. During the next decade, he was seen in guest spots in a number of popular television series, including *Kojak*, *Police Story*, and *Murder, She Wrote*. But he was never seen in another feature film. During the late 1980s, Stevens moved back to Spain — this time for good. On September 15, 1994, at the age of 71, the actor died of cancer in Majores, Spain.

Mark Stevens deserves a solid spot in the annals of Hollywood history if for no other reason than his sense of determination and fortitude. Able to accurately assess the potential of his career, Stevens donned a never-say-die demeanor and struck out on his own rather than continue performing in poor-quality films. By so doing, he was able to cultivate his talents as a director, producer, and writer, resulting in several films worth watching today.

"It might sound strange coming from me," he once laughed, "but I don't like to act. I'm not a very good actor, and I'm not kidding myself about it."

Film Noir Filmography

The Dark Corner. Director: Henry Hathaway. Producer: Fred Kohlmar. Running time: 99 minutes. Released by 20th Century-Fox, April 9, 1946. Cast: Mark Stevens, Lucille Ball, Clifton Webb, William Bendix, Kurt Kreuger, Cathy Downs, Reed Hadley, Constance Collier, Eddie Heywood and His Orchestra, Molly Lamont.

The Street with No Name. Director: William Keighley. Producer: Samuel G. Engel. Running time: 91 minutes. Released by 20th Century-Fox, July 14, 1948. Cast: Mark Stevens, Richard Widmark, Lloyd Nolan, Barbara Lawrence, Ed Begley, Donald Buka, Joseph Pevney, John McIntire, Howard Smith, Walter Greaza, Joan Chandler, Bill Mauch, Sam Edwards, Don Kohler, Rober McGee, Vincent Donahue, Phillip Pine, Buddy Wright, Larry Anzalone, Robert Karnes, Robert Patten.

Between Midnight and Dawn. Director: Gordon Douglas. Producer: Hunt Stromberg. Running time: 89 minutes. Released by Columbia, October 2, 1950. Cast: Mark Stevens, Edmond O'Brien, Gale Storm, Donald Buka, Gale Robbins, Anthony Ross, Roland Winters, Tito Vuolo, Grazia Narciso, Madge Blake, Lora Lee Michel, Jack Del Rio, Phillip Van Zandt, Cliff Bailey, Tony Barr, Peter Mamakos, Earl Brietbard, Wheaton Chambers, Frances Morris.

Cry Vengeance. Director: Mark Stevens. Producer: Lindsley Parsons. Running time: 83 minutes. Released by Allied Artists, February 1954. Cast: Mark Stevens, Martha Hyer, Skip Homeier, Joan Vohs, Douglas Kennedy, Don Haggerty, Cheryl Callaway, John Doucette.

References

Ames, Walter. "Mark Stevens, Man of Many Talents, Doesn't Like to Act." *Los Angeles Times*, August 5, 1956.
"Bankrupt, Says Actor Stevens." *Hollywood Citizen-News*, February 24, 1962.
Biography of Mark Stevens. RKO Radio Studios, August 17, 1945.
Biography of Mark Stevens. 20th Century-Fox, circa 1946.
Emerson, Faye. "TV Toughie Mark Stevens: Butter-and-Egg Man?" Publication Unsourced, October 5, 1954.
"Ex-Wife Files Suit Against Mark Stevens." *Hollywood Citizen-News*, March 19, 1964.
Heimer, Mel. "Why TV's Martin Kane Is Allergic to Trench Coats." *Los Angeles Examiner*. June 13, 1954.
Henry, Marilyn. Let Us Not Forget Mark Stevens. *Classic Film Collector*, circa 1977.
Hopper, Hedda. "Mark Stevens—He's Been Thru the Mill." *Chicago Sunday Tribune*, July 13, 1947.

_____. "Stevens Couple May Reconcile." Publication Unsourced, September 24, 1947.

Johnson, Erskine. "Mark Stevens." *Los Angeles Daily News*, April 28, 1951.

"Mark Stevens Hurt in Film." Publication Unsourced, November 30, 1951.

Obituary. *Variety*, October 3, 1994.

Parsons, Louella O. "Actor Mark Stevens and Wife Reconciled." *Los Angeles Herald-Examiner*, September 24, 1947.

_____. "Mark Stevens Reconciliation Fails; Wife to Ask Divorce." *Los Angeles Examiner*, February 14, 1948.

_____. Title Unsourced. *Los Angeles Examiner*, November 23, 1947.

"Romance of Actor with Hedy Ended." *Los Angeles Daily News*, September 24, 1947.

Stevens, Mark. "The Role I Liked Best." *The Saturday Evening Post*, March 18, 1950.

Thomas, Bob. "Return of Male Stars Worries Film Newcomer." *Hollywood Citizen-News*, March 8, 1946.

"UA to Finance, Release Pic for Mark Stevens, Who Is Giving Up Acting." *Variety*, November 25, 1955.

PAUL STEWART

"You seem like a reasonable man. Why don't we make a deal? What's it worth to you to turn your considerable talents back to the gutter you crawled out of?" — Paul Stewart in *Kiss Me Deadly* (1955)

Paul Stewart was once described as a Madison Avenue version of Humphrey Bogart — dapper yet sinister, ruthless and deadly, but with a sense of style. A co-founder of the American Federation of Television and Radio Artists (AFTRA) and an original member of Orson Welles' *Mercury Theater on the Air*, Stewart not only found fame on the radio, in film, and on stage, but in television as well, both in front of the camera and behind the scenes. He was seen during his screen career in such blockbusters as *Citizen Kane* (1941) and *Twelve O'Clock High* (1949), as well as seven films noirs—*Johnny Eager* (1942), *Champion* (1949), *The Window* (1949), *Edge of Doom* (1950), *Appointment with Danger* (1951), *Loan Shark* (1952), and *Kiss Me Deadly* (1955).

Born Paul Sternberg in New York City on Friday, the 13th of March 1908, the talented and prolific actor was the only son of the owner of a mercantile textile business and his wife, Nathalie Nathanson, a former concert pianist. A performer since his adolescent years, young Paul made his theatrical debut at the age of 11, singing and dancing in *Kiddy Kapers of 1919* at the Palm Gardens in New York, and later performing in local little theater groups. His early experience also included a school production of *Rosie from Paris*, where his portrayal of an "unctuous, mustachioed villain" served as an initiation for the heavies he would play in years to come. Despite his affinity for the stage, however, he enrolled in Columbia University after attending high school, with aspirations of becoming a lawyer. But by the time he graduated, his sights were determinedly set on a career in the field of entertainment.

Altering his last name to "Stewart," the actor quickly found work on Broadway, appearing in his first hit, *Subway Express*, in the mid-1920s, followed by a series of successful plays that included *Two Seconds* and *East of Broadway*, and the Theater Guild production of *Wine of Choice*. He also demonstrated a knack for comedy when he replaced comic Milton Berle in *See My Lawyer*. During the summers, Stewart was an active performer on the "Straw Hat Circuit"— a group of small, regional little theaters that gained their nickname because their busy summer seasons drew attention from the better-established, urban theaters. Two of his biggest successes in this field were his performances in *Burlesque* with Gypsy Rose Lee in Saratoga, New

York, and *The Petrified Forest* in White Plains, New York, in the Duke Mantee role that would later serve as Humphrey Bogart's first screen hit.

In 1932, Stewart expanded his performing repertoire to the medium of radio when he secured a staff position at WLW in Cincinnati, where his many duties included actor, writer, producer, announcer, and sound effects man. After 13 months, he returned to New York, where he was heard on a variety of top-rated radio programs over the next several years, including the long-running *The March of Time*.

According to Stewart's press biographies, the actor was responsible for introducing "boy wonder" Orson Welles to radio when he recommended him for a part on *The March of Time* in 1935; the two men developed a close association and in 1938, Stewart became a cast member of Welles' *Mercury Theater on the Air*, in an acclaimed performing troupe best known for its 1938 broadcast of "The War of the Worlds." The realistic depiction of an invasion from Mars in a small New Jersey town terrified many listeners and required an apology from Welles the following day. The broadcast, on which Stewart served as associate producer, was "largely Paul's work," according to Mercury Theater co-founder John Houseman, but the actor "never really received any kind of credit" for its astounding impact.

Around this time, Stewart took a break from his busy performing schedule to marry Peg LaCentra, a radio and big band singer who had performed with Artie Shaw and Benny Goodman, and would later, on screen, dub the singing voices of such stars as Ida Lupino in *The Man I Love* (1946) and *Escape Me Never* (1947), and Susan Hayward in *Smash-Up: The Story of a Woman* (1947). The couple had no children, but remained married until Stewart's death nearly a half-century later.

With his radio career still in full swing, Stewart appeared in Welles' acclaimed 1941 stage version of Richard Wright's novel *Native Son*, then teamed with Welles again for

his film debut in *Citizen Kane* (1941), portraying the oily valet of the film's protagonist, Charles Foster Kane. The following year, he was seen in a small role in his first film noir, *Johnny Eager* (1942), starring Robert Taylor and Lana Turner.

This feature focused on the relationship between the title character (played by Taylor), a vicious gangleader who uses his cab driving job as a front for his lawless activities, and Lisbeth Bard (Turner), an idealistic sociology student. Lisbeth also happens to be the stepdaughter of district attorney John Farrell (Edward Arnold), who has issued an injunction to halt the opening of the Johnny's illegal dog track. Despite his growing feelings for Lisbeth, Johnny implicates her in a fake murder so that he can blackmail Farrell, but by the story's end, Johnny has turned over a new leaf; placing his life in danger to prove Lisbeth's innocence, he is gunned down in the street.

In this feature, Stewart was seen in the relatively small but pivotal role of Julio, a mobster who is used by Johnny in his blackmail scheme; during a staged fight with Julio, Johnny tells Lisbeth to shoot his opponent, and she does, later suffering a mental breakdown when she believes she has actually committed murder. ("Hey, I should be on the stage," Julio crows after the successful enactment. "I'm a good actor, eh?") Later, Julio resurfaces, double-crossing Johnny and going to work for his rival, Lew Rankin (Barry Nelson). In the final climactic scene, Johnny waylays Julio in order to prove to Lisbeth that she did not kill him — when Julio tries to flee, Johnny shoots him, but Johnny himself is later killed by Rankin's hoods and police. Stewart's performance earned notice from several critics; the reviewer for *Variety* found that he did "full justice to [his] assignment," and the critic for *The Hollywood Reporter* wrote: "From the stage, Paul Stewart stands out ... as Julio."

After *Johnny Eager*, Stewart returned to New York to do his part in the war effort by joining the Office of War Information (OWI), a U.S. government propaganda agency that documented the country's mobilization during the early years of World War II. During his service in the OWI, Stewart served as narrator for *The World at War*, the only full-length motion picture issued by the federal government, and produced more than 1,000 recordings for the troops abroad. He also resumed his stage career during this period, and was given two leaves of absence by the OWI to return to Hollywood for *Mr. Lucky* (1943), starring Cary Grant, and *Government Girl* (1943), a wartime comedy with Olivia deHavilland and Sonny Tufts.

At the war's end, Stewart turned his interests behind the camera and landed a contract to direct films at Paramount Pictures. But in two years, his sole assignment was directing a segment of *Variety Girl* (1947), the studio's all-star tribute to the philanthropic organization, Variety Clubs International.

"I started going to psychiatrists, just to pass the time," Stewart said in a 1950 interview. "I even took up clay modeling. Finally, I stayed away from the studios for two solid months. Nobody said a thing." He was finally given the job of directing *Burning Journey*, a boxing saga slated to star Edward G. Robinson, but the studio later developed a case of "cold feet," and abandoned their plans to make the movie. (It would be made a year later by independent producer, Bob Roberts, as the John Garfield starrer *Body and Soul*.) Stewart was then hired by RKO Studios to direct *Christabel Caine*, starring Joan Fontaine, but the film was shelved by the studio and, disheartened by his experiences, Stewart returned to New York, where he made his directorial debut for the stage play *The Stars Weep in New York*.

Finally, after a six-year absence from the big screen, Stewart returned to Hollywood to triumphantly resume his acting career in *The Window* (1949), his second film noir.

One of the sleepers of the year, *The Window* centered on Tommy Woodry (Bobby Driscoll), a young boy whose overactive imagination is a constant source of frustration to his parents (Arthur Kennedy and Barbara Hale). When Bobby announces one night that he has seen a murder committed in an upstairs apartment, his parents adopt a "boy-who-cried-wolf" stance and force him to apologize to the couple he accused of the deed. But Bobby, for once, was telling the truth — when the killers, Joe and Jean Kellerson (Stewart and Ruth Roman), realize that their crime was witnessed, they track the youngster to an abandoned building where, after a suspenseful chase, Mr. Kellerson falls to his death and his wife is apprehended by police.

Among the cast of excellent performers, Stewart was especially memorable as the murderous neighbor, particularly in the scene in which he first encounters Tommy alone in his apartment. Throughout his exchange with the youngster, Kellerson exhibits a frighteningly friendly demeanor, with a cold smile and steely eyes that reveal the danger lurking behind the façade. ("What's the matter with you, Tommy?" Kellerson says. "Don't you like me? Have I ever done anything to you? What are you running around telling stories for?") The film was an unexpected box-office hit, and Stewart was hailed for his menacing performance, with Charles J. Lazarus of *Motion Picture Herald* labeling his role as "excellently played," and the *New York Times* critic writing that Stewart and Roman "play the Kellersons with just the right show of fear and desperation."

Stewart's success in *The Window* led to a spate of film offers, and after an appearance as "Doc" Kaiser in the blockbuster war drama *Twelve O'Clock High* (1949), he was cast in a trio of films noirs—*Champion* (1949), *Edge of Doom* (1950), and *Appointment with Danger* (1951). In the first, produced by Stanley Kramer and directed by Mark Robson, Stewart played Tommy Haley, the manager of a heartlessly ambitious prize-fighter, Midge Kelly (Kirk Douglas). As the film follows Midge's humble beginnings and Haley's unflagging efforts that take the fighter to the top of his game, Midge uses and discards his wife, Emma (Ruth Roman), and his disabled brother, Connie (Arthur Kelly). Ultimately, he even gets rid of Haley, trading in his loyal manager for a chance to fight in the champi-

onship bout. ("This is a celebration," Haley tells Connie after learning of Midge's plans. "Midge is getting a shot at the title and he's getting himself a new manager…. What right did I have to expect anything else? I know the racket. I'm too old to believe in fairy tales.") Midge wins the championship but later, in a rematch, he is badly battered by his opponent, Johnny Dunne (John Day)— although Midge emerges the winner, he dies in his dressing room following the fight, as Haley looks on in pity.

After earning raves for his realistic portrayal of the manager in *Champion*, Stewart was seen in *Edge of Doom* (1950), portraying Craig, a small-time hood who is suspected in the killing of a local parish priest. Even after he admits that he was robbing a local movie house at the time of the murder, Craig is identified by an elderly woman and arrested for the crime. As it turns out, however, the murder was committed by a neighbor of Craig's, Martin Lynn (Farley Granger), a luckless young man who, grief-stricken after his mother's death, impulsively bludgeoned the priest when he refused to provide her with a "grand funeral." Although he is initially silent when police pin the murder on Craig, Mar-

tin is later plagued by "the voice of conscience" and ultimately confesses his crime.

Stewart's next noir, *Appointment with Danger*, found the actor portraying still another character from the other side of the tracks, this time a ruthless gangleader, Earl Boettiger, who is planning a $1 million heist of a postal truck. (While Boettiger is seldom seen inflicting violence by his own hand, his callous nature is clearly revealed in one scene when he calmly watches one of his henchmen beat another to death with a bronze baby shoe.) The gang is infiltrated by undercover postal inspector Al Goddard (Alan Ladd), but the planned robbery is nearly botched and the mobsters take a local nun (Phyllis Calvert) as a hostage. During a meeting at an abandoned shack, the nun inadvertently blows Goddard's cover, but before Boettiger can carry out his plans to shoot the agent, police arrive and Boettiger is killed.

Stewart racked up more raves for his portrayals in his latest two noirs; for his appearance in *Edge of Doom*, the *Los Angeles Times*' Philip K. Scheuer praised his "stand out" execution of his role as the two-bit hood, and the critic for the *New York Times* wrote that his was one of the film's best performances. Similarly, after the release of *Appointment with Danger*, Stewart was lauded by *Variety*'s critic, who found that he "dominates the crooks," and the *New York Times* reviewer, who called him "slickly sinister as the gang chief."

Although most of his screen time to date had been spent playing a variety of criminals, Stewart viewed his typecasting with amusement, later telling reporters that he'd hoped his "tough good looks" would lead to starring roles in Hollywood.

"But I came along on the cusp of that trend," he said. "It was going out of fashion and I got stuck as a heavy. I played subtle heavies, assistant heavies, stylish, rich heavies. People know my face, but not my name."

Continuing a trend he'd started in the late 1940s, Stewart commuted frequently between New York and Hollywood, directing or starring in a number of Broadway plays including *Sing Me No Lullaby, Twilight Walk,* and *Mister Roberts,* and appearing in such films as the five-stories-in-one comedy *We're Not Married* (1951); *Deadline U.S.A.* (1952), a hard-hitting newspaper drama starring Humphrey Bogart; and *The Bad and the Beautiful* (1952), the superb story of a ruthlessly ambitious film producer, featuring Kirk Douglas and Lana Turner.

"We're the main support of the airlines, anyway — I guess I've been back and forth 10 times this year," Stewart joked in a 1950 interview. "[My wife and I] correspond a lot, and we talk on the phone every Sunday, making a list of the things we want to discuss beforehand. Runs into a big expense, in time."

In 1952, Stewart returned to the realm of film noir in *Loan Shark,* where he played Lou Donnelli, a top henchman in a loan sharking operation. When local tire factory employee Joe Gargen (George Raft) joins the organization, Donnelli is immediately suspicious of his motives, but his doubts are brushed aside by his boss, Vince Phillips (John Hoyt), and Gargen is allowed to head up a lucrative operation involving a laundry delivery service. It turns out, however, that Donnelli was on target — Gargen was hired by the tire factory's general manager to infiltrate the gang: "You been real sharp, peeper, but you never conned me for a minute," Donnelli tells Gargen. "Come on — I'm gonna take you down and show you how the boilers work in the laundry. You never really inspected them. I been thinkin' about the boiler gag for a long time. You're gonna be the cleanest stiff in town." Gargen manages to get the jump on Donnelli, however, and guns him down, along with Phillips and, ultimately, the organization's leader, who turns out to be a bespectacled accountant named Walter Karr (Larry Dobkin). Upon its release, the film earned lukewarm reviews, with the critic for the *New York Times* writing that the film, "while nothing special, could have been a lot worse." Stewart's performance was viewed more favorably, however; *Variety*'s reviewer proclaimed that the actor and co-stars Dobkin, Hoyt, and Russell Johnson "put over

their respective chores as members of the racket," and in the *New York Times,* the critic wrote that Stewart and his fellow supporting players "contribute some telling punches of their own."

On the right side of the law for a change, Stewart starred as a compassionate detective in the outstanding Stanley Kramer production of *The Juggler* (1953), with Kirk Douglas and Milly Vitale; a sportswriter in *The Joe Louis Story* (1953); and a Korean war POW in *Prisoner of War* (1954), starring Ronald Reagan and Steve Forrest. But he returned to ruthless crime and the shadowy world of film noir with his final feature from the era, *Kiss Me Deadly* (1955). One of film noir's quintessential offerings, this film starred Ralph Meeker as private eye Mike Hammer, who encounters a series of violent characters after the torture-murder of a young hitchhiker he picks up (Cloris Leachman). Among those who cross Hammer's path is Carl Evello (Stewart), a refined but powerful gangster, who warns Hammer against continuing his pursuit, later kidnaps him, and winds up with a knife in the ribs for his troubles. Hammer ultimately learns that the young hitchhiker's death was tied with a leather-bound box referred to as "the great whatsit," which reportedly contains valuable radioactive material, and the film abruptly ends with a fiery conclusion shortly after the box is opened.

Stewart's role as the unflappable, steely-eyed gangster earned mention in a few reviews, including one that termed him "up to standard." But by now, the actor had turned his talents to the small screen — from the 1950s through the 1980s, he would appear in such top-rated programs as *Alfred Hitchcock Presents, Perry Mason, Wagon Train, It Takes A Thief, Hawaii Five-O, Matt Helm, Cannon, Mannix, The Rockford Files,* and *Remington Steele.* Beginning in the mid-1950s, he served as director on a number of series as well, including episodes of *Playhouse 90, The Twilight Zone, The Defenders, Hawaiian Eye, Peter Gunn,* and *The Mod Squad.* After several years behind the camera, however, Stewart grew frustrated with the changing times and the modern techniques of the actors he was responsible for directing.

"I call them 'do-it-yourself' actors because they take no direction and play the role the way they 'feel' it," Stewart said in 1958. "The actors seem more concerned with their movements than the meaning of the lines. An actor doesn't look at a girl when he tells her he loves her. Instead, he scratches his head, bites his fingernails, and looks out the window. This is realism? Even the westerns are looking different — if it keeps up, the only straight performers will be the horses."

Alongside his television duties, Stewart continued acting in feature films — during the remainder of the decade, he was seen in *The Cobweb* (1955), a box-office flop despite its direction by Vincente Minelli, producing duties by John Houseman, and a cast that included such luminaries as Richard Widmark, Gloria Grahame, Lauren Bacall, and Charles Boyer; *Hell on Frisco Bay* (1955), a crime melodrama starring Alan Ladd and Edward G. Robinson; and *King Creole* (1957), a vehicle for Elvis Presley that is considered to be the best of his films.

Stewart continued his work in both television and movies during the next two decades; the most memorable included *A Child is Waiting* (1963), starring Burt Lancaster and Judy Garland, who was excellent in a rare non-singing role; *In Cold Blood* (1967), the gripping dramatization of Truman Capote's best-selling novel; *Fat City* (1972), an off beat drama directed by John Huston; *The Day of the Locust* (1975), which focused on the seamy side of Hollywood during the 1930s; and *W.C. Fields and Me* (1976), a biopic of the famed comedian in which Stewart portrayed Florenz Ziegfeld.

Although Stewart suffered a heart attack in 1974, while filming *Bite the Bullet* (1975) in Charma, New Mexico, the actor continued accepting small roles through the early 1980s. His last film was Paul Mazursky's *Tempest* (1982), based on the Shakespearean play. After several years of ill health, he died on February 17, 1986, in Cedars-Sinai Medical Center in Los Angeles. He was 77 years old.

With a career that spanned six decades and included appearances in countless productions for radio, television, the stage, and film, as well as well-received efforts behind the camera, Paul Stewart may have had, as he termed it, an "unknown face," but his contributions are undeniable. In a memorial tribute held four days after his death, fellow SAG board member Bert Freed offered an ideal summation of the actor's life and career.

"His humor was always there," Freed said. "There was a glitter in his eyes. You could see the giant of a man, but it was always behind that mild, wry smile of his, looking sardonically at the world around him, but with great love and humanity.... He had it all — the talent, the human compassion, the wit, the bravery, the righteous rage. You name it, at the appropriate time, he'd always have it. And he'd never cease giving it. His life was a glowing, memorable performance."

Film Noir Filmography

Johnny Eager. Director: Mervyn LeRoy. Producer: John W. Considine, Jr. Running time: 102 minutes. Released by MGM, February 19, 1942. Cast: Robert Taylor, Lana Turner, Edward Arnold, Van Heflin, Robert Sterling, Patricia Dane, Glenda Farrell, Barry Nelson, Henry O'Neil, Charles Dingle, Cy Kendall, Don Costello, Paul Stewart. Awards: Academy Award for Best Supporting Actor (Van Heflin).

Champion. Director: Mark Robson. Producer: Stanley Kramer. Running time: 99 minutes. Released by United Artists, January 1949. Cast: Kirk Douglas, Marilyn Maxwell, Arthur Kennedy, Paul Stewart, Ruth Roman, Lola Albright, Luis Van Rooten, John Day, Harry Shannon. Awards: Academy Award for Best Film Editing (Harry Gerstad). Academy Award nominations for Best Actor (Kirk Douglas), Best Supporting Actor (Arthur Kennedy), Best Black and White Cinematography (Frank Planer), Best Score (Dimitri Tiomkin), Best Screenplay (Carl Foreman).

The Window. Director: Ted Tetzlaff. Producer: Frederic Ullman, Jr. Running time: 73 minutes. Released by RKO, August 1949. Cast: Barbara Hale, Bobby Driscoll, Arthur Kennedy, Paul Stewart, Ruth Roman. Awards: Best Mystery Film of the Year award from the Mystery Writers of America. Academy Award for Outstanding Juvenile Actor

(Bobby Driscoll). Academy Award nomination for Best Editing (Frederic Knudtson).

Edge of Doom. Director: Mark Robson. Producer: Samuel Goldwyn. Running time: 99 minutes. Released by RKO, August 3, 1950. Cast: Dana Andrews, Farley Granger, Joan Evans, Robert Keith, Paul Stewart, Mala Powers, Adele Jergens, Harold Vermilyea, John Ridgeley, Douglas Fowley, Mabel Paige, Howland Chamberlain, Houseley Stevenson, Sr., Jean Innes, Ellen Corby, Ray Teal, Mary Field, Virginia Brissac, Frances Morris.

Appointment with Danger. Director: Lewis Allen. Producer: Robert Fellows. Running time: 89 minutes. Released by Paramount, May 9, 1951. Cast: Alan Ladd, Phyllis Calvert, Paul Stewart, Jan Sterling, Jack Webb, Stacy Harris, Henry Morgan, David Wolfe, Dan Riss, Harry Antrim, Paul Lees.

Loan Shark. Director: Seymour Friedman. Producer: Bernard Luber. Running time: 79 minutes. Released by Lippert, May 23, 1952. Cast: George Raft, Dorothy Hart, Paul Stewart, Helen Westcott, John Hoyt, Henry Slate, William Phipps, Russell Johnson, Benny Baker, Larry Dobkin, Charles Meredith, Harlan Warde, Spring Mitchell, Margie Dean, Ross Elliott, Robert Bice, Robert Williams, Michael Ragan, Virginia Caroll.

Kiss Me Deadly. Director and Producer: Robert Aldrich. Running time: 105 minutes. Released by United Artists, May 18, 1955. Cast: Ralph Meeker, Albert Dekker, Paul Stewart, Maxine Cooper, Gaby Rodgers, Wesley Addy, Juano Hernandez, Nick Dennis, Cloris Leachman, Marian Carr, Jack Lambert, Jack Elam, Jerry Zinneman, Percy Helton, Fortunio Bonanova, Silvio Minciotti, Leigh Snowden, Madi Comfort, James Seay, Mara McAffee, Robert Cornthwaite, James McCallian, Jesslyn Fax, Mort Marshall, Strother Martin, Marjorie Bennett, Art Loggins, Bob Sherman, Keith McConnell, Paul Richards, Eddie Beal.

References

"Actor Paul Stewart Has Heart Attack in Charma. *Boxoffice*, June 10, 1974.

Biography of Paul Stewart. NBC Biography, October 10, 1944.

Biography of Paul Stewart. Paramount Pictures, circa 1958.

Biography of Paul Stewart. RKO Radio Pictures, Inc., December 29, 1947.

Biography of Paul Stewart. Warner Bros. Studio, December 2, 1956.

"Character Actor Dies." *Los Angeles Daily News*, February 18, 1986.

"Friends Pay Tribute to Paul Stewart, 'An Actor's Actor.'" *Screen Actor News Hollywood*, April 1986.

Hill, Gladwin. "Nice Work If You Don't Try to Get It." *New York Times*, January 29, 1950.

"Hollywood Veteran, Welles Collaborator, Paul Stewart Dies." February 18, 1986.

"Ill and Injured." *Variety*, June 3, 1974.

Nolan, J.E. "Films on TV." *Films in Review*, August/September 1970.

Obituary. *The Hollywood Reporter*, February 19, 1986.

Obituary. *Variety*, February 18, 1986.

"Paul Stewart Dead at 77." *AFTRA*, Spring 1986.

"Paul Stewart Is Dead at 77; Stage, Screen and TV Actor." *New York Times*, February 19, 1986.

"Paul Stewart, 'Juggler' Nemesis." *New York Post*, May 26, 1953.

"Paul Stewart, 'Stylish Heavy' in Many Movies." *Chicago Tribune*, February 19, 1986.

"Rites Today for Actor Paul Stewart." *Los Angeles Times*, February 21, 1996.

Scheuer, Philip K. "Marriage of Acting Pair Spans Nation." *Los Angeles Times*, December 25, 1949.

Soble, Ronald L. "Veteran Character Actor Paul Stewart Dies at 77." *Los Angeles Times*, February 19, 1986.

BARRY SULLIVAN

"You punks. You cheap, ten-buck thugs. Go home to Cornell and tell him to wipe your noses.... How dare you put your filthy hands on me." — Barry Sullivan in *The Gangster* (1947)

In films and television, Barry Sullivan was a successful, prolific performer, with appearances in nearly 80 movies, starring roles in four series on the small screen, and guest spots on countless television programs, from *Playhouse 90* to *The Love Boat*. But off screen, Sullivan had a rocky personal life characterized by stormy marriages and bitter divorces, and, after several years of secrecy, he revealed that his only son, Johnny, had been born mentally retarded. During a span of four decades, the often outspoken performer was seen in such memorable big screen fare as *The Great Gatsby* (1949), *The Bad and the Beautiful* (1952), *Earthquake* (1974), and *Oh, God!* (1977), and starred in a total of six films noirs: *Suspense* (1946), *The Gangster* (1947), *Framed* (1947), *Tension* (1949), *Cause for Alarm* (1951), and *Loophole* (1954).

Patrick Barry Sullivan was born on August 29, 1912, in the Bronx, New York, to realtor Cornelius Daniel Sullivan and his wife, Ellen. One of six brothers, Sullivan attended several schools as a child, including St. Nicholas of Tollentine Parochial School, St. Regis Preparatory School, and Fordham Preparatory School, leaving each "by mutual consent," he once said.

"I finally graduated from none of them," Sullivan said. "I had plenty of credits, but they weren't put together right."

At the age of 17, Sullivan left home and landed a job as a doorman at the Palace Theater, attending night school to obtain his diploma and playing semi-professional football with a team in Long Island. Deciding that he wanted to become a lawyer, Sullivan enrolled at Temple University on a football scholarship, where he first developed an interest in acting.

"The drama coach saw me in a football team minstrel show and offered me a part in a school play," Sullivan recalled in a 1969 interview. "Suddenly, I was an actor."

Sullivan, who dropped his first name because he thought "it made me sound like a professional Irishman," was seen in several school productions, including a leading role in Philip Barry's *Holiday*. After leaving Temple, Sullivan honed his acting craft on such radio programs as the *Myrt and Marge Show* and *Portia Faces Life*, then landed his Broadway debut in January 1936, playing Capt. Lynch in *I Want a Policeman*. This role was followed by a walk-on in the Alfred Lunt–Lynn Fontanne production of *Idiot's Delight*, and a small part in *St. Helena*. Later that year, Sullivan was cast in the role of a cadet in the smash Broadway play *Brother Rat*, and after five months, replaced actor Eddie Albert in the lead. Notable as Sullivan's first big hit,

Brother Rat was also significant for personal reasons—while performing in the road version of the play, he met actress Marie Browne, and on August 13, 1937, the two were married in Tijuana, Mexico. Sullivan and Marie went on to have two children, Johnny and Jennie.

Professionally, Sullivan was seen during the next several years in a series of plays, many of them flops including *All That Glitters*, *Eye on the Sparrow*, and *Yankee Fable*, opposite Ina Claire. He also spent a season of summer stock in Cohasset, Massachusetts. The experience gained by the budding actor at the small theater proved to be invaluable.

"I played leading romantic roles in 10 successive plays during 10 successive weeks," Sullivan told the *Boston Post* in 1956. "I got so I could learn a part in a few days, and many different kinds of parts."

Finally, in 1942, Sullivan landed a role in the play that would lead him to the big screen. Unable to serve in World War II because of a shoulder injury dating from his football days, Sullivan was performing on Broadway in *Johnny 2 × 4* when he attracted the notice of a Paramount talent scout and was offered a contract. Sullivan "grabbed the offer" and the following year was cast in *High Explosive* (1943), with Chester Morris and Jean Parker. This mediocre programmer was followed by such films as *And Now Tomorrow* (1944), a glossy soaper starring Loretta Young as a deaf woman who falls in love with her doctor; *Rainbow Island* (1944), a popular South Sea comedy with Dorothy Lamour; and *Duffy's Tavern* (1945), which flopped at the box office despite a cast that included Bing Crosby, Paulette Goddard, Alan Ladd, Veronica Lake, and Barry Fitzgerald. But it wasn't until after the expiration of his Paramount contract that Sullivan had his first starring role, his first big hit, and his first film noir, *Suspense* (1946).

Here, Sullivan portrayed Joe Morgan, a former promoter from Chicago who describes himself as "always sort of between jobs. I'm the guy that swung and missed." Joe's luck changes when he is hired to sell peanuts at a Los Angeles ice show run by Frank Leonard

(Albert Dekker), and is quickly promoted as the assistant to Frank's right-hand man, Harry (Eugene Pallette). Although his old Chicago girlfriend, Ronnie (Bonita Granville), arrives on the scene, Joe only has eyes for the star of the ice show, Roberta (Belita), who also happens to be Frank's wife. When Frank is believed killed in an avalanche at his remote mountain cabin, Joe takes his place as head of the ice show, but Roberta is haunted by guilt and is reluctant to continue their affair. Later discovering that Frank is still alive, Joe kills him in self-defense, and after Roberta insists that he turn himself in to police, Joe concocts a scheme to murder her during a dangerous ice show stunt. At the last minute, Joe has a change of heart and abandons his plan, but when he leaves the stadium, the jilted Ronnie is lying in wait and shoots him. Viewing Joe's dead body, Harry remarks with a touch of irony, "He shoulda stuck to peanuts."

Although the impact of *Suspense* is somewhat diminished by Belita's interminable skating performances, the film was a well-executed thriller and earned approval from one reviewer as "gripping drama from start to finish." For his performance, Sullivan earned mostly good reviews; although the *New York Times'* Bosley Crowther panned him as "sour and truculent," he was hailed by Lloyd L. Sloan in the *Hollywood Citizen-News*, who wrote: "Barry Sullivan, in the ambitious young man role, gives a top performance which should earn him a place on filmdom's star roster."

Continuing in the realm of the dark, Sullivan followed *Suspense* with two more films noirs in 1947, *Framed* and *The Gangster*. The first feature centered on an elaborate plan cooked up by bank vice-president Stephen Price (Sullivan) and his waitress-lover, Paula Craig (Janis Carter), to embezzle $250,000 from the bank, find a man who physically resembles Stephen, murder him by pushing his car over a cliff, and escape with the cash by passing off the dead man as the banker. The nefarious couple finds their victim in Michael Lambert (Glenn Ford), an unemployed min-

ing engineer passing through town, and the scheme proceeds with only one hitch — after getting Michael drunk, Paula bludgeons her lover, sending his body over the cliff instead. Although she manages to convince Michael that he was responsible for the deadly deed, the engineer later realizes Paula's duplicity and in the film's final scene, sets her up for capture in the bank after she collects the cache of stolen funds. Upon the film's release, Sullivan was mostly overlooked in favor of the more substantial roles played by Ford and Craig, but the picture was applauded by critics, with W.E. Oliver terming it a "tight and suspenseful mystery melodrama" in the *Los Angeles Herald Express*, and the *Los Angeles Times'* Edwin Schallert labeling it a "thriller-diller."

Next, in *The Gangster*, Sullivan starred as Shubunka, a neurotic, scar-faced mobster who reveals his outlook in the film's opening: "I worked the rackets. Dirty rackets. Ugly rackets. I was no hypocrite — I knew everything I did was low and rotten, I knew what people thought of me. What difference did it make? What did I care? I got scarred, sure. You get hurt a little when you fight your way out of the gutter." Tortured by his irrational jealousy over his singer girlfriend Nancy (Belita), and threatened by a local rival, Shubunka is further troubled when his corrupt lifestyle is condemned by the wholesome young cashier of the ice cream parlor he frequents. Despite his resolve to hang on to his territory, Shubunka is ultimately betrayed by Nancy, and dies in the gutter, gunned down during a driving rainstorm by an unseen assailant.

While *The Gangster* offers a number of interesting character portraits, the film was panned by most reviewers, including Virginia Wright of the *Los Angeles Daily News*, who found that the feature "suffers from a confused and over-written script." Wright was similarly unimpressed with Sullivan's performance, writing that he "plays the title role with only an occasional relaxing of his facial muscles," and the critic for the *New York Times* agreed, describing the actor as "stern of face and tight-lipped." The actor rebounded somewhat, with a starring role as a racketeer in his sole film of 1948, *Smart Woman*, then earned praise the following year for his performance as a selfish, adulterous husband in MGM's *The Great Gatsby* (1949). His well-received performance earned Sullivan a contract with Metro and he was promptly cast in *Tension* (1949), his fourth film noir.

As this film opens, Sullivan's oddly dubbed character, Lt. Detective Collier Bonnabel, addresses the audience, demonstrating with a rubber band his theory that "there's only one thing that breaks cases wide open — tension." The complex plot of this feature centers on the unfaithful Claire Quimby (Audrey Totter) and her unassuming drug store manager spouse, Warren (Richard Basehart). When Claire's well-to-do lover, Barney Deager (Lloyd Gough), turns up dead, Bonnabel heads up the investigation, focusing his efforts on a traveling salesman known as Paul Sothern. As it turns out, Sothern is actually Warren, who had assumed the alternate identity as part of an elaborate scheme to murder Deager, but found himself unable to go through with the deed. Suspecting that Warren's wife is the murderer, Bonnabel actively romances her and in the film's climax, craftily tricks her into revealing her guilt in the crime. ("You let me down, baby. And I thought you were such a smart girl, too," Bonnabel tells her. "It was a good try, Claire. You almost made it.") Fast-paced and well-written, *Tension* was inexplicably savaged upon its release; Floyd Stone of *Motion Picture Herald* complained that it "lacks the ingredients of the positive crime film: chase, violence, and crowning, rapid action," and panned Sullivan's performance, calling him "affected, and the result is to make the spectator wonder whether the detective is clever or ineptly venal." The *New York Times*' Bosley Crowther was only slightly more kind, but while he noted the film's "capable cast," the critic dismissed the production as a whole, writing that "a much better title for this picture would be 'Patience,' presuming such a thing."

After *Tension*, MGM cast Sullivan in a series of supporting roles in *Nancy Goes to Rio* (1950), a fluffy musical starring Ann Sothern; *Grounds for Marriage* (1950), a comedy about a doctor and his opera singing ex-wife; *The Outriders* (1950), a rather conventional western with Joel McCrea; *A Life of Her Own* (1950), a tedious Lana Turner starrer; and *Cause for Alarm* (1950), his fifth film noir. This feature starred Loretta Young as Ellen Jones, a housewife whose insanely jealous husband, George (Sullivan), is recuperating from a heart ailment. Exacerbating George's fragile condition is his irrational belief that Ellen is having an affair with his doctor, and that the two are plotting his demise: "You must think I'm very stupid," George tells his wife. "Don't you think I know you're in love with him? … You're not as subtle as you think you are, Ellen. First I thought it was just an infatuation, but now I realize it's more serious — serious to the point where my life is more in danger from your heart than mine." As "insurance" against his wife's plans, George pens a letter to the local district attorney in which he describes his suspicions in great detail. After requesting that Ellen mail the letter, George triumphantly reveals its contents to his stunned wife, and promptly drops dead from a heart attack. The tension-filled remainder of the picture involves Ellen's frantic efforts to retrieve the letter before it reaches its destination, but in the rather dissatisfying climax, the letter is returned to her by the postman — it lacked sufficient postage.

After earning praise from one critic for "handl[ing] his rather precarious assignment quite well" in *Cause for Alarm*, Sullivan was loaned to RKO for one of the best roles of his career, the estranged husband of Bette Davis in *Payment on Demand* (1951). The actor later fondly recalled his experience working with his famed co-star.

"I thought I was pretty good until I first did a film with Bette Davis. If you work with slobs you get sloppy too. But when you're with someone like Bette, you stand on your head to do better," Sullivan said in 1954. "With Bette, each scene is a new challenge and she responds to it in terms of spontaneous combustion. She is terrific."

Back at MGM, the actor was again seen to good advantage in the box-office smash *The Bad and the Beautiful* (1952), portraying a director double-crossed by a ruthless producer (Kirk Douglas), and *Jeopardy* (1953) — the last film under his Metro contract — a taut drama in which his character is trapped under a pier at high tide while his wife (Barbara Stanwyck) enlists the aid of a criminal to save his life. During the summer of 1953, Sullivan took a break from filmmaking to tour with Viveca Lindfors in the comedy *Bell, Book and Candle*, and later that year was seen on the small screen opposite Sylvia Sidney in "As the Flame Dies" on *Ford Theater*. Back in Hollywood, Sullivan starred with Dorothy Malone in his final film noir, *Loophole* (1954).

Praised by one critic for its "terse, economical direction," *Loophole* featured Sullivan as Mike Donovan, a luckless bank teller falsely suspected of theft when he discovers a cash shortage of $49,000. Despite being cleared by police, Donovan is fired from his job and his life goes from bad to worse as he is stalked by a relentless bonding company investigator (Charles McGraw), is forced to sell his house, and loses a series of jobs, finally winding up as a taxi cab driver. ("It's great, isn't it," Donovan bitterly tells his wife. "First they put you in jail, then they say you're innocent, then they fire you, and then they put a tail on you. Sure, everything's going to be just dandy.") By chance, Donovan later encounters the real thief, bank teller Herman Tate (Don Beddoe), and although he is shot by Tate's money-grubbing girlfriend (Mary Beth Hughes), he manages to subdue them both and is later reinstated in his position at the bank. For his performance, Sullivan was praised in *Variety*, whose reviewer included him in his mention of the film's "competent cast," and by the critic for the *New York Times*, who noted "the good performances of the major actors ... who blend with the other ingredients into an enjoyable whole."

After *Loophole*, Sullivan returned to his Broadway roots, replacing Henry Fonda as Lt. Barney Greenwald in *The Caine Mutiny Courtmartial*. Shortly after joining the hit production, Sullivan shared his reaction to landing the role, stating that he had only 10 days to prepare.

"There just wasn't time to be scared," Sullivan told *New York Daily Mirror* columnist Sidney Fields. "When I could breathe again, I realized it was my first play here in 12 years and I had an awful lot of nerve. But a Herman Wouk wrote the play, a Charles Laughton directed me, and my only concern was to prove neither had wasted their time on me."

Sullivan not only proved his worth on Broadway, but also in the televised version of the play when he reprised his role the following year on *Ford Star Jubilee*, earning an Emmy nomination for Best Actor in a Single Performance (he lost to co-star Lloyd Nolan). Throughout the remainder of the 1950s, and for the next two decades, Sullivan built a second career on the small screen, guesting on such popular programs as *Alfred Hitchcock Presents*, *Perry Mason*, *It Takes a Thief*, *Night Gallery*, *McCloud*, *Hawaii Five-O*, *Cannon*, *The Streets of San Francisco*, *Kung Fu*, *Quincy*, *The Bionic Woman*, *Charlie's Angels*, *The Love Boat*, and *Little House on the Prairie*. He also starred in four series, *The Man Called X* (1956-57), *Harbormaster* (1957-58), *The Tall Man* (1960–62), and *The Road West* (1966-67); appeared in such mini-series as *Rich Man, Poor Man Book II* (1976), *Once an Eagle* (1976), and *Backstairs at the White House* (1979); and fulfilled a longtime interest in directing by helming episodes of several shows, including *Highway Patrol* and *Harbormaster*.

"I think I'd rather direct than anything," Sullivan once said. "I think if you want to say something, you can come closer to it as a director than anywhere else in this medium."

While Sullivan was building his television repertoire, he managed to find time for such stage productions as *The World of Carl Sandburg*, in which he toured with Bette Davis, and *Too Late the Phalarope*, a critically acclaimed but short-lived South African racial drama. He was also seen in a number of feature films, including *Queen Bee* (1955), playing the spouse of domineering Joan Crawford;

Strategic Air Command (1956) a box-office hit highlighted by breathtaking air footage; *Forty Guns* (1957), an intriguing western co-starring Barbara Stanwyck; *Another Time, Another Place* (1958), a tearjerker in which he portrayed the fiancé of Lana Turner; *Seven Ways from Sundown* (1960), a tiresome Audie Murphy starrer; *A Gathering of Eagles* (1963), a wartime drama with Rock Hudson and Rod Taylor; *Pyro* (1964), an odd thriller where he starred as an engineer bent on revenge against his ex-lover; *Harlow* (1964), a dreadful biopic starring Carol Lynley in the title role of the 1930s film star; *An American Dream* (1966), which focused on a TV commentator who accidentally causes the death of his shrewish wife; *This Savage Land* (1969), in which he portrayed a Civil War-era widower; and *Tell Them Willie Boy Is Here* (1970), an interesting western starring Robert Redford and Robert Blake.

Although Sullivan's multifaceted career was continuing at a steady pace, the same could not be said of his rocky personal life. In 1957, after 20 years of marriage, the actor and his wife were divorced, with Marie Sul-

livan testifying that the split stemmed from Sullivan's repeated absences from their home.

"Barry was gone for about a year and when he returned he began to take frequent business trips to the East," Marie said in June 1957. "Finally he said he didn't want to be married to me and he had no intention of returning to me or the family."

Sullivan married again in July 1958, this time to Birgitta Hall, but just a few months later, the actor announced that he and the voluptuous Swedish actress were separated, terming the union a "rather silly" affair that lasted only "ten minutes."

"It just didn't work," Sullivan said. "She's a nice girl and I'm not a bad fellow. We gave it a try and it just didn't work." The couple eventually reunited, but Sullivan's troubles continued when he was arrested the following year after police spotted him speeding and driving "erratically" along the Pacific Coast Highway. The actor, who was reportedly "antagonistic and not cooperative" when stopped by patrolmen, later pleaded guilty and was fined $263. Then, in June 1958, Birgitta Hall filed for divorce, claiming that Sullivan was "given to violent fits of temper." Although Hall later dropped her suit, she filed for divorce again in 1960; this suit, for the first time, noted that the couple had a five-year-old daughter, Patricia, born during Sullivan's marriage to his first wife. After yet another reconciliation, the couple's stormy union finally ended in April 1961.

Soon after his divorce from Hall was finalized, Sullivan courageously revealed a family secret that had been kept from the public for nearly 20 years—his oldest child, Johnny, was mentally retarded and had been under the care of doctors since the age of four.

"It's a worldwide problem, and too many cases are hidden in attics. The more people know about the problem, the more openly they face the problem, the greater the medical progress will be in helping other Johnnies," Sullivan told *Los Angeles Mirror* columnist Erskine Johnson in June 1961. "At first we thought it couldn't be Johnny. It must be us. Then the brain-wave test told us the truth.

Our friends never did quite understand our feelings. They kept telling us how brave we were, or that it was God's will, or they didn't mention it at all. We tried to keep it a secret at first, until I learned what people forget — that there are rewards." Sullivan later served as honorary chairman of the National Association of Mental Health and joined a parents' organization that raised funds for research and worked to improve conditions at state institutions.

Meanwhile, in August 1962, Sullivan made a third trip down the aisle; wife number three was 23-year-old Egyptian actress Desiree Sumara. But this union was doomed from the start and three years later, Sumara filed for divorce, claiming that Sullivan "never hugged or kissed me or showed me any affection. He was highly argumentative and at other times was silent for days. I used to cry all the time and had to seek medical attention."

When Sullivan wasn't making news because of his rocky relationships, he was providing hot copy with his strongly worded rants against the changing times in Hollywood. In a 1964 interview in the *Los Angeles Times*, Sullivan blasted modern film producers, labeling them "schnook heads."

"They don't know anything. They don't know how to read. They don't know how to think. In essence, I think they're a bunch of slobs," Sullivan said. "True, there are some who have some blood in them. They're interested in what they're doing. They're not just interested in having some so-called stars up to the home for a cocktail party.... Producers are scared. They're out-of-their heads scared. They just try to live, most of them. You can't go through the business that way."

And two years later, Sullivan focused his contempt on the television industry, stating in *Variety* that many producers for the small screen "become producers because they are shrewd promoters, manipulators, or salesmen who put a package together — and then they don't know what to do with it."

Despite the actor's vehemently expressed opinions, Sullivan continued to appear in such feature films as *The Candidate* (1972), in which he provided the narration; *Earthquake* (1974), a popular disaster film with a star-studded cast including Charlton Heston, Ava Gardner, Lloyd Nolan, and Lorne Greene; *Oh, God!* (1977), an entertaining comedy with George Burns in the title role; and *Caravans* (1978), an Iranian desert epic starring Anthony Quinn. He concentrated most of his energies on the small screen during this period, appearing in a variety of made-for-television movies, including *Night Gallery* (1969), which was helmed by a young man who, in his television directing debut, made a solid impact on Sullivan.

"I just finished a movie with a 22-year-old director, Steven Spielberg, that I flipped over," Sullivan said in the *New York Post*. "[But] his hair's a little long."

After a small role in *Casino* (1980), a television movie starring Mike Connors, Sullivan retired from performing. Out of the public eye for more than a decade, and suffering for several years from a respiratory ailment, the actor died in his Sherman Oaks, California, home on June 6, 1994, at the age of 81.

Throughout his lengthy and distinguished career, Barry Sullivan demonstrated an admirable ability to transform setbacks into successes and tragedy into triumph. A true star of stage, screen, and television, he remains one of the underrated gems of his day, and a noteworthy contributor to the era of film noir.

Film Noir Filmography

Suspense. Director: Frank Tuttle. Producers: Maurice and Frank King. Running time: 101 minutes. Released by Monogram, June 15, 1946. Cast: Belita, Barry Sullivan, Albert Dekker, Eugene Pallette, Bonita Granville, Edith Angold, George Stone.

The Gangster. Director: Gordon Wiles. Producers: Maurice and Frank King. Running time: 84 minutes. Released by Allied Artists, October 1947. Cast: Barry Sullivan, Belita, Joan Lorring, Akim Tamiroff, Henry Morgan, John Ireland, Fifi D'Orsay, Virginia Christine, Sheldon Leonard,

Leif Erickson, Charles McGraw, John Kellogg, Elisha Cook, Jr., Ted Hecht, Jeff Corey.

Framed. Director: Richard Wallace. Producer: Jules Schermer. Running time: 82 minutes. Released by Columbia, May 25, 1947. Cast: Glenn Ford, Janis Carter, Barry Sullivan, Edgar Buchanan, Karen Morley, Jim Bannon, Sid Tomack, Barbara Wooddell, Paul Burns.

Tension. Director: John Berry. Producer: Robert Sisk. Running time: 95 minutes. Released by MGM, January 11, 1950. Cast: Richard Basehart, Audrey Totter, Cyd Charisse, Barry Sullivan, Lloyd Gough, Tom D'Andrea, William Conrad, Tito Renaldo.

Cause for Alarm. Director: Tay Garnett. Producer: Tom Lewis. Running time: 74 minutes. Released by MGM, January 29, 1951. Cast: Loretta Young, Barry Sullivan, Bruce Cowling, Margalo Gillmore, Bradley Mora, Irving Bacon, Georgia Backus, Don Haggerty, Art Baker, Richard Anderson.

Loophole. Director: Harold Schuster. Producer: Lindsley Parsons. Running time: 79 minutes. Released by Allied Artists, March 12, 1954. Cast: Barry Sullivan, Charles McGraw, Dorothy Malone, Don Haggerty, Mary Beth Hughes, Don Beddoe, Dayton Lummis, Joanne Jordan, John Eldredge, Richard Reeves.

References

"Actor Barry Sullivan Divorced." *Los Angeles Examiner*, June 26, 1957.

Alpert, Don. "Sullivan's Irish Up Over Producers and Assorted Schnooks and Slobs." *Los Angeles Times*, February 2, 1964.

"Barry Sullivan." *Limelight*, September 22, 1960.

"Barry Sullivan and Bride Separating." *Hollywood Citizen-News*, September 16, 1958.

"Barry Sullivan Divorced." *New York Herald Tribune*, June 27, 1957.

"Barry Sullivan, 81, A Leading Actor in Movies and TV." *New York Times*, June 8, 1994.

"Barry Sullivan to Sing." *New York Journal-American*, July 31, 1958.

"Barry Sullivan Weds Egyptian Screen Beauty." *Los Angeles Times*, August 6, 1962.

"Boosts Film's Good Guys." *New York Morning Telegraph*, June 18, 1953.

"Busy Barry." *New York Times*, March 14, 1954.

Carroll, Harrison. "Sumara, Sullivan in Rift." *Los Angeles Examiner*, August 30, 1963.

Churchill, Reba and Bonnie. "Actor Tests New Sound Technique." *Beverly Hills Newslife*, February 17, 1954.

_____. "Barry Sullivan Teams with Shelley Winters in Film." *Beverly Hills Newslife*, December 2, 1953.

Creelman, Eileen. "Barry Sullivan of 'And Now Tomorrow' Talks of His Latest Paramount Pictures." *New York Sun*, December 9, 1944.

"Desiree Leaves Barry Single and 'Confused.'" *New York Daily News*, August 5, 1962.

"Drunk Driving Trial for Sullivan." *Los Angeles Examiner*, January 3, 1959.

Field, Rowland. "Along Broadway." *Newark Evening News*, July 14, 1954.

Fields, Sidney. "Sullivan Becomes Greenwald." *New York Daily Mirror*, June 22, 1954.

"Film Star Sullivan Hit by Divorce." *Los Angeles Examiner*, May 24, 1957.

"Gita Doesn't Want Divorce." *Los Angeles Examiner*, September 17, 1958.

Graham, Sheiliah. "Barry Sullivan Pulls No Punches." *Indianapolis Star*, June 27, 1954.

Herridge, Frances. "'Caine Mutiny Court Martial' Sexy?" *New York Post*, August 23, 1954.

Hopper, Hedda. "Stage's Barry Sullivans Agree to Part." *Los Angeles Times*, March 17, 1957.

Holt, Toni. 'I Went Berserk After I Knew My Son Was Retarded,' Says Actor Barry Sullivan." *The National Tattler*, May 19, 1974.

Johnson, Erskine. "Barry Sullivan Tells Why Son Johnny Can't Talk." *Los Angeles Mirror*, June 23, 1961.

Kaufman, Dave. "'Hack' Producers Bug Barry; CBS Readies Replacements." *Variety*, September 20, 1966.

Norton, Elliot. "Actor's Big Gamble." *Boston Post*, September 16, 1956.

Obituary. *The London Times*, June 15, 1994.

Parsons, Louella O. "'Mellerdrama' Preferred, Says Barry Sullivan." *Pictorial TView*, February 19, 1956.

Robbins, Jack. "Barry Sullivan: He's with the Kids." *New York Post*, February 22, 1969.

Schallert, Edwin. "Sullivan High on Filmland." *Los Angeles Times*, April 10, 1955.

Smith, Cecil. "Barry Sullivan Wants to Direct." *Los Angeles Times*, February 17, 1958.

"Sullivan's Wife Sues for Divorce." *Los Angeles Examiner*, June 3, 1959.

"Swedish Actress Wife Sues Barry Sullivan." *Los Angeles Examiner*, June 3, 1959.

Thirer, Irene. "Barry Sullivan's One Legit Actor Who Likes Hollywood." *New York Post*, December 6, 1944.

_____. "One-Night Stand? Not for the Sullivan Boy." *New York Post*, March 4, 1944.

Thomas, Kevin. "Actor Barry Sullivan Survives Myriad Film Style Changes." *Los Angeles Times*, May 14, 1966.

"Unkissed Wife Plea Divorces TV, Film Star." *Hollywood Citizen-News*. January 19, 1965.

Wald, Richard C. "Good By to 'Phalarope,' Sullivan Goes Homeward." *New York Herald Tribune*, November 18, 1956.

"Wedding Day Postponed by Couple." *Los Ange-les Times*, August 5, 1962.

Wilson, Earl. "'Youthful' Barry Sullivan." *New York Post*, February 18, 1969.

WILLIAM TALMAN

"You haven't got a chance. You guys are gonna die, that's all. It's just a matter of when."— William Talman in *The Hitch-Hiker* (1953)

To modern audiences, William Talman is best known as the luckless district attorney Hamilton Burger, who never won a case against TV's popular defense attorney, Perry Mason. But Talman's talent extended far beyond his ability to depict his character's frustration and annoyance at being outwitted in the courtroom week after week. The actor showed an equal mastery for stage and screen acting, screenwriting, directing, and producing, and early in his career, even demonstrated a proficiency for dancing and singing. Talman also evinced an inner fortitude that allowed him to overcome a number of personal setbacks, including a pair of rancorous divorces, child custody battles, and a widely publicized arrest that threatened to end his career. While he only appeared in 19 films over a span of 18 years, Talman made a decisive mark in the era of film noir, with memorable performances in *Armored Car Robbery* (1950), *The Racket* (1951), *City That Never Sleeps* (1953), and *The Hitch-Hiker* (1953).

William Whitney Talman, Jr., entered the world on February 4, 1917, with the proverbial silver spoon in his mouth. His father, an electrical engineer and auto parts manufacturer, raised William and his younger brother, Tom, in fine style in their home of Detroit, Michigan.

"[He made] enough to send me to school in a limousine each day," Talman once recalled. "That meant I had to fight my way in and out."

Talman first exhibited an interest in acting while attending the Cranbrook School in Bloomfield Hills, Michigan, where he was one of the co-founders of the school's Dra-

matics Club. He continued to participate in drama activities as a public speaking major at Dartmouth College, but in the first of many near-disasters in Talman's life, his secondary schooling was permanently interrupted during his sophomore year.

"I was enamored of a girl at Smith [College] and decided one weekend to call on her because a freshman offered to lend me 'his' car. I didn't know he had borrowed it from a girl at Bennington," Talman related to *TV Guide* in 1963. "A bus forced us off the road, we hit a tree. Well, a boy who was with us was killed instantly and we went first to the hospital and then to jail."

According to the actor, the student who had loaned him the car told authorities that the vehicle was stolen, and although the matter was later straightened out, Darmouth officials "asked me to resign," Talman recalled. He was invited to return the following year, but Talman declined. Instead, he spent the next few years in a series of widely varying pursuits, including traveling to Canada and England with the Moral Re-Armament evangelism movement, teaching tennis at the Belvedere Club in Charlevoix, Michigan, working in the Wayne County district attorney's office, and serving as a dancing emcee in nightclubs around the country. During these years, Talman also landed his first professional acting job, in *The Ghost of Yankee Doodle* at the University of Michigan Drama Festival in Ann Arbor, Michigan.

After urging from a friend, Talman saved enough money to travel to New York, where he worked in a number of summer stock productions, as well as the road company of

Of Mice and Men. He debuted on Broadway in *Beverly Hills*, but the show was a flop. Talman followed this play with several more short-lived productions before being cast in the lead role in *Spring Again* in 1941. But Talman was able to perform in the successful show for only a week before he was drafted into the Army. (He was replaced in the production by his understudy, Kirk Douglas, whose well-received performance served to launch his successful Hollywood career.) During his four-year service in the Army Signal Corps, Talman continued his penchant for varied activities; he directed more than 100 shows for servicemen, tried his hand at playwriting, and coached the boxing team for his unit, which won the Army's Western Pacific Boxing Championship in Manila in 1945. Talman also found time to marry New York actress Lynne Carter while on furlough in September 1942. The two went on to have a daughter, Lynda, in 1948.

Upon his discharge from the Army in 1946, Talman wasted no time in resuming his acting career; just two weeks after returning to New York, he was cast opposite his wife in *Dear Ruth*, a popular Broadway production that ran for 40 weeks. He also starred with Lynne in the long-running play *A Young Man's Fancy*, demonstrated his singing ability in a musical entitled *Yokel Boy*, directed his first professional show at the Cliff Summer Theatre in Long Island, New York, and was seen in several stock productions, including a well-received version of *John Loves Mary*. Between engagements, he widened his realm of experience by working as a stage manager.

In 1949, Talman's career took an unexpected change of direction when he traveled to Hollywood as a representative of the Actor's Equity Council to correlate the Screen Actor's Guild with Equity and the American Federation of Radio Artists. On the day before his scheduled return to New York, he was approached by a talent scout from RKO, invited to take a screen test, and signed to a contract. Upon Talman's move to Hollywood, however, studio head Howard Hughes failed to put him to work.

"Hughes was in one of his blue, or inactive periods," Talman later said. "I sat 13 months before they used me."

Instead, the actor was loaned to Paramount for his screen debut in *Red, Hot and Blue* (1949), a lively Betty Hutton musical that gave Talman a rare opportunity to show off his comedic talents. The following year, he was seen in his first film for his home studio, *The Woman on Pier 13* (1950), originally released as *I Married a Communist*. A heavy-handed anti–Communist melodrama, the film lost $650,000 at the box office, and Talman fared little better with a loanout to Universal for a routine Audie Murphy western, *The Kid From Texas* (1950). He did find success, however, with a brief return to the stage, directing and producing *Honest John* at the Las Palmas Theater in Los Angeles, and back at his home studio, he was seen in a standout role in his first film noir, *Armored Car Robbery* (1950). Here, the actor portrayed Dave Purvis, a callous criminal who masterminds a scheme to rob an armored car at a Los Angeles ballpark. The flawlessly executed crime is disrupted when local detectives show up and gunfire leaves one cop dead and one of the robbers, Benny McBride (Douglas Fowley), severely wounded. Although Purvis and his henchmen escape, the gangleader later kills Benny when the injured man insists on medical treatment, and the other hoods are ultimately hunted down by police. After abducting and shooting a rookie detective (Don McGuire), Purvis attempts to flee with the money and Benny's showgirl wife (Adele Jergens), but he meets a grisly end at a local airport when he is struck and killed by a departing airplane. For his role as the heartless Purvis, Talman was praised in *Variety* for "put[ting] plenty of color into [his] heavy assignment."

After *Armored Car Robbery*, Talman remained in the noir realm, this time on the right side of the law in *The Racket* (1951). Here, Talman played a highly regarded police officer, Bob Johnson, who is described by one character as the "best young cop on the force — honest, decent, plenty of guts." After he successfully identifies a man involved in a local murder, Johnson is put on special assignment by his boss, Capt. Tom McQuigg (Robert Mitchum), a no-nonsense cop determined to bring to justice his nemesis, Nick Scanlon (Robert Ryan). But when Scanlon pays a visit to the police station in search of McQuigg, he encounters Johnson instead, and kills the young officer during a scuffle. McQuigg finally gets his man by the film's end, however, when the gangster is gunned down while trying to escape through a station house window. While this hard-hitting noir was mostly dominated by Mitchum and Ryan, Talman was singled out in *Variety* for his "strong work" as the rookie cop.

Although his screen career was in full swing, Talman was not as successful in his personal life. In the fall of 1951, the actor filed for divorce from his wife, who promptly countersued, charging extreme cruelty. In the divorce hearing the following year, Lynne Talman told the court that her husband's neglect had left her "unable to concentrate on my career."

"About two years ago, he lost interest in me and our home, staying away and being highly critical when he was there," she said. "If we had guests, he would remain in his room, or leave soon after they arrived."

In May 1952, Lynne was awarded custody of the couple's three-year-old daughter, Lynda, and Talman was ordered to pay her 24 percent of his gross income. Lynne was also allowed to keep $75,000 in securities that the actor had given her early in their marriage. (Nearly a decade later, in 1960, Talman would attempt to gain legal custody of his daughter, as well as to modify the 1952 divorce agreement. He would be unsuccessful in both endeavors.) Meanwhile, Talman wasted no time in giving marriage another try; shortly after his divorce, he married Barbara Reed, a former actress who had appeared in such films as *Three Smart Girls* (1936), *Sorority House* (1939), and *Death Valley* (1946). Talman and Barbara later had two children, Barbara in 1953, and William III in 1954.

On screen, after playing a jet pilot in a

war adventure, *One Minute to Zero* (1952), Talman starred as the villain in back-to-back films noirs, *City That Never Sleeps* (1953) and *The Hitch-Hiker* (1953). The first takes place on a single night in Chicago, skillfully weaving together the lives of such characters as Johnny Kelly (Gig Young), a disillusioned cop planning to quit the force; Johnny's mistress, Sally (Mala Powers), who is determined to escape her seedy existence as a showgirl; Gregg Warren (Wally Cassell), who works as a department store "mechanical man" and carries a torch for Sally; Hayes Stewart (Talman), a former magician turned burglary expert; Penrod Biddel (Edward Arnold), a ruthless criminal attorney; and Lydia (Marie Windsor), Biddell's wife and Stewart's mistress. As the film's intertwining plots unfold, Stewart attempts to extort a $100,000 payoff from Biddel in exchange for damaging papers he has stolen, but he is forced to shoot the lawyer when Biddel pulls a gun. Stewart later kills Johnny's sergeant father and his mistress, Lydia, before falling to his death on the electrified "third rail" of the city's elevated train tracks.

Although *City That Never Sleeps* was

panned in the *New York Times* for its "strict, cardboard cops-and-robbers style, with dialogue to match," Talman was hailed for his role as the murderous burglar, with one critic calling his performance "the most persuasive of the entire lot, conveying the sizzling restraint of a truly fine performer." He earned similar raves for his second film noir of the year, *The Hitch-Hiker*, where he played Emmet Myers, a vicious serial killer who terrorizes a pair of fishing buddies (Edmond O'Brien and Frank Lovejoy) who pick him up on the road. During the nightmarish trip, the killer provides a glimpse into his persona when he bitterly tells the men, "Nobody ever gave me anything. So I don't owe nobody. My folks were tough. When I was born, they took one look at this puss of mine and told me to get lost. Well, I didn't need 'em. I didn't need any of 'em. Got what I wanted my own way." The two men are forced at gunpoint to drive to Mexico, and their plans to escape are dashed when they learn that Myers suffers from a paralyzed eye that remains open even when he is sleeping. The tension-filled journey finally comes to an end, however, when a diligent Mexican officer tracks the trio to a small village and captures Myers as he is trying to flee.

Directed by actress Ida Lupino, *The Hitch-Hiker* was praised by one reviewer for its "71 terror-stricken minutes," and Talman's performance was universally applauded; the *New York Times* critic reported that the actor "makes the most of one of the year's juiciest assignments"; Philip K. Scheuer wrote in the *Los Angeles Times* that audiences were "held captive by William Talman"; and Lowell E. Redelings of the *Hollywood Citizen-News* characterized the actor as "simply magnificent."

As the midpoint of the decade approached, Talman entered one of his busiest and most creative periods. No longer under contract to RKO, he worked as a freelancer, appearing in 10 films between 1955 and 1957, including *Crashout* (1955), where he played one of six convicts who escape from prison on a quest for a fortune in gold coins; *Big*

House U.S.A. (1955), a hard-hitting crime drama in which he again played a escaped felon; *Two-Gun Lady* (1956), where he starred opposite Peggie Castle; and *Hell on Devil's Island* (1957), in which he was seen as a crooked prison overseer. He also co-wrote (with Norman Jolley) and starred in *I've Lived Before* (1956), a drama about reincarnation, and *Joe Dakota* (1957), a slow-moving western notable primarily because there were no shots fired throughout the film. In addition to his feature film work, Talman guested on several television series, including *Screen Directors Playhouse* and *Trackdown*, before landing the role that would catapult him to nationwide fame — Hamilton Burger on *Perry Mason*. In this wildly popular CBS-TV series starring Raymond Burr in the title role, Talman's character never won a court case, and over time, the actor expressed a minor degree of frustration over the constant ribbing he received because of it.

"I am a little tired of the cracks," he said in 1958. "If you watch the series, you will discover that Mason has always defended an innocent party. At the close, he not only frees the innocent but exposes the guilty. The viewer must assume that on the other days of the week, Hamilton Burger prosecutes these people and obtains convictions. Anyway, Mason *has* to win. That's what the television series is about. Moreover, whoever heard of Matt Dillon losing a fight on *Gunsmoke*?"

But just a few years after Talman offered this rationale, he faced a real-life legal battle that eclipsed any drama he faced on the small screen. In the early morning hours of March 13, 1960, the actor was arrested in a Hollywood party raid, along with seven others, by officers who charged that the revelers were "high on marijuana." According to authorities, an undercover officer had been invited to the party and arrived to find everyone "in the nude." Police also said they found one marijuana cigarette stub, several "prepared marijuana smokes," and a quantity of loose marijuana in bedroom closets, the bathroom medicine chest, and in other locations throughout the apartment. Talman denied any knowledge of the presence of the drug and insisted that he had only stopped at the apartment to "have a social drink."

Deputy District Attorney John Loucks decided against charging the actor with possession of marijuana, asking, "How could a person have marijuana in his possession when he didn't have a strip of clothes on his body?" Loucks chose, instead, to charge Talman and the seven others with lewdness and vagrancy. After his arrest, Talman told reporters that the incident "is going to ruin me"—and he was relatively accurate in his gloomy prediction. Just four days later, the actor was summarily fired from the cast of *Perry Mason* by CBS-TV officials, who announced that the character would be recast. (They later reversed this stance, claiming that Talman had not been fired, but that the option on his contract had simply not been renewed because the show's format had changed and would no longer depict the role of the district attorney). And although the actor's June 1960 trial was halted after just three days (the presiding judge proclaimed that "it isn't against the law to go around a house without clothes on"), CBS refused to rehire the actor.

After being dropped from *Perry Mason*, Talman made ends meet by writing several teleplays under an assumed name, but even after being vindicated by the court, he was unable to find work on CBS or any other network. Shortly after the end of the trial, the actor was offered a role on NBC's *Bonanza*, but Talman claimed that the offer was rescinded after pressure from the top brass at CBS.

"I don't want to be the center of a controversy," Talman told *Los Angeles Examiner* columnist Charles Denton in August 1960. "But what in the name of heaven can I do now except point a finger at these people and say, 'Look what they're doing to me?' I thought that when a man had a fair hearing in court and was cleared, he could at least go back to where he started. But it hasn't worked that way. To me, that's the main issue in this whole mess.... What does it mean for a man to be

acquitted in court if everyone treats him as if he were guilty?"

During the next several months, letters poured in from fans demanding the actor's return, CBS officials were urged to rehire Talman by Raymond Burr and the show's producer, Gail Patrick Jackson, and numerous newspaper columns were written in Talman's defense. In a typical column, *Los Angeles Mirror Television and Radio* Editor Hal Humphrey passionately declared that "Hollywood has sentenced [Talman] to an indefinite period of unemployment for a crime he didn't commit. Talman isn't in jail.... He might be better off in jail, though, because he can't find any work."

Finally in December 1960, nine months after his arrest, Talman was quietly rehired as Hamilton Burger on *Perry Mason*. The actor later claimed to harbor no bitterness about the experience, and he remained with the show until the series ended in 1966. But Hamilton's return to the popular series did not spell the end of his personal setbacks. In 1959, the actor's wife, Barbara Reed, had filed for divorce, charging Talman with cruelty and desertion and testifying that "he hadn't shown me any affection since 1958." In August 1960, in the midst of the controversy surrounding Talman's arrest, Barbara was awarded custody of the couple's two children, along with $700 a month in support. Talman regained custody in 1961, however, when Barbara turned the children over to her ex-husband and moved to Mexico. (Two years later, the former actress committed suicide, leaving a note indicating that she had been in ill health.) Talman's troubles continued in the early 1960s when a Los Angeles judge ruled that he had to continue paying his first wife, Lynne, 24 percent of his income; at that time, he had already paid her nearly $250,000 since their 1952 divorce.

"Could you urge your readers to send money?" Talman wryly joked in *TV Guide*.

But, in what was perhaps the sole bright spot in the actor's life during this period, Talman took a chance in 1961 on a third trip down the aisle; wife number three was Peggy

Flanigan (who, incidentally, was one of those arrested with Talman at the party raid a year earlier). By all accounts, this union was a happy one, and produced two children, Timothy in 1963 and Susan Marie in 1965.

After *Perry Mason* left the air, Talman participated in a 22-day USO tour of Vietnam and Thailand, appeared in guest spots on such television series as *The Wild, Wild West* and *The Invaders*, and — in his first feature film in more than a decade — was seen in *The Ballad of Josie* (1968), a mildly pleasant comedy-western starring Doris Day. Sadly, shortly after filming his role as an attorney for the latter production, Talman was diagnosed with lung cancer. A three-pack-a-day smoker for many years, Talman promptly began radiation treatments, but learned the following year that he was also suffering from an inoperable brain tumor. Determined to make the most of the remainder of his life, the actor set out with his wife, their two children, and her two youngsters from a previous marriage, for a two-month tour of Europe. Shortly after their arrival in London in early August 1968, however, Talman fell ill and the family was forced to return to the United States. A few weeks later, on August 30, 1968, Talman died after a heart attack at West Valley Community Hospital. He was 53 years old.

In addition to the feature films and television appearances from Talman's 20-year career, the actor also left behind a poignant public service commercial for the American Cancer Society that was filmed just six weeks before his death. Surrounded by his wife and children, and seated next to a picture of Raymond Burr, Talman reminded viewers that Burr "used to beat my brains out on TV every week for about 10 years."

"You know, I didn't really mind losing those courtroom battles. But now I'm in a battle right now I don't want to lose at all because if I lose it, it means losing my wife and those kids you just met," Talman said. "So take some advice about smoking and losing from someone who's been doing both for years. Before I die, I want to do what I can do to leave a world free of cancer for my children."

Although a handful of television stations found the commercial too graphic, most aired the 60-second spot just as Talman had filmed it. His courageous message left a powerful impact, even on his widow, Peggy.

"After Bill died, I still continued smoking," Peggy said in a 1970 interview. "Then, one night, the children and I were watching *Lassie* and Bill's commercial came on. Little Timmy turned to me and said, 'Mommy, Daddy said to stop smoking.' And I did, right then and there."

While his talent and versatility was all too often eclipsed by his personal woes, William Talman nonetheless managed to exhibit, particularly in his film noir performances, that his was a talent worth recognizing. However, it is his spirit of perseverance and his concern for his fellow man in the face of his own mortality that provides an even more admirable legacy.

Film Noir Filmography

Armored Car Robbery. Director: Richard Fleischer. Producer: Herman Schlom. Running time: 67 minutes. Released by RKO, June 8, 1950. Cast: Charles McGraw, Adele Jergens, William Talman, Douglas Fowley, Steve Brodie, Don McGuire, Don Haggerty, James Flavin, Gene Evans.

The Racket. Director: John Cromwell. Producer: Edmund Grainger. Running time: 88 minutes. Released by RKO, December 12, 1951. Cast: Robert Mitchum, Lizabeth Scott, Robert Ryan, William Talman, Ray Collins, Joyce MacKenzie, Robert Hutton, Virginia Huston, William Conrad, Walter Sande, Les Tremayne, Don Porter, Walter Baldwin, Brett King, Richard Karlan, Tito Vuolo.

City That Never Sleeps. Director and Producer: John H. Auer. Running time: 90 minutes. Released by Republic, August 8, 1953. Cast: Gig Young, Mala Powers, William Talman, Edward Arnold, Chill Wills, Marie Windsor, Paula Raymond, Otto Hulett, Wally Cassell, Ron Hagerthy, James Andelin, Thomas Poston, Bunny Kacher, Philip L. Boddy, Thomas Jones, Leonard Diebold.

The Hitch-Hiker. Director: Ida Lupino. Producer: Collier Young. Running time: 71 minutes. Released by RKO, April 29, 1953. Cast: Edmond

O'Brien, Frank Lovejoy, William Talman, Jose Torvay, Sam Hayes, Wendell Niles, Jean Del Val, Clark Howat, Natividad Vacio, Rodney Bell, Nacho Galindo, Martin Garralaga, Tony Roux, Jerry Lawrence, Felipe Turich, Joe Dominguez, Rose Turich, Orlando Veltran, George Navarro, Jun Dinneen, Al Ferrara, Henry Escalante, Taylor Flaniken, Wade Crosby, Kathy Riggins, Gordon Barnes, Ed Hinton, Larry Hudson.

References

"Actor Talman's Ex-Wife Dies." *Hollywood Citizen-News*, December 12, 1963.

"Actor Talman to Be Treated for Cancer." *Hollywood Citizen-News*, September 29, 1967.

Adams, Val. "Good Loser Gets a Double Drubbins." *New York Times*, April 24, 1966.

Baessler, Paul. "Winless for Six Years, Burger Keeps Smiling." *Los Angeles Herald-Examiner*, July 11, 1963.

Besler, Lee. "Bill Talman Tells His 'Desperate' Strait." *Los Angeles Mirror*, December 6, 1960.

Biography of William Talman. RKO Radio Studios. November 3, 1952.

Biography of William Talman. USO Public Relationships Department, July 24, 1967.

"Child Custody to TV Actor Talman." *Hollywood Citizen-News*, March 21, 1961.

"Custody Bid Dropped by Talman." *Hollywood Citizen-News*, January 11, 1961.

Dallos, Robert E. "Perry Mason's TV Foe, Dead of Cancer, Left Antismoking Film." *New York Times*, September 13, 1968.

Denton, Charles. "Ex-'D.A.' Bill Talman Has Say in Court of Public Opinion." *Los Angeles Examiner*, August 15, 1960.

Engels, Mary. "She Carries on His Crusade." *New York Daily News*, March 19, 1970.

"Film Pair Greet Second Child, Son." *Los Angeles Examiner*, July 28, 1954.

Fuller, Tyra. "Now Busy Bill Talman Has No Film Scheduled." Publication Unsourced, circa 1949.

Gebhart, Myrtle. "Business Trip Brought Film Fame." *Boston Post Magazine*, October 2, 1949.

Gehman, Richard. "He Never Comes in First." *TV Guide*, April 27, 1963.

Humphrey, Hal. "Controversy Over Anti-Cancer Film." *Los Angeles Times*, October 21, 1968.

_____. "Erle Stanley Gardner Speaks on Case of the Ostracized D.A." *Los Angeles Mirror*, August 18, 1960.

_____. "Perry Mason's DA Officially Dead, but Still Looks for Job." *Los Angeles Mirror*, August 3, 1960.

Hyams, Joe. "Perry Mason 'D.A.' Fights Own Case." *New York Herald Tribune*, August 22, 1960.

Ladd. Bill. "When Perry Mason Wins, So Does the Prosecutor, Says Man Playing Role." *Louisville Courier-Journal*, November 2, 1958.

Lembke, Bud. "Mason's DA Loses Another Case." *New York Post*, August 24, 1960.

"Lynne Carter Divorced from 'Critical' Mate." *Los Angeles Times*, May 9, 1952.

"Lynne Carter Wins Divorce from Actor." *Los Angeles Examiner*, May 9, 1952.

"Morals Charges Against Talman, Others Dropped." *Los Angeles Times*, June 18, 1960.

Obituary. *Newsweek*, September 23, 1968.

Obituary. *Variety*, September 3, 1968.

"'Perry Mason' D.A., 4 Girls Seized in Nude Dope Raid." *Los Angeles Examiner*, March 14, 1960.

"'Perry Mason' D.A. Freed on Morals Charge." *New York Herald-Tribune*, June 18, 1960.

"'Perry Mason' D.A. Jailed in Hollywood Party Raid." *Los Angeles Times*, March 14, 1960.

"Talman Alimony Extended." *Los Angeles Examiner*, January 11, 1961.

"Talman Gets 'Perry Mason' Role Back." *Los Angeles Times*, December 9, 1960.

"Talman Hints Court Fight to Save TV Job." *Los Angeles Times*, March 19, 1960.

"Talman's Pen Also Poison, Webs Rule; Adopts Pseudonym." *Variety*, August 18, 1960.

"The Legacy of a Dying Actor: An Anti-Smoking Commercial." *New York Post*, September 13, 1968.

"TV Actor Undergoes Surgery." *Hollywood Citizen-News*, September 28, 1967.

"Wife Divorces William Talman." *Los Angeles Examiner*, August 24, 1960.

ROBERT TAYLOR

"I'll handle your business for you, Rico — I'll even protect your hoods for you, but I refuse to eat with you. Because you're a slob." — Robert Taylor in Party Girl (1958)

Known as "The Man with the Perfect Face," Robert Taylor was more than just that. The popular actor of film and television was also, by all accounts, a Hollywood rarity — a nice guy.

"When one thinks of his extraordinary good looks, he had every right to be a bit spoiled," a co-star once said of the actor. "But not Bob. He was unassuming, good-natured, and had a wonderful sense of humor."

While Taylor was adored by fans for his handsome visage and lauded by friends for his affability, however, his capability as a thespian was often overlooked. Particularly in his early career, Taylor's on-screen performances were largely ignored by critics, who — much to the actor's dismay — concentrated instead on his "pretty boy" looks. Nonetheless, the actor managed to demonstrate in such films as *Camille* (1936), *Three Comrades* (1938), and *Waterloo Bridge* (1940), that his cinematic contributions extended far beyond his famed widow's peak and exquisitely formed features. His talent was also shown to good advantage in his six film noir appearances: *Johnny Eager* (1942), *Undercurrent* (1946), *The High Wall* (1947), *The Bribe* (1949), *Rogue Cop* (1954), and *Party Girl* (1958).

The handsome screen star was born on August 5, 1911, in Filley, Nebraska, saddled with the rather graceless moniker of Spangler Arlington Brugh. In 1918, the Brugh family moved to Beatrice, Nebraska, where Spangler attended elementary and high school, excelling in sports and developing an affinity for the cello. After high school, Spangler enrolled in Doane College in nearby Crete, with plans to follow in his father's career path as a doctor. Instead, with his mother's encouragement, the young man continued to pursue his interest in the cello, and during his Christmas and summer vacations in 1930 and 1931, Spangler performed on local radio sta-

tion KMMJ with a musical trio known as the Fly Swatters. His love for the instrument was so great, in fact, that when his music teacher at Doane transferred to Pomona College in Claremont, California, Spangler followed him there.

Although he later admitted that he could not remember why, Spangler joined the drama club at Pomona College, appearing in such school productions as *Camille*, *The Importance of Being Earnest*, and *M'Lord the Duke*. During his senior year, while appearing in *Journey's End*, he caught the attention of MGM casting director Ben Piazza, who offered Spangler free acting lessons at the studio. Although he turned down the offer, Spangler enrolled at the Neely Dixon Dramatic School in Hollywood after his graduation, and a short time later he inked a seven-year agreement with Metro at a starting salary of $35 a week. The studio's first order of business was to change the young man's name to a more marquee-friendly moniker, and Robert Taylor was born.

Taylor's initial screen appearances were loan-outs to other studios; the first was to 20th Century-Fox for *Handy Andy* (1934), starring Will Rogers, followed by *There's Always Tomorrow* (1934) at Universal, in which he played the son of Frank Morgan. Back at his home studio, Taylor played a bit part in *Buried Loot* (1934), the first in the series of *Crime Does Not Pay* shorts; a small role in *A Wicked Woman* (1934), a passable melodrama with Jean Parker and Charles Bickford; and his first lead in *Times Square Lady* (1935), where he starred opposite Virginia Bruce.

"I was awful. The worst actor in the world," Taylor said years later. "[But] I was lucky. I had it good compared with the kids of today. When I started … they put me in B pictures until I learned to act a little. You could do that in those days; keep on making terrible pictures that nobody ever saw until you learned."

Taylor was obviously a fast learner — he made an impact on critics and audiences alike in *Society Doctor* (1935), and became an overnight star when he was paired with Irene Dunne in Universal's *Magnificent Obsession* (1935), a three-hankie weeper that was a hit with moviegoers and critics alike. After his triumphant performance in this feature, Taylor began appearing with some of Hollywood's most popular leading ladies, including Janet Gaynor in *Small Town Girl* (1936), Joan Crawford in *The Gorgeous Hussy* (1936), and Loretta Young in *Private Number* (1936). Like most of Taylor's co-stars, Young spoke later of the actor's professionalism and down-to-earth demeanor.

"I worked with Bob Taylor just after the big furor about him got underway, and he was being hailed as the new great lover," Young said. "I don't know what I expected him to be like, but I found him a surprisingly normal person, neither fussed nor conceited. He was simply doing his work and letting matters take their own course. It's always easy to get along with anyone like that."

Another of Taylor's co-stars during this period was Barbara Stanwyck, with whom he was teamed in *His Brother's Wife* (1936), a hit romantic drama helmed by W.S. Van Dyke. Off screen, Taylor and Stanwyck were a hit as well, providing an ideal illustration of the adage that opposites attract. As pointed out by columnist Louella Parsons, Stanwyck was "big city, [Taylor] was small town. She was decisive; he was a dreamer. Barbara was a few years his elder; he was exceptionally young for his age." Despite their differences, however, Taylor and Stanwyck began a highly publicized romance that would culminate with their marriage on May 14, 1939.

Meanwhile, Taylor was fast becoming one of MGM's most celebrated performers; his weekly salary was increased to $3,500, he received an estimated 30,000 pieces of fan mail each month, and film exhibitors voted him the fourth biggest box-office star of 1936 (after Shirley Temple, Clark Gable, and the team of Fred Astaire and Ginger Rogers). In another testament to his sudden fame, a reporter from the *London Observer* proclaimed that "1936 will go on record as the year of Edward VIII, the Spanish war, and Robert Taylor."

Taylor's star continued its vertical ascent with his portrayal of Armand Duval in *Camille* (1936), with Greta Garbo in the title role. In this hit film, Taylor struck just the right note of lovesick devotion and touching pathos, causing one reviewer to grudgingly admit that he "avoids the callousness of previous Armands." Although he was only 25 years old, Taylor more than held his own with the luminous Garbo, later giving the credit for his performance to his co-star and the film's director.

"[Some] people tell me it's my best performance, and if it is, I can thank her and director George Cukor," Taylor said. "You can't work with a woman like that without catching a spark from her, and Cukor is an expert at bringing out the best in actors."

After such lightweight fare as *Personal Property* (1937) with Jean Harlow, and Fox's *This is My Affair* (1937), a re-teaming with Barbara Stanwyck, Taylor starred alongside Maureen O'Sullivan and Vivien Leigh in *A Yank at Oxford* (1937); earned acclaim for his "splendid" performance in the touching drama *Three Comrades* (1938); and portrayed a boxer who accidentally kills a man in the ring in *The Crowd Roars* (1938). For the latter film, Taylor refused to use a stunt double, training at his ranch home with professional fighters.

"When I read over the script for this picture, I was enthusiastic about the part," Taylor said in a 1938 interview. "I decided I wouldn't just give an imitation of a fighter; I'd be one."

For the next few years, Taylor's career witnessed a slump as he continued to battle his "pretty boy" label (he was once asked by a reporter if he had hair on his chest, and another speculated on whether his eyelashes were longer than Greta Garbo's). His films during this period included *Lucky Night*

(1939), a humdrum comedy with Myrna Loy, and *Lady of the Tropics* (1939), a box-office flop co-starring Hedy Lamarr. But the actor rebounded in 1940 with *Waterloo Bridge*, playing a wartime soldier who has an ill-fated romance with a ballerina, portrayed by Vivien Leigh. Taylor would later consider the film as his favorite, stating that "it came at a time when I didn't think I was a good actor. When I saw the picture, I was surprised — along with everybody else."

After starring roles in *Billy the Kid* (1941), notable primarily as the actor's first Technicolor film, and *When Ladies Meet* (1941), in which he demonstrated a deftness for light comedy, Taylor was seen in the title role of his first film noir, *Johnny Eager* (1941). In taking on one of the first "heavy" roles of his career, however, Taylor encountered resistance from MGM head Louis B. Mayer.

"When I was at Metro, playing those romantic leads ... I got hold of the *Johnny Eager* script and I felt I had to do it. Louis B. Mayer screamed and roared and wept," Taylor recalled years later. "I was changing the image he had built up for so many years, I was his 'son,' he was looking out for my best interests and so on. Well, we finally got Mayer to agree to my doing *Johnny Eager*. And since it was a gangster picture, it changed my whole life from that point on. I wasn't a romantic lead anymore. I was an actor."

As Johnny Eager, Taylor played a slick ex-con who works as a taxi driver to mask his criminal activities, which include plans to open a dog racing track. Standing in the way of Eager's project is district attorney John Farrell (Edward Arnold), who is the stepfather of a young sociology student with whom Eager comes in contact. When Farrell's stepdaughter, Lisbeth Barr (Lana Turner), falls in love with Johnny, the polished hood implicates her in a staged murder so that he can blackmail Farrell into lifting his injunction against the dog track. Emotionally shattered, Lisbeth suffers a breakdown and Johnny has a change of heart, admitting that he loves her and confessing the truth about the fake murder. Lisbeth refuses to believe him, however,

and Johnny puts his life in jeopardy to prove that she is innocent — after placing Lisbeth in the care of her former fiancé, Johnny is gunned down by members of a rival gang and police.

Upon the release of *Johnny Eager*, Taylor earned rave reviews; the critic for *Variety* termed his performance "soundly socked and ... very convincing," and the reviewer for *The Hollywood Reporter* wrote: "Robert Taylor plays Johnny Eager to show he isn't a star to be stupidly typed. He is brilliant in projecting a relentless mobster, hard as nails and twice as sharp." The latter also offered high praise for the film itself, calling it "a picture to rank with *Little Caesar*, *Scarface*, and *Public Enemy No. 1* as a smash box office attraction."

While Taylor was altering his on-screen persona, however, his life behind the scenes was in turmoil. For some time, his marriage to Barbara Stanwyck had been strained, due in part to the filming schedules that frequently kept the couple apart. The union was nearly fractured during the shooting of *Johnny Eager* when Taylor became involved with the 20-year-old Turner, telling reporters that he "was never known to run after blondes, [but] Lana was the exception." Taylor reportedly even considered leaving his wife, but years later, Turner said that she "would never be responsible for breaking up a marriage, however unhappy it was. I wasn't in love with Bob, not really. Oh, we'd exchanged kisses, romantic passionate kisses, but we'd never been to bed together. Our eyes had, but not our bodies." A short time later, however, Taylor and his wife began construction on a new house in Beverly Hills, and Stanwyck put a temporary lid on the swirl of rumors by asking the press, "Does that sound like we're getting a divorce?"

Professionally, as part of MGM's contribution to the war effort, Taylor next starred in *Stand by for Action* (1942), with Charles Laughton and Brian Donlevy, and *Bataan* (1943), in which he earned acclaim for his "first-rate" portrayal of a tough-as-nails sergeant. He was also seen as an orchestra conductor who falls in love with a Russian girl

in *Song of Russia* (1943), a film to which Taylor reportedly objected because of what he
considered to be the film's pro–Communist
message. After this feature, Taylor enlisted as
a lieutenant in the Naval Air Corps but, at
age 32, he was judged too old too fly and
served instead as a flying instructor. During
his service, Taylor also directed 17 training
films and provided the narration for the battle film *The Fighting Lady* (1943), earning
praise from one reviewer for his "stern, self-
effacing voice with no trace of the movie
star."

Taylor's first two features following his
November 1945 release from the Navy were
back-to-back films noirs, *Undercurrent* (1946),
with Katharine Hepburn and Robert
Mitchum, and *The High Wall* (1947), where
he starred opposite Audrey Totter. In *Undercurrent*, Taylor played Alan Garroway, a successful inventor and businessman who marries a college professor's daughter, Ann
Hamilton (Katharine Hepburn), after a whirlwind romance. Before long, Alan reveals an
obsessive hatred for his brother, Michael
(Robert Mitchum), who has not been seen
for several years. Although Alan maintains
that Michael disappeared after he was caught
stealing from the family business, Ann learns
more about her brother-in-law by speaking
to several of his friends and finds herself falling in love with a man she has never met. As
it turns out, Michael left the company after
suspecting that Alan murdered a engineer
who was working on an invention and made
a fortune from his plans. After Michael later
resurfaces and reveals his plans to tell Ann
the truth, Alan realizes that his wife no longer
loves him and plots to kill her. Taking Ann
on a horseback ride, Alan tries to force her
over a steep cliff, but his plan backfires and
he is trampled to death.

Next, in *The High Wall* (1947), Taylor
starred as Steven Kenet, a pilot who is admitted to a psychiatric hospital after confessing that he has strangled his wife, Helen
(Dorothy Patrick). Suffering from a subdural
hematoma that causes blackouts and painful
headaches, Kenet undergoes an operation and

reveals that he cannot remember the circumstances of his wife's death. A doctor at the
hospital, Ann Lorrison (Audrey Totter), uses
drug therapy to jog Kenet's memory, and he
eventually realizes that his wife was actually
killed by her employer, Willard Whitcombe
(Herbert Marshall), with whom she was having an affair. Unable to prove that he is innocent, Kenet escapes from the hospital and,
with Lorrison's help, manages to slip through
a police cordon and enter Whitcombe's apartment: "I'll kill you before anyone gets here,"
Kenet tells him. "There's nothing they can do
to me but send me back to the asylum. The
law says I'm insane. Not responsible. You
fixed that." As Kenet subdues Whitcombe,
Lorrison administers a "truth serum" and
Whitcombe admits his guilt, emerging from
the effects of the drug to find that his confession has been witnessed by police.

Taylor's performances in both *Undercurrent* and *The High Wall* were viewed favorably by critics. The *New York Times*' Bosley
Crowther judged that he "accelerates a brooding meanness" in *Undercurrent*, and Lloyd
Sloan of the *Hollywood Citizen-News* praised
his "splendid" portrayal, writing that Taylor
"run[s] the gamut from tender love scenes to

unrestrained hysterics." Similarly, of *The High Wall*, Crowther wrote: "Taylor can look fiercer than any nut we know."

During this period, Taylor made headlines when he was called to testify before the House Un-American Activities Committee (HUAC), as part of its investigation into Communist-related activities in the entertainment industry. In his testimony before the committee, Taylor stated that he knew of several people in Hollywood who "act an awful lot like Communists."

"I can name a few who seem to sort of disrupt things once in a while," he testified. "Whether or not they are Communists I don't know. One chap we have currently, I think, is Howard Da Silva. He always seems to have something to say at the wrong time." Taylor went on to claim that the script for his 1943 movie *Song of Russia*, written by Richard Collins and Paul Jarrico, was pro–Communist, as was a tune in the film by Yip Harburg. "If I had my way," Taylor said, "they would all be sent back to Russia or some other unpleasant place!" Ultimately, Da Silva, Collins, Jarrico, and Harburg would each find themselves blacklisted in the Hollywood community. (Decades after his testimony, and nearly 30 years after his death, Taylor's revelations before the committee would resurface to taint his memory — because of his testimony, a petition was circulated in 1990 demanding that the actor's name be expunged from the Robert Taylor Building on the old MGM lot [now owned by Lorimar Productions]. As a result, the building was renamed after director George Cukor.)

On the big screen, meanwhile, Taylor was seen in his fourth film noir, *The Bribe* (1949), co-starring John Hodiak and Ava Gardner (with whom the actor reportedly had a brief affair). This feature focused primarily on a quintet of characters: Rigby (Taylor), a federal agent sent to infiltrate an illegal war surplus ring in Central America; Tugwell and Elizabeth Hintten (Hodiak and Gardner), an American couple suspected of involvement in the ring; A.J. Bealer (Charles Laughton), a member of the ring who is desperate for money to finance a foot operation; and Carwood (Vincent Price), a mining engineer who is actually the mastermind of the lucrative scheme. After numerous plot twists — including a furtive romance between Rigby and Elizabeth, Elizabeth drugging her lover after being blackmailed by Bealer, and Carwood's murder of Tugwell — Rigby confronts the gang leader and guns him down in the midst of a carnival fireworks display. Although it was the weakest of Taylor's six noirs, the actor earned favorable reviews for his performance, with *Variety*'s critic writing that he "pleases as a federal cop," and the reviewer for *The Hollywood Reporter* opining that Taylor "is convincing as the government man."

With the onset of the 1950s, Taylor was seen in a number of films of varying quality, from *Ambush* (1950), a passable western with Arlene Dahl, to *Quo Vadis* (1951), a sweeping, big-budget epic shot on location in Rome. One of the highest grossing films of the year, *Quo Vadis* also served to be the undoing of Taylor's marriage when rumors linked him romantically with bit player Lia DeLeo. News of the alleged affair eventually reached Barbara Stanwyck, who flew to Rome and threatened Taylor with a divorce. Although the actress later admitted she was only trying to frighten her spouse, Taylor called her bluff and the popular twosome ended their 13-year marriage on February 25, 1952. (Stanwyck never remarried, and later referred to Taylor as the only man she would ever love.)

In one of the biggest hits of his career, Taylor starred in 1952 in *Ivanhoe*, playing a Saxon knight alongside co-stars Elizabeth Taylor, Joan Fontaine, and George Sanders. He followed this costumer with another the following year, *Knights of the Round Table* (1953), in which he played Lancelot opposite Ava Gardner's Guinevere, and *All the Brothers Were Valiant* (1953), a rousing adventure tale with Ann Blyth and Lewis Stone (in the last film of his career). Throughout the remainder of the decade, he was seen in a mixed bag of features, including *I Love Melvin* (1952), a musical in which he was briefly seen in a dream sequence; *Ride, Vaquero* (1953), a sweeping western in which he was again teamed with Ava Gardner; *Valley of the Kings* (1954), notable primarily for the rumored off-screen romance between the actor and his co-star, Eleanor Parker; *The Adventures of Quentin Durward* (1955), a popular costumer set in 15-century France; *D-Day, the Sixth of June* (1956), a rare loanout to Fox; *The Power and the Prize* (1956), a humdrum drama with Mary Astor and Burl Ives; and *Tip on a Dead Jockey* (1957), a sluggishly directed crime mystery co-starring Dorothy Malone and Gia Scala. Taylor was also seen during this period in his final two films noirs, *Rogue Cop* (1954) and *Party Girl* (1958).

In the first, Taylor starred as a crooked police detective, Chris Kelvaney, who earns extra cash by performing various duties for a mobster named Dan Beaumonte (George Raft). The lucrative association between Chris and Beaumonte is shattered, however, when Chris' younger brother, rookie cop Eddie (Steve Forrest), refuses to back off of his identification of a murderer with ties to Beaumonte. After Chris tries to exact a promise from the mobster that Eddie will not be hurt, he gets into a brawl with Beaumonte and one of his hoods (played by Alan Hale, Jr., best known as the Skipper from TV's *Gilligan's Island*), and Beaumonte later has Eddie killed by an assassin, Langley (Vince Edwards). Determining to avenge his brother's death, Chris gains valuable information from Beaumonte's ex-girlfriend (Anne Francis), but she, too, is murdered by Langley. Chris manages to capture the gunman, and sets a trap for Beaumonte with the help of a fellow detective, Sid Myers (Robert Ellenstein). The plan nearly backfires when Chris is severely wounded in a shootout, but just as Beaumonte is about to run over Chris with his car, he is shot and killed by Myers. Described in one review as a "rugged yarn," *Rogue Cop* was a hit with audiences and critics alike, and Taylor once again walked away with numerous plaudits for his performance. In the *New York Times*, Bosley Crowther judged that the film was "very well acted by Robert Taylor in the somewhat disagreeable title role"; Howard McClay wrote in the

Los Angeles Daily News that the actor "turn[ed] in a good study of a policeman who turns crooked"; and in the *Los Angeles Times*, Philip K. Scheuer declared: "With the greatest of ease, Robert Taylor makes the switch from knighthood to night 'hood.'"

Taylor was back on the fringes of the law in his final film noir, *Party Girl*, playing 1930s-era attorney Thomas Farrell, a self-described "mouthpiece for the mob — guardian angel for punks and gunmen." Farrell's chief client is mob leader Rico Angelo (Lee J. Cobb), from whom Farrell tries to extricate himself after falling for a local showgirl, Vicki Gaye (Cyd Charisse). Against his better judgment, Farrell agrees to Rico's request to defend a psychotic young hood, Cookie LaMotte (Corey Allen), setting off a chain-reaction of events that include Farrell's arrest for bribing a juror, LaMotte's escape from jail and subsequent murder, and Farrell's exposure of Rico's illegal activities to authorities. After learning of Farrell's betrayal, the mobster kidnaps Vicki, threatening to disfigure her face with acid unless Farrell changes his story. Farrell agrees, but when police arrive on the scene, Rico is shot and accidentally douses himself with the acid before falling from an upper-story window to his death. For his performance in this rare color noir, Taylor earned praise from several critics, including the reviewer for *Variety*, who said he "carries considerable conviction as the attorney, suave and virile"; and Lynn Bowers of the *Los Angeles Examiner*, who called Taylor and Charisse "about as decorative a pair of stars as one would want, although Taylor is not playing this one on looks only." The critics were less impressed, however, with the overall production; the reviewer for the *Hollywood Citizen-News* judged that there was "too much triteness — too much of the familiar sights and sounds of past gangster films," and in the *Los Angeles Times*, Philip K. Scheuer wrote: "I have read reviews which insist that this gangster melodrama of Chicago in the 30s is satire, but it seems to me that most of the laughs occur in the wrong places and are, as we say, unintentional."

While he wasn't on screen, Taylor met the woman who would become wife number two, German-born model and actress Ursula Schmidt-Hut Thiess. Divorced with two young children, Ursula met Taylor on a blind date a few months after his split from Stanwyck, and the two were married on May 24, 1954. They would later purchase a 113-acre ranch in the Mandeville Canyon area where they raised quarter horses, cows, chickens—and two children of their own, Terence, born in 1955 and Tessa, in 1959. Taylor and Ursula would remain together until the actor's death.

Meanwhile, Taylor's appearance in *Party Girl* had marked the end of his 24-year relationship with MGM, the second longest of any actor at the studio (Lewis Stone was the longest contractee at nearly 30 years). Taylor did, however, ink a short-term agreement with his old studio, entitling him to two more pictures, which included *The House of the Seven Hawks* (1959), filmed on location in England and Holland. But at this point in his career, and upon the urging of his neighbor, actor-director Dick Powell, Taylor turned his sights to the small screen, landing the starring role on *The Detectives*. Also known as *Robert Taylor's Detectives*, the popular crime show aired on ABC from 1959 to 1961, then ran for another year on NBC.

"Television is a lot of fun," Taylor said. "You go in and get it done. No time is wasted, as in the movie business."

Back on screen after *The Detectives*, Taylor was seen in a series of films that included *Cattle King* (1963), his final film for MGM; *Miracle of the White Stallions* (1963), a dismal wartime drama released by Disney; and *A House is Not a Home* (1964), a tiresome biopic about the life of 1920s bordello madam Polly Adler. He also starred during this period in *The Night Walker* (1965), a horror film that reunited him with first wife Barbara Stanwyck.

"Any actor who would turn down a chance to play opposite Barbara Stanwyck, under any circumstances, would have to be out of his head," Taylor told reporters. "She's certainly one of the pros in the business."

Around this time, it was announced that NBC-TV would launch *The Robert Taylor Show* in the 1963-64 season, starring Taylor as a trouble-shooter for the Department of Health, Education and Welfare in Washington. Although six installments of the series were filmed, however, the show was canceled and the episodes were never aired. According to stories that later surfaced, federal officials were reportedly unhappy with the advance episodes that were viewed, and claimed that the series did not accurately reflect the work of the department. At the time of the cancellation, however, Taylor expressed confusion over the show's abrupt termination.

"We weren't sure why [the series was canceled]," Taylor said in a 1964 interview in the *New York Post*. "We had the full cooperation of the Department of Health. Perhaps the station was afraid we'd get involved with cigarettes and drugs, and after all, they are among the biggest TV sponsors."

The actor did return to television in 1966, replacing Ronald Reagan as host of the long-running western series *Death Valley Days*. As he had throughout his career, the actor earned praise for his professionalism and affability on the show's set.

"Mr. Taylor was one of Hollywood's true gentlemen," said former stuntman Neil Summers in his 1987 book, *The First Official TV Western Book*. "He never forgot your name and was at all times a gracious man to the crew and his fans."

After two years, Taylor left *Death Valley Days*, returning to the big screen for a cameo appearance as a rancher in *Where Angels Go ... Trouble Follows* (1968), starring Rosalind Russell, and a starring role alongside Charles Boyer in *The Day the Line Got Hot* (1968). A fairly likable comedy, the latter film would be Taylor's last. In the summer of 1968, the actor was diagnosed with lung cancer following surgery for a fungus infection known as valley fever. After having most of his right lung removed during the operation, Taylor struggled valiantly against the disease, but he died at age 57 on June 8, 1969.

Undeniably one of Hollywood's most beloved male stars, Robert Taylor seemed to take neither himself nor his profession too seriously, a behavioral rarity that probably contributed to his high regard throughout the Hollywood community. Delivering the eulogy at Taylor's funeral, Ronald Reagan perhaps summed up the actor's life best when he called him "one of the truly great and most enduring stars of the Golden Era of Hollywood."

"Perhaps each one of us has his own different memory," Reagan said, "but I'll bet that somehow they all add up to 'nice man.'"

Film Noir Filmography

Johnny Eager. Director: Mervyn LeRoy. Producer: John W. Considine, Jr. Running time: 102 minutes. Released by MGM, February 19, 1942. Cast: Robert Taylor, Lana Turner, Edward Arnold, Van Heflin, Robert Sterling, Patricia Dane, Glenda Farrell, Barry Nelson, Henry O'Neil, Charles Dingle, Cy Kendall, Don Costello, Paul Stewart. Awards: Academy Award for Best Supporting Actor (Van Heflin).

Undercurrent. Director: Vincente Minnelli. Producer: Pandro S. Berman. Running time: 114 minutes. Released by MGM, November 28, 1946. Cast: Katharine Hepburn, Robert Taylor, Robert Mitchum, Edmund Gwenn, Marjorie Main, Jayne Cotter, Clinton Sundberg, Dan Tobin, Kathryn Card, Leigh Whipper, Charles Trowbridge, James Westerfield, Billy McLain.

The High Wall. Director: Curtis Bernhardt. Producer: Robert Lord. Running time: 100 minutes. Released by MGM, December 25, 1947. Cast: Robert Taylor, Audrey Totter, Herbert Marshall, Dorothy Patrick, H.B. Warner, Warner Anderson, Moroni Olsen, John Ridgeley, Morris Ankrum, Elisabeth Risdon, Vince Barnett, Jonathan Hale, Charles Arnt, Ray Mayer, Dick Wessell, Robert Emmet O'Connor, Celia Travers, Mary Servoss, Bobby Hyatt, Eula Guy, Jack Davis, Tom Quinn.

The Bribe. Director: Robert Z. Leonard. Producer: Pandro S. Berman. Running time: 98 minutes. Released by MGM, February 3, 1949. Cast: Robert Taylor, Ava Gardner, Charles Laughton, Vincent Price, John Hodiak, Samuel S. Hinds, John Hoyt, Tito Renaldo.

Rogue Cop. Director: Roy Rowland. Producer: Nicholas Nayfack. Running time: 87 minutes. Released by MGM, September 17, 1954. Cast: Robert Taylor, Janet Leigh, George Raft, Steve Forrest, Anne Francis, Robert Ellenstein, Robert F. Simon, Anthony Ross, Alan Hale, Jr., Peter Brocco, Vince Edwards, Olive Carey, Roy Bancroft, Dale Van Sickel, Ray Teal.

Party Girl. Director: Nicholas Ray. Producer: Joe Pasternak. Running time: 99 minutes. Released by MGM, October 28, 1958. Cast: Robert Taylor, Cyd Charisse, Lee J. Cobb, John Ireland, Kent Smith, Claire Kelly, Corey Allen, Lewis Charles, David Opatoshu, Kem Dibbs, Patrick McVey, Barbara Lang, Myrna Hansen, Betty Utey, Jack Lambert.

References

"Acting Just Job to Taylor." *New York Morning Telegraph*, August 27, 1964.

Alexander, Linda. "Robert Taylor: Still a Star." *Classic Images*, November 1994.

Biography of Robert Taylor. ABC Television Network, July 1959.

Bowers, Ronald L. "Robert Taylor." *Films in Review*, January 1967.

Buckley, William F. "Idol Who 'Named Names,' Still an Idol." *New York Daily News*, February 1, 1990.

Calanquin, Leon V. "The Saga of Robert Taylor." *Classic Images*, September 1987.

DuBrow, Rick. "Taylor Has No Plans for Retirement." *New York Morning Telegraph*, July 20, 1961.

Graham, Sheilah. "Bob Taylor, Non Method Actor." *New York Mirror*, June 19, 1960.

Hale, Wanda. "'Farmer' Taylor Has Fun." *New York Daily News*, July 27, 1964.

Harris, Leonard. "Robert Taylor Gives Up." *New York World-Telegram and Sun*, August 24, 1964.

Herridge, Frances. "Robert Taylor's a Heavy in 'House.'" *New York Post*, July 24, 1964.

Mann, Roderick. "Onetime Film Idol: 'I Was the Worst.'" *New York World-Telegraph and Sun*, August 29, 1962.

Mishkin, Leo. "Bob Taylor Envisions 'Change' in His Long Career in Films." *New York Morning Telegraph*, April 21, 1966.

Obituary. *Variety*, June 11, 1969.

Parsons, Louella O. "By Accident, a Star Again." *Cosmopolitan*, September 1954.

"Robert Taylor." *Screen Thrills Illustrated*, October 1963.

"Robert Taylor Has Cancer." *Newark Evening News*, December 3, 1968.

"Robert Taylor Recuperates." *New York Times*, October 15, 1968.

"Robert Taylor's Unseen Series." *Newark Sunday News*, June 15, 1969.

Stein, Herb. "Taylor Enjoys Sensible Living." *New York Morning Telegraph*, April 5, 1963.

"Straight-Talking Trouper." *New York Herald Tribune*, November 6, 1960.

Wagner, Laura. "Robert Taylor: Matinee Idol." *Films of the Golden Age*, Summer 1999.

——— LAWRENCE TIERNEY ———

"Anybody who puts the finger on me is living on borrowed time."— Lawrence Tierney in *Shakedown* (1950)

Lawrence Tierney was once likened to the renowned fictional character Dr. Jekyll–Mr. Hyde.

"When he's sober, he's serious, thoughtful, ambitious," a 1951 newspaper account revealed. "When he's drunk, he's close to crazy."

With his portrayal of Depression-era gangster John Dillinger in the late 1940s, Tierney rose to instant fame, but he fell from Hollywood favor with equal rapidity when his screen career was eclipsed by his stormy, violent, and often bizarre personal life. Arrested more than 20 times for crimes varying from public drunkenness to assaulting a waiter with a sugar bowl, Tierney quickly transformed from a promising actor to what one columnist termed a "rowdy screen actor who has been decisioned, knocked out, and fouled by John Barleycorn." But while he appeared in fewer than 50 films (and only 23 of those between 1943 and 1956), Tierney offered a memorable, menacing presence to four films from the era of noir: *Born to Kill* (1947), *The Devil Thumbs a Ride* (1947), *Shakedown* (1950), and *Female Jungle* (1956).

Tierney was born in Brooklyn, New York, on March 15, 1919, one of three sons of the chief of police of the New York Aqueduct Guards. (His two brothers, Scott Brady and Edward Tierney, later followed their sibling onto the big screen.) A top student and star sportsman at Boys' High School in Brooklyn, Tierney won an athletic scholarship to Manhattan College, attending for two years before quitting to work as a sandhog on a Hudson River Tunnel. His entrance into the field of acting, however, is a matter of debate. According to one account, Tierney was waiting for a female companion one night outside a theater stage entrance when the manager spotted him, mistook him for an actor, and offered him a job on the spot. Later, while performing a bit part in a play produced by the Blackfriars, a New York experimental acting group, Tierney was seen by an RKO talent scout, who arranged for a screen test and offered the actor a contract with the studio. Another version claims that Tierney took a modeling job with the John Powers agency as a lark. Asked by a co-worker to accompany him to New York's RKO offices, Tierney was tested, signed to a contract, and promptly shipped off to Tinseltown.

The route to RKO notwithstanding, Tierney made his screen debut for the studio in 1943, appearing in a minor role as an FBI man in *Government Girl*, starring Olivia de Havilland, followed by *The Ghost Ship* (1943), an atmospheric horror film with Richard Dix. He was next seen in RKO's teenage melodrama *Youth Runs Wild* (1944), starring Bonita Granville and Kent Smith; *The Falcon Out West* (1944), one of 11 films in the whodunit series; *Those Endearing Young Charms* (1945), a lighthearted romantic comedy starring Laraine Day; *Back to Bataan* (1945), a big-budget war epic; and *Mama Loves Papa* (1945), a dreary comedy that flopped at the box office. Few of Tierney's features during this period made much of an impact, but his big break was just ahead. On loan to Monogram Studios, Tierney was cast in the title role of *Dillinger* (1945), a low-budget biopic that was made in only three weeks and earned the actor a total of $300, plus $75 in overtime work.

Although the story bore little resemblance to the facts of the infamous gangster's life, the film was Tierney's ticket to instant fame.

It was around this time, however, that Tierney began to make news for his exploits off screen. On May 22, 1945, the actor was arrested for public drunkenness, and a few weeks later, on June 5, 1945, he was arrested on the same charge. On both occasions, Tierney was ordered to pay a $25 fine. After a third arrest on July 27, 1945, in what police called "a strangling condition," Tierney was sentenced to 10 days in the county jail.

The actor's troubles continued the following year. In January 1946, Tierney was involved in a brawl with William Kent, stepson of the owner of the Mocambo nightclub, during a party at the home of artist John Decker. The following month, the actor was charged with assault and battery after punching actor Paul DeLoqueyssie, and in March, the actor was arrested near the Mocambo after a second fight with Kent.

"I was quietly enjoying a drink when Kent came in and began making abusive remarks to me," Tierney told the press. "I'd have gotten things settled properly if the cops hadn't come."

Following the altercation at the Mocambo, Tierney was fined $100 and announced that he was "going on the wagon for good." But it wasn't long before he was in trouble with the law again. In August 1946, the actor showed up at the Hollywood Receiving Hospital with a gash on his neck and right index finger, claiming that he received the injuries when he slipped from the glass top of a table while adjusting a light fixture. Upon questioning from attendants, Tierney reportedly became "belligerent," and was arrested once again for drunkenness. For this incident, Municipal Judge Eugene Fay fined Tierney $50, sentenced him to five days in the local city jail, and placed him on a year's probation, during which he was ordered to refrain from driving or drinking intoxicants.

"You are one of those people who can't handle liquor," the judge told Tierney. "Someone has to jolt you to your senses. You've got to make up your mind to quit, or you'll end up as a drunkard such as you'll see in Lincoln Heights jail. They were once as good-looking, straight, and youthful as you are. You're headed for the same fate that has overtaken them."

Between arrests, Tierney managed to find time to star in several features, including *Badman's Territory* (1946), a box-office hit in which he portrayed Jesse James; *Step By Step* (1946), a humdrum chase film; *San Quentin* (1946), a manhunt saga co-starring Barton MacLane; and his first two films noirs, *Born to Kill* (1947) and *The Devil Thumbs a Ride* (1947). In *Born to Kill*, Tierney portrayed Sam Wild, described by one character as "the quiet sort, and yet you get a feeling if you step out of line you'd get your teeth kicked down your throat." Psychotic and paranoid, Sam — as the title individual who is "born to kill" — racks up no fewer than four murders during the course of the film, including his girlfriend (Isabel Jewell), his best friend (Elisha Cook, Jr.), and his lover, Helen Trent (Claire Trevor). Although Helen is aware of his murderous nature, she is perversely attracted to Sam, despite her engagement to a local steel heir (Phillip Terry), and even after he marries her wealthy foster sister (Audrey Long): "Your roots are down where mine are," Sam tells Helen in one scene. "I knew that the first time I saw you." By the time Helen comes to her senses about Sam, it is too late — when he learns that she has contacted the authorities, Sam kills Helen just before he is gunned down by police.

Notwithstanding his tendency to be what director Robert Wise termed "a bit unstable" during the filming of *Born to Kill*, Tierney turned in a frighteningly memorable performance as Sam Wild, resulting in one of film noir's most disturbing, yet riveting, characters. He continued demonstrating his homicidal habits in his next noir, *The Devil Thumbs a Ride*, which begins as Tierney's character, Steve, robs and murders the night manager of a bank. Fleeing town, he hitches a ride with Jimmy Ferguson (Ted North), a traveling salesman headed home to his wife in Los

Angeles. Along the way, Steve convinces Jimmy to give a ride to two women — Carol (Nan Leslie) and Agnes (Betty Lawford) — then avoids a roadblock and runs down a motorcycle cop who gives chase. And when Jimmy wants to turn around and check on the injured officer, Steve shrewdly talks him out of it: "That'd be stupid," he says. "With cops, seeing is believing, and nothing else. Beside, Fergie ... you're a married man. With those dames, you wouldn't stand a chance either. Look — let's go to that beachhouse you told us about. And then tomorrow when the whole thing's cooled down, I'll be glad to go to the police station with you and make a report of the whole thing." Despite his smooth promises, however, Steve has other plans — once at the beachhouse, he flattens the tires to Jimmy's car, disables the telephone, and murders Carol when she rejects his advances. Using his skills as a forgerer to convince a local sheriff that *he* is Jimmy Ferguson, Steve almost succeeds in a clean getaway, but when Jimmy's wife shows up, Steve is forced to flee, willingly accompanied by Agnes. Ultimately, Steve meets a violent end on the road, shot down by police who have identified him as the bank manager's killer.

Although *The Devil Thumbs a Ride* stands up today as an excellent example of film noir, it was panned by critics, including the *New York Times*' Bosley Crowther, who wrote: "It is pictures like these which give the movies a black eye and give us a pain in the neck." Tierney displayed a similar distaste for the film; years after its release, the actor admitted that he "didn't like [it] at all."

"I never thought of myself as that kind of guy," Tierney said in a 1998 interview in *Scarlet Street* magazine. "I thought of myself as a nice guy who wouldn't do rotten things. But obviously that miserable son of a bitch in the film would! I hated that character so much, but I had to do it for the picture."

Despite his formidable portrayals in his two films of 1947, Tierney's reputation off screen continued to nosedive. In an interview in February of that year with *Los Angeles Daily News* columnist Earl Wilson, the luckless actor

claimed that he was "off the sauce for a long time, but not necessarily forever."

"Haven't had a drink in three weeks," Tierney said. "When I drink, I drink a lot of it, and when I drink a lot of it, I'm just as likely as not to climb a wall." Unable to stay on the wagon, however, the actor quickly racked up more arrests for drunkenness and disturbing the peace, and found himself behind bars, sentenced to 90 days at the county honor farm. After serving 47 days of the sentence, Tierney was released on parole, once again vowing to quit drinking.

"I feel great," he said upon his release. "Besides doing the work — hoeing, digging, and milking — I even got in a little road work. I had already joined Alcoholics Anonymous, and I talked a lot of AA with some of the other prisoners. This time I'm really getting on the program."

But by now, the actor's mounting brushes with the law had begun to take their toll on his career. He only appeared in one film during the remainder of the decade, a tautly directed thriller entitled *Bodyguard* (1948), instead spending most of his time in and out of further troubles. In early 1948, the actor was sued for $100,000 by a bartender who charged that Tierney knocked him unconscious, causing him to suffer impairments to his sight and hearing. (The matter was later settled out of court.) The following January, Tierney was driven to the county jail by a cab driver who claimed that the actor had repeatedly lunged at the steering wheel and had become abusive and threatening before passing out in the vehicle. After this incident, Tierney was given "one more chance" by Judge Henry H. Draeger, who fined the actor $150 and handed down a 90-day suspended jail sentence.

"You have come a long way in motion pictures," the judge told Tierney. "You are a success in your profession. However, you do not appreciate its advantages.... I am going to give you one more chance to demonstrate the faith the public has in you is not misplaced."

But the actor failed to heed the judge's

stern admonishment. In May 1950, Tierney caused a disturbance while sitting ringside at the Ocean Park boxing arena when he grabbed a beer bottle from a vendor's tray. When officers confronted the actor, he reportedly pointed the bottle at them and said, "Stick 'em up!" His antics earned Tierney yet another trip to jail, after which he was given a $50 fine and sentenced to two years of summary probation. Later that year, he was arrested for assault after an incident involving actress Jean Wallace.

"Larry called and asked if I would be interested in playing with him in a play," Wallace told columnist Louella Parsons. "We talked about the part and then I offered to drive him home. Suddenly he became wild and started to scream."

Meanwhile, back on screen after a two-year absence, Tierney starred in a mediocre mystery, *Kill or Be Killed* (1950), then returned to realm of noir in his third film from the era, *Shakedown* (1950). This feature centered on an unscrupulous newspaper photographer, Jack Early (Howard Duff), whose venal exploits include befriending a local mobster, Nick Palmer (Brian Donlevy), and securing information that allows him to take photographs of Palmer's rival, Harry Coulton (Tierney), during the commission of a robbery. After blackmailing Coulton with the damaging pictures and pocketing $25,000, Early reveals that Palmer was his source of information. Later, when Coulton seeks revenge on Palmer by planting a bomb in his car, Early not only takes pictures of Coulton in the act of the crime, but he also photographs the car just as it blows up, which catapults him into national prominence. Early's tactics catch up with him, however, when he blackmails Coulton again, this time forcing the gangster to aid him in committing a robbery at a charity affair. During the ball, Coulton guns Early down and as the photographer's last, irony-filled act, he snaps a picture of his killer just before he dies.

After earning mention for his "good job" in *Shakedown*, Tierney was seen in *The Hoodlum* (1951), a passable gangster film co-star-

ring his younger brother, Edward, and *Best of the Badmen* (1951), featuring Robert Ryan and Claire Trevor. But Tierney's film roles that year paled in comparison with his increasingly erratic behavior off screen. In one incident, which took place on June 21, 1951, Tierney and a male companion entered the yard of Frances Naylor, a resident of West Los Angeles. According to Naylor, the two men refused to leave the premises, and when she let her dog out of the house to frighten them away, Tierney "kicked [the dog] so hard I thought he had broken her neck." Reportedly, when Naylor's 25-year-old son, John, attempted to "repulse the unwanted visitors," he, too, was kicked by Tierney, sustaining a broken jaw in the process. At his trial on the resulting battery and peace disturbance charges, Tierney testified that he never kicked John Naylor, and only struck him because he was threatening the actor with a large butcher knife.

"I hit him with my hand," Tierney said. "I hit him twice. When somebody has a knife,

I'm going to hit as hard as I can." He was later found not guilty on the charge of disturbing the peace, but was found guilty of battery, for which he was sentenced to 180 days in jail (half of the sentence was suspended; he later served 74 of the 90 days remaining). But the case wasn't over — on the day that the verdicts were announced, John Naylor filed a civil suit against the actor, seeking $30,587.50 in damages. The suit was finally settled in January 1954, with Tierney agreeing to pay Naylor $5,000.

Tierney's downhill slide continued when he was arrested a few months after the Naylor trial for disturbing the peace. According to news accounts, around 6 A.M. on October 9, 1951, Tierney was spotted inside Saint Monica's Church in Santa Monica, "wandering about in his bare feet." When police arrived, Tierney screamed, "You can't take me! I'm in sanctuary!" then leapt over pews of worshippers gathered for early Mass and fled into a side room. Police barricaded the actor in the room and called his brother, Edward, but when his younger sibling arrived, Tierney punched him in the face. Ambulance attendants and officers finally quieted Tierney, strapped him with leather restrainers, and took him to the Los Angeles Neurological hospital for "mental treatment."

"Lawrence is a sick boy," Edward Tierney told the press. "He needs treatment."

No charges were filed against Tierney in the church incident, but two weeks later, he was arrested on a common drunk charge after entering a Los Angeles bar in his sock feet, and offering to "whip anybody in the house." Officers J.B. Evans and D.B. Weld — to whom Tierney gave his occupation as "bum"— quoted the actor as saying, "I can hold my liquor. I've been drinking double shots for three days without any sleep at all and I can still carry on a conversation." For this charge, Tierney was placed on probation and gave the judge his "word of honor" that he would not drink again.

For nearly a year, Tierney managed to stay out of trouble, and appeared in two of his best films during 1952 — The Bushwhackers, a Civil War–era western starring John Ireland, and The Greatest Show on Earth, a lavish, star-studded circus epic that won the year's Academy Award for Best Picture. The film's director, Cecil B. DeMille, was reportedly so impressed with Tierney's performance that he asked for him to be put under contract at Paramount Studios. But before the agreement could be inked, Tierney was in trouble again. The planned contract was canceled, and for the remainder of the decade, Tierney appeared in only three more films, including his final film noir, Female Jungle (1956). Here, in a rare appearance on the right side of the law, Tierney portrayed Sgt. Stevens, an alcoholic cop determined to unearth the killer of a film actress who was strangled outside a bar where he was found drunk. During his investigation, Stevens encounters a variety of offbeat characters, including Claude Almstead (John Carradine), the dead woman's foppish press agent; Alec Voc (Burt Kaiser), a moody caricaturist; and Candy Price (Jayne Mansfield, in her film debut), a nyphomaniac who is having an affair with Voc. Although all signs initially point to Almstead as the guilty party, it turns out that the real killer was Voc, who was blackmailing the actress. Filmed on a shoestring budget (Mansfield was reportedly paid only $150 for her role) and suffering from a thoroughly implausible plot, Female Jungle came and went with little notice.

By the late 1950s, Tierney's career appeared to be all but over. But the decrease in his screen time seemed to have no effect on his appearances in the press. Between 1957 and 1964, the actor was involved in numerous scrapes, including an incident in August 1957 when he was charged with burglary after kicking in the door of a young woman's apartment, and a 1958 run-in with two police officers that one reporter described as a "wild-kicking, free-swinging fracas." The latter incident, which took place outside of a bar where the actor had been refused more alcohol, was Tierney's third brush with the law within a 12-hour period.

"We arrived at 12:05 A.M. to find Tierney loud, boisterous and filthy-mouthed," a police officer told reporters. "We placed him under arrest, but he began to resist. He punched me about the head and body several times, then kicked me in the groin.... We were forced to use the stick on him."

Tierney's other troubles included a brawl with two drinking buddies in front of a crowd of holiday shoppers in December 1959; an arrest in 1961 after he tried unsuccessfully to crash a party thrown by actress Elizabeth Taylor and her then-husband Eddie Fisher; a charge of battery in July 1962 when actor Dimitrios Georgopoulous claimed that Tierney threw hot coffee and whiskey on him at a Hollywood restaurant; and a 1963 disturbance in a Hollywood Boulevard drug store during which Tierney struck a waiter in the face with a sugar bowl and was, in turn, conked on the back of the head with a metal cream dispenser. The actor also earned a conviction for third degree assault in 1964, after a cab driver charged that Tierney tried to choke him.

"The whole beef could have been settled for $1.45. That's what the cabbie wanted but I wasn't going to pay because I didn't like the way he was driving," Tierney explained. "So this cop comes along and says, 'Why don't you pay him the $1.45?' and I said, 'What the hell are you, a collection agency?' and the first thing you know I was under arrest. I just reached over the cabbie's shoulder to turn off the ignition and he said I was trying to strangle him. But all that's academic because they found me guilty anyway."

During this period, the actor was also arrested on several occasions for drunk driving and public drunkenness, including one in January 1960, just hours after police discovered the dead body of his mother, Marie, with a bottle of sleeping pills nearby. And in a departure from his usual misdeeds, he was fined $80 in 1967 for shoplifting a sweater from a department store in Paris. In many of the news accounts, Tierney was described in mocking and contemptuous terms; one reporter stated that Tierney "once portrayed Dillinger on the screen and apparently never got over it," while another wrote an article that began: "Lawrence Tierney, Hollywood's Brooklyn boy, got in a fight again, yesterday morning early, ho, ho, hum-m-mm."

In the years during Tierney's absence from the screen, the actor made ends meet with a series of odd jobs including construction work and driving a hansom cab. He also appeared on a handful of television programs, including *Naked City* and *Adventures in Paradise*, and finally returned to feature films in 1963 with *A Child is Waiting*, a critically acclaimed drama produced by Stanley Kramer, directed by John Cassavetes, and starring Burt Lancaster. He was also seen in a minor role in *Exorcism at Midnight* (1966), a weak, low-budget horror film with an unknown cast, and *Custer of the West* (1968), a mediocre biography of General George Custer. By the early 1970s, the actor was publicly seeking film work.

"Basically, I need a job. I'm alive, but not doing well," Tierney said in an interview in *The National Enquirer*. "I had a big problem with alcohol, but I don't drink anymore. I began drinking very heavily and getting into trouble. I used to hit the headlines ... with all this nonsense — bad behavior, drunken brawls. I'd like to do a film — a good film. I'm a good actor, and I'm ready to go. But reputations are hard to live down."

A short time later, Tierney was cast in a small role as a hospital guard in *Such Good Friends* (1971), a so-so satire starring Dyan Cannon, but he didn't appear on screen again until 1975, when he played an FBI agent in the forgettable crime drama, *Abduction*. Between these features, the actor nearly lost his life when he was stabbed in the abdomen during an altercation outside a New York bar, and he was back in the news two years later when he was questioned in connection with the death of a 24-year-old woman who reportedly leapt from a fourth-floor window minutes after Tierney's arrival at her apartment. (No charges were filed against Tierney, who told police that the woman was "very upset about something.")

Tierney's long-stalled career finally began to look up during the 1980s. After small parts as a bartender in *Gloria* (1980), a coffee shop patron in *Arthur* (1981), and a carriage driver in *Nothing Lasts Forever* (1984), the actor was featured as a police lieutenant in *Prizzi's Honor* (1985), which was nominated for numerous Academy Awards, including Best Picture. This appearance led to a series of roles in such pictures as *Murphy's Law* (1986), starring Charles Bronson; *Tough Guys Don't Dance* (1987), in which he was a standout in a cast that included Ryan O'Neal, Isabella Rosellini, and Wings Hauser; and *The Horror Show* (1989), a rather dreadful fright flick. He was also seen on the small screen in such series as *Fame, Tales from the Darkside, Hunter, Star Trek: The Next Generation*, and *Hill Street Blues*, in which he played the recurring role of a police sergeant in numerous episodes.

The actor fared even better in the 1990s. He was seen on the big screen in *Reservoir Dogs* (1992), where he was prominently featured as the leader of a gang of thieves; *A Kiss Goodnight* (1994), in which he played a police detective; *Junior* (1994), a mediocre comedy starring Arnold Schwarzenegger as the world's first pregnant man; and *2 Days in the Valley* (1996), a underrated crime drama with Danny Aiello, James Spader, Glenne Headley, Paul Mazursky, and Eric Stolz. Tierney was also heard as the voice of Rick in three animated children's features in 1996, *Toto Lost in New York, Christmas in Oz*, and *Who Stole Santa?*; guested on a variety of television series including *Seinfeld, Silk Stalkings, L.A. Law, ER*, and *Star Trek: Deep Space Nine*; and appeared in several made-for-television movies, including *Dillinger* (1991), this time playing a sheriff, and *Casualties of Love: The Long Island Lolita Story* (1993), starring Alyssa Milano.

In 1998, Tierney portrayed the small role of Hollis Vernon "Grap" Stamper in the big-budget disaster film, *Armageddon*, starring Bruce Willis and Ben Affleck. It was the actor's final role. In February 2001, after a series of strokes, Tierney was hospitalized in a Hollywood nursing home, and he died there in his sleep the following year, on March 26,

2002. (Tierney was reportedly survived by a daughter, Elizabeth.)

Sadly, Lawrence Tierney's talent as an actor was far overshadowed by his volatile life away from the camera, and his legacy will be that of a heavy-drinking brawler who destroyed his own career just as he was beginning to explode on the cinematic scene. But on the silver screen, in the dark and shadowy world of the film noir, he will forever remain one of the era's most intimidating, terrifying, and unforgettable characters.

Film Noir Filmography

Born to Kill. Director: Robert Wise. Producer: Sid Rogell. Running time: 92 minutes. Released by RKO, May 3, 1947. Cast: Claire Trevor, Lawrence Tierney, Walter Slezak, Philip Terry, Audrey Long, Elisha Cook, Jr., Isabel Jewell, Esther Howard, Kathryn Card, Tony Barrett, Grandon Rhodes.

The Devil Thumbs a Ride. Director: Felix Feist. Producer: Herman Schlom. Running time: 63 minutes. Released by RKO, March 1947. Cast: Lawrence Tierney, Ted North, Nan Leslie, Betty Lawford, Andrew Tombes, Harry Shannon, Glenn Vernon.

Shakedown. Director: Joe Pevney. Producer: Ted Richmond. Running time: 80 minutes. Released by Universal-International, September 23, 1950. Cast: Howard Duff, Brian Donlevy, Peggy Dow, Lawrence Tierney, Bruce Bennett, Anne Vernon, Stapleton Kent, Peter Virgo, Charles Sherlock.

Female Jungle. Director: Bruno Ve Sota. Producer: Burt Kaiser. Running time: 70 minutes. Released by AIP, June 1956. Cast: Lawrence Tierney, John Carradine, Jayne Mansfield, Burt Kaiser, Kathleen Crowley, James Kodl.

References

"Actor Fined $80 in Paris Shoplifting." *Hollywood Citizen-News*, February 28, 1967.
"Actor Jailed 5 Days to See Drunks' Fate." *New York Post*, October 9, 1946.
"Actor's Arrest Ordered." *New York Times*, April 23, 1957.
"Actor Tierney Arrested for 16th Time. *New York Post*, August 9, 1955.
"Actor Tierney Booked Again." *Los Angeles Examiner*, October 15, 1950.

"Actor Tierney Found Guilty." *New York Daily News*, April 21, 1964.

"Actor Tierney Found Guilty in Battery Case." *Los Angeles Times*, August 16, 1951.

"Actor Tierney in New Fight." *Los Angeles Examiner*, February 25, 1948.

"Actor Tierney in Rerun-In with Cops." *New York Daily News*, October 18, 1963.

"Actor Tierney Is Held, Girl Asserts He Kicked in Door." *New York Herald Tribune*, August 26, 1957.

"Actor Tierney Released After 74 Days in Jail." *Hollywood Citizen-News*, May 12, 1952.

"Actor Tierney Settles Damage Suit." *Los Angeles Daily News*, January 12, 1954.

"Brawl Costs Tierney $600." *Los Angeles Examiner*, November 21, 1946.

"Dillinger Star Is Stabbed." *New York Post*, January 19, 1973.

Kalech, Marc and Juffe, Mel. "Lawrence Tierney and a Suicide." *New York Post*, June 21, 1975.

"Lawrence Tierney Is Confined Claiming Sanctuary in Church." *New York Herald Tribune*, October 9, 1951.

"Lawrence Tierney Put on Liquor Probation." *Los Angeles Times*, November 24, 1951.

McKay, Rick. "Crack-Up: The True Story of a Hollywood Tough Guy." *Scarlet Street*, Fall 1998.

Mok, Michael. "Larry Tierney Has Court Rerun, Without Commercials." *New York Daily News*, April 30, 1964.

Parsons, Louella O. "Jean Explains Tierney Trip." *Los Angeles Examiner*, October 16, 1950.

Rascoe, Burton. "Lawrence Tierney's Big Problem." *The American Weekly*, August 10, 1947.

"Reduced Charge Puts Tierney on Probation." *Los Angeles Times*, May 25, 1950.

Smith, Robert G. "Dillinger Star Lawrence Tierney: My Battle with Booze." *National Enquirer*, March 21, 1970.

"Tierney Brawls, Moiseyev Merry." *Los Angeles Mirror*, June 29, 1961.

"Tierney Enters Not Guilty Plea." *Los Angeles Times*, May 12, 1950.

"Tierney Free, Takes Pledge." *Los Angeles Examiner*, June 19, 1947.

"Tierney Gets in Brawl." *Hollywood Citizen-News*, July 20, 1962.

"Tierney Gets Lecture, 'One More Chance.'" *Los Angeles Daily News*, January 6, 1949.

"Tierney Guilty on New Counts." *Los Angeles Examiner*, May 10, 1947.

"Tierney Jailed Again." *Hollywood Citizen-News*, July 21, 1962.

"Tierney in Psycho Ward After Chase." *Los Angeles Daily News*, October 8, 1951.

"Tierney Rides Cab to Jail and Gets Booked." *Los Angeles Times*, January 5, 1949.

"Tierney Lays Quitting to Vitality Lack." *Hollywood Citizen-News*, July 28, 1951.

"Tierney Leaps Pews, Slugs Kin." *Los Angeles Examiner*, October 9, 1951.

"Tierney's in Again for Battling Cops." *New York Journal-American*, October 14, 1958.

"Tough Tierney Brawls Anew." *Newark Evening News*, October 14, 1958.

Wilson, Earl. "Tierney, On Wagon, Still Has Troubles." *Los Angeles Daily News*, March 3, 1947.

GEORGE TOBIAS

"How many times I gotta say it — there's no percentage in smartenin' up a chump."
— George Tobias in *The Set-Up* (1949)

Despite a career that spanned five decades and included roles in nearly 60 feature films, George Tobias is best known to modern audiences as Abner Kravitz, the pipe-smoking, long-suffering neighbor on television's popular series, *Bewitched*. His small screen success notwithstanding, Tobias showed his versatility on the big screen in comedy as well as drama, announcing early in his film career that he couldn't be "typed."

"There aren't enough similar kinds of film stories to be made," Tobias said. "I'll be wearing a mustache in some of them and a beard in others. It'll be Tobias playing the roles, but I want to play them so the people won't recognize me, so they'll think I'm somebody else."

In addition to performances alongside such stars as James Cagney, John Garfield, and Gary Cooper, Tobias offered his talents to four films from the era of noir: *Nobody Lives Forever* (1946), *The Set-Up* (1949), *Southside 1-1000* (1950), and *The Tattered Dress* (1957).

The actor once tagged "the man of a thousand bit parts" was born on July 14, 1901, on the Lower East Side of New York. At an early age, Tobias became enamored with horses, and it developed into a love that he maintained for the rest of his life.

"I remember the horse-drawn street cars on First Avenue, the livery stables, the horse-drawn carriages," Tobias recalled in a 1967 interview in *TV Guide*. "When I was a kid, I used to tie a stocking on my belt for a tail and I'd crawl on my knees under the table kicking people and neighing like a horse. My first job was stable boy at the Black and White Riding School in Brooklyn. Then I was a riding master on the Borscht Circuit in the Catskills."

Although Tobias' parents, Samuel and Yetta, were repertory players in the Yiddish theater, they had high hopes that their son would pursue a profession as a doctor, lawyer, or a merchant. But it wasn't to be. One fateful day in 1916, Tobias' older brother, Benjamin, a student at New York's Neighborhood Playhouse, informed his sibling that the company was seeking a bit player for their upcoming production, *The Mob*. Tobias auditioned and, at the age of 15, made his debut in the play as an old sea captain. After several years with the Neighborhood Playhouse, Tobias joined the Provincetown Players, appearing in *The Hairy Ape*, and a short time later landed a role in the Broadway production of *What Price Glory?* He remained with the cast from 1924 to 1926, then went on to appear in such plays as *The Road to Rome* and *The Gray Fox*, and the Theater Guild productions of *Elizabeth the Queen* with Alfred Lunt and Lynn Fontanne, and *Red Dust*, with Franchot Tone. In 1934, he joined the Theater Union, a group devoted to producing plays about the working class, portraying a class-conscious sailor in *Sailors of Catarro* and an American miner in *Black Pit*. For his performance in the latter, he earned praise from one critic for adding "a welcome note of mirth to the proletarian drama."

Between productions, Tobias worked at a variety of odd jobs, not to earn extra cash, but to hone his skills as a performer.

"I worked in car shops, foundries, on boats, in factories, just about every place, because I wanted to be an actor," Tobias said in 1940. "I knew I wasn't good looking enough to be a leading man, so I worked around with people of every nationality to pick up their accents and mannerisms. I remembered every one. My folks thought I was crazy, doing that hard work just to be an actor. Once in a while I used to think so, too, but not now."

Tobias' talent for mastering dialects paid off in 1936 when he won raves for his portrayal of a Russian ballet master in the hit George Kaufman–Moss Hart play *You Can't Take it With You*. After the run of this production, Tobias spent two years in the popular Cole Porter musical *Leave It To Me*, starring Mary Martin. Around this time, Hollywood beckoned, and Tobias was tapped for a role in MGM's *Another Thin Man* (1939), the third in the series starring William Powell and Myrna Loy.

"I accepted the offer, even though I'd never considered pictures. Anyway, I thought, if nothing actually happened, it would mean a free trip to the coast," Tobias said. Upon his arrival in Tinseltown, however, William Powell fell ill and the picture was postponed; instead, he was offered a role by MGM in a 'B' picture. "I told my agent I didn't think I ought to go into a 'B' picture, and he said, 'What's the matter with Bs?' and I said I'd heard they weren't good for anybody. So he said, 'If you can get enough of them to do, they're plenty good.' So I said okay, it's your bread and butter as well as mine. And I went into it."

The 'B' picture was *Maisie* (1939), which turned out to be a hit for the studio, a successful comeback vehicle for star Ann Sothern, and the start of a busy career for Tobias. After staying with MGM for *Ninotchka* (1939), which carried the tagline, "Garbo Laughs!"; *They All Come Out* (1939), a crime drama that marked the directorial debut of Jacques Tourneur; and *Balalaika* (1939), a Nelson Eddy starrer, Tobias signed a long-term contract with Warner Bros. In the next year, he appeared in 10 features for his new studio, including the Humphrey Bogart–George Raft hit, *They Drive by Night* (1940), in which he played a Greek produce buyer; *Torrid Zone* (1940), one of seven films Tobias would make with James Cagney; *The Man Who Talked Too Much* (1940), an inferior remake of the 1932 Warren William feature, *The Mouthpiece*; *Calling All Husbands* (1940), a mediocre comedy with Florence Bates; and *Saturday's Children* (1940), the first of seven features in which Tobias would appear with John Garfield (who became one of the actor's closest friends).

Tobias maintained his frenetic shooting pace during the next several years, playing a variety of roles in such features as *The Strawberry Blonde* (1941), starring James Cagney and Rita Hayworth; *The Bride Came C.O.D.* (1941), an amusing comedy with Cagney and Bette Davis; *Sergeant York* (1941), with Gary Cooper in the title role of the World War I hero; *Yankee Doodle Dandy* (1942), which won an Academy Award for star James Cagney; *My Sister Eileen* (1942), based on the hit Broadway play; *Mission to Moscow* (1943), a wartime drama directed by Michael Curtiz; *Captains of the Clouds* (1942), where Tobias played a French-Canadian bush pilot; *This Is the Army* (1943), a star-studded musical tribute to the war effort with a cast that included Ronald Reagan, Joan Leslie, Alan Hale, Rosemary DeCamp, and songwriter Irving Berlin; and *Between Two Worlds* (1944), starring John Garfield.

"They keep me plenty busy at Warner's," Tobias said, "and that's the way I like it. When I reported to the studio ... I said I wanted to work. They took me at my word. I'll take as many roles as the studio will give me. I want to set a record."

Despite this pronouncement, Tobias drastically slowed down his film schedule in 1945 and 1946, appearing in only a handful of features, including his first film noir, *Nobody Lives Forever* (1946). As this feature opens, notorious gambler Nick Blake (John Garfield) is returning to his home in New York after being injured in the war. Upon learning that he has been swindled out of his

$50,000 savings by his girlfriend, Toni (Faye Emerson), and her new lover, Nick pulls up stakes and moves to Los Angeles with his henchman, Al Doyle (Tobias). Along with Al, local hood Doc Ganson (George Coulouris), and an old friend, Pop Gruber (Walter Brennan), Nick takes part in a scheme to extort money from a wealthy widow, Gladys Halvorsen (Geraldine Fitzgerald). When Nick falls for the widow, he calls off the plan, but Ganson kidnaps Halvorsen, resulting in a gun battle that not only ends in Ganson's death, but Pop's as well.

As Nick's faithful sidekick, Tobias effectively combined his talent for both drama and comedy, particularly in a scene in which Al subtly convinces his partner to join Pop in fleecing the widow: "At the time, I thought you were crazy for nixing it — but I guess you were right," Al tells Nick after he initially turns Pop down. "That proposition is a big one ... a guy has to keep in hand in. You been away a long time, Nick. A guy can lose his touch awful quick. Listen, Nick — if you never wanna work another deal, it's okay with me. We got plenty of dough — right now. Only it's a shame to see a top guy like you throw away his talent." Although Tobias earned good notices for his performance in the film, however, *Nobody Lives Forever* was a disappointment at the box office.

After loan-outs to MGM for *Gallant Bess* (1946), a wartime drama about an army horse taken home by a solider, and to RKO for *Sinbad the Sailor* (1947), starring Douglas Fairbanks, Jr., Tobias appeared in his last film under his Warner's contract, *My Wild Irish Rose* (1947), based on the life of composer Chauncey Olcott. He was next seen in Eagle-Lion's routine romance *Adventures of Casanova* (1948), starring Arturo de Cordova, then returned to film noir with back-to-back features, *The Set-Up* (1949) and *Southside 1-1000* (1950).

In the first, which takes place during a single night at the Paradise City boxing arena, Tobias played Tiny, the oily manager of boxer Stoker Thompson (Robert Ryan). Unbeknownst to Stoker, Tiny has accepted a $50 payoff from a local gangster named Little Boy (Alan Baxter) to ensure that the aging fighter will lose the night's upcoming match: "The guy's blown a hundred fights already without anybody's help and he ain't gonna need none tonight," Tiny tells Stoker's trainer, Red (Percy Helton).

Despite Tiny's confidence in Stoker's defeat, however, he is forced to reveal the deal to the boxer before the final round of the match when it becomes apparent that Stoker is winning. ("You gotta lay down, Stoker," Tiny says in desperation. "It's supposed to be in the bag. There's 20 bucks in it for you, maybe 30.... Look — this is Little Boy's fix — he's payin' us to go in the tank. You gotta go down, Stoker — you gotta! Go down on the first good punch, stay down, take the count, and let's get outta here.") Stoker refuses to throw the fight and finishes off his opponent, but the triumph will be his last in the ring — after Stoker's victorious win, Little Boy's henchmen beat him in an alley behind the boxing ring and break his hand, ending his career. Hailed by one critic as a "real dilly" and a "sizzling melodrama," *The Set-Up* is considered one of the best fight pictures ever filmed and earned favorable reviews for To-

bias, who was praised in the *New York Times* for his "crisp, believable performance."

Next, as Reggie in *Southside 1-1000*, Tobias portrayed a member of a powerful counterfeiting ring headed by hotel manager Nora Craig (Andrea King), whose imprisoned father engraves the counterfeit plates from his cell. The gang is infiltrated by undercover Treasury officer John Riggs (Don DeFore), but Riggs' cover is blown, leading to a gun battle and the capture of most of the members of the gang. Nora manages to flee with a $100,000 cache of money, but she is caught by Riggs in a freight yard and, trying to throw the officer to the tracks below, falls to her death instead. As the unconscionable Reggie, Tobias portrayed his nastiest noir character; his ruthlessness was best demonstrated in a scene in which he escorts a luckless businessman (Barry Kelley) to a meeting on an upper floor of a high-rise building. In the middle of the corridor, Reggie is joined by another member of the gang and the two toss the man from a window, with Reggie covering his mouth as he screams and casually tossing his hat after him. Although *Southside 1-1000* was mostly overlooked by critics, Tobias' implacable, stone-faced performance remains one of his most memorable.

Off screen, Tobias had by now gained a reputation in Hollywood as "the last of the old-time bachelors." The never-married actor once claimed that, in the start of his career, he was too poor to get married.

"Then I went through a period where I was too busy, and now I'm too rich," Tobias said, with typical good humor. "Don't get me wrong, I'm not a woman-hater. To me, friendship is the greatest thing in the world, and if I'd marry a gal, I'd lose a friend. Oh, I've had gals who want to fuss after me or cook me a dinner, and that's when I say, 'Look I'll cook for you.' There's nothing I can't cook. In all those pictures, I never got the girl and they never got me. On or off screen, I never got caught."

Professionally, Tobias' cinematic output began to dwindle with the onset of the 1950s; his most notable features were *Ten Tall Men*

(1951), a Burt Lancaster western that scored at the box office; *Rawhide* (1951), another western, this one starring Tyrone Power and directed by Henry Hathaway; *The Glenn Miller Story* (1954), with James Stewart in the title role of the popular bandleader; and *The Seven Little Foys* (1955), an entertaining musical biography of Eddie Foy, in which James Cagney reprised his *Yankee Doodle Dandy* role of George M. Cohan. Away from the big screen, Tobias found time to return to Broadway, offering an acclaimed performance as Stosh in the hit production of *Stalag 17* in 1952, and appearing with Don Ameche and Hildegarde Neff in 1955 in *Silk Stockings*, a musical version of *Ninotchka*.

Back in Hollywood, Tobias reprised his *Silk Stockings* role for the 1957 film version, starring Fred Astaire and Cyd Charisse, then appeared in his final film noir feature, *The Tattered Dress* (1957). This feature starred Jeff Chandler as James Cordon Blane, an unscrupulous criminal attorney who is self-described as a defender of "racketeers, dope peddlers, and panderers." In a highly publicized case, Blane wins an acquittal for a wealthy resort town resident who murdered his wife's lover, primarily due to his savage cross-examination of the town's sheriff, Nick Hoak (Jack Carson). Humiliated by Blane's treatment, Hoak accuses the attorney of bribing a juror, Carol Morrow (Gail Russell), who is Hoak's mistress. When Blane is acquitted of the charges, Hoak pulls a gun on Blane as he leaves the courtroom, but in an ironic twist, the sheriff is himself shot and killed by Carol.

As Billy Giles, Tobias played a former comic who was successfully defended for murder 10 years earlier by Blane. ("How can he make an audience laugh?" one character says of Giles' faded career. "They look at him and remember how he emptied a revolver into his wife and her lover.") Now a staunch ally of the attorney, Billy unearths evidence that can support Blane's claim of innocence, but he meets a fiery end when Hoak forces his car off the highway.

After his supporting performance in *The Tattered Dress*, Tobias returned to his old home studio, Warner Bros., for *Marjorie Morningstar* (1958), starring Natalie Wood in the title role. But by now, Tobias was growing disillusioned with the changes in Hollywood, and the film marked the start of a five-year screen absence for the actor.

"I'm not in love anymore. The love is gone, understand? This is my trade and I do my job," Tobias told *Los Angeles Times* reporter Don Alpert. "I'll tell you what is wrong now. What is wrong with all the arts— the greats— they're all gone. Where are you going to find a Wally Beery? A Charlie Chaplin? A Barrymore or a Gable?"

Tobias was also critical of the improvisational "Method" acting technique that had taken Hollywood by storm, calling it "one of the greatest rackets."

"I was there at the inception of the whole damn thing," he said. "They would stand in a corner, holding the bridge of their nose or some damn thing, thinking and getting in the mood…. What a difference between then and now. In those days, you could relax. Everybody was happy. If they couldn't get the first take, they took it in the second take or the third or the fourth. Today, everything is so hectic, with people falling all over themselves."

Turning his sights to the small screen, Tobias landed a role on the popular ABC series *Adventures in Paradise*, set in the South Pacific. He remained with the show for two years, from 1959 to 1961, and was also seen in guest spots on such programs as *Laramie*, *Overland Trail*, *The Deputy*, *The Rebel*, and *The Untouchables*. He returned to feature films for the 1963 production of *A New Kind of Love*, a disappointing comedy despite a cast that included Paul Newman, Joanne Woodward, and Thelma Ritter. He was also seen in the western feature *Bullet for a Badman* (1964), with Audie Murphy and Darren McGavin, and *Nightmare in the Sun* (1964), a weak crime drama notable only as the first feature film directed and produced by veteran actor Marc Lawrence. But Tobias' best-known role was just ahead — Abner Kravitz, the world-weary neighbor on *Bewitched*, next-door neighbor to a modern-day witch (played by Elizabeth Montgomery) and husband of the ever-nosy Gladys. One of ABC's longest-running sitcoms, the popular series was seen from September 1964 to July 1972; Tobias remained with the show throughout its entire run, and in 1977 reprised his role in a guest spot on the short-lived follow-up series *Tabitha*, which focused on Samantha's now-adult daughter.

During the run of *Bewitched*, Tobias took time out to appear in the big-screen productions of MGM's *The Glass Bottom Boat* (1966), a popular Doris Day comedy, and Warner Bros.' *The Phynx* (1970), a dreadful spy spoof that featured cameo appearances by a host of veteran Hollywood performers including Joan Blondell, Patsy Kelly, George Jessel, Andy Devine, Ruby Keeler, Maureen O'Sullivan, Butterfly McQueen, Pat O'Brien, and Rudy Vallee. Tobias was also seen during his *Bewitched* years on such television series as *Perry Mason*, and after the show left the air, he appeared on a number of top-rated programs, including *The Waltons* and *Starsky and Hutch*.

In the early 1970s, Tobias retired from performing, preferring to spend his time on his remote ranch, located 135 miles from Hollywood.

"I've got my ranch, my horses, my guns," Tobias said. "When I'm coming down the road late at night and my dogs are barking, it's all nice and peaceful. I know there's nobody who's going to say, 'You're late!' and 'Where ya been?' I get me a log going in the fireplace and light up my pipe and God, it's wonderful. People think I'm lonely. I'm the happiest guy in the world. How can I be lonely? I can always sit on the side of the road and whittle."

One of Tobias' last public appearances was in the fall of 1979, when he played in the Don Sutton Celebrity Golf Tournament in Calabasas, California. By that time, he was battling cancer, and the following year, on February 27, 1980, Tobias died at Cedars Sinai Medical Center at the age of 78. In a footnote

that might have amused him, Tobias continued to make the news after his death when the car carrying his body from the medical center to a local mortuary was stolen by two men.

"But they left running and screaming when they noticed the body in the back seat," a Los Angeles detective told reporters. "They really became unglued."

Although today's audiences frequently associate George Tobias with his television work, his contribution to films, particularly in his prolific heyday, is worth remembering. His low-keyed comedic portrayal of Abner Kravitz aside, he offered notable portraits in numerous screen gems, particularly in such films as *The Set-Up* and *Southside 1-1000*. And while Tobias often viewed his profession as merely a job, he left no doubt that acting was one of his greatest joys.

"It's just a way of earning a living," he once said. "My fun comes from the living."

Film Noir Filmography

Nobody Lives Forever. Director: Jean Negulesco. Producer: Robert Buckner. Running time: 100 minutes. Released by Warner Bros., November 1, 1946. Cast: John Garfield, Geraldine Fitzgerald, Walter Brennan, Faye Emerson, George Coulouris, George Tobias, Robert Shayne, Richard Gaines, Dick Erdman, James Flavin, Ralph Peters.

The Set-Up. Director: Robert Wise. Producer: Richard Goldstone. Running time: 72 minutes. Released by RKO, March 29, 1949. Cast: Robert Ryan, Audrey Totter, George Tobias, Alan Baxter, Wallace Ford, Percy Helton, Hal Fieberling, Darryl Hickman, Kenny O'Morrison, James Edwards, David Clarke, Phillip Pine, Edwin Max.

Southside 1-1000. Director: Boris Ingster. Producers: Maurice and Frank King. Running time: 73 minutes. Released by Allied Artists, November 2, 1950. Cast: Don DeFore, Andrea King, George Tobias, Barry Kelley, Morris Ankrum, Robert Osterloh, Charles Cane, Kippee Valez.

The Tattered Dress. Director: Jack Arnold. Producer: Albert Zugsmith. Running time: 93 minutes. Released by Universal-International, March 14, 1957. Cast: Jeff Chandler, Jeanne Crain, Jack Carson, Gail Russell, Elaine Stewart, George Tobias, Edward Andrews, Philip Reed, Edward C. Platt, Paul Birch, Alexander Lockwood, Edwin Jerome, William Schallert, Joseph Granby.

References

Alpert, Don. "Old-Timer George Tobias: Is This the Face of a Method Actor?" *Los Angeles Times*, September 13, 1963.

Bacon, James. "The Guy Who Played Cagney's Best Friend." *Los Angeles Herald-Examiner*, February 28, 1980.

Biography of George Tobias. Paramount Pictures, January 1955.

Biography of George Tobias. RKO Radio Pictures, March 11, 1946.

Biography of George Tobias. Warner Bros., March 17, 1969.

Copeland, Elizabeth. "Tobias Anxious to Play as Many Roles as Possible." *Richmond (Virginia) News Leader*, March 23, 1941.

Drake, Herbert. "Names in Lights." *New York Herald-Tribune*, July 26, 1936.

Dunning, Jennifer. "George Tobias Dies, Veteran Actor, 78." *New York Times*, February 29, 1980.

"Finds 'Try, Try Again' Pays, Even in Hollywood." *New York Herald-Tribune*, July 28, 1940.

Gautschy, Dean. "Tobias Dodges Trip to Altar." *Los Angeles Herald-Examiner*, January 12, 1963.

"Greek Barber in New Film Is Also a Lasso Artist." *Brooklyn Daily Eagle*, February 16, 1941.

Herridge, Frances. "Tobias Knows Accent, Not Language." *New York Post*, February 13, 1956.

Hobson, Dick. "The Last of the Old-Time Bachelors." *TV Guide*, May 20, 1967.

"Mr. Tobias's Beard Is Real but Nobody Believes It." *New York Post*, December 26, 1936.

Obituary. *Newsweek*, March 10, 1980.

Obituary. *New York Daily News*, February 28, 1980.

Obituary. *Variety*, March 5, 1980.

"Out in the Open." *Variety*, June 16, 1937.

"Role of Blimp Weighty Problem for Tobias." *New York Morning Telegraph*, February 9, 1942.

Thirer, Irene. "Serious Screen Comic." *New York Post*, August 6, 1941.

"Tobias and His Lariat and the Elusive Calves." *Brooklyn Daily Eagle*, October 26, 1941.

"Tobias Credo: 'Give Me Parts; Others Can Have the Billing.'" *New York Herald-Tribune*, May 5, 1946.

"Valor Prize for Tobias." *New York World-Telegram*, May 4, 1937.

"Vehicle with Actor's Body Stolen — Briefly." *Los Angeles Times*, February 29, 1980.

Wallace, Ed. "A Real Manhattan Cowboy Gallops Home." *New York World-Telegram*, August 9, 1941.

Wolf, Patricia. "Shocked Thieves Find Actor's Body in Car." *Los Angeles Herald-Examiner*, February 28, 1980.

REGIS TOOMEY

"All you smart guys are prize suckers and I don't have to be too bright to trip you up. All I have to do is watch and wait. Sometimes not so long, either." — Regis Toomey in *Cry Danger* (1951)

Regis Toomey once jokingly referred to himself as "the undertaker's friend" — before his career-changing role as a soda jerk in Frank Capra's *Meet John Doe* (1941), Toomey had portrayed a string of hapless film characters who, alternately, had fallen from a building roof, been murdered with a tomahawk, shot in the back, scalped, drowned, and smashed to smithereens in a dive bomber attack.

"I began to think I was Calamity Toomey," the actor said.

But the actor managed to survive both on screen and off, and during his 50-year career, he appeared in nearly 200 films — including appearances in a total of eight films noirs and featured roles in five: *Strange Illusion* (1945), *The Big Sleep* (1946), *The Guilty* (1947), *I Wouldn't Be in Your Shoes* (1948), and *Cry Danger* (1951).

Born in Pittsburgh, Pennsylvania, on August 13, 1898 (some sources say 1902), Regis Toomey was one of four children of Francis X. Toomey, a mill hand, and his wife, Marie Ellen. As a student in the Pittsburgh public schools, Toomey found that he was often picked on because of his name, forcing him to prove that he wasn't a "sissy." (His brother, Ord, no doubt suffered a similar fate.)

"I never won a fight," Toomey said in a

1941 interview. "So I found it was better to talk fast and run."

Later, as a student at the University of Pittsburgh, Toomey put his "fast talking" experience to good use and joined the debating team, as well as the school's Cap and Gown Club, for which he was frequently cast as the "leading lady" in the all-male revues. Abandoning his initial plans to pursue a law career, Toomey set his sights on the field of acting, gaining experience in summer stock at Pittsburgh's Empire Theater. But after graduating from the University of Pittsburgh, Toomey was unable to land an acting part and, instead, became a salesman with a steel firm, using his salary to finance night courses in drama at the Carnegie Institute of Technology.

In 1924, following two years at Carnegie Tech, Toomey decided to try his fortune in the Big Apple. Just four days after his arrival in New York, he won an understudy role in Arthur (uncle of Oscar) Hammerstein's production of *Rose Marie*. The assistant choreographer with the production was a dancer named Kathryn Scott — on January 14, 1925, Toomey and Scott were married, and would go on to enjoy one of Hollywood's longest lasting marriages.

Shortly after his marriage to Kathryn, Toomey snagged the juvenile lead in a London production of *Little Nellie Kelly*, and remained abroad to appear with James Gleason in *Is Zat So?* Upon his return to the United States, he found no trouble finding roles in Los Angeles and San Francisco, and was seen in such plays as *Twinkle, Twinkle* with Joe E. Brown, *Moonlight*, and *Hit the Deck*. While appearing in the latter production, Toomey was spotted by producer-director Roland West, who cast him in his first film, *Alibi* (1929), starring Chester Morris. After the premiere of this popular gangster film, Toomey signed a long-term contract with Paramount–Famous Players–Lasky and for the next several years was seen in lead roles opposite some of Hollywood's biggest names, including Constance Bennett in *Rich People* (1929); William Powell and Jean Arthur in

Street of Chance (1930); Gary Cooper in *A Man from Wyoming* (1930); Mary Astor and James Cagney in *Other Men's Women* (1931); Clara Bow in *Kick In* (1931); Barbara Stanwyck in *Shopworn* (1932); and Loretta Young in *She Had to Say Yes* (1933).

In the early 1930s, Toomey left Paramount in order to freelance, but after several years, his star began to wane. By 1936, according to one columnist, "he had run through a long series of drunks and heavies and nobody wanted him anymore. From $1,500 a week, his wage went to zero." Undaunted, Toomey hired a new agent, who decreased the actor's asking price and quickly began to find small parts for his client. In 1941, Toomey hit pay dirt when he played a minor but memorable role in Frank Capra's *Meet John Doe*; portraying a soda jerk, Toomey delivered a heartfelt speech that the critic for the *New York Morning Telegraph* termed "one of the most gripping, most intensely dramatic movie scenes of the year."

After *Meet John Doe*, Toomey signed a seven-year contract with Warner Bros. (One of his first assignments with the studio made motion picture history — in *You're in the Army Now* [1941], Toomey shared a kiss with actress Jane Wyman that, at 185 seconds, was the longest on-screen kiss to date.) Throughout the decade, Toomey was seen in a number of popular features, including *They Died With Their Boots On* (1941), starring Errol Flynn and Olivia deHavilland; *Sister Kenny* (1946), with Rosalind Russell in the title role; *Spellbound* (1945), directed by Alfred Hitchcock; *Station West* (1948), a western starring Dick Powell and Jane Greer; and *Come to the Stable* (1949), an appealing holiday movie with Loretta Young and Celeste Holm.

Also during this period, Toomey began his appearances in a series of films noirs, beginning with the Ella Raines–Franchot Tone starrer *Phantom Lady* (1944), in which he delivered a total of two lines as an unkempt detective. The following year, he essayed a significantly more substantial role in *Strange Illusion* (1945), a minor noir offering where he portrayed Dr. Vincent, a kindly physician who serves as a sounding board for college student Paul Cartwright (Jimmy Lydon). Plagued by a recurring nightmare and egged on by an overactive imagination, Paul suspects that his would-be stepfather, Brett Curtis (Warren William), is actually a murderer who is after his widowed mother's fortune. When aspects from his nightmare actually begin to take place, Paul displays increasingly erratic behavior, giving Curtis the opportunity to have a psychiatrist friend, Professor Muhlbach (Charles Arnt), suggest that the boy be admitted to his sanitarium. Working with Dr. Vincent, Paul decides to accept the doctor's recommendation in the hopes of finding evidence against Curtis, and before long the two learn that Curtis is actually a man named Barrington who murdered his wealthy first wife and teamed with Muhlbach to kill Paul's father. After confronting Professor Muhlbach with his knowledge, Paul manages to escape from the sanitarium and track down Curtis, who injures the young man during a struggle but is ultimately shot and killed by police.

After this rather offbeat feature, Toomey appeared in 1946 in his third noir in as many years, the notoriously convoluted *The Big Sleep*. Here, Toomey was seen as Bernie Ohls, a crafty homicide detective and friend of private eye Philip Marlowe (Humphrey Bogart). It is Bernie who refers Marlowe for a job working for Gen. Sternwood (Charles Waldron), the millionaire father of two daughters, the youngest of whom (Martha Vickers) is being blackmailed by an unknown source. Soon after Marlowe takes on the case, bodies begin piling up — the first being that of the Sternwood's chauffeur. "They seem to be a family that things happen to," Bernie tells Marlowe in one scene. "There's a big Packard belonging to one of them washing around in the surf off Lido Pier. And I almost forgot — there's a guy in it." Characterized by numerous plot twists and a conglomeration of memorable characters, *The Big Sleep* depicts a deluge of double-crosses and no less than seven murders before Marlowe finally gets his man — and Sternwood's older, level-headed

daughter, Vivian (Lauren Bacall) in the bargain. With one critic describing the film as a "fast-moving murder mystery without time for a yawn," *The Big Sleep* was cheered by moviegoers and critics alike. In *Time* magazine, the reviewer recommended the feature as "wakeful fare for folks who don't care what is going on, or why, so long as the talk is hard and the action harder"; *Cue*'s critic judged that it blended "blackmail, murder, kidnapping, mayhem, and assorted skullduggery"; and in the *Los Angeles Times*, Edwin Schallert wrote, "There's an A-1 cast throughout, with such ladies as Martha Vickers ... and Dorothy Malone stealing the spotlight now and then, while John Ridgely, Regis Toomey, Bob Steele, [and] Elisha Cook, Jr., nearly all of whom do unusual roles, help to build up the picture's impact."

Next, Toomey was featured in *The Guilty* (1947), a low-budget noir that centered on an unusual love quartet between working stiff Mike Carr (Don Castle), his emotionally unstable roommate Johnny Dixon (Wally Cassell), and the identical twin Mitchell sisters, Linda (the good one) and Estelle (the bad one), both played by Bonita Granville. Although Dixon originally dated Estelle, he dumped her in favor of Linda, but was unable to ignore Estelle's blatant attempts to lure him back. Carr, meanwhile, begins dating Estelle, but becomes suspicious when he sees her sporting a gold bracelet that was a gift from Dixon. When Linda turns up missing, Detective Heller (Toomey) enters the picture, focusing his investigation on Dixon, particularly when Linda's body is found after being beaten, strangled, partially stuffed into an incinerator, and concealed in a gravel-covered barrel. Despite warnings from Carr, Dixon goes on the lam, but it appears that the murder was actually committed by Alec Trenholt (John Litel), who lived for several years as a boarder in the twins' home. Six months later, however, Carr returns to the house where Linda was killed and encounters Detective Heller, who arrests him for the murder — it turns out that Carr was insanely jealous of Estelle's continuing relationship with Dixon and killed Linda in a murderous rage, thinking that she was her twin sister. Based on a story by Cornell Woolrich, *The Guilty* was released to mostly unimpressive reviews; the critic for the *New York Times* completely dismissed it as "an unpretentious and bland addition to the season's mysteries," and although the *Los Angeles Daily News*' Marie Mesmer stated that the film's killer was "very cleverly concealed until the end," she also wrote, "The film has an idea, [but] it isn't backed up with enough weighty and believable content to stretch beyond a passable melodrama." As for Toomey, he merely earned mention in one notice, along with Litel, as "round[ing] out the featured cast."

The actor fared only slightly better in his next noir, *I Wouldn't Be in Your Shoes* (1948), which was also adapted from a work by Cornell Woolrich. In this B-grade Monogram feature, the actor was once again seen as a detective, this time offering aid to a young married couple, Tom (Don Castle) and Ann (Elyse Knox), who are struggling to make a living as a dance team. When a discarded pair of Tom's dance shoes are identified as clues in a local murder, Tom is arrested and convicted for the crime, but Ann

and Toomey's Judd continue to search for evidence that will clear Tom's name. Ultimately, they emerge successful in their determined quest, but in a surprise twist, it turns out that Tom actually was the killer. After this box-office disappointment, Toomey was seen in yet another noir feature, *Beyond the Forest* (1949), but his role as the father of a passel of children was limited to only a few minutes on screen.

As the 1950s began, Toomey continued to play minor roles in films of varying quality — *Mrs. O'Malley and Mr. Malone* (1951), in which he portrayed a newspaper reporter, was a fun murder mystery starring Marjorie Main, while *Frenchie* (1951) was a weak remake of *Destry Rides Again* (1939), with Shelley Winters and Joel McCrea in the roles originally played by Marlene Dietrich and James Stewart. Toomey was also seen in small parts in *Showboat* (1951), *Tomahawk* (1951), and *The Tall Target* (1951) before returning to the shadowy world of film noir for his final two appearances in the era. In the meatier of the roles, Toomey was featured as Lt. Gus Cobb in *Cry Danger* (1951), which opens as Cobb is awaiting the arrival of Rocky Mulloy (Dick Powell), who was recently released from a five-year prison stretch for a murder and $100,000 robbery that he did not commit. Although Rocky's release was secured after an ex–Marine, Delong (Richard Erdman), provided him with an alibi, Cobb continues to suspect Rocky's involvement in the crime, telling him, "I'm going to keep a tail on you, Rocky. Twenty-four hours a day.... If I get you again, the Army, Navy, and the Marines won't be able to help you." With his alleged partner in the crime, Danny Morgan, still in prison, Rocky works with Delong to find the real killer, but along the way he falls in love with Danny's wife, Nancy (Rhonda Fleming). Meanwhile, after several attempts on his life, Rocky uncovers proof that a local mobster, Castro (William Conrad), was behind the robbery and murder, but he also learns, to his dismay, that Danny was actually involved in the crime and that Nancy has been in possession of her husband's share of the stolen money all along. At the film's end, Rocky turns Nancy over to Cobb, telling him with regret that "she's already packed." In this feature, the actor turned in one of his best performances and his role was singled out as "nicely played" in the *New York Times*. After this top-notch offering from the era, Toomey was seen in the last film noir of his career, *The People Against O'Hara* (1951), but here, he portrayed the minor role of a police department radio technician, most of which was viewed from the back of his head.

During this period, between film assignments, Toomey began making guest shots on a variety of programs on the small screen. He specialized primarily in western series, such as *Cheyenne*, *The Virginian*, *Rawhide*, *Maverick*, *The Adventures of Jim Bowie*, *Bronco*, and *Texas John Slaughter*, but he also guested on such top-rated series as *Perry Mason*, *Green Acres*, and *The F.B.I.* In addition, the prolific actor was a regular performer on a total of seven series between 1954 and 1965, *Hey Mulligan*; *Richard Diamond, Private Detective*; *Dante's Inferno*; *Petticoat Junction*; *Burke's Law*; *Shannon*; and *The Mickey Rooney Show*.

In feature films, Toomey continued to find work, but most of the pictures were fairly forgettable. Notable exceptions were *The High and the Mighty* (1954), starring John Wayne; *Guys and Dolls* (1955), a hit musical with Marlon Brando and Frank Sinatra; and *Voyage to the Bottom of the Sea* (1961), an entertaining science-fiction feature. Toomey appeared in only a handful of films in the 1970s, including *Won Ton Ton, The Dog that Saved Hollywood* (1976), a satirical comedy that bombed at the box office despite a spate of cameos from such veteran performers as Alice Faye, Walter Pidgeon, Ann Rutherford, William Demarest, Victor Mature, Rudy Vallee, Jackie Coogan, Rhonda Fleming, Stepin Fetchit, and Huntz Hall. Toomey's last big-screen role was a police chief in another poorly received film, *C.H.O.M.P.S.* (1979), starring Wesley Eure and Valerie Bertinelli.

On October 12, 1991, more than a decade after his last screen appearance, Toomey died of natural causes at the Motion Picture and Television Hospital in Woodland Hills, California. He was 93 years old. Shortly before his death, he had received a visit from former President Ronald Reagan, a longtime friend who had appeared with the actor in the 1937 feature *Submarine D-1*.

With a screen career that took him from leading man status to one of Hollywood's most reliable character performers, Regis Toomey may not have had one of the screen's most recognizable names, but he certainly had one of its most familiar faces. Whether he was playing an uncompromising gumshoe, a suave man-about-town, a ruthless gangster, or a crusading lawyer, Toomey always delivered.

Film Noir Filmography

Phantom Lady. Director: Robert Siodmak. Producer: Joan Harrison. Running time: 87 minutes. Released by Universal, February 17, 1944. Cast: Franchot Tone, Ella Raines, Alan Curtis, Aurora, Thomas Gomez, Fay Helm, Elisha Cook, Jr., Andrew Tombes, Jr., Regis Toomey, Joseph Crehan, Doris Lloyd, Virginia Brissac, Milburn Stone.

Strange Illusion. Director: Edgar G. Ulmer. Producer: Leon Fromkess. Running time: 84 minutes. Released by PRC, March 31, 1945. Cast: James Lydon, Warren William, Sally Eilers, Regis Toomey, Charles Arnt, George H. Reed, Jayne Hazard, Jimmy Clark, Mary McLeod, Pierre Watkin, John Hamilton, Sonia Sorrel, Vic Portel.

The Big Sleep. Director and Producer: Howard Hawks. Running time: 118 minutes. Released by Warner Bros., August 31, 1946. Cast: Humphrey Bogart, Lauren Bacall, John Ridgely, Martha Vickers, Dorothy Malone, Patricia Clarke, Regis Tomey, Charles Waldron, Louis Jean Heydt, Elisha Cook, Jr., Sonia Darrin, Bob Steele, James Flavin, Thomas Jackson, Thomas Rafferty, Theodore Von Eltz, Dan Wallace, Joy Barlowe.

The Guilty. Director: John Reinhardt. Producer: Jack Wrather. Running time: 71 minutes. Released by Monogram, March 22, 1947. Cast: Bonita Granville, Don Castle, Wally Cassell, Regis Toomey, John Litel, Ruth Robinson, Thomas Jackson, Oliver Blake, Caroline Andrews.

I Wouldn't Be in Your Shoes. Director: William Nigh. Producer: Walter Mirisch. Running time: 70 minutes. Released by Monogram, May 23, 1948.

Cast: Don Castle, Elyse Knox, Regis Toomey, Charles D. Brown, Rory Mallinson, Robert Lowell, Bill Kennedy.

Beyond the Forest. Director: King Vidor. Producer: Henry Blanke. Running time: 97 minutes. Released by Warner Bros., October 22, 1949. Cast: Bette Davis, Joseph Cotten, David Brian, Ruth Roman, Minor Watson, Dona Drake, Regis Toomey, Sarah Selby, Mary Servoss, Frances Charles.

Cry Danger. Director: Robert Parrish. Producers: Sam Wiesenthal and W.R. Frank. Running time: 79 minutes. Released by RKO, February 21, 1951. Cast: Dick Powell, Rhonda Fleming, Richard Erdman, William Conrad, Regis Toomey, Jean Porter, Jay Adler, Joan Banks, Gloria Saunders, Hy Averbach, Renny McEvoy, Lou Lubin, Benny Burt.

The People Against O'Hara. Director: John Sturges. Producer: William H. Wright. Running time: 102 minutes. Released by MGM, September 5, 1951. Cast: Spencer Tracy, Pat O'Brien, Diana Lynn, John Hodiak, Eduardo Ciannelli, James Arness, Yvette Duguay, Jay C. Flippen, William Campbell, Richard Anderson, Henry O'Neill, Arthur Shields, Louise Lorimer, Ann Doran, Emile Meyer, Regis Toomey, Katherine Warren, Paul Bryar, Peter Mamakos, Perdita Chandler, Frank Fergusson, Don Dillaway, C. Anthony Hughes, Lee Phelps, Lawrence Tolan, Jack Lee, Tony Barr.

References

Biography of Regis Toomey. ABC Television Network, circa 1963.

Biography of Regis Toomey. Paramount Studios, December 1951.

Biography of Regis Toomey. Samuel Goldwyn Productions, circa 1955.

Chapman, John. "Hollywood." Publication Unsourced, April 6, 1941.

Obituary. *Variety*, October 14, 1991.

Othman, Frederick C. "Toomey Finally Lives Through Entire Movie." *New York Morning Telegraph*, June 24, 1941.

"Regis Toomey, 93; Actor Was in More Than 200 Movies." *Los Angeles Times*, October 13, 1991.

"Regis Toomey, Actor in Films, Dies at 93." *New York Times*, October 16, 1991.

"Toomey Meets John Doe and His Stock Goes Up." *New York Morning Telegraph*, March 5, 1941.

―――― **HAROLD VERMILYEA** ――――

"Somebody's going to shoot you sooner or later."— Harold Vermilyea in *Chicago Deadline* (1949)

Grey-haired and chubby-cheeked, with an unassuming air, Harold Vermilyea was a late arrival to the screen scene, and didn't stay long — after making his Hollywood film debut at the age of 57, the stocky performer appeared in a total of only 15 features. Among these films, however, were such gems as *Gentleman's Agreement* (1947) and *Miracle of the Bells* (1948), and during his years on screen Vermilyea was seen alongside such stars as Alan Ladd, Bing Crosby, and Burt Lancaster. In addition, Vermilyea possesses a unique distinction in the era of film noir — a full third of his movies were made during the era: *Sorry, Wrong Number* (1948), *The Big Clock* (1948), *Manhandled* (1949), *Chicago Deadline* (1949), and *Edge of Doom* (1950).

The actor who was frequently compared to character actor Gene Lockhart was born in New York City on October 10, 1889, the son of building contractor Eugene Vermilyea and his wife, Anna Dolano, a former Broadway actress. According to sources, Vermilyea was also a descendant of Jahannes Vermilje, one of the Dutch settlers of Nieuw Amsterdam. Despite an early interest in acting, Vermilyea was discouraged by his father from entering the profession and instead, after receiving his schooling in New York and England, he studied stenography and typing. His clerical proficiency earned him a job as secretary to United States Senator Robert Owen from Oklahoma and later to playwright Augustus Thomas, author of such Broadway productions as *Arizona*, *The Harvest Moon*, and *Indian Summer*.

Vermilyea's association with Thomas rekindled his desire to pursue an acting career and the playwright assisted him in landing a job with a stock company at New York's Wadsworth Theater. A short time later, in 1914, the actor made his Broadway debut in *The Lion and the Mouse*, followed by *Get-Rich-Quick Wallingford*, written by George M. Cohan, and the Cohan-produced *It Pays to Advertise*, where Vermilyea succeeded future screen actor Grant Mitchell in the lead role.

With the onset of World War I, Vermilyea enlisted in the Army, serving in France for two years with the Army Ambulance Service. Following his discharge, he resumed his relationship with Cohan, starring in the national tour of *A Tailor-Made Man*. During the next two decades, Vermilyea became a household name on the Broadway stage with appearances in nearly 30 productions, including *The Enemy*, starring Walter Abel and Fay Bainter; *Hobohemia*, penned by Sinclair Lewis; *The Youngest*, with Verree Teasdale and Genevieve Tobin; *A Man With Red Hair*, which featured a young Edward G. Robinson; *Boy Meets Girl*, a hit comedy produced by George Abbott; *The Pure in Heart*, which closed after only seven performances; and *Bad Manners*, whose cast included Margaret Sullavan. During these years, Vermilyea also took time to appear in his first film, playing a bit part in the Frederic March starrer *Night Angel* (1931), which was filmed at Paramount's studio in Astoria, New York.

In the late 1930s, Vermilyea gave up the stage and turned to radio, spending the next five years on a variety of programs, including *The Kate Smith Hour*, *The Royal Gelatin Hour*, and *The Rudy Vallee Hour*, on which he played a leading role. He also appeared on numerous soap operas, including the longrunning *Stella Dallas*. Too old to serve in World War II, Vermilyea contributed to the war effort by acting as director of the American Theatre Wing's Victory Players.

Vermilyea returned to Broadway in 1944, earning acclaim for his portrayals of a lisping Gestapo agent in *Jacobowsky and the Colonel*, and a southern congressman in *Deep*

Are the Roots, both directed by Elia Kazan. His standout performance in *Jacobowsky* caught the notice of Hollywood producer-writer Richard Maibaum, who convinced the actor to take a four-week leave from the stage to appear in his upcoming feature film, *O.S.S.* (1946), a wartime drama starring Alan Ladd.

"I like the prospect of going to Hollywood. Salary is nice, too," Vermilyea said, although he complained upon his arrival that he was "almost done in" by the cross-country airplane flight to Tinseltown. "I'm too old for this sort of nonsense. Next time I'll take the train!"

Although Vermilyea's serio-comic portrayal of a secret operative in *O.S.S.* attracted widespread notice, one columnist wrote that "few in Hollywood knew his name, fewer knew his background, and there wasn't even one portrait of the man to be found in any studio files." But that was about to change. Vermilyea was quickly signed to a contract with Paramount and the following year was loaned to Fox for one of his best features, *Gentleman's Agreement* (1947), starring Gregory Peck as a writer who poses as a Jew for an article he is writing on anti–Semitism. The following year — the busiest of his screen career — Vermilyea was seen in RKO's touching drama *Miracle of the Bells* (1948), starring Fred MacMurray, and was back at Paramount for five features, including *The Emperor Waltz* (1948), a Bing Crosby musical; *The Sainted Sisters* (1948), with Veronica Lake and Joan Caulfield; and *Beyond Glory* (1948), a box-office hit starring Alan Ladd. He was also featured that year in his first two films noirs, *The Big Clock* (1948) and *Sorry, Wrong Number* (1948).

The rather complex plot of *The Big Clock* centers on a murder committed by media mogul Earl Janoth (Charles Laughton), who kills his mistress, Pauline (Rita Johnson), after she laughingly berates him during an argument ("You'd be pathetic if you weren't so disgusting," she says). Leaving Pauline's apartment, Janoth spies a shadowy figure and realizes that the man can connect him to the murder. In an effort to find the man, Janoth assigns the staff of his crime magazine to un-earth the killer, not knowing that the man in the hallway was his own editor, George Stroud (Ray Milland), who'd been out with Pauline earlier on the night of her death and tries to mask his own involvement. Meanwhile, a spate of leads are turned up by George's staff, which includes art critic Don Klausmeyer (Vermilyea), who manages to uncover a piv-otal clue in the person of a dotty local artist (Elsa Lanchester). In the film's climax, George points the finger at Steve Hagen (George Macready), Janoth's assistant, and partner in the cover-up, who promptly reveals that Jan-oth is the real killer. In desperation, Janoth shoots Hagen and tries to flee, but instead falls down an elevator shaft to his death.

After being singled out in the *Hollywood Citizen-News* for "lend[ing] topnotch support to the principals" in *The Big Clock*, Vermilyea played a significant role in his second film noir, *Sorry, Wrong Number*. This tension-filled feature starred Barbara Stanwyck as Leona Stephenson, a shrewish and domineer-ing heiress who is bedridden because of a heart condition and keeps in contact with the world through the telephone. One evening, while trying to locate her husband, Henry (Burt Lancaster), Leona overhears two men discussing their plans for the imminent mur-der of a woman, but the telephone connec-tion is lost before the potential victim is named. Trying without success to report the would-be crime to authorities, Leona becomes increasingly frantic after she talks to Henry's former girlfriend (Ann Richards) and an ap-prehensive chemist, Waldo Evans (Vermi-lyea). As it turns out, Henry has teamed with Evans in a lucrative scheme to steal and sell drugs from the pharmaceutical company owned by Leona's father (Ed Begley). The profitable scheme goes awry, however, when Henry is blackmailed for $200,000 by a for-mer partner and can only obtain the money by arranging to have his wife killed — the de-tails of which were discussed in the conver-sation Leona overheard. Before the murder can be carried out, Henry experiences a change of heart and warns Leona to escape, but it is

too late, and he is forced to listen on the tele-phone as the killer approaches her bedside. For his performance as Mr. Evans, Vermilyea was praised by several reviewers and the film was a box-office smash upon its release, with the critic from *Variety* terming it "a real thriller," and the reviewer for *Cue* proclaim-ing: "For sheer, unadulterated terror, there have been few films in recent years to match the quivering fright of *Sorry, Wrong Number*." Vermilyea followed this hit with appearances in two more noirs, *Manhandled* (1949) and *Chicago Deadline* (1949).

In the first, Vermilyea played his first and only true noir heavy, a mercenary and, ultimately, lethal psychiatrist named Dr. Red-man. As the feature begins, Redman is listen-ing as a patient, Alton Bennett (Alan Napier), recounts a recurring nightmare in which he kills his wealthy wife, Ruth (Irene Hervey). Taking notes during Bennett's recitation is Redman's secretary, Merl Kramer (Dorothy Lamour). Days later, Redman murders Mrs. Bennett and takes her jewels, only to have them stolen by sleazy private detective Karl Benson (Dan Duryea), a neighbor of Merl's. Redman later retrieves the jewels from Ben-son at gunpoint, but he is killed in a grisly scene when Benson runs him over with his car. Benson then attempts to pin Mrs. Ben-nett's murder on Merl and even tries to throw her from the roof of their apartment build-ing before police finally catch up to him. Al-though *Manhandled* was justifiably panned as a "cheap, sensational hodgepodge of in-credible melodramatics," Vermilyea turned in a chilling performance as the determined and deadly doctor.

Vermilyea's second noir of the year, *Chi-cago Deadline*, focused on the efforts of news-paper reporter Ed Adams (Alan Ladd) to un-cover the circumstances that led to the death of a young woman found in a run-down hotel room. Taking the woman's address book be-fore police Lt. Jack Anstruder (Vermilyea) arrives on the scene, Ed finds a series of in-dividuals who knew her, including mobster Solly Wellman (Berry Kroeger), small-time hood Blacky Franchot (Shepperd Strudwick), and wealthy industrialist G. G. Temple (Gavin Muir). Refusing to reveal his resource to Anstruder, Adams continues pursuing the case, doubling his efforts after Blacky is murdered. Ultimately identifying Solly as the killer, Adams guns the mobster down during a parking garage shootout, and later burns the address book at the woman's memorial service. For his performance as the frustrated cop, Vermilyea earned mention by Ann Helming of the *Hollywood Citizen-News*, who wrote that he was "good in a supporting role." Helming held a less favorable view of the film itself, however, claiming that "the plot spreads out in more directions than an octopus," and in the *New York Times*, Bosley Crowther dismissed the feature as "a lurid adventure tale." A vastly different opinion was offered by the *Los Angeles Examiner*'s Lynn Bowers, however, who found that the film was "as exciting a story as you're likely to see hereabouts," and that the "performances of the brilliant cast are top caliber."

In 1950, Vermilyea was seen in only two features, *Born to Be Bad* (1950), starring Joan Fontaine as a goldigging schemer, and *Edge of Doom* (1950), the last of his five films noirs. Here, the actor played Father Kirkman, a parish priest whose rather cold nature is revealed in an early scene when he is told that a woman has arrived to see him on an urgent matter. "Have her wait," the priest says, continuing to drink his tea. "Everything is always urgent." Kirkman's character is further illuminated when a young man, Martin Lynn (Farley Granger), tells him his mother has died and insists that she be given a "fine funeral." Kirkman refuses, gently at first but with more vehemence as Martin becomes increasingly agitated. "You're overwrought, boy—calm yourself! You haven't the money for a big funeral and that's the end of it. I've been patient with you, but there's nothing more to say.... For the last time, I'm telling you the answer is no, no, no!" Overcome with rage, Martin picks up a crucifix from the priest's desk and bludgeons him to death, fleeing the rectory shortly before the body is found by Kirkman's assistant, Father Roth

(Dana Andrews). Faced with the growing suspicions of police and Father Roth during the next few days, Martin tries to mask his involvement, but by the film's end, alone with his mother's body in the chapel, he finally admits his guilt in the crime. While Vermilyea turned in a good performance as the callous priest, the critic for the *New York Times* found that his role was "only sketchily developed in the film." The same reviewer went on to acknowledge "the shock effect" of the scene where Vermilyea's character is murdered, but he added that "the horror of the deed tends to become diluted in the rush of consequences ... which gives *Edge of Doom* the appearance of being contrived."

In his final two feature films, Vermilyea was seen in a pair of comedies for Universal, *Katie Did It* (1951), starring Ann Blyth and Mark Stevens, and *Finders Keepers* (1952), with Tom Ewell and Julie Adams. Away from the big screen, Vermilyea concentrated on the medium of television during the next several years, appearing on such programs as *Danger*, *Lux Video Theatre*, *Man Against Crime*, *Studio One*, and *Philco Television Playhouse*.

On January 8, 1958, Vermilyea died of a heart attack at his New York home. The 68-

year-old actor never married and had no survivors.

Because most of his acting career was spent on the Broadway stage and in radio, Harold Vermilyea is often unrecognized today, but he managed to fashion a body of screen work that provides a fine representation of his talent. Once described as possessing "a mobile face which can be either cherubic or sinister," Vermilyea played a diverse series of screen roles during his all-too-brief tenure on the big screen, from frightened chemist to steely murderer, earning a well-deserved place in the Hollywood history books.

Film Noir Filmography

Sorry, Wrong Number. Director: Anatole Litvak. Producers: Hal B. Wallis, Anatole Litvak. Running time: 98 minutes. Released by Paramount, September 1, 1948. Cast: Barbara Stanwyck, Burt Lancaster, Ann Richards, Wendell Corey, Harold Vermilyea, Ed Begley, Leif Erickson, William Conrad, John Bromfield, Jimmy Hunt, Dorothy Neumann, Paul Fierro. Awards: Academy Award nomination for Best Actress (Barbara Stanwyck).

The Big Clock. Director: John Farrow. Producer: Richard Maibaum. Running time: 93 minutes. Released by Paramount, April 9, 1948. Cast: Ray Milland, Charles Laughton, Maureen O'Sullivan, George Macready, Rita Johnson, Elsa Lanchester, Harold Vermilyea, Dan Tobin, Henry Morgan, Richard Webb, Tad Van Brunt, Elaine Riley, Luis Van Rooten, Lloyd Corrigan, Margaret Field, Philip Van Zandt, Henri Letondal, Douglas Spencer.

Manhandled. Director: Lewis R. Foster. Producers: William H. Pine and William C. Thomas. Running time: 97 minutes. Released by Paramount, May 25, 1949. Cast: Dorothy Lamour, Dan Duryea, Sterling Hayden, Irene Hervey, Philip Reed, Harold Vermilyea, Alan Napier, Art Smith, Irving Bacon.

Chicago Deadline. Director: Lewis Allen. Producer: Robert Fellows. Running time: 87 minutes. Released by Paramount, November 2, 1949. Cast: Alan Ladd, Donna Reed, June Havoc, Irene Hervey, Arthur Kennedy, Berry Kroeger, Harold Vermilyea, Shepperd Strudwick, John Beal, Tom Powers, Gavin Muir, Dave Willock, Paul Lees.

Edge of Doom. Director: Mark Robson. Producer: Samuel Goldwyn. Running time: 99 minutes. Released by RKO, September 27, 1950. Cast: Dana Andrews, Farley Granger, Joan Evans, Robert Keith, Paul Stewart, Mala Powers, Adele Jergens, Harold Vermilyea, John Ridgeley, Douglas Fowley, Mabel Paige, Howland Chamberlain, Houseley Stevenson, Sr., Jean Innes, Ellen Corby, Ray Teal, Mary Field, Virginia Brissac, Frances Morris.

References

"A Man of Whom Hollywood Never Heard." *New York Herald-Tribune*, May 26, 1946.
Biography of Harold Vermilyea. Paramount Studios, February 1948.
Cohn, Herbert. "Harold Vermilyea Going to Hollywood, But Aspiring Young Actors Needn't Fret." *Brooklyn Eagle*, February 2, 1946.
"Harold Vermilyea, Actor, Dies at 68; Appeared in 32 Plays on Broadway." *New York Times*, January 9, 1958.
"H. Vermilyea, Actor 40 Years." *New York Herald-Tribune*, January 10, 1958.
Obituary. *Variety*, January 15, 1958.

CLIFTON WEBB

"If you come a little bit closer, my boy, I can just crack your skull with my stick."
— Clifton Webb in *Laura* (1944)

Elegant and urbane, with a caustic wit and a supercilious air, Clifton Webb possessed a wide-reaching talent that not only encompassed his triumphs on the stage and the screen, but also extended to accomplishments as a dancer, painter, and opera singer as well.

"Short of a dog-and-pony show," a friend of the actor's once said, "there isn't much he hasn't successfully essayed."

In addition to his renown as a performer, Webb was also characterized by an attention to fashion that made him a regular choice on annual "best-dressed" lists, and an uncommonly close relationship with his mother, Mabelle, with whom he lived until her death at age 90. It was Mabelle, in fact, who was photographed alongside Webb when the sophisticated thespian arrived in Hollywood in 1944 for his first screen talkie and one of his most famous films — the classic noir feature *Laura*.

The tall, lean, and impeccably groomed actor was born Webb Parmalee Hollenbeck on November 11th in Indianapolis, Indiana. The year of his birth is in question; although it is most likely that he was born in 1893, sources report a range from 1889 to 1896. Little is known about the actor's father, as well, except that he was a local businessman. According to legend, Webb's mother Mabelle — who was reportedly only 14 when the future actor was born — left Webb's father when he failed to share her affinity for show business. ("We never speak of him," Mabelle once said. "He wasn't interested in the theater.")

Moving to New York, Mabelle enrolled "young Webb" (as she called him throughout his life) in dancing school, and when he was seven years old, he attracted the attention of Malcolm Douglas of the Children's Theater. He made his professional debut in *The Brownies* at Carnegie Hall in 1900, followed by the title role in *Oliver Twist* and a featured part in *The Master of Carlton Hall*. It was in the latter production that the actor learned his initial lesson about the level of competition that often existed in his profession.

"An old actor was cast as my father and we had a scene together in which he was downstage with his back to the audience while I read my big speech," Webb recalled in a 1948 interview with Hedda Hopper. "One night he pulled the old gypsy switch on me and worked around until he was way up at the backdrop. I stopped cold and said (I fear, quite audibly), 'Will you please go back where you belong?' He was so surprised he returned to his marks in a very docile fashion."

Upon Webb's graduation from grammar school, his ambitious mother enrolled him in art school, where he excelled as a painter and gave his first exhibition at the age of 14. But while one critic labeled Webb a "juvenile genius," the actor later said that he grew tired of painting and began to study voice instead, making his grand opera debut in *Mignon* with the Aborn Opera Company in Boston. He followed this production with appearances in a variety of operas and operettas, including *Madame Butterfly*, *La Boheme*, *Hansel and Gretel*, and *The Purple Road*. But it wasn't long before the talented performer was ready to move on to another creative arena.

"After I'd mastered some 24 operative roles in various languages, the dance craze came along," Webb said in 1949. "I ditched the opera to make a reputation as a dancer."

Earning acclaim over the next several years, Webb toured the country in a ballroom dancing act; opened the Webb Dance Studio, with his mother serving as secretary-manager; and displayed his fancy footwork in a variety of musicals, beginning with *Love O' Mike* in 1917, and followed by such productions as *Listen Lester* with Irene Bordoni; *Sunny* with Marilyn Miller; *She's My Baby*, with Beatrice Lillie; and *Treasure Girl* with Gertrude Lawrence. He was also in such straight dramatic productions as *Meet the Wife* co-starring Mary Boland, and *As You Were* with Ruth Donnelly, but he found his greatest success on the musical-comedy stage; after his well-received impersonations of Mahatma Gandhi and Douglas Fairbanks, Jr., in *As Thousands Cheer*, Webb was labeled by one critic as "the most versatile of all American revue artists." Also during this period, the actor found time to appear in small roles in several silent feature films, including *Polly with a Past* (1920), where he played a bit part, and *Heart of a Siren* (1925), starring the "too-beautiful girl" Barbara LaMarr, in one of the last films before her death at the age of 29.

Throughout the actor's rise to fame on the stage, Webb's mother was a constant presence, offering advice, negotiating contracts, and providing support. It was also Mabelle who gave the actor his new moniker ("She happened to be driving through Clifton, New Jersey one day," Webb recalled. "She liked the name because it had good rhythm"), and one columnist would later note that Mabelle Webb "has been the dominant influence in his career."

"She never was a stage mother, never one of those objectionable creatures who shove their offspring under producers' noses, show them off, or clamor for attention — what she gave me was confidence, encouragement, and help," Webb once said. "She's a great person, a genuinely remarkable character — not a bit like Whistler's mother, who never did anything but sit around and say, 'When are you going to finish this damn picture?'" (In later years, after the actor's success in Hollywood, Webb and Mabelle would be tagged "the closest mother-and-son act in show business," with Mabelle accompanying Webb to Tinseltown parties and premieres, frequently being included in the actor's newspaper and magazine interviews, and co-hosting Webb's lavish gatherings in the Beverly Hills house where they lived together.)

In 1935, shortly after his success in *As Thousands Cheer*, Webb was beckoned to Hollywood by MGM, where executives planned to star him in a picture opposite Joan Crawford. Although he remained in California for nearly two years— earning a salary of $3,500 a week — the film never materialized.

"I learned upon my arrival that a sinister malady called 'story trouble' had afflicted the picture," Webb later recalled. "It was like a glorious vacation in never-never land — I didn't do a stick of work. But an actor must act, and although I had a wonderful time, darling, simply wonderful, I wasn't working, so I wasn't happy. So after sitting around for 18 long months, conscience-stricken over the king's ransom they were paying me, I returned to New York."

Back in the Big Apple, Webb wasted no time in returning to the stage, starring in such long-running productions as *The Importance of Being Earnest*, *The Man Who Came to Dinner*, and *Blithe Spirit*, which played more than 650 performances in New York and London. It was during the nationwide tour of the latter production that Webb received an offer that would represent a turning point in his career — he was approached by director Otto Preminger for the role of caustic newspaper columnist Waldo Lydecker in *Laura* (1944).

"I was all set to take the show up to Vancouver, B.C.— that's British Columbia, darling, not Before Christ," Webb quipped, "when this marvelous thing came up and there was simply no turning it down." Before the cameras began to roll, Webb signed a five-year contract with the studio producing the film, 20th Century–Fox.

In this stylish offering from the film noir era, the voice of Webb's Lydecker is the first that is heard, as he intones, "I shall never forget the weekend that Laura died." The woman to whom he refers is Laura Hunt (Gene Tierney), described by Lydecker as "the best part of myself," who has been killed by a shotgun blast to the face in the living room of her home. Investigating the murder is detective Mark McPherson (Dana Andrews), who finds himself becoming obsessed with the beautiful victim as he grows to know her through Lydecker; her indolent, would-be fiancé, Shelby Carpenter (Vincent Price); and her aunt, Ann Treadwell (Judith Anderson). As McPherson continues his investigation, he learns the bulk of Laura's past from Lydecker, who appointed himself her mentor and fell in love with her, using his column and a variety of other resources to keep her potential suitors at bay. McPherson also discovers that, despite his ostensible devotion to Laura, Shelby was secretly romancing both Ann Treadwell and a young model, Diane Redfern, from the advertising agency where he and Laura worked.

Stymied in his search for Laura's killer, McPherson is stunned when the object of his increasing obsession returns unharmed after a weekend in the country, and it is revealed that the dead woman is actually Redfern, who had been taken to Laura's apartment by Shelby. Although he initially suspects Laura's involvement in the crime, McPherson soon deduces that the real culprit is none other than Lydecker who, unable to thwart Laura's plans to marry Shelby, was driven to end her life and mistakenly killed Redfern instead. Before Lydecker can be nabbed by police, however, he gains access to Laura's home and, realizing that she has fallen for McPherson, determines to carry out his original plan. ("Do you think I'm going to leave you to the vulgar pawing of a second-rate detective who thinks you're a dame?" Lydecker asks her. "Do you think I could bear the thought of him holding you in his arms, kissing you, loving you?") Before he can fire, however, Laura shoves past him and McPherson breaks through the door, gunning down Lydecker, who dies with Laura's name on his lips.

A smash-hit at the box office, *Laura* earned raves from critics, who hailed the film as a "smart and sophisticated" melodrama and praised the performances of the outstanding cast. The majority of the accolades, however, were heaped on Webb's memorable portrait of the acerbic Waldo Lydecker; those offering the most effusive praise included Lowell E. Redelings of the *Hollywood Citizen-News*, who opined that Webb's "superior work adds the finishing touch to a finished photoplay — a job sanded to a satin smoothness and polished to a high gloss," and Dorothy Manners, who wrote in the *Los Angeles Examiner*, "*Laura* is really Clifton Webb's picture. Webb's — and Otto Premminger. The Messrs. Preminger and Webb apparently put their heads together and said, 'Let's show them what a really worldly, cynical sophisticate looks like when he is the real article.' The result is the brilliant, completely sparkling performance by Webb as the rapier-witted columnist and art connoisseur who becomes the ill-fated 'Laura' patron and Svengali." (These well-deserved laurels were accompanied by Webb's nomination for an Academy Award for Best Supporting Actor, but he lost, unfortunately, to Barry Fitzgerald for *Going My Way* [1944].)

After his triumph in *Laura*, Webb remained in the realm of film noir for his second and final feature from the era, *The Dark Corner* (1946), starring Mark Stevens and Lucille Ball. Here, as Hardy Cathcart, the actor portrayed an art gallery owner who, like Waldo Lydecker — and Webb himself — was possessed of a haughty countenance and a brittle wit. His persona is revealed early on when, at a lavish party in his home, Cathcart cordially greets an overweight, overly bejeweled guest, then snipes to his companion, "The wife of the Austrian critic — she always looks like she's been out in the rain, feeding the poultry." Along with Cathcart, the film's principal characters include the gallery owner's beautiful and much-younger wife, Mari (Cathy Downs); a refined but crooked attorney, Tony Jardine (Kurt Krueger); private detective Bradford Galt (Stevens), who recently served a two-year prison stretch in San Francisco after being framed for manslaughter by Jardine; Galt's faithful secretary-turned-girlfriend, Kathleen (Ball); and "White Suit," (William Bendix), a mysterious, self-described "private dick."

As the story begins, Galt is led to believe that he is being harassed by Jardine, but it is later revealed that Cathcart, after learning that the attorney is having an affair with his wife, has hired White Suit to goad the detective into murdering Jardine. When this plan fails, Cathcart orders White Suit to kills Jardine himself and stage a scene that points the finger of blame at Galt. As Galt and Kathleen frantically search for the source of the frame job, Cathcart arranges a meeting with White Suit to deliver the payment for his job but, instead, pushes him from an upper story window to his death. Ultimately, Galt learns that Cathcart is behind the entire scheme and tracks him to his gallery, where he encounters Mari and informs her of Jardine's murder. Meanwhile, Cathcart confronts Galt at gunpoint, planning to make him victim number three, but before he can pull the trigger, Mari recovers from her shock and empties a gun into her husband's body. After the film's release, Webb was applauded for his performance, with the *Los Angeles Examiner*'s James O'Hara writing that, "in his first appearance since *Laura*, [Webb] delivers the same polished performance that with a single movie won him a top rating as a superb character man." But while the review in the *New York*

Times noted that the actor "has another chance to indulge his talent for acerbic characters," the paper's critic further observed that "if Mr. Webb doesn't change his style soon, his admirers are likely to grow impatient."

Despite this warning, Webb was seen in a similar role in his third film, *The Razor's Edge* (1946), in which he portrayed a snobbish expatriate. His performance earned the actor his second Academy Award for Best Supporting Actor, but he went home empty-handed again, this time losing to double amputee Harold Russell for *The Best Years of Our Lives* (1946).

"I will never get my hopes up again. It's too much of a disappointment when you lose," Webb told columnist Louella Parsons. "But if there is any compensation in losing, I was glad to lose to Harold Russell, and I wrote and told him so. He deserved to win."

Shortly after the release of *The Razor's Edge*, Webb returned to Broadway for *Present Laughter*, a Noel Coward comedy in which he starred opposite Jan Sterling. Back in Hollywood after a five-month run with the play, Webb found that he was ready for a change from the string of acid-tongued characters he'd depicted on the screen, and found the

perfect vehicle in *Sitting Pretty* (1948). In this entertaining comedy, the actor starred as Lynn Belvedere, a prissy genius who becomes a babysitter, convinced that he has all the answers on child-rearing (including that children should chew each mouthful of food 27 times). Webb caused a sensation in the role, delivering such a believable portrayal that letters poured in from parents around the country, seeking his advice.

"This must be my punishment for remaining a confirmed bachelor," Webb said later. "Ever since I dumped the bowl of oatmeal on [co-star] Roddy McCaskill in *Sitting Pretty*, I have been called on for assistance in rearing the bubble-gum youth of this nation. Every time the mailman comes, he brings me letters from anxious mothers wanting to know by return mail whether they should spank Junior or ask the police department to give him a good stern lecture."

Webb's performance also resulted in the actor's third Academy Award nomination, but this time around, he lost to Laurence Olivier in *Hamlet* (1948). According to an often-repeated anecdote, a Hollywood producer stopped Webb at a restaurant to congratulate him on the public's response to *Sitting Pretty*, adding, "I don't suppose you'll be speaking to us small fry now that you've had this big success." Webb reportedly affixed the gentleman with a frosty gaze and rejoined, "My dear man — I have *always* been a success. One more will not unsettle me." The actor would later film two sequels to *Sitting Pretty*, *Mr. Belvedere Goes to College* (1949) and *Mr. Belvedere Rings the Bell* (1951), but neither was as good as the original.

By now, in addition to the fame he achieved through his first four film appearances, Webb was developing a reputation throughout the Hollywood community as one of the best-dressed gents in town. He was also credited with having introduced a number of fashion innovations into the American man's wardrobe, including the white messcoat dinner jacket, the double-breasted vest, and the red carnation boutonniere. Nearly every newspaper and magazine story written about the actor included a section devoted to his elegant taste in clothes; in an article in *Coronet*, it was reported that the actor owned "what is perhaps the finest and most extensive wardrobe in Hollywood. He admits to having 65 suits custom-made of the finest materials. He doesn't buy shoes by the pair or clothes by the suit, but by the dozens.... Much of his spare time and many of his happiest hours are spent in tailoring shops where, a friend relates, he noses through the bolts of material like a well-mannered bird dog."

"Clothes are like relatives to Webbie," an actress friend of Webb's was quoted in the same article. "They're something he has to live with, and he doesn't want any that will embarrass him."

Webb's reputation as a clothes horse was rivaled, however, by his distinction as a popular party-giver and party-goer, and he enjoyed a distinguished circle of friends that included writer W. Somerset Maugham (whom he affectionately called "Willie"), director George Cukor, and actress Lillian Gish. The celebrated functions hosted by Webb at the Beverly Hills house he shared with his mother featured what one columnist called "the creme de la creme of Hollywood society."

"He is an entertainer with a sound and worldly appreciation of success," a *Los Angeles Examiner* columnist wrote in the early 1950s. "At one of his parties last spring, Cole Porter played the piano for Cobina Wright, Gene Tierney, and Joan Bennett. In another corner Charles Brackett, who wrote the sensational *Sunset Boulevard*, was talking to Barbara Paley (Mrs. Astor's sister) and Charles K. Feldman about Gloria Swanson. Louis Jourdan talked with Mrs. Laddie Sanford about her husband's polo ponies, and at 10:30, Marion Davies made a splendid entrance, wearing diamonds worth over a hundred thousand dollars."

Meanwhile, back on the screen, Webb starred in one of his best-loved films in 1950, *Cheaper by the Dozen*, about real-life efficiency expert and father of 12, Frank Gilbreth, and was seen in supporting roles throughout the decade in a number of well-received films. He played a silent screen star-turned-college professor in the amusing comedy *Dreamboat* (1952); a snobbish socialite redeemed through tragedy in *Titanic* (1953); a suave American writer living in Rome in *Three Coins in the Fountain* (1954); a shrewd businessman selecting a successor for a top company position in *Woman's World* (1954); a greedy millionaire in *Boy on a Dolphin*; and a prissy 1890s-era bigamist in *The Remarkable Mr. Pennypacker* (1959). During this period he was also offered a role alongside Fred Astaire in *The Band Wagon* (1953), but reportedly turned it down, according to one columnist, "because [he was] used to top billing by now, and refused to take second billing to anyone, even Fred Astaire."

Although Webb continued to accept film assignments, he was frequently in ill health during the latter part of the 1950s; during the filming of *Boy on a Dolphin* in Greece, the actor was hospitalized with pneumonia, and three years later, an "undisclosed illness" forced him to step out of a role in *Journey to the Center of the Earth* (1959) (he was replaced by James Mason). But he weathered a far worse blow in October 1960 when his mother, Mabelle, suffered a heart attack and died at the age of 90. By all accounts, Webb was shattered by the loss and experienced such a lengthy and reclusive period of mourning that playwright Noel Coward began referring to him as "the world's oldest living orphan."

Following his mother's death, Webb appeared in only one more film, *Satan Never Sleeps* (1962), a mediocre drama in which he starred with William Holden as a priest in 1940s Communist China. During the next several years, Webb continued to be plagued by illness, undergoing surgery to correct an abdominal aneurysm in January 1963 and going under the knife again in May 1966 to remove an intestinal block. A few months after the second surgery, on October 13, 1966, Clifton Webb suffered a heart attack and died at his Los Angeles home, almost six years to the day after the passing of his mother. At his side was his longtime secretary Helen

Matthews, who later told the press, "I just don't think Clifton could face the thought of another anniversary of his mother's death." (Interestingly, just seven months after Webb's death, his Beverly Hills house was purchased by television producer Doug S. Cramer and his wife, and for years afterward, stories circulated around Hollywood that the residence was "haunted" by Webb and Mabelle. "I happened to be sitting across from [Cramer's mother] one night when she stared talking about strange happenings in the former Webb home," columnist James Bacon wrote in December 1969. "She was sleeping in Clifton's old bedroom and went to bed one night with a clean ashtray on the table beside the bed. When she awoke in the morning, there were about ten cigarette butts in the astray. They were Kents, Clifton's brand. Then another time, she looked out the window and saw an old woman in flimsy veils dancing on the lawn. This was Mabelle, Clifton's mother, of course.... Clifton may not be alive, but he still lives in Beverly Hills.")

With only 20 films in 18 years to his credit (all for 20th Century-Fox), Clifton Webb's unforgettable portrait of Waldo Lydecker succeeded in catapulting him into the nation's consciousness, and he remained there throughout his film career. The relative brevity of his career makes it even more impressive that Webb was able to create such a variety of memorable characters, and his modern-day fans still continue to enjoy the images he left behind. In a tribute that appeared shortly after Webb's death, *Los Angeles Herald Examiner* reporter Frank Lee Donoghue summed up the respect that admirers held of the multifaceted performer, accurately predicting that his impact would last for years to come.

"It is not likely that the day will ever come," Donoghue wrote, "when Broadway and Hollywood, and London's Mayfair as well, will cease to recall the legends, the successes, and the happy idiosyncrasies which made Clifton Webb one of the most glittering personalities of stage and screen."

Film Noir Filmography

Laura. Director and Producer: Otto Preminger. Running time: 88 minutes. Released by 20th Century-Fox, October 11, 1944. Cast: Gene Tierney, Dana Andrews, Clifton Webb, Vincent Price, Judith Anderson, Dorothy Adams, James Flavin, Clyde Fillmore, Ralph Dunn, Grant Mitchell, Kathleen Howard. Awards: Academy Award for Best Cinematography (Joseph LaShelle). Academy Award nominations for Best Director (Otto Preminger), Best Supporting Actor (Clifton Webb), Best Screenplay (Jay Oratler, Samuel Hoffenstein, Betty Reinhardt), Best Art Direction (Lyle Wheeler, Leland Fuller, Thomas Little).

The Dark Corner. Director: Henry Hathaway. Producer: Fred Kohlmar. Running time: 99 minutes. Released by 20th Century-Fox, April 9, 1946. Cast: Mark Stevens, Lucille Ball, Clifton Webb, William Bendix, Kurt Kreuger, Cathy Downs, Reed Hadley, Constance Collier, Eddie Heywood and His Orchestra, Molly Lamont.

References

"Abdominal Surgery Set for Actor Clifton." *Los Angeles Herald-Examiner*, January 4, 1963.

"Actor Clifton Webb Dies." *New York World Journal Tribune*, October 14, 1966.

Bainbridge, John. "Mr. Belvedere & Mr. Webb." *Life*, May 30, 1949.

Berch, Barbara. "Clifton Webb's Feats." *New York Times*, July 29, 1945.

Blumenfeld, Ralph. "Clifton Webb Dies on the Coast." *New York Post*, October 14, 1966.

Carroll, Harrison. "Clifton Webb, Abroad for Film, Felled by Illness." *Los Angeles Herald-Express*, October 26, 1956.

"Child-Psychologist Mantle Is Thrust on Clifton Webb." *New York Herald-Tribune*, March 26, 1950.

"Clifton Webb Has a Problem." *New York Morning Telegraph*, April 3, 1950.

"Clifton Webb Home Purchased." *Hollywood Citizen-News*, May 5, 1967.

"Clifton Webb Rites Tuesday." *New York Daily News*, October 15, 1966.

"Clifton Webb, 72, Dies on Coast; Movies' Dignified Mr. Belvedere." *New York Times*, October 15, 1966.

Donoghue, Frank Lee. "Clifton Webb — Unforgettable." *Los Angeles Herald-Examiner*, October 16, 1966.

"Film Star Clifton Webb Dead at 69." *San Francisco Chronicle*, October 14, 1966.

Flyte, Sebastian. "Clifton Webb." *Los Angeles Examiner*, circa 1950.

Graham, Sheilah. "Clifton Webb Now Recluse." *Hollywood Citizen-News*, July 22, 1961.

Greenletter, Horace. "'I'm Not Mr. Belvedere,' Exclaims Ace Babysitter." *Los Angeles Daily News*, April 6, 1950.

"Heart Attack Kills Actor Clifton Webb." *Oakland (California) Tribune*, October 14, 1966.

Hopper, Hedda. "Clifton's Sitting Pretty." *Chicago Tribune*, July 25, 1948.

_____. "Clifton Webb Ill in Greece." *Los Angeles Times*, October 27, 1956.

_____. "Hospitalized for Bronchitis." *Los Angeles Times*, June 1, 1946.

Larsen, Dave. "Clifton Webb, 76, Suave Star of Screen, Dies at His Home." *Los Angeles Times*, October 14, 1966.

Martin, Pete. "Hollywood's Self-Confessed Genius." *Saturday Evening Post*, April 16, 1949.

Morris, Mary. "Song-Dance-and-Party Man." *PM*, November 11, 1945.

"Mrs. Mabelle Webb, Actor's Mother, Dies." *Los Angeles Examiner*, October 18, 1960.

Parsons, Louella O. "Clifton Webb." *Los Angeles Examiner*, April 23, 1950.

_____. "Clifton Webb: Hollywood's Bachelor Homebody." *Los Angeles Examiner*, December 12, 1954.

_____. "In Hollywood with Louella O. Parsons: Clifton Webb." *Los Angeles Examiner*, circa 1947.

"Rambling Reporter." *The Hollywood Reporter*, November 19, 1991.

"Rites Tomorrow for Clifton Webb; 69-Year Career Covered Most Showbiz." *Variety*, October 17, 1966.

"Services for Clifton Webb on Tuesday." *San Francisco Chronicle*, October 1966.

Scheuer, Philip K. "Unique Screen Character Developed by Clifton Webb." *Los Angeles Times*, March 28, 1948.

Scott, John L. "Clifton Webb Stirred by Greece Adventure." *Los Angeles Times*, March 17, 1957.

Skolsky, Sidney. "Tintypes: Clifton Webb." *Hollywood Citizen-News*, February 19, 1959.

Stinson, Charles. "Clifton Webb: He's Smooth on Angles." *Los Angeles Times*, September 7, 1958.

Traine, Leslie. "Clifton Webb Says 'Yes!'" *Movieland*, circa 1945.

Ward, L.E. "Clifton Webb." *Classic Images*, September 1984.

"Webb Forced to Quit Film Role." *New York Journal-American*, June 18, 1959.

Wood, Thomas. "Clifton Webb: Gentleman Actor." *Coronet*, July 1954.

JACK WEBB

"You gonna take this Maxie's word? If somebody gave him a bible, he'd steal it." — Jack Webb in *Appointment with Danger* (1951)

The first four bars from the theme music of the long-running television show *Dragnet* are all that is needed to summon an image of the taciturn Los Angeles police sergeant, Joe Friday. His alter ego, Jack Webb, not only starred in the series, but also produced and directed it (along with its radio predecessor), and it is the one production with which he is most closely and immediately associated. But Webb was seen in nearly 20 films between 1948 and 1966, including a critically acclaimed performance in *The Men* (1950), and appeared during his screen career alongside such notables as Marlon Brando, William Holden, and Charlton Heston. He was also featured in supporting roles in four films noirs: *He Walked by Night* (1948), *Dark City* (1950), *Sun-set Boulevard* (1950), and *Appointment with Danger* (1951).

John Randolph Webb was born on April 2, 1920, in Santa Monica, California, the only child of Samuel and Margaret Webb. When Webb was two years old, his Jewish father and Catholic mother divorced, and he and Margaret moved in with her mother in an area of Los Angeles the actor would later describe as "too poor to steal in."

"In our neighborhood, everybody was just as poor as we were. No Cadillacs ever went up and down the street — just a lot of penny-ante bootleggers," Webb said once. "My mother and grandmother worked when they could find it, but most of the time we were on relief. So was everyone else."

As a child, Webb developed pneumonia, which turned into bronchitis and, later, asthma, forcing his mother and grandmother to frequently carry him so that he would avoid exertion. Instead of playing stickball or cops-and-robbers with the neighborhood boys, Webb spent much of his time drawing pictures, listening to the radio, or reading in the local library.

At Belmont High School, where he was president of his senior class, Webb became interested in drama and frequently appeared in school productions. After graduating, he was awarded an art scholarship to the University of Southern California, but he declined, choosing instead to help support his family by working at a men's clothing store. During the next four years, Webb worked his way up from clerk to store manager, taking time out to appear in various radio programs on local stations.

In 1943, Webb joined the Army Air Force as an aviation cadet. Stationed at Camp St. Cloud in Minnesota, he took preflight training and for a short time piloted B-26 bombers. He also wrote, directed, and served as master of ceremonies for two USO variety shows. After being granted a dependency discharge in 1945, he went to work for station KGO in San Francisco, where he was the disk jockey for an early morning show, *The Coffee Club*, and for 26 weeks played the role of a tough detective in *Pat Novak for Hire*.

Returning to Los Angeles in 1947, Webb married a young singer and actress, Julie London, who is perhaps best remembered for her 1955 single, "Cry Me a River." The two first met prior to the war, when Webb was employed at the clothing store (London also worked there, as an elevator operator), and they later had two daughters, Stacy in 1950, and Lisa in 1952. Career-wise, Webb was heard on a number of radio programs, including *Johnny Modero: Pier 23*, *The Whistler*, and *This Is Your FBI*. Webb's radio performances led to his 1948 screen debut, a bit part in *The Scar* (also known as *Hollow Triumph*), a low-budget film noir feature. The film was produced by actor Paul Henreid, who starred in

a dual role as con artist Johnny Muller and psychiatrist Victor Bartok. Learning that he is a dead-ringer for the doctor, Johnny hatches a scheme to assume Bartok's identity, but later winds up murdered by hoods who mistake him for the doctor.

Webb next played his first supporting role in a film noir, portraying a forensics expert in *He Walked By Night* (1948). This fast-paced feature tells the story of Ray Morgan (Richard Basehart), a brilliant, psychopathic thief who kills a police officer during an attempt to rob an electronics store. Evading authorities by monitoring police calls and frequently altering his modus operandi in order to throw authorities off his trail, Morgan ultimately meets his end during a tense chase through the drainage system canals beneath Los Angeles.

Although Webb earned little mention by critics for his performance in *He Walked by Night*, the film nonetheless represented a significant turning point in the actor's career. During filming, Webb met Sgt. Marty Wynn, who was assigned by the Los Angeles Police Department to serve as the movie's technical advisor; it was Wynn's suggestion for a radio program based on actual police cases that gave Webb the idea for *Dragnet*. With the cooperation of the Los Angeles Police Department, the actor studied police procedures, techniques, and terminology; accompanied detectives on police calls; and even attended classes at the police academy to learn about criminal law. Assisted by Wynn and Los Angeles detective Jack Donohoe, Webb fashioned a sample story, initially planning to call it *The Cop* or *The Sergeant*. He later settled on the title, *Dragnet*, and also created the series' now-familiar epilogue, telling listeners that the dramatized case was true, and that "the names were changed to protect the innocent."

The first episode of *Dragnet* was aired as a summer replacement on NBC radio on June 3, 1949, with Webb starring as the terse-talking, no-nonsense Sgt. Joe Friday, and Barton Yarbrough playing his partner, Ben Romero. Within two years, *Dragnet* was one of radio's most popular shows. Harriet Van Horne of the *New York World-Telegram and Sun* hailed it as "one of radio's more intelligent (and less bloody) crime programs," praising the show's "emphasis on the people who enforce the law rather than on those who break it."

While working on *Dragnet*, Webb found time to accept a bit part in *Sword in the Desert* (1949), starring Dana Andrews, then was applauded for his "excellence" in portraying one of his finest roles, a wisecracking paraplegic in *The Men* (1950), which starred Marlon Brando in his film debut. After this triumphant appearance, Webb was seen in three consecutive films noirs: *Dark City* (1950), *Sunset Boulevard* (1950), and *Appointment with Danger* (1951).

In *Dark City*, Webb portrayed Augie, a small-time racketeer who joins with his partners Danny Haley (Charlton Heston, in his first film) and Barney (Ed Begley) to fleece a naive salesman in a poker game. Distraught after losing $5,000, the salesman, Arthur Winant (Don DeFore) commits suicide, and the three gamblers find that they are being stalked by Winant's psychotic brother, Sidney (Mike Mazurki). The mean-spirited Augie is at first cocky and arrogant ("Since when did you start running things?" he asks Danny), but he changes his tune when Barney is murdered. "We're in this together," he shakily tells Danny after showing up at his apartment. "I sat around in the lobby for — I don't know — hours, I guess. Saw a lot of funny-looking characters and it made me kinda jumpy." As it turns out, Augie's "jumpiness" was justified — he becomes Sidney Winant's next victim. Before Danny can become the third, however, he works with police to set himself up as a decoy, luring Sidney to his room and nearly losing his life before the killer is shot by police.

After being singled out as "noxious as a low coward" in *Dark City*, Webb was seen in a featured role in his second noir, the classic *Sunset Boulevard*, which told the story of a down-on-his luck writer, Joe Gillis (William Holden), and the faded silent movie star

Norma Desmond (Gloria Swanson), with whom he becomes romantically — if reluctantly — involved. Webb portrayed Artie Green, Joe's wisecracking pal, described by one character as "as nice a guy as ever lived." Artie's niceness notwithstanding, his fiancée, Betty Schaefer (Nancy Olson), only has eyes for Joe, but their budding romance is nipped when Norma learns of the affair. After dramatically threatening suicide, Norma throws a permanent monkey wrench in Joe's plan to leave her when she puts a bullet in his back. Although most critics focused their attention on the standout performances of Holden and Swanson, Webb earned notice by several reviewers, including Darr Smith of the *Los Angeles Daily News*, who wrote that Webb and the film's supporting cast were the "real flesh and blood inhabitants of this picture."

In his final film noir, *Appointment with Danger*, Webb played his biggest role of the era, gang member Joe Regas. Along with fellow hoodlum George Soderquist (Henry Morgan), Joe is responsible for the murder of a United States postal inspector, which was witnessed by a local nun, Sister Augustine (Phyllis Calvert). Determined to find the killers, the dead man's co-worker, Al Goddard (Alan Ladd), infiltrates the gang, but his cover is inadvertently blown by the nun after she is abducted by Joe. Goddard kills Joe during a fight, but he runs out of bullets in the midst of a gun battle with the gang's leader, Earl Boettiger (Paul Stewart). Just as Boettiger is about to finish off Goddard, the police arrive, and the gang leader is killed. As Joe Regas, Webb essayed his most nefarious noir character; in one scene, he vehemently insists on killing Sister Augustine in order to prevent her from identifying him, and in another, he beats his weak-willed partner to death with a bronze baby shoe. For his portrayal, he earned mention in the *New York Times* for his "competent" performance and in *Variety* for his "capable assist on menace."

By now, Webb was in the midst of plans to expand his successful series to the small screen. In late 1951, *Dragnet* premiered on NBC-TV with a story called "The Human

1955, and Best Male Personality in 1954). And Webb continued to capitalize on the show's popularity. Three years after the television premiere of *Dragnet*, he produced and starred in the screen version.

"All this space — all this time — a whole hour and a half," Webb said of the *Dragnet* film. "I hope we've been able to do something effective with it. Frankly, I'm cramped on TV — there's just not enough time in 22 minutes to show any real emotion, any play of feeling.... It's too fast, too choppy. Luckily, our actors are among the best in the business — I'm amazed at what they've been able to do."

By now, Webb had become known for his conscientious attention to detail, drive for perfection, and tireless, 12-to-14-hour work days. But his professional ambitions had taken a toll on his married life, and after a brief separation, Webb's wife, Julie London, filed for divorce.

"It was my fault. I never could adapt myself. I never got home on time for dinner. When I did get there, I was usually too tied up with my own problems to be a companion for my wife," Webb admitted in a December 1953 interview. "I never saw the kids except for two minutes in the morning, when I left for the studio, and on Sunday.... I can't stop working, or worrying about the show. I'd go crazy if I tried. So our marriage got to the point where love wasn't enough."

In their 1954 divorce settlement, London was given custody of the couple's daughters and was awarded $300,000 in cash, $18,000 a year alimony, jewelry, a car, and $50,000 in house furnishings. The following year, Webb married again, this time to Dorothy Towne, whom he first met when she acted as a bit player in a *Dragnet* episode. But this union was a stormy one from the start, characterized by public spats and numerous separations, and the couple divorced two years later.

"Dorothy is a fine girl, and I have the deepest respect for her," Webb said in 1956. "But it is senseless to remain together when we are unhappy."

Bomb," which served as a preview of the regularly televised Thursday night show. (Barton Yarbrough reprised his role as Ben Romero, but he died shortly after the airing of the pilot and was replaced by several actors, including Barney Phillips and Herb Ellis, before Ben Alexander took on the role of Officer Frank Smith until the series' end in 1959.) The show was an instant hit and introduced a series of icons and parlances to the American popular culture, including the program's theme music and its opening, "This is the city, Los Angeles, California," and such frequently uttered phrases as "My name's Friday ... I'm a cop," and "Just the facts, ma'am." The show was also characterized by the stamp of Webb's company, Mark VII Productions, whose distinctive trademark — a perspiration-drenched hand hammering a stencil — was the final shot after the credits.

Webb, who was praised by one reviewer for his "complete disdain for the clichés of the conventional crime show," was rewarded for his efforts with numerous accolades — he received the Look TV awards in 1953 and 1954 for Best Director, the Billboard award for Best Actor in 1954, and was nominated for four Emmy awards (Best Actor in 1953, 1954, and

The actor gave marriage a third try in 1958, marrying former Miss USA Jacqueline Loughery, but after six years, this marriage, too, ended in divorce. For Webb, the fourth time would be the charm — his 1980 marriage to Opal Wright lasted until the actor's death.

Professionally, Webb was back on the big screen in 1955, starring in the title role of *Pete Kelly's Blues*, which he also produced and directed. He took on the same duties for his next two films, *The D.I.* (1957), an uncompromising portrait of a tough Marine drill instructor, and *-30-* (1959), in which he played the managing editor of a newspaper. Both were realistic, true-to-life dramas that were well-received by critics and moviegoers alike.

"I'm trying to give the effect of taking a wall away from any city room in the country to let audiences look inside," Webb said of the latter film. "There won't be a single movie cliché about newspapers. No one will rush in shouting, 'Stop the presses!' And the editor doesn't say, 'I've got a story that'll bust this town wide open.' Also out are reporters with press cards stuck in their hat bands."

By the time *Dragnet* ended its television run in September 1959, Webb had already produced three other series for the small screen, but none were successful. *Noah's Ark*, a drama focusing on two veterinarians, starred Paul Burke and Vic Rodman, and ran on NBC from September 1956 to February 1957; *Pete Kelly's Blues*, with William Reynolds in the title role, was seen on NBC from April 1959 to September 1959; and *The D.A.'s Man*, a half-hour crime show featuring John Compton, ended in August 1959 after an eight-month run. Webb had high hopes, however, for his next series for Mark VII, *General Electric True*, a half-hour anthology focusing on themes of heroism.

"Our stories will try to use the same approach that was so successful with George M. Cohan," Webb said. "We want to show that Americans can be patriotic and heroic people. If we're accused of being flag-wavers, so much the better. That is exactly what we're aiming for."

But this series, too, ended after only a year, leading many to speculate that the failure of Webb's recent shows was due to his on-screen absence.

"That's not for me to say," Webb said in 1960. "The reason I haven't gone into another series is simple. I didn't want to wear out my welcome. Another thing, I know my limitations as an actor, and I want to stay within those limitations. Shakespeare is hardly for me. I act when I can handle the part, and I take out the rest of my energies on producing and directing."

Webb was back on the big screen the following year, however, with a rare comedy appearance in *The Last Time I Saw Archie* (1961), which he also produced and directed. After this feature, Webb concentrated solely on his television projects and in 1963, he signed on as head of production for Warner Bros. Television, which named him producer of the long-running series *77 Sunset Strip* in the hopes that he could regain the show's former popularity. Webb promptly changed the series' snappy theme music, replaced the show's director with actor William Conrad, and changed the entire cast, with the exception of star Efrem Zimbalist, Jr.

Despite Webb's good intentions, the ratings on the show plummeted, and the actor was abruptly and unceremoniously dumped by Warners in December 1963. His attorney, Jacob Shearer, told reporters that Webb had received a note "notifying him that his services would not be required until further notice." Two weeks later, Webb filed suit against Warners, contending that the company had illegally broken a three-year contract under which he was to be paid $150,000 per year. The suit was settled out of court in September 1964, with Warners agreeing to pay Webb a weekly salary of $3,000 during the remainder of the contract.

Following the Warner Bros. debacle, Webb entered a kind of self-imposed professional exile, but he returned three years later with a tried-and-true series: *Dragnet*.

"There's been a breakdown in our morals, a total disregard for constituted authority," Webb said in 1966, "and I hope a series like

Dragnet can do something to help restore respect for the law."

With Webb once again starring as the laconic Joe Friday, *Dragnet '67* premiered on January 12, 1967, this time co-starring Harry Morgan as Friday's partner, Bill Gannon. Produced and directed by Webb, the show's second television incarnation dealt with such topical issues as drug use and student dissidence, and was another hit, lasting until 1970. A year after this much-needed jumpstart to his career, Webb premiered *Adam-12*, which focused on the daily activities of two LAPD officers (Martin Milner and Kent McCord). This successful series was seen on NBC for four years, and Webb enjoyed another hit with a hospital drama, *Emergency!*, which premiered as a mid-season NBC replacement in January 1972 and ran until September 1977. Among the stars Webb hired for the latter show was his ex-wife, Julie London, and her second husband, Bobby Troup.

"She was a hell of an actress, people forget, before she became a singer," Webb explained. "That's why I hired her."

Throughout the 1970s, Webb produced several made-for-television movies, including *Hec Ramsey* (1972), *Chase* (1973), *The Log of the Black Pearl* (1975), and *Little Mo* (1978). He also continued to serve as producer or executive producer for a number of television series under the Mark VII banner, but none achieved the success of *Adam-12* or *Emergency! The D.A.*, starring Robert Conrad, Harry Morgan, and Julie Cobb (daughter of Lee J. Cobb) ran from 1971 to 1972; *Escape*, a semi-documentary series narrated by Webb and chronicling close calls with danger, was canceled after four episodes; *Chase*, a crime show focusing on a special police unit, aired from September 1973 to August 1974; *Sierra*, about a National Park Service search-and-rescue team, was seen opposite the popular CBS drama *The Waltons* and ended after 13 weeks; *Mobile One*, a drama about a movie television news unit starring Jackie Cooper, lasted less than one season; and *Project U.F.O.*, based on unexplained cases in the U.S. Air Force's UFO files, ran from February 1978 to

January 1979. The latter series would be Webb's last.

On December 23, 1982, after complaining of severe stomach pains and lapsing into unconsciousness, Jack Webb suffered a fatal heart attack in his West Hollywood home, at the age of 62. He was later buried with full LAPD honors, and the badge number used for so many years by Joe Friday, Number 714, was retired by the department. In addition, after Webb's death, the Los Angeles Police Department established the Jack Webb Awards, given each year to honor citizens who support law enforcement.

Jack Webb's death brought to an end one of the most prolific and innovative careers in television history. Given the popularity in recent years of "reality" television shows and series focusing on otherworldly phenomena, it is clear that Jack Webb was a man ahead of his time, and long after his death, his pioneering influence has been demonstrated on such television programs as *NYPD Blue*, *The X-Files*, and *ER*. And today, decades after *Dragnet* and Joe Friday first entered the nation's consciousness, they have maintained their popularity, impact, and appeal. A revival of *Dragnet* appeared in syndication during the 1989-90 television season, and a feature-length version of the show was released in 1987, starring Dan Aykroyd as Friday, and featuring Harry Morgan in a reprisal of his role as Bill Gannon. The phenomenon of *Dragnet* was even cited during the late 1990s, as part of the investigation into possible financial and legal improprieties of then–President William Clinton. The special counsel appointed to look into the case, Kenneth W. Starr, defended his oft-criticized techniques by comparing himself to Joe Friday.

"You all are too young to remember a wonderful program called *Dragnet*," Starr told reporters in April 1998. "'Just the facts, ma'am,' Jack Webb would say. I had the pleasure of meeting Jack Webb. And that's something I always remembered, 'Just the facts.'"

(Webb's widow, Opal, later scoffed at Starr's comments. "When I saw him say that, I just had to laugh," Opal said. "I can imagine

Jack looking at me and saying, 'He's got to be kidding!' He would have hit the ceiling.")

Beyond the specter of Joe Friday, however, Jack Webb will be remembered as a talented and driven actor, producer, and director, as well as an admired and well-respected man.

"Jack had kind of a dour expression and laconic speech and did not appear to be a terribly affectionate man on Dragnet," co-star Harry Morgan said after the actor's death. "In reality, he was just the opposite.... He was a man of great warmth, generosity, and affection."

And those are just the facts.

Film Noir Filmography

The Scar. (Original release title: *Hollow Triumph*) Director: Steve Sekely. Producer: Paul Henreid. Running time: 82 minutes. Released by Eagle-Lion, October 1948. Cast: Paul Henreid, Joan Bennett, Eduard Franz, Leslie Brooks, John Qualen, Mabel Paige, Herbert Rudley, Paul E. Burns, Charles Trowbridge, Ann Staunton, Mack Williams, Franklin Farnum, Morgan Farley, Joel Friedkin, Renny McEvoy, Phillip Morris, Tom Stevenson, Benny Rubin, Charles Arnt, Sid Tomack, Jack Webb.

He Walked by Night. Director: Alfred Werker. Producer: Robert Kane. Running time: 79 minutes. Released by Eagle-Lion, February 6, 1949. Cast: Richard Basehart, Scott Brady, Roy Roberts, Whit Bissell, Jimmy Cardwell, Jack Webb, Bob Bice, Reed Hadley.

Dark City. Director: William Dieterle. Producer: Hal Wallis. Running time: 98 minutes. Released by Paramount, October 18, 1950. Cast: Charlton Heston, Lizabeth Scott, Viveca Lindfors, Dean Jagger, Don DeFore, Jack Webb, Ed Begley, Henry Morgan, Walter Sande, Mark Keuning, Mike Mazurki, Stanley Prager, Walter Burke.

Sunset Boulevard. Director: Billy Wilder. Producer: Charles Brackett. Running time: 115 minutes. Released by Paramount, August 10, 1950. Cast: William Holden, Gloria Swanson, Erich von Stroheim, Nancy Olson, Fred Clark, Lloyd Gough, Jack Webb, Cecil B. DeMille, Hedda Hopper, Buster Keaton, Ann Q. Nilsson, H.B. Warner, Franklyn Farnum, Sidney Skolsky, Ray Evans, Jay Livingston. Awards: Academy Awards for Best Art Direction-Set Decoration/Black and White (Hans Dreier, John Meehan, Sam Comer, Ray Moyer), Best Score/Drama or Comedy (Franz Waxman), Best Story and Screenplay (Charles Brackett, Billy Wilder, D.M. Marshman Jr.). Academy Award nominations for Best Picture, Best Director (Billy Wilder), Best Actress (Gloria Swanson), Best Actor (William Holden), Best Supporting Actor (Erich Von Stroheim), Best Supporting Actress (Nancy Olson), Best Black and White Cinematography (John F. Seitz), Best Film Editing (Arthur Schmidt, Doane Harrison).

Appointment with Danger. Director: Lewis Allen. Producer: Robert Fellows. Running time: 89 minutes. Released by Paramount, May 9, 1951. Cast: Alan Ladd, Phyllis Calvert, Paul Stewart, Jan Sterling, Jack Webb, Stacy Harris, Henry Morgan, David Wolfe, Dan Riss, Harry Antrim, Paul Lees.

References

Belser, Emil. "Sergeant Friday Really Gun-Shy." *New York Morning Telegraph*, June 9, 1954.

Fields, Sidney. "Jack Webb: Everything — Except Happiness." *New York Daily Mirror*, January 4, 1954.

Geller, Andy. "'Dragnet' Widow: Starr's Clueless." *New York Post*, April 25, 1998.

Graham, Sheilah. "Just a Fact — Webb to Wed Next Week." *New York Daily Mirror*, January 3, 1955.

Hawn, Jack. "Jack Webb: 'An Original.'" *Los Angeles Times*, December 29, 1982.

Hyams, Joe. "Jack Webb Barks at Film Crew, Too." *New York Herald Tribune*, April 23, 1957.

_____. "Webb Explains Switch to Movies." *New York Herald-Tribune*, January 31, 1961.

"Jack Webb in Settlement." *New York Herald Tribune*, April 16, 1954.

"Jack Webb Is Dismissed as Warner's TV Chief." *New York Times*, December 20, 1963.

"Jack Webb Marries Actress." *New York Times*, January 12, 1955.

"Jack Webb's Co. Files in D.C. vs. Writers Guild." *Variety*, May 2, 1973.

"Jack Webb, Second Bride Call It Quits." *New York Post*, November 13,1955.

"Jack Webbs Part Again." New York Herald Tribune, March 1, 1957.

"Jack Webb Takes 4 Flops in Stride." *New York World Telegram*, October 15, 1960.

"Jack Webb to Remarry." *New York Times*, June 6, 1958.

"Jack Webb, Wife No. 2 Call It Quits." *New York Daily News*, October 18, 1956.

Jamison, Barbara Berch. "Spinning a Wider Webb." *New York Times*, August 8, 1954.

Kaufman, Dave. "Webb Sez Vidpix Producers

Gotta 'Retool Thinking,' Show More Courage." *Variety*, November 5, 1968.

Lowrey, Cynthia. "Jack Webb: 4 Hats and All Professional." *New York Post*, August 16, 1967.

Malnic, Eric. "Jack Webb, Sgt. Friday of TV, Dies." *Los Angeles Times*, December 24,1982.

McManus, Margaret. "Webb Eyes TV in '62 Despite 2 Setbacks." *New York World Telegram*, May 27, 1961.

Muir, Florence. "Hollywood." *New York Daily News*, December 14, 1966.

Parsons, Louella O. "Jack Webb's New Marriage Formula." *Pictorial TView*, August 17, 1958.

Prial, Frank J. "Jack Webb, Laconic Sgt. Friday on TV 'Dragnet' Series, Is Dead." *New York Times*, December 24, 1982.

Scott, Vernon. "Webb's Dragnet Hauls in Heroes." *New York World-Telegram and Sun*, July 18, 1963.

_____. "Webb Stars as '30' Editor." *Newark Evening News*, August 14, 1958.

_____. "Webb Vows He'll Make Honest Newspa-

per Movie." *New York World-Telegram and Sun*, August 17, 1959.

Skolsky, Sidney. "Tintypes: Jack Webb." *New York Post*, June 11, 1961.

"The Jack Webbs Divorced." *New York Times*, November 26, 1953.

Thomas, Bob. "Facts from Webb." *Newark Evening News*, June 12, 1961.

Tregaskis, Richard. "The Cops' Favorite Make-Believe Cop." *The Saturday Evening Post*, September 26, 1953.

"Webb Ready to Wave the Flag." *New York Herald-Tribune*, August 19, 1962.

"Webb Settles with Warner's." *New York Times*, September 9, 1964.

Williams, Robert. "Just the Facts on Jack Webb." *New York Post*, December 20, 1953.

Wood, Thomas. "Jack Webb Leads a Jazz Band." *New York Herald Tribune*, May 22, 1955.

Zolotow, Maurice. "The Names Have Not Been Changed." *The American Weekly*, September 19, 1954.

ORSON WELLES

"Some people can smell danger. Not me." — Orson Welles in *The Lady from Shanghai* (1948)

Orson Welles has been labeled a genius with such frequency that the term has become somewhat clichéd. But for a man of his astounding creativity, few other words in the English language would do as well. During the first 15 years of his career alone, Welles gained fame as one of the greatest theatrical directors of his time; launched a nationwide panic as a result of one of his radio broadcasts; and wrote, directed, and produced what is now regarded as one of the finest films ever made. Along the way, he also demonstrated prowess as a magician, cartoonist, author, scenic designer, and musician.

"How many folks do you know who, at the age of thirty, have done so many things?" Hedda Hopper wrote of Welles in a 1944 article. "All the ingredients for greatness are here, but will he ever reach the goal he's striving for? Only time will tell. But to me, Orson Welles has only scratched the surface of Orson Welles."

Throughout the remainder of his life, Welles continued "scratching the surface" of his talent, serving as writer, narrator, director, producer, or star of numerous plays and television shows and nearly 80 films, including such classics as *Jane Eyre* (1944) and *The Long, Hot Summer* (1958). He also made a significant contribution to film noir, with five widely varying features from the era to his credit: *Journey Into Fear* (1942), *The Stranger* (1946), *The Lady from Shanghai* (1948), *The Third Man* (1949), and *Touch of Evil* (1957).

Born George Orson Welles on May 6, 1915, the future "boy genius" was the younger of two sons of Richard Head Welles, an inventor and manufacturer from a wealthy Virginia family, and his wife, Beatrice Ives, a gifted pianist who reportedly was once imprisoned for her activities as a suffragette. Many stories abound regarding the early years of Orson Welles, several told by Welles himself. Among other legendary tales, it is said that Welles was a musical virtuoso by the age of three, an expert magician and water colorist by four, sat up nightly reading Balzac at the age of eight, and played King Lear before he was 10. While many of the accomplishments attributed to the young Welles were fabrications, they also contain a grain of truth; the boy was unusually gifted in numerous areas, and was, by all accounts, doted upon by those around him.

"I was spoiled in a very strange way as a child, because everybody told me from the moment I was able to hear, that I was absolutely marvelous," Welles once said. "I never heard a discouraging word, for years. I didn't know what was ahead of me."

Welles' parents separated when he was six years old and he remained with his mother, who encouraged his budding talent on the piano and the violin. But when Beatrice Welles died of a liver disease two years later, Welles' musical aspirations came to an abrupt end.

"I stopped playing immediately," he said. "It was a kind of traumatic shock from [my mother's] death combined with, I think, essential laziness— the delight of not having to go on doing those scales. And [I] abandoned my career in music — that's what I was supposed to be destined for."

Now in his father's care, Welles was enrolled at the Todd School for Boys in Woodstock, Illinois, where he took an interest in dramatics and participated in school productions as an actor, director, designer, and scenic artist. In 1928, Welles' father died of heart and kidney failure, and the boy's upbringing was taken over by Dr. Maurice Bernstein, a physician who had known Welles since his birth. Upon his graduation from Todd, Welles eschewed his guardian's wishes to send him to a university, studying instead for a year at the Chicago Art Institute, and later deciding to embark on a painting tour of Ireland. Investing in a donkey and a cart, the 16-year-old Welles traveled the countryside for several months, winding up in Dublin where he presented himself at the famous Gate Theater and announced that he was an acclaimed performer with the New York Theater Guild. His tale was not believed, but he reportedly performed during an audition with such "demoniac authority" that he was hired as the Duke of Wurtemberg in the theater's production of *Jew Suss*. After making his professional debut in October 1931, Welles spent the next several months in Dublin, playing smaller parts in such productions as *The Dead Ride Fast*, *The Archdupe*, and *Death Takes a Holiday*.

Returning to the United States the following year, Welles found that his plan to take Broadway by storm was a dismal failure. Instead, he went back to Woodstock, Illinois, where he teamed with his former Todd School headmaster, Roger Hill, in co-editing acting editions of *Julius Caesar*, *Twelfth Night*, and *The Merchant of Venice*. Welles wasn't away from the stage for long, however. In 1933, he joined Katharine Cornell's acting company, portraying Mercutio in the road tour of *Romeo and Juliet*, and the following year he returned to Woodstock to launch a summer theater festival. During the festival, Welles made what many consider to be his first film (but which he later dismissed as little more than a "home movie"), entitled *Hearts of Age*. Welles' "co-star" in *Hearts of Age* was 18-year-old Virginia Nicholson, a participant in the theater festival. After a whirlwind romance, Welles and Nicholson were married on Christmas Day 1934. They went on to have a daughter, Christopher, in March 1938, but the union was on shaky ground for several years (exacerbated by Welles' reported affair with a ballerina), and the two were divorced in February 1940.

Meanwhile, after debuting on Broadway in late 1934 in *Romeo and Juliet*, where he played Tybalt and spoke the choral prologue, Welles met director-producer John Houseman, who offered him a role in his upcoming production of *Panic*, the Pulitzer Prize–winning play by Archibald McLeish. When Houseman was later put in charge of the Federal Theatre Project's Negro People's Theater, he hired Welles as co-director, and the two men produced a highly acclaimed, all-black version of *Macbeth*.

"I wanted to give the black actors a chance to play classics without it being funny. Or even exotic," Welles once said. "My great success in my life was that play. The opening night, there were five blocks in which all traffic was stopped. You couldn't get near the theater in Harlem. Everybody who was anybody in the black or white world was there. And when the play ended, there were so many curtain calls that finally they left the curtain open and the audience came up on the stage to congratulate the actors. That was magical."

Under the auspices of the Federal Theatre Project, Welles and Houseman later produced *Dr. Faustus*, starring Welles in the title role, and *The Cradle Will Rock*, then withdrew from the project to form their own company, the Mercury Theater. In November 1937, Welles co-produced a modern-dress version of *Julius Caesar*, a wildly successful Mercury production that later earned a Broadway run, as well as other well-received plays including *Shoemaker's Holiday*, *Heartbreak House*, and *Danton's Death*. Because of the expense required for the vast scale of the Welles-Houseman productions, however, Welles turned to the medium of radio to make ends meet. After reprising his role of the scheming banker in the radio version of *Panic*, and earning praise for his "splendid purple-velvet voice," Welles found himself in great demand over the airwaves. His radio work during the next several years included performances on such programs as *The March of Time*, *Fall of the City*, *The Three Ghosts*, *The Poison Death*, *The Phantom Voice*, *The Silent Avenger*, *The White Legion*, *The Bride of Death*, *My Little Boy*, and *The Open Window*. He also served as the uncredited voice behind the popular series *The Shadow*.

"I used to go by ambulance from one radio station to another, because I discovered there was no law in New York that you had to be sick to travel in an ambulance," Welles recalled in a 1982 BBC documentary. "So I'd hire the ambulance and I would go from CBS to NBC and they'd hold an elevator for me. I'd go to the fifth floor, go into the studio,

whichever I was booked for. I'd say, 'What's the character?' They'd say, '80-year-old Chinaman,' and I'd go on and do the 80-year-old Chinaman. And then rush off somewhere else."

In 1938, Welles convinced executives at CBS to hire the entire Mercury Theater company to present a series of radio plays adopted from famous novels. Named the Mercury Theater on the Air, the group consisted of such stellar performers (and future film stars) as Agnes Moorehead, Paul Stewart, and Ray Collins, and presented plays that included *Dracula*, *The Count of Monte Cristo*, *The 39 Steps*, and *A Tale of Two Cities*. But the group's most famous broadcast by far took place on October 30, 1938, when Welles aired his version of H.G. Wells' *The War of the Worlds*, presented in the format of a news broadcast report of an invasion from Mars. Although three announcements were made during the broadcast that emphasized the program's fictional nature, the production caused a nationwide panic. According to an account that appeared the following day in the *New York Times*, the trepidation experienced by listeners took various forms—innumerable calls were placed to area police stations; one citizen stopped his wife just as she was about to swallow a vial of poison; prayer vigils were held in countless churches; and many individuals were treated at hospitals for "shock and hysteria." After the furor from the broadcast died down, the 22-year-old Welles reported that he was "just stunned" by the reaction.

"Everything seems like a dream," he said, offering an apology to the listening public. "It was the Mercury Theater's own radio version of dressing up in a sheet and jumping out of a bush and saying 'boo!' I don't think we'll choose anything like this again."

The highly publicized broadcast eventually became Welles' ticket to Hollywood—after the spring 1939 Mercury stage production of *The Five Kings* turned out to be an expensive failure, Welles accepted an offer from RKO president George J. Schaefer. The unprecedented agreement called for Welles to write, direct, produce, and star in two films, with RKO relinquishing all rights to alter the pictures without Welles' approval.

"This superb contract only happened because I didn't much want to make a movie," Welles said later. "I thought the only way I'd possibly make it was without anybody interfering. So I asked for things nobody ever had.... I was given a limited budget, but unlimited control, and the studio wasn't even allowed to see the rushes, if you can believe such a thing."

Welles' first film was *Citizen Kane* (1941), featuring such Mercury Theater veterans as Joseph Cotten, Agnes Moorehead, Everett Sloane, Ruth Warrick, Dorothy Comingore, and Ray Collins. A thinly veiled depiction of real-life newspaper magnate William Randolph Hearst, the film earned unanimous critical acclaim, but did poor business at the box office due to limited distribution and a delayed release by RKO. Still, *Citizen Kane* earned a total of nine Academy Award nominations, including four nods for Welles—Best Picture, Best Director, Best Actor, and Best Original Screenplay—making him the first person in Hollywood history to earn nominations in those four categories. Along with Joseph Mankiewicz, Welles won the Oscar for Best Screenplay and today, more than six decades after its release, the picture is considered one of the best films produced in the annals of cinema. At the time he made *Citizen Kane*, Welles was only 25 years old.

After *Citizen Kane*, Welles briefly returned to New York to stage the acclaimed adaptation of Richard Wright's *Native Son*, then returned to Hollywood where he wrote, produced, and directed *The Magnificent Ambersons* (1942), again utilizing Mercury players Joseph Cotten, Ray Collins, and Agnes Moorehead (in an outstanding performance that earned her an Academy Award nomination). After shooting ended on the picture—but before editing was complete—Welles was asked by Nelson Rockefeller, then-U.S. coordinator of Inter-American Affairs, to serve as a goodwill ambassador to South America by making a film about the Carnival celebration

in Rio DeJaneiro. Entitled *It's All True*, the film was to combine documentary footage of the Carnival with three dramatized short stories. But the picture would never be made and would, in fact, spell the end of Welles' association with RKO.

"RKO asked to see the rushes," Welles said in the BBC documentary. "They see a lot of black people and the reaction is, 'He's just shooting a lot of jigaboos jumping up and down.' They didn't even hear the samba music, because it hadn't been synched up. They made a great publicity point of the fact that I had gone to South America without a script and thrown all this money away. I never recovered from that attack."

Meanwhile, RKO executives had promised Welles that a movieola and editors would be sent to him in South America so that he could complete the final editing on *The Magnificent Ambersons*. The studio never followed through on this agreement—instead, approximately 45 minutes of the film was cut and was never seen again. Viewing the film's finale as "too downbeat," the studio also reshot a different ending with stars Cotten and Moorehead.

"They destroyed *Ambersons* and the picture itself destroyed me," Welles later said. "I didn't get a job as a director for years afterwards."

During the period before his departure for South America, Welles had co-written and co-starred in a film with Joseph Cotten, *Journey Into Fear* (1942), his first film noir. (Like *Ambersons*, *Journey Into Fear* was later edited without the input of Welles, who maintained that some of the film's plot points were eliminated, resulting in an often-perplexing picture: "At one marvelous moment, a man who's been killed in the third reel, looks through a porthole," Welles said in 1982. "So naturally it confuses you.")

Journey Into Fear centers on a multifarious set of characters, including Howard Graham (Cotten), a munitions expert visiting Istanbul; Col. Haki (Welles), the head of the secret police; Kuvetli (Edgar Barrier), a Turkish police agent posing as a tobacco salesman; Banat (Jack Moss), a hired killer; and Muller (Eustace Wyatt), the architect of a Nazi plot who describes himself as a "good German." When Graham is nearly killed by an assassin's bullet during his trip to Istanbul, Haki arranges for his return to America, with Kuvetli installed on the ship to ensure his safe passage. Aboard the ship, however, Kuvetli is murdered and Graham is later captured by the Nazis. He manages to escape, but he is pursued by Muller and Banat onto the ledge of a building during a driving rainstorm. Haki emerges to shoot Muller, and Graham ultimately manages to turn the tables on Banat, pursuing him until he falls from the ledge to his death. For his role in this often-bewildering but nonetheless interesting noir, Welles was praised in *Variety* as "above-par," and the critic for the *New York Times* wrote that the actor's "fine flair for melodrama is stamped on every scene." The latter reviewer also judged, however, that "Welles' characterization of the Turkish police chief is the only one which is overdrawn."

While Welles was still in South America in 1942, RKO underwent a shakeup that resulted in the resignation of George Schae-fer, who had engineered Welles' contractual arrangement, and the hiring of Charles Koerner (who vowed to institute the studio's new policy of "showmanship not genius"— a direct reference to Welles). In the wake of the debacle involving *It's All True*, Koerner issued a statement to the press that read in part: "Accordingly, because space was urgently needed for those engaged in current production, RKO requested representatives of Mr. Welles to make available offices which had been occupied by them.... Disagreements that have existed between RKO and Orson Welles and his Mercury Productions have culminated in the necessity of his leaving the RKO-Pathé lot." And with that, Welles' days as the "boy genius" of the RKO lot came to an unceremonious conclusion.

Out of a job and rejected on medical grounds for service by the United States Army, Welles spent the next two years airing a series of radio broadcasts called *Hello Americans*, and entertaining service personnel with the Mercury Wonder Show, during which he demonstrated his talent in the art of illusion. One of the performers initially slated to appear in Welles' USO act was 24-year-old actress Rita Hayworth (she was later replaced by Marlene Dietrich), who had recently risen to fame in such features as *Blood and Sand* (1941) and *You Were Never Lovelier* (1942). Welles had met Hayworth several months earlier, and before long, the two were an item. Dubbed "Beauty and the Brain" by the press, they were married on September 7, 1943, and although Hollywood wags insisted that the marriage of two such different personalities couldn't last, the union seemed—for a while, at least—a solid one.

After his marriage to Hayworth, Welles returned to the big screen, starring opposite Joan Fontaine in *Jane Eyre* (1944), an engrossing interpretation of the classic Charlotte Brontë novel. He spent the next year writing a political column for the *New York Post* and serving as director, narrator, and star of two plays for the CBS radio series *This Is My Best*. Only mildly diverted by these activities, Welles was eager to resume his familiar position behind the camera, and he got the chance in 1946 when International Pictures signed him to direct and star in *The Stranger* (1946), his second film noir. Here, the actor portrayed a Nazi war criminal, Franz Kindler, who poses as a college professor in Hartford, Connecticut, and puts the finishing touches on his masquerade by marrying Mary Longstreet (Loretta Young), the daughter of a Supreme Court judge. Kindler's well-planned facade begins to shatter, however, when he is trailed to Hartford by Wilson (Edward G. Robinson), a member of the Allied War Crimes Commission. At first, Mary is vehemently skeptical when Wilson reveals her husband's atrocities ("It's a lie," Mary insists. "He's not one of those people!"), but she later accepts the truth and confronts Kindler during a tense scene in the town's clock tower. As the townspeople gather below, Mary shoots Kindler and he falls to his death, impaled on a revolving mechanism connected to the tower.

Although *The Stranger* was hailed by one critic as a "socko melodrama," reviewers dissented in their views of Welles' performance. The critic for *Variety* had nothing but praise for the actor, noting the "uniformly excellent cast" and stating that Welles, Robinson, and Young had "turn[ed] in some of their best work." The *New York Times'* Bosley Crowther disagreed, however, writing that Welles essayed "a boyishly bad acting job in a role which is highly incredible ... the performance of Mr. Welles in the title role is one of the less convincing features of this film." Crowther was equally unimpressed with the production itself, sniping that "the whole film ... comes off a bloodless, manufactured show. The atom-bomb newsreels on the same bill are immeasurably more frightening."

Following *The Stranger*, Welles returned to Broadway to stage *Around the World*, a lavish musical adaptation of Jules Verne's *Around the World in 80 Days*, but the critically acclaimed show failed to excite audiences and Welles' lost an estimated $350,000 on the production. Back in Hollywood, he managed to recoup some of his financial

losses by providing the narration for *Duel in the Sun* (1946), starring Jennifer Jones, and *Battle for Survival* (1947), and serving as producer, narrator, and actor in the *Schlitz Summer Playhouse* series on CBS radio. But by now, Welles had more serious affairs with which to contend — affairs of the heart.

In December 1944, Welles and wife Hayworth had welcomed a daughter, Rebecca, but in the ensuing years, their marriage had started to deteriorate, hastened in part by Welles' frequent absences and feverish devotion to his career. Hayworth reportedly turned to alcohol to quell her growing suspicions about her husband's fidelity, and she herself engaged in a brief affair in 1945 with singer Tony Martin. The couple formally separated the following year, although Welles made it clear in an interview with columnist Florabel Muir that he desired a reconciliation.

"I love Rita for what she is exactly," Welles said. "I don't want to change her one little bit.... Rita looks and acts like a friendly, gentle, gay little thing, but in reality she has a will of iron. I hope she will not act too hastily in discussing our status with lawyers."

Although Hayworth had announced her intentions to seek a divorce, she agreed to star in Welles' latest project, his third film noir, *The Lady From Shanghai* (1948). "I made an agreement and I'll stand by it," she told the press. "I owe it to Orson."

The *Lady From Shanghai* starred Welles as Michael O'Hara, an Irish seaman who finds himself in a situation of nightmarish proportions when he meets and falls in love with a beautiful stranger, Hayworth's Elsa Bannister: "Once I'd seen her," Michael says, "I was not in my right mind for quite some time." Hired by Elsa as a crew member on her yacht, Michael encounters a slew of quirky characters including Elsa's psychologically and physically impaired husband, Arthur (Everett Sloane), touted as "the world's greatest criminal attorney"; Sidney Broom (Ted De Corsia), who has been hired by Arthur to spy on his wife; and Arthur's business partner, George Grisby (Glenn Anders), who secretly lusts after Elsa. Although he plans to run away with Elsa at the trip's end, Michael instead finds himself involved in a convoluted plot that results in his arrest for the murders of Broom and Grisby. Defended by Arthur, who plans to ensure his conviction, Michael escapes, discovers that Elsa was responsible for the death of Grisby, and confronts her in a House of Mirrors at an abandoned amusement park. In the film's famous climax, Arthur locates the couple there, and he and Elsa engage in a lengthy gun battle that ultimately ends in both their deaths.

Despite Welles' high hopes for *The Lady from Shanghai*, the entire experience was a dismal one for the actor. Shortly after production ended, on November 10, 1947, Hayworth was granted a divorce from Welles and later told reporters that she was "tired of being a 25 percent wife.... He's interested in everything about himself and nothing about his wife." And the release of the film the following year invited a spate of reviews that were nearly universal in their distaste. *Variety*'s critic complained that the plot was "often foggy of purpose and confusing to follow"; the reviewer for *Boxoffice* dismissed Welles' "none-too-convincing Irish brogue"; and in the *New York Times*, Bosley Crowther wrote that Welles "has a strange way of marring his films with sloppiness." But although Welles himself later stated that the picture was "an experiment in what not to do," *Shanghai* did manage to earn a handful of favorable reviews, with the critic for *Cue* finding that it offered "a new level of excitement," and the *Film Daily* raving, "*The Lady from Shanghai* is tense dramatic entertainment loaded with surprises and departing vividly from orthodox treatment. Each time Welles does a film he composes a complete new text on the form. His new bag of tricks on display is inventive, imaginative, full of surprises."

After Welles' divorce from Hayworth, the actor produced, directed, and starred in Republic's low-budget production of *Macbeth* (1948). Shot in just three weeks, the film is seen today as a triumph, but upon its release, it was panned by critics and moviegoers stayed away in droves.

"It was done as a B-picture, a quickie," Welles said. "I thought I'd have a great success with it, and that I'd be allowed to do all kinds of difficult things, as long as they were cheap ... [but] it was a big critical failure. It was the biggest critical failure I ever had."

The following year, Welles rebounded from this disappointment with a relatively minor, but undeniably memorable role in *The Third Man* (1949), his fourth film noir. A British thriller directed by Carol Reed, this film centers on Holly Martins (Joseph Cotten), an American writer who travels to Vienna at the request of his friend, Harry Lime (Welles), arriving in time for Harry's funeral. Informed that Harry died after being struck by a car, Holly is stunned to hear his friend described by a law officer as "the worst racketeer that ever made a dirty living in this city." Seeking more information about Harry's death, Holly garners conflicting stories; in one version, he is told that two men carried Harry to the side of the road after the accident, and in another, he hears of a "third man" who was on the scene. Ultimately, Holly not only discovers that Harry faked his own death and is, in fact, still alive, but also that he was the mastermind of a nefarious scheme that involved stealing penicillin, diluting it to increase its volume, and selling it to patients who subsequently suffered tragic consequences. At the film's end, Harry is tracked through the sewers of Vienna by Holly and a horde of police; Holly is the first to find his friend, and after Harry gives him a nearly imperceptible nod of consent, Holly fatally shoots him.

In his small but pivotal role as the elusive Harry Lime, Welles earned rave reviews after the release of *The Third Man*, and the film was a worldwide hit. But by now, Welles had grown anxious to return to directing, and he began focusing his energies on what would be his most ambitious project to date, his version of Shakespeare's *Othello*. The production, however, turned out to be more than Welles bargained for. After contracting with an Italian film company to provide the financing for the picture, Welles traveled with his cast to the west coast of Africa, only to learn after his arrival that the Italian backers had gone bankrupt.

"We had no money, and we were in Africa," Welles recalled, "and we had no costumes, nothing."

Welles essayed a Herculean effort to complete the film, earning money by appearing in such features as *The Black Rose* (1950), starring Tyrone Power, and *Trent's Last Case* (1952), a British mystery, then returning to *Othello*'s various locations throughout Europe to resume shooting. The film ultimately took two years to complete, and despite numerous cast changes, it was finally released in 1952. Labeled a "flawed masterpiece," *Othello* went on to win the Grand Prix at the Cannes Film Festival.

Deciding to leave Hollywood behind, Welles relocated to Europe and dived headfirst into a number of varied projects; in 1953, he starred in the CBS television production of *King Lear*; performed on two BBC radio productions, *Song of Myself* and *Queen of Spades*; and wrote the libretto and designed the sets and costumes for a London ballet, *The Lady in the Ice*. He was seen on British television in 1955, serving as producer and host of *The Orson Welles Sketchbook* and *Around the World with Orson Welles*. Also that year, he directed and starred in his blank-verse adaptation of *Moby Dick*, transforming the Duke of York Theater, one critic wrote, into "a house of magic." On the big screen, he was seen in a number of foreign productions, including *Royal Affairs in Versailles* (1953), shot in France with Claudette Colbert and Jean-Pierre Aumont, and *Trouble in the Glen* (1954), a British comedy co-starring Margaret Lockwood. During this period, he also wrote two novels, *Une grosse legume* and *Mr. Arkadin*, which he adapted into a 1955 film.

Along with his many professional activities, Welles found time to romance Countess di Girfalco, Paola Mori, who played his daughter in *Mr. Arkadin*. On May 8, 1955, after the release of the film, Welles and Mori were married in London, and Mori spoke frankly to the press about her relationship with the famed performer.

"I know what people say about him," Mori told a reporter for *The Daily Express*. "Moody ... erratic ... difficult. 'Act with him,' they said, 'and you'll be sick in bed with liver trouble. He's impossible.' Instead, I am marrying the man. You see, I know how to cope with him.... It is not that Orson is abnormal — he is supernormal. The secret is finding out how normal he is underneath the super."

Mori apparently unearthed the secret; the couple welcomed Welles' third daughter, Beatrice, in November 1955, and despite a rather public affair carried on for many years between Welles and sculptor Oja Kodar, he and Mori remained together until his death in 1985.

Career-wise, Welles continued to throw himself into his many projects, including an acclaimed portrayal as Father Mapple in John Huston's *Moby Dick* (1956); a guest spot on the popular television series *I Love Lucy*, on which he demonstrated his ongoing fondness for magic; and providing the narration for the CBS television production of *The Fall of the City*. Then, in 1957, after a self-imposed exile of nearly a decade, Welles returned to Hollywood to direct and star in his final film noir, *Touch of Evil*.

This dark entry in the realm of noir opens with one of Welles' most spectacular sequences, a three minute, 20-second, continuous shot that ends with the explosion of a car near the Mexican border. The explosion — which killed a local millionaire and his female companion — serves as the catalyst for uniting a motley group of individuals on both sides of the law, including Hank Quinlan (Welles), a small-town detective renowned for his "game leg" that acts as the tool for his unerring intuition; Hank's loyal best friend and fellow cop Pete Menzies (Joseph Calleia); Mike Vargas (Charlton Heston), a Mexican narcotics investigator who witnessed the scene of the explosion; Mike's American bride, Susie (Janet Leigh), who demonstrates a steely sense of fortitude in the face of a number of dire circumstances; and "Uncle Joe" Grandi (Akim Tamiroff), a local racketeer whose mobster brother is being investigated by Vargas. Interweaving a number of plot points, *Touch of Evil* focuses on Quinlan's investigation of the car explosion and his swift arrest of a young Mexican man, Manolo Sanchez (Victor Millan), for the crime; Vargas's realization that Quinlan has planted evidence to support his "intuition" regarding Sanchez' guilt; and Grandi's attempts to discredit Vargas by involving his wife in a drug-related scandal. Ultimately, Grandi winds up dead at the hands of Quinlan, Vargas proves to Menzies that Quinlan has been planting evidence in his cases for years, and in the film's final showdown, Vargas and Menzies kill each other during a gun battle. Ironically, after Quinlan's death, it is revealed that the man arrested for the car bombing had confessed to the crime.

For his memorable portrayal as Quinlan, Welles was applauded by numerous critics, including the reviewer for *Variety*, who praised his "unique and absorbing performance"; the *Hollywood Citizen-News* reviewer, who cited his "brilliant" acting; and the critic for *Boxoffice*, who wrote, "It is Orson Welles who steals the show with his superb acting. His portrayal of a thoroughly despicable character will remain in the minds of action fans long after the show has ended." The notices for the overall production were mixed, however. Howard Thompson predicted in the *New York Times* that "nobody, and we mean nobody, will nap during *Touch of Evil*," and the *Boxoffice* reviewer maintained that the film "packs a terrific punch that will have audiences on the edge of their seats." But *Variety*'s critic, while noting that the feature "smacks of brilliance," added that "it takes more than good scenes to make a good picture," and Kay Proctor of the *Los Angeles Examiner* dismissed it as "an incredible, hoked-up mish-mash of dope, dynamite, murder, crooked cops, brutality, rape frames, double-crosses, triple-crosses-you name it, the picture's got it!"

As with nearly every Welles-directed

film since *The Magnificent Ambersons*, *Touch of Evil* was edited without Welles' involvement.

"It's never been explained," he said. "They loved the rushes. Every day the head of the studio came to me and wanted me to come to the office and sign a deal for several pictures ... then they saw a rough cut of it and they were so horrified that they wouldn't let me in the studio. And nobody's ever explained what horrified them.... It was too dark for them, too strange, I think ... a little too tough, a little too black. But that's a guess. I just don't know." (Interestingly, in 1998, more than 40 years after the initial release of the film, *Touch of Evil* was re-edited and re-released by October Films to comply with a 58-page letter penned by Welles to Universal studio executives in which he described his desired changes.)

In 1958, Welles was a standout as a brutish Southern landowner in *The Long, Hot Summer*, a steamy drama starring Paul Newman and Joanne Woodward, and offered several more memorable performances during the next few years, including the liberal advocate Jonathan Wilk in *Compulsion* (1958), and the tax-plagued film director in *The V.I.P.'s* (1963), but he didn't appear behind the camera again until 1962, when he directed *The Trial*, based on the novel by Franz Kafka. Starring Anthony Perkins, the film was released to mixed reviews and was criticized by some who felt that Welles misinterpreted Kafka's story.

Never at a loss for work, Welles divided his time between television and feature films during the next two decades; one of his most notable roles was his portrayal of Falstaff in *Chimes at Midnight* (1966), which many consider to be his greatest performance. Welles also considered the film — which he wrote and directed — as his favorite.

"If I wanted to get into heaven on the basis of one picture," he once said, "that's the one I would offer up."

Other memorable features included *Is Paris Burning?* (1966), in which he played the Swedish consul; *A Man for All Seasons* (1966), a critical and commercial hit that won the Academy Award for Best Picture; *The Immortal Story* (1968), a beautiful fable starring and directed by Welles; and his final directorial effort, *F for Fake* (1973), an unusual documentary-style film in which he served as narrator. (The film also featured his longtime mistress Oja Kodar.) Upon its release, *F for Fake* was acclaimed by critics, but Welles was disappointed by the lack of enthusiasm from audiences.

"The failure of *F for Fake* was one of the big shocks of my life," he said in 1982, "because I really thought I was on to something."

In his later years, most of Welles' projects involved the use of his distinctive voice; he was heard on such television programs as *Around the World* (1961), *Continental Classroom: Out of Darkness* (1962), *The Silent Years* (1971), *Future Shock* (1971), *Survival: Magnificent Monsters of the Deep* (1976), and *A Woman Called Moses* (1978), and numerous feature films, including *Start the Revolution Without Me* (1970), *Bugs Bunny Superstar* (1975), *The Double McGuffin* (1979), *The Man Who Saw Tomorrow* (1980), *Genocide* (1981), and *Almonds and Raisins* (1984). Never one to turn down a respectable job, Welles also served for several years as the TV pitchman for Paul Masson wines.

In the 1970s, between Welles' numerous projects, he began work on a film called *The Other Side of the Wind*, which told the story of a famous moviemaker (played by John Huston) and his struggle to find financing for his film. He was still working on the picture when he died of a heart attack on October 9, 1985. He was 70 years old.

Toward the end of his life, Welles was showered with numerous accolades, including an honorary Academy Award in 1970, the American Film Institute Life Achievement Award in 1975, and the French Legion d'Honneur in 1982. They were much-deserved honors for one of the screen's greatest talents, both in front of the camera and behind it. While he was known as much for his eccentricities and demanding personality as for his talent, it cannot be disputed that Orson Welles was truly a creative genius whose like will never be seen again.

"Working with him was never very long on an even keel — it was either up or down," said director Robert Wise, who worked as a film editor on *Citizen Kane* and *The Magnificent Ambersons*. "Marvelously exciting, stimulating, maddening, frustrating.... He could one moment be guilty of a piece of behavior that was so outrageous it would make you want to tell him to go to hell and walk off the picture, [and] before you could do it, he'd come up with some idea so brilliant that it would literally have your mouth gaping open, so you never walked.

"You stayed."

Film Noir Filmography

Journey Into Fear. Director: Norman Foster. Producer: Orson Welles. Running time: 71 minutes. Released by RKO, March 18, 1943. Cast: Joseph Cotten, Dolores Del Rio, Orson Welles, Ruth Warick, Agnes Moorehead, Everett Sloane, Jack Moss, Jack Durant, Eustace Wyatt, Frank Readick, Edgar Barrier, Stefan Schnabel, Hans Conreid, Robert Meltzer, Richard Bennett, Shifra Haran, Herbert Drake, Bill Roberts.

The Stranger. Director: Orson Welles. Producer: Sam Spiegel. Running time: 95 minutes. Released by RKO, July 21, 1946. Cast: Edward G. Robinson, Loretta Young, Orson Welles, Philip Merivale, Billy House, Richard Long, Konstantin Shayne, Martha Wentworth, Byron Keith, Pietro Sosso.

The Lady from Shanghai. Director and Producer: Orson Welles. Running time: 86 minutes. Released by Columbia, June 10, 1948. Cast: Rita Hayworth, Orson Welles, Everett Soane, Glenn Anders, Ted De Corsia, Erskine Sanford, Gus Schilling, Carl Frank, Louis Merrill, Evelyn Ellis, Harry Shannon, Wong Show, Sam Nelson.

The Third Man. Director and Producer: Carol Reed. Running time: 104 minutes. Released by London Films, 1949. Cast: Joseph Cotten, Orson Welles, Alida Valli, Trevor Howard, Paul Hoerbiger, Ernst Deutsch, Erich Ponto, Siegfried Breuer, Hedwig Bleibtreu, Annie Rosar, Herbert Halbik, Alexis Chesnakov, Wilfrid Hyde-White, Paul Hardtmuth, Nelly Arno, Jenny Werner, Leo Bieber, Frederick Schreicher, Paul Smith, Martin Boddey. Awards: Academy Award for Best B/W Cinematography (Robert Krasker). Academy Award nominations for Best Director (Carol Reed), Best Editing (Oswald Hafenrichter).

Touch of Evil. Director: Orson Welles. Producer: Albert Zugsmith. Running time: 95 minutes. Released by Universal-International, May 21, 1958. Cast: Charlton Heston, Janet Leigh, Orson Welles, Joseph Calleia, Akim Tamiroff, Joanna Moore, Marlene Dietrich, Ray Collins, Dennis Weaver, Victor Millan, Lalo Rios, Valentin de Vargas, Mort Mills, Mercedes McCambridge, Wayne Taylor, Ken Miller, Raymond Rodriguez, Michael Sargent, Zsa Zsa Gabor, Keenan Wynn, Joseph Cotten, Phil Harvey, Joi Lansing, Harry Shannon, Rusty Wescoatt, Arlene McQuade, Domenick Delgarde, Joe Basulto, Jennie Dias, Yolanda Bojorquez, Eleanor Corado.

References

Andrews, Colman, with Terrail, Patrick. "Orson Welles on a Lifetime of Great L.A. Eating." *Los Angeles Magazine*, August 1981.

"A Screen Genius Returns." *The London Times*, May 6, 1985.

Belcher, Jerry. "Orson Welles, Theatrical Genius, Found Dead at 70." *Los Angeles Times*, October 11, 1985.

Biancull, David. "Welles' Runs Dry." *New York Post*, December 3, 1992.

Bogdanovich, Peter. "Is It True What They Say About Orson?" *New York Times*, August 30, 1970.

"By Orson Welles: But Where Are We Going?" *Look*, November 3, 1970.

Canby, Vincent. "The Undiminished Chutzpah of Orson Welles." *New York Times*, March 2, 1975.

Cotten, Joseph. "Orson and Me." *Los Angeles Magazine*, September 1985.

Duning, Decla. "Energy Machine." *Los Angeles Times Sunday Magazine*, December 24, 1939.

Ebert, Roger. "Orson Welles Dead." *Chicago Sun-Times*, October 11, 1985.

Greenberg, Abe. "Of Orson Welles, Poseur or Genius?" *Hollywood Citizen-News*, May 5, 1966.

Harmetz, Aljean. "30 Directors Honor Orson Welles." *New York Times*, October 21, 1981.

Hopper, Hedda. "Rita Hayworth Again Leaves Orson Welles." *Los Angeles Times*, March 13, 1947.

_____. "Rita Hayworth Becomes Bride of Orson Welles in Quiet Rite." *Los Angeles Times*, September 8, 1943.

Lahr, John. "The Wonder Boy." *The New Republic*, March 17, 1986.

Leaming, Barbara. "The Unfulfilled Promise." *New York Times Magazine*, July 14, 1985.

MacDonald, Dwight. "Orson Welles and His Magic Steam Engine." *Esquire*, July 1963.

Maxwell, Elsa. "The Wacky World of Orson Welles." *The American Weekly*, March 18, 1956.

McBride, Joseph. "The Lost Kingdom of Orson Welles." *The New York Review*, May 13, 1993.

McCarthy, Todd. "Orson Welles, Renaissance Man of Film, Stage, Radio, Dies at 70." *Variety*, October 16, 1985.

Minoff, Philip. "Notes on TV." *Cue*, October 29, 1953.

"No One to Fill Welles' Seat." *New York Daily News*, October 12, 1985.

Norton, Thelma. "The Will to Power in Orson Welles Films." *Classic Images*, November 1982.

"O'Brien, Geoffrey. "A Touch of Ego." *Village Voice*, October 15, 1985.

"Orson Welles Marries Italian Countess-Actress." *Los Angeles Times*, May 9, 1955.

"Orson Welles' Revolution Is Still in Progress." *New York Times*, October 20, 1985.

"Orson Welles, Theatrical Genius, Found Dead at 70." *Los Angeles Times*, October 11, 1985.

Othman, Frederick C. "Orson Fumbles, but Gets Ring on Rita." *Los Angeles Herald*, September 8, 1949.

Parsons, Louella O. "Rita Hayworth Rift Rumored." *Los Angeles Examiner*, March 12, 1947.

"Posters for Profit." *New York Times*, May 5, 2000.

Quindlen, Anna. "The Magnificent Orsons." *New York Times*, September 15, 1985.

"Rita Hayworth Files Suit to Divorce Orson Welles." *Los Angeles Times*, October 2, 1947.

"Rita Hayworth Will Return to Welles; Tony Martin Sad." *Los Angeles Examiner*, September 22, 1946.

"Ross, Don. "Welles Is Back in Full Crisis." *New York Herald Tribune*, January 8, 1956.

Sarris, Andrew. "Exit Orson." *The Village Voice*, October 29, 1985.

Schallert, Edwin. "Welles Remains a Mystery Man." *Los Angeles Times*, October 9, 1955.

Shaffer, Rosalind. "Films' Quadruple Threat, Orson Welles, in Limelight with His Latest Romance." *Hollywood Citizen-News*, September 11, 1943.

Shivas, Mark. "Guess Who's Coming to Dinner Now?" *New York Times*, November 26, 1972.

Skolsky, Sidney. "Tintypes: Orson Welles." *Hollywood Citizen-News*, May 7, 1941.

Siskel, Gene. "Legend of Film, Orson Welles, 70." *Chicago Tribune*, October 11, 1985.

Sorel, Edward. "Movie Classics—*Citizen Kane*." *Esquire*, October 1980.

Tynan, Kenneth. "Orson Welles." *Show*, October 1961.

Vidal, Gore. "Remembering Orson Welles." *The New York Review*, June 1, 1989.

Weiss, Hedy. "Remembering Orson Welles." *Chicago Sun-Times*, October 13, 1985.

"Welles Inducted into the Legion of Honor." *Los Angeles Herald-Examiner*, February 23, 1982.

Wilmington, Michael. "Orson Welles: Giant of Cinema, Maker of Myths." *Los Angeles Times*, October 20, 1985.

Yentob, Alan. "Orson Welles." *The London Observer*, October 13, 1985.

Documentary

"The Orson Welles Story." An Arena/BBC Presentation. Copyright 1982.

RICHARD WIDMARK

"You know what I do to squealers? I let 'em have it in the belly so they can roll around a long time, thinkin' it over." — Richard Widmark in *Kiss of Death* (1947)

There was little about Richard Widmark's humble career beginnings that would hint at his ability to portray the chillingly psychotic gangster in *Kiss of Death* (1947). Shy and reserved, Widmark worked as a college professor a decade before he shocked moviegoers by pushing an elderly, wheelchair-bound woman down a flight of steps, all the while suffusing theaters with his trademark maniacal laugh. Following this memorable film debut, Widmark went on to become one of Hollywood's most respected performers, and an archetypal noir actor with roles in seven superb examples of the era. In addition to *Kiss of Death*, Widmark starred in *The Street with No Name* (1948), *Road House* (1948), *Night and the City* (1950), *Panic in the Streets* (1950), *Don't Bother to Knock* (1952), and *Pickup on South Street* (1953).

Richard Widmark was born in Sunrise, Minnesota, on December 26, 1914, the first of two sons of Mae Ethel and Carl Widmark, a traveling salesman. Because of his father's job, Widmark moved frequently as a child, living in Sioux Falls, South Dakota; Henry, Illinois; and Chillicothe, Missouri, before settling over a bakery his father purchased in Princeton, Illinois.

"I suppose I wanted to act in order to have a place in the sun," Widmark said once. "I'd always lived in small towns, and acting meant having some kind of identity."

Widmark had been what he termed a "movie nut" since the age of three, but as a student at Princeton Township High School, he appeared in only one school production.

"I don't recall having any interest in acting, [but] what I had discovered early on was that I enjoyed talking in public," Widmark said in a 1987 interview in *Parade* Magazine. "I started giving three-minute speeches in my freshman English class. I loved doing it because I was very shy, and yet, when I got up before an audience, I felt comfortable. Then one day I addressed the whole student body and talked for about 10 minutes. All of a sudden, I was making them laugh, I was making them listen, and I felt very powerful. It was an exhilarating feeling."

While at Princeton Township, Widmark participated in numerous extracurricular activities, including serving as senior class president, playing on the football team, working on the newspaper staff, and delivering the commencement speech for his 1932 graduation. He planned to put his affinity for talking to good use as a lawyer, and enrolled at Lake Forest (Illinois) College as a pre-law major, attending on a four-year combination athletic-academic scholarship. While there, however, Widmark was taken under the wing of the school's drama coach, who encouraged him to pursue an acting career. After graduating in 1936, Widmark remained at the college for two years as a professor, teaching speech and drama.

In 1938, Widmark headed for New York, where a former college classmate-turned-radio producer gave him a job on the radio series, *Aunt Jenny's Real Life Stories*. His background proved to be an ideal complement for radio and the actor went on to appear on numerous programs, including *Big Sister*, *Stella Dallas*, *Pepper Young's Family*, *Front Page Farrell*, *Grand Central*, *The March of Time*, *Manhattan at Midnight*, *Cavalcade*, and *Inner Sanctum*.

"Sometimes I appeared on the air from morning until midnight. Often did eight a day. After each one, I scrammed to a waiting taxi and was driven at a fast clip a few blocks to another station, where I slid in like a ballplayer, on my line with the red hand on the clock," Widmark told a reporter in 1948. "I seldom knew the plots of those soap operas. I memorized my own lines in the taxis. They paid me $1500 a week for it, so I didn't care what happened to Uncle Ezra or Cousin Eddie. And I learned a thing or two about character, voice, and the microphone on that treadmill."

With the onset of World War II in 1941, Widmark attempted to join the U.S. Army but was rejected for service because of a perforated eardrum. Instead, during the war years, the actor entertained servicemen as part of the American Theatre Wing, served as an air raid warden, and made appearances for the Office of War Information. A year after being turned down by the Army, Widmark married Ora Jean Hazlewood, whom he had met while both were students at Lake Forest, and who was later one of his students. The couple, who had a daughter, Anne, in 1945, went on to enjoy one of Hollywood's most enduring marriages.

"I waited until I was old enough to know what I wanted before I married and that helps," Widmark once said of their union, which lasted until Jean's 1997 death of complications from Alzheimer's Disease. "Besides, most of the women I meet are actresses, and Jean is so refreshingly different, I always look forward to getting home to her. I just like my wife a lot. After I was married, I just figured, 'Well, that's it.' I never thought beyond that."

In 1943, Widmark debuted on Broadway in *Kiss and Tell*, playing a young Army Air Corps lieutenant. Later that year, he was seen in a short-lived run of a William Saroyan play, *Get Away Old Man*, and in 1944 he was featured in *Trio*, a controversial play that touched on the theme of lesbianism. The play was closed after 67 performances by the License Commissioner, but not before Widmark was praised in the *New York Herald Tribune*, who wrote that his "tense underplaying sustains the most faltering moments of the play." He went on to star in a series of what he called "prestige flops," including *Kiss Them for Me* in 1945, *Dunnigan's Daughter* in 1946, and the Chicago production of *Dream Girl* in 1947. But he got his long-awaited big break when Hollywood director Henry Hathaway visited New York to cast the role of vicious hood Tommy Udo, for his new film, *Kiss of Death* (1947).

"Hathaway didn't want me," Widmark said in 1987. "I have a high forehead; he thought I looked too intellectual. But [20th Century-Fox head] Darryl Zanuck wanted me to test. For the test, I wore a wig that brought my hairline way down like an ape. But Henry sat on the test. Finally the production manager sent it to Zanuck. My getting the part didn't make Henry too happy. He gave me kind of a bad time."

Cast in a supporting role in this, his first film noir, Widmark caused a sensation. As Udo, he all but stole the picture from star Victor Mature, making a memorable mark with his trademark high-pitched laugh, carrying out such despicable deeds as pushing a wheelchair-bound woman down a flight of stairs, and illustrating his psychotic bent with suitably menacing dialogue. "We're going to have some fun together. Lots of fun, just like we used to," Udo says in one scene. "You got a wife and kids, ain't ya, pal? They're gonna have some fun, too. I'm gonna enjoy meetin' your family. Kids like to have fun. We'll all have some fun together. You and me. And your wife. And your kids. From now on, lots of fun."

The story of *Kiss of Death* focuses on career criminal Nick Bianco (Mature), who gains his exit from prison after providing damaging information on a number of fellow hoods, including Udo. After settling down with a new wife (Coleen Gray) and gaining custody of his two young daughters, Nick begins to turn his life around, only to find himself in jeopardy when Udo is acquitted on a murder charge. Fearing for his own life as well as the safety of his family, Nick sets an elaborate trap for his vicious nemesis, nearly losing his life when Udo shoots him several times before he himself is killed by police. Hailed by critics, including one who said he played Udo with "horrible, unctuous emphasis," Widmark was rewarded for his efforts with an Academy Award nomination for Best Supporting Actor. He lost, however, to Edmund Gwenn in *Miracle on 34th Street*.

"I thought, 'Geez, this is easy,'" Widmark laughingly recalled 40 years later. "I haven't come close since."

Now under a seven-year contract with Fox, Widmark was promptly cast in a trio of villainous roles: one of a group of malcontent Civil War veterans who become outlaws in *Yellow Sky* (1948), an intellectual gangleader in *The Street with No Name* (1948), and a vengeful proprietor bent on murder in *Road House* (1948) — the latter two marking the actor's swift return to film noir.

The Street with No Name starred Mark Stevens as Gene Cordell, an undercover agent investigating the murder of a woman during a nightclub holdup and the gang member who was suspected of the killing. Posing as a drifter with a police record, Cordell successfully infiltrates the highly organized gang run by Alec Stiles (Widmark), who is characterized by his frequent use of a nose inhaler, his obsession with avoiding airborne germs, and his meticulous selection of the members of his gang: "I'm building an organization along scientific lines," Stiles tells Cordell. "I need men who know their way around, who can get by. That's why I screen you ... like in the Army. Only I pick my own recruits." Although Cordell manages to gain Alec's confidence, he is later marked for murder when his cover is blown by the gangleader's inside man at

the police department. Alec's clever scheme to have Cordell shot by police backfires, however, and after a chase through a manufacturing plant, Alec is gunned down by Cordell.

In Widmark's second noir of the year, *Road House*, the actor played Jefty Robbins, a road house proprietor who falls for singer Lily Stevens (Ida Lupino) soon after hiring her for his club. Jefty's feelings are unrequited, however; Lily is drawn instead to club manager Pete Morgan (Cornel Wilde), and when the two announce their plans to leave town together, Jefty frames Pete for theft. After persuading the judge to release Pete into his custody, Jefty soon reveals the rationale behind his seemingly benevolent act: "We're just one big happy family," he tells the couple. "Lily singing in the bar, Pete living upstairs — just the way it was. We're twins from now on, kid — where I go, you go. And just suppose I was mean? Suppose you tried to marry Pete and leave town? Or [Pete], suppose you got mad and tried to slug me? One word to the judge and that's all, brother. Ten years in the pen. Oh, what a set up!" Later, Jefty forces the couple into accompanying him on a trip to his remote cabin, where he continues to wreak his maddening brand of psychological torture, ultimately announcing his intention to kill them both. But his plans finally come to an abrupt and permanent end when, during a struggle with Pete, Jefty is shot and killed by Lily.

Widmark earned raves for his performances in both of his 1948 noirs. After the release of *The Street with No Name*, the reviewer for *Variety* proclaimed the actor "the backbone of the film," and wrote that "his looks and personality have the latent menace of a loaded automatic." The *Los Angeles Daily News*' Frank Eng agreed; while praising the efforts of co-stars Stevens and Lloyd Nolan, the critic judged that "it is Richard Widmark who seizes the opportunity to walk off with the plaudits of the crowd." The actor earned similar accolades for his portrayal of the psychotic club owner in *Road House*—the *New York Times*' critic said that he did "an excellent job (complete with chilling laughter)," and Fred Hift of *Motion Picture Herald* gushed: "There is no need to stress the acting skill of Richard Widmark. Once again audiences are treated to his spine-chilling laugh as a man gone insane with hate and jealousy. He is superb. There are few actors that so well manage to portray the outer manifestations of a twisted mind."

Following this string of bad-boy roles, Widmark found his fame on the rise, with numerous fan magazines featuring such articles as "Shy College Professor Becomes Film Toughy," "Something New In Gangsters," and "Respectable Villain." He also discovered that his performances were beginning to elicit strong reactions from moviegoers.

"It's weird, the effect actors have on an audience. With the roles I played in those early movies, I found that quite a few people wanted to have a go at me," Widmark recalled in 1987. "I remember walking down the street in a small town and this lady coming up and slapping me. 'Here, take that, you little squirt!' she said. Another time I was having dinner in a restaurant when this big guy came over and knocked me right out of my chair."

But moviegoers would have been surprised to learn that Widmark was the antithesis of the characters he portrayed, possessing a sensitive nature and maintaining a staunch opposition to guns and violence of any kind.

"I won't have a gun in my house," he once said. "I don't hunt, and the one time I went fishing, I caught a little trout. I took him to the basement to scrape him. I called him George. It broke my heart that I had caused his death."

In 1949, Widmark was finally given the opportunity to play a sympathetic role in *Down to the Sea in Ships*, starring Lionel Barrymore, followed by his first top-billed role in *Slattery's Hurricane*, in which he played a roguish daredevil pilot. The following year, he offered another memorable performance, playing a psychotic racist opposite Sidney Poitier in *No Way Out* (1950), then starred in two more films noirs, *Night and the City* (1950) and *Panic in the Streets* (1950).

In the first — set in London — Widmark was Harry Fabian, who suffers with what is described by one character as "a highly inflamed imagination, coupled by delusions of grandeur." Constantly embroiled in unsuccessful get-rich-quick schemes, Harry stumbles on what appears to be a sure-fire plan when he gains the trust of famed Greco-Roman wrestler Gregorius (Stanislaus Zbyszko) and his protégé Nikolas (Ken Richmond). Before long, Harry successfully arranges a potentially lucrative bout between Nikolas and a local fighter known as the Strangler (Mike Mazurki), despite the objections of Gregorius' son, Kristo (Herbert Lom), who controls the town's fight game. ("You're very sharp, Mr. Fabian," Kristo tells him. "You've done a very sharp thing. Maybe even sharp enough to cut your throat. You've made my father believe in you, but I know you. Born a hustler, you will die a hustler.") Harry's dream of a big payoff quickly dies, however, when the Strangler goads Gregorius into an impromptu fight and the older wrestler suffers a fatal heart attack. The enraged Kristo puts a price on Harry's head, and the luckless promoter meets an ignominious end when he is caught and killed by the Strangler. Once again, Widmark was hailed for his performance; in a typical review, the critic for *Variety* wrote that the actor delivered "one of his finest portrayals, lending absolute conviction to his role of the hustler who betrays everybody he has any dealings with."

Next, in *Panic in the Streets*—labeled by one critic as a "crackling, exploding strip of cinematurgy"—Widmark played his sole noir role in which he was on the right side of the law. Here, he portrayed Dr. Clinton Reed of the United States Public Health Service, who fights the skepticism of his superiors in an effort to halt the spread of a potentially deadly pneumonic plague: "This morning, right here in the city, your police found the body of a man who was infected with the disease," Reed says of a bullet-riddled corpse discovered by authorities. "Everyone who came in contact with the body has been inoculated ... all but one—the man who killed him. If the killer is incubating pneumonic plague, he can start spreading it within 48 hours. Shortly after that, you'll have the makings of an epidemic." Focusing his search around the New Orleans docks, Reed faces resistance and suspicion from the residents, but he ultimately locates the prime carrier of the virus, a sadistic hood by the name of Blackie (Jack Palance). After a chase through a coffee warehouse—during which a guard is killed and Reed is conked on the head—police manage to subdue Blackie and the crisis is averted.

After earning mention for his "competent performance" in *Panic*, Widmark was next seen in a series of widely varying roles, including a Marine lieutenant in *Halls of Montezuma* (1951), commander of an underwater demolition team in *The Frogmen* (1951), a parachuting forest fire fighter in *Red Skies of Montana* (1952), a killer who is apprehended by an old friend in the "Clarion Call" segment of *O. Henry's Full House* (1952), and a bon-bon manufacturer in his first comedy, *My Pal Gus* (1952), for which he was praised in *Variety* for "showing both good comedy feeling as well as the more touchingly dramatic flavor required in the final scene." In his fourth film of 1952, Widmark was back to the realm of film noir, starring with Marilyn Monroe and Anne Bancroft in *Don't Bother to Knock* (1952).

This dark and often frightening film features a mélange of distinct characters, including Nell Forbes (Monroe), who spent three years in an asylum after the death of her boyfriend led to a suicide attempt; Nell's uncle, Eddie (Elisha Cook, Jr.), an elevator operator who finds Nell a babysitting job in the hotel where he works; and Jed Towers (Widmark), a cynical pilot and hotel guest who has just been dumped by his long-suffering girlfriend, Lyn Lesley (Anne Bancroft, in her screen debut): "I wouldn't marry you even if you wanted me to," Lyn tells Jed. "[It's] the way you treat people. The way you think about them. All you can focus on is the cold outside of things, the simple facts. Not any causes or whys or wherefores. Oh, you're sweet. And you're fun. And you're hard. And you lack something that I ask for in a man—an understanding heart." The lives of the principal players intertwine within the walls of the hotel, reaching a climax when Nell confuses Jed with her dead lover and accuses the young girl in her charge with coming between them. After the girl is found by her mother, bound and gagged, Nell wanders in a daze to the hotel lobby and purchases a pack of razor blades, planning to finish the deed she attempted three years earlier. She is stopped, however, when Jed makes his way through the gathered crowd and convinces the girl to surrender to police. Jarred by his harrowing experience with Nell, Jed is a transformed man by the film's end, and the final reel sees him reuniting with Lyn to start a new future. Despite Widmark's well-done performance, *Don't Bother to Knock* was the least successful of his seven films noirs, and the critic for *Variety* wrote that Widmark's role "offers him little opportunity, but he handles the part with his customary glibness."

After being briefly suspended by Fox

executives for refusing to accept a role in a film entitled *The Number*, Widmark was seen in two war films, *Take the High Ground!* (1953), on loanout to MGM, and *Destination Gobi* (1953), co-starring Don Taylor. He followed these with his final film noir, *Pickup on South Street* (1953), an absorbing feature co-starring Richard Kiley and Jean Peters. As the film begins, Widmark's character, Skip McCoy, steals the wallet of a subway train passenger (Peters), setting in motion a series of events that lead to murder and the exposure of a Communist spy network. It turns out that the stolen wallet held microfilm containing military secrets that the woman, Candy, was unknowingly transporting at the behest of her boyfriend, Joey (Kiley). After discovering the value of the stolen property, Skip first attempts to land a $25,000 payoff for its return, but his priorities soon change; transformed by his love for Candy, and determined to avenge the murder of a pal by the name of Moe (Thelma Ritter), Skip tracks Joey down and turns him into police.

Widmark's role as the grifter in *Pickup on South Street* was a particularly violent one — in an early scene, Skip knocks Candy unconscious after finding her lurking in his waterfront shack, then revives her by dousing her with the contents from a bottle of beer. And later, as described by *New York Times* critic Bosley Crowther, "at one moment, Widmark ... is smothering this lady with hot kisses [and] the next moment he is slapping her with her handbag and knuckle-dusting the side of her jaw. Oddly enough, this is treatment that Miss Peters seems to adore. She not only thrills to his caresses (of both sorts), but comes back for more." Although Crowther groused about the picture's "brutish climate," however, he did manage praise for Widmark's performance, including the actor in his sweeping comment that the film's cast did "very well."

Widmark finished out his contract with 20th Century-Fox in 1954, starring that year in *Hell and High Water*, a rather implausible tale about efforts to stop an atomic bomb threat in the north Pacific; *The Garden of Evil*,

a weak adventure yarn with Gary Cooper and Susan Hayward; and *Broken Lance*, an overly dramatic western that was a remake of Fox's earlier hit, *House of Strangers* (1949). The actor declined to re-sign with Fox, stating that he preferred to freelance.

"I knew I had to get away from Fox," he said in a 1961 interview. "I was being switched around from movie to movie without getting a chance to do much that I liked."

On his own, Widmark appeared in a mixed-bag of films that ranged from first-rate to downright lousy. Features such as Columbia's *A Prize of Gold* (1955), which effectively combined action and comedy, and *The Last Wagon* (1956), a fast-paced Fox western, were certainly worth the price of admission. Less worthy was *The Cobweb* (1956), an overblown soaper that failed to attract audiences despite a star-studded cast (including Lauren Bacall, Gloria Grahame, Charles Boyer, and Lillian Gish), a renowned director (Vincente Minelli), and a top-flight producer (John Houseman). Taking matters into his own hands, Widmark established his own production company, Heath Productions (after his daughter's middle name), stating that "the actor is just the bloke who fronts for all the machinery."

"I'm having fun with my company," Widmark told columnist Sheilah Graham in 1957. "I went into acting because I didn't want to be a businessman, and here I am in business. It's hard work, of course, but interesting to go back to between making pictures for major studios. The main thing is to find a story."

Widmark found his story in *Time Limit* (1957), which focused on the court martial of a major charged with collaborating with the enemy while a POW in a Korean prison camp.

"I saw the play in New York, and liked it very much," Widmark said in 1961. "Warner Brothers had a pre-production deal on the play, they owned the script, but it was at the time when they were getting very afraid to do small pictures because television was coming in very deeply. So I was able to buy it."

Helmed by actor Karl Malden in his directorial debut, released through United Artists, and starring Widmark and Richard Basehart, the film was well-received by critics and audiences alike. Widmark lashed out in the media, however, when a film clip of the movie was censored when it was aired on Dave Garroway's NBC-TV *Today* show in October 1957. The clip was televised during an interview between Garroway and Widmark, and eliminated by NBC censors was a line in which an officer's wife says, "My husband has been home for five months and six days and, in all that time, we have never been to bed together." Widmark was told that the line had been cut by the network in the interest of "good taste."

"It's hard to accept the network's point of view when the air channels are busy claiming that a happy marriage really depends on a special deodorant or a favorite toothpaste," Widmark said after the broadcast. "No, they are horrified at the suggestion that married people do or don't sleep together. It's time the networks grew up."

Other films produced under the Heath banner were *The Trap* (1959), a tense thriller featuring compelling performances by Widmark and Lee J. Cobb, and *The Secret Ways* (1961), a cloak-and-dagger melodrama that had more than a few unintentionally humorous moments. Filmed on location in Europe, the latter was a critical and financial bomb, and after its release, Widmark frankly admitted that he had learned from the experience.

"I would never try to go with a complete German unit again, I'd bring my own crew either from England or America. There was a constant tug all the time for the five months we were over there making the film," Widmark said, adding that he planned to appear in one picture for a major studio each year, while making his own picture every year through Heath, on a "smaller, simpler scale." But *The Secret Ways* would be the last film produced by Widmark and the actor later called moviemaking "a ruthless, nasty, cutthroat business."

Between the pictures produced through Heath, Widmark had continued to star in such features as *Saint Joan* (1957), which received a lukewarm reception from critics; *The Tunnel of Love* (1958), in which he played the philandering husband of a childless wife; and *Two Rode Together* (1961), a passable western co-starring James Stewart and directed by John Ford. Widmark later recalled his experience on the latter film as one of the most fun-filled of his career.

"We all had tin ears," Widmark recalled with amusement in 1987. "I'm deaf in one ear, Jimmy's deaf in the other, and Ford was nearly deaf in both. It was four months of the three of us going, 'What? What? What?'"

Also during this period, Widmark starred in *Judgment at Nuremberg* (1961), an outstanding dramatization of the real-life prosecution of Nazi war criminals; *How the West Was Won* (1962), a sweeping western saga in which Widmark was praised for making a "vital impression"; *Flight From Ashiya* (1964), a tired adventure about a group of shipwreck survivors off the coast of Japan; and *The Long Ships* (1964), a dreadful adventure spectacle that re-teamed Widmark with his *No Way Out* co-star, Sidney Poitier, who played a Moorish leader. (Advertisements for the film heralded it as Poitier's "first non–Negro role," and the distinguished actor later remarked: "To say it was disastrous is a compliment.")

Widmark fared better with his next outing with Poitier, *The Bedford Incident* (1965), a tense adventure about the peace-time monitoring of Russian submarines by U.S. destroyers, and was shown to good advantage as a one-eyed Confederate officer in *Alvarez Kelly* (1966). And although he returned to cinematic mediocrity in *The Way West* (1967), a clichéd western noteworthy only as the film debut of Sally Field, he rebounded the following year with a first-rate portrayal of a tough New York detective in *Madigan* (1968), which focused on a tough New York cop. Widmark later reprised his role in 1972 on a television series of the same name, which ran for one season on NBC. Having eschewed television appearances for most of his career (with the exception of a 1955 guest spot on *I Love Lucy*, where he played himself), Widmark changed his tune in the early 1970s. In addition to *Madigan*, the actor was seen in several made-for-television movies during the next two decades, including *Vanished* (1971)—for which he was nominated for an Emmy award, losing to George C. Scott for *The Price—Brock's Last Case* (1973), *The Last Day* (1975), *Mr. Horn* (1979), *All God's Children* (1980), *Blackout* (1985), *A Gathering of Old Men* (1987), and *Cold Sassy Tree* (1989).

Now approaching his 60s, Widmark began to appear in smaller roles on the big screen, but he took this reality in stride.

"Psychologically, there is an adjustment that you have to make as you get older," Widmark said in a 1986 interview in *Us* magazine. "You're used to being the number-one fella, and all of a sudden you're standing around and you're looking at the number-one fella, and you realize, 'Oh I'm the number six fella.' The name of the game is survival."

And Widmark continued to survive. During the 1970s and 1980s, his best films included *When the Legends Die* (1972), which focused on the plight of the American Indian; *Murder on the Orient Express* (1974), featuring an all-star cast that included Albert Finney, Lauren Bacall, Ingrid Bergman, and Sean Connery; *Twilight's Last Gleaming* (1977), a political thriller with Burt Lancaster and Charles Durning; *Coma* (1978), an eerie science-fiction thriller based on the Robin Cook bestseller; and *Against All Odds* (1984), which was a hit at the box office despite Widmark's dismissal of his role as a ruthless lawyer as "a lousy part. It was a cliché." Not all of Widmark's films during these years were so well-received, however — he was also seen in *The Swarm* (1978), a laughable disaster film whose cast included such stellar Hollywood veterans as Olivia deHavilland, Henry Fonda, Fred MacMurray, Jose Ferrer, Lee Grant, and Ben Johnson; and *Hanky Panky* (1982), an unfunny comedy starring Gene Wilder and his future wife Gilda Radner. Widmark's last feature film to date was *True Colors* (1991), in which he was featured as a

U.S. senator. He was also interviewed for the 1997 television documentary *Big Guns Talk: The Story of the Western*.

Although Widmark has not been seen on screen in more than a decade, his contribution to films has not been forgotten or gone unappreciated. In 1990, The National Board of Review of Motion Pictures presented the actor with its highest honor, the D.W. Griffith Career Achievement Award, a well-deserved accolade that served to illuminate the talent, versatility, and longevity that Widmark possesses.

An intensely private man, Widmark has given relatively few interviews throughout his career, and has taken great pains to ensure his privacy as well as that of his family.

"If you don't do a lot of interviews and you want to keep your life separate from your profession, people think you're a little nuts or stupid," Widmark told *Us* magazine in 1986. "I'm [against] all these Barbara Walters-type interviews where people get on TV and tell all in great detail. I don't care about someone else's inside life. They can work it out for themselves. You say all that to the public and really, what's left for you? Whaddya got? There's got to be something for you and your family that everybody in the world doesn't have to be in on."

Still, the actor has always maintained that he found that "place in the sun" that he sought growing up in Princeton, Illinois, and, looking back on his career, he expresses a genuine sense of satisfaction.

"My life turned out great," he once said. "I've seen the world, met wonderful people. I have absolutely no regrets. I've had a hell of a good time."

Film Noir Filmography

Kiss of Death. Director: Henry Hathaway. Producer: Fred Kohlmar. Running time: 98 minutes. Released by 20th Century-Fox, August 27, 1947. Cast: Victor Mature, Brian Donlevy, Coleen Gray, Richard Widmark, Karl Malden, Taylor Holmes, Howard Smith, Anthony Ross, Mildred Dunnock, Millard Mitchell, Temple Texas. Awards: Academy

Award nominations for Best Supporting Actor (Richard Widmark), Best Original Story (Eleazar Lipsky).

The Street with No Name. Director: William Keighley. Producer: Samuel G. Engel. Running time: 91 minutes. Released by 20th Century-Fox, July 14, 1948. Cast: Mark Stevens, Richard Widmark, Lloyd Nolan, Barbara Lawrence, Ed Begley, Donald Buka, Joseph Pevney, John McIntire, Howard Smith, Walter Greaza, Joan Chandler, Bill Mauch, Sam Edwards, Don Kohler, Roger McGee, Vincent Donahue, Phillip Pine, Buddy Wright, Larry Anzalone, Robert Karnes, Robert Patten.

Road House. Director: Jean Negulesco. Producer: Edward Chodorov. Running time: 95 minutes. Released by 20th Century-Fox, November 7, 1948. Cast: Ida Lupino, Cornel Wilde, Celeste Holm, Richard Widmark, O.Z. Whitehead, Robert Karnes, George Beranger, Ian MacDonald, Grandon Rhodes, Jack G. Lee.

Night and the City. Director: Jules Dassin. Producer: Samuel G. Engel. Running time: 95 minutes. Released by 20th Century-Fox, June 9, 1950. Cast: Richard Widmark, Gene Tierney, Googie Withers, Hugh Marlowe, Francis L. Sullivan, Herbert Lom, Stanislaus Zbyszko, Mike Mazurki, Charles Farrell, Ada Reeve, Ken Richmond.

Panic in the Streets. Director: Elia Kazan. Producer: Sol C. Siegel. Running time: 96 minutes. Released by 20th Century-Fox, August 4, 1950. Cast: Richard Widmark, Paul Douglas, Barbara Bel Geddes, Walter Jack Palance, Zero Mostel, Dan Riss, Alexis Minotis, Guy Thomajan, Tommy Cook. Awards: Academy Award nomination for Best Motion Picture Story (Edna and Edward Anhalt).

Don't Bother to Knock. Director: Roy Ward Baker. Producer: Julian Blaustein. Running time: 76 minutes. Released by 20th Century-Fox, July 1952. Cast: Richard Widmark, Marilyn Monroe, Anne Bancroft, Donna Corcoran, Jeanne Cagney, Lurene Tuttle, Elisha Cook, Jr., Jim Backus.

Pickup on South Street. Director: Samuel Fuller. Producer: Jules Schermer. Running time: 83 minutes. Released by 20th Century-Fox, June 17, 1953. Cast: Richard Widmark, Jean Peters, Thelma Ritter, Murvyn Vye, Richard Kiley, Willis B. Bouchey, Milburn Stone, Henry Slate, Jerry O'Sullivan. Awards: Academy Award for Best Supporting Actress (Thelma Ritter).

References

Arneel, Gene. "Widmark Loves Films, Not Film Biz; Raps Japanese Showmen's 'Deceit.'" *Variety*, November 7, 1962.
Avins, Mimi. "Old Pro." *Us*. January 27, 1986.
"'Bad' Influence on Daughter." *New York Morning Telegraph*, December 1, 1952.
Biography of Richard Widmark. NBC Radio, January 22, 1943.
Biography of Richard Widmark. United Artists Corp., circa 1956.
Churchill, Reba and Bonnie. "More Villains If You Please." *Beverly Hills Newslife*. February 2, 1955.
Crichton, Kyle. "Young Man with a Sneer." *Collier's*, April 16, 1949.
Demaris, Ovid. "Bad Guy." *Parade*, February 22, 1987.
"Dilemma for Dick." *Movie Stars Parade*, October 1952.
Gebhart, Myrtle. "Shy College Professor Becomes Film Toughy." *Boston Post Magazine*, December 26, 1948.
Graham, Sheilah. "Hollywood." *The Daily Mirror*, March 17, 1957.
_____. "Widmark — Movie Tough Guy — Is Mild-Mannered in Real Life." *Buffalo Evening News*, June 4, 1949.
Guernsey, Otis L. "A Tip to Actors— Be Tough." *New York Herald-Tribune*, June 12, 1949.
"Honor for Widmark." *The Hollywood Reporter*, February 5, 1990.
Hopper, Hedda. "New Pattern Bad Man!" *Chicago Sunday Tribune*, circa 1948.
_____. "Richard Widmark Roles Memorable. *Los Angeles Times*, November 23, 1958.
"Man with the Maniacal Laugh." *San Francisco Chronicle*, September 28, 1947.
"Respectable Villain." *New York Post Home News*, July 25, 1948.
"Richard Widmark." *Limelight*, July 21, 1960.
"Widmark Is an Ex-Professor." *Syracuse Herald-Journal*, July 14, 1948.
Widmark, Richard. "Creating Without Compromise." *Films and Filming*, October 1961.
"Widmark Swims Against H'wood Tide; Blasts Blockbuster Trend." *The Hollywood Reporter*, February 4, 1959.
Williams, Bob. "Widmark Blasts TV Gag on Film's 'Sex' Dialogue." *New York Post*, October 22, 1957.

CORNEL WILDE

"You don't always get the chance in this life to do what you should."— Cornel Wilde
in *Storm Fear* (1956)

Curly-haired with a sensuous gaze, Cornel Wilde starred in such memorable pictures as *A Song to Remember* (1945) and *The Greatest Show on Earth* (1952) during his 50 years on the big screen. But he achieved an even greater measure of success and respect behind the camera, directing and producing numerous films, including the highly acclaimed *The Naked Prey* (1966). As an actor, Wilde was seen in nearly 50 features, offering some of his best performances in features from the noir era: *High Sierra* (1941), *Leave Her to Heaven* (1945), *Road House* (1948), *Shockproof* (1949), *The Big Combo* (1955), and *Storm Fear* (1956).

Cornelius Louis Wilde began his life on October 13, 1915, in New York City — not in Budapest, Hungary, as some sources claim — the younger of two children born to Louis and Renee Wilde. Although more than one colorful account exists regarding Wilde's early life, the most frequently cited version states that his Hungarian-born father, an army officer, worked in New York as an exporter for a European perfume and cosmetics firm. Called back to Hungary to serve in World War I, Louis Wilde took his family with him, returning to New York at the war's end. Attending Townsend Harris High School in New York, the younger Wilde graduated at age 14, but had to postpone his plans for college because his father had fallen ill. The family again returned to Hungary, where Louis received government-funded medical care; during this second stay in Europe, Cornelius Wilde traveled extensively, took up fencing, and became fluent in several languages, including Italian, French, German, and Russian.

When the family relocated to New York in the early 1930s, Wilde enrolled in New York City College as a pre-med student, financing his tuition by working as a toy salesman at Macy's and an advertising salesman for a

French language magazine. Between work and school, Wilde also found time to train for the United States fencing team for the 1936 Olympics and, after finishing his four-year college course in three years, was offered a scholarship to the College of Physicians and Surgeons at Columbia.

Several versions also abound regarding Wilde's next course in life. One account states that after Wilde paid his initiation fee at Columbia, he suddenly decided to spend his summer vacation "trying out stock." Another claims that, prior to enrolling at Columbia, Wilde encountered an old friend who told him about a Broadway play that was seeking to cast a juvenile role and suggested that he try out for the part. According to still another account, the actor had developed a "lure" for the theater and auditioned for Theodora Irvine, of the Irvine Acting Theater. Despite his nervousness during the reading, Wilde was given a scholarship, and chose the acting school instead of Columbia.

The path he took notwithstanding, Wilde abandoned his plans for a medical career, turned down a spot on the U.S. fencing team, and appeared in the mid-1930s in *Moon Over Mulberry*, shortening his first name to Cornel. The play ran for more than 300 performances, and Wilde's portrayal was singled out by the reviewer for *Women's Wear Daily*, who wrote: "The boy played by Wilde is projected stiffly, but the youth, under able direction, should show promise."

During the next few years, Wilde gained experience in several plays, including *Love Is Not Simple* with Ina Claire, *Having Wonderful Time*, *Jeremiah*, *Antony and Cleopatra*, *Pastoral*, and *White Plume*. Also during this period, Wilde met an attractive 17-year-old by the name of Patricia Knight — reportedly, in a booking agency — but he was unable to convince the aspiring actress to agree to a date until he suggested that she test with him for a stage role.

"Much as she disliked me, she couldn't resist that, because she was looking for work," Wilde said. In 1937, Wilde and Knight were married, and in 1943, had a daughter, Wendy.

Adding radio work to his repertoire, Wilde continued to act in a series of unsuccessful plays, but in 1939 he caught the attention of famed actor Laurence Olivier, who was preparing for a Broadway revival of *Romeo and Juliet* with his then-wife, Vivien Leigh. Olivier hired Wilde for dual duty — portraying the character Tybalt, and serving as technical advisor for the play's fencing sequences. The cast traveled to Hollywood for rehearsals, where Olivier was slated to begin work on *Pride and Prejudice* (1940).

"Between rehearsals I chanced to meeting Paramount's casting director Boris Kaplan on the street. He asked what I was doing and I told him," Wilde said in a 1944 interview. "His eyes popped. He suggested a screen test. It was made — but Paramount didn't sign me up. So I got myself an agent, and he took that test to Warner Bros."

Wilde signed with Warners, and after the short-lived run of *Romeo and Juliet* (it closed after just 36 performances), he returned to Hollywood for a bit part in *The Lady With Red Hair* (1940), starring Miriam Hopkins and Claude Rains. In Wilde's second film, *The Perfect Snob* (1941), he moved up to fourth billing when he replaced actor John Shelton, who had fallen ill.

"On one day's notice I got the role," Wilde later recalled. "I even used John Shelton's wardrobe."

Following a minor role in *Knockout* (1941), a boxing drama starring Arthur Kennedy, Wilde was cast in his first film noir, *High Sierra* (1941), an outstanding early example from the era starring Humphrey Bogart as ex-convict Roy "Mad Dog" Earle. After serving an eight-year prison stretch, Earle teams up with his former cronies to rob a California resort hotel, aided by a pair of minor-league hoods, Red (Arthur Kennedy) and Babe (Alan Curtis), and the resort's young

clerk, Louis Mendoza (Wilde). Despite the gang's intricate planning, the heist goes awry, beginning when Earle is forced to shoot a security guard and Mendoza insists on fleeing with the gang ("You've got to take me with you, I couldn't face the police now," Mendoza says. "I never thought you'd have to shoot somebody!") During the getaway, Red and Babe are killed in a fiery car crash and after being captured by police, the jittery Mendoza identifies Earle, resulting in a statewide manhunt. As a crowd of curiosity-seekers gather, Earle is cornered while trying to escape into the High Sierra mountains, and is finally gunned down by police.

Although Wilde's minor role was overlooked by most reviewers, the actor later said the film had a significant impact on his later assignments.

"It was a small part — just about five days' work, and it ruined me," Wilde said. "Whenever a role as a villain came up, they'd say: 'Oh, yes, we could use that heavy in *High Sierra*.' After having been pushed around by Bogart in *High Sierra*, I was slugged and kicked by Dennis Morgan in *Kisses for Breakfast*. The other characters might have gotten kisses for breakfast, but I, as the villain with the moustache, got kicks instead."

After getting "kicked around" in *Kisses for Breakfast*, Wilde received a similar treatment from Warner Bros.— he was unceremoniously dropped from his contract. Years later, the actor said that he would have faced "starvation if my agent hadn't had enough faith in me to keep Pat and myself in groceries." After testing at nearly every studio in Hollywood for the next six months, Wilde was finally signed by 20th Century-Fox and he was promptly cast in the war drama, *Manila Calling* (1942); a comedy-drama with Ida Lupino, *Life Begins at Eight-Thirty* (1942); and a Sonja Henie starrer, *Wintertime* (1943). Unable to serve in World War II because of an earlier back injury, the actor also spent time during this period entertaining servicemen at the famed Hollywood Canteen.

In 1945, Wilde was loaned to Columbia for his first starring role, playing composer

Frederic Chopin in *A Song to Remember*. But the actor admitted that he was not the original choice for the role.

"When the part of Chopin came along, I begged for a test. The powers that be wouldn't consider it," Wilde told columnist Hedda Hopper in 1954. "'You can't play a consumptive musician,' they argued. 'You're too healthy.' For three months they tested practically everybody in town, then let me take a whack at it. I had to make four tests before I convinced them."

Although the actual music in *A Song to Remember* was recorded by renowned musician Jose Iturbi, Wilde practiced the piano for 400 hours over a four-month period to perfect the technique needed to portray Chopin. ("Every moment I wasn't on the set, I was working at the piano," Wilde said.) The film received mixed notices upon release; the reviewer for *Newsweek* wrote that "the film's best performance is that of a comparative newcomer, Cornel Wilde, as the troubled Pole," but in an especially scathing review, critic James Agee called the movie "as infuriating and as funny a misrepresentation of an artist's life and work as I have ever seen." The critics' views of the film notwithstanding, *A Song to Remember* was a box-office hit and earned for Wilde an Academy Award nomination for Best Actor. He lost, however, to Ray Milland in *The Lost Weekend* (1945.)

After Wilde's appearance in *A Song to Remember*, he became what he termed "a classical costume actor," and was instantly cast in another costumer, *A Thousand and One Nights* (1945). This entertaining spoof was followed by Wilde's return to film noir in *Leave Her to Heaven* (1945), co-starring Gene Tierney and Jeanne Crain. Here, Wilde starred as novelist Richard Harland, whose marriage to the beautiful and enticing Ellen Berent (Tierney) nearly becomes his undoing. Jealous of anyone or anything that detracts Richard's attention from her, the psychopathic Ellen allows her husband's invalid brother to drown, causes the miscarriage of her baby, and, unable to hold on to Richard, commits suicide and leaves clues that point

to her sister, Ruth (Jeanne Crain), as her killer. But it is not until Richard takes the stand during Ruth's trial that his wife's true nature comes to light: "Yes, she was that sort of monster," he replies in response to the vehement questioning from the prosecuting attorney (Vincent Price). "A woman who sought to possess everything she loved. Who loved only for what it could bring her. Whose love estranged her own father and mother. Whose love possessed her father until he couldn't call his soul his own. Who, by her own confession to me, killed my brother, killed her own unborn child. And who is now reaching from the grave to destroy her innocent sister. Yes, she was that sort of monster." Although Richard's revelations ultimately lead to Ruth's acquittal for murder, his impassionate speech during the trial results in an ironic twist — because of his failure to report Ellen's role in his brother's death, Richard is sentenced to two years in prison for conspiracy. The film ends on an upbeat note, however, when Richard is released after serving his time to find Ruth waiting for him.

For his role as the luckless spouse, Wilde earned mixed reviews; Lowell Redelings, of the *Hollywood Citizen-News*, wrote that Wilde "comes off nicely," and the critic for *Film Daily* raved that *Leave Her to Heaven* marked his "coming-of-age as an actor." Other critics, however, were not so kind — the reviewer for *Motion Picture Herald* found the actor "too tame" in comparison with the showier performance of Gene Tierney, and in the *New York Herald Tribune*, Howard Barnes sniped, "Cornel Wilde is given the rather hapless assignment of the lunatic lady's poor husband. He plays the role with chin up. The trouble is that he looks just about the same, whether his partially paralyzed brother is allowed to drown or he is fighting a suicide's post-mortem charge in the witness stand." This rather dim view notwithstanding, Wilde in later years named *Leave Her to Heaven* as one of his favorite films.

"Beautiful, good cutting, offbeat characters," he said. "That one I really liked."

Wilde next returned to costume pictures,

starring in *Centennial Summer* (1946), a pleasant musical set in 1876 Philadelphia, and *The Bandit of Sherwood Forest* (1946), in which he played the son of Robin Hood.

"Believe me, I rebelled against some of these pictures," Wilde said in 1960. "I was constantly under suspension for refusing parts. I fought very hard not to do *The Bandit of Sherwood Forest*, but in the end my money ran out."

After a loan-out to Columbia for the critical and financial bomb, *It Had to Be You* (1947), co-starring Ginger Rogers, Wilde landed a starring role in the much-ballyhooed *Forever Amber* (1947), playing opposite Linda Darnell. But this lavish costumer was another box-office disappointment. Although the actor found himself being typecast in period pictures, however, he tried to make the most of the situation by utilizing the "method" technique espoused by famed acting coach Lee Strasberg, with whom Wilde had briefly worked before the start of his film career.

"I became interested in motivations. In one of these costume pictures, I was playing someone described as a likable rogue. It was one of the usual two-dimensional characters, so I decided to find out what he did for a living," Wilde once recalled. "It didn't say in the script.... So I asked the producer. He bellowed, 'What the hell does it matter?'"

The actor was back in yet another costume feature in 1948, re-teamed with his *Amber* star Linda Darnell in *The Walls of Jericho*, but returned to a current-day setting with two films noirs in as many years, *Road House* (1948) and *Shockproof* (1949). In the first, Wilde played Pete Morgan, manager of a road house near the Canadian border who becomes involved in a lethal love triangle involving the club's owner, Jefty Robbins (Richard Widmark) and singer Lily Stevens (Ida Lupino). Despite Jefty's attraction for Lily, she falls for the club's manager, but when the two announce their plans to marry, the unstable Jefty puts in motion a plan of revenge that ends when he is shot and killed by Lily. "I guess it couldn't be helped," Pete says at the film's end. "It was either Jefty or us."

Wilde's next noir, *Shockproof*, marked his only film appearance with his wife, Patricia Knight. Here, the actor portrayed Griff Marat, a parole officer who falls in love with parolee Jenny Marsh (Knight), recently released from prison after a five-year stretch for murder. Torn between her feelings for Griff and her loyalty to her former lover, Harry Wesson (John Baragrey), Jenny accidentally shoots the latter during a scuffle and goes on the lam with Griff. The now-married couple set up house in a remote town and Griff finds a job working on an oil well, but their relationship begins to deteriorate under the strain of their growing paranoia and fear of discovery. Finally, believing that their identities have been discovered by a neighbor, Jenny and Griff agree to turn themselves in, only to learn that Harry Wesson is still alive. In the rather disappointing climax, Wesson is asked by police to identify his shooter, and he states that the shooting was accidental.

Of Wilde's two latest noirs, he earned his best notices for his performance in *Road House*; he was singled out by Fred Hift in *Motion Picture Herald* for "render[ing] able support," and *Variety*'s critic found that he "impresses favorably in a rough-and-tumble he-man role." After returning to the stage in 1949 to star opposite his wife in the Cape Playhouse production of *Western Wind*, Wilde was seen in his first western, *Two Flags West* (1950), co-starring Joseph Cotten, followed by a starring role as an American sailor in *Four Days Leave* (1950), which was filmed in Switzerland. The following year, however, it was Wilde's personal life that took center stage. For several years, Wilde's marriage to Patricia Knight had been a stormy one, characterized by public spats and frequent separations. In August 1951, Knight obtained a Reno divorce, and less than a week later, Wilde married 25-year-old actress Jean Wallace, who had previously been wed to Franchot Tone. The couple later had a son, Cornel Wallace Wilde, and remained together until their divorce in 1981.

Career-wise, Wilde was seen in one of his most popular features in 1952, the big-budget circus epic, *The Greatest Show on Earth*, in which he played a French aerialist known as The Great Sebastian. Years later, Wilde admitted that he was forced to overcome a lifelong fear of heights in order to play the role.

"I had to get up on a 35-foot platform and get the trapeze in motion," Wilde said. "I did have a terrible fear of heights, but that certainly got me over it. I wanted the part desperately."

Also that year, Wilde appeared in an entertaining swashbuckler, *At Sword's Point* (1952), which had been shelved by RKO since its filming two years earlier. Here, Wilde was given an opportunity to demonstrate his fencing prowess, but the actor later recalled that his screen battles often resulted in a variety of injuries.

"Although I had fenced in national and international competitions for many years, the fights I find most dangerous are those involving swords, spears, lances, etc., especially if the combats are on horseback," Wilde said once. "I have been hurt several times in sword fights, generally because my opponent had to learn fencing for the first time in his life and then memorize a difficult routine which had

to be done at considerable speed to look good…. I have been pierced and cut many times on various parts of the body."

When his contract with Fox expired, Wilde signed with Columbia, but was cast during the next two years in such run-of-the-mill features as *California Conquest* (1952), a wildly inaccurate depiction of the territorial struggle between the United States, Mexico, and Russia; *Saadia* (1953), a drama set in Morocco that offered an odd combination of romance, bandit raids, and witchcraft; and *Main Street to Broadway* (1953), a weak romantic comedy highlighted only by cameo appearances of such veteran stars as Tallulah Bankhead, Louis Calhern, and Ethel and Lionel Barrymore (in his last film). The actor fared better, however, in *Woman's World* (1954), a first-rate picture focusing on three business executives vying for the top spot in their company, and *The Big Combo* (1955), his fifth film noir.

In *The Big Combo*, Wilde starred as police detective Leonard Diamond, who is torn between his obsession with a ruthless mobster known as Mr. Brown (Richard Conte), and his love for Brown's weak-willed socialite girlfriend, Susan Lowell (played by Wilde's real-life wife, Jean Wallace). Continually frustrated in his efforts to nab Brown, Diamond's determination increases when a botched attempt on his life results in the death of his sometime lover, Rita (Helene Stanton), and he uses the painful incident to convince Brown's first wife (Helen Walker) to provide damaging information about the mobster: "What about the girl he had killed three days ago?" Diamond asks. "Did she deserve to die, too? Someone he didn't know, never met, never saw. They took 11 bullets from her body. And the following morning Miss Lowell had breakfast with him. He ordered bacon and two eggs. Tell her, Susan. Tell her how he ate his bacon and eggs while he looked at the papers. And saw the body of this girl lying in the morgue." Meanwhile, after first deflecting an attempted coup by his right-hand man (Brian Donlevy), Brown later murders his two henchmen and plans to flee the country with

Susan, but Diamond corners him in an airplane hangar and, with Susan's aid, finally captures his nemesis at the film's end.

Although *The Big Combo* is regarded today as one of film noir's must-see offerings, it earned mixed notices from critics; *Variety*'s reviewer found that the feature depicted "grim melodramatics that are hardhitting despite a rambling, not-too-credible plot," and the critic for the *New York Times*' panned it as "a shrill, clumsy and rather oldfashioned crime melodrama with all hands pulling in opposite directions." The *Times* reviewer expressed similar disdain for Wilde's performance, writing that he "plays his murkily defined role with uncertain vigor, and small wonder." After the release of the film, Wilde formed his own company, Theodora Productions, and announced plans to make a series of films on which he would serve as director.

"It's a good thing for an actor to branch out into producing and directing," Wilde said. "Looks don't last forever and these are the jobs in which look count for nothing. I am now able to express my own artistry at last."

Wilde was given his first opportunity to express his artistry when he directed his final film noir, *Storm Fear* (1956), an underrated feature with such fascinating characters as Charlie (Wilde), a lifelong hood characterized by his callousness toward those who love him and a psychologically engendered stuttering condition; his disapproving, healthchallenged brother Fred (Dan Duryea), Fred's wife, Elizabeth (Jean Wallace), who is Charlie's former lover, and their adolescent son, David (David Stollery); Hank (Dennis Weaver), Fred and Elizabeth's hired man, who is secretly in love with Elizabeth; and two members of Charlie's gang, an amiable B-girl named Edna (outstandingly played by Lee Grant), and Benjie (Steven Hill), a violent sociopath. Set in a remote, snow-covered area in the mountains, the story begins when Edna, Benjie, and Charlie — suffering from a gunshot wound in the leg — arrive at Fred and Elizabeth's home, seeking refuge following a

bank heist. Unbeknownst to the boy, David is actually Charlie's son; capitalizing on David's admiration for him, and even manufacturing a story about the circumstances that led to his life of crime, Charlie convinces the youngster to lead the gang over the treacherous mountains to the state highway on the other side. During the trek, Edna is left for dead when Benjie pushes her over a ridge; David shoots Benjie when the hood takes the cache of money and brutally beats Charlie; and Charlie is mortally wounded by Hank, who has been stalking the trio. In the film's final scene, Charlie admits to David that he is "no good ... just a bum," but begs his son with his last breath to never forget him. After the film's release, the critic for the *New York Times* complained that Wilde "should have been a nice guy and ... doesn't come across as a heel," but the feature marked a first-rate directorial debut for the actor and his portrayal of Charlie remains one of his most memorable.

During the next two decades, Wilde produced, directed, and starred in numerous films, including an auto racing drama, *The Devil's Hairpin* (1957), which he also co-wrote; *Maracaibo* (1958), which balanced a romantic plot with an action story about a raging oil well fire; *Sword of Lancelot* (1963), a portrait of the love story of Sir Lancelot and Queen Guinivere; *The Naked Prey* (1966), a harrowing adventure tale of a white hunter pursued through the jungle by African natives; *Beach Red* (1967), a wartime saga costarring Rip Torn; *No Blade of Grass* (1967), a futuristic story of a world consumed by famine; and a deep sea adventure, *Shark's Treasure* (1975), which was also written by Wilde. In several of the features (excepting *The Naked Prey*, *Beach Red*, and *Shark's Treasure*), Wilde's wife, Jean, served as co-star, and *No Blade of Grass* was the sole Wilde production in which the actor did not appear.

One of the most prolific stars-turnedproducer in Hollywood, Wilde enjoyed financial success with several of his features, and *The Naked Prey* earned particular praise, hailed as "an artistic achievement" in *Variety*, and "one of the most exciting chase movies" by reviewer Judith Crist. Wilde's war drama, *Beach Red*, was also well-received, with Howard Thompson of the *New York Times* terming it a "nimbly piloted ... graphic, unflinching and honest drama of men in combat."

Between focusing on his own films, Wilde managed to find time to make rare appearances in other feature productions, including the title role in *Omar Khayyam* (1957); a cameo role in the Dick Van Dyke starrer, *The Comic* (1969); a Viking warrior in *The Norseman* (1978); and D'Artagnan in *The Fifth Musketeer* (1979). Beginning in the 1950s, he was also seen in guest spots on such television series as *I Love Lucy*, *General Electric Theater*, *Kraft Suspense Theater*, *Night Gallery*, and *Murder, She Wrote*, and an odd made-for-television movie, *The Gargoyles* (1972).

In the late 1980s, Wilde was diagnosed with leukemia. Three days after his 74th birthday, on October 16, 1989, he died in Cedars-Sinai Medical Center in Los Angeles. Enterprising and hard-working to the end, at the time of his death he was planning a sequel to his acclaimed film *The Naked Prey*, and working on his autobiography.

While Cornel Wilde gained fame in front of the camera, it was his work behind the scenes that provides him with his greatest legacy. Numerous actors formed their own production companies during the 1950s and 1960s, but many never made a single film. Wilde not only produced, directed, and starred in eight features, but managed to make money on several, and certainly earned acclaim and respect for his vision. Late in his life, Wilde appropriately summed up his life and his motivation:

"I realized long ago that I could not depend on luck to bring me success," the actor said. "I worked hard, extra hard to improve my chances by increasing my abilities and my experience. It was my goal to accomplish, in my life, something of value and to do it with self-respect and integrity."

Film Noir Filmography

High Sierra. Director: Raoul Walsh. Producer: Hal B. Wallis. Running time: 100 minutes. Released by Warner Bros., January 4, 1941. Cast: Humphrey Bogart, Ida Lupino, Alan Curtis, Arthur Kennedy, Joan Leslie, Henry Hull, Barton MacLane, Henry Travers, Elisabeth Risdon, Cornel Wilde, Minna Gombell, Paul Harvey, Donald MacBride, Jerome Cowan, John Eldredge, Isabel Jewell, Willie Best, Arthur Aylsworth, Robert Strange, Wade Boteler, Sam Hayes.

Leave Her to Heaven. Director: John M. Stahl. Producer: William A. Bacher. Running time: 110 minutes. Released by 20th Century-Fox, December 25, 1945. Cast: Gene Tierney, Cornel Wilde, Jeanne Crain, Vincent Price, Mary Phillips, Ray Collins, Gene Lockhart, Reed Hadley, Darryl Hickman, Chill Wills, Paul Everton, Olive Blakeney, Addison Richards, Harry Depp, Grant Mitchell, Milton Parsons. Awards: Academy Award for Best Color Cinematography (Leon Shamroy). Academy Award nominations for Best Actress (Gene Tierney), Best Sound Recording (Thomas T. Moulton), Best Interior Decoration/Color (Lyle Wheeler, Maurice Ransford, Thomas Little).

Road House. Director: Jean Negulesco. Producer: Edward Chodorov. Running time: 95 minutes. Released by 20th Century-Fox, November 7, 1948. Cast: Ida Lupino, Cornel Wilde, Celeste Holm, Richard Widmark, O.Z. Whitehead, Robert Karnes, George Beranger, Ian MacDonald, Grandon Rhodes, Jack G. Lee.

Shockproof. Director: Director: Douglas Sirk. Producer: S. Sylvan Simon and Helen Deutsch. Running time: 79 minutes. Released by Columbia, 1949. Cast: Cornel Wilde, Patricia Knight, John Beragrey, Esther Miniciotti, Howard St. John, Russell Collins, Charles Bates.

The Big Combo. Director: Joseph Lewis. Producer: Sidney Harmon. Running time: 89 minutes. Released by Allied Artists, February 13, 1955. Cast: Cornel Wilde, Richard Conte, Brian Donlevy, Jean Wallace, Robert Middleton, Lee Van Cleef, Earl Holliman, Helen Walker, Jay Adler, John Hoyt, Ted De Corsia, Helen Stanton, Roy Gordon, Whit Bissell, Steve Mitchell, Baynes Barron, James McCallion, Tony Michaels, Brian O'Hara, Rita Gould, Bruce Sharpe, Michael Mark, Philip Van Zandt, Donna Drew.

Storm Fear. Director and Producer: Cornel Wilde. Running time: 88 minutes. Released by United Artists, February 1, 1956. Cast: Cornel Wilde, Jean Wallace, Dan Duryea, Lee Grant, David Stollery, Dennis Weaver, Steven Hill, Keith Britton.

References

Ankerich, Michael G. "Cornel Wilde; His Painful Lessons on Survival." *Classic Images*, January 1989.

Bahrenburg, Bruce. "Star Rediscovered." *New York Times*, circa 1967.

Cassa, Anthony. "The Cornel Wilde Story." *Hollywood Studio Magazine*, June 1980.

"Cornel Wilde at MGM: Will Produce-Direct 'Blade of Grass' Novel." *Variety*, November 5, 1969.

"Cornel Wilde Producing." *Variety*, December 17, 1958.

"Cornel Wildes Are Divorced." *New York Times*, August 31, 1951.

"Cornel Wilde, 74, Athletic Actor, Director, Producer." *Chicago Sun-Times*, October 17, 1989.

"Cornel Wilde Weds Jean Wallace." *New York Times*, September 5, 1951.

"4 New Members at Newport Casino." *New York Journal American*, July 17, 1938.

Flint, Peter B. "Cornel Wilde, 74, a Performer and Film Producer." *New York Times*, October 17, 1989.

Garrett, Gerard. "The Costume Cavalier Gets Up to Date." *The Evening Standard*, July 1, 1960.

Gebhart, Myrtle. "She Has a Boston Accent." *Boston Post Magazine*, June 6, 1948.

"Good-Will Man." *Newark Evening News*, January 3, 1965.

Graham, Sheilah. "Cornel's Wild Adventure." *New York World-Telegram and Sun*, June 12, 1965.

Hale, Wanda. "Actor Produces Film, and Dream Comes True." *New York Daily News*, August 18, 1963.

"Honeymoon for Wildes." *New York Morning Telegram*, September 6, 1951.

Hopper, Hedda. "That Wilde Man." *Chicago Tribune Magazine*, September 19, 1954.

Mosby, Aline. "Confesses He Was Slipping." *New York Morning Telegram*, January 29, 1952.

Kaminsky, Stuart .M. "Interview: Cornel Wilde." *Film Reader*, January 1977.

Scott, Vernon. "Cornel Wilde Film Maverick." *New Jersey Record*, April 15, 1975.

Sterritt, David. "Treasure-Hunting Star." *The Christian Science Monitor*, October 1, 1975.

Thirer, Irene. "Cornel Wilde Practiced the Piano 400 Hours, Till His Hands Bled, to Get the Role of Chopin." *New York Post*, September 9, 1944.

_____. "Wilde's 'Lancelot' Set for Palace." *New York Post*, September 8, 1963.

"Wilde and Wife to Star in Own Independent Film." *New York Herald Tribune*, January 18, 1955.

"Wilde Doings." *New York Times*, December 24, 1972.

"Wilde Night on Via Veneto: Actor in Nightclub Scuffle." *New York Post*, September 26, 1960.

Appendix A:
FREQUENTLY NOIR, BRIEFLY SEEN

Many of the actors in the film noir era of the 1940s and 1950s were "repeat performers," but seldom received prominent billing and often were not credited at all. Still, these obscure actors served an integral role in the dark features of this realm. Frequently serving as nameless policemen or hoods, they crop up in these films again and again, providing a valuable backdrop to the nefarious goings-on at the forefront of the silver screen.

This section of *Bad Boys* focuses those actors who are frequent noir contributors, but were usually only briefly seen on screen — each appeared in at least seven films noirs, but seldom, if ever, earned higher than seventh billing. There are exceptions; some of the actors had one or more featured roles in their repertoire of noir films, but they primarily served a secondary function, complementing the landscape that comprises film noir.

JAY ADLER

A member of the noted Adler theatrical family, Jay Adler was born in New York on September 26, 1896, one of seven children of Jacob Adler, a celebrated star of the Yiddish theater, and his actress-wife, Sara. Like his siblings, Stella, a noted acting coach, and Luther, an actor of stage, screen, and television, Jay Adler was drawn to the theater from an early age. After appearing in both Yiddish and English language productions, including

such Broadway shows as *Golden Boy* and *Blind Alley*, Adler made his film debut in *The Saint in New York* (1938), the first entry in the popular, long-running series. Over the next three decades, he appeared in nearly 40 films; the most successful included *The Prisoner of Zenda* (1952), starring Stewart Granger; *Love Me or Leave* Me (1955), a James Cagney-Doris Day vehicle; and *Lust for Life* (1956), featuring Kirk Douglas as famed painter Vincent Van Gogh.

Wait (1954), *Murder is My Beat* (1955), *The Big Combo* (1955), *Crime of Passion* (1957), and *Sweet Smell of Success* (1957). Although most of his parts in these films were minor ones — including portrayals of a bellboy, hotel desk clerk, and bartender — Adler enjoyed his most significant role in *99 River Street*, in which he portrayed Christopher, an unscrupulous jewel fence.

In the late 1940s, Adler expanded his performing repertoire to include the medium of television, and was seen during the next 10 years in such series as *Your Show Time*; *Richard Diamond, Private Detective*; *Mr. Lucky*; *The Untouchables*; *Wanted: Dead or Alive*; *The Twilight Zone*; *The Fugitive*; and *Perry Mason*.

Adler's last screen appearance was in *Macon County Line* (1974), produced by and starring Max Baer, Jr. (best known for his role as Jethro in *The Beverly Hillbillies*). In failing health for several years, he died at the age of 82 on September 23, 1978, at the Motion Picture and Television Hospital in Woodland Hills, California. He was survived by Luther and Stella, two other sisters, and his daughter, Pearl McCord.

"It was natural for all of us to gravitate toward the stage when we grew up," Adler said in a 1940 interview. "We were brought up in the midst of great acting ... we all had great pride in mother and dad, and I think each of us had a secret hope that we would be as great as they — but none of us, in my opinion, has made that grade."

Adler was also seen in some of film noir's finest offerings: *Cry Danger* (1951), *The Mob* (1951), *Scandal Sheet* (1952), *The Turning Point* (1952), *99 River Street* (1953), *The Long*

References

"Name of Adler Rarely Misses Broadway Cast." *New York Herald Tribune*, November 24, 1940.
Obituary. *The Hollywood Reporter*, September 26, 1978.
Obituary. *Variety*, September 26, 1978.

MORRIS ANKRUM

Morris Ankrum was born on August 28, 1896, in Danville, Illinois, one of two children of Horace and Caroline Ankrum. As a youth, Ankrum was bitten by the acting bug when he attended his first play, *Wildfire*, at Chicago's Great Northern Theater. (Coincidentally, Ankrum would make his professional stage debut in the same theater, years later,

in *The Green Goddess*, starring George Arliss.)

Moving with his family to California as a child, Ankrum attended Berendo Elementary School and Los Angeles High School. After graduating from the University of California at Berkeley with a degree in law, Ankrum passed the California Bar examination, and later became an associate professor in economics at the University of California at Los Angeles. Also during this period, he started a little theater group in Berkeley and worked as a teacher and director at the famed Pasadena Playhouse. Following his acting bow with George Arliss in the mid-1920s, Ankrum went on to make numerous stage appearances during the next decade, including roles in *Ghosts*, starring Minnie Fiske; *Gods of the Lightning*, with Sylvia Sidney; and *Within the Gates*, starring Lillian Gish. He also portrayed King Henry IV in Orson Welles' Mercury Theater production of *The Five Kings* in 1939.

By now, Ankrum had expanded his performing repertoire to include films; after bit parts in *Reunion in Vienna* (1933) and *Stand Up and Cheer!* (1934), he was billed as Stephen Morris in several episodes of Paramount's Hopalong Cassidy series, including *Hopalong Cassidy Returns* (1936), *Trail Dust* (1936), *Hills of Old Wyoming* (1937), and *North of the Rio Grande* (1937).

"Coming to Hollywood, it was a year of Westerns and only Westerns," Ankrum once remarked.

Off screen during the latter part of the decade, Ankrum returned to Hollywood in 1940, broadening his cinematic horizons in a wide variety of films, including such hits as *Tales of Manhattan* (1942), featuring Edward G. Robinson and Rita Hayworth; *The Human Comedy* (1943), which Ankrum once cited as his favorite picture; *Thirty Seconds Over Tokyo* (1944), an all-star war epic; *See Here, Private Hargrove* (1944), with Robert Walker in the title role; and *The Harvey Girls* (1946), a tuneful Judy Garland starrer.

In addition to these features, Ankrum was also seen in a total of eight film noir features, beginning with a role as an assistant district attorney in an early noir entry, *I Wake Up Screaming* (1942). He was also seen in *The Postman Always Rings Twice* (1946), *Undercurrent* (1946), *Lady in the Lake* (1947), *The High Wall* (1947), *The Damned Don't Cry* (1950), *In a Lonely Place* (1950), and *Southside 1-1000* (1950). Ankrum's best film noir role

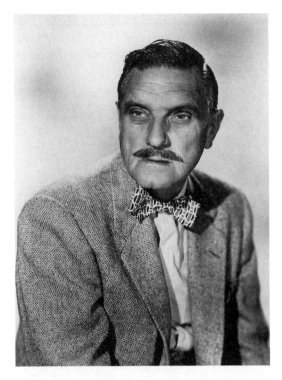

came in the latter production, in which he was fifth-billed as a ailing, aging convict who uses his ever-present Bible as a vessel for smuggling counterfeiting plates to a phony priest.

When his film noir phase ended, Ankrum could most often be found in such science fiction features as *Rocketship X-M* (1950), *Flight to Mars* (1951), *Invaders from Mars* (1953), and *Earth vs. the Flying Saucers* (1956), or westerns including *Cattle Queen of Montana* (1954), where he played the father of Barbara Stanwyck; *Walk the Proud Land* (1956), in which he depicted one of the numerous generals of his career; and *Frontier Gun* (1958), starring John Agar and Joyce Meadows. During this period, Ankrum also guested on countless television series, mostly westerns including *Cheyenne, Maverick, The Rifleman, Death Valley Days, Rawhide,* and *Bronco*, and in a rare non-western program, he portrayed the recurring role of a judge on the *Perry Mason* series.

In late August 1964, Ankrum fell ill with an acute case of trichinosis; a week later, on September 2, 1964, he died at Huntington

Hospital in Pasadena, California. The 68-year-old actor was survived by his wife of more than 30 years, Joan Wheeler, and his two children, David and Carrie.

References

Biographical Information. Metro Goldwyn Mayer Pictures, circa 1943.

Obituary. *The Hollywood Reporter*, September 3, 1964.

Obituary. *Variety*, September 3, 1964.

DON BEDDOE

Don Beddoe was a marvel. During a performing career that spanned seven decades, Beddoe appeared in a total of nearly 200 films; in one year alone, the actor was seen in a whopping 27 features. Among these features were 12 examples from the film noir period, where Beddoe depicted everything from a mild-mannered thief to an ill-fated police detective.

Although it is known that Donald T. Beddoe was born in Pittsburgh, Pennsylvania, on July 1st, the exact year of his birth is a bit of a mystery. Some sources say that the actor was born as early as 1888, while others put his year of birth at 1903. This discrepancy notwithstanding, Beddoe — son of a prominent oratorio tenor by the same name — spent a number of his early years in London and later attended the University of Cincinnati.

Beddoe taught for a time on the faculty of his alma mater, and reportedly was interested in pursuing a career in journalism, but he was also drawn to the theater and joined Stuart Walker's stock company in Indianapolis ("I knew from the very outset that I'd never get a part or hold an audience with my looks, so I learned to act," Beddoe said once). In 1929, the actor made his Broadway debut in *Nigger Rich*, joining a cast that included Spencer Tracy, and later was seen in such productions as *Penny Arcade* (1930), which served to launch James Cagney's screen career; *Man Bites Dog* (1933), with Dennie Moore and Victor Killian; *The Blue Widow* (1933), featuring Queenie Smith; and *Nowhere Bound* (1935) with Fred Kaufman. Although most of his plays were flops, Beddoe hit the jackpot with *The Greeks Had a Word for It* (1930), a comedy that ran for more than 250 performances. According to several sources, Beddoe also appeared in a number of silent films (and "didn't like them"), but no evidence of specific features is available.

Aside from his possible silent features, Beddoe was first seen on the big screen in the late 1930s, when he played small parts in such films as *The 13th Man* (1937), a 'B' mystery; *My Son Is Guilty* (1939), a programmer starring Bruce Cabot; and *Golden Boy* (1939), starring William Holden in the title role of the violinist-turned-boxer. Signing a contract with Columbia, he was also seen in several entries in the studio's *Lone Wolf* and *Blondie* series before leaving Hollywood to serve in the Army Air Corps during World War II.

Back on screen, most of Beddoe's features consisted of programmers and low-budget quickies, but he was seen in a number of well-received films including *Winged Victory* (1944), based on the smash-hit Moss Hart play; *O.S.S.* (1946), starring Alan Ladd; *The Best Years of Our Lives* (1946), the award-winning post–WWII drama; *The Farmer's Daughter* (1947), with Loretta Young in the title role; *Cyrano De Bergerac* (1950), starring Jose Ferrer; *Carrie* (1952), starring Jennifer Jones in the title role; *The Big Sky* (1952), a Howard Hawks–directed western; *River of No Return* (1954), with Robert Mitchum and Marilyn Monroe; *Night of the Hunter* (1955), again starring Mitchum, this time as a murderous preacher; *The Joker Is Wild* (1957), featuring Frank Sinatra as 1920s entertainer Joe E. Lewis; *Pillow Talk* (1959), a witty sex comedy with Doris Day and Rock Hudson; and *Papa's Delicate Condition* (1963), starring Jackie Gleason and based on the book by former silent film star Corinne Griffith.

Alongside these features were Beddoe's film noir offerings, beginning with *Calcutta* and *They Won't Believe Me* in 1947. After these, he was seen in *Gun Crazy* (1950), *Southside 1-1000* (1950), *Caged* (1950), *The Enforcer* (1951), *The Unknown Man* (1951), *The Racket* (1951), *Scandal Sheet* (1952), *Don't Bother to Knock* (1952), *The Narrow Margin* (1952), and *Loophole* (1954). Beddoe played his most memorable noir roles in the latter two; in *The Narrow Margin*, he was Gus Forbes, a

detective who is gunned down by hoods while escorting a government witness from her home, and in *Loophole* he portrayed Herman Tate, an unassuming teller who steals nearly $50,000 from a bank, allowing another employee (Barry Sullivan) to take the rap.

In addition to his prolific film career, Beddoe was seen in numerous guest spots on the small screen; from the early 1950s to the early 1980s, the actor appeared on some of television's most popular shows, including *The Lone Ranger, Death Valley Days, Perry Mason, Maverick, Zorro, Alfred Hitchcock Presents, Bonanza, Petticoat Junction, Gunsmoke, Bewitched, Mayberry R.F.D., Mannix, Maude,* and *Little House on the Prairie.* He was also a regular on the short-lived television series *The Second Hundred Years* (1966-67), starring Arthur O'Connell, and played Constable Warren in the 1977 television production of *Our Town*, with Hal Holbrook, Ronny Cox, and Robby Benson. During his later years, he supplemented his income from acting by developing a second career in real estate.

Beddoe's last screen appearance was in the 1985 feature *Nickel Mountain*, in which he played a rural doctor. Six years after this role, the twice-married actor died in Laguna Hills, California. Depending on which source is to be believed, he was anywhere from 88 to 102 years old at the time of his death.

References

"Beddoe in 'Three for Tonight.'" *New York Times,* October 14, 1954.
"Father Malachy's Miracle." *Playbill,* November 17, 1957.
"Juvenile Scores in Carnival Play on St. James Bill." *Boston Advertiser,* October 10, 1928.
"Married Here Monday." *New York Sentinel,* May 9, 1944.
Obituary. *The Big Reel,* September 1991.

WHIT BISSELL

Whitner Notting Bissell was born on October 25, 1909, in New York City. One of his earliest acting experiences came while he was a student at the University of North Carolina at Chapel Hill, where he performed with the school's Carolina Playmakers, which presented plays both on campus and throughout the country. In addition to Bissell, the group's alumni included such future film notables as Louise Fletcher and Andy Griffith.

As a young man, Bissell debuted on Broadway in 1943 in *Holy Matrimony*, which was followed by a variety of well-received productions, including *Hamlet*, starring John Gielgud in the title role; *The Star-Wagon*, with Burgess Meredith and Lillian Gish; *Room Service*, produced by George Abbott; *Two on an Island* with Luther Adler and Betty Field; and *Café Crown*, directed by Elia Kazan. He made his film debut in 1943, with a bit part in *Destination Tokyo*, a popular wartime film starring Cary Grant and John Garfield. He went on to appear in nearly 100 films, including such box-office hits as *Riot in Cell Block 11* (1954), *The Caine Mutiny* (1954), *The Desperate Hours* (1955), *Gunfight at the O.K. Corral* (1957), *The Defiant Ones* (1958), *The Time Machine* (1960), *The Magnificent Seven* (1960), *Birdman of Alcatraz* (1962), *Hud* (1963), *Airport* (1970), *Pete 'n Tillie* (1972), and *Soylent Green* (1973). Bissell also developed a cult following after his appearances in a series of horror movies, including *The Creature from the Black Lagoon* (1954), *I Was a Teenage Werewolf* (1957), and *I Was a Teenage Frankenstein* (1957); as well as his role as a military officer on the short-lived but wildly popular science fiction television series, *The Time Tunnel*. For his contributions to these productions, Bissell received the Life Career Award from the Academy of Science Fiction, Fantasy, and Horror Films in 1994.

In addition to his recurring role on *The Time Tunnel*, Bissell was seen in guest spots on television programs covering all genres, from westerns to science fiction, and comedy to drama. Among other series, he appeared on *You Are There*, *Science Fiction Theater*, *The Californians*, *The Rifleman*, *The Untouchables*, *Perry Mason*, *Wagon Train*, *The Outer Limits*, *The Fugitive*, *Petticoat Junction*, *Star Trek*, *I Dream of Jeannie*, *Here's Lucy*, *Cannon*, *Harry O*, *Quincy*, *The Bionic Woman*, *The Incredible Hulk*, and *The Dukes of Hazzard*. His final television appearance was a reprisal of his role as *The Time Tunnel*'s Lt. General Heywood Kirk in *Aliens from Another Planet* (1982).

Slight of build, with fine features and a mild manner, Whit Bissell does not immediately come to mind when conjuring images of film noir performers. Yet, Bissell was featured in nearly a dozen of the films noirs of the 1940s and 1950s: *Somewhere in the Night* (1946), *Brute Force* (1947), *A Double Life* (1947), *Canon City* (1948), *Raw Deal* (1948),

He Walked by Night (1948), *The Killer That Stalked New York* (1950), *Convicted* (1950), *Side Street* (1950), *The Turning Point* (1952), and *The Big Combo* (1955), Of these, Bissell made his biggest impact in *Brute Force*, where he was seen as a bespectacled prison inmate who hangs himself after learning that his wife has divorced him, and *Canon City*, in which he played an edgy escaped convict.

On March 5, 1996, at the age of 1986, Bissell died at the Motion Picture and Television Fund Hospital in Woodland Hills, California. The actor had suffered from Parkinson's Disease and been confined to a wheelchair for several years. He was survived by four children from three marriages—a son, Brian, and three daughters, Kathy, Victoria, and Amanda.

"It was a good life," Bissell said in a 1996 interview with the *Los Angeles Times*. "The challenge of breathing something special into every role you played. For an actor, just being at work made you feel alive."

References

Biography of Whit Bissell. Twentieth Century-Fox Studio, November 29, 1945.

Jankiewicz, Pat. "The Wit and Wisdom of Whit Bissell." *Filmfax*, September 1990.

Mott, Patrick. "Bissell Blasts Hogan Support From Weaver." *The Hollywood Reporter*, October 8, 1975.

"Mrs. Bissell's Services Held Here Yesterday." *Beverly Hills Citizen*, January 14, 1958.

Obituary. *Los Angeles Times*, March 8, 1996.

Obituary. *New York Times*, March 11, 1996.

Obituary. *Variety*, March 7, 1996.

Oliver, Myrna. "Whit Bissell; Movie, TV Character Actor." *Los Angeles Times*, March 7, 1996.

"Whit Bissell Denied SAG Panel's Backing; Nine Petitions OK'd." *Variety*, September 8, 1977.

PETER BROCCO

Peter Brocco was born on January 16, 1903, in Reading, Pennsylvania, and first performed on the stage at age 11, when he played the Fool in a local production of *King Lear*. He later worked in community theater in Reading, and although he studied theology at Tufts College in Massachusetts, he focused his efforts on a theatrical career after his graduation.

Heading for New York, Brocco quickly found work on the Broadway stage — his first appearance was as a corpse in *Peter Ibbetson*, starring Basil Rathbone and Violet Cooper. His subsequent roles in New York were more substantive, however, and he was seen with famed stage actor Walter Hampden in *Cyrano DeBergerac*, as well as *Hamlet*, *Immortal Thief*, *Henry V*, and *An Enemy of the People*. During the Depression, Brocco worked with the Federal Theatre Project in New York, making ends meet by taking on such jobs as dishwasher, gardener, and handyman.

Brocco made his screen debut in 1932,

playing a wireless operator in *The Devil and the Deep*, a deep sea drama starring Tallulah

Bankhead, Charles Laughton, and Gary Cooper. He didn't appear on screen again until the 1947 feature *Lone Wolf in Mexico*, one of a 19-episode series about a crime-solving jewel thief. With a film career that ultimately spanned seven decades, Brocco's best-known films included *The Great Caruso* (1951), *The Prisoner of Zenda* (1952), *I'll Cry Tomorrow* (1955), *Spartacus* (1960), *Elmer Gantry* (1960), and *One Flew Over the Cuckoo's Nest* (1975). His last screen appearance was in 1991, in the Danny DeVito starrer *Other People's Money*.

The actor's 80-plus films included a total of 10 films noirs: *The Reckless Moment* (1949), *The Undercover Man* (1949), *Tension* (1949), *The Breaking Point* (1950), *The Killer That Stalked New York* (1950), *His Kind of Woman* (1951), *Roadblock* (1951), *The Narrow Margin* (1952), and *Rogue Cop* (1954). In most of these, Brocco played such bit parts as the "Bank Heist Man" in *Roadblock* or the "Technician" in *Tension*. He played his most significant role in the first-rate feature, *The Narrow Margin*, portraying Vincent Yost, a steely but refined hood who attempts to bribe a detective into handing over the witness he is escorting across the country. He also turned in a memorable performance as the self-confident murderer, Wrinkles Fallon, in *Rogue Cop*.

From the early 1950s through the 1980s, the distinguished actor was a frequent guest on some of the most popular series on the small screen, including *The Adventures of Superman*, *I Love Lucy*, *Perry Mason*, *The Twilight Zone*, *The Outer Limits*, *The Dick Van Dyke Show*, *I Dream of Jeannie*, *Lost in Space*, *The Man from U.N.C.L.E.*, *Bewitched*, *The Big Valley*, *Mission Impossible*, *Star Trek*, *Happy Days*, *The Rockford Files*, *Hill Street Blues*, and *St. Elsewhere*.

In the mid-1970s, the actor developed a debilitating eye condition known as macular deterioration, which left him partially blind, but he continued to appear in both television and feature films until shortly before his death from a heart attack on December 27, 1992.

References

Baker, Elizabeth Wirt. "First Person: Peter Brocco." *California Living*, September 25, 1983.
Biography of Peter Brocco. Avco Embassy Pictures, 1974.
Biography of Peter Brocco. Jay Bernstein Public Relations, circa 1975.
Biography of Peter Brocco. *Performing Arts*, Summer 1973.
Biography of Peter Brocco. Warner Bros. Studios, circa 1983.
Obituary. *The Hollywood Reporter*, January 7, 1993.
Obituary. *Variety*, January 4, 1993.
"Peter Brocco; Veteran Performer in Movies, Theater, Television." *Los Angeles Times*, January 1, 1993.

——— CHARLES CANE ———

A stage veteran with roots in vaudeville and burlesque, Charles Cane appeared in small roles in nearly 70 films, including 12 from the noir era: *The Dark Corner* (1946), *Dead Reckoning* (1947), *Framed* (1947), *The Dark Past* (1948), *In a Lonely Place* (1950), *Southside 1-1000* (1950), *Convicted* (1950), *Scandal Sheet* (1952), *Kansas City Confidential* (1952), *The Big Heat* (1953), *Crime Wave* (1954), and *The Killing* (1956). In most, Cane was unbilled, and in all but two, he was seen as an officer of the law. He was singled out for his performance in *Dead Reckoning*, however; in *The Hollywood Reporter*, Jack D. Grant wrote, "Charles Cane is excellent as a police lieutenant."

Cane was born on April 18, 1899 (some sources say 1905), in Springfield, Missouri, the son of Charles Cannefax, a salesman, and his wife, Martha. After attending Clark Elementary School and Soldan High School in St. Louis, Cane enlisted in the Army, but injured his spine and spent two years in a plaster cast. During his lengthy convalescence, Cane studied singing and later enrolled in New York's Damrosch School of Music.

After debuting on stage as a chorus boy in *Bunch and Judy*, starring Fred Astaire, Cane went on to play the baritone lead in the Shuberts' production of *Artists and Models*, then formed his own vaudeville act, a comedy routine billed as Deagon and Cannefax, which toured the United States and England for eight years. Later, he landed a role in the road company of the Theatre Guild's production of *The Time of Your Life*, featuring William Bendix; during the show's two-week run in Los Angeles, Cane decided to try his hand on the silver screen and debuted in a bit part in *Sucker List* (1941), an entry in MGM's *Crime Does Not Pay* short subject series. During the next two decades, he was seen in such films as *The Big Street* (1942), featuring Lucille Ball and Henry Fonda; *Mr. Lucky* (1943), starring Cary Grant; *Mrs. Parkington* (1944), with Greer Garson in the title role; *Born Yesterday* (1950), a first-rate vehicle for Judy Holliday; and *Marty* (1955), which earned an Academy Award for Ernest Borgnine.

In the early 1960s, Cane abandoned his acting career; his final screen performances were in a series of westerns: *A Day of Fury* (1956), an offbeat oater starring Dale Robertson as an aging gunfighter; *Gun Battle at Monterey* (1957), a box-office flop despite a cast headed by Sterling Hayden, Ted De Corsia, and Lee Van Cleef; and *The Gambler Wore a*

Gun (1961), a remake of *The Lone Gun* (1954). Off screen for more than a decade, Cane suffered a stroke in 1973 and died at the Motion Picture Television Country Home and Hospital in Woodland Hills, California, on November 30, 1973. He was 76 years old.

References

Biography of Charles Cane. Offices of Samuel Goldwyn, circa 1946.
"Charles Cane's Rites Saturday." *Los Angeles Herald*, December 7, 1973.
Obituary. Variety, December 3, 1973.

ANTHONY CARUSO

Dark, brawny, and ominous, Anthony Caruso could always be counted on to add a touch of menace to the screen. Born on April 7, 1916, in Frankfort, Indiana, Caruso moved as a child with his family to Long Beach, California, and began his acting career while still in high school, where he was a standout in school productions. His acting ability earned the young man a scholarship to the prestigious Pasadena Playhouse, but Caruso opted instead to hone his craft with a local stock company, the Hart Players. He performed in 104 productions over a two-year period with the company, then accepted the Pasadena

most substantial — film noir role came in the noir classic, *The Asphalt Jungle*, where his prowess as a safecracker provided a sharp contrast to his proud pronouncements concerning his infant daughter. He was also a standout as the sadistic henchman of an exiled mobster in *His Kind of Woman*, where he administered a beating with a brass belt buckle to the bare-backed Robert Mitchum.

With appearances in nearly 100 films during his screen career, Caruso was seen in such top-notch offerings as *Watch on the Rhine* (1943), *The Story of Dr. Wassell* (1944), and *Pride of the Marines* (1945), in which he played a rare sympathetic role. In addition to his frequent casting as a hood, Caruso also often portrayed characters of ethnic origin — his many characters included Nat Cucci in *Sunday Punch* (1942), Jose Santos in *Star in the Night* (1945), Miggleori in *Objective, Burma!* (1945), Pinky Luiz in *Don't Gamble with Strangers* (1946), Lieutenant Massaoud in *Desert Legion* (1953), Chavez in *Fort Algiers* (1953), Marcus Vizzini in *Joe Dakota* (1957), Santiago Santos in *The Wonderful Country* (1959), Rocco in *Young Dillinger* (1965), Don Da Vinci in *Meet Johnny Barrows* (1976), and Don Carlos in *The Legend of Grizzly Adams* (1990), his final big screen role.

Playhouse scholarship, and was instrumental in launching the first Pasadena Playhouse Shakespearian Summer Festival.

After his tenure with the Pasadena Playhouse, Caruso joined the Federal Theatre Project, in New York, a component of President Franklin D. Roosevelt's Works Progress Administration (WPA). With the Federal Theatre, Caruso was seen in a variety of productions, including *Judgment Day, Loyalties, Having Wonderful Time, Blind Alley*, and *Winterset*. Funding for the Federal Theatre Project was discontinued in 1939, but Caruso had been spotted by talent scouts from 20th Century-Fox, who cast him in a small role as a mobster in his film debut, *Johnny Apollo* (1940).

The role of the heavy was one that would stand Caruso in good stead throughout his career, particularly in the realm of film noir. The actor appeared in seven films from the era: *The Blue Dahlia* (1946), *They Won't Believe Me* (1947), *The Undercover Man* (1949), *Scene of the Crime* (1949), *The Asphalt Jungle* (1950), *His Kind of Woman* (1951), and *Baby Face Nelson* (1957). Caruso's finest — and

Caruso also enjoyed a prolific television career. Beginning in the early 1950s and for nearly three decades, he was seen in hundreds of television series, including *The Adventures of Superman, The Lone Ranger, Zorro, Death Valley Days, Maverick, Gunsmoke, Perry Mason, Rawhide, The Untouchables, The Addams Family, The Wild Wild West, Gomer Pyle U.S.M.C., Green Acres, It Takes a Thief, The F.B.I., Mission: Impossible, Ironside, The Streets of San Francisco*, and *The Incredible Hulk*.

Frequently praised as a "devoted family man," Caruso married stage actress and singer Tonia Valenti in 1942, and went on to have two children, Antonio and Valentina. After a lengthy illness, the actor died on April 4, 2003, at his Brentwood, California, home. His death came just days before his 87th birthday.

References

"Anthony Caruso: One of Hollywood's Busiest Character Actors." *The Hollywood Diary*, September 1, 1961.
"Anthony Caruso, Villain of Western Films." *Chicago Sun-Times*, April 7, 2003.
Biography of Anthony Caruso. *TV and Movie Western*, March 1960.
"Junior Guild to Honor Actor Anthony Caruso." Press Release, Junior Guild of Saint Anne's Maternity Home, August 1987

JOHN DOUCETTE

Born in Brockton, Massachusetts on January 21, 1921, John Doucette was once described as "one of Hollywood's best supporting players." When Doucette was a child, his family moved to Los Angeles, California, where he indulged his early interest in acting at Lincoln High School, appearing in his first play at the age of 15. Later, the actor was trained at the Pasadena Playhouse, and made his film debut in 1947, in *Road to the Big House*, a prison drama starring John Shelton and Ann Doran.

During the next eight years, Doucette was seen in 12 films noirs: *Ride the Pink Horse* (1947), *Canon City* (1948), *I Wouldn't Be in Your Shoes* (1948), *The Crooked Way* (1949), *Criss Cross* (1949), *Convicted* (1950), *The Breaking Point* (1950), *Strangers on a Train* (1951), *The Big Heat* (1953), *Cry Vengeance* (1954), *New York Confidential* (1955), and *House of Bamboo* (1955). In these, he normally portrayed "heavy" roles, including several prison inmates and, in one film, simply a "thug." In *Cry Vengeance*, however, he was seen in a rare role on the right side of the

law, playing a sensitive cop who tries to save an embittered former detective from self-destruction. But it was in his series of performances as criminals with "psychological problems" that Doucette was most likely to be recognized.

"I try to make people feel sorry for me even though I'm no good," he said in 1959. "Once I played a crook who got the mumps."

In a film career that included more than 130 films and lasted nearly 40 years, Doucette was seen in a number of box-office blockbusters, including *The Fountainhead* (1949), *Winchester '73* (1950), *High Noon* (1952), *There's No Business Like Show Business* (1954), *The Last Time I Saw Paris* (1954), *Peyton Place* (1957), *Cleopatra* (1963), *True Grit* (1969), and *Patton* (1970). He also enjoyed a prolific television career, with most of his appearances coming on such westerns as *The Lone Ranger*, *The Range Rider*, *Adventures of Wild Bill Hickok*, *Annie Oakley*, *Gunsmoke*, *Cheyenne*, *Broken Arrow*, *Wagon Train*, *Rawhide*, *The Big Valley*, *Kit Carson*, *Bat Masterson*, *Cisco Kid*, *How the West was Won*, and *The Virginian*. Doucette was also a regular on the series *Lock Up* during its year-long run from 1959 to 1960, and on *The Partners*, from 1971 to 1972. (The latter, a sitcom starring Don Adams, was canceled in mid-season, unable to compete against the popularity of *All in the Family*.) His final role was in the 1982 television drama, *Heart of Steel*.

The father of five girls and three boys, Doucette died of cancer on August 16, 1994, at his home in Cabazon, California. He was 73 years old.

References

"Baddies Behind Bars." *TV Guide*, August 12, 1959.
"John Doucette." *Western Clippings*, September-
October, 1994.

"John Doucette Dies; Veteran Character Actor."
The Hollywood Reporter, August 19-21, 1994.
Obituary. *Los Angeles Times*, August 19, 1994.
Obituary. *New York Times*, August 16, 1994.
Obituary. *Variety*, August 29, 1994.

JAMES FLAVIN

With appearances in more than 400 films, James Flavin once earned the honor of having roles in more motion pictures than any other living screen actor. Best known for his "colorful, side-of-the mouth portrayals" of tough-talking lawmen, the prolific actor was born on May 14, 1906, in Portland, Maine.

As a young man, Flavin's interest lay far away from the stage; a graduate of West Point, he was also an All-American guard on the 1924 Army football team. Two years after his triumph on the gridiron, however, Flavin turned to acting, appearing in a number of stock productions in Portland, then heading for Broadway. Following several successful plays, including *Sweet Adeline* with Helen Morgan in 1929, Flavin caught the attention of Hollywood talent scouts and signed on with Universal Studios. In his first year on the big screen, Flavin was seen in eight films, including *The Air Mail Mystery* (1932), an adventure serial in which he starred as aviator Bob Lee. Co-starring with Flavin in the series was actress Lucille Browne; after a whirlwind romance, the two were married and remained together for more than 30 years.

Flavin quickly found himself in great demand, and was seen in bit parts and minor roles in more than 300 features throughout the 1930s and 1940s. Among these were such hits as *King Kong* (1933), in which he played Briggs, the Second Mate; *Baby Take a Bow* (1934), with Shirley Temple; *'G' Men* (1935), starring James Cagney; *My Man Godfrey* (1936), the hilarious screwball comedy with William Powell and Carole Lombard; *Blondie* (1938), the first entry in the long-running series; *Union Pacific* (1939), a sweeping western starring Barbara Stanwyck and Joel McCrea; *The Grapes of Wrath* (1940), John Ford's classic epic; *Knute Rockne, All American* (1940), with Pat O'Brien in the title role; *Yankee Doodle Dandy* (1942), featuring James Cagney in his Academy Award–winning role; *Heaven Can Wait* (1943), a charming romantic comedy starring Don Ameche; and *A Stolen Life* (1946), which starred Bette Davis in the dual role of twin sisters. In the vast majority of his many films, Flavin was seen as a police detective, street cop, or prison guard.

The actor also made his mark during these years in film noir, appearing in 13 features from the era: *High Sierra* (1941), *I Wake Up Screaming* (1942), *Laura* (1944), *Mildred Pierce* (1945), *Conflict* (1945), *The Strange Love of Martha Ivers* (1946), *The Big Sleep* (1946), *Nobody Lives Forever* (1946), *Nightmare Alley* (1947), *Nora Prentiss* (1947), *The Velvet Touch* (1948), *Armored Car Robbery* (1950), and *Destination Murder* (1950). He enjoyed his best role in the last of these; as

Lt. Brewster in *Destination Murder*, he played a police detective who helps to capture a crafty murderer, portrayed by Hurd Hatfield.

Between film assignments, Flavin found time for frequent appearances in such television series as *The Lone Ranger*, *I Love Lucy*, *Alfred Hitchcock Presents*, *The Untouchables*, *Mr. Ed*, *The Addams Family*, *It Takes a Thief*, and *The Brady Bunch*. He was also seen as a regular on two series, *Man with a Camera*, which starred Charles Bronson and featured Flavin as a New York City police lieutenant, and *The Roaring Twenties*, an hour-long adventure series.

Although he was seen in fewer roles as he neared his 70s, Flavin continued to make sporadic appearances; in 1967, he was seen with fellow film noir veterans Jeff Corey and Charles McGraw in *In Cold Blood*; played a wisecracking reporter in the Broadway revival

of *The Front Page* in 1969; had a small part as a priest in *The Barefoot Executive* (1971), a comedy starring Kurt Russell; and played President Dwight D. Eisenhower in the television movie *Francis Gary Powers: The True Story of the U-2 Spy Incident* (1976). The latter was his last appearance. On April 23, 1976, Flavin suffered a ruptured aorta and died in Los Angeles, just days short of his 70th birthday. His wife, actress Lucille Browne, died two weeks later.

References

"Flavin Is Honored For Record 418 Film Roles." *Back Stage*, September 12, 1969.
"James Flavin Cast in 'Square Needle.'" *Los Angeles Times*, February 13, 1951.
"James Flavin, 69, Character Actor." *New York Times*, April 23, 1976.
Obituary. *Variety*, April 26, 1976.

BYRON FOULGER

Despite a prolific film career than spanned four decades, Byron Foulger could most aptly be described as the man in the background. Although he appeared in more than 230 films, most of his roles were unbilled, while others identified him by occupation only, including "Justice of the Peace," "coroner," "orderly," "druggist," and "morgue clerk." Still, the unassuming character actor was associated, however briefly, with such hit Hollywood features as *The Prisoner of Zenda* (1937), *You Can't Take It with You* (1938), *Union Pacific* (1939), *Sullivan's Travels* (1942), *The Lost Weekend* (1945), *Samson and Delilah* (1949), and *The Long, Hot Summer* (1958).

Born on August 27, 1899, in Ogden, Utah, Foulger began his acting career on the stage, appearing in such Broadway productions as *Medea*, *The Trial of Joan of Arc*, *Iphigenia in Aulis*, *Mr. Faust*, and *Candida*. (All five productions also featured fellow noir performer Moroni Olsen.) Foulger made his screen debut

in 1934, playing a bit role in the Katharine Hepburn starrer *The Little Minister*. From there, the bespectacled actor was seldom idle; during the next decade, he appeared in an average of 21 films each year, reaching his zenith in 1944, when he was seen in small parts in a whopping 29 features. He was also a frequent performer in film noir, with roles in 13 features: *When Strangers Marry* (1944), *Ministry of Fear* (1944), *Scarlet Street* (1945), *Cornered* (1945), *Deadline at Dawn* (1946), *The Postman Always Rings Twice* (1946), *Suspense* (1946), *Dead Reckoning* (1946), *They Won't Believe Me* (1947), *He Walked by Night* (1948), *They Live by Night* (1949), *Dark City* (1950), and *Union Station* (1950). Of these, his showiest role came in *They Live by Night*, where he played the amiable, loquacious owner of a mountain cabin briefly used as a refuge by the film's stars Farley Granger and Cathy O'Donnell.

Complementing Foulger's productive film vocation was an equally busy career on the small screen. Beginning in the late 1940s, he was seen on some of television's most popular series, including *The Lone Ranger*, *I Love Lucy*, *Maverick*, *The Twilight Zone*, *Hazel*, *Gunsmoke*, *Perry Mason*, *Wagon Train*, *The Andy Griffith Show*, *Get Smart*, *Green Acres*, *The Monkees*, *The Wild Wild West*, and *Adam-12*. He also played a recurring role on *Petticoat Junction* as Wendell Gibbs, and on *Captain Nice* as the hero's father who was always pictured behind a newspaper.

"The only parts of me ever shown are the feet and the top of my head, and I never have more than a line or two of dialog to learn," Foulger said during the run of the short-lived 1967 series. "I wouldn't like to devote the rest of my life to sitting behind a newspaper, but the pay is good and I have a stand-in and a big dressing room."

On April 4, 1970, shortly after filming his role as a minister in the feature film *Cockeyed Cowboys of Calico County* (1970), Foulger died of what was ruled a "heart malfunction." The 70-year-old actor was survived by his wife, actress Dorothy Adams, and a daughter, Rachel Ames.

References

Humphrey, Hal. "A Character Actor the Fans Can't See." *Los Angeles Times*, February 20, 1967.

Obituary. *Variety*, April 7, 1970.

STEVEN GERAY

Born on November 10, 1904, in the Czechoslovakian city of Uzhorod, Steven Geray entered the world as Istvan Gyergyay, the son of a wealthy textile manufacturer and landholder. As a teenager, Geray's sights were focused on a career as a violinist, and he made his professional debut in a concert at Budapest's Academy of Music. Despite favorable notices, however, Geray abruptly altered his vocational aspirations, deciding instead to move to Paris and become a painter.

"But I soon discovered I couldn't draw," Geray once admitted.

Urged by friends from Budapest, Geray next opted to try his luck on the stage; after appearing as Aloysha in a production of *The Brothers Karamazov*, the actor joined the Hungarian National Theatre, playing in a variety of plays for the next several years. He was later seen in such London productions as *Let's Be Gay*, *Silver Swan*, and *Let's Pretend*, as well as several British feature films, and made his Hollywood debut in the 1935 musical *Dance Band*, starring Charles "Buddy" Rogers.

In addition to character roles in such popular films as *Phantom of the Opera* (1943), *Spellbound* (1945), *All About Eve* (1950), and *Gentlemen Prefer Blondes* (1943), Geray was seen in 12 features from the film noir era: *The*

Mask of Dimitrios (1944), *Cornered* (1945), *Gilda* (1946), *Deadline at Dawn* (1946), *So Dark the Night* (1946), *The Dark Past* (1948), *In a Lonely Place* (1950), *A Lady Without Passport* (1950), *The Second Woman* (1951), *The House on Telegraph Hill* (1951), *Affair in Trinidad* (1952), and *New York Confidential* (1955). Of these, he was most prominently featured in *The Mask of Dimitrios* (1944), in which his character commits suicide after being double-crossed in a financial deal by

the scheming title character; *Cornered*, where he played a wealthy, ill-fated Nazi collaborator; *So Dark the Night*, in which he was top-billed as a Parisian detective who discovers that he suffers from a split personality; and *Gilda*, which featured the actor as Uncle Pio, a brutally honest casino washroom attendant who ultimately kills the film's villain, Ballin Mundson (George Macready).

Under contract for several years to Columbia Studios, Geray also enjoyed a measure of success on the small screen, appearing in such television series as *Sky King*, *The Adventures of Superman*, *Zane Grey Theater*, *Perry Mason*, *The Untouchables*, *Voyage to the Bottom of the Sea*, *I Dream of Jeannie*, and *The Time Tunnel*. After playing Dr. Rudolph Frankenstein in his final feature film, *Jesse James Meets Frankenstein's Daughter* (1966), Geray retired from acting; several years later, on December 26, 1973, he suffered a fatal heart attack, leaving behind his second wife and two children.

References

"Barbara Goodall Sues Husband." *Los Angeles Times*, September 24, 1943.
Biography of Steven Geray. Columbia Studios, circa 1947.
Obituary. *Variety*, December 28, 1973.

REED HADLEY

Once described as possessing a "boyish, disarming, beguiling smile," and "sexy, rugged masculinity," Reed Hadley was known as much for his distinctive voice as his handsome looks.

The performer who experienced success on the radio, stage, television, and screen was born Reed Bert Herring in Petrolia, Texas, on June 25, 1911. Relocating frequently because of his father's job as an oil driller, Hadley attended elementary school in Columbiana, Ohio, and Bennett High School in Buffalo,

New York, where he first became interested in dramatics. After graduating, Hadley enrolled at the University of Buffalo with plans to study law, but when financial constraints forced him to withdraw after his first year, he refocused his energies on acting.

Working by day in a local department store, Hadley became active in the Buffalo Studio Theatre Player's Group, and later headed for New York City, where he played two roles in the hit Broadway production of *Hamlet*, starring John Gielgud. When the play closed,

Hadley used his deep, well-modulated voice to land a series of radio jobs, including lead roles on such popular programs as *Silver Theatre*, *Cavalcade of America*, and *Big Town*. He also continued to hone his acting skills in stock companies in Mt. Kisco and Rochester, New York, and Madison, Connecticut, appearing in *Death Takes a Holiday*, *The Petrified Forest*, and *Spring Dance*, among other productions.

Hadley added feature films to his performing repertoire in the late 1930s, making his screen debut in *Hollywood Stadium Mystery* (1937), starring Neil Hamilton and Evelyn Venable. During the next several years, he would be seen in small roles in such popular features as *Calling Dr. Kildare* (1939), an early entry in the series starring Lionel Barrymore and Lew Ayres; *The Bank Dick* (1940), an hilarious W.C. Fields vehicle; *Ziegfeld Girl* (1941), featuring Judy Garland and Lana Turner; and *Now, Voyager* (1942), the classic three-hankie weeper starring Bette Davis. He also starred in the title role of the Republic Pictures serial, *Zorro's Fighting Legion* (1939), and returned to his roots on the radio, starring for several years in the popular series, *Red Ryder*. In 1943, Hadley also began lending his distinctive voice to the big screen,

serving as narrator for such films as *Guadalcanal Diary* (1943), *Buffalo Bill* (1944), *The Last Bomb* (1945), *13 Rue Madeleine* (1946), and *Walk a Crooked Mile* (1948).

The actor's voice was also an integral part of five of the eight films noirs with which he was associated; he served as narrator for *The House on 92nd Street* (1945), *T-Men* (1947), *He Walked by Night* (1948), *Canon City* (1948), and *The Killer That Stalked New York* (1950). In each, Hadley provided the familiar, authoritative tone that was so well-suited to the documentary style of noir. In front of the camera, Hadley also appeared in three additional noirs: *Leave Her to Heaven* (1945), in which he portrayed a physician; *The Dark Corner* (1946), where he was a police lieutenant; and *The Brasher Doubloon* (1947), in which he was again seen as a doctor. His fairly substantial role in *The Dark Corner* was singled out by several reviewers, including James O'Farrell of the *Los Angeles Examiner*, who wrote: "Reed Hadley, acting the inevitable 'man from headquarters,' offers a genuine reading of the part that fires it with a tinge of originality."

With the onset of the 1950s, Hadley turned to the small screen, playing featured roles on two series, *Racket Squad* in 1950 and *The Public Defender* in 1954, and guesting on such shows as *The Restless Gun*, *Rawhide*, *Bat Masterson*, *Perry Mason*, and *Green Acres*. Hadley's feature film appearances dwindled drastically during the decade that followed; of his five films during the 1960s, he served as narrator for two, *Gunfight at Comanche Creek* (1964) and *The Fabulous Bastard from Chicago* (1969). He also played a small role in *The St. Valentine's Day Massacre* (1969), portraying Hymie Weiss.

Hadley's last feature film appearance was in *Brain of Blood* (1972), in which he played a fallen Arab leader whose brain is transplanted into the body of a scientist's deformed lab assistant. It was hardly a fitting conclusion to a distinguished career. Two years later, on December 11, 1974, Hadley suffered a fatal heart attack at the age of 63. He was survived by his wife of 34 years, Helen Hampton Hadley, and their son, Dale.

References

Biography of Reed Hadley. 20th Century-Fox, May 7, 1943.

McClay, Howard. "Reed Hadley." *Los Angeles Daily News*, July 16, 1952.

Obituary. *Variety*, December 13, 1974.

HARRY HARVEY

Born on January 10, 1901, in Indian Territory, Oklahoma (now Oklahoma City), Harry Harvey used his intrinsic musical talent to springboard into an early career as a performer. After playing the trombone in a church band in Fort Worth, Texas, when he was 16 years old, Harvey was hired as a trombone player in Gus Hill's Honey Boy Minstrels, remaining with the popular performing troupe for two seasons. In 1920, Harvey signed on with Lasses' White Minstrels, and later appeared on the burlesque circuit in a revue called *Laffin' Thru*.

Harvey joined the cast of the Golden Rod Show Boat on the Mississippi River in 1923, and for the next several years, played in stock companies throughout the midwest, in Louisville, Kentucky, and in New York. After appearing in the road company of the hit 1934 musical *Hit the Deck*, Harvey caught the eye of a Hollywood talent scout and the following year, he transferred his talents to the silver screen in such small parts as a cab driver in *One More Spring* (1935), a photographer in *Dr. Socrates* (1935), a bailiff in *Under Your Spell* (1936), and a mail clerk in *Public Enemy's Wife* (1936). During his early years, he also played reporters in a number of films, including *Behind the Green Lights* (1935), *The Moon's Our Home* (1936), *Born to Fight* (1936), *Theodora Goes Wild* (1936), *Kid Galahad* (1937), *Border Café* (1937), *Special Agent K-7* (1937), *Gangster's Boy* (1938), *The Spy Ring* (1938), *Stanley and Livingstone* (1939), *Pop Always Pays* (1940), *Three Girls About Town* (1941), and *War Against Mrs. Hadley* (1942). Never at a loss for work, Harvey was seen in an average of 12 films a year, with his busiest year coming in 1946, when he was seen in 17 features.

Among Harvey's multitudinous movies were 10 films noirs, the majority of which were released by RKO studios, with whom the actor signed a long-term contract in 1945: *Crack-Up* (1946), *Nocturne* (1946), *Crossfire* (1947), *They Won't Believe Me* (1947), *He Walked by Night* (1948), *The Accused* (1948), *They Live by Night* (1949), *The Reckless Moment* (1949), *Convicted* (1950), and *The Big Carnival* (1951). Unbilled in most of the films, Harvey's best role was in *They Won't Believe Me*, where he played the judge presiding over the case of a man (Robert Young) accused of murdering his wife.

In addition to his feature film work, Harvey enjoyed a measure of fame on the small screen, guesting on numerous television series, primarily such westerns as *The Lone*

Ranger, The Gene Autry Show, The Range Rider, Adventures of Wild Bill Hickok, Annie Oakley, The Life and Legend of Wyatt Earp, Tales of Wells Fargo, Maverick, Colt .45, Wagon Train, The Virginian, Laredo, Branded, Cimarron Strip, The Guns of Will Sonnett, Gunsmoke, Lancer, and *Bonanza.* He also appeared as a regular on four series, *The Roy Rogers Show,* where he played Sheriff Tom Blodgett in 1951; *It's a Great Life,* starring Frances Bavier and Barbara Bates, from 1954 to 1956; *Man Without a Gun,* which ran during the 1957 season, in which he portrayed Mayor George Dixon; and *It's a Man's World,* where he was seen as Mr. Stott from 1962 to 1963.

Harvey began to slow down his frenetic work pace in the 1960s, appearing in only a handful of feature films and made-for-television movies; the most notable of these were the big screen productions of *Pollyanna* (1960), with Hayley Mills in the title role; *Cat Ballou* (1965), starring Lee Marvin and Jane Fonda; *The Trouble with Angels* (1966), a delightful comedy starring Rosalind Russell and Hayley Mills, and directed by Ida Lupino; and *Airport* (1970), the big-budget, star-studded disaster movie based on Arthur Hailey's best-selling novel. After a small role in the fittingly titled *Columbo: Swan Song* in 1974, Harvey retired from acting. He died just over a decade later in a nursing home in Sylmar, California, at the age of 84. His only son, television director and actor Harry Harvey, Jr., preceded the actor in death, but the veteran performer was survived by several grandchildren and great-grandchildren.

References

Biography of Harry Harvey. RKO Radio Studios, August 30, 1945.
Obituary. *Variety,* December 2, 1985.

BARRY KELLEY

Barry Kelley was once described as "a big, burly guy whom you could hardly have avoided if you've been going to movies at all lately." Indeed, during a two-year span early in his film career, the actor appeared in featured roles in nearly 20 pictures, playing everything from detectives to hoods.

Born on August 19, 1908, in Chicago, Illinois, Edward Barry Kelley was educated at the city's Goodman School of Theatre, from which he graduated in 1930. After honing his craft in a variety of stock company plays, Kelley debuted on Broadway in the 1934 production of *Within the Gates,* a long-running drama with a cast that included Lillian Gish and Morris Ankrum. He was later seen in such stage hits as *Hamlet,* featuring John Gielgud and Judith Anderson; *The Wingless Victory,* starring and produced by Katherine Cornell; *The Star-Wagon,* where he was originally cast as a thug and was later promoted to replace co-star Kent Smith; and *Oklahoma!,* starring Howard Da Silva and Celeste Holm. Kelley also stepped into the lead role of the smash-hit *Born Yesterday* when Paul Douglas left the production for a career on the screen.

After a year in *Born Yesterday,* Kelley, too, made the trek to Hollywood, where his first film, *Force of Evil* (1948), also marked his initial foray into the realm of the film noir. During the next seven years, Kelley appeared in an additional 10 noirs, *The Undercover Man* (1949), *Knock on Any Door* (1949), *Too Late for Tears* (1949), *The File on Thelma Jordon* (1949), *The Asphalt Jungle* (1950), *Southside 1-1000* (1950), *The Killer That Stalked New York* (1950), *711 Ocean Drive* (1950), *The Long Wait* (1954), and *New York Confidential* (1955). Despite a penchant for meeting untimely screen deaths, Kelley was seen to his greatest advantage in *The Undercover Man,* where he played a crooked district attorney who is murdered by the syndicate after he makes a deal with an IRS tax investigator; *The Asphalt*

Jungle, in which he was a standout as a corrupt cop; *711 Ocean Drive*, in which he was a wire service operator who gets bumped off by a disgruntled bookie; and *Southside 1-1000*, where he portrayed a businessman involved with a lucrative counterfeiting scheme who is shoved from the upper story window of an office building.

In addition to his film noir features, Kelley was seen during his career in such popular fare as *Ma and Pa Kettle* (1949), starring Marjorie Main and Percy Kilbride in the title roles; *Mr. Belvedere Goes to College* (1949), featuring Clifton Webb as a know-it-all babysitter; *Flying Leathernecks* (1951), a World War II saga starring John Wayne and directed by Nicholas Ray; *Carrie* (1952), the well-done adaptation of a Theodore Dreiser novel; *Trial* (1955), which featured Glenn Ford as an attorney defending a Mexican boy of murder; *The Joker Is Wild* (1957), starring Frank Sinatra as entertainer Joe E. Lewis; *The Manchurian Candidate* (1962), in which he portrayed the secretary of defense; and *The Love Bug* (1968), an amusing Disney comedy about a car with a mind of its own. Kelley also was a frequent presence on the small screen, guesting on such series as *Gunsmoke, Bonanza, The Untouchables, The Fugitive, Perry Mason,* and *The Beverly Hillbillies*, and serving as a cast member on *Big Town, Pete and Gladys, Mr. Ed,* and *Petticoat Junction.*

On June 5, 1991, just two months after the death of his wife, Kathleen, Barry Kelley

died at the Motion Picture Home and Hospital as a result of congestive heart failure. He was survived by his daughter, Gayle, and his sister, Virginia.

References

Obituary. *Los Angeles Times*, June 22, 1991.
Obituary. *The Big Reel*, September 1991.
Obituary. *Variety*, July 1, 1991.
Smith, Darr. "Barry Kelley." *New York Daily News*, January 15, 1951.

JOHN KELLOGG

John Kellogg took the long way around to the silver screen. Born in Hollywood, California, on June 3, 1916, Kellogg attended Beverly Hills High School, then worked in a gas station while attending drama classes in the evenings. After a half-hearted effort to crash the gates of the local studios proved fruitless, the young man hitchhiked to New York, where he roomed for a while with the actor later known as Tom Drake.

Kellogg's first acting break came when he joined a summer stock company in Cohasset, Massachusetts, known as the South Shore Players. Spotted by a scout for the famed Shubert brothers, Kellogg was hired for the lead role in his Broadway debut, *Honor Bright.* Although the show was a flop, the actor went on to land parts in such productions as *Dance Night, Escape By Night,* and the road tour of *Brother Rat.* His performance as the male

lead in the latter production led to his return to his hometown for his first film role, playing the brother of the title character in MGM's *Young Tom Edison* (1940). During the next few years, he was seen in small roles in such features as 20th Century Fox's *High School* (1940), a vehicle for Jane Withers; Warner's *Knockout* (1941), a well-done boxing saga starring Arthur Kennedy; United Artists' *To Be or Not to Be* (1942), a first-rate comedy-drama directed by Ernst Lubitsch; and RKO's *Pride of the Yankees* (1942), starring Gary Cooper in the poignant biography of baseball star Lou Gehrig.

After serving two years in the Marine Corps during World War II, Kellogg returned to Hollywood for a series of films that included *A Walk in the Sun* (1945), a war film starring Dana Andrews; *Without Reservations* (1946), with Claudette Colbert and John Wayne; *Suddenly, It's Spring* (1947), a pleasant comedy featuring Fred MacMurray and Paulette Goddard; *Station West* (1948), starring Jane Greer as the operator of an old west gambling den; *Twelve O'Clock High* (1949), a hit wartime adventure with Gregory Peck and Dean Jagger; *Samson and Delilah* (1949), starring Victor Mature and Hedy Lamarr in

the title roles; *Tomorrow is Another Day* (1951), starring Ruth Roman and Steve Cochran as fugitive lovers on the lam; *Come Fill the Cup* (1951), featuring an outstanding performance by James Cagney as an alcoholic newspaper reporter; *Rancho Notorious* (1952), a Fritz Lang-directed western starring Marlene Dietrich; and *The Greatest Show on Earth* (1952), Cecil B. DeMille's circus extravaganza featuring such stars as Charlton Heston, Cornel Wilde, Gloria Grahame, James Stewart, Betty Hutton, and Dorothy Lamour.

Also during this period, Kellogg made his mark in the realm of film noir. Having appeared as a reporter in his first noir, *Among the Living*, in 1941, the actor was seen in roles in seven more features from the era between 1946 and 1951: *Somewhere in the Night* (1946), *The Strange Love of Martha Ivers* (1946), *Johnny O'Clock* (1947), *Out of the Past* (1947), *The Gangster* (1947), *House of Strangers* (1949), and *The Enforcer* (1951). Aside from the menacing, small-time hoods he portrayed in *The Gangster* and *The Enforcer*, Kellogg's best noir role by far came in *Johnny O'Clock*, in which he played Charlie, the loyal friend of the title character, who turns out to be not quite so loyal. (In Kellogg's best scene in the film, he is asked by O'Clock why he "fingered" him, and Charlie passionately rejoins, "Why shouldn't I? Johnny O'Clock with the girls. Johnny O'Clock with the clothes. 'Here, Charlie, boy — here's a bone, here's a shirt, here's a bed.' A cop comes in — who gets pushed around? Charlie. Where's Johnny O'Clock? Where he always is — lookin' out for himself. I did like you do — I traded you in for someone who could do me some more good.")

Throughout the 1950s and 1960s, Kellogg's film appearances dwindled as he concentrated most of his energies on a busy television career. Beginning in the late 1940s, the actor was seen on such small screen favorites as *The Lone Ranger*, *The Adventures of Superman*, *Maverick*, *The Untouchables*, *Gunsmoke*, *Bonanza*, *The Outer Limits*, *The Fugitive*, *The Wild, Wild West*, *Alias Smith and Jones*, *St. Elsewhere*, and *Wiseguy*. He also appeared on the hit series *Peyton Place* during the 1966-67 season, and was featured in such made-for television movies as *The Doomsday Flight* (1966), *The Silence* (1975), and *Blind Justice* (1986). Between these projects, Kellogg found time to return to his roots on the stage, performing in such productions as *Salvation on a Shoestring* in 1955, *Uncle Vanya* in 1956, and *Memphis is Gone* in the late 1970s. His performance in the latter play was praised by one critic as "highly dedicated craftsmanship carried to a transcendental level."

Although Kellogg enjoyed a fair amount of success in his career as an actor, his personal life did not always run a smooth course. Twice married and twice divorced, the actor made headlines in 1947 when he was arrested on a felony wife beating charge, and was back in the news in 1952 when both of his ex-wives, actress Linda Brent and singer Helen Shirley Kellogg, sued him for failure to pay alimony and child support payments. While the actor protested that he was getting "a lot of attention for a man with only 13 cents in his pocket," Kellogg was sentenced to five days in jail.

Kellogg continued to work professionally into the 1980s, when he was seen in the feature films *Violets Are Blue* (1986), in which he portrayed the father of actress Sissy Spacek, and *Orphans* (1987), a well-done drama starring Matthew Modine and Kevin Anderson as orphaned brothers. Kellogg's final acting performance came in the 1989 made-for-television movie, *Jacob Have I Loved*.

After more than a decade away from the limelight, John Kellogg died on February 22, 2000, of complications from Alzheimer's Disease. He was survived by his three children, Sharon, Cheryl, and Steven.

References

"Actor Sentenced on Alimony Pay Delay." *Los Angeles Examiner*, July 30, 1952.
Biography of John Kellogg. RKO Radio Studios, May 23, 1950.
"Each of Actor's Ex-Wives Sends Him to Lockup." *Los Angeles Times*, July 30, 1952.
Obituary. *Los Angeles Times*, March 9, 2000.
"2 Ex's Slap Actor in Jail Over Alimony." *Los Angeles Daily News*, July 29, 1952.

EMILE MEYER

Once described as "the toughest man on the border," Emile Meyer was born on August 18, 1910, in New Orleans, one of four children of Bernard Meyer and his wife, Mary. After graduating from St. Alysius High School, Meyer embarked on several money-making ventures, including a fried pie business, a lumber and piling company, and a trucking business. None was successful. Later, he worked as an insurance salesman, cab driver, longshore paymaster, and safety engineer for the federal government.

"There is absolutely nothing in my background that would indicate I should be an actor," he said once.

In 1948, Meyer decided to try his hand on the stage, and was first seen in a produc-tion of *The Petrified Forest* at Le Petit Theatre du Vieux Carre, a local little theater company. The following year, Meyer was recommended to Elia Kazan when the famed director came to New Orleans to film *Panic in the Streets* (1950). Meyer won a small role as a ship's captain in the film, his screen debut and his entry into the world of film noir.

In addition to *Panic in the Streets*, Meyer appeared in seven other films noirs over the next decade: *The Big Night* (1951), *The Line-Up* (1958), *The Mob* (1951), *The People Against O'Hara* (1951), *Shield for Murder* (1954), *Sweet Smell of Success* (1957), and *Baby Face Nelson* (1957). Of these, his biggest part was his fourth billing as a police captain in *The Shield for Murder*, where his character demonstrates

unflagging loyalty toward a cop who turns out to be crooked. Perhaps his most memorable noir performance, however, was in *The Sweet Smell of Success*. In this film, Meyer was singled out by one reviewer, who wrote that he "comes through quite effectively as a brutal, corrupt detective."

Although Meyer frequently portrayed heavies, he claimed that his acting specialty was "humane cops."

"But I get to play them so seldom," he once said. "I guess I just look mean, because whenever a producer needs a real louse, I get a call."

Aside from his work in film noir, Meyer was seen in such films as *Carbine Williams* (1952), *Shane* (1953), *The Man with the Golden Arm* (1955), *The Blackboard Jungle* (1955), *Move Over, Darling* (1963), *The Outfit* (1973), and his final feature, *The Legend of Frank Woods* (1977). He was also seen in such television drama series as *The F.B.I.* and *Perry Mason*, and westerns including *Annie Oakley*, *Death Valley Days*, *The Restless Gun*, *Broken Arrow*, *Maverick*, *Colt .45*, *Bat Masterson*, *Wichita Town*, *Rawhide*, and *Bonanza*.

After suffering from Alzheimer's disease for several years, Emile Meyer died in Covington, Louisiana, on March 19, 1987, at the age of 76. He was survived by four children.

References

Biography of Emile Meyer. Columbia Studios, October 21, 1957.

Biography of Emile Meyer. Paramount Studios. April, 1952.

Obituary. *Variety*, April 1, 1987.

ROBERT OSTERLOH

Only a scant amount of biographical information could be unearthed on Robert Osterloh, but no discussion of film noir actors would be complete without his inclusion.

A talented performer whose film career spanned four decades, Osterloh was born on May 31, 1918, and debuted on the big screen in the 1948 film noir feature *The Dark Past* (1948), starring William Holden and Lee J. Cobb. During the next decade, he was seen in nine additional noirs: *Criss Cross* (1949), *The Undercover Man* (1949), *White Heat*

(1949), *Gun Crazy* (1950), *Southside 1-1000* (1950), *A Lady Without Passport* (1950), *711 Ocean Drive* (1950), *The Prowler* (1951), and *Baby Face Nelson* (1957). His showiest noir roles came in *White Heat* and *711 Ocean Drive*. In the former, he played Tommy Ryley, a cellmate of psychotic gangster Cody Jarrett (James Cagney), who is shot in the back by the gangster as he tries to surrender to police at the film's end. (It is also Tommy who delivers the news to Cody that his beloved mother is dead.) The latter film featured Osterloh as Gizzi, who commits a murder-for-hire, only

nie and Patricia Neal; *The Well* (1951), a tense racial drama; *The Wild One* (1953), starring Marlon Brando as the rebellious, leather-jacketed motorcycle gang leader; *Riot in Cell Block 11* (1954), a gritty prison film co-starring noir veterans Neville Brand, Emile Meyer, and Whit Bissell; *Invasion of the Body Snatchers* (1956), where Osterloh was seen as an ambulance driver; and *Inherit the Wind* (1960), featuring Spencer Tracy and Fredric March.

In the 1950s, Osterloh also launched a successful television career, appearing in such popular series as *Wagon Train*, *Perry Mason*, *The Rifleman*, *The F.B.I.*, and *Ironside*. His last big screen appearance was in the Clint Eastwood starrer, *Coogan's Bluff* (1968), in which he played a deputy.

Osterloh died in Los Osos, California, on April 16, 2001. He was 82 years old.

to be killed himself after trying to parlay the murder into a blackmail bonanza.

In addition to his film noir credits, Osterloh was seen during his career in such features as *The Day the Earth Stood Still* (1951), a hit science-fictioner starring Michael Ren-

References

"Robert Osterloh." Internet Movie Database: www. imdb.com.

———— JOHN RIDGELY ————

Born John Huntington Rea on September 6, 1908, John Ridgely attended elementary school in Hinsdale, Illinois, and the Kemper Military Academy in Boonville, Missouri, before enrolling at Stanford University. During his college years, Ridgely participated in numerous athletic activities, including basketball, ice hockey, and track, and honed his budding acting skills in such plays as *The Goose Hangs High*, *So This Is London*, and *The Bride*.

After graduating from Stanford in 1931, Ridgely headed for California, where he spent the next several years as a performer with the famed Pasadena Playhouse, performing in a wide variety of productions, including *Lost Horizon*, *Not for Children*, *Cock Robin*, *The Music Master*, and *Paths of Glory*. Spotted by

a Warner Bros. talent scout while appearing in the latter play, Ridgely landed his first screen role, playing a steward in the Evelyn Venable starrer, *Streamline Express* (1935). Signing a long-term contract with Warners, Ridgely was seen in such popular features as *They Won't Forget* (1937), which brought Lana Turner into the public eye; *They Made Me a Criminal* (1939), a hard-hitting drama starring John Garfield; *Dark Victory* (1939), starring Bette Davis as a doomed socialite; *They Drive By Night* (1940), featuring Humphrey Bogart and George Raft as truck driving siblings; *They Died With Their Boots On* (1941), starring Errol Flynn as General George Custer; *The Man Who Came to Dinner* (1942), a delightful comedy with Bette Davis and Monty Woolley; and *Arsenic and Old Lace* (1944),

detective Philip Marlowe (Humphrey Bogart). Despite the showier roles of his co-stars, Ridgely was singled out by several critics for his performance, including Edwin Schallert of the *Los Angeles Times*, who included Ridgely in his praise of the film's "A-1 cast," and the *Los Angeles Daily News*' Virginia Wright, who wrote: "John Ridgely, as the big-time gambler, is another good bit of casting against type."

After ending his contract with Warners, Ridgely's most successful features included Paramount's *A Place in the Sun* (1951), starring Montgomery Clift and Elizabeth Taylor, and Cecil B. DeMille's circus extravaganza, *The Greatest Show on Earth* (1952). The actor was also seen in 1954 on the short-lived daytime television serial *Woman with a Past*, starring Constance Ford. His appearance on the soap opera would be his last performance, however; plagued by a chronic heart condition, Ridgely was forced to retire from acting, and died on January 18, 1968, at the age of 59. He was survived by his wife, Virginia, and a son, John.

starring Cary Grant and directed by Frank Capra.

After making his debut in the era of film noir with *Danger Signal* (1945), Ridgely went on to appear in *The Big Sleep* (1946), *Nora Prentiss* (1947), *Possessed* (1947), *The High Wall* (1947), *Border Incident* (1949), and *Edge of Doom* (1950). His most prominent role, and one of the best of his career, came in *The Big Sleep*, where he portrayed Eddie Mars, the polished gambler who winds up on the losing end when he butts heads with private

References

Biography of John Ridgely. Paramount Studios, circa 1945.
Obituary. *The Hollywood Reporter*, January 25, 1968.
Obituary. *Variety*, January 24, 1968.

ROY ROBERTS

Early in his professional life, Roy Roberts was at a crossroads, forced to choose between a vocation as a baseball player or an actor. He opted for the latter, and went on to earn acclaim as a stage performer, appear in nearly 100 motion pictures, and develop a successful third career on the small screen.

Once described as possessing "a rugged determination and a lot of vitality and tal-

ent," Roberts was born on March 19, 1900, in Tampa, Florida, and reportedly shed his "bothersome" Southern accent by studying Shakespeare. As a young man, however, he used his athletic skills to play for two years as a catcher with a semi-professional baseball team in his home town. Although his prospects of advancing into the major leagues were promising, Roberts received an offer to appear in a local stock company production, which paid considerably more than he was receiving on the baseball diamond.

"And so," a columnist wrote in 1936, "he turned in his catcher's mitt and his uniform and donned grease paint."

For the next several seasons, Roberts appeared with stock companies throughout the country, including a group called The Original Williams Company, a tent-show troupe traveling through small towns in the South. He also operated his own company in Baltimore, Maryland, for nearly a year. After his Broadway nod in the 1931 production of *Old Man Murphy*, Roberts appeared in the popular musical *Everybody's Welcome*, featuring the Ritz Brothers; *The Inside Story*, with Brian Donlevy and Louis Calhern; *The Body Beautiful*, which closed after less than five performances; *Ladies and Gentlemen*, with Helen Hayes; *The Old Foolishness*, with Sally O'Neill; *My Sister Eileen*, with Shirley Booth; and *20th Century* alongside William Frawley and Dennie Moore.

After more than a decade on the stage, Roberts turned his talents to the big screen, debuting in the popular wartime drama, *Guadalcanal Diary* (1943), starring Preston Foster. Over the next 43 years, he appeared in a number of cinema favorites, including *The Sullivans* (1944), a wartime drama starring Anne Baxter; *A Bell for Adano* (1945), with John Hodiak and Gene Tierney; *My Darling Clementine* (1946), the John Ford-directed version of the gunfight at O.K. Corral; *Gentleman's Agreement* (1947), where he played a hotel manager who refuses to give a room to Gregory Peck; *Joan of Arc* (1948), starring Ingrid Bergman in the title role; *House of Wax* (1953), a popular Vincent Price horror film; *It's a Mad Mad Mad Mad World* (1963), a star-studded, fun-filled romp; and *Chinatown* (1974), directed by John Huston and starring Jack Nicholson.

Some of Roberts' best features, however, were among the 10 films noirs in which he appeared: *Strange Triangle* (1946), *Nightmare Alley* (1947), *The Brasher Doubloon* (1947), *Force of Evil* (1948), *He Walked by Night* (1948), *Chicago Deadline* (1949), *The Reckless*

Moment (1949), *The Killer That Stalked New York* (1950), *I Was a Communist for the FBI* (1951), and *The Enforcer* (1951). His most substantial noir role came in *Force of Evil*, in which he portrayed a ruthless syndicate leader named Ben Roberts, and *The Enforcer*, where he teamed with assistant district attorney Humphrey Bogart to nab an elusive mobster. After his run of film noir movies, Roberts returned to his roots on the stage, appearing with Joe E. Brown in the musical comedy, *Carnival in Flanders*. Despite writing and direction by Preston Sturges, however, the play was short-lived and one reviewer commented that Roberts "deserved better from scripter Sturges."

While continuing his frequent appearances in feature films, Roberts began a prolific television career in the early 1950s, guesting on a wide variety of shows including *My Little Margie*, *The Adventures of Rin Tin Tin*, *The Lone Ranger*, *Perry Mason*, *Rawhide*, *The Deputy*, *The Dick Van Dyke Show*, *The Twilight Zone*, *The Addams Family*, *Green Acres*, and *Family Affair*. He was also a cast member on eight separate series, *The Gale Storm Show*, *McHale's Navy*, *Gunsmoke*, *Petticoat Junction*, *The Beverly Hillbillies*, *Peyton Place*, *Bewitched*, and *The Lucy Show*.

Roberts' last appearance was in the entertaining Disney film, *The Strongest Man in the World* (1975). Shortly after the film's release, on May 28, 1975, Roberts suffered a fatal heart attack and died in Los Angeles at the age of 75.

References

Coleman, Robert. "'Carnival in Flanders' Is a Lavish Extravaganza." *New York Daily Mirror*, September 10, 1953.

"Football Player at Work." *New York Post*, March 30, 1942.
"He Was a Second Fiddle." *Brooklyn Daily Eagle*, July 26, 1936.
"Ringside Seat." *Playbill*, November 22, 1938.
Ross, George. "So This Is Broadway." *New York World-Telegram*, December 2, 1937.
"Roy Roberts in Toronto." *New York Post*, June 26, 1940.
"Rush of July Openings for Barn Theatres." *New York Daily News*, June 26, 1940.
"The Old Foolishness." *Playbill*, December 20, 1940.

DEWEY ROBINSON

Noted for his numerous gangster portrayals, as well as his appearances in more than 200 feature films, Dewey Robinson was born in New Haven, Connecticut, on August 17, 1898. After serving in World War I, Robinson began his performing career in New York, serving as a regular in the Marx Brothers musicals of the 1920s and making his screen debut in the Tallulah Bankhead vehicle *Tarnished Lady* in 1931.

During the remainder of his career, Robinson appeared in an average of 10 pictures each year, portraying a range of such colorfully identified characters as the "Bust-in-the-Nose Man" in *Grand Slam* (1933), a waterfront diner wanting salt in *Bureau of Missing Persons* (1933), the burly man in the Turkish bath in *Havana Widows* (1933), a lemonade stand man in *Professor Beware* (1938), a soldier collecting signatures in *Juarez* (1939), the silent guy in the jail cell in *Tin Pan Alley* (1940), and the fifth member of the Ail and Quail Club in *The Palm Beach Story* (1942). Unbilled in most of his films, the actor was also seen in a mixed bag of vocations; in addition to frequently playing small-time hoods, Robinson also played a spate of bartenders, truck drivers, prison guards, butlers, butchers, fighters, street cleaners, doormen, bouncers, and cab drivers.

Of his numerous features, Robinson's most popular included such hits as *Blonde Venus* (1932), starring Marlene Dietrich; *Sullivan's Travels* (1942), directed by Preston Sturges and featuring Veronica Lake and Joel McCrea; *Casablanca* (1942), the classic Humphrey Bogart starrer; and *Father of the Bride* (1950), with Spencer Tracy in the title role. He was also seen in small parts in nine features from the film noir era: *When Strangers Marry* (1944), *Murder, My Sweet* (1944), *Scarlet Street* (1945), *Suspense* (1946), *The Gang-*

ster (1947), *I Walk Alone* (1948), *Tension* (1949), *Dark City* (1950) and *Roadblock* (1951). Each of his noir roles was unbilled; his most significant came in *Murder, My Sweet,* where he played the bar owner who gets knocked around by the hulking Moose Malloy (Mike Mazurki).

Robinson's prolific career as a bit player was derailed in 1950 when he was struck by a hit-and-run driver in Beverly Hills, suffering a skull fracture and severe internal injuries. Later that year, on December 11, 1950, the actor suffered a fatal heart attack, leaving his wife, Louise. He was 52 years old.

References

"Dewey Robinson, Character Actor, Dies in Las Vegas." *Los Angeles Times,* December 13, 1950.

"Dewey Robinson Hit by Auto. *Los Angeles Examiner,* March 25, 1950.

Obituary. *Variety,* circa December 1950.

HARRY SHANNON

Born on a farm in Saginaw, Michigan, on July 13, 1890, Harry Shannon was a natural performer, known from an early age for his singing and dancing prowess. At the age of 15, the future character actor of stage and screen landed his first professional job when he was tapped to replace an ailing juvenile in a traveling repertory show. Leaving his farm life behind, Shannon wound up in New York, where he later made his Broadway debut in Harry Clay Blainey's *Child Slaves of New York.*

During the next several years, Shannon honed his skills as a musical comedy performer, working in a wide variety of venues, including the "chautauqua" circuit, carnivals, burlesque, and vaudeville. Around 1910, he joined the Morosco Company at the Burbank Theater in Los Angeles, appearing with such stage notables as Marjorie Rambeau and Walter Catlett, and was later seen in such Broadway hits as *Oh, Kay!* with Gertrude Lawrence; *Laugh, Clown, Laugh,* starring Lionel Barrymore; *Hold Everything,* featuring Bert Lahr and Victor Moore; *Simple Simon,* starring Ed Wynn; and *Mrs. O'Brien Entertains,* featuring Gene Tierney and Robert Williams.

In the late 1920s, Shannon was seen in *From Hell Came a Lady,* presented by actor Joseph Schildkraut's Theatre Guild in Los Angeles. Spotted by producer-director Bryan Foy, Shannon was cast in a number of Foy's

experimental talking pictures, and later appeared with Charles "Buddy" Rogers in *Heads Up* (1930), the first all-talking feature produced by Paramount at its studio in Astoria, New York.

During his film career, Shannon appeared in more than 100 pictures, including such memorable features as *Citizen Kane* (1941), where he played the father of the film's title character; *Random Harvest* (1942), a popular tearjerker starring Ronald Colman and Greer Garson; *The Sullivans* (1944), based on the real-life story of a family of brothers killed in World War II; and *Mr. Blandings Builds His Dream House* (1948), an enjoyable comedy with Cary Grant and Myrna Loy. He was also seen in 11 films noirs: *This Gun for Hire* (1942), *Crack-Up* (1946), *Night Editor* (1946), *The Devil Thumbs a Ride* (1947), *Nora Prentiss* (1947), *The Lady from Shanghai* (1948), *Champion* (1949), *Where Danger Lives* (1950), *The Killer That Stalked New York* (1950), *Witness to Murder* (1954), and *Touch of Evil* (1958). Most of his film noir roles depicted lawmen, most notably the detective in *The Devil Thumbs a Ride* who stalks a psychopathic killer played by Lawrence Tierney. In a departure from his usual noir appearances, however, he turned in a well-done performance in *Champion* as a diner owner who forces a "shotgun" wedding between his daughter (Ruth Roman) and the man she loves (Kirk Douglas).

Shannon's numerous film appearances were complemented by his television work, which included guest spots on *I Love Lucy*, *Alfred Hitchcock Presents*, and *The Untouchables*, as well as numerous western programs including *Have Gun, Will Travel, Death Valley Days, Rawhide, Cheyenne, Colt .45, Gunsmoke, Bat Masterson*, and *The Dakotas*.

Even into his 70s, Shannon continued to work in such feature films as *Summer and Smoke* (1961), with Geraldine Page, and *Wild in the Country* (1961), an Elvis Presley starrer. On July 27, 1964, two years after the release of his last movie, *Gypsy* (1962), Shannon was found dead in his home. He was survived by his wife, Louise.

References

Biography of Harry Shannon. RKO Radio Pictures, June 26, 1942.
Biography of Harry Shannon. Warner Bros. Pictures, February 1, 1962.
"Harry Shannon Funeral Rites to Be Friday." *Los Angeles Times*, July 29, 1964.
Obituary. *Los Angeles Herald-Examiner*, July 30, 1964.

ART SMITH

After finding success on the Broadway stage, Art Smith was in the midst of a promising and prolific film career when he was blacklisted as part of the Communist witch-hunts of the 1950s. Until that grim chapter in cinema history impacted his life, Smith had appeared on screen with such stars as Burt Lancaster, Robert Montgomery, and Robert Ryan, and was seen in an even dozen films noirs.

Arthur Gordon Smith was born on March 23, 1899, in New York City, the only child of actor-theater manager Norman Lincoln, and his wife, Jane Smith, an actress and accomplished pianist. As a child, young Smith's parents moved frequently; for a while, his father managed a theater in Portland, Oregon, and later, the boy attended Queen Anne High School in Seattle, Washington.

Interested in performing from an early age, Smith studied acting at the Goodman Theater in Chicago, making his professional debut as Puck in *A Midsummer Night's Dream* in 1926. Although he held down a variety of jobs to make ends meet–including construction and factory work–Smith was singularly focused on an acting career and was first seen on Broadway in November 1929, appearing alongside Bette Davis in the long-running drama *Broken Dishes*. During the next several years, Smith was a constant presence on the Broadway stage; some of his most highly acclaimed appearances came through his association with New York's famed Group Theatre, including *Awake and Sing!*, *Waiting for Lefty*, *Golden Boy*, and *Rocket to the Moon*. For his performance in the latter, Smith won a New York Critics Award and was praised by the *New York Times* critic for his "tremendous insight and force of emotion."

After first appearing on screen in a bit part in the 1934 war feature *The Fighting Ranger*, Smith moved to Hollywood in the early 1940s, landing minor roles in such features as *Government Girl* (1943), a mild comedy starring Olivia deHavilland; *None But the Lonely Heart* (1944), which featured a well-received performance by Cary Grant; and *A Tree Grows in Brooklyn* (1945), a touching story of a New York family in the early 1900s. Then, after playing a supporting role in *Brute Force* (1947), Smith spent the next several years appearing in a series of features from the film noir era: *Framed* (1947), *Body and Soul* (1947), *T-Men* (1947), *A Double Life* (1947), *Ride the Pink Horse* (1947), *Caught* (1949), *Manhandled* (1949), *Quicksand* (1950), *In a Lonely Place* (1950), *Try and Get Me* (1950), and *The Killer That Stalked New York* (1950). Smith's initial noir performance as the sympathetic but liquor-soaked prison doctor in *Brute Force*, was singled out by several critics, including Harrison Carroll of the *Los Angeles Evening Herald Express*, who said his role was "well-handled," and the *Hollywood Citizen-News*' Lloyd L. Sloan, who included the actor in his mention of the supporting cast members who "merit high praise." In addition to this role, Smith was also prominently figured in *Ride the Pink Horse*, in which he played a determined detective trailing star Robert Montgomery; *In a Lonely Place*, where he portrayed the loyal agent of an emotionally and physically explosive screenwriter (Humphrey Bogart); and *Quicksand*, where he was seen as a cantankerous, deceitful, and potentially deadly garage owner.

During this period, Smith was also seen in such well-done pictures as *Letter from an Unknown Woman* (1948), a lavish tearjerker starring Joan Fontaine; *The Next Voice You Hear* (1950), which focuses on a couple whose lives are changed when they hear the voice of God on the radio; and *The Painted Hills* (1951), an entertaining Lassie adventure. He also returned to Broadway, appearing with Fredric March and Morris Carnovsky in *An Enemy of the People* (1950) and with Celeste Holm and Kevin McCarthy in *Anna Christie* (1952). But around this time, Art Smith found his entire career in jeopardy when he was accused of Communism during the House Un-American Activities Committee (HUAC) hearings; Smith was not only condemned for lending his name to at least nine Communist causes between 1934 and 1949, but he was identified as a Communist by director Elia Kazan, and Group Theatre founder and playwright Clifford Odets. (Ironically, Odets' May 1952 testimony before the HUAC came just one month after Smith closed in the playwright's successful Broadway revival of *Golden Boy*.)

Smith returned to Broadway in 1957, in the original cast of *West Side Story*, followed by *A Touch of the Poet* in 1958 and *All the Way Home* in 1959. Two years after the latter production, Smith was seen in his first feature film in nearly a decade, *The Hustler* (1961), playing a bit part as a pool room attendant. Two years later, he was back on screen in *The Moving Finger* (1963), but this crime drama starring Lionel Stander was Smith's last film.

On February 24, 1973, three years after appearing in the television production of *Do

Not Go Gentle Into That Good Night, Smith suffered a fatal heart attack at a nursing home in West Babylon, New York. The 73-year-old actor was survived by his son, Craig Gordon Smith.

References

"All the Way Home." *Playbill*, November 30, 1960.
"Art Smith." *Aware Bulletin*, July 15, 1955.
"Art Smith, Stage Actor, Dead; Won Acclaim in Play by Odets." *New York Times*, February 28, 1973.
"A Touch of the Poet." Cast Questionnaire, circa 1958.
"Home is the Hero." *Playbill*, September 22, 1954.
Lockridge, Richard. "The New Play." *New York Sun*, March 19, 1942.
Obituary. *Variety*, March 7, 1973.

RAY TEAL

Perhaps best known to modern audiences for his 13-year portrayal of Sheriff Roy Coffee on the television series *Bonanza*, Ray Teal was born on January 12, 1902, in Grand Rapids, Michigan. Teal was enrolled at the University of California for a short time, where he played the saxophone in the school's band, and he later appeared in a number of productions at the Pasadena Playhouse. Upon graduation, Teal toured the South in a one-man show and worked as emcee at theaters in New York, Los Angeles, and Toronto, before making his screen debut in *Western Jamboree* (1938), a Gene Autry vehicle that was the first in a long series of Teal's appearances in westerns. These included *Pony Post* (1940), *Cherokee Strip* (1940), *Wild Bill Hickok Rides* (1942), *They Died With Their Boots On* (1942), *Apache Trail* (1942), *Canyon Passage* (1946), *Cheyenne* (1947), *Whispering Smith* (1948), *Streets of Laredo* (1949), *Winchester '73* (1950), *Ambush* (1950), *Ambush at Tomahawk Gap* (1953), *Apache Ambush* (1955), *The Oklahoman* (1957), *Saddle the Wind* (1958), *Cattle King* (1963), and his final film, *Chisum* (1970).

Between westerns, Teal found time to play minor roles in a total of 19 films noirs: *Decoy* (1946), *Brute Force* (1947), *The High Wall* (1947), *Dead Reckoning* (1947), *I Wouldn't Be in Your Shoes* (1948), *Raw Deal* (1948), *Road House* (1948), *Scene of the Crime* (1949), *The Asphalt Jungle* (1950), *Convicted* (1950), *Edge of Doom* (1950), *Southside 1-1000* (1950),

Gun Crazy (1950), *Quicksand* (1950), *Where Danger Lives* (1950), *The Big Carnival* (1951), *Captive City* (1952), *The Turning Point* (1952), and *Rogue Cop* (1954). With the exception of the occasional prisoner or guard, Teal portrayed policemen in each of his noir films; of these, the most noteworthy was the lawman on the wrong side of the law in *The Big Carnival*. Here, Teal memorably played a corrupt sheriff who makes a deal with an unscrupulous reporter (Kirk Douglas) in an effort to boost his chances for re-election.

Teal could also be glimpsed in a variety

of other first-rate films, including *Kitty Foyle* (1940), which featured Ginger Rogers in her Academy Award-winning role; *Strange Cargo* (1940), a spiritual drama starring Joan Crawford and Clark Gable; *Sergeant York* (1941), with Gary Cooper in the title role; *Woman of the Year* (1942), a Spencer Tracy–Katharine Hepburn comedy; *The Best Years of Our Lives* (1946), the Academy Award–winning drama with Fredric March and Myrna Loy; *Carrie* (1952), an outstanding adaptation of Theodore Dreiser novel; *About Mrs. Leslie* (1954), a moving melodrama featuring Shirley Booth and Robert Ryan; *Inherit the Wind* (1960), starring Spencer Tracy and Fredric March; *Judgment at Nuremberg* (1961), a powerful postwar drama; and his final film, *The Liberation of L.B. Jones* (1970), a popular "black exploitation" film. In most of his films, Teal's roles amounted to little more than bit parts, and many were unbilled. Still, the actor maintained that he was pleased with the path his career had taken.

"Usually I'm nameless," he said. "Sometimes I wear beards or wigs, sometimes no— but I have the face nobody recognizes or remembers. It's my fortune. I'm safe in this business just so long as no one recognizes me."

Aside from his appearances in more than 200 films, Teal was a regular performer on television as well. In addition to his long-time association with *Bonanza*, the actor was seen in guest spots in such western fare as *The Lone Ranger*, *Cheyenne*, *Frontier*, *Broken Arrow*, *Gunsmoke*, *Maverick*, *Laramie*, *Wagon Train*, and *The Rifleman*. He also appeared on *Alfred Hitchcock Presents*, *The Twilight Zone*, *Perry Mason*, *I Dream of Jeannie*, and *Green Acres*.

In 1974, Teal made his final television appearance, portraying a judge in *The Hanged Man*. Two years later, on April 2, 1976, he died in Santa Monica, California, following a long illness. He was 70 years old.

References

Biography of Ray Teal. Paramount Studios, circa 1950.

Obituary. *Variety*, April 5, 1976.

"Ray Teal, Lawman in Western Films, Bonanza TV Series, Dies." *Los Angeles Times*, April 3, 1976.

SID TOMACK

With appearances in only 34 films over a span of three decades, Sid Tomack was better known for his television work, which included recurring roles on such series as *My Friend Irma* and *The Life of Riley*, as well as multiple appearances on *Perry Mason* and *The Adventures of Superman*. Still, Tomack managed to make his mark in the realm of film noir, with appearances in *Framed* (1947), *A Double Life* (1947), *The Scar* (1948), *Force of Evil* (1948), *House of Strangers* (1949), *Abandoned* (1949), *Side Street* (1950), and *Appointment with Danger* (1951). In each, he played minor, sometimes unbilled parts, including a bartender, a jewel fence, and a trainman, and in three of the films, he was seen as a waiter.

Born on September 8, 1907, in Brooklyn New York, Tomack began his career as part of a vaudeville song-and-dance team called "Sid Tomack and Reis Brothers." He later honed his craft as a performer by serving as the master of ceremonies at resorts in New York's Catskill Mountains, and in his first feature film, *A Wave, a WAC, and a Marine* (1944), he appeared as himself. Most of Tomack's film appearances between 1947 and 1951 were in his film noir features, but he was also seen during this period in such pictures as *I Love Trouble* (1948), starring Franchot Tone; *Boston Blackie's Chinese Adventure* (1948), the next-to-last feature in the 14-episode Columbia series; and *The Fuller Brush Girl* (1950), with Lucille Ball in the title role.

In addition to his roles as Jim Gillis in *The Life of Riley* in 1949, and Al in *My Friend Irma* in 1952, Tomack also appeared on such television series as *The Adventures of Superman* and *Perry Mason*. He also continued his big screen appearances throughout the 1950s, playing a carnival barker in *The Hoaxters* (1952), a bartender in *These Wilder Years* (1956), a nightclub waiter in *The Opposite Sex* (1956), and a reporter in *The Space Children* (1958). His final film was *Sail a Crooked Ship* (1961), a comedy starring Robert Wagner. On November 12, 1962, the actor died of a heart ailment at the age of 55, leaving behind his wife, Virginia Ledell, two sons, Michael and Peter, and a daughter, Karen.

References

Obituary. *New York Times*, November 14, 1962.
Obituary. *Variety*, November 21, 1962.

TITO VUOLO

During his 16-year Hollywood career, Tito Vuolo was seen in a series of ethnic roles, portraying waiters, vendors, barbers, and store owners. In a number of his features, however, he managed to rise above his stereotyped material, turning in performances that showcased his unique talents. Many of these memorable portrayals were provided in the actor's 12 film noir features.

A native of Naples, Italy, Vuolo was born on March 22, 1893. He began performing as a child, working at the age of 10 in a local circus, where he sang comedy songs between acts. After sailing to America at the age of 14, Vuolo took singing lessons, planning to pursue an opera career, but later joined a vaudeville act with the Keith Circuit. Several years later, when Vuolo married, he formed an act with his wife — the two were billed as Vuolo and Narciso, "the highest-priced Italian couple in the business."

Vuolo made his legitimate stage debut with an Italian company, in a translation of *The White Sister*. He was later seen in a number of Italian productions, as well as several Pirandello plays, based on the works by Sicilian playwright Luigi Pirandello. He was first seen on Broadway in *Pasquale Never Knew*, which opened in March 1938 — and closed after three performances.

"My, was that an awful flop!" Vuolo said in a 1941 interview. "The notices were the worst I ever see."

After this inauspicious beginning, Vuolo was seen in such stage productions as *Once Upon a Night*, *The World We Make*, *The Big Story*, and *Mr. and Mrs. North*, in which he played the part of a janitor. When the screen rights to the latter play were bought by MGM, Vuolo was invited to Hollywood to reprise his role but, instead, he "found himself on the set of *The Shadow of the Thin Man*," a columnist reported. Five years later, Vuolo appeared in the televised version of *Mr. and*

Mrs. North (1946), and the following year was seen in the first of his many films noirs, *Kiss of Death* (1947), starring Victor Mature and Richard Widmark. This feature was followed by *T-Men* (1947), *I Wouldn't Be in Your Shoes* (1948), *Sorry, Wrong Number* (1948), *Cry of the City* (1948), *House of Strangers* (1949), *Between Midnight and Dawn* (1950), *Southside 1-1000* (1950), *The Man Who Cheated Himself* (1950), *The Enforcer* (1951), *The Racket* (1951), and *The Killing* (1956). He was perhaps most memorable as the father of a young girl involved with a criminal in *Cry of the City*, and as a luckless taxi driver, Tony Vetto, in *The Enforcer*, who recognizes a killer in his cab and is murdered for his troubles.

In addition to Vuolo's film noir features, he was also seen in a number of box-office hits during the 1940s and 1950s, including *The Bishop's Wife* (1947), a holiday favorite starring Loretta Young; *Mr. Blandings Builds His Dream House* (1948), an amusing comedy with Cary Grant and Myrna Loy; *Flamingo Road* (1949), a Joan Crawford starrer; *Everybody Does It* (1949), a comedy with Paul Douglas and Linda Darnell; and *The Great Caruso* (1951), which depicted the life of opera star Enrico Caruso.

Vuolo's last screen performance was in the 1957 feature, *20 Million Miles to Earth*, a so-so science fictioner in which he was seen as a police commissioner. Five years later, on September 14, 1962, Vuolo died of cancer in Los Angeles, California. He was 69 years old.

References

"A Bell for Adano." *Playbill*, December 6, 1944.
Dalrymple, Jean. "Circus and Stage Jobs Prove The Making of One American." *New York Times*, April 20, 1941.
"Johnny on a Spot." *Playbill*, January 8, 1942.
"Mr. and Mrs. North." *Playbill*, January 12, 1941.
"Shubert Comedy Set." *New York Herald-Tribune*, December 5, 1941.
"The Italian Point of View." *New York Post*, January 15, 1940.

Appendix B:
LAST WORDS
FROM THE
BAD BOYS

Film noir is rife with some of the most memorable and quotable lines in motion picture history. Along with noir's distinctive characters, shadowy presentation, labyrinthine plot tangles, and cynical, hopeless tone, it is the hard-boiled dialogue that makes it such a fascinating era of filmmaking. Even the lesser offerings from the period fairly crackle with snappy lines and unforgettable comebacks.

The spicy words and phrases that are intertwined throughout the films noirs of the 1940s and 1950s cover a wide range, from vicious threats, to deep despair, to heavy cynicism. This section of *Bad Boys* provides a smattering of these noteworthy lines, divided into categories that delineate their various types.

Regarding Dames

"Young woman, either you have been raised in some incredibly rustic community, where good manners are unknown, or you suffer from the common feminine delusion that the mere fact of being a woman exempts you from the rules of civilized conduct. Or possibly both." — Clifton Webb in *Laura*

"You don't really think I could be in love with a rotten little tramp like you, do you?" — Zachary Scott in *Mildred Pierce*

"I didn't know they made 'em as beautiful as you are, and as smart — and as hard." — Dan Duryea in *Too Late for Tears*

"Nothing personal, sister. How about a deal? You let my brother off the hook — *you* keep the rock and I'll keep *him*." — Robert Ryan in *The Racket*

"I know you like a book. You're a no-good, nosy little tramp — you'd sell out your own mother for a piece of fudge, but you're smart along with it." — Sterling Hayden in *The Killing*

"That is quite a dish. I wonder what her angle is." — Van Heflin in *The Prowler*

"With a woman like you, a man always runs a risk." — Vincent Price in *The Las Vegas Story*

"It was the bottom of the barrel and I scraped it, but I didn't care. I had *her*." — Robert Mitchum in *Out of the Past*.

"I must say, for an intelligent girl, you've surrounded yourself with a remarkable collection of dopes." — Dana Andrews in *Laura*

"A dish — 60-cent special. Cheap, flashy, strictly poison under the gravy." — Charles McGraw in *The Narrow Margin*

"You're pretty hard to resist. You're beautiful. With that sweet, innocent face, I was beginning to believe all those lies." — Alan Ladd in *Calcutta*

"She's my life, Mama. She's good and she's beautiful. And when a man tells me he will hurt her, this man I must kill, Mama." — Richard Conte in *Cry of the City*

"She was a charming, middle-aged lady with a face like a bucket of mud. I gave her a drink. She was a gal who'd take a drink if she had to knock you down to get to the bottle." — Dick Powell in *Murder, My Sweet*

"You have her. We want her. How much? As simple as that." — Peter Brocco in *The Narrow Margin*

"If this were fiction, I would fall in love with Vera, marry her, and make a respectable woman out of her. Or else she'd make some supreme, class A sacrifice for me — and die." Tom Neal in *Detour*

"Dames are always pulling a switch on you." — Dana Andrews in *Laura*

"I had no illusion about deceiving you — you have the feline perception that all women have." — Albert Dekker in *Kiss Me Deadly*

"What a beautiful picture. Moonlight. Sagebrush. My wife with a stranger." — Vincent Price in *The Las Vegas Story*

"Just pay me off and I'm quiet. But use cash. Don't try to pay me off with pitch handed to you by this cheap piece of baggage." — Steve Brodie in *Out of the Past*

"She was cool. Like somebody making funeral arrangements for a murder not yet committed." — Dick Powell in *Murder, My Sweet*

"People aren't safe with women like you in the world, and people have to be protected." — Lloyd Nolan in *Lady in the Lake*

"Mr. Scranton, when you see her, will you tell her I love her? No, don't tell her I love her. Tell her to go home and forget me. Tell her to forget me." — Frank Lovejoy in *Try and Get Me*

"Mice — they're all for ya as long as you're in the chips. I never seen a dame yet that's still around when you hit the skids." — Wallace Ford in *The Set-Up*

"You know when a woman loves you like that she can love you with every card in the deck and then pull a knife across your throat the next morning." — Van Heflin in *Johnny Eager*

"What's the matter, baby? I'm not gonna hurt ya. Now go and read your comic books like a good girl." — James Cagney in *White Heat*

"Last night, comin' home all dolled up, makin' a big play. You thought it'd work, didn't ya? Thought you had me all tied up. Like a knot. So no matter what you did, I wouldn't do anything. You got me to trust you, didn't ya? ... What'd you do with my money?" — John Garfield in *He Ran All the Way*

"I don't think I'll have to kill her. Just slap that pretty face into hamburger meat, that's all." — Sterling Hayden in *The Killing*

"One thing I can't stand is a dame that's drunk.... She's got the shakes, see. So she has a drink to get rid of them. That one tastes so good, so she has another one. First thing you know, she's stinko again." — Edward G. Robinson in *Key Largo*

"Flossie had looks, brains, and all the accessories. She was better than a deck with six aces. But I regret to report that she also knew how to handle a gun. My gun." — John Hoyt in *Brute Force*

"You're a beautiful dame, Iris. One of the best I've seen. And you treat me like it was Christmas Eve. But no thanks. I see through you like those silk dresses you wear." — Richard Conte in *New York Confidential*

"What kind of dame *are* you?" — Mickey Rooney in *Quicksand*

Forewarned Is Forearmed

"Don't get cute with me." — Howard Da Silva in *The Blue Dahlia*

"You make one more cute move and see how long you'll live." — Dick Powell in *Cry Danger*

"One bad move outta you and I'll put you on your back for good." — Jack Webb in *Appointment with Danger*

"Be still or I'll snap your arm like a wishbone." — Ted De Corsia in *The Naked City*

"The first guy that talks or tries to identify anyone is gonna get a headache he can't cure." — Alan Ladd in *Appointment with Danger*

"Get out of here before I knock your brains in." — Dick Powell in *Johnny O'Clock*

"One of these days you're gonna start pickin' me apart and I'll slap you out from between your ears." — Robert Taylor in *Johnny Eager*

"If you so much as look cross-eyed at anybody, I'll blow the back of your skull out." — Neville Brand in *D.O.A.*

"Touch my truck and I'll climb into your hair." — Richard Conte in *Thieves' Highway*

"Go on, sit in any chair you wanna sit in. If you don't like that one, take another one. I want you to consider yourself my guest. We'll have a couple of drinks. And then I'm gonna knock your teeth out." — William Bendix in *The Glass Key*

"Do me a favor, Castro, while I'm on the phone. Try to jump me. I'd love nothing better than shooting you right in the belly." — Dick Powell in *Cry Danger*

"People lose teeth talkin' like that. You want to hang around, you'll be polite." — Humphrey Bogart in *The Maltese Falcon*

"You like to shoot? So do I. So I'm warnin' you, don't try anything smart with me." — William Talman in *The Hitch-Hiker*

"Get outta here while you can still walk." — Glenn Ford in *The Big Heat*

"Nobody gets me — nobody. Nobody gets me 'til I get you. You know that, don't you? You're gonna sweat, Tino. You're gonna sweat blood. And then I'm gonna put a bullet right between your eyes." — Mark Stevens in *Cry Vengeance*

"Coppers — always with the strong-arm stuff. If I meet this monkey without his badge ..." — John Kellogg in *Johnny O'Clock*

"You got a long nose. Why don't you keep it to yourself?" — Mark Stevens in *The Street With No Name*

"I don't like people that play games. Tell your boss — when you wake up." — Humphrey Bogart in *The Big Sleep*

"I'll put this right through your skull if you get up before I tell you." — Dick Powell in *Cry Danger*

"You haven't seen the day when you can throw me out on the junk pile. I'll be back ... I've been around a long time — I know all the angles. Who do you think you are? You can't stop me. Nothing will stop me." — Barry Sullivan in *The Gangster*

"Look, creep. Don't ever touch me again.... I'll kill you if you ever touch me again." — Mark Stevens in *Cry Vengeance*

"I want him to be fully conscious. I don't like to shoot a corpse. I want to see the expression on his face when he knows it's coming." — Raymond Burr in *His Kind of Woman*

"I'm gonna take a smack out of him right now. I'd give my right arm to smash his face in. I can't stand the sight of it." — Elisha Cook, Jr. in *The Gangster*

"You got a head on your shoulders. Now take it outta here before I bust it." — Sheldon Leonard in *Somewhere in the Night*

"I'd just as soon see you all with your guts hanging out." — John Garfield in *The Breaking Point*

"You're in the same boat that I am, but you're gonna be in it dead." — Lloyd Nolan in *Lady in the Lake*

"You ever cross me again, or look like it, I'll bury you. Now beat it." — John Garfield in *Nobody Lives Forever*

"I'm sorry I can't give you a choice of food, Steve. But it won't make much difference. You're not going to live long enough to get any nourishment out of it." — Raymond Burr in *Desperate.*

"You do that again and I'll kick your face in." — Edmond O'Brien in *D.O.A.*

"I kept remembering that pretty face of yours, Jardine, all the time I was in hock. If you're not sharp, you're not going to have that pretty face. You're not going to have any face at all."— Mark Stevens in *The Dark Corner*

"I'm givin' you a chance to blow. If you decide to stick, I'll shoot the first one that don't do as I tell them."— Humphrey Bogart in *High Sierra*

"If I ever catch you around here again, they'll have to pick you up with a sieve."— Victor Mature in *I Wake Up Screaming*

"Say, I'll bet that new bride of yours is pretty. How 'bout it, Steve? You going to the police? While you're there, we'll have the missus. I don't care what you tell them. But if Al doesn't walk out of that police station by midnight, your wife ain't going to be so good to look at."— Raymond Burr in *Desperate.*

"All right, let's play 20 questions. You answer them correctly, maybe I won't knock your teeth out."— Mark Stevens in *The Dark Corner*

"Niles. I killed a policeman. I'll kill you. Makes no difference."— Richard Conte in *Cry of the City*

"For a nickel, I'd grab him. Stick both thumbs right in his eyes. Hang on 'til he drops dead." — Richard Widmark in *Kiss of Death*

"Listen gay boy, you don't run around knocking off state's attorneys— it isn't being done this year. If Stewart gets a scratch on him, they'll hunt you down like a sewer rat."— Robert Taylor in *Party Girl.*

"You ever hear of a game called Russian Roulette? It's supposed to show how much nerve you have. Six chambers. One bullet ... You want to play some more?"— Dick Powell in *Cry Danger*

"You stick this in the back of your filthy brain and keep it there. We're gonna keep minding your business until you and your gorillas are tucked away in cages where you belong."— Edmond O'Brien in *Between Midnight and Dawn*

"We're goin' right on being pals, you and me. We're gonna have some fun together. Lots of fun, just like we used to. You got a wife and kids, ain't ya, pal? They're gonna have some fun, too. I'm gonna enjoy meetin' your family. Kids like to have fun. We'll all have some fun

together. You and me. And your wife. And your kids. From now on, lots of fun."— Richard Widmark in *Kiss of Death*

Doom, Despair, and Agony

"Everything's gone wrong."— Fred MacMurray in *Pushover*

"This is bad."— John Garfield in *Nobody Lives Forever*

"It's just that you're the only one left. Even my mother turned me out. Without you, I'm nothing. Finished. Dead."— Richard Conte in *Cry of the City*

"No sooner do I get my head above water when somebody pushes me down again."— John Garfield in *The Breaking Point*

"I got a feeling something's closing in on me. I don't know what it is."— Mark Stevens in *The Dark Corner*

"All my life I've been running. From welfare officers, thugs, my father ... I'm a dead man." — Richard Widmark in *Night and the City*

"Whichever way you turn, fate sticks out a foot to trip you."— Tom Neal in *Detour*

"People do things they don't mean sometimes. Things just happen."— Frank Lovejoy in *Try and Get Me*

"You know how it is early in the morning on the water? Everything's quiet, except for the sea gulls— a long way off. Then you come ashore, and it starts— and in no time at all, you're up to your ears in trouble. And you don't know where it began."— John Garfield in *The Breaking Point*

"A marriage to a woman who accepted my love, yet despised me so thoroughly she resorted to murder ... I feel stripped bare. Degraded." — Brian Donlevy in *Impact*

"I wake up in the night sweating and there's no way out. No way out."— John Garfield in *The Breaking Point*

"I've got a feeling I'm right behind the eight ball. Something's going to happen."— Mark Stevens in *The Dark Corner*

Questions, Questions

"How come a nice guy like you is a cop?" — Ted De Corsia in *The Big Combo*

"What do I have to do to make you understand the way I feel about you — rob a bank?" — Howard Duff in *Shakedown*

"How does it feel, dying in the dirty middle of somebody else's love affair?" — Lloyd Nolan in *Lady in the Lake*

"Am I dumb, or is someone trying to cover up something?" — William Talman in *The Racket*

"Did you ever want to forget anything? Did you ever want to cut away a piece of your memory or blot it out? You can't, you know." — Tom Neal in *Detour*

"What's wrong with the law that we can't touch him? Oh, I know — our kind of laws are designed to protect the innocent. It's not enough that we know a man is guilty — we have to *prove* it." — Roy Roberts in *The Enforcer*

"You arresting me? I don't think so." — Vincent Price in *The Bribe*

"Is this what you folks do for amusement in the evenings? Sit around toasting marshmallows and calling each other names? Sure, if you're so anxious for me to join in the game, I'd be glad to. I can think of a few names I'd like to be calling you myself." — Orson Welles in *The Lady from Shanghai*

"A wife and two kids, eh, Weiss? There are a couple of boys in town I might speak to about them. How would you like to have the wife and two kids worked over?" — Barry Kelley in *711 Ocean Drive*

"You talk about values — what kind of values do you think I have now? How do I know what's right?" — Glenn Ford in *Convicted*

"What's that church stuff do for ya, anyway?" — John Garfield in *He Ran All the Way*

"You think I'm funny? I don't like to be laughed at." — Robert Ryan in *Beware, My Lovely*

"I wanted him here alive — what happened? I told you to go without guns. Which one of you changed my mind?" — Richard Conte in *The Big Combo*

"How much does a policeman earn? Three, four hundred dollars a month? We offer you a fortune. And what do we ask in return? That you point her out and turn the other way…. We'll get her whether you give her to us or not, so don't take too long. It'd be a shame if you missed your opportunity." — Peter Brocco in *The Narrow Margin*

"Are you a man, or what? Trying to gyp and double-cross, but with no guts for it. What's inside of you? What's keeping you alive?" — Sterling Hayden in *The Asphalt Jungle*

"Do you mind if I laugh in your face?" — Dick Powell in *Johnny O'Clock*

Self-Assessment and Actualization

"I just wanna be somebody." — Richard Widmark in *Night and the City*

"Twenty years ago when Kubik ordered me that job, I shoulda thrown it in his face. He showed me a plush, lined rat-hole and I crawled in and made it my home." — Richard Conte in *The Brothers Rico*

"Sure, the suckers all give me sour looks. The minute they stop I'm worried, see, because then I know I'm not on my toes. And that's where I'm stayin'. Ready to hit the first guy that's fool enough to try and cross me in the first place." — Robert Taylor in *Johnny Eager*

"I don't know what your troubles are, but I have my own." — Leon Ames in *Lady in the Lake*

"I don't trust anybody." — Alan Ladd in *This Gun for Hire*

"I never confuse business with sentiment. Unless it's extremely profitable, of course." — Clifton Webb in *The Dark Corner*

"I'm a natural-born suspect. It's because I'm not the conventional type." — Vincent Price in *Laura*

"All I've got left to peddle is guts. I'm not sure I got any — I have to find out." — John Garfield in *The Breaking Point*

"I don't like gambling very much. I don't like being at the mercy of those little white squares that roll around and decide whether you win or lose. I like to have the say-so myself." — Lawrence Tierney in *Born to Kill*

"I do like a man who tells you right out that's he's looking out for himself. Don't we all? I don't trust a man who says he's not." — Sydney Greenstreet in *The Maltese Falcon*

"There's just one idea man in this outfit. Me. I do the thinking. I give the orders." — Richard Widmark in *The Street With No Name*

"Quit the act. I know you too well. We're the same kind of people. The same kind of dirt." — Robert Taylor in *Rogue Cop*

"I thought by this time I'd have the world on fire." — John Garfield in *The Breaking Point*

"I know newspapers backwards, forwards, and sideways. I can write 'em, edit 'em, print 'em, wrap 'em, and sell 'em. I can handle big news and little news. If there's no news, I'll go out and bite a dog." — Kirk Douglas in *The Big Carnival*

"For 16 years I've been a cop — for 16 years I've been living in dirt and take it from me, some of it's bound to rub off on you. You get to hate people. Everyone you meet." Edmond O'Brien in *Shield for Murder*

"Just because I was a wrestler, everybody thinks I'm dumb. I'm not dumb. I'm smart." — Ted De Corsia in *The Naked City*

"I was happy. I was contented following orders, until you came sneaking around with your big ideas. Telling me how we could take the old man for all the money — the places we were going to live. Making me the hottest hood in town." — William Talman in *City That Never Sleeps*

"I'm not a violent man, Mr. Peters. As a matter of fact, I hate violence. But there are times when the most peace-loving simply must do it. And this may be one of them." — Peter Lorre in *The Mask of Dimitrios*

"The only thing I ever wanted was to be a good cop, but they got to me. Oh, they got to me good. Now there's only one thing I want." — Mark Stevens in *Cry Vengeance*

"I didn't like the feeling I had about her. The way I wanted to put my hand on her arm. The way I kept smelling jasmine in her hair. The way I kept hearing that song she'd sung. Yeah —

I was walking into something, all right." — Humphrey Bogart in *Dead Reckoning*

"I'd give my soul to take out my brain, hold it under the faucet and wash away the dirty pictures you put there today!" — Kirk Douglas in *Detective Story*

"I told you — I forget things. Sometimes when I start out in the morning, I tell myself, 'Remember to come back here tonight — this is where you live.' But I can't remember." — Robert Ryan in *Beware, My Lovely*

"Nothing kills me. I'll die in Stockholm like my great-grandfather, age 93. I'm not scared of anyone — including you." — John Hoyt in *The Big Combo*

"Decency and integrity are fancy words, Ellen, but they never kept anybody well fed. And I've got quite an appetite." — Howard Duff in *Shakedown*

"You don't snuff out 10 years of my life with a pinch of your fingers. If that's your idea, you don't know me as well as you think you do." — Leon Ames in *The Velvet Touch*

"I assure you I could never throw a lovely body from a moving car. My artistic temperament wouldn't permit it." — Humphrey Bogart in *In a Lonely Place*

"I've been in so many towns, so many places — I can't ever remember anyone caring about me. I don't think I ever loved anyone. And I know no one ever loved me." — Robert Ryan in *Beware, My Lovely*

"I didn't like to think about it. But by then, I'd done just what the cops would say I did. Even if I didn't." — Tom Neal in *Detour*

"You're insane. You're out of your mind. Me too." — Kirk Douglas in *The Strange Love of Martha Ivers*

"Listen, sweetheart — I have a way of getting people to do what I want 'em to do." — Howard Duff in *Shakedown*

"Oh, boy — am I in a mess." — Mickey Rooney in *Quicksand*

Sizing Up the Other Guy

"Genius — you're just a chiseler out for a soft buck. You're not crooked and you're not straight.

You take what you can get where you can get it, but you don't want any trouble. You'll die at age 66 in bed with three grand in the bank, but you'll never be an operator." — Ted De Corsia in *Slightly Scarlet*

"I'm worried about you, Joe. Somewhere in your bloodstream you've got a crazy bug. And it's swimming upstream night and day. Get a cure. Or you'll kill us all." — Paul Stewart in *Appointment with Danger*

"You know, I don't know whether you're a bright young man or a liar. People that lie to me aren't very bright." — Brian Donlevy in *Shakedown*

"I'm only a little fool. I'm an amateur at it. You're a professional." — Joseph Cotten in *The Third Man*

"I thought you knew all the answers. I thought you was a wise guy from way back." — Edward G. Robinson in *Key Largo*

"All I got workin' for me are a lot of dumbheads. They'd have a tough time figuring out how to get across the street." — Robert Ryan in *The Racket*

"I always said it's a pleasure talkin' to a sharp guy. You don't waste breath. Precious thing, breath." — John Ireland in *Raw Deal*

"It was a set-up. He put a leash around my neck. He used me like a bloodhound to track down my brother … dirty, stinkin' animal!" — Richard Conte in *The Brothers Rico*

"I'm sorry for him — the poor, demented fellow seems to have nothing to look forward to. Except lifetime in a padded cell. He'd be better off dead." — Herbert Marshall in *The High Wall*

"I'd hate to take a bite out of you. You're a cookie full of arsenic." — Burt Lancaster in *Sweet Smell of Success*

"So that's your hero, huh, Tony? He breaks out of jail, fools the cops. Talks big with a gun in his hand. But look at him, Tony. His leg shot full of holes, fever going up. No place to go, no place to sleep — just run, run, run 'til he can't run any more. Escape. Escape to where? Look at him, Tony. He's a dead man." — Victor Mature in *Cry of the City*

"Our friend Shorty was the kind of crook that nobody likes, not even me, who am rather broadminded about such things." — Fred Clark in *Ride the Pink Horse*

"He was my friend. No, he wasn't my friend, but he was a nice man." — Peter Lorre in *The Mask of Dimitrios*

"Look, Stevenson — size doesn't count in our business. We all know you're a big, strong guy. We all know you can fight. But this isn't the way you're going to settle the little difference our organization happens to have with you." — William Conrad in *Sorry, Wrong Number*

"The more pain you inflict, the more pleasure you get. That's why you'd never resign from this prison. Where else would you find so many helpless flies to stick pins into?" — Art Smith in *Brute Force*

Brilliant Observations and Casual Commentary

"Fate, or some mysterious force, can put the finger on you or me for no good reason at all." — Tom Neal in *Detour*

"Matrimony is a state I don't recognize. It's not love — it's pots and pans and a conversational fistfight every Saturday night, with a paycheck as the purse." — Howard Duff in *Shakedown*

"You'd think that the people in this town would have something to do than figuring out ways to get rid of each other." — Broderick Crawford in *Black Angel*

"Of all the 14-karat saps. Starting out on a caper with a woman and a dog." — Humphrey Bogart in *High Sierra*

"Newspaper readers forget fast — it goes in one eye and out the other." — William Conrad in *The Racket*

"In your crowd, a polite 'no' is enough. In mine, it isn't. The only kind of a 'no' they understand is from the end of a gun." — Steve Cochran in *The Damned Don't Cry*

"He twisted my neck like I was a ten-cent rag doll." — Jack Palance in *The Big Knife*

"The cheaper the crook, the gaudier the patter."— Humphrey Bogart in *The Maltese Falcon*

"How I detest the dawn. The grass always looks as if it's been left out all night."— Clifton Webb in *The Dark Corner*

"Every time I run into something worthwhile, it's married." Barry Sullivan in *Suspense*

"Knocking over newspapermen just isn't being done this season."— Lawrence Tierney in *Shakedown*

"Cops have no friends. Nobody likes a cop. On either side of the law. Nobody."— Robert Ryan in *On Dangerous Ground*

"It's gettin' so you can't tail a guy anymore without havin' the cops jump on ya. This town's going to the dogs."— Percy Helton in *The Crooked Way.*

"Just like the old days— blazing guns and big, black limousines."— Regis Toomey in *Cry Danger*

"I don't like certain kinds of private dicks— I never did. I never met one yet that wasn't a crook."— Lloyd Nolan in *The Lady in the Lake*

"Imagine me in on this cheap rap. Big man like me. Picked up just for shovin' a guy's ears off his head. Traffic ticket stuff."— Richard Widmark in *Kiss of Death*

"Your old man made his money in oil, and that made you an heiress. I never knew my father, or anybody I could call that. I had to make mine myself. Well, I'm making it. But there's someone who's always trying to take it away. You either protect what you've got or you've got nothing."— Steve Cochran in *The Damned Don't Cry*

"You had sidewalks and lawns out in front— my old man's idea of success was a buck twenty an hour, union scale."— Van Heflin in *The Prowler*

"Nick hated me. He'd cut my throat for a nickel."— Mickey Rooney in *Quicksand*

"When an impoverished character, unendowed with any appreciable virtues, succumbs to a rich man's wife, it must be suspected that his interest is less passionate than pecuniary."— Clifton Webb in *The Dark Corner*

"You guys are soft. You know what makes you that way? You're up to your necks in IOUs. You're suckers. You're scared to get out on your own. You always had it good, so you're soft. Well, not me. Nobody ever gave me anything. So I don't owe nobody.... Got what I wanted my own way. When you got the know-how and a couple of bucks in your pocket, you can buy anything. Or anybody. Especially if you got 'em at the point of a gun. That really scares 'em."— William Talman in *The Hitch-Hiker*

Words of Wisdom

"You can't just go around killin' people whenever the notion strikes you — it's not feasible."— Elisha Cook, Jr., in *Born to Kill*

"Everyone's out to get you. Remember that."— Paul Stewart in *Edge of Doom*

"Never underestimate a man because you don't like him."— Everett Sloane in *The Big Knife*

"Everybody's got a price— all you gotta do is find out what it is."— Broderick Crawford in *New York Confidential*

"Look — you're here on a free ride. Don't come to the party and give away drinks."— Jack Webb in *Appointment with Danger*

"Everybody has something to conceal."— Humphrey Bogart in *The Maltese Falcon*

"Any cop that'll shake you down is a cop that'll kill ya — and just for the fun of it, too. Don't ever forget that."— James Cagney in *Kiss Tomorrow Goodbye*

"The time comes when a man's got to stop running away and face things. Or else go on running for good."— Steve Cochran in *White Heat*

"A shrewd man never asks questions until he has gathered enough information to be able to distinguish between lies and truth."— George Macready in *A Lady Without Passport*

"It may sound hard but sometimes, in order to be happy, you have to be a little ruthless."— Zachary Scott in *Danger Signal*

"Take a look around you. See that busboy over there? He steals from the waiter. The waiter steals from the owner. And the owner gyps the government. Nobody's handing out any free lunches in the world." — Richard Conte in *New York Confidential*

"The biggest mistake I made before was shooting for peanuts. Five years have taught me one thing: anytime you take a chance, you better be sure the rewards are worth the risk, 'cause they can put you away just as fast for a ten dollar heist as they can for a million dollar job." — Sterling Hayden in *The Killing*

"It's a rich world. But it hates to give. You gotta take. Somewhere out there, someone owes you something. All you gotta do is have the nerve to collect." — Paul Stewart in *Edge of Doom*

"One thing you gotta learn, kid. You gotta look and act like other people." — Howard Da Silva in *They Live By Night*

"Don't play God just because you've got a gun." — Sterling Hayden in *Suddenly*

Penetrating Put-downs

"You'd lie to your own mother on her death bed." — Edmond O'Brien in *Between Midnight and Dawn*

"For six bits, you'd hang your mother on a meat hook." — Mark Stevens in *The Dark Corner*

"You'd sell your own mother if she was worth anything." — John Garfield in *The Breaking Point*

"When you're slapped, you'll take it and like it." — Humphrey Bogart in *The Maltese Falcon*

"Joe, tell the man I'm going to break him so fast he won't have time to change his pants. Tell him the next time I see him he'll be down in the hotel lobby crying like a baby and asking for a ten dollar loan. Tell him that. And tell him I don't break my word." — Richard Conte in *The Big Combo*

"George, that's the first time anyone thought enough of you to call you a shark. If you were a *good* lawyer, you'd be flattered." — Everett Sloane in *Lady from Shanghai*

"Nobody's your pal now. You're dead. Lay down." — John Kellogg in *Johnny O'Clock*

"Joe, the man has reason to hate me. His salary is $96.50 a week. The busboys in my hotel make better money than that." — Richard Conte in *The Big Combo*

"You're dead, son. Get yourself buried." — Burt Lancaster in *Sweet Smell of Success*

"You got a sewer for a mind. One day you're gonna fall in." — Richard Conte in *House of Strangers*

"You're so lucky … if this were a movie, you'd have been on the floor ten times." — Jack Palance in *The Big Knife*

"You must have been kissed in your cradle by a vulture." — Kirk Douglas in *Detective Story*

"You got a soft job and good pay. Stop thinkin' about what might have been. And who knows — you may live to die in bed." — Richard Conte in *The Big Combo*

"Loyalty — that's something you can't buy. Half the pigs that work for us can't even spell it." — Broderick Crawford in *New York Confidential*

"You took my job. You took my hotel. You thought you could push me right off the earth. You punk." — Brian Donlevy in *The Big Combo*

"I wouldn't touch you with sterilized gloves." — Victor Mature in *I Wake Up Screaming*

"I wouldn't give you the skin off a grape." — Richard Widmark in *Kiss of Death*

BIBLIOGRAPHY

Agan, Patrick. *Is That Who I Think It Is?* Vol. 1. New York: Ace, 1975

_____. *Is That Who I Think It Is?* Vol. 3. New York: Ace, 1976.

_____. *Whatever Happened To* —. New York: Ace, 1974.

Alleman, Richard. *The Movie Lover's Guide to Hollywood.* New York: Harper and Row, 1985.

Amberg, George. *New York Times Film Reviews,* 1913-1970. New York: Arno, 1971.

Austin, John. *Hollywood's Unsolved Mysteries.* New York: Shapolsky, 1990.

Barraclough, David. *Hollywood Heaven.* New York: Gallery Books, 1991.

Baxter, John. *The Gangster Film.* New York: A.S. Barnes, 1970.

Boller, Paul F., and Davis, Ronald L. *Hollywood Anecdotes.* New York: Morrow, 1987.

Bookbinder, Robert. *Classics of the Gangster Film.* Secaucus, New Jersey: Citadel, 1985.

Brode, Douglas. *The Films of the Fifties.* Secaucus, New Jersey: Citadel, 1976.

_____. *Lost Films of the Fifties.* Secaucus, New Jersey: Citadel, 1988.

Brunette, Peter, and Peary, Gerald. "Tough Guy: James M. Cain Interviewed." *Film Comment,* May-June 1976.

Buller, Richard. "James M. Cain: The Hollywood Years, 1944-1946." *Hollywood Studio Magazine,* November 1985.

Capra, Frank. *The Name Above The Title.* New York: Macmillan, 1971.

Clarens, Carlos. *Crime Movies.* New York: W.W. Morton and Company, 1980.

Connor, Edward. "Cornell Woolrich on the Screen." *Screen Facts,* 1963.

Copjec, Joan, ed. *Shades of Noir.* London: Verso, 1993.

Crowther, Bosley. *The Great Films: Fifty Golden Years of Motion Pictures.* New York: Putnam, 1967.

Crowther, Bruce. *Film Noir: Reflections in a Dark Mirror.* London: Columbus, 1988.

_____. *Hollywood Rajah.* New York: Henry Holt and Company, 1960.

Davis, Ronald L. *The Glamour Factory.* Dallas, Texas: Southern Methodist University Press, 1993.

DeCarlo, Yvonne, with Warren, Doug. *Yvonne: An Autobiography.* New York: St. Martin's Press, 1987.

Dooley, Roger. *From Scarface to Scarlett.* New York: Harcourt Brace Jovanovich, 1979.

Dorian, Bob, with Dorothy Curley. *Bob Dorian's Classic Movies.* Holbrook, Massachusetts: Adams, 1990.

Eames, John Douglas. *The MGM Story.* New York: Crown, 1982.

_____. *The Paramount Story.* New York: Crown, 1985.

Endres, Stacey, and Cushman, Robert. *Hollywood at Your Feet.* Los Angeles, California: Pomegranate, 1992.

Finch, Christopher, and Rosenkrantz, Linda. *Gone Hollywood.* Garden City, New York: Doubleday, 1979.

"Film Noir: The Dark Age of American Cinema, 1944-1955." A Two-Unit Extension Course (AMSX 320), Cal-State Fullerton, Fullerton, California, circa 1990.

Fox-Sheinwold, Patricia. *Gone but Not Forgotten.* New York: Bell, 1982.

_____. *Too Young to Die.* New York: Crescent, 1991.

Geisler, Jerry, as told to Pete Martin. *Hollywood Lawyer: The Jerry Geisler Story.* New York: Simon and Schuster, 1960.

Gelman, Barbara, ed. *Photoplay Treasury.* New York: Crown, Inc., 1972.

Griffith, Richard. *The Movie Stars*. Garden City, New York: Doubleday, 1970.

Hannsberry, Karen Burroughs. *Femme Noir: Bad Girls of Film*. Jefferson, North Carolina: McFarland, 1998.

Herbert, Ian, ed. *Who's Who in the Theatre*. 16th ed. Detroit, Michigan: Gale, 1981.

Higham, Charles, and Greenberg, Joel. *Hollywood in the Forties*. New York: Barnes, 1968.

Hirsch, Foster. *The Dark Side of the Screen: Film Noir*. New York: Da Capo, 1981.

Hopper, Hedda. "Hedda Hopper Picks Films Stars of 1951." *Chicago Tribune*, circa 1950.

Katz, Ephraim. *The Film Encyclopedia*. New York: Crowell, 1979.

Kleiner, Dick. *Hollywood's Greatest Love Stories*. New York: Pocket, 1976.

Kobal, John. *People Will Talk*. New York: Knopf, 1985.

Lamparski, Richard. *Whatever Became Of...?* 2nd ser. New York: Crown, 1968.

_____. *Whatever Became Of...?* 3rd ser. New York: Crown, 1970.

_____. *Whatever Became Of...?* 4th ser. New York: Crown, 1973.

_____. *Whatever Became Of...?* 8th ser. New York: Crown, 1982.

_____. *Whatever Became Of...?* 9th ser. New York: Crown, 1985.

_____. *Whatever Became Of...?* 10th ser. New York: Crown, 1986.

_____. *Whatever Became Of...?* 11th ser. New York: Crown, 1989.

Levin, Martin, ed. *Hollywood and the Great Fan Magazines*. New York: Harrison House, 1970.

Lloyd, Ann, and Fuller, Graham, eds. *The Illustrated Who's Who of the Cinema*. New York: Macmillan, 1983.

Lyons, Barry. "Fritz Lang and the Film Noir." *Mise-en-Scene*, circa 1970.

Maltin, Leonard, ed. *Leonard Maltin's Movie Encyclopedia*. New York: Penguin, 1994.

Maxfield, James F. "Out of the Past: The Private Eye as Tragic Hero." *New Orleans Review*, Fall and Winter 1992.

McCarty, John. *Hollywood Gangland*. New York: St. Martin's, 1993.

_____. *Thrillers: Seven Decades of Classic Film Suspense*. Secaucus, New Jersey: Citadel, 1992.

McClelland, Doug. *Forties Film Talk*. Jefferson, North Carolina: McFarland, 1992.

McNeil, Alex. *Total Television*. New York: Penguin Books, 1996.

Miller, Rex. "Film Noir." *The Big Reel*, August 1995.

Mordden, Ethan. *The Hollywood Studios*. New York: Fireside, 1988.

Moses, Robert, ed. *Classic Movie Companion*. New York: Hyperion, 1999.

Norman, Barry. *The Story of Hollywood*. New York: Nal Books, 1987.

O'Donnell, Monica M., ed. *Contemporary Theatre, Film and Television*. Vol. 4. Detroit, Michigan: Gale, 1987.

_____, and O'Donnell, Owen, eds. *Contemporary Theatre, Film and Television*. Vol. 5. Detroit, Michigan: Gale, 1988.

Ottoson, Robert. *A Reference to the American Film Noir*. Metuchen, New Jersey: Scarecrow, 1981.

Palmer, R. Barton. *Hollywood's Dark Cinema: The American Film Noir*. New York: Twayne Publishers, 1994.

Parish, James Robert. *Hollywood Character Actors*. New York: Arlington House, 1978.

_____. *Tough Guys*. New York: Rainbow Books, 1976.

_____, and Bowers, Ronald L. *The MGM Stock Company: The Golden Era*. New York: Bonanza, 1972.

_____, and Leonard, William T. *Hollywood Players: The Thirties*. New York: Arlington House, 1976.

_____, and Stanke, Don E. *The All-Americans*. Carlstadt, New Jersey: Rainbow Books, 1977.

Peary, Danny. *Cult Movies 3*. New York: Fireside, 1988.

_____, ed. *Close-Ups: The Movie Star Book*. New York: Simon and Schuster, 1978.

Pickard, Roy. *The Hollywood Story*. Secaucus, New Jersey: Chartwell, 1986.

Polan, Dana. "Film Noir." *Journal of Film and Video*, Spring 1985.

Pratley, Gerald. *The Cinema of Otto Preminger*. New York: Barnes, 1971.

Quinlan, David. *The Illustrated Encyclopedia of Movie Character Actors*. New York: Harmony, 1985.

Ragan, David. *Movie Stars of the '40s*. New Jersey: Prentice Hall, 1985.

_____. *Movie Stars of the '30s*. New Jersey: Prentice Hall, 1985.

_____. *Who's Who in Hollywood, 1900-1976*. New Rochelle, New York: Arlington House, 1976.

Robertson, Patrick. *Film Facts*. New York: Billboard Books, 2001.

Sattin, Richard. "Joseph H. Lewis: Assessing an (Occasionally) Brilliant Career." *American Classic Screen*, November-December 1983.

Scheuer, Steven H. *The Movie Book*. Chicago, Illinois: Playboy, 1974.

Schickel, Richard. *The Stars*. New York: Bonanza, 1962.

Schrader, Paul. "Notes on Film Noir." *Film Comment*, Spring 1972.

Schultheiss, John. "The Noir Artist." *Films in Review*, January 1989.

Selby, Spencer. *Dark City: The Film Noir*. Jefferson, North Carolina: McFarland, 1989.

Shipman, David. *The Great Movie Stars: The Golden Years*. New York: Bonanza Books, 1970.

_____. *The Great Movie Stars: The International Years*. New York: St. Martin's, 1972.

Silver, Alain, and Ursini, James, eds. *Film Noir Reader*. New York: Limelight, 1996.

_____, and Ward, Elizabeth, eds. *Film Noir*. 3rd ed. New York: Overlook, 1992.

Sperling, Cass Warner and Millner, Cork, with Jack Warner, Jr. *Hollywood Be Thy Name: The Warner Brothers Story*. Rocklin, California: Prima Publishing.

Stephens, Michael L. *Film Noir: A Comprehensive, Illustrated Reference to Movies, Terms and Persons*. Jefferson, North Carolina: McFarland, 1995.

Thomas, Nicholas, ed. *International Dictionary of Films and Filmmakers. Volume Three–Actors and Actresses*. 2nd ed. Detroit, Michigan: St. James, 1992.

Thomas, Tony. *The Films of the Forties*. Secaucus, New Jersey: Citadel, 1975.

_____, and Solomon, Aubrey. *The Films of 20th Century-Fox*. Secaucus, New Jersey: Citadel, 1985.

Twomey, Alfred E., and McClure, Arthur F. *The Versatiles: A Study of Supporting Character Actors and Actresses in the American Motion Picture*. New York: Barnes, 1969.

Vermilye, Jerry. *The Films of the Thirties*. Secaucus, New Jersey: Citadel, 1982.

_____. *More Films of the Thirties*. Secaucus, New Jersey: Citadel, 1989.

Welch, Julie and Brody, Louise. *Leading Men*. New York: Crescent, 1985.

Wilson, Ivy Crane, ed. *Hollywood in the 1940s: The Stars' Own Stories*. New York: Ungar, 1980.

Zinman, David. *Fifty Classic Motion Pictures*. New York: Crown, 1970.

Documentaries

"American Cinema: Film Noir." A New York Center for Visual History Production, in co-production with KCET and the BBC. NYCVH, Copyright 1994.

"Hollywood: The Golden Years" (Episode Five). A BBC Television Production in association with RKO Pictures. BBC, Copyright 1987.

INDEX